# THE BLUE GUIDES

Albania
Austria
Belgium and Luxembourg
China
Cyprus
Czech and Slovak Republics
Denmark
Egypt

FRANCE
France
Paris and Versailles
Burgundy
Loire Valley
Midi-Pyrénées
Normandy
South West France
Corsica

GERMANY
Berlin and Eastern Germany
Western Germany

GREECE
Greece
Athens and environs
Crete

HOLLAND
Holland
Amsterdam

Hungary
Ireland

ITALY
Northern Italy
Southern Italy
Florence
Rome and environs
Venice
Tuscany
Umbria
Sicily

Jerusalem
Malta and Gozo
Mexico
Morocco
Moscow and St Petersburg
Portugal

SPAIN
Spain
Barcelona
Madrid

Sweden
Switzerland

TURKEY
Turkey
Istanbul

UK
England
Scotland
Wales
London
Museums and Galleries
   of London
Oxford and Cambridge
Country Houses of England
Gardens of England
Literary Britain and Ireland
Victorian Architecture in
   Britain
Churches and Chapels
   of Northern England
Churches and Chapels
   of Southern England
Channel Islands

USA
New York
Boston and Cambridge

D0920163

TEIL DER SEITENANSICHT

*Restored elevation of the Temple of Zeus, Olympia*

BLUE GUIDE

# GREECE

Robin Barber

*Maps and plans by John Flower*

**A&C Black**
London

**WW Norton**
New York

Sixth edition 1995

Published by A & C Black (Publishers) Ltd
35 Bedford Row, London WC1R 4JH

© Robin Barber 1995

All rights reserved. No part of this publication may be reproduced or used in any form
or by any means—photographic, electronic or mechanical, including photocopying,
recording, taping or information storage and retrieval systems—without permission of
the publishers.

The rights of Robin Barber to be identified as author of this work have been asserted
by him in accordance with the Copyright, Designs and Patents Act, 1988.

Maps and plans by John Flower

A CIP catalogue of this book is available from the British Library.

ISBN 0-7136-3250 X

Published in the United States of America by
WW Norton and Company, Inc
500 Fifth Avenue, New York, NY 10110

Published simultaneously in Canada by
Penguin Books Canada Limited
10 Alcorn Avenue, Toronto, Ontario M4V 3B2

ISBN 0-393-31273-9

The author and the publishers have done their best to ensure the accuracy of all the
information in Blue Guide Greece; however, they can accept no responsibilty for any
loss, injury or inconvenience sustained by any traveller as a result of information or
advice contained in this guide.

**Robin Barber** was born in Chapel en le Frith, Derbyshire, in 1940. At present Senior
Lecturer in Classics at Edinburgh University, he is an MA (Classics) and PhD of
St Andrews University and holds the Oxford Diploma in Classical Archaeology. He
has travelled in Greece for over 30 years, five of which were spent there, first as Greek
State Scholar (for research in Aegean archaeology), then as Assistant Director of the
British School at Athens. He has done fieldwork in Crete and the Cyclades and
published numerous articles on Greek art and archaeology. His book *The Cyclades in
the Bronze Age* appeared in 1987 and, in a Greek translation, in 1994. He is also author
of *Blue Guide Athens*. Amongst particular Greek enthusiasms, he would count the
poems of G. Seferis, the rebetika songs of Sotiria Bellou and walking in the countryside.

The publishers and the author welcome comments, suggestions and corrections for the next edition of Blue
Guide Greece. Writers of the most informative letters will
be awarded a free Blue Guide of their choice.

Printed and bound in Great Britain by
Butler & Tanner Ltd, Frome and London

# PREFACE

In producing this further revision of Blue Guide Greece, I am even more conscious than before of debts owed to the efforts and kindness of others. Foremost once again is Ann Thomas whose companionship, support, indefatigable good humour and willingness to track down the most elusive and recondite pieces of information have ensured that this work is much fuller and more accurate than it would otherwise have been. To Dick and June Elliott I am also very greatly indebted, for putting at my disposal the knowledge gained in many visits to Greece and spending parts of their holidays researching on my behalf. Dick has also helped with proof reading and the maps. Similarly Kenneth and Brenda Collier made many helpful suggestions and followed up queries for me on the ground; and Božidar and Svetlana Slapšac toured some of the Ionian islands on my behalf. There follows a list, incomplete as I must sadly admit, of some of the many others who have helped in variety of different ways in the preparation of this volume. I am particularly aware of the omission of an enormous Greek contingent, many of whose names I never knew or omitted to record, who gave me directions, information, suggestions, encouragement and, as often as not, hospitality. It is their contribution above all which has kept me going in what has at times seemed an impossible task and I hope particularly that they will benefit, in however small a way, from the greater knowledge and understanding of their country that this book may generate.

Bill Allen, Militsa Alvanitidhou, Michael Angold, Tony Beck, Elinor and Christopher Bevan, Michael Boyd, John Camp, Hector and Elizabeth Catling, Nicolas Coldstream, John Coleman, Richard Clogg, Ian Cunningham, Glenys Davies, Martin Davies, Katie Dhimakopoulou, Dick and June Elliott, Lisa French, Elizabeth Gebhard, M. J. Grond, John Ellis Jones, Olga, Tasos and Zoë Hadjianastasiou, David Hardy, Gregory Karafillis, Jonas Lehrman, Peter Lock, Eleanor Loughlin, Toula Markettou, Jim McCredie, Catherine Morgan, Jamie Morton, Francis Pagan, Kostas Papayiannis, Anna Pariente, Stavros Pateras, Jackie Pearson, Fiona Pitt-Kethley, Hans Pohlsander, John Prag, Jane Rabnett, the Ross family, the Samaras family, Angeliki Sakhini, Eric Salzen, Henk Schrama, Babette Sigalas, Karin Skawran, the Taylor family, Miltiadhis Tsamis, Anna and Gilles Touchais, Yiannis Tsedhakis, Malcolm Wagstaff, Harriet Blitzer Watrous, Philip Wharmly, Hector Williams, Penny Wilson-Zarganis, Nancy Winter and P. Zoridhis.

In addition staff of the Dhimarkía or Nomarkhía at the following places gave substantial help either in person or by correspondence: Aiyio, Arta, Florina, Kastoria, Larissa, Serres, Thebes. In Britain I gratefully acknowledge the help of the Greek National Tourist Organisation.

At A&C Black, the editing and production process has been overseen by Gemma Davies and Judy Tither: John Flower has made his usual invaluable contribution both in amending plans and maps, and producing new ones.

My general policy has been to include in the text anything, of whatever period, that might be of interest to the visitor. Since space is always at a premium, items of lesser importance or of interest to a more limited audience are often mentioned very briefly and without detailed directions to their location. I would be interested to know whether readers find this satisfactory, since it requires some additional research on the visitor's part.

Coverage of the city of Athens has been considerably abbreviated in this volume since a recent and detailed description can be found in Blue Guide Athens (3rd. edition, 1992). Comments would be welcomed on the desirability of dividing coverage of Greece into several smaller volumes, since this seems a likely consequence of new discoveries and of the increasing body of information about the country's historical monuments.

# Acknowledgements

For permission to reproduce photographs and drawings the publishers would like to thank Agra Publications; E. Forbes-Boyd; American School of Classical Studies at Athens: Agora Excavations; B. T. Batsford Ltd; Benaki Museum, Athens; Board of Trustees of the Victoria and Albert Museum; The British Museum; British School at Athens; Cambridge University Press; Cultural Foundation of the National Bank of Greece; Deutsches Archaologisches Institut Athen; Ecole Française D'Athènes; Ekdotike Athinon S.A.; Dr J. Ellis Jones; Gannadius Library, American School of Classical Studies; Manolis Korres; National Historical Museum, Athens; The National Museum of Copenhagen, Department of Near Eastern and Classical Antiquities; Osterreichische Akademie der Wissenschaften *and Johannes Koder;* Prestel Verlag, Munich; Thames and Hudson Ltd; Universite Libre de Bruxelles; Yale Univesity Press.

# Blue Guides

The Blue Guide series began in 1918 when Muirhead Guide-Books Limited published Blue Guide London and its Environs. Findlay and James Muirhead already had extensive experience of guide-book publishing: before the First World War they had been the editors of the English editions of the German Baedekers, and by 1915 they had acquired the copyright of most of the famous 'Red' Handbooks from John Murray.

An agreement made with the French publishing house Hachette et Cie in 1917 led to the translation of Muirhead's London guide, which became the first 'Guide Bleu', Hachette had previously published the blue-covered 'Guides Joanne'. Subsequently, Hachette's Guide Blue 'Paris et ses Environs' was adapted and published in London by Muirhead.

In 1931 Ernest Benn Limited took over the Blue Guides, appointing Russell Muirhead, Findlay Muirhead's son, editor in 1934. The Muirheads' connection with the Blue Guides ended in 1963, when Stuart Rossiter, who had been working on the Guides since 1954, became house editor, revising and compiling several of the books himself.

The Blue Guides are now published by A & C Black, who acquired Ernest Benn in 1984, so continuing the tradition of guide-book publishing which began in 1826 with 'Black's Economical Tourist of Scotland'. The series continues to grow: there are now more than 60 titles in print, with revised editions appearing regularly, and new titles in preparation.

# CONTENTS

# Maps and plans

# EXPLANATIONS

## Type
The main routes are described in large type. Smaller type is used for branch-routes and excursions, for historical and preliminary paragraphs, and (generally speaking) for descriptions of minor importance.

## Distances
Distances (placed in front of the place-name) are given cumulatively from the starting-point of the route or sub-route in kilometres and miles; on diversions from a route (placed *after* the place-name), they are specific to that place from the point of divergence from the route. Road distances have been calculated where possible from the km posts on the roads themselves, otherwise from measurement on official maps; constant realignments make it certain that these distances will vary slightly from those measured by motorists on their milometers. A Greek asked a walking distance will always give the answer as a walking *time*. Archaeologists, however, invariably use metres and the site plans are accordingly scaled in metres.

## Asterisks
Asterisks indicate points of special interest or excellence.

## Abbreviations
In addition to generally accepted and self-explanatory abbreviations, the following occur in the Guide:

| | |
|---|---|
| A', B' | tou Protou (i.e. 'the first'), the second, etc. |
| A.J.A. | American Journal of Archaeology |
| Akr. | Akroterion (i.e. Cape) |
| Ay. | Ayios, Ayia, etc. (Saint or Saints) |
| B.C.H. | Bulletin de Correspondance Hellénique |
| B.S.A. | Annual of the British School at Athens |
| c | circa |
| C | century |
| dr(s) | drachmas(s) |
| fl. | floruit |
| Hdt. | Herodotus |
| Hesp. | Hesperia |
| J.H.S. | Journal of Hellenic Studies |
| Leof. | Leoforos (Avenue) |
| N.T.O. | (see below) |
| Od. | Odhos (Street) |
| Plat. | Plateia (Square) |
| R. | rooms |
| Rest. | restaurant |
| Rte | route |
| Thuc. | Thucydides |
| EOT (NTO) | Ελληνικός Οργανισμός Τουρισμού (National Tourist Organisation. |
| KTEA (KTEL) | Κοινόν Ταμείον Εισπράξεων Λεωφορείων (Joint Pool of Bus Owners). |
| O.T.E. | Οργανισμός Τηλεπικοινωνιων Ελλάδος (Greek Telecommunications Organisation). |

# THE MONUMENTS OF ANCIENT GREECE

by **Nicolas Coldstream**

# A. The Monuments in their Historical Setting

### The Stone Age

The earliest vestige of human life in Greece—earlier than the emergence of Homo Sapiens himself—consists of a fossilised skull of Neanderthal type found near Salonika. Of the more developed food-gathering culture of Palaeolithic Greece one can now get a clear impression from three cave sites in the Louros valley, Epirus: recent excavations there have revealed occupation going back to c 40,000 BC, and a Mousterian flint industry similar to those of Balkan Europe.

The first impulses towards farming, towards the domestication of animals, and towards the foundation of settled villages came to Greece from Anatolia. The oldest farming communities in Greece—and indeed in Europe—were centred round the fertile plains of Thessaly and Macedonia. An Early Neolithic settlement at Nea Nikomidhia near Veroia (7th–6th mill. BC) shows traces of large rectangular houses, and displays several links with Anatolia in its artefacts. The later stages of Neolithic culture are best represented at Sesklo and Dimini, both near the land-locked gulf of Pagasae. At Sesklo (6th–5th mill. BC) the lack of fortifications and the manufacture of elegant painted and burnished pottery bear witness to a peaceful and flourishing agricultural civilisation, while the importation of obsidian from the island of Melos proves the existence of trade even at this remote period. The rectangular houses, with walls built of mud brick, were founded on a stone base which remains their only visible memorial to the visitor today. At the neighbouring village of Dimini (founded c 3400 BC) concentric rings of fortification reveal a more turbulent state of affairs; in these unsettled conditions the rise of centralised authority is suggested by the building of a spacious house on the summit of the mound, whose pillared porch, leading into the main hall, foreshadows the Mycenaean megaron.

### The Early Bronze Age (c 2800–2000 BC)

In the ensuing centuries, while Thessaly relapsed into provincialism, the centre of civilisation moved southward. With the arrival of fresh influences from Anatolia (c 3200–2800 BC), the inhabitants of the Aegean world learned the use of copper alloyed with tin to make bronze. They spoke a pre-Hellenic language, to which some non-Greek features in Greek place names (such as -nth- and -ss- in Corinth, Knossos) are generally attributed. Most settlements of this period lay on the eastern seaboard of the Peloponnese and of Central Greece, in the Cyclades, and in Crete. On the mainland the most impressive Early Helladic site is at Lerna in the Argolid, where the imposing House of Tiles, evidently an important seat of administrative authority, is the earliest known building of monumental proportions in the Aegean area. Even more progressive was the Early Minoan culture of Crete, perhaps owing to its proximity to the advanced civilisations of the Near East: contact had already been established with the Old Kingdom of

Egypt at the very beginning of the Bronze Age. The Cycladic islands, very sparsely settled in Neolithic times, now enjoyed one of the most dynamic and creative periods in their history; this is the period of the well-known marble idols. The islanders made especially rapid progress in metalworking skills, and played an active part in exchanges both with the mainland and with Crete.

## The Middle and Late Bronze Age: The Palatial Civilisations of Crete and Mycenae (c 2000–1100 BC)

Soon after 2000 BC the unity of the Aegean world was broken for several centuries. Invaders, usually identified with the first Greeks, swept over the mainland in two waves (c 2200 and c 2000 BC) destroying the main centres of Early Helladic civilisation: meanwhile the Minoans, who suffered no such disruption, gradually extended their influence over the Cyclades.

The focus of Cretan power now moved to the centre of the island, with the foundation of the three palaces at Knossos, Phaestos, and Mallia. The similarity of their layout, and their lack of effective defences suggest the growth of a single organised kingdom, which established a 'pax Minoica' in the Aegean by the exercise of an overwhelming supremacy at sea, unchallenged until the emergence of the Greek mainland as an important power in the 16C BC.

All three palaces were frequently rebuilt after periodical destructions by earthquake, reaching their most advanced form in the 16C BC; yet their basic plan was never radically altered, consisting of a vast network of rooms grouped asymmetrically round a central court, often rising to three storeys. The intricacy of Minoan palaces, which in the impressionable minds of later Greek visitors gave rise to the fanciful legend of the Labyrinth, was demanded by a monarchy that was at once theocratic and bureaucratic: all the reins of authority, whether political, religious, or commercial, were held within the palace walls. The spaciousness of the state apartments and the secure privacy of the domestic quarters supplied the essential needs of princely dignity. Under the same roof, the most skilful artisans plied their crafts under royal supervision. The magazines, with their ordered rows of earthenware pithoi, stored the royal reserves of oil, wine, corn, and other commodities, whose management required the use of writing: at first a system of hieroglyphs was evolved (c 2000–1660 BC), gradually superseded by a more convenient syllabic script, Linear A (c 1900–1450 BC). Neither of these scripts can yet be read. Finally the presence of small shrines and purificatory areas within the palaces reminds us that Minoan kings could also act as High Priests.

By the beginning of the Late Bronze Age (c 1550 BC) the Minoans had attained the summit of their power. Minoan outposts had been planted in the Cyclades (notably at Phylakopi on Melos and at Akrotiri on Thera), on Kythera (Kastri), on Rhodes (Triandha), and at Miletus: Minoan wares had been exported to the markets of Cyprus, Syria, and Egypt: after c 1500 BC, Minoan emissaries began to appear in Egyptian tomb paintings of the XVIIIth Dynasty under the name of Keftiu, bearing costly gifts of friendship to the Pharaohs. On the Greek mainland, Minoan influence was probably confined to the artistic sphere; it is first seen in the astounding wealth of gold vessels, jewellery and weapons in the shaft graves at Mycenae (c 16C BC), and continues in the rich offerings of the 15C tombs at Vapheio and in the Pylos area. The Minoan style was frequently adapted to scenes of war and hunting—subjects that were foreign to Minoan taste, but congenial to the martial temper of the mainlanders.

Around 1500 BC the volcanic island of Thera erupted in a truly catastrophic manner and devastated many major centres in Minoan Crete. The mastery of the Aegean world steadily passed from Crete to the rising power of Mycenae—a process that was accelerated by the irretrievable wreckage of the palace at Knossos c 1380 BC, whether by human or natural agency: but even before this date some form of mainland control over the Cretan metropolis is clearly indicated by the appearance of a new script in the Knossian archives (Linear B) which has been deciphered as an early form of Greek. Likewise, by the end of the 15C BC, Mycenaean traders had taken over the Minoan overseas outposts, and after this date, the commercial initiative in the Mediterranean from Sicily to Egypt had passed into Mycenaean hands.

In the 14–13C BC Mycenae assumed the hegemony of the Aegean world, giving her name to the advanced civilisation in which she played the predominant part. Not that impressive memorials of the period are lacking in other parts of Greece: Messenia, Boeotia, Attica, and Laconia were all heavily populated, and it is to Pylos that we turn for the best preserved palace on the mainland (13C BC). The Linear B archives from there suggest that the king of each district (*wanax*) stood at the head of his own highly organised feudal system. In the *Iliad* of Homer we are told that these local rulers, in their turn, were obliged to supply contingents for foreign ventures like the supreme command of Agamemnon, king of Mycenae, who was regarded as *primus inter pares*.

At Mycenae the pattern of settlement is typical of many other areas. On a low rocky eminence, fortified by a ring of massive Cyclopean masonry, dwelt the king and his court. His palace was smaller than the Cretan prototype, but more symmetrically designed. Not far below, an intricate complex of shrines ('The House with the Idols') also combines Minoan and mainland features. Outside this citadel lived the king's subjects in contiguous villages, each with its own cemetery hewn in the rock: the royal dynasty were buried in the monumental tholos (or 'beehive') tombs, one of the chief glories of the age: elsewhere only in Egypt was such veneration paid to the illustrious dead. Far beyond the limits of this lower town, the king's gaze could range over the flourishing settlements of the Argive plain (such as Prosymna, Argos, and Dendra), past the citadel at Tiryns, down to the sea at Nauplia, which, together with the little port at Asine, guarded the entrance to his kingdom from foreign invasion.

Around 1200 BC began the demise of the Mycenaen civilisation which has been attributed to a variety of causes: economic collapse, internal conflict, disastrous changes of climate, local earthquakes, and land invaders from the North, possibly equated with the Dorians of ancient Greek tradition. Against the menace of hostile incursion, impressive defence works were constructed: the fortification of the Perseia spring at Mycenae, the galleries at Tiryns, and the stairway to the spring under the Acropolis at Athens, three marvels of military engineeing, all belong to this date. Pylos succumbed to an early foreign attack (c 1200 BC): Mycenae and Tiryns were devastated, and by 12C BC, after further assaults, lay in ruins. Significantly for the future course of Greek history, Athens survived the ordeal unscathed. Many of her Ionian kinsmen took refuge on her soil before finding new homes across the Aegean on the western seaboard of Asia Minor (11–10C BC). These colonists were the vanguard of a movement which was eventually to spread Hellenic civilisation all round the shores of the Mediterranean: but in these pages we cannot follow their fortunes, being concerned exclusively with the monuments of the mother country.

## The Hellenic City-State: c 1100–27 BC

The commotions at the end of the Bronze Age destroyed once again the unity of Aegean civilisation, and ushered in a Dark Age. Isolation from the eastern Mediterranean was never complete, as is apparent from the varied exotica found in the rich cemeteries of Lefkandi in Euboea. Most parts of Greece, however, were cut off from the outside world through loss of sea communications. Reduced to parochial poverty and isolated from one another by mountain barriers, the Greeks were for a time forced to rely on the resouces of their own poor soil, whose tillage became easier with the invention of iron tools.

From the 8C BC onwards, with the revival of sea-borne commerce and the recovery of prosperity, Greece was divided into several hundred small communities, variously governed. Some, never fully urbanised (for example, in Thessaly), retained a loose organisation by tribes (ethné); others, as in Boeotia and Achaea, made common cause in leagues; but the more progressive Greeks developed the fully autonomous city-state (polis), which was to presevere for many centuries as the most dynamic unit of Greek society. Athens became an exceptionally large polis by effecting the union of all Attica, but even so her territory was no larger than an average English county. In the 5C BC, when all freeborn male Athenians possessed the franchise, the citizen roll numbered about 40,000, all of whom were entitled to vote in person at the meetings of the Assembly; among other cities, only a handful could muster more than 10,000. Plato fixed the number at 5040 for his ideal state: Aristotle thought that all citizens should know one another personally.

For the siting of a Hellenic City, three things were indispensable: an effective water-supply, access to arable land, and above all an easily defensible position, since relations between neighbouring states were seldom cordial. At first the acropolis served as a fortress in times of danger: later, whole cities were fortified. Athens and Thebes both grew up round typical Mycenaean strongholds: in the Peloponnese, where the Dorians tended to avoid the main Mycenaean centres, the cities of Corinth and Argos were protected by yet more massive citadels. The Spartans, trusting in their military prowess, dispensed with both natural and artificial defences and chose an exposed site in the Laconian plain. In times of peace, after the disappearance of monarchical rule, the acropolis was usually set apart for the worship of the patron deity. By the end of the 6C BC, temples had been built over the ruins of the Bronze Age palaces at Athens, Mycenae, Tiryns, and Knossos: after the sack of the Athenian acropolis by the Persians in 480 BC, the cult of Athena was glorified by a series of monuments that became the wonder of Greece.

With the rise of democratic and oligarchic governments, the agora became the true centre of public life. Here, in a level square expanse at the very heart of the city, political and commercial business could be conducted; here, too, men could seek congenial company in their idle moments, enjoying the opportunities for free and leisured discussion from which Greek thought derives its originality. All round the square, buildings grew up in a more or less haphazard fashion, depending on the whim of the people and the balance of the treasury at any given time: it was not until the Hellenistic period that the agora was subjected to organised planning. The stoa, or open portico, which offered shelter from the sun and rain, became an essential component in the architecture of the agora: behind the long colonnade, where philosophers did much of their teaching, the interior could be divided into a large number of rooms suitable for shops, offices, banks, or market-stalls. By the 2C BC, the Athenian agora was virtually surrounded by stoas, of which one, that presented by Attalos II of Pergamon (mid-2C BC), has been restored as a museum. Other buildings were devoted to the smooth working of Athenian democracy: the Bouleuterion housed the Council of 500 who prepared the business of the full Assembly of citizens: in the round building known as the Tholos, a standing committee drawn from their numbers (the Prytaneis) remained on duty, in order to deal with any emergency that might arise. The Assembly, too numerous to be accommodated in the Agora, met on the Pnyx, where a bank of earth converted the rocky hill into an artificial theatre. For the same reason, public spectacles were removed from the agora at an early date: hence the construction of theatres, stadia, and gymnasia, usually sited on the outskirts of the city, and sometimes outside its walls.

The nucleus of the Greek theatre was the circular orchestra, or 'dancing-place', since drama had originally evolved from the ritual dances to the god Dionysos at country festivals. For the seating of the spectators, full advantage was taken of natural contours; the auditorium (theatron), with its tiers of stone seats, enclosed the orchestra on three sides, and, if necessary, was banked up at the ends by retaining walls (analemmata). In the 5C BC, the great age of Attic tragedy and comedy, the spectators were seated on earth banks or wooden benches, and temporary stages of wood and canvas were thought sufficient. Stone seating did not become usual until in 4C BC, while raised stone-built stages were probably an innovation of the Hellenistic period. It was left for Roman architects to bind the stage and auditorium into a singe structure by throwing vaults over the side passage (parodoi) between the two: in the course of this transformation, both the auditorium and the orchestra assumed a semicircular shape.

The stadium and gymnasium were designed for athletic contests and athletic practice respectively. The word *stadion* originally meant a unit of distance equivalent to c 180m (200 yards), the length of the normal foot-race; where possible (as at Athens and Epidaurus) the course was sited in a long and shallow trough between two hills, and the spectators were placed on the banks either side. The familiar simicircular end (sphendone) and the idea of stone seating were borrowed from the theatre in Hellenistic times: monumental entrances (as at Delphi) were a Roman contribution. The gymnasium usually assumed the form of a large square court, surrounded by colonnades. Besides its original function as an athletic training ground, it inevitably became a social centre, like a miniature agora. The close relation between the physical and spiritual aspects of Greek education (gymnastike and mousike) becomes apparent when we recall that Plato adopted the name of the neighbouring gymnasium (Academia) in naming his own School of philosophy.

In contrast to the splendour of public buildings, private houses were modest and unpretentious. In the islands, walls were constructed entirely of rough stone; on the mainland, the usual material was mud brick, placed on a rubble foundation. A complete town of the 8C BC, with spacious square rooms, has been recently excavated at Zagora on the island of Andros. For the Archaic period (7–6C BC) the steeply terraced hill-town overlooking the harbour of Emborio on Chios offers the fullest evidence. The excavation of Olynthus has furnished the ground plan of a Classical residential suburb (c 430–348 BC) laid out with streets intersecting at right-angles, under the influence of Hippodamus of Miletus, who first designed cities on a grid

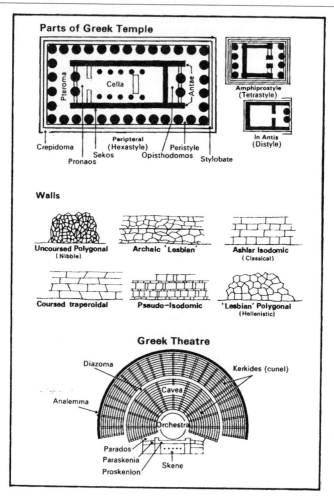

**Parts of Greek Temple**

Pteroma · Cella · Antae · Amphiprostyle (Tetrastyle) · In Antis (Distyle)

Crepidoma · Pronaos · Sekos · Peripteral (Hexastyle) · Opisthodomos · Peristyle · Stylobate

**Walls**

Uncoursed Polygonal (Nibble) · Archaic 'Lesbian' · Ashlar Isodomic (Classical)

Coursed traperoidal · Pseudo-Isodomic · 'Lesbian' Polygonal (Hellenistic)

**Greek Theatre**

Diazoma · Kerkides (cunei) · Cavea · Analemma · Orchestra · Parados · Paraskenia · Skene · Proskenion

system: the houses were approximately 18m square, with rooms looking out on to a small courtyard. A greater degree of comfort is found in the mansions of the wealthy businessmen of Hellenistic Delos (mainly 2C BC) where the courtyard has acquired a handsome peristyle of marble columns, and the floors are often decorated with colourful mosaics: but not until Roman times do houses become really sumptuous.

Among the most permanent and impressive of Hellenic monuments are the walls of fortification, which frequently survive in an excellent state of preservation on sites where little else is to be seen. Full circuits became normal in the 5C BC, equipped with towers at regular intervals; with the steady improvements in siege engines, rebuilding was often necessary. Exceptionally fine are the walls of Messene, founded in 370 BC, after the liberation of Messenia from the Spartan yoke. Here the walls were built in their full height and thickness with squared stone blocks, and carefully fitted, as was customary until the Roman period, without any mortar or cement. Such walls were unusually extravagant; the usual practice was to build the parapets and the battlements in mud brick, and to fill the interior with rubble, restricting the fine masonry to the outer surfaces. The fortification of a city was regarded by Aristole as an essential part of its adornment; and among the rich variety of masonry styles, none is more satisfying to the eye than the polygonal method of walling, which enjoyed an especial vogue before c 450 BC, before it became fashionable to lay the blocks in regular courses. At Oiniadai in Akarnania, a complete polygonal circuit (c 450 BC) survives: more accessible are the forts at Eleutherae and Aegosthena, both excellent examples of the regular isodomic style (early 4C BC). The visitor to Eleusis will find a good series of fortification and terrace walls, dating from the 8C to the 4C BC.

**The Hellenic Sanctuary**. In addition to the temples and the shrines within the city, the countryside of ancient Greece abounded in holy places of all kinds, varying in extent from a simple enclosure with an altar to the great Panhellenic sanctuaries of Olympia and Delphi. Many such shrines give evidence of worship far back into prehistoric times, ultimately owing their sanctity to the awe-inspiring beauty and majesty of their scenery. Sometimes the surroundings reflected the attributes of the god: thus mountain peaks were sacred to Zeus, while Poseidon was judiciously worshipped on stormy capes.

Since the offering of sacrifices played such a predominant part in the official cult of the Olympian gods, the altar was an indispensable component of even the smallest shrines; set out in the open air and surrounded by a sacred precinct (peribolos), the altar was always the main centre of public veneration. The temple was usually a later addition, whose purpose was to house the image of the god, and not to be a place of congregational worship like the Christian church—here though, an exception is provided by the famous cult of Mysteries at Eleusis, where the secret ceremonies of initiation were confined to the darkness of the Telesterion.

A sanctuary might also acquire a monumental columnar entrance (propylon) and a stoa to provide lodgings for priests, or to house stalls where pilgrims might purchase suitable votive offerings. For local shrines such as the Sanctuary of Aphaia on Aegina, or the Argive Heraion, no further buildings were necessary. By contrast, the great Panhellenic sanctuaries of Olympia and Delphi, which attracted to their religious festivals thousands of visitors from all over the Greek world, needed many of the administrative buildings found in a large city: a bouleuterion and a prytaneion (town hall) as well as a stadium, a gymnasium, and sometimes a theatre also. Furthermore, the Greek states strove with one another not only for prizes at the quadrennial games, but also in the magnificence of their monumental dedications, which might take the form either of small votive chapels ('treasuries') or of imposing groups of sculpture. Such intense rivalry was always a powerful stimulant to the vitality of Greek art; later, when the Pax Romana put an end to the animosities between the city-states, the Hellenic spirit lost much of its creative impulse.

## The Graeco-Roman Period: 27 BC–AD 330

The political independence of the Greek city-states came to an end in 27 BC, with the incorporation of the province of Achaea into the Roman Empire. Long before this date, Rome had begun to absorb the civilising influence of Greek literature, art, and thought: she now repaid her debt by maintaining unbroken peace for the next three centuries. She made little attempt to impose her own way of life on her Greek subjects: not only did Greek remain the official language of the Eastern Mediterranean, but many of the cities of old Greece were allowed to retain their local autonomy, and the responsibility for their own upkeep. In AD 160 the traveller Pausanias, whose *Description of Greece* is a valuable source for the study of Greek monuments, found the main cities and sanctuaries in a flourishing condition, although some of the ancient sites were already desolate. Greece remained a peaceful backwater until the ruinous devastations of the Heruli (267) temporarily shattered her security.

Under Roman rule, Corinth became the administrative capital of the province of Achaea, and today her ruins offer the best impression of a spacious and thriving Graeco-Roman city. Elsewhere in the south, there is a scarcity of typically Roman monuments—of triumphal arches, imperial baths, and amphitheatres: in their stead, Greek magistrates and Greek architects preferred the simplicity of the propylon, the gymnasium, and the old-fashioned theatre, albeit in its Roman form (a characteristic example is the Odeum of Herodes Atticus at Athens). But in the north, where Hellenic culture had not penetrated so deep, there is a greater abundance of typically Roman architecture, especially in the later years of the Roman Empire: one may cite the Arch of Galerius at Salonica (c AD 300), the extensive forum of Philippi, and the purely Roman foundation of Nicopolis. A well-appointed Roman town on the island of Kos, where several mural paintings are preserved, has more in common with the sumptuous cities of Asia Minor than with the Greek mainland.

Athens, though shorn of all political power, still played the part of a university town, and remained a great artistic centre. Her sculptors took the lead in attempting to satisfy the insatiable appetite of Roman collectors. Not content with the universal practice of copying famous Classical works Athenian artists specialised in elegant pastiches of the Classical Style of the 5–4C BC: especially worthy of note are the lively Neo-Attic reliefs in the Piraeus Museum, and a fine group of Attic sarcophagi in the Salonica Museum (AD 2–3C). The more typically Roman work (idealised statues of emperors, and realistic portraits of private individuals) is best represented in the Museums of Corinth and Heraklion.

# B.   The Monuments in their Artistic Aspects

## Minoan and Mycenaean Art

**I. Architecture**. In the absence of separate buildings reserved for religious worship, the architectural genius of the Aegean Bronze Age found its fullest expression in royal places and royal tombs. The conception of a building as a work of art stems from the older civilisations of Egypt and Syria, whence many of the typical features of Minoan palaces are derived: for example, the careful dressing of stone into large square blocks, the decorative use of stucco, the elaborate system of drainage through earthenware pipes, and, above all, the grouping of rooms round a central court.

After the Early Helladic House of Tiles at Lerna, the Greek mainland offers no further monumental architecture until the rise of Mycenaean civilisation. The palaces of Mycenae, Tiryns, and Pylos (14–13C BC) all owe much to Crete in the complexity of their plan, but there has been one notable modification: the central position is now occupied not by a large court as in Crete, but by a large suite of state rooms in the form of the ancestral megaron—a type of house whose history can be traced back to the Neolithic period, and which was much favoured by the first Greeks who invaded the mainland in c 2200 and c 2000 BC. Its palatial form is as follows: from a relatively small court, a pillared porch (aithousa) leads into an anteroom (prodomos) which in turn gives access to the spacious square throne room (domos) with a low central hearth, round which four wooden columns support the roof. Since all three rooms have the same breadth, and since the doors are all aligned on the same axis, the megaron introduced an element of symmetry lacking in the Minoan prototype, but prophetic of later Greek architecture.

The royal tholos tomb is the most original, and the most distinguished, of Mycenaean architectural forms. A monumental passage (dromos) leads into a domed funerary chamber, whose masonry rises by corbelled courses, until the gap is closed at the apex: the chamber was then covered by a mound of earth, and the dromos filled in. Among the nine examples at Mycenae, three stages of its development may be followed. One of the earliest is the 'Tomb of Aegisthus' (early 15C BC) whose chamber is nearly all constructed of rubble, except the door-way, which is lined with rather larger masonry and crowned by a massive lintel. The enormous weight of the superstructure led the architects of the second group (of which the Lion Tomb, c 1450 BC, is typical) to leave a relieving triangle above the lintel: at the same time some attempt was made to dress the stones of the chamber. The climax of the series is represented by the superb 'Treasury of Atreus' (c 1300 BC): here the whole design is translated into handsome ashlar masonry and the façade is elaborately decorated: the portal was flanked by a tall pair of attached half-columns tapering downwards like their Minoan prototypes; a smaller pair stood at either side of the relieving triangle, which was filled in and covered with friezes of sculptured rosettes and spirals in green and stone. A close relationship exists between the structure of this façade and that of the contemporary Lion Gate, where the walling is also in ashlar technique, and the famous heraldic lions occupy the relieving triangle. Elsewhere the circuit of the citadel is mainly of Cyclopean construction, i.e. composed of roughly dressed boulders, the crevices being filled with small stones.

**II. Painting and Pottery**. Enough has survived of Aegean fresco painting to establish it as one of the major arts of the late Bronze Age, developed initially by the Minoans for the interior decoration of palatial buildings. Since the pigments were applied when the plaster was still wet, a rapid and sure touch was essential. Where his Egyptian contemporary preferred to linger lovingly over anatomical details, the Minoan artist obtained a lively effect from a few summary, impressionistic strokes; after the surface had dried, details could be touched up in tempera. Most frescoes in Crete fall into three classes: floral and rocky landscapes with birds or animals; miniature human scenes portraying animated crowds of men at women at seasonal religious festivals; and more monumental compositions, containing humans at life size. Sexes are effectively distinguished by the use of red paint for men, and white for women; in the landscapes, the background of flowers and rocks is usually repeated along the upper border. In the Minoan houses at Akrotiri on Thera all three classes are represented among the numerous frescoes found in excellent condition under the volcanic overlay of c 1500 BC. The Spring Fresco presents pairs of swallows greeting one another, against a landscape of red lilies growing out of volcanic rocks. The miniatures are represented by the Ship Fresco, packing five harbour towns and hundreds of human figures into a microcosm of island life. Most striking among the larger frescoes is the vast composition in the Xeste 3 shrine, showing scenes of religious initiation extending round the walls of two storeys. A preference for white backgrounds and firm outlines distinguishes the Theran school from the Cretan, in which figures are more often distinguished by masses of contrasting colours; there is, however, the same love of naturalism which enlivens the contemporary pictorial art of Minoan Crete in the 16C BC. Firm outlines are also characterstic of the frescoes in Mycenaean palaces (14–13C BC), but the taste is now for more formal compositions, and more stylised renderings of the figures. Although some themes were taken over from Minoan tradition, others reflect the more warlike and aggressive temperament of the mainlanders: for example, the battle scene at Pylos, the boar hunt at Tiryns, and the long frieze round the megaron at Mycenae showing warriors and horses preparing for battle.

Before the earliest frescoes were painted, Minoan potters had already attained a high peak of excellence in the polychrome Kamares ware, named after the cave-sanctuary high on the eastern flank of Mt Ida where it was first noted, and often imported to the Cyclades. In the best period (19–18C BC) the decoration is applied in red and white to a dark ground, and the designs strike a subtle balance between curvilinear abstract ornament and stylised plant motives. Minoan pottery of the 16C and 15C BC, which deeply influenced the style of early Mycenaean ware, owes much of its decoration to the influence of free painting, although the potter was always guided by the shape of the vase in his choice of ornament. For this reason human figures and animals were avoided, whereas after c 1550 BC, when the decoration began to be applied in dark paint on a light ground, flowers and marine subjects could be accommodated in their most naturalistic form; the octopus became a special favourite, since its elastic shape could be adapted to suit any large surface. Such extreme naturalism was short-lived: by the late 15C BC the floral and marine motives on the Palace Style jars from the Knossos area and from the Greek mainland began to assume a regular and symmetrical form. After 1400 BC, when the artistic initiative passed to the mainland, they gradually degenerate into abstract linear patterns. Larger phases, however, sometimes carry pictorial decoration, the chariot team being a favoured subject.

**III. The Plastic Arts**. Some life-sized female statues in terracotta, in a Minoan style of c 1550–1450 BC, have been recovered from a sanctuary at Ayia Irini on the Cycladic island of Kea; otherwise, no monumental statues survive from the Aegean Bronze Age. Smaller figures, however, have a long history. A nude female statuette from Lerna, gracefully natural in its pose, shows that even in Neolithic times a lump of clay could be transformed into a thing of beauty: the marble idols of the Cyclades (2500–2000 BC), more austerely stylised, belong to the same artistic milieu. Most Mycenaean figurines in terracotta are crude and mass-produced, but the contemporary ivories are of high quality; a group in ivory from Mycenae, portraying two women and a child (15C BC), is remarkable for its humanity and tenderness.

Minoan artists, working for Mycenaean patrons, were consistently successful in the techniques of relief in metal, where their plastic skill could be combined with their innate pictorial talent. Their complete mastery of this medium is displayed in the two magnificent gold cups from the tholos at Vapheio (15C BC), both depicting the hunting of wild bulls: with a frame only 10cm high, full justice has been done to a tense and dramatic theme, and the majesty and ferocity of the animals has been superbly caught. We are also reminded of Minoan free painting by the pictorial use of precious metals in the daggers from the shaft graves of Mycenae, where gold and silver are inlaid in a background of dark alloy, and minor details are incised: their free and naturalistic style makes it seem likely that they were the work of Cretan smiths, at a time when the mainland was just beginning to succumb to the spell of Minoan civilisation (c 1550 BC).

In the plastic arts both the Minoans and the mainlanders achieved their finest results when working on a small scale. Among their most valuable legacies are the sealstones and gold signet rings, which in a largely illiterate world were used as a means of identification. In the hands of Minoan craftsmen their engraving became a highly developed pictorial art: their subjects vary from intimate studies of animal and bird life to detailed representation of cult scenes, which supply us with our main source of information on the obscure topic of Minoan and Mycenaean religion.

## Hellenic Art

**I. Architecture**. The chief glory of Greek architecture is the Doric temple. Clay models from Perachora (8C BC) and the Argive Heraion (7C BC) reveal its embryonic form, which resembled the domestic megaron of prehistoric times: a columnar porch (pronaos) led into a long hall (cella) which housed the image of the god: the roof gables were steeply pitched, and must have been thatched. In the earliest temples the roof of the pronaos was already supported by columns, arranged either between the forward continuations of the side walls (in antis) or, less commonly, in a free-standing colonnade across the front (prostyle). Behind these columns a single entrance gave access to the cella, and remained its only source of lighting: if necessary, the wooden beams of the ceiling were supported by one or two rows of internal columns. (The latter arrangement was eventually preferred, since a single row down the centre would interfere with the setting of the cult statue.) Behind the rear wall of the cella, the pronaos was often duplicated by a second porch, the opisthodomos. Since the walls of the cella were at first built of mud brick on a timber frame, the larger temples from c 700 BC onwards were protected from the rain by a continuous veranda with an outer row of columns all round the building (peripteron).

Both the columns and the superstructure (entablature) were originally constructed of wood, and many of their characteristic features, when later translated into stone, recall the original material. Doric columns were placed directly on the upper foundations (stylobate) without any base, and tapered upwards like tree-trunks, with a pronounced convex curve (entasis): their broad and concave flutes, meeting each other at a sharp angle, might have resulted from the use of a rounded adze to shape a wooden log. Their capitals consist of two parts: a round cushion with a curved profile (echinus), supporting a square abacus. The entablature above the peripteron comprises the plain architrave, the typically Doric frieze where square metopes, sometimes bearing relief sculpture, alternate with grooved triglyphs (representing wooden beam-ends), and the projecting cornice (geison), whose two members, horizontal and sloping, frame the triangular pediments at the façades.

In the Heraion at Olympia (c 600 BC), although the columns and entablature were originally of wood, all these essential elements of the Doric order were already present: the temple had attained a monumental maturity at a time when secular builing was still in its infancy. In the next two centuries its proportions were considerably improved, but the basic plan remained unaltered. Soon after, perhaps owing to the oppressive weight of the newly

## Doric

## Ionic

## Greek Orders of Architecture

| | | |
|---|---|---|
| A. | Pediment | f. Frieze |
| B. | Entablature | g. Triglyphs |
| C. | Column | h. Metopes |
| D. | Crepidoma | i. Regulae & Guttae |
| a. | Acroterion | j. Architrave or Epistyle |
| b. | Sima | k₁ Capital (Doric) |
| c. | Geison or Cornice | k₂ Capital (Ionic) with Volutes |
| d. | Tympanum | l. Abacus |
| e. | Mutules & Guttae | m. Echinus |

| | |
|---|---|
| n₁ | Shaft with flutes separated by sharp arrises. |
| n₂ | Shaft with flutes separated by blunt fillets |
| o. | Bases |
| p. | Stylobate |
| q. | Euthynteria |
| r. | Stereobate |

**Corinthian Capital**

**Pergamene Capital**

invented clay roof-tiles, the whole structure was translated into limestone. At first the new medium was treated with caution: the monolithic columns of the temple at Corinth (c 540 BC), the earliest in Greece that still remain standing, are extremely stout and closely bunched: their capitals are as broad as possible, so as to diminish the span of the massive architrave lintels. Further experience brought greater confidence: the columns became progressively taller, thinner, and more widely spaced, the capitals narrower and lighter: both tended to lose their curved profile. Limestone shafts were most conveniently built up in drums, and their appearance was improved by a coat of stucco: but even so they could not vie either in beauty or strength with the marble that the Athenians had begun to quarry from Mt Pentelikon, at the end of the 6C. Thereafter, beginning with her Treasury at Delphi (c 490 BC), Athens used marble for her religious buildings. Further aesthetic progress was made in the 5C with the beginning of the temple's ground plan: the cella was now furnished with increasing elaboration, and the cult statue was often flanked (as at Aegina) by a two-storeyed colonnade. The splendour of the façades was immeasurably enhanced by the magnificent groups of pedimental sculpture of Aegina (c 500–480 BC) and of the Temple of Zeus of Olympia (c 460 BC). After 200 years of experiment, the Doric style reaches its climax in the Parthenon, finished in 438 BC. Apart from the superlative excellence of the famous sculptured decorations, a new subtlety is introduced by the rising curves of stylobate and entablature, and the inwardly slanting axis of the peripteral columns.

After the perfection of the late 5C, progress on purely Doric lines was hardly possible: but stagnation was happily averted, since mainland architects had begun to interest themselves in other styles. The Ionic order, first evolved across the Aegean in the 6C, had already found mature expression in the grandiose and ebullient temples of Artemis at Ephesus and in the Heraion of Samos, both surrounded by a double peripteron. The Ionic of Attica assumed a more restrained form, illustrated by the Erechtheion and the Temple of Nike (last quarter of 5C): apart from their well-known volute capitals, Ionic columns differ from Doric in their elaborately moulded bases, their slimmer shafts, and their deeper fluting: the architrave is divided into three shallow horizontal slabs, with a continuous frieze above, often bearing sculptured decoration. Doric and Ionic elements were often successfully married, especially by Attic architects: inside the Propylaea tall and graceful Ionic colonnades were happily combined by Mnesikles with a massive Doric exterior; his colleague Iktinos introduced Ionic sculptured friezes outside the cella of the Parthenon, and round the interior of the Temple of Apollo at Bassae (c 450–420 BC). This remote highland sanctuary also preserves the earliest known Corinthian capital: the Corinthian order (which differs from the Ionic only in the acanthus capital) was subsequently much exploited in the interiors of 4C BC buildings, reaching great heights of delicacy in the Temple of Athena Alea at Tegea and in the Tholos at Epidaurus. Its use on a gigantic scale in the double peripteron of the Temple of Olympian Zeus at Athens (174 BC–AD 138) reflects the more flamboyant taste of a later epoch; but even in Hellenistic times the Doric order was never wholly ousted, appearing in extremely attenuated form in the Temple of Isis on Delos. This is one of the few religious buildings of this period which survived to any height: in the secular field, however, the versatility of the Hellenistic architect is attested by many *stoas* (best represented by that of Attalos in Athens, c 150 BC), by the gabled façades of Macedonian built tombs, and by the ingenious octagonal water-clock in Athens, known as the 'Tower of the Winds' (c 40 BC).

**II. Sculpture**. Greek monumental sculpture began under the influence of Egypt in the 7C BC, when life-size statues of marble and limestone were first made in Crete, in the Peloponnese, and in the Cyclades. Attica entered the field with the kouros from Sounion (c 600 BC), first of a long line of nude male figures offered at tombs or dedicated at local shrines. In this great work, nearly twice life-size, we are inevitably reminded of Egyptian proto-types by the stance (left foot forward), by the rigidity of the arms, by the stylised wig, and by the stiffness of the whole conception: but whereas the Egyptians directed their chief attention to the undulating surfaces of the skin, the sharp transitions of the early Attic statue show a determination to clarify the bone structure underneath. After this ambitious start, the kouroi from Volomandra (c 560 BC), Anavysos (c 530 BC), and Ptoön (c 510 BC), illustrate the gradual process made by 6C sculptors in defining the anatomy of the human body at rest. With each generation, the transitions at the neck, the hips and the knee-caps are more convincingly rendered and the modelling becomes more rounded and assured. By the time of the Kritian Boy (c 480 BC) complete anatomical mastery has been attained: the body has become an organic whole, no longer the sum of its parts. The parallel series of korai (the maiden votaries of Athena dedicated on the Acropolis) reveals another facet of the archaic genius: the power to create harmonious patterns from the gay and elaborate Ionian draperies that came into fashion at the court of the Athenian tyrant Peisistratos and his sons: none, however, is more beautiful than the vivacious Peplos Kore (c 530 BC) who still wears the plainer Doric dress.

Archaic sculptors devoted much of their thought to the decoration of temples and treasuries. Ionic friezes and Doric metopes were both adorned in relief: friezes invited continuous narrative scenes, like the Battle of the Gods and Giants on the Siphnian Treasury at Delphi (c 525 BC) while the square metopes were more suitable for detached episodes, such as the Labours of Herakles, and other single combats. In the triangular pediments, the sculptures were carved in the round and attached to the background by iron dowels: the awkward shape of the field presented a stern challenge to the artist's power of grouping his figures in an effective ensemble, and thus forced him to depart from the rigidly frontal pose of the free-standing statues. Here, too, battle scenes made good compositions. The early 'Hydra' and 'Triton' pedimental groups from the Acropolis (c 570–560 BC) show Herakles engaged with scaly monsters whose tails fit conveniently into the lower angles: more ambitiously, a later group from the Acropolis showing the Battle of Gods and Giants (c 520 BC) and the groups from Aegina (c 500–480 BC) were entirely constructed from human figures, embattled and closely entwined, either striding, falling, kneeling, crouching, or lying wounded in the corners. The Lapiths and Centaurs from the West pediment at Olympia (c 460 BC) bring this spirited tradition to a tempestuous climax.

With such valuable experience behind them, the sculptors of freestanding statues in the Early Classical period (c 480–450 BC) boldly departed from the archaic frontal stance. The Kritian Boy (c 480 BC) is allowed to relax, with the weight of the body unevenly divided; in place of the typical archaic smile, the features have assumed the noble severity also found in the Apollo at Olympia, who calmly presides over the struggle between Lapith and Centaur. Other masterpieces of this period are two bronze statues, the Delphic Charioteer (c 475 BC) and the Poseidon of Artemision (c 460 BC); the contrast between the static repose of the charioteer and the dynamic energy of the god emphasises the tremendous vitality of this versatile generation. In a century when the finest sculptors worked in bronze, it is a tragedy that so few life-size bronze originals of this time survive. Pheidias

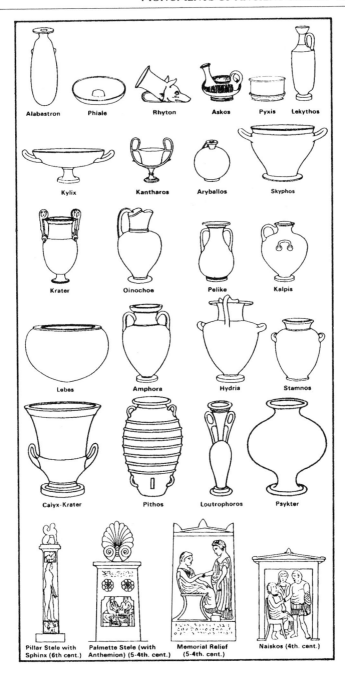

Alabastron    Phiale    Rhyton    Askos    Pyxis    Lekythos

Kylix    Kantharos    Aryballos    Skyphos

Krater    Oinochoe    Pelike    Kalpis

Lebes    Amphora    Hydria    Stamnos

Calyx-Krater    Pithos    Loutrophoros    Psykter

Pillar Stele with Sphinx (6th cent.)    Palmette Stele (with Anthemion) (5-4th. cent.)    Memorial Relief (5-4th. cent.)    Naiskos (4th. cent.)

of Athens and Polykleitos of Argos represent the high noon of classical sculpture in the middle and third quarter of the 5C BC. Two over-life-size bronze warriors of commanding presence, recovered from the sea off Riace in Calabria and now in the Reggio museum, have been attributed to the hand of Pheidias. Otherwise, for our knowledge of the genius of these sculptors, we were largely dependent on the marble copies—and art critics —of Roman times: however accurate the copies, and however discerning the critics may have been, we can only contemplate the achievement of the great masters through the eyes of a later age. We know that Pheidias superintended the building and the adornment of the Parthenon; yet few, if any, of the existing sculptures can have been chiselled by his own hand, and all would have been considered minor works in comparison with his colossal gold and ivory (chryselephantine) cult images of Athena Parthenos and of Olympian Zeus, both irretrievably lost. Nevertheless we can get some idea of the serene majesty of his style from such Parthenon marbles as still remain in Athens: from the gods and horsemen of the frieze, and from the fine and vigorous metope (Lapith and Centaur) that still remains in position at the SW corner of the Temple: although their features are still idealised, the figures are realistically posed, and their drapery falls in natural folds. In the next generation, the Nike of Paionios at Olympia (c 420 BC) and the reliefs from the Nike Balustrade at Athens (c 410 BC) illustrate a novel fashion for windswept diaphanous garments, through which the outline of the body can be clearly discerned.

In the 4C sculpture lost much of its monumental quality, and began to express the moods of individual human beings. The style of Praxiteles is well-known to us from his Hermes at Olympia (c 360 BC), while a bronze original in Athens, the Marathon Youth, may belong to his school: the softer outlines, the completely relaxed pose, the unprecedented wealth of detail in the modelling, and above all the gentle, dreamy expression of the eyes and mouth are all typical of the new spirit. His contemporary Skopas, to whose hand, or influence, the surviving heads from the Temple at Tegea are attributed, specialised in studies of violent emotion. Lysippos was renowned for the creation of a completely realistic athletic type, less heavily built than before and with a smaller head. These new proportions are embodied in the Agias at Delphi (c 320 BC); more moving, perhaps, is a work of great beauty and pathos which reflects his style: the tombstone (stele) from the Ilissos (Athens, No. 869) showing a father lamenting the death of his son, killed while hunting.

Lysippos was of the few privileged artists who were commissioned to execute portraits of Alexander the Great, and in the Hellenistic period individualistic portraiture reached a high level of achievement. A fine early example is the brutally realistic bronze bust of the boxer Satyros from Olympia (c 330 BC): later Greeks artists found a ready market among the Italian business men on Delos (c 100 BC), whose features they rendered with extreme candour. The scope of themes was vastly enlarged: foreign racial types, childhood, old age, and deformity all came within the sculptors' repertoire. The spirited Boy Jockey from Artemision (c 220 BC), who is clearly not of Hellenic stock, is a typical subject: characteristic, too, is his pose, which offers a satisfactory composition from every viewpoint. Whatever the aesthetic merit of this work, technical virtuosity could hardly be carried further.

**III. Painting and Pottery**. The decoration of clay vases deserves an honourable place in the annals of Greek art for two reasons: first because the potter's craft preserves the only continuous artistic link between the Mycenaean and Hellenic civilisations; secondly, with the loss of almost all free painting of the finest period (6–4C BC), the art of vase-painting remains almost the sole witness to the pictorial talent of the Greeks.

After the collapse of Mycenae Athens became the chief source of ceramic ideas. In the Dark Age the decoration of pottery is severely abstract, but always relevant to the shape. On Protogeometric vases (11–10C BC) the patterns are mainly confined to neat sets of concentric circles and semi-circles derived from the slovenly spirals of the latest Mycenaean: in the full developed Geometric style (9–8C BC) the ornament becomes rectilinear in character, and the meander assumes the leading rôle. Representational art is reborn towards the end of the period (c 750 BC) when huge vases, which served as grave markers, bear stylised funerary scenes. Each region has its own local style.

The renewal of contact with the Near East ushered in an Orientalising phase (7C BC) when Greek potters borrowed the fauna and flora of Syro-Phoenician art and adapted them for their own purposes. Corinth seized the initiative in art as well as in commerce, and created a delicate miniature style ('Protocorinthian') based on animal friezes, lotus-flowers, and palmettes: when humans appear, mythical scenes may sometimes be recognised. On small vases the technique known as black-figure was first perfected: figures were first drawn in silhouette (as in Geometric times), and then elaborated with incised detail; and finally touches of colour were added in purple or white. Other Orientalising figured styles arose in Attica ('Protoattic'), Laconia, the Cyclades, and Rhodes: all could match the vitality of Protocorinthian drawing, but none could excel its purity of line. In each of these regional schools, the details were at first rendered in outline, but by the end of the 7C the black-figure technique had been universally adopted under the influence of Corinth.

In Attica, where the most ambitious potters had cultivated a wild and grandiose style (best illustrated by the 'Polyphemus' amphora in Eleusis, c 660 BC) the arrival of incision imposed a salutary discipline: on a late Protoattic masterpiece, the Nessos amphora in Athens (c 610 BC), Attic grandeur is tempered by Corinthian refinement; out of this promising union grew the mature Attic Black-figure style of the 6C BC, when Athens retrieved the artistic and commercial initiative from Corinth, and eventually established a monopoly in the production of fine figured pottery. Animal friezes were now subordinated to scenes of human action, depicting the narratives of Greek mythology: the most popular themes were provided by the cycle of the Trojan war, the Labours of Herakles, and the revels of Dionysos with his attendant rout of satyrs and maenads. Black-figured drawing reached the limits of its potentialities in the work of Exekias (c 540–525 BC), who succeeded in endowing his figures with a new spiritual quality: the calyx-krater in the Agora Museum is a worthy example of his quiet and reflective manner.

The invention of the Red-figure technique (c 530 BC) allowed the painter greater freedom of expression. The colour scheme was now reversed, the figures being left in the orange tone of the clay, while the background was filled in with lustrous black; inner details could be rendered in brown or black paint, depending on the strength of the solution. By c 500 BC the finest artists were using the new technique, and had begun to lay the foundations of European representational drawing. A passionate interest in the structure of the human body led them to vary the pose of their figures: vigorous experiment with three-quarter views and foreshortened limbs introduced for the first time the illusion of a third dimension. At the same time the repertoire of themes became greatly extended, as scenes from daily life took their place beside heroic and dionysiac subjects.

Red-figured vase painting reached its highest level of achievement in the first quarter of the 5C BC, when the new medium had been fully mastered: the figures on these late archaic vases are drawn with a supple vigour that makes most subsequent work look somewhat staid and academic by contrast. With the rapid advance of sculpture and free painting after c 475 BC, the decoration of pottery was gradually reduced to a minor art, which no longer attracted artists of the front rank. A distinguished exception here is the work of the Achilles painter (c 450–430 BC) who specialised in the production of oil-flasks (lekythoi) for funerary use, decorated in subdued matt colours against a white background. His figures, isolated and statuesque, reflect the classical serenity of the Parthenon sculptures, with which they are contemporary, and enable us to visualise something of the grandeur of classical free painting. But in the 4C the figured decoration of pottery became a degenerate art, and in Attica it had died out in c 320 BC.

Tantalising glimpses of figured mural painting in the 4–3C BC are offered by the built tombs of western Macedonia. Scenes in the three royal tombs of the Great Tumulus at Vergina represent the late Classical flowering of this monumental art, already enlivened by a daring use of chiaroscuro. On the façade of the Great Tomb at Lefkadhia, the scene of Judgement in Hades, with its four statuesque figures, is a masterpiece of early Hellenistic times. Slighter work of the 3C BC may be seen on the Thessalian painted gravestones (stelai) in Volos museum.

**IV. Minor Arts**. Terracotta figurines were usually offered as votives at sanctuaries, representing either the deity or the worshippers. They were always freely modelled until the early 7C BC, when the introduction of the clay mould from the eastern Mediterranean eventually led to mass production. Archaic and Classical terracottas follow the current sculptural style, sometimes brightly coloured. The most frequent subjects are seated goddesses and standing draped women; types of unusual interest are jointed dolls (5–4C BC) and masked actors from Middle and New Comedy (4C BC). Outstanding among Hellenistic figurines are the draped females in the Tanagra style, named after the Boeotian city where they were first noted, but initially made in Athens and imitated in many other Greek centres. Realistically portrayed in the fashionable dress and hair style of their time, the women are less stereotyped than earlier figurines, and possess an alluring grace and charm.

Bronze figurines, cast in solid metal, were also initially associated with sanctuaries. Geometric figures of horses and men, sometimes attached to the ring handles of vast tripod cauldrons, are prominent among the early votives at Olympia and Delphi, followed by the Archaic shield bands of Olympia which present mythical scenes in relief. Because of their small scale, bronze figurines of the Archaic and Classical periods often show a greater freedom of pose than contemporary statues. Archaic reclining banqueters and Classical female dancers are typical subjects, and figurines may also serve as handles for mirrors or large vessels. Hellenistic bronze figurines share the extreme virtuosity and accomplishment of larger statues.

After the Dark Age the art of seal-engraving was recovered in the 8C BC. A square Argive Geometric class, using various soft stones, was succeeded by the ivory disc seals of Corinth (7C BC) on which the designs recall the finesse of Protocorinthian pottery. The Island gems of Melos, meanwhile, revive the shapes and sometimes the motifs of Minoan prototypes. Shortly before 550 BC East Aegean workshops appear to have led the way in introducing gems in the form of Egyptianising scarabs, using hard stones such as cornelian, chalcedony and rock crystal. Thus began a gem-engraving tradition of surpassingly high achievement, culminating in the work of Dexamenos of Chios in the late 5C BC. By then the scarab had been replaced by the scaraboid with domed back, and the gems were often placed on swivels to serve as bezels for metal finger rings. The fixed intaglios of Classical rings, whether on inset stones or cut into the metal, display less subtlety of modelling. An innovation of the Hellenistic period, pursued further in Roman times, was the engraving of cameos, exploiting differently coloured layers of onyx.

Coinage, invented in the Lydian kingdom of western Asia Minor, became established in Greece during the 6C BC. Silver was the preferred metal, even for the smallest denominations; electrum and gold were rare alternatives. Each minting city chose its own obverse and reverse designs from patron deities, heroes and creatures associated with local cults or myths; thus on Athenian coins a helmeted head of Athena occupies the obverse, and her owl the reverse with the first three letters of the city's name. As with the gems, the engraving of intaglios on the two bronze dies, between which the coins were punched, called for consummate skill and artistry. Local pride and conservatism might require the retention of the same emblems over several centuries; but, as old dies wore out, new ones kept pace with current sculptural styles. Alexander the Great, in the mints of his expanding empire, created an important precedent in introducing his own head on the obverse, gradually replacing that of Herakles who had been adopted by his predecessors as an appropriate hero for the Macedonian kingdom. His example was followed by the rulers of the large Hellenistic kingdoms and, eventually, by Roman emperors; it was left to the Romans, however, to devise reverse designs for imperial propaganda.

# BYZANTINE ART AND ARCHITECTURE IN GREECE

by **Professor Karin M. Skawran**

The Byzantine monuments which are discussed here lie within the limits of the Greek state as it exists today. The limitation to Greece is arbitrary since no frontiers between this area and the rest of the Byzantine world existed. Greece today is a varied territory which comprises the mountainous end of the Balkan peninsula, a fringe of western islands, including Corfu (Kerkyra) and the numerous Aegean islands extending to Crete, Rhodes and the coast of Asiatic Turkey.

The mainland is so fragmented by mountains and inlets of the sea that, formerly, many of the settled areas were largely dependent, like the islands, on sea communications. But regional isolation, when sea travel was perilous, was offset by the impact of direct seaborne contact with the capital at Constantinople in normal times, when the Aegean also provided sea-lanes between East and West.

Athens, with only modest local resources, was particularly vulnerable and, despite its central position, did not during the Byzantine period enjoy the dominant position it does today. Thessaloníki, on the other hand, sustained by the fertile Macedonian plains at the gateway to the Balkan hinterland, enjoyed an easy land link with the capital across the rolling hills of Thrace. Significantly it was here, at Ferai near the present Turkish frontier, that a prince of the imperial house founded the Monastery of Kosmosoteira and, not far away, on the precipitous peninsula of Mount Athos, arose the greatest of all Orthodox monastic communities. In Thessaloníki itself, the second city of the Empire, the **Panayia ton Khalkeon**, as well as the recently uncovered 12C frescoes in Osios David, bear the strongest imprint of metropolitan influence.

Westward, the same arterial link, the Via Egnatia, continued more precariously through the Albanian mountains to the Adriatic coast and thence by sea to the West. Nevertheless in the Greek part of this region, centres such as Kastoria usually share a similar local character with their neighbours of the Balkan fringe.

South of Mount Olympus the settlements around the plain of Thessaly form another entity which, apart from the **Koimesis** church at Kalambaka (Church of the Dormition), preserves little from the height of the Byzantine period. Further S the central Pindus range effectively bisects the country, leaving the entire territory of Ioannina and Arta to Navpaktos isolated to the W. To the E, the Boeotian plain nourished one of the richest silk industries of the Empire.

Close by, isolated by the summits of Helicon, which shut off this plain from the Gulf of Corinth, stands the great Monastery of Holy Luke (**Osios Loukas**). Southward of the Isthmus and the Argolid, in the adjoining territories of Thebes, Athens and Corinth (all three commercial and administrative centres of importance) was the heartland of the Greek province in Byzantine times.

Beyond the fertile plains of Argos, a tangle of mountains fills the northern Peloponnese. With their offshoots, the towering range of Taygetos and the lower mass of Parnon, these mountains leave only restricted areas for prosperous settlement: upland Arcadia; the Laconian plain that nourished Lacedaemon (the ancient Sparta), later to be abandoned for the greater security of nearby Mistra; the smiling land of Messenia, preserving in the **Zoödhokhos Piyi** at Samarina one of the most sophisticated churches in Greece, and, to the NW, the plains of Elis and Achaea, extending to the port of Patras at the entrance to the Gulf of Corinth. Yet it is in the remote regions that most of the surviving monuments are to be found: in eastern Laconia at Yeraki, the sea-girt stronghold of Monemvasia, and in the rugged peninsula of Mani.

Nearby Kythera always provided a stepping-stone to Crete and, like that large island, could offer a port of call for traffic from E to W, a circumstance of which some of their early frescoes remind us (in Kythera, the Cave chapel of Ay. Sophia on the N coast, near Milopotamos and Ay. Demitrios near Pourko; in Crete, Ay. Eutykhios and the Catholicon of the Monastery of Myriokephala near Rethymnon).

The Dodecanese and Rhodes itself, the gateway to the Aegean from the E, have little to offer, with the important exception of Patmos, where the fortified **Monastery of St John the Divine** boasts some of the finest frescoes of the Middle Byzantine period. The other islands off the Asiatic coast—Samos, Chios and Lesbos—marked stages on an important sea route to the capital. Chios especially, in the **Nea Moni**, boasts an imperial foundation and preserves other fine churches.

The Cyclades, despite their central position in the Aegean, could still be isolated, and in some cases even rendered uninhabitable, by the piracy with which the islands were often plagued. Nevertheless, in the sheltered interior of **Naxos**, recent exploration has brought to light some of the earliest church frescoes surviving in Greece (Ay. Artemios; the Cave church of the Nativity of the abandoned Monastery of the Kaloritissa near Sangri; Ay. Kyriaki near Apeiranthos). Santorini has an imperial foundation in the frescoed church of **Panayia tis Gonias**. In contrast few painted churches have as yet been reported from the western islands, even from the largest, Corfu (Kerkyra) (Ay. Merkourios, near the village of Ay. Markos and Ay. Nikolaos, Kato Korakiana).

## The Early Christian period (4–7C)

Long-lasting peace and security resulted in the building of a large number of churches and the conversion of some pagan temples into Christian churches. Over the past years, archaeologists have uncovered the remains of over 300 basilicas, either *extra muros* or within city boundaries, as at **Philippi** and **Amphipolis** (Macedonia), in **Nicopolis** (Epirus), **Thebes** (near Volos) and **Corinth**. In Thessaloniki some of these early basilicas have been fully preserved. Their vast proportions and grandeur were never again equalled.

In the 5C, after the edicts by Theodosius II and Valentinianus III, all pagan temples were closed or converted into **Christian churches**, e.g. the Parthenon, the Erechtheion, the Theseion and many others in Athens; the workshop of Pheidias at Olympia; the Athena temple at Tegea; the Galerius Mausoleum (Rotunda) in Thessaloniki; as well as sanctuaries on the islands of Naxos, Sikinos and Kea. Only a few buildings have been assigned to the 4C (basilica at Epidaurus) and only a few have been preserved from the end of the 6th to the middle of the 7C. It seems that this period witnessed the restoration and rebuilding of churches from the previous centuries.

During this Early Christian period the basilican type of church predominated. It is normally characterised by its longitudinal groundplan and was approached on the W through a colonnaded *atrium* (outer courtyard). On its E side the *narthex* (vestibule) was entered through two doors, which in turn gave access to the *naos* (church proper) through a *trivelon* (three-arched arcade, supported by two columns). The interior of the basilica consisted of a central nave, usually wood-roofed and raised above the side aisles to incorporate a clerestory. The nave was separated from the aisles by arched colonnades. In the E it terminated in a semicircular apse which usually protruded on the exterior. There are several variants of this type with a transverse aisle at the eastern end as at Philippi, Nicopolis, the Ilissos in Athens, and Panormos in Crete. In some of these churches the transverse aisle protrudes on the N and S sides, terminating in lateral apses. This cloverleaf type of groundplan can be found in Epirus (Paramithia, Dodona) and central Greece (Klapsi).

Five-aisled basilicas with a transverse aisle are rare (Ay. Diemitrios in Thessaloniki and the basilicas in Epidaurus and Nicopolis); so also are basilicas with a domed centralised cross layout (Thasos, Paros). Basilicas with a central cupola developed in the 6 and 7C in Philippi (Basilica B) and in Athens, Paros and Gortyna (Crete). Variants are the octagonally planned basilica in Philippi and the inscribed-cross type of groundplan of Osios David in Thessaloniki.

Much of the lavish decoration which characterised the interior of these basilicas consisted of sculptural decoration, particularly on the capitals, cornices and on the chancel screen (*iconostasis*), which separated the *naos* from the sanctuary, as well as on the *ambo* (lectern). The floor and the lower part of the walls were covered in marble, while the upper sections were decorated with mosaics. This is particularly evident in the basilicas of

Thessaloniki. Here one can witness the transition from the late phase of ancient art to a purely Byzantine style, for example in the dome mosaics of the **Rotunda of St George** (5–6C). Two or three figures of saints, depicted frontally and in a strict hieratic pose, have been placed in front of elegant stage-like façades, reminiscent of Hellenistic art. The impressionistic-painterly style of these mosaics also strongly recalls the late phase of ancient art. In the **Acheiropoietos** church, apart from the beautifully preserved marble floor of the nave, colourful mosaics adorn the soffits of the arches of the colonnades. The images of plant and bird life bear Christian symbolic connotations. The apse mosaic of **Osios David** (5–7C) and the magnificent wall mosaics of **Ay. Demitrios**, are characterised by their purely Byzantine style and can be compared with the mosaics in Ravenna.

### The period from mid-seventh to mid-ninth centuries

During this period Greece experienced dark times. The Empire was impoverished by economic crises and thrown into turmoil by the invasions of tribes from the N and by the Arabs who, from the beginning of the 7C, had invaded the country and had settled on the coasts of North Africa, Egypt and Syria. They occupied Crete in 823. Trade routes by sea were cut off and there was little building activity. Many buildings of previous periods had been destroyed by earthquakes in 521 and 551, and had fallen victim to the invaders. The Iconoclastic movement of the 8th and 9C also had devastating results, especially for painting. Most images depicting holy personnages were destroyed. Some non-figurative paintings in the remoter areas of Eurytania (Episkopi); Naxos (Ay. Artemios; Ay. Kyriaki); Mani (Ay. Prokopios), Crete and Ikaria are considered to be late survivals of the Iconoclast tradition.

### The mid-ninth to twelfth centuries (Middle Byzantine period)

The liberation of Crete (961) and the victory of Basil II over the Bulgars (1018) resulted in a renewed building activity during this period. The monastic movement also experienced a new height. On Mount Athos several large monasteries and churches were built.

Thebes in Boeotia, the capital of the *thema* Hellas (administrative centre and seat of the *strategos,* the civil and military governor of southern Greece) developed as an important administrative, economic and artistic centre. Its silk industry became famous, as did the orientalising style of some of its stone sculpture. The one-aisled Ay. Ioannis Theologos (872) was built by Basileos, a well-known dignitary. Another dignitary was responsible for the Panayia church in **Skripou** on the site of ancient Orchomenos. Important churches were erected also in Eurytania (the Episkopi church, today submerged underwater and its frescoes moved to the Byzantine Museum, Athens) and the churches on Skyros (895) and in the vicinity of Thessaloniki (Peristera, c 871).

This cultural revival lasted through the region of the Comnenes in the 12C to the conquest of Constantinople by the Crusaders in 1204 and the foundation of the short-lived Latin Empire (1204–61).

Here and there, a few of the great wood-roofed basilicas, which had been almost universal in the early period, survived the hiatus created by the Slav migrations and Arab supremacy at sea. One of them, the **Panayia Acheiropoieitos** in Thessaloniki, was partially redecorated in this period. Like the converted temples such as the Parthenon itself, they ensured among the builders of the much less ambitious churches of the later period a frequent preference for the three-aisled basilican form, particularly for metropolitan churches (Koimesis church, Kalambaka). These later basilicas, usually of smaller dimensions, either retained the colonnades of their prototypes, as in the **Taxiarchis Mitropoleos** at Kastoria, or, when columns were lacking, substituted arcades on masonry piers, as in **Ayioi Anargyroi** in the same town and the Basilica at Servia. In some cases columns and piers alternated, as at Kalambaka and Ay. Stephanos at Kastoria. Sometimes lack of timber imposed the substitution of masonry vaults over both nave and aisles, often without clerestory windows, so providing greater scope for painted decoration, as in Ay. Ioannis Theologos, Naxos and Ay. Pandeleimon, Crete.

For smaller churches, especially in the early phase of recovery and in more remote regions, the simplest type of chapel prevailed: a single rectangular chamber with an apse, either with a pitched roof of timber and tiles (Ay. Nikolaos Kasnitzi at Kastoria) or spanned by a masonry vault (as in Ay. Prokopios, Mani). A variant common to both classes provided twin apses opening from the single chamber, either wood-roofed (Ay. Merkourios, Corfu) or vaulted, as in Ay. Pandeleimon, Ano Boularioi, Mani.

Even in Salonica, despite the example of the great Rotunda which was converted into a church in the 5C, church-builders were slow to adopt the system of roofing with vaults and domes, developed in Byzantium under Justinian and of which Greece preserved only one contemporary example in the great church at **Paros**. **Ay. Sophia** in Thessaloniki, a domed square enclosed by a vaulted ambulatory which was built in the eighth century, is transitional in both form and date, for it was constructed when Greece was largely swamped by migrations.

As the recovery of the province proceeded, what was to be the classic form of the domed church in our period crystallised in the capital: the inscribed-cross domed type. This was a square hall of modest size with a small central dome carried on four piers, or, ideally, columns and abutted by four radiating barrel-vaults with lower domical or cross-vaults (sometimes small domes) over the corner bays, the whole preceded by a *narthex* or vestibule at the W and screened on the E from the tripartite sanctuary. This last comprised the central *bema* with the altar flanked by the *prothesis* for the preparation of the sacrament on the N and the *diaconicon* or sacristy on the S. This architectural scheme provided, at no great distance from the worshipper, ample surfaces for figural decoration in support of the teaching of the Church, and its standardisation led to a large measure of uniformity in the arrangement of the subjects represented.

Closer ties with the capital, particularly in the 11 and 12C, were reflected in the Greek church-builders' gradual rejection of the basilica in favour of this and other domed forms. The classic type was introduced in Greece sometimes quite unchanged and with columns, not piers, as in the **Panayia ton Khalkeon**, Thessaloniki and the **Theotokos** church, Osios Loukas. More often it was modified by adjustments to the basilica tradition. The square and strictly centralised *naos*, the church proper, was often elongated and the corner bays tended to retain the barrel-vaults which had covered the aisles of the vaulted basilicas. Frequently the *naos* and the sanctuary were telescoped so that the E vault abutting the dome covered the *bema*, its flanking corner bays became the *prothesis* and *diaconicon*, and the *iconostasis* was moved to line up with the pair of columns supporting the eastern arch of the dome, as at Episkopi, Santorini. This telescoping of *naos* and sanctuary was more usually achieved by retaining only the two western columns of the classic type and by supporting the E side of the dome on the two solid walls of the originally separate sanctuary. This simplified plan was frequently adopted for Greek churches from the late 11C and is found in many parts of the country, for instance in the church of Samarina, Messenia;

Ay. Iason and Sosipatros, Corfu; it was very popular in the Mani (Ay. Stratigos, Ano Boularioi; Episkopi, Tigani).

In many of the earlier domed churches, instead of the isolated columns of the classic Constantinopolitan type, solid walls pierced by openings separate the corner bays (Episkopi, Eurytania; Metamorphosis near Koropi, Attica; Protothronos, Naxos).

In some regions and on the islands small domed churches of the most elementary inscribed-cross type are found. In these simple, one-aisled chapels the N and S cross-arms appear internally only as shallow arched recesses, as in several Naxos examples, like Ay. Kyriaki, Ay. Yioryios, and Ay. Pakhomios, all in the vicinity of Apeiranthos. The cruciform character of the superstructure is usually quite apparent from the outside, and where it is not, a dome has been set somewhat arbitrarily above the middle of a simple vaulted one-aisled chapel (Ay. Eutychios in Crete). The free-standing cross plan was also sometimes used for domed churches of modest size, as in the **Panayia Damiotissa**, Naxos. The related triconch type with lateral apses in place of the side-arms of the cross occasionally occurs, though not in any painted church of our period; the **Panayia Drosiani**, Naxos is an earlier example. The Koubelidiki in Kastoria is a 10C triconch church and contains frescoes from a later period.

Most Middle Byzantine churches in Greece of the foreign types are of small dimensions. To meet the needs of some major monastic foundations such as Nea Moni on Chios and Osios Loukas, their founders could use a more ambitious formula, what may be called the large-dome type. In these churches the dome covers the whole span of the square *naos*, the corners of which are bridged by squinches to form the octagonal base of the large dome, as at Nea Moni, Chios and in others on the same island. In an enlargement of this type, barrel-vaulted arms extend from the four cardinal arches to an outer rectangle of which the corner spaces are filled with chapels, for instance in Ay. Sophia, Monemvasia and Ay. Nikolaos 'sta Kambia', near Orchomenos. In one case, the Catholicon of Osios Loukas, the surrounding chapels carry galleries.

From the overall architectural types we may pass to some significant component features. The *narthex* is not always present in the Greek churches. When it occurs in earlier buildings it is roofed in the simplest way with a continuous transverse barrel-vault, as in the Episkopi church, Eurytania. Later, the normal arrangement in domed churches was to differentiate a central bay by roofing it at a higher level, with a vault running east-west. In the Mani the wall between the west cross-arm and the *narthex* is frequently suppressed and the west vault continues unbroken from the dome to the west wall of the *narthex*. The central bay of the *narthex* is thus included in the main body of the church, giving it the elongated proportions of a basilica, as in Ay. Stratigos, Ano Boularioi. Very rarely a gallery is added over the *narthex*: in the Panayia ton Khalkeon, Thessaloniki (with domes over the outer bays), and in the much smaller church of Ay. Stephanos, Kastoria. The outer vestibule (*exonarthex*) is almost unknown. Exceptionally, the Samarina church has an elegant portico with a domed belfry flanked by bays with domical vaults. These domical vaults are used in the same church in the western corner bays; like the groined cross-vaults used in the Crypt of Osios Loukas and Ay. Nikolaos 'sta Kambia', they belong to the central Byzantine tradition. In Greece these forms seldom supplanted the almost universal barrel-vaults either in the cross-arms or in the corner bays.

A preference for unified surfaces and neat contours in the Greek churches contrasts with the more articulated façades favoured in the capital and followed in the Panayia ton Khalkeon. Occasionally, however, the form of the lateral cross-arm is repeated as a buttressing arch on the façade, for instance in the Theotokos church, Osios Loukas.

The semicircular apse and the cylindrical dome drum characterise the earlier churches in Greece and they were never altogether abandoned. The use of poor building stone imposed their retention in some remote places, as in the apse of Ay. Stratigos, Ano Boularioi, Mani; Ay. Ioannis Theologos and Ay. Kyriaki in Naxos; for it was easier to build rounded forms than polygonal ones in rubble construction. Semi-hexagonal apses and octagonal dome drums appeared earlier in major churches where brick and dressed stone were used, for instance in the Theotokos church, Osios Loukas. Such examples led to the increasing use of angular forms. In Greece from the early 11C onwards, the octagonal domes took on a special form: the horizontal cornice was suppressed and the arched cornices of each face of the octagon, for example, rising from colonnettes at the angles, form the characteristic arching eaves-line, as in Ay. Stratigos, Mani.

Differences in masonry techinque characterise particular areas. Construction in brick alone, common in Constantinople, is rare in Greece outside Thessaloniki (Panayia ton Khalkeon and the apse of the Catholicon of Osios Loukas). On the other hand, the use of stone alone is uncommon except in the islands, for instance in Ay. Yioryios Diassoritis and in the Panayia Dhamiotissa, Naxos. Mixing the two materials, the mainland builders from the second half of the 10C onwards make use of the *cloisonné* treatment in which the individual squared stones are enclosed by tile-like bricks in both vertical and horizontal joints. This basic walling system is fully developed in the Theotokos church, Osios Loukas. For a time cut bricks were used in the vertical joints to make decorative motifs, often based on Greek letters or the Arabic cufic script, as in the Taxiarchis Mitropoleos and Ay. Anargyroi, Kastoria, and the Theotokos, Osios Loukas. In the Mani brick, and with it the *cloisonné* masonry technique, makes its first appearance in Ay. Stratigos. In some Middle Byzantine churches, for instance in Ay. Iason and Sosipatros, Corfu and Ay. Sozon, Yeraki, it is common to use the *cloisonné* technique only in the upper courses, for such prominent features as the dome and the framing of windows. Usually façades were crowned with a dentil frieze, consisting of a series of bricks placed at an angle. A reaction to over-ornate brickwork led to the appearance of neat ashlar façades in the 12C, as in Ay. Nikolaos 'sta Kambia'.

Until the early 11C the arcade type of window was most frequently used in Greek churches. This type, in which the lights of a double or triple window are arched separately in brick at the same level, recalls the window arcades of the Early Christian basilicas. Its use is continued in the lower series of windows of the east end of the Catholicon of Osios Loukas. In the course of the 11C the arcade-type window was gradually replaced by the grouped type. In this the whole window is embraced in a single arch within which the individual lights are arched separately. In three-light windows of this type the central light is sometimes arched at a higher level. This grouped form of window is often flanked by blind half-arches of brick. The type appears perhaps for the first time in Greece in the dome of the Theotokos church, Osios Loukas. In the 12C it was used almost exclusively, for instance in the Evangelistria, Yeraki; but stone dressings gradually replaced those of brick, both in the window arches and elsewhere in the building. The *tympanum* of this grouped type of window was sometimes filled with designs imitating cufic lettering, but later simple geometric designs were preferred, as in the Evangelistria, Yeraki.

Glazed bowls set in mortar appeared as a type of façade ornament during the 11C and were generally used during the 12th, notably in the Mani, (Episkopi, Tigani).

## Church decoration

Some description has already been given of the adornment of Pre-Iconoclastic buildings (above; Early Christian period). One of the major developments following the overthrow of the Iconoclasts was the establishment of a **standard programme** for the distribution of religious images in church decoration. The decoration of the interior of the domed Middle Byzantine church was conditioned by the conception of the space it enclosed as a reflection of the cosmos. It had its own heavenly sphere in the dome and a more terrestrial region in the lower part of the church. In an hierarchic system the images were assigned to a higher and lower level as seemed appropriate. This cosmological-hierarchic order derives, it now seems, from the neo-Platonic writings of the Pseudodionysios Areopagita composed at the end of the 5C or the beginning of the 6C. The domed inscribed-cross type of church with its centralised plan was perfectly suited to the hierarchic arrangement required for the chosen representations, and it gave a formal unity to the spiritual conceptions which inspired this programme. Three factors determined its development: the requirement of theological instruction, the architectural forms available for decoration, and the survival in some degree of pre-Iconoclast traditions. But, above all, it was the architecture of the standard type of church which determined the elements of an ideal scheme of arrangement. In considering these we have to distinguish between mosaic churches in which the lower parts of the wall are sheathed with marble revetments, and the more humble painted churches in which these lower parts provided additional space for figural decoration, though here, in the lowest register, marble was often imitated in fresco. Although the principal Christian images *per se* had long since been standardised, the evolution of their arrangement since the Early Christian period had been crippled by a theological controversy. The Iconoclasts' ban on religious images had virtually obliterated the earlier traditions, necessitating the foundation of an almost entirely new programme in which images were in accord with the architecture they adorned, and at the same time conformed with the concepts of Greek Orthodox theology.

No complete and homogeneous church decoration from the period immediately following Iconoclasm has survived in the capital, and our knowledge of the iconographic programmes of churches in Constantinople is based on some problematical reconstructions derived from contemporary descriptions and on a few surviving fragments. Photius' description of the mosaics of 864 in the Church of the Virgin of the Pharos attests the prevalence of isolated figures in a restrained and hierarchic ensemble. *Christ Pantocrator* was figured in the summit of the dome, a host of Angels in its radiating gores; the *Virgin Orans* in the apse; and elsewhere Apostles, Prophets, Bishops and Martyrs. No narrative scenes are mentioned. It appears that the first post-Iconoclastic schemes were rather simple with isolated figures arranged in an hierarchic manner, limited to the dome with its drum and pendentives, the apse and the higher vaults. It is safe to say also that these early programmes set the course for the full development of the Middle Byzantine system in which narrative scenes and other complex figural compositions found a place. Already in the time of Basil I, if not earlier, the mosaic decoration of the Church of the Holy Apostles in Constantinople embraced a full narrative cycle of the Life of Christ. Moreover, it is clear that in the central dome the figure of Christ portrayed 'as if he were the sun', was surrounded by the Apostles accompanied by the Virgin, in a representation of the Ascension. Since the Ascension prefigures the Second Coming of Christ as Supreme Judge, it does not differ theologically from the more usual bust of the *Pantocrator*, a more abstract dogmatic symbol of Christ in Glory after the Ascension.

In the 'classic' decorative programme of the Middle Byzantine period, the dome, the apse and the higher vaults are reserved for the depiction of the most sacred personages. The bust of *Christ Pantocrator* was the most favoured image for the summit of the dome. His image formed the centre, formally and spiritually, around which the rest of the images in the church were arranged in a strictly hierarchic manner. The *Pantocrator* was accompanied in the zone below by a Celestial Host, while standing Prophets were represented between the windows of the drum, and the Evangelists commonly in the pendentives. The *narthex* usually has its own heavenly zone: Christ *Pantocrator* appears above the door leading to the nave, and if there were domes, they contained the bust of the Virgin or that of Christ Emmanuel.

Almost invariably the conch of the apse was reserved for the image of the Virgin (sometimes accompanied by two worshipping Archangels), either enthroned with the Child on her lap or standing (as the *Hodegetria*) with the Child on her arm, or alone with arms unpraised as Intercessor (*Orans*).

The appropriate place for the Communion of the Apostles was near the altar, often on the wall below the conch of the apse. Likewise the Bishops, conceived as participating in the Liturgy, belong to this area and are depicted in the lowest register of the apse wall and sometimes extending along the lateral walls of the sanctuary. Deacons also belong to the same liturgical programme and occur therefore in the sanctuary, usually just outside the apse. Overtones of the Liturgy are also expressed in the themes adopted for other parts of the church.

The Ascension commonly fills the *bema* vault, while the rest of the scenes from the Life of Christ, usually limited to the twelve major episodes of the Festival Cycle, are depicted outside the sanctuary on the vaults and the upper surfaces of the walls. These narrative scenes are arranged more or less chronologically, starting with the Annunciation in the eastern part of the church and ending with the Dormition of the Virgin, usually on the west wall. Ideally the twelve scenes from the Festival Cycle are: the Annunciation, the Nativity, the Presentation, the Baptism, the Transfiguration, the Raising of Lazarus, the Entry, the Crucifixion, the *Anastasis* (Harrowing of Hell), the Ascension, the *Pentecost* and the Dormition of the Virgin. To these were sometimes added subordinate cycles illustrating Christ's Passion (the Last Supper, the Washing of the Feet, the Betrayal, the Descent from the Cross and the Incredulity of Thomas), the Infancy of Christ (his Parents, the Adoration of the Magi and the Flight into Egypt), Christ's Miracles, the Life of the Virgin or that of a favoured Saint.

There were no strict rules governing the distribution of isolated figures, although they were arranged according to the rank assigned to them by the Church. Holy Physicians, like the Deacons, were usually admitted to the sanctuary, while Holy Monks, Female Martyrs and canonised Emperors were commonly relegated to the *narthex*. Sacred Warriors and Martyrs were figured in the nave in relatively high positions where such were available, while half-figures and busts of Saints in medallions often decorated the soffits of arches.

The decoration of wood-roofed basilicas inevitably required a different distribution of the images. In the Sicilian basilica, for example, the

*Pantocrator* was transferred to the conch of the apse, which automatically became the most sacred focal point of these churches, and the Virgin, together with the adoring Archangels, was moved to the next zone below. Bishops were retained in the lowest zone or zones of the apse wall, while the narrative and other cycles were distributed in two long series on the side walls of the nave.

These were the classical schemes of decoration adopted in Middle Byzantine churches, against which the programmes followed by the Greek fresco painters must be judged.

## Late Byzantine art (thirteenth to fifteenth centuries)

In 1204 Greece was conquered by the Franks and the Empire split into several political and cultural centres which largely developed independently from the capital. Fortified cities developed, such as Mistra and Moukhli in the Peloponnese and Arta in Epirus. Their newly established independence contributed towards a competitive spirit which also affected their artistic activities.

In architecture slight adjustments and changes were made to the existing basilican and domed-inscribed cross types of groundplan. Buildings from this period are characterised by their more elegant and narrow proportions and by their exterior brick and tile ornamentation. Architectural additions to the main church building resulted in their more complex appearance. The basilica, especially in Euboea and Epirus, underwent a late development. The transept was widened and raised above the other aisles, emphasising the characteristic cross-shape of the basilica during this period.

As a result of the declining economic situation of the Empire, mosaic decoration was gradually replaced by fresco painting. In the monastery church of **Porta Panayia** in Thessaly mosaic decoration has been reserved for the *iconostasis*, and in the **Paregoritissa** in Arta only the *Pantocrator* in the dome was executed in mosaic. Similarly, mosaics adorn the upper parts of the walls of the Apostle church in Thessaloniki, while the rest of the church is decorated with frescoes (1310).

Despite the gradual decline of the Empire, the painting during this late phase is characterised by an exceptional vitality and a dynamic revival of classical prototypes. On the islands and in the more remote regions of Greece, however, the more conservative, linear style, witnessed in the mosaics at Osios Loukas, predominated.

During this period Thessaloniki and the neighbouring Balkan countries developed as the important centres for monumental painting. After a period of stagnation (1330–60), painting in Constantinople gave fresh impetus to the art. Largely retrospective in character, it tended to revive the more painterly and humanist style of classical art. This style is perhaps best reflected in the fresco painting at **Mistra** which is characterised by its idealisation, elegance and lyrical sophistication. Crete, during the 14th and 15C, fell under the influence of the painting in Constantinople and gradually developed a distinctly **Cretan school** of painting which dominated Greek painting during the 16th and 17C.

# POST-BYZANTINE MONUMENTS: FRANKISH, VENETIAN AND OTTOMAN GREECE

by **Peter Lock**

## History of Frankish and Venetian Greece

Western influences on Greece go back to the 11C. Western travellers like the monk Benedict of Peterborough and the Spanish Jew Benjamin of Tudela visited the land in that century and recorded their impressions of it. But, all-too-often, the contacts were violent and were motivated by greed rather than by scholarship or tourism. The Norman conquerors of southern Italy sought to expand their dominions across the narrow Straits of Otranto and in the years 1081–84 seized Corfu and raided as far as Larissa in Thessaly. Pressure was renewed in 1146 when Thebes and Corinth were sacked and silk-workers forcibly taken from those cities and settled in Sicily.

To balance the Norman threat the Byzantine rulers resorted to the age-old policy of setting barbarian against barbarian. They signed a treaty with the Venetians in which the unique Venetian commodity, naval power, was enlisted against the common Norman foe in return for commercial advantages within the empire (1082). In turn the Venetians became dangerous and had to be restrained by the introduction of commercial rivals from the other Italian mercantile republics of Amalfi, Genoa and Pisa to whom trading concessions were granted during the course of the 12C. By 1200 the West had considerable political and commercial aspirations in the eastern Mediterranean, whilst the actions of Richard I of England in seizing Cyprus from the Byzantine authorities in April 1191 while on his way to the Third Crusade (1189–93) showed how easily lands might be gained in the East.

With the Fourth Crusade (1202–04) Greece lost what unity it had as part of the Byzantine Empire, a unity that was not to be restored until the Turkish conquests of the 1450s/70s and its incorporation in the Ottoman Empire.

After the sack of Constantinople by the Crusaders on 12 April 1204 and the establishment of the Latin Empire of Romania there, the former provinces of the Byzantine Empire were partitioned amongst the Venetians and the other Crusaders, who came mainly from France and Germany. The Republic of Venice, eager to consolidate its predominance in the carrying-trade of the Levant, acquired harbours such as Methoni and Koroni and the bulk of the Aegean islands, all strategic bases that would protect its sea-lanes to Alexandria, Alexandretta, Cyprus, and the ports of Asia Minor and the Black Sea. In many of the islands the Republic, whilst maintaining suzerainty in its own hands, was content to leave direct rule to ambitious Venetian families like the Orsini and Tocci who ruled as Dukes of Cephalonia, and the Sanudi and Crispi who ruled the Cyclades as Dukes of the Archipelago. The Greek mainland was left to Frankish barons from Flanders, France and Germany who divided up the land as it was conquered into feudal states owing vague and various allegiance to the Frankish King of Thessaloniki (to 1223), then to the Latin Emperor of Constantinople (to 1260) and thereafter to the Capetian, Aragonese and Angevin rulers of western Europe. Elements of the former Byzantine

Empire survived around Nicaea and Trebizond in Asia Minor and in the Despotate of Epirus in NW Greece.

Of the various Frankish states the most important were the Duchy of Athens and Thebes (1205–1460), the Principality of Achaia (1205–1432), and the various scattered Venetian possessions with various dates from 1205 to 1715 in the Aegean and to 1797 in the Ionian islands. Late-comers were the Knights of St John, who moved from Cyprus to Rhodes in 1310 and remained there until their expulsion by the Turks in 1522, and the Genoese, who had taken no part in the Fourth Crusade but who acquired colonies from the revived Byzantine Empire after 1261. Edward Gibbon dismissed '…the obscure and various dynasties that rose or fell on the continent or in the isles', but they are worthy of brief separate consideration to set the monuments in their political and patronage framework.

The Lordship (after 1260 the Duchy) of Athens and Thebes was granted to the Burgundian Otho de la Roche in 1205. This feudal unit retained its identity long after the passing of the Franks, forming the core of the Turkish Sanjak of Attica, Boeotia and Euboea. The splendour of the court at Thebes and the excellence of the French spoken there was much-written about by western visitors. The Frankish dynasty was overthrown in 1311 by the Catalan Company, a band of mercenaries, who, after fighting in Sicily and in Asia Minor, were employed by the Frankish Dukes and fell out with their employer over payment. The Franks were annihilated at the Battle of the Kifisos (somewhere near the modern Levadhia railway station), a battle in many ways analogous to the Battle of Bannockburn fought in 1314.

The Catalans owed allegiance to the Crown of Aragon. Besides indulging in acts of piracy against the Venetians, they extended the territory of the Duchy to the north, incorporating Neo-Patras, and built up Daulis (La Dablia) and Levadhia as important urban centres. In their turn the Catalans were replaced in 1381 by the Florentine banking family, the Acciaioli. The Acciaioli ruled the Duchy until 1460 and its final annexation by the Turks. The Florentines not only built the fine tower that stood by the Nike bastion on the Acropolis (demolished in 1874 and now visible only in paintings, some of which are in the Ethnike Pinakotheke, Athens) but also introduced Albanians into central Greece to re-populate the Duchy. Their descendants are still found in the area and many still speak an Albanian patois.

In the Peloponnese the Principality of Achaia with its centre at Andravidha (Andreville) was set up by two adventurers from the Champagne, William de Champlitte and Geoffrey de Villehardouin. On Champlitte's death (1209) Geoffrey assured the Principality for himself and his heirs. However, by 1278 the male line had failed and the Principality was ruled by bailes appointed by the Angevin monarchs in Naples. At this time of weakness Byzantine authority was reviving in the Peloponnese. Starting in 1262 with the regaining of Mistra, Old Maina, and Monemvasia, by 1432 the Byzantine Despotate of the Morea did in fact govern the whole of the Peloponnese with the exception of the Venetian bases at Methoni, Koroni, Argos, Lepanto and Nauplia. The Byzantine restoration was short-lived for by 1461 the Despotate had succumbed to the Turks.

The Venetians gained the islands and many coastal bases in the partition of 1204 and continued to add to those possessions throughout the period. However, the *Stato da Mar* fluctuated considerably in extent as it encountered and attempted to contain the Turkish threat. Crete, purchased in 1204, remained Venetian until 1669 despite many revolts. It was important for sugar, corn and horses. Euboea, acquired in 1209 was held until 1470. Its capital Chalkis (Negroponte) was the main base for naval patrols in the Aegean. Koroni and Methoni were important supply points on the route to Syria. They both fell to the Turks in 1500. Argos was acquired in 1388 and lost in 1463; Nauplia gained in 1388, lost 1540, regained 1686 and finally lost in 1715. This fluctuation of fortune and empire is well-reflected in Athens. Acquired in 1394, it was regained by the Acciaioli in 1402; raided in 1464, it was gained for the last time in 1687 when the forces of the Holy League, led by the Venetian Francisco Morosini and largely Venetian-inspired, captured Athens and held it for a year. This last Crusade in the Near East cost the Parthenon its roof. Despite the latter-day Crusade Venice was not strong enough to hold on to its resurrected Greek empire and in 1718 the Peloponnese together with Tinos, the last island in Venetian occupation, fell to the Turks.

Finally, the occupation of Rhodes by the Knights of St John in the years 1310–1522 has been mentioned above. Genoese possessions on the Greek islands should also be noted. They included Chios, rich in mastic, which was held until 1566 and also Lesbos, Samos and Thasos, all of which had passed into Turkish hands by the 1470s.

Frankish and Venetian Greece was swept away by the Turkish conquest of the 15C. Its legacy to Greece might be summed up as some loan-words in the modern Greek language, a certain amount of literature such as the *Livre de la Conquête*, the *Chronicle of the Morea* and, perhaps most important of all, the *Erotokritos* of the Veneto-Cretan Vitsentzos Kornaros (1553–1617), and a very considerable body of archaeological remains in the landscape. There had been no mass conversion to Roman Catholicism, no union of the Roman and Orthodox Churches, no adoption of Gothic styles of architecture and no substantial emigration from the West to Romania. The Franks remained a tiny minority.

## The Monuments of Frankish and Venetian Greece

The study of the monuments of Post-Byzantine Greece is hampered by the absence of firm historical evidence and by the lack of careful excavation of a well-stratified medieval site that might lead to a tighter dating of the pottery of the period and hence to closer dating of other sites with which it is associated. This vagueness is reflected in the tiny amount of Frankish and Venetian material displayed in museums. Examples of pottery, terracotta, and coinage may be chanced upon in museums all over Greece. However, there are small displays in the Agora and Benaki Museums in Athens, and in the museums at Chalkis, Corinth, Mistra, Nauplia and Rhodes. The Byzantine Museum in Athens, too, has some icons in its collection that reflect Frankish influence. Fragmentation is the keynote of the period, evident not only in its political history (outlined above) but also in the monuments themselves. The monuments, especially fortifications, were adopted and adapted by the successive rulers of the land, often causing an architectural confusion difficult to disentangle.

Firm documentary evidence of the fiscal and legal transactions of these Post-Byzantine regimes does not appear to have survived in any quantity and so only a very few of the buildings have even approximate dates based on documentary evidence. Thus it is known that the Castle of Chlemoutsi was constructed between 1220 and 1223 since the means by which it was financed were sufficiently high-handed to warrant Papal excommunication and so to deserve mention not only in the Papal archives but also in the *Chronicle of the Morea*. Likewise the destruction of the Benedictine monastery of Nôtre Dame at Issova by the Greeks in 1264 (and hence the dating of its construction to the first quarter of the 13C) was recorded because soon after this sacrilegious act those same Greeks were routed by a small

Frankish force apparently led by Our Lady of Issova mounted on a white horse. It is, then, on the chance mention of a building in the medieval accounts of the impious and the scandalous that the architectural historian is forced to rely.

An examination of styles, of plans, and of materials can shed some light on differentiating and dating the Frankish, Venetian and Turkish monuments but this is not as straightforward as at first it might appear. With regard to Christian religious buildings, Gothic was and is a foreign style in Greece and as such it stands out as distinctive from the traditions of Byzantine architecture with its emphasis on the rounded form. There is almost no complete Gothic structure in Greece with the exceptions of the church of Nôtre Dame at Issova (Benedictine), Ayia Sophia at Andravidha (Dominican) and Ayia Maria at Zarnaka (or Zarnaka; Cistercian). At the first two churches there are both lancet and tracery windows, ogeed piscinae, diagonal ribbed-vaulting, and Gothic moulding is evident in the corbels and string courses. Not only is Zarnaka the most ruinous of the trio but the builders of the Cistercian Order were limited by their Rule as to the amount of display that they might indulge in. Nonetheless, there are the remains of foliated capitals and an intriguing keystone carved with a 'green man'—a type common in late medieval northern Europe. The masonry of these churches consists of small regular ashlar throughout although at Andravidha tile slips have been used in the joints—a typical Levantine construction technique.

More often it would appear that Gothic features were added to existing Byzantine buildings. This is particularly noticeable at the Monastery of Daphni where a 14C Cistercian porch, complete with pointed arches contrasts with the rounded, brick-decorated Byzantine openings immediately behind it. Ayia Paraskevi in Chalkis is a Byzantine basilica with added ribbed-vaulting and much Frankish foliated carving on keystones, capitals and corbels. Ayia Maria at Gastouni is another Byzantine church, this time with a Gothic doorway, whilst the Church of the Koimesis at Khalandritsa has a squared (i.e. Frankish) east end. Finally, Frankish tomb-chests, without effigies or other decoration but set in wall-niches with pointed arches, occasionally appear in the midst of Byzantine churches. The best examples may be seen at Ayios Yioryios, Akraifnion, Ayia Paraskevi, Chalkis, and Ayios Yioryios in the Castle of Yeraki. Existing Byzantine churches would seem, then, to have been used by the Franks. The requirements of the Latin liturgy as expressed in the church plans of Western Europe seem to have been sacrificed to convenience.

The needs of defence have seldom respected monuments in Greece and adaptation and repair by successive builders are both features of the fortifications. Poor historical documentation makes it impossible to identify exclusively Frankish, Venetian, and Turkish structures. Masonry styles are of little help since the re-use of Classical blocks, rubble masonry and a liberal use of tile slips in the joints were employed from late Roman to modern times in Greece. This makes it unwise to assume that what looks old is necessarily so.

In general the typical 13C Frankish castle is composed of baileys around a central keep with square flanking-towers in the curtain wall. This lay-out is commonly found in castles in the areas of Frankish occupation from Bodhonitsa and Levadhia to Kalamata and Old Navarino but perhaps most significantly at Chlemoutsi, the most-securely dated of early Frankish castles. This layout represents no departure from north European and Byzantine military planning of the 12th Century. However, circular flanking-towers do appear at some Frankish sites in the 13C and make a striking contrast wth Byzantine towers. Fine examples may be seen at Argos, Castel Franchi at Nauplia and at Chlemoutsi. Frankish castles are often sited on the summits of precipitous and isolated hills which not only removed the necessity for massive circuit walls but also raises questions of the reasons for and the means of their construction.

Venetian fortifications provide interesting contrasts with those of the Franks mainly with regard to siting and plan. Unlike the mountain fastnesses of the Franks Venetian fortifications were sited with reference to the sea and the need to protect a harbour as the first and last resort of succour and supply. As a result they have massive landward defences with ingeniously protected gateways. They also well illustrate the adaptation of traditional medieval defences to artillery fortification with the addition of bastions, escarpments and cavaliers. These features may best be seen at Koroni, Methoni and Nauplia.

Post-Byzantine archaeology in Greece has suffered from neglect. What there is of it has tended to concentrate upon the military sites at the expense of towns, houses, rural settlement, and communications. Of these topics virtually nothing is known. Houses must have formed the great majority of buildings yet few medieval houses are known and their general typology is not worked out. Some 12C house-plans from the excavations at Athens and Corinth would indicate groups of modest rooms around a central courtyard, whilst at Mistra only the Laskaris mansion has received attention. The old city of Rhodes provides the most evocative medieval townscape. Of medieval rural settlement some attention has been given to the free-standing towers of the central Greek countryside which may, perhaps, represent the centres of Frankish fiefs, whilst abandoned village settlements still await study. The medieval road and bridge network is equally unknown (a fine Frankish bridge complete with a chapel on one of its piers survives at Karytaina). There is a great need to record these monuments and for the deliberate excavation of both medieval military and domestic sites.

## The Turkokratia and its monuments

The Turkish occupation (1460–1830) was for Greece a time of oppression and neglect. Many Turkish monuments were destroyed during and in the aftermath of the bitter War of Independence (1821–30) and there is still a disinclination to study the monuments of this period. Few Moslem monuments now survive intact except in Thrace and the old city of Rhodes where Turkish communites still exist. The atmosphere of Turkish settlements in Greece is best evoked by the towns of the north, especially Dhidhimotikhon, Kastoria, Kavalla old town, Kozani and Xanthi.

Most mosques lie in ruins or have been put to secular use after the removal of the minarets. Most notable and accessible of this latter group are the Tzisdharaki mosque in Monastiraki Square, Athens, built in 1759, the nearby Fetiche mosque at the corner of the Roman agora and the mosques in Chalkis (1470), Dhidhimotikhon, Kavalla and Nauplia. Also in Athens and in Nauplia are 18C medresses or Islamic schools. Just opposite the gateway to the Athens medresse is the so-called Tower of the Winds, which became in the 18C a tekke or headquarters for an order of dervishes. An early 19C Islamic charitable foundation is represented by the Imaret at Kavalla, an impressive grouping complete with fountains, a mosque, pointed arches and patinated copper domes. This was originally an old-people's home, built and endowed by the city's most famous son, Muhammad Ali (1769–1848) who was Ottoman governor of Egypt from 1805 to

1848, in which period this former Macedonian tobacco-merchant turned his Pashalik into a royal dynasty.

With regard to the fortifications there are few purely Turkish sites to be seen. They generally show an elaborate, even fussy plan, and construction with the needs of artillery warfare in mind. These best examples are at Rion (1499), New Navarino (1573) and the Karababa at Chalkis (1686). For the rest there has been adaptation and repair of existing structures often difficult to distinguish. Masonry styles are similar to those of the Franks and Venetians, and the Turks too used pointed arches occasionally distinguishable by the 'L-shaped' jointing in the soffit. Brick fan-vaulting is another pointer to Turkish workmanship. Some fine examples of this may be seen in the Castle of the Morea at Rion.

In towns the Turks seem to have occupied the defended areas like the former acropolises, leaving the Greeks in the lower towns or the suburbs. The ruined Turkish bath-houses and other buildings within the walls of the former Venetian fortress of Methoni should be contrasted with the small but lively later Greek settlements just outside the walls. The traveller George Wheler, visiting Chalkis in 1676, described how only the Turks lived within the city walls whilst 18C prints show the Parthenon being jostled by Turkish streets and houses. Acrocorinth too has remains of Turkish bath-houses, a mosque and other buildings within its walls. Fountains were an important part of the Turkish town and examples survive at Koroni, Nauplia and Old Corinth. In the countryside 19C travellers make it clear that there were Turkish estates all over Greece, even if they were not particularly dense on the ground. Many were described as consisting of towers surrounded by mud huts. They seem to have left no trace in the archaeological record. Just what they looked like is unknown, although the travellers seem to have had no difficulty in differentiating them from Frankish towers. Bridges too, mainly of 18C date, may be found all over Greece but especially fine examples should be sought in Epirus near Zagori and Konitsa.

The artefacts of the Turkokratia are seldom displayed and less often studied. The Benaki Museum, Athens, contains some Turkish material though not found in Greece. However, the various folk museums now springing up all over Greece do give some impression of the material culture of the subject population in the latter days of the Turkokratia. Nonetheless, the archaeology of Turkish Greece is still almost a virgin field.

# GREEK VERNACULAR ARCHITECTURE: AN OUTLINE

by **Peter Lock**

Vernacular architecture has been defined as the study of traditional domestic buildings, traditional in the sense that their plan, construction, ornament and materials reflect the social and economic life of a region at a particular time. Conservatism and localism are its predominant features, and country towns and villages its most sympathetic environment. The shape and the physical nature of Greece and its islands have produced both a wide variety of regions and a diversity of influences on the builder. Since prehistoric times the narrow cultivated valleys separated from each other by barren mountains have produced self-contained units of settlement whilst its tapering landmass has produced climatic and vegetational regions as diverse as the continental climate and deciduous and coniferous forest communities of the north to the Mediterranean climate and maquis of the Peloponnese. The visitor would be well advised to bear these points in mind during the examination of traditional buildings in a particular area.

The study of vernacular architecture in Greece is of fairly recent generation and owes much to the work of Professor Charalambos Bouras and his students at the National Polytechnical University in Athens. Much of their work can be seen in the admirable regional guides to Greek traditional architecture published by the Melissa Press, Athens. The work of recording by drawing and photography is urgent. Since the 1960s there has been much rebuilding and renewal in the towns and villages of rural Greece. In towns like Thebes, Lavadhia and Patras development has destroyed for ever the pre-neo-Classical buildings of the mid 19C, whilst in the villages the traditional long-houses, still being built up to the 1940s have been relegated to store-houses or incorporated in modern concrete structures. The visitor must remember that unlike other monuments these are private properties and the permission of the owner must be obtained to look and photograph. Leaving aside the Frankish, Venetian and Turkish structures on Rhodes, the Peloponnese, Crete and the islands together with the neo-Classical buildings in the principal cities, all of which might be regarded as foreign imports and the architecture of power, albeit like the 18C towers of the Mani or the free-standing towers of the medieval countryside the products of local craftsmen working with traditional materials, what can be said in general terms of our current knowledge of the vernacular architecture of Greece ?

First the long-house seems to be the most widely distributed traditional form and second the chronology of surviving buildings seems to go back only two or three centuries. This may well be the result of the disturbed history of Greece in the late 17C, consequent population movements and the desire to avoid the attention of Venetian and Turkish tax officials. Certainly the Venetian governors of the Peloponnese in the years 1685–1715 noted the preference of the Greeks to live in huts (*kalive*) rather than spend money on houses for these very reasons. There was certainly an enormous destruction of housing during the War of Independence (1821–33), but this alone does not account for the disappearance of houses of the 17C and before. Travellers like the Reverend John Hartley noted that, 'In the chief towns, and in a multitude of the country villages, not a dwelling remained entire.' This was in the Peloponnese. In the Argolid one-third of the villages were destroyed. Yet in nearby Navplio, which perhaps suffered the least of any town, the predominant architecture belongs to the 18C and early 19C and not earlier. However this might have been, the earliest standing structures, usually to be found in mountain villages, go back no more than some 250 years. Indeed the bulk of surviving long-houses seem to date from the 19C, some surviving from after the War of Independence which brought land redistribution and land grants to Greek farmers but the bulk of surviving rural housing dates to a period of rebuilding around the 1880–90s. Documentary evidence for these attributions is virtually nonexistent and buildings incorporating date-stones generally belong to the period 1920–40. Instead the student must rely upon the oral testimony of the owner, most of which seem to be surprisingly accurate as to year and builder.

From this same source something of the use of rooms and the organisation of life in a rural long-house can be obtained. The favoured form, both in small town and village, was the single-storeyed long-house, although an additional storey might be added in the mountains to exploit declivities in the landscape. A rough guide to their dimensions in 10–12 metres long and 3–4 metres wide, 2 metres to the eaves-drip with a wall-thickness of one metre. Accommodation comprised two or three rooms separated by a through entrance. At one end goats and sheep might be kept and dairying carried on. This latter activity is usually marked by fireplaces and smaller windows; at the other end the family would eat and sleep, cupboards recessed in the walls at this end are a feature and some of the fireplaces from the late 19C were built for display despite their modest environment. In some houses the through passage itself was the site of the fire. Social and economic differentiation is recognisable in these features. The alignment of the long-house was usually north–south providing a shady spot on either side of the house depending on the passage of the sun. A small cobbled area was provided by the through doors for outside work. The environs of the house should not be ignored and note should be taken of any wells, bread-ovens, olive presses and storage areas for wine, crops and animal fodder.

The earlier the structure generally, the less the ornament. Not surprisingly most attention was focused on the door surround. From this the principal entrance of the two opposing doors may be discerned. In general, buildings dating to the later 19C have round-headed doors looking to all intents and purposes very Romanesque. The early 20C rural dwelling of a more prosperous owner may well display neo-Classical influences. In rural settlements the development of the settlement may be discerned from its buildings. Starting around an original plataia, often with an old church and a number of long-houses, the development downhill to a modern road, neo-Classical shops and cafenia are often noticeable. In such settlements in the years before the First World War the advent of the two-storey town house is noticeable. It is usually in a prominent position in the plataia or new second plataia if the settlement has expanded, often with a surrounding balcony at first floor level, a date-stone and the rural version of the neo-Classical. Such houses are often to be found in villages clustered around a larger centre and may well represent the work of a builder of that centre. For the rest, the traditional long-house with its one-metre plus thick walls, rough undressed masonry and crudely dressed roof timbers of just a beam and two joists every two metres and locally made tiles resting on reed insulation, if available, have all the hallmarks of local craftsmen. So, too, do the materials used; stone predominates in such a mountainous country, but in the valleys of the large rivers and in marshy areas like Lake Kopais and the Pylos area mudbrick long-houses may be noticed. Some have suggested that the long-house tradition goes back to Classical times. It certainly goes back beyond the 19C. In deserted settlements in which the Greek countryside abounds, the foundations of two-roomed long-houses with just one entrance facing out to a walled yard and no recessed fireplace may be noted. Here there are no occupants to question, only the evidence of sherd scatters. These would seem to suggest a rough date of 14–17C for such forms with the earliest three-roomed long-houses with opposing entrance belonging to the later 17C and persisting down to this century. In-coming groups like the Albanians from the 14C and those Greeks settled after the various exchanges of population in the early part of this century have all lived in long-houses, so too have the nomadic Sarakatsani in their long rectangular animal shelters or tenda.

Aside from the central style, the variety of the Greek vernacular tradition, albeit belonging to the last two centuries, makes it necessary to select a few special cases as worthy of the attention of those with limited time. The Pelion peninsula in Thessaly separates the Gulf of Volos from the Aegean

Sea and has a variety of settlement patterns and an astonishing stock of timber and stone dwellings of the 19C. These range from mansions with a fine range of internal wooden fittings, external galleries and the occasional tower-house adapted and extended to 19C tastes down to the home of the small-holder, in the long-house tradition but with the same emphasis on high-quality wooden construction. The island of Hydra in the Saronic Gulf provides a range of merchant houses closely dated to the half century between 1770 and 1820. The merchants of Hydra town and nearby Kaminia built themselves mansions which both externally, in window forms and roof lines, and internally, in the amenities provided, recreated the houses which they saw in Venice and other ports of northern Italy from which they carried grain from the Black Sea. On the islands attention is focused upon the town house and the ingenious uses of locally available materials in external decoration and roofing. On Kimolos, Thera and Antiparos, the shortage of timber has resulted in the use of local stone built up in corbelled domes as roofs. Space is at a premium and the need to preserve agricultural land very much to the fore. The towns on the islands of Santorini, Keos, Andros and Tinos are well worth visiting. On Chios, Naxos, Andros and Tinos the interplay of Byzantine, Italian and Turkish influences on decorative motifs are particularly noticeable and provide material for much interesting speculation. The dove-houses on the last two last-named islands are particularly evocative in this pursuit. It must be stressed that the above is a selection of the picturesque and structurally striking. Vernacular architecture of high quality is to be found everywhere in Greece. From the materials, roof-form, house stock and plan and the settlement form, much ready information is to be gained of the climate, geology and agriculture of the surrounding area, whilst the present repair of the buildings will be an indicator to modern economic conditions and present rural priorities.

Our knowledge of Greek vernacular architecture will only increase with the accumulation of data from all the regions of the peninsula. This will depend upon interesting Greek scholars, school-teachers and private individuals of the educational and touristic value of vernacular architecture and the urgent need to record this vanishing past before it is lost.

# MODERN GREEK HISTORY

by **Richard Clogg**

The Greeks were the first of the subject peoples of the Ottoman Empire to gain independence, achieving sovereign statehood in 1830. The reasons for this are several. The enormous coastline of the Greek lands and islands, coupled with a strong nautical tradition, rendered the Greeks more open to European influences than their more landlocked Balkan neighbours. During the eighteenth century Phanariot Greek grandees acquired considerable influence over the conduct of Ottoman diplomacy and amassed wealth and status as rulers of the Danubian Principalities of Wallachia and Moldavia, the core of present day Romania. Greek merchants during the eighteenth century came to dominate much of the commerce of the Ottoman Empire. Like the Phanariots, most of these were too comfortably locked into the existing status quo to offer direct support to the embryonic national movement. Nonetheless the benefactions of rich merchants to schools and libraries; the subsidies they provided for publications; and, above all, the scholarships they gave to young Greeks to study in the universities of Europe, laid the foundations of the intellectual revival that was such a significant feature of the decades leading up to the outbreak of armed revolt against the Ottoman Turks in the 1820s.

In western Europe, Greek students, besides imbibing the intoxicating ideas of the Enlightenment and the nationalist doctrines emanating from the French Revolution, were made aware of the extent to which the language and culture of the ancient world were universally revered by the educated in Europe. On their return to the Greek lands they strove to inculcate an understanding of this incomparable heritage in their fellow countrymen, most of whom at this time thought of themselves as Orthodox Christians rather than Greeks. It was during the first decade of the 19C that Greeks began to give their children (or to adopt for themselves) the names of the worthies of ancient Greece, much to the chagrin of the Orthodox Church, which equated classical antiquity with paganism. The foremost Greek intellectual of the age, Adamantios Korais (1748–1833), himself a very distinguished classical scholar, urged the study of the ancient authors as well as the preservation of the physical remains of antiquity.

The decades before 1821 witnessed the birth of the 'language question', the prolonged, divisive and at times violent debate as to the form of Greek appropriate to a regenerated Greece. Some looked to the supposed purity of Attic Greek of the 5C BC as a model; some championed the spoken or 'demotic' language of the people (itself, given the timespan involved, remarkably little changed from the koine Greek of New Testament times). Others, among them Korais, advocated a middle way and it was their view which prevailed. The dominance of *katharevousa* (literally 'purifying') Greek as the official language of the state and of education was only ended as recently as 1976.

The groundwork for an armed revolt against the Turks was laid by the *Philiki Etairia* (Friendly Society). This secret society was founded in 1814 in Odessa by three young Greeks, fired by the example of Rigas Velestinlis (1757–98) who, in the late 1790s, had sought in vain to inspire a Balkan-wide revolt. Gradually the conspiracy spread throughout the Greek world. When Count Ioannis Capodistrias (1776–1831), the Corfiote Greek who served as Tsar Alexander I of Russia's foreign minister, declined the leadership, his place was taken by General Alexander Ypsilantis (1792–1828), another Greek in the Russian service.

An invasion of the Danubian principalities in February 1821 by Ypsilantis was soon followed by an uprising in the Peloponnese, as the conspirators sought to exploit the Ottoman Sultan Mahmud II's preoccupation with destroying the power of Ali Pasha, the Muslim Albanian warlord who held sway over much of mainland Greece. Ypsilantis' incursion was soon crushed, but the Peloponnesian uprising met with greater success. Much of the military muscle of the revolt was provided by the klefts, essentially bandits, while the Greeks soon secured control of the sea. Foreign philhellenic volunteers, the poet Byron among them, also made their way to Greece.

It was not long, however, before dissension in the Greek ranks and the Sultan's acquisition of powerful new allies threatened the insurgents. But the Greek cause was saved by the Powers. These had initially been indifferent to the cause of Greek liberty but had become increasingly concerned at the threat to stability (and commerce) posed by the revolt. It was the destruction of the Ottoman fleet by a combined British, French and Russian fleet at the battle of Navarino in 1827 that was to ensure that some kind of Greek state came into existence. While negotiations continued as to the extent of its boundaries, Count Capodistrias served as president until his assassination in 1831.

The powers imposed as his successor King Otto (1815–67) of the Bavarian Wittelsbach dynasty, and put themselves forward as the guarantors of the new state (an ambiguous status that was a pretext for meddling in its internal affairs) whose independence was formally recognised in 1830. In deference to the enthusiasm of Greek nationalists for the classical past, the capital was moved to Athens, at that time little more than a village, but soon to be endowed with a university and many other public buildings built in a handsome neo-Classical style.

The borders of the new state left many more Greeks still under Ottoman rule than within the newly established kingdom, whose frontiers embraced the Peloponnese, part of southern Roumeli and some of the nearby islands. The **Megali Idea**, the grandiose 'Great Idea' of uniting Greek populations widely scattered throughout the Near East within the bounds of a single state, with Constantinople as its capital, was to be the motive force of Greek foreign policy during the nineteenth and early twentieth centuries, and was indeed to dominate much of the country's domestic politics to the detriment of much-needed reforms.

The problems that faced the new state were daunting. Not only was the country devastated by almost ten years of intermittent fighting but the infrastructure of a state was almost wholly lacking. During the early period of his reign King Otto relied heavily on Bavarian advisers. This alienated many veterans of the war who felt cheated of the spoils of victory. Otto's failure to concede a constitution was another source of the resentment which precipitated the virtually bloodless coup of 3 September 1843, the first of many political interventions by the military.

The constitution which Otto was forced to concede in 1844 was a liberal document for its time but the king and the politicians on whom he relied were soon able to subvert its spirit. Representative institutions had not developed organically over centuries as they had in western Europe but had been imported wholesale and grafted on to a traditional society with very different a value system. Powerful local notables dominated the new parliament, dispensing favours and patronage in return for votes. They were consumed with the desire for office, for control of the government machine was essential if their clients-cum-voters were to be rewarded. In an economically backward country, the state was a major source of employment, as it has continued to be until the present day. It was not long before the discontents which had culminated in the coup of 1843 surfaced once again. These resulted in Otto's enforced departure from Greece in 1862, again as a result of military intervention.

His successor, George I (1845–1913), a member of the Danish royal family, was to reign for almost fifty years. As a kind of dowry, and in the vain hope of dampening Greece's vaunting Irredentist ambitions, Britain in 1864 ceded the Ionian islands (Corfu among them), a British protectorate since 1815. This was the first accession of territory since Greece became independent. The second, an indirect consequence of the crisis that convulsed the Balkans during the 1870s, came in 1881 when the Turks grudgingly ceded the rich agricultural province of Thessaly and a part of Epirus.

In 1864 a new, and still more liberal, constitution was adopted, but the politics of the early period of King George's reign continued in their traditional mould. Elections were frequent, and changes of administration still more so, as politicians engaged in the frantic pursuit of the spoils of office. From the late 1870s onwards there was, however, an important evolution towards a more stable two-party system, with power alternating

**The Expansion of the Greek State, 1832–1947**

between the reform-minded, if uncharismatic, Kharilaos Trikoupis (1832–96) and the demagogic, populist (and popular) Theodoros Deliyannis (1826–1905). Trikoupis believed political and economic modernisation to be the essential precondition of territorial expansion. Deliyannis, for his part, believed that Greece's problems would be solved once a 'Greater Greece' had come into being. Economic problems, culminating in the effective bankruptcy of the state in 1893, were one of the factors behind the great wave of emigration, principally from the Peloponnese and to the United States, that got under way in the 1890s and which contributed to the emergence of a diaspora which has established itself in many parts of the world, and particularly in the United States and Australia.

Deliyannis was in power when in 1896 the Cretans launched one of their periodic uprisings aimed at bringing about the *enosis* or union of the 'Great Island' with the kingdom. This gave rise to the 'Thirty Day' war with Turkey, the outcome of which was a rapid and humiliating defeat for Greece. The lesson of the war was clear: Greece confronted the Ottoman Empire without allies at her peril.

Defeat in 1897 contributed to the climate of revulsion towards the old politicians that was one of the factors (another was a renewed demand for 'enosis' on the part of the Cretans) that precipitated the coup launched in 1909 by the disgruntled officers and non-commissioned officers of the Military League. Eleftherios Venizelos (1864–1936) was now projected to the forefront of the political stage. Venizelos, who had made his reputation in the politics of his native island of Crete, which had been granted autonomous status after the 1897 war, was acceptable to the military as someone who had not been compromised by the petty politics of the kingdom. Once elected, with a massive majority, in 1910, Venizelos embarked on an ambitious programme of political, economic and military modernisation.

It was Venizelos who laid the foundation for Greece's spectacular successes in the Balkan wars of 1912–13. In October 1912, Greece joined with Montenegro, Serbia and Bulgaria, to attack the Ottoman Empire. Greece, Bulgaria and Serbia had hitherto been rivals in an increasingly bloody struggle to lay claim to the territory of Ottoman Macedonia, a byword for ethnic complexity. The Greeks made sweeping gains. A number of Aegean islands, including Chios, were captured, as was Thessaloniki, now the second city of Greece, which had also been covetously eyed by the Bulgarians. The newly acquired territories included the monastic republic of Mount Athos, a bastion of Orthodoxy founded in Byzantine times, on the easternmost of the three fingers of the Chalkidiki peninsula.

As a consequence of the Balkan wars, Greece's land area increased by two thirds. Venizelos, the architect of these spectacular gains, was idolised. Under his charismatic leadership, Greece now appeared to be well placed to become the leading power in the Eastern Mediterranean. When King George I was assassinated by a madman in 1913, nationalist enthusiasts called for his successor Crown Prince Constantine (1868–1922) to be crowned not Constantine I (as he was) but Constantine XII, so as to emphasise Greece's claim to be the heir to the Byzantine Empire, whose last Emperor had been Constantine XI Palaiologos. Within the space of ten years, however, the unity and sense of purpose that Venizelos had forged during his first premiership were to give way to division and disarray, and the heady dreams of a revived Byzantium were to vanish in devastating military defeat in Asia Minor.

The immediate cause of the 'National Schism', as it came to be known, was the quarrel between King Constantine and Venizelos over the country's alignment during the First World War. Venizelos was an enthusiastic champion of the Entente Allies (Britain, France and Russia), while the king, whose emotional sympathies lay with the Central Powers (Germany and Austria-Hungary), believed Greece's interests would best be served by neutrality. Disagreements over foreign policy were but one dimension of the schism. There was also conflict between modernisers and traditionalists; between champions of a 'Greater' Greece and advocates of a 'small but honourable' Greece; between the inhabitants of 'New' Greece, whose inhabitants venerated Venizelos as their liberator, and the royalist conservatives of 'Old' Greece, the heartland of the original kingdom. The conflict led Venizelos in 1916 to establish a rival government, based in Thessaloniki, a move that brought the country to virtual civil war. In 1917 Britain and France ousted King Constantine from the throne and Venizelos now returned to power in Athens as prime minister of a country formally united but bitterly divided against itself.

Venizelos rapidly brought Greece into the war on the side of the Entente and, in 1919, at the Paris Peace Conference received the reward for his unswerving devotion, namely permission to occupy Smyrna (Izmir) and a large swathe of western Asia Minor which, with its large Greek population, had long been the object of Irredentist aspirations. But the army had been undermined by political divisions and the invasion had acted as the catalyst for the Turkish nationalist movement headed by Mustafa Kemal (Atatürk).

In 1922 the Greek armies were driven into the sea and Smyrna, with its large Greek and Armenian population, was burnt. Those Greek civilians in Asia Minor who had not fled with the retreating Greek armies were compulsorily exchanged for Muslims living in Greece.

In Greece a military coup drove King Constantine once again from the throne and the influx of some 1,300,000 refugees (from Russia and Bulgaria as well as from Asia Minor) gave a powerful stimulus to the establishment of a republic in 1923. Greece's inter-war history is a tale of confusion, with the army, and the refugees, acting as the arbiters of political life. Venizelos' last administration between 1928 and 1932 provided a period of relative stability but the country was badly effected by the world slump. Antagonism between supporters of Venizelos and of the exiled King George II (1890–1947), who had succeeded to the throne in 1922, became ever more bitter as Venizelists in the armed forces launched two unsuccessful coups, in 1933 and 1935. In the wake of the latter King George was restored to the throne following a fraudulent plebiscite. The king's hopes of healing the Venizelist/royalist divide were to be critically undermined by the fact that it was the very small communist party that held the balance of power in the hung parliament that emerged from the elections of 1936. The ensuing political confusion was exploited by an arch-conservative (and hitherto insignificant) politician, General Ioannis Metaxas (1871–1941), to establish a dictatorship. The 'Regime of the Fourth of August 1936' was an authoritarian, paternalist and unpopular dictatorship, with some fascist trappings, which enabled the diminutive dictator to vent his spite against politicians in general and communists in particular.

The time of the communists was to come during the Second World War when, having been a marginal factor throughout the inter-war period, they were to become the dominant political force. Greece became embroiled in the Second World War when, in October 1940, Metaxas, reflecting the national mood, rejected a humiliating Italian ultimatum which was the prelude to an outright invasion. Within a short time the Greek armed forces had pushed the Italians back into Albania, whence the invasion had been launched, and had liberated a large swathe of southern Albania with its substantial Greek minority. But the euphoria engendered by the victorious Albanian campaign during the winter of 1940/41, which had shown that the Axis war machine was not invincible, was to be dissipated in the bitterness of defeat when, in April 1941, the Germans invaded Greece. They rapidly overran the Greek forces and the British expeditionary force that had been sent to their aid. Within less than two months mainland Greece and Crete, which it had been intended to hold as an impregnable stronghold, had been overcome and the King and his government had been forced to flee. The tripartite (German, Italian and Bulgarian) occupation was extremely harsh. A fearful famine during the winter of 1940/41 cost 100,000 lives, while, in 1943, much of Greece's Jewish community was wiped out. Vicious reprisals were imposed for acts of resistance.

The communists took an early lead in organising such resistance and rapidly built up a commanding influence through the establishment of the National Liberation Front (EAM) and the National People's Liberation Army (ELAS). With the assistance of a British Military Mission, some notable acts of resistance were accomplished, notably the destruction in November 1942 of the Gorgopotamos railway viaduct, a rare occasion when EAM/ELAS co-operated with its main non-communist rival EDES. But, as during other periods of grave national crisis, the period of the occupation was to be characterised by dissension. This culminated in internecine fighting between the resistance movements during the winter of 1943/44.

Although this confrontation was patched up, it prefigured the armed clash in December 1944 between ELAS and the British forces that had accompanied the government-in-exile on its return to Greece on liberation in October 1944. The settlement of the December 1944 conflict did not endure and during 1945 and 1946 the country slid towards outright civil war, a bitterly fought conflict in which the old schism between Venizelists and anti-Venizelists was to be overlaid by a new division between communists and anti-communists.

During the civil war of 1946–49, the communist Democratic Army received considerable logistical support from the newly established communist regimes in Yugoslavia, Albania and Bulgaria. The national government in Athens, in turn, received massive military and economic aid from the US. The national army gradually established military superiority and, in the late summer of 1949, the defeated remnants of the Democratic Army were forced into a bleak exile in Eastern Europe and the Soviet Union.

Greece was on a war footing for much of the decade of the 1940s, just as she had been for much of the period 1912–22. But, although delayed, the process of post-war reconstruction was remarkably rapid, and the overall standards of living rose markedly, even if the political wounds of the civil took a generation to heal and political instability gave rise to a military dictatorship that comprehensively misruled the country between 1967 and 1974, employing methods that were by turn brutal and absurd. Paradoxically it was the common experience of resistance to the junta that contributed significantly to the healing of the breach between the far left and the right.

The Colonels' dictatorship collapsed in 1974, in the wake of its disastrous attempt to topple Archbishop Makarios of Cyprus, who had become president of the island when it had gained its independence from Britain in 1960. The junta's coup in turn precipitated the Turkish occupation of northern Cyprus. Konstantinos Karamanlis (1907-), a prominent conservative politician, was summoned from exile to oversee the restoration of democracy. A referendum resulted in a decisive vote against a restoration of the monarchy, which had been abolished by the Colonels, thereby bringing an end to the reign of Constantine II (1940-). Besides consolidating Greece's newly restored democratic institutions, Karamanlis devoted much energy to securing Greece's accession to the European Community.

In 1981, Greece entered the Community as its tenth member. Not only is Greece the only member state in which Orthodoxy is the prevailing religion, but, during four or more centuries of Ottoman rule, the Greeks had been largely insulated from the great historical movements that have had such a powerful influence on the evolution of Western Europe. 1981 also saw the election of the country's first socialist government with the victory of the Panhellenic Socialist Movement (PASOK), headed by Andreas Papandreou (1919-). The peaceful transition in power from right to left seemed to presage a new stability in the political system. If Greece's future clearly lay in a united Europe, many problems remained in the economy, in relations with Turkey and with her Balkan neighbours.

# GREEK FOLK ART

by **Jane Cocking**

The folk arts of Greece are among the most decorative and fascinating in Europe, reflecting the environment in which they are produced with beauty of style and technique. This introduction aims to answer the questions, what exactly is folk art, who made it, and for what purpose, and what can it tell visitors about the country through which they are travelling? There will follow a brief description of the main categories of folk art in Greece together with some suggestions as to where to see or purchase examples of the various crafts.

The primary feature of any item of folk art is that it is an object which can fulfil a practical purpose as well as being as decorative. Whether or not the item is actually used for that purpose is not important. A decorated wooden spoon is definitely a piece of folk art, as is an embroidered cushion or a carved distaff; even large pieces of carving on the wall of a house usually serve some architectural purpose. They are all basically functional objects which, either decorated or undecorated, were in daily use.

Greek folk art may be divided roughly into the professional and the domestic. The former comprises items made by artisans who have had some apprenticeship or training, however informal. They are often characterised by the need for specialist and frequently relatively costly equipment requiring financial investment. They may also involve a continuous process which necessitates an investment of time in order to be in attendance at specific moments during that process. These arts often developed a guild structure and a common craft identification and frequently became associated with specific families.

Included in the professional category are stone carving, metal work, architectural woodcarving and some forms of pottery. This last reinforces the point that objects of folk art are both decorative and functional. For example, traditional Rhodian plates painted with designs are items of folk art. They are capable of serving as plates and yet they are frequently used to decorate island homes. A plain pithos however, is also the product of the potter's workshop, but is only functional and not decorative. The pithos therefore, is an example of folk craft and not folk art.

Domestic arts are defined by their lack of specific timed processes. They may be taken up and set down as other duties allow, they are usually carried out in the home and they require little specialist equipment. As the items produced are often those that are actually used in the home, rather than being purely decorative, they are likely to need constant replacement. It is easier to produce such items oneself rather than to order them from an independent source. Such arts include basketry, weaving, embroidery and pastoral woodcarving. This last epitomises the difference between professional and domestic folk arts. Pastoral work includes all small items such as walking sticks, distaffs and spoons which can be carved and whittled intermittently. This contrasts with its professional counterpart, architectural woodcarving, which requires planning and possibly co-ordination with other workers.

In general, items of folk art are made by their users. Even professionals are usually only producing for their own community. There is no intention of exporting goods. Domestic workers are even more obviously producing for their own needs. The personal nature of the objects is highlighted by the fact that they have frequently gained significance in the family as they grow older, for sentimental and not financial reasons. For example, many pieces of embroidery found in 20C homes consist of several fragments from different items sewn together to form a whole. This is because, as embroidery began to die out, daughters who did not do as much work as their mothers divided their relatives' embroideries and then, left with several small pieces, sewed them together for greater use and personal value. What had been an individual's possession had become a family heirloom.

The raw materials of folk art are usually locally produced and therefore readily available. Imported raw materials are only used to supplement local supplies and not to replace them as a matter of preference. This has two results: it underlines the idea of the actual character and appearance of folk art being dictated by local conditions, and it throws light on the position of folk art in society. It is something which is done as a matter of course and tradition which does not have great material value (for example, a blanket made from locally produced wool and dyed using natural dye stuffs gathered in the vicinity). This is completely different from an item of 'high art' which may involve the planned import of rare and costly materials.

Greek folk art also bears all the recognised hallmarks of ethnographic expression. Items are anonymous, very rarely is work actually 'signed'. This is for two main reasons. First, there is no thought of an artist conceiving an original idea and executing it for its own sake. Second, there is no reason to sign a piece of work that was either for use by the family of the creator or a member of a relatively small community where all items of a certain type were the work of one man; for example, copper objects were all made by the coppersmith. It is highly unlikely that there would be more than one specialised worker in such a field in the district.

The second hallmark is tradition. Designs and techniques changed and developed very slowly as they were passed down from generation to generation. For example, the French traveller Savary criticised the women of Kimolos for what he regarded as the ugliness of their dress. He received the reply, 'Our grandmothers were clad in the same way, we do but follow the custom'.

Finally, items of folk art are spontaneous, they are completely entrenched in the lives of the people who create and own them; they are not the result of a conscious desire to fulfil a perceived need.

Greek folk art embodies all of these general characteristics and one more of its own, regionalism. Before 1947 different parts of Greece had very different histories as they fell variously under the influence of the Ottoman Empire, Venice, Genoa and their local representatives. The folk art of the area reflects this well. It falls technically and stylistically into nine different divisions: Epirus, Macedonia, Sterea Ellas, Attica, Peloponnese, Skyros and the northern islands including Paros, the Cyclades, the Dodecanese and Crete. These divisions coincide with the historical pattern of the country as well as with other features such as dialect; for example, Paros, while geographically in the Cycladic group, has both a dialect and style of folk art which have far more in common with the Sporades with which it shares a common historical heritage.

In view of this regional differentiation it is possible to identify the origin of a piece on stylistic grounds. For example, Cycladic embroidery incorporates repeated diaper designs and tightly twisted thread while the Dodecanese is characterised by separate individual motifs and heavy flock silk.

Attribution on stylistic grounds raises the question as to whether intermarriage and travel between regions caused the actual movement of objects of folk art and the mingling of styles. Population movement did not take place as a result of historical and environmental factors and this led to certain anachronisms. For example, Robert Pashley in his *Travels in Crete* (1837) described a girl who spent some time living in Naxos for 'protection and security during the war in Crete'. When she returned to her native village where Pashley met her she still wore the Naxian costume and worked Naxian embroidery. This, he says, annoyed her family and made her extremely conspicuous.

A further example of the transmission and mingling of designs is found in the village of Apeiranthos on Naxos today. Many of the inhabitants are the descendants of several families who migrated from Crete during the 19C and they still speak with a marked Cretan accent. The traditional textiles which are being worked there are based on Naxian techniques used together with Cretan designs.

In spite of such relatively isolated examples, a definite sense of regional identity was preserved in most places and it would require a very large-scale migration to produce a significant alteration in the style of the folk art being found in a given area worked either by immigrants or natives.

It has been mentioned before that one of the main characteristics of folk arts in general is that they are made of locally available raw materials, and in an area so clearly divided into various regions as Greece this dictates one of the most interesting features of the subject, the diversity of different categories produced in different areas. For example, metalwork is much more common in the north where silver (in the north-west) and copper (in the north-east) are more readily available than further south. Similarly, thickly wooded areas are characterised by heavy carved panelling in the vernacular architecture which is absent in stone houses of the more sparsely wooded islands. There are certain exceptions to this general rule, often in the case of relatively easily transportable light textile fibres. For example, Crete produces large amounts of woven and embroidered textiles made of wool, cotton, silk and linen. That the island definitely produced large quantities of silk, cotton and wool is shown by 19C local records and consular documents. Linen however, proves to be more difficult; in the late 19th and early 20C it is known that it was imported on a large scale from the Ionian islands for semi-industrial uses and presumably some of the surplus found its way onto the home market. However, prior to this it seems quite possible that flax was produced in small subsistence quantities in areas such as the Lasithi Plain in the east and the White Mountains in the west.

Decoration is obviously an important aspect of folk art. Together with the purpose of items of folk art and the raw materials from which they were made, the designs and motifs are a reflection of the environment in which they were worked. Designs and motifs epitomise folk art in the way in which they are passed down from generation to generation by word of mouth. Nor are they passed on to specific individuals alone; they are part of a communal heritage which is available to the mass of the population in some form.

Folk art is definitely decorated and not designed. Motifs are arranged over a surface rather than the worker using an overall scheme which involves the preconceived idea of a link between the form of the object and the style in which it is decorated. This is often illustrated by the way in which designs and motifs are arranged on the item, for example, by covering the whole thing with a single repeated motif, starting at one edge and working over to the next.

Designs rarely change even when they are worked on pieces completely different in form and style. Designs on pottery from Rhodes remain basically the same whether they are worked on high necked jugs, square bottles or tiles. Similarly the same designs are used in the same area on all types of media.

The origins of the designs used in Greek folk art fall into three basic categories: those taken from personal experience, which are usual in peasant art; the more geometric designs that are repeated throughout the piece and seem to be part of a general Mediterranean heritage but are particularly common in Greece; and those which are a direct result of outside influences.

In the first group the workers were influenced by their natural surroundings, for example in depictions of flowers and birds. Human figures appear infrequently, but when they do are usually engaged in some activity, for example an Epirote wedding or Cycladic dancer. Geometric motifs fall into the simple and the complex. The simple ones are common in folk art throughout the world but the more complex ones are the result of local interpretations of basic motifs which are unlikely to be repeated elsewhere.

The third category of motifs, those which are copies of motifs indigenous in other areas, is particularly characteristic of Greek folk art. It is reasonable to assume that in the case of Greece the motifs did not emerge spontaneously, but were passed along some identifiable route of communication. The Mediterranean has always been a water-way that united people rather than kept them apart, and as various areas of Greece fell under a succession of foreign rulers the motifs from those cultures were absorbed into the common heritage. Examples of this process in action are the Anatolian rose spray found in Crete and in the Cyclades, the Turkish pomegranates in Epirote work and the south Italian peacocks and mermaids in the Ionian Islands and Crete. In each case the rudiments of the design are picked up either by copying imported objects or by personal teaching. However, as the new designs are worked using local raw materials they assume a slightly different appearance in each region.

To look at Greek folk art in greater detail it is necessary to examine the various crafts and their basic characteristics individually.

## Pottery

One of the most common forms of folk art throughout Greece, it is particularly highly decorated with vivid red, blue and green floral designs in Epirus and the Dodecanese, quite possibly in imitation of high-quality Isnik wares. Peloponnesian material is characterised by a greenish glaze and green and yellow watery designs. Unglazed wares with incised decoration are also common throughout the area.

## Textiles

Possibly the next most common form. Woven and embroidered textiles are found throughout Greece, although embroidered pieces are more often seen in the south than the north where the climate dictated heavier woollen pieces both for clothing and for home insulation. Textiles have been particularly susceptible to imported foreign designs. As a result they are often the most accurate indicators of the degree of foreign influence exerted on a given area. Classic examples are the embroidered textiles of Crete which include Byzantine double-headed eagles, Italian sirens and Turkish tulips, admirably reflecting the island's history.

## Metalwork

Most metal objects tend to be easily portable or costume items. This is largely as a result of their high value and the need to be able to carry them easily if a hasty move were required. These are the most difficult items for which to establish a chronology as they have been the frequent victims of melting down and reforming.

## Woodwork

One of the most varied forms of folk art, woodwork decorates a wide range of pieces and more than any other form illustrates homogeneity of design throughout Greece.

## Stone-carving

A less common form of folk art, stonework designs do not tend to develop but remain highly stylised or very representative of imported designs.

## Wall-painting

More common in the north than the south, wall-painting is relatively rare, but where it does exist provides excellent evidence of life at the time of its creation.

# Museums

There is a rapidly growing number of folk art museums throughout Greece, ranging from the large national collections to small village exhibitions. The following is a minute selection of some of the larger ones.

## Benaki Museum, Athens

A vast private collection including a wide range of folk art. The collection of island embroideries is particularly fine.

## Museum of Folk Art, Plaka, Athens

A beautifully displayed collection of textiles, woodwork and some metal-work. Pieces are well labelled and illustrated with photographs.

## Peloponnesian Folklore Foundation

(Winner of the Small Museum of Europe Award.) An excellent display illustrating textile processing and different forms of textile techniques. The upper floor houses an extensive collection of mainland costumes.

## Museum of Macedonian Folklore, Thessaloniki

A wide collection of objects, well displayed, providing a clear insight into the way folk art represents regional history.

## Folk Museum of Epirus, Ioannina

A smaller collection of Epirot objects, including some particularly beautiful costumes.

# Buying Folk Art

In some areas it is possible to purchase items (pottery and textiles in particular) in the areas in which they are still being made, the most reasonable value usually being obtained from village craftsmen selling from their own premises. In the case of older items it is probably best to find dealers in the larger towns, away from the main centres of tourist activity, where it is still possible to find good pieces at relatively low prices.

# PRACTICAL INFORMATION

## Introduction

This section of the Guide is designed to help prospective visitors to Greece choose the route best suited to their requirements and to enable them to travel as comfortably and effectively as possible once they arrive. Readers should note that the 'Practical Information' section includes much advice (e.g. on methods of travel within Greece, or on site and museum hours) which is vital to successful travel and is not repeated subsequently.

### Sources of Information

Information about any matter to do with visiting Greece can be obtained from the **National Tourist Organisation of Greece** (in Greek, EOT) which has offices in **London** (4 Conduit St W1R D0J), **New York** (645 Fifth Avenue), **Los Angeles** (611 West Sixth Street) and **Chicago** (168 North Michigan Avenue). There are also branches in **Canada** (1300 Bay Street Toronto, and 1233 Rue de la Montagne, Montreal) and **Australia** (51–57 Pitt Street, Sydney), as well as other countries. Regional leaflets and the regularly revised General Information about Greece are available at all these offices.

Two English-language monthlies (published in Athens but available in Britain, from Alsos Books (see Books about Greece, below) or BAS Overseas Publications Ltd, Unit 1C, 159 Mortlake Road, Kew, Surrey, TW9 4AW) are invaluable for planning travel both to and within Greece, since they contain an extremely wide range of information. They are *Greek Travel Pages* (price in Athens c £8, 1994) and *Hellenic Travelling* (£6.50). These publications give details of air, rail and bus travel, hotel information (not below C category) and much other useful matter (customs, shop hours, etc.). The English magazine *Time Out* is useful for cut-rate travel, including buses. In the USA, the *New York Sunday Times* may be consulted. See also below under Travel In Greece etc.

For accommodation, the detailed and comprehensive *Guide to the Greek Hotels*, published annually in mid-March by the Hellenic Chamber of Hotels (price in Athens, £8, 1994) gives information about hotels of all categories, with prices.

### Maps

Maps of Greece are notoriously unreliable, although those published by major foreign motoring organisations and long-established map firms are now usually adequate for the major roads. Sheets obviously geared for the holidaymaker, whether published in Britain or Greece, are best avoided. The most useful maps, although rather small in scale and requiring a knowledge of the Greek alphabet, are those published in book form by Kapranides and Fotis, in association with the Greek Motoring Organisation (ELPA). In Britain these can be obtained from Alsos Books (see Books about Greece). In Greece they are quite widely available in bookshops, though you should be sure that you are being sold the current edition: over 20 have now been published and a new version appears annually. These books also contain a host of useful information of other kinds.

Contoured maps at 1:200,000 (mostly compiled in the 1960s) are available for each nome (equivalent to a British county) and can be purchased from the Ethnikí Statistikí Ipiresía tis Elládhos, 14 Likoúrgou (the offices are well hidden, in an arcade, but don't give up!), Athens 112, and nowhere else. Some sheets which were revised in 1972 show ancient sites. Certain coastal areas are well covered by Greek Naval Charts which can be bought at the Hydrographic Office.

Larger scale maps of certain areas are available from the Army Geographical Service at 4 Evelpídhon (Pedhíon tou Areos) on Monday, Wednesday and Friday mornings only.

A specialist map stockist in Britain is Stanfords, 12 Long Acre, Covent Garden, London WC2.

# Travel to Greece

## By Air

This is the quickest and most convenient method of getting to Greece and can be relatively cheap. **Scheduled flights** are operated by British Airways, PO Box 10, Heathrow Airport, Hounslow, Middlesex TW6 2JA, tel. 0345 222111 (from London and, less frequently, Manchester) and Olympic Airways, 11 Conduit St, London W1R 0LP, tel. 0171 409 3400 (London only), with several flights a day in summer, including some direct services to Thessaloniki, Corfu, Rhodes, and Crete. The cheapest fares usually apply to trips of not more than one month's duration, where the ticket is booked well in advance and no change at all is permitted to the dates or times. As there are frequent changes in fare structures, current information should be sought from experienced travel agents, who are more willing than the airlines to divulge the existence of the cheaper fares. Summer fares are usually higher than winter, and travel at weekends slightly more expensive than on weekdays. Other European and American airlines also operate regular scheduled services to Athens.

**Charter flights** operate from many regional airports (as well as from London) and to a considerable variety of destinations within Greece. While these are mainly intended for buyers of complete package holidays at rates which include accommodation, it is also possible to use them for travel only (with a nominal charge for accommodation). These flights are not necessarily very much cheaper than the cheapest fares on scheduled flights and may involve travelling at inconvenient times. On the other hand, they may allow direct travel from a local airport to the precise destination and, especially out of season, seats are often sold at discount prices when booked close to the departure date.

In Athens, all foreign airlines use the East Terminal at Ellinikon Airport, while Olympic Airways operates from the West Terminal. It is worth remembering that, since the internal services are also based there, Olympic is the only airline whose flights from abroad do not require a change of terminal when onward air travel to another destination within Greece is intended.

## By Rail

Unless using a student Inter-rail ticket (of limited duration), rail travel is no longer cheap and, unless the cost is further inflated by the purchase of sleepers, not very comfortable. The direct routes are from Northern European ports via France and Italy, or via Belgium/Holland and Germany and Austria into former Yugoslavia, though at present there are **no passenger services through to Greece**. Couchettes or sleepers, if required, should be booked well in advance. Those who dislike the antiseptic nature of air travel may well consider taking the train to an Italian port followed by a boat crossing to Greece (see below). Time-table and other information about rail travel is available from British Rail Travel Centres (best at the larger stations).

## By Sea

There is no regular direct passenger line from Britain to Greece, which would in any case require a good deal of time. There are however a substantial number (less frequent out of season) of passenger/car ferry services from Adriatic ports (Brindisi, Bari, Ancona and, less frequently, Venice) to Patras (often via Corfu and/or Igoumenitsa), with onward bus connections to Athens, or direct to Piraeus through the Corinth canal. The Brindisi–Patras route takes about 20 hours, via Corfu and Igoumenitsa; the others correspondingly longer. Amongst the companies providing these services are Fragline (Brindisi), Adriatica (Brindisi, Venice), ANEK (Ancona, Trieste), Charitos (Brindisi), European Seaways (Brindisi), Ventouris (Bari), Marlines (Ancona), Strintzis Lines (Ancona), Minoan Lines (Ancona), Hellenic Mediterranean Lines (H.M.L.) (Brindisi). Some routes continue to Turkey, Cyprus, the Levant or Egypt.

## By Road

The shortest overland route, **not practicable at present**, is c 3150km (1950 miles), via southern Germany, Austria and former Yugoslavia and takes an absolute minimum of four days. For the trip to be enjoyable a more leisurely drive is preferable, perhaps following the Adriatic coast (considerably longer). Alternatively, car ferries may be used from one of the Italian ports mentioned above (the Brindisi route is the fastest, but not necessarily the most pleasant). Motorail services from a Channel port or Paris to southern France or Italy (Milan best) reduce the strain of driving. The services (including route and customs information, and bookings) provided by the AA and RAC are essential. For the Greek motoring organisation (ELPA), see below.

## By Bus

This is the cheapest (and least comfortable) method of getting to Greece. Vehicles travel either direct (**not at present**) from a Channel port, or via one of the Adriatic ferries. There may or may not be night stops en route. The apparent economy may not be real when the cost of food and accommodation is taken into account. Travellers should be certain to choose a reliable operator. Information may be obtained from the Victoria Coach Station in London, student travel agencies, or newspaper advertisements (see above). The journey takes about 3–4 days.

## Travelling Formalities

**Passports** (British Visitors' Passports are valid) are the only travel document necessary for British nationals to travel in Greece. Application forms are available from any Post Office. Full passport requests may take some time to process and several weeks should be allowed. Those wishing to stay in

Greece for longer than three months must apply, at the end of that period and not before, for a *permis de séjour* (adhía paramonís; in Athens at the Aliens' Bureau, 173 Leofóros Alexándras; in the provinces at regional bureaux or the local police station). They may be required to submit proof of financial self-sufficiency.

## Customs

Normal EEC regulations on import/export of goods, alcohol, tobacco, etc. apply. Valuable items (especially electronic equipment) may be entered in the passport and re-export required (or else payment of import tax) at the end of the period of stay. This restriction always applies to private cars. Those wishing to keep a foreign-registered car in Greece for more than four months must apply for a permit from the appropriate customs department (in Athens 14 Od. Frantzí, Athens 117 42), when an extension of up to 9 months may be granted according to circumstances.

## Currency

Drs 100,000 in Greek currency may be imported by foreign nationals but the amount of travellers' cheques, etc. is not limited. Foreign banknotes of value higher than 1000 U.S. dollars must be declared on arrival. Any foreign currency, in whatever form, whose re-export may be desired on departure, must be declared on arrival. The export limits are Drs. 20,000 for foreign visitors; foreign currency up to $1000, unless arrangements have been made on arrival (see above).

# Travel Within Greece

## Sources of Information

The two publications cited above (*Greek Travel Pages* and *Hellenic Travelling*) remain indispensible. Also useful is the ELPA road atlas. *The Week in Athens*, available from the National Tourist Organisation, is free and has information about entertainments in Athens and travel. The National Tourist Organisation of Greece has offices in various towns. The Athens centre is within the National Bank of Greece branch in Sintagma Square (2 Karayióryi Servías). It distributes much travel information in duplicated sheets, answers queries and can deal with hotel bookings. The *Guide to Greek Hotels* can be purchased here. A less crowded alternative office is close by, in the General Bank at 1 Ermoú. The former Tourist Police have now been replaced as a separate organisation by members of the ordinary police force who staff information desks in police stations. The central organisation in Athens has a good general telephone enquiry service (dial 171). The Greek Motoring Organisation (ELPA) has a similar enquiry service (dial 174). Foreign languages are spoken and all kinds of information provided. For enquiry services offering information about specific methods of travel only, see below.

## Organised Travel

Details of the numerous cruises and coach tours of various durations may be acquired from any of the sources of information mentioned above.

## Sea Travel

Sea travel plays a large part in Greek transport with most ships now carrying cars as well as passengers. Most lines are based on Piraeus but travellers in more distant parts of Greece should investigate services originating in, for example, Thessaloniki, Kavalla, Patras, Rhodes, or Crete. A useful source of up-to-date and usually reliable information is the daily commercial shipping paper *Naftemborikí* (Ναυτεμπορική) which includes a complete list of the following seven days' domestic sailings from Piraeus and other main ports, also international arrivals and departures. Ability to read names in Greek is obviously necessary. Note also that π.μ. (p.m.) = English a.m. and μ.μ. (m.m.) = English p.m. Day-of-departure information about timings, which should **always** be checked before travelling, can be obtained in Athens from a recorded service (dial 143) or the Piraeus Port Authority (dial 108). Outside Athens, the most reliable information will be that provided by the local port authority (Limenarkhíon or Limenikós Stathmós; Λιμεναρχείον, Λιμενικός Σταθμός). A useful list of their telephone numbers is provided in the ELPA road atlas. They are the only reliable way of checking boat services in distant places, though some knowledge of Greek may be required. Travel agents tend to promote services operated by companies whom they represent.

**Booking** may be done in advance at travel agencies (many in central Athens, particularly the Omonia area) or, especially in smaller places, the agency (praktoríon) of the boat company concerned. It is best to choose the boat on which to travel from an independent source, as not all agencies have tickets for all boats and they naturally emphasise their own vessels. Be sure to choose the most direct route. Some services (especially to the Cyclades and Dodecanese) make many more stops and take much longer than others. A useful survey of boat services throughout Greece is R.F. Poffley, *Greek Island Hopping* (Thomas Cook, 1994, regularly updated).

There are four main **classes**: first, second, tourist and third (= deck); some vessels have a luxe class. Classes are officially assigned according to the quality of the available accommodation. Thus relatively few boats have all the four main classes and some do not have a first class at all. Most boats have cabins only in the first (and second) classes. No supplement is charged for cabins but there is no reduction if they are not available. To ensure a berth, it is necessary to have cabin and berth numbers entered on the ticket by the issuing agency. Vague promises that one will be available on the day are not enough. Decks of boats become very crowded and uncomfortable in the summer and, whatever the class, it is often more comfortable to travel inside. Cabins are a great benefit on night (or even long day) crossings, but can be stuffy on older boats. On long-distance ferry services, cars need to be booked well in advance. For short crossings in local waters, it is necessary only to turn up and join the queue.

## Air Travel

Air travel in Greece is provided by the extensive internal network of Olympic Airways. There are flights to many destinations and long distances can often be covered much more effectively by this means of travel, which is cheap by British standards. The frequency of flights obviously varies a good deal with the destination.

**Booking** may be done at any office of or agent of Olympic Airways in Greece or abroad, though the fastest service is provided by those with a computer terminal. Advance booking is essential in the summer season (especially to the islands and other popular holiday areas). There is an extremely efficient and useful telephone booking system (in Athens dial 9666666; or via any office or agent). An intending traveller can be entered on the flight list simply by making a phone call; you will be given a date and time by which the ticket must be collected and paid for (again at any Olympic office or agent). If the booking is not taken up in time it automatically lapses, without cost to the customer.

## Railways

Greece was the last country in Europe to take up railway development (after 1881) and railways play only a small part in the country's transport system. A line from Athens to Piraeus was constructed in 1867–69 and electrified in 1904, but the main Piraeus–Athens–Larissa line was built only in 1902–09, and did not reach Thessaloniki until 1916. The first international express (Simplon–Orient) ran in July 1920. The track and rolling stock have recently been substantially improved. The former Peloponnesian Railway (SPAP) is now administratively part of the state railway system but has a separate terminus in Athens and is of metre gauge only. The services are generally punctual but slow on account of the terrain. For the tourist the Peloponnesian Railway provides a convenient (and, south of Corinth, very attractive) approach to, e.g. Argos, Patras, Olympia, Tripolis, and Kalamata. **Booking** should be done in advance to secure a seat, at stations or a network of in-town booking offices.

## Road Travel

**Long distance buses** are operated by Joint Pools of Bus Owners (Κοινόν Ταμείον Εισπραξείων Λεωφορείων; KTEL). In Athens these have been further grouped for operation in two main terminals, situated in the outskirts of Athens and served by city buses from central points. Each still has its own booking-office (praktoríon). Bookings (preferably in advance, and in any case before boarding the bus to ensure a numbered seat) may be made by telephone; the booking-offices are listed in the telephone directory under TAMEION, or more conveniently in one of the sources of information (above): a recorded list of Athens numbers is available over the telephone by dialling 142. With a booked seat it is not necessary to appear more than a few minutes before scheduled departure time when luggage is stowed.

Buses keep well to schedule. The promoters have strictly-interpreted agreements about the places they serve. A bus from Kalamata may take passengers between that town (or its dependent nome) and any other place along its route to (say) Athens; it may not pick up intermediate passengers beyond Tripolis and Corinth, which, being in different nomes, are the province of KTEL. The traveller who intends to board a long-distance bus at the roadside needs some knowledge not only of schedules but of the nome boundaries, and should work out beforehand the name of the KTEL required (this is always prominently displayed on the front of the bus even if the destination sometimes is not).

**Local services.** Most villages, however remote, are served by a bus based on the nearest town of any size. Small villages may be served once or twice daily, or less frequently. Timings are designed to suit local markets and schools, not visitors, and the return trip may involve a night's stay.

**Advice on bus travel**: those relying on buses as their main form of transport are most strongly urged to make the bus station or office (often, in a small place, the local café) their first port of call, immediately on arrival anywhere. A timetable of departures will often be prominently displayed and plans can be made. It is well worth postponing the compelling attractions of bed or refreshment in order to avoid missing the once-weekly bus (perhaps leaving early the following morning) to a much-desired destination.

**City services**. Buses and some trolley routes serve the capital between about 05.30 and midnight, with some all-night routes. Though frequent, they are often very crowded. Similar systems are operated in Thessaloniki and other large towns. There is a flat fare over a large area of the centres and suburbs of major cities (in Athens Drs. 75, likely soon to rise to Drs. 100, in early 1995). Tickets are purchased in advance from bus company kiosks or designated agents and cancelled in machines on entry. Failure to do this renders the passenger liable to a fine of 20 times the fare. Supplements are charged on night services.

## Taxis

Metered taxis are numerous and cheap in the towns. There is a minimum fare of Drs 200. Supplements (Drs 200) are payable for journeys originating at any major public transport terminal; also for large quantities of luggage (Drs 500). Supplements for radio taxis called to a private house or hotel are Drs 200 and 500, respectively. Outside the city boundary, a higher tariff applies. At busy times and with (or sometimes without) the permission of the original hirer, the driver may pick up other passengers going in roughly the same direction. Enquiry is made by shouting one's destination through the window. A deduction should be made for such passengers when they reach their destination, since the fare shown on the meter will be that from the original point of hire. This may not always be easy to negotiate but, at peak hours, it is probably worth ignoring the relatively small mark-up.

In country areas, meters are not always fitted but there is a standard tariff which may or may not be publicly displayed or adhered to, and an agreement as to the fare should always be made in advance. If in doubt, enquire the price from several drivers. Travellers are advised to make good use of taxis which, judiciously employed, can enable you to see far more than might otherwise be possible in the time, where public transport is lacking, and at relatively modest cost. They can, quite often, work out cheaper than a hired car. For not-too-distant excursions, an arrangement can be made for the driver to return later, at a specified time, at a total fare less than that for two single journeys.

## Hire Cars, etc

There are numerous car hire companies in Greece (lists in the main Sources of Information and from the National Tourist Organisation). Airports of any size have representatives of the larger companies. On the other hand some sizeable centres (Kastoria and Kozani are examples) may have no such provision. Hire in Greece is relatively expensive, though the cost varies enormously according to season, length of hire, company and booking circumstances. In 1994 the best bargains were for cars booked in advance from Britain through one of the major companies (e.g. Hertz, Holiday Autos; c £170 per week for a small car). On the spot, where rates are substantially higher, the cheapest rate is achieved by taking a full week's hire, with unlimited mileage. Three-day unlimited mileage rates are also available; otherwise the cost is calculated by adding a charge per kilometre to a modest daily rate. Some travel firms offer inclusive packages with flight, and car on arrival; others provide the option of car hire at rates similar to those offered by UK-based firms. Reductions can sometimes be negotiated at quieter periods. When calculating rates from hire company leaflets, you should be sure to include taxes (usually high—about 20 per cent) and any charges for additional insurance cover which may be desired. In spite of the cost, the advantages to be gained in terms of extra mobility and access to remoter areas often make it an attractive option, particularly if costs can be shared.

**Scooters** and **bicycles** can often be hired in tourist resorts. Great care is required with scooters; accidents are a serious hazard on unsurfaced roads.

## Motoring

Driving (on the right) is conducted in a competitive spirit which can be alarming to the visitor and accords Greece the dubious distinction of having one of the highest accident rates in Europe. Nevertheless, outside the large cities, the roads are not crowded and motoring is pleasant. City traffic can always be avoided by leaving at quiet times of day. Petrol stations are plentiful on main roads but may be infrequent in remote areas. It is unwise to count on finding petrol easily after 19.00 or at weekends. Larger towns will always have one or two stations open; information from local papers, the police or tourist information sources. Parking is difficult in towns where there are often wide restrictions (frequently ignored). Private motorists can get road maps, information etc. from the Greek Motoring Organisation (ELPA: ΕΛΠΑ). The Athens headquarters is at the Athens Tower, 2 Od. Mesogeíon, and there are regional offices in all towns of any size, as well as some mobile trailers. The roadside assistance and rescue service (dial 104, in Athens) is extremely efficient and has reciprocal arrangements with other European motoring organisations. The ELPA telephone information bureau (dial 174, foreign languages spoken) has already been mentioned. An alternative, and equally efficient nationwide rescue service is Express (234 Leofóros Singroú; Drs 17,000 for 6 months subscription).

## Walking

Walking in the Greek countryside is one of the greatest pleasures to be had, partly for the natural surroundings; partly for the seemingly endless supply of friendly, helpful and hospitable people that you are likely to encounter. It is virtually impossible to plan walks in any detail, since large scale maps showing footpaths are not generally available. However, since for many country people walking is the main form of travel, paths and old paved trackways (calderímia) are numerous and directions may be sought locally (for useful words, see below on finding archaeological sites). Directions may often be somewhat confusing (both in reality and because of language problems) and it is advisable to ask continually, if in any doubt at all. Unfamiliar hazards may be fierce dogs (who usually retreat when stones are picked up), snakes and swarming bees. Since the terrain can be rough and twisted ankles always a danger, some may prefer not to walk alone in remote areas.

# Accommodation and Food

## Hotels (Ξενοδοχεία: Xenodhokhía)

Lists of hotels can be found in various Sources of Information (see above). The most comprehensive is the *Guide to the Greek Hotels*. Other publications tend not to list hotels in categories below C.

There are six official categories: **L** and **A–E**. Even in country districts modest but modern hotels are to be found almost everywhere. The de Luxe hotels are of international standard and almost all have restaurants; their rooms all have private bathrooms and air-conditioning. In all hotels of class **A**, most of classes **B** and **C**, and many of class **D** a proportion of rooms (sometimes all) have private bath or shower. Many Greek hotels do not have restaurants. Hotels classed **D** or **E** may have no public rooms and sometimes only cold water, though their standard of cleanliness and service is often adequate. (**F–A** = Furnished Apartments).

Charges are fixed annually by the Government. Hoteliers may not exceed the maximum permitted figure; the charge appropriate to each room, quoted with service and taxes included, is entered in a notice fixed usually to the inside of the door, and on a summary table displayed at the reception. Central heating or air conditioning is always extra. Considerable reductions can be obtained in November–March, and at other times in quieter areas. In general large hotels in seaside resorts are closed in winter, except where the place is an important town, e.g. Corfu, Navplion.

Despite the official categorisation, hotels can still vary widely. In Greece, as elsewhere, many hotels at popular sites and beach resorts are geared to package tours and coach groups rather than to the unexpected overnight guest. Furthermore some hotels can legally insist on demi-pension terms, thus tying the visitor to their usually unimaginative restaurants. In the provinces a universal-type basin plug and a stock of toilet paper can still be useful. It is difficult to get single rooms; single occupation of a double room is usually charged at 80 per cent of double price.

Charges vary considerably, even within each category, so that a cheap B-class hotel can be less expensive than a dearer C. It is thus worth investigating establishments which seem at first sight likely to be too expensive. Provincial hotels are often substantially cheaper than those in large towns or major tourist centres. In 1994 (also applicable winter 1994/5), a twin room in a good middle-range C class hotel, with private bath, cost about £17.50 (accommodation only). It is advisable to inspect the accommodation before making a definite agreement. Hoteliers are always willing to show rooms and respect an adverse decision.

**Rooms**. Where no hotel accommodation is available it is often possible, especially in holiday resorts or tourist centres, to find rooms either in specially built letting blocks (Rooms for Rent is an ubiquitous sign) or in private houses. The former are really modest hotels. The rooms quite often have a private bathroom and there is usually a fridge and kitchen, where food can be kept or prepared. In the islands, people often meet boats with offers of such accommodation; otherwise help may be sought from the police tourist officer or the local café.

**Motels**, of which there are a growing number, and seaside **Bungalow-hotels** have the same classification system as hotels.

**Youth Hostels**. The Greek Youth Hostel Association (4 Odhós Dhragat-saníou, Athens) is affiliated to the International Youth Hostels Federation. Its hostels may be used by members of any affiliated association. Accommodation is usually simple and members are obliged to keep early hours; stay is generally limited to five days. There are hostels in Athens, Delphi, Patras, Ioannina, Thessaloniki, Mikonos, Corfu, and Iraklion, also smaller ones elsewhere. In Athens are the YWCA (11 Od. Ameríkis) and the YMCA (28 Od. Omírou), maximum stay 10 days, meals extra. In July and August the Polytechnic School in Athens also accommodates groups of students.

**Car-camping sites** are run by the NTOG (modest charges) at Voula, Killini, Patras (Ayia), Kamena Vourla, Thessaloniki, Asprovalta, Kavalla,

Khalkidiki (Kriopiyi, Paliouri, and Kalandra), Fanari, Alexandroupolis, and on Mt Olympos (Skotina). An up-to-date list can be obtained from the Athens office. Elsewhere there are many private camping sites.

# Food

## Dining Out

In the larger centres a few restaurants and de luxe hotels offer an international cuisine. Well-prepared Greek dishes, however, are greatly to be preferred to emulation of alien styles. The basic ingredients are usually excellent and, since all Greeks eat out frequently, there is a wide choice of places. Travellers are well advised always to choose establishments crowded with locals, where the food will be better (and cheaper) and the atmosphere livelier.

## Restaurants (Εστιατόρια: Estiatória)

In Athens lunch is usually taken between 13.00 and 16.00 (earlier on Sunday) and dinner (generally the more important) between 20.00 and 23.00 (summer 21.00 and 01.00), though hotels catering particularly for foreigners conform more closely to Western times. Outside Athens hours also tend to be earlier. Estiatória display at the entrance a bill of fare, showing their category (L, A–D) and the prices of each dish, both basic and with tax and service included. There are usually translations into English. Fixed price and table d'hôte meals are rare. A service charge is added by law so that any gratuity to the waiter (on the plate) is a recognition of personal service. A wine boy (mikrós, but often an older man), however, receives only what is left for him on the table (c 5 per cent).

The distinction between a restaurant proper and a Ταβέρνα is no longer so clear, but in general the **tavérna** is less formal, patronised for a convivial evening rather than for luncheon, and partly at least out of doors; its fare is uncompromisingly Greek. An **exokhikón kéndron** (ΕΞΟΧΙΚΟΝ ΚΕΝΤΡΟΝ; 'rural centre') combines the functions of café and taverna in a country or seaside setting. The simplest kind of meal, consisting of milk, coffee, bread, butter, honey, etc., can be had in a **galaktopoleíon**, or dairy, though these are fast disappearing. Here in provincial towns the visitor will find the nearest equivalent to breakfast obtainable. A **zakharoplasteíon**, or pâtisserie, sells pastries and confectionery, with drinks of all sorts, though larger establishments in the cities serve also light meals (generally not cheap). They increasingly resemble the French café, and for younger generations are replacing the traditional Greek kafeneion (see below). The **ouzerí** serves mezédhes (a series of small dishes often including sea food, such as octopus or prawns), traditionally with ouzo, but most offer other drinks as well. Fast-food establishments have also invaded Greece.

Restaurants and taverna meals of comparable standard are considerably cheaper than in Britain. The pattern of meals is also less stereotyped, the sharing of portions being quite usual; it is essential to order each course separately as several dishes ordered together may arrive together. In tavernas it is usual to visit the kitchens to choose dishes, and in waterside tavernas it is customary to select fish from the ice; this will then be weighed, the price appearing on the menu per kilo. The oily content of most Greek food is too exuberant for some tastes, though the local wine is a good counteragent. Frozen foods (still rare in Greece) must be indicated by law on the menu with the letters KAT.

Good table wines (see further below; unresinated, *arretsínoto*), both red and white, are obtainable in bottle everywhere and some of the better-known have a nation-wide distribution. Retsína, the resinated white wine characteristic particularly of Attica and the Peloponnese, has lost some of its former popularity as other wines have improved. It can always be obtained in bottle, but the traditional can or jug from the barrel is preferable, when available. This can be more refreshing and less soporific in the heat of the day with an al fresco meal. Beer (of Bavarian type) is brewed in Greece and other lagers are brewed under licence or imported. Tap water is generally safe in Greece, but mineral waters from spas such as Loutraki are readily available.

## Food and Wine

The favourite Greek apéritif is *oúzo*, a strong colourless drink made from grape-stems and flavoured with aniseed; it is served with *mezé*, snacks consisting of anything from a simple slice of cheese or tomato or an olive to pieces of smoked eel or fried octopus. As in Italy the Greek meal may begin with a foundation course of rice, such as *piláfi sáltsa*, or of pasta (*makarónia*), perhaps baked with minced meat (*pastítsio*) or with *tirópita* (cheese pie). Alternatives are soup or hors d'oeuvre, the latter being particularly good. *Taramosaláta* is a paste made from the roe of grey mullet and olive oil. *Tzatzíki* consists of chopped cucumber in yoghourt heavily flavoured with garlic. The main course may be meat (κρέας, kréas), or fish or a dish on a vegetable base, baked (τού φούρνου, too foúrnu), boiled (βραστό, vrastó), fried (τηγανιτό, tiganitó), roast (ψητό, psitó), or grilled (σχάρας, skháras). The chef's suggestions will be found under ΠΙΑΤΑ ΤΗΣ ΗΜΕΡΑΣ (piáta tis iméras; dishes of the day). *Moussaká* consists of layers of aubergines, minced beef, and cheese, with butter and spices, baked in the oven. Foreign dishes may appear in transliteration, e.g.: Εσκαλόπ (escalope), Σνιτσελ Χολσταῖν (Schnitzel Holstein), Μπιντόκ αλα Ρους (Bintok à la Russe), Κρέμ καραμελέ (crème caramelle), Σαλάτ ντέ φρουῖ (salade de fruits). Many sweets have Turkish names, and shish kebab is frequently used as a synonym for *souvlákia*, pieces of meat grilled on a skewer. Also cooked in this fashion is *kokorétsi*, which consists of alternate pieces of lamb's liver, kidney, sweetbreads, and heart, wrapped in intestines. When not grilled, meat is often stewed with oil in unappetising chunks. Greek cheeses tend to monotony; the ubiquitous *féta* is better eaten—peasant-fashion—with black pepper, oil and *rígani* (oregano) than on its own. In country areas local produce should be requested. Sweets, however, are elaborate and varied, though more often eaten separately than as a course of a meal. Among the most popular are *baklavá*, composed of layered pastry filled with honey and nuts; *kataîfi*, wheat shredded and filled with sweetened nuts; and *galaktoboúreko*, pastry filled with vanilla custard.

## Wine (κρασί: Krasí)

Wine in Greece is generally good and stronger than the wines of France. Wines are of two basic types—resinated and unresinated. *Retsína*, flavoured with resin from pine trees, is most characteristic of the south, and to the trained palate varies as much in taste and quality as do unresinated wines. Although much is bottled, retsína is better drunk young from the cask. Rosé varieties (κοκκινέλλι), are locally popular. There is a large variety of wines, white (άσπρο, áspro), red (μαύρο, mávro, literally black), or rosé (κόκκινο, kókkino, literally red). There are good draught red wines from Nemea, Rhodes and Corfu. It is invidious to recommend bottled wines from the vast range available but some of the following may be sampled: Hymettus (red and white), Santa Elena (white), Pallíni (white), Vílitsa (white), Zítsa (white, semi-sparkling), Sámaina (white), Castel Daniélis (red), Tsántali (white, rosé), Chevalier de Rhodes (red), Náoussa (red), Robólla (white). The latter three are rather more expensive but no Greek wine is costly by British standards. The champagne of Rhodes is pleasant. The wines of the Carras estate are also good. Sampling local wines is a great pleasure. Most wine shops stock a reasonable range. In Athens the shop of a large wine co-operative at 73 Odhós L. Riankoúr (off Od. Panórmou, between Alexándras and Kifissías) has an interesting selection.

The **menu** which follows contains a large number of the simpler dishes to be found:

OPEKTIKA (orektiká), Hors d'oeuvre

Διάφορα ορεκτικά (dhiáfora orektiká), Hors d'oeuvre variés
Ταραμοσαλάτα (taramosaláta), see above
Ντολμάδες Γιαλαντζή (dolmádhes Yalantzí), Stuffed vine leaves served hot with egg-lemon sauce
Ντολμαδάκια (dolmadhákia), Cold stuffed vine leaves
Ελιές (elliés), Olives

ΣΟΥΠΕΣ (soúpes), Soups

Σούπα αυγολέμονο (soúpa avgholémono), Egg and lemon soup
Σούπα από χόρτα (soúpa apó hórta), Vegetable soup
Μαγειρίτσα (maghirítsa), Tripe soup generally with rice (Easter speciality)
Ψαρόσουπα (psarósoupa), Fish soup

ZYMAPIKA (Zimárika), Pasta and Rice dishes

Πιλάφι σάλτσα (piláfi sáltsa), Pilaf
Σπαγέτο σάλτσα μέ τυρί (spagéto sáltsa me tirí), Spaghetti
Μακαρόνια (makarónia), Macaroni

ΨAPIA (psária), Fish

Στρείδια (strídhia), Oysters
Συναγρίδα (sinagrídha), Sea bream
Μπαρμπούνια (barboúnia), Red mullet
Μαρίδες (marídhes), Whitebait
Αστακός (astakós), Lobster
Γαρίδες (garídes), Scampi (Dublin Bay prawns)
Καλαμαράκια (kalamarákia), Baby squids
Κταπόδι (ktapódhi), Octopus
Λιθρίνια (lithrínia), Bass

ΛΑΔΕΡΑ (ladherá), Vegetables or XOPTA (khórta), Greens

Πατάτες τηγανιτές (patátes tiganités), Fried potatoes
Φασολάκια φρ. βουτ. (fasolákia fr. voútiro), Beans in butter

Μπιζέλια (biséllia), Peas
Ντομάτες γεμιστές ρύζι (domátes yemistés rízi), Stuffed tomatoes

ΑΥΓΑ (avgá) Eggs

Ομελέτα Ζαμπόν (Omelétta Zambón), Ham omelette
Αυγά Μπρουγέ (avgá 'brouillé'), Scrambled eggs
Αυγά α λά Ρούζ (avgá 'à la Russe'), Eggs with Russian salad

ΕΝΤΡΑΔΕΣ (entrádhes), Entrées

Αρνάκι φασολάκια (arnáki fasolákia), Lamb with beans
Μοσχάρι (moskhári), Veal
Σηκοτάκια (sikotákia), Liver
Κοτόπουλο (kotópoulo), Chicken
Χήνα (khína), Goose
Παπί (papí), Duck
Τζουτζουκάκια (tsoutsoukákia), Meat balls in tomato sauce
Κοτολέτες Χοιρινές (kotoléttes khirinés), Pork cutlets

ΣΧΑΡΑΣ (skháras), Grills

Σουβλάκια από φιλέτο (souvlákia ápo filéto), Shish Kebab (see above)
Μπριζόλες μοσχ. (brizóles moskh.), Veal chops
Κεφτέδες σχάρας (keftédhes skháras), Grilled meat balls
Γουρουνόπουλο ψητό (gourounópoulo psitó), Roast sucking-pig
Παϊδάκια Χοιρινά (païdhákia khiriná), Pork chops

ΣΑΛΑΤΕΣ (salátes), Salads

Ντομάτα σαλάτα (domáta saláta), Tomato salad
Μαρούλι (maroúli), Lettuce
Ραδίκια (radhíkia), Radishes
Κολοκυθάκια (kolokithákia), Courgettes
Αγγουράκι (angouráki), Cucumber
Αγκινάρες (ankináres), Artichokes
Μελιτζάνες (melizánes), Aubergines (eggplants)
Πιπεριές (piperiés), Green peppers
Ρώσσικη (Russikí), Russian

ΤΥΡΙΑ (tiriá), Cheeses

Φέτα (féta), Soft white cheese of goat's milk
Κασέρι (kasséri), Hard yellow cheese
Γραβιέρα (graviéra), Greek gruyère
Ροκφόρ ('Roquefort'), Blue cheeses generally

ΓΛΥΚΑ (gliká), Sweets

Χαλβά (Halvá)
Μπακλαβά (baklavá) see above
Καταΐφι (kataḯfi)
Γαλακτομπούρεκο (galaktoboúreko)

Ρυζόγαλο (rizógalo), Rice pudding
Γιαούρτι (yiaoúrti), Yoghourt

ΦΡΟΥΤΑ (froúta), Fruits

Μήλο (mílo), Apple
Μπανάνα (banána), Banana
Αχλάδι (akhládhi), Pear
Πορτοκάλι (portokáli), Orange
Κεράσια (kerásia), Cherries
Φράουλες (fráoules), Strawberries
Δαμάσκηνα (dhamáskina), Plums
Ροδάκινα (rodhákina), Peaches
Βερύκοκα (veríkoka), Apricots
Πεπόνι (pepóni), Melon
Καρπούζι (karpoúzi), Water-melon

**MISCELLANEOUS**

Ψωμί (psomí), Bread
Βούτυρο (voútiro), Butter
Αλάτι (aláti), Salt
Πιπέρι (pipéri), Pepper
Μουστάρδα (moustárdha), Mustard
Λάδι (ládhi), Oil
Ξίδι (xídhi), Vinegar
Γάλα (ghála), Milk
Ζάχαρι (zákhari), Sugar
Νερό (neró), Water
Παγωμένο (pagoméno), Iced
Παγωτό (paghotó), Ice Cream
Λεμόνι (lemóni), Lemon

The traditional Greek **café** (ΚΑΦΕΝΕΙΟΝ) of the provinces is an austere establishment usually thronged with men for whom it is both local club and political forum. Coffee (καφέ) is always served in the 'Turkish' fashion with the grounds. It may be drunk heavily sweetened (variglikó), medium (métrio) or without sugar (skhétto). Cafes displaying the sign ΚΑΦΕΝΕΙΟΝ– ΜΠΑΡ (café-bar) also serve drinks. There are now also many more modern, if less colourful, cafés.

# General Information

## Prices

These change and relative values alter so frequently in accordance with fluctuations in the exchange rate that prices are rarely quoted in the following pages, though some general estimates of the relative costs in comparison with those prevailing in the UK are given. The cost of living in Greece is much closer to that of western Europe than was previously the case but, in some respects (e.g. restaurant meals, fruit and vegetables) is substantially cheaper.

## Season

Climatically the best months to visit Greece are April to mid-June and September to October. At more popular places the season extends from March with heavily booked hotels. In July and August beaches are crowded, and the temperature even there may be uncomfortable (average max. 32°C, min. 22°). During the not infrequent heat-waves shade temperatures may exceed 38° in Athens and 43° in Thessaly. March and November and later often have surprisingly warm days with long hours of sunshine, but in the earlier part of the year the sea is rarely warm enough for swimming. Equally it can be rainy with chilly evenings until well into April. In winter Athens has very changeable weather, bitter winds and squally rain alternating with dazzling sunny intervals, so that a heavy overcoat and sunglasses may be needed together; but snow (though commonly visible on the surrounding hills) rarely settles in the city. The Aegean islands enjoy milder winters, while the mountainous inland regions of the mainland share the general rigours of the Balkans.

## Language

A knowledge of ancient Greek is a useful basis, but no substitute, for the study of modern Greek. Apart from the unfamiliarity of modern pronunciation many of the commonest words (e.g. water, wine, fish) no longer come from the same roots. Fluency in modern Greek adds greatly to the ease and pleasure of travelling, but English is understood everywhere on the main tourist routes. A knowledge of at least the Greek alphabet is highly desirable, however, since street names, bus destination plates, etc., may otherwise be unintelligible. A smattering of Greek is much appreciated and certainly ensures greater contact with local people. A successful modern introduction to Greek, which has the advantage of subject matter related to life in Greece today, is D. A. Hardy, *Greek language and people* (BBC publications, 1983 and many reprints; cassettes available but not essential).

The Greek alphabet now as in later classical times comprises 24 letters:

Α α, Β β, Γ γ, Δ δ, Ε ε, Ζ ζ, Η η, Θ θ, Ι ι, Κ κ, Λ λ, Μ μ, Ν ν, Ξ ξ, Ο ο, Π π, Ρ ρ, Σ σ ς, Τ τ, Υ υ, Φ φ, Χ χ, Ψ ψ, Ω ω.

**Vowels**. There are five basic vowel sounds in Greek to which even combinations written as diphthongs conform: α is pronounced very short; ε and αι as e in egg (when accented more open, as in the first e in there); η, ι, υ, ει, οι, υι have the sound of ea in eat; ο, ω as the o in dot; ου as English oo in pool. The combinations αυ and ευ are pronounced av and ev when followed by loud consonants (af and ef before mute consonants).

**Consonants** are pronounced roughly as their English equivalents with the following exceptions: β = v; γ is hard and guttural, before a and o like the English g in hag, before other vowels approaching the y in your; γγ and γκ are usually equivalent to ng; δ = th as in this; θ as th in think; before an i sound λ resembles the lli sound in million; ξ has its full value always, as in ex-king; ρ is always rolled; σ (ς) is a sibilant as in oasis; τ is pronounced half way between t and d; φ = ph or f; χ, akin to the Scottish ch, a guttural h; ψ = ps as in lips. The English sound b is represented in Greek by the double consonant μπ, d by ντ. All Greek words of two syllables or more have one accent which serves to show the stressed syllable. The classical breathing marks are still sometimes written but have no significance in speech. In the termination ον, the n sound tends to disappear in speech and the ν is often omitted in writing.

## Calendar and Time

Greece abandoned the Julian calendar only in 1923 so that even 20C dates can be in Old or New Style. All moveable festivals are governed by the fixing of Easter according to the Orthodox calendar. Greece uses Eastern European Time (2 hours ahead of G.M.T.); π.μ.—a.m. and μ.μ.—p.m. When making an appointment it is advisable to confirm that it is an 'English rendezvous', i.e. one to be kept at the hour stated. The siesta hours after lunch (often late) should not be disturbed by calling or telephoning.

## Manners and Customs

The more formal conventions of Greeks should be observed. The handshake at meeting and parting is de rigueur, and inquiry after the health taken seriously. The correct reply to καλώς ωρίσατε (kalós orísate: welcome) is καλώς σας βρήκαμε (kalós sas vríkame: glad to see you). To the inquiry τί κάνετε; (tí kánete; how do you do?) or πως είσθε; (pos íste; how are you?) the reply should be καλά, ευχαριστώ, και σείς (kalá efkharistó, ke sis): well, thank you—and you?—or έτσι καί έτσι (etsi ke etsi), so-so. General greetings are Χαίρετε (khérete; greetings, hallo) Γειά σας (yásas; hello, goodbye-lit: your health) and Στό καλό (sto kaló; keep well), both useful for greeting strangers on the road. Περαστικά (perastiká) is a useful word of comfort in time of sickness or misfortune meaning 'may things improve'. Except in the centre of Athens it is still customary to greet shop-keepers, the company in cafés, etc., with καλημέρα (kaliméra: good day) or καλησπέρα (kalispéra: good evening). Σας παρακαλώ (sas parakaló: please) is used when asking for a favour or for information, but not when ordering something which is to be paid for, when Θά ήθελα (tha íthela; I should like) is more appropriate. The Greek for yes is ναί (né) or, more formally, μάλιστα (málista); for no, όχι (ókhi). Αντίο (Addío), goodbye, so long, in Greek has none of the finality of its Italian origin.

In direct contrast to English custom, personal questions showing interest in a stranger's life, politics, and money are the basis of conversation in Greece, and travellers must not be offended at being asked in the most direct way about their movements, family, occupation, salary, and politics, though they will usually find discussion of the last singularly inconclusive.

By Greek custom the bill for an evening out is invariably paid by the host; the common foreign habit of sharing out payment round the table is looked upon as mean and unconvivial, and visitors valuing their 'face' will do it discreetly elsewhere. A stranger is rarely allowed to play host to a native.

It is not good manners to fill a wine-glass, nor to drain a glass of wine, the custom being to pour it half full and keep it 'topped up'. Glasses are often touched with the toast εις υγείαν σας, your health (generally shortened in speech to the familiar yásas or yámas, or, to a single individual, yásou); they are then raised to the light, the bouquet savoured, and the wine sipped before drinking (thus all five senses have been employed in the pleasure).

When visiting a Greek house you may formally be offered preserves with coffee and water; this should not be refused. Strictly to conform to custom the water is drunk first, the preserves eaten and the spoon placed in the glass, and the coffee drunk at leisure. Payment must, of course, never be offered for any service of hospitality. An acceptable way of reducing an obligation is by making a present to a child of the house. Equally hospitality should not be abused; those offering it, especially in the countryside, frequently have less resources than their foreign guests—even the proverbially poor student.

The 'Volta', or evening parade, universal throughout provincial Greece, has no fixed venue in Athens. Fasting is taken seriously in Lent.

## Health

Climate and unfamiliar food can cause problems. Elementary precautions are obvious: avoid overexposure to the sun (which burns even when a sea breeze makes it seem cool), and too much oily food. It is advisable to carry one or two patent remedies. Rice and lemon juice are good for upset stomachs. Chemists can advise on other medicines. Dog bites need immediate treatment by a doctor.

## Public Holidays

Offical public holidays in Greece are: New Year's Day; 6 January (Epiphany); Kathará Dheftéra ('Clean Monday'), the Orthodox Shrove Day; 25 March (Independence Day); Orthodox Good Friday, Easter Monday, 1 May; Ascension Day; 15 August (Assumption); 28 October 'Okhi' day (see below); Christmas Day; and 26 December (St. Stephen). In addition Athens celebrates the feast of her patron saint, St. Dionysios the Areopagite (3 October), and some other cities a patronal festival.

**Carnival** after three weeks' festivities reaches its peak on the Sunday before Clean Monday with processions and student revels. The tradition is strong in Patras, Naoussa, and in Athens is centred on Plaka. Procession of shrouded bier on Good Friday (Epitáfios); 'Christos anésti' (Christ is risen) celebration, with ceremonial lighting of the Paschal candle and release of doves, in front of churches at midnight preceding Easter Sunday, followed by candlelight processions and 'open house'. Roasting of Paschal lambs and cracking of Easter eggs on the morning of Easter Day. These ceremonies are performed with public formality in the capital. **Okhi Day**, commemorating the Greek 'no' (όχι) to the Italian ultimatum of 1940, is celebrated with remembrance services and military processions, especially in Thessaloniki.

## Postal Services

For the main post offices (Ταχυδρομεία: Takhidhromía) in Athens, see Athens. Provincial post offices close at 14.00 and do not open at weekends. Apart from their usual services, post offices now change travellers' cheques. Letter boxes (γραμματοκιβότια) are painted yellow and may be marked εσωτερικά (inland), εξωτερικά (abroad), or επείγοντα (express). Postage stamps are obtainable at some kiosks and shops as well as at post offices (10 per cent surcharge). The charge for express letters is reasonable and usually ensures delivery in the UK two days after posting. A registered letter is ένα συστημένο γράμμα (éna sistiméno grámma). There are often considerable delays to post (especially postcards) in the summer season and internal mail is not exempt from problems. Correspondence marked Poste Restante (to be called for) may be sent to any post office and collected by the addressee on proof of identity (passport preferable). A small fee may be charged. The surname of the addressee should be clearly written, and no Esq. added. **Parcels** are not delivered in Greece. They must be collected from the post office, where they are subject to handling fees, full customs charges, and often to delay. The bus companies operate an efficient internal parcels service from their own offices.

## Telephones

The Greek telephone and telegraph services are run by a public corporation, the Οργανισμός Τηλεπικοινωνίων Ελλάδος (O.T.E.; always referred to by its acronym—ό, té), which is quite separate from the postal authority. All large towns have a central office of the company, with call boxes and arrangements for making trunk and international calls and sending telegrams. Most villages have an O.T.E. centre, which may be a local café. If not, the hours are likely to be restricted. Major offices have a 24-hour service.

Long-distance calls can also be made from ubiquitous public card phones, most hotels, many kiosks and any other establishment which has a meter (μετρητή; metrití) attached to the telephone. The meter records the number of units and payment is made accordingly. The availability of metered phones means that it is not usually necessary to visit an O.T.E. centre to make a long-distance call (either domestic or international). The charge per unit is fixed—lowest at O.T.E., slightly higher at kiosks and shops; highest in hotels. The cheap rate is 22.00–06.00 (U.K. calls) and 23.00–08.00 (U.S A.). Current (January 1995) rates are Drs 96 and 226 per minute (cheap rates to U.K. and U.S.A.), the normal charge being c 1/3 more. The cheap rate period within Greece is 22.00–08.00. There is international direct dialling. Otherwise, for Greek long-distance calls, dial 132; international 161; telegrams: domestic 155, international 165. Police 100. Time 141 (in Greek).

Local calls can be made from card-phones, and many kiosks, shops, etc.

## Banks

Banks are open Monday to Friday (except public holidays) from 08.00 to 14.00 (13.30 Friday). Some banks in the centre of Athens (especially Sintagma Square) are open for longer hours and part of the weekend. This is occasionally the case also in some holiday resorts. **Bureaux de Change** are operated by some travel agents and hotels will often change money, though it is advisable to ensure that the proper rate is being offered and that commission charges are not excessive. Post offices may also be used (see above). Travellers' cheques are undoubtedly the easiest way of carrying funds. Money can be withdrawn from banks using major credit cards and these are accepted by bank machines, although only in the larger centres. The Visa network is more extensive than Mastercard. Leading credit cards are accepted by a fair number of commercial establishments but are sometimes regarded with suspicion.

## Shops

Shops are open in summer 08.00–13.30 and 17.30–20.30 on Tuesday, Thursday and Friday; 08.00–14.30 only, on Monday, Wednesday and Saturday. In winter 08.30–13.30 and 17.00–20.00 on Tuesday, Thursday and Friday; 08.30–14.30 on Monday, Wednesday and Saturday. Supermarkets have a special status, opening 08.00–21.00 daily, except Sunday. Some kinds of shop (e.g. dry cleaners) never open in the evening or on Saturdays. Outside Athens, hours are more flexible. In large towns chemists take turns to offer a 24-hour service; duty chemists in Athens are listed in *The Week in Athens*, or may be discovered by dialling 173 on the telephone.

The Periptero (Περίπτερο), or kiosk, developed from a French model, is a characteristic feature of Greek life. Selling newspapers, reading matter, postcards, cigarettes, chocolate, toilet articles, film, postage stamps, etc., some kiosks are open for about 18 hours a day.

## Museums and Archaeological Sites

Sites of any significance are usually signposted and the area enclosed. There is normally an admission charge which varies with the importance of the place concerned. Students are allowed reduced prices on production of a valid identity card. *Bona fide* foreign students of any branch of classical studies can obtain a free pass through their institutions. Opening hours of sites and museums vary according to the season, the importance of the antiquities and local conditions. All museums (but not sites) close on Mondays. For small sites/museums, it is advisable to reckon on opening hours 08.30–13.00 for absolute safety. In fact the closing time is usually about 15.00 and, at the more important centres, as late as 17.00 for museums and 19.00 for sites. The National Tourist Organisation in Athens provides an information sheet on opening hours, as do the travel guides. Both sites and museums are closed on 1 January, 25 March, Good Friday morning, Easter Day and Christmas Day. Hours are restricted on Christmas Eve, New Year's Eve, 2 January, 5 January, the last Saturday of Carnival, Thursday in Holy Week, Easter Tuesday. Private galleries etc. fix their own hours which are often limited to short periods on two or three days a week. At major sites, where the number of visitors can detract considerably from your pleasure in the tourist season, it is best to start at opening time in the morning, before the large parties arrive.

In general photography (with hand cameras) is free on archaeological sites, and permitted (except where unpublished material is on display) in museums on purchase of a second ticket for the camera. ΑΠΑΓΟΡΕΥΕΤΑΙ (apagorévetai) means forbidden. Set fees (not cheap) are charged for using tripods, etc.

The Greek Antiquities Service treats its visitors' safety as their own responsibility. Visitors should beware of unfenced trenches and unrailed heights. The nature of archaeological remains ensures the maximum number of objects that can be tripped over. It is particularly dangerous to move about while reading or sighting a camera.

No guide-book to Greece has the space to give detailed directions to every remote or minor site. These stand, unfenced and unmarked, often some way from the modern village that has taken upon itself their ancient name (proven or supposed). Help beyond that given in the text can usually be had from locals with the use of the following vocabulary: *yiá* (towards) *ta arkhaía* (ancient things), *to kástro* (any fortified height), *tis anaskafés* (excavations), *to froúrio* (medieval castle). Country peasants rarely have any idea of periods of chronology, whereas intelligent school-boys some-times have a good knowledge of their local antiquities. Licensed guides are available in Athens, and on some major sites; casual offers of guidance are better politely declined in Athens and Piraeus, but can be disinterested and invaluable elsewhere.

Orthodox churches may be visited at any reasonable hour; when they are closed, as is now often the case, inquiry should be made for the key; if the church is isolated, in the nearest village. Women are not permitted to enter the sanctuary.

## Antiquities

The regulations to protect Greece's heritage are strictly enforced. Importation of antiquities and works of art is free, but such articles should be declared on entry so that they can be re-exported. Except with special permission, it is forbidden to export antiquities and works of art (dated before 1830) which have been obtained in any way in Greece. If a traveller's luggage contains antiquities not covered by an export permit, the articles are liable to be confiscated and prosecution may follow. Note that the use of metal detectors is strictly forbidden in Greece and it is an offence to remove any object, however seemingly insignificant, from an archaeological site.

## Equipment

Most people require sunglasses in Greece, even in winter. Strong suncream, a sunhat, and caution in exposing oneself to the sun are important particularly in the summer. A pocket compass can be useful, since many directional indications in the Guide are given by compass-points. Carrying a small pair of binoculars is also highly recommended. Those travelling informally should consider taking a small camping stove for hotel-room breakfasts, etc. It is a good idea to carry washing powder, a few clothes pegs and a strong piece of string for a temporary clothes line. An electric torch is useful. Some form of mosquito repellant should be carried (though it may not be needed): small electrical devices are available from all chemists, and packs of combustible coils ('spirales') for conditions where there is no electricity.

Diving and underwater photography are not permitted in most parts of Greece.

## Newspapers

The *Athens News* is published daily and *Greek News* weekly on Fridays, in English. Foreign newspapers are obtainable at central kiosks in Athens late on the day of publication (and the following day at other major tourist centres) at two to three times the home price. *The Athenian*, a well-produced monthly magazine in English, has articles on various aspects of Greek life and culture and useful information about entertainment, restaurants and basic services in the capital. The weekly *Athinórama* (Αθηνόραμα; Thursdays, in Greek) has comprehensive information about all forms of entertainment (including gastronomic) in Athens, for those with a knowledge of Greek.

## Weights and Measures

The French metric system of weights and measures adopted in Greece in 1958, is used with the terms substantially unaltered. Thus μέτρο, χιλιόμετρο (khiliómetro), etc. Some liquids are measured by weight (κιλό etc.), not in litres. The standard unit of land measurement, the *stremma*, is equal to ¼ acre.

# Note on Transliteration

As Col. Leake wrote 150 years ago 'It is impossible in any manner to avoid inconsistency' in dealing with the transliteration of Greek place-names. The policy adopted in this text has been to use one system for modern place names, and another for those of ancient times, though even this causes problems where names which have remained the same may be spelt differently according to context.

Names of modern localities have been transliterated in accordance with the phonetic system codified by the Permanent Committee on Geographical Names (E. Gleichen and J.H. Reynolds, *Alphabets of Foreign Languages*, P.C.G.N. for British Official Use, London 1951, pp. 52–56), used alike by NATO and by professional and archaeological journals. Though this results sometimes in visual ugliness, and for those with a knowledge of Greek increasing irritation (disguising the familiar apparently unnecessarily: thus Khloï), it has three merits: a great measure of alphabetical consistency for indexing; easy cross-reference to most official maps and to original excavation reports; and the possibility for non-Greek-speakers of producing a recognisable pronunciation. Where the result has seemed too *outré* and where there is a recognised and familiar English version (e.g. Rhodes), this has been used at least in all subsidiary references.

Ancient names have been given in the traditional English form used by classical scholars and archaeologists, preferring the purely English form where this exists (e.g. Aristotle, Homer), and the Latin form where this has become accepted everyday English usage: e.g. Boeotia, not Boiotia; Plato, not Platon. In other instances the form nearest to the ancient Greek has generally been preferred (with k for κ, rather than the misleading c), and (e.g.) Sounion rather than Sunium.

This duality, though producing the inconsistencies noted above between ancient and modern (e.g. respectively ch and kh for χ), highlights the pitfall that the modern place bearing the equivalent of a Classical name is not necessarily in the location of its ancient counterpart. Where they are coincident, some compromise is necessary: it is well for Christians to remember the Beroea of St. Paul, but advisable when journeying there to think of the modern town as Vérria.

It should be pointed out that, until the recent designation of demotic Greek as opposed to katharevousa (formal Greek) as the state language, place names had often both a katharevousa and a demotic form (αι Αθήναι, η Αθήνα for Athens). Formal versions of place names may occasionally linger on old signs. The final -v of neuter names, is almost always omitted. Neither modern form is necessarily the ancient form: thus, Thorikos, anciently ή Θόρικος has become ό Θορικός. In addition **all** place-names, like other nouns, decline; this often produces a change of stress as well as of inflexion. Some places have their more familiar spoken form in the accusative (given, where thought desirable, in the text), though they appear on maps in the nominative; places ending in -on often drop the 'n' in speech, sometimes the whole syllable. Street names are in the genitive when called after a person, e.g. Ermou (of Hermes), also in the genitive when leading to a place, e.g. Patission (to Patissia). As in English, a church may be spoken of by the name of its saint in the nominative or genitive. In the vexing instance where the Greek name is in itself a transliteration from Roman characters, each example has been treated on its apparent merits. Thus Βερανζέρου (which in Greek pronunciation bears little resemblance to the Fr. *Béranger*) has been rendered Veranzérou; Βύρωνος similarly has been rendered Víronos by sound since Lord Byron properly appears in Greek literary criticism as Μπά ϋρον. Names of modern Greeks have been rendered where possible as their owners transliterated them or as arbitrary custom has demanded.

No consistency can be attempted in the language or spelling of hotel names, since they are often chosen quite arbitrarily themselves. What is displayed on the building is likely not to correspond with the name listed in the hotel guide—only experience can help in the realisation that (e.g.) Ilios, Helios, and Soleil designate the same hotel (Ηλιος), or that Mont Blanc and Lefkon Oros are one and the same.

In this book, at its first mention, a place-name is given also in Greek, where the difference from English may make this an aid to reading maps and road signs. On main roads signposts are printed in Greek and Roman characters (but inevitably not in a consistent transliteration). In the Guide, accents have been put on transliterated place names at their main entry, since they show pronunciation stress. For the sake of economy they have sometimes been omitted elsewhere, though an attempt has been made normally to accent words which travellers may need to use for asking directions; the names in the index are fully accented. Ancient names, if accented, have been given their modern stress, where this may be a help in asking directions. Breathings are not normally given. Accents on initial vowels are not given, in accordance with modern practice.

# Bibliography

### Archaeological Sources
R.J. Stillwell (ed.), *The Princeton encyclopaedia of Classical sites* (Princeton University Press, 1976). For further information and references to publications on sites mentioned in the text. *British School at Athens/Society for the Promotion of Hellenic Studies *Archaeological Reports*, an annual, and somewhat technical, survey of recent discoveries in Greece and its ancient colonies. Enquiries to the Secretary, Hellenic Society, 31–34 Gordon Square, London WC1H 0PY. For those with some knowledge of Greek, there is an excellent popular 3-monthly periodical, *Arkhaiología* (ΑΡΧΑΙ–ΟΛΟΓΙΑ) available from kiosks and shops in Greece, or by subscription from Arkhaiologia, 3 Od. Khrístou Ladhá, Athens 102 37.

### Prehistory
*Sinclair Hood, *The home of the heroes* (Thames and Hudson, 1967); *The arts in prehistoric Greece* (Pelican History of Art series, 1978; Yale University Press).

### Ancient History
*A.R. Burn, *A traveller's history of Greece: the Pelican history of Greece* (Pelican, 13th rev. ed., 1982).

### Art and Architecture
*C.M. Robertson, *A shorter history of Greek art* (Cambridge University Press, 1981). *A.W. Lawrence (rev. R. A. Tomlinson), *Greek architecture* (Pelican History of Art series, 1983; Yale Univesity Press). *D.E. Strong, *Roman art* (Pelican History of Art series, 1976; Yale University Press). *F. Sear, *Roman architecture* (Batsford, 1982). *D. Talbot Rice, *Art of the*

*Byzantine era* (Thames and Hudson, 1963). *J. Beckwith, *Early Christian and Byzantine art* (Pelican History of Art series, 1979, 2nd. ed.; Yale University Press). *R. Krautheimer, *Early Christian and Byzantine architecture* (Pelican History of Art series, 1986, 4th. ed., with S. Ćurčić; Yale University Press).

### History
W. Miller, *The Latins in the Levant* (J. Murray, 1908). J. Campbell and P. Sherrard, *A history of modern Greece* (Cambridge University Press, 1968). R. Clogg, *A concise history of Greece* (Cambridge University Press, 1992).

### Anthropology
J. du Boulay, *Portrait of a Greek mountain village*, (Oxford Monographs on Social Anthropology, Oxford, 1974).
J.K. Campbell, *Honour, Family and Patronage: a study of insititutions and moral values in a Greek mountain community*, (Oxford Monographs on Social Anthropology, Oxford, 1964).

### Other Guides
*Mark Ellingham et al., *Greece: the Rough Guide*, 1992 (5th. ed.). Useful for practical information. *P. Hetherington, *Byzantine and Medieval Greece* (John Murray, 1991). Restricted to the Mainland and not comprehensive, but nonetheless useful in a neglected field. *B. de Jongh (rev. John Gandon), *The Companion Guide to Mainland Greece* (Collins, 1989). Historically evocative.

### Other
R. and M. Clogg, *Greece* (Oxford World Bibliographies, 1980), gives bibliographical information on a wide variety of Greek topics, ancient and modern. R. Clogg (ed.), *Greece in the 1980s* (Macmillan, 1983), aspects of life in contemporary Greece. K. Andrews, *Athens* (Methuen Cities of the World Series, 1967), not easy to obtain but one of the best books ever written about Greece: a sensitive and finely written appreciation of Athens and its people. Osbert Lancaster, *Classical landscape with figures* (John Murray, 1975), rather dated, but witty and penetrating about the country and its inhabitants. *Dilys Powell, *An affair of the heart* (M. Haag, 1983), a sentimental but understanding book about Greek village life as observed by the author during her husband's excavations at Perakhora in the 1930s. Melissa Publishing House (Athens); various authors, *Greek traditional architecture*. 50 chapters (extensively illustrated), available *separately or in 8 collected volumes covering the different regions of Greece. In Greek and English, also some in German, A. Huxley and W. Taylor, *Flowers of Greece and the Aegean* (Chatto and Windus, 1977). Hellmut Baumann (tr. W. T. & E. R. Stearn), *Greek wild flowers and plant lore in ancient Greece* (The Herbert Press, 1993). *Miles Lambert-Goćs, *The wines of Greece* (Faber, 1990). For walkers: *T. Salmon, *The mountains of Greece, A walker's guide*. (Cicerone Press, rev. ed., 1993); *G. Sfikas, *The mountains of Greece*. (Efstathiadhis, Athens, 1979/1982). Titles marked * are obtainable in paperback, though some such works on art and architecture are not particularly cheap.

Other books relating to specific areas and sites are mentioned at the appropriate points in the main text.

**Bookshop**. Alsos Books, 14 Ashbridge Street, London NW8 8DH; tel. 0171 724 6774; fax 0171 724 5294, is recommended for all books about Greece, and particularly for obtaining works published in Greece.

# I ATHENS

Readers should note that the monuments of Athens and its environs are fully described in Blue Guide Athens (3rd edition, 1992). The commentary given here is abbreviated for routes within the city of Athens.

**ATHENS**, capital of the Hellenic Republic, is set in a bowl of mountains (*Hymettos* (S)—modern Imittós, *Parnes* (N)—modern Párnitha, *Pentelikon* (E)—modern Pendéli), with the sea and its port of Piraeus to the W. The modern city was laid out in the 19 and 20C by Bavarian architects of King Otho. Still prominent in the plain, in spite of urban development, are the Acropolis and other hills including Lykabettos (modern Likavittós).

'Odhós' (Street) is often omitted in addresses, here as in modern Greek. Otherwise the abbreviation 'Od.' may be used.

**Note** that fuller information about facilities in Athens is included in *Blue Guide Athens and Environs*.

**Airport** at **Ellinikó**, 9.5km SE on the coast for both international and domestic flights (two terminals, separately approached). Express bus no. **91** (blue and yellow double decker) connects both airports with central Athens (Síntagma Sq.) and Od. Stadhíou, near Omónia Sq. Every 30 minutes from 06.00–21.00; less frequently at other times. Express bus no. **19** connects both airports with Piraeus (Karaïskáki Sq.). Every 1 or 2 hours, 05.00–20.20. Direct bus of Olympic Airways from West Airport to Olympic Town Terminal in Od. Singroú. Other local bus services pass close to the entrance to the West Airport; the East is some distance from the main road.

**Arrival by Sea** at Piraeus (see Rte 12); Athens can be reached in 25 minutes by the Electric Railway, by bus, or taxi (approx. 10 x bus fare).

**Railway Stations**. **Lárissa** (2, 1), in the NW of the city, for the standard-gauge line to Thebes, Lárissa, Thessaloníki, and Idhoméni (connecting via Gevgelija and Belgrade with the European trunk lines, though note that these routes are not operating passenger services at present). **Peloponnísou** (2, 1), adjoining Lárissa to the SW, for the metre-gauge line to Corinth and the Peloponnese. Booking offices at stations or, in town, Karólou 1, Sína 6 (Panepistimíou), Filellínon 17. Access by bus **405** from Leof. Alexándras, trolley **1** from Leof. Amalías or Panepistimíou for Lárissa Station; bus **047** from Od. Menándrou (Omónia) or **057** (Panepistimíou) for Peloponnísou. **Omónia** (3, 3 underground), Omónia Sq., for the Greek Electric Railway (abbreviated in Greek ΕΗΣ) to Piraeus and Kifisiá (see below).

**Hotels**. Athens has numerous hotels in all classes. Several of the higher class hotels are located in the area of Síntagma Sq., more modest round Omónia. Pláka (streets near Síntagma), Thissíon and the area S of the Acropolis (Od. Mitséon etc.) are locations worth trying.

For hotels in the hills and near the sea, see Rtes 13 and 15.

**Flats** (apartments), rated as A or B class hotels, can be rented by the week.

**Youth Hostels**. 1 Ay. Meletíou (170 beds; open always); 2 Alexándras (220 beds; July–Sept only); 20 Ioulianoú (82 beds); 5 Kipsélis (180 beds); 4 Patissíon. For general information, apply to Greek Association of Youth Hostels, 4 Dhragatsaníou. YMCA, 28 Omírou; YWCA, 13 Ameríkis.

**Restaurants** (lunch usually between 12.30 and 3pm; dinner between 8.30 and midnight). International food and décor (not cheap) at **L** class hotels. Otherwise, for up-to-date guidance consult current periodicals, e.g. *The Athenian*, *Athinórama* (the latter in Greek), or *Blue Guide Athens*.

**Tavernas** (some open evenings only, 8.30 or 9 to 1am or later) are ubiquitous. Many in Plaka cater for tourists; others (e.g. behind the Hilton, on the slopes of Lykabettus, or in the suburbs) have a more local atmosphere. In summer Athenians often dine farther out in Attica.

**Zakharoplastéia** (Patisseries). Among the best known are Zonar's, 9 Panepistimíou and Floca, 4 Koraî and 118 Leofóros Kifissías.

**Cafés** (Kafenéia) are numerous. Those in or near the main squares and avenues cater mainly for tourists.

**Post Office** (3, 5; all services, including cables) 100 Aiólou (corner of Omónia Sq.), open Monday–Friday 07.30–20.00, Saturday 07.30–14.00; branch offices: Síntagma, at Othonos/Níkis; Omónia Sq. (underground); also in Patriárkhou Ioakhím, etc. The Síntagma office only is open on Sundays (09.00–13.00). **OTE Centres**: 85 Patissíon, (open 24 hrs); also 15 Stadhíou; 53 Sólonos; 7 Kratínou (these 07.00 or 08.00 to 22.00 or midnight).

**Police Office** (Aliens Dept.), 173 Alexándras. **Tourist Police**. There is an excellent telephone service (tel. 171; English spoken).

**Information Bureaux**. National Tourist Office, 2 Karayeóryi Servías (in National Bank of Greece); 1 Ermoú (in General Bank); 4 Stadhíou; in booking hall of Omónia Underground Stn; and at the Airport. Royal National Foundation, 9 Filellínon. Note also the Tourist Police Telephone Service (above) and a similar provided by the Greek motoring organisation, ELPA (ΕΛΠΑ), tel. 174.

**Street plans** of central Athens are available from the National Tourist Organisation and from booksellers and kiosks in Athens. The Greek motoring organisation (ELPA) in conjunction with the publishers Kapranídhis and Fótis, produces an excellent book of street plans of the city and suburbs, with index, and there are other similar publications (e.g. by K. Daravíngas).

**Leaflets, Newspapers, Magazines**. The National Tourist Organisation (see above) publishes (weekly, free) *The Week in Athens* in English and French. The *Athens News* is published daily in English, and *Greek News* weekly, also in English. The *Athenian*, a well-produced monthly magazine in English, has articles on various aspects of Greek life and culture and useful information about entertainment, restaurants and basic services in the capital. The weekly *Athinórama* (Αθηνόραμα; Thursdays, in Greek) has comprehensive information about all forms of entertainment (including gastronomic) in Athens, for those with some knowledge of Greek.

**Travel Agents**. Trans Hellenic, 36 Voúlis; Alfa, 12 Vas. Sofías; Ghiolman and Hellas, 7 and 14 Filellínon; American Express, 2 Ermoú; Wagons-lits/Cook, 2 Kar. Servías; Hermes en Grèce and CHAT 4 Stadhíou; and many others, including Astória, 104 Aiólou (7th. floor). The Periyítiki Léskhi, 12 Polytekhníou, organises excursions to many places difficult of access by public transport.

**Shipping Offices**, mostly in Piraeus (Rte 12). Also in Athens: Hellenic Mediterranean Lines at 28 Amalías, Strintzis Lines, 48 Amalías.

**Airline Offices**. British Airways, 10 Othonos (Síntagma); Olympic Airways, 6 Othonos, 3 Kotopoúi (Omónia Sq.), 96 Singroú (coach terminal and bookings) for telephone bookings: 9666666; TWA, 8 Xenofóndos; Air France 4 Karayeóryi Servías; Lufthansa, 11 Vas Sofías (Síntagma) Qantas 104 Eólou (Omónia).

**Taxis** (ranks in main squares). Surcharges operate from a public transport terminal, during night hours and at holiday periods. See Practical Information.

There are now several firms operating radio-taxis. These are generally reliable and the supplement is modest (Drs. 200 from a private house, Drs. 300 from a hotel), though the telephone lines can be very busy. Up-to-date and other numbers from magazines or daily papers.

**Electric Railway**. Frequent metropolitan service from Kifissiá via Omónia to Piraeus in 40 minutes. Intermediate halts (S of Omónia): Monastírion (2, 8), Thissíon, (2, 8), Petrálona, El. Venizélos/Távros, Kallithéa , Moskháton, Néon Fáliron; N of Omónia: Victoría, Attikí, Ayios Nikólaos, Káto Patíssia, Ayios Elefthérios, Patíssia, Perissós, Pevkákia, Néa Ionía, Iráklion, Iríni (for Olympic Stadium), Maroússi, KAT (Accident Hospital).

**Transport tickets**. For electric railway tickets may be bought from stations. For ordinary buses and trolleys tickets are purchased from bus company kiosks near main bus stops, also from many ordinary kiosks (periptera), or shops (often newsagents) bearing the sign (ΠΩΛΟΥΝΤΑΙ ΕΙΣΙΤΗΡΙΑ). The traveller is responsible for cancelling the ticket by inserting it in one of the orange machines on board buses or trolleys or at railway station barriers. Failure to do this results in an instant fine (frequently and summarily imposed) of 20 times the standard fare. Supplements are charged on night bus services.

**City and Suburban Buses** (KTEL 1–6 of Athens, plus yellow trolleys). Owing to the one-way traffic system, outward routes through the city seldom coincide with the return journey; between the Omónia area and Síntagma Sq., traffic goes N by Leof. Panepistimíou (Venizélou), S by either Stadhíou or Akadhimías. As an approximate guide (see maps for destinations and departure points), the first digit of the bus number indicates its general destination, as follows: **0**, Central Athens; **1**, coastal suburbs S towards Vouliagméni; **2**, S suburbs on slopes of Hymettos; **3** and **4**, SE and E to central and eastern Attica; **5**, Kifissiá and N suburbs; **6** and **7**, NW and **8**, W towards Dhafní; **9**, SW to Piraeus. For other routes in the vicinity of Athens, see below. Among the most useful routes are:

(a) **Within the city. 2/11/12** (trolleys). Pangráti–Síntagma–Patíssia (Museum); **022**. Marásleion–Gennádhion Library–Plat. Káningos; **023**. Votanikós–Assómaton–Monastiráki–Síntagma; **040** (green bus). Piraeus–Síntagma (Od. Filellínon); **049**. Piraeus (Dhimotikó Théatro)–Omónia (Od. Athinás); **051**. Od. Veranzérou–Akadhimía Plátonos (Plato's Academy); **230**. Od. Ippokrátous–Akadhimías–Akrópolis–Thissíon.

Minibuses. **100** Zínonos (near Omónia)–Márnis–Akadhimías–Síntagma–Sofokléous–Zínonos. **200** Pédhion Areos (Leof. Alexándras)–Exárkheia–Menándrou–Kolokotróni–Kolonáki–Vas. Sofías–Perikléous–Athinás–3 Septemvríou–Pédhion Areos.

(b) **Suburban and Attica. 115**. Leof. Olgas–Várkiza; **118**. Olgas–Vouliagméni; **121**. Olgas–Ay. Nikólaos–Glifádha; **122**. Olgas–Ano Voúla; **224**. University–Kaisarianí; **421**. Od. Vasiléos Irakleíou–Museum–Palaiá Pendéli; **503**. Káningos–Varibóbi; **538/589**. Káningos–Kifissiá; **603**. National Library–Psikhikó. From Piraeus, **109**. Piraeus–Glifádha–Voúla.

To Soúnion (via coast or inland), Lávrion, Pórto Ráfti, Markópoulo/Vravróna, Kálamos/Amphiáraion, Oropós, and places in E Attica, from 14 Od. Mavromatéon (3, 1). To Marathon, Rafína, Ayía Marína/Rhamnous from 29 Mavromatéon/Leof. Alexándras (3, 1). (To central and SE Attica, also from Thissíon.)

To Mégara from Thissíon (6, 3).

To Eleusis from Plat. Koumoundoúrou (2, 6).

**Telephone numbers** for enquiries for specific local destinations can be obtained (in Greek) by dialling 185.

**Long-Distance Bus Stations**. Services to the Peloponnese, Macedonia, Epirus, and the Ionian Islands from 100 Kifissoú (reached in 15 min. by bus 051 from Menándrou, near Plateía Ayíou Konstandínou (below Omónia), buses also from Síntagma).

Services to Euboea, Central Greece, and Thessaly from 260 Liossíon (reached by bus 024 from Leof. Amalías or Panepistimíou).

**Booking** is possible by 'phone, provided tickets are collected by a specified time before you travel. Advance booking is essential at busy periods, if you wish to travel on a specific service. In any case tickets must be bought before boarding the bus to ensure a numbered seat. **Telephone numbers** for enquiries and/or bookings for specific long-distance destinations are available (in Greek) by dialling 142.

**Car Hire** (self-drive). Hertz, 12 Singroú; Avis, 48 Amalías; Hellascars, 7 Stadhíou; Budget, 90 Singroú; Holiday Autos, 8 Singroú, etc. List available from NTOG.

**Embassies, Legations, and Consulates**. British, 1 Ploutárkhou (4, 8); United States, 91 Leof. Vas. Sofías (5, 6); Australia, 37 D. Soútsou; Canada, 4 Yennadhíou.

**English Church**, St Paul's (7, 5), Odhós Filellínon, services on Sun at 8, 9 and 10am; special times on Saints' days. **American Church** (4, 5; St Andrew's), 66 Sína; **Roman Catholic Church** (4, 7; St Denis), Leof. Panepistimíou (Venizélou).

**Banks**. Head Offices: Bank of Greece, 21 Panepistimíou (Venizélou); National Bank of Greece, 86 Aiólou; Commercial Bank of Greece, 11 Sofokléous; Ionian and Popular Bank of Greece, Pesmazóglou/Panepistimíou (Venizélou), etc. Normal hours 08.00–14.00 (Fridays, 13.30). Of many branches with exchange facilities, several near Síntagma Sq. are open additional hours: National, 2 Karayeóryi Servías (Monday–Friday 14.00–21.00pm, Saturday and Sunday 08.00–20.00); Ionian and Popular, 2 Mitropóleos (Monday–Friday 14.00–17.30pm, Saturday 09.00–12.30);

Commercial, 11 Panepistimíou (Venizélou) (Monday–Saturday 14.00–15.30, Sunday 09.00–midnight).

**Learned Institutions**. British School at Athens, 52 Souidhías; British Council, 17 Kolonáki Sq., with library; American School of Classical Studies, and Gennádhion Library, 54 and 61 Souidhías; American Library at Hellenic-American Union, 22 Massalías; Greek Archaeological Society, 20 Panepistimíou (Venizélou); Direction of Antiquities Services, Bouboulínas; École Française d'Archéologie, 6 Dhidhótou; Institut Français d'Athènes, 29 Sína; Deutsches Archäologisches Institut, 1 Fidhíou; National Library see Rte 10; Municipal Library, Odhós Kleisthénous; Parliament Library, Parliament Building; Benakios Library, 2 Anthímou Gázi; Royal Research Institute (Byzantine and Modern Greek studies), 4 Leof. Vas. Sofías; College of Music, 35 Piraiós; Foreign Press Service, 3 Zalokósta.

**Clubs**. Automobile and Touring Club of Greece (ELPA/ΕΛΠΑ, Pírgos Athinón, Vas. Sofías/Mesogeíon; Hellenic Alpine Club, Plat. Kapnikaréas; Greek Youth Hostels Association, 4 Dhragatsaníou.

**Duty chemists** are listed in The Week in Athens and daily papers, or dial 173 on the telephone.

**Booksellers**. Eleftheroudhákis, 4 Níkis; Kaufmann, 28 Stadhíou, also 11 Voukourestíou; Pantelídhis, 9 Ameríkis; Andrómeda (excellent specialist Classics and Archaeology), 46–50 Mavromikhaïli; Protoporía, 3–5 Gravías (Greek); Foliá tou Vivlíou (in arcade), 25/29 Panepistimíou; second-hand shops at lower end of Ippokrátous.

**Theatres**. **Winter Season** (October–May): Ethnikón (National Theatre Company), Ay. Konstandínou; Olympía (Lirikí Skiní), 59 Leof. Akadhimías, opera and operetta; Arts (Tékhnis), 44 Odós Stadhíou, and others. **Summer Season** (June–September) in the Odeíon of Herodes Atticus; and other outside venues, including Lykabettos.

**Concerts**. Athens State Orchestra (Monday) in winter at Pallas, 1 Vourkourestíou; in summer at the Odeion; recitals at Parnassos Hall (Od. Chr. Ladá). Hall of the Friends of Music, Vasilíssis Sofías. **Son et Lumière**, lighting of the Acropolis viewed from the Pnyx. **Folk Dances** in the Philopappos Theatre.

**Popular Music**. Apart from public concerts, in Boites. There is normally no entrance charge but drinks are more expensive, to compensate; e.g. Zoom, 37 Kidhathenaíon, Pláka, Zígos, 22 Kidhathenaíon, Kíttaro, 48 Ipírou/Akharnón; also at expensive night-clubs along the coast towards Glifádha.

**Rembétika**, the traditional music of the dispossessed (comparable in content to the American blues) is enjoying a new popularity. The most famous old-timer still singing (not in summer) is Mikhaïlis Dhaskalákis at Pikérmi, Attica (22km from Athens, on the road to Rafína, Rte 21). The same system of payment applies as at boites, though charges are rather higher. Programmes at these traditional establishments do not begin until c 23.00 and the main singer rarely appears before half past midnight. Similar music can be heard from contemporary groups in a boite setting at such centres as Rembetikí Istoría, 181 Ippokrátous. Other establishments offer music in the ordinary folk tradition, each usually performing works from one area of Greece, e.g. To Armenáki, 1 Patriárkhou Ioakeím, Távros (islands), Kríti, Ay. Thomás, Ambelókipi (Crete).

**Cinemas** are numerous and cheap. The principal houses (many with films in English) are in Stadhíou and Panepistimíou.

**Sport. Tennis** at Athens Tennis Club, Leof. Olgas; Panellínios, Odhós Mavromatéon. Swimming, open-air pool Leof. Olgas. Indoor pool, 277 Patissíon. **Golf** at Varibóbi; also at Glifádha. **Sailing**: information from Sea Horse, tel. 8952212/8956733. **Racecourse** at Fáliron Delta (bottom of Singroú). **Motor Racing**, Acropolis Rally (late May) for touring cars starts and ends in Athens; Autumn Rally in November. Football (mostly Sunday afternoons) at Leof. Alexándras (PAOK or Panathenaïkós); Néon Fáliron (Olimpiakós); Néa Filadhélfia (AEK or Athlitikí Enosis Konstantinoúpolis).

**Festivals**. Athens Festival of Music and Drama, June–August; Blessing of the Waters at Epiphany (6 January) in Plateía Dhexamení after procession from St Dionysios the Areopagite just to the S; Feast of St Dionysios (3 October); Anniversary of 1944 Liberation (12 October), hoisting of National Flag on Acropolis; Easter candlelight procession on Lykabettos. **Wine Festival** at Dhafní (Rte 16) in September.

# HISTORY OF ATHENS

## Ancient History

Occupation of the Acropolis goes back to the Neolithic period. In Mycenaean times (1600–1200 BC) there was a palace and fortified citadel there. The union of Attica under Athens probably took place in the 8C and the Geometric art style of the area became dominant in Greece. For most of the 7 and 6C Athens was governed by tyrants (the Peisistratids) who embellished the city architecturally. Athenian Archaic pottery was exported throughout the Greek world. Major social and economic reforms were instigated by Solon (early 6C). The tyrants were overthrown at the end of the 6C and a more democratic system of government developed (Kleisthenes). In 498 Athens and Eretria responded to an appeal to help the Greek cities of Ionia (Asia Minor) in their revolt against Persian domination. The result was the first Persian invasion of Greece, defeated at the Battle of Marathon (490). Ten years later the Acropolis was sacked in a further Persian attack, but the invaders were repulsed after the Battles of Salamis and Plataea. In the 5C Greek drama reached its maturity in Athens.

During the 5C the Delian League of allies against the Persians was transformed into an Athenian empire and the Athenians under Perikles used communal funds to beautify their city. Increasing rivalry between Athens and Sparta finally resulted in the Peloponnesian War (431–404 BC) which ended in the defeat of Athens. The city's authority revived in the early 4C but subsequently succumbed to that of the Macedonian kingdom under Philip II. Athens was well treated by Alexander the Great but had a chequered history under his successors. The city came under Roman control in the 2C but retained a privileged position, though sacked by Sulla in 86. Subsequently Hadrian spent long periods in Athens (120–128 AD) and was responsible for many public buildings, as later was Hérodes Atticus. It remained a leading educational centre until the schools of philosophy were closed by Justinian in AD 529.

## Later History

In the 3–6C AD Athens suffered from Barbarian raids. It was of little importance in the Byzantine period. After the fall of Constantinople in 1204, the city came under Frankish rule for about 100 years. Subsequent control by Sicilians, Florentines and Venetians ended when Athens was annexed to the Ottoman empire in 1456. In 1687 the Parthenon was shattered during a Venetian bombardment of the Turkish position on the Acropolis. Visitors to Athens in the 17 and 18C began to research and publish the city's antiquities. Thirteen years after the outbreak (1821) of the War of Independence Athens became the capital of a liberated Greece.

During the first world war the city was occupied by French and British troops. The population was swollen by the exchange of Greek and Turkish nationals in 1923. Athens was occupied by German forces from 1941–44.

# 1

# From Síntagma Square to the Acropolis and the Agorá

Bus 230 (from Akadhimías or Síntagma to Thissíon) stops below the Acropolis. A more interesting approach (on foot) is from the N through Plaka.

The most conspicuous feature of Síntagma (or Constitution) Square, from which the Greek Constitution was proclaimed in 1843, is the old **Royal Palace**. This lies to the E, beyond Leofóros Amalías and is now the seat of the **Greek Parliament**. In front is a **Memorial to the Unknown Soldier**, with a ceremonial guard. In antiquity the **Mouseion** (Garden of the Muses) was hereabouts.

Southwards along Amalías is the attractive **National Garden**, originally belonging to the Palace. On the other side of the road (right) are the **Russian Church** (Sotíra Likodhímou; c 1031) and the **English Church** (St Paul's; 1843). At no. 36 is the **Jewish Museum**. The **Zappeion Gardens** (left) have the Zappeion exhibition hall (1874–78). Beyond Leofóros Olgas (S of Zappeion) is the **Arch of Hadrian** (c 132 AD). Behind is the Sanctuary of Olympian Zeus (Rte 7).

To the W Od. Lissikrátous leads into Plaka. At the end ran the **Street of the Tripods**. Tripods, given for success in dramatic contests, were displayed here, often on top of columns or structures. The **Monument of Lysicrates** (334 BC) is a well preserved example—a circular marble structure in the the Corinthian order, with sculptural decoration and an inscription on the architrave. Beyond, at the site of the **Odeion of Perikles**, a large hall with interior columns used for musical performances at the Panathenaic Festival, you can turn left into Od. Thrasíllou to meet the broad Od. Dhioníssou Areopayítou which runs along the S side of the Acropolis. Opposite, on the corner of Od. Makriyánni, is the Centre for Acropolis Studies (see Rte 2). On the right, past the Odeion of Perikles, is the **Temenos of Dionysos Eleutherios** of which the most important element is the **Theatre of Dionysos** dating from the 6C but rebuilt in stone in the 4C and substantially altered (including the shape of the orchestra) in the Hellenistic and Roman periods. The front row of seating consisted of 67 thrones for dignitaries. Other monuments on the higher slopes include, further W, an **Asklepieion**.

The Theatre of Dionysos was linked to the Roman **Odeion of Herodes Atticus**, to the W, by the long (163m) **Stoa of Eumenes**, endowed by King Eumenes II of Pergamon (197–159 BC). This was built against a terrace wall with arches which supported the **peripatos**, a roadway round the acropolis. The Odeion was built in honour of Regilla, wife of Herodes, who died in AD 160. It has the typical shape of a Roman theatre, a well-preserved façade with entrances and niches for statues, and is used annually for performances of the Athens festival.

Beyond the Odeion a drive (right) approaches the Acropolis. Ahead a panoramic avenue circles Mouseion Hill to the Philopappos Monument (Rte 3). The main road, now Leofóros Apostólou Pávlou, continues (c 1km) to the W entrance of the Agora and Thissíon.

# 2

# The Acropolis

The Acropolis rock (156m; 91m above the general level of the city below) has been occupied since prehistoric times. In the Late Bronze Age (c 1600–c 1200) it was the site of a Mycenaean palace with massive fortifications. In the Archaic period it was at times the residence of tyrants, as well as a religious centre. In the Classical period its functions were entirely religious. The finest buildings were erected the later 5C following the defeat of the Persians. It was captured as a stronghold by Franks, Venetians and Turks who were succeeded by a Bavarian garrison (till 1835). Excavation and reconstruction began in the 18C and continue today, with particular effort being devoted to protecting the monuments from atmospheric pollution.

**Approaches** by paved road (cars prohibited) from Dhionnísou Areopayítou (Rte 1) or by paths from the Agora and Areopagus or from Plaka and the N slope. **Note** that it is no longer possible to enter the individual ancient buildings.

Tickets are sold at the **Beulé Gate**, a defensive structure of c 280 AD built of material from the earlier choregic monument of Nikias. Above, a high plinth belongs to the **Monument of Agrippa**. Originally a Hellenistic monument with a quadriga on top, it later carried statues of Antony and Cleopatra and finally (after 27 BC) of Marcus Agrippa. You then climb to the **Propylaia**, a monumental gateway designed by Mnesikles and built c 437–432 to replace an earlier version. The structure is almost entirely of Pentelic marble. The inner and outer central façades are Doric. The columns in the passage are Ionic. The N wing (called Pinakotheke after the pictures seen there by Pausanias) was probably a ritual dining room with couches. The S wing consists only of a curtailed façade, which provides a visual balance, though there was no room to build behind without encroaching on the precinct of Athena Nike. Two halls at the inner (E) side of the structure were planned but never built.

The charming **Temple of Athena Nike** in the Ionic order stands on a bastion to the S of the propylaia. The bastion conceals a Mycenaean predecessor, part of the defensive system. A naïskos stood there before the temple was built c 427–424. The badly preserved frieze (copy) depicts deities and scenes of Greeks and Persians in combat. The temple platform was surrounded by a sculpted marble parapet with figures of winged Victory (Nike) including the famous Sandalbinder (Museum).

Turning to the left beyond the propylaia you pass the area of the projected N hall, then the ground where stood the chapel of the Frankish dukes (demolished 1860). Beyond Late Roman cisterns, at an angle of the wall, descends a flight of steps used by the Arrhephoroi (maidens in the service of Athena). Also on this slope of the Acropolis was a Mycenaean stairway and concealed spring chamber. The Acropolis wall further on is constructed of blocks from the entablature of the Old Temple of Athena. Beyond the Erechtheion, built into the wall, are drums from the unfinished older Parthenon destroyed by the Persians in 480. You reach the Belvedere.

Returning, in front of the Parthenon are the remains of the circular Ionic **Monopteros of Rome and Augustus**, mentioned by Ciriacus of Ancona. The path continues W along the massive Wall of Kimon (restored). The W front of the Parthenon, approached by steps partly rock-cut and partly built, was

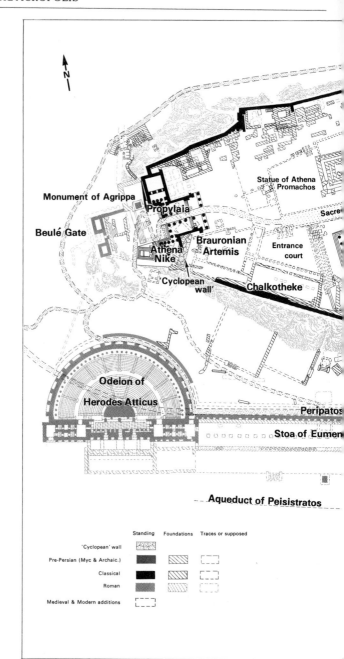

Standing     Foundations     Traces or supposed

'Cyclopean' wall

Pre-Persian (Myc & Archaic.)

Classical

Roman

Medieval & Modern additions

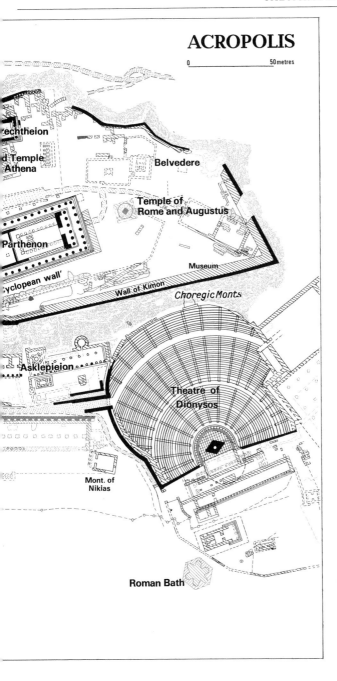

# ACROPOLIS

0                 50 metres

rechtheion

d Temple
Athena

Belvedere

Temple of
Rome and Augustus

Parthenon

Museum

cyclopean wall'

Wall of Kimon

*Choregic Monts*

Asklepieion

Theatre of
Dionysos

Mont. of
Nikias

Roman Bath

preceded by an Entrance Court with, on the S side, the **Chalkotheke** or Magazine of Bronzes. To the W was the **Sanctuary of Artemis Brauronia**, a stoa with two projecting wings. To the W is a fragment of the **Mycenaean wall** and, beyond, a corner of the earlier propylaia.

40 paces in front of the Propylaia are the remains of the base of the **Statue of Athena Promachos** by Pheidias, erected c 458 BC as a memorial of the Persian wars. It was 9m high and visible from Cape Sounion.

The **Parthenon** itself (built 447–438 BC; the sculpture completed in 432), the cardinal feature of the refurbished Acropolis, is remarkable for its materials (chiefly Pentelic marble), its sculptures and the subtlety of its design. Pheidias was in overall charge of the project and was solely responsible for the chryselephantine cult statue. Basically a Doric building, it has several unusual features. Although it was the grandest building on the Acropolis it was not the most important ritually. The Erechtheion was the focus of the Panathenaic procession as the repository of the oldest and most revered (wooden) statue of Athena.

The Parthenon was larger than most Doric temples (8 x 17 columns) and had more sculpture (all 92 metopes were decorated, as well as both pediments and, most unusually, a continuous Ionic frieze running round the outside of the building within the colonnade).

Various additions were made in later antiquity. In the 6C it was turned into a church. From 1204–58 it followed the Latin rite as cathedral of the Frankish dukes. It was later converted into a mosque. In 1674 Jacques Carrey, a painter in the entourage of the Marquis de Nointel, made drawings of the sculptures (many now lost). In 1687 it was blown up in a Venetian bombardment, when used by the Turks as a powder magazine. The results were disastrous. Pieces of sculpture were removed at various times, most notably by Lord Elgin in 1801. Restoration started in 1834–44; the current programme in 1983.

The subjects of the sculptures were **East Pediment**: Birth of Athena (springing fully armed from the head of Zeus); **West Pediment**: Contest between Athena and Poseidon for possession of Attica; **Metopes**: (some uncertain) Battle of Lapiths and Centaurs (S), Gigantomachy (E), Amazonomachy (W), Trojan War; **Frieze**: Panathenaic procession, probably adapted to depict (on the E end) the reception into divine company of the heroes of the Battle of Marathon.

Most of the Parthenon sculptures are in the British Museum. Substantial sections are in the Acropolis Museum. Some are in the Louvre.

Between the Parthenon and the Erechtheion are the foundations of the Archaic (c 529 BC) **Old Temple of Athena**, destroyed by the Persians, though the opisthodomos survived in use as a treasury.

The **Erechtheion**, designed to succeed the Old Temple of Athena as the joint shrine of Athena and Poseidon-Erechtheus and finally completed c 395, is an extremely complex building. Its interior layout remains uncertain because of later alterations. The surrounding precinct contained altars and other sacred places. The style is Ionic but the central unit has a normal entrance at only one end (E) because at the W the building is two-storeyed due to the steeply sloping site. There are porches on both N and S. The N had an ornamental doorway, refurbished in Roman times; the S is the famous **Caryatid Porch**, whose roof is supported by caryatids standing on a parapet. The frieze course consists of dark Eleusinian limestone against which the (now fragmentary) relatively small-scale sculptures would stand out.

The **Acropolis Museum** at the SE corner of the site is particularly rich in Attic sculpture. The Archaic pedimental sculpture in the first three rooms is outstanding, as are the votive figures of korai in the fourth. Room 5 has pediments from the Old Temple of Athena; Room 6: important works of the Early Classical ('Severe') style. Room 7 has models of the Parthenon pediments and fragments of the originals. Room 8: sections of the Parthenon frieze; also Nike figures from the Nike parapet and bits of the Erechtheion frieze. Room 9 includes caryatids from the Erechtheion.

# 3

# The Areópagus, Mouseíon, Pnyx, and Hill of the Nymphs

The saddle linking the Acropolis to the Areopagus spur to the W may have been the site of the original Agora. The **Areópagus** gave its name to the council of nobles which became in early times both senate and supreme judicial court. With the rise of democracy it declined. Below to the N are the ruins of the 16C church of St Dionysos the Areopagite, also remains of Mycenaean chamber tombs. The Cave of the Furies where the final scene of the Eumenides of Aeschylus took place was traditionally located here.

Returning via the Acropolis approach road to Leofóros Dhionísou Areopayítou, to the SW is the Dionysos restaurant behind which paths (also a road) mount the tree-clad slopes of the **Mouseíon Hill** (148m), always a key point in the fortifications of Athens and the site of a Hellenistic fort. On the summit is the **Monument of Philopappos** (AD 114–116) built by the Athenians in honour of C. Julius Antiochus Philopappus, a prince of Commagene (N Syria), who had a distinguished career both as an Athenian citizen and as a Roman consul and praetor. The sculptures depict Philopappus and members of the Commagene royal family.

A paved path descends in the direction of the observatory. The area contained many houses in antiquity. The path reaches the modern drive which also serves the Philopappus theatre. Here is the chapel of Ayios Dhimitrios Loumbardhiaris, refurbished in the 1950s. Above rises the hill of the **Pnyx** (109m). Near the top (NE; path from the chapel) is the meeting place of the Athenian Assembly under the democracy. The original arrangement where the seating faced N and the speaker's rostrum S was later reversed. Stoas etc. at a higher level may have been part of a 4C Panathenaic stadium. To the N is the **Hill of the Nymphs** (104m) crowned by the **observatory** (1842). There are old and new churches of Ayia Marina.

Descending past the observatory to Leofóros Apostólou Pávlou, to the right is an overgrown excavated area and to the left an entrance to the Agora excavations.

Leofóros Apostólou Pávlou continues NW, leaving the sweep of the main road, beside gardens with a bus terminal, to Ayios Athanásios. Along Od. Eptakhálkou (left) a footbridge crosses the railway to the entrance gate to the Kerameikos (Rte 4).

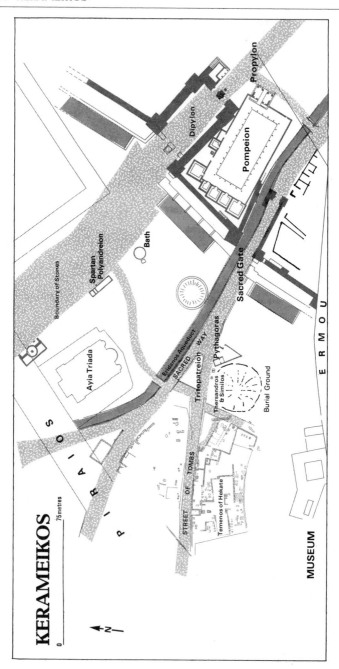

# KERAMEIKOS

0 ————— 75metres

N

Propylon

Pompeion

Dipylon

Sacred Gate

Bath

Spartan
Polyandreion

Boundary of Stones

Ayia Triada

Eridanos Aqueduct

SACRED WAY

Tritopatreion

Pyrthagoras

Thersandros
& Similos

Burial Ground

STREET OF TOMBS

Temenos of Hekate

P I R A I O S

E R M O U

MUSEUM

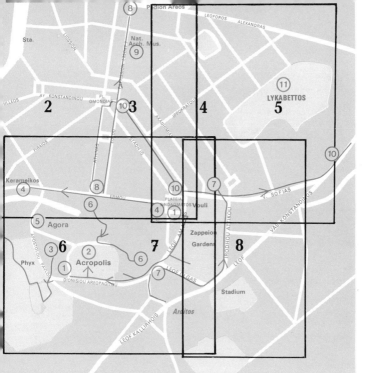

The numbers in circles refer to routes in the text.

# Key page
# to
# Map numbers

| 0 | 100 | 200 | 300 | 400 yards |
|---|-----|-----|-----|-----------|
| 0 | 100 | 200 | 300 | 400 metres |

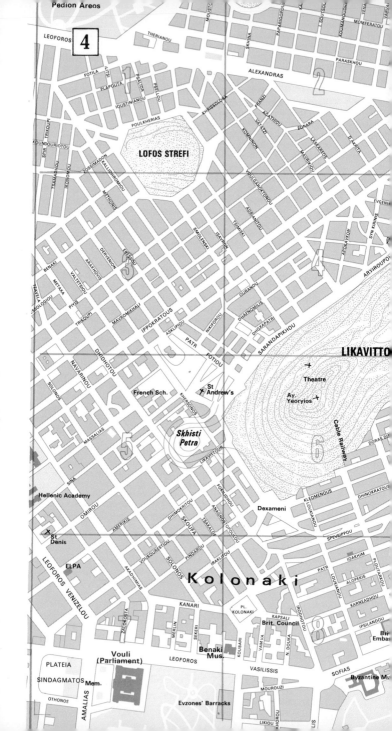

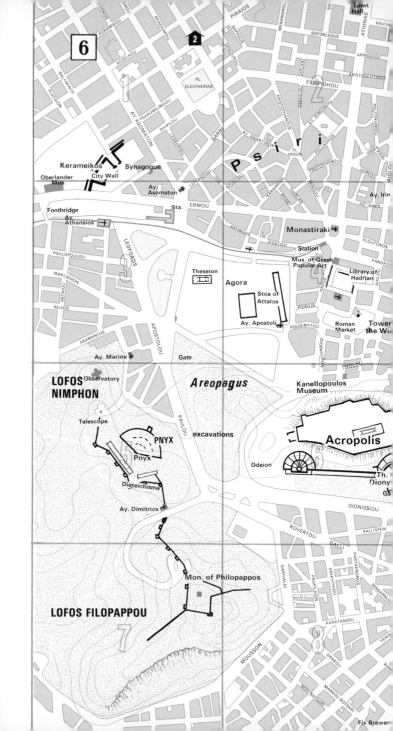

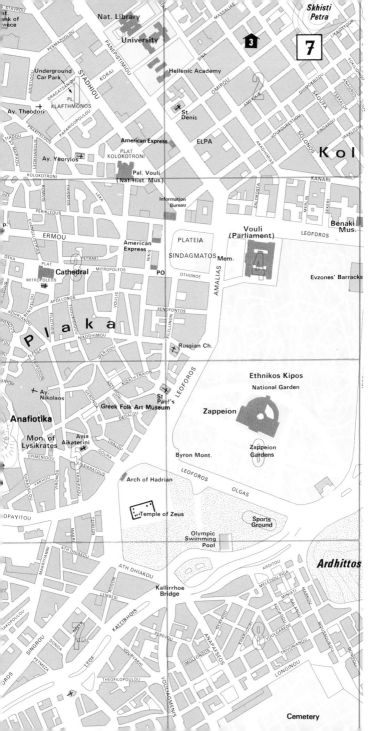

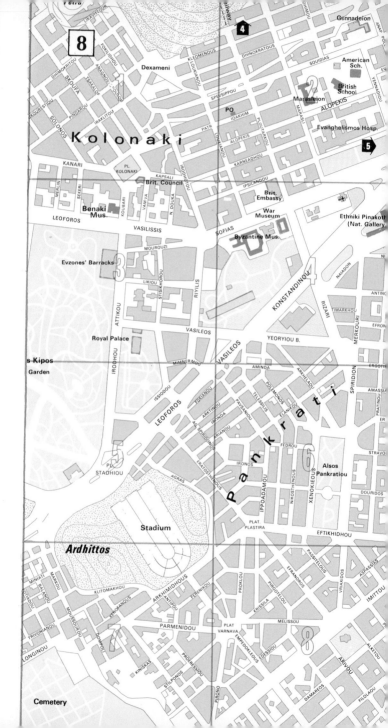

# 4

# From Síntagma Square to the Agorá and the Kerameikós

Bus no. 026 from Amalías, via Mitropóleos, returning via Ermoú

Odhós Ermoú descends straight W from Síntagma. To the S, in a square off the parallel Od. Mitropóleos, is the **cathedral** (or Metropolis; 1840–55). Nearby is the tiny 12C **Small Metropolis** or old cathedral. Both buildings reuse old material. In the centre of Ermoú is a small square with the charming 11–13C **Kapnikaréa**, the university church. You cross Od. Eólou (Rte 8) with the Acropolis towering to the S and pedestrian precincts to the N. Ermoú passes through Monastiráki Square and continues W. To the left is a major junction, close to Thissíon station on the electric railway; to the right, further on, the entrance to the **Kerameikos** excavations (excellent guidebook by U. Knigge available in English translation (1991)). The area includes the remains of the Dipylon and Sacred Gates, parts of the walls of Athens and an important cemetery area outside with the **Demosion Sema**, the burial place of Athenian heroes and notables. Inside the walls the Inner Kerameikos, towards the Agora, was the home of potters and smiths. At the gates converged important routes—from Piraeus, Eleusis and Boeotia, and many travellers entered the city at this point.

*Kerameikós. Funeral plot with grave stelai, etc*

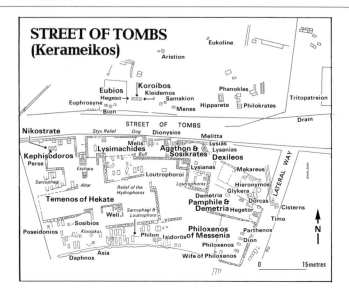

**STREET OF TOMBS (Kerameikos)**

Through the entrance to the site there is a plan of orientation on a prominent mound. A path descends to the **city walls**, with the **Sacred Gate** spanning both the Sacred Way to Eleusis and the Eridanos stream. The space between the two gates was occupied by the **Pompeion**, a place of preparation for ceremonial processions. The structure was rebuilt in the Roman period. The **Dipylon** was a double gateway, as the name implies, either side of a court. The cemetery area was outside the Dipylon, along the roadsides. The most striking remains are the burial plots to either side of the so-called Street of the Tombs. Sculpted stelai are prominent. There is a cast of the stele of Dexileos, killed in the Battle of Corinth in 394 BC.

The **Oberlaender Museum** has funerary sculpture, the contents of graves and a particularly fine and important collection of pottery of the periods Sub-Mycenaean to Proto-Attic.

The **Academy**, made famous by Plato's school of philosophy, was a sacred wood, c 2 stadia in diameter, situated at the end of an avenue 6 stadia from the Dipylon. The site (most easily reached by bus 051 from Od. Veranzérou, and bounded by Odd. Thenaías and Alexandreías) was identified by a boundary stone found in 1966. The remains (an Early Helladic house, a Geometric heroön, parts of an archaic (?) circuit wall, a 4C colonnaded court and a Roman gymnasium and baths) and their surroundings are disappointing.

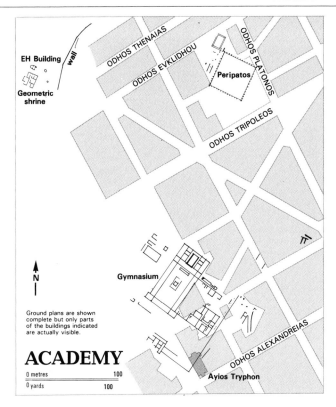

**EH Building**

ODHOS THENAIAS

ODHOS EVKLIDHOU

ODHOS PLATONOS

wall

**Peripatos**

**Geometric shrine**

ODHOS TRIPOLEOS

N

**Gymnasium**

Ground plans are shown complete but only parts of the buildings indicated are actually visible.

**ACADEMY**

0 metres 100

0 yards 100

ODHOS ALEXANDREIAS

**Ayios Tryphon**

# 5

# The 'Theseíon' and the Agorá

**Approaches to the Agorá**.

1. At the SW corner from Leofóros Apostólou Pávlou (near Thissíon terminus of bus 230, see Rte 1).

2. On N side by bridge over electric railway from Od. Adhrianoú.

3. On S side below the acropolis, near church of Holy Apostles.

There is an excellent Guide to the Excavations and Museum published in English by the American School of Classical Studies (4th edition, 1990); also a booklet *The Athenian agora: a short guide* (Excavations of the Athenian Agora, Picture Book no. 16, 1976). The upper gallery of the stoa of Attalos has models showing the Agora at different stages of its development.

The Doric temple, often called **Theseion**, crowning the low knoll of Kolonos Agoraios on the W side of the Agora, was in fact a temple of Athena and Hephaistos (Theseus is depicted in some of the sculptures). It was probably built c 449 BC. Thanks to its adaptation and use as a Christian church

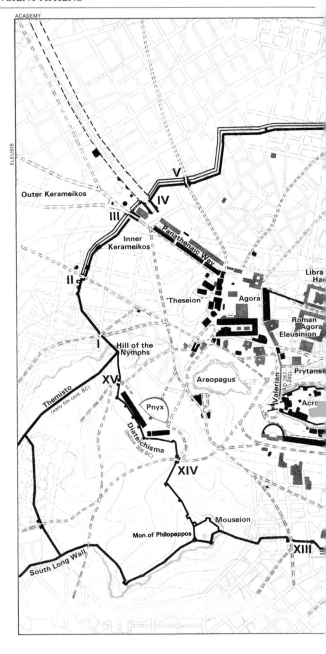

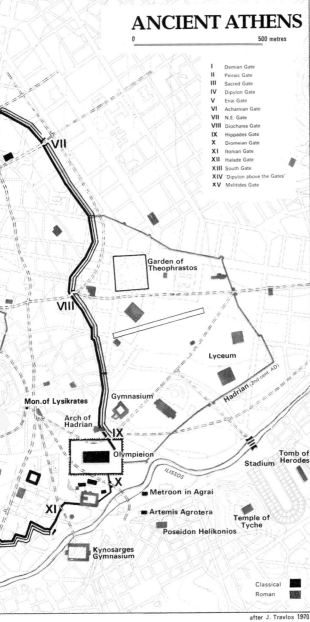

# ANCIENT ATHENS

0 ————————————————— 500 metres

| I | Demian Gate |
|---|---|
| II | Peiraic Gate |
| III | Sacred Gate |
| IV | Dipylon Gate |
| V | Eriai Gate |
| VI | Acharnian Gate |
| VII | N.E. Gate |
| VIII | Diochares Gate |
| IX | Hippades Gate |
| X | Diomeian Gate |
| XI | Itonian Gate |
| XII | Halade Gate |
| XIII | South Gate |
| XIV | 'Dipylon above the Gates' |
| XV | Melitides Gate |

VII

Garden of
Theophrastos

VIII

Lyceum

Hadrian (2nd cent. AD)

Gymnasium

Mon. of Lysikrates

Arch of
Hadrian

IX

Olympieion

Tomb of
Stadium    Herodes

X

ILISSOS

Metroon in Agrai

XI

Artemis Agrotera

Temple of
Tyche

Poseidon Helikonios

Kynosarges
Gymnasium

Classical ■
Roman ▨

after J. Travlos 1970

between the 7C and 19C AD, it has survived better than any other antique building in Greece.

The **Agora** was the public centre of the ancient city—a place for meetings social or otherwise, marketing, public administration and the operation of the legal system. From the 6C BC when the area ceased to be used as a cemetery, buildings to serve these various purposes grew up round the 'square' over a long period of time, and eventually encroached upon it. Only with the aid of period plans or models is it possible to get an idea of the nature of the Agora in antiquity.

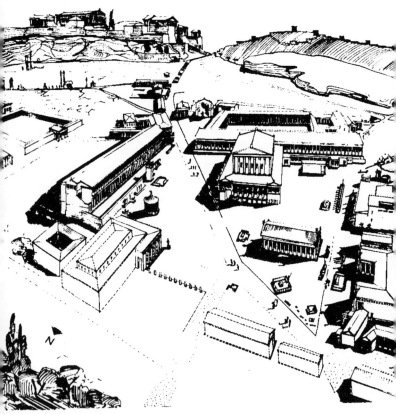

*Athens Agora. Reconstruction of area in 2C AD*

Near the SW corner of the excavated area is a boundary stone of the Agora inscribed in lettering of the 5C BC. The SW side of the Agora was the first to acquire public buildings. The **tholos**, evident now only from its circular floor, replaced an earlier building c 465 BC. It housed the Prytany or duty committee of the State Council as well as various official items (standard measures etc). To the NW are the foundations of the **new bouleuterion** or Chamber of the Council which prepared legislation for the Assembly. It had semicircular rows of seats, unlike its predecessor to the E (the old bouleuterion), which was subsequently used as an archive store. An earlier structure antedated both. Further N the **Metroön** took its most sophisticated form in the Hellenistic period when the complex was fronted by a colonnade. It housed a temple of the Mother of the Gods and archive repository. Outside are the bases for various statues. The fine masonry of the **great drain** (5C) can be seen; also the long base of the **Monument of the Eponymous Heroes** (of the Athenian tribes) which served too as an official notice board. N of the Metroön were the small Archaic **temples** of Apollo Patroös and one of Zeus and Athena. At the N end are two important **stoas**. The first is that of **Zeus Eleutherios** built c 430, Doric with Ionic interior columns, also marble Nike acroteria. Beyond, in the railway cutting, are the remains of the **Stoa Basileios** (or Royal Stoa) only identified in 1970. It was the headquarters of the Royal Archon and housed the statutes of Solon and Draco. In front is the 'lithos' (stone) where the archons took their oaths of office. The building probably dates to c 500 BC. Two porches were added c 400. Somewhere near Hipparchos was assassinated in 514 BC by Harmodios and Aristogeiton. Outside the fenced area, in a building plot on the other side of the street, are the excavated remains of the **Stoa Poikile** (or Painted Stoa), the first of the buildings on the N side of the Agora to be investigated (1980). Built c 460 it is named from the magnificent paintings which originally decorated the walls. It also contained shields captured from the Spartans at Sphakteria (example in museum). The stoa was Doric, with Ionic columns in the interior. In the area were many herms.

Within the archaeological site but largely obscured by the railway cutting is the **Peribolos of the Twelve Gods**, identified by an inscription: there is a ground altar to the S. The site of the **Temple of Ares**, a Classical building moved in the Roman period to this site from elsewhere, is marked in gravel. To the S are two huge interrelated structures, the **Odeion of Agrippa** (c 15 BC) and a much later (c 400 AD) **gymnasium**. The **Panathenaic Way** is marked by stone water channels and the bases of unidentified monuments.

The E side of the Agora is closed by the **Stoa of Attalos**. The original building was erected by Attalos II, King of Pergamon 159–138 BC, and contained shops. The stoa, reconstructed on its original foundations in 1953–56 at the expense of private donors from the USA, was dedicated as the Agora Museum by King Paul in 1956. Earlier finds below included a Classical lawcourt and Mycenaean and Protogeometric graves. The façade had Doric columns below and Ionic (with a balustrade) above. In front of the centre are a rostrum and a donor's monument. The interior has been somewhat modified to allow the installation of the excellently arranged **museum** of finds from the Agora.

S of the stoa is the so-called **'Valerian' Wall**, a Roman fortification using materials from buildings partly destroyed in the Herulian sack of AD 267. The wall follows the line of the façade of the destroyed **Library of Pantainos** erected before AD 102. Between the Library and the Stoa of Attalos a street led E towards the Roman market (see Rte 6).

Near the SE gate is the **Church of the Holy Apostles**, restored to its form of c 1020. There are 17C wall paintings in the narthex. Beneath and to the E are foundations of a **nymphaion**. Earlier on this site was the **mint** of Athens. To the N, bordering a roadway, are the remains of a **fountain house**. The road ran along the back of the first **south stoa** which formed the S side of the Agora from the 5C to the 2C BC. At the W end a large square foundation may be that of the **Heliaia lawcourt**. The south side of the Agora was remodelled in the 2C BC, with the construction of the enormous **middle stoa**, the second version of the south stoa and other elements forming a south square. The earlier layout of the area has been obscured by the Roman gymnasium.

# 6

# Pláka

The derivation of the name (recent) is uncertain. The area lies between Ermoú and the N/NE slopes of the Acropolis. Most of the buildings date from the mid 19C. Some have been excellently restored. The modest buildings of **Anafiótika** are charming.

Monastiráki Square opens from the S side of Ermoú (see Rte 4). At the SE corner is the former **Mosque of Tzistarákis** built in 1759; its minaret razed after 1821. Used for years as a prison, it became the Museum of Greek Popular Art in 1918. Recently reopened, the good displays are mainly of modern and traditional ceramics.

E and W run Pandróssou with tourist shops and Iféstou, less sophisticated and still specialising in metal goods, the latter descending to Plateía Avissinías, the site of the flea market.

Beyond the mosque stands a façade of the Library of Hadrian (see below). This W wall had a simple porch standing forward of the marble wall. To either side of the porch (the section N of the porch surviving) were seven unfluted columns with Corinthian capitals. To the left, the **Gate of Athena Archegetis**, a four-columned Doric portico, forms the main entrance to the Roman Market (below). A worn inscription on the architrave records contributions of Julius Caesar and Augustus. Outside the enclosure (entrance at NE) is the **Tower of the Winds** (properly the Horologion of Andronikos Kyrrhestes) of the 2 or 1C BC. It served the triple purpose of sundial, waterclock and weathervane. The building (in marble) is octagonal, each face marking a cardinal point and adorned with a relief of the appropriate wind. A semicircular turret attached to the S face was a reservoir for working the waterclock. It was originally surmounted by a revolving bronze triton. In Turkish times it was occupied by dervishes.

Below extends the rectangular **Roman Market** (c 111m x 96m) of which the S part has been excavated. It was a large paved peristyle court, with a propylon at the SE (for the W gate see above), and blocks of rooms behind the colonnades. At the edge of the site is a mosque and, on the corner of Od. Aiólou, the gateway of the former **medresse** (seminary). In Dhiogénous is a **Museum of Greek Folk Music** (1991). Along Aiólou is the **Library of Hadrian** (closed; see also above, this route, for the W façade), here with Corinthian columns buttressing the E wall. The building consisted of a walled enclosure (122m x 82m) with a cloistered court. The Library was contained in a room on the E side. The interior was probably a garden.

Across the square and reached via Adhrianoú and Mnesikléous is the 14C church of the **Metamórfosis** (or Sotiráki). Nearby is the **Kanellopoulos Museum** (English catalogue) in a restored 19C mansion. It contains a varied collection of antiquities and is particularly rich in bronzes. Od. Theorías runs to the entrance of the Acropolis.

To the N in Od. Thólou is the **Old University** (1837–41) recently restored to be a Museum of the University. Further on is **Ayioi Anárgyroi**, remodelled in the 17C and at the corner of Pritaníou the Byzantine chapel of **Ayios Nikólaos Rangavás**. Above Pritaníou is the remaining part of the neighbourhood of **Anafiótika** with narrow alleys and tiny houses in the style of island villages. It was built in the 19C by immigrant workers drawn to Athens for the construction of the new capital. The first two houses were put up (illegally) by families from the island of **Anáfi**.

Descending to Adhrianoú and turning left into Kidhathenaíon you find at no. 17 the **Museum of Greek Folk Art** (free; closed Monday), with an outstanding collection of embroidery. Síntagma is to the NE.

# 7

# From the Arch of Hadrian to the Benáki Museum

Behind the Arch of Hadrian (Rte 1) is an archaeological park (entrance in Vasilíssis Olgas) surrounding the Temple of Olympian Zeus. **Ancient houses** are overlain by a large **Roman bath**. Part of the **Themistoclean wall** can be seen with the **Hippades Gate**. There is a late 5C AD **basilica** built of Classical fragments. The **Sanctuary of Olympian Zeus** occupies an artificial terrace supported by a peribolos. The temple is the largest is Greece. Begun in the Archaic period, it took 700 years to complete in the course of which Corinthian was substituted for the original Doric.

S of the Olympieion ancient remains have almost all been obliterated by urban development. The river Ilissos has suffered likewise. The **Kynosarges gymnasium** was hereabouts. To the SE (via Od. Anapáfseos) is the main modern cemetery of Athens (Próto Nekrotafío) with much fine funerary sculpture and the tombs of eminent Greeks and some foreigners (including the archaeologists Schliemann and Furtwangler).

In the triangle formed by the E edge of the Olympieion and the Avenues Ardhittoú and Olgas are the Olympic swimming pool, the tennis club and the Ethnikos Athletic Club. Olgas and Ardhittoú join below the hill which was in antiquity *Ardettos*. On the opposite height, beyond the stadium, is the probable Tomb of Herodes (not accessible). The **stadium** occupies a natural valley between these two hills. It was restored 1896–1906. It may have originated under Lycurgus in 330 BC (but see Pnyx, Rte 3). As restored it has an athletic track (at high level) and, on the E side, a tunnel admits competitors and officials from the changing rooms.

Opposite the stadium Od. Iródhou Attikoú runs between the E side of the National Garden and the modest former **Palace**, residence of the king after the restoration of 1935 and more recently of the president. At the top of the street is Vasilíssis Sofías, and opposite the **Benáki Museum** (8, 3; at present closed for refurbishment and extension, though the Museum shop is open) containing the impressive fruits of 35 years eclectic collecting by Antoine Benaki. The chronological and geographical range is exciting, though Greek material is naturally prominent.

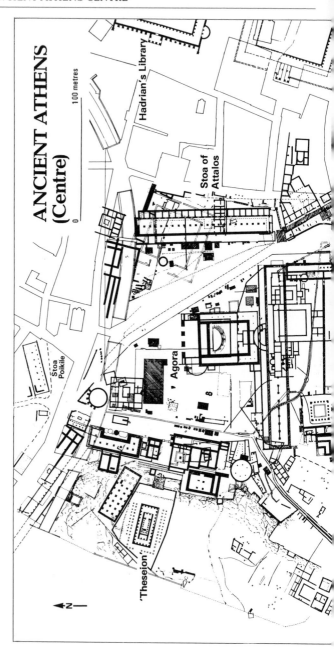

Acropolis

Wall of Valerian

THEORIAS

*Areopagus*

Dörpfeld's excavations

'Prison'

LEOF: APOSTOLOU PAVLOU

after J. Travlos with permission of the American School of Classical Studies, Athens.

# 8

## From Monástiraki to the National Museum

From Monastiráki (Rte 6) the broad, busy and exciting Odhós Athinás, with vegetable and meat markets, leads straight to Omónia Square. Take the narrower Od. Aiólou, parallel to the E, a popular shopping street, now largely pedestrianised. To the right is **Ayía Iríni** (excellent choir). 450m further, Plateía Dhimarkheíou (formerly Kótzia) has the **Town Hall** (Dhimarkeíon) on the W, facing the National Bank of Greece. On the S side is a mansion by Ziller. Excavations have revealed the foundations of the National Theatre (demolished in 1938) and many relics of the ancient city.

Athinás leads directly into **Omónia** (Concord) **Sq.** (Ομόνοια), the name commemorating the reconciliation of two warring 19C political factions. It is a focus of commerce and communications. There is a central fountain and, beneath, the main station of the Electric Railway with a busy concourse (shops, post office, bank etc). Immediately to the left Od. Piraiós begins its straight course to the port. A little to the E, Od. Patissíon (officially Ikosiokhtó Oktomvríou, or 28 October St.) passes W of Plateía Káningos (bus terminals), where a statue of Canning recalls his services to Greek independence. On the E side of Patissíon is the **Polytekhneíon** (a University teaching technical subjects and Fine Arts) designed by Kaftandzoglou and built of Pentelic marble in 1862–80. Passing the National Archaeological Museum (gardens; cafés; Rte 9) you reach the **Plateía Areos**, at the SW corner of the **Pédhion Areos**. At the S side of the park are War Memorials and at the NE end the former military academy (Evelpídhon), now law courts.

# 9

## National Archaeological Museum

**Approaches**. **Trolley-bus/bus** no. 2, 12 or 3 from Síntagma Sq. to the museum which is in Odhós Patissíon (Rte 8), 450m N of Omónia Sq., and a short walk from Plateía Kánningos. **Electric railway** (1 stop) from Monastiráki to Omónia. No direct service from the Acropolis.

**Admission**. Closed Monday. A printed catalogue to the sculpture (1968) and good illustrated souvenir volumes are available in English; guide to the prehistoric collections, at present only in French and German. These and slides and postcards are sold in the entrance hall.

**Cafés**. In gardens outside Museum and, within, off the central atrium (stairway from entrance hall or via Room 20)—not cheap.

**Shop**. In basement, with access from entrance hall. Casts and replicas of objects in the museum collections are sold; also good site and museum guidebooks published by the Ministry of Culture; videos.

The **National Archaeological Museum** (3, 2; Εθνικό Αρχαιολογικό Μουσείο) contains an outstanding collection of material from the whole of Greece, though new finds now go to the appropriate regional museums. The museum was erected in 1866–89, and a large E wing added in 1925–39.

Directly opposite the entrance are the prehistoric galleries. The main hall contains Mycenaean finds, in particular the amazing riches from the shaft graves at Mycenae including the famous gold masks. Amongst many other spectacular objects are inlaid daggers from Shaft Grave IV, gravestones (stelai) with relief decoration, and decorated gold cups from Vaphio (Lakonia). Galleries to the left and right contain respectively Neolithic/Early Bronze Age and Cycladic material.

Returning to the vestibule you enter the N wing where the first rooms have chiefly Archaic sculpture. The massive Sounion kouros is in Room 8. Classical sculpture is from Room 14. In 15 is the spectacular bronze Poseidon (or Zeus) from Cape Artemision. Several rooms are entirely devoted to grave and votive stelai. Room 20 includes later copies of the chryselephantine Athena Parthenos of Pheidias. Room 21, on the central axis of the building, has a 2C copy of the famous 5C Diadoumenos of Polykleitos and a fine Hellenistic bronze of a horse and jockey (also from Artemision).

Here you can turn left to Gallery 34 which connects the old and new wings of the museum. The area is arranged to recall an open-air sanctuary. At the end you turn left into Room 36 which contains the Karapanos Collection, especially rich in bronzes (Dodona is very well represented). Room 37 (bronzes) includes the 4C Marathon Boy. Beyond are the recently opened Egyptian galleries. The Helène Stathatos collection will be housed in this part of the museum.

The first floor is also accessible from the end of Gallery 34 but you can first return to the main sequence of rooms in the old building. Rooms 22–28 contain Late Classical sculpture, including the interesting but fragmentary finds from the Temple of Asklepios at Epidaurus. Rooms 29 and 30 are devoted to the Hellenistic period and Rooms 31–33 (not all open) to Roman sculpture.

The first floor (access from Gallery 34, above) has an exhibition of finds from the remarkable prehistoric settlement (excavated from 1967) at Akrotiri on Thera. Especially interesting are the well-preserved frescoes. This floor however is almost entirely devoted to the enormous and spectacular collection of **ancient pottery**. The quantity is so great that the most remarkable pieces do not obviously stand out. Room 1 has Prehistoric to Geometric; Rooms 2 and 3 Orientalising; Room 4 Early Black Figure, also metopes from the Temple of Apollo at Thermon; Room 5 Mature Black Figure; Room 6 Further Black Figure, also Red Figure (from 530 BC); Room 7 Mature Red Figure; Room 8 White-ground Lekythoi; Room 9 Red Figure and White-ground; also the Niinion pinax from Eleusis.

The fine **Numismatic Collection** (only a small selection displayed) is in the S wing. The **Epigraphic Collection** is entered from Od. Tosítsa.

# 10

# From Omónia Square to Ambelókipoi

The route follows one of three main arteries (Odd. Akadhimías, Panepistimíou, Stadhíou, all one-way) from the area of Omónia to the area of Síntagma/Leofóros Vasilíssis Sofías, the latter continuing to Ambelókipoi. **Trolley bus** no. 3 takes the route described via Akadhimías and Vasilíssis Sofías, returning via Panepistimíou. Other **suburban buses**, from Plateía Káningos or the Academy, take similar routes. Stadhíou is one-way in the direction of Síntagma and, although followed by bus and trolley routes, none of them continues into Vasilíssis Sofías.

Odhós Stadhíou, busy with good shops and some impressive buildings, is aligned on the distant (and invisible) stadium. Half way along (right), at the W corner of Plateía Klafthmónos, is the fine 11–12C Byzantine church of **Ayioi Theódoroi**. At the SE **King Otho's Palace** has become a **Museum of the City of Athens**. Farther on (right) is Plateía Kolokotróni with an equestrian statue of Kolokotronis and, behind, the **Old Parliament Building** (Palaiá Voulí; 1858–74), now the **National Historical Museum** (08.30–15.00; closed Monday), with an extensive and interesting collection of portraits, arms, and relics, especially of the War of 1821–28.

Shortly beyond, the street bends to enter the lower side of **Síntagma Square** (Rte 1). For continuation, see below.

If you take the alternative Od. Panepistemíou (University St.; officially Leofóros Eleftheríou Venizélou), you pass (right) the **Arsákeion** built for a girls' school and training college (1836, rebuilt 1848; see Rte 15), and until recently used as law courts, soon to be the Supreme Court.

Farther on an important group of buildings is fronted by formal gardens. In the centre is the **University** (Πανεπιστήμιο; 3, 6; 1839–42). In front are statues of Gladstone, Capodistrias, the philologist Koraï, the poet Rhigas and the patriarch Gregory.

To the left is the **National Library** (3, 6; 1887–91; Adm. free daily, except holidays, 09.00–13.00 & 17.00–20.00).

On the far side of the University is the **Hellenic Academy** (3, 6; 1859). Colossal figures of Athena and Apollo are set on two Ionic columns in front. Seated figures of Plato and Socrates are either side of the entrance.

Just beyond are the Byzantine-style **Eye Hospital** (Οφθαλμοιατρείο), the Italianate **Roman Catholic church** (1870), dedicated to St Denis. Opposite is the **Bank of Greece**. Beyond (left; no. 22) the **Archaeological Society** (founded 1837), **Schliemann's House** has an inscription on the loggia (ΙΛΙΟΥ ΜΕΛΑΘΡΟΝ: Palace of Troy). It is to house the Numismatic Museum.

At the NE corner of Síntagma you turn left beside the Parliament into Leofóros Vasilíssis Sofías, lined on the N with embassies and ministries. From the left enters Leofóros Akadhimías.

Immediately behind the University, in Akadhimías, an attractive former hospital is now a cultural centre. At no. 50 (in the Pink Building) is the **Theatre Museum** (entrance in Sína; Mon–Fri 09.00–15.30).

You pass the **Benaki Museum** (Rte 7). To the left the fashionable district of Kolonáki (see below) rises on the S slope of Lykabettos.

The ***Byzantine Museum** (4, 8; 08.30–15.00, closed Monday) occupies the **Villa Ilissia**, built in 1848 for the eccentric Sophie de Marbois, duchesse de Plaisance (1785–1854). This is Greece's main museum of Byzantine antiquities, with a rich collection. Outside are various items of sculpture and architecture. The interior rooms on the ground floor are mainly devoted to reconstructions of various types of Early Christian and Byzantine church, with appropriate furnishings, and other contemporary finds. The upper floor has a fine collection of ikons and frescoes.

Adjacent is the imposing **War Museum** (adm. free; 09.00–14.00, closed Tuesday). It contains material illustrating Greek military activity from prehistoric times to the present day.

Beyond the next cross-roads (left) a small public garden (café) fronts the **Evanghelismós Hospital**, founded in 1881 (extended 1983). Behind are the **Marasleion**, a secondary school and teachers' training college, and the British and American Schools (5, 5).

The excellent and imposing **Gennadeion Library** is a little higher up the S slope of Lykabettos. Close by, to the SE, is the formerly monastic **Moní Petráki**, now a theological seminary.

The conspicuous **Hilton Hotel** (5, 7) stands at the important junction of Leofóros Vasilíssis Sofías with Leofóros Konstandínou.

On the corner of the latter street, opposite the Hilton Hotel, is the **Ethnikí Pinakothíki** (National Picture Gallery) and **Aléxandros Soútzos Museum** (closed Monday). This museum is devoted to 19 and 20C Greek painting and sculpture. It is not a museum of contemporary Greek art, which is represented in the Vorrés Museum in Paianía (tel. 664-2520) and the Pierídhes Museum in Glifádha (tel. 894-8287), see Rtes 13 and 17B. The permanent collection consists primarily of 19 and 20C Greek art, although there are some European acquisitions.

Nearly 1km farther out (left) is the imposing **Hall of the Friends of Music** (opened 1992). Just before this, a lane leads off (l.) into the **Párko Eleftherías**, with an Arts Centre (Κέντρο Τεχνών: exhibitions; pleasant café). Next is the **United States Embassy**. The road continues to **Ambeló-kipoi**, where it meets Leofóros Alexándras, a dual highway from Pedhion Areos (Rte 8). Before that, below the 'Athens Tower' (Pírgos Athinón), the road to Marathon and the Mesogeion branches right (Rte 17B).

# 11

# Lykabettos (Likavittós)

The ascent of Lykabettos (on foot from the SW) takes c 45 minutes from Síntagma Square, via Kolonáki Square and a stepped path from the top of Od. Loukianoú.

The easiest route is by the **funicular railway**, further E, at the top of Od. Ploutárkhou, reached by bus 023 from the Academy or Od. Kanári.

The approach from the N (turnings off Od. Asklipíou, bus 026 from Panepistimíou) or, higher, by the 'Periferiakó Likavittoú' from Dhexamení (see below) gives access by road and paths first to the Likavittós Theatre (plays and concerts in summer), then by stepped path to the summit.

**Lykabettos** (Λυκαβηττός; in modern Greek **Likavittós**; 4, 4) is the highest (277m) of the hills of the **Anchesmos** range. It now rises like a steep island from a sea of houses. The slopes are wooded and there are informal paths as well as the standard approaches.

A wireless station of the Royal Hellenic Airforce occupied the W slopes until 1961. In 1941 this was the operations centre of the Greek Air Force and formed King George's last HQ on the mainland before he retired to Crete in the face of the German advance. The ceremonial cannon are sited here.

From the SW and the Benáki Museum (Rte 7) the short Od. Koubári leads to Kolonáki Square (Plateía Kolonakíou or, more properly, Filikís Etaireías), centre of the most fashionable district of Athens. To the right (SE corner) is the **British Council** (library, lecture hall) which also has offices on the opposite side of the square.

Beyond the main British Council building, Od. Kapsáli leads to (right) Od. Neofítou Doúka where, at no. 4, is the **Goulandris Museum of Cycladic and Ancient Greek Art** (1986; 10.00–16.00 (15.00, Sat); closed Tuesday). The museum has fine objects of ancient art from prehistoric to Roman times and is particularly rich in marble figurines and other material of the Cycladic Early Bronze Age; also temporary exhibitions in its new extension, an adjacent mansion designed by Ziller.

Above NE corner of Kolonáki Square, is the Roman **Dhexamení**, or reservoir of the acqueduct of the old town. It was recommissioned in 1840 and subsequently restored. Here at Epiphany takes place the ceremony of the Blessing of the Waters. Above the Dhexamení you can get access (via Od. E. Rogkákou) to the series of streets which provide a continuous route (known as the Periferiakó Likavittoú) round the mountain, and access to/from various points of the city. Near Dhexamení also is the top of Od. Loukianoú and the start of the zigzag path to the little 19C chapel of Ayios Yeoryios on the **summit** of Lykabettos (tourist pavilion offering meals and snacks), which provides a magnificent *panorama of Athens and Attica. The funicular railway gives a direct approach to the summit.

On the N side in Od. Dhidhótou, off Asklipíou, is the **École Française d'Athènes**, the oldest archaeological school in Greece (1846). Above here, steep streets lead to the Periferiakó and the upper slopes of Lykabettos.

# 12

## Néo Fáliro and Piraeus

**Approaches from Athens. By rail**, by the Piraeus Electric Railway (ΕΗΣ) from Omónia, 11km in 20 minutes. Trains every 7 minutes.

**By road**. The shortest route to Piraeus (9km) is by the old Odhós Piraiós, followed by bus 049 from Omónia Sq., via the industrial suburbs of Petrálona and Réndis. The ΕΗΣ bus 040 (green) from Síntagma Sq. takes Leofóros Singroú, then diverges via Kallithéa to reach Fáliron Bay at Tzitzifiés. The pleasantest route (11km) is by Leofóros Singroú and Fáliron Bay, described below.

From the Olympieion (Rte 7) the broad Leofóros Andréas Singroú (7, 7) runs straight to the coast, passing large international hotels and between **Kallithéa** and **Néa Smírni** (New Smyrna), to reach Faliron Bay at (6km) the **racecourse**. You turn right along the shore, with much reclaimed land. 7km **Tzitzifiés** (Hotels, C) is noted for tavernas with bouzouki music.

In Phaleron Bay the Athenians beached their triremes until the beginning of the 5C BC.

8km **Néo Fáliro**, or **New Phaleron** (Hotels C, and others). The **Anglo-French Cemetery**, behind the Karaïskakis Stadium, N of the railway station, contains monuments to sailors who died in Piraeus in 1855–59. The area is now dominated by the vast (126m x 28m) and impressive boat-shaped **Stadium of Peace and Friendship**, completed in 1985 for concerts and indoor sport. From New Phaleron you follow the railway and Odhós Skilítsi to meet the old Athens–Piraeus road (Pl. 8) or, by Odhós Tzavéla and Plat. Ippodhamías, reach the central harbour of (11km) **Piraeus**.

**PIRAEUS** (Πειραίευς), now **Piraiévs**, is, as in Classical times, the port of Athens. With suburbs it is the third largest town in Greece (476,304). The SW part of its peninsula, called **Akti**, is joined to the E part by an isthmus which separates the Great Harbour (**Kantharos**) from the circular **Zea** (or Pashalimani). Farther E, below the hill of **Kastella** (*Munychia*) is the still smaller harbour of **Tourkolimano** (also Mikró Limáni). The spine of the peninsula divides the modern town into the more fashionable quarter to the S, and E, well supplied with restaurants etc., and a commercial sector surrounding the main harbour.

The modern town follows the rectangular plan of its ancient predecessor, whose visible remains are scanty. The museum, the port and the topography are of considerable interest. A recent study of the ancient city is R. Garland, *The Piraeus*, 1987. Recent discoveries can be traced through *Archaeological Reports*, see Bibliography.

**Arrival by Sea**. Customs and passport formalities generally on board (none from Greek ports). On departure for abroad, passports and customs at the central passenger terminal on the quay. Taxicabs plying to addresses in Athens are entitled to double fare.

**Shipping Quays. Akti Poseidhónos** (Pl. 3) to Aegina, Poros, Idhra, and Spetsai; **Plateía Karaïskákis** (Pl. 3) to most other Greek destinations; **Aktí Miaoúlis** (E end; Pl. 7) to Italy, Turkey, and other ports beyond Greek frontiers; (W end) for ocean liners. **Zéa** (Pashalimáni; Pl. 11) for hydrofoils for Idhra, Spetsai etc.

**Railway Stations**. ΕΗΣ (Pl. 3), for Athens and Kifissia; ΣΠΑΠ (Pl. 3), for Corinth and the Peloponnesus; ΟΣΕ (Pl. 2) for Thessaloníki.

**Restaurants** along waterfront at Tourkolímano (seafood, some expensive), also on Akti Themistokléous.

**Post Office** (Pl. 7), Odhós Fílonos. **Tourist Police** at corner of Aktí Miaoúlis and Filellínon.

**Buses**. From Electric Railway Station; 20 (circular) to Kastélla and Tourkolímano; also to Néo Fáliro, Passenger Terminal. From Plateía Koraî (Pl. 7); **040** (green) to Athens (Filellínon); 904/905 (circular) to Akte. From Leofóros Ethnikís Antistáseos (Pl. 7) to Athens (Omonia; **049**), Glifádha (**149**) and suburbs. From Plateía Karaïskáki (Pl. 3) to Piraeus suburbs.

**Shipping Offices**. Adriatica, 85 Aktí Miaoúlis; Karageorgis, 26–28 Aktí Kondhíli; Epirotiki, 87 Aktí Miaoúlis; Hellenic Mediterranean Lines, Electric Station Building: Mediterranean Sun Lines, 5 Sakhtoúri; Strintzis Lines, 26 Aktí Posídhonos; Ventouris Lines, 91 Piraiós; Minoan Lines, 28 Aktí Posídhonos.

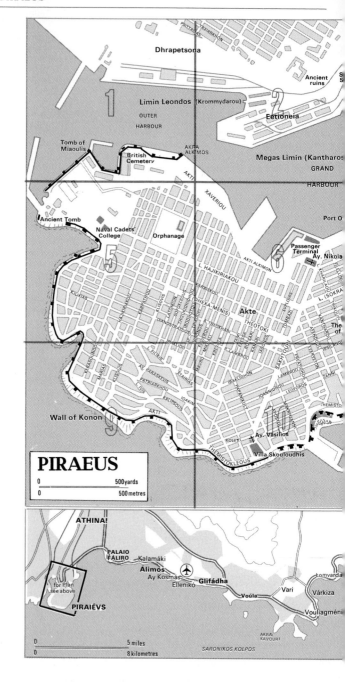

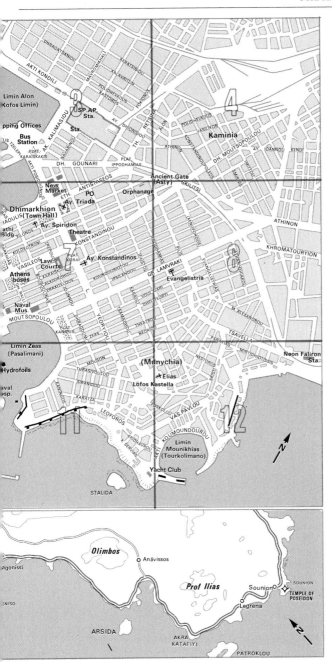

**Shipping Services** (quays see above). Argossaronikos to Aegina (2–3 times per hour), continuing (many times daily) to Methana and Poros, and (3–4 times daily) to Idhra, Ermioni, and Spetsai; twice weekly to Leonidhi. Also to Aegina by hydrofoil (hourly). Aegean services daily (usually except Sunday) to Siros, Tinos, Mykonos (1–3 times), Samos, Chios, Mytilene, Kos, Rhodes (1–3 times), and Crete. From 2 to 5 times weekly to many other Aegean Islands, the Ionian Islands, Brindisi, Venice, Istanbul, etc. **Hydrofoils**, from Zea to Kea, Kithnos; Poros, Idhra, Spetsai, Leonidhi, Monemvasia, etc.

**Car Hire.** Hertz, 9–11 Ay. Nikolaos, facing Passenger Terminal (Pl. 6).

**Festival.** Blessing of the Waters at Epiphany (6 January).

**History.** Piraeus became the major Athenian naval base under Themistocles. Munychia was fortified by Hippias c 510; the larger fortification system begun in 493. In the 5C Piraeus had a cosmopolitan population consisting largely of Metics (μέτοικοι), or resident aliens, who controlled much of its manufacture and trade. Piraeus was a Macedonian and Roman base and commercial centre. After Alaric's raid in 396 it declined. In medieval times the city was known as *Porto Leone* and by the Turks as Aslan-liman. Resettled by islanders after 1834, it grew rapidly through the 19C. The refugee influx of 1922 further increased the population. In the Second World War the port was put out of action on the first night of the German air attack (6 April 1941) when ammunition ships blew up. It now provides a port of call for most shipping lines operating in the E Mediterranean and is the focus of Greek services to the islands. The opening scene of Plato's *Republic* is laid in Piraeus, at the house of the aged Kephalos.

## Defences of Ancient Piraeus

The **Long Walls**, sometimes called the 'Legs' (τὰ σκέλη), formed part of the original fortification scheme of Themistocles. The **First** or **Northern Long Wall** (7km long) ran from Athens to Piraeus, the **Second** or **Phaleric Long Wall** (6.5km long) from Athens to the E end of Phaleron Bay. The walls were completed c 456 BC. (Thuc. I, 108). A **Third** or **Southern Long Wall**, parallel with the first and the same length, was built by Kallikrates under the direction of Pericles to guard against the possibility of a surprise landing in Phaleron Bay. The Northern and Southern Long Walls, starting from two points in the outer wall of the Piraeus, converged to within 183m of each other and then ran parallel to the region of Pnyx hill (comp. Rte 3). Between them ran a road. A second road, probably the 'carriage-road' (ἁμαξιτός) mentioned by Xenophon (*Hellenica* II, 4, 10), ran outside the Northern Long Wall. The direct modern road (Odhós Piraiós, above) follows the Northern Long Wall for much of its course, the Electric Railway the Southern Long Wall. Sections of both can be seen between the Karaïskákis Stadium and Odhós Piraiós (left) and in front of the Klostoufantourgoú School.

The Themistoclean **city wall** guarded all three harbours; fortified entrances to each, forming part of the circuit, were probably closed by chains. The full circuit was 60 stadia (Thucydides II, 13). The rebuilding of the walls is usually credited to Konon (Xenophon, Hell. IV, 8), though an inscription has shown that this was started before his victory at Knidos and the work was probably finished only after 346 (Demosthenes XIX, 125). The defences were shortened on the N side but the circuit was extended round the whole of Akte.

Under Pericles the **city** itself was laid out by Hippodamos of Miletus on a chess-board plan with a spacious agora at the centre. Boundary stones have been found. **Ship-sheds** were numerous and prominent and there were dry docks. Lycurgus constructed a naval arsenal or skeuotheke (Σκευοθήκη) in the harbour of Zea, designed by the architect *Philo* in 346–329 BC.

Odhós Skilítsi and Odhós Pílis, the extension of Tzavélas (see above), converge by Plateía Ippodhámou, from which roads lead W to the Electric Railway Station and SW to the main harbour.

Just off Skilítsi, c 90m E of Plat. Ippodhámou, are the remains of the **Asty Gate**, where the Hamaxitos, or 'carriage-road' (see above), entered the city. Many neighbouring buildings incorporate classical masonry from the Long Walls.

At the heart of maritime Piraeus at the E angle of the **Great Harbour** stands the **Dhimarkhíon** (Pl. 7), or Town Hall, in front of which is a clock, a local landmark ('to rolói'). Immediately in front is Aktí Poseídhonos. To the SW is Aktí Miaoúlis with liner berths (adm. restricted) and the **passenger terminal** (Pl. 6). Here and in **Plateía Karaïskákis** to the N are the offices of shipping companies.

The modern harbour corresponds very nearly to the ancient *Kantharos* ('goblet'), which was divided, then as now, between naval (N) and commercial (S) shipping. Roughly where the old passenger terminal now stands, five stoas lined the quay. Traces of one of them have been found c 140m from the quay SE of the custom house; other traces of the **Emporion** are visible in the foundations of the church of **Ayia Triadha** (Pl. 7).

NORTH-WESTERN QUARTER. Only limited traces of Classical buildings remain on the peninsula of Eëtioneia.

From the Town Hall Leofóros Yeoryíou tou Prótou leads shortly to the **Tinan Gardens**, laid out in 1854 by a French admiral. Opposite stands the **cathedral** (Pl. 7; **Ayía Triádha**). On the corner of Odhós Fílonos in July 1959 was discovered the unique collection of bronze statuary now in the Piraeus Museum, perhaps part of Sulla's loot, awaiting shipment to Rome. Farther on in Plateía Koraḯ is the **Municipal Theatre**. The broad Leofóros Iróön Polytekhníou (Ἡρώων Πολυτεχνείου) leads SW along the spine of the peninsula, between pleasant gardens; streets at right angles lead (right) to Akti Miaoúlis and (left) to Zéa (see below). In the N angle of Odd. Skouzé and Filellínon, an archaeological park has Roman houses and shops of the 2–6C AD.

At No. 38 Odhós Filellínon (Pl. 6) is the newly refurbished **Archaeological Museum**, with interesting material, excellently displayed. Outstanding are the large-scale bronzes (upstairs), including the superb **\*\*Piraeus Kouros**, an Athena and an Artemis; fine **\*Neo-Classical reliefs of Amazonomachies from Kifissia, c AD 200; and a massive funerary monument from Kallithea with relief (Amazonomachy, Zoömachy) and free-standing commemorative sculptures, c 400 BC.

Next to the museum are the scanty remains of the Hellenistic **Theatre of Zea**.

In a building plot at Ipsilándou 170, near the junction with Bouboulínas, is a section of the skeuotheke or **Arsenal of Philo** (see above) found in 1988. The architect's complete specification for the building was found in 1882 (model in the Naval Museum).

You reach the ancient harbour of *Zea* (or Pashalimáni; Pl. 11), a land-locked basin connected with the sea by a channel c 200m by 100m, lined on either side by the ancient walls, which terminate at the inner end of the channel in two short moles. The port had 196 **ship-sheds**, spread fanwise round the bay; many traces of these may be seen, particularly in the basement of a block of flats on the E side. On the W side is a new outer yacht basin. Hydrofoil services (except those for Aíyina) leave from here.

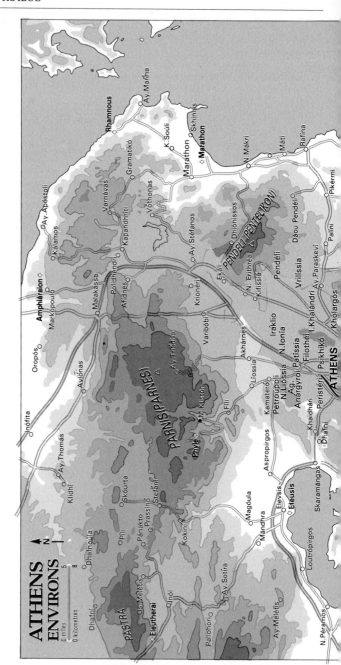

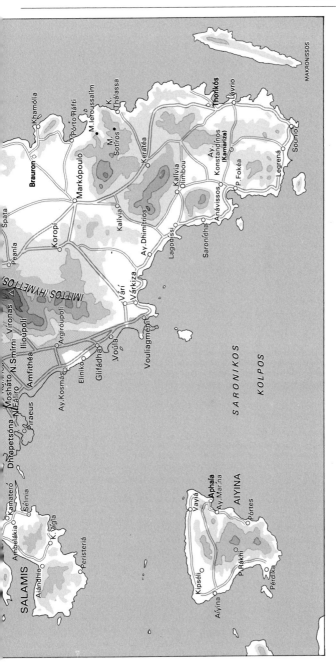

Behind the reclaimed shoreline below Akti Themistokléous a new **Naval Museum of Greece** (ΝΑΥΤΙΚΟΝ ΜΟΥΣΕΙΟΝ ΤΗΣ ΕΛΛΑΔΟΣ) faces a formal garden in which are displayed guns, conning towers, torpedo tubes, etc. The main door is to the right, but entrance more normally to the left. Opposite the main entrance the building incorporates part of the Themisto-clean wall. Displays and objects illustrate the history of the Greek marine.

In the other direction the shaded Plateía Kanáris (Pl. 7) is a favourite promenade.

The promontory to the SE was perhaps the site of *Phreattys*.

On the neck of the peninsula is the site of the **Asklepieion**, or Sanctuary of Asklepios Munychios (reliefs).

The road to Néo Fáliro here leaves the shore and passes below **Kastélla**, with ancient quarries. The Hill of Munychia (85m; 10 minute walk), the acropolis of Piraeus, commands all three harbours and *views of Phaleron Bay and the Saronic Gulf. It has been used as a military strongpoint in both ancient and modern times. The modern chapel of **Ayios Elias**, near the summit, marks the site not of the Temple of Artemis Munychia but of **Bendis**, a celebrated sanctuary. About 90m W is the upper entrance to a flight of 165 steps, known as the **Cavern of Arethusa**, which leads to the stuccoed subterranean galleries that held the water supply of the citadel (65.5m deep). On the W slope of the hill (discovered in 1880, but now covered up) was the ancient **Theatre of Dionysos** referred to by Thucydides (VIII, 93). To the E is the **Veákio**, a modern open air theatre. From Munychia, Leofóros Yeoryíou tou Prótou (see above) descends to the main harbour.

Keeping to the cliffs you descend past the **Yacht Club of Greece** (Ναυτικός Ομιλος Ελλάδος), on the site of the fortress of Hippias and the Temple of Artemis Munychia. The picturesque yacht basin of **Tourkolímano** (Pl. 12) retains the form it had as the ancient port of Munychia. It was protected by two long moles, each ending in a lighthouse tower and had slips for 82 triremes, of which some foundations can be seen under water to the N and S. The name Tourkolimano seems unlikely to survive a chauvinist campaign to change it to **Mikrolímano**.

The return to either Zea or the Great Harbour can be made by bus No. 904/905 (circular route).

The rocky and usually deserted S coast of the **Akte Peninsula** is pleasant to *walk, especially in the late afternoon.

The anticlockwise route is best. It can be shortened by taking bus No. 904/905 (circular route from Plat. Koraî) to the point S of the Naval School, where it emerges on the shore. From there Zea can be reached on foot in 1 hour.

The W extremity of the peninsula, once a royal park, is now a restricted naval area. On the most northerly point, the ancient promontory of **Alkimos** (Pl. 1), once stood the great **marble lion** (probably from Delos) that was inscribed in runes by Harald Hardrada and gave to Piraeus its alternative names of Porto Leone and Porto Draco. The lion was removed to Venice by Morosini in 1687. About 275m W of Alkimos are some graves of English soldiers and a **Monument to Andreas Miaoulis** (1769–1835), the admiral. Behind are quarries and, to seaward of the lighthouse, a rock-hewn grave traditionally known as the Tomb of Themistocles and a poros column, re-erected in 1952, that marked the S entrance to the harbour.

Leofóros Iróön Polytekhníou is continued to the W by Leofóros Khatzikiriá-kou to the **Naval School** (Pl. 5), from where Akti Themistokléous follows the indented S shore of the peninsula. The **Wall of Konon** is visible in its lower courses for most of the way, often supporting small tavernas. A short section of the **Wall of Themistocles** survives to the SE of the **signal station** (56m) which crowns the highest point of the peninsula.

# II ATTICA

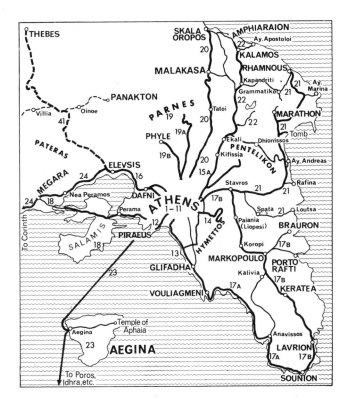

The name of **ATTICA** (Αττική; Attikí), the region which surrounds Athens, is probably derived from the word ἀκτή (akte), 'promontory' or 'peninsula', literally 'the place where the waves break'. It became an entity with the *synoecism* (amalgamation) of the old Mycenaean centres during the late-Geometric period. Geographically Attica is a roughly triangular peninsula which ends in Cape Sounion; its base, c 50km wide, is the almost continuous mountain barrier from the bay of Aigosthena, in the W, to the channel of Euboea, in the E. This consists of the ranges of Pateras, Kithairon, and Parnes and the coastal hills of Mavrovouni. This barrier formed the ancient boundary between Attica and Boeotia, with disputed areas around the three passes: the Megarid, Eleutherai, and Diakria. Possession of Salamis and the Megarid secured the W approaches, which are effectively cut off from the Peloponnese by the great Yerania range. Athens itself, protected by the inner ring of Aigaleos, Pentelikon, and Hymettos, but connected by easy roads with the plains beyond, is the natural centre of the region. Many of the Attic mountains, in the time of Pausanias crowned by images of the gods, are now surmounted by ugly radar stations, with restricted access to their summits.

Modern Attica became a separate administrative entity in 1899 when it was detached from Boeotia. The boundaries have been altered several times since. There are now two nomes: Attikís and Piraiós. Attikis consists of two eparchies: Attica proper and the Megarid. Piraios has five: Piraeus itself (which, however, includes Salamis and Spetsai); Aegina; Idhra; Kithira; and Troezenia. Greater Athens, comprising part of the eparchy of Attica and part of the eparchy of Piraeus, enjoys special administrative status within its territory.

Among features of interest are the coastal resorts SE of Athens; the hill resorts to the N; Mt Hymettos; the monasteries of Kaisariani and Dhafni; the Mesogeia with the site and museum of Brauron; and Sounion. Archaeologically rewarding also are Marathon, Eleusis and Aegina; also, a little farther away, the Amphiaraion at Oropos, and Rhamnous. With a car, it is possible to combine two or three places in one day. Bus services are extensive and frequent to many places, though they radiate from central Athens and are little help to those in seaside hotels. In the season there are coach excursions to the main sites. The area can be very pleasant for walking, though expanding towns, military zones, and spreading villa development are ever-increasing obstacles. The countryside is carpeted with flowers in spring, also a good season to enjoy the crisp air and clear Attic light.

Rtes 13–16 contain excursions which can be made by public transport leaving every few minutes from Central Athens; they are possible at any time of day without advance planning. The later routes require some organisation but can each be made in a single day from Athens. In Rtes 19, 20, and 22 the old roads out to the N are described, since they give easier access to remains of historical interest, every day more hidden in suburbia; in each case a faster route is via the Athens–Thessaloniki Highway.

Useful guides to this area are L.D. Loukopoulou, *Attika* (National Bank of Greece) 1973 and C. Bouras et al., *Churches of Attica*, 1970.

# 13

# The Attic Coast to Vouliagméni

**Road**, dual carriageway, 25km (15½ miles). **Buses** (Prefix 1) every 15 minutes from Síntagma Sq. to Edhém and Ayios Kosmás (133); from Leofóros Olgas, regularly, to Glifádha, Vouliagméni etc. The distances below are measured from Síntagma Sq.

The **West Coast of Attica**, in Classical times a flourishing region with many demes, degenerated into insignificance at an early date, and for centuries lay neglected and difficult of access. The discovery of medicinal springs near Glifádha and Vouliagméni after the First World War led to the foundation of bathing resorts, and in recent years the coast has been developed as the summer playground of Attica. The hinterland, a bare stony tract, is less developed but the coast is very crowded in July–August.

From the Olympieion to (6km) the racecourse, see Rte 12. The broad new highway turns left along the coast, whose conformation has been changed by land reclamation. The rocky headland that closed Phaleron Bay to the E, once identified with Cape Kolias (see below), is more likely the site of ancient *Phaleron* itself, which is usually placed near the Chapel of St George.

The ancient deme of Phaleron, the original port of Athens, was connected with the capital by the Phaleric Long Wall. Traces of this have been found on the hill, and the foundations of a mole in the sea. The Spartans, tricked by the exiled Alkmaeonids into invading Peisistratid Athens, were defeated in the neighbouring plain.

7km **Palaió Fáliro** (Παλαιό Φάληρο: Hotels B, C, D; restaurants), or **Old Pháleron**, a seaside resort (61,371 inhab.) with a water-sports stadium and swimming pool, extends E along the shore. To the left in the **Phaleron War Cemetery**, stands the Athens memorial, dedicated in May 1961, to 2800 British dead of 1939–45, who have no known grave in Greece or former Yugoslavia. The more direct approach from Leoforos Singrou comes in from the left. 9.5km **Kalamáki** (Hotels A, B, C, D; tavernas) has views of Hymettos. 11km **Alimós** (Hotel B), with a marina, corresponds to the ancient *Halimous*, birthplace of Thucydides (471–c 400 BC), whom Macaulay called 'the greatest historian that ever lived'. Some ancient building remains have been found; the clay of this area was highly valued by Athenian potters. Along the shore are summer amusements. 13km A turning (left; signs to Mesogeíon Avenue and Olympic stadium) skirts the airport and joins a major new by-pass of Athens which leads through the S suburbs on the foothills of Mt Hymettos, to debouch in Odhós Mesogeíon, on the NE side of the city (Rte 17B). The promontory of **Ayios Kosmás** is named after a 19C chapel, whose conventual buildings are now a taverna. The headland probably represents the ancient *Kolias Akra*, where many wrecked Persian ships were washed ashore after the Battle of Salamis.

Excavations by Prof. G. Mylonas in 1930–31 produced no signs of ships but showed that the coast has sunk since Classical times. On the E side of the headland and in the sea below were found remains of two separate periods, Early and Late Helladic. Stone house walls are visible. The cemetery along the E shore is Early Bronze Age. The graves show affinities with Cycladic types. Trade in Melian obsidian may have encouraged the contact. The site came to a violent end c 1900 BC. In Mycenaean times it was a fortified village, subsequently abandoned in the 12C BC. The Classical sanctuary of Aphrodite seen by Pausanias may lie beneath the chapel.

To the right of the road is the **National Athletic Centre**; to the left extends **Athens Airport**, named after (12km) **Ellenikó**. The terminal building, begun in 1961, was one of Eero Saarinen's last works.

17km **Glifádha** (Γλυφάδα; Hotels L, A, B, C, D; restaurants), a flourishing seaside resort (63,306 inhab.) with sandy beaches and an 18-hole golf course, owes its foundation in 1920 to the discovery of medicinal springs. Prospective visitors should be aware that the flight path to the airport lies over the town. Near the Antonopoulos Hotel are the ruins of an Early Christian basilica said to commemorate St Paul's supposed first landing in S Greece at this spot. At Vasiléos Yeoryíou 29 is the **Pieridhes Gallery of Modern Art** (open daily 11.00–20.00; tel. 8948287). Leofóros Grigoríou Lambráki (left) connects with the inland route from Athens.

The old inland road, a little shorter, has been upgraded and extended eastwards beyond Voúla. It leaves central Athens S of the Olympieion, crosses the Ilissos near the Kallirrhoë (8, 5) and turns S. Beyond (3km) Ayios Dhimítrios, a pleasant modern church, Mt Hymettos, previously hidden by suburbs, is well seen to the left. 5m **Trákhones** (the ancient deme *Euonymon*) has a theatre of the mid-4C BC with an unusual rectangular orchestra (cf. Thorikos) suggesting an earlier origin. To see this, you must turn right at lights into Odhós Arkhaíou Theátrou.

A turning to the West Terminal (Olympic Airways) follows immediately (further lights) and access roads to the new by-pass (see above) lead off to the left. You pass the airport itself and, farther on, an entrance to the Greek Air Force base, followed immediately by the access road to the East Terminal (foreign airlines).

A right fork serves Glifádha, joining the coast by Astir Beach. At the S end of Hymettos lay ancient *Aixone*, where the Thesmophoria, celebrated by women in the Temple of Demeter, provided Aristophanes with the theme for a play; Aixone has been identified with Glifádha.

Beyond the airport (c 3km) the little church of Ayios Nikolaos is a landmark (right) by traffic lights. A left turn at the following lights allows you to bear right and join Odhós Proódhou to begin an excursion to the remarkable stalactite Grotto of Pan, Apollo, and the Nymphs (the **Vari Cave**) overlooking Vári. You continue along Odhós Imittoú (extension of Proódhou) and climb into the hills. Beyond the cemetery of Ano Voúla (c 4.5kms from the main road) you pass through a disused metal gateway and 200m further, a dirt road diverges (right) on a corner. The track leads to a hill (c 10 minutes) where it divides (keep right) and you soon reach the cave, visible just below the road to the right, its mouth covered by a metal grill. The descent needs non-slip shoes and care. A rope would give added confidence. A wall of rock divides the grotto into two chambers. The larger chamber, in which is a spring of clear water, contains the curious Relief of Archidamos, by whom the grotto appears to have been decorated. The figure holds a hammer and chisel, with which it is working at some indefinite object cut in the rock. Likewise cut in the rock are a primitive altar of Apollo Hersos, a headless seated goddess, and a much defaced head of a lion. The cave was excavated by the American School in 1903 (A.J.A. 7 (1903)), when votive reliefs representing Hermes and the Nymphs, Pan playing the syrinx, etc., of the 4–3C BC were found as well as coins and deposits proving occupation from c 600 to 150 BC and in the 4C AD.

At the S foot of the hill, below and visible from the cave (15 minutes scramble), a Classical farmhouse was explored by the British School in 1966 (B.S.A. 68 (1973)). The lower courses of the walls survive and the plan can be easily made out. This is the so-called 'Vari House'.

Obtrusively visible from the cave, and dominating the plain beyond the farmhouse is the Military Academy at Vari (see Rte 17A).

The main road continues to join the coastal route at Voúla (see below).

On the promontory of **Alikí** (right) late-Mycenaean chamber-tombs have been explored. As you cross the boundary of (19km) **Voúla** (Hotels A, B, C, D; restaurants) the main orthopaedic hospital of the Athens area lies to the left. Voula is a garden city (17,998 inhab.) of summer villas; the beach and camping site are controlled by the NTOG. In Ano Voúla, to the E and to be identified with the ancient deme of *Halae Aixonidae*, a variety of ancient structures have been excavated, including farm and country houses, terrace and boundary walls and roads with kerbs. Leofóros Váris–Várkizas leads off left to connect with the end of the inland route from Athens. Here has been found an important ancient cemetery (at Pigadhákia) and a fort on the hill of Kastrí. The main road passes behind (22.5km) **Kavoúri** (Hotels A, B, C), crossing the peninsula of **Kamínia** to Vouliagméni. Two wine-trading galleys (of the 4C BC) were found in 1960 lying in five fathoms off the islet of **Katramonísi**.

The three-tongued promontory, which forms the seaward end of the Hymettos range, was famous in antiquity as **Cape Zoster** ('girdle'), strictly the name of the central tongue (now **Cape Lomvárdha**). Here Leto unloosed her girdle before the birth of Apollo and Artemis (see Paus. I, 31, 1). The 6C **Sanctuary of Apollo Zoster**, unearthed in 1925–26 at the neck of the central tongue, has been absorbed by the garden of the Astir Palace hotel; the attendant building of the same period, later enlarged, discovered in 1936, may be the priests' house or a pilgrims' hostel. Herodotus (VIII, 107) tells how, after the battle of Salamis, the Persians mistook the rocks of the headland for Greek ships. The uninhabited island of **Fléves** (the ancient *Phabra*) lies 1.5km off the cape.

25km **Vouliagméni** (Βουλιαγμένη; Hotels L, A, B, C; inc. luxury flats; restaurants), the most fashionable seaside resort in Attica (3450 inhab.), has a large yacht marina. It takes its name from a picturesque **lake** (bathing) of warm, green water enclosed by the sheer limestone rocks of the E cape of Kaminia. Its brackish, sulphurous waters help cases of rheumatism, neuritis, arthritis, and skin diseases. The overflow from the lake runs underground to the sea and bubbles up from the sea bottom, raising its temperature for some distance. The fine sandy beaches (open all year) enclosed by the three headlands have been efficiently equipped by the NTOG (good restaurants).

From Vouliagméni to **Soúnion**, see Rte 17A.

# 14

# Kaisariní and Hymettos

**Road**, 15.5km via Kaisariní, to the prohibited area, c 3km before the summit of Hymettos. **Bus** (No. 224 from the University) in 20 minutes to the suburb; the monastery is 30 minutes further on foot.

**Hymettos** (Υμηττός, in modern Greek **Imittós**), famous for its sunset glow, its honey, and its marble, is the range of hills, 16km long, that shuts in the Attic plain on the SE, almost reaching the sea at Cape Zoster. It is divided by the Pirnari Glen into Great Hymettos (Μεγάλος Υμηττός; 1027m) and Lesser or Waterless Hymettos (Ανυδρος Υμηττός), of which the highest point is Mávro Voúni (804m). The **Kakórrhevma Gorge** runs from below the summit towards the suburbs of Zoödhókhos Piyí and Pankráti which have encroached high on the W slopes; the steeper E side dominates Liópesi. The mountain is almost treeless and the aromatic plants and shrubs which produced the best food for bees are less widespread than in Classical times, though terebinth, juniper, thyme, sage, mint, lavender, etc., can still be found.

The Hymettian bee has migrated to Pentelikon and Tourkovouni. The violet colour which now, as in antiquity, suffuses the mountain at sunset is peculiar to Hymettos (cf. the 'purpureos colles' of Ovid, below). Hymettian marble (so-called Kara marble) was quarried in antiquity on the W side of the mountain, close to the Kakórrhevma Gorge and approximately on the site of the ruined **Convent of Karyaes**. Near the Convent of St John the Hunter (Rte 17B), at the N end of the ridge, are modern quarries.

From a little E of the Hilton Hotel (5, 8) a shrinking pine copse marks the bed of the Ilissos between the suburbs of Zográfou and Kaisariní. Leofóros Vasiléos Alexándrou to the S of the wood is the main approach road to the suburb of **Kaisariní**. Beyond, you cross the Athens by-pass and climb to (5.5km) **\*Moní Kaisarianís** (341m), an 11C monastery, closely confined at the end of the ravine amid the welcome shade of cypress, pine, and plane trees. Here since pagan times shrines have marked the source of the Ilissos.

On the brow of the hill just above the monastery is a famous fountain, known in ancient times as *Kyllou Pera*; its waters were supposed to cure sterility. There was a temple of Aphrodite nearby and the spot was made famous by Ovid in the well-known lines of the *Ars Amatoria* (III, 987) describing the sad legend of Cephalus and Procris. The spring supplied Athens with drinking water before the construction of the Marathon Dam. It feeds a fountain on the outside E wall of the monastery where the water gushes from a ram's head (cast; the Archaic original is now in the Acropolis Museum). Fragments built into the walls belong to an earlier Christian basilica, probably of the 5C.

The present structure is first mentioned in the 12C. The name is sometimes thought to be derived from Caesarea, perhaps the source of its original ikon. In 1458 when the Sultan Mehmed II visited newly conquered Athens, the Abbot of Kaisarianí was chosen to deliver up to him the keys of the city, in recognition of which the convent was exempted from taxation by the Turks. Until 1716 it was independent of the Metropolitan and had a school and a celebrated library (moved to Athens and destroyed in the War of 1821). It was noted also for its honey. Deserted in the 18C, it is now a national monument. During the Second World War the secluded ravine was used by the Germans for the execution of hostages. The monastery was restored in 1956–57; the church is still a focus of pilgrimage on Ascension Day.

The conventual buildings (entered from the far side), grouped round a pretty court, include a **mill** and **bakery**, and a **bath-house**, now restored after use as an oil-press. The **refectory** has a finely moulded Roman lintel over the door and a domed kitchen. The **church**, built of stone with brick courses, is in the form of a Greek cross. The dome is supported on Roman columns. The **parecclesion** (dedicated to St Anthony) was added in the 16C, the **narthex** in the 17C, and the **belfry** in the 19C. The frescoes, apart from those by Ioannis Ipatos (Peloponnesian, 1682) in the narthex, are in a 17–18C Cretan style. A tomb in the crypt was explored in 1950.

The area round the monastery has been discretely provided with picnic tables, and some paths laid out among the trees.

The road crosses a bridge over a gully, then swings left to a saddle below a rocky outcrop with a sudden view of the whole of Athens. It then climbs to (9km) the pretty **Moní Asteríou** (548m), another 11C monastery, restored in 1961. A path descends in c 1.5km to **Ayios Ioánnis Theológos**, a Byzantine church above the suburb of Goudhí (Rte 17B). You reach (10km) Mávra Vrákhia (646m) a col 3km N of the summit. The col is marred by a radar station, but with access to the summit prohibited, is the best vantage point on Hymettos, with a wide view over the Mesogeia and to the plain of Marathon. The road climbs S but the view is westward only, across Salamis to the Peloponnese. At 15km the asphalt ends, though it is possible to continue round the mountain on rougher surfaces to the cave above Paiania on the E (Rte 17B).

The summit (1027m) was crowned in Classical times with a statue of Zeus. Remains of an altar were found in 1939, and a cave has yielded ancient pottery.

# 15

# Kifissiá and Pentelikon (Pendéli)

## A. From Athens to Kifissiá and Ekáli

**Road**. 14km (9 miles). Buses 538/539 from Plateía Kánningos every few minutes to Kifissiá. From Kifissiá to Ekáli and Ayios Stéfanos, buses 508, 509, 512, 552. The nearer suburbs are served by many local routes.

**Railway**, 16km, by Piraeus Electric Railway (ΕΗΣ) from Omónia Square.

Leofóros Vasilíssis Sofías (Rte 10) from Sindagma Sq. and Leofóros Alexándras from Omónia Sq. meet at **Ambelókipoi**, 2km from Sindagma. You take the left fork and follow Leofóros Kifissías. To the left rises **Tourkovoúni** (338m), the ancient *Anchesmos*. On the E slope is (6km) **Psikhikó** (Ψυχικό), a garden suburb. Here at Benaki Hall is **Athens College**, a co-educational boarding school on an American pattern, founded in 1925; its Greek pupils, many from overseas, are taught bilingually in Greek and English. It has a modern theatre, where productions (including visiting artists) are often open to the public. Next to it is the **Arsakeion**, a progressive girls' school removed c 1930 from a site near the University. 6.5km. Turning (right) to Néa Pendéli, see below. 8km. **Filothéi** (Φιλοθέη), a model suburb built by the National Bank of Greece in 1930–35, with film studios, is favoured by foreign residents. Roads lead W to Néa Ionía and E to Ayía Paraskeví (Rte 17B). 9km There is a turning (right) for the **Olympic Stadium**. Completed in 1982, the stadium, which is set in 250 acres, seats 80,000 spectators. It has an indoor sports hall, training fields, tennis courts, an Olympic training centre and accommodation for 320 competitors. The 1996 Olympic games, for which it was designed, were not awarded to Greece. For visitors without cars, access is either by the electric railway from central Athens (Omónia, etc.) to the new station of Eirene (Iríni) or by any Kifissiá bus (and 500m walk). The main highway passes to the right of (12km) **Maroússi** or **Amaroúsi** (Hotel D), the ancient *Athmonia*, which derives its name from a temple of Artemis Amarousia. It is notable for its potteries and local clay (though some is now imported). Off the old road, **Anávryta College** (originally a boarding school), started on the model of Gordonstoun in 1947 by Jocelyn Winthrop Young, occupies the former Singros estate.

In the main square is a bust, by Tombros (1961), of Spiros Louis, the local shepherd who won the first modern marathon race at the Olympic Games of 1896.

The small church of Ayios Dhimítrios has 17C frescoes by the painter-priest Dhimítrios.

The Tsaroúkhis Foundation (signs; open daily, except Tuesday, 09.00–14.00; tel. 8062637) has a collection of works of the famous modern artist (1910–89).

You pass (left) the large KAT (Kéntron Atikhimáton or Accident Centre) hospital and soon enter (14.5km) **KIFISSIÁ** (Κηφισσιά; 268m Hotels L, A, B, C), an attractive and popular 'garden city' (39,166 inhab.) on the SW slopes of Pentelikon. The summer temperature averages 10° lower than in the city, and the shade of its pine trees gives welcome relief from the glare of Athens. Menander was a native of Kifissiá, and here Herodes Atticus had a villa, a visit to which inspired Aulus Gellius to write his rambling *Noctes Atticae*. Now, as in Roman times, the town is a favourite retreat of the Athenians in summer. It is the seat of the Metropolitan of Attica and Megaris.

The suburb has many **hotels**, mostly in the higher categories, and mainly in the Kefalári area. There are also excellent **zakharoplasteia** and numerous **restaurants**. Kifissiá and the northern suburbs generally are pleasant places to eat, especially in summer, when there are also direct buses to bathing resorts. In Kifissiá also is the **Goulandrís Natural History Museum**, at Odhós Levídhou 12.

In December 1944 Tatoî aerodrome (occupied by the RAF in October) was evacuated in face of the ELAS rising and British air headquarters set up in the Pentelikon and Cecil hotels in Kifissiá, already cut off from Athens. ELAS attacked on 18 December and forced the garrison to capitulate. On the 20th the survivors (c 600 officers and men) began a forced march, together with civilian hostages, largely on foot through Central Greece. RAF aircraft tracked their progress through Thebes, Levadhia, Lamia, and Larissa to Trikkala, dropping supplies wherever possible. At Lazarina (Rte 47C) in the

Pindos on 23 January an exchange of prisoners was arranged and the airmen repatriated from Volos.

The road enters Plateía Platánou. On the left gardens descend to the station; the road to Kefalári forks right. On this corner (right) a shelter covers four **Roman sarcophagi**, with reliefs, perhaps from the family vault of Herodes (busts of Herodes and of Polydeukion, his pupil and cousin, were found in 1961 in a garden near the church of Panayia tis Xidhou, a short way N of the Plateia. Subsequent discoveries, 1972–74, have revealed more sculpture and a probable bath building. All may be from the villa of Herodes Atticus; cf. above). **Kefalári**, a district of villas, gardens, and hotels, takes its name from a small and usually dried up stream, which, after rain, is a source of the Kifissos. The place is fast expanding into the foothills of Pentelikon, and it is possible to walk to Moní Pendéli and the ridge of the mountain.

From the N end of Kifissiá a road branches left towards Tatoî and Dhekélia (cf. Rte 20).

The main road continues NE to **Kastrí**, above which (right) an ancient fort crowns the NW spur of Pentelikon, and (20km) **Ekáli** (Hotel C), a pleasant summer resort amid pine woods, which has adopted the name of an ancient deme situated farther NE.

Immediately N of Ekáli a road (right) leads to (3km) **Dhiónisos**, ancient *Ikaria*, where Dionysos is alleged to have been entertained by Ikarios, and the grateful god of wine instructed his host in the cultivation of the grape. At 5km there is a turning (left; 550m) for the Sanctuary of Dionysos (left) discovered by the American School in 1888. At 10.5km **Ayios Pétros** (café) has a fine view over Marathon Bay. The road descends to Néa Mákri (Rte 21).

# B. From Athens to Moní Pendéli

**Road**, 16km (10 miles). Buses 422, 425, 426, 427 (Palaiá Pendéli) from Odhós Vasiléos Iraklíou (behind National Archaeological Museum).

From Athens to (6km) Psikhikó, see above. Soon after you take the right fork to (10km) **Khalándri** (Χαλάνδρι; Hotel C on the road to the N), a pleasant suburb occupying the site of *Phyla*, birthplace of Euripides (480–406 BC). The ancient orgies of the 'Great Goddess' (probably Mother-Earth) at Phyla antedated the mysteries at Eleusis. About 1km S the chapel of **Panayía Marmariótissa** covers the remains of a Roman tomb. At 14.5km is a turn (left) for **Néa Pendéli** (buses 423, 427), continuing to Maroussi (4km), via **Melíssia**, with film studios. A little further (right) is a rustic villa (now a taverna) built by the Duchesse de Plaisance.

16km **Moní Pendéli**, a monastery founded in 1578 and now one of the richest in Greece, is shaded by a cluster of lofty white poplars. The buildings are modern, but the chapel contains 17C paintings. The main church has important modern frescoes by Rállis Kopsídhis in the narthex. In the basement of the monastery are displays illustrating the history of education in Greece under Turkish rule, in which the church played a leading role. The road curves round the monastery grounds and ends at a large open space (bus terminus; tavernas); in the centre is the chapel of **Ayía Triádha**, near which traces of terraces mark the site of *Palaia Pendeli*, the ancient deme of Penteli. A little to the S of the convent (on a by-road towards

Stavrós) stands the **Palace of Rodhodhaînis**, built in a Gothic style for the Duchesse de Plaisance by Kleanthes. Here she died (1854) and is buried. It was restored in 1961 as a royal residence, and is now the setting for concerts on some evenings in the summer.

**PENTELIKON** (Το Πεντέλικον; modern Pendéli), the mountainous range enclosing the Attic plain on the NE, runs for 7km from NW to SE. Its ancient name was *Brilessos* (Βριλησσός), but by Classical times it had come to be called Pentelikon after the township of *Pentele* where the famous marble quarries lay. The principal summit (Kokkinarás; 1110m), to the NW, like that of Hymettos, has been disfigured by an ugly radar station and is inaccessible. Vayáti (1007m), the secondary summit, 500m SE, can still be climbed, as can the little platform between them, the site of the statue of Athena mentioned by Pausanias.

About 1.5km NE of the monastery are the **ancient quarries** which lie SE of the summit. Because of the complexity of the modern quarry road system the approach is obscure and you are advised to take a guide or consult the excellent *From Pendeli to the Parthenon* by M. Korres (Greek edition, Athens, 1993; English translation 1995). One approach is via the Nea Pendeli road (cf. above), turning right after c 500m into Od. Perikléous which gives access to the mountainside. This route can also be joined from the monastery or from Palaia Pendeli.

At least 25 quarries can be made out at a height of 700–1000m. Their exploitation, though begun c 570 BC, was unimportant before the 5C BC, and became general in Pericles' day. The crystalline rock of Pentelikon yielded the fine white marble which was used for many of the most important buildings, also for sculpture. It superseded Hymettian marble and poros for architectural purposes, though never quite ousted Parian marble, which is easier to chisel, for sculpture. The rich golden tint that age gives to Pentelic marble is due to the presence of iron oxide. The stone yielded by the modern quarries at Dhiónisos, on the N slope of Pentelikon, is less white.

Sections can be seen of the ancient **paved ways**, down which the cut blocks were transported on wooden sledges. The holes on either side held bollards round which steadying ropes were wound. The **Quarry of Spiliá** (700m), close by such a paved road, was worked out by the ancients. In the NW corner is a large **stalactite grotto** containing twin chapels. The S unit contains some relief decoration with crosses, angels, eagles and an inscription, suggesting use as a place of worship in the pre-Ikonoclastic period. To the N a domed chapel of the abbreviated cross type was subsequently added. The S chapel has frescoes from c 1225, including a representation of the Melismos in the apse and a portrait of Michael Choniates, bishop of Athens between 1182 and 1204. The N chapel also has fresco decoration. Remains of walls and inscriptions at the entrance mark a monastery of Byzantine date that survived the Frankish period. 400m higher (NNE), near other quarries, is a cave, site of a Sanctuary of the Nymphs, which produced fine reliefs. From Spilia, the climb to the ridge takes c 75 minutes.

The *view, one of the broadest in Attica, is remarkable for its vast expanse of water, visible in all directions except NW. To the N rises the pyramidal Dhirfis, while on the E lie Euboea, Andros, and Tinos. The Plain of Marathon is partly hidden by an intervening spur. To the SE the sea is studded with islands; across the valley to the S the ridge of Hymettos runs down to the sea; on the SW Athens spreads over the plain. Far to the S are the mountains of Milos, 150km away.

# 16

# From Athens to Eleusis (Eléfsis)

**Road**, 22km (14 miles), by the Ierá Odhós to Eléfsis (Elefsína), via (11km)
Dhafní. Buses: no. 864, every 15 minutes, from Plateía Koumoundhoúrou
(Eleftherías) (2, 6) for Dhafní (20 minutes) and beyond to Eléfsis (45 minutes);
bus 026 from Síntagma Sq., etc. to Plateía Koumoundhoúrou and Votanikós;
buses also from Piraeus.

The first 5 or 6km are heavily industrialised and extremely tedious on foot.

The faster but unrewarding Leofóros Athinón (taken by all long-distance buses),
which forms the initial section of the highway to Corinth, runs almost parallel, c 1km
to the N. It is reached from Omónia Sq. by Ayíou Konstandínou and Akhilléos streets
(2, 5) and, after crossing Leofóros Kifissoú by a new flyover near the Peloponnesian
bus station, joins the Sacred Way just beyond the conspicuous mental hospital (right)
at Dhafní. Beyond Asprópirgos you must diverge (right) onto the old road; the Corinth
highway now by-passes Eléfsis.

**By rail to Eléfsis** (SPAP), 27km in 35–45 minutes. The line runs N through haphazard
suburban settlements to (10km) **Ano Liósia**, where it curves SW. Beyond a large army
transport depot it traverses a narrow valley, passing through a gap in the **Dema** (τὸ
Δέμα; 'the Link'), or **Aigaleos-Parnes Wall**, a westward-facing rampart that follows an
undulating course for 4.5km along the watershed. The S two-thirds are built in various
styles of masonry (cf. B.S.A. 52, 1957) in 53 short sections separated by 50 sally-ports
and two gateways. Farther N the wall is crude and continuous. There are two signal
(?) towers. The wall is apparently military and may date from the Lycurgan period. A
**house**, of the late 5C BC, laid out round a court, was excavated in 1960 just N of the
railway. The sparsely inhabited valley between the Aigaleos ridge and the foothills of
Parnes is dotted with beehives. Emerging into the Thriasian Plain (see below) at (23km)
**Asprópirgos**, with a huge oil refinery, the line joins the road on the outskirts of (27km)
**Eléfsis**.

From Omónia Square (3, 3) Odhós Piraiós leads to (1km) the Kerameikos
(Rte 4). The Ierá Odhós preserves both the name and very largely the
original course of the **Sacred Way** (Ἱερά Ὁδός) followed by initiates from
Athens to Eleusis, though nowadays few indications remain of the tombs
and shrines described at length by Pausanias. Sections of the road itself
have been regularly uncovered in excavations: in 1984, roadworks over a
distance of 5km led to such discoveries and to the location of tombs which
lay beside. From the Kerameikos the narrow road passes the noisy industrial area of **Votanikós**. The **Botanic Gardens** (Βοτανικός Κήπος) (2km; left),
with its tall poplars, contain the Agricultural School of Athens University.
A little farther on, **Plato's olive-tree** (now merely a bus stop!) used to recall
the famous grove that once bordered the Kifissos from Kolonos to the sea.
3km **Ayios Sávas** (right), a medieval church near the conspicuous naval
signal station, stands on the site of a Temple of Demeter supposed to
commemorate the spot where she rewarded the hospitality of Phytalos by
giving him the first fig-tree. The walls incorporate Classical and Byzantine
marble blocks. Farther on, a by-road (right) passes the **Hydrographic Office**
of the Greek navy, and joins Leofóros Athinón. You cross Leofóros Kifissoú,
the extension to Piraeus of the National Highway, with the canalised
Kifissos, some way W of its ancient bed. The country opens out amid sparse
olives on approach to the comparatively low ridge of **Aigaleos** (Αιγάλεως),
the W horn of the natural amphitheatre that surrounds Athens. On the right

is the conical hill of **Profitis Ilias** (189m), surmounted by a chapel. From this point, when coming from the W, you get a first sudden view of Athens, especially striking at sunset. The new highway (see above) joins the ancient road at **Dhafní**.

The **Monastery of Daphní** (or **Dhafní**; camping site), surrounded by a high battlemented wall, stands to the S of the junction. Both church and walls incorporate ancient materials from a **Sanctuary of Apollo**, on the same site, mentioned by Pausanias but destroyed c AD 395. The convent owes its name to the laurels (δάφναι) sacred to Apollo, which once flourished in the neighbourhood.

**History.** The monastery, founded in the 5C or 6C, was dedicated to the Virgin Mary. It was rebuilt at the end of the 11C, but sacked by Crusaders in 1205. In 1211 Otho de la Roche gave it to the Cistercians, who held it until 1458. Two Dukes of Athens, Otho himself and Walter de Brienne, were buried here. The convent was reoccupied in the 16C by Orthodox monks until its abandonment in the War of Independence. Restorations were made in 1893 after the building had been used in turn as barracks and lunatic asylum. The structure was strengthened in 1920, and a more elaborate restoration was undertaken after the Second World War.

The fortified enceinte and a few foundations inside near the NE corner survive from its earliest Christian period. Of the 11C monastic buildings only some foundations of the great **refectory** can be seen on the N side. The pretty **cloister** (restored), S of the church, dates from the Cistercian period, with the addition of 16C cells. Round it are displayed sculptural fragments, Classical and Byzantine. The two sarcophagi, ornamented with fleurs-de-lys and Latin crosses, are sometimes supposed to be of the Frankish dukes.

The *church is a fine example of Byzantine architecture of c 1080, with an added exo-narthex, which was restored in 1961 to the later form given it by the Cistercians. The pointed arches and crenellations contrast not unpleasingly with the reused Classical pillars. The truncated W tower on the N side bore a Gothic belfry. The three-light windows of the church are separated by mullions and surrounded by three orders of brickwork. The lights are closed by perforated alabaster slabs. The drum of the dome has round engaged buttresses between each of its 16 windows. You enter from the cloister by the S door. The interior is noted for its *mosaics, which, though fragmentary in comparison with their original extent, have no rivals in S Greece; indeed, apart from those at Osios Loukas in Phokis, none nearer than Thessaloniki. Most complete are those on the S side of the narthex, portraying the Presentation of the Virgin and the Prayer of Joachim and Anna. On the vault of the dome is a celebrated representation, uncompromisingly stern, of Christos Pantokrator, on a gold ground. The frieze, round the drum below, depicts saints and prophets. Finely preserved on the pendentives are the Annunciation, Nativity, Baptism, and Transfiguration. On the W side of the N choros, the Entry into Jerusalem has interesting perspective effects (note the little boys' foreshortened feet). In the bema, or sanctuary, though the Virgin above the apse is fragmentary and the vault is empty, the flanking Archangels are well-preserved. Of the frescoes that once adorned the lower walls of the church, four are still comparatively clear. The **crypt** has recently been cleared.

**Wine Festival** (September–October, daily in the evening; sometimes rather rowdy) in grounds and pine woods. Entrance fee covers *ad lib.* tasting of 60 or more wines, folk dancing, etc.

Beyond Dhafní construction of the wide modern highway required blasting and major earthworks, so that the now intermittent traces of the Sacred Way

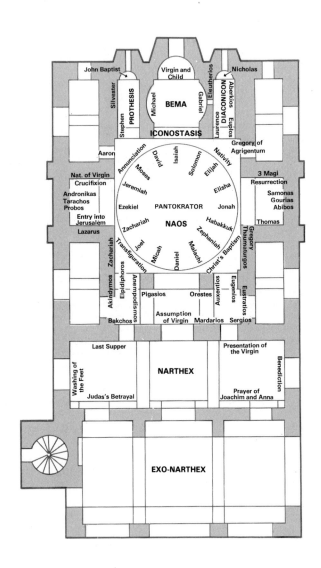

John Baptist

Virgin and Child

Nicholas

Silvester

PROTHESIS

Michael

**BEMA**

Gabriel

Eleutherios

Aberkios

Euplos

DIACONICON

Stephen

Laurence

**ICONOSTASIS**

Gregory of Agrigentum

Aaron

Annunciation

David

Isaiah

Solomon

Elijah

Nativity

Moses

Elisha

Nat. of Virgin

Crucifixion

Jeremiah

3 Magi

Resurrection

Andronikas
Tarachos
Probos

Ezekiel

**PANTOKRATOR**

Jonah

Samonas
Gourias
Abibos

Entry into
Jerusalem

**NAOS**

Zachariah

Habakkuk

Thomas

Lazarus

Joel

Zephaniah

Micah

Daniel

Malachi

Christ's Baptism

Zachariah

Transfiguration

Gregory
Thaumaturgos

Akindymos

Elpidiphoros

Anempodismos

Pigasios

Orestes

Auxentios

Eugenios

Eustratios

Bakchos

Assumption
of Virgin

Mardarios

Sergios

Last Supper

Presentation of
the Virgin

Washing
of
the Feet

**NARTHEX**

Benediction

Judas's Betrayal

Prayer of
Joachim and Anna

**EXO-NARTHEX**

# DAPHNI

0       3 metres

must be sought first to the left then to the right. A mile beyond the monastery (right) are the scanty foundations of a **Temple of Aphrodite**.

In the face of the wall of rock behind are several niches for votive statuettes with mutilated inscriptions below them. Remains are visible also of 'the wall of unwrought stones that is worth seeing' (Pausanias, I, 37, 7). This wall, which was outside the precinct of Aphrodite, at its SE corner, was built of rough blocks of stone and was over 9m thick; it may have been part of an ancient fort. The Sacred Way, uncovered here during the excavation of the temple in 1891–92, ran between the temple and the wall.

The road descends towards the Bay of Eleusis, landlocked by the island of Salamis and horribly industrialised. At 14.5km it reaches the shore and swings abruptly right (N).

To the left a road leads in 1.5km to **Skaramángas** (Hotels C), with the **Hellenic Shipyards**, founded in 1956 by Stavros Niarkhos, on the site of naval yards destroyed during the Second World War. The complex was taken over by the State in 1985. The first ship to be built here, a 25,000-ton tanker, was launched in 1960. The graving dock, opened in 1970, can accommodate vessels up to 250,000 d.w. tons, and is the largest in the Mediterranean. The **Naval Training Headquarters** is for conscripts of the Royal Hellenic Navy. A coastal road continues round the Skaramángas Hills (270m; a spur of Aigaleos) to **Pérama** (8km; see Rte 18), the starting-point of the ferry to Salamis.

The modern road along the **Paralía Aspropírgou** or Asprópirgos shore, which for a long time occupied the ancient causeway of the Sacred Way, has been widened by land reclamation. On the right are the **Límnes Koumoundhoúrou**, now salt marshes and ponds but anciently the *Rheitoi* streams, which formed the fish preserves of the Eleusinian priesthood, and marked the boundary between Athens and Eleusis. You are now skirting the Thriasian Plain, so called from the ancient deme of *Thria*.

The **Thriasian Plain**, stretching for c 14.5km along the Eleusinian Gulf, is usually identified with the Rarian or Rharian Plain, in Greek myth supposedly the first to be sown and the first to bear crops; here Demeter made the ground lie fallow while her daughter remained in the underworld. The plain is now one of the most highly industrialised areas in the country; its oil tanks, chimneys and cargo quays combine with the heavy motor traffic to make the last 6.5km of the Sacred Way the least romantic road in Greece. Salamis is usually obscured by dust and sulphur fumes.

18km The **Government Nautical College** (500m left) trains captains of the merchant navy. 18.5km. Turning (right) to Asprópirgos (1.5km; see above). At 21km you fork right (signposted 'No toll road') from (and pass under) the main highway. To the left of the old road, c 200m beyond a group of cypresses, by a well ('Kaló Pigádhi'), are four complete arches of a **Roman bridge**, which carried the Sacred Way across the Eleusinian Kifissos. The bridge, 5.5m wide and c 46m long, built of poros, probably dates from AD 124 when Hadrian was initiated into the Eleusinian mysteries. A hundred feet of the Sacred Way have been uncovered to the W. At the entrance to Elefsis is the desecrated chapel of **Ayios Zakharías**, where the famous relief of Demeter and Kore was found.

22km **ELEUSIS** (Ελευσίς, usually accusative, Elefsína; Hotel C), an expanding industrial town (22,793 inhab.) with cement, petro-chemical, and steel works, is occupied also with shipbuilding and the manufacture of soap and olive oil. The ancient city of *Eleusis*, birthplace of Aeschylus (525–456 BC) and home of the Sanctuary of Demeter and of the Eleusinian Mysteries, was situated on the E slopes of a low rocky hill (63m) which runs parallel with and close to the shore. The **Sacred Way**, of which large sections have been traced (paved and with kerbs), led direct to the sanctuary. It lies left of the modern road at the entrance to the town, but the modern approach to the site is signposted from the centre. The extensive excavations of the sanctuary, which had a continuous history from Mycenaean to Roman times, are of great interest but, apart from the telesterion and museum, the remains are not always easy to appreciate.

**History.** The legendary foundation of a city at Eleusis by Eleusis, a son of Ogygos of Thebes, before the 15C is substantiated, at least chronologically, by existing remains of houses (Middle Helladic II), dated to the 18–17C BC. Tradition tells of wars between the Athenians and Eleusinians in heroic times, resulting in the deaths of Erechtheus and of Immarados, son of Eumolpos. Eumolpos was reputed to be the first celebrant of the mysteries of Eleusis. The introduction of the cult of Demeter is ascribed by the Parian Chronicle to the reign of Erechtheus (c 1409 BC) and by Apollodoros to that of Pandion, son of Erichthonios (c 1462–1423). The first shrine (?) on the sanctuary site is dated by sherds to the Late Helladic II period, though there is nothing concrete to connect it with Demeter. The 'Homeric' Hymn to Demeter (late 7C BC) gives the orthodox version of the institution of the mysteries by Demeter herself (cf. below). The city seems to have been a rival of Athens until it came under firm Athenian sway about the time of Solon. Henceforward the cult grew and the sanctuary was constantly enlarged. Its reputation became panhellenic and initiation was opened to non-Athenian Greeks. Rebuilding was carried out by Peisistratos, who doubled the size of the area and enclosed it with a strong wall; but his work fell victim to the Persian invasion. Kimon initiated the reconstruction which was completed under Pericles. His telesterion was to survive with modifications to the end. Eleusis suffered heavily under the Thirty Tyrants, who here established a fortified base against Thrasyboulos, massacring those who opposed them. The sanctuary was extended again in the 4C BC. The town remained a stronghold throughout the Macedonian period. Under the pax Romana the sanctuary was adorned with a new gate. The Imperial transformation of Eleusis probably began under Hadrian. In AD 170 the sanctuary was sacked by the Sarmatians, but was immediately restored at the expense of Marcus Aurelius. At his initiation in 176 the Emperor was allowed to enter the anaktoron, the only lay person so honoured in the whole history of Eleusis. The Emperor Julian was initiated, completing his sanctification (according to Gibbon) in Gaul; Valerian (253–60) reorganised the defences of the site in the face of threats from Barbarian tribes (Goths and Herulians); Valentinian allowed the Mysteries to continue, but Theodosius' decrees and Alaric's sack were jointly responsible (c 395) for their end. The town was abandoned after the Byzantine period and not reoccupied till the 18C.

The Homeric **Hymn to Demeter** sets down the anciently accepted mystique of the cult's divine foundation. While gathering flowers, Persephone (Kore, or the Maiden), Demeter's daughter, was carried off by Hades (Pluto) to the nether regions. Demeter, during her quest for Persephone, came to Eleusis, where she was found resting, disguised as an old woman, by Metaneira, consort of King Keleos. After her first disastrous attempt to reward the king's hospitality by immortalising his son Demophon, Demeter revealed her identity and commanded Keleos to build a megaron in her honour. To this she retired, vowing that she would neither return to Olympos nor allow crops to grow on earth until Kore was delivered up. Finally Zeus commanded Hades to return Persephone, but because she had eaten pomegranate seeds while in the underworld she was bound to return there for part of every year. Before leaving Eleusis, Demeter broke the famine and gave to Triptolemos, second son of Keleos, seeds of wheat and a winged chariot, in which he rode over the earth, teaching mankind the use of the plough and the blessings of agriculture.

Candidates for initiation were first admitted to the **Lesser Eleusinia** which were held in the month of Anthesterion (February–March) at Agrai, in Athens, on the banks of the Ilissos. Being accepted as Mystai (initiates), they were allowed to attend the Greater Eleusinia, which took place in Boëdromion (September), and lasted nine days, beginning and ending in Athens. For them a truce was declared throughout Hellas. During the seventh night the qualified Mystai became Epoptai. These annual celebrations (*teletai*) consisted of a public secular display and a secret religious rite. The former, the responsibility of the Archon Basileus and his staff, took the form mainly of a **procession** (*pompe*) from Athens to Eleusis. The religious rite was entirely in the hands of the Hierophant and priesthood of Eleusis, hereditary offices of the Eumolpids and the Kerykes. The most important officials included the Dadouchos (torchbearer) and the Hierokeryx (herald). The procession took place on the fifth day. It was headed by a statue of Iacchos, a god associated with the cult, and the *hiera*, or sacred objects, were carried in baskets (*kistai*). During the Peloponnesian War, when no truce was declared, the procession was reduced; for some years after the Spartan occupation of Dekelia the pompe went by sea. In 336 BC the news of the destruction of Thebes by Alexander the Great caused the only recorded instance of the procession's cancellation after it had set out.

The fundamental substance of the **Mysteries**, the character of the sacred objects displayed, and the nature of the revelation experienced were never divulged. Alcibiades was condemned to death in absentia (though later reprieved) for parodying part of the Mysteries; Aeschylus was almost lynched on suspicion of revealing their substance on the stage. It is thought probable that a pageant (*dromena*) was performed representing the action of the Hymn of Demeter. Initiation carried with it no further obligation, but seems to have been spiritually uplifting. Cicero derived great comfort from the experience.

Eleusis attracted the attention of western travellers from Wheler (1676) onwards. E.D. Clarke carried off a statue to Cambridge in 1801. The propylaea were uncovered in 1812 by the Society of the Dilettanti. Systematic excavations, started by the Greek Archaeological Society in 1882, were greatly extended by Konstantinos Kourouniotes in 1917–45, especially after the Rockefeller Institution had provided a grant in 1930. Both the earlier work and that done since the war by G.E. Mylonas, A.K. Orlandos, and J. Travlos are admirably summarised in Mylonas, *Eleusis and the Eleusinian Mysteries* (1962).

A good idea of the layout and complexity of the excavations can be gained from the terrace in front of the prominent 19C chapel. Visitors with limited time can then investigate the forecourt, the two propylaea, the telesterion, the SE walls, and the museum. A full exploration of the remains takes the best part of a day and requires some scrambling. Care should be taken on the acropolis, where there are unfenced cisterns.

The **excavations** lie at the foot and on the E slopes of the acropolis and include the greater part of the **Sanctuary of Demeter and Kore** and its dependencies. This was protected on three sides by the main city wall and separated from the city on the fourth side by a dividing wall. As you pass the entrance gate the **Sacred Way** changes from a modern to an ancient paved road, which ends on the **Great Forecourt** before the city walls. This spacious square formed part of the new monumental entrance planned probably in the reign of Antoninus Pius. Here the *mystai* gathered in order to perform the necessary acts of purification before entering the sanctuary. From the square the Great Propylaea led directly to the sanctuary; to left and right triumphal arches led towards the main gate of the town and to the visitors' quarter of baths, hotels, and recreation centres.

Many of the marble blocks to be seen in the Great Forecourt came from the buildings that defined its limits. To the left are the remains of a **fountain**. Beyond it stood a **triumphal arch**, one of two (see above) faithfully copied from the Arch of Hadrian at Athens. The foundations remain; its gable has been reassembled in front; the inscription (replaced near by) reads 'All the Greeks to the Goddesses and the Emperor'. Close to the NE corner of the Great Propylaea is the sacred well that passed throughout Classical times for the **kallichoron**, or **Well of the Fair Dances**. The well-head, beautifully fashioned in polygonal masonry with clamps, probably dates from the time of Peisistratos. Mylonas has suggested that this is, in fact, the **Parthenion**, or **Well of the Maidens**, mentioned in the Hymn as the place where Demeter sat to rest. The name kallichoron may have been transferred to it from the well near the telesterion after the importance of the Parthenion had been centred on the 'Mirthless Stone' on which she sat (cf. below).

In the centre of the court are the scanty remains of the **Temple of Artemis Propylaia and of Poseidon**, amphiprostyle in form and constructed in marble. It must have been

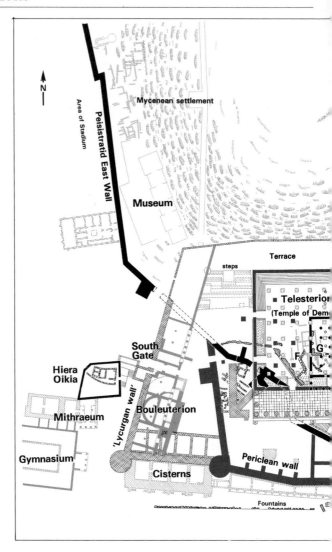

quite new when described by Pausanias. The **altar** to the E was presumably dedicated to Artemis, that to the N probably to Poseidon, while at the NW corner is an **eschara**, constructed in Roman tiles, on remains proving that the sacred nature of the spot goes back to the 6C BC. The rectangular area that interrupts the pavement beyond the eschara has been identified with the **Temenos of the Hero Dolichos**; beneath the houses outside the enclosure are extensive remains conjectured to be of a **pompeion**.

The **Great Propylaea**, built in Pentelic marble on a concrete core by Marcus Aurelius or his predecessor, is a close copy of the propylaea at Athens, both in plan and dimensions. It is approached by six marble steps and faces NE.

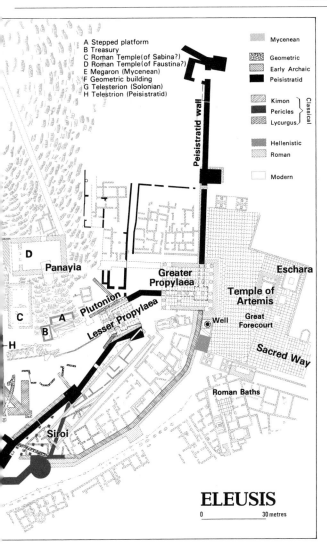

A Stepped platform
B Treasury
C Roman Temple(of Sabina?)
D Roman Temple(of Faustina?)
E Megaron (Mycenean)
F Geometric building
G Telesterion (Solonian)
H Telestrion (Peisistratid)

Mycenean

Geometric

Early Archaic

Peisistratid

Kimon
Pericles — Classical
Lycurgus

Hellenistic

Roman

Modern

Peisistratid wall

D

Panayia

Greater
Propylaea

Eschara

Temple of
Artemis

Plutonion

Great
Forecourt

Well

C  A

Lesser Propylaea

B

H

Sacred Way

Roman Baths

Siroi

**ELEUSIS**

0          30 metres

Reassembled on the pavement in front are two of the six Doric **columns** of the façade and the **pediment** with its central medallion bust of (?) Marcus Aurelius. Parts of the entablature are assembled to the right of the steps. The bases of the six Ionic columns that flanked the central passage are in situ. The transverse wall was pierced by five doorways: the threshold of the small one to the left shows the greatest wear. At some time of danger (? under Valerian) the Doric colonnade was closed by a thick wall; the single door that then gave entrance has left a roller groove in the pavement.

Crosses scored on the pavement probably derive from Christian fears of pagan spirits.

The gateway covers a corner tower of the Peisistratid enceinte. To the W this remained the city's fortification in later times; to the E a later wall enclosed a Classical extension to the city, while the Peisistratid circuit continued to serve as the peribolos of the sanctuary. Between the two walls are numerous small buildings dating mainly from the time of Kimon. The area between the two propylaea seems to have been a level forecourt in Roman times.

The **Lesser Propylaea** which face N and form the entrance to the innermost court, were vowed to the goddesses by Cicero's friend Appius Claudius Pulcher in his consulship (54 BC) and completed after his death by two nephews. The structure consisted of two parallel walls, each 15m long, with Ionic attached columns, which enclosed a passage 10m wide. This is divided into three at its inner end by two short inner walls (parastadia) parallel to the exterior walls. Forward of the doors, whose supporting rollers have left prominent grooves, were antae; the bases in front of them supported two Corinthian columns. The inner façade had caryatids instead of columns. Portions of the inscribed architrave and frieze are recomposed at the side. The frieze is composed of triglyphs and metopes, both carved with emblems of the cult.

You now enter the inner **Precinct of Demeter**, for two thousand years an area forbidden to the uninitiated on penalty of death. To the right is the **Plutonion**, a triangular precinct of the 4C BC, enclosing a cavern sacred to Pluto (Hades). A shrine was built at its mouth in the Peisistratid era; the surviving foundations are of a temple completed in 328 BC (a dated inscription has been found referring to the purchase of its wooden doors). Following the **processional road**, you come next to a rock-cut **stepped platform** (Pl. A) which adjoined a small building, perhaps a **treasury** (Pl. B). The platform may have served as a stand from which the start of a sacred pageant was watched; Mylonas suggests that the **'Mirthless Stone'** (Agelastos Petra) may be identified with the worked piece of rock that here projects above the pavement of the Roman sacred way. The levelled terrace beyond the treasury supported a **temple** (Pl. C) possibly dedicated to Sabina, wife of Hadrian, on whom the Greeks had conferred the title of New Demeter. Between this and the treasury is a **thesauros** (offertory box) hewn from a boulder. You ascend to the large square platform on which stood the Hall of the Mysteries.

The first shrine decreed by Demeter 'beneath the citadel and its sheer wall upon a rising hillock above the Kallichoron' occupied a limited site on ground which sloped steeply away. As each enlargement of the sanctuary was undertaken, it became necessary to extend the artificial terrace on which it stood. Consequently each shrine in turn escaped complete destruction by being buried under the next. The result is an archaeological palimpsest of rare completeness but baffling complexity.

The great **telesterion**, the Hall of Initiation and the Mysteries, is an almost square chamber 53m by 52m, partly cut out of the rock of the acropolis and partly built on a terrace. The existing remains appear to be those of the Periclean rebuilding (with the addition of the Portico of Philo), as finally remodelled by Marcus Aurelius. On each of the four sides were eight tiers of seats, partly cut in the rock and partly built up; these were interrupted at six points only, for two doors on each of the disengaged sides. The hall accommodated 3000. Six rows of seven columns each supported the (? wooden) roof; they were in two tiers separated by an epistyle (possibly with a frieze). The bases of most remain; one of them has as its top course a reused block of the 1C AD, showing the extent of the Roman restoration. In the centre, on a site it had occupied from the first, was the **anaktoron**, or holy of holies, a small rectangular room roofed somehow by Xenokles with an opaion, or lantern, of which no trace has survived. By the side of the anaktoron stood the throne of the hierophant. Externally the solid walls, broken only by doorways, must have enhanced the air of mystery. Later the SE face was fronted by the **portico of Philo**, whose pavement and massive supporting wall (18 courses of masonry) form one of the most prominent features of the site. This was completed, according to Vitruvius, in the reign of Demetrios of Phaleron. The huge prostoön had a colonnade of twelve Doric columns by two, which were left unfluted. An ancient **well** cut into the rock below may be the original kallichoron (cf. above).

Excavations have revealed traces of at least six earlier structures on the same site. The **Mycenaean megaron** (remains of two walls in the NE half of the hall) was a chamber c 17m square. This was replaced by a Geometric structure, a Solonian telesterion, and again by the **Telesterion of Peisistratos**, which occupied the NE corner of the final structure. This hall had five rows of five columns each, with a portico on the NE front, and was destroyed by the Persians. Kimon incorporated the ruins into a rectangular hall, designed round the old anaktoron, and with seven rows of three columns each. It was apparently not finished. Pericles probably instigated a grander design by which the building again became square, doubling that of Kimon. This was first entrusted to Iktinos, whose plan to support the roof on only 20 columns (foundations visible) had to be abandoned for technical reasons. The design was replaced by another by Koroibos, which was completed after his death by Metagenes and Xenokles. Lycurgus may have ordered the Portico of Philo. The L-shaped foundations that extend beyond the E and S corners show that earlier plans for building a peristyle were started. After the Sarmatian sack, the Romans restored the interior with somewhat makeshift columns and extended the NW side another six feet into the rock.

From the Portico of Philo the **court** of the sanctuary, a level artificial terrace, extended to the E and S. This had been built up and enlarged with each successive reconstruction, generally using the fortification wall of the previous sanctuary as a retaining wall for the new. The greater part of the late-Classical fill has been removed to show the successive stages, making apparent the steepness of the natural contour. Sections of the **Wall of Peisistratos** are roofed with corrugated iron to preserve their upper part constructed in unbaked bricks. A stretch immediately below the centre of the Portico of Philo shows where Kimon filled the Persian breach in the mud-brick wall with limestone masonry in alternately large and small courses (pseudo-isodomic), based directly on the Peisistratean socle. The inner face is rough and evidently retained a fill of earth. Within this wall parts of an Archaic polygonal terrace wall may be seen. Beyond the Peisistratean corner-tower are the remains of a Kimonian **gate**. This was later blocked by the Periclean **siroi**, where the first-fruit offerings were stored; five of its piers are very prominent.

The S side of the court was bounded in the 5C by the **Periclean wall**, the function of which was minimised in the following century when the sanctuary was extended to the new **south wall** of Lycurgus. Against the inside face of this are some remains identified with successive rebuildings in Hellenistic and late-Roman times of a **bouleuterion**, or chamber of the city council. Outside the Lycurgan **south gate** is a trapezoidal precinct surrounded by a wall (see below). Within this wall are the foundations of a **hiera oikia**, a Geometric house sacred to the memory of a hero; the building was destroyed early in the 7C, but remained a scene of religious rites into the Archaic period. Beyond are some traces of a **Mithraeum**. From outside the extreme S corner of the precinct you get an instructive panorama of contrasting types of ancient wall building.

Looking towards the museum you see the perfectly fitted polygonal masonry (6C) of the peribolos of the Sacred House. To the right is the **'Lycurgan' wall** (? 370–360 BC), one of the best preserved examples of ancient fortification, with both a square and a round **tower**. On four slightly receding courses in pecked Eleusinian stone are set tooled courses in yellow poros; this is probably a conscious matching of the Periclean style. Beyond the corner the wall is masked by ruined Hadrianic cisterns. Farther on, the **Periclean east wall**, like the Lycurgan, has a separate socle, here rusticated, while the upper part shows traces of bevelling.

On either side of the telesterion a flight of steps was cut in Roman times to give access to a wide **terrace**, 6m above the hall floor. You climb the S steps to the **museum**, which houses the important but relatively few works of art found at the site. Outside the entrance are a Roman sarcophagus (c AD 190) in marble with a well-carved representation of the Kalydonian boar-hunt (the lid does not belong); two representations in white marble of torches, c 2.5m high; a capital from the Lesser Propylaea; and a fine head of a horse. ROOM I (to the right). Copy of the 'Niinnion Tablet', a red-figured votive pinax now in the Athens Museum; the figures are believed to be performing rites from the Mysteries, the only known representation. Reconstruction of one corner of the geison of the Peisistratid telesterion; Archaic kouros (c 540 BC); running girl from a pediment of c 485 BC. In the centre, huge Proto-Attic *amphora (7C BC), depicting Odysseus blinding Polyphemos and Perseus slaying Medusa. Dedication reliefs: marble stele, Demeter seated with (probably) Hekate (c 475 BC); stele (411 BC) depicting a fight between Athenian cavalry and Spartan hoplites. Decree of 421 BC concerning the construction of a bridge over the Rheitoi (see above), with relief.

ROOM II (entrance-hall) contains a cast of the most famous Eleusinian relief, now in the Athens Museum. Facing the door is a *statue of Demeter (headless and armless), perhaps by Agorakritos of Paros, pupil of Pheidias (420 BC); behind is the fragmentary relief of Lakratides (1C BC), showing Triptolemos setting out in his chariot; the statue of Persephone is Roman. Relief: Demeter on the 'Mirthless Stone' approached by votaries. ROOM III. Heads and statues, including Asklepios, dedicated by Epikrates (320 BC), found in a field. ROOM IV has a model of the site at two stages of its development (Peisistratid and Roman). Roman statuary: *Antinoos, represented as a youthful Dionysos standing by the Delphic omphalos; Tiberius as pontifex maximus; small and delicate Herakles.

ROOM V. Caryatid in the form of a kistephore (basket-carrier) from the inner parastade of the Lesser Propylaea (its fellow is in the Fitzwilliam Museum, Cambridge); green stole, in a good state of preservation, from a burial of the 5C BC (the only linen cloth surviving from the Classical era); Amphora of c 610 BC from Megara by the Chimaera painter; inhumation burials, including that of a boy in a larnax (terracotta coffin); decree reliefs. ROOM VI. Vases of all periods from 1900 BC to AD 450, including a plain Mycenaean vase with a Linear B inscription (? an unidentified Cretan place-name) which recurs on the Knossos tablets; kernoi, the characteristic sacred vessels of the cult.

Other remains, on the acropolis and outside the walled circuit are mostly of more specialised interest.

Beyond the museum are some prehistoric (Middle and Late Helladic) and Roman buildings. Late Helladic material has been found on the **acropolis**, from which there is a pleasant view towards Salamis. There is an important prehistoric cemetery. On the plateau beyond are Hellenistic remains. The Frankish tower that formerly crowned the W height fell victim to the quarrying activities of the cement factory. At the E point of the acropolis a **chapel** (Panayia) with a detached belfry occupies part of a platform on which, in Roman times, stood a **temple** (Pl. D), probably dedicated to Faustina, wife of Antoninus Pius.

From the chapel you can descend to the Lesser Propylaea, NW of which are some ruins of a Roman house perhaps having belonged to the Kerykes, one of the hereditary priestly families. Farther off is the **Asty Gate** of the Peisistratid enceinte; its plan, uncovered by Travlos in 1960, is well preserved; still further W lay the **Megarian Gate**. The wall is not preserved but part of the ancient road from **Eleusis** to **Megara** has been found there. The **Roman quarter** to the E of the Great Forecourt is interesting for its bathing establishments with piped water and a great drain with brick vaults and manholes at regular intervals. Further SW, against the outer face of the Periklean wall and its Lycurgan extension, are rows of Roman fountains and cisterns. Part of the Mycenaean settlement has been located recently in Od. Nikolaîdhou, opposite. In the town, near the church of Ayios Yeoryios, another **Roman bath**, partially excavated in 1959, proved to be one of the largest discovered in Greece (time of Hadrian).

Many discoveries of all periods are continually made in excavations in building plots in the town. In 1977 parts of Roman (?) harbour installations were identified and what may be a terrace wall of the 'dolicho' (3C–2C BC racecourse).

# 17

# From Athens to Soúnion

The excursion to Soúnion, seldom omitted by visitors to Athens, is generally made by the coast road. The old inland road however has much to recommend it and allows many interesting diversions.

## A. By the Coast Road

**Road**, 70km (43½ miles). Buses from Odhós Mavrommatéon (stop also in Od. Filellínon) c hourly take passengers for destinations beyond Várkiza. Half-day excursions by coach (CHAT, etc.). Buses (No. 145 etc.) for Várkiza depart from Leofóros Olgas.

To (25km) **Vouliagméni**, see Rte 13. The road continues 'en corniche' winding along the rocky *coast. The pine-clad slopes, once renowned for game, are fast being replanted with hotels and bungalows. 31km **Várkiza** (Hotels A, B, C), with camping sites, a sandy beach (NTOG), a marina, and water-sports. The place gave its name to the Agreement of 1945, whereby the organisations ELAS and EAM were demobilised and disarmed, bringing the first Communist rising to an end.

A little farther on a road leads inland to **Vári** (1.5km), a village amid pines (for the Vari Cave and House cf. Rte 13). Leaving Vári in the direction of Koropí (Rte 17B), the road crosses a flat plain, dominated (left) by the Military Academy, or **Officer Cadets' School**, the Sandhurst of Greece. In addition to military leaders, it trained naval cadets until 1846 and civil engineers in 1870–87. Founded at Navplion in 1828 by Capodistrias, the academy was transferred first to Aegina, then in 1837 to Piraeus. In 1894 it moved to the **Evelpídhon** building (now lawcourts) in central Athens (Pedhion Areos). It has been in its present location since 1981. Cadets wear a dark blue uniform, with yellow collar and bands and white gloves.

About 700m beyond the further limits of the Academy, opposite the first of two boat yards, a road climbs straight towards the summit of **Kiáfa Thíti** above the village of Thítsi. On the top are the recently excavated remains of a fortified prehistoric stronghold where finds include Middle Helladic and Mycenaean. A Byzantine church overlies earlier buildings.

35km. The **Bay of Lomvárdha** may represent the harbour of the Attic deme of *Lamptrai*, sited due N on the slope of Hymettos. Churches mark the seaward ends of roads from Koropí (Rte 17B). 42km **Lagonísi** (Hotels L, A, B) is a bungalow resort. Mt Panion, to the NE, is lost behind the Attic **Olimbos** (Olympus; 486m), a pyramidal hill which is skirted by the road. Beyond (46km) **Saronís** (usually Saronídha; Hotel B) are the large Eden Beach and Alexander Beach hotels. The little island of **Arsídha** lies close to the coast off the **Bay of Anávissos** (Hotels A, B, C). The new Athens racecourse is to be constructed here. A by-road leads left to the hamlet (1.5km), where the celebrated kouros was found and an important Geometric and Archaic cemetery has been excavated, then passes between Olimbos and Panion to Kalívia (16km; Rte 17B). Off (60km) **Cape Katafíyi**, which has a fine panorama of the Saronic Gulf, lies the uninhabited **Gaidhouronísi**, known to Strabo as *Patroklou Charax*, the palisade of Patroclus. There are some remains of the 3C fortifications built here by Patroclus, admiral of Ptolemy II, who commanded the Egyptian fleet sent to help the Athenians against Antigonus Gonatas in the Chremonidean War. 64.5km **Legrená** (Hotels B).

70km **Cape Soúnion**, known also as **Cape Kolónes** (Κάβο Κολώνες), is a precipitous rocky headland rising 60m from the sea. The low isthmus which joins it to the mainland separates the sandy and exposed bay of Soúnion (Hotels A, B, C), a developing resort, from the rocky but sheltered haven to the E. On the highest and furthest point of the headland are the columns of the ruined Temple of Poseidon (see below), which give the headland its alternative name. The visitor wishing to share Byron's experience of 'Sunium's marbled steep, Where nothing save the waves and I may hear our mutual murmurs sweep' should visit the site out of season and in the morning. On Sundays and towards sunset it is overrun by coach parties.

The township of *Sounion* (Σούνιον; Lat. *Sunium*), whose wealth was proverbial in Classical times, stood at the head of the bay of the same name, where regattas were held in honour of Poseidon. After the battle of Salamis the Athenians here dedicated a captured Phoenician ship (one of three; Hdt. VIII, 121). Some years before, the Aeginetans had seized the sacred Athenian *Theoris*, the ship that conveyed the sacred envoys (Θεωροί to Delos, while it lay at Sounion (Hdt. VI, 87). The town was a port of call of the corn ships from Euboea to Piraeus. The Athenians fortified it during the Peloponnesian War and, in 413 BC (Thuc. VIII, 14), the entire headland was enclosed, the promontory forming the citadel. The inhabitants were noted for harbouring runaway slaves whom they often enfranchised without question. On one occasion a strong gang of slaves seized the fortress and devastated the neighbourhood. Terence mentions Sunium as a haunt of pirates. It was a favourite resort of the corsairs, one of whom, Jaffer Bey, is supposed to have destroyed some of the columns of the temple. One of three of the crew who escaped the foundering of a Levantine trader here was the second mate and poet, William Falconer, who immortalised the incident in *The Shipwreck* (1762).

The remains on the W half of the promontory now form an archaeological precinct. The Temple of Poseidon was measured by Revett in 1765 and by the Dilettanti Society in 1812. Byron carved his name on a pillar. The site was excavated by Dörpfeld in 1884 and by the Greek Archaeological Society in 1899–1915. In 1906 two colossal kouroi were found in the debris to the E of the temple. Since 1958 some columns have been re-erected.

The whole acropolis was enclosed by a double **Fortification Wall**, c 500m long and strengthened at intervals by square towers. It formed a semicircle from the Bay of Soúnion on the NW, where part is well preserved, to the S cliff edge. Its SE angle enclosed the **Temenos of Poseidon**, a precinct supported on the N and W by a terrace wall. This was entered on the N side by Doric **propylaea**, built of poros and marble in the 5C, the axis of which is aligned with the E front of the temple.

A square room to the W separated the gate from a **stoa**, which extended along the peribolos wall. Its foundations have collapsed in the far corner, but five bases remain of six interior columns that divided it lengthwise. A second stoa, running N–S, abuts on the first at the W.

The *Temple of Poseidon**, near the edge of the cliff, forms a conspicuous landmark from the sea. From a distance it presents a dazzlingly white appearance that proves illusory at closer hand: the columns are of grey-veined marble quarried at **Agriléza** (5km N by an ancient road), where bases of columns of the same dimensions can still be seen. The attribution to Poseidon was confirmed by an inscription. On stylistic grounds Prof. Dinsmoor ascribed the design of the temple to the architect of the Hephaisteion at Athens, with a date of c 444 BC. It stands on the foundations of an earlier structure in poros stone, founded shortly before 490 BC and unfinished at the time of the Persian invasion. The Doric peristyle had 34 columns (6 by 13), resting on a stylobate of 31.1m by 13.4m. Nine columns remain on the S side and six (four re-erected in 1958–59) on the N side, with their architraves. The columns are unusual in having only 16 instead of the normal 20 flutes. The sculptural arrangement also departed from the normal custom, an Ionic frieze (see below) lining all four sides of the interior space in front of the pronaos (cf. the Hephaisteion). The external metopes were left blank (perhaps because of the exposed nature of the site); the pediments, which were sculptured, had a raking cornice with a pitch of 12½° instead of the more usual 15°.

The INTERIOR had the usual arrangement of pronaos, cella, and opisthodomos. Both pronaos and opisthodomos were distyle in antis. There survive only the N anta of the pronaos, with its adjacent column, and the S anta, which was reconstructed in 1908.

Thirteen slabs of the frieze, in Parian marble, stand to the E of the approach path. The sculpture, much eroded, is believed to illustrate a contest of Lapiths and Centaurs, the Gigantomachia, and exploits of Theseus (cf. the *Hephaisteion*).

The *view from the temple over the sea is striking. To the E lies Makronisos; about 11km S the rocky island of Ay. Yeoryios, the ancient *Belbina*. The nearest islands to the SE are **Kea, Kithnos**, and **Seriphos**, to the S of which, on a clear day, even **Melos** can be made out. To the W is **Aiyina**, in the centre of the Saronic Gulf, with the E coast of the Peloponnese behind.

Beyond the tourist pavilion on a low hill commanding the isthmus on the N, are the remains of a small **Sanctuary of Athena Sounias**. The temple was noted by Vitruvius for the irregularity of its plan, with an Ionic colonnade along the E and S sides of the structure of c 450 BC. The cella was 5.9m by 3.8m, with four columns in the middle arranged in a square. The cult statue stood at the back. A little to the N are the remains of a small Doric temple, distyle prostyle, probably dedicated to the hero Phrontis.

# B. Via the Mesógeia

**Road**, 64.5km (40 miles). 12km Stavrós.—18km Paianía.—24km Koropí.—30km Markópoulo.—40km Keratéa.—55km Lávrion.—64.5km Soúnion. **Buses** from Odhós Mavromatéon every hour (more frequently on Sundays and holidays) to Lávrion (in 1½ hours; taking passengers for Keratéa and beyond only); usually continuing after an interval to Soúnion; also to Markópoulo (half-hourly; three times daily from Markopoulo to Brauron) and Pórto Ráfti (hourly). To Paianía (Liópesi; nos 125, 310) and to Koropí (nos 307, 308), every 20 minutes from Thissíon.

From the centre of Athens to (2.5km) **Ambelókipoi**, see Rte 11. You take the right fork (Odhós Mesogeíon). The N foothills of Hymettos appear intermittently above the suburban development. In trees (right) stands the **Police College**. The S bypass (Rte 13) joins Mesogeíon by an underpass. At (4km) **Goudhí** the University of Athens has its Ilíssia precinct. Above stands Ay. Ioannis Theologos (Rte 14). At (6.5km) **Kholargós**, which bears the name of the native deme of Pericles (c 490–429 BC), you pass (left) the huge administrative HQ of the Greek army, known locally as the Pentagon (Pentágono). Mt Pentelikon rises behind. 6m **Ayía Paraskeví**. The Nuclear Research Centre (which includes amongst its activities the analysis of archaeological artefacts), designed by a British company and opened in 1961 by King Paul, bears the name of Democritus, the first scientist to propound an atomic theory. The headquarters of the Greek broadcasting services (EPA and ET) are also here. A by-road leads (right; 2km) to **Moní Ayios Ioánnis Kinigós**, the monastery of St John the Hunter (view); its 12C church has a strangely supported dome and a 17C narthex (festival, 26 July). At (12km) **Stavrós**, by a radio-telephone station, you round the N spur of Hymettos, leave the Marathon road which is carried forward on a flyover, and turn S into the Mesogeía.

The **Mesógeia** (τὰ, anciently ἡ, Μεσόγεια, 'the inland'), which lies between Hymettos and the Petalion Gulf, is watered by two seasonal rivers: the Valanaris entering the sea S of Rafína and the Erasinos near Vráona. Its red clay is the most fertile soil in Attica, producing good wine, much of which is flavoured with pine resin to produce the retsina favoured by Athenians. *Brauron* was important in antiquity; the modern capital is Koropí. Many of the attractive little churches have frescoes by Yeoryios Markos and his school.

15km **Gliká Nerá** was the site of a Mycenaean chamber tomb cemetery. 18km **Paianía** (also Liópesi; *Kanakis Taverna in a lemon-grove at the N end), a straggling village (9710 inhab.) in pleasantly wooded country, has readopted the name of the birthplace of Demosthenes (c 384–322 BC), identified with some remains to the E. Here is the **Vorrés Museum** (open weekend mornings only), a seven-acre complex which combines modern with traditional architecture and gardens. The buildings contain traditional artefacts, prints and pictures relating to modern Greek history and (in a specially designed gallery) a collection of modern painting and sculpture. To the S of the village is the church of **Ayios Nikólaos Chalídhou** which has unusual decoration in the dome (12C). A by-road (signposted) leads to the **Koutoúki Cave** (open daily; guided tours; tasteless gift shop). You bear right off the new road which leads direct to Markopoulo for (24km) **Koropí**, the liveliest village (12,790 inhab.) in the Mesogeia, which is surrounded by vineyards; retsina vats are prominent. By-roads lead (right) to the coast. SE of the village is the church of **Metamórphosis Sotíras**, with late 10C/early 11C frescoes. Interesting is the dome decoration which includes

the Pantocrator, the symbols of the Evangelists, Seraphim and Cherubim.
30km **Markópoulo**, a busy and prosperous centre (6716 inhab.) is noted for
its bread. By the conspicuous **church**, whose interior is enlivened with
encaustic illustrations of the lives of various saints, diverges the road to
Brauron and Pórto Ráfti.

FROM MARKÓPOULO TO PÓRTO RÁFTI, 8km (through bus from
Athens). 2.5km By-road to Vráona (see below). About 5km S rises **Mt
Mirenda** (613m). Between road and mountain, near a medieval watch-
tower, lay the ancient deme of *Myrrhinous*, where Artemis Kolaïnis, the
bird goddess, was worshipped. Inscriptions to Artemis were found on the
site in 1960–61, after the Greek Archaeological Service had explored 26
tombs, mostly of the 8C BC, uncovered a section of prehistoric road, and
confirmed the existence of a Shrine of Pythian Apollo. From this area in
1972 came also the superb kouros and kore (Phrasikleia) now in Athens
Museum. 6km Track (right) to **Prasiai**, see below.

6.5km **Pórto Ráfti** has one of the best natural harbours in Greece, though
it is little used. The beautiful bay is unequally divided by the narrow rocky
spit of **Ayios Nikólaos** (tavernas), off which lies the islet of **Prasonísi**. It is
protected on the seaward side by the islets of **Ráfti** and **Raftopoúla**. On Ráfti
is a colossal seated marble statue of the Roman period, popularly known as
the 'tailor' (ράφτης), whence the modern name of the harbour. The statue,
which is female, may represent Oikoumene and has served as a beacon-
light. Helladic and Byzantine sherds have been noted on the steep slopes
of both islets. From the beach, the last in Attica to remain in Allied hands,
6000 New Zealand troops were evacuated in April 1941. Various traces of
ancient buildings have been found, including (at **Natso**) what seem to be
remains of the Shrine of Delian Apollo mentioned by Pausanias. Scholars
locate ancient *Prasiai* on the S slopes of the bay, where 22 Mycenaean tombs
were found in 1894–95.

From *Prasiai* the annual Theoria, or sacred embassy, set out to Delos in the ship believed
to be that in which Theseus returned triumphant from Knossos. Here Erysichthon, an
envoy of Delos, who died on his return journey, was buried, and here came the
mysterious first-fruits of the Hyperboreans on their way from central Europe to Delos.

The bay is closed on the S by the peninsular headland of **Koróni**, anciently
*Koroneia*. Its acropolis and an unbroken long wall with nine towers within
the isthmus formed a **fortress**. Excavated in 1960 by the American School,
this is proved by coins of Ptolemy II Philadelphus to be an Egyptian
encampment of the Chremonidean War (? 265–261 BC). In this war the
Athenians threw in their lot with Egypt and Sparta in an unsuccessful bid
to free themselves from Macedonian domination. On the N side of the bay
at Dhrívlia (in a grove c 200m inland from a prominent sea-side kiosk) are
the remains of a three-aisled Early Christian basilica of the 5C. This area is
dominated by the precipitous **Peratí** (307m), with unexplored caves. The
road continues beneath the hill past two tavernas to **Ayios Spiridón** (the
bus terminus, 2km from Ayios Nikolaos; Hotel C), 10 minutes beyond
which, above the banks of a stream, is the huge **necropolis** of chamber
tombs (Late Helladic III C), excavated and published by Prof. Sp. Iakovidhis. You can continue round the shoreward side of Perati (taverna) to
Brauron (c 8km; see below).

From Ay. Spiridon a boat can be hired to visit Ráfti (see above; rocky disembarkation
and stiff climb).

The by-road to **Vraóna** (*Brauron*), 6km from Markópoulo, diverges from the Pórto Ráfti road (see above). A square **tower** (left; c 1km from the road), beyond the fork, is Frankish. Farther on (left) are the interesting remains of an Early Christian **basilica**. You pass a by-road (left) which ascends to the prominent Hotel Mare Nostrum and continues to Loútsa and Rafína.

The name Vraóna (Βραώνα) is a medieval corruption of Βραύρων, but the ancient name is being readopted as Vravróna.

**Brauron**, one of the twelve ancient communities antedating the Attic confederation, is situated in the broad and marshy valley of the subterranean Erasínos c 1.5km from the sea. The district apparently comprised the townships of *Halai Araphenides* (now Loútsa, a little to the N) and *Philiadai*. Peisistratos had estates in the neighbourhood. The attractive **Sanctuary of Artemis Brauronia** (08.30–15.00 Tue, Wed, Sat, Sun) lies just beyond the Loutsa fork at the foot of a low hill, immediately below the little late-Byzantine chapel of Ayios Yeoryios.

The site can be reached by bus (for Hamólia) three times daily from Markópoulo which has a regular service from Athens. Alternatively the 304 service (also 305, 316) from Thissíon to Artemis or Néa Loútsa terminates at the Hotel Mare Nostrum (above), c 30 minutes walk away (less if the intervening valley is dry).

Beyond the chapel a small **shrine** marked the entrance to a cavern, the roof of which fell in the 5C BC. This seems to have been venerated in Archaic times as the **Tomb of Iphigeneia**. Other tombs probably belong to priestesses of Artemis.

Tradition relates that Iphigeneia brought to Brauron the image of Artemis which she and Orestes stole from Tauris (Euripides, *Iphigeneia in Tauris*, 1446–67). In one version she is virtually identified with the goddess and performs the ritual sacrifice of her brother; in another she herself dies at Brauron. A wooden image was taken by the Persians from Brauron to Susa. In Classical times the savage rites had been moderated, and Artemis was worshipped in her function as protectress of childbirth. The Brauronia was a ceremony held every four years, in which Attic girls between the ages of five and ten, clad in saffron robes, performed rites which included a dance where they were dressed as bears (cf. Aristophanes, *Lysistrata*, 645). The connection between bears, childbirth, and Artemis recalls the legend of Callisto, but the purpose of the ritual remains mysterious. In the late 4C BC the site suffered from flooding and by the time of Claudius it was deserted, for Pomponius Mela (*De situ Orbis*, II, 3) claims that Thorikos and Brauron, formerly cities, are now but names. Excavations, carried out with difficulty in the waterlogged valley by the Greek Archaeological Society under John Papadhimitriou in 1946–52 and 1956–63, show occupation since Middle Helladic times (earliest on hill above).

On the lower ground, discovered in 1958, are the remains of a Doric **temple** of the 5C BC, measuring c 20m by 10m, the foundations of which stand on rock-hewn steps (? the 'holy stairs' of Euripides). Here were discovered dedicatory reliefs in coloured terracotta, bronze mirrors, and votive jewellery. Many of these had been deposited in a sacred pool (now dry) below the temple. Adjoining the temple is a huge Π-shaped **stoa**, built before 416 BC, in which have been found inscriptions recording it to be the 'parthenon' of the arktoi, or 'bears'. It had nine dining-rooms (remains of tables and dining couches). Part of the colonnade (note the tall pillars which would have supported votive reliefs) and entablature was re-erected in 1962. Just to the W is a remarkable stone **\*bridge** of the same period. Inscriptions record other buildings (gymnasium, palaistra, stables etc.) which have not been found.

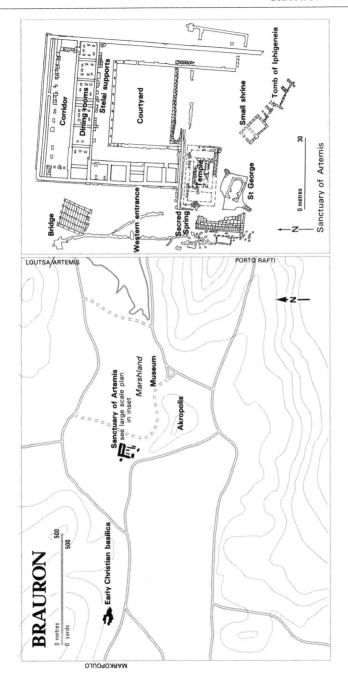

The large well-arranged site museum (round the next bend of the road) has marble statues and heads of little girls and of boys, also very fine 4C marble reliefs. There are numerous dedicatory offerings from the sanctuary—vases, figurines, mirrors, jewellery, etc. Models reconstruct the appearance of the site. Here also are Geometric finds from Anavyssos and important LHIII C pottery from Perati.

Past (2km) the museum is a right fork to Pórto Ráfti (7km from Brauron), while the left branch terminates at Hamólia (3km, camping).

The main road by-passes (34km) **Kalívia** (7357 inhab.), with attractive churches. Inscriptions suggest that the ancient deme of *Prospalta* was in the vicinity. Outside the village is the church of the **Panayia Mesosporitissa** (11–13C) then (1.3km from centre) **Ayios Petros**, which has a portrait of Michaelis Choniates, bishop of Athens. The halo shows that the picture was executed after his death and the frescoes must therefore date to after 1220. About 1.5km SW, on a by-road to Anávissos (16km; Rte 17A), is the pretty **Taxiarkhis**, a deserted monastic church built over an Early Christian basilica. The 18C frescoes have earlier (some 13C) below. At the 36th kilometre post a track leads (left) to **Ayios Yeoryios**, a Byzantine church with reused Ionic capitals. The countryside becomes more hilly. To the left rises Mt Mirenda (see above), to the right the double crest of **Panion** (651m), known locally as Keratovoúni (the horned mountain). Its steep E summit dominates (40km) **Keratéa**, a prosperous village (6712 inhab.), with orchards, vineyards, and good water, where Chateaubriand suffered from sunstroke. The church of **Ayia Kyriaki** has 12C frescoes signed by 'Georgios'. From Keratea a road descends to the **Convent of the Palaioimerologítai** (Adherents of the Old Calendar), 8km E, above the exposed beach of Kakí Thálassa. The new main road to Lavrion swings left; you keep to the old (right). The little mining hamlet of (50km) **Pláka** lies below the top of the next ridge (168m), where there is a view down towards the **Bay of Thorikós**, reached by a zigzag descent. The new road joins our route, just before modern Thorikos.

Dominating the bay (1.5km NE of the road), is the conical hill of **Velatouri**, the acropolis of ancient *Thorikos*. Towards the sea is the promontory of Ayios Nikolaos, which divides Portomandri, to the S, from Frankolimani, a smaller bay to the N, protected by Cape Vrisaki. This deep refuge is half-way between Piraeus and Rhamnous.

The mines of Thorikos are now known to have been exploited in the third millennium BC. In the Mycenaean period legend suggests dynastic ties with Athens (its king, Kephalos, married Prokris, daughter of Erechtheus). Thorikos was fortified in 412 BC as a defensive outpost of the Laurion mines (cf. Xenophon Hell. i. 2, 1). It was deserted after the Classical period but there are signs of renewed settlement in late antiquity (4–6C AD).

The site is reached from the road by turning left at a prominent sign (PPC: Public Power Corporation) and again at a smaller sign to 'Ancient Theatre of Thorikós'. The most significant remains of the Classical township lie at the S foot of the hill. One **tower** from the fortification system survives, standing to a height of c 3.5m. Higher up is the **theatre**, unique in its irregular plan, which awkwardly follows the natural slope. The first orchestra was laid out with a retaining wall in the Archaic period. In the mid 5C the theatre had 21 rows of seats; a century later it was extended to provide room for a further 12 rows, some of which may have had temporary seats. At that point the theatre would have accommodated about 6000 spectators. The **cavea** forms an irregular ellipse and is divided by two stairways, almost

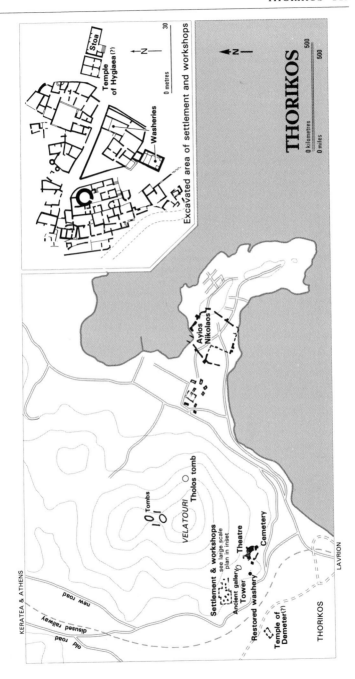

THORIKOS

0 kilometres 500

0 miles 500

Excavated area of settlement and workshops

Stoa

Temple
of Hygiaea (?)

Washeries

0 metres 30

Ayios
Nikolaos

VELATOURI

Tombs

Tholos tomb

Settlement & workshops
see large scale
plan in inset

Ancient gallery

Theatre

Tower

Cemetery

Restored washery

Temple of
Demeter (?)

THORIKOS

LAVRION

KERATEA & ATHENS

new road

disused railway

old road

parallel, into three sections, the central one nearly rectangular, those at either end sharply curved. The seats are roughly hewn. The lower rows were approached from below; the upper via two ramps set against the marble retaining wall of the structure. The W ramp is pierced by a corbelled passage. The narrow W parodos is bounded by a small **Temple of Dionysos** in antis (rock-cut foundations, a few blocks, fragments of mosaic floor). This faces across the rectangular orchestra towards the foundations of a large **altar**. Below the theatre has been recently excavated an Archaic and Classical cemetery whose **tombs** are grouped round small funerary monuments. To the W of this the hillside was quarried for construction of the theatre. Above the quarry is a restored ore washery, with a gallery (locked) beyond.

Many such **washeries** have been found in the Lavrion area. They were used for grading the crushed ore-bearing rock from the local mines. A rectangular water tank (often with a cistern behind) has small perforations in its front wall to release jets of water into long sloping wooden troughs with cross partitions (none of these have survived). The heaviest (richest) fragments were retained in the highest partitions, while the remainder were caught lower down or (if light and valueless) swept away by the water. A broad 'table' in front of the tank and troughs was used for drying the material. Round the table ran a water channel with settling tanks at the corners. The water used in the washing process escaped into this, was clarified and could be reloaded into the main tank when it reached the end of the circuit.

A good deal of excavation has been undertaken in an area c 100m NW of the theatre, where 7C houses were converted into workshops (including washeries) for processing the metal ores mined close by in the late 5C or early 4C. Several of the complexes include thick-walled round 'towers', perhaps for the dry storage of grain above ground level. A late Archaic double **Temple** (probably) **of Hygiaea** and small adjacent stoa can also be seen here.

The remains of a peripteral Doric **temple**, possibly of Demeter and Kore, of unusual design, with 7 columns on the fronts and 14 at the sides, unearthed in 1812 c 1km W of the theatre, have been covered again. Much of its materials were transported to Athens in Augustan times and re-erected in the SE corner of the agora.

On the **acropolis** the most impressive remains are of prehistoric tombs, though evidence of Early Helladic and Mycenaean settlement has also been found and the area was the acropolis of the Classical town below. Parts of cemeteries of the Geometric and later periods have been found on the S slopes. Excavations are of the Greek Archaeological Society in 1890 and 1893; and recently of the Belgian Mission. On the E side of the nearer summit is a Mycenaean tholos tomb (III), excavated in 1893, whose chamber was 8.61m high. Further N are four other Mycenaean tombs. One has a domed interior, another an unusual oblong form. A tumulus nearby somewhat resembles those found at Marathon.

The maritime fortress of 412 BC occupies the isthmus between the two harbours to the W of the church.

About 5km offshore lies the island of **Makrónisos**, anciently called *Helena*, from a tradition that Helen rested here on her flight with Paris. Used after the civil war of 1946 as a detention centre, it is now uninhabited except by shepherds in summer. Part of an Early Bronze Age settlement has been excavated.

54km **Lávrion** (Λαύριον), known in the 19C as *Ergasteria* because of its workshops, is a scattered industrial town of 8846 inhabitants, which owes its existence to the neighbouring mines and its name to the ancient district

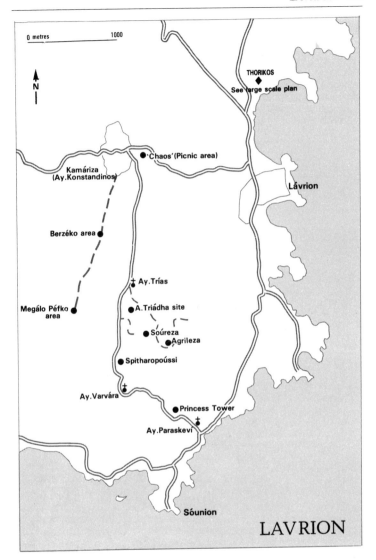

of *Laurion*. Control of the silver mines of Laurion contributed hugely to Athens' commercial and political greatness; the Athenian silver coinage ('Laureot owls') had prestige all over the world. There is an interesting **Mineral Museum** in a 19C building, originally belonging to the French mining company, off the main road on the W side of town.

The mines were exploited in prehistoric times; Aeschylus alludes in the *Persae* (235) to the Θησαυρὸς Χθόνος. The decision of the Athenians in 483 BC to finance the building of a fleet with the surplus yield of the mines laid the foundations of their naval supremacy, and by the time of Pericles the industry had reached the peak of its prosperity. As a result of the Spartan presence at Dekelia in 413, the mines were closed. Though they were reopened c 355, perhaps partly due to Xenophon's treatise on mines as a neglected source of revenue, and lasted another four centuries, they were never again as important. Pausanias refers to them in the past tense and for centuries they lay neglected. Modern exploitation, very largely the result of French initiative, was in the hands of three companies: one French (reconstituted after disputes about government royalties in 1873), one Greek (1860), and one American. The modern mines were concerned principally with the extraction of cadmium and manganese, and, to a lesser degree, with reworking the ancient slag-heaps for lead. The last mines closed in the late 1970s, though imported ore was processed for about another ten years. Just to the north of Lavrion, the old French smelting works, revived briefly by a Greek company in the 1980s, is proposed for restoration as a monument of industrial archaeology. The synthetic textile mills are important.

The best preserved **ancient mines** are situated to the S of **Kamáriza** (Ayios Konstandínos), a village about 5km to the W of Lavrion (sign on N outskirts).

The mines anciently belonged to the State, which granted them on perpetual leases to contractors. They were worked by slave labour. Over 2000 ancient shafts have been

*Washery for metal ores. Reconstruction by J. Ellis Jones.*

found, some perpendicular (18–122m deep) and some sloping. The roofs of the galleries (24–46m deep) were supported either by artificial piers or by natural ore-bearing pillars left in the rock. The removal of these pillars, which was dangerous, was punishable by death. Ventilation shafts carried off the bad air. Some miners' lamps and other relics have been found. In various places chains of huge **cisterns** and ore-washeries (see Thorikos) and furnaces are to be seen.

From **Kamáriza** two routes lead S. On the far (W) side of the village a road gives access to sites in the Berzeko valley and at Megalo Pefko. More accessible are the remains described here, reached via the more easterly road (turn left in village by wayside shrine). The tarmac road passes a huge natural pit in the limestone ('Khaos') and between traces of ancient and modern mine working to (3km) the church of Ayía Triádha. A partly excavated washery and open cistern (with later lime kiln inserted) can be seen on the S side of the church, and a ruined modern industrial complex beyond. If you continue 500m SW on the tarmac road from the church and turn left downhill to a parking place, steps descend to an impressively large tract of excavated ancient mining remains at the head of a valley. These include a tower built over a washery, a series of interconnected cisterns, washeries and associated workrooms, and some pits. Other (unexcavated) remains of washeries etc. lie further down the valley. Returning to the tarmac road, you can continue S and SW along a high ridge, reforested. To the left, near the road, are an excavated grave terrace and a small washery with associated compound (cistern, ore-grinding boulder 'tables'). Opposite, further from the road, is a large washery compound. Further along the road are houses and the church of Ayía Varvára (ancient stele on left). You can then descend (E), passing (left) the **Princess Tower** farmhouse site (low stub of round tower in enclosure) to reach the coast road 2km from Sounion.

Another route from Ayía Triádha church is by a track (from E end of church, behind fenced garden) leading directly S along the E flank of Agrileza valley. You skirt the high fence of a modern factory compound and reach (at 1km; right) a downturn to the ancient site of **Soureza** which has three impressive washery complexes with cisterns (fenced enclosure). A short distance further S you reach the site of **Agrileza** (excavated by the British School 1977–83): first, to the right of the track, is the **Golden Pig Tower** (2m high) and an excavated washery in compound. Beyond (left) is an unexcavated compound, with two cisterns and surface indications, then another (excavated and fenced), with washery, adjacent cistern and rooms round two terraced yards. Below the track to the right is a fine walled cistern with internal staircase. The track, now difficult to follow, descends, leading eventually to the coast midway between Lavrion and Sounion (c 3.5km from Agrileza).

Beyond Kamáriza the road continues to the W coast at Anávissos (14km from Lavrion).

From Lavrion a boat (daily in summer, pm) departs for the island of **Kéa**, sometimes continuing to Kíthnos.

The road continues S at some distance from the sea. On the W are moderate wooded hills. Above the coast (Hotel B) are summer villas.

At (59km) Pashalimáni on the coast below can be seen some remains of a Greek and Roman harbour **town** with an agora and metal working establishments.

The columns of the Temple of Poseidon are seen on the skyline as you join the coast route at the approach to (64.5km) **Soúnion.**

# 18

# Sálamis

The crescent-shaped island of **Sálamis** (ΣΑΛΑΜΙΣ; usually accusative Salamína; 93 sq. km) lies in the N of the Saronic Gulf close inshore. Its NW coast is less than 1km from the coast of Megaris, and its NE coast is separated from the mainland of Attica by the Strait of Salamis, scene of the famous battle. The island thus turns the Bay of Eleusis almost into a lagoon. Salamis with 22,567 inhabitants, mainly of Albanian descent, forms part of the eparchy of Piraeus. Its soil is dry and rocky and, though a few vineyards and cornfields are found in the plains, the climate is unhealthy. The highest point is **Mavrovouni** (404m). According to Strabo the ancient capital originally lay on the S coast opposite Aegina; this was moved before Classical times to the E coast; the modern capital is on the W side of the island at the head of the Bay of Kouloúris. Salamis is famous for its battle and important as a naval base, but it is somewhat run-down, heavily populated with holiday homes, and archaeological remains are meagre. Military establishments impede a close study of the scene of the battle, the best general view of which is still obtained from Xerxes' vantage-point behind Perama (below).

**History.** In Mycenaean times *Salamis* seems to have had dynastic connections with both Aegina and Cyprus. The Homeric catalogue records a contribution of twelve ships led by Telamonian Ajax. In the 7C the island was disputed between Athens and Megara. It was annexed to Athens as a cleruchy by Solon, the Athenians going so far as to forge an extra line of Homer in support of their claim. In 480 BC the Athenians evacuated Athens and, with Salamis as base, entrusted themselves to their 'wooden walls'. After 318 BC Salamis surrendered to the Macedonian Cassander, but in 229 BC it was recovered for Athens by Aratos, when the Salaminians were expelled in favour of new colonists.

**Approaches.** From Athens in 35 minutes by frequent bus nos 841, 842 from Plateía Koumoundhoúrou (Eleftherías) (or from Piraeus by frequent bus no. 843 from Electric Railway Station) to Pérama on the S coast of the Skaramangas peninsula. The road runs through the sprawling industrial town of **Níkaia** (87,587 inhab.), which extends NW of Piraeus to the Aigaleos hills, and passes below the supposed vantage-point from which Xerxes watched the Battle of Salamis. 15km **Pérama** has shipyards where trawlers, tugs, and coastal vessels are built. The buses terminate at the quay, whence ferries (c ½ hourly) cross the Strait of Salamis to the island; to **Paloúkia** (cars taken), via the N side of the island of Ayios Yeoryios, for the town of **Sálamis** (2km; bus every 10 minutes); to **Kamateró**; and to a landing-stage E of Ambelákia for **Selínia**. The crossings take c 15 minutes. Buses serve all main points on the island.

The **Battle of Salamis** was fought about 22 September 480 BC. The tactics of the battle and the fundamental identification of the island of Psyttaleia (Ψυττάλεια) are still the subject of scholarly disagreement. Most commentators identify Psyttaleia with Lipsokoutáli, a view excellently argued by A.R. Burn (*Persia and the Greeks*, 1962) and by Paul W. Wallace (A.J.A., 1969). N.G.L. Hammond (J.H.S., 1956) identified Psyttaleia with Ayios Yeóryios and Lipsokoutáli with Atalante. This may be thought to accord better with the accounts of Herodotus (VIII, 70–94) and of Aeschylus who fought in the battle and describes it in the *Persae* performed eight years later. The general strategy of the battle is not in doubt though Athenian tradition seems as usual to have exaggerated the disparity between the opposing forces.

Salamis was a key point in Themistocles' plan of defence against the Persians and in the event a decisive one. While all Athenian women and children were evacuated to Troezen, Salamis was to receive the old men and exiles (who were ordered to return).

An attempt to stem the Persian advance was to be made with half the allied fleet at Artemision while the remaining Athenian triremes with the reserves of the fleets of Sparta, Corinth, and Aegina were to lie off Salamis. Before the action the Persians were in Phaleron Bay. The news that they had despatched an army by land towards the Isthmus alarmed the Peloponnesians who had to be persuaded against retiring on Corinth. Xerxes' plan to bottle the Athenians in the Skaramangas strait or force them into open water to the E by building a pontoon boom across the strait itself was foiled by Cretan archers. Themistocles, hoping to force an immediate battle in the narrows, where he would have the advantage, organised a leak of information to Xerxes that the Peloponnesians intended to retreat. Under cover of darkness the Persians put into operation a new plan to encircle the supposedly disunited Greeks; Psyttaleia was occupied; a squadron of 200 Egyptian ships was despatched to block the W strait between Salamis and Megara; and the remaining ships were drawn up in a line right across the E exit. The Persian plan seems to have been to surprise the Greeks, while they were still drawn up on the beaches at dawn, and capture their base. Xerxes himself set up a silver throne on Aigaleos, 'the rocky brow that looks o'er sea-born Salamis', whence he could watch the battle. Aristides, the exiled rival of Themistocles, who succeeded in slipping through to the Greek fleet from Aegina, was the first to bring the news of the investment. His statement was confirmed by a Tenean deserter. The forewarned Greeks, who now had no alternative but to fight, embarked before dawn, retired apparently in flight before the advancing enemy and formed up in hiding behind a promontory. When they emerged in battle order the advantage of surprise was with them. With more manoeuverable ships, lower in the water, they made deadly use of the technique of ramming. As Themistocles had foreseen, the Persians became hopelessly confused; Artemisia, queen of Halicarnassos, was seen to sink one of her allies' ships. 'Their multitude became their ruin' (Aeschylus). The Corinthian contingent (70 ships) under Adeimantos was later said by Athenian gossip to have taken no part in the battle, perhaps because was executing a feint withdrawal or shadowing the Egyptian squadron.

At the critical moment a force under Aristides captured Psyttaleia, making the victory complete. The fleet of Aegina is said to have distinguished itself most, and next the Athenians. Although the battle did not become such a legend to the Athenians as Marathon, it is much more entitled to rank as one of the 'decisive battles' of the world. To the Persians Marathon was merely the defeat of a punitive expedition, Salamis the overthrow of a royal scheme of conquest.

To the N of **Paloúkia** the **arsenal**, the most important naval station in Greece, extends round the Bay of Arapi, cutting off access to the NE part of the island. From Paloúkia one road leads S to **Ambelákia**, near which (1.5 km; at Palaiomagoúla on the Kynosoura promontory) a stone mound 20m in diameter has been identified as the **Tomb of the Fallen** of the great battle, and crosses the base of the **Kamateró peninsula**, the site of Classical *Salamis* (few traces) to **Selínia**, a villa resort. Alternatively you can travel W to **Sálamis**, or **Kouloúri**, the chief town of the island, at the head of a deep bay on the W coast. Much of the area is a rash of bungalows. In the bay, since the laying up in 1959 of ships from Far Eastern waters, the Japanese pearl oyster has been found: attempts to cultivate it are being made at Batsí (Megálo Péfko). A road skirts the bay to the straggling village of **Aiándeio**; at the entrance to the village roads lead E to **Kakí Vígla**, **Peráni** and **Peristéria**, hamlets on the coast; also S over the mountain to (6.5km) **Ayios Nikólaos** and then down to the coast.

Beyond Sálamis the road crosses the island's NW peninsula. 8km The **Moní Faneroméni**, or Convent of the Apparition of the Virgin (Φανερωμένη), has a remarkable fresco of the Last Judgement. Nine glazed bowls built into the exterior fabric are 13C–16C AD and include two Corinthian and two Italian pieces. The monastery is crowded with pilgrims on 4 September and there are traditional processions in Passion week. Néa Péramos (Rte 24) is seen across Vasiliká Bay. At (10km) **Stenó** was formerly the landing-stage of the Megaris ferry.

To the S of the road, overlooking St George's Bay just below the ridge, is a long fortification wall, identified in 1960 by the American School with the fort of *Boudoron*, built by the Athenians in the 5C to keep watch over Megara, and ravaged in 429 BC by the Peloponnesian fleet.

You can return to Salamis town by continuing S and E, with possible diversions along the N coast of the Gulf of Salamis, opposite Aiandeio.

# 19

# Mount Parnes

**Mount Parnes**, in Greek **Párnis Oros** (Πάρνης Ὄρος; often Párnitha, accusative), the rugged mountain range to the NW of Athens, forms the central part of the massif dividing Attica from Boeotia. Radar stations disfigure some of the heights. It is defined at the E end by the Diakria, or 'Upland', the lowest exit from the Attic plains, and on the W by the pass between Mt Pastra, its W extension, and Kithairon. Parnes thus extends some 40km from E to W. Its wildness is clearly evident from the air. The area remains sparsely populated, scored by ravines, and, except where the slopes are clothed in forests of pine or oak, exposed to the elements. Wolves and bears, seen in Roman times, are no longer found, but sheepdogs may cause problems. The mountain is crossed by only one main road suitable for normal vehicles (via Dhekelia; see Rte 20), though the ancient route to Thebes by way of Phyle and Pyli is passable with care. Walkers intending to make expeditions should take provisions and a compass; a tent is also useful, since to the W of Phyle there is no hotel nearer than Thebes, and, except on the two approaches described below, public transport can be reached only on the Thessaloniki highway or at Avlon Station to the N, or on the Thebes road to the S. The SE slopes are now easily accessible and have been developed for winter sports. The W forts (Panakton etc.) are more easily visited from the Thebes road (Rte 41).

By car the two routes below may be combined without returning to Athens by using the link road through Akhárnai to Ano Liósia.

## A.  To Ayía Triádha and the summit

**Road** to **Grand Hotel Parnes**, 35km (22 miles); bus no. 714 to Ayía Triádha (twice daily) from Odhós Sourmelí. 736 (Sundays only; hourly, 09.00–21.00) to terminus (then by telepherique) from Odhós Sourmelí (Plateía Váthis, below Archaeological Museum; 2, 4). ('Parnis' is signposted via Odhós Akharnón and the National Highway, which you leave after 10km to join the road described below c 1.5km N of Akhárnai.)

From Plateía Váthis, NW of Omónia Sq., Odhós Liossíon (**Railway Museum** at No. 310; open Wednesday 17.00–20.00, Friday 10.30–13.30) passes under the National Highway at (5.5km) **Tris Yéfires** ('Three Bridges'), in the natural 'gap' where the road and two railways cross the Kefissos. At (6km) **Ayioi Anáryiroi** the Fíli road diverges left (see below). You bear right and after c 2km pass a knoll (left) marked by some medieval remains; this is possibly the hill occupied by the Peloponnesian army under King Archidamos in 431 BC, when it ravaged the Athenian Plain. The frustrated Acharnians, prevented by Pericles from defending their lands, were later prominent in opposing the peace party in their desire for revenge (see Aristophanes). 12km **Akhárnes** (Αχάρναι, Hotels C, D), or **Meními̇dhi**, in modern as in ancient times is a large deme surrounded by vineyards. Its Classical inhabitants engaged in charcoal-burning on Parnes. Here in 1932 was found a marble stele of the 4C engraved with the 'Oath of Plataia'. For Menidhi Tomb, see Rte 20. The road climbs gradually at first, then in steep turns, offering ever broader views over the plain of Attica. At (33km) **Ayía Triádha**, a little mountain resort amid pine woods, the bus terminates. The road divides: to the right on a spur with a superb *panorama is (2.5km farther) the Grand Hotel Mont Parnes (L; cable-car, casino, swimming pool, tennis courts, cinema, etc.); to the left you can reach (3km) the **refuge** of the Greek Alpine Club (1165m) and the entrance to the radar station (no adm.) that crowns (7km) **Karábola** (1413m), the summit of Párnes.

Within a few yards of the top a sacrificial pyre, explored in 1959–60, yielded pottery and 3000 knives of the period 1000–600 BC. This discovery probably locates one of the two altars to Zeus mentioned by Pausanias.

To reach the **Cave of Pan** turn left in Ayía Triádha just before a conspicuous café then, after 300m, left at a sign to Cave of Pan. The road winds down into the gorge of Moní Klistón. After 7.7kms, at the lowest point of the road, is a path on the right bank marked with red blazes. This crosses to the left bank, climbs and then descends very steeply to the **Cave of Pan** which forms the locale of Menander's 'Dyskolos'. (This site has often proved very difficult to find and you are advised to take a guide or get instructions from a previous visitor). Across the gorge (SW) rises the wooded spur of **Kalamára**, a hump with sheer sides anciently called *Harma* because, when seen from Athens, it resembled a chariot. The Pythiasts watched for lightning to play on its summit as a signal for the departure of the sacred mission to Delphi. A covering of cloud is today taken as a sign of rain.

# B. To Phyle (Filí)

**Road.** 31km (19½ miles) through the village of Filí (bus no. 723, 734 from Plateía Váthis (Odhós Sourmelí); 2, 4) and on to Moní Klistón and the fortress of Phyle.

To (8km) **Ayioi Anáryiroi**, see above. You bear left in company with the Peloponnese railway, beyond which can be seen a castellated mansion (Pírgos tis Vasilíssis), once a model farm of Queen Amalia. The house is now a training school and camp for Boy Scouts. 12km **Ano Liósia** (railway station; see Rte 16) stands in the gap between Aigáleos and Párnes. You ascend through a defile to (18.5km) **Filí** (Φυλή), a village (formerly Khasiá) in a hollow, which has readopted the ancient name. The road enters the gorge of **Potámi Goúras** and then climbs to (22.5km) **Moní Klistón**, correctly Panayia ton Kleiston (Our Lady of the Gorges), an old convent with a 14C church rebuilt in the 17C. There is a school and a terrace with a fine view down into the gorge. A fountain in the court bears the date 1677.

For **Phyle** you ignore the turning to Moní Kleistón and continue upwards to (31km) the fortress which lies (left) on a prominent flat-topped hill. It can also be reached on foot (c 2 hours) by leaving the main road (left) at the entrance to the gorge and, after c 15 minutes, ascending to the right up a ravine; but the route is difficult to find.

The fortress (649m) crowns a precipitous triangular platform projecting forward from a summit some 5m higher. It dominated alternative defiles of the ancient direct route from Thebes to Athens (of strategic value only for a comparatively small force) and looks out over the whole Athenian plain. It apparently replaced an earlier fort (see below) in the 4C BC; it was garrisoned by Kassander and subsequently dismantled and ceded to the Athenians by Demetrios Poliorketes.

The main entrance is on the E side. The enclosure has a pentagonal plan. To the W and SW the defences have crumbled, but elsewhere the well-preserved walls stand to the sixth course of squared blocks. Of five towers, four were square and one round. Like Eleutherai and Rhamnous, the fort had no water supply within the walls; in the neighbourhood and also near a spring, 20 minutes NE, are remains of houses.

A road, indifferent but passable, continues along an ancient course to the Plateau of Skourta, in which stand **Píli** (24km from Filí) and **Pánakton**. Many ancient sites, including watchtowers presumably belonging to the Attica-Boeotia frontier of classical times have been located in a recent survey (1986–). From Píli the Skhimatári–Thebes road can be joined at various points. Thebes is at least 12 hours walk further

About 1.5km to the NE of Phyle is another summit, on which are considerable remains of polygonal masonry. These are sometimes thought (Chandler J.H.S. 46 (1926)) to mark the post which Thrasyboulos captured in 403 BC after his expulsion from Athens by the 30 Tyrants and defended with 70 men against 3000. Hence he proceeded to the capture of Piraeus.

# 20

# From Athens to Tatóï and Skála Oropoú

**Road**, 50km (31 miles). **Local buses** (no. 505, etc) infrequently from Kifissia terminal to Tatóï and Varibóbi; frequently from Plateía Káningos to Kifissia (buses 538, 539). **Buses** to Skála Oropoú via the Kifissia road (Rte 15), joining this route at Malakássa, twice daily from Odhós Mavromatéon. Skála Oropoú and the ferry to Eretria are reached more directly by the National Highway and a new road diverging at 34km; **buses** hourly from Od. Mavromatéon. For the Menídhi Tomb, take bus 722 (Kókkinos Mílos B) from Od, Akharnón/Avérof; stop by tomb.

You leave central Athens by the Patissia road (Rte 8), passing the National Archaeological Museum. 5km **Patíssia** (Πατήσια) is a favourite suburban resort of the Athenians. Its name (*padishah*, Sultan) may derive from from the fact that under the Turks the land was crown property. 6km **Alissídha**.

Above **Perissós**, 2.5km NE, on the NW slope of Tourkovoúni, is the **Omorphi Ekklesia**, or 'beautiful church', dedicated to St George in the 12C. It has mural paintings by a Salonican artist of the 14C, when the S chapel was added; the narthex is more recent.

You bear left (into Od. Khalkídhos) across the Piraeus Electric Railway, then right (into Leofóros Dhekélias), to pass through (7km) **Néa Filadhélfia**, a planned refugee suburb. The road divides W of the AEK football stadium.

The left fork (Od. Píndhou) leads to Akhárnes (5km; Rte 19), crossing in turn the old Lavrion railway, the National Highway, and the Kifissos. In **Likótripa** (2.5km), up the hill beyond the cemetery, to the right of the road, is the tumulus covering the **Menídhi Tomb**, a Mycenaean tholos tomb excavated by the German School in 1879. The finds are in the National Museum. For public transport, see above.

You continue NE on Leofóros Dhekélias. It becomes Od. Tatóïou and swings left. On the hill of Nemesis (left of road) was the Mycenaean settlement to which the Menidhi tomb belonged. Beyond (10.5km) **Koukouváounes**, you cross the National Highway, then the Kifissos. Near (14.5km) **Dhekélia station**, on the State Railway, is **Tatóï Airfield**, a Hellenic Air Force base and flying school. 19km **Varibóbi** (Βαρυμπόμπη; Hotels L, B, C) where you join a road from Kifissia, is noted for its golf course. About 1.5km NW are the ruins of the so-called **Tomb of Sophocles**. The road ascends towards the pass.

24km **Tatóï**, known also by its ancient name of *Dekelia* (mod. Dhekélia), is beautifully situated amid oak-woods in the entrance to the pass of Klidhí ('key'). To the right the former **Summer Palace** stands in a fine park, a good example of scientific afforestation on uncongenial soil. Local antiquities from the royal estate were gathered together into a small museum by George I; this was destroyed by fire in 1916 but the surviving objects, together with later finds from the area, have been described by the Princesses Sophia and Irene (1959–60). At Tatóï were born George II (1890) and King Alexander (1893). The **mausoleum** of George I and Alexander (d. 1920) stands on the hill called **Palaiókastro** above the village (left), where are the ruins of a Spartan fortress constructed in 413 BC. George II and King Paul are also buried at Tatóï.

Ancient *Dekelia* (Δεκέλεια) guarded the easternmost of the three passes over Parnes, the vital route by which food from Euboea reached Athens. By this pass Mardonius retreated into Boeotia before the battle of Plataia. On the advice of the renegade Alcibiades, the Spartans captured the pass in 413 BC and built a fortress (see above), initiating the blockade by land which, after the naval victory of Lysander at Aegospotami, led to the surrender of Athens. **Hadrian's aqueduct**, lengthened and restored by the Ulen company, runs S from Tatóï to a reservoir below Lykabettos.

The defile passes between the two hills of **Strongilí** (right) and **Katsimídhi** (850m). On the latter are traces of an Athenian fort, built in the 4C to guard the pass. The wooded uplands resound to the clonking of sheep bells. Beyond (32km) **Ayios Merkoúrios**, a chapel with a spring, the steep zigzag descent has a superb *view across the Euripos to Euboea. In the foreground are the railway and the highway to the north, which you cross at (37km) **Malakássa**. The road winds through upland scrub, then descends in more wooded country, with good views of the Strait of Euboea, to (50km) **Skála Oropós** (Hotels C; tavernas), or more correctly **Skála Oropoú** (Σκάλα Ωρωπού), on the site of the ancient *Oropos*. From its shallow bay a ferry (frequent) provides the shortest connection between Athens and Euboea. From the beach King Constantine I embarked in 1917 for Messina on his way to exile in Switzerland.

Ancient *Oropos* was important to Athens as the nearest accessible place of embarkation with a short sea passage to Euboea. To it came ships bringing vital corn supplies and cattle for the capital. According to Dikaiarchos, the Oropians were rapacious and ill-mannered; their customs officers were especially notorious. The town fell alternately under Thebes and Athens, with intervals of independence.

Many finds of ancient buildings (including an Early Christian basilica, near the ferry terminal) have been made in recent years in the town and its suburbs (Lagovoúni, Néa

Palátia)—parts of the city wall, cemeteries, a stoa—but no full discussion has yet been published. A building in the town has been assigned for a new Archaeological Museum.

Diodoros records that in 402 BC the Thebans moved the Oropians 7 stades inland, presumably from Skála to the site of modern Oropós.

The modern village of **Oropós**, 5km inland to the SW, has a 17C church. Lignite mines are worked in the neighbourhood.

Road from Skála to the **Amphiáraion**, see Rte 22. Car ferry (frequent) to **Erétria**.

# 21

# From Athens to Marathon. Rhamnous

**Road** to Marathon (Marathóna), 42km (26 miles). 12km Stavrós.—27km Turning for Rafína (3km right).—30km Turning for Ayios Andréas (2km right).—38km Marathon Tomb.—42km Marathón.—47km Káto Soúli.—51.5km Turning (right) to Ayía Marína (2.5km).—58km Rhámnous (Rhamnoúnda).

**Bus** to Marathón from Odhós Mavromatéon (half-hourly mornings, hourly thereafter) in c 1 hour, continuing (regularly) to Grammatikó (see below) or (7 times daily) to Káto Soúli (½ hour more); also four times daily to Ayía Marína (best for Rhámnous; ferry to Néa Stíra, Almiropótamos) also to Rafína and Néa Mákri (both half-hourly). To Spáta, frequently from Thissíon, bus 304, 305.

From Athens to **Stavrós**, see Rte 17B. You leave the Mesogeion road to the right at a flyover, cross the old Lavrion railway, and pass a modern church surrounded by cypresses and a cemetery. *Gargetos*, birthplace of Epicurus (341–270 BC) lay hereabouts. 15km **Pallíni**, formerly Kharvati and now marked by a radio station, has readopted the name of Classical *Pallene*, which had a noted temple of Athena. It was associated with the legendary victory of the Heraklids over Eurystheus and with Theseus' defeat of the Pallantids. Here c 545 BC Peisistratos, returning from exile in Macedonia, defeated an Athenian force to make himself finally master of Athens. The local white wine is well known.

13km Turn for **Spáta**, a large village, c 6.5km SE, in a wine-producing district. Mycenaean chamber-tombs excavated by Stamatakis in 1877 produced interesting finds, especially ivories (National Museum). Here will be situated the second airport for Athens. Contracts will soon be awarded (1994). The special tax added to airline tickets to fund this enterprise is known, rather charmingly, as the 'Spatósimo'. Beyond Spáta, on the coast, is the popular beach of **Loútsa**, now often known as **Artemis** (or Artemídha; Hotel D; tavernas), identified by an inscription as *Halai Araphenides*. Here in 1956 were discovered remains of a **Dionysion** and a **temple** of Artemis Tauropolos and (1975–76) a possible **propylon** (originally 5C BC) to the sanctuary.

You pass (right) a tomb of partisans executed in 1942. 22km **Pikérmi** (Hotel C; restaurants) is noted for the discovery of fossil remains of the neo-Tertiary period. The finds, which include the dinotherium, the largest fossil known, are now in the natural history museum of Athens University. The 16C nunnery of Ayia Filothei is now a private house. The district is rich in vineyards and olive-groves, and the scenery attractive. The summit of Pentelikon, until now skirted by the road, is hidden behind an intervening spur. Along the road here in April 1941 British troops abandoned their transport before embarking. Near (24km) **Drasesa Bridge**, where the road crosses the Megálo Rhévma, some English tourists, including Lord Muncaster, were captured by brigands in 1870. The scandal attending the subsequent murder of four of them at Dilessi in Boeotia caused energetic steps to be taken to suppress brigandage. 27km Turning (right) for Rafína.

**Rafína** (Hotels C, D, E), site of the ancient deme of *Araphen*, is 3km away on the sea (bathing). Its small but busy harbour (new quays) is connected by steamer with Karistos (Euboea) and with Andros, Tinos, Siros, Paros and Naxos; also intermittently other destinations including the N Aegean and Dodecanese. A heavy swell hampered evacuation here in 1941. On the height of **Askitarió** (2km S) are the remains of an Early Helladic town (explored in 1955).

On the outskirts of Rafína there is a turn (right) for (8km) **Artemis (Loútsa)** (see above), (15km) **Brauron** and **Pórto Ráfti** (23km from Rafína; Rte 17B).

On the wooded SE slope of Pentelikon, sharp left opposite the junction for Rafína, stands the conspicuous sanatorium of the **Moní Dáou Pendéli**. The convent, founded in the 10C, was refounded in 1963 after being deserted since 1690. A huge dome, borne on six columns, crowns the church, which shows many Eastern features. The 13C narthex dates from its Frankish period which ended in 1456. The woods are scored by fire lanes. Here, in a **German Military Cemetery** approved in 1962, have been concentrated the German dead of the campaign in Greece (1941–44).

The road approaches within 2kms of the shore to cross the ridge where **Xilokeratiá** (268m), the last spur of Pentelikon, descends to the sea. On the descent behind the attractive shore of **Máti** (Hotels A, B, C), the whole Bay of Marathon is seen across the woods that back **Ayios Andréas** (2km right), a popular bathing place with tavernas, where some remains of the ancient harbour have been found. 32km **Néa Mákri** (Hotels B, C, E), popular for bathing and with some classical remains, stands at the seaward end of a road that follows the N slope of Pentelikon from Ekáli via Dhiónissos (Rte 15A). It has a large Neolithic settlement and may be the site of *Probalinthos*, whose name is of pre-Greek origin. The road passes between **Mt Agriliki** and the small marsh of **Brexisa** (see below) into the Plain of Marathon.

The **Plain of Marathon** claims attention both for the famous battle and for archaeological discoveries, particularly those made in 1969–70. Geographically the plain, 10km long and 2.5–5km wide, extends in crescent form round the Bay of Marathon from the **Kynosura Promontory** (with an unidentified acropolis) in the N to Cape Kavo in the S. On the landward side it is shut in by the stony mountains that 'look on Marathon'. These are of moderate height but rise abruptly from the plain. **Stavrokoráki** (310m), the most northerly, is separated from **Kotróni** (235m) by the torrent bed of the **Kharadra**, which descends from the Marathon Lake past the modern village of Marathon to the sea. Geologists suggest that it would have been a negligible obstacle in the plain in Classical times. Between Kotroni and **Aforismós** (573m) runs the **Valley of Avlona**. The valley is joined at the village of Vraná (possibly the ancient Marathon) by the Rapentosa Gorge. This defile runs NNE from the hamlet of Rapentósa between Aforismos and **Agriliki** (556m), the mountain forming the southern barrier of the plain. Agriliki has rubble walls that may date from the Mycenaean period.

In the N of the plain the **Great Marsh** (Μεγάλος Βάλτος; nowadays criss-crossed by drainage canals) stretches from Stavrokoraki to the base of the Kynosura Promontory, where it ends in the small salt-water lake of **Drakonera**. The **Little Marsh (Brexisa)** at the S end is probably a

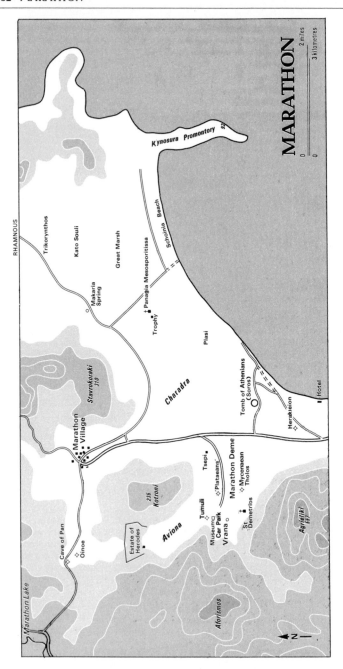

MARATHON

post-Classical formation; it is now partially drained and occupied by a United States forces radio station and the Golden Coast Hotel B.

**Battle of Marathon.** After the easy destruction of Eretria the Persians crossed to Attica. Datis, their general, was probably influenced in his choice of the Bay of Marathon by Hippias, whose father had landed here successfully 50 years before. Meanwhile the Athenians, after despatching Pheidippides post haste for Spartan aid, marched to Marathon and encamped in the Sanctuary of Herakles, a strong position astride the mountain track from Athens and commanding the only road. The Persian numbers, not stated by Herodotus and grossly exaggerated by later Athenian tradition, are now thought not to have exceeded two divisions of infantry (? 24,000 men) and a small force of cavalry. The Athenians received unexpected aid from Plataia, which sent its whole available force, perhaps 1000 strong, to join the 8000–9000 men of Athens. The command was vested in the Polemarch, Kallimachos, whose staff of ten generals included Miltiades (the traditional architect of the victory), and perhaps Themistocles and Aristides.

Four days passed, the Persians being unwilling to attack the strong Athenian position, the Athenians loath to leave it without the expected Spartan reinforcements. Believing he had failed to lure the Athenian army down into the plain, Datis re-embarked his cavalry to move on Athens by sea, sending a land force forward to cover the operation. Seeing them within striking distance, probably soon after dawn on 12 September 490 BC, Miltiades gave the word for action. He had left his centre weak and strongly reinforced his wings; the right wing, the place of honour, was led by Kallimachos; on the left wing were the Plataians. The Greek hoplites advanced rapidly across the mile of No Man's Land before the surprised Persians could get their archers properly into action, possibly helped by tree cover (Prof. Burn has pointed out the similarity of tactics used at Bannockburn). The Athenian wings were successful, while their weak centre was pierced by the Persians. The wings then enveloped the Persian centre which broke. In the ensuing rout the Persians fled to their ships. Many of them were caught in the Great Marsh. They lost 6400 men, while the Athenian dead numbered only 192, including Kallimachos. All were buried on the spot. A runner is said to have been sent to Athens, where he died of exhaustion after announcing the victory.

The Persian fleet, having lost only seven ships, put out to sea in an attempt to surprise Athens; but Miltiades, by a rapid march, reached Athens first, and the Persians sailed back to Asia. The battle proved that the long-dreaded Persians were vulnerable and was 'the victory of which the Athenians were proudest'. The Spartan army arrived in time to view the battlefield on the following day. Of the many legends that accrued to Marathon perhaps the best known are those of the ghostly assistance of Theseus and of Pan. The impressive silence of the plain is said to resound at night to the clash of arms and the neigh of steeds (though it is almost certain that no cavalry took part). Unsolved mysteries connected with the battle include the flashing of a shield on Pentelikon (Hdt. VI, 115). The most detailed modern appraisals are by Burn (*Persia and the Greeks*) and in *Journal of Hellenic Studies* (vol. 52, 1932), but these and even Kendrick Pritchett's *Studies in Ancient Topography* II (1969) need to be considered in the light of continuing finds.

## The Archaeological Sites

As you enter the plain, there is first a road (right) across the Brexisa Marsh to the Golden Coast Hotel (see above), just to the S of which, on an island of solid ground are fragments of Roman masonry, usually thought to be the family mausoleum of Herodes Atticus (AD 101–177, a native of Marathon), and earlier remains have been located in the area. A little farther along, a second road (right) is signposted 'Marathon Tomb' (350m; large car park; café). This **Sorós**, 10m high and c 180m round, marks the graves of the 192 Athenians who fell in the battle. The top of the mound has a view of the battlefield. At the foot is a marble bas-relief, copied from the 'Warrior of Marathon'. The 'tombstones with the names of the fallen arranged according to tribes', which Pausanias (I, 32, 3) tells us were set over the Sorós, have disappeared.

Contrary to usual practice, the fallen at Marathon were buried where they fell in token of their outstanding valour. Excavations undertaken in 1890 confirmed the ancient tradition attaching to the Sorós: ashes and calcined bones, as well as small black-figured lekythoi of the early 5C, were discovered. Obsidian arrowheads found on the surface by Schliemann six years earlier, which led him to attribute a much earlier date to the mound, may have been used by the Ethiopian archers (Hdt. VII, 69). No graves have been located of the slaves, who are said to have fought for the first time at Marathon. It is probable that Pausanias was right that the Persian dead were merely flung into an open trench. For the Tomb of the Plataians, see below

The Soros road continues to the shore (Hotels A, C; cafés) where a road leads N along the beach for c 1km to the site of **Plasí**, a slight rise 100m inland, excavated in 1969–70 and again in 1979. Here are an Archaic peribolos of polygonal stones, possibly belonging to a shrine and, nearby, a settlement with chiefly prehistoric and early Iron Age finds. This may be the site of the ancient deme.

You return to the main road, where c 1.5km farther on a road forks back to the hamlet of Vraná (3km; signs to Mouseion Marathona). About 100m down this road (right), largely covered by a hangar is the **Tsépi Vraná** site, a large EH cemetery (closed) containing carefully arranged and well-built cist graves. Vases found, as well as the graves themselves, are of Cycladic type. Between here and Vrana extends NW the Avlona valley, where (2.5km) a huge walled enclosure is known from an inscription on the ruined gateway to have belonged to Herodes Atticus. At 2.5km (right) is a large tumulus (reached by path from the museum, 300m farther), excavated in 1969–70 and probably the **Tomb of the Plataians** who fell at Marathon, which Pausanias records as a separate memorial. The identification is not certain. The mound, constructed entirely of stones, contains two circles of pit graves; skeletons found were mostly of young men, and the pottery in the graves is contemporary with that in the Athenian Soros. Just N of the museum, under a large shelter, are grave circles consisting of paved slabs, each circle containing stone tombs of MH–LH date. The skeleton of a Przewalski-type horse occupies a separate tomb but this is probably a later intrusion. Another circle stands in the open.

The **museum** has five rooms. You turn right. ROOM A, Neolithic pottery from the Cave of Pan (see below). ROOM B, cases 4–5, finds from the Early Cycladic cemetery (Tsepi); case 6, from Middle Helladic tumuli (Vrana); cases 7–8, from Geometric graves. ROOM Γ, vases etc. from the Tombs of the Athenians (case 10) and Plataians (case 11); bronze cinerary urn; boundary stones and inscribed stelai. ROOM Δ, Classical grave stelai and furnishings; rare bronze mirror with wooden covers; objects from various cemeteries; Panathenaic amphorae. In the centre is part of the trophy (ionic capital etc.) erected by the Athenians (?) at Mesosportissa to celebrate the victory of Marathon. ROOM E, Hellenistic and Roman finds, including an inscription concerning Herodes Atticus, and an Egyptianising 'kouros' of 2C AD.

About 1km SE of the museum, the small chapel of **Ayios Dhimítrios** stands alone just above the foot of Agriliki; close by are the remains of an open-air precinct, c 140m square, identified in 1954 by Prof. Sotiriades with the celebrated sanctuary of Herakles (see above). On the plain, 1km from the chapel, in a small grove of low trees, is a tholos tomb (Mycenean II; locked): it yielded a gold cup, and the complete skeletons of two horses were buried beneath the dromos. Also in the vicinity of the church are the foundations of the funerary peribolos of Gyles of Probalinthos and his family.

The main road continues N past the Rhamnous turn. 42km **Marathón** (commonly Marathóna), a sprawling agricultural village. At the entrance is a marble platform with flag poles, the starting-point for annual marathon races.

FROM MARATHON TO KAPANDRÍTI, 20km (12½ miles), occasional buses to Grammatikó. Beyond Marathon the road climbs via (5km) **Ano Soúli** to (8km) **Grammatikó**.—14km. **Varnávas**, on the slope of Mavrovouni, has a Frankish tower.—20km **Kapandríti**, see Rte 22.

FROM MARATHON TO MARATHON LAKE, 8km (5 miles). A road leads W from Marathon to Marathon Lake (Rte 22), passing below the site of ancient *Oinoe*, part of whose cemetery has been excavated at Skáliza. At Oinoë in 1957 Papadimitriou discovered the **Cave of Pan and the Nymphs** of Marathon, described by Pausanias and identified by an inscription of 60 BC found in situ. The cave (no adm.) seems to have been a place of cult from Neolithic times to the end of the Bronze Age, after which it was deserted until the 5C BC. Herodotus tells of the resurgence of the worship of Pan following his aid to Pheidippides before the Battle of Marathon.

To reach **Rhamnous** you take the **Káto Soúli** road (right) at the entrance to Marathon village, and follow the foot of the hills. At 46km there is a turn (right) to **Skhoiniá**. It has a long sandy beach and has become a bungalow resort. 47km **Káto Soúli**, where (left) are vestiges of the walls (3C AD) of ancient *Trikorythos*. You cross a lonely upland valley with barren hills on either side. 51.5km Fork; to the right lies the little seaside hamlet of **Ayía Marína** (regular ferries to Néa Stíra and Almiropótamos in Euboea). You bear left and rise gradually to (58km) **Rhamnous**.

**Rhámnous** (commonly Rhamnoúnda), is one of the least spoilt sites in Attica, worth visiting as much for its romantic isolation and the beauty of its setting as for its archaeological interest. The name was derived from the prickly shrub (ῥάμνος) which still grows in the neighbourhood. In more recent times the fortress was known as Ovriókastro, a corruption of Εβραίων κάστρον (Jews' Castle).

The headland was famous as early as the 6C BC for the worship of Nemesis. Its small cove provided shelter on an otherwise inhospitable coast for ships about to pass the dangerous narrows of Ayía Marína. Later a fortress was built to watch over navigation in the Euripos. This gained importance in 412 BC after the Athenian loss of Dekelia, when Rhamnous became the port of entry for food from Euboea, since it offered the only route wholly on Attic soil that did not involve passing the narrows. Rhamnous was the birthplace of the orator Antiphon (b. 480 BC), whose school of rhetoric was attended by Thucydides. The sanctuary was first described by the Dilettanti Society in 1817; partially excavated by Staïs in 1890–94; and re-examined by A. Orlandos in 1922–23 (B C H, 1924). The fortress was described by J. Pouilloux *Le fortresse de Rhamnonte* (1954). Since 1975 extensive reinvestigation has been directed by V. Petrakos (author of *Rhamnous; a concise guide*, Athens, 1983). A small site museum is accessible only by special permission.

Nemesis was the compensating goddess, measuring out happiness and misery. She took especial care of the presumptuous, punishing 'hubris', the crime of considering oneself master of one's own destiny. She was known also by the surnames of 'Adrastia' ('inescapable') and of Rhamnousia, from her sanctuary at Rhamnous. Associated with the worship of Nemesis was Themis, the goddess who personified law, equity, and custom.

Most of the site, apart from the area of the temples, has been closed to the public for some years. The full description is here retained in the hope that access will soon be restored.

At the head of a glen is an artificial platform, 45m wide, constructed in the 5C BC of large blocks of local marble laid horizontally. Nine courses are exposed at the NE corner. The sacred precinct thus formed contains the remains of two temples, an altar, a stoa and a small fountain house. Although none of the visible remains are earlier than the 5C, both votive offerings and rooftiles of the early 6C show that there was ritual activity from that time.

The smaller **temple** (of Themis?) was built on a virgin site in the early 5C. It measures 10.7m by 6.5m and consists merely of a cella in antis with a Doric portico of two columns. The walls which stand to c 1.8m are built of large polygonal blocks of white marble. Two marble seats (casts *in situ*) dedicated to Themis and Nemesis and three statues from the cella with inscribed pedestals (found in 1890) are in Athens. The building continued in use (as a treasury/storeroom) into the 4C AD.

The first **Temple of Nemesis**, nearer the sea, was constructed at the end of the 6C BC in poros limestone as a Doric building, distyle in antis. This temple was probably destroyed by the Persians and replaced by the structure whose remains are still visible. This successor is a Doric peripteral building with six columns by twelve, the last of four sometimes ascribed to the so-called 'Theseum architect'. According to Dinsmoor, it was probably begun on the Festival Day of the Nemesieia (Boedromion 5; i.e. 30 September) 436 BC, and is known by an inscription to have been rededicated to the Empress Livia, probably by Claudius in AD 45. The interior had the usual arrangement of cella, pronaos and opisthodomos in antis. The unfinished fluting on the remaining drums of six columns (S side) suggests that the building was never completed.

Fragments both of the cult statue of Nemesis (including a colossal head, now in the British Museum) and of its base have been found. The statue (c 421 BC) was in Parian marble and the work of Agorakritos. Pausanias believed it to have been made from the very marble brought by the Persians for use as a victory monument and incorrectly attributed it to Pheidias. The base (partly reconstructed, in the museum) has carved decoration on three sides, showing Leda introducing Helen to her real mother, Nemesis.

Still within the precinct are, to the E of the temple, the foundations of an altar; to the N the scanty remains of a stoa of the 5C (34m long) which originally had wooden columns in its façade. In front of the stoa was a small fountain house, with a two-columned porch. Opposite the precinct, on the other side of the road, are the foundations of a large Hellenistic structure.

Descending the rocky glen N towards the sea (**access not permitted at present**) you reach in 10 minutes an isolated hill girdled with the picturesque enceinte (c 1km in circuit) of the ancient town. The lower part of the south gateway is well preserved, as are short portions (3.7m high in places) of the walls, in ashlar masonry of grey limestone. Nine towers of the fortress can be made out. Recent work has been done on the E gate and four others, smaller, have also been located. There is a shrine of Aphrodite by the road leading in from the E gate to a small open square. Within the town also are some remains of another **temple** and other shrines, a **gymnasium**, and an inner citadel. A sanctuary of Amphiaraos lies outside, to the NW.

Visible beside the road below the temples are the substantial remains of some of the funerary enclosures (**periboloi**—see R. Garland in BSA 77 (1982) and illustration above under Athens, Kerameikos), with which it was lined. These were topped with sculptured stelai etc. and inscriptions commemorating the dead. The line of the road can be traced back towards the entrance beyond the custodian's hut and the remains of other enclosures, less well preserved, made out.

A rough track (not recommended, but passable with a tough car) continues the line of the road by which you approached the site and comes (after 3km) to a wider but indifferent unsurfaced road which, partly utilising an abandoned mineral railway (loading installations on the coast), ascends from Grammatikó (8km; 1½ hours on foot).

# 22

# From Athens to Marathon Lake, Kálamos, and the Amphiáraion

**Road** to the Amphiáraion, 49km (30½ miles); to Marathon Lake, 31km (20¼ miles). **Buses** (9 daily) to Kálamos (45km; for the Amphiáraion) from Odhós Mavromatéon; from Kifissiá terminal, to Stamáta (bus 507); from Plateía Kánningos to Kifissiá, buses 538, 539.

From central Athens to (20km) **Ekáli**, see Rte 15. You continue N, passing the road to Dhiónisos (Rte 15). 1km beyond the Dhiónisos turn, another road leads (right) in 2km to **Stamáta** where, on the hill of **Mygdhaléza** (2km to the N) an Early Christian basilica and associated buildings were excavated in 1977. The complex, probably built in the 5C AD, like the nearby settlement, incorporated Classical masonry and inscriptions and may be on the site of the ancient deme of *Hekale*, where Theseus instituted a festival to Zeus in memory of the priestess who sheltered him on his way to fight the Bull of Marathon. *Plotheia* was also hereabouts. 22.5km **Dhrosiá** (Hotels C, D) is another upland resort.

At (24km) **Ayios Stéfanos** a road (right) leads in 9km to Marathon Lake (tourist pavilion) and on to Marathon (Rte 21).

**Marathon Lake** (in Greek **Límni Marathónos**) is an irregular sheet of water (c 243 hectares) formed by impounding the Kharadhra and Varnava torrents. It supplies some of the needs of Greater Athens, though since the Second World War its capacity has had to be augmented by artificial inflows from Parnes, the Boeotian lakes etc. The **dam**, built by the Ulen company of New York in 1925–31, at the SE end of the lake, consists of a curved concrete wall 285m long, 47m wide at the base, and 4m wide at the top. It is claimed to be the only dam in the world faced with marble. A roadway runs across. The height above the river bed is 54m, with an elevation of 227m above sea-level. At the downstream side is a marble replica of the Athenian Treasury at Delphi, which serves as an entrance to the inspection galleries.

At Ayios Stéfanos you can, after 1km, join the Athens–Thessaloniki highway, leaving it again at the Kapandríti exit. Alternatively you can take the Marathon Lake turning, then bear left almost immediately in Ayios Stéfanos, rounding the station (**Oion**) on the left and crossing the line, to continue by the old road running parallel with the highway. Seen to the left is modern **Afídhnes** (also Kioúrka), where the church of Ay. Theodoroi has 13C frescoes beneath later paintings; to the right, at the N end of Marathon Lake, beyond the new works which control the entry of waters piped from N Parnes, is a hill (Kotróni) with some ancient walls to be identified either with Classical *Aphidna* or with *Oion*.

Theseus hid Helen at *Aphidna* after carrying her off from Sparta. Her whereabouts were divulged by the inhabitants of Dekelia to her brothers, Castor and Pollux, who laid siege to Aphidna and rescued her. Aphidna was the home of Kallimachos, polemarch at Marathon.

After (36km) **Kapandríti**, where you join a road from Grammatikó (Rte 21), the pleasant road winds over tree-clothed hills to (45km) **Kálamos**, the small centre (329m) of a well-watered and wooded region above the Gulf of Euboea. A prehistoric settlement has been located at Vlastó.

The road continues to (5km farther) **Ayioi Apóstoloi** (Hotels B, C; restaurants), originally a fishing village, now a seaside resort.

From Kálamos a road descends in loops to the **Amphiáraion** (4km) in the Mavrodhilisi ravine. On foot the site can be reached in 25 minutes by the old path (difficult not to lose), shaded by pines, which crosses the road several times. The road must be followed for the last 100m as the entrance lies beyond the bridge that crosses the stream. Approach by the road is less uncertain and not unpleasant.

The **\*Amphiaraion**, or **Sanctuary of Amphiaraos**, founded in honour of the healing god, was at once an oracle and a spa. It occupies a sheltered and sunny situation, well suited to a resort of invalids, on the left bank of a wooded glen, watered by a mountain torrent. In spring anemones carpet the site.

The sanctuary (illustrated guide, *The Amphiaraion of Oropos* (1992) by V. Petrakos) commemorated the elevation to divinity of Amphiaraos, the great seer and warrior of Argos, who fought as one of the seven against Thebes. On the defeat of this expedition he fled, pursued by Periklymenos, but the earth opened and swallowed him up, together with his chariot, near Thebes. His cult was adopted by the Oropians and concentrated here near a spring famed for its healing properties. Mardonius came to consult the oracle before the battle of Plataia. Whoever wished to consult the god sacrificed a ram and lay down for the night, wrapped in its skin, in the portico allotted for the purpose, and there awaited the revelations to be made in dreams. The process of incubation (**ˊἐγκοίμησις**) was very similar to that practised in the Asklepieion. The cure did not, however, wholly depend on these miraculous communications, for there were medical baths in the precinct. After a cure, the patient had to throw gold or silver coins into the sacred spring. The excavations (1927–30) of the Greek Archaeological Service were interrupted by the death of Leonardos, the excavator. Some restoration has been effected since 1960.

Descending the path parallel to the stream, you see (right) the little **Temple of Amphiaraos**, a Doric building of the 4C, with a pronaos and a cella divided into three by parallel colonnades. The foundations, partly eroded by the stream, have been restored. The base of the cult statue is still in position. The back wall was joined by a porch (door marks in the threshold) to the priests' lodging. Ten metres from the temple is the **altar**, on which the ram was sacrificed; and below the altar the **Sacred Spring**, into which the coins were thrown. Its waters were drunk from shells, many of which have been found. Above the altar is a terrace with a line of over 30 inscribed **pedestals** of statues, mostly Roman. On a line with these are the remains of a long bench. In front is the **museum** (rarely open; enquire at entrance to site), containing numerous inscriptions, a curious early herm, torsos and, in the back court, reassembled architectural members of the temple and stoa. Beyond are the remains of the **enkoimeterion**, a long stoa, erected c 387 BC, with 41 Doric columns on the façade and divided internally into two long galleries by 17 Ionic columns. It had a small room at either end, possibly reserved for women patients. Along the walls ran marble benches, resting on claw feet, on which the patients submitted to the process of

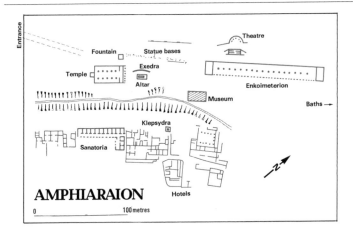

**AMPHIARAION**

0                                        100 metres

incubation. Behind the stoa is a small **theatre**, with a circular orchestra and seating for 300 spectators. Five marble **thrones** with scroll ornaments are preserved. The **proskenion** (restored) has eight Doric columns surmounted by an epistyle with a dedicatory inscription. Beyond the stoa were the **baths**. On the opposite bank of the stream are some confused remains of the accommodation provided for patients and part of a **klepsydra**, or water-clock, its bronze plug mechanism visible.

A new road continues to **Skála Oropós** (Rte 20), c 12km NW.

# 23

# Piraeus to Spétses

**Boats** from Piraeus (opposite the Dhimarkhíon) to Spétsai (Spétses) in 4–5 hrs, calling at Aíyina (1¾ hrs). Méthana (2 hrs), Póros (2½ hrs), Idhra (3¾ hrs), and Ermióni (4¾ hrs). Not every boat calls at every port. In summer 4–5 times daily to Idhra and Spétses; 10–12 times to Póros; several times per hour to Aíyina (gap between mid-morning and early afternoon). Extra services at weekends. Aíyina boats sometimes continue to Néa Epídhavros. Also (by launch) to Ayía Marína and Souvalá (Aíyina) direct.

**Express service** ('Flying Dolphin'—Hydrofoils) from Piraeus (Zea; Pl. 11), twice daily to Póros (1 hr), Idhra (1½ hr), and Ermióni (1¾ hr); 4 times to Idhra, Spétses (1¾ hr), and Pórto Khéli (2 hrs); daily to all these ports continuing to Návplio (4 hrs); also service continuing to ports on the Peloponnesian coast and/or Monemvasía (3¾ hr; see Rte 32), or to Kíthira (5 hrs) and Neápolis (5¾hrs). From the main port c 10 times daily to Aíyina in 35 minutes. Bookings may be made at Wagons-Lit Cook at 2 Karageórghi Servías (Síntagma). Routes and frequencies vary seasonally.

**By Car**. Only residents with a special permit may have cars on Spétses. However the island can be reached by driving to Kósta on the Argolic peninsula (where cars may be left by the landing-stage) and taking the ferry.

To explore the islands and the Argolic peninsula, five or six days are needed. From Póros (via Galatá), Ermióni (via Kranídhi), or Spétses (via Pórto Khéli) it is possible to reach Návplio by bus.

Within the day a round cruise (without landing) can be made to Spétses, or a superficial visit may be made to any one island; organised day trips (CHAT, etc.) briefly visit Aíyina, Póros, and Idhra.

# A.   From Piraeus to Aíyina (Aegina)

The boat passes down the centre of the **Great Harbour** of Piraeus with liner berths to the left and commercial wharves to the right. The prominent square building on the Akte peninsula is the Hadjikiriakou Orphanage. You pass between the remains of the ancient moles; from the **Outer Harbour** the W landmarks of the Akte peninsula (Rte 12) are clearly visible. The channel opens out into the Saronic Gulf (Saronikós Kólpos), the skyline of which, on a clear day, seems filled with mountains. The long islet of **Lipsokoutáli**, with naval installations, is usually taken to be the ancient *Psyttaleia*, though some recent theories about the Battle of Salamis have thrown doubt on this (Rte 18). To the W rise the scrubby hills of **Salamis**, backed by the higher peaks beyond Megara. Astern the scars of Pentelikon are prominent and the Attic coastline is visible as far as Vouliagmeni and the islet of Fleves. As you draw level with the lighthouse on the S point of Salamis, you see the sugar-loaf of Acrocorinth backed by the frequently snowy cap of Killini filling the W end of the Saronic Gulf. Ahead rises Aíyina; the temple of Aphaia can just be made out high up on the left. The boat passes E of **Eleoúsa** and heads towards the low Akr. Plakakia, the NW cape of Aíyina (lighthouse). Away to starboard appear the five Dhiaporioi Nisoi, the ancient Isles of Pelops. We turn S into the Strait of Metopi, the shallow channel that separates Aegina from **Angístri**. The jagged peaks of Méthana rise ahead to the right of Moní. A solitary column (see below) marks the promontory guarding (27km) the port of Aíyina.

**AIYINA** or **AEGINA** (Αἴγινα; the stress is on the first syllable), a triangular island of 86 sq. km, occupies the centre of the Saronic Gulf, almost equidistant from Attica and Argolis. With Angístri and the small attendant islets to the W it forms nowadays an eparchy (12, 430 inhab.) of the nome of Piraios. The sea approach is difficult because of the sunken rocks and reefs that surround it. Water is supplied by wells. Much of the W part consists of a plain which, though stony, is well cultivated with pistachio nuts and, farther S, with citrus fruits. The interior of the island is mountainous, pine-clad to the NE, and with pleasing landscapes, while at the S corner rises the magnificent conical mountain, **Oros** (531m), the finest natural feature of the island. The climate is delightful and the island is popular as a holiday area, though relatively unspoilt. The local industries include pottery: sponge-fishing was also formerly important. The two-handled porous water-jars (kanátia), common in Athens, are made here. In addition to pistachio nuts, olives, vines, almonds, and figs are cultivated.

**History**. Notwithstanding its small size, the key position of Aegina in the Saronic Gulf ensured her early importance. The name probably derives from a divinity (Hellenised as Aigaios) imported from Anatolia by Early Helladic invaders speaking a Lycian dialect, but Neolithic finds make it certain that the island was occupied as early as the end of the 4th millennium BC. About 2000 BC the inhabitants were supplanted by a Bronze Age people, probably of IndoEuropean race, speaking an Aeolian or Arcadian dialect and worshipping Poseidon. The island was an important trading centre in the Middle Helladic period. Thereafter it shares the Mycenaean culture of the mainland. Later legend tells of its only hero-king, Aiakos, son of Zeus and Aegina, who afterwards became one of the three judges of the Underworld. His sons Peleus and Telamon had to flee for the murder of their half-brother Phokos; Telamon afterwards became king of Salamis. A Dorian invasion brought the Thessalian cult of Zeus Hellanios. Aphaia seems to have been a variant of the Mother-Goddess from Crete, perhaps imported during the early Iron Age.

Possibly abandoned for two centuries before 950 BC, the island was recolonised probably from Epidauros (Herod, VIII, 46). Its infertile soil combined with its geographical situation spurred the inhabitants to maritime enterprise. At the end of the 8C it enjoyed parity with fellow members of the Kalaurian League, and was apparently no longer subject to Argos. By the 7C the Aeginetan marine was predominant in the Hellenic world. The island was noted for pottery and especially for the quality of its bronze-founding. The system of coinage introduced in Argos by Pheidon (c 656 BC) was probably borrowed from Aegina (rather than the other way about); indeed coinage very likely first reached Europe by way of the island. Its silver coins became the standard in most of the Dorian states, and in the 6C Aegina was a major centre of Greek art. Aeginetan merchants set up a temple to Zeus at the founding of Naukratis on the Nile; one, Sostratos, according to Herodotus (IV, 152) had also sailed to Spain. Their harbour was crowded with merchant ships (Thuc., V, 53) and the Aeginetan navy grew to a formidable size, exciting the jealousy of Athens. Solon's laws prohibiting the export of corn from Attica were probably directed mainly against Aegina, which henceforward, whatever its alliance, was always anti-Athenian. Aristotle calls it 'the eyesore of Piraeus' ('Rhet.', III, 10, 7); Herodotus (V, 82) adduces a mythical feud, and may be historically unreliable about the war between Athens and Aegina (? 488–481) in which the Athenians were worsted.

At Salamis (480 BC) the Aeginetans atoned for any previous homage to Persia by distinguishing themselves above all other Greeks, and the battle marked the zenith of their power. As a member of the Spartan League, Aegina was protected from attack until the reversal of Kimon's policy, when the Aeginetans were quickly defeated by the Athenians in two naval battles. In 457 BC the city was humiliated after a siege (Thuc., I, 108). At the beginning of the Peloponnesian War the Athenians expelled the inhabitants and established a cleruchy. The scattered remnants were allowed to return in 404 from their exile in Thyrea (where the Spartans had accommodated them), but Aegina never recovered from this blow. It passed with the rest of Greece to Macedon and afterwards to Attalos of Pergamon. In Byzantine times it constituted a joint bishopric with Keos. Paul of Aegina, celebrated for a treatise on medicine and surgery, was born here in the 7C AD. Saracen raids caused the inhabitants to shift the capital inland (see below) where it remained until the 19C. After 1204 the island was a personal fief of Venetian and Catalan families until, in 1451, it passed to Venice. Captured and laid waste in 1537 by Khair-ed-Din (Barbarossa), it was repopulated with Albanians. Morosini recaptured it for Venice in 1654, and it became one of the last Venetian strongholds in the E, being ceded to Turkey in 1718. In 1826–28 the city was the temporary capital of partly liberated Greece, and here the first modern Greek coins were minted. Many of the present inhabitants are descended from families who came at this time from the Peloponnese, or from refugees who fled here from Chios and Psara.

The modern town of **Aíyina** (6373 inhab.; Hotels A–E; restaurants on the quay), near the NW corner of the island, occupies part of the site of the ancient city, which extended much farther to the N. It still has buildings erected during the presidency of Capodistrias, to whose memory a statue stands in the main square. From the sea the most conspicuous features are two churches: Ayios Nikólaos, and the cathedral on the quay. The modern harbour, oval in shape and crowded with picturesque caïques, corresponds with the ancient **commercial harbour**. Its moles were rebuilt by Capodistrias on the ancient foundations. The S mole marked the S limit of the ancient city, forming an extension of its walls. The N mole bears a tiny white chapel of typical Aegean design. Beyond the N mole remains of rectangular quays of the ancient **military harbour** (Κρύπτος Λιμήν) can be seen beneath the surface of a smooth sea.

It was protected on the N by a low promontory (Kolónna; 10 minutes from the quay), which formed the citadel, fortified from Neolithic to Christian times. In the Classical period at least it was within the enceinte which was continued seaward from farther N by a breakwater. The **museum**, to the right on entry to the archaeological site, is at present (1994) closed: it suffered a serious theft in 1992. ROOM 1. Models of the prehistoric 'white house' on the Kolonna site and of a prehistoric furnace; ROOM 2. Early and Middle Bronze Age pottery, much of it resembling Cycladic; some Anatolian forms; sword and gold from an MBA grave; ROOM 3. Mycenaean pottery and figurines; ROOM 4. Marble and poros architectural fragments, sculpture and inscriptions including a boundary stone from the temenos of Apollo and Poseidon and an inscription naming the goddess Aphaia; ROOM 5. Archaic and Classical reliefs and a 5C sphinx; ROOM 6. Geometric, Archaic and Classical pottery including (in case to right) the fine Orientalising 'Ram Jug' (Odysseus and companions escaping from the Cyclops); ROOM 7. Relief with chariot; minor sculptures, bronzes, Roman lamps, altar; ROOM 8. Sculptural fragments; COURT. Various fragments of relief sculpture and architecture. Beyond the museum are the main **excavations**.

German excavations by G. Welter in 1924 beneath the temple showed remains of a building about a century earlier, below which again were late-Mycenaean houses. Work has been greatly extended W and S of the temple since 1969, with the discovery of the substantial remains of an Early–Late Helladic fortified settlement, whose remains now dominate the area. Of the **Temple of Apollo** (formerly attributed to Aphrodite), all that remains are a lone column, without its capital, from the opistho-domos, and some scanty poros foundations of polygonal masonry. The temple (Doric, 6 columns by 12), built c 520–500 BC, was superseded by a late-Roman fortress, fragments of which survive on the seaward side; the area was quarried during the rebuilding of the harbour.

To the SE a square structure of Archaic date is possibly the **Aiakeion** (shrine of Ajax). To the NW of the temple a circular structure is thought to accord with Pausanias' description of the **Tomb of Phokos**. At the end of the cape near the water, some scanty Pergamene remains are perhaps those of an **Attaleion**.

The quay has a Tourist Information Office (open only in the season). At its S end is the **Panayitsa** (1806), cathedral of the Metropolitan of Idhra, Spétses, and Aíyina. Inland from the quay is the post office and the former museum which, although closed, retains in its courtyard inscriptions, architectural fragments and reliefs.

Beyond the post office, you reach Odhós Ayíou Nikoláou which leads past the medieval **Márkelon Tower** to **Ayios Nikólaos**, a modern church. Behind this are some remains of an Early Christian basilica. A street running N leads shortly to **Kanáris' House**, once occupied by the hero of Khios. Some of the local houses are given over to the processing of sponges. In the S part of the town (Od. Aféas) is the former **orphanage**, built by Capodistrias for children orphaned by the War of Independence and, since 1854, used successively as barracks and prison and now a folk museum. Below the courtyard is an ancient catacomb.

Farther on (5 minutes) is the **Faneroméni** (18C), with the remains of a basilica over a crypt. On the coast road, opposite the cemetery is the **House of Trikoúpis**, where both Kharilaos Trikoupis (1832–96), the statesman, and Spyridion, his historian father, lived for a short period. To the left of the main road to the Temple of Aphaia and Ayía Marína (see below; bus stop Assómatos on Ayia Marina route and about a 15 minute walk, or about ¾ hr E from the town centre), is the **Omorfi Ekklesía**, a church of 1282 built of antique materials and dedicated to St Theodore. Its frescoes (somewhat later) are well preserved.

Buses and taxis to the Temple of Aphaia and elsewhere, from beyond the W end of the quay.

The principal excursion is to the Temple of Aphaia (by Ayía Marína bus). The road runs through pistachio plantations, and vineyards dotted with olive and fig trees. 6.5km **Palaiokhóra** (left), capital of the island from the 9C until 1826, was rebuilt twice after destruction by Barbarossa (1537) and by the Venetians (1654). Covering the bare hillside are the ruins of more than 20 churches and monasteries (contact guardian for access), survivors from the 13C and later, some with stone ikonostases and reasonably preserved frescoes. A ruined castle crowns the summit. Below this ghost town is a monastery containing the embalmed body of Ay. Nektários (Anastasios Kefalas; 1846–1920), Metropolitan of Pentapolis and the first saint to be canonised (1961) by the Orthodox Church in modern times. 8km **Mésagros**. From this village a road leads to the N coast and then through **Souvalá** (Hotels C, D), a pleasant fishing village with radio-active springs, back to Aíyina. At 10.5km the road bears right and climbs.

12km. The **\*Temple of Aphaía** stands on a pine-clad hill with a splendid view over the Saronic Gulf. Erected at the end of the 6C or in the early years of the 5C on the site of two earlier temples, it has been called 'the most perfectly developed of the late Archaic temples in European Hellas'. In 1956–60 fallen columns and part of their entablature were re-erected, though lightning caused damage to the SW corner in 1969.

The temple was explored in 1811, when its sculptures were removed to Munich (see below). Bavarian excavations undertaken in 1901–03 by Furtwängler in order to complete these groups proved the dedication to Aphaia, the Aeginetan equivalent of the Cretan goddess Britomartis. The shrine had previously been attributed first to Zeus Panhellenios and later to Athena. Numerous fragments were recovered (D. Öhly) in 1969 and subsequent years of the earlier Archaic temple's polychrome stonework.

You pass through the **outer peribolos wall**. To the right are remains of ritual dining rooms and the priests' quarters; three stucco baths served for purification rites. The artificial **terrace** on which the temple stands is approached by a **propylon** of the 5C, with an unusual arrangement of pilasters on the façade. To the E are the foundations of the latest **altar**, from the base of which a **ramp** rises to the **stereobate** of three steps on which the temple stands.

The **temple** is now roped off to preserve the remaining traces of the red stucco which originally covered the floors of the pronaos and cella. It is Doric peripteral hexastyle, with 12 columns on the flanks. The local lime-

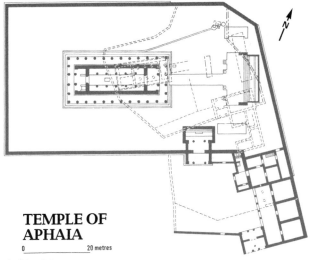

# TEMPLE OF APHAIA

0 ———————— 20 metres

after Welter and others

stone used was coated with a thin layer of stucco and painted. Of the original 32 columns, 24 now stand. They are three Doric feet in diameter at the base and axially spaced at eight feet. The corner columns are thickened for optical effect. All the shafts are monolithic, except for three adjacent columns on the N flank which are built up of drums, presumably in order to leave a gap until the last moment to facilitate the erection of the interior. The architrave is well preserved and the whole entablature has been restored at the W end of the N side by the replacement of the triglyphs, metopes, and cornice. The sekos is divided into a cella with pronaos and opisthodomos in antis. Two columns survive of the **pronaos**, which once housed figureheads of Samian triremes captured at Kydonia. Marks can be seen on the columns where the entrance was closed off with a high grille.

The **cella**, the walls of which have been partly rebuilt, was divided internally by two colonnades of five columns each; above an epistyle a second row of smaller superposed columns carried a flat ceiling. Seven of the interior columns have been restored to place with three of the upper shafts; their taper is continuous. At a later date aisle floors were put in at triforium level, approached presumably by wooden stairs. The position of the cult statue (fragment of the acrolithic arm in the National Archaeological Museum in Athens) is shown by marks in the floor where a railing stood round it. The doorway from the opisthodomos is not central and was pierced after a solid cross-wall was started.

The pedimental sculptures were of Parian marble. Seventeen statues found by Cockerell and von Hallerstein in 1811 were acquired by Ludwig I of Bavaria and, after 'restoration' by Thorvaldsen in Rome, sent to Munich, where they remain. The scenes represented two combats before Troy in the presence of Athena. Parts of a third and a fourth group (now in Athens and Aíyina museums) have since come to light; these are believed to have been deliberately removed but the reason is unknown.

At the NE corner of the terrace is a cistern which caught rainwater from the roof; it connects with a 'cave' which was built as a cistern for the Archaic temple.

To the W of the temple is the excavation house and an interesting architectural museum (not yet open to visitors) with finds from recent excavations, in particular the (painted) façade of the archaic temple.

Beyond the temple the road descends to **Ayía Marína** (Hotels A–E, most closed in winter), a resort on an attractive bay, used by cruise ships to disembark passengers for Aphaía and served in summer by launches from Piraeus. The road is being extended S to join the W coast at Pérdhika.

FROM AIYINA TO OROS (3 hrs). You take the Pérdhika road (bus), which leaves the town by the S quay and skirts the shore, and follow it as far as (6km) **Marathón**. From here a path runs inland to **Pakheiá Rákhi**. A road (unfinished) continues to **Anitsaíon**. 1.5km along the road, a track (right) leads to the church of **Taxiárkhis**, on the site of substantial Hellenistic remains. These include a great stepped road (visible from the road below) which climbs to a rectangular **terrace** supported by stepped polygonal retaining walls. From there a staircase, 7m wide, gives onto a second area with a hypostyle structure. There are two connected cisterns higher up.

From the chapel an arduous path ascends the N slope of the pyramid to the summit. **Oros** (The Mountain), known also as **Ayios Ilías** and to the ancients as *Panhellenion*, is a conspicuous landmark (531m) from all over the Saronic Gulf. The gathering of clouds on its peak is a sure sign of rain, a phenomenon noted in antiquity. Near the summit was a settlement (13C BC) whose people may have introduced the cult of Zeus Hellanios (the rainbearer) from Thessaly and which came to the violent end suffered by so many Mycenaean sites. It was reoccupied in the Geometric period. The Oros commands a splendid *view; nearly the whole island is visible, rising apparently from the midst of a vast lake encircled by an almost continuous coastline. You can return by descending to **Anitsaíon** and following the road through **Pórtes** to **Ayía Marína** on the coast. Below Pórtes, a track (left) leads to the **Panayía Khrisoleóntissa**, an isolated monastery of 1600 whose church, enlarged in 1806, has a remarkable ikonostasis.

From Marathón the road continues to (9km) **Pérdhika** (Hotels B, D), where a track leads to the S point of the island. Here stands the monastery of **Ayía Triádha**, built by Ay. Nektarios (see above). The islet of **Moní**, offshore from Pérdhika, has a camp site and tourist pavilion. That of **Angístri**, larger and with several villages and accommodation, is pleasant for bathing. Daily boats (20 minutes from Aíyina town); more frequently in summer.

# B.  From Aíyina to Póros

Leaving Aíyina, the boat heads S to pass through the Vathi Strait. To port (E) the islet of **Moní** (above) has a prominent lighthouse; to starboard (W) the tree-clad **Angístri** hides **Kíra**. Beyond Moní and the conspicuous Mt Oros, the SE coast of Attica becomes visible to the E all the way to Sounion. About 6km S of Aíyina is **Petrokáravo**, a dangerous isolated rock, used for target practice. You pass close below the terraced hillsides of **Méthana**, a peninsula connected by an isthmus less than 300m across with the mainland of the Peloponnese. The name, properly ἡ Μεθάνα, was corrupted as early as Pausanias to Τά Μέθανα.

The interior consists of the bare ridges of **Mt Khelóna** (742m), an extinct volcano.

Strabo gives an imaginative or derivative account of the seismic disturbance that gave birth to the mountain, which Pausanias places in the reign of Antigonus Gonatas. The peninsula, which was by confusion called *Methone* even in early texts of Thucydides (as Strabo mentions), was fortified by the Athenians as early as 425 BC in the Peloponnesian War. The fortifications, traces of which are visible, were strengthened during the Ptolemaic occupation (3C BC).

The little port of (44km) **Méthana** (1054 inhab.; Hotels B, C, D, E; rooms) has the usual attractions of a watering-place. The warm sulphur springs, used in the cure of rheumatic and allied affections, give the name **Vromolímni** ('stinking shore') to the village on the hillside above. **Nisáki**, a rocky islet connected by a causeway with the waterfront, is charmingly planted with pines and oleanders. Both here and on the Thrioni plateau above Vromolimni are traces of ancient walling.

A bus (occasional) follows a coastal road to Galatás, passing close to *Troezen*.
A pretty walk (or road) leads via (40 minutes) **Stenó** on the isthmus to the W slope of the peninsula where, below the village of **Megalokhóri**, are (2½ hrs) the remains of the acropolis of ancient *Methana*. The *view from **Kaïméni Khóra** ('the burnt village'; 45 minutes farther) is delightful: across the Bay of Methana the majestic Mt Ortholithi (1114m) and Mt Arachnaion (887m) rise sheer from the water. The crater is 30 mins. further. Above the village is an ancient tower. The tiny chapel of the **Panayía Krasáta**, on the W point of the peninsula, was erected by a wine merchant saved from shipwreck; wine is said to have been used to mix the mortar. The W branch of the road, towards Kounoupítsa has fine views to the N and W.

The boat enters the narrow right-angled strait dividing Poros from Troezenia and in 2½ hrs from Piraeus reaches the town and port of (51.5km) Poros.

**PÓROS**, an island about 10km long from E to W, is separated from the mainland by a strait (350m across at its narrowest; ferry). The name (πόρος) means both strait and ferry. The island was known in antiquity as *Kalauria*, and was the headquarters of the Kalaurian League. The interior is occupied by low rocky hills wooded with pines. The scenery and climate are delightful and the island is a favourite summer resort of the Athenians.

**History**. The **Kalaurian League** was a historically shadowy maritime confederation, formed c 7C BC under the aegis of Poseidon. Its members included Athens, Aegina, Epidauros, Troezen, Hermione, Nauplia, and Prasiai (in Attica), together with Boeotian Orchomenos. Under the Turks Poros was practically independent. Here in 1828 were held the conferences of the British, French, and Russian plenipotentiaries entrusted with the task of settling the basis of the Greek kingdom (**Protocol of Poros**). In 1831 the independent islanders, under the leadership of Idhra, took up an attitude of open hostility to the arbitrary government of Capodistrias and established a 'Constitutional Committee'. The national fleet of Greece, including the frigate *Hellas* (flagship) and the steamship *Karteria*, lay in Poros harbour. Capodistrias gave orders for this to be made ready for sea, but Admiral Miaoulis, acting under the orders of the Hydriot government, seized the fleet and the arsenal. On 13 August 1831, Miaoulis, rather than hand over the fleet to the Russian Admiral Ricord, blew up the flagship *Hellas* and the corvette *Hydra*.

The town of **Póros** (3273 inhab.; Hotels, B, C, E) lies on the strait, opposite the village of Galatá on the Peloponnesian coast. The small volcanic peninsula on which it is built was once the island of *Sphaeria*, named after Sphaeros, the charioteer of Pelops. A low isthmus and bridge now join it to the island. The first naval arsenal of independent Greece was established here in 1830 and survived until 1877, when it was closed in favour of Salamis. The buildings now house the **Petty Officers' Naval Training School** (Κέντρον Εκπαιδεύσεως Ναυτοπαίδων), the Greek Dartmouth. On the shore stands an obelisk to the memory of Frank Abney Hastings, buried in Poros. The island is the summer base of the reconstructed ancient trireme *Olympias* (tests and occasional open day). There is a small archaeological and historical **museum** (08.45–18.00, except Sun 09.30–14.30; closed Mon) with material from the island (*Kalauria*) and adjacent mainland (chiefly *Troizen*).

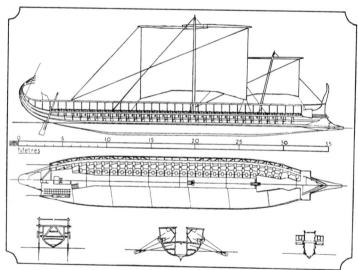

*General arrangement of the reconstructed trireme*

The view across the strait, with its busy small boats, is delightful: Galatá (see below) is backed by a long range of green hills. To the left is the **Lemonodhásos**, a picturesque spot where lemon groves grow amidst water-mills. The conspicuous fort above was built by forced labour during the German occupation.

From the quay the short road continues beyond the Naval School (see above), crosses the causeway, and follows the coast to the E, passing (2.5km) several summer seaside hotels. 4km The **Monastery of Zoödhókhos Piyí** is beautifully situated in a verdant glen above the Sirene Hotel (B), where there is a beach and tavernas (bus).

Before the monastery a new road encircling the heights to the E mounts through the pinewoods to the plateau of **Palátia**, where the ruins of the **Sanctuary of Poseidon** are picturesquely situated in a saddle between the highest hills of the island, c 550m above the sea (*view). The ancient city of *Kalauria* was situated near by, and the sanctuary was the headquarters of the Kalaurian League. Excavations in 1894 by the Swedish archaeologists Wide and Kjellberg showed that the entire precinct was built in the 6C BC on the site of a sanctuary that dates back to Mycenaean times. The scanty remains of the **Temple of Poseidon** show it to have been a Doric peripteral hexastyle (6 by 12 columns), built of blueish limestone. Here Demosthenes, seeking sanctuary in 322 BC, was cornered by Antipater's emissaries and took poison. The inhabitants buried him with honour in the precinct and Pausanias saw his grave. To the SW of the temple four **stoas** formed a quadrangular precinct.

The summit of the island (*views) is reached by turning left onto the road outside the sanctuary. A further left turn (motorable track) as the road bends leads to a watchtower on the summit.

## FROM PÓROS TO TROEZÉN (AND NÁVPLIO). Ferry in 5 minutes to

Galatás (Hotels B, C, D) on the mainland; then **road** (level walking but little shade; bus, see below) and by-road to (9km) (**Troezén**; pron. Trízina; formerly Dhamalá).

Buses twice daily to **Troizen**, several other services pass (6.5km) **Ayios Yeóryios** on their way to Methana, Lesia, etc., making it possible with a little planning to ride most of the way in both directions. An alternative is to take a small boat to (1 hour) Kelenderis, the ancient mole of Troizen in the Bay of Vidhi, and to walk from there to Troizen in 40 minutes. Daily buses continue beyond Ayios Yeoryios, via (22km) **Dhrióp**i, and (41km) **Trakheiá**, to (60km) **Ligourió** (Rte 29), passing close to the Hieron of Epidauros, and then to (85km) **Návplio**.

The road runs W, soon leaving the coast and passing through orange and lemon groves. At 4km a rough mule path (left), though shorter, is little quicker. Near the beginning of (6.5km) **Ayios Yeóryios** a by-road ascends to (9km) **Trízina** (refreshments), a village lying below the N shope of **Mt Aderes** (719m), the ancient *Phorbantion*. It occupies part of the site of *Troezen* (Τροιζήν), the ancient capital of the small and fertile territory of Troezenia. To the S between the deep ravines of Ayios Athanásios (E) and the Yefíri (W) rises an isolated hill (313m; view), on which a Frankish tower marks the site of the acropolis. The principal ancient ruins, however, lie to the W of the village.

*Troezen* appears early in legend as the birthplace of Theseus. It was here that Poseidon made the horses of Hippolytos, his son, to take fright and drag their master to his death. Orestes was purified at Troezen after his matricide. In 480 BC when the Persians occupied Athens, the Troezenians gave hospitality to Athenian refugees. The famous stele detailing Themistocles' plan of evacuation was found here. The Athenians captured the city in 457–446. In the Peloponnesian War the Troezenians sided with Sparta. Their city was a member of the Kalaurian League. The Franks established a barony and a bishopric here. The Third Greek National Assembly, at which Capo-distrias, the Corfiot foreign minister of Russia, was elected President of Greece, was held at Troizen, in March 1827. In May of that year, the **Constitution of Troezen**, usually known as the charter of the liberties of Greece, was published, though it was put into immediate abeyance at the time. This was the third of the 'constitutions', the others being those of Epidauros (1821) and of Astros (1823).

The proverbial expression 'a bishop of Damala', signifying one whose cupidity has made him overreach himself, springs from the story commemorated in local song of a medieval bishop surprised by a Barbary corsair and sold into slavery while trying to catch fish bigger than some which had been presented to him.

The scanty but scattered remains (sign in village), exposed by the French School in 1890 and 1899 and re-examined by the German Institute in 1932, lie near three ruined Byzantine chapels incorporating ancient fragments. You come first to the so-called **Theseus Stone**, then (left fork; 10 minutes) to the remains of the city walls with a fine **tower**, 13m square and 10m high, with a postern and a staircase. The lower half is ancient, the upper medieval. From here there is a path along the course of an ancient aqueduct to the gorge of Yefiraíon, spanned by the picturesque single-arched **Devil's Bridge** (Yéfira tou Dhiavólou). The surroundings are cool and pleasant and it is possible to swim.

Of the other remains the most interesting (15 minutes W of the tower; right fork at the Theseus Stone) is a building c 30m square, consisting of a colonnaded court surrounded by rooms and, on the W side, a hall with benches and a channelled floor. This has been identified by Welter as an **enkoimeterion** and the building may therefore be an **Asklepieion**. Beyond this, the deserted **Palaiá Episkopí**, or bishop's palace (or church), is perhaps the site of the **Temple of Aphrodite Kataskopia** ('Peeping Aphrodite'). Pausanias records such a temple built on the spot where the amorous Phaedra used to watch Hippolytos at his manly exercises; their graves were in its precinct.

From **Galatás** a road, with good views to **Idhra**, leads in 41km to **Ermióni** (Rte 23D). Inland of (30km) **Thermísia** is a 14C fort built by Walter of Brionne.

# C.  Ídhra (Hydra)

From Poros the boat heads SE. The Strait of Poros is guarded at the E end by the tiny island of **Boúrdzi**, where there are conspicuous remains of a medieval fortress; then rounds **Cape Skilli**, the ancient Skyllaeon, off which lie the rocky Tselevínia. Ahead extends Idhra, separated from the Argolic peninsula by the sea of Ermione (Ermionis Thalassa).

**ÍDHRA** or **HYDRA**, the ancient *Hydrea*, is a long narrow island, with inhospitable shores, largely barren of vegetation and short of water. Everywhere mountainous, it rises to 590m in Mt Klimaki. The island, with the islet of Dhokós, near which an Early Bronze Age wreck has been investigated, constitutes an eparchy of the nome of Piraios, most of its 2387 inhabitants are concentrated in its only town. There are no motor vehicles. Since its discovery as a location for film-making, the island has become a fashionable artists' colony and retreat of intellectuals and has attracted also a less orthodox fringe. In season the level of tourism can be oppressive. An international puppet festival has been held in July in recent years.

In antiquity *Hydrea* belonged to the inhabitants of Hermione, who sold it to Samian exiles. They gave it in trust to the Troezenians whilst they went on to Crete. During the centuries of Turkish rule, enterprising refugees from Albania and the Peloponnese settled in Hydra to escape the exactions of the Turkish governors. The Hydriots became practically self-governing, paying no taxes but supplying sailors for the Turkish fleet. Their mercantile marine flourished, carrying corn to France through the British blockade of the French Revolutionary wars, and by 1821 the island had a population of 40,000 and a fleet of 150 merchantmen. After a month's vacillation in 1821, they threw themselves heart and soul into the War of Independence, merchant families, notably that of Koundhouriotis, converting their trading vessels at their own expense into men-of-war. Among the many Hydriot naval commanders of the war were Tombazis, Tsamadhos, Voulgaris, and Miaoulis, the commander-in-chief. Among their famous descendants are Admiral Paul Koundhouriotis (1855–1935), hero of the war of 1912, later regent and president of Greece, and Demetrios Voulgaris (1802–77), prime minister in 1855. The islanders, however, never recovered from their patriotic efforts in the War of Independence and the commercial centre moved to Syros. A staple 'industry' used to be fishing for sponges off the North African coast; tourism has now become the main source of income.

72km. The town of **Ídhra** (2279 inhab.; Hotels A, B, C, D; accommodation always difficult; rooms must often be sought in private houses), which is hidden until the last moment on approach from the sea, rises in an amphitheatre on the slopes of the steep hills that enclose its deep natural harbour. Its character is formed by the imposing mansions, built in the late 18C for the great Hydriot families by Venetian and Genoese architects. They are unusual in Greek island architecture for their individuality, their size, and their sloping tiled roofs. Many retain their ancient doors of cypress and are gaily colour washed. The **Houses of George Koundhouriotis** and **Lazaros Koundhouriotis**, both with relics of the war of 1821–28, are shown on application, by courtesy of family descendants. A Merchant Navy Training School occupies the **House of Tsamadhos**; adjacent is a small **museum** of Hydriot archives. The **House of Tombazis** shelters an international hostel for artists run by the Athens School of Fine Arts. The 17C conventual **Church of the Dormition of the Virgin** (Koimísis Theotókou) has a notable screen; the monastic cells are occupied as municipal offices. Narrow lanes succeeded by paths lead upward past **Ayios Ioánnis**, a church with 18C frescoes, to (1 hour) the twin convents of **Ayía Efpraxía** (nuns) and **Profítis Ilías** (monks) just below the summit (595m) dominating the town.

To the E of the town a coast path leads in 40 minutes via the village of **Mandráki** (Hotel A, closed in winter), with a deserted naval boatyard, to the dying monastery of **Ayía Triádha** (1704). At the E end of the island (2 hrs more) is the more flourishing **Monastery of Zourvas** (43 monks).

To the W of the town a path follows the N shore to (¾ hr) **Kamíni**, where on Good Friday the epitaphios is borne in procession into the sea. The path continues to (½ hr) **Vlíkhos**. A few poor and stony beaches break the rocky inaccessibility of the coast (bathers do better to hire a boat). A medieval bridge and some offshore islets provide points of interest on the way to (1½ hrs) **Mólo**. At (2½ hrs) **Episkopí**, on a plateau, scanty Byzantine remains have been found.

# D.   From Ídhra to Spétses

From Idhra some boats turn along the N coast of the island and pass directly through the Petassi Strait, which separates it from Dhokos (see below), to Spetses (96km). Others cross first to (88.5km) **Ermióni** (Hotels B, D, E), c 19km W on the mainland where **Petrothálassa**, **Plépi**, and **Saládhi** on the neighbouring coast have huge holiday hotels. The little town (2334 inhab.) stands at the base of a spit of land, which separates the two excellent natural anchorages that gave to *Hermione* its ancient importance. On the promontory, which has been laid out as a park, are some foundations of a **Temple of Poseidon**. A mosaic exposed near the school belonged to a complex of Early Christian buildings dependent upon a **basilica** of the 6C.

A chasm in the neighbourhood was supposed in ancient times to be a short cut to Hades, avoiding the Styx. The frugal Hermionians accordingly put no passage-money in the mouths of their dead.

S of Ermióni is the monastery of **Ayioi Anargyroi** whose church and fine frescoes may be 16C.

Buses connect Ermióni with **Galatás** (Rte 23B) and with **Kranídhi** (Rte 29).

From Ermióni the boat passes between the sparsely populated island of **Dhokós** and the promontory of **Mouzáki** which protects Ermióni on the S. To the S of Dhokós lies the island of **Trikéri**. Rounding Cape Milianos (*Kolyergia*; remains of a temple and a tomb), you drop anchor at Spétses, capital of the island of the same name.

**SPÉTSES**, a small oval island 6.5km long with 3603 inhabitants, comes directly under the eparchy of Piraios. The central ridge of the attractive and healthy island rises gently to 291m. Spétses, the ancient *Pityoussa*, or pine tree island, was the first of the archipelago to revolt from the Turks in April 1821, and her sailors distinguished themselves in the war by their ferocity. The anniversary of the naval engagement of 8 September 1822, when Spetsiot brigs and fireships repelled a superior Ottoman force, is celebrated by a regatta.

The clean and tastefully built town of Spétses (Hotels A–E) is a fashionable resort, favoured by the Athenians in summer. Transport is provided by carriage or donkey. The **Dapia**, or fortified point, just by the jetty, is a historic small square where the main cannon battery was deployed. Cannon still decorate its walls. It now forms the modern Plateia, with many cafés. Here the rising of 1821 was planned. The port offices on the right occupy the Chancellery of the time. The family mansion of Hadzi-Yiannis Mexis, the first Archon of Spetses, houses a **museum** of relics of the war, including a casket containing the bones of Bouboulina, local heroine of the struggle. The house in which she lived is behind the Dapia. The he four churches of the town are interesting. The bishop's seat, once in the church of the **Assumption**, is now in **Ayios Nikólaos**: during the revolution the church was monastic, and Napoleon's brother Paul occupied one of its cells. Outside the town is the **Anargírios and Koryialénios School of Spetses**, founded in 1927 but now closed. This Greek 'public school' was organised on English lines. The island was once the home of John Fowles and inspired the setting of *The Magus*.

To the E of the town the old harbour of **Limáni** is closed by a promontory, on which stands the little chapel of **Panayía Armádhas**, built to commemorate a naval victory over the Turks in 1822. Farther on is the nunnery of **Ayioi Pándes**. The beach of **Ayía Paraskeví**, on the S side of the island, is the scene on 26 July of a panegyric. **Ayioi Anárgyroi** beach, a short distance to the E, can be reached by bus or boat.

**Spetsopoúla**, a small island off the SE coast of Spetsai, belongs to Stavros Niarkhos, the shipowner.

**Ferry and motor boats** to Kósta and Portokhéli on the Peloponnesian coast, whence buses to Kranídhi and Návplio. In summer boats also to Návplio; excursions to Monemvasía; tour of the island by boat in 2½ hrs.

# 24

# Athens to Corinth (Kórinthos)

The **Athens–Corinth Toll Highway** replaces much of the older road which mostly follows the course of the railway. The new road is straighter and more level and avoids level-crossings (a notorious hazard before); but with the dangers have also gone the charming proximity to the sea. The narrow bends of the Kakí Skála (see below) no longer need to be negotiated. Here is described the **Old Road**.

**Road**, 81km (50½ miles) 23km **Elefsís**. Fork left beyond the town.—42km **Mégara**.—63km **Ayioi Theódhoroi**.—75km **Corinth Canal**.—81km **Corinth**.

**Buses** every 30 minutes from 100 Od. Kifissoú.

**Railway** (SPAP). 91km (56½ miles). 9 trains daily in c 2 hours.

From Athens to (23km) Elefsís, see Rte 16. Beyond the town you bear left from the Thebes road (Rte 41), pass large ammunition factories, and reach the shore. The **Trikérato**, the jagged SE end of the Pateras range (known in ancient times as Kerata, 'Horns') formed the ancient boundary between Attica and Megaris. It ends in a small cape, below which are the Elefsis shipyards. The road crosses the cape and continues en corniche with fine views across the landlocked bay to Salamis.

29km **Loutrópirgos** (Hotel D) is a pleasant resort with villas. 31km **Megálo Pévko**. 35km **Néa Péramos** (6868 inhab. Hotel C) founded as a refugee settlement, has artillery and commando schools. The road now crosses the fertile **Plain of Megaris**, planted with vines and olives. 42km **Mégara** can be by-passed, but its twin hills are seen to the right.

**Mégara**, chief town of the eparchy of Megaris, with 20,403 inhabitants, rises on the slopes of two moderate hills, **Karia** (E, 270m) and **Alkathoös** (W, 287m). These heights, the twin citadels of the ancient city, are reached by turning right off Od. 28 Oktomvríou, just before the railway station, and ascending Od. Khr. Moraíti which passes through Plateía Iróön, overlying part of the site of the agora. The street plan of the town reflects its ancient state. Of the many buildings described by Pausanias (I, 39–44), only the **Fountain of Theagenes** survives, above and to the right of Plateía Iroön, in Od. Krínis. It was cleared in 1958; the large reservoir had a roof supported on columns. On the slopes of Alkathoös are fragments of a Temple of Athena built into one of several interesting churches. Numerous traces of Megara's past have been discovered in rescue excavations—including a section of the 4C city wall, with towers, on the S side of the town, near the Agricultural Co-operative (Γεωργικός Συνεταιρισμός) and before the railway station (Od. 28 Oktomvríou). A Hellenistic workshop and two cellars with pillars, characteristic of the houses of ancient Mégara, can be seen in the grounds of the High School (Yimnásion)—but little of note is visible. Many ancient blocks are built into chapels and houses, which are still constructed of the white mussel-stone mentioned by Pausanias. Underground chambers are a feature of the ancient houses here. There is an archaeological collection on the W side of the town (not open) and a new museum is projected.

A lively and colourful fair is held on Easter Tuesday on the open space NW of the town, near the chapel of Ayios Ioánnis. The traditional dance ('trata': seinenet) is performed.

**History**. Though the Homeric catalogue treats Attica and Megaris as a whole, in the Geometric period *Megara* was independent. Her woollen industry prospered and she planted colonies as far W as Megara Hyblaea (728 BC) and as far E as Selymbria, Chalcedon, and Byzantium, founded according to tradition by Byzas c 660. About 640 BC Theagenes, a popular leader, made himself tyrant. Rivalry with Athens for possession of Salamis led to strife with Kylon, his son-in-law, and the island fell c 570 to Peisistratos. Possibly about the same time Perachora was finally lost to Corinth. The invasion of Megaris by Mardonius marked the W limit of the Persian advance; 3000 Megarians fought at Plataia. In 461, menaced by Corinth, Megara formed a short-lived alliance with the Athenians, who built long walls to protect her access to the port, Nisaea. She soon reversed her policy, encroached on sacred Eleusinian land, and murdered an Athenian envoy. Pericles' decree of 432, excluding Megarians from Attic markets and harbours, was one of the prime causes of the Peloponnesian War. During the war the Athenians invaded Megaris twice yearly until in 427 Nikias seized Minoa, then an island connected to the mainland by a causeway, and established a close blockade not a mile from the city. Though the acropolis of Nisaea and the long walls fell in 424, the city itself was never taken. It has never been of much importance since, Pausanias remarking of the Megarians that 'they were the only Greek people whom even the Emperor Hadrian could not make to thrive'. Their fortifications nevertheless survived to be repaired in the 5C AD.

Megara was the birthplace of Theognis (c 570–485), the elegiac poet, and of the sophist Eukleides (450–380), a disciple of Socrates, who founded the Megarian School of philosophy.

The well, still in use, 15 minutes N of the town, must be the **Fountain of the Sithnidian Nymphs**. The chapel of **Ayios Nikólaos**, at the seaward end of Odhos Pákhi, marks the site of the ancient harbour of *Nisaea*. **Palaiókastro**, bearing a Venetian tower, to the W, may represent the acropolis of Nisaea; the hill of **Ayios Yeóryios** (chapel), to the E, with ancient walls, is probably *Minoa*, though some authorities have sought to place this farther E beyond the modern harbour of **Pákhi** (tavernas).

A road crosses the isthmus to (16km) **Alepokhóri** on the Bay of Aigósthena. At 2.5km a turning to the left leads to the monastery of **Ayios Hierótheos** (3.5km after a further left fork), where the church of the **Panayía Kyparissiótissa** (one-aisled) has recently-cleaned frescoes in the dome. At Alepokhóri there are impressive remains of *Pagai*, a fort held by the Athenians in 459–445 BC. The track from here to Aigósthena (Rte 41) provides a strenuous but rewarding walk.

From Mégara a road across Yeráneia to Loutráki was constructed during the German occupation. This follows the line of an ancient road (visible in places) but is itself now derelict. From the saddle between the gulfs there is a magnificent *view.

Beyond Mégara the **Yerania Mountains** (Γεράνεια Ορη; 1370m), the forest-clad range which stretches from the Gulf of Alkionídhon to the Saronic Gulf, forms a natural barrier between Central Greece and the Peloponnese. The road at first runs high above the sea, with a panoramic *view of the Saronic Gulf. From the Malouris Petra (near the 48th km post) Ino leapt into the sea with Melikertes.

At **Mármara**, 260m above sea level and 1½–2 hour walk W of Mégara are the remains of a sanctuary of Zeus Aptesios (B.C.H. 1983). The road descends almost to sea-level by the Kakí Skála (Κακή Σκάλα; 'Evil Staircase'), a narrow tortuous pass under the vertical cliffs. Above tower the **Skirónidhes Pétres** or Skironian Rocks.

In antiquity the road occupied a ledge high up the cliff. The Megarians attributed its construction to their polemarch, Skiros, one of the first settlers in Salamis. The Athenians told of Skiron, a robber who, after despoiling travellers, kicked them into the sea to be eaten by a turtle; he met a like fate at the hand of Theseus. Hadrian made the road passable for chariots, but the route was as dangerous as ever in the 19C. It could always be blocked in time of emergency. The Peloponnesians obstructed it on receiving news of Thermopylae; a section was blown up in the War of Independence.

The road enters a little plain that backs the sandy coast (bathing). 63km **Ayioi Theódhoroi** (Hotels A, B, C, D) is noted for its crystallised fruits. The district of **Mulki** occupies the site of *Krommyon* (fl. 8C–3C BC), where Theseus slew the wild sow. Out in the gulf lies **Evraionísi**, an islet fortified by the Franks.

You now cross the Plain of Sousaki, marred by oil refineries but with good views of the Peloponnesian mountains ahead: prominent in the foreground, the jagged N face of the Onia Mountains and the sugar-loaf of Acrocorinth; in the distance the great cone of Killini. The **Isthmus of Corinth**, a low, flat, and barren tract of limestone, less than 100m at its highest point, connects the Peloponnese with the rest of Greece. It is 16km long and barely 6.5km wide at its narrowest point. 73km **Kalamáki**, a little port (ferry to Isthmia; Rte 25C), on the site of ancient *Schoinous*, lies 1km to the left at the entrance to the Corinth Canal. Soon after the turn the old road joins the main highway just beyond the toll point. You then pass the turning to Loutráki and Perakhóra (Rte 25F), and cross the **\*Corinth Canal** on a bridge only 33m long but over 60m above the water. The bridge was doubled in 1974 by the addition to the E of a similar structure supplied by a Stockport company. The railway bridge is close to the right.

The ancients used to drag small ships across the Isthmus by the Diolkos (Rte 25D), but the idea of piercing a canal dates at least from the time of Periander, and was periodically revived by Greek and Roman rulers. Caligula had the isthmus surveyed and Nero actually started operations in AD 67, using 6000 Jewish prisoners sent by Vespasian from Judaea. The work was stopped by the insurrection of Vindex in Gaul. Its traces, investigated by the French School (B.C.H. 1884), were obliterated by the building of the modern canal in 1882–93.

This is nearly 6.5km long, 25m wide, and 8m deep. It is protected at each end by breakwaters, those at the W end 240m long, enclosing the port of **Poseidonia**. The central part of the canal runs in a cutting through the rock, 87m deep. It is quite straight and there are no locks. A current of 1–3 knots necessitates a cautious passage. The canal can accommodate comparatively large vessels, and shortens the distance from Piraeus to Brindisi by c 320km. German parachutists captured the bridges over the canal on 26 April 1941, thus severing communications between the retiring British forces.

The new road to Epidauros (Rte 25C) diverges left. At the top of a low rise the Bay of Corinth comes into view with the W end of the canal, Loutráki, and the heights of Perakhóra. You fork right for (81km) Corinth (Rte 25). Those bound direct for Ancient Corinth can bypass the modern town by continuing on the Highway for a further 5km and taking a signposted turn before the next toll-point.

# III THE PELOPONNESE

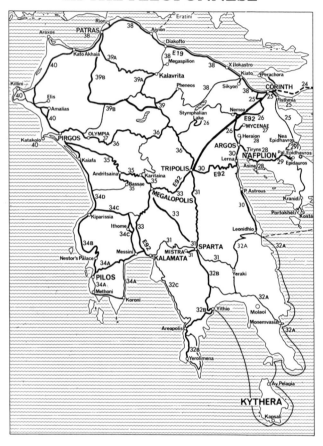

The **PELOPONNESE**, or **Pelopónnisos**, forms the S extremity of the Balkan peninsula. Joined to the mainland of Greece by an insignificant isthmus, it was known to the ancients as the Island of Pelops (ἡ Πελοπόννησος); its medieval name, The Morea, was probably derived not from a fanciful likeness to the leaf of the mulberry-tree (μόρον), which it does not resemble in the least, but from the fact that the mulberry flourished in the country. The modern division into the seven nomes of Argolis (E), Corinthia (NE), Achaea (N), Elis (NW), Messenia (SW), Laconia (SE), and Arcadia (inland, N centre) roughly corresponds to the ancient regional division. The largest towns are Patras and Kalamata. The scenery of the Peloponnese combines beauty and grandeur and its archaeological interest is unsurpassed.

The N coast, ending in **Cape Dhrepanon**, opposite Navpaktos, is separated from the mainland of Greece proper by the long narrow Gulf of Corinth, and is comparatively free from indentations. To the S the peninsula sends out the three long tongues of land, separated by the Messenian and

Laconian Gulfs, which give it a distinctive shape. These end (from W to E) in **Cape Gallo** (the ancient Akritas), fringed by the Oenoussae Islands: in **Cape Matapan** (Tainaron), the southernmost point of continental Greece: and in **Cape Malea**, off which lie the islands of Elaphonisi, Kythera, and Antikythera. A fourth but less obtrusive tongue, fringed with islands and ending in **Cape Skilli** (Skyllaion), stretches SE between the Gulf of Navplion and the Saronic Gulf. Off the NW coast lie the Ionian islands of Zante and Kephalonia. The maximum length of the peninsula is 212km (from Cape Dhrepanon to Cape Matapan); its greatest width is 216km, but road distances tend to be longer both in distance and time than this might indicate, owing to the terrain. The new highway from Corinth to Tripolis has greatly reduced travelling time to the central Peloponnese.

An irregular series of mountains, encircling Arcadia, forms the backbone of the country, with articulations almost reaching to the sea in all directions. The highest peaks of this central group are **Zereia** (the ancient Kyllene; 2378m), **Aroania** or Chelmos (2355m), and **Olonos** or Erymanthos (2224m). These form a natural barrier across the peninsula from E to W. To the N of Erymanthos **Mt Voïdia** or Panakhaïkon (1929m) rises above Patras. Two important chains run S from the Arcadian group. The long range of **Taiyetos**, with **Ayios Ilias**, the highest mountain in the Peloponnese (2408m) separates the Messenian Plain from the Laconian Valley and ends in Cape Matapan. The parallel chain of **Parnon** (1940m), continuing the E mountain wall of Arcadia (culminating in **Artemision**, 1772m), closes the Laconian Valley on the E, reaches to Cape Malea, and reappears in the hills of Kythera.

Practically the only low-lying portions are the isthmus and shores of the Bay of Corinth; the coastal district of Achaia and Elis from Patras to Pirgos, with the vale of Olympia; and the plains or valleys of Messenia, Laconia, and Argos, at the head respectively of the Gulfs of Korone, Laconia, and Navplion. A feature of Arcadia is the bleak Plain of Tripolis, lying 610m above the sea. The vale of Olympia is watered by the **Alpheios**, the longest and most famous river in the peninsula; the Messenian Plain by the **Pirnatsa** or Pamisos, the most copious; the Valley of Laconia by the **Eurotas**; and the Argolic Plain by the seasonal **Panitsa** or Inachos. The **Elean Peneios** flows into the Channel of Zante. The whole of the N coast is seared by small torrents, generally dry but occasionally sweeping the road into the sea. A feature of the plateaux of the interior is the number of *katavóthrai* (καταβόθραι), swallow-holes into which the rivers disappear underground; they are common in Arcadia. The only natural lakes are **Pheneos** and **Stymphalos**, both now virtually dry, but there are hydroelectric reservoirs behind the Peneios and Ladon dams.

**Communications** in the main are excellent and the major sites can be toured with ease and comfort, either by public transport or by organised coach tour. The 4–5 day tours (from Athens) allow those with limited time (or inclination) to see more than would otherwise be possible by private car. The Argolid is readily accessible by train as also is Olympia (via Patras): the Arkadian route between Corinth and Kalamata is particularly attractive. Intending visitors to the SW can conveniently fly direct to Kalamata. The new road from Corinth to Tripolis allows fast access to the heart of the Peloponnese. In spite of these facilities for swift travel, longer periods spent exploring remoter areas and their antiquities bring commensurate rewards.

**History.** The Peloponnese was inhabited at least as early as the Mesolithic period (Franchthi Cave, 11th millennium BC). The population increased in Neolithic and Early Helladic times (3rd millennium BC), but neither archaeology nor tradition gives certain indications of the origin or language of its people. From them perhaps come the non-Hellenic place-names ending in ινθος-, -οσος, and -ηνη (e.g. Corinth,

Mycenae). They were probably of Asiatic origin. Their implements were of stone, then copper, and later of bronze. Their existence is probably mirrored in the legendary Pelasgoi of Herodotus. Remains of typical Early Helladic sites can be seen at Zygouries and Lerna.

Towards the end of the 3rd millennium, in Early Helladic III, a violent upheaval may mark the arrival of new racial groups, of Indo-European stock, possibly the first Greek-speaking people, since their culture develops without a break into the Mycenaean civilisation, which is now known to have written records in Greek. The following Middle Helladic period had a characteristic wheel-made grey monochrome pottery ('Minyan') and developed another ware with matt-painted decoration. Their houses were small, with a characteristic horseshoe plan, with a hearth in the centre of the largest room and an open porch; the scheme is the prototype of the later megaron. Their dead were buried (originally without or with few offerings) in a contracted position in cist graves. Their traditions survive in the hero legends of Perseus, Herakles, etc. Middle Helladic remains have been excavated at Lerna, Asine, and Mycenae. The contents of Grave Circle B, now in Athens, give a good idea of the art of the end of this period of development (c 1550 BC). Thereafter the mainland becomes influenced by Middle Minoan civilisation, though utilising Cretan ideas in an individual way.

Rapid development marks the Late Helladic period—the widespread civilisation known to Homer as Achaean and to us as Mycenaean because both archaeology and tradition confirm that its focus was at Mycenae. The other main centres of the Peloponnese were at Argos and Pylos. No danger seems to have threatened from abroad, quite the reverse if the references to marauders from Ahhiyawa (found on the Hittite tablets) indeed refer to the activities of the Achaeans in Asia Minor.

A wave of Greek-speaking people from the N, the so-called Dorian Invasion, brought widespread destruction to the Peloponnese. Classical historians attributed this break to the return of the Herakleidai, descendants of an earlier Mycenaean dynasty (which included Herakles) exiled by the Pelopid rulers of Mycenae before the Trojan War. This was a political upheaval of a very violent kind which put back civilisation several centuries, but cultural and racial continuity was evidently not affected for Attica seems not to have been occupied by the Dorians and is neither less nor more Greek than the Peloponnese. Arcadia is said never to have been subordinated to either Achaeans or Dorians. The dispossessed Achaeans supposedly resettled in the N in the area which perpetuates their name to the present day.

The recovery of the Peloponnese is associated with the change from the Bronze to the Iron Age, and the slow development of new technology and more sophisticated arts. Argos was particularly important at this stage.

The early recorded history of the Peloponnese deals with the rise of Sparta (Rte 31). From 337 BC when the Synedrion of Corinth confirmed Philip of Macedon as leader of the Greek world, the historical centre of the Peloponnese becomes Corinth (Rte 25A). After the sack of Corinth in 146 BC, the peninsula formed part of the Roman senatorial province of **Achaea**; this was temporarily joined in AD 15–44 to Macedonia.

The Peloponnese was ravaged in AD 267 and 395 by the Goths and by Alaric. Placed by the Constantinian reorganisation in the diocese of Macedonia, the province enjoyed (alone of Eastern provinces) proconsular rank. Ecclesiastically it remained subject to Rome (under the Metropolitan of Thessalonica), sending only one bishop (of Corinth) to Ephesus (431). By 457 the Peloponnese had a number of bishops and Corinth had become a metropolitan see. In 540 the Huns penetrated to the gates and Justinian refortified the Isthmus; the W shores were attacked by Totila's Ostrogoths in 549; but in the Peloponnese the ancient era survived into the 6C. Widespread earthquakes devastated the peninsula in 522 and 551.

Avar and Slav incursions submerged the Peloponnese c 587, bringing two centuries of barbarism. Plague wrought havoc in 746–47. In 805 the Morea (as it was now called) became a Byzantine 'theme', and under the Orthodox church slowly refined and assimilated the Slav elements, although predominantly Slav pockets survived in the Taiyetos region far into Frankish times and the Mani remained aloof as ever. New menaces soon arose in the Saracen corsairs, beaten off in 881, and the Bulgars, who penetrated the Morea in 924–27 and in 996. In general the 11C was a period of reconstruction and prosperity, during which Venetian merchants began to acquire the trading privileges that they developed throughout the 12C.

A year after the fall of Constantinople in 1204 William de Champlitte landed in the western Peloponnese. Assisted by Geoffrey de Villehardouin, he conquered the Morea and divided it up into 12 fiefs among various barons of France, Flanders and Burgundy. Geoffrey de Villehardouin, who became in 1210 Prince of Morea (or Prince of Achaea), governed the country with moderation. In 1261 Michael III Palaeologus regained Monemvasia, the Maina, and Mistra, where he installed a Byzantine 'Despot'. The house of Villehardouin lasted till 1301, when Isabella Villehardouin married Philip of Savoy. Philip became Prince of Morea, sharing his sovereignty with the Marshal of St Omer. In 1318 the principality passed to the Angevin House of Naples, which held it insecurely till 1383. The Venetians occupied Methone, Argos, Nauplia, and Navarino; and Nerio Acciaioli established himself in Corinth, Argolis, and Achaea.

The Byzantine Palaeologi gradually won back the Peloponnese by means of matrimonial and other alliances. In 1453 two rival despots, Demetrius Palaeologus at Mistra, and his brother Thomas at Patras, simultaneously appealed to Turkey for help against the Albanians, who were devastating the country. The Turkish general Turakhan, after assisting, proceeded to conquer the two brothers. In 1458 Mehmed II ordered the invasion of the Morea under Omar, son of Turakhan. In 1460 the conquest was completed. The Venetian coastal settlements were abandoned in 1573. Francesco Morosini reconquered the peninsula in 1685–87, and in 1699 it was ceded to Venice by the Treaty of Carlowitz. In 1715 Ali Pasha retook it for Ahmed III, and the Treaty of Passarowitz gave it back to Turkey. In 1770 an insurrection led by Orloff was repressed.

In 1821 the War of Independence was begun in the Peloponnese by the action of Germanos, Archbishop of Patras. The same year Peter Mavromichales, Bey of the Maina, took the field, his example being followed by Kolokotronis, a celebrated klepht of the Morea, and by other chieftains. Tripolis fell in October 1821. In 1822 Kolokotronis defeated Dramali in the defile of Dervenaki and took Corinth; in 1823 Nauplia fell. The Greeks suffered a set-back in 1825, when Ibrahim Pasha invaded the Morea with an Egyptian army; but some months after the battle of **Navarino** (1827) the French landed in the Gulf of Korone, under General Maison, and Ibrahim fled. The Turks evacuated the country in October 1828, and the French withdrew soon afterwards. In 1831 an insurrection of the Mainotes, who resented sinking their independence even in liberated Greece, was suppressed by Bavarian troops. In the Second World War British troops were evacuated from Navplion, Monemvasia, and Kalamata; a notable naval engagement was fought off Cape Matapan; and Kalavrita suffered one of the more atrocious reprisals of the war.

# 25

## Corinth (Kórinthos) and its environs

### A. Corinth

**CORINTH**, in Greek **KORINTHOS** (Κόρινθος; Hotels C, D, E), or New Corinth, capital of the nome of Korinthia and seat of a bishop, is a modern town of 27,412 inhabitants, situated on the Bay of Corinth. 2.5km W of the Corinth Canal. It dates only from the destruction of Old Corinth by earthquake in 1858. The new town was wrecked in its turn in 1928 and rebuilt on antiseismic principles. It seems to turn its back on the sea and offers little to the visitor; swimming is best to the W of the town. **Old Corinth** (Hotel A; Rooms), or Arkhaía Kórinthos, now a mere village, occupies part of the site of the ancient city. Its little square, with a fountain, lies 5.5km to the SW of

*View of Corinth c 1700. Engraving*

New Corinth (frequent bus) or can be reached in minutes from the main Patras highway.

The *ancient city* lay below the N slopes of the mountain of **Acrocorinth** (575m), its almost impregnable citadel. Its commanding position between two seas early made it a centre of commercial intercourse between Europe and Asia: cautious traders preferred the safe portage of the isthmus to the dangerous voyage round the Peloponnese. In addition, the renowned Isthmian Games, which were held every other year in the neighbourhood, further increased its importance. At its zenith Corinth is said to have had a population of 300,000; the number of slaves is put by Athenaeus as high as 460,000. The city had two important harbours: *Lechaion*, on the Bay of Corinth, joined to the town by long walls, and *Kenchreai*, on the Saronic Gulf—hence the epithet 'bimaris' Corinthus. In addition, there was the less important port of *Schoinous*.

The ancient inhabitants, whose worship of Aphrodite was characteristic, were notorious, in an age of licence, for their vices. The Greek proverb, latinised by Horace '*Non cuivis homini contingit adire Corinthum*', is usually taken to mean that not everyone could afford to go and join in this reckless profligacy. On this uncongenial soil St Paul founded a church during his 18 month sojourn in the city. Peculiarly apposite, therefore, is his reminder to the Corinthian citizens that 'evil communications corrupt good manners' (I Cor. 15, 33). The First Epistle offers a vivid picture of the internal troubles of the early Church.

Corinth has given its name to an architectural order (the Corinthian capital having been invented according to Vitruvius by Kallimachos in the 4C BC; but see Olympia), and in modern times, to the currant (Κορινθιακή σταφίς), which was first cultivated in the neighbourhood. In England the 'Corinthian' of the early 19C was a sporting gentleman riding his own horse or sailing his own yacht; today the adjective survives as the name of a yacht club.

**History**. The name *Korinthos* is of pre-Greek origin and the vicinity of Corinth has been occupied continuously since the 5th millennium. The longest break seems to have followed a disaster contemporary with the destruction of the House of the Tiles at Lerna (Rte 30; Early Helladic II). The Homeric city of *Ephyra* ('The Lookout'), home of Medea, Sisyphus, and Bellerophon, may be located at Korakou nearer the coast; Mycenaean settlements in Corinthia were subordinate to the Argolid. The site of

Classical Corinth was refounded by the Dorians. Towards the end of the 8C the historical last king of a semi-mythical line gives place to the oligarchy of the Bacchiadai, under whom Corinth became a mercantile power. Overpopulation may have occasioned the foundation of colonies at Corcyra and Syracuse (c 734), but Corinthian prowess at sea is attested by the tradition that Ameinokles of Corinth built ships for Samos in 704, by the finding of typical Protocorinthian pottery (aryballoi, alabastra, skyphoi) all over the Mediterranean, and by the naval battle of 664 against her revolting colony Corcyra (at which, according to Thucydides, the trireme was introduced into Greek waters). In the mid-7C the Bacchiads were overthrown by Kypselos, who devoted 30 years to the development of trade and industry.

Under his son Periander, one of the Seven Sages, who reigned for 44 years (629–585), the city reached a level of prosperity that it maintained under Psammetichos, his nephew, and the moderate oligarchy of merchants who overthrew him. New colonies were founded on the Ambracian Gulf, Leukas was occupied, and Corcyra reconquered. The Isthmian Games were founded or reorganised. Trade in bronzes and vases expanded to Egypt and Mesopotamia, to the Black Sea and to Spain. The Corinthians are credited with the invention of the pediment and its decoration.

During the Persian War the city served as Greek headquarters and her forces were represented in the major battles. The increasing commerce of Athens robbed Corinth of her foreign markets. She failed to prevent Athens from annexing Megara (457 BC) and for the remainder of the 5C found herself, not always happily, in the Spartan camp. The war in 434 BC between Corinth and Corcyra was a cause of the Peloponnesian War, in which Corinth supported the Syracusans against the Sicilian expedition. After the death of Lysander she joined Thebes, Athens, and Argos against her former ally, but fared badly in the ensuing Corinthian War (395–387). At Corinth, after 362, Xenophon wrote the *Hellenica*. In 346 Timophanes seized power only to be killed by his brother Timoleon, who was later to achieve fame as the saviour of Sicily from the Carthaginians.

Corinth shared in the defeat of Chaironeia (338 BC) and received a Macedonian garrison. At the Synedrion of Corinth, the following year, the Greek world ratified the leadership of Philip of Macedon, and after his assassination, of Alexander, in the campaign against Persia. The city flourished under a century of Macedonian rule. To this period belongs the Corinthian painter Euphranor, who practised in Athens c 336 BC. The Cynic philosopher Diogenes (412–323) ended his days in Corinth as tutor to the sons of Xeniades. Aratos expelled the Macedonian garrison in 224 BC and united Corinth to the resuscitated Achaean League. In 146, after the defeat of the League by the Romans, the defences of Corinth were mercilessly razed to the ground by Mummius and his ten legates. It lay desolate until, in 44 BC, Julius Caesar planted on

*The Defeat of Dramali. Engraving*

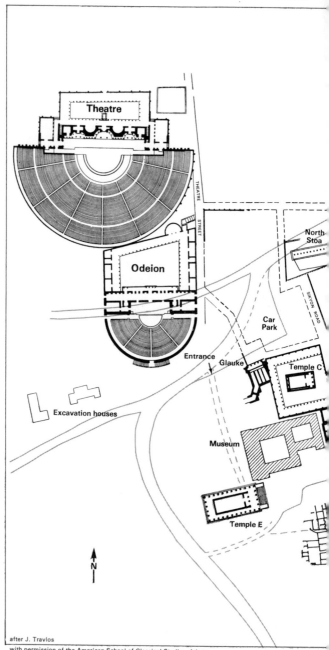

after J. Travlos

with permission of the American School of Classical Studies, Athens.

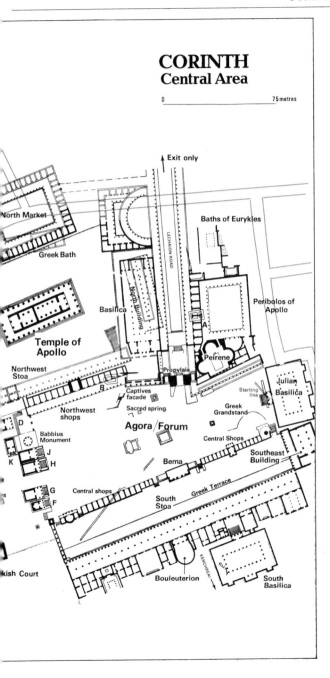

# CORINTH
## Central Area

0              75 metres

Exit only

North Market

Greek Bath

Baths of Eurykles

LECHAION ROAD

Basilica

North Building

Peribolos of
Apollo

Temple of
Apollo

Peirene

Northwest
Stoa

Propylaia

A

Captives
facade

Starting
line

Julian
Basilica

B

Sacred spring

Greek
Grandstand

Northwest
shops

Agora / Forum

Babbius
Monument

Central Shops

D

J

H

K

Bema

Southeast
Building

G

Central shops

Greek Terrace

F

South
Stoa

kish Court

Bouleuterion

KENCHREAI

South
Basilica

its site a colony of veterans, the *Colonia Laus Julia Corinthiensis*, which soon achieved splendour and importance as the capital of the province of Achaia. The luxury and dissipation of Corinth again became a byword. St Paul spent 18 months in Corinth in the proconsulship of Gallio (c AD 51–52), plying his trade of tentmaker in company with Aquila and Priscilla (Acts, XVIII, 3). Gallio refused to be judge of complaints about Paul, laid before him by the local Jews. Nero's proclamation of Greek independence at Isthmia was rescinded by Vespasian, but Corinth, embellished by Hadrian (with an aqueduct from Lake Stymphalos) and by Herodes Atticus, became the finest city in Greece.

Though it survived the ravages of the Herulians in AD 267 and of Alaric in 395, Corinth suffered from disastrous earthquakes in 522 and 551, and its decline set in. After a final period of prosperity in the 11C, it was sacked by the Normans in 1147 and the rest of its history is one of successive captures. Its masters included Villehardouin (1212), the Acciaioli (1358), the Palaeologi (1430), the Turks (1458), the Knights of Malta (1612), and the Venetians (1687). In 1715 it was retaken by the Turks: the siege of Corinth is the one described by Byron. The victory of Kolokotronis over Dramali to the S opened the way to Corinth, which fell into Greek hands after a short siege; Dramali himself died here and the remnant of the Turks was evacuated by sea.

**Ancient Corinth** occupied a large area on a rocky plateau (60m) between its citadel and the sea. The Long Walls started at the top of Acrocorinth, included the city, and ended at the port of Lechaion (see below). The actual length of the city walls does not, however, tally with the measurements of Strabo (viii, 6, 21–22). The principal excavation area lies close to the village cross-roads.

The excavations and museum need at least half a day; with a car it is possible to combine Corinth, Acrocorinth, Lechaion, Isthmia, and the Diolkos in one day's visit but, if possible, it is better to spend two or three days in the area. Perachora should not be missed.

Entrance to the archaeological site and museum is from the car park above the odeion. There is an exit from the Lechaion road (where this description terminates) which leads into the modern village close to the square. The **odeion**, **theatre**, and **Asklepieion** do not lie within the fenced archaeological site and may be visited either before or after. They are closer to the entrance and are therefore here described first.

Across the road from the site entrance is the **odeion**, a Roman construction cut largely from the rock, resembling in plan that at Pompeii. It held c 3000 spectators. Built towards the end of the 1C AD, it was reconstructed (c 175) by Herodes Atticus; the interior was totally destroyed by fire and after AD 225 was again restored as an arena or beast-pit by cutting away the lowest rows of seats. Even after a further destruction in 375 by earthquake, the building was patched up to serve until Alaric's holocaust. Adjacent to the N is the **theatre**, with a similar but even longer history. Founded in the 5C BC, it ended by presenting *naumachiae* (mock sea-battles). Here the multitude acclaimed Aratos of Sikyon after his nocturnal capture of Acrocorinth (243 BC). The **cavea** of the Greek period is well preserved because the Romans filled it in with earth to produce a steeper rake before rebuilding the seating; the central part has been excavated. In 1925–29 wall-paintings of gladiatorial scenes were found on the late-Roman barrier round the arena; they have since perished. An inscription, scratched in the plaster, was also found recording the story of Androcles and the lion. In the **orchestra** several levels of pavement can be distinguished.

To the E of the stage buildings is a paved square. An inscription on a paving block records that Erastus laid the pavement at his own expense in return for the aedileship. This is probably the Erastus known to St Paul (Romans, xvi, 23). On the E side of the street, opposite the square, Roman buildings may have included taverns for those attending performances.

About 500m N of the theatre are the remains of the **Asklepieion**, which stood at the edge of the bluff just within the city wall (cars may get close by taking the road which runs immediately below the Xenia Hotel). A useful guide-booklet, published by the American School, is *Cure and cult in ancient Corinth* (1977). Rock cuttings show that a small prostyle tetrastyle Doric temple of the 4C BC stood in the centre of a colonnaded court. Except on the N side the spaces within the colonnades are too narrow to have been an ambulatory and probably sheltered the dedications of the cured. Many ex-votos are now in the museum. Near the entrance to the precinct is a stone offertory box in which copper coins were found. Behind and below the W wall of the sanctuary lies the health centre itself, arranged round a lower court. Off the E side of its peristyle are three rooms, that to the S still with its stone benches; they were probably dining rooms. Over them was a great hall, which closed the W end of the upper court. The S and W walks of the peristyle have access to draw-basins of the **Fountain of Lerna**, fed by four large reservoirs which extend S into the rock. Another copious supply of water, c 180m E, is known as the **Baths of Aphrodite**. Here a Turkish staircase and some fortifications date from the late 17C. (These sites are all individually fenced by barbed wire but there is still a reasonable view.)

A road leads W between the odeion and the theatre to the site of a **Roman villa** (2km), discovered in 1925 and protected by a shelter (key at the museum). Some of the mosaics from its five rooms have been removed to the museum. More important are the excavations (15 minutes on foot farther SW) in the *Kerameikos*, or **Potters' Quarter**, on the W edge of the plateau. Remains of workshops and storerooms of the 7–4C lie inside the Archaic city wall (? 7C). Through them run the massive foundations of the Classical **fortifications**. The later wall with remnants of towers and gates may be traced to the gates of Acrocorinth (see below).

You return to the car park and the entrance to the main site. Beyond the ticket office the path leads to the museum.

En route (left) is a cubic mass of rock, in which are cut the four large reservoirs that formed the **Fountain of Glauke**, a construction similar to the Peirene fountain (see below). Pausanias (II, 3, 6) attributes its name to Glauke, Jason's second wife, who is supposed to have flung herself into it to obtain relief from the poisoned robe sent her as a wedding-present by Medea. Roman alterations, the decay of the roof in medieval times, and the earthquake of 1928 have all but obliterated its porticoed façade and three drawbasins. The reservoir, which was fed by a small conduit from the base of Acrocorinth, had a storage capacity of c 64,000 litres (14,000 gallons). Adjoining the fountain to the E is a colonnaded precinct, the entrance to which faced the Sikyon road. Within the court stood a somewhat earlier temple (C), perhaps the **Temple of Hera Akraia**, though not (needless to say) that on whose altar the citizens of Corinth slew the children of Medea.

The **museum**, endowed in 1931 by Ada Small Moore in memory of her father, a Philhellene of Chicago, was extended in 1950. A break-in and thefts in 1991 have necessitated some rearrangment of the exhibits.

In the ENTRANCE COURT: part of a dolphin from the Fountain of Poseidon. VESTIBULE. Restored mosaic. Two griffins attacking a horse (c 400 BC, one of the earliest known Greek pebble mosaics); head of Herodes Atticus.

To the right opens the GREEK GALLERY, arranged to show the rise of Corinth from a small settlement to an important manufacturing city-state. (By the door is a case of finds from the Sanctuary of Demeter and Kore, recently excavated, including a large terracotta figure.) Archaic period: sphinx of limestone (6C BC); inscribed stone from the sacred spring reading in Archaic Corinthian letters 'Sanctuary boundary; do not come down. Fine 8 drachmai'; forepart of a horse (? part of a metope from the Temple of Apollo); small altars, Doric capital, etc., from the potters' quarter.

The cases contain locally-made vases showing the progression of style from Protogeometric (case 8), through Geometric (9–11), to Protocorinthian (cases 12–13; 725–625 BC), known throughout the Mediterranean; the aryballos shape occurs frequently (fine example showing two warriors fighting). Cases 13–15. *Ripe Corinthian pottery (625–550 BC) is at its best in the first 25 years.

Head of a fallen Amazon from a fragmentary terracotta group; painted sphinx; bronze helmet of Corinthian type; sarcophagus of the 5C BC containing the bones and grave furniture of a youth. Cases 22–24. Black-figured ware (550–450 BC) in imitation of the Attic style which was capturing all the markets, compared with vases imported from Attica (kylix signed by Neandros). The black glaze did not adhere firmly to the local Corinthian clay. Case 25. Decorated terracotta altars and relief plaque with gorgon. Cases 26–28. Corinthian and imported Attic red-figured pottery (500–350 BC); Attic and Corinthian black-glaze pottery; Hellenistic vases; pottery from other sites. Cases 29 and 21. Late Classical and Hellenistic terracottas. In centre cases: figurines and moulds; lamps and other items.

Across the vestibule is the ROMAN AND POST-CLASSICAL GALLERY. Statues from the Julian basilica, representing members of the Gens Julia, including Augustus as Pontifex Maximus (c AD 13); head of Nero. In Case 46, marble statuette of Aphrodite (copy of the cult statue of the Akro-korinthos shrine in the Roman period); also Byzantine and Roman glass. Three mosaics (2C AD) from a villa outside the NW wall. Roman copies of Classical heads from the theatre, probably the Sappho of Silanion and the Doryphoros of Polykleitos; also of an Artemis of the 5C, and of a Tyche. Fragment of a large relief of dancing Maenads (neo-Attic, 1C AD). Head of Dionysos (after Praxiteles). Colossal figures from the 'Captives' Façade'. Fragmentary sarcophagus of Hadrian's day with reliefs of the departure of the Seven against Thebes and the death of Opheltes. Roman copy of an athlete (after Myron or Kalamis).

Heads of Antoninus Pius (33), Caracalla (34) as a youth of eighteen. 35. Woman with her hair in braids. *43. Head, a rare example of its period (4C AD). 44–46. Marble statues of emperors or governors (6C AD), the third recut from an earlier work. Sgraffito and incised pottery of the 12C and 'Protomajolica' ware (finds so far paralleled only at Athlit in the Holy Land). Case 52. Byzantine pottery; wooden lute of 10C.

In the CLOISTER. Frieze reliefs from the theatre (Hadrianic rebuilding), representing the Labours of Herakles and an Amazonomachia; the goddess Roma, on a base with other statues from Temple E; Byzantine decorative carvings; inscription reading Συναγώγη Εβραίων (Jewish synagogue; 3C AD or later), and a head of Coptic type, perhaps of Egyptian sandstone and imported in the 4C or 5C AD. In the NW corner of the courtyard is a base inscribed to Regilla (probably the wife of Herodes Atticus). The **Asklepieion Room** (opened on request) contains finds from the Asklepieion, the site of which (to the N; see above) may be seen from the window. They include typical ex-votos, Early Christian gravestones, and a cache of silver and weapons of the early 19C.

Immediately to the right on leaving the museum you pass the foundations of **Temple E**, an early Imperial building of imposing proportions, possibly the Capitoleum or the Temple of Octavia. Parts of the entablature are displayed on the platform. S of the temple part of the Roman *decumanus* has been exposed.

In the SE part of the temple temenos, immediately S of the museum, recent excavations have thrown light on the medieval history of Corinth. In particular a **Frankish court** (gravelled) has a church at the N end and partly colonnaded structures on the W and E. The complex was probably destroyed in the Catalan attack on Corinth in 1312 but refurbished for use in the 15–18C. The area has produced coins, jetons, and important deposits of medieval pottery.

Opposite Temple E the path leads directly to the excavation. Before the gate (left) is a display of architectural fragments including column capital types (Doric, Ionic, Corinthian, from left to right along the back wall).

Steps descend to the site. It is best first to make for the **Temple of Apollo**, prominent on a knoll to the left, one of the oldest temples in Greece and the most conspicuous monument on the site. The temple, of the Doric order, had a peristyle of 38 columns (6 by 15). Seven adjacent columns remain standing, five on the W front and two more on the S side; the five that form the corner support part of their architrave. Four further columns lie where they fell; foundations remain of four others removed by the Turkish owner in 1830. The shafts are monoliths, c 7m high and 1.8m in diameter at the base, of rough limestone. The lower side of the fallen columns shows the well-preserved Greek stucco and the thicker plaster of a Roman restoration. They have 20 flutes. Their flat archaic capitals are characteristic of the mid-6C BC.

The naos had two unequal chambers separated by a wall, with a distyle portico *in antis* at either end. Two rows of interior columns supported the roof. The foundations of a statue base have been found in the W chamber, near the partition wall. In the SW corner of the pronaos was found a rectangular strong-box lined with waterproof cement.

The precinct of the temple has been cleared, exposing slight but important remnants of an earlier temple (7C) which has some similarities with the Archaic temple at Isthmia (see below).

Below to the N, partly obscured by the modern road, lie the remains of the **north market**, a rectangular peristyle surrounded by shops. Some mosaic pavements survive. The market was rebuilt and used in Byzantine times. Earlier, a Greek **bath house** stood on the site. Extending to the W was the long **north stoa**; some of its coloured terracotta antefixes are in the museum. The gold necklace and hoard of 51 gold staters of Philip and Alexander the Great found here are in the National Archaeological Museum at Athens.

To the S, there is a good overall view of the so-called **agora**, more accurately the **forum**, since what we see is a Roman market-place. Its vast extent (c 210m by 90m) was determined by the existence of the south stoa (see below). The Greek and Hellenistic agora may have been elsewhere since no earlier buildings of importance have been found below the area between the temple hill and the south stoa. This seems to have been occupied by a race-course and various cult places. In a radical Roman replanning the area was transformed into two unequal but more or less level terraces, the upper part being c 4m higher at the centre. The division between the two was marked at first by a terrace wall; later, shops were erected in front of this.

The **West Side** of the forum was bounded by a row of shops, fronted by a colonnade (an inscription on the entablature relates to a repair after an earthquake in AD 375). Through the middle of these (now seen to the right) you entered the site. Set forward of the shops were six **Roman temples** and a monument, all now so ruined as to mean little to the layman.

From excavation and the description of Pausanias these have been identified from S to N as a **Temple of Venus Fortuna** (Pl. F); the **Pantheon** (Pl. G); two **temples**, erected by Commodus, perhaps to Hercules (Pl. H) and to Poseidon (Pl. J), the latter replacing the Poseidon fountain seen by Pausanias; the **Babbius Monument**, a rotunda on eight Corinthian columns, of which some members are set up at the side of its square concrete base; the **Temple (?) of Clarian Apollo** (Pl. K); and a **Temple of Hermes** (Pl. D). These identifications have recently been disputed (*Hesperia* 44 (1975) 25–9). In Frankish times the forum area was covered with houses. Over Temples D, J, H, K etc., and to the E was built a monastic complex (of St John). Like the Frankish structures described above this was destroyed in the Catalan sack.

The **South Side** of the forum (the administrative centre of the Roman province of Achaea) is closed by the **south stoa**, the largest Classical secular building in Greece, dating originally from the 4C BC. It had already been reconstructed before 146 BC. Facing the forum was a double colonnade with 71 Doric columns in front and 34 Ionic columns in the middle. Some columns have been collected and restored to position. The rear of the building was transformed in Imperial times.

In its original form it was divided into a row of 33 shops, each with another room behind. All but two of the front compartments had a well, supplied from the Peirene system. From the number of drinking cups recovered from the wells, it is thought that the 'shops' served chiefly as places of refreshment and the wells as refrigerators. A second floor, reached by stairs at either end, probably served as night quarters, and the stoa is believed to have been a huge hostelry built to house delegates to the Panhellenic Union which Philip of Macedon convened at Corinth. The building was restored in Julian times, but in the 1C AD most of the rear half was demolished to make way for administrative buildings; the colonnades remained. The Greek form is best observed

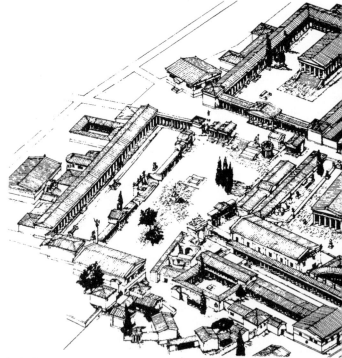

*Corinth. Restored view of the ancient city in the Roman period*

at the W end, where at one point Greek walls stand to a height of 2.75m; a section of the roof has been reconstructed from tiles found in the wells.

From the NW corner of the stoa a Roman foundation wall extends at right angles to the building; on it stand archaic columns, taken possibly from the Temple of Apollo, and across the top a water channel supplied a basin.

The Roman administrative buildings begin near the W end of the stoa where a square hall may be the **Duovirs' Office**; this was later encroached on by a **bath-house** (well-preserved hypocaust). Towards the centre of the stoa, two shops retained their function in the Roman reconstruction; finds from here included a well-preserved head of Serapis in gilded marble, a base inscribed with the full name of the Roman colony, and the remains of a cash box with coins showing the place to have been destroyed by fire c AD 267, perhaps in a Herulian raid. Next are the **bouleuterion**, or council chamber. Its curved stone benches have been replaced in position. Through the centre of the stoa a paved **road** led S towards Kenchreai. To the E (under cover) is a beautiful marble fountain. The next section of the stoa was turned into a forecourt, through which, by a marble stairway and porch, was reached the **south basilica**. This was similar to the Julian basilica (see below) and, like it, once adorned with Imperial statues. Next is the presumed **Office of the Roman Governor**, with an antechamber, floors of marble veneer, and (in the antechamber) the base of a statue inscribed to a procurator of the Emperor Trajan. The third hall in from the E end of the stoa was probably the **Office of the Agonothetes**, who directed the Games

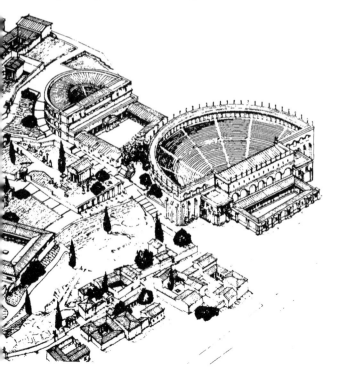

at Isthmia. Here (beneath a shed) are a mosaic of a victorious athlete standing before the goddess of good fortune (Eutychia), and the restored roof section (see above). Two further mosaics of Dionysiac scenes are farther S under another shelter.

In front (c 3m) of the south stoa you cross the line of a low terrace wall below the level of the Roman pavement. Cuttings suggest that this supported over 100 monuments, all probably carried off to Rome during the century following the sack in 146 BC. Pausanias mentions marble or bronze statues (reproductions perhaps) of Zeus, Athena, Aphrodite, Ephesian Artemis, Apollo, and Hermes, as well as gilded wooden statues of Dionysos with faces painted red. During the period of ruin a cart road passed diagonally across the forum (traces at the E end of the wall).

The Upper Forum was the administrative centre of the Roman province of Achaea. The **south-east building** (right) had a marble Ionic colonnade. It was rebuilt three times and may have been the *tabularium*, or archive respository of the Roman colony. In front stands a prominent **circular pedestal** with a truncated shaft.

The **East End** of the forum is closed by the **Julian basilica**. The well-preserved remains are of a crypto-porticus which formed the base of a Corinthian basilica of the Augustan period. Four imperial portrait statues were found here.

In front of the basilica the Roman pavement has been removed to expose an earlier Greek one. It is as well to keep in mind this difference in levels as otherwise the relationship of Greek to Roman buildings is hard to understand.

Parallel to the building and partly underlying its projecting entrance porch is the starting-line of a **race course**, preserved for its entire length of 18m and with places for 16 contestants. An earlier starting-line with a different orientation lies beneath it. To the S is a curved retaining wall which perhaps supported a judges' grandstand. These remains may be connected with the Hellotia, a Corinthian festival mentioned in the 13th Olympian Ode of Pindar.

From a circular pedestal, whose function is unknown, a line of buildings extended W, dividing the lower from the upper forum. Its central feature was the **bema**, a monumental rostra upon which Roman officials appeared before the public. Since later a Christian church was built above its ruins, this may be the place where Gallio, the Roman governor, refused to act upon Jewish accusations against the Apostle Paul. To right and left of the rostra extended rows of **shops**, replaced in Christian times by a flight of steps running the whole length of the forum. In the centre of the lower forum are the foundations of an **altar** and of an elevated **grandstand**.

**North Side**. Almost opposite the bema, towards the centre of the north side, where the Lechaion road enters the agora, stood the **Captives' Façade**, an elaborate two-storey structure of Parian marble. The lower storey consisted of Corinthian columns; the upper storey had at least four Atlantes of barbarian captives (portions in the museum). This constituted the final screen of the basilica flanking the Lechaion road (see below), from which it was separated by an open court.

Adjoining is the **Triglyph Wall**, a low terrace wall decorated with a triglyph frieze, originally painted. It bore tripods and statues, and a surviving base of dark Eleusinian limestone has the signature of Lysippos. Of the two openings for stairways which divide the wall into three sections, one leads down to the **sacred spring** (closed by a grating; key with the custodian). The spring, which had two bronze lion's head spouts (5C BC—one now on display in the E room of the museum), was originally in the open air, but was transformed into an underground chamber when the surrounding ground level was raised. It apparently ran dry and was unknown to the

Romans, being covered by a later basin fed by a conduit. On the terrace to the N of the Triglyph Wall, and connected with it by an elaborate tunnel, was a small **oracular shrine**. The tunnel, entered by a secret door disguised as a metope between the triglyphs, probably housed the 'oracle'—a priest who pronounced through a small hole below the floor of the shrine. The whole of this area was sacred and public access was forbidden; a minatory inscription has been found on its boundary (see above, museum).

To the W stood the colonnade of the 15 **north-west shops** (3C AD). The large central shop, with its stone vault intact, forms the most conspicuous element of the forum; the concrete vaults of the others have fallen. Behind, the **north-west stoa**, in poros, over 90m long, earlier formed the N boundary of the forum. The front had Doric columns and the interior Ionic. The front stylobate is well-preserved and many columns are still in position (3C BC).

Returning past the Captives' Façade, you pass through the **propylaia**, the gateway to the agora (which *you* use as an exit). Originally a long shallow building, in poros, with a large central arch and two smaller ones on each side, the portal was replaced in the 1C AD by a typical Roman triumphal arch in marble, surmounted in the time of Pausanias by two gilt bronze chariots bearing Helios and his son Phaethon. Little remains beyond the foundations of the later arch and a portion of the façade of the earlier one. From the road the approach to the propylaia is by a flight of three steps, a landing and a larger staircase.

The **Lechaion road** led into the city from its N port (see below). An impressive monument to Roman town planning, 12m wide, paved and drained in the 1C AD, it remained in use for centuries. Steps at its steepest part seem to have precluded use by wheeled traffic. To the right, at the foot of the steps which descend from the propylaia, is the *****Fountain of Peirene**, the lower one of that name, the upper being on Acrocorinth, a natural spring of immemorial antiquity, which has been so much elaborated and remodelled that it looks like an artificial fountain. The water is stored in four long reservoirs fed by a transverse supply tunnel. The reservoirs are hidden by a fountain-house, with a six-arched façade, 'with chambers made like grottoes, from which the water flows into a basin in the open air' (Paus. II, 3, 3). This basin measures 9m by 6m and is sunk below the level of the court of the fountain.

*Peirene* 'was a woman who was turned into a spring of water by the tears she shed in bewailing her son Kenchrias, whom Artemis had unwittingly killed' (Paus, II, 3, 2). The fountain-house has undergone several modifications. In front of the reservoirs are three deep draw-basins, immediately behind the six chambers of the arcade. Before the arcade was built, the front wall of the basins formed a parapet over which the water was originally drawn in jars. Then the clear space in front of the draw-basins was divided into the existing six chambers. Later (3C BC) Ionic columns were erected on the old parapet of the draw-basins, which ceased to be accessible. When Corinth was rebuilt by the Romans the old façade was masked by a new two-storey poros façade—the present series of stone arches. Their engaged Doric columns supported an architrave and a second storey of engaged Ionic columns. This arrangement was continued at right angles to the façade and made to enclose a court 15m square. At the same time the open-air fountain was built in the courtyard. Towards the end of the 1C AD the walls of the court were lined with marble. In the 2C AD the court was remodelled (probably by Herodes Atticus) to the form which exists today with massive vaulted apses on three sides. About the same time the arched openings of the façade were narrowed so as to allow of blind arches between each of them, giving 11 arches instead of six. The front walls of the chambers were reinforced and the side walls decorated with paintings of fish swimming in dark blue water (best preserved in Chamber 4). Finally, in early Byzantine times a row of columns was built across the

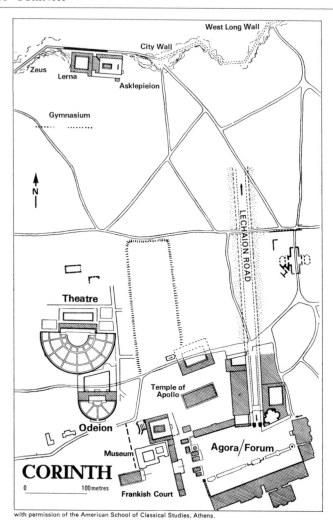

with permission of the American School of Classical Studies, Athens.

façade, and alterations were made to the court. An iron pipe now taps the fountain for the villagers' use.

Corinth was known in verse and to the Delphic oracle as 'the city of Peirene'. Euripides mentions its 'august waters' (*Medea*, 68).

Immediately to the N is the **Peribolos of Apollo**, an open court 32m by 23.5m, surrounded by a marble Ionic colonnade, 5m wide, upon a stylobate of Acrocorinthian limestone. Some columns have been re-erected and parts of the epistyle assembled. The heavy foundations in the centre may have supported the bronze statue of Apollo mentioned by Pausanias. A dyeing works occupied the NE quarter in the 5C BC. Below runs the overflow of Peirene, which served the quarter as a main sewer. On the W side, by the Lechaion road, are the foundations of a small Greek **temple** (Pl. A) of the

4C BC; this was soon replaced by an open shrine in which a covered statue faced its altar across a pebble pavement.

Off the S side of the peribolos is an apse, which has been cut into by the E apse of the Peirene court. At an earlier level are scanty remains of a Doric hexastyle **stoa** and, near the foot of the steps ascending to the Peirene court, some basins from the earliest water system of the Tyrants.

Also on the E side of the road and extending below the modern village are some remains of a great bath of the Imperial era, perhaps the **Baths of Eurykles** praised by Pausanias as the finest in the city. To the S, is a **public latrine** with some seats *in situ*.

The W side of the road is mainly occupied by a terrace on which are the foundations in poros of a **basilica** of the 1C BC, 64m by 23m, possibly a judgement hall. This was later rebuilt in marble on a larger scale and with a façade on the agora (see above). The basilica terrace was supported at the E by the rear wall of a colonnade which masks 16 small shops. A flight of steps leads through one of the S shops to the extensive though indistinct remains of a **Greek market** of the 5C BC, which lies deep underneath the basilica.

You return to the road and ascend to the exit from the site, leaving to the left the remains of a square **Roman market**, with colonnades and shops (later replaced by a semicircular court) which is still partly concealed under the modern road.

To the E of the village are some vestiges of an **amphitheatre** of the 3C AD, of the **Isthmian Gate**, and of the Early Christian **Basilica of Kranneion**, with a martyrium, that existed in various forms from the 5C to Frankish times. This lay just within the **Kenchreai Gate**, where sections of city wall can be traced.

To the S of the village, just below the road to Acrocorinth and on its lower slopes, can be seen a **Sanctuary of Demeter** excavated since 1968 by the American School. The sanctuary dates back to the 7C BC, and among the finds has been a marble head of the 2C from a cult statue of the goddess. There is an excellent booklet, *Demeter and Persephone in Ancient Corinth* (1987).

# B.  Acrocorinth (Akrokórinthos)

**Approach**. A road climbs from the museum to the gate, where there is a tourist pavilion. On foot the visit requires at least 3 hours. From the museum a track leads due S to a cluster of houses below the **Fountain of Hadji Mustapha**; from there a path winds up to the right round the W face of the mountain to (1 hr) the outer gate.

*Acrocorinth (Ακροκόρινθος), the Acropolis of Corinth, the limestone mountain (575m) which rises precipitously to the S of ancient Corinth, is among the strongest natural fortresses in Europe. The citadel was the goal of all who aspired to the domination of the Peloponnese and it changed hands many times. The summit is enclosed by a wall not less than 2.5km in circumference and the only approach is defended by a triple line of fortification. To this construction Byzantines, Franks, Venetians, and Turks contributed; but their walls and towers stand mainly on ancient foundations.

In the Frankish invasion Acrocorinth was besieged by William de Champlitte for three years (1205–08); its defender, Leo Sgouros, flung himself to his death in 1208, but the citadel continued to resist Geoffrey de Villehardouin and Otho de la Roche until 1210, when Theodore Angelos fled to Argos with the church treasure of Corinth.

You cross a dry moat, once spanned by a drawbridge, to the first of the three gateways which are connected by ramps. The **outer gate** is largely Turkish, while the **middle gate** is a Venetian rebuilding of a Frankish structure; traces of ancient walls can be seen. The **inner gate** is flanked by massive square towers, that to the right little altered since the 4C BC. The gateway incorporates reused Byzantine columns and had a portcullis worked from an upper room. Students of military architecture should not miss the well-preserved **fortifications** to the N or the Frankish **inner keep** to the right above the gates. Visitors pressed for time may prefer to take the path across more gently rising ground amid an overgrown jumble of ruined Turkish houses, Byzantine chapels, and brick-vaulted cisterns, to the S circuit wall of the citadel. Here, near ruined Turkish barracks at the SE corner, is the **Upper Peirene Spring**. The subterranean well-house is covered by a vaulted roof of Hellenistic date (protected above by modern concrete). A stairway leads down to a pedimented entrance screen and continues below water level. The water, which is clear and cold (but *not* safe for drinking), is 3.5m–4.5m deep and has never been known to retreat beyond the screen. The higher of the two summits of Acrocorinth, due N of Peirene, bore in turn a **Temple of Aphrodite**, a small basilican church, a watch tower, a cloistered mosque, and a paved Venetian belvedere. The worship of Aphrodite, the Syrian Astarte, was accompanied by religious prostitution, and the temple is said to have been served by a thousand sacred courtesans. Little remains now but the *view, one of the finest in Greece. It was described by Strabo and extends on a clear day from Aiyina and the Parthenon in the E almost to Navpaktos in the W, embracing most of the Saronic Gulf and the whole of the Gulf of Corinth.

The N horizon is bounded, from E to W, by Salamis, the hills of Megara, Kithairon, and Yeraneia. The Perakhora peninsula is prominent in the foreground, then the distant peaks of Helikon, Parnassos, Ghiona, and the mountains of Aetolia. On the S side of the Gulf, Killini blocks a more distant prospect to the W; farther SW the sharp point of Artemision is conspicuous; to the S Mycenae is hidden amid the ranges of Argolis. The

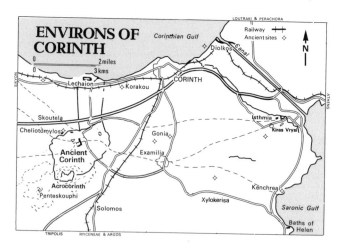

ENVIRONS OF CORINTH

tiny Frankish castle of **Pendeskoúphi** (Mont-Escorée: bare mountain) boldly crowns the nearest precipitous height of Kastraki.

# C. Isthmia and Kenchreai (Kekhriés); also for Epidauros

**Road,** diverging (right) from the main road to Athens c halfway between New Corinth and the Canal bridge; coming from Athens the *second* turning (left; for Epidauros) after the canal.—7km Isthmia.—12km Kekhriés (ancient *Kenchreai*).—69km Epídhavros (Epidauros; Sanctuary of Asklepios).

The **Ancient Road** ran E from the agora to Examilia, where it divided, the left branch making directly for Isthmia while the right branch led to Kenchreai.

From New Corinth you follow the Athens road, join the main highway, then fork right for **Kirás** (sometimes Krias) **Vrísi**, passing substantial traces of the **Isthmian wall**, which extends for c 9.5km across the narrowest part of the isthmus. The fortification which follows a natural line of low cliffs, can be traced for practically its whole length. The best preserved section is that immediately E of the Isthmian Sanctuary (see below), where it is 7m high and 2.5m thick. The remains belong to the original construction of 410–420 AD and to repairs of the time of Justinian. Sections of the Classical trans-Isthmian wall mentioned by Herodotus and of a Hellenistic rebuilding of it have been traced in the countryside NW of Kenchreae.

Above Kiras Vrisi (path beside Venetsianos mini-market), on the ridge of **Rákhi**, are the recently excavated remains of an interesting 4–3C settlement (evidence for olive oil production and beekeeping) which apparently met a violent end (slingshots). There was also an Archaic/Classical shrine (? of Demeter) on the site. Beyond the village you approach the Isthmian Sanctuary which stands (left) on a natural terrace between the village and the Isthmian wall.

The **Sanctuary of Poseidon at Isthmia** has a history of cult activity going back to the 11C BC. One of the four Panhellenic sanctuaries celebrated in the Odes of Pindar, it was later famous for its games. Like those of Olympia, Nemea, and Delphi, the games appear originally to have honoured the funeral of a particular hero.

Tradition tells of Melikertes, son of Athamos and Ino. When his mother leapt with him into the sea from the Molurian Rock (Rte 24), the drowned boy was landed on the Isthmus by a dolphin. Corinth was undergoing a famine and an oracle declared that this would stop only when the Corinthians gave the boy fitting burial and honoured him with funeral games. His name was changed to Palaimon and the Isthmian Games instituted in his honour. The oracle later declared that, to prevent the famine returning, the games must be perpetual.

Disregarding legend, which ascribes their foundation to Poseidon, the Sun, or Sisyphos, and Attic tradition, which gives the honour to Theseus, it would appear that the games were instituted about the time of Periander, the date of the first Isthmiad usually being given as 582 BC. They were held in the 2nd and 4th year of each Olympiad. Their organisation was in the hands of Corinth until its destruction in 146 BC, when it passed to Sikyon; the venue of the games was probably transferred. They reverted to Corinth after the refoundation of the city by Julius Caesar. The Athenians originally had the place of honour while the Eleans were excluded. In 288 BC the Romans were allowed to compete. The athletic contests were second only to those at

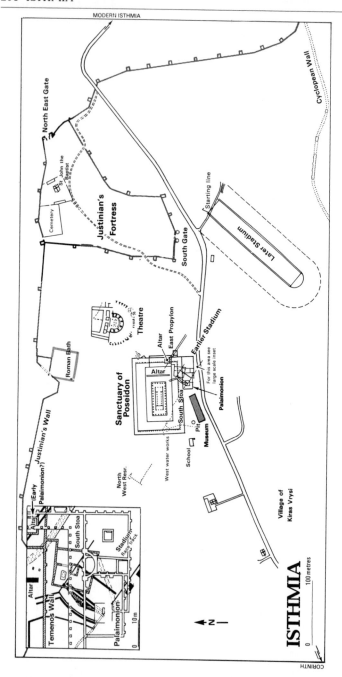

MODERN ISTHMIA

North East Gate

Cyclopean Wall

St. John the Baptist

Cemetery

Justinian's Fortress

South Gate

Starting line

Later Stadium

Theatre

Altar

East Propylon

Earlier Stadium

Roman Bath

Sanctuary of Poseidon

Altar

Palaimonion

For this area see large scale inset

South Stoa

Pit

Museum

Justinian's Wall

(Early Palaimonion?)

Altar

North West Resr.

West water works

School

Village of Kiras Vrysi

Altar

Temenos Wall

South Stoa

Stadium Race track

Palaimonion

10 m

**ISTHMIA**

N

0          100 metres

CORINTH

Olympia, which they resembled. Musical events were added by the late 5C BC, on the model of the Pythian games.

At the games of 336 BC Alexander the Great was nominated leader of the Greeks against Persia; at the games of 196 BC Flamininus declared the independence of Greece; and here in AD 66 the second proclamation of independence was made by Nero. Scientific excavation of the site was begun in 1952 by the University of Chicago under Oscar Broneer and work continues under Prof. E. Gebhard.

By the road stands the **museum**, so well supplied with explanatory plans and photographs that it is best visited first. The first section is devoted to Isthmia itself: panathenaic amphorae; athletic equipment including *halteres* (jumping weights); two *perirrhanteria* (restored); tiles and paintings from the Archaic temple (7 by 18 columns). Beyond are finds from Kenchreai, notably panels in *opus sectile* (glass mosaic) depicting a harbour town (these were found packed in crates and may have been imported from Egypt; they were damaged in an ancient earthquake); wooden doors; sculptured ivory plaques with male seated figures. There are also finds from the sanctuary and settlement at **Rakhi** (see above).

The site entrance, just beyond the museum, skirts a wall built of roof tiles from the Archaic temple of Poseidon and leads (right) to the square foundation in *opus incertum* of the Roman **Palaimonion**. The temple had a circular open colonnade of eight columns, which is depicted on local coinage of the Antonine period. It is centred over a water basin of the early stadium, which tradition evidently took to be the tomb of Palaimon. The earliest (Hadrianic) version of the temple may have been the 'altar', over which the **east stoa** was subsequently built.

Alongside, beneath the **south stoa**, the open end of the **earlier stadium** (constructed 575–550 and removed c 300 BC) has been uncovered. The triangular pavement, scored with radiating grooves, is part of a **starting gate** (? 5C) for 16 runners of the kind alluded to by Aristophanes (*Knights* 1159). A starter, standing in the pit, operated traps (*balbides*) hinged to wooden posts, by means of cords running in the grooves under bronze staples.

On level ground immediately to the N are the remains of the second **Temple of Poseidon**, a 5C Doric structure which had a peristyle of 6 columns by 13. In the words of its excavator, 'the casual visitor will marvel chiefly, perhaps, at the thoroughness of its destruction' (O. Broneer). An earlier Archaic temple (built 690–650 BC) on the same site and particularly interesting for its early use of dressed stone, is of great importance for the history of Greek monumental architecture. It had a peristyle of 7 by 18 columns and wall-paintings. It was completely destroyed by fire. Another mysterious fire in 390 BC damaged the later building (Xen. 'Hell.', IV, v, 4), which was afterwards re-roofed. A colossal statue, unearthed in 1952, formed part of a cult group of Poseidon and Amphitrite of the Antonine period.

The sanctuary became derelict after the sack of Corinth and traces of a wagon road can be seen passing across its altar. Reorganisation was undertaken in the middle of the 1C AD. In the second half of the 2C AD the **temenos** was extended and the temple area surrounded by stoas, the cost of which was defrayed by the high priest, P. Licinius Priscus.

The **theatre** is situated in an artificial hollow midway between the precinct and the Isthmian wall. Virtually nothing remains of the building originally constructed in the early 4C BC and several times modified. Its roof tiles are stamped with the name of Poseidon or with a dolphin and trident. Here Nero sang hymns in honour of the Isthmian deities Poseidon and Amphitrite, Melikertes and Leucothea. Cult caves can be seen at the NE corner of the central temenos.

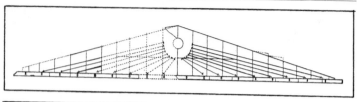

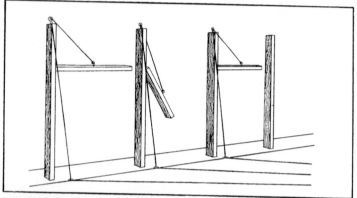

Isthmia. The starting gate

At present visible only from the fence are the remains of huge Roman **baths**, in which excavations since 1975 have uncovered the great hall with a superb mosaic floor, an elaborate hypocaust, and traces of an earlier pool.

On the opposite side of the road, in an obvious gully to the SE of the sanctuary, is the **later stadium**, larger than the first and orientated roughly at right angles to it. This was in use from c 300 until 146 BC. The starting line at the open end was discovered in 1961. On the slope beyond the stadium are traces of a **cyclopean wall** of the end of the Mycenaean period. Its function is uncertain.

A prominent feature of the area is a late antique **fortress**, constructed of materials pillaged from the sanctuary. This irregular enclosure abutting the Peloponnesian side of the wall was taken by early excavators to be the peribolos of the sanctuary itself. Its identity was established by a British examination in 1933; and full excavation has been undertaken by the University of California since 1967. The south gate and two adjacent towers have been cleared, and the junctions of the fortress with the Isthmian wall investigated.

The road continues past turns (left) to the modern hamlet called **Isthmia** (Hotel A) at the E end of the canal. This is served by a minor road direct from the main canal bridge and has access to a second bridge, lowered under water for the passage of ships, which connects with the older Athens road. On the coast to the E (Kavos) are substantial traces of Byzantine settlement. Round a headland (5km farther on, on the Epidauros coast road) lies **Kenchreai** (modern Kekhriés). Here the ancient S port of Corinth, on the Saronic Gulf, was investigated by both land and underwater excavations in 1963 (Indiana University and University of Chicago, under Robert Scranton). The S harbour mole can be seen clearly, extending into the sea. It has a system of warehouses (1–5C AD), also partly visible but continuing under the modern road. At the shoreward end of the mole are the remains of a Christian church with some mosaics (covered) and a Sanctuary of Isis (now mostly underwater). From the latter came the remarkable panels in glass *opus sectile* (now in the Isthmia Museum) with Nilotic and architectural panoramas, as well as large full length portraits of Homer, Plato and others. These items were sealed in the sanctuary after an earthquake c AD 375, along with wooden furniture, a pulley block, bone and ivory decoration, etc.

The N mole can be seen a few minutes' walk away at the other side of the harbour. Near it are the remains of a substantial Roman brick building of the 2C AD, possibly the Sanctuary of Aphrodite mentioned by Pausanias. On the hill behind is an extensive Roman necropolis, including a monumental Early Roman mausoleum. To the N of the road are remains of a number of Roman structures excavated in a rescue operation by the Greek Archaeological Service in 1976. Insubstantial traces of the pre-Roman city can be traced on the low hills further to the N. St Paul commends to the Romans (16, 1) one Phoebe of Kenchreai who may have been the bearer of the epistle itself.

Beyond **Kekhriés** (beach; rooms) the excellent and attractive Epidauros road (occasional cafés; some buses between Corinth and Ligourio/Nafplion) passes below **Stanotópi**, the E spur of Mt Oneion, with remains of a fort of the 4–3C BC. At (13km from Corinth) **Loutró Elénis** (Hotels B, C) a hot sea spring (Helen's Bath), known to Pausanias, is still in use. **Galatáki** (Hotel B), ancient *Solygeia*, 2km inland, has remains of an Archaic Temple of Apollo. After (15km) **Káto Almirí**, with a Mycenaean chamber tomb cemetery, the road climbs inland to pass through sparsely populated pine-clad countryside, with views down to the sea. At 32km there is a turn to **Kórfos** (left; 10km; Hotels B, C, D) on the coast. At 43.5km, immediately to the left of the road is the attractive **Moni Agnountas**, a fortified monastery of the ?10C, later altered. Its church of the Koimesis tes Theotokou has frescoes. At 48.5km an alternative (and slightly shorter) route to Ligourio and Nafplion diverges to the right. **Néa Epídhavros** (Hotels C, E) lies to the right, its port to the left of the road, which continues close to the sea with views of the Methana peninsula and the islands of the Saronic Gulf. 53km Turn (left) to **Palaiá Epídhavros** (Hotels B, C, D; see Rte 29), with a ferry to Aiyina and Piraeus. At 66km there is a junction, right for **Ligourió** and Nafplion; left for the **Sanctuary of Asklepios** (Rte 29) and access to Kranidhi, Ermioni, Methana, Galata etc. (Rtes 23B, D, 29.)

# D.   The Diolkos

Near the W end of the Corinth Canal excavations in 1956–62 uncovered a long stretch of the **Diolkos**, the paved slipway across which ships were winched in ancient times from Poseidonia on one gulf to Schoinous on the other.

A well-preserved section (?6C BC), including traces of the dock at the entrance, can be seen (left) by the car ferry linking Corinth with Loutraki.

# E.   Lechaion (Lékhaio)

The site lies to the right of the Corinth–Patras road, c 4km W of Corinth, beyond the prehistoric (EH) hill site of **Korakou** excavated by the American School in 1916. You turn right just beyond the turning (left) for Ancient Corinth towards **Paralía Lekhaíou**.

**Lechaion**, the ancient N port of Corinth, can be identified by the clear outline of its (silted up) artificial harbour. Here in 396 Stilichon disembarked his punitive expedition against the Gothic invaders of the Peloponnese. Excavations between the harbour and the sea since 1956 have uncovered the complete ground plan of a vast **basilica**, c 186m by 46m, built in the reign of Marcian (450–457) and extended under Justin I some 70 years later. It may have been dedicated to St Leonidas and the Virgins, who were martyred by drowning off Corinth by Decius. The church was ruined in the earthquake of 551, after which the **baptistery**, to the N of the narthex, served for worship for two or three centuries. Much of the marble pavement survives and some exquisite capitals; fragments of coloured glass have been recovered.

# F.   Loutráki and Perachora (Perakhóra)

**Road**, 33km (20½ miles), asphalted to Vouliagméni and cars can be taken to within 400m of the Heraion. **Buses** frequently to Loutráki, every two hours from Loutraki to Perakhóra village, continuing occasionally in high summer to Vouliagmení. Walkers from Loutraki who are willing to swim a few yards can follow a delightful cliff path (3 hrs) direct to the Heraion, keeping seaward of the lake.

From Athens by bus (8 daily in 1½ hrs) or by train (5 daily in 1½–2 hrs), to Loutraki; occasional weekend excursions to the Heraion by the Periyitiki Leskhi of Athens (see Practical Information).

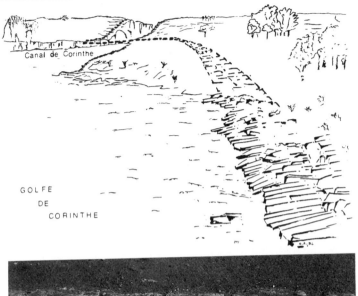

*The Diolkos. Restored line of the trackway, and actual section with wheel-ruts*

From Corinth you take the Athens road, cross the canal and, beyond the bridge, turn left to (9.5km) **Loutráki** (Λουτράκι; Hotels A–E), one of the principal spas in Greece, situated at the E end of the Bay of Corinth and sheltered by the towering Yerania Mountains. Like its ancient predecessor *Therma*, the town (9388 inhab.) gets its name from the hot springs that issue from the mountainside only a few yards from the sea. Their saline waters (30–31°C) are used both internally and externally in cases of dyspepsia, arthritis, and liver complaints. The sea-front is attractively laid out with eucalyptus and exotic shrubs.

A long steep climb to the NW rises above (12km) a chalet hotel on the shore, with splendid views over the Bay of Corinth. You pass below a monastery and reach a small plain about 305m above the sea, dominated to the N by a sheer crag. 22.5km **Perakhóra** is the local village centre (1296 inhab.). From the little museum (at present closed because of earthquake damage), a road leads W through olives, then descends a valley to the Fishing Club (spring) at the NE corner of **Lake Vouliagméni**, the ancient *Eschatiotis*, separated from the sea by a narrow spit through which a channel was cut c 1880. An Early Helladic settlement (by the lake) and Mycenaean chamber tombs (at Skáloma) have been excavated. Skirting the N shore of the lake, you come to a group of tavernas, to the right of which, fed by a catch-pit, is a well-preserved **cistern** (? 4C BC) still in use. Larger cisterns near by, with staircases descending 30m into the ground, are more difficult to inspect. Ancient *Perachora* occupied the greater part of the narrowing peninsula to the W. This was anciently called *Peraion* or Πέρα Χώρα, 'the country beyond the sea' (as seen from Corinth), and commands, as even Acrocorinth does not, the entire Gulf. All around jagged rocks tumble towards the sea, except where a valley descends to the sheltered cove which attracted the mariners of the ancient world. The ⋆view extends to the heights behind Navpaktos, 105km away, where a bend in the straits make the gulf seem like a huge lake ringed by mountains. Predominant to the N are Helikon and Parnassos; to the S, Killini.

**History**. Only slight traces of occupation have been found from the Middle Helladic and Mycenaean periods, at which time, according to Plutarch, Perachora belonged to Megara. In the Geometric period, presumably under Argive influence, a Heraion was founded, but the site flourished as a Corinthian town mainly in the Archaic and Classical periods when Corinth, as an independent city state, dared not allow it to fall into other hands. In the Corinthian War of 391–390 BC Agesilaos of Sparta captured the place; Xenophon, who served on the Spartan side, describes the brief campaign (Hell., iv, 5). Except for shepherds, the site has been deserted since Roman times, but its remains have suffered from stone robbers from the opposite coast. Perachora was excavated in 1930–33 by Humfry Payne and the British School; recent excavations by R.A. Tomlinson.

The road ends at a plateau (parking space). A high-level path leads from there E to the lighthouse, where polygonal walling suggests the existence of a fortified acropolis.

A lower path takes you to the pretty harbour with the remains of a **Sanctuary of Hera Akraia**. The site was excavated by the British School in 1930–33 (the venture charmingly described by Dilys Powell in *An affair of the heart* and *The traveller's journey is done*): numerous votive offerings were probably the dedications of passing mariners. Only foundations remain: a section of the earliest temple (apsidal, Geometric period), and nearby the narrow rectangular temple which succeeded it in the 6C. There may have been an intermediate building of which nothing has survived. Associated with the temple is a fine triglyph altar, whose decoration is a Doric frieze. To the W of the temples was an enclosed area (so-called 'agora') which had a stoa in the 5C. E of the temples, an L-shaped Doric stoa was constructed in the 4C BC.

The small chapel of Ay. Ioannis, originally overlying the apsidal temple and moved in 1933, is visible to the E up the valley. A path leads by the church to a prominent oval water cistern of Hellenistic date and, immediately to the S of this, the remains of ritual dining-rooms, such as are regularly associated with Greek sanctuaries. The path continues upwards to the temenos of **Hera Limenia**, a walled enclosure within which is a rectangular temple or treasury of the mid 8C BC. Here were found numerous votive offerings (many now displayed in Athens). Immediately to the W of the temenos was a sacred pool, now dry, into which offerings were thrown, possibly prior to consultation of the oracle which is said by Strabo to have existed at the site.

About 300m E of the temenos a circular structure, 28m in diameter, has been excavated since 1982. The edifice, belonging to the Classical period, was waterproofed, doorless and has a floor which slopes inward towards the centre—features which suggest that it was a water collection tank. It is almost certainly the monument mentioned by Xenophon (Hellenica, IV, 5. 6) as the place where King Agesilaos of Sparta sat reviewing his war booty in 392 BC.

Bathers from the cove should not go beyond its mouth (danger of currents and sharks).

# 26

# Corinth to Mycenae (Mikínes), Argos, and Návplio

## (also to Trípolis direct by new road)

**Road**, 60km (37¾ miles). 18km Khiliomódhi.—29km. Turn for Neméa.— 39km. Turn for Mycenae (Mikínes).—48km. Argos.—54km Tiryns (Tírintha).—60km **Návplio**. This route is served by the Athens–Navplio **Buses** (hourly in 2½ hrs), and as far as Argos by some other Athens–Peloponnese services; from Corinth to Navplio in 1½ hours, every 90 minutes; frequent local service between Argos and Navplio.

**New Road Corinth–Tripolis** (direct), 84km (52 miles).—7km Junction beyond Ancient Corinth (also for Navplio and Argos by old road). 18km Spathovoúni (toll).—27km Neméa.—47km Stérna (exit for Argos).—57km Kaparéli.—60km Artemísion Tunnel (1400m).—70km Nestáni (exit for Vítina and Olympia).—81km End of road.—84km Trípolis.

The new road has no petrol stations and no other access points apart from those specified above. There are numerous lay-bys. When travelling N (or retrospectively) there are good views of the fortifications of Acrocorinth. Between Spathovoúni and Nemea, extensive ancient quarries can be seen to the right of the road. The road is excellent for gaining fast access to the central (and East) Peloponnese but avoids the Argolid completely.

**Railway**, SPAP 5 times daily to Navplio, 65km (40 miles) in c 1½ hr; Argos, 53km, in c 1 hour; through trains from Athens. To Mycenae, 43km in c 50 minutes.

This route crosses the nome of **Argolis**, the easternmost of the divisions of the Peloponnese. Bordered on the N by Corinthia and on the W by the mountains of Arcadia, it consists of the Argolic plain (see below) and a mountainous peninsula, the fourth and least conspicuous tongue of the Peloponnese, which separates the Gulf of Navplion (the ancient Argolic Gulf) from the Saronic Gulf. The modern province corresponds roughly to the ancient **Argolid** less the islands off its E coast (Poros, Hydra, and Spetsai), which nowadays fall under Attica. The modern capital is Navplion which provides the most comfortable and convenient centre for exploration. The region is of the greatest archaeological importance, including Mycenae, Tiryns, Argos, and Epidauros as well as many other significant (though less visited) sites, both Classical and Mycenaean. A useful arcaheological guidebook, locally available, is V. Lambrinoudakis, *Argolida*, n.d. (c 1993).

From modern Corinth the Argos road runs SW through vineyards. To the right rises Acrocorinth. Both road and railway climb the wooded valley between the Oneia hills (563m; left) and Mt Skiona (700m). 13km **Athíkia station**; in the village, 4km SE, was found the Apollo of Tenea, an archaic kouros, now in Munich. At (18km) **Khiliomódhi** (1634 inhab.) a road branches left to the **Pass of Ayionóri** (8km) with a medieval castle repaired by Morosini, and continues by Prósimna to the plain of Argos. By this road Dramali succeeded in fighting his way out of the plain of Argolis, at the cost of a further 1000 men, two days after his defeat at Dhervenaki (see below). The scanty remains of **Tenea** lie near this road at Klénia 1.5km S of Khiliomódhi.

The inhabitants of Tenea claimed to be Trojans brought captive by the Greeks from Tenedos. Oedipus, who had been exposed as a child by his father, was brought up here by the shepherd Polybos. The town sent out most of the colonists of Syracuse. It sided with Rome in 146 BC and so escaped the destruction of Corinth. A man from Asia, contemplating a move to Corinth, asked the oracle's advice, and received the unexpected reply, 'Blest is Corinth, but Tenea for me'.

The road passes N of (25km) **Ayios Vasílios**. Above the village (1.5km left) are the remains of a medieval castle; and a little to the E, off the road to Klénia (see above; signposted), the low hill of **Zygouries**, a Bronze Age settlement excavated in 1921–22 by the American School, with good examples of Early Bronze Age housing. To the NW is the truncated top of **Mt Fokas**, the ancient *Apesas* (872m). You now enter the territory of **Kleonai** the ruins of which lie 3km NW.

'Well-built' *Kleonai* (*Iliad*, II, 570) was 80 furlongs from Corinth on the prehistoric road over the hills to Argos. Its site (well-fortified, as Strabo remarks) occupies an isolated hill overlooking the valley of the Longos. Off a by-road (right) a track, initially signposted, leads in the general direction. To the left are the foundations of a **Shrine of Herakles**. Ploughed-out blocks and washed-down sherds cover a wide cultivated area. It is possible to continue from Kleonai to ancient Nemea.

The road becomes increasingly shut in by hills as it reaches the summit (392m) near (30km) **Neméa-Dhervenákia** station. Straight ahead is a road for Nemea. Our route turns left to cross the track. Then a branch road doubles back (left; signed Dhervenakia) to (c 1.5km) a chapel in a grove beside a spring. Above stands a colossal statue of Kolokotronis, victor in the battle of 1822 (see below).

At 31km another road diverges (right) to modern **Neméa** (9.5km), formerly Ayios Yeoryios, situated at the S end of Trikaranon (727m). Here (2.5km S) is the monastery of Vrákhos (1633). The site of ancient *Nemea* is at **Iráklion**, a village only 4km along this road. It lies on a lonely little plateau (364m), 4km long and 1km wide, watered by the river Nemea (or Koutsommati), which flows into the Gulf of Corinth. The area is dominated by Mt Fokas, with an ash altar of Zeus on the summit. The valley of Nemea is celebrated for its red wine. The N part has been recently surveyed by American archaeologists. Like Olympia, Nemea was a sacred precinct and not a city, though Strabo speaks of the village of Bembina as being close by. Near here Herakles slew the Nemean lion. In the cypress grove surrounding the Temple of Zeus (now partially replanted in ancient pits) were celebrated biennially the **Nemean Games**, one of the four great Panhellenic festivals.

According to one legend of Roman date the Games were instituted by Herakles after he had slain the Nemean lion, but in Classical times the foundation myth involved the death of the infant prince Opheltes in whose honour the Argive Adrastus and the Seven Against Thebes held the first games. The festival was managed by the people of Kleonai from the time of their historical foundation in 573 BC until the late 5C when the games appear to have been moved to Argos. Returned to Nemea in c 330 BC, the games remained under Argive control and were removed again to Argos in the 3C probably never to return to Nemea. Excavation has suggested there was no occupation between Mycenaean times and the 8C, and little activity until the 6C.

The French School studied the temple in 1884 and 1912; the site was partly excavated by the American School in 1924–27, and again in 1964. Large-scale excavation (now completed) took place from 1974. There is an excellent guidebook, S.G. Miller and others, *Nemea. A guide to the site and museum* (1990); and another to the stadium: S.G. Miller, *The ancient stadium of Nemea*, n.d. (c 1994).

The **stadium** can be seen to the left of the approach road just after the first sight of the temple is obtained. In 1992–93 it was landscaped and opened to the public. Of embanked earth, it occupies a partly natural hollow. The starting line is *in situ* and a stone water channel surrounds the course. Foundations of a judges' stand and distance markers are visible. The **entrance tunnel** (c 320 BC), approached through a courtyard building of uncertain function, has graffiti (boys' names) written by admirers.

You continue down the main road to the outskirts of the village, where a lane (right) leads to the main site. The **museum** (car park; 08.45–15.00 Tues–Fri, 09.30–11.30 Sun, closed Mon; same hours for site), opened in

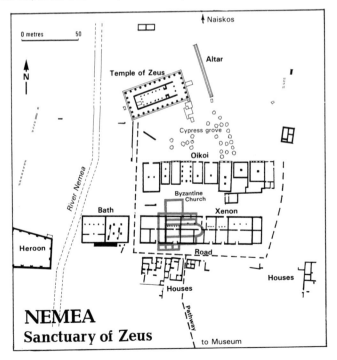

1984, has models of the site, a comprehensive display of finds, architectural elements (in the court) and a display of early travellers' views and accounts of Nemea; also finds from other sites in the area.

Leaving the museum, you turn right and pass through the site to begin at the central structure.

The **Temple of Nemean Zeus**, a Doric peripteral hexastyle (6 columns by 13), was built between 340 and 320 BC of locally quarried stone, on the site of an earlier sanctuary. Its columns are unusually slender; three remain standing, one from the peristyle and two from the pronaos, still supporting their architrave. The drums of many other columns lie in order as they have fallen as the result of deliberate destruction at various times from the 4C AD to the 13C. The roof had already fallen before Pausanias saw it. Other column drums are now lined around the site, having been studied and inventoried for a possible reconstruction of the temple which has begun on the crepidoma of the N side. The lowest course of the cella is sufficiently well preserved to show that it had a pronaos in antis but no opisthodomos. Within the cella 14 columns enclosed the central space, while to the W, between the colonnade and the wall, and below the floor level, is an **adyton**, or secret inner chamber, approached by a flight of crude steps. Parallel to the façade are the foundations of a long narrow **altar** of unusual type.

To the SE of the temple stood a row of nine *oikoi*, or **treasuries**, seen by their foundations to be about twice the size of those at Olympia, and dating to the early 5C.

Parallel and farther to the SW is a **bath house** of the late 4C, the bathing chamber of which was protected by a shelter in 1925 but is still often waterlogged. Beyond (left), is a rectangular structure of the late 4C whose central wall re-used a pedestal (now in the museum) bearing a dedicatory inscription of Aristis, son of Pheidon of Kleonai, who four times won the pankration in the Nemean Games in the mid 6C. The building, which had at least five separate entrances from a roadway to the S, is believed to have been a **xenon** (or hostel). Overlying its middle section is a large Christian **basilica** (6C AD) constructed of great blocks taken from the temple, and refloored in terracotta in the 12C. The screen and sanctuary floor are of limestone blocks from a monument of the 4C BC. The apse and narthex can be traced, and on the N side, a baptistry with a large font: there are graves of the same period nearby. The mound which covered these remains had earlier been supposed to cover the 'Tomb of Opheltes'. The latter has now been identified with an enclosure W of the bath house. It consists of a large five-sided compound of the early 3C which lies over a curvilinear predecessor of the 6C, and surrounded a series of altars.

S of the xenon stretches of the terracotta aqueduct which carried water to the bath house are visible, and farther S a line of large houses, perhaps for the priests.

On the hill of **Tsoúngiza**, immediately W of the Sanctuary of Zeus, is a Neolithic and Bronze Age settlement.

FROM NEMÉA TO TRÍPOLIS. 102km (63miles). The road leaves modern **Nemea** (no signs; ask for road to **Psári**) and crosses the plain of Phliasia (305m; with an Ottoman castle on the **Polífégi** peak at the S end), passing (3.5km, right) the site of *Phlious* (commonly Phlioúnda) which is marked by a small chapel (Panayía Rakhiótissa; ?13C, with interesting constructional features) on a ridge, round which are scattered the somewhat indeterminate remains, recently re-examined by the American School. They include a theatre and a large colonnaded court, between the chapel and the road. After **Galatás** (11km; an alternative lower route, left, to Platani and Skoteini) the road climbs (retrospective views), via **Aïdhónia**, with an interesting cemetery of Mycenaean chamber tombs (looted objects were recovered from New York by legal action in 1993) to the pleasant village of **Psári** (23km). Just beyond Psári a by-road leads in 7km to **Kiónia** and Lake Stymphalos (Rte 38).

32km Turn (left) for **Aléa**. Ancient *Alea* 3km E of the modern village, on a hill above a valley, has fine 4C fortifications on the acropolis. The road continues amid mountain scenery, by-passing **Skotiní** (46km), then descending to **Kandhíla** (62km) and the plain of Orchomenos.

71km (right) An asphalt road (unmarked) climbs in 2km to the hamlet of **Kalpáki** which lies at the SE foot of the acropolis, on the site of the lower city of ancient *Orchomenos*. The track proceeds through the village, climbs the mountainside (keep right) and becomes a footpath leading to the main site.

Arcadian Orchomenos occupied a strategic position on the midland route between N and S Peloponnese. Homer calls it 'rich in sheep' (πολύμηλος; *Iliad II*, 605). Herodotus tells us that 120 Orchomenian soldiers fought at Thermopylae and 600 at Plataia. Just before the first battle of Mantinea (418 BC) the Athenians and Argives besieged and took the city. The scattered remains excavated in 1913 by the French School include the foundations of two **temples** (Apollo and Aphrodite, and, higher up, Artemis Mesopolitis), a stoa of the agora, cisterns, and a small **theatre**, but the situation of the site is more impressive than its remains. The acropolis (936m) stands at 245m on an almost isolated hill dividing the plain into two halves. On the E a narrow defile connecting the two parts of the plain is guarded on either side by ruined Venetian watch-towers. The *view is extensive. To the SW across the plain towers Mainalon, while farther SE you see into the Plain of Mantinea. The fields, under waving corn, seem like a patchwork quilt whose colours change with the passing clouds. To the N loom the high peaks round Mt Feneos.

Near Orchomenos is the church of **Ayios Nikolaos sta Kambia'**, with a frescoed crypt of **Ayía Varvára** beneath. Together they reproduce at a small scale the architecture of Osios Loukas of which this monastery was a dependency. The crypt is of the inscribed-domed cross plan with ten groin-vaulted bays with barrel-vaulted extensions E and W. The frescoes in the crypt are assigned to the 12C.

Off the main road to the right **Khani Anésti** is a pleasant stopping place (restaurants).

75km Turn (left) for the Byzantine church of the Dormition (Koimesis tes Theotokou) which incorporates earlier material. The Argos road turns S into the **Pass of Dhervenáki** (Δερβενάκια), the ancient 'Pass of the Tretós', between the twin summits of **Mt Tretos**, the 'perforated' mountain (τρητός), so called because it is honeycombed with caves. Road and railway descend the rocky defile. Nearby, on 6 August 1822, Kolokotronis caught the army of Dramali, which was retreating from the plain of Argolis. The Turks left 4000 men dead on the field, and though a few cavalry fought their way through to Corinth, Dramali and the remainder retreated to try an alterna-tive route (see above). From the S outlet of the pass you look into the plain of Argos.

The view is generally hazy. To the left the bare summits of **Ayios Ilias** (809m), **Zara** (660m) and **Euboia** (535m) overshadow the acropolis of Mycenae. On the right Argos sprawls below its mountain citadel while the E Arcadian mountains rise behind, **Artemision** reaching 1772m, and **Ktenia** 1599m. In the centre, beyond the ruins of Tiryns, the battlemented acropolis of Akronavplion rises for a moment above the blue line of the Argolic Gulf.

Near (38.5km) **Fíkhtia** are the remains of two ancient watchtowers. Just beyond (left) are the turning for **Mycenae** (4km; Rte 27) and **Mycenae station**. The road runs down the middle of the Argolic Plain.

The **Argolic Plain** is triangular, extending from a base of c 19km on the Argolic Gulf to an apex at Mt Tretos; to the E and W it is hedged in by barren mountains. The plain is watered by the capricious **Panitsa** (the ancient *Inachos*), the **Xerias** (*Charadros*), and other seasonal streams. Their dryness was attributed in antiquity to the anger of Poseidon because Inachos allotted the country to Hera. Hence Argos is 'very thirsty' in Homer (πολυ–δίψιον Ἄργος). Close to the sea, however, the land is marshy, and between the marshes and the upper part of the plain is the fertile tract of land which was famed for the horses bred in its pastures (Ἄργος ἱππόβοτον, *Iliad*, II, 287; 'aptum equis', Horace, *Odes*, I, 7, 9).

43.5km **Koutsopódhi** lies among olive-groves, vineyards, and cotton and tobacco fields. 44.5km Access road (right) to the new Corinth–Tripolis motorway. You cross the Panitsa and the wide bed of the Xerias.

48km **ARGOS** (Ἄργος; Hotels C, D, E), the seat of an eparchy, is a prosperous town of 21,901 inhabitants situated in the centre of the Argolic plain just W of the Xerias and 8km from the sea. Local industries include cattle breeding and tobacco growing. The modern town occupies the site of the ancient city, at the foot of its two citadels ('*duas arces habent Argi*', Livy). The ancient importance of Argos is reflected in the fact that in Homer 'Argive', like 'Danaan' and 'Achaean', is a synonym for 'Greek'. Argos is often ignored by tourists, but although some of the antiquities are of rather specialised interest, the museum is interesting and well laid out and the town has several interesting buildings either restored or in the process of restoration (the town hall, the market building, the Kapoditria barracks).

**History.** *Argos*, which traditionally traced its foundation to Pelasgians from another Argos in the north, was occupied from the Early Bronze Age. Here the mythical Danaos fled from his brother Aegyptos. Adrastus of Argos, who led the Seven against Thebes to restore his son-in-law Polyneices to his throne, was the sole survivor of that disastrous expedition. Diomedes, successor of Adrastus and next to Achilles the bravest hero in the Greek army, led the Argive contingent in the Trojan War.

After the Dorian invasions had superseded the power of Mycenae, Argos aspired to the predominant position in the Peloponnese for over four centuries. Her last great king, Pheidon, led an army to the banks of the Alpheios and restored the Olympic Games to Pisa. He was the first to introduce coinage and a new scale of weights and measures into continental Greece. His defeat of the Lacedaemonians at Hysiae (c 668 BC) marked an early round in the long struggle with Sparta for the E seaboard of Laconia. In 550 Sparta defeated Argos and annexed Argive Thyreatis. An attempt to retrieve this loss was crushed c 494 BC at Sepeia, near Tiryns, when Kleomenes I routed an Argive army. The defence of Argos by the poetess Telesilla is probably legendary. The city took no part in the Persian Wars and resented the participation of Mycenae and Tiryns. A renewal of the struggle against Sparta enabled her to destroy her former dependencies in 468 BC. Ten years later Argos is in alliance with Athens and adopting democratic government. During the Peloponnesian War, in 420, Athens, Argos, Elis, and Mantinea formed a league, but the defeat of the allies in 418 by the Lacedaemonians at the First Battle of Mantinea and an oligarchic rising in Argos effectively put that city out of the war.

Argos was an ally of Corinth in the Corinthian War (395–386). She helped to defeat the Spartans at the Second Battle of Mantinea (362 BC). Pyrrhus attacked Argos in 272 BC; he was killed in the abortive street-fighting after being felled by a tile thrown by an old woman from a rooftop. In 229 BC Argos temporarily joined the Achaean League, and after 146 BC was included in the Roman province of Achaia.

The city became a bishopric in the 5C and was elevated to the rank of metropolis in 1088. It withstood the Franks for seven years before surrendering in 1212; thenceforward its history is bound up with that of Navplion. The Turks ravaged it in 1397. In the War of Independence the seizure of the Larissa by Demetrios Ypsilantis caused the retreat of Dramali (comp. above). Ypsilantis' 'National Convention' of 1821 met at Argos before its removal to Epidauros, and here in 1829 Capodistrias convened the Fourth National Assembly which concentrated power in his hands. The city was sacked by Ibrahim Pasha in 1825 and occupied by the French in 1832 after a fight with armed bands had caused the last bloodshed of the war.

The Argive school of sculpture was famous. Its best known member was Polykleitos (fl. 452–412). It was said that, while Pheidias made the noblest statues of gods, Polykleitos was unsurpassed for his statues of men.

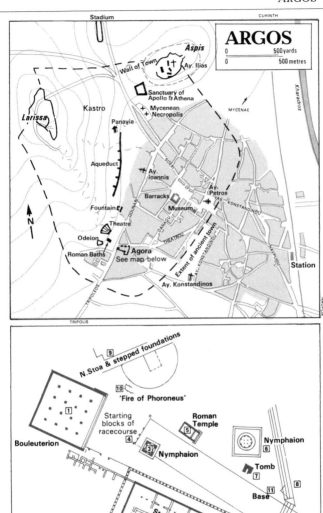

Agora plan

The modern town covers much of the area of the ancient city. Systematic explorations outside the town were made in 1902–30 by Wilhelm Vollgraff, a Dutch archaeologist and member of the French School. Since 1952 further excavations have been made on these and other sites by the French School and the Greek Archaeological Service has been active.

In the **Plateía Ayíou Pétrou** stands the church of St Peter (1859), patron saint of Argos. Within, the modern woodwork is carved in a traditional style.

To the SW is the **museum**. FOYER. Mosaic; large Geometric vases, giant burial pithos. GROUND FLOOR GALLERY. Middle Helladic, Mycenaean, and Geometric pottery and bronze objects from tombs. Bronze *helmet and cuirass of the late Geometric period. *Krateutai* (fire-dogs) in the shape of triremes (bronze); spits; pottery fragment showing Odysseus and Polyphemos (7C BC); red-figured vase by Hermonax showing Theseus and the Minotaur; terracotta figures playing blind man's buff; lyre (6C BC; restored) made of the shell of a tortoise and ibex horns. Upstairs: Roman sculpture including statues from the baths; mosaic floor.

Stairs lead down to the LERNA ROOM with important pottery finds of Lerna I–VII, excavated by J.L. Caskey from 1952; they range from Early Neolithic through to Mycenaean. Terracotta statuette (c 4500 BC); seal impressions. Early Helladic ceremonial hearth (restored). On the TERRACE outside are large well-preserved mosaics of the 5C AD (Seasons; Months; Bacchus; Hunting scenes).

The square beyond the museum was an animated open **market** and a covered market building. From here Odhos Tsókri, the old **bazaar**, provides the shortest approach to the **Aspis** (see below).

You take the Tripolis road to (1km; left) the **agora** (see Marchetti in B.C.H. 1994).

The sanctuary of Apollo Lykeios mentioned by Pausanias (from which came the title *Lykeios Agora*) has not been found, but blocks from it may have been incorporated in later alterations to the bouleuterion. Archaic houses (sometimes visible in lower levels) were demolished to make way for the public buildings of the Classical period. Many of these were altered in Roman times and following destructions caused by the Heruls 267 AD or the Goths in 395. The 18 temples recorded by Pausanias were probably destroyed by the Goths. In the 5C AD the public buildings fell into disuse.

The archaeological site is divided by the main road at the point where it turns S towards Tripolis. The large excavated area E of the road is of somewhat specialised interest. Nearest the road are the lower courses of a Roman **bouleuterion** (Pl. 1), originally 5C, whose roof was carried on 16 Ionic columns. To the SE is a large rectangular complex (Pl. 2), with the remains of **colonnades** to N, W and E. The section of the colonnade immediately E of the bouleuterion was a later addition. In the 5C BC the interior was an open **court**: in the 1C AD baths (their brick construction prominent) were built in the W part and the E section was converted into a **palaistra** (some column bases from the court, and mosaics of later date, survive). Opposite the NW corner of the stoa, and E of the bouleuterion, is a square 1C AD **nymphaion** (Pl. 3) of brick within a stone surround. This was built over a racecourse (cf. Athens and Corinth) three of whose **starting blocks** (Pl. 4) survive beside the nymphaion. The start incorporated a *hysplix* (starting mechanism, cf. Isthmia): there were 18 lanes, each c 1m wide. NE are the poros foundations of a building of the Hellenistic period which was later rebuilt as a **Roman temple** (Pl. 5; base of cult statue (?) visible). To the E are the untidy remains of another **nymphaion** (Pl. 6), identified as such by inscriptions on the surviving architrave. The circular superstructure over a cistern is formed out of an earlier building on the same site. S of this is a **tomb** (Pl. 7) of the 2C AD which had rich finds. Further on is the recently discovered marble **base** (Pl. 11) of a substantial monument (? Hadrianic) of fine marble construction. The E side of the site is bounded by the extensive **drainage channels** (Pl. 8) for carrying off the water which flooded down from the hills above. The original open channel of massive limestone blocks was succeeded by watercourses which were roofed with brick vaults in the Roman period.

Back near the entrance to the site, N of the bouleuterion, another **stoa** (?), 4C in origin, has been recently excavated. Attached to it is a circular **stepped foundation** (Pl. 9). A large base within this is composed of reused blocks from a triglyph altar and a Roman honorific base. Originally used for choral performances in honour of Apollo and/or meeting of the old Council of Eighty, it was later converted into an ornamental pool. S of this a trapezoidal enclosure defined by well preserved limestone posts (of reused archaic material) enclosed carbonised remains and may be the **Fire of Phoroneus** (Pl. 10) mentioned by Pausanias. Its archaic predecessor belonged to the **Seven against Thebes**.

To the W of the main road, the path to the site lies above the original approach road to the theatre. To the S of the ancient road are the impressive remains of a temple of the 1C AD, perhaps of Asklepios and/or Serapis, remodelled as a **bath building** in the 2C AD. In antiquity a monumental stepped **entrance** projected 18m from the façade, joined to the street by a passage. The apse of the W end is preserved to roof height. The layout can best be seen from the hillside to the S of the theatre. The *frigidarium* was equipped with three plunge-baths and the establishment had three *calidaria* with marble-faced baths. In the **crypt** below the apsidal reception hall are three sarcophagi. Many architectural fragments and sections of mosaic floor (much now covered over) testify to the original splendour of the building. Sections of the hypocaust heating system can be seen.

Cut into the side of the hill above is the **theatre**, which accommodated c 20,000 spectators and is thus rivalled in size on the Greek mainland only by those at Dodona, Megalopolis and Sikyon. It dates from the end of the 4C BC or a little later, but was twice remodelled in Roman times.

In the S parodos is a small relief of the Dioscuri. The **orchestra**, 25.5m in diameter, was paved in blue and white marble in the 4C AD when it was turned into a waterproof basin for the staging of naval contests. The late Roman modifications to the stage have been removed to reveal the foundations of the Greek **skene**, largely destroyed in the 2C during the Imperial reconstruction. The wings of the **cavea**, which were built on artificial banking, have disappeared, but 81 rows of seats remain in the rock-cut centre section. Two (later three) **diazomata** and seven flights of steps, not placed regularly, divided the seating. The surviving seats of honour in the front row include an imperial **throne** probably of the time of Gratian. The cavea was covered by an **awning**, supported on wooded poles set in large square holes cut into the back rests of the seats, every 10–14 rows. In the theatre two national conventions met in the War of Independence (see above).

To the S are some remains of the **aqueduct** that brought water for the *naumachiae*. Fragments of 4C walling here probably upheld a road leading to the theatre. Farther on a **Roman odeion** of the 1C AD (later restored) covers vestiges of a second **theatre** antedating the larger one farther N. Fourteen curved rows remain of the Roman seating. The straight banks of the Greek structure, originally of some 35 rows, probably constituted the meeting-place of the Argive assembly. To the S of the Odeion are remnants of an **Aphrodision** which survived from the Archaic period to c AD 405.

From the modern reservoir above the theatres a tiring zigzag path (better used for the descent) leads up in 45 minutes to the **kastro** (see below), a fortress crowning the ancient Larissa.

Skirting the base of the Larissa you approach the **Deíras**, the ridge joining the Larissa to the Aspis; the ancient road from Argos to Mantinea passed through a gate on this ridge. The convent of Panayía tou Vrákhou (Virgin of the Rock; left, above) stands on the site of a Temple of Hera Akraía. The rounded hill of Ayios Ilías which rises to the NE of the ridge is the ancient *Aspis* ('Shield'), the original citadel of Argos, which lost its importance when the Larissa was founded. At its SW foot Vollgraff discovered a **Mycenaean necropolis**, which was more fully explored in 1955–59. Twenty-six chamber tombs and six shaft graves have come to light as well as a Middle Helladic building of the early 2nd millennium. About 140m NW the **Sanctuary of Apollo and Athena** forms a long rectangle divided into four terraces.

On the W is a **great court** with a stone altar, and bases of tripods and statues. A rock-cut staircase of 10 steps, 27.5m wide, leads to the central terrace, which contained the **Temple of Pythian Apollo** or **Apollo Deiradiotes** (Apollo of the Ridge) and the **manteion** or oracle, a rectangular building of unbaked bricks on a stone foundation. A large Byzantine church was built on this spot. To the E, on a lower terrace, was a **round temple** or tholos, and on an upper terrace was the **Temple of Athena Oxyderkes** (Sharp-eyed Athena), supposedly dedicated by Diomedes 'because once when he was fighting at Ilium the goddess lifted the darkness from his eyes' (*Iliad*, V, 127). Here also was a large cistern. The **stadium** lay farther N outside the wall.

The summit of the **Aspis** (100m) is crowned by the little chapel of Ay. Ilías. Here the Argives had a small **acropolis**, built over the remains of a Bronze Age settlement discovered by Vollgraff and now being reinvestigated.

The polygonal 6C **walls** of the Hellenic fortress describe an oval round the chapel. They were built on the remains of the prehistoric enceinte (Middle Helladic), except in the NE where they formed a triangular salient with two square towers and four posterns. Within the walls, against the E wall and round the chapel, are two groups of **Pre-Mycenaean houses**, in ashlar bonded with clay. To the S and W a group of Macedonian buildings surrounds an Archaic **temple**. A conspicuous hexagonal **tower** marks the junction of the acropolis and city walls.

From the Deiras a road runs W before climbing steeply to the summit of the **Lárissa** (276m) the principal citadel of Argos. The **ancient citadel** was formed of two concentric enceintes, an outer wall of Hellenic masonry (5C) having been added to the polygonal work of the 6C which protected the Archaic acropolis. Sections of antique masonry can be traced in the medieval *\*kastro*, which was built largely on the old foundations by the Byzantines and Franks and enlarged by the Venetians and Turks. The 5C wall survives on the NW of the outer enceinte, while the polygonal wall is best seen on the NE side of the **keep**. This fine medieval structure incorporates fragments from a Temple of Zeus Larisaos and a Temple of Athena, the poros foundations of which were excavated in the court by Vollgraff. Traces of Mycenaean wall and a votive deposit of the 8C BC were also found.

The view embraces the whole Argolid and the Gulf of Navplion. Far to the E rises Arachnaion. Immediately to the W is **Mt Lykone**, crowned by the remains of a small temple of Artemis Orthia; behind rises Artemision. To the N the flat summit of Mt Fokas is conspicuous.

You can descend by one of two paths, neither distinct and both steep. The more westerly passes close to some traces of the **town walls**, while that to the E passes a rock-cut relief of a horseman and a snake to reach a rectangular **terrace** supported by a polygonal wall. At its NE corner is a relief of seated divinities. Vollgraff identified the place with the **Kriterion**, or Judgement Place, where Hypermnestra was condemned by her father Danaos for refusing to kill her husband; at a later date it supported a fountain.

From Argos to the Heraion, see Rte 28C; to Lerna and Tripolis, see Rte 30. Buses (office in Od. Kapodistríou) every ½ hour to **Navplion**; hourly to **Corinth** and **Athens**; to **Tripolis** (once daily each by old and new roads) and **Kalamata**, etc.; also five daily to **Mycenae**; for **Sparta**, and **Yithion**, etc., change in Tripolis.

Road and goods line continue across a fertile plain which supplies the markets of Athens with vegetables. 53km. Turning (left) for Khónika, (Argive Heraion), Dhendrá and Mycenae (Rtes 27, 28). 54km **Tiryns** (modern Tíryntha). The massive walls of the ancient city (Rte 28B) are seen to the left. 60km **Návplio**, see Rte 28A.

# 27

## Mycenae (Mikínes)

**Approaches. Road**. From Corinth or Návplio to Fíkthia (Rte 26) or from Návplio via Tiryns and Khónika (Rte 26). From Fikthia (bus stop from Athens) a good by-road climbs (4km) to the village of Mikínes and the Lion Gate. Daily **Coach tours** from Athens (less frequent in winter). Several **buses** per day from Argos and Návplion.

**Railway** to Mycenae station, see Rte 26. Then, on foot (4km), as below.

From Fíkhthia or the near-by railway station of Mycenae the road leads E to (2km) **Mikínes** (formerly Kharváti; Hotels B, C, E, Rooms). 2km further on is the archaeological site, where there is a huge car-park just below the Lion Gate. The fencing makes it more difficult to appreciate the skilful siting of the fortress and the magnitude of Mycenaean conception as a whole. However, out of tourist hours, a better sense of the human scale in comparison with the rugged and difficult terrain can still be obtained by approaching on foot.

A by-road (asphalt, but rough in places) leads from Mikínes to Khónika (for the Argive Heraion) and Tiryns (Rte 28C).

**MYCENAE** (Μυκναι), in modern pronunciation *Mikínai*, a city known to archaeology as the centre of the great Helladic civilisation and to tradition as the capital of Agamemnon, lies 15km from the sea, half-hidden in a mountain glen or recess (μύχος), between **Mt Ayios Ilias** (750m) on the N and **Mt Zara** (600m) on the S. Its position oversees the landfall in the Gulf of Navplion and controls the natural roads N through the mountains to Corinth and the Isthmus. The city, which Homer calls 'rich in gold' (πολύχρῡσος) and 'well-built' (ευκτίμενον πτολίεθρον) and 'broad-streeted' was proverbial in Classical times for its wealth. At its zenith Mycenae consisted of a fortified administrative centre probably with further settlement outside the walls. The acropolis, the residence of its kings (who enclosed within its walls the tombs of some of their predecessors), stands on an almost isolated hill skirted by two deep ravines which fork from the mouth of the glen, the **Kokoretsa** running W and the **Khavos** SW. From the NW corner of the acropolis a long narrow ridge runs S parallel to the Khavos. In the slopes of this ridge are the tholos or beehive tombs which Pausanias mistook for treasuries and, in part overlying these, the less important ruins of Hellenic buildings from the 3C BC.

**Excavations**. The earliest systematic excavations, which uncovered the first circle of shaft graves, were initiated in 1874–76 by Schliemann, who was succeeded by Stamatakis. In 1886–1902 digging was continued by the Greek Archaeological Society under Tsountas. Extensive excavations in 1920–23, 1939 by the British School at Athens under Prof. Alan Wace showed that some of the interim conclusions reached by Evans and Myres about the chronology of Mycenae were ill-founded. Wace resumed excavations in 1950–55; in 1951 work of restoration and preservation was begun on behalf of the Greek government. Since 1952, when Grave Circle B was excavated, the Greek Archaeological Society has been actively engaged at Mycenae, with extensive investigations undertaken by Prof. G.E. Mylonas. Lord Wm. Taylour directed British excavations after Wace's death, first in collaboration with J. Papadhimitriou, then with G.E. Mylonas.

**History**. Archaeological evidence shows that the site was first occupied in the 6th millennium BC and had an unremarkable Neolithic and Early Helladic culture to c 2000 BC. The extent of Middle Helladic settlement is unclear but a large cemetery consisting of groups of cist tombs extended to the W in the nearest rock soft enough to be dug. In the middle of this area, during the Late Helladic I period (c 1550 BC), six large shaft graves were dug for a ruling family; a further 14 shaft graves, forming another group farther from the citadel, are slightly earlier.

The earliest of the tholos tombs seems to date from the following century, and this type of interment continues to 1300 BC, showing a progressive structural development culminating in fine architecture. Nine such tombs have been discovered at Mycenae; they must have belonged to people of high status and seem to bear the same relationship to the contemporary chamber tombs as the shaft graves do to the cist tombs. Soon after 1350 BC a Cyclopean enceinte was constructed, and the Palace and most of the buildings within replanned on a more lavish scale. This first circuit was extended c 1250 BC to include Grave Circle A within the fortification and, at the same time, the Lion Gate replaced an earlier and differently aligned entrance system. The walls of this new 'West enceinte' cut through the original cemetery of the area. This, the period of greatest prosperity, was interrupted by a violent earthquake, which was followed by only partial rebuilding. Fifty years later (c 1200 BC) the site was devastated by fire: at about the same time the final element of the fortification system was built—the north-east extension, which protected the site's water supply. At or after the end of the 12C a further fire destruction occurred, after which the citadel was abandoned until the early Iron Age, though the walls remained virtually intact. Then a small township developed which sent contingents to fight at Thermopylae and Plataea; this fell to the jealousy of Argos in 468 BC and the site was again left waste. Later the walls were repaired and a Hellenistic town spread over the W ridge. Mycenae's most important period, however, begins c 1650 BC and ceases c 1100–1050 BC with the fall of the civilisation to which it gives name.

**Mycenaean Civilisation**. Towards the end of the Middle Helladic period a sudden stimulus apparently influences the previously unremarkable mainland culture. The contents of the shaft graves at Mycenae (already a dominant centre) suggest the existence of a sophisticated and dynamic aristocracy with very considerable wealth. The technique and artistry of the finds is highly accomplished. The dead of the previous generation were much less lavishly provided. The theory that Minoan conquerors or colonists were responsible for the form of burial, the use of gold, and the warlike accoutrements alike being foreign to Minoan custom; Helladic building types continue unchanged by Cretan influence. A later theory that the riches of these graves were loot from Minoan Crete brought back when Helladic warriors destroyed the Old Palaces also has little to commend it. There is no evidence of gold on this scale in Crete whereas contemporary documents in Egypt record that there it was 'like dust beneath the feet'. The Egyptian pharaohs of the XVIII dynasty paid their commanders in gold. At the time of the shaft-graves (c 1600 BC onwards) the Egyptians were seeking aid from overseas in their struggle against the Hyksos. It is possible that the heavily-armed Achaean warriors fought as mercenaries on the Nile, when they brought back to Mycenae the Egyptian belief in life after death, the fashion for golden death-masks, and provision of elaborate grave-goods (comp. the representations of cheetah, and the ostrich eggs, among the finds). Legend attributes an Egyptian origin to the hero Danaos. This explanation however is also speculative.

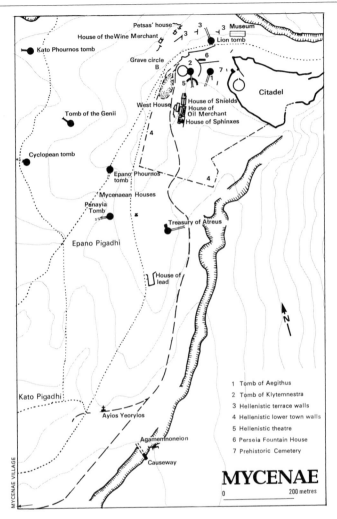

Petsas' house

House of the Wine Merchant

Kato Phournos tomb

Grave circle B

Museum

Lion tomb

Tomb of the Genii

West House

House of Shields
House of
Oil Merchant
House of Sphinxes

Citadel

Cyclopean tomb

Epano Phournos tomb

Mycenaean Houses

Panayia Tomb

Epano Pigadhi

Treasury of Atreus

House of lead

N

Kato Pigadhi

Ayios Yeoryios

Agamemnoneion

Causeway

1 Tomb of Aegithus
2 Tomb of Klytemnestra
3 Hellenistic terrace walls
4 Hellenistic lower town walls
5 Hellenistic theatre
6 Perseia Fountain House
7 Prehistoric Cemetery

# MYCENAE

0          200 metres

MYCENAE VILLAGE

Nevertheless, in Late Helladic I (early 16C BC), Mycenaean culture does assume in addition many Minoan characteristics in its pottery, jewellery, representation of bulls, and the symbols of the double-axe, the sacred pillar and horns of consecration, associated with a cult of the Mother Goddess. Relations may have led to dynastic marriages; this would account for the presence in female tombs on the mainland of engraved gold seal-rings of a type exactly paralleled in Crete. For whatever reason, Mycenaean craftsmen learned from Minoan masters new techniques.

The following period (LH II; 15C BC) sees the expansion of Mycenaean civilisation all over mainland Greece, with considerable trade farther afield. It seems likely that Knossos itself and other Cretan palaces fell to mainland aggression c 1450. The graves of this period have mostly been plundered and the architecture obscured by later rebuilding so that less of it is known than of the periods before and after. It is characterised by the earlier tholos tombs and represented artistically by the splendid contents of three such tombs found intact at Vaphio, Midea (Dendra), and Pylos. The presence of amethyst and amber beads proves that trading relations already existed with Egypt and the Baltic. The vases are finely made and decorated. The large 'palace-style' vases as well as the beehive tombs typify the insolent exuberance of the age.

The full tide of Mycenaean influence (LH III) is reached in the 14C. This period is particularly characterised by its fine architecture, of which there are substantial remains. Houses have basements for storage and several rooms. Royal dwellings, with more than one storey and frescoed walls, have become palaces indeed. Accounts are kept in writing, though so far no evidence has come to light of literary composition. The cities are linked by roads and chariots are used.

The ruler of Mycenae seems to have been the overlord of a loose federation of considerable extent. Immediately subordinate strongholds in the Argolid included Tiryns, Midea and Asine. The whole of the Peloponnese was under the dominion of Mycenae. Her cultural influence extended to Attica, Aegina, Boeotia, Euboea, Thessaly, the Ionian Islands (except perhaps Corcyra), Aetolia, Phokis, and the islands of the Aegean. Even Crete which had largely inspired the civilisation of Mycenae was now subordinated to the younger nation. The principal gates of mainland citadels, which previously faced the hinterland, are rebuilt to face the coast as Mycenaean interests of trade or conquest reach out to the confines of the Mediterranean. There was a vigorous export and import trade with Cyprus and the Levant and on to Egypt. The S Sporades appear to have had settlers. Mycenaean objects have been found in Macedonia, in the Troad, and on the W coast of Anatolia. Ugarit on the Syrian coast had a Mycenaean trading post.

The almost total eclipse of Mycenaean civilisation over the whole area has not yet been adequately explained (see V.R. d'A. Desborough, *The Greek Dark Ages*, 1972). A surge of defensive building in the later 13C, in particular the ensuring of a secret water-supply at Mycenae, Tiryns, and Athens, suggests either an external threat or civil war. Many important Mycenaean sites suffered destruction towards the end of the 13C. The majority of smaller settlements are abandoned at this time, except in Achaea, the Ionian Islands, the E Aegean, and Cyprus, where they increase (presumably reflecting an influx of refugees). Before 1100 BC there was a second wave of disasters throughout the region which effectively ended a whole way of life. The 'Dorian Invasions' of Classical historians, internal risings, famine, pestilence, change of climate, seismic disaster, have all been suggested as the reason, none of them by itself accounting for all the conflicting archaeological evidence. What is indisputable is that the continuity of civic life was disrupted and material progress set back for four centuries.

**Homer, Mycenae, and the Trojan War**. The visitor to Mycenae can hardly avoid the attempt to fit the Homeric stories into the archaeological setting. The historical trustworthiness of Homer was first questioned by Herodotus and the consistency of the texts by Zoilus of Amphipolis. Quite apart from questions of authorship, date of composition, or unity of the transmitted text, 'there remain many anachronisms in language and in social customs and inconsistencies in the narrative of the poems (whether internal, as between the 'Catalogue of Ships' and the rest of the *Iliad*, or external, as between the *Iliad* and the *Odyssey*, or between Homeric and actual geography, in the description of Ithaca), which have to be accounted for' (*A Companion to Homer*). Recent finds in Mycenaean archaeology, however, have proved the persistence of Mycenaean traditions in Homer in matters of armament, social and burial customs, and religion, of which evidence had wholly vanished by Classical times. The decipherment of Linear B tablets found on Mycenaean sites has thrown new light on some of the problems.

Finds at Troy show that the site was destroyed twice during the period of Mycenaean hegemony in the Aegean but there is still no conclusive proof that the Mycenaeans were responsible.

A copy exists of a letter from a Hittite ruler to the king of Ahhiyawa (? Achaea) about events in Lycia; the Homeric letter from the king of Argos to the king of Lycia (*Iliad*, VI, 168–69) may be part of the same correspondence. Myrtilos, the charioteer of Oinomaos, bears a name suggesting that he was a Hittite expert from whom the Greeks learned the art of the chariot. The Attarssyas with a hundred chariots who harried the Hittites in the 13C was perhaps a member of the house of Atreus. Hittite documents record Mycenaean activity in Asia Minor amounting to a large-scale expedition.

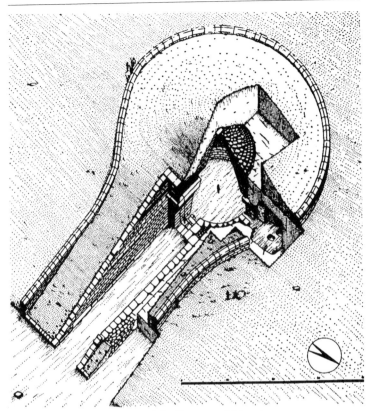

*Mycenae. Isometric view of the Treasury of Atreus*

Whether or not this is to be connected with any of the archaeological evidence for destructions at Troy, it implies a fleet and a single leader. The Catalogue of Ships in *Iliad* II reproduces the basic form of Mycenaean lists found in Linear B tablets, and is taken by some scholars to be a quoted document from the Bronze Age. Aulis, where the ships assembled, has a Mycenaean cemetery. It seems, therefore, that a historical 13C Mycenaean king who led a large expedition to Asia Minor, contributed largely to Homer's Agamemnon.

It is probable, however, that the story of the siege of a maritime town, defended by people whose background is known, belongs to Mycenaean tradition as early as the 16C BC (note the siege rhyton, Athens Museum). This is confirmed by the discovery on tablets found at Pylos, Knossos and Mycenae, of many names that are given in the *Iliad* to Trojan warriors. This traditional story was elaborated for generations in the different Mycenaean kingdoms, gathering later exploits, with changes of locale and dramatis personae, and sometimes of fashion and armament; it could have then been given a new eastern setting when Troy was attacked by an expedition led by a king of Mycenae.

Chronological problems are also raised by the *Odyssey*, the action of which is set after the Trojan War. The correspondence between objects (e.g. Nestor's cup; 'the wrought mixing bowl of solid silver doubled with gold about the rim' given by Menelaus to Telemachus; etc.) described by Homer and those discovered in Mycenaean excavations is sometimes close, though the Homeric object may be more typical of a period before the Trojan War or placed in juxtaposition with an anachronistic object. However, the ascribed provenance of Achaean riches accords with archaeological probability, as when Menelaus mentions his adventures in Egypt and claims to have 'seen Ethiopians in their native haunts'; Polybus of Egyptian Thebes had given him ten talents in gold. It seems that events from several periods of Mycenaean adventure may be telescoped in the *Odyssey* into one ancestral epic; the Egyptian expedition, the Trojan War, and the voyages of colonists to the W Mediterranean. The series of treacheries, improper marriages, and acts of revenge that characterise the Homeric dynasty of Mycenae, and supplied the basis for the embroideries of Classical drama, may actually have happened in the 16C BC (see below).

From Mikínes the road up to (2km) the acropolis of Mycenae runs below an older track which follows some remains of a Turkish aqueduct and overlooks the ravine of the Khavos, or Chaos. The prehistoric road from Mycenae to Prosymna traversed this ravine by a **bridge** and causeway, the ruins of which may still be seen. The ancient road lies below and to the E of the modern just below the chapel of **Ayios Yeoryios**, in the cemetery of which is buried Humfry Payne (1902–36), excavator of Perachora.

To the left, the old track follows the ridge back to the village, passing the **Kato Pigádhi**, the ancient lower well of the city, 'modernised' in 1940 and still in use. An upper well, **Epáno Pigádhi**, lies 500m farther N between the late-Helladic cemetery of Kalkani and the Panayia Tomb.

The modern road continues to skirt the Atreus Ridge, cutting through a large chamber tomb. Farther on a massive wall of undressed stone supports a wide paved terrace built of packed boulders fronting the so-called *Treasury of Atreus, or **Tomb of Agamemnon**. An architectural masterpiece, as well as being the largest and best-preserved of the tholos tombs, this is also one of the latest, being dated by constructional style and pottery finds to c 1350 BC. The connection with Atreus (the father of Agamemnon) is speculative.

**Tholos** or **beehive tombs** are characteristic of the periods Late Helladic II to IIIA at Mycenae but are found over a longer period elsewhere. Over 100 have been located in widely separated parts of Greece. They are usually composed of two parts, the **dromos**, or approach, an unroofed passage cut horizontally into the hill, and the **tholos**, which formed the actual tomb. This was of masonry, built into a circular excavation in the hill, and rising in a cone like a beehive to about the same height as the diameter of the floor. The top of the cone projected above the slope of the hillside and was covered with earth. Occasionally, as in the 'Treasury of Atreus', an additional chamber, rectangular in shape, opened from the tholos.

At Mycenae nine such tombs have been discovered, all outside the fortifications. Unlike the shaft-graves on the acropolis they had all been plundered, with the result that less is known about their contents. Architecturally the tholos tombs at Mycenae fall into three groups, showing a progressive structural development, marked in particular by the increased use of dressed stone and the placing of a relieving triangle above the lintel. They may be dated between c 1520 and 1300 BC. The Treasury of Atreus is the finest example of the third group.

By the time of Pausanias the original purpose of these structures had been forgotten and they were taken for underground treasuries. The discovery of six skeletons in the tomb at Menidhi (Athens) placed the question of their purpose beyond all doubt.

The tomb is built into the E slope of the ridge. From the artificial **terrace** (see above), you pass through traces of the **enclosing wall** that barred the entrance. The **dromos** is 35m long and 6m wide; its walls, which naturally rise as it penetrates the hillside, are built of great squared blocks of breccia laid in horizontal courses and water-proofed behind with a lining of clay. At the end of the approach is a **doorway** nearly 5.5m high tapering slightly towards the top. The lintel is formed of two large slabs of stone, of which the inner one is 8m long, 5m wide, and 1m thick, with an estimated weight of 120,000kg. Above a triangular space lightens the weight borne by the lintel. On either side of the doorway, on a square stepped base (still in position), stood an engaged half-column of dark green limestone. Parts of the shafts and of the carved capitals have been found; a few of these are in Athens Museum, but the greater part is in the British Museum. Above, smaller columns flanked the facing of ornamental coloured bands that masked the 'relieving triangle'; some rosso antico fragments of this façade are also in London. They derive probably from quarries at Kiprianó near Cape Matapan (see B.S.A. 1968). The entrance passage is 5m deep; in the middle a stone threshold has pivot holes on which the double doors were swung. The bronze nails that held the doorframe and fixed the wood or bronze covering of the threshold are still in place.

The **tholos** is a circular domed chamber, 13m high and 14.5m in diameter, formed by well-fitting blocks of breccia in 33 concentric courses, joined without mortar and gradually diminishing in height. The blocks vary from 1.25m–2.15m in length. Each course overlaps the one immediately below it (corbelling), the topmost course being closed by a single block which, unlike the keystone of an arch, could be removed without endangering the stability of the structure. The overlaps have been cut away, so that the interior presents a smooth unbroken surface curved both horizontally and vertically. The floor is natural rock. From the third course upwards are rows of holes in regular order, some of them with their original bronze nails; these were bored to receive bronze rosettes as at Orchomenos. The outside of the dome was wedged with smaller stones.

A much smaller doorway, 2.8m high and 1.3m wide, similarly surmounted by a triangular opening, leads from the N side of the beehive chamber into a **rock-cut chamber**, 8.25m square and 5.8m high. The walls may have been lined and decorated with sculptured slabs as at Orchomenos. In the centre is a circular depression.

On the thyme-covered ridge to the W (view) are remains of a settlement of Late Helladic date. The excavations of 1955 showed the walls to be the terraces of outlying villas ('House of Lead', 'Lisa's House', etc.), not fortifications; earlier theories of a fortified prehistoric 'lower town' have been abandoned. Just below the conspicuous **Panayía Chapel** is the **Panayia Tomb**, another tholos chamber (of the second group), discovered by Tsountas in 1887; it lacks its upper part. A hundred metres farther N is a tholos of the first group, known as the **Epano Phournos Tomb**.

To the N of the **Treasury of Atreus** are the remains of houses belonging to the Mycenaean settlement outside the citadel.

Rounding a corner beyond the Treasury of Atreus you cross an area of confused Hellenistic ruins surrounded by a wall, the course of which can still be traced. Farther on (right) are the excavated foundations of several **houses**, probably of wealthy merchants of the 13C BC; all were destroyed by fire. The names given them by the British excavators derive from the objects discovered. Construction is of rubble packed with clay. This supported a timber frame filled in with brick.

In the **House of Sphinxes** were found ivory plaques depicting sphinxes and nine Linear B tablets which had fallen from an upper room. The **House of the Oil Merchant**, adjoining to the N, contained (N room) 11 large pithoi and an installation for warming them. Thirty-eight written tablets came to light amid the burnt ruins. Across a narrow lane, the **House of Shields** yielded carved ivories, many in the shape of the figure-of-eight shield. The **West House**, adjoins the House of the Oil Merchant.

At the N end of the ridge the road turns E towards the citadel. On the left is the level **car park**; in the angle of the road (right) lies **Grave Circle B**, discovered by accident in 1951 and excavated in 1952–54 by the late John Papadhimitriou and others.

Though archaeologically one of the most important of discoveries at Mycenae there is not a great deal to see. The enclosure, bounded by a wall similar to that of the larger grave circle on the acropolis (see below) and containing 25 graves, 15 of them shaft graves, lay partly beneath the road, while the section to the E had been overlapped by the vault of the Tomb of Klytemnestra. The bodies had been buried over a period of years with objects of ivory, gold, bronze, and rock crystal, though less sumptuously than the burials of Grave Circle A. The burials are thought to date from c 1650 BC. Grave Rho, now roofed, is a built tomb, inserted into the cemetery later, in the 15C BC.

In the dip below (right; footpath) are two tholos tombs. The **Tomb of Klytemnestra** was partially excavated by Mrs Schliemann in 1876 and more fully explored by the Greek Archaeological Society in 1891–92. It is of the normal type without a side-chamber, and is built on the same principle as the Treasury of Atreus, though a little smaller. From the refined architecture it is thought to be the latest of the tholos tombs (c 1300 BC). The upper 18 courses of its dome, destroyed probably by Veli Pasha, were restored in 1951. The **dromos** (65m long) contained a circular depression which seems to have been a woman's grave, as gold trinkets and bronze mirrors were found in it. The **doorway** is recessed and was flanked by fluted half-columns. Here can be clearly seen how the ornamental façade that covered the relieving triangle was supported. Above the dromos traces of a small **theatre** of the Hellenistic period show that by then the existence of the tholos had been forgotten. Only one semicircle of seats can be clearly made out.

The so-called **Tomb of Aegisthus**, farther E, was excavated by the British School in 1922. This is on the same plan, but both the style of construction (rubble walls) and the pottery found within align the tomb with the first group (c 1470 BC), though an earlier (Middle Helladic) date has since been proposed; the collapse of the tholos was due to the weakness of the material. It had been looted before the Hellenistic period.

On the other side of the modern road, in the N slope of the ridge, is the **Lion Tomb**, a tholos of the second group. Its dome has collapsed. Over to the left is **Petsas' House**, where a store of over 600 unused pots, ranged in sizes, was unearthed.

The road now reaches the **\*acropolis**, built on a triangular hill (278m) of which the N side is c 320m long and the others c 180m. In its present form, the enceinte with the Lion Gate, the palace, and most of the houses within, represents the result of architectural developments over a period from c 1350–c 1200 BC. The **walls** are preserved for their whole extent. There is a gap in the middle of the precipitous S slope where there was no need of fortification. They follow the contours of the rocks and in general vary in height between 4.5m and 10.5m, reaching 17m in the middle of the SW side. The thickness mostly varies from 3m to 7m but in places on the N and SE sides they are as much as 10–14m wide. There were two gates and a sally-port.

Three different styles of construction may be distinguished. The 'Cyclopean' walls are of huge blocks of dark limestone, shaped only roughly if at all. This masonry takes its name from the tradition that the original walls, like those of Tiryns, were built by the Cyclopes. The two gateways, with their towers and approach walls, are in squared blocks of breccia, hammer-dressed and in regular courses like the later tholos tombs. This gives extra strength and dignity to the entrances to the city. The so-called Polygonal Towers are built of finely-jointed polygonal blocks of breccia; these and the short sections of wall repaired with similar but curved blocks date from the reoccupation of the 3C BC.

The famous **\*Lion Gate** stands at the NW angle of the acropolis. It is reached by an approach 14.5m long and 9m wide, formed on the left (NE) side by a salient of the fortification wall and on the right (SW) side by a tower or bastion projecting from the wall. This tower commanded the right

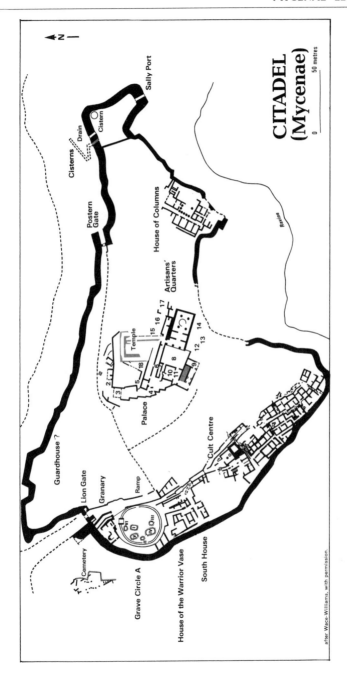

**CITADEL
(Mycenae)**

0                    50 metres

N

Sally Port

Cisterns

Drain

Cistern

Postern
Gate

House of Columns

Ravine

Artisans'
Quarters

Temple

Palace

15  16  17

18

2

3

4

5

8

9

10

11

12  13  14

Cult Centre

Guardhouse ?

Lion Gate

Granary

Ramp

Cemetery

Grave Circle A

House of the Warrior Vase

South House

after Wace-Williams, with permission.

or unshielded side of anyone that approached. The gateway, unlike the entrances to the tholos tombs, has monolithic gateposts (3.2m high) which slope inwards to provide an opening that narrows from 3.1m at the bottom to 2.9m at the top. Across these, and probably mortised to them, is placed a massive lintel, 4.5m long, 1.9m thick, and 1m high in the centre, diminishing in height towards the sides. In the lintel and threshold are pivot-holes for double doors, and sockets in the side posts show where a wooden bar held them closed. The pavement (no longer visible) was scored to give foothold and rutted on either side for chariot-wheels.

Above the lintel a triangular slab of grey limestone, 3.7m wide at the base, 3.1m high, and 0.6m thick, fills the relieving triangle. Carved in relief on it is a pillar supported by two lions (more properly, perhaps, lionesses), which rest their front paws on the two joined altars that constitute its base. Their heads have disappeared. The pillar, which tapers downwards, supports an abacus, and probably has a religious significance. A seal found at Mycenae depicts a similar device, perhaps the badge of the city or of its royal house; in this representation a dove rests on top of the pillar.

Within the gate (right) is the **granary**, so-called because pithoi of carbonised wheat were found during its excavation. The building, which was of two storeys, was perhaps in fact a guard-house.

From the gate the main route climbed by a ramp to the Palace, at first in a SE direction, then N following the line of the wall. Its surface was dug away in Schliemann's excavations, but the massive embanking walls of the ramp remain. The terrace-wall to the N, designed to support the higher ground above, is a modern reconstruction.

To the right is **Grave Circle A**, the Royal Cemetery, a circular enclosure 27m in diameter, consisting of a double ring of dressed slabs 0.9m–1.5m high and 0.9m apart. The space between the two concentric rings appears to have been filled originally with rubble; the top was covered with horizontal slabs, of which one is in place, showing the mortise-and-tenon joints. The entrance, formed by a well-made opening in the circle, 3.7m wide and lined with slabs, is opposite the Lion Gate. Ten sepulchral stelai and a small round altar were found over the graves. The stelai, now in the National Museum at Athens, bear crude sculptures in low relief, most of them showing men in chariots fighting or hunting.

Within this enclosure are six **Shaft Graves**, cut perpendicularly in the rock at a depth of 7.5m. They vary considerably in size, but all were floored with pebbles and lined with rubble masonry; they appear to have been covered with slabs, which had collapsed beneath the weight of the soil above. In the tombs were found 19 skeletons; the bodies had been interred in a contracted position, not burnt. The burial furnishings, which constitute one of the richest archaeological discoveries ever made, are splendidly displayed in Athens.

Archaeologists date these tombs to the end of the Middle Helladic and early Late Helladic periods, and postulate a 16C royal house, which they call the 'Shaft Grave dynasty'. The cemetery, of which the graves form part, lay outside the early citadel; when the later enceinte was planned the common graves were treated with scant respect and even looted, while this royal group was incorporated within the walls and replanned as a monument. The circle was renewed and the entrance moved from the W to the N. The stelai were lifted and replaced, and an altar installed in the centre.

These were presumably pointed out to Pausanias as the graves of Agamemnon and his companions; the locals adding, following a tradition that goes back to Homer, that the murderers Klytemnestra and Aegisthus were buried outside the walls as they were considered unworthy of burial within. It was Schliemann's unshakeable belief that what he had found was in fact the grave of 'all those who on their return from Ilium were murdered by Aegisthus after a banquet which he gave them'. The belief was fortified by the contents of Grave III, in which were the skeletons of two infants wrapped in sheets of gold together with the remains of three women. Schliemann inferred that these were Cassandra with her two attendants and the twins that she had borne to Agamemnon. For a short time it seemed that Homer might after all be shown to be documentary history.

The grave circle is however undoubtedly centuries earlier than any possible date for the siege of Troy. Just as Homer describes customs (e.g. cremation) which are quite foreign to Mycenae at any period, so he seems also to have fused more than one period of Mycenaean events into one anachronistic saga. Malory's treatment of the Arthurian legends may be compared.

The characteristic shape of the inlaid daggers found here and at other Mycenaean sites is curiously echoed in the dagger-shaped marks cut in the trilithons of Stonehenge, the construction of which has elements in common with the final arrangement of the Mycenaean monument; no satisfactory theory yet accounts for what are perhaps coincidences.

To the S of the royal cemetery several groups of buildings have been uncovered; the remains represent only their basement level, drained and strongly built in stone to support a brick and timber floor above. They were constructed over the Middle Helladic cemetery in the 13C BC. The first group consists of the **Ramp House**, the **House of the Warrior Vase**, named after the famous vase found here by Schliemann, and the **South House**.

Further S is **Tsountas' House**, so-called from its first clearance by the Greek archaeologist in 1886. Further work here in 1950 and in 1970–72 shows the complex to consist of an elaborate shrine, with a separate house on the lower two terraces to the W. Work on the intervening area, the only unexcavated part of the citadel with any depth of deposit, began in 1953 and was completed by a Helleno-British team under Professor Mylonas and Lord William Taylour. The area includes a large handsome hall with a covered passage leading to it and, on the lower terraces, two roughly built shrines which contained unusual clay idols and coiled snakes, a unique fresco and fine ivories (mostly displayed in the Navplion Museum). This section is now known as the **Cult Centre**. Further S still is another area of well-built and well-arranged basements.

From the ramp a modern path follows the contour of the hill to the domestic entrance of the **Palace**. Two guard rooms (Pl. 1, 2) precede a cobbled court, where the column bases of the **propylon** are seen. An **inner gate** (4) gave access to a long corridor (6) and to the state quarters, the official entrance to which was, however, on the S side. These centre round the **Great Court** (8). In Mycenaean times a **grand staircase** (9) led the visitor via an **anteroom** (11) to a room (10) whose use is uncertain. It may have been a throne room, a guest suite or a control post and archive room. From the E side of the Great Court a **porch** (12) and **vestibule** (13) lead into the **megaron** (14), a room 12.7m by 11.8m, in the centre of which was the sacred **hearth**. Four wooden pillars supported a roof; the bases are still visible. The rooms to the N are believed to represent the private apartments; a small one (17) with a red stuccoed bath is pointed out as the place of Agamemnon's murder. The topmost point is overlaid by scanty remains of a **temple** rebuilt in Hellenistic times with material from an earlier structure of the Archaic period. The view takes in the Argolid with the Larissa of Argos prominent.

E of the Palace on the lower terraces are important buildings, now considered to form an E wing of the Palace. The first is the artisans' quarters, an open corridor with workshops opening off on either side. Below, in the SE angle of the citadel, lies the so-called **House of Columns** which has close similarities to the palace of Odysseus as described in the Odyssey. Beyond are two groups of storerooms. Farther E is the heavily fortified late extension of the acropolis with a sally-port and a **secret cistern**, of the kind now known at both Athens and Tiryns, approached by a passage through the wall and descending stairs. A little to the W is a **postern gate** of the same period as the Lion Gate.

# 28

# Návplio, Tiryns (Tírintha) and the Argive Heraíon (Iraío)

Quite apart from its own charm, Navplio is the best centre for excursions in the Argolid. With a hired car, it is possible to make a superficial tour of Tiryns, Argos, Mycenae, and the Heraion in one day. If more time is available, it is better to take four days, one for Navplio and its surroundings, two divided between Tiryns, the Heraion, Mycenae and Argos, with a fourth for the visit to Epidauros (Rte 29).

## A.  Návplio

**NAVPLIO** (Ναύπλιο, pron. Návplio), called by the Venetians *Nápoli di Romanía*, is the chief town (11,897 inhab. Hotels A–E) of an eparchy and the capital of the nome of Argolis. Its delightful situation near the head of the Argolic Gulf and the splendid examples of late-medieval military architecture make it one of the most attractive towns in Greece. Originally walled, the quiet city huddles along the N slopes of a small rocky peninsula, crowned by the citadel of Its-Kale (85m), towards which narrow streets, lined with old houses attractively balconied and shuttered, rise from the quay. On the SE the conspicuous fortress of Palamidhi (215m) dominates the peninsula.

Facing away from the open sea, Navplio provides the safest harbour on the coast of Argolis, with some trade in tobacco, currants, and cotton. Though the seat of a bishop and a military station, the town has lost the importance it once had as the temporary capital of Greece, and is frequented mainly as a holiday resort.

**Restaurants**. On quay; in Plateía Iatroú; in and behind Plateía Sindágmatos. **Cafés** in same areas.

**Tourist Police**. Fotomára and Singroú (off Pl. Nikitára to SW). **Police**. Od. A. Paráskhou.

**Buses**. From Plat. Nikitára (various positions in SW corner) to Tiryns and Argos (frequent); to Corinth and Athens (frequent); to Trípolis and Sparta (8), also Yíthion etc. (2–4); to Toló (for Asine) (frequent, less so in winter); to Ligourió, Asklepieíon, Palaiá Epídhavros, Néa Epídhavros (2–6); to Kranídhi (for Ermióni and Spétses) and Galatá (for Póros) (3–4)).

**Railway station**. On quay opposite corner of Odd. Polizoídhou and Bouboulínas.

**Swimming**. Below the Xenia Hotel (to the S).

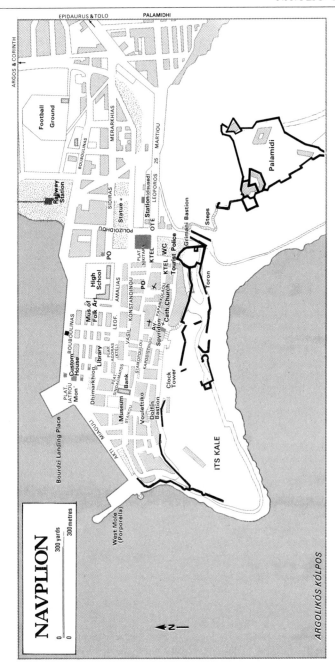

**History**. Palaeolithic remains have recently been found on Akronavplion, and a Neolithic cave site in the area. In Mycenaean times *Nauplia* may have been, as its name suggests, the naval station of Argos. The legend later grew of a mythical founder Nauplios, son of Poseidon by Amymone, daughter of Danaos. A descendant of Nauplios, Palamedes, is said to have invented lighthouses, the art of navigation, measures and scales, and the games of dice and knucklebones, in addition to introducing the letters Y, Φ, X and Ψ into the alphabet of Cadmus (historically anachronistic). He was slain by his fellow-Greeks in the Trojan War on a false charge of treachery for playing a trick on Odysseus. About 625 BC Nauplia, previously a member of the maritime League of Kalauria, fell to Argos. The Nauplians fled to Messenia, where the Lacedaemonians gave them Methone. The town was again deserted in the time of Pausanias, who saw only walls, a sanctuary of Poseidon, the harbour, and the Spring of Kanathos.

Nauplia is mentioned as a trading-post in 11C Venetian annals. After the fall of Constantinople (1204), it remained for a time in Byzantine hands, the governor Leon Sgouros vainly trying to create here the nucleus of a Greek kingdom. In 1210 the town was taken by Geoffrey de Villehardouin, who gave it, with Argos, to Otho de la Roche. It remained an appanage of the Dukes of Athens, but on the fall of Athens to the Catalans in 1311 stayed loyal to the Brienne family. In 1388 Nauplia was bought from Marie d'Enghien by the Venetians, whose first task was to recover it from the hands of Theodore Palaeologos of Mistra. Turkish sieges were repelled in 1470, in 1500 when Bayezid II attacked in person, and for 14 months in 1538–39, but in 1540 Nauplia became the Turkish capital of the Morea. Count Königsmark, Morosini's lieutenant, recovered it for Venice in 1686, and until recaptured by the Turks in 1715 it became capital of the kingdom and seat of the Bp. of Corinth. Morosini died within sight of the walls in 1694. After its recapture Ahmed III visited Nauplia in person. As a consequence of a temporary occupation of Nauplia by the Russians in 1770, the capital was removed to Tripolis.

During the War of Independence Nauplia was the most important fortress in the Morea, its two strongholds being regarded as impregnable. The Greeks laid siege for over a year in 1821–22; a few months after the rout of Dramali they seized Palamidhi, and the town capitulated. Later the two citadels were for a time in the hands of rival Greek chieftains, who indulged their passion for civil war at the expense of the luckless inhabitants, until Adm. Codrington and Sir Richard Church intervened. The town escaped destruction and in 1828 Capodistrias, the regent, moved his provisional seat of government here from Aegina. In 1831, Capodistrias was assassinated outside the church of St Spiridon. Otho, first king of Greece, disembarked at Nauplia in 1833 after the ratification of his election in 1832 at Pronoia, remaining till the government was removed to Athens in 1834. The insurrection of the garrison here helped to bring about his abdication in 1862.

At Nauplia on 26 April 1941 the British evacuation of 6685 men and 150 nurses was chaotic in the darkness and many men were lost when the transport *Ulster Prince* ran aground, blocking the harbour entrance. *Hyacinth*, trying to free her, fouled the tow wire in her screw, and *Slamat* was sunk by dive bombers. Two destroyers (HMS *Diamond* and *Wryneck*) were also lost.

The bus terminus (and disused railway station) are at the N foot of Palamidhi, where two squares and a park divide the suburb of Pronoia from the town. In the E square stands a vigorous **Statue of Theodore Kolokotronis** by Lazaros Sokhos (1901), and in the W a marble figure of Capodistrias. To the NW, the **High School**, the first to be founded in liberated Greece, faces the building (now the Institut Français) in which it was installed by King Otho in 1833. In the centre of this square stands a **Monument to Demetrios Ypsilantis**. Behind the High School, with an entrance in Od. Vasiléos Alexándrou, is the new **Museum of the Peloponnesian Folklore Foundation**, winner of the European Museum of the Year award in 1981 for its fine displays. The foundation was set up in 1974 under the directorship of Mrs I. Papantoniou and based on her extensive collection of Greek folk art. It now comprises a research centre and library in Athens and the museum in Navplio. The foundation sponsors projects in all areas

*Arrival of King Otho at Navplio, 1833*

of folklore and folk art studies and publishes the periodical *Ethnográfika*. This Folk Museum (09.00–14.30, closed Mon and all February) occupies an attractively restored neo-Classical house. The ground floor is devoted to a display of the techniques involved in the production of folk textiles in Greece, beginning with a historical introduction to the subject. All the processes from raw fibre to the finished item are illustrated. Of special interest are the looms, the more unusual types of weaving (e.g. tablet and band weaving) and the display in the final case of the inner room which shows highly decorated folk art items re-used as ecclesiastical vestments. The upper storey contains the museum's collection of folk costumes and other memorabilia. There is a small museum shop.

Close by, in Leof. Amalías, is the restored building of the first **Military Academy** of Greece (1828).

Odhós Vasiléos Konstandínou, the narrow main street, thronged during the evening volta, leads from the main square (see above) to Plateía Sindágmatos, the centre of the town. In the SW corner is the ex-Mosque of **Vouleftikó**, in which the first Greek parliament met in 1827–34. It is said that this building, the medresse behind it (now the museum store), and the second mosque in the square (now a cinema) were erected by one family in expiation of a crime.

The **Archaeological Museum** occupies the upper floors of a dignified Venetian building of 1713, once a naval depot. FIRST FLOOR. Unique and virtually complete *suit of Mycenaean armour found in a tomb at Dhendra in 1960. Neolithic pottery from the Franchthi Cave. Early to Late Helladic pottery from sites in the Argolid (including Grave Circle B at Mycenae), that of LH I–II showing marked Minoan influences in shape and decoration; stele from Grave Circle B with incised figure of a horseman; terracotta idols mainly from the Citadel House shrine at Mycenae (various types of figures, snakes) plus the 'Lord of Asine'; fragments of frescoes from Tiryns and Mycenae; Mycenaean lamp from Midea; sherd inscribed in Linear B. SECOND FLOOR. Sub-Mycenaean *helmet from Tiryns; finds of the

Geometric period and later; votive discs (7C BC) with painted scenes; grotesque masks (8C) from Tiryns and Asine; the 'Tiryns Inscription'; sole inscription found at this site until the surprising discoveries of December 1962; figurines and votive objects; Panathenaic amphorae; black-glazed krater (4C); Hellenistic terracotta bath.

The **quay** commands a fine view across the bay to the mountains of Argolis. In the Plateía Iatroú in front of the **Custom-House** is the **Monument to the French**, a marble obelisk erected in 1903 in memory of General Fabvier, Admiral de Rigny, and others, who fell in the War of Independence. Aktí Miaoúli, a wide promenade on the site of the old town walls (demolished 1929–30), leads to the **west mole**, built on the foundations of the 'porporella', or underwater stone barrier, that once protected the entrance to the harbour. It also ringed the islet of **Boúrdzi** (450m offshore), on which stands the **Castel Pasqualigo**, erected by the Bergamasque architect Antonio Gambello in 1471, and many times modified. It was used in the 19C as a retreat of the execrated public executioner. From the W mole a path follows the **Bastion of the Five Brothers** (Πενταδέλφια), the only surviving part of the circuit wall begun in 1502, to the W end of the peninsula. Here, high up, can be seen a postern gate and a few steps of the ascent cut by Morosini's galley-slaves in 1686. You follow the S side of the peninsula towards the little bay of Arvanitía in the neck of the isthmus, now a bathing place (adm. charge). Above tower the crags of *Its Kalé* (Turkish: Üç Kalè), the 'three castles' (Greek, Frankish, Venetian) that constituted **Akronávplion**.

A fortress has existed on the site since antiquity. The original walls of polygonal masonry (still visible from below on the N side) have provided the foundation for each successive rebuilding. The decaying walls were partly restored by the Venetians in 1394–1409 and the lower *Castello del Torrione*, designed by Gambello (see above), added c 1477–80. This now supports the Xenia Hotel. After the erection of the town wall in 1502 the upper castle was allowed to fall into disrepair until 1701–04 when Dolfin strengthened its entrances. Within, the former untidy but historic ruins have given way to hotels and tourist installations, but good views can be had from the panoramic road. From the far end long flights of steps within the **Baluardo Dolfin** descend to the **Porta Sagredo** of 1713, above the main square. On the S side of Akronavplion, traces of Palaeolithic occupation were found in 1973.

In the lower town Odhós Kapodhistríou has surviving Turkish fountains. On its N side is the charming Venetian portal of the church of **Ay. Spiridon**, built in 1702, outside which Count John Capodistrias was assassinated in 1831 by George and Constantine Mavromichales; the mark of the bullet fired by Constantine is still shown near the entrance. A little higher up the slope, the **Metamorphosis** (Transfiguration), a Venetian conventual church returned by King Otho to the Roman rite after it had served the Turks as a mosque, contains a curious register of Philhellenes.

The **Fortress of Palamidhi** (Παλαμήδειον; 215m) stands on the summit of a lofty and almost inaccessible rock commanding the whole of the Argolid and with a •view of the surrounding mountains. On foot it is reached by a dizzy climb of some thousand steps requiring stamina even in cool weather; best in the morning. A road now climbs the S side (via Od. 25 Martíou; see below). The name preserves the legend of Palamedes, but the difficult terrain seems to have inhibited building here until the governorship of Agostino Sagredo, when, to a design of Ant. Giaxich, a Dalmatian engineer (wounded at Argos, 1695), the fortress was built by Lasalle in 1711–14. The **caponier**, or covered way, was erected a little earlier to provide a protected retreat from the hill to the city. The complex fortification, entered by a series of gates bearing the Lion of St Mark, consists of outworks and ramparts connecting three independent fortresses, in ascending order named **San Girardo** (the patron saint of the Sagredo), **San Nicolò**, and **Sant'Agostino** (after the podestà).

Palamidhi, inadequately garrisoned, fell after eight days' siege in 1715. The poet Manthos of Ioannina, who was present, slanderously attributed its fall to the betrayal of its plans by Lasalle. More recently the forts were renamed after Greek heroes and Fort Miltiades (S. Nicolò) served as a convict prison. Kolokotronis was incarcerated here.

The new road up the SE slope of Palamidhi passes close to a Mycenaean cemetery of rock-hewn chamber-tombs.

The PRINCIPAL LOCAL EXCURSION is to Toló (9.5km; bus). You take the Epidauros road. After 250m a sign points (right) to the **Bavarian Lion**. This was carved in the rock by order of Ludwig I of Bavaria to commemorate his soldiers who died in an epidemic at Tiryns in 1833–34. In this suburb of **Prónoia** in 1832 the National Assembly ratified the election of Prince Otho to the throne of Greece.

1km Turning (right) to the **Ayía Moní**, or nunnery of Zoödhókhos Piyí, founded by Leo, Bishop of Argos; its elegant church dates from 1149. The curious fountain (1836) in the garden, decorated with reliefs and fed by an ancient conduit, is reputed to occupy the site of the Kanathos, a spring in which Hera annually renewed her virginity.

At 3.5km, beyond the hamlet of **Areia**, you turn right off the Epidauros road.

At 6.5km a tarmac road forks left, passes **Dhrépano** (Hotels B, C) at the head of a long marshy inlet, then skirts the coast to **Iria** (27km), whose scattered remains attest a Mycenaean origin and Classical history; this road continues via **Stavropódhi** to join Rte 29. You keep right, pass through the village of modern **Asíni**, then, ignoring a turn to Dhrépano (left), arrive at the rocky headland (Kastráki) on which stand the ruins of *Asine*. A path leads past a small chapel.

*Asine* was occupied from the Early Helladic period; later by migrants from N Greece, Dryopians according to Strabo. The inhabitants sided with the Spartans in their invasion of Argos after the First Messenian War, and afterwards fled to Messenia, settling at Korone (Rte 34A). The place was deserted until the 2C BC when it again became a fortified township. The Swedish excavations of 1922–30 were the idea of Crown Prince (later King) Gustav Adolf, who himself took part. The results were published in English (Stockholm, 1938). Excavations were resumed in 1970.

The **lower town** has imposing sections of Hellenistic ramparts on the N side, with a gate and piece of paved road. Within were found widespread traces of Early Helladic occupation, foundations of many houses of the Middle Helladic and Late Helladic periods, and of Roman baths, as well as Venetian additions to the fortifications (Morosini landed at Tolo in 1686). Geometric and Hellenistic remains survive on the **acropolis**. The wild flowers are varied. A Middle Helladic and Mycenaean necropolis was explored on Mt Barbouna (below). Protogeometric and Geometric (including fortifications) finds were also made.

Beyond the site, the road turns W, skirting the sandy shore at the foot of Mt Barbouna (91m) to (9.5km) **Toló** (Hotels B, C, D), a summer resort with camp-sites. The bay is protected by islets. There is a better beach E of the site.

Among other places accessible by local bus is **Ayios Adhrianós**, 5km NE, where in 1962 a site was located on a hill-top to the NW (remains of Cyclopean walls; chapel on temple foundations above a cave), perhaps to be identified with ancient *Lessa* (though this is claimed for each of three other forts on the Ligourio road).

# B.  Tiryns (Tírintha)

**Tiryns** (mod. Tírintha) is 4km from Navplio on the level road to Argos (Rte 26). After 1.5km appear on the right the two limestone hills of Ayios Ilias (111m and 213m), each crowned by a chapel; these hills were used as quarries by the builders of Tiryns. Farther on is the penal **Agricultural College** founded by Capodistrias. In 1926 in a field belonging to the college was discovered the so-called 'Treasure of Tiryns'. The site lies just beyond to the E of the road.

The citadel of **\*\*TIRYNS** (ΤΙΡΥΝΣ) (good guide by German Archaeological Institute, *Führer durch Tiryns*) occupies the summit of a low rocky height known inevitably as Palaiókastro (27m), the lowest and most westerly of a series of isolated knolls rising like islands from the flat plain. It is separated from the sea (now c 1.5km distant) by reclaimed marshland. The fortress-palace is enclosed by cyclopean walls, the finest specimens of the military architecture of the Mycenaeans. Homer speaks of 'wall-girt Tiryns' (Τίρυνθα τειχόεσσαν; *Iliad*, II, 559); Pindar admires the 'Cyclopean doorways' (κυκλωπία πρόθυρα; Frag. 642); and Pausanias compares the walls of Tiryns with the pyramids of Egypt. The palace within is more complex than those at Mycenae and Pylos. The unfortified city lay in the surrounding plain.

**History**. *Tiryns* was inhabited before the Bronze Age; the earliest people may have been lake-dwellers in the marsh. In one legend Tiryns is the birthplace of Herakles and the base of operations for his labours (*Apollodoros*, II, iv, 12). The fortifications in their present form belong to the 13C BC though they may have had predecessors. Despite its size and wealth, Tiryns seems always to have been secondary to Argos or Mycenae. Though it continued to be inhabited through Geometric times and sent a contingent to Plataia in 479, the place was never again important. It was destroyed by Argos in 468 BC. It became a fortress in the Hellenistic period and the strength of the walls proved an attraction in Byzantine times, when a church was built in the great forecourt. The site was explored by Schliemann and Dörpfeld in 1884–86. There was considerable reconstruction of fallen walls in 1962–64; the long-delayed discovery of the water-supply in 1962 by the late N. Verdelis has led to further investigation of the lower enceinte, continued in recent years by the German Archaeological Institute.

The fortress is most impressive from below. The summit on which it stands has the form of a waisted oblong 299m long and from 20m to 34m wide, descending from S to N in three terraces. The whole of the area is enclosed by the \***walls**, nearly 700m in circuit, which are built of two kinds of limestone, red and grey, in irregular blocks of different sizes, laid as far as possible in horizontal courses. The stones, the largest of which are estimated to weigh over 14,000kg, are partially hammer-dressed; smaller stones bonded with clay mortar fill the interstices. Round the lower citadel the walls are 7m–8m thick; round the irregular upper citadel, where their line is broken by towers, salients, and re-entrant angles, they vary in thickness from 5km–11km, in places containing galleries and chambers. They stand to about half their original estimated height of 20m.

The main entrance was in the middle of the E wall. A smaller entrance opened in the great semicircular bastion that projects on the W side, and there were three posterns in the lower citadel.

Admission is by a new gate from the by-road (E) to the steep and ruinous **ramp** (Pl. 1), c 5m wide, which formed an approach practicable for chariots. Its disposition exposed the visitor's right or unshielded side to the defenders as at Mycenae and necessitated at the top a sharp turn. The **main entrance** (Pl. 2) opened in the outer wall, here 7.5m thick. The original opening of c 5m has been reduced to 2.5m by later masonry; there is no trace of a gate. You are now in a long passage running N and S between the inner and outer walls. To the right, passing a square niche below an arch (probably a guard post), it leads down to the lower citadel (see below). 50m to the left is the **outer gateway** (Pl. 3), of similar size to the Lion Gate at Mycenae. In the monolithic threshold are holes for the pivots of folding doors, and in the rebated gateposts are bolt holes, 15cm in diameter, allowing a cross-bar to be shot home into the wall. The right gatepost is intact, the left one is

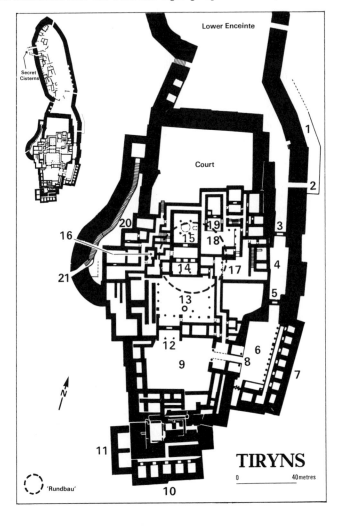

Lower Enceinte

Secret Cisterns

Court

TIRYNS

'Rundbau'

0     40 metres

N

broken, and the lintel has disappeared. Beyond, the passage widens to form a **barbican** (Pl. 4), narrowing again to a point where an **inner gate** (Pl. 5) probably guarded the oblong *Courtyard* (Pl. 6). Here, to the left, in the thickness of the outer wall, is the first of the two series of *galleries and chambers* for which the fortress is specially noted. The **E gallery**, fronted by a colonnade, had a corbelled vault and communicated by six doors with six vaulted **chambers** (Pl. 7), each 3.4m square.

Opposite opens the **great propylaia** (Pl. 8), a double porch divided by a wall, in which was a single doorway. Between antae within and without stood wooden columns, the stone bases of which are still in position. The gateway supersedes an earlier one. From the inner porch a narrow passage leads off direct to the smaller megaron (see below).

You enter the **forecourt** (Pl. 9) of the palace, from which remains of a Byzantine church have been removed; it is bounded on three sides by the fortress walls and the complex of *casemates* built into them. You descend by a covered staircase, with a right-angled bend in the middle, to the vaulted **S gallery** (20m long, 5m high, and 1.5m wide) at a level 7m below that of the court. The sides narrow to a loophole in the E wall by which it was lit. Five doorways open from the gallery into rectangular vaulted **chambers** (Pl. 10). On the SW side a rectangular **tower** (Pl. 11), with a frontage of 19m, enclosed two cisterns.

The **Royal Palace** is reached from the N side of the forecourt by the **smaller propylaia** (Pl. 12). The earliest version of the palace in this form dates to the 14C BC. There was an important Middle Helladic building here but no architectural remains of LH I–II have survived. Its present layout belongs to c 1250 BC. The site was destroyed by fire in c 1200 BC but continued to be occupied. The walls of the palace stand to a height of only 0.5m–1m; above this limestone base they were of sun-dried brick, the whole being then covered by stucco and decorated with frescoes. The huge stone thresholds of the doors remain *in situ*; the floors are of concrete made of lime and pebbles. In the colonnaded court (Pl. 13) is a round sacrificial altar. A **porch** (Pl. 14), with two columns and elaborate benches, gives access by triple doors to an ante-chamber, and then through a door (closed in antiquity only by a curtain) to the **megaron** (Pl. 15), or great hall. In the centre is a circular clay hearth, 3.4m in diameter. The roof was supported by four wooden columns, set on stone bases, which had an open lantern to give light and let out the smoke. The base of the throne is well preserved and the painted floor intact in places. The walls were frescoed with scenes of a boar hunt and a life-size frieze of women. Reached from the ante-chamber is the **bathroom** (Pl. 16), with a floor composed of one huge limestone monolith 4m by 3m.

The apartments described above are duplicated on a smaller scale behind and to the E (outer court, Pl. 17; inner court, Pl. 18; smaller megaron, Pl. 19; and ancillary buildings), sometimes thought to be women's quarters, though a recent study (by K. Kilian) suggests that a double megaron arrangement was typical of advanced Mycenaean palaces. Behind is a large open court separated by the massive inner wall from the lower enceinte. In the Early Helladic period, a massive round building, c 28m in diameter and with walls 4–5m thick (possibly a granary), occupied the hilltop. It was two-storeyed and roofed with terracotta tiles. This is now concealed beneath the megaron and court. The **lower enceinte** has been intensively investigated by the German Archaeological Institute (Prof. K. Kilian) in recent years. The area was occupied as early as Neolithic times and substantial remains of Early Helladic buildings have been discovered. The massive fortifications, however, were only built in the later 13C. About 1200 BC there was a catastrophic destruction, probably by earthquake, after which the layout of the buildings was completely changed. The most interesting discoveries (not yet accessible) are of a cult room of 12C date, with a predecessor on the same site, and associated ritual equipment, including large numbers of terracotta figures of various types. There is also much evidence of industrial activity, including metal working.

From a square tower to the W of the rear court a well-preserved **·secret stair** (Pl. 20) winds down within a massive bastion to an inconspicuous corbelled **postern gate** (Pl. 21). You can leave the fortress, turn right, and skirt the outer walls. At the NW angle of the lower enceinte two secret passages lead steeply downward through the walls from inside to two **underground cisterns** fed by springs. There are comparable arrangements at Mycenae and on the acropolis at Athens, but the Tiryns passages were discovered by accident only in 1962. Stones covering the cisterns were found (only, unfortunately, after some had been moved) to bear Archaic inscriptions shallowly cut in *boustrophedon* c 600 BC.

In the immediate vicinity of the palace, settlement remains of the Early Helladic and Mycenaean periods have been investigated, also a Dark Age and Geometric cemetery. About 1.5km E of the palace, on the W side of the hill of Profitis Ilias, is a Mycenaean tholos tomb.

# C.  The Argive Heraíon (Iraío)

**Approaches**. Road from Argos to (7.5km) Khónika, a village with a 12C church (restored 1963), then (c 1.5km farther) to the site. Road from Mycenae to Khonika, see above Rte 27. Via Ayia Triádha and/or Tiryns, see below. **Bus** from Navplio and Argos to Khonika (several). The view is clearest in the evening.

The **Heraíon of Argos**, or Sanctuary of Hera, dedicated to the tutelary goddess of the Argolid, was common to Argos and Mycenae. An imposing complex of ruins, usually ignored by visitors, the sanctuary occupies a spur (Palaiókastro; 128m) projecting SW and commands a fine view over the plain of Argos.

The site was discovered in 1831 by the Philhellene, General Thomas Gordon, who dug here in 1836; its excavation in 1892–95 constituted the first major work of the American School (under Charles Waldstein). Further work was done by Carl Blegen in 1925–28; and a chance discovery led to a short but profitable season in 1949 by P. Amandry and J. Caskey (Hesperia XXI). The summit of the hill was first occupied in Early Helladic times. Pausanias refers to the area by the name *Prosymna* and in the surrounding slopes Blegen dug many tombs from Neolithic to Late Mycenaean in date. At the Argive Heraion Agamemnon is fabled to have been chosen leader of the Trojan expedition. Hither from Argos Kleobis and Biton drew the chariot of their mother in the story told

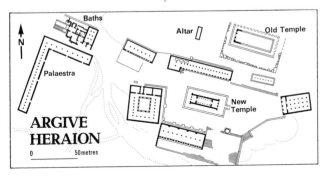

by Solon to Croesus (Herod I, 31). The old temple was burnt down in 423 BC by the carelessness of the aged priestess Chryseis.

The Archaic and Classical sanctuary is built on three terraces, above which is the Helladic settlement. A path, to the right, leads to the **Upper Terrace**, supported by a massive retaining wall in conglomerate, which has all the appearances of Mycenaean workmanship but is believed to date from the Late Geometric period. The surface of the terrace is paved and almost perfectly level. On it are traces of the stylobate of the **old temple**, perhaps the earliest peripteral building of the Peloponnese, dated to the first half of the 7C. In the Doric style (6 by 14 columns), its upper structure may have been of wood and unburnt brick.

In the centre of the **Middle Terrace** stands the poros stereobate of the **new temple**, erected c 420–410 BC by Eupolemos of Argos. This was a Doric peripteral building (6 by 12 columns) in which was set up a chryselephantine statue of Hera by Polykleitos, said to have deserved comparison with the Olympian Zeus of Pheidias. Pausanias claims to have seen here also the ancient *xoanon* in pearwood removed by the Argives from Tiryns in 468 BC, a bejewelled golden peacock dedicated by Hadrian, and a purple robe offered by Nero.

The buildings bounding this terrace have many unexplained features. Below the wall that supports the upper terrace is the **north stoa**, believed (on the evidence of surviving capitals which do not certainly belong to it) to date from the 6C BC or even earlier. The foundations are of limestone and the blocks forming the rear wall are well squared. In the centre are statue bases and at the W end a basin, lined with cement, is connected to an elaborate water-supply system. The **north-east building**, dating from the end of the 7C, was altered at a later date. The **east building** is a mid-5C rectangular structure in poros with a portico and a triple row of interior columns. The **west building**, one of the earliest examples known of a peristyle court (late 6C), has three rooms leading off its N side; it may have been a banqueting place. To the NW are further foundations, possibly belonging to a late monumental entrance. Farther W are a large Roman bathing establishment and a palaestra.

The **south stoa**, at the third level below the retaining wall of the middle terrace, shows the finest workmanship of any building on the site, and is dated to the mid- 5C. It is now suggested that what were formerly thought to be flights of steps leading up to the S stoa and past it on the E side to the temple, are in fact Archaic retaining walls of stepped construction (*analemmata*).

The site guard will show a well-preserved tholos tomb c 200m below the main site.

The Middle Helladic and Late Helladic cemeteries of **Prosymna**, explored by Blegen, are in the hillsides to the NW at approximately the same contour height as the upper terrace.

From Khonika a road continues NE to (9km) **Berbáti** (which has readopted the name Prósimna; but see above). Here in 1936–37 the Swedish Institute explored a cemetery of Mycenaean chamber-tombs and an EH–LH settlement.

Recent work in the area has identified two Mesolithic sites (in the Kleisoura Gorge), also Mycenaean farmsteads.

Another road runs SE from Khonika to (5.5km) **Ayía Triádha** (formerly Merbaka) where it meets a better road from Argos (7km) and another from Tiryns (6km). The village, which has an attractive 12C church (with Late Byzantine paintings), is said to derive its earlier name from William of Meerbeke, Latin Archbishop of Corinth (fl. c 1280), who translated various Greek medical classics. Turning E for a further 5km you can reach **Dhendrá** (on foot a more direct track from Khonika avoids Merbaka). Here (on a slope NW of the village) the Swedish Institute dug an unrobbed tholos tomb in 1926–27 (LH IIIA; finds in Athens) and, in 1937–39, richly furnished Mycenaean chamber-tombs surrounding it (gold cups, remains of wooden coffin, etc.). Another tomb dug in 1960 yielded the Mycenaean ceremonial armour now in Navplion museum. The cemetery belongs to the Bronze Age settlement of *Midhéa*, the acropolis of which stands 30 minutes E of Dhendrá (road in 1km from **Mídhia** village); it has a cyclopean enceinte (late 13C BC) with impressive walling and gates. The site, founded much earlier in the Bronze Age, was destroyed by earthquake and fire c 1200 BC but occupation continued on a significant scale in LH IIIC. There is a much later phase of use in the 4C AD. Excavation and restoration work is in progress.

# 29

# Návplio to Epidauros (Epídhavros) and the Argolic Peninsula

**Road**, 30km (19 miles) to Epidauros; 94km (59 miles) to Kósta, for Spetses. Buses, see Rte 28. The Epidauros sanctuary is called locally Ieró Ligouríou and is not at either Néa or Palaiá Epídhavros (see below).

Leaving Návplio you enter the valley which separates the slopes of Palamidi, on the S, from the bare waterless range of Arakhnaion, to the N. Its highest point rises to 1199m but the most striking peak is the lower Mt Arna (1079m) above Ligourió. The view is much better on the return journey when the serried ranges of the Peloponnese rise ahead. Just after the 14km stone, 50m before a modern bridge at a sharp corner, above the road (left) is the corbelled arch of a massive **Cyclopean bridge**, perhaps of the 5C BC but probably of Mycenaean origin. A little farther on (left) rises **Kazárma**, a small but precipitous hill (280m) with some remains of a **citadel** of the 5C with walls standing to 6m in polygonal masonry (road/track left after Cyclopean bridge). Below it, near the road, are the remains of a **tholos tomb** (fenced). A second 4C fortress stands conspicuously above the road at (16km) **Kastráki** (left; 430m road access from Arkhadhikó). 27km The decayed church of **Ayía Marína**, to the left, occupies the site of an Ionic temple of Athena. Nearby are the scanty remains of a pyramidal structure of the 4C BC, believed to be a guard-house. 27km **Ligourió** (Λιγουριό; Hotels C, D), with 2182 inhabitants, has several Byzantine churches, of which the most interesting (on our road, beyond the centre) incorporates small fragments from the Tholos in the sanctuary (see below).

From Ligourió a road continues NE through a defile, then divides. The left branch joins the new road from the Corinth Canal (Rte 25C) just short of **Néa Epídhavros** (13km; Hotels C, E; occasional ferry from Piraeus), where the first 'National Assembly' met on 20 December 1821 to declare the independence of Greece ('Constitution of Epidauros'). Above the town (1381 inhab.) are ruins of the Frankish castle of Nicholas de Guise, Constable of the Morea. The right branch leads to **Palaiá Epídhavros** (9km; Hotels B, C, D), with a little harbour (ferry to Aiyina and Piraeus). The ancient city of *Epidauros* stood on the head-land to the S of the harbour. Cyclopean walls still stand and a group of Mycenaean chamber tombs was excavated in 1888. There have been sporadic discoveries of remains of Archaic–Roman date.

Submerged buildings have been identified and a *Theatre of Dionysos excavated in 1972 with 10 kerkides and 18 rows of seats (late 4C BC), many inscribed with names of citizens who endowed the seating.

You bear right in Ligourió and 2.5km farther on left for the Sanctuary of Epidauros. The right branch continues through the peninsula (see below).

30km The **Hieron of Epidauros** (Ierón Ligouríou), or **Sanctuary of Asklepios**, is situated in a broad and lonely valley between Mt Velanídhia, the ancient *Titthion* (858m), on the NE, and Mt Kharáni, the ancient *Kynortion*, on the SE. The site was both a religious centre and a fashionable spa. In addition to the temples and colonnades devoted to the cult of Asklepios (or Æsculapius) and the festivals associated with the sanctuary, there were dwellings for the priest-physicians, hospitals for the sick, sanatoria for the convalescent, and hotels and places of amusement for the healthy. In Roman times baths were added, fed by reservoirs which collected water from the local springs.

In extent the Sanctuary compares with Delphi or Olympia, but apart from the theatre, the ruins themselves are not well preserved, although an extensive restoration project is in progress. The pine-clad setting is charming despite the artificial landscaping and paraphernalia of the festival. The road passes between the stadium and the fenced part of the site (entrance gate, left; car park, right), then enters the main gate (no cars). Within are (right) a **tourist pavilion** (refreshments) and the **Xenia Hotel** (B), and (left) the Museum. The road and paths continue to the theatre where the description (below) starts.

**History**. The worship of Apollo at the Epidaurian sanctuary seems to go back into the mists of time, that of Asklepios being grafted on not earlier than the Archaic period. It superseded that of Apollo by the 4C, by which time Epidauros had become established as the 'birthplace' of Asklepios. The cult seems to have originated in Homeric times in Thessaly, possibly at Trikke, and to have been carried S via Phokis and Boeotia, but first attained prominence at Epidauros in the 6–5C spreading from there to Athens. Kos (Rte 75A) always claimed a Trikkan origin. Some of the medical as opposed to magical expertise of Asklepios may have filtered through Asia Minor and Kos from Egypt. The Ptolemaic Greeks identified with their own hero-god Asklepios Imhotep (lived c 2780 BC), the Egyptian genius and deified physician, around whose tomb at Sakkara the first healing sanctuary grew up. The fame of the sanctuary at Epidauros reached a peak in the 4C BC when, perhaps, magic and faith were giving place to more scientific treatment.

The Hieron belonged to the city of Epidauros (see above) and was in charge of an annually elected priest of Asklepios, assisted by recorders, choristers, police, and other officials. Recovered patients gave costly offerings and votive inscriptions. Every four years, nine days after the Isthmian Games, an athletic and dramatic festival known as the *Asklepieia* was celebrated.

Livy and Ovid both tell how Rome, ravaged by an epidemic in 293 BC, sent for the sacred serpent from Epidauros. The sanctuary was despoiled by Sulla in 86 BC and the loot distributed among his soldiers.

The excavations, begun in 1881, became the life's work of P. Kavvadias. The French School also excavated just after the Second World War, J. Papadhimitriou in 1948–51 and V. Lambrinoudhakis in recent years.

The *theatre, one of the best-preserved Classical buildings in Greece, dates from the 4C BC and seems to have escaped alteration until recent years, when judicious restoration has been carried out. The building is on the World Heritage List. It is now the centre of an annual summer festival of drama. Its acoustics are unusually perfect, the slightest whisper or rustle of paper from the orchestra being clearly audible from any of its 14,000 seats. The **cavea**, c 114m across, faces N. It has 55 rows of seats, 34 below the diazoma and 21 above. The lower block is divided into 12 wedges by 13 staircases; the upper block has 23 stair-cases. The seats of honour were of red, the ordinary seats of white limestone. The two flanks of the theatre were supported by poros retaining walls, recently restored. The **orchestra** is a complete circle 20m in diameter, the circumference of which is marked by a ring of limestone flags. The floor was of beaten earth. In the centre is the round base of the **thymele**, or altar. Between the circle and the front row of seats is a semicircular paved depression, 2.1m wide, placed to collect rainwater. Access to the theatre is by two **parodoi**, passing through double doorways (restored) with pilasters embellished with Corinthian capitals. The foundations of the **stage** can be seen when they are not covered by temporary wooden scenery.

Above the theatre (direct access to the road barred by fencing) is the interesting **Sanctuary of Apollo Maleatas**, intensively excavated since 1974 and recently

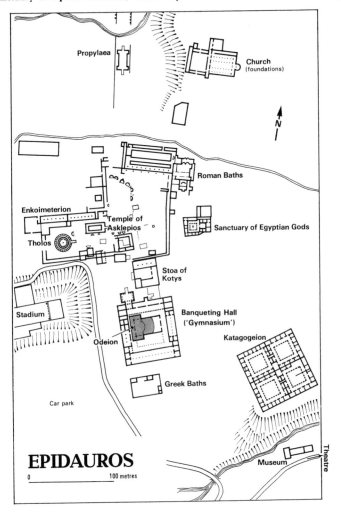

Propylaea

Church
(foundations)

N

Roman Baths

Enkoimeterion

Temple of Asklepios

Sanctuary of Egyptian Gods

Tholos

Stoa of Kotys

Stadium

Banqueting Hall ('Gymnasium')

Katagogeion

Odeion

Greek Baths

Car park

**EPIDAUROS**

0           100 metres

Museum

Theatre

conserved. Best access is via a good dirt road (1.8km) from behind the tourist pavilion: to reach it leave the car park at the NE corner, just before the police post and post office hut. Keep right at doubtful junctions on the hillside. The site gates are immediately to the left of the track. On entry, some **prehistoric houses** lie to the left. You leave the cistern to the right, pass by the side of the nymphaion and enter the sanctuary proper. To the left, below the hill with the prehistoric houses, a Mycenaean **terrace** was converted into an open air temple-shaped enclosure in the Roman period. Next to it is the Classical **Temple of Apollo**, overlying an Archaic predecessor. In front, at a lower level, are remains of earlier **altars**, going back to the Mycenaean period (votives). The N side of the area is bounded by the remains of a Hellenistic **stoa**, on a **buttressed terrace** of splendid masonry. In the centre is the 4C **altar** and other structures. On the E side is an entry staircase beside which is a rectangular **Temenos of the Muses**, with a back wall of rough stones recalling the caves frequented by the Muses. The site may have been damaged in c 80 BC by pirates. It was refurbished in the 2C AD at the expense of one Antoninus (see main sanctuary). To this period belong the remarkable and well-preserved vaulted *cistern and the nearby **nymphaion** which it fed. Also of the Roman period, behind the Temenos of the Muses and outside the main sanctuary area, are a complex priests' house and a propylon with stepped approach.

The **museum** is most conveniently visited before the excavations. To right and left of the entrance are two Corinthian columns from the interior colonnade of the tholos and two Ionic columns from the abaton. ROOM I. Inscriptions recording miraculous cures; Roman statuary; surgical instruments; building *stelai* with accounts for the Tholos and Temple of Asklepios. ROOM II. Sculpture (mostly casts) from pediments; reconstruction of the entablature of the propylaia. ROOM III. Reconstructions: part of the Temple of Asklepios (380–375). Pavement of the tholos, a curious building of which two different conjectural versions are illustrated by drawings; it was built c 360 BC possibly by Polykleitos the Younger. Corinthian capital, section of circular wall, ornate ceiling, and decorated doorway, all from the same building and finally a reconstruction of its entablature.

The **excavations** lie to the NW. You come first to the remains of a large square building, probably the **katagogion**, a hotel comparable with the Leonidaion at Olympia. It had four cloistered courts from each of which opened 18 rooms. The polygonal walls stand to a height of 0.6m and most of the threshold blocks are in place.

To the W are the ruined Greek **baths**. The **gymnasium** (usually so-called but more probably a ceremonial **banqueting hall**), a huge colonnaded court, with exedrae and other rooms off it, survives only in one course of the outer walls. The two rooms at the SE and SW corners have off-centre doorways for the convenient insertion of dining couches and the large E hall preserves traces of stone couch- supports with dowel holes in their upper surfaces. The Romans built an **odeion** in the court, of which considerable portions of the brick-built auditorium and stage buildings survive. This may indicate that the courtyard was the location of musical and theatrical ritual in earlier times. The whole base of the **great propylaia** of the gymnasium, at the NW corner, is preserved with its pavement and ramp, though the Doric colonnade has vanished. The indeterminate ruins to the NE may be of the **Stoa of Kotys**, a building originally of unburnt brick that collapsed and was rebuilt (along with other parts of the sanctuary) by a Roman senator Antoninus, probably the Emperor Antoninus Pius.

The most important group of buildings in the Hieron now opens out to E and W; this was the area that the Byzantines walled and converted into a rectangular fortress. At the SE corner, immediately N of the stoa, is the little Greek **Temple of Themis**, with an unidentified Roman building beyond. Turning to the W, you find the foundations of the **Temple of Artemis**, a Doric prostyle building with six columns on the front (4C BC). Almost adjoining on the N is a large rectangular building which may have included the original **abaton**, where patients slept expecting the visitation of the god and a cure by miraculous dreams. It was replaced in the 4C by another building (see below) and this site altered in Roman times. Various inscribed bases may be seen to the N, which probably bordered the sacred grove.

The **Temple of Asklepios** is approached by a paved path and ramp. The temple was a Doric peripteral hexastyle, with 6 columns by 11, about 24m long, and dating from c 370 BC. Nothing, however, remains but foundations and the fragments in the museum.

A *stele* found in 1885 supplies many details of the method and cost of construction. The work was supervised by the architect *Theodotos* and the temple took 4 years and 8½ months to build. The sculptor *Timotheos* made the models for the pedimental sculptures and may have been responsible for some of them, though other artists were certainly involved. The doors were of ivory and the cult statue in gold and ivory was by *Thrasymedes of Paros*. According to Pausanias Asklepios was represented seated on a throne, grasping a staff in one hand, and holding the other over the head of the serpent; a dog crouched by his side. Two marble reliefs, possibly copies of the statue, were found (now in Athens).

To the S of the temple is the **Great Altar of Asklepios**, and farther S, crossed by the line of the Byzantine wall, are the foundations of a small building which may be the **Epidoteion**, or sanctuary of the bountiful healers.

The most interesting building after the theatre is the **tholos**, or **rotunda** (reconstruction project in progress), built c 360–320 BC by the same Poly-kleitos, a more florid and elaborate construction than the corresponding buildings at Delphi and Olympia. Nothing is left but the foundations, but a very good idea of the appearance of the building may be obtained from the partial reconstructions, drawings, and plans in the museum (see above). The foundations consist of six concentric walls, in conglomerate, with a maximum diameter of 22m.

The rotunda stood on a stylobate of three steps. The three outer foundation walls supported an outer peristyle of 26 Doric columns, in poros, stuccoed and painted; the main circular wall of the building with a large portal flanked on either side by a window; and an interior colonnade of 14 marble columns with fine Corinthian capitals. The three inner foundation walls form a miniature labyrinth, the purpose of which, as indeed of the whole building, is obscure. A sacred well or a snake pit are among possibilities; more likely perhaps is that it was the focus of a chthonic cult of Asklepios. Above the labyrinth was a spiralling chequered pavement in black and white marble. The ceiling was coffered, carved, and painted. Lion's head gargoyles were regularly placed at the edge of the roof, on the apex of which was a carved floral acroterion.

To the N of the tholos and forming the N side of the area enclosed by the Byzantines, is a line of two adjacent stoas, each 10m deep, now reduced to their foundations. Their combined length was nearly 71m; the W colonnade was built, owing to the slope of the ground, in two storeys, so that its upper floor continued the level of the single storey of the E colonnade. The two together comprised the **abaton**, or **enkoimeterion**, the place of incubation. One or two of the benches which lined the walls and joined the columns still survive. A staircase of 14 steps led up to the second storey. In the E colonnade were found tablets (now in the museum) inscribed with accounts of miraculous cures. In the SE corner is a **well**, 17m deep; in the SW corner an underground passage. The well was sunk in the 6C BC and incorporated in the 4C building.

Turning N you leave on the right a large Roman **thermal establishment** fed by water from Mt Kynortion and reach the main **propylaea** of the sanctuary with part of the **sacred way** from the town of Epidauros. The limestone pavement and the ramps leading to the great gate are in good condition. To the S among the trees are some indistinct remnants of a large and very early basilican **church** with double aisles and a large atrium. Skirting the boundary fence, to the W, you pass a small **Temple of Aphrodite** and a huge **cistern** of Hellenic date.

You can now cross to the **stadium**, laid out in a natural declivity during the 5C BC, with seats partly cut from the rock and partly built up in masonry. The starting and finishing lines survive, c 180m apart, and the construction, without sphendone and with an inclined entrance tunnel, somewhat resembles its counterpart at Olympia. A stone water channel with basins at intervals surrounds the track.

TO KRANÍDHI, PORTOKHÉLI AND KÓSTA (for Spétses). Returning to the main road (at 28km; see above) you turn left and continue S and E. Beyond (43km) **Trakheiá** a road branches (left) to Méthana and Galatás (see Rte 23B); while c 1.5km farther on a by-road (right) leads back to Navplio via Iria (see Rte 28A). Continuing S, you cross the scrub-covered W flank of Mt Dhidhima (1074m), and from a saddle (488m) have a *view across the Argolic Gulf.

64km **Dhídhima**, which with its mountain preserves an ancient name, lies below in the centre of a circular plain. 76km A road leads (right) to **Koiládha** (4km), an active fishing and boat-building village. In the **Fránchthi Cave**, on the N side of the bay, a stratigraphical sequence going back to the Palaeolithic period (8th millennium BC) has been discovered, including, at the bottom of the Mesolithic deposit, the earliest complete skeleton found in Greece. There is also obsidian from Melos in the Mesolithic levels. This is a key site for the study of the Early and Middle Neolithic in Europe.

80km **Kranídhi** (Hotels C) is the market centre (3959 inhab.) of the peninsula. The Greek senate removed here in 1823 following their rupture with the executive. The chapel of the Ay. Triádha (Holy Trinity) has frescoes by John of Athens, dated to 1244. These include the Ascension and the Hospitality of Abraham. Ermioni (Rte 23D) lies 8km E.

Passing through fine stone-pines you reach (87km) **Portokhéli** (Hotels A, B, C, D), on the N side of an inlet. The remains on the S side of the harbour have been equated with *Halieis*, settled by refugees from Tiryns after 479 BC. Here, from 1962–68 and subsequently, the American School of Classical Studies explored the ancient site which is now partly underwater. The fortification system is visible on the acropolis and its continuation has been traced beneath the sea. The lower town was laid out, in the 4C BC, on a grid plan with typical small courtyard houses; the higher zone is earlier in date and unplanned. The agora and an industrial quarter have been identified. To the SE of the town were found graves of the 6C–4C BC, one group covered by a tumulus.

Many huge summer hotel complexes have been built on the adjacent coasts; there is a ferry to Spétses (40 minutes).

Turning left round the E side of the bay the road approaches (93km) **Kósta** (Hotels B), also developed as a holiday resort. Ferry to Spétses (several times daily in 15 minutes); also (more expensive) constant motor boats.

# 30

# Argos to Trípolis

**Road**, 61km (38 miles), one of the best in the Peloponnese, with good mountain scenery.—10km Lérna.—29km Akhladhókambos.—61km Trípolis. Bus daily in 4 hours.

For direct road from Corinth to Tripolis, avoiding Argos, see Rte 26.

**Railway**, 69km (43 miles), 3 trains daily in 1½ hours, all starting from Athens (add 2½–3 hours; see Rtes 24, 26).

Leaving Argos by the road past the theatre (see Rte 26), you turn S, skirting the hills that hem the Argolic plain.

On the outskirts of the town, 1.5km beyond the theatre, a right turn (signed 'Ellinikon Pyramids') can take you to **Kókla** (turn left at sign to Panayia Koklas) where some unplundered tombs of an important Mycenaean cemetery of LH I–II date were excavated in 1981–82. Nine chamber tombs and five pit graves were located, but the most important was a tholos tomb with a plastered and painted doorway and rich finds which included gold and silver vessels. Burials in one tomb included four small horses. Most of the tombs are covered. The settlement (unexcavated) is nearby.

5km By-road (right) to **Kefalári** (2.5km W), a shaded village (restaurants) at the foot of the precipitous Mt Khaon, where the Kephalari, the ancient *Erasinos*, issues from the rocks. The ancients thought that the waters came under-ground from Lake Stimfalos (51km NW; Rte 38). The spring (Kefalóvrisi) forms a pool, above which open two caverns, dedicated to Pan and Dionysos. The larger resembles an acute Gothic arch and extends c 60m into the mountain; the smaller one has been converted into the chapel of the Panayia Kefalarítissa. The ancient festival of *tyrbe* (disorder) is recalled by the modern festival on 18 April. Nearby prehistoric remains and a fine large basilican church of the 6C, probably dedicated to St Paul, were excavated and covered.

About 2km SW of Kefalári (road by church, signposted Ellinikó) on a hillock stands the impressive **Pyramid of Kenkreai**, the more complete of the two pyramids in the Argolid. The interesting structure is of hard local limestone, laid roughly in courses, with both squared and polygonal blocks. A corbelled arch, at the SE corner, gives access by a blind corridor to an inner rectangular room. The pyramid was excavated in 1901 by Wiegand who concluded that it was not, as Pausanias believed, the polyandrion of the Argives who fell at Hysiae. Louis Lord re-examined it (Hesperia 1938) and takes it to be a late-4C BC guard house used by patrols.

To the right Mt Ktenias, the ancient *Kreopolon*, rises to 1599m; Mt Pontinos, its easternmost spur, closes the Argolic Plain, extending to within 300m of the sea. On its summit rise the ruins of a Frankish **castle**, occupying the site of a house of Hippomedon and a temple of Athena Saïtis.

The vigorous defence of the narrow gap below on 25 June 1825 by Demetrios Ypsilanti with 227 men against a much larger force of Egyptians checked the advance of Ibrahim Pasha on Navplio after his capture of Tripolis. From the shore here in 1941 General Maitland Wilson, Commander-in-Chief Greece, departed by flying-boat to reorganise the continuing struggle in Crete. The Germans added three forts to defend the gap.

10.5km **Míloi** (Μύλοι, the mills) lies between Mt Pontinos and the sea, on the site of ancient *Lerna*. Here in a sacred grove of plane-trees were celebrated the Lernaean mysteries in honour of Demeter, and here Herakles slew the Hydra. At the S end of the village, to seaward of the road and on a mound fortified by the Germans in 1943, stands the conspicuous concrete shelter protecting the excavations made by the American School under J.L. Caskey in 1952–58. There is a useful short guide book in English. The **site** was occupied from the 4th millennium BC to the close of the Mycenaean period, and is one of the most important in Greece for remains of the Early Helladic period. The **fortifications** are virtually unique for their period. The **House of Tiles**, so-called from the extensive remains of its rectangular terracotta roof tiles, is one of the most elaborate EH buildings yet found. A palace, or administrative centre of the corridor-house type, it is 25m long and 12m wide and had two storeys. It was destroyed by fire at the end of EH II, so helping to preserve its mud-brick walls. The EH III levels had some pottery from Troy, whereas the Middle Helladic settlement, which here seems to follow without any violent upheaval, has pottery imports from near Niš (Balkan) as well as from Crete and the Cyclades. Two Mycenaean royal shaft graves (robbed in antiquity) cut through the House of Tiles. Geometric graves have been found to the SW of the site.

You pass (left) a road to Astros (20km S) and Leonidhi (66.5km), etc, also providing an alternative route to Tripolis (70.5km from Argos, see below).

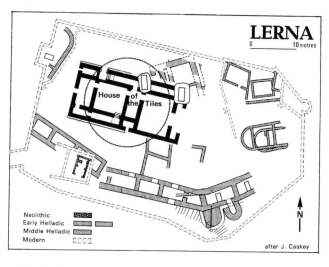

**LERNA**

0         10 metres

House of the Tiles

Neolithic
Early Helladic
Middle Helladic
Modern

N

after J. Caskey

The coast on the Astros road is pleasant. At 7km **Xeropigádhi** has rooms and facilities. Beyond (10km) is the Pournos headland with Classical watchtowers, near ancient *Dini*. At 14km you can keep left for **Parálion Ástros** (Hotels C, D) attractively situated on the sea, with a medieval fort (also some earlier remians) on the promontory, beyond which the road continues via **Ayios Andréas** and **Tíros** (Hotels C, D, at harbour) and then via **Kosmás** (a further 30km) to **Yeráki** (Rtes 32A, 31; 50km from Leonidhion, for Sparta and/or Monemvasia. Alternatively you can turn inland for (20km) **Ástros** (Hotel D), an agricultural centre (2459 inhab.), growing olives and fruit, and especially noted for peaches. It belongs to Kynouria, an eparchy of Arcadia. Here in 1823 was held the Second National Assembly called by various Klepht leaders of the insurrection to revise the constitution of 1821. There is a newly arranged **Archaeological Museum** (by the gymnasion; sign in the village square; 09.30–14.00, closed Monday) in a delightfully refurbished school building (1810) with a lovely garden. It contains excellent sculpture (mostly Hellenistic and Roman) and architectural fragments from the Villa of Herodes Atticus at Loukou (see below) and some other material from Kynouria. Amongst the sculptures are two fine grave reliefs, one of a naked warrior resting his arm on a herm. Other reliefs show Hermes and nymphs and feasting heroes. There is a staute of Antinous and portraits of Commodus and (probably) Aelius Verus. Grave goods from Classical-Roman cemeteries at Ellinikon, SW of Astros (? ancient *Thyrea*) include bronzes and relief decorated avses. There is a little Mycenaean and Geometric material; also some coins, and Byzantine moulds. In the garens is a Roman sarcophagus lid with a reclining figure.

The main Tripolis road (good surface; pleasant route) continues beyond the museum. After 4km, immediately left of the road, is the delightful **Moní Loukoús**. Part of a Roman acqueduct faces you on the short climb to the monastery. The church is a foundation of c 1100 and has a complete cycle of (later) frescoes. The compound is lovely and contains various architectural remains of the ancient town of *Eua*, important in the Roman period, but an earlier foundation (? *Thyrea*). Pausanias saw a shrine of Polemokrates, grandson of Asklepios and sculptures of the divine family have been found. 200m to the N of the monastery, in a fenced enclosure (no adm.) on the other side of the main road, substantial building and other remains, including a nymphaion and mosaic floors, belonged to the **Villa of Herodes Atticus**, whose existence is attested by other sources. The site promises to be of great interest when excavations are complete.

The road continues, climbing steadily through attractive, though subsequently barer landscape, via **Káto Dholianá**, **Prosília** and **Stádhio** (for Tegea and Episkopi), to Tripolis (40km from Astros; see below).

**Ellinikó**, 14km SW of Astros, on a more southerly road to Tripolis, has Hellenistic fortifications.

The road turns W, climbing Merovitsa, the S spur of Mt Ktenias, by steep, but well-engineered and protected, hairpin bends, with splendid retrospective *views of the Argolic Gulf. The railway runs farther S in the red gorge of Kiveri, into which the road crosses by (21km) a saddle c 610m high (*view; café c 3km farther on). The valley opens out on the hairpin descent (springs).

At 18km (left) there is a turning to (25km) **Akhladókambos** (Αχλαδόκαμ–πος; 520m), a village (844 inhab.) on the hillside, with its railway station (273m) in the fertile valley below. The place gets its name from the wild pear (αχλαδιά) which once grew on the mountain slopes.

Just before the village, on a ridge to the left, are the ruins of *Hysiai*, where the Argives defeated the Lacedaimonians in 669–668 BC. The town lay on the frontier between Argos and Tegea, and was destroyed by the Lacedaimonians in 417 BC. Its acropolis is marked by good polygonal walling.

Towards the head of the valley the vegetation becomes scrubby and alpine. On a hill near the summit (780m) are the remains of *Moukhli*, a Byzantine fortress used by the Franks and destroyed in 1460. You enter Arcadia.

At (50km) **Ayioryítika** (Αγιωργίτικα) the railway is rejoined after its tortuous detour (far to the S) round Parthenion (1215m), now to the left. On Parthenion's slope a sanctuary once marked the spot where Pan promised the runner Pheidippides that he would aid the Athenians at Marathon.

52km **Stenó**, watered by the Sarandapotamos, lies amid rolling cornfields of the Plain of Tripolis. An interesting find of Early Bronze Age metallurgical kilns was made here.

The **Plain of Tripolis**, a monotonous plateau enclosed by an amphitheatre of barren mountains, really consists of two adjoining level tracts, the **Plain of Tegea** in the S and the **Plain of Mantinea** in the N. About 30km long from N to S and with a maximum width of 16km, it averages 655m above sea-level and suffers extremes of temperature with violent hail and thunderstorms in summer. Vines, wheat, and barley are grown, but, apart from the mulberry, the plateau is now almost treeless. There are several marshes, but few rivers or streams; such as exist mostly disappear into swallow-holes (*katavothrae*). The plain was famous in antiquity for the three Arcadian cities of Mantinea, Tegea, and Pallantion.

**61km TRIPOLIS** (Τρίπολις; Hotels B, C, D, E), the capital (22,429 inhab.) and only large town of the nome of Arcadia, is the chief centre of communications in the Peloponnese. It lies in a bleak situation at the S foot of Mt Apano Krepa (1559m), a peak of the Mainalon range. A modern manufacturing town, it is also the seat of a bishop.

**Buses**. The main bus station is in Plateía Kolokotróni. Important destinations include Athens (13 daily), Argos and Navplio (4), Patras (1), Pirgos (3), Megalopolis (9), Andritsaina (2). Buses for Sparta (11; for Monemvasia, Gytheion, etc.) and for Kalamata (12; also for the Mani and Messenia) leave from two separate cafés near the railway station).

**Railway**. Station on the SE edge of town To Athens 3 daily in 4 1/2 hours; to Kalamata 3 daily in 2 3/4 hrs.

**History**. Tripolis was founded, under the name of *Droboglitza* or *Hydropolitza* about the 14C to take the place of the three derelict cities of the plain (above) and the eparchy to which it belongs still keeps the name of Mantineia. Later it was called *Tripolitza* (in Turkish *Tarabolussa*) and became in 1770 the fortified capital of the Pasha of the Morea. It was taken in 1821 by Kolokotronis, when the Turkish population was massacred, and retaken in 1824 by Ibrahim Pasha, who completely destroyed the town in the retreat of 1828. It revived after 1834.

The most attractive features are the squares, with animated cafés beneath their trees, and the saddlery and harness shops in the streets joining them. Some of the shops and cafés in the sidestreets (especially in and around Od. Taxiárkhon) have kept their traditional style. There are a theatre and cultrual centre (exhibitions etc.) in Od. Ethnikís Anitistáseos, the latter opposite the hige Plateía Areos (cafés).

Just off the main square (signs) is an excellent **Archaeological Museum** (opened 1986), formerly the Panarcadian Hospital, designed by Ziller. ENTRANCE HALL. Inscriptions and reliefs (mainly Hellenistic and Roman) from various sites in Arcadia. Noteworthy are herms, one of normal form from Mantineia, others with pyramidal heads, a peculiarly Arcadian type; large fragment of 4C funerary monument from Mantineia, with acanthus and spiral decoration; seated Archaic figure from Asea (in alcove). SCULPTURE GALLERY (right of entrance). Reliefs and freestanding sculpture (Archaic to Roman). A Classical funerary relief shows a woman and an athlete with strigil; lower part of Archaic relief showing warrior with shield and spear; two Roman reliefs from Villa of Herodes Atticus at Loukou; Hellenistic satyr; head of Aphrodite; head of colossal statue; small 4C seated figure of Demeter holding an apple. The adjoining room is devoted to small objects (mainly Archaic and Classical) from Arcadian sanctuaries: Gkortsouli, Akova, Tripiti, Likokhia etc. Many well-conserved bronzes (dress ornaments, pins, jewellery), small votive vases, numerous terracotta votive figures (many Archaic) and plaques. GALLERY TO LEFT (of entrance hall). On right, photographs of excavations and a fine display of vases (LHIIIB2-C), also bronze weapons and jewellery, from the Mycenaean chamber tomb cemetery at Palaikastro Gortynias (excavated 1985). To left, important material (primarily Early Helladic) from the LN–LH settlement at Sakovouni, Kamenitsa, Gortynia—pottery, obsidian and flint, worked and unworked deer horn, important EH votive figurine, other minor terracotta objects. In a WING at this end of the museum, with various small galleries opening off, is more pottery from Palaikastro; Geometric vases (including grave markers) from Melia (Mantineia); marble heads (in passage, some from Tegea); Hellenistic pottery and interesting wooden vessels from Megalopolis; finds from a Hellenistic cemetery at Mantineia, including a small terracotta statue of Attis dancing. Major statuary includes a Roman copy of a seated Athena; standing female figure (Hellenistic, from Mantineia).

BASEMENT. In the hall, various items of sculpture, including two floral acroteria from the 2C Temple of Despoina at Lykosoura; 5C inscription of sacred law from Mantineia on part of a column; Lakonian relief of seated man holding a cup; other reliefs of Poseidon (?5C); grazing horse (4C). In gallery to right, more photographs of and finds from the Palaikastro cemetery (see above), including bronze weapons, obsidian, scraps of gold leaf. Objects in small side rooms include coins; bronze vessels and other finds from Classical cemetery at Mantineia; bronze vessels from Mantineia and Orchomenos, one inscribed with a dedication; Archaic and Classical bronze stamp seals from Tegea, also terracotta and minor bronze votives and red-figure pottery. To left are two rooms with sculpture: (1) examples of reliefs showing figures reclining at funerary feasts, with food and snakes (symbolic of underworld); damaged head from Tegea of the school of Skopas; Roman figures of the great and small Herakleiotissa types. (2) Late Roman funerary *stelae*; Hellenistic fragment with Erotes holding cymbals; part of 4C relief of seated Zeus with eagle under seat; Hellenistic heads of Asklepios; Roman (Trajanic) portrait head of woman with characteristic hairstyle; 4C votive column with relief decoration and inscriptions to Artemis and Athena. In a side room, Roman glass and pottery from Megalopolis and other Arcadian sites. In GARDEN, outside, sculptures, mainly Hellenistic and Roman funerary reliefs.

Buses of KTEL 6 Arkadias go from the bus station to (8km) **Aléa** (no refreshments), formerly Piali, the site of ancient *Tegea*. One of the oldest and most important cities in Arcadia, *Tegea* occupied a large area and its few remains are scattered.

The largest city in the plain, Tegea waged a long war with Sparta until beaten into submission c 560 BC as a vassal-state. The Tegeans sent 500 men to Thermopylae and 1500 to Plataia, and after the Persian wars tried unsuccessfully to throw off the yoke of Sparta with Argive aid. In the Peloponnesian War the Tegeans sided with Sparta. In 370 BC, after the battle of Leuktra, Tegea joined the Arcadian League, and at the second battle of Mantinea (362 BC) fought on the side of Thebes against Sparta. In 222 BC Tegea became an unwilling member of the Achaean League. Still a flourishing city in the time of Strabo and in the time of Pausanias, Tegea was destroyed by Alaric in the 5C AD. The city was refounded by the Byzantines, and under the name of *Nikli* it became one of the most important centres in the Morea. In 1209 Geoffrey de Villehardouin here established a barony. Tegea was the birthplace of *Atalanta*, the fleetest runner of the age and the heroine of the Calydonian boar-hunt.

The site was excavated by the French School in 1889–90, 1902, and 1910 and by the Greek Archaeological Service in 1965. For renewed work, see below.

In the village the bus stops outside a well-arranged little **museum**, reconstructed in 1967 (some objects now moved to Tripolis) and recently refurbished and extended. CENTRAL ROOM. Marble thrones from the theatre; Hellenistic female statues. ROOM TO LEFT. Sculpture from the Temple of Athena Alea, from the workshop of Skopas: head of Telephos or Herakles; two torsos of Nike Apteros (not Atalanta); torsos of heroes from the pediments; architectonic decoration from the temple. ROOM TO RIGHT. Six herms conjoined; head of Herakles. Relief from a sarcophagus, depicting Achilles and the corpse of Hector. Reliefs: lion, lioness; funeral feast. INNER ROOM, beyond, in cases: Geometric bronzes from Asea,

Classical vases, terracotta and bronze statuettes; fragment of Daedalic relief; terracotta votives and plaques; Geometric and Archaic bronzes, both in the round and repoussé; funeral stelai; Early Helladic pots.

In three minutes you reach (near the church of Ayios Nikolaos) the **Temple of Athena Alea**, excavated in 1889 and 1902. New research and excavations (1990, Norwegian Institute and others) have identified traces of the Archaic temple (late 7C) and discovered Late Geometric and Archaic votives. There is evidence for metallurgical activity in the sanctuary. Two successive apsidal structures were probably even earlier temples. Some Mycenaean finds suggest prehistoric cult activity. It was one of the most famous sanctuaries in Greece; here two kings of Sparta, Leotychides and Pausanias, took refuge, as well as Chryseis, the careless priestess of the Argive Heraion. After the Archaic temple was burnt down in 395 BC, the rebuilding was entrusted to Skopas of Paros. The new temple had a Doric peristyle of 6 columns by 14, and an internal colonnade of Corinthian half-columns, with Ionic above. The substructure is virtually complete; many fragments of fallen column survive. There was an open court to the N. The pediments were decorated with sculpture (? by Skopas), fragments of which survive in the local museum and in the National Museum at Athens. The E pediment represented the Hunt of the Calydonian Boar, with figures of Meleager, Theseus, Atalanta, and Ankaios. The W pediment depicted the Fight of Telephos and Achilles on the banks of the Kaikos in Mysia.

20 minutes further N is **Palaiá Episkopí** (refreshments), a pleasant wooded area which is the site of the annual (August) Peloponnesian Exhibition. This also incorporates athletic contests, dancing displays and a fair. There is a **Folk Museum** in a large building by the road (the Tegean Domestic School). A huge church of 1888 overlies the Byzantine basilica of *Nikli* (fragments are rebuilt into the walls, and ancient mosaic ikons are venerated). These structures partly overlie the ancient **theatre**, rebuilt in marble by Antiochus IV Epiphanes (175–164 BC). The retaining wall of the **cavea** has been cleared: the stage building was to the W. Opposite the W door of the church an avenue leads through the great park. At the far side are remains of an Early Christian **basilica** (of Thyrsos) whose **mosaics** (enclosed but visible, best seen by obtaining key from the Alea Museum) of the 12 months of the year are the most substantial surviving feature. Off the same avenue but nearer the church the **medieval wall** carries an inscription and busts commemorating a meeting of the International Olympic Commission here in 1934. Behind the wall, and N of the church, a recently excavated area is hard to interpret unaided. Medieval houses were found in the upper levels. Below (the curve of its central and northern apses visible, close to remains of the theatre at the E side of the site) was a large **Early Christian basilica**. The narthex contained mosaics (covered). The basilica was probably destroyed in the Slav incursions of the 7C AD. Beyond this building (towards the medieval wall) were later built a small Byzantine church and a **bath building**. At the S side of the area part of the stylobate of the S stoa of the ancient **agora** (3C BC +) can be made out. To the NE stands another section of the **medieval wall**.

A long avenue leads directly to the main Tripolis–Sparta road at **Kerasítsa** (see below), where the bus stops.

The marble for the Tegea temple sculptures came from **Dholianá**, c 10km SE as the crow flies. The quarries are accessible from **Mavríki**, 13km by road from Tegea. The scanty remains of the 6C Temple of Artemis Knakeatis are on a shelf just below the summit of Psili Korfi (1520m).

FROM TRÍPOLIS TO MANTINEA (MANTÍNIA), 12.5km. The road for Pirgos and Olympia runs NNE across the plain. To the left is the long range of Maenalos with the village of **Merkovoúní** on the hillside. The cornfields give place to vineyards producing a celebrated non-resinated red wine. You approach the narrow gap (1.5km wide) between the projecting spurs of Maenalos and Mt Ktenias that marked the ancient frontier between Tegea and Mantinea. On a shoulder of (6km) Mytika (left) are the ruins of a square **watchtower** of polygonal masonry doubtfully identified as the *Skopí* ('look-out') from which the dying Epaminondas watched the Second Battle of Mantinea. This district, once covered by an oak wood, was called *Pelagos* ('the sea'), thus satisfying the oracle's prediction that Epaminondas should beware of the sea. Here were fought several great battles (see below). At 4km is the hamlet of **Khánia Skopís**. About 2km further a link to the Corinth motorway diverges right.

At 9.5km is a by-road (right) into the **Plain of Mantinea**, where the marella cherries used in the manufacture of 'Vissinádha', a popular soft drink, are grown. 2.2km beyond the turn the road passes over a low bridge and through the S fortifications. 700m further, to the left, is an eccentric church (1972), a Minoan-Classical-Byzantine folly dedicated to Ay. Photeini, with other curious monuments in its grounds. Opposite, approached by a fenced avenue, are the most substantial remains of ancient *Mantinea*.

*Mantinea* (629m), one of the most important Arcadian city-states, was the inveterate rival of Tegea, and its whole history is coloured by this mutual antagonism based probably on disputes over water-supply. The acropolis, occupied from prehistoric times, was 1km N on the hill of **Gortsoúli** (see below), known to the ancients as *Ptolis*. On top of the hill was an Archaic shrine. In the Peloponnesian War the Mantineans were generally allies of Athens, the Tegeans being on the side of Sparta. After the Peace of Nikias in 421 BC Mantinea joined Athens, Argos, and Elis in the quadruple alliance that led up to the **First Battle of Mantinea** (418 BC), described in Thuc. 5. 64–74.

In 385 BC King Agesipolis, at the head of the Lacedaemonian army, besieged and took Mantinea after undermining the mud-brick fortification walls with the help of the dammed-up waters of the Ophis. He razed most of the city to the ground and dispersed the population. After the battle of Leuktra the Mantineans, with the help of Thebes, returned to their city, and built the extensive fortifications whose ruins we see today. They rearranged the course of the Ophis so that it became a protection instead of a danger. The foundation in 370 BC of the Arcadian League was due to the efforts of *Lykomedes*, a native of Mantinea, but six years later the Mantineans themselves seceded from it and openly joined the Spartans.

At the **Second Battle of Mantinea** (362 BC) Tegea, the ancient ally of Sparta, fought on the side of Thebes, while Mantinea shared in the defeat of her former enemy, Sparta (Xen. Hell., 7, 5, 18–27). Epaminondas was mortally wounded in the moment of triumph and the battle marked the end of the fourth and last Theban invasion of the Peloponnese. Joining the Achaean League the following century the Mantineans fought against Agis IV and helped to defeat Kleomenes III at Sellasia. Revolting against Macedonian dominance of the Achaean League, the city was captured in 222 BC by Antigonos Doson, who changed its name to *Antigoneia*, a name it kept until Hadrian's time. In 208 BC occurred another 'Battle of Mantinea', in which the Achaeans under Philopoemen defeated the Lacedaemonians, Philopoemen killing the tyrant Machanidas with his own hand (see Polybius, 11.11). An excellent exegesis of the three battles is in Pritchett, *Studies in Ancient Greek Topography* II.

The excavated buildings (in two fenced compounds only one of which is accessible) are roughly in the centre of the walled circuit (see below). In a new project, the layout of the site is being plotted with use of ground-penetrating radar. Most of the visible remains are Roman (note concrete construction) but parts of earlier structures are visible. The path comes first to a small **theatre**. Immediately beyond (E) is the **agora**, crossed by narrow paved roads and bounded by stoas on the N and E. To your left is the stylobate of the N **stoa**, with some column settings. Beneath semicircular Roman foundations (perhaps of an **Exedra of Epigone** who is known from inscriptions to gave paid for refurbishment of the agora) can be distinguished walls of an earlier phase of the agora. Beyond are workshops (?). Immediately E of the *skene* of the theatre the foundations of two Roman temples lie between the remains of narrow paved roads. There are three further temples here, one to the N and two to the S. Ancient sources mention temples of Hera, of Zeus Soteros and of a bouleuterion (council house). Two small 'wings' project from it into the agora: between them were statue bases. The building was later divided longitudinally, with a colonnade in the S façade. The E end became a temple for emperor worship. The foundations of the E stoa of the agora and its associated buildings are in the further enclosure. Additional stoas and other buildings were constructed to the SE, probably in the 2C AD, perhaps paid for from the bequest of Eurykles. A Byzantine church was found further SE.

Tombs (late Classical to Roman) belonging to the site have been excavated at Mília nearby, and at Tripití, an Archaic shrine.

The ˙walls of Mantinea, though no longer stadning to any height, are among the best examples of Greek period fortification. They are contemporary with the walls of Messene (c 370 BC), and may have been built be the same theban architects. The circuit is almost entire, elliptical in form, with a perimeter of nearly 4km. The walls, encircled by the diverted but now dry Ophis, are built of large square or polygonal blocks; up to four courses are still standing. The curtain wall was 4m thick. There were over 120 square towers, placed about 26m apart, and 10 gates, defended in various ways.

If you continue along the road from the site entrance, the road again cuts the line of fortifications, visible to the right (track) opposite the first house (left). 700m further a narrow road (right) climbs in 1.5km (sign) to the 'Panayia Gortsouli'. From the summit, a pleasant spot, there is an excellent view of the site and the line of the fortifications can be partly traced (binoculars useful).

FROM TRÍPOLIS TO VITÍNA VIA ALONÍSTAINA, 36km (23 miles). The road leaves Tripolis to the W, passing (5km) within 1km of **Selimna**, where the Russo-Greek forces gathered in the 1770 insurrection. The route continues NW below the sullen slopes of Mainalon. 15km **Daviá**. A local 'Palaiókastro' marks the site of ancient *Mainalos*, with a medieval fortress. A temple with painted terracotta sculpture and architectural decoration was found here in 1972. The road divides (left, see Rte 36); the right branch continues round Mainalon to (27km) **Alonístaina**, a pretty mountain village founded c 1300 amid wooded crags.

37km Vítina, see Rte 36.

# 31

# Trípolis to Sparta, Mistrá

Road to Sparta (Spárti), 63km (39 miles) with views of wild grandeur, and then to Mistrá, 6km farther.—**Buses** from Athens, via Trípolis, to Sparta, about 9 times daily in 4 hours; from Sparta to Mistrá, see below.

A straight road runs across the plain of Tegea. 5km **Ayios Sóstis**, on the old road to the left, occupies the acropolis of *Tegea*; the main ruins (Rte 30) of the ancient city lie to the left at (8km) **Kerasítsa**. The road climbs into rocky hills with views back to the marshy Lake Taka, drained by swallow-holes. 14km **Manthiréa** (780m; formerly Kamári) has adopted the new name from *Manthyrea*, one of the nine original townships of Tegea. 19km petrol station (restaurant; 854m). The road crosses an intermittently cultivated upland plain, then descends S to the Kleisoura Pass, the long defile that provides the best approach to Lakonia, though we have already entered the modern nome. At the S end is a **memorial** to 118 Spartans of the resistance movement who were killed by the Germans on 26 November 1943. Climbing out of the defile, the summit (831m) of the pass at 42km is crowned by a modern defence post. The road descends a ridge with *views of the Taiyetos and Parnon ranges.

At 49km the site of ancient *Sellasia* appears (right) on a hill now crowned by a chapel of Ayios Konstandinos. At the Battle of Sellasia in 221 BC Antigonos Doson routed the Spartan forces of Kleomenes III. The young Philopoemen of Megalopolis distinguished himself in the allied Achaian force.

The twisting descent reaches (59km) **Kladhás**, where the tributary Oenous is crossed. Shortly after, a long iron bridge carries the road across the Evrotas into (63km) Sparta. (For turnings to Yeraki and Megalopolis near the Evrotas crossing, see below and Rte 33.)

**SPARTA** (224m; Hotels B, C, D, E), in Greek **Spárti** (Σπάρτη), the capital of Lakonia, seat of the Metropolitan of Sparta and Monemvasia, and the agricultural centre (13,011 inhab.) of the Evrotas valley, dates only from 1834. Laid out with broad streets on the Diktynnaion Hill (see below), the town has a striking position at the foot of Taiyetos and is protected on the E by the more distant Parnon. Cool breezes blow, especially in the early evening when the sun disappears behind the mountains. The olive and orange groves which produce its main livelihood are all around and, if its buildings lack architectural merit, they are not so high as to spoil the spectacular mountain views.

Ancient Sparta, or *Lakedaimon*, occupied a vast triangular area on the right bank of the Evrotas including six low hills: the *Kolona*, the *Acropolis*, the *Hill of Argive Hera*, the *Issorion*, the *Diktynnaion*, and the *Hill of Armed Aphrodite*. During the period of its greatness the city remained unwalled, since the natural strength of its position and the bravery of its soldiers were considered sufficient protection. The inhabitants dwelt in a group of five scattered townships, separated by gardens and plantations. Sparta had few of the magnificent public buildings that adorned other Greek cities and its scanty remains—as Thucydides foretold—reflect little of its ancient status.

**Buses** from Od. Vrasídhou opposite Hotel Menelaíon to Athens (2), Tripolis (3), Corinth (7); Kalamata (2), Monemvasia (1), Yithion (5), Areopolis, etc. (1); also to Yeraki (2) and other Lakonian villages; from Od. Leonídhou to **Mistrá**.

**History and Institutions**. Though some traces of LHIIIB occupation have been found on the acropolis, Homeric *Sparta* seems to have been elsewhere, perhaps at *Therapnai* near the Menelaion, while Kouphovouno, to the SW, was occupied from Neolithic times. The most important Bronze Age site (unexcavated) may have been at Paliopyrgi, near *Amyklai* (also with prehistoric finds) and close to the rich Vapheio tholos tomb. *Lakedaimon* was a Dorian foundation and developed in its later history those traditions and customs least suited to urban progress. These fossilised into a constitution which by Classical times was unique among city states. Tradition ascribes it to the reforms of Lycurgus (for whom many dates have been argued in the 9C–7C), but its developed form may not be earlier than the end of the 7C BC. The inhabitants of Lakedaimonia were divided into three classes; Spartans, or more correctly Spartiates, Perioikoi, and Helots, of whom only Spartiates had citizen rights.

The government of the state was composed of the five *ephors*, the *gerousia*, or council of elders, the two *kings*, and the *apella*, or assembly of citizens over 30 years old. The gerousia consisted of 28 citizens over 60 years old and the two kings. They prepared necessary legislation and put it to the assembly. The ephors were elected annually and while in office were the most powerful men in Sparta, although final decisions of war and peace were in the hands of the gerousia and the apella. The kings were under the control of the ephors and the only power they retained was command of the army in the field. All citizens could attend the assembly, but its power was limited to accepting or rejecting proposals put to it by the gerousia.

Our knowledge of the Spartan 'caste' system is limited to its state as evolved by the Classical period. The *Spartiates*, whose numbers may never have exceeded 10,000, were the rulers of Lakedaimonia. Each was given an estate of public land which was cultivated by slaves, leaving the Spartiate to spend his whole life in military and public service. From birth he was subject to stern discipline. Weak or deformed children were left to die on Taiyetos. Stronger children remained with their mothers until their seventh birthday. Their education in camps was supervised by young soldiers and discipline enforced by pack leaders; drill exercises and brutal competitive games figured largely. At 20 the Spartiate entered the army proper (perhaps after a period in the *krypteia*, or secret police, which was at intervals let loose upon the Helots). He was expected to marry but continued to live in barracks and to eat in a mess on prescribed rations supplied from his own estate. He became a full soldier-citizen at the age of 30.

*Perioikoi*, or 'dwellers around', lived in a number of villages in Laconia and neighbouring Messenia. They had no citizen rights but were free-men. Their only duty to the state was to serve, when called upon, as hoplites. The *Helots* were serfs and completely under the control of the Spartiates, whom they always greatly outnumbered. They consisted of the descendants of former inhabitants of Laconia and of surviving Messenians who were enslaved. They were obliged to cultivate the Spartiate's estates and to deliver the required produce from them.

Though the system itself had all the characteristics least acceptable to the 'democratic' ideal, either ancient or modern, the Spartan regime seems to develop its ruthlessly illiberal and wholly militaristic nature only about the time of the Persian wars. From the Geometric period to the 6C Spartan arts flourish; pottery, sculpture in bronze, and basic architecture, though never opulent, keep pace with those of other cities. The music and dancing of her festivals are famed. In the 7C poetry flourishes with the native Kinaithon, Terpander of Lesbos, and Tyrtaios. By the 5C every setback—the numerical inadequacy of the ruling caste, the earthquake of 464 BC, the chronic Messenian discontent—is countered only by greater austerity. This policy was superficially successful while the war machine functioned and the quality of Spartan troops made up for their dwindling numbers, but did nothing in the long run to stave off the inevitable effects of depopulation and an outmoded economy.

Spartan expansion began near the end of the 8C with the attack on the fertile territory of Messenia. This conquest was later followed by a long revolt of Messenians (685–668). After the region had been subdued Sparta began to increase her power in the Peloponnese. A long war with Tegea (c 600–560) showed that expansion was possible only by dominating vassal allies not by annexation. By the end of the century Tegea and Thyreatis were subdued and the **Peloponnesian League** instituted with Sparta at its head. Argos, the only neighbouring state that could hope to defy Sparta, was decisively defeated at Sepeia c 494.

Sparta took no part in repelling the first Persian expedition, but in 480–479 added to her prestige by the exploit of Leonidas at Thermopylae and the victory of Plataia under Pausanias. The later intrigues of Pausanias in Byzantium and the campaign of Leotychides in Thessaly, both opposed by Athens, showed Sparta that better policy lay in maintaining strength in the Peloponnese; control of the Aegean was left to Athens. In 464 the Helots revolted and only outside aid saved the state from destruction. The imperialism of Athens in the second half of the 5C forced the Greeks to turn to Sparta as their champion.

The Peloponnesian War ended with the defeat of Athens, leaving Sparta the most powerful state not only of the mainland, but also in the Aegean, where she waged an unsuccessful war with Persia. The Greeks were already finding Sparta a worse master than Athens and in 395 she was attacked by a coalition led by Athens, Thebes, Corinth, and Argos. Although Sparta triumphed on land (at Corinth), her fleet was defeated at Knidos in 394 and all hopes of an overseas empire were abandoned. With the peace of 386, Sparta kept her position by forcing the Persian terms on the rest of the cities. A powerful new enemy soon arose in Thebes; Theban hoplites, using new tactics, at Leuktra in Boeotia (371 BC) broke for ever the legend of Spartan invincibility. Epaminondas of Thebes invaded Laconia and reached the outskirts of Sparta itself. To keep Sparta powerless Messenia was revived as an independent state, the Arcadian League was formed, and a chain of fortresses was founded encircling Sparta's N frontier.

The Achaian League and the Macedonians continued the campaign against Sparta. In 295 BC Demetrios Poliorketes all but captured the city, and in 272 Pyrrhus could easily have taken it after defeating the Spartans in the field. Kleomenes III abolished the ephorate and ruled as a tyrant in a vain attempt to restore Spartan hegemony, but was utterly defeated at Sellasia. Sparta became a dependency of Macedon, regaining momentary independence only under the tyrants Machanidas (207 BC) and Nabis (195–192). After Nabis' assassination Philopoemen forced Sparta to join the Achaian League, razed the city walls, and repealed the laws of Lycurgus.

Under the Romans Laconia had a period of prosperity in the 2C AD as a province of Achaia and under Septimius Severus was even allowed to revert to a Lycurgan regime. The city was destroyed in AD 396 by Alaric and when the Slavs invaded in the 9C the population migrated to the Mani. The Byzantines refounded a town under the name **Lakedaimonia**, but by 1248 it had lost all importance to Mistra and disappears from history until 1834. Excavations, undertaken by the British School in 1906–10 and 1925–29, were resumed in 1988.

The course of the **city walls** has been traced for most of the 10km circuit. The walls of Sparta were a feature of her decline. The first defences were made in 307–295 BC and supplemented when Pyrrhus threatened the city in 272. By 218 walls and gates existed. These were strengthened by Nabis against Flamininus, pulled down by the Achaians in 188 and rebuilt by Appius Claudius Pulcher in 184 BC.

The centre of Sparta is a large flagged and arcaded **plateia**, scene of the evening volta. To the E is the **museum**.

VESTIBULE. Stelai and inscriptions once bearing inlaid votive sickles of iron, dedicated to Artemis Orthia by boy-victors in ordeal contests; 218. Stele retaining its sickle. ROOM 1 (right). Roman mosaics from Sparta. ROOM 2. Architectural fragments from the Amyklaion; reliefs of the heroised dead; Archaic reliefs, including Helen and Menelaus; terracotta figurines, plaques, also pottery from the Sanctuary of Zeus, Agamemnon and Alexandra-Cassandra (Ayia Paraskevi, Amyklai). ROOM 3. *Leonidas in marble (5C), upper part of a superb warrior statue, perhaps the memorial raised to Leonidas on his reburial at Sparta (it inspired the modern memorial at Thermopylae); 440. Stele of Damonon, victor in chariot races, with a long mutilated inscription recording the circumstances of its dedication (5C BC); colossal heads of Hera (?Archaic) and Herakles (Hellenistic); other Archaic and Classical freestanding sculpture; votive stelai and inscriptions.

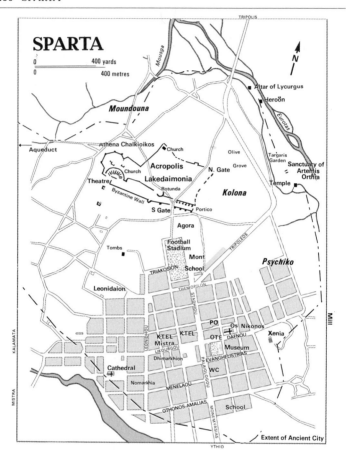

ROOM 4 (left). Masks in terracotta, lead votive figurines and limestone reliefs from the Sanctuary of Artemis Orthia; kraters and amphorae showing Spartiate warriors in combat; statuary representing Herakles; Archaic bronze ⋅figurines; pottery and other votives from the shrine of Athena Chalkioikos and from the Menelaion and Amyklai; burial pithoi and craters with relief decoration. ROOM 5. Mainly Hellenistic and Roman sculpture, including Archaising. Head of Artemis; Hermes; torso of Asklepios; Dioscuri; wild boar in steatite; 307. Fragmentary relief from a sarcophagus; 717. Triglyph and two metopes from the acropolis; clay votive model of a Roman galley found in the sea off Cape Malea. ROOM 6 (= stair). New finds from Diros Cave. Pottery, stone, bone and terracotta. ROOM 7 (upstairs). Prehistoric finds (pottery, bronzes and figurines) from various sites in Lakonia, mostly cemeteries and including Pellana (two large palace-style jars), Epidauros Limera, Palaikastro Gortynias; photographs of site at Pellana.

The ruins of ancient *Sparta* lie N and NE of the modern town. You take Odhós K. Palaiológou which continues as Stadhíou. At the top stands a modern memorial to Leonidas. His tomb lay near the theatre, where the broken statue believed to represent him was found. To the left of the sports stadium a track leads through olive-groves to the S gate of the **acropolis**, the highest of the low hills of Sparta (20m above the plain). Its walls were built between AD 267 and 386 and completed on the E side after the Slav invasion in the 8C. Here was the centre of Byzantine Lakedaimonia. The contour of the summit has been altered by a modern reservoir and the view is obscured by trees. Immediately inside the gate is a brick-built Roman portico. In its developed form (2C AD) it was c 188m long and 14.5m wide and, at least partly, double fronted, extending as a monumental revetment to the acropolis hill from a round building on the W—and may have continued along the E side. The façades probably had Doric columns whose archaising characteristics may copy those of a much earlier predecessor. To the E there are barrel vaulted chambers (visible in recent excavations to the W; some with facilities for the provision of water) at the lower level. Part of the E section was radically transformed in the 11–12C AD, perhaps into the monastery of Ayios Nikon Metanoeites which is known from sources to have included a double fronted stoa. Late houses were built over the W end of the structure. Following the left hand lane from the gate along the crest of the hill past two ruined 11C churches, you reach (below; left) the **theatre** built in the side of the hill in the 2C or 1C BC. Next to the theatre at Megalopolis it is the largest in Greece, but much of its masonry went into late fortifications or was quarried for Mistra. New excavations are in progress. The theatre, which was used for public meetings as well as theatrical performances, had a movable stage building which was pushed

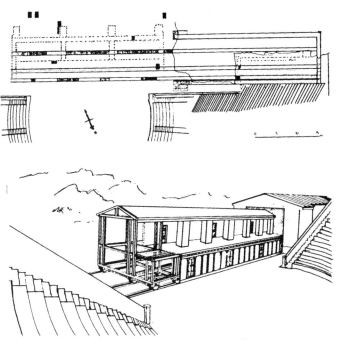

*Sparta,Theatre. Top: plans of tracks for moving stage.*
*Bottom: restoration of mobile stage building*

into position on wheels. The grooves of the tracks can be made out. The E parodos wall has more than 30 inscribed blocks, bearing lists of magistrates of the 2C AD.

The terrace to the N produced in 1907 remains from the **Temple of Athena Chalkioikos**, a building lined with bronze plates, legendarily associated with Aristomenes' defiant gesture at the beginning of the first Messenian revolt, when he came by night to hang up a shield with an insulting dedication; and later with the vindictive and sacrilegious treatment accorded to King Pausanias when he sought sanctuary here. Today nothing can be seen.

From the bend in Odhós Tripóleos a path descends to the **Sanctuary of Artemis Orthia**, scene of the endurance tests by flogging that featured in the upbringing of Spartan boys. The sanctuary existed in the 10C BC, and in Archaic times comprised a walled enclosure with an **altar** on the E side and a small **temple** on the W. In the 2C AD the whole complex was reconstructed and a Roman theatre built to accommodate spectators. There seem in earlier days to have been other contests of milder sort; singing, oratory, and rougher games for boys of 10 and upward. Farther N along the Evrotas are a **heroön** and a huge stone **altar**.

Numerous discoveries in emergency excavations beneath the modern town have attested to its prosperity in the Roman period when it had a regular plan and many fine houses with mosaics, etc.

Excursions may be made to the sites of the *Menelaion* (5km) and the *Amyklaion* (8km). For the first, you cross the Evrotas, turn right on the Yeraki road. At 4.5km a road (signed 'Menelaion') leads left to the chapel of **Ayios Ilias**. Follow the path beyond straight for c 20 minutes. On the hill are three platforms on which stood the **Menelaion**, or Shrine of Menelaus and Helen, whose identification, originally based on the records of Pausanias, has recently been confirmed by the discovery of dedications inscribed to both. Its ruined masonry is imposing and the view superb. Just below the summit to the NE are Mycenaean remains uncovered in 1910 and since 1973. These consist of a 'mansion' of which three structural phases have been distinguished; the first on the lower terrace only, the second and third involving additional elements on the terrace immediately above. The arrangement of rooms in all phases closely resembles that of the developed Mycenaean palaces (cf. below, Palace of Nestor at Pylos), though on a more modest scale. Mansion 1, dated to the 15C BC, is one of the earliest of such complexes so far known. The site was destroyed by fire in c 1200 BC. There are other Mycenaean remains in the vicinity, suggesting that the site covered a large area.

From the centre of Sparta the Yithion road leads to modern **Amíkles**, where you turn left at a sign 'Amyklyon' to **Ayía Kiriakí**, a chapel on the site of the **Amyklaion**, excavated by the German School in 1925. The sanctuary surrounded the Tomb of Hyakinthos, which was crowned by an archaic statue of Apollo seated on a chryselephantine throne. Here the great festival of the Hyakinthia took place in July. The place is firmly identified by an inscription, but the remains are not illuminating. The site however seems to have had continuous occupation since Mycenaean times (and Hyakinthos is a pre-Greek deity). The church of **Ayía Paraskeví**, to the S, may occupy the site of the **Sanctuary of Zeus, Agamemnon and Alexandra-Kassandra**, from which a huge Archaic votive deposit with hero-reliefs was unearthed close by in 1956.

*Amyklai*, the ancient capital of the Mycenaeans in Laconia, probably lay nearby at **Palaiopíryi**, the largest Late Helladic settlement (unexcavated) yet discovered in Laconia, and close to the **Vaphio** tholos tomb (guide necessary), source of the famous gold cups in Athens. Mycenaean finds (chamber tombs) have also been made at Spilákia.

The EXCURSION TO MISTRÁ (8km W) is essential. Buses regularly (see above), though with a long midday interval. The road runs W to the foot of Mt Taiyetos, crossing a luxuriant region, thick with orange, fig, and mulberry trees. The eroded mountain sides are scored with *langádhes* (deep gorges), each with its torrent. The gorge of **Paróri**, the gloomiest and most forbidding ravine, has been identified with the *Apothetai* where the Spartiates used to expose their weakly children. It may also be the *Kaiadas*, or criminal pit, from which Aristomenes made a miraculous escape (but see below, Tripi). To the N of Parori is the Gorge of Mistra, at the entrance to which is a hill with the ruins of the medieval city. You pass through modern Mistrá, where a 19C mansion is being restored as a **folk museum**.

**MISTRÁ** (Μυστράς), a purely medieval town in its ruin, has been likened to a Byzantine Pompeii, though it has a nearer parallel in Les Baux in Provence. Churches, monasteries, palaces, and houses line the narrow winding streets. The situation alone would make it an enchanting spot, but within its walls are preserved some of the finest examples of 14–15C Byzantine architecture in Greece, and the numerous wall-paintings, although sometimes badly damaged, are among the most characteristic of their kind. An impregnable fortress crowns the summit.

**History**. On the hill of *Mezythra*, 5km from medieval Lakedaimonia, William de Villehardouin built a fortress in 1249 to protect the town from the marauding Slavs of Taiyetos. Mezythra was corrupted by the Franks to *Mistra*, which in the French dialect of the time meant 'mistress'. Villehardouin, taken prisoner in 1259 at Pelagonia by Michael Palaiologos, was forced after three years captivity to surrender Mistra, together with Monemvasia and Maina, by way of ransom. The Greeks, using Mistra as a base, drove the Franks into Elis, but were completely defeated in 1265 in the defile of Makriplagi near Gardiki and William returned to Laconia. The inhabitants of Lakedaimonia had meanwhile settled on the hill of Mistra under the protection of the fortress.

After 50 years of strife the Greeks reconquered the greater part of the Morea. Monemvasia gave way in importance to Mistra and here from 1349 the peninsula was governed by a Despot, either a son or brother of the emperor (often his heir presumptive). The despots were successively Manuel Cantacuzene (1349–80); Matthew, his brother (1380–83); and Demetrios (1383–84). Here after his abdication in 1354 John VI Cantacuzene lived with his sons as the monk Ioasaph Christodoulos (died 1383). The Cantacuzenes were followed by the Palaiologi; Theodore I Palaiologos (1384–1407), who became a monk and was succeeded by his nephew, Theodore II (1407–43); Constantine Dragatses (1443–48) who succeeded to the Imperial throne to be the last Emperor of Byzantium; and Demetrios (1448–60), whose unedifying squabbles with his brothers gave the Turks their opportunity. In 1400–42 Mistra was the home of the philosopher Gemistos Plethon, the rediscoverer of Plato. Cardinal Bessarion (1389–1472), the illustrious scholar of Trebizond, attended his lectures in 1423.

Mistra passed to the Turks in 1460, though it was temporarily invested in 1464 by Sigismondo Malatesta of Rimini, then in the service of Venice. From 1687 to 1715 the city was in the hands of the Venetians when it reached its second peak of prosperity. Its population reached 42,000. The main industry was silkworm culture. On the return of the Turks the town rapidly declined. It was burnt in 1770 by Albanian troops after the Mainotes had captured it for Orloff, and again in 1825 by Ibrahim's soldiers. After the refounding of Sparta in 1834 Mistra was virtually abandoned. The French School saved the site from complete ruin in 1896–1910, but it served as a battlefield in 1944 between various partisan forces. The last 30 families were moved by the Greek Archaeological Service in 1952, and wholesale reconstruction was undertaken, initially by Prof. A. Orlandos.

The ruins rise on the N and E side of the hill. They are in three zones. The **kastro** occupies the summit; below to the N is the walled **upper town** (Khora), the houses of which cluster around the Despot's palace; below again extends the **lower town** (Katokhora), added somewhat later, which includes the cathedral. The parapets and upper sections of defence walls are generally Turkish refurbishings. A modern road ascends the hill to a point above Ayia Sophia (car park), providing the easiest approach to the kastro. It is best to enquire below whether this entrance is open. The bus stops at the main gate.

You enter the **lower town** by a restored gate and turn right.

The **cathedral of Ayios Dhemetrios** (Metrópolis), built (or perhaps rebuilt) in 1309 by the Metropolitan Nikephoros Moschopoulos, stands in a spacious court in which are an antique sarcophagus and a fountain dated 1802. The basilica was altered in the 15C when the upper part was replaced by five domes after the model of the Aphentiko. As a result the paintings in the nave have been cut in two. The arcade of the marble ikonostasis has remarkable fretwork carving; the cornice above was added in the 15C. The 17C walnut throne is richly carved. In the floor is a two-headed marble

eagle that possibly commemorates the coronation here of the Emperor Constantine XII (see above). The paintings are ascribed to ten different artists in three periods. Those in the N aisle (portraits of saints, torture and burial of St Demetrios, sufferers from dropsy and leprosy) are shown by their symmetry and repose to be the earliest works. S aisle, prophets, life of the Virgin, miracles of Christ, more realistic (14C). Narthex, also 14C but by a different hand, Last Judgement.

Adjoining the cathedral is the **museum**, formed by Gabriel Millet (died 1954), who did so much to save Mistra from further ruin. It contains decorative fragments, mostly from the churches. Marble relief of Christ; fragments of a lintel with the monogram and arms of Isabella de Lusignan. Little survives of the **Episcopal Palace**, part of which gave place to monastic cells in 1754.

Above and to the left stands the 14C **Evangelistria**, a simple mortuary chapel (two ossuaries) with good sculptural detail (notably ikonostasis). You diverge (right) from the main street for the **Vrontokhion**, a great monastic complex, cultural centre, and burialplace of the Despots. It has two churches, both built by the Archimandrite Pachomios, the first *Ayii Theodori (c 1296) being the latest of the churches in Greece built with a central octagon (cf. Daphni, on a larger scale). It was restored in 1932. Farther on is the attractive **Aphentikó**, or **Panayia Hodegetria**, dating from 1310 but much restored since it was largely pulled down in 1863. It was the earliest church at Mistra built to a composite plan, a fusion of the basilica and the cross church with domes, an idea revived from earlier practice. It has four small cupolas and a central dome (rebuilt), with a beautiful bell-tower.

The INTERIOR is remarkable for its proportions, its purity of line, and the carved ornamentation. The marble facings have disappeared. In a side chapel on the N side of the narthex is the tomb of Theodore II, with (above) frescoed portraits of him in the robes of despot (Aphentis) and the habit of a monk. Here also the tomb of Pachomios. In the corresponding S chapel the walls have copies of chrysobuls detailing the foundation, properties, and privileges of the monastery. The *frescoes, in bold colour, include the miracles of Christ (narthex); group of martyrs (in NW chapel); and a panel of St Gregory, the illuminator of Armenia (in the apse). The ruined **cells** and the **refectory** can be identified.

Beyond the Evangelistria the road passes under a machicolated Gothic archway and higher up divides: the left branch leads to the Pantanassa, which is described on the descent. By the right branch you enter the **upper town** by the **Monemvasia Gate**, pass below a tall 15C house with arcades and machicolations, skirt a small **mosque**, and reach the square in front of the Despot's palace.

The **Palace of the Despots** (*Anaktora*), a rare example of a civic Byzantine building, is an extensive ruin dating from various periods. The wing nearest to the mosque may have been erected under the Franks (13C) and had two successive additions under the Cantacuzenes. In the 14C the Palaiologi added the fourth building in the line and, in 1400–60, the immense vaulted audience-hall at right angles; its façade was painted and its flamboyant windows are framed in poros mouldings and covered with stucco. The hall was heated by eight chimney-pieces. Behind the palace are other official buildings which extend to the massive **Nauplia Gate**, protected by an external redoubt.

Visitors who are pressed for time should here turn back and make directly for the Pantanassa and Perivleptos.

To the W of the palace, beyond a small **Turkish bath** is the church of **Ayia Sophia**, built in 1350 by Manuel Cantacuzene as the katholikon of the Zoödhotos monastery. It was used as the palace chapel and here are buried Theodora Tocco, wife of Constantine (died 1429) and Cleopa Malatesta, wife of Theodore II (died 1433). There survive remains of the ikonostasis, of the pavement, and of the refectory and cells. The paintings were preserved by Turkish whitewash. There is a fine view from the porch.

From here you continue to ascend, passing under a small aqueduct, to the **kastro**, built in 1249 by William de Villehardouin and repaired and refortified along existing lines by the Turks, so that the plan remains Frankish even though much of the masonry is later. The **keep** (564m) commands a magnificent *view, well demonstrating its strategic importance.

On the descent you can pass Ayia Sophia and through ruined houses (right) to the so-called **Little Palace**, a spacious Byzantine house of early date, then down steps to **Ayios Nikolaos**, a curious building of the Turkish period with a modern roof.

The **Pantanassa**, the most beautiful of the churches of Mistra, was built in 1365 by Manuel Cantacuzene and enlarged in 1428 by John Frangopoulos, protostrator (minister) of Constantine Palaiologos. It now belongs to a nunnery. In plan the church resembles the Aphentiko, but the proportions are more slender. It is orientated N–S. A broad flight of steps leads to a picturesque loggia commanding a fine view over the Evrotas valley. Over the narthex is a gallery reached by an external staircase and opening into the Gothic tower (splendid *view). The side galleries are continued over the aisles as far as the apses.

The paintings in the body of the church are late, with the exception of the fine portrait of Manuel Chatsikis (1445) in the narthex. Those in the galleries are more decorative. Under the W gallery is a happy combination of architectural lines and painted ornament (fine head of a prophet on the NW pendentive); in the NW cupola is a vigorous Patriarch. Note also Palm Sunday, with children playing; Annunciation; and Presentation in the Temple.

You descend a path (unsigned) on the open flank of the hill to the **Monastery of the Perivleptos**, named on a plaque over its entrance (1714). The **church** (latter half of the 14C) in stone and brick, with pentagonal apses and an octagonal dome, has the pure style of three centuries earlier. Below the E end is an unusual little chapel with a tiled pavement. To the S of the church is a square battlemented tower, richly ornamented on its E face. The *frescoes give a good idea of the ikonography of a 14C Byzantine church. The dome has retained its Pantokrator. Above the side entrance, Dormition of the Virgin; in the Prothesis chapel to the left, Divine Liturgy, celebrated by Christ and the angels; in the bema, Ascension; in the vaulting of the S transept, Nativity; in the W nave, Transfiguration (note the silhouette of Christ); in the S aisle, Childhood of the Virgin.

Returning towards the main gate you pass (right) the 18C **House of Krevatas**, a vast mass of ruins. The chapel of **Ayios Ioannis** lies outside the walls near the **Marmara Fountain**. On the inner path which leads back to the Metropolis are the two small churches of **Ay. Yeoryios** (962, restored 1953) and **Ay. Christophoros** (14C, restored 1954).

FROM SPARTA TO YERÁKI, 40km (25 miles), gently undulating through cultivated country; bus. You take the Tripolis road and beyond the bridge turn right. Soon after there is a turning to **Khrísafa** (Χρύσαφα; 20km), where the churches of the Chrysaphiótissa (1290) (sign in village; church 1km beyond) and Ayii Pándes (1367) both have wall paintings. Other churches include Koímesis tes Theotókou (14C), Ayios Ioánnis Pródhromos (14C), Ayios Dhimítrios (1641). The Moní Prodhrómou dates from 1625. At **Tsákona** to the N of this road are some remains of a **Sanctuary of Zeus Messapios**. Also N of the road ( at c 7km) is a turn to the monastery of Ayioi Saranda (1620). The ruins of its predecessor in the vicinty include a cave church (key at monastery) with 13–15C frescoes. Above the cave is the rock-cut *askitario* of Timiou Prodhromou with 13C frescoes.

You continue along the left bank of the Evrotas. At **Skoúra** the road turns E. 2km N of Skoura, at **Melathriá**, on the hill of Profítis Ilías, is a cemetery of Mycenaean chamber tombs. Beyond (24km) **Goritsá** is a distant view towards Yeraki across a wide valley. 40km **Yeráki** (Γεράκι), a large village (1638 inhab.), not much visited, occupies the site of ancient *Geronthrai*. Its imposing acropolis (591m) has walls in the cyclopean style, best preserved on the N and E. They were investigated in 1905 by the British School and certainly date from Mycenaean times; theyhey may even have Middle Helladic origins. A small **museum** contains local finds.

About ½ hour SE by road on a long detached ridge of Parnon stands medieval **Geraki**, one of the original 12 Frankish baronies, with remains of 15 small medieval churches. It is best to contact the phylax in the village (enquire at cafés in the main square) for directions and to open the churches which are nearly all locked. The **kastro**, at the N end of the ridge (easy path in 20 minutes to summit), was built by Jehan de Nivelet in 1254. It has fine views of Parnon and Taiyetos. **Ayios Yeóryios**, the basilican castle chapel (13C), has a florid Gothic shrine recalling South Italian work. The W door of the **Zoödhókhos Piyí** (1431), and the shrine in **Ayía Paraskeví**, both lower down the slope, have rude incised and sculptured decoration in a local Gothic idiom. During cleaning in 1964, frescoes of the late 12C were found in the **Evangelístria**; particularly interesting are those in the dome. **Ayios Sózon**, built over an Early Christian basilica, has frescoes of the same period. **Ayios Athanásios** has been over-restored (dome rebuilt). The church at the extreme S end of the ridge has a mural painting representing Joshua attacking a city of the Amorites. Other noteworthy buildings are **Ayios Ioánnis Chrysóstomos** (13C) and **Ayios Nikólaos** (14C).

FROM SPARTA TO KALAMÁTA, 60km (37½ miles) over the *Langadha Pass. 2 buses daily. The road is steep with hairpin bends, needing care in bad weather, and provides marvellous views of the Taiyetos and into Messenia on the W. 5km Superb view of Mistra (left). At 7km the road starts to climb, and at (9km) **Trípi** (Hotel D) enters the Langadha Gorge. To the S, near the modern hotel Kaiadas is one of the places claimed as that where the Spartans exposed weakly children. Recovery of human remains from a cave nearby support the identification. After 16km the road passes into Messenia amid fir forests. There are superb views of the Taiyetos peaks, often snow-capped. 24km Hotel (B). At the summit (1524m), a little farther on, is a tourist pavilion. 35km **Artemísia**. The road descends a gorge but, at 48km, climbs a steep zigzag to a col, from the top of which is a fine view down to Kalamata. The road enters Kalamata by the frourion; for the centre you keep the river to the right.

# 32

# Southern Laconia (Lakonía)

The predominantly mountainous region S of Sparta is one of the less visited parts of Greece, although the area between Sparta and Monemvasia and from Leonidhi, across Mt Parnon, to Yeraki is now more accessible with improved roads. Nevertheless, in the Taiyetos and Parnon ranges transport is less readily available; haste is impossible, accommodation limited and sometimes primitive. Visitors will, however, be rewarded by superb scenery and unexpected traces of the past. For Byzantinists Monemvasia, best approached by sea, is imperative. Yithion is a quiet and pleasant seaside town. The coastal settlements from Kiparissi to Monemvasia can be reached by road but the sea approach is described here since it is both more pleasant and easier. Southern Laconia has escaped several incursions which afflicted the rest of the country. The Maniots claim never to have been conquered by Slav or Turk, the Tzakonians to have survived from remoter times still; but claims by either to be indigenous are exaggerated or at best unproven. Certainly both peoples display characteristics of their own and are very resistant to change.

A useful article on the antiquities of the area, by Wace and Hasluck, is in B.S.A. 1914. For Mani, see P. Greenhalgh and E. Eliopoulos *Deep into Mani*, 1985.

# A.  From Piraeus (Peiraía) by sea

**Ferry** weekly to Monemvasía in 6–8¾ hours, continuing either to Kíthira and Andikíthira direct, or via Neápolis and Kíthira to Yíthion (in 22¾ hrs) as described below. Some timetables continue to W Crete.

**Hydrofoil** ('Flying Dolphin') daily in summer (3½ hrs to Monemvasia) as far as Neapolis, sometimes to Kasteli, in western Crete.

NB. Where two times are given those in *brackets* refer to hydrofoils. The smaller ports do not have direct services.

Leaving Piraeus the ship heads due S for Cape Skillaion, passing E of Aiyina and between Idhra and the mainland of Argolis (Rte 23). Trikkeri and Spetsopoula are left to starboard, then it heads W across the open sea.

4 hours (3 hrs) **Skála** is the landfall for **Leonídhi** (Λεονίδι), the chief town (3804 inhab. Hotels C, D, E) of Kynouria, an Arcadian eparchy which is separated from the hinterland by the abrupt ranges of **Mt Parnon**, a long and sparsely populated range rising to 1936m, without low passes. Wolves are still found here. A large wooded tract was designated as a game reserve in 1961.

FROM LEONÍDHI TO YERÁKI VIA KOSMÁS, 50km (31 miles), imperfect asphalt, except for 3km between Kosmás and Yeráki which is adequate. In Leonidhi the road (signs to Sparti) turns inland past a memorial to the dead of a battle (1949) in the civil war, climbs to pass below the **Moní Elónas**, crossing Parnon (spectacular scenery) to Kosmas and Yeraki (Rte 31). The road is steep but passable with care and worth the effort.

4½ (3½) hrs **Kaaríssi** (Κυπαρίσσι; Hotels C), ancient *Kyphanta*, a charming village 2km inland from the sea with its picturesque harbour (**Paralía**) and adjacent village of **Mitrópolis** occupying an olive-planted plateau backed by dramatic mountains. This is one of the few points where the forbidding Lakonian coast does not rise sheer from the sea. On a sharp bend in the main road above Kiparissi, a striking rock cleft has springs and other remains almost certainly of an Asklepieion (B.S.A. 1914) mentioned by Pausanias (path signed Panayia sto Vrakho; none beyond to highest spring and sanctuary terrace). Immediately S of Paralia, twin peaks linked by a saddle have Archaic/Classical (W) and medieval (E) **fortifications**, the latter also a ruined Byzantine church. The road beyond the Asklepieion (daily bus to Molaoi), narrow and imperfect, climbs steeply into the interior.

The ship follows the rugged and lonely seaboard. The white Evangelistria Monastery is backed by a hill crowned with three round fortress towers. 5½ (4) hours **Yéraka** (or Limin Ierakos; limited rooms), the harbour of Ierax, an attractive mountain village 3.5km inland, is enchantingly situated on a narrow fjord. Dominating the entrance on the N, immediately above the village, is the fine acropolis of *Zarax*, of whose ancient history little is known (B.S.A. 1914), with Archaic/Classical walls and towers, an interesting gate to the small inner acropolis, and several later churches and other buildings. The fortifications were probably reused in medieval times. To the S there is a (mainly unsurfaced) road to Monemvasia; to the W, beyond the inland village (occasional small bus, not daily), there is a minor road inland to **Reikhéa** (for Molaoi, bus connection).

8½ (3½) hours **MONEMVASÍA** (Μονεμβασία; Hotels A, B, C, D, E), aptly described as the Gibraltar of Greece, owes its name to the single approach (μονή ἔμβασις) by which it is reached from the landward side. Called by our old writers *Malmsey*, by the Venetians *Napoli di Malvasia*, and by the French *Malvoisie*, it was once famous for its export of wine. Situated at the seaward end of a forbidding rocky promontory, at least from Byzantine times there was an upper and a lower town—the former occupying the summit of the promontory, the latter its S slope. The buildings were altered and extended by successive holders of the site. The Byzantine Lower Town, which has been substantially restored in recent years, now houses 78 of the present inhabitants of the area, most (768) of whom live in **Yéfira**, the mainland township. Modern and ancient settlements are linked by a succession of causeway, bridge (renewed 1889), and roadway round the S side of the rock. The modern harbour is N of the casueway. A useful book is A.G. and H.A. Kaligas *Monemvasia* (1986) in the Greek Traditional Architecture series.

**History**. The promontory was anciently called *Minoa*, a name that hints at Cretan influence. After the Slav invasion it became a refuge for the Greeks of Laconia and, under the name of *Monemvasia*, developed into an important fortress and flourishing port. In 1147 it repulsed an attack by the Normans of Sicily and thereafter was nearly always the last outpost of the Morea to fall to succeeding waves of conquerors. In 1249 William de Villehardouin took it after a siege of three years, but he had to give it up in 1262, with Mistra and the Maina, to Michael Palaiologos, in payment of his ransom. Monemvasia became the tenth see in the empire, the commercial capital of the Byzantine Morea, and enjoyed special exemptions and trading privileges. The town later came into the hands of the Pope (1460–64), of the Venetians (1464–1540 and 1690–1715), and of the Turks (1540–1690 and 1715–1821). In 1564 the Turks repelled an attack of the Knights of Malta. Monemvasia was the scene in April 1821 of a particularly odious massacre of the surrendered Turkish garrison. From here in 1941 c 4000 men of the 6th NZ brigade were successfully evacuated. Malmsey, or Vin de Malvoisie, was originally the name of the celebrated red and white wines shipped from Monemvasia, though produced in Tinos and other Aegean islands.

The end of the approach road (20 minutes on foot) is barred by the impressive W wall of the **Lower Town**, with towers and bastions, which descends straight from the Upper Town to the sea. There is a narrow gate. The houses are closely packed and the streets steep, narrow, and intricate. The present 'agora' probably reflects the main Byzantine street and artisans' area. Of the surviving churches, most notable is the **cathedral**, the largest medieval church in Lakonia, dedicated to *Elkómenos Chrístos* (Christ in chains). It dates from the reign of Andronikos II, who in 1293 elevated the see to metropolitan rank. The portal was rebuilt of Byzantine fragments in 1697. Massive piers with pointed arches support the heavy barrel-vaulted nave and aisles. Opposite, **Ayios Pávlos**, built in 956 and transformed by the Turks, serves as a **museum** of marble fragments, including a Frankish tombstone of 1245 and a 16C font. Just above stands the decayed **Panayía Kritikia** (or Mirtidiotissa) and farther on, near the sea, the **Panayía Chrysaphítissa**, attractively restored and whitewashed. Nearby is the large **Ayios Nikolaos** (1703). Other churches include a double building dedicated to **Ayioi Demetrios and Antonios, Ayia Paraskevi, Ayioi Saranda** and the **Panayia Katelhoumena.**

You wind up a fortified zigzag to the **Upper Town**, or *Goulá*, entered by a tunnel that still has iron-bound gates. The original entrance was via a path and a gate on the N side of the promontory: this was blocked by the

Turks with what the Venetians came to call the *Muro Rosso*. The remains within cover an area of c 600 x 200m. A new plan is being prepared and some of the buildings cleaned. The overall layout is difficult to make out. There were probably originally two streets, running the length of the site. Most of the ruins are of houses, which were grouped in enclosures. They incorporate architectural features of various periods, e.g. Venetian arches. On a high point to the N is a fortified acropolis with a wall and four towers. The Turks built a second fort at the E end of the site. The best preserved building is the church called **Ayia Sophia** (but most probably the Panayia Hodegetria), origianlly the katholikon of a monastery. Set on the edge of a cliff, with a fine view, it was founded by Andronikos II. The plan similar to that at Daphni. It was restored in 1958. The exo-narthex is a Venetian addition. The five doorways have sculpted marble lintels. Four frescoed medallions survive in the squinches, above which a 16-sided drum of impressive proportions supports the dome. The church also contains fragments of frescoes assigned to the early 13C; in the sanctuary, the Ancient of Days (vault), hierarchs; in medallions in the drum of the dome, busts of saints; in the narthex, above the entrance to the nave, Christ Pantokrator between worshipping angels. Three large cisterns probably belong to the Ottoman period (there are many smaller, earlier examples). One of these, the so-called **galera**, has been cleaned.

About 5km N of the town (leave by Neapolis/Molaoi road and turn right after 3km (sign Ayios Ioannis), then right onto asphalt road), at the point where the road reaches the shore, is the hill crowned by the remains (fortifications most prominent) of the Epidaurian colony of **Epidauros Limera**, one of the free Laconian cities. Beyond the site the asphalt ends but the road continues unsurfaced to Yeraka (8km further; see above).

FROM MONEMVASÍA TO SPÁRTA (SPÁRTI). **Road**, 95km (59 miles). Regular buses to **Molaoí** and Sparta in c 3 hours; by changing at Tarapsa, it is possible to reach Yithion and even the Mani the same day; 2 through buses daily to Athens in 6 hours.

From Monemvasia a road runs N along the sandy shore of Ayía Kiriakí, turning inland short of Epidauros Limera (see above) into a stony valley of scrub. At 12km the road from Velies and Neapolis (41km) comes in from the left. 17km **Sikéa** (1084 inhab.) stands (left) on a hill above the road. You cross a plain cultivated with olives, leaving on the left a turning for Papadhiánika and Plítra (near ancient *Asopos*, mostly submerged). 22km **Moláoi** (usually Moláous; Hotels D), a well-watered market town (3010 inhab.) below a ravine on the E slope of an isolated hill (914m), has remains of a fortress and a Byzantine church.

Among low stony hills the road passes below the Monastíri tis Kanganiás (1km left) and leaves (31km) a turning for **Apidhéa** (3km right), with a 14C church and traces of the walls of ancient *Kome*. 35km Crossroads with routes to Apidea (right) and opposite S to Likovrisi, Elaia etc.

3km **Likóvrisi** (Hotel C). 8km **Kokkiniá** (hamlet with two cafés). On the prominent hill of Kastraki (ascend in ½ hour by the left of two tracks opposite camping site before cafés) are the remains of a **Temple of the Mother of the Gods** (excavated 1988–). Beyond Kokkinia, to the right of the road, is an interesting Roman *columbarium*. Much of ancient *Akriai* here is now beneath the sea. The road continues to (14km) **Elaía**, (23km) **Asopos** etc.

45km **Vlakhióti** (Βλαχιώτη), a depressing village (2279 inhab.), is connected by road with Yeraki (17km). Among rice and cotton fields (3km left) lie traces of *Helos*, by tradition the first town to be enslaved by the Spartans, providing an etymology for the word 'Helot'. Many traces of prehistoric occupation have also been noted near **Astéri**, to the S. The road passes the old church of Paniyirístra and crosses the Evrotas. 47km **Skála** (Hotels D, E) is the modern market (3181 inhab.), of the plain. 62km **Krokeaí** (1288 inhab) was famed in antiquity for its stone quarries (Lapis Lacedaemonius). The ancient town lay to the SE of its modern counterpart and the quarries beyond. At (72km) **Khání Tárapsa** you join the main Sparta–Yithion road (Rte 32B). 95km **Sparta**, see Rte 31.

The boat next passes Cape Kamili, a low narrow promontory, beyond which rises Cape Maléa, the S extremity of Laconia. The cape, the 'Formidatum Maleae caput' of Statius, was dreaded by mariners. Doubling the cape, you reach (11 hours from Piraeus) **Neápolis** (Hotels B), a small town (2469 inhab.) on the Voiatic Gulf. This and the peninsula are named after the free-Laconian town of *Boiai*, some remains of which can be seen near the shore to the S. A museum is destined to house finds from the Pavlopetri site (MH–LH), to the N, investigated by Cambridge University in 1967–68, mostly under-water. The gulf is closed on the W opposite Pavlopetri by **Elafónisos** (Hotels B), anciently a promontory named Onugnathos (ass's jaw) and now separated from the mainland by a strait c 400m wide. After calling at its little port, the boat heads S to Kithira.

**Kíthira** (Κύθηρα), or *Kythera*, known to the Venetians as *Cerigo*, and historically one of the Ionian Islands (Rte 56), has more recently been administered as an eparchy of Piraios. It has an air service to Athens (7 times weekly in May–Oct). With Andikíthira (see below) it has 3091 inhabitants. Kithira, 32km long by 19km broad, is separated from Elafonisos by a channel 8km wide. The surface of the island is rocky but the hills do not exceed 503m. It is mostly uncultivated, but some parts produce corn, wine, and olive-oil. The honey is much esteemed.

**History**. In remote antiquity *Kythera* is said to have been called *Porphyrousa* from its abundant murex. The Phoenicians may have developed its purple industry and introduced the worship of Syrian Aphrodite, but in the first half of the 2nd millennium BC it was a Minoan colony. In the Iliad Amphidamas and Lykophron are native to Kythera. In the Peloponnesian War the island guarded the S seaboard of Lakedaimonia until subdued by Athens in 424. It became a Venetian possession in the late 13C, having previously been under Byzantine rule. After the Fourth Crusade it suffered from pirate raids, the inhabitants being sold into slavery by Barbarossa in 1537. In 1715–18 it passed into Turkish hands but from 1719–97 was again controlled by Venice, thereafter sharing the fortunes of the Ionian islands (Rte 56) until 1864. The Greek island, at first linked with Lakonia, is now administered by Attica. Its population has halved in the last century and its economy is now dependent on migrants in Australia. Some 850 British troops got away via Kithira in 1941 after the mainland was completely in German hands.

Its weekly ferries from Piraeus call first at **Ayía Pelayía** (11–13 hrs) in the NE, also linked by the island's main road with Khora (26km) via Potamos, then at Kapsáli at the S end of the island. There is a daily local service from Yithion and Neapolis.

13–15 hours **Kapsáli** is 3kms by road from **Khóra**, or **Kíthira**, the chief place (226 inhab.), which stands on a narrow ridge 500m long, terminating at the SE end in a precipitous rock crowned by a medieval **kastro** with a museum. There is a small hotel and a few rooms are available locally. Visitors should be aware that accommodation can be extremely difficult to find in season.

Interesting are the stalactite caverns and the Minoan colony site of **Kastri**, near **Avlémonas** (24km from Khora; summer camping site at Palaiópolis) on the wide E bay. It was occupied as a trading post c 2000–1450 BC; the British School excavation here in 1964 also showed Neolithic, Roman and Early Byzantine occupation. Palaiokastro, farther inland, is believed to be the site of ancient Kythera. Here the church of Ayios Kosmas incorporates Doric capitals traditionally associated with a sanctuary of Aphrodite.

Also on the E coast, some 9km from the village of **Pótamos** is the large deserted Byzantine site (recently reinvestigated) of **Palaiochóra** (30km from Khora), with a fortified enceinte, houses and church.

On the W coast, near **Milopótamos** and a few hundred metres W of the village, is an early 16C **castle**. Near the same village (c 2.5km S, to the right of the road to Khora) is a cave which has been transformed into a simple one-aisled chapel dedicated to **Ayía Sophía** and her daughters the Saints Elpis, Pistis and Agape (Hope, Faith and

Charity). The well-preserved frescoes which decorate the stone ikonostasis are 11–early 12C.

To the N (c 6km) of Khora, in the village of **Livádhi**, is a church of **Ayios Andreas**, of domed-inscribed cross type with an irregular three-naved basilican appearance. Fragments of frescoes from three periods (9C, 11C and early 13C) have been distinguished.

About 37km to the SE of Kithira and nearly half-way to Crete is the little island of **Andikithira** (Αντικύθηρα), or Cerigotto (14 hours from Piraeus, weekly), known as **Líous** to its 70 inhabitants. Like Crete it has undergone upheavals in recent times: along the entire coastline runs a dark band, rising to a height of c 3m above the present sea-level, with furrows formed by a dozen successive sea levels. The chief place is the hamlet of **Pótamos**, 1.5km NE of which, on the headland of Palaiokastro, are the walls (5–3C BC) of **Aigilia**, chief place of Classical Antikythera.

In the channel between Kithira and Andikithira are the remains of a wreck of the 1C BC which produced bronzes and marbles now in the National Museum.

# B. From Sparta (Spárti) to Yíthion and the Máni (Alika)

**Road**, 101/123km (63/76 miles). **Bus** 5 times daily to Yíthion; once daily to Areópolis, Dhíros, Alika.—24km Kháni Tárapsa.—46km Yíthion.—73km Areópolis. Thence alternative routes to Alika: 2km S of Areópolis, a turn (left) leads to the E coast to join the main S road at Alika via (85km) Kótronas.—109km Láyia.—123km Álika. The W coast road continues from Areópolis to (79km) Pírgos Dhiroú.—97km Yeroliména.—101km Alika.

**Sparta**, see Rte 31. The road runs S through orange groves, crossing one tributary of the Evrotas after another. Before and after (5.5km) **Amíkles** (formerly Sklavokhóri), it passes the hills of Ayia Kiriaki and Palaiopiryi, both to the left. (For local antiquities see Rte 31.) 8km Turning (right) for **Palaiopanayía** from which a steep but driveable track leads to the climbers' refuge at **Ayía Varvára** (c 27km) on Taiyetos. From the refuge (1399m) the summit of Taíyetos (2400m; Profitis Ilias) can be climbed.

The road continues through olive groves and mulberry plantations. 14km Turning to **Xirokámbi** (3km; right) where the torrent is spanned by a single-arched bridge in Hellenistic polygonal masonry.

23.5km Turning for **Vasiláki** (4km, right) where the church of Ayios Ioannis Prodhromos has 13C frescoes. The road ascends the low Vardhou-nokhoria Hills, which run E from the Taiyetos. To the right is the village of Tarapsa, just before (24.5km) **Kháni Tárapsa** (refreshments), where the road divides. Left is the main road to Monemvasia (Rte 32A). Our road continues to ascend through wooded country. From the summit (300m) there are fine views of the Helos Plain and the Lakonian Gulf. On the descent is (35.5km) modern **Aiyíes** where a turn to **Ayios Nikolaos** (13km) gives access (rough track from plateia, and path) to the castle of **Bardounia**, guarding a pass over Taïyetos. Near the village of Límni (right) are the ruins of *Aegeiai*, which had a temple to Poseidon by a lake.

45km **Yíthion** (Γύθειον; Hotels A, B, C, D), or Gytheion, the ancient and modern port of Sparta, is the second largest town (4239 inhab.) in Lakonia and the seat of an eparchy. Olives, oil, and valonia are its chief exports. It has a pleasant promenade and is connected by ferry with Piraeus (see Rte 32A), also with Kithira and W Crete.

The inhabitants of *Gytheion* claimed Herakles and Apollo as joint founders; Classical tradition speaks of Minyan colonists and Phoenician traders in purple-dye. The town became the naval arsenal and port of Sparta, and was sacked by the Athenian admiral Tolmides in 455 BC. Epaminondas besieged it in vain. Nabis rebuilt and fortified the site. Gytheion was the most important city of the free-Laconian League. At *Kranaë* Paris and Helen spent their first night together.

The modern town behind the waterfront is largely on reclaimed land. The **ancient city** was to the N. The **theatre** (excavated 1891) can be seen c 250m from the N end of the sea front (signs). In the orchestra, a large well-like structure is not recorded in reports. Above, various Roman buildings, including a bath (to be preserved) have been found. The **museum** contains a few local antiquities. The island of **Marathonisi**, the ancient *Kranaë*, is a low rocky islet (connected by causeway). The church is on ancient foundations. The Pírgos tón Grigorákidhon has been restored and is to be used as a local **Historical and Ethnological Museum**. Some prehistoric finds have been made.

The remainder of this route lies through the highland region known as the **Mani** (Μάνη), or *Maina*, occupying the last 30m of the Taïyetos range as far as Cape Matapan. The area is known locally as **Kakavoúlia** or **Kakóvouna**. The mountains are treeless and almost barren, though olives thrive and the ground is laboriously cultivated wherever a terrace can be contrived. The population is distributed in small villages, often perched on apparently inaccessible mountain ledges. The Outer Mani is described in Rte 32C. Inner or Deep Mani lies beyond Areopolis.

It was extensively settled in the Neolithic period and there is some archaeological evidence of activity in Mycenaean times, through to the 9C BC. Urban settlements are known to have existed since Homeric times when *Messe, Las* and *Oitilo* contributed ships to the expedition against Troy. The Dorians established small city states which later became satellites of Sparta. In the decline of Sparta they organised their towns into the Confederation of Free Laconians, whose independence was recognised by Augustus while the rest of the Peloponnese was subject to Rome. Their descendants acquired the name of Maniotes and continued in the same independent spirit. They clung to paganism until the reign of Basil I (867–86). Many elaborate churches were built in the 10–12C, providing evidence of new prosperity. The Frankish invaders of the mid 13C built or restored fortresses. With the restoration of Byzantine rule the area acquired new importance. Reinforced by refugees during the Slav invasions, they lived in clans commanded by chieftains and did not welcome strangers. Blood feuds were common and families built towers of refuge. The Turks failed to subdue the area, recognising its principal chieftain as 'Bey of the Maina' owing nominal allegiance to the Porte. The Maniotes eagerly joined the Orloff rising and in the War of Independence when the family of Mavromichales produced one of its most famous generals (Petrobey). In 1834, however, the Maniotes strongly resented merging their independence in the new kingdom and were with difficulty subdued.

Beyond Yíthion the road at first runs SW along the coast affording views across the Lakonian Gulf to Kíthira. 2km To the left is the hill of **Mavrovoúni** with an attractive village (rooms; restaurants) and, on the summit by the church of Trión Ierarchón, the **medieval castle** of Yithion, known locally as *To kástro tou Goulá*.

After Mavrovouni, by the 5th km stone from Yithion, a prominent sandy hill (Skina; right) has Mycenaean chamber tombs. The road crosses the fertile and marshy plain of Passava and then turns inland through woodland. On many of the hills stand medieval towers.

53km On a hill above the road is the ruined Frankish **Castle of Passava**, built in 1254, and incorporating fragments of ancient Greek masonry. The fine enceinte is best reached by a path starting from just before the sign to the village of **Hosarió**. This was probably the site of Classical *Las*, but no

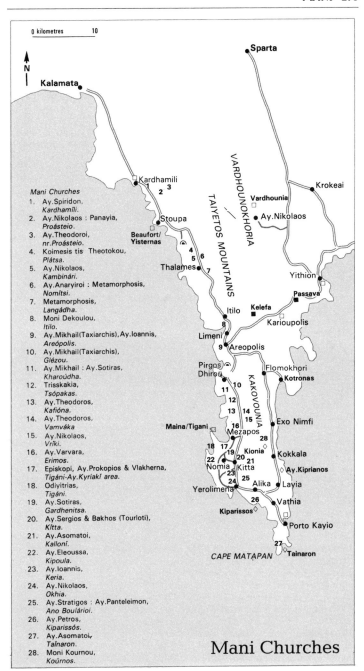

0 kilometres 10

N

**Sparta**

**Kalamata**

Kardhamíli
1
2 3

**Krokeai**

VARDHOUNOKHORIA

**Vardhounia**

Stoupa

**Ay.Nikolaos**

Beaufort/
Yisternas

TAÏYETOS MOUNTAINS

4
5 6
Thalames
7

**Yithion**

Itilo
8
**Kelefa**

**Passava**

Limeni

Karioupolis

9 **Areopolis**

Pirgos
Dhirou

**Flomokhori**

10
11
12
13 14
15

KAKOVOUNIA

**Kotronas**

**Exo Nimfi**

**Maina/Tigani**

16
Mezapos
28

18 17
19
22 20 21
Nomia 23
24 25
Yerolimena

Kionia

**Kokkala**

**Ay.Kiprianos**

Kitta

Alika
**Layia**

26
**Vathia**

**Kiparissos**

**Porto Kayio**

27
CAPE MATAPAN **Tainaron**

Mani Churches

1. Ay.Spiridon,
   *Kardhamíli.*
2. Ay.Nikolaos : Panayia,
   *Proásteio.*
3. Ay.Theodoroi,
   *nr.Proásteio.*
4. Koimesis tis Theotokou,
   *Plátsa.*
5. Ay.Nikolaos,
   *Kambinári.*
6. Ay.Anaryiroi : Metamorphosis,
   *Nomítsi.*
7. Metamorphosis,
   *Langádha.*
8. Moni Dekoulou,
   *Itilo.*
9. Ay.Mikhail(Taxiarchis),Ay.Ioannis,
   *Areópolis.*
10. Ay.Mikhail(Taxiarchis),
    *Glézou.*
11. Ay.Mikhail : Ay.Sotiras,
    *Kharoúdha.*
12. Trisskakia,
    *Tsópakas.*
13. Ay.Theodoros,
    *Kafióna.*
14. Ay.Theodoros,
    *Vamváka.*
15. Ay.Nikolaos,
    *Vríki.*
16. Ay.Varvara,
    *Erimos.*
17. Episkopi, Ay.Prokopios & Vlakherna,
    *Tigáni-Ay.Kyriakí area.*
18. Odiyitrias,
    *Tigáni.*
19. Ay.Sotiras,
    *Gardhenitsa.*
20. Ay.Sergios & Bakhos (Tourloti),
    *Kítta.*
21. Ay.Asomatoi,
    *Kalloní.*
22. Ay.Eleoussa,
    *Kipoula.*
23. Ay.Ioannis,
    *Keria.*
24. Ay.Nikolaos,
    *Okhia.*
25. Ay.Stratigos : Ay.Panteleimon,
    *Ano Boulárioi.*
26. Ay.Petros,
    *Kiparissós.*
27. Ay.Asomatoi,
    *Taínaron.*
28. Moni Kournou,
    *Koúrnos.*

**Mani Churches**

Mycenaean remains have so far come to light to justify identification with Laas of the *Iliad*.

Beyond (56km) **Karioúpolis**, probably founded as a stronghold in the 6 or 7C AD, with a castle and a fortified settlement of C 1800, a picturesque defile emerges high above **Liménio**, the harbour of Areopolis. The road from Oitilo is joined on the bare grey slopes of Profitis Ilias (813m). 71km Turn for **Kelefá** (5km; right), near which (signed track from village) is the huge walled frontier post erected by the Ottomans in the 17C to control the Maniotes. 73km **Areópolis** (Αρεόπολις; Hotels A, B, C), a constricted village (759 inhab.) of tower houses, is the chief centre of the Mani. The church (Taxiárkhis), dating from 1798, has primitive reliefs of martial saints. Ayios Ioannis has a full series of frescoes.

The landscape S of Areopolis is dominated by the Kakavoulia and Sangias (1218m) which rises between Pirgos Dhirou and Kotronas on the E coast. It is dotted with tower-houses and primitive barrel-vaulted chapels (probably 9C); the domed Byzantine churches date mainly from the 11C and 12C. At 75km a turn (left) leads to the E coast.

79km **Pírgos Dhiroú** has a small tourist pavilion, from which a road leads (in 4km) to the **Bay of Diros** (refreshments; bathing). Here two spectacular ˙caverns, **Vlikádha** (or Glifádha; adm. daily, incl. boat on underground lake) and **Alepótripa** ('fox-hole'; closed temporarily) were opened to the public in 1963; both have stalactites and stalagmites and are lit by electricity. Alepotripa has yielded extensive Neolithic finds. There is a **museum** of Neolithic material. At **Glézou** (80km, left), the church of the **Taxiárkhis** dates from the 11C (façade rebuilt). At 87km a turn to the left at **Bríki** is the best approach to **Vamvárka**, where the church of Ayios Theodhoros is dated by an inscription to 1075. At 88km, a road (right) leads to (1km) **Erimos**, with the domed cruciform church of **Ayía Varvára** (1150), distinguished by its fine proportions and masonry. **Mézapos**, possibly the site of Homeric *Messe*, lies on the coast. On the promontory of Tigani, (W) of the same bay, stands the **Castle of Maina**, the Frankish fortress erected by William II de Villehardouin in 1248. An earlier wall with three towers on this promontory may be Mycenaean. A considerable portion of the ramparts remain. There are the ruins of one of the largest (22m by 15m) and earliest Christian basilicas (5–6C). To reach it turn right at 91km to **Stavrí** and the conical hill of Ay. Kiriakí (45 minute walk). On this road a right turn past the hamlet of **Ay. Yeóryios** leads to the 12C church of **Episkopí**, once the seat of the Bishopric of Maina. It stands on a hillside with a view across the Bay of Mésapos to the peninsula of **Tigáni**. The fine frescoes are mainly 12C, with a Last Judgement in the narthex. It has been restored.

92km **Koíta**, now almost depopulated, was reported by Leake to have almost 100 families and 22 towers. Above Koita the decayed church of Ay. Asomatoi has a carved marble iconostasis. 96km (left) in **Káto Boularioí** is the Anemodhoura **tower**, one of the earliest towers (possibly 1600), built of huge dry stones tapering to the top. There is also the well-preserved late 18C tower of the Mantouvalos family. Just above Ano Boularioí is the cruciform 11C church of **Ay. Stratigos**, its dome supported by Roman Ionic columns. It contains an almost complete cycle of frescoes (mainly 12C).

97km **Yeroliména**, a small fishing village where boats no longer call. At (101km) **Alika** there are two inscribed stelai in the square. One is the dedication to Gaius Julius Laco by the Union of Free Laconians, the other to an 'excellent citizen' named Tanagros from his own 'City of the Tainarians'. Here the road divides; the S road continuing to Portokayio (see below) and the left fork to the E coast.

FROM ALIKA TO PORTOKÁYIO, 12km (7½ miles). The road continues S. At 2km, on the coast, is **Kipárissos**, ancient *Kaenipolis*, one of the most important cities in the Messenian Gulf in the 1C AD and later. There are extensive remains round the two bays of Almirós and Psaroliméni and up to the village of Alika. On a headland, the Hill of Metamórphosis, stands a ruined 19C tower surrounded by fragments of marble, possibly the site of Pausanias' *Megaron of Demeter*; there are remains of a monumental building to the W. By the beach the church of **Ay. Paraskeví** incorporates ancient marble and pieces of columns possibly from the Temple of Aphrodite mentioned by Pausanias. Behind the church is a massive inscribed stele in honour of the Emperor Gordian. In the olive groves SE are the ruins of the basilica of **Ay. Petros** (early 6C), incorporating ancient material. The jambs of the W door are two inscribed stelai, to the Empress Julia Domna and to a generous citizen Lysicrates.

The road follows the coast before climbing steeply inland to (5km) **Váthia**, a village of tower-houses standing on a hill. The N.T.O. has restored some of the tower-houses as pensions. The road continues to climb with spectacular views N up the coast to **Cavo Grosso** before rounding a headland to a dramatic section cut into the cliff with a precipitous drop to a long narrow plateau high above the sea (view S to Cape Matapan, ancient *Tainaron*).

At 10km a turn (left) leads 1.5km through a small gorge full of cypress and citrus to the 16C Turkish **castle** of Portokáyio, perched high on a cliff edge overlooking the almost circular Bay of Portokáyio, the name of which is a corruption of the Venetian 'Quaglio' (quails). The road curves E towards the isthmus. Below (right) between two sandy inlets, is **Porto Marmári** (or Akhíllion), ancient *Achilleion*, with restored tower houses and the remains of a medieval castle. On the highest point of the isthmus (left) is the prominent tower of Khárakes.

The road descends steeply to (12km) the small sandy beach of **Portokáyio**, ancient *Psamathoús*. Tainaron can be reached on foot (1 hour) from the highest point of the road before it descends to Portokayio. A path (right) meets an unsurfaced but adequate road from Porto Marmári which gives direct access to the Poseidon Sanctuary. Otherwise, keeping Vathi Bay on the left, walk on a descending path along a scarp; take the right fork and continue S to the shoulder of the promontory of Livádhi, which forms the bottom end of Vathí Bay. Over the low saddle is the hamlet of **Kokkinóyia** and, below, the Bay of Asomatos. The chapel of Asomatos on the headland occupies the site of the famous **Temple of Poseidon** (5C BC), part of the extended shrine of Poseidon Tainarios where the Free Laconians had their religious headquarters. The large blocks on the N wall formed part of the ancient temple. On a pebbly beach (left) is the cave of the Oracle of Poseidon mentioned by Pausanias. There are remains of a religious complex attached to the oracle which was still in use during the late Roman period. In the bay (right) are numerous cisterns which inspired the name of **Pórto Khísternes**. In the next small bay to the S is a pebble mosaic. The track continues (½ hour) to the lighthouse at the tip of **Cape Matapan**. Cape Matapan has much the same latitude as Gibraltar and is thus the second most southerly place on the European mainland. Off Cape Matapan, on 28 March 1941, four Italian ships were sunk or damaged by a British contingent under Admiral Cunningham.

You continue left towards the E coast through a valley skirting the southern tip of the Kakavoúlia and cross the watershed (view of the Laconian Gulf) to (115km) **Láyia** (bus to Sparta daily), 400m above sea level. Now depopulated, it was once the main town of SE Mani. There are some fine towers.

At 118km (500m before the village of **Dhimarístika**) the main road cuts across an ancient road from the harbour of Kiprianós to the marble quarries of rosso antico (Tainarion marble) highly prized in antiquity and used (*inter alia*) in the decoration of the Treasury of Atreus at Mycenae. The quarries were exploited by an Italian company before the First World War. The road loops down through scattered towered settlements (view N to the great promontory of Stavrí) to (125km) the small harbour of **Kokkála** (beach, rooms).

At 128.5km there is a turn (left) to **Nímfi** (500m) where a steep path up the Kournós ravine leads to the monastery of the Panayia and the ancient shrine of Kiónia (500m beyond; 1½ hours from Nímfi). Below the monastery is a circular cistern incorporating ancient material. The cistern has a constant water supply from a spring above the monastery. Water was supplied to the sanctuary and settlement of **Kionia**. Situated on a high plateau 480m above sea level are the foundations of two Doric temples built in local grey limestone. The larger (peripteral) temple dates from the second half of the 2C BC, the smaller (in antis) from the Augustan period. There are extensive remains of a settlement with cisterns, a cemetery with rock-cut reliefs and a fortified acropolis. Magnificent views E to Cape Malea and SE to Kithira.

The road continues with the grey, barren Kakavoulia rising steeply to the W, punctuated by sombre ravines and towered villages. Across a small coastal plain with olives and cypress the high towers of **Flomokhóri** (138km) are visible. At 139km is a right turn to the delightful small fishing village of (3km) **Kótronas**, ancient *Teuthrone* with a sandy beach (rooms). On the small peninsula of Skopá to the SW are the remains of a Byzantine **fortress**. To the E, on the high point of Stavrí Peninsula, are remnants of **fortifications** associated with Spartan defences during the Corinthian War. The road climbs to (140km) **Loukadhiká**, with its once-fortified citadel, and turns W through a pass with oaks and cypress opening onto the cultivated plain of (144km) **Pírrikhos** which still bears its ancient name. According to Pausanias the city derived its name either from Pyrrus, the son of Achilles, or from the god Pyrrichos who was one of the Kouretes. Beyond, the road descends through a valley, with a view of the Bay of Dhiros, to join (149km) the Areopolis–Yerolimena road, 2km S of (151km) **Areópolis**.

# C.   From Kalamáta to Areópolis

**Road**, 76km (47½ miles). No road in Greece offers more spectacular coastal scenery. Most of this route lies in Messenia. **Buses** daily to Itilo and Areópolis.

**Kalamáta**, see Rte 34A. You leave the town along the seafront (or bypass) by the E suburb of Yiannitsánika. 7km Almiró (Hotel B), villa resort of Kalamáta, and Káto Sélitsa, where Mount Kalafi rises steeply from the sea, both form part of the commune of **Vérga**. The narrow gap was blocked by a wall, the 'Mandhra tis Verghas', in 1826 and the Mani successfully defended against Ibrahim's ravaging army. The road now climbs inland with many turns (*views first over Cape Kitries to the Messenian Gulf, then inland to the Taïyetos). **Avía**, on the shore, may be the *Hire* of the *Iliad*. The road passes below **Sotiriánika**, whose castle is conspicuous from Kalamata but seen only in retrospect from the road. A concrete arch over the wild wooded Kóskaras Defile replaces an old packhorse bridge, best seen from the steep hairpin bends on the far side.

20km **Kámbos** (537 inhab.), with a conspicuous church, a tholos tomb (dug in 1888), and vestiges of an ancient temple, is dominated by the **Castle of Zarnata**. Best reached from the next village **Stavropiyí** (keep left in village), this is a huge Frankish enceinte (before 1427) with a Turkish keep built by Achmet Kiuprili in 1670. It was captured by stratagem in 1685 by Morosini. The kastro rests on polygonal foundations, perhaps of *Gerenia*. The S wall was torn down during the disturbances of 1943–49 and further damage done by earthquake in 1947. The Byzantine church of Zoödhókhos Piyí has a carved wooden templon. Farther on, the square battlemented Tower of Koumoundhouráki crowns a second height.

Beyond the next summit, the descent affords a tremendous *view right down the Mani: Kardhamili in its little plain of olives is seen below as from the air. Venitiko Island, off Cape Akritas, is evident across the Gulf. 36km **Kardhamíli** (Καρδαμύλη; Hotels B, C), a seaside village of 429 inhabitants, perpetuates the name of *Kardamyle*, one of the seven cities that Agamemnon offered to Achilles to appease his wrath. It was transferred by Augustus from Messenia to Laconia. The medieval **castle** (300m inland, visible from road to the N; signs in main street to 'Old Kardhamíli') incorporates ancient masonry. It houses a tower complex of the Mourtzinos family and an 18C Venetian church with some interesting exterior carving. Here Kolokotronis set up his headquarters in 1821 prior to the seizure of Kalamata. The acropolis (path from church starting through a fine gateway) has rock-cuttings of probably Mycenaean date. Offshore is a fortified islet.

The road, cut from the rock, clings to the coast. It passes below **Proásteio**, near which (turn right at the end of the village) is the ruined 11C monastic church of **Ayios Nikolaos** and its 13C successor dedicated to the Ayioi Theodoroi, with 13C paintings. 41km **Stoúpa** (formerly Lévktron) by the sea has largely replaced the inland village. Ancient *Leuktra*, a free Laconian city, may have occupied the curious table-top hill above the village. The acropolis became Castle Beaufort c 1250, built by William de Villehardouin.

46km **Selínitsa**, or Ayios Nikólaos, off the main road by the sea, has a prominent war memorial. At **Ayios Dhimítrios**, to the S, is a stalactite cave. Beyond **Rínglia** the road crosses a ravine and climbs continuously. **Plátsa** and the succeeding villages have Byzantine **churches** and arcaded foundations incorporating ancient fragments. Amongst them are Ayios Nikolaos Kambinari, S of Platsa, 11–12C; Ayios Ioannis Prodhromos (Platsa), 12C with frescoes of several periods; Ayioi Anargyroi (Nomitsi), 12–13C with 14C frescoes; Metamorfosis (Thalames), 12–13C, with 14–15C frescoes; Ayios Sotir (Langadha), 11C as are some of the frescoes. The isolated church of Ayios Dhimitrios, on a spur above Platsa, commands a superb view to the N. **Thalámes** (or Koutifári) is proposed as the site of ancient *Thalamai* and has a small **Museum of the Mani**, with local artefacts, maps etc.

The tower-houses of (56km) **Langádha** rise in terraces. Here the church of the **Metamorfosis** by the road is 9C and has exterior decoration and fine frescoes, now being gradually revealed from beneath a plaster covering. **Trakhíla**, with a cave, is seen on the coast below. The road enters Laconia, Areopolis appears across the Limenion Gulf and the wilder ranges of Inner Mani rise ahead. 70km **Oítilo** (Οίτυλο; Hotel A), or Vitylo, a village making a potent unresinated wine, was the capital of the Mani before Areopolis. Its name survives unchanged from Homeric times. Here Napoleon I put in on his way to Egypt. The village is divided by the Ravine of Milolangadho, the boundary between Outer and Inner Mani, from **Kelefá** (Rte 33B). The road continues with superb views via **Liménio** (restored tower houses) to (76km) **Areópolis**.

# 33

## Trípolis to Kalamáta

**Road**, 95km (59 miles), bus in 2¾ hours.—34km Megalópolis.—95km Kalamáta.

**Railway**, 123km in 2½ hours. To Léfktro, formerly Biláli, junction for Megalópolis, in 1 hour; to Zevgolatió, junction for Kiparissía, in 2 hours.

You leave Tripolis from the central square (Vas. Yeoryíou; signs to Kalamata) and head SW, passing a smaller square with a market. 4.5km By-road to **Valtétsi** (6.5km) where in 1821 Khurshid Pasha's Turks, marching to the relief of Tripolis, were defeated by Kolokotronis. 6km **Mákri** crossroads (village 1km right); to the left, signpost to modern **Pallantio** (4km). After c 1km on that road, beyond a quarry, a forest track (right) leads up the cypress covered slopes in front of Mt Kravari, the ancient *Boreion* (1143m), where are the modest remains of *Pallantion*: foundations of three temples of Archaic and later date (one of them beneath the church of Ayios Yiannis) and traces of the city walls.

According to legend, 60 years before the Trojan War, King Evander, the son of Hermes by an Arcadian nymph, founded from *Pallantion* a colony by the river Tiber. The name of the Palatine hill reflects his native town, and Pallantion was accordingly regarded as the mother-city of Rome itself. When Megalopolis was founded, Pallantion dwindled to a village, but Antoninus Pius, in memory of Evander, restored its civic status and privileges. It was explored by the Italian School in 1940. Just SE of the ruins are the remains of an embankment, of rammed earth encased with stone, that served both as a dyke against the waters of the Taka Marsh and as a frontier barrier against Tegea.

About 1.5km to the SW of Pallantion (also accessible from the Kaloyerikos pass, via the railway line) a chapel of the Metamorfosis overlies a **temple** which may be that of Athena and Poseidon mentioned by Pausanias. The site was quarried by the inhabitants of Valtetsi in the 19C.

The road now climbs the Pass of Kaloyerikos (810m; fine retrospect of the Plain of Tripolis), and descends into the dreary plain of Asea. The high range of Taïyetos is seen to the S. 16.5km **Aséa** station (654m) lies 3km below its village, near the springs that form the source of the Alpheios.

An isolated hill 150m NE of the station and to the right of the road inland to Epano Asea is the acropolis of ancient *Asea*, shown by Swedish excavations in 1936–38 to have had a continuous existence from Neolithic to Middle Helladic times and to have been reoccupied in the Hellenistic period. Some remains can be seen. Beyond (3km) Epáno Aséa, on the slopes of Mt. Ayios Ilias (and close to the church of the same name) are remains of a **temple** which is another candidate for that of Athena and Poseidon (see above).

17.5km A left turn leads (in 15km) to the Megalopolis–Sparta road (see below). The railway draws away to the S to pass, after **Marmariá**, below the site of the ancient *Oresthasion* on the long ridge that runs N from Mt Tsempero (1252m). The line crosses the hills through a gorge, then descends by wide loops through Leondhári (see below) to **Léfktro** (formerly Bilali), junction for Megalopolis. The road surmounts the ridge (view) and descends in zigzags to the plain.

The **Plain of Megalopolis**, the great W plain of Arcadia, is about 30km long from N to S and 16km wide. With an average altitude of 427m, it has a much more temperate climate than the Plain of Tripolis. It is pleasantly wooded and well watered by the Alpheios, while the outlines of the encircling mountains make a fine background.

34km **Megalópolis** (Μεγαλόπολις; 427m; Hotels C, D) is a small modern town (4646 inhab.) with, about 1km N, the widespread but unrewarding ruins of the 'Great City', in antiquity both chief town of the surrounding district and capital of the federated states of Arcadia. The city straddles the Hellison, one of the seven tributaries of the Alpheios, the federal capital (*Oresteia*) occupying the nearer bank while the municipal city lies across the river. The view and atmosphere are marred by the large power station which dominates the area.

**History**. When the Pan-Arcadian League was formed after Leuktra, Arcadia lacked a capital city. Mutual jealousies precluded the choice of any existing city, and a new site was selected. Its position was determined by Epaminondas of Thebes in accordance with his concept of a strategic barrier to contain the Spartans, the other bastions of which were to be Messene, Mantineia, and Argos. The 'Great City' (ή Μεγάλη Πόλις) as it was called by the Greeks (Megalopolis being a Roman corruption), was built in 371–368 BC, and populated by wholesale transplantation from 40 local villages and smaller migrations from Tegea, Mantineia, etc. The League had a federal Council of 50 members and an Assembly called the Ten Thousand, which met in the Thersileion at Megalopolis: the executive power was held by a Strategos who had an army of 500 Eparitoi at his command. The confederation soon broke up; Mantineia withdrew in 364 after the League had tampered with the sacred treasuries at Olympia, and in 362 half the Arcadians fought with the Spartans against Thebes. The inhabitants of Megalopolis had to be prevented from returning to their former homes by Pammenes' Theban soldiers. Spartan attempts to reduce the city were foiled in 353 with Theban aid and again in 331 when Megalopolis sided with Macedon. Having joined the Achaean League in 234, the city again suffered Spartan attack; saved once by a hurricane, it was sacked in 223 BC by Kleomenes III. Two-thirds of the population escaped to Messenia under the leadership of Philopoemen (253–183 BC), almost the only great man produced by Arcadia, returning two years later after Kleomenes' defeat at Sellasia. Strabo quotes an unknown comic poet to the effect that 'the Great City was a great desert', and Pausanias found it 'mostly in ruins', though under the later emperors it was the seat of a bishop. It finally disappeared in the Slav invasion. Besides Philopoemen, the only native of note is Polybius (204–122 BC), the historian.

Megalopolis was excavated by the British School in 1890–93, and the School has undertaken a survey project in the area in recent years. Ploughing has seriously damaged much of the site, which is principally interesting for the theatre. This is reached from the Andritsaina road, which passes through the ancient city (left turn just before the bridge over the river).

The **theatre**, which is built up against the N side of a hillock, 100m from the river, was the largest in Greece. It dates, in its original form, from the 4C BC, but is later than the Thersileion. The **cavea** is divided by 10 stairways and two diazomata, to make 59 rows of seats for c 21,000 spectators. The lowest tiers are well preserved. The **orchestra** is 30m in diameter. The place of the W parodos is taken by a **skenotheke**, or property room. The portico of the Thersileion seems to have served also as a permanent skene for the theatre. The stone **stage**, adorned by 14 marble columns between antae, is a Roman addition.

The **Thersileion** is perhaps the most elaborate example known of the square hall. Measuring 52.5m by 66.5m, it had five concentric rows of columns, set parallel to the outside walls and arranged on radials from a tribune offset from centre. The bases of the columns remaining *in situ* show that the wooden floor sloped down towards the tribune, above which the roof line was probably broken by a lantern. Facing the theatre and originally separated from the hall only by piers (later by a continuous wall with doorways), was a Doric prostyle portico with 14 columns beneath a single pediment. The building was destroyed in 222 BC and not rebuilt.

Beyond the river the **Sanctuary of Zeus Soter** and the **Stoa of Philip**, demarcating the agora, are now barely identifiable. Sections of the town wall have been found. For the continuation of the road to Andritsaina, see Rte 35.

Perhaps the most interesting excursion from Megalopolis (after that to Bassae; Rte 35) is to the finely situated site of **Lykósoura** (or Likósoura; 14km). You take the Kalamáta road (see below) and just beyond the Alpheios branch right on to a road which is asphalted as far as the second village (**Apidhítsa**), where you again branch right, and at 11km left. The museum is visible on a saddle to the left; immediately below, a rough track forks left. The site is fenced; key from hamlet below. The **museum** contains inscriptions and much of the colossal cult statues by Damophon (casts of heads, which are in Athens). The site is more interesting below the museum. There are considerable remains of a prostyle **temple** with a side door on the S of the cella (cf. Bassae). In front is a **stoa**, and in the hillside (S) a stepped retaining wall.

From Likósoura a good road leads to **Líkaion**, (4km) where it continues unsurfaced to **Ano Karyés** (7.5km). Turn left just before the village (dangerous in wet weather) and ascend past the stadium, hippodrome and stoas (11km) to the summit (14km from Likósoura; fine views) of Mt Lykaion (1407m), in antiquity the centre of a primitive cult of Zeus involving rainmaking, human sacrifice, werewolves, and athletic games. Within its precinct neither man nor beast cast a shadow. The summit is a conical mound, the great sacrifical pyre which, with the precinct below, was excavated in 1903. Below are column bases seen by Pausanias which originally supported golden eagles. On the S side of Mt. Lykaion (at 1195m) is a sanctuary of Pan. Access is also possible from the Andritsaina–Bassae road, via **Nédha** to Likaion (surfaced to Nedha, unsurfaced beyond).

From Megalopolis the Kalamata road runs SW, crossing (36km) the Alpheios; just beyond the bridge (right) is the by-road to Lykosoura (see above). 47km **Paradhísia** guards the approach to the **Makriplayi Pass** (600m), the main route of communication between Arcadia and Messenia. **Kháni Vídhi** marks the summit of the pass. Here is a by-road (left) to **Kheirádhes** (3km) where a path continues in one hour to 'Kókkala' on a W spur of Taïyetos, where the ruined old fortress on ancient foundations (? *Ampheia*) is the Byzantine and Frankish **Castle of Gardhiki**, near which William de Villehardouin and Ancelin de Toucy, marching from Kalamata in 1265, beat the forces of the Great Domestic of the Eastern Empire. The road winds down with views across the tree-covered Plain of Steniklaros (Rte 34C); Mt Ithome appears behind Meligala to the SW.

At the foot of the descent, turnings (right) first to Kiparissia and then to ancient *Ithome* (Rte 34C), as the road runs straight across the plain through thick olive groves. The copious springs near (74km) **Ayios Flóros** were considered by the ancients to be the source of the Pamisos proper before it joined the Mavrozoumenos.

82km **Palaiókastro** (1km E of the road) is the site of Classical *Thouria*, a city destroyed in 464 BC by the Spartans and rebuilt by Epaminondas. It was given by Augustus to Laconia to punish the Messenians for siding with Antony. The Classical remains are at the N end of a long ridge in which many Mycenaean tombs have been found: this may be the place known to Homer as *Anthea*. Modern **Thouría** is 3km farther along the road.

At 90km is the junction with the road from Messini (Rte 34A). 95km **Kalamáta** (see below).

FROM MEGALÓPOLIS TO SPARTA (SPÁRTI), via Georgítsi, 68km (42miles). A slow but spectacular road, high along the N shoulder of Taïyetos.

The road runs S via (5km) Léfktron (see above). 11km **Leondári** (Λεοντάρι), a medieval village, 1.5km SW of its station, occupies a commanding position on the top of the hill (578m) forming the N end of the Taïyetos range and overlooking a narrow pass separating Arcadia from Messenia. The Frankish **castle** is in ruins. Here Thomas Palaiologos was defeated by the Turks in 1460; the inhabitants fled to Gardhíki only to be massacred there. The little two-domed church of the Apóstoloi (14C) was converted into a mosque. Near it is the smaller 12C church of Ayios Athanásios. About 2.5km NW of Leondári, on the left bank of the Xerillas, are the scanty vestiges of *Veligostí* (Βελιγοστή), important in Byzantine times. It is reached from the bridle-path that leads in 1¾ hours between the Samara Hills and Mt Ellenitsa to Paradhísia (see below).

Beyond Leondari routes lead S to the scattered villages (Dhirrákhi, etc.) on the W slopes of Taïyetos. 22km Junction for (4km, left) **Skortzinós**, with a frescoed 14C church of the Taxiarkhs and beyond, **Káto Aséa** (see above). You turn right for (24km) **Kiparíssi**. Continuing the road crosses the Arcadian frontier before (32km) **Longaníkos**, a narrow mountain village. The church of Profitis Ilias has a restored painting of St George from a Byzantine church dedicated to the saint. 39km **Georgítsi** (Hotel C), with fine views of the upper Eurotas valley. 44km Left turn for **Pellána**.

The village of **Pellána** is 4km from the main road. About 800m beyond the plateia (rough road between kafeneions) a small sign points right to 'Mycenaean Tholos Tombs'. They (5) are in fact rock-cut chambers of tholos shape. One is the largest so far found and the site in general is informative and interesting. The finds are in Sparta Museum.

46km **Kastóri**.

The road descends to (68km) **Sparta** (Rte 31).

# 34

# Messenia (Messinía)

**Messinia**, one of the six ancient countries of the Peloponnese and one of its seven modern nomes, is bounded on the N by Elis and Arcadia, on the E by Laconia, and on the S and W by the Ionian Sea. The region consists mainly of the SW peninsula of the Peloponnese, containing the triangular mass of high ground that culminates in Aigaleon. To the E of this range lies the fertile Messenian Plain watered by the Pamisos, the largest river in the S Peloponnese: to the N and NE are secondary plains; and the natural boundaries lie along Xerovouni and Taïyetos. The capital and principal trading port is Kalamáta.

In Homer Messenia belonged to the Neleid princes of Pylos, of whom the most famous was Nestor, while the E part was included in the joint kingdoms of Agamemnon and Menelaus. In the Dorian invasion Messenia was assigned to Kresphontes. The original inhabitants absorbed their conquerors and their prosperity excited the envy of Sparta. In the **First Messenian War** (? 743–724 BC) the Spartans conquered the country and, notwithstanding the devotion of Aristodemos the Messenian king, captured the fortress of Ithome, reducing the inhabitants to the condition of Helots. A rebellion known as the **Second Messenian War** (or First Messenian Revolt; ? 685–668 BC) was with great difficulty suppressed, when the fort of Eira was captured. The hero of this was Aristomenes, 'the first and greatest glory of the Messenian name'. Many of the Messenians emigrated to Sicily, where, in 493 BC, their descendant Anaxilas of

Rhegium captured Zancle and renamed it Messana (now Messina). The **Third Messenian War** (or Second Messenian Revolt) in 464–455 BC had far-reaching consequences. The Athenians, who had sent an expeditionary force to help the Lacedaemonians, were rudely dismissed. After the fall of Ithome they therefore befriended the exiled Messenians, settling them in Naupaktos. It was these Messenians who in 425 BC aided the Athenians at the siege of Sphakteria. After the battle of Leuktra in 371 BC, Epaminondas repatriated the Messenians and founded for them the city of Messene. They remained independent till the Roman conquest in 146 BC.

The ancient topography of the area has been the subject of intensive study by the University of Minnesota Messenia Expedition since 1958 and is now published.

# A.  From Kalamáta to Pylos (Pílos)

**Road**, 51km (31½ miles). **Bus** several times daily in 1½ hours, some continuing to Khóra and Kiparissía.

**KALAMÁTA** (Καλαμάτα; Hotels A–E) a manufacturing town and port (43,625 inhab.) amid groves of citrus fruit trees is the best base for expeditions in Messenia. The capital of the nome of Messenia, it is the focus of local communication and has air, rail, and coach services from Athens. The centre stands a long mile from its harbour, once the principal outlet for exports from the Peloponnese. Kalamata olives have a high reputation and figs are dried, processed and packed. Kalamata claims to be the first Greek city to have revolted against the Turks in 1821. In 1941 it was forced to surrender after the Royal Navy had put to sea to meet an Italian threat and 7000 allied troops fell into enemy hands.

On 14 September 1986 a severe earthquake caused loss of life and serious damage to Kalamata and nearby villages. Damage is still visible and demolished buildings have in some cases been replaced by prefabricated.

**Airport** at **Asprókhoma** (8km NW), with daily service to Athens.

**Railway** to Athens 6 times daily in 6½–7½ hours; to Kiparissia, Pirgos, and Patras, etc. **Car Park** in Plat. Venizélou, near station.

**Post Office**, Iatropoúlou 4.

**Buses** of KTEL 4 Messenias (Od. Artémidhos 96) to Athens (10), via Tripolis and Corinth; also to Koroni (8); to Pilos (10), Khora (5), and Kiparissia (3); to Kardamyle, Oitilo (3), etc. Also to Sparta (3), Patras (2), Thessaloniki (1).

**Ferry**. To Kastélli (Crete).

**Car Hire**. Stavrianós, 89 Nédhontos; Theodhorakópoulos, 2 P. Késari.

**Tourist Police**. Aristoménous/Frantzí.

The centre is the Plateía Vasiléou Yeoryíou B', the tree-lined broadening of Odhós Aristoménous, the long main street. Ayioi Apóstoloi, farther N (closed since earthquake), has a Byzantine core of 1317. Odhós Ipapandís, lined with exotic trees, leads N to the cathedral church of **Tis Ipapandís** (1859). Steps mount to the **kastro** (closed), erected by Geoffrey I Villehardouin in 1208 on the acropolis of ancient *Pharai*. There are traces of walls as far back as Mycenaean times. The castle consists of an outer enceinte, an inner redoubt, and a keep.

A Byzantine double enceinte had already fallen into disuse before 1204, and in 1208 its church was encased within the walls of the new keep. The castle was held by the Villehardouins for nearly a century and here William (1218–78) was born and died. It

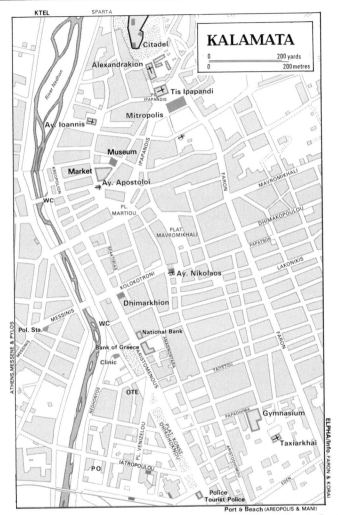

KALAMATA

| 0 | 200 yards |
| 0 | 200 metres |

KTEL   SPARTA

Citadel

Alexandrakion

Tis Ipapandi

IPAPANDIS

Mitropolis

Ay. Ioannis

Museum

Market

Ay. Apostoloi

WC

PL. MARTIOU

PLAT. MAVROMIKHALI

Ay. Nikolaos

Dhimarkhion

Pol. Sta.

WC

National Bank

Bank of Greece

Clinic

OTE

Gymnasium

Taxiarkhai

PO

Police
Tourist Police

Port & Beach (AREOPOLIS & MANI)

was captured by the Slavs in 1293 but won back, and passed by marriage to Guy II, Duke of Athens in 1300. Florentines and Angevins held the site in turn until it passed to the Palaiologoi in 1425. Held by the Venetians during the first Turko-Venetian war (1463–79), it was sacked by them in a raid in 1659. The Turks blew up a part in 1685 and the Venetians continued its demolition.

Two fine old houses of the Benaki and Kyriakou families, near the church of Ayios Ioannis, house an **Archaeological Museum** (closed since earthquake) containing a good Roman mosaic, Byzantine ikons, and relics of the War of Independence; also the Swedish finds from Malthi.

In the E suburbs is the interesting (originally 12C) cemetery church of **Ayios Kharálambos**, two storeyed and partly underground.

*Kalamáta. Benaki family house ('arkhontikó')*

At **Akovítika**, a hamlet 3km due W of Kalamata, S of the railway, an important EH building was discovered in 1969.

From Kalamata to the Mani, see Rte 32C; to Sparta, see Rte 31.

You take the Tripolis road and after 5km bear left. Beside the branch railway, the road passes the airport (also a military air base), then crosses the fertile marshes of the Markaria plain and the Pamisos to (8.5km) **Messíni** (Μεσσήνη; Hotels), principal town (6453 inhab.) of its eparchy. A centre of rice production, locally called Nisí, it should not be confused with the ancient city (Rte 34C) whose name it has adopted. From its vast square buses ply to many Messenian villages. Olives and figs alternate with vines and fruit-trees. San Agostino Beach Hotel (B) lies to the S of (14km) **Análipsis**. Near (19km) **Rizómilos** investigations by the University of Minnesota on an eroded hill-top (Nikhória) have shown occupation throughout the Bronze Age and later.

A branch road (left) approaches the Messenian Gulf, with views to the mountains of the Mani. At (6km) **Petalídhi**, a small port (1113 inhab.) on the W shore of the Gulf of Kalamata, on 30 August 1828, General Maison landed 14,000 French troops, causing Ibrahim Pasha's immediate evacuation of the Morea. Just behind the town rises the acropolis (some remains), perhaps of ancient *Aepeia*, renamed by Epimelides (c 370 BC) after Koroneia, his native town in Boeotia, whence the later corruption *Korone*. Its inhabitants migrated farther S in the middle ages (see below) and the town was repopulated in the 19C by Maniots. The whole coast to modern Koroni comes into view, while to the W rise the pretty cypress-dotted foothills of Mt Likódhimon (957m). The road runs above the sea. At **Longá**, 1.5km W of (18km) **Ayios Andréas** remains of four successive **temples** mark the site of a temple of Apollo Korythos. 25km **Kharakopió**. A road (right) crosses the S part of the promontory, via **Finikoúndha** to Methoni.

29km **Koróni** (Hotels B–E), a picturesque medieval town (1794 inhab.) stands on a promontory at the foot of a Venetian castle. The antique remains (breakwater, cisterns, walls, etc.) are of *Asine*, a colony planted by perioikoi from Argive Asine. The derelict site was reoccupied in the Middle Ages by the inhabitants of Korone (now Petalidhi, see above), hence its modern name. This was corrupted by Frankish conquerors into *Coron*. In 1206 after a year's tenure the Franks had to cede it to the Venetians. Coron was attacked from the sea in 1428 by the Turks. In 1500, the inhabitants, demoralised by the news from Methone (see below), mutinied and gave in to the Turks only to be banished to Kefalonia. Andrea Doria captured Coron in 1532 for the Holy Roman Empire but, being besieged in turn by Khair-ed-din Barbarossa, was taken off with the inhabitants in a squadron of Sicilian ships, leaving the empty town to the Turks. It fell in 1685 to Morosini who massacred its 1500 defenders. Its final period (1718–1828) under Turkish rule was ended by General Maison.

The principal points of interest in the **castle** are the reused Classical masonry in the outer curtain; the Gothic entrance gate; the great talus of the E scarp moulded to the rocky bluff; the SE and SW artillery bastions, probably Turkish work; and the Byzantine wall of reused fragments which divides the inner from the outer court.

Messenia ends (11km SW) in Cape Gallo, the ancient *Akritas*, off which lies the rocky uninhabited islet of **Venetikó** or Theganousa. Methoni is 32km NW.

To the W of Rizómilos the road is crossed by torrents and may be difficult after rain. It closely follows the course of a prehistoric road explored in 1962 and suggested to be that taken by the Homeric heroes between Sparta and Pylos. Beyond (31km) **Kazárma** (alternative route to Khóra, Rte 34B, right in 21km) oak woods clothe the hill slopes. At (36km) **Soulinári** there is a turning (right) for **Kremmídhia** (3km further), with tholos tombs (overgrown). At 39km, the road summit (488m) has a view over Navarino Bay; to the right begins the Venetian aqueduct (also visible further on to the left) which feeds a Turkish fountain at Pilos. 48km Junction with the Kiparissía road (see below).

50.5km **PYLOS** (Πύλος; Hotels B, C, D), pronounced Pílos, known locally as Neókastro, and more familiar to foreigners as **Navarino**, is the chief town (2014 inhab.) of the eparchy of Pilia. The clean and attractive little town, built with arcaded streets by the French in 1829, rises from the S shore of Navarino Bay at the foot of a promontory (N end of Mt St Nicholas, 484m) on which a castle guards the S entrance to the bay. It is the most pleasant base from which to explore Southern Messenia.

**History**. This site was not occupied in antiquity. In 1572 the Turks built a fortress on Mt St Nicholas which was called Neokastro to distinguish it from the Palaiokastro to the N of the bay (see below). The name of **Navarino**, locally obsolete, is probably a Venetian corruption of *Ton Avarinon* (Castle 'of the Avars'), originally given by the Byzantines to the old castle and carried over to the new castle during the Venetian occupation of 1686–1718. In 1825 Ibrahim Pasha made it the centre of his operations in Messenia, which he utterly devastated. The intervention of the powers in 1827, the consequent battle of Navarino (see below), and the imminent arrival of French troops brought about Ibrahim's evacuation of the Morea in September 1828. The town dates from General Maison's occupation and has attracted to itself the Classical name of *Pylos*, causing still further confusion (see below).

The Plateía Trión Navárkhon, planted with planes and limes, has a memorial (1927) to Admirals Codrington, de Rigny, and von Heyden, who commanded respectively the British, French, and Russians at Navarino. The **museum** includes contents of Hellenistic tombs at Yialova, and Mycenaean finds from Koukounara (9.5km NE; 1958–59).

The interesting Turko-Venetian fortress of **Neokastro** (restored) to the SW is reached in ten minutes by the shore (ascend steps beyond school and follow path beside walls) or from the Methoni road, along which are remains of its Turkish aqueduct. The fortress consists of a large crenellated enceinte, enclosing a citadel with six bastions, and with an attractive domed mosque converted into a church. There is a small hotel beyond. The outer bastion, to the SW, with a platform above the sea, gives a good view of the enceinte as a whole and commands the entire bay; the best view is from the keep. The citadel was rebuilt in 1829 by the French and was in use as

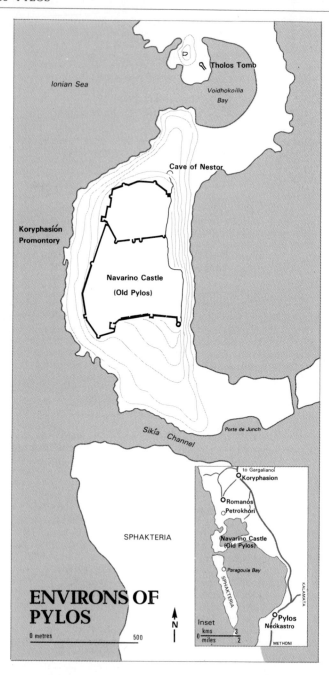

Ionian Sea

Tholos Tomb

Voidhokoília Bay

Cave of Nestor

Koryphasíon Promontory

Navarino Castle

(Old Pylos)

Sikía Channel

Porte de Junch

SPHAKTERIA

**ENVIRONS OF PYLOS**

0 metres    500

N

to Gargalianoí

Koryphasion

Romanós

Petrokhóri

Navarino Castle
(Old Pylos)

Paragoúla Bay

SPHAKTERIA

KALAMÁTA

Pylos
Neókastro

Inset
kms
0    3
miles
2

METHONI

a prison until recent years; it now shelters a Boy Scout headquarters. There is a display of material relating to the War of Independence. A museum with similar emphasis is in preparation, with displays of material from underwater excavations.

**Buses** to Methóni, Kalamáta, Gargalianoí, etc.

**Navarino Bay** forms a magnificent natural harbour, 5.5km long (N–S) and 3km wide, with a depth of 12–30 fathoms (22–55m). Its W side is formed by Sphakteria (see below). The only practicable entrance, on the S, is 1190m wide and divided into unequal channels by the islet of Pilos and the Tsikhli-Baba Rocks. On the islet are a lighthouse and the **French Monument**, erected in 1890 when the remains were transferred here from the mainland cemetery of fallen from Navarino and from the Morea Expedition of 1828–30. In the centre of the harbour a low rock called Khelonaki ('small tortoise') is crowned by the **Memorial to the British Sailors**.

**Battle of Navarino.** The Treaty of London (6 July 1827) provided that Great Britain, France, and Russia should guarantee the autonomy of Greece, under the suzerainty of Turkey, without breaking off friendly relations with the Porte. Their fleets were, without open hostilities or bloodshed, to intimidate Ibrahim Pasha into withdrawing the Turkish and Egyptian fleets from the Morea. A wide discretion was left to the senior admiral (Codrington). The allies called for an armistice; the Greeks promptly accepted but the Turks rejected the demand. On 20 October the allied fleet of 26 sail (11 British, 7 French, 8 Russian), mounting 1270 guns, entered the Bay of Navarino, which sheltered the Turko-Egyptian fleet, numbering 82 warships, 2438 guns, and 16,000 men. After an ultimatum to Ibrahim Pasha demanding his withdrawal from the Morea, a few shots fired by the Turks brought about a general action. At nightfall the Ottoman fleet, reduced to 29 ships, had lost 6000 men. The allies lost 174 killed and 475 wounded, but not a single ship. The news of this unexpected victory was received in England with mixed feelings (being referred to in the King's speech of 1828 as 'an untoward event'), in Russia with ill-concealed satisfaction, and in France with frank delight. Prince Metternich denounced the action as 'an unparalleled outrage'.

The uninhabited island of **Sphakteria**, or Sfayiá, which all but closes the bay on the W, is 4.5km long and 450–900m wide. The uneven interior of the island is covered with thickets. On the harbour side the cliffs, 30–90m high, are precipitous. The highest point, Ay. Ilias (168m), near the N end, is partly surrounded by a ruined **Cyclopean wall**—the 'ancient wall made of rough stones' (Thuc. iv, 31), where the Spartans made their last stand (see below). In favourable weather you can cross in a small boat from Pilos to the S end of Sphakteria and cruise up its E coast. At the S end of the island is the **Tomb of Capt. Mallet**, a French officer killed in the War of Independence. Farther N is the **Grotto of Tsamadhas**, named after a Greek officer; beside it is the **Monument of Santorre di Santa Rosa** (1783–1824), the Tuscan philhellene. Below the clear waters farther N the wrecks of Turkish ships can sometimes be seen. You land in the Bay of Panagoula in the middle of the E coast. Here, near a chapel, is the **Monument to the Russian Sailors** with an additional inscription of 1960.

A path ascends in ten minutes to a plateau with two brackish wells. Here for 72 days in the summer of 425 BC 420 occupying Spartans held out against an Athenian force under Demosthenes and Kleon. When the 292 survivors eventually surrendered, the myth that Spartans always fought to the death was broken. Thucydides describes the affair in great topographical detail which can easily be related to the terrain. Sphakteria was long famous as a nest of pirates and it is said to be the scene of Byron's 'Corsair'.

Passing the Tortori Rocks, at the NE end of Sphakteria, you cross the practically useless Sikia channel, which is only a few feet deep. By prior arrangement with the boatman, you can land at the foot of the Koryphasion

Promontory, near the remains of an ancient break-water called **Porte de Junch** (des joncs: 'rushes') by the Franks and 'Zonchio' by the Venetians. A path leads up in ½ hour to the acropolis of **'Old Pylos'**, surmounted by a Venetian castle. It seems probable that here also was the harbour town of the prehistoric Palace of Nestor (see below).

Strabo records that some of the inhabitants of Messenian Pylos 'at the foot of Mt Aigaleos' (see below) moved to this site, which the Spartans called *Koryphasia* (Thuc. IV, 3) from κορυφή ('summit'). Its occupation by the Athenians in 425 BC was the first act in the drama of Sphakteria.

From the 6C to the 9C AD Pylos was the home of a colony of Slavs and Avars: hence its name *Avarinos* or *Navarinon* (see above). In 1278 Nicholas II of St Omer built a castle here. In 1353 the Genoese captured a fleet under its walls. In 1381 it was occupied by Gascon and Navarrese adventurers; to the latter is sometimes attributed the origin of the name of Navarino. The castle was purchased by the Venetians in 1423 and fell to the Turks in 1501. After it had been bombarded by Don John of Austria in 1572 it was superseded by the Neokastro and known as **Palaiokastro**. Its capture in 1686 by Morosini and Königsmark ended its utility.

The spacious **castle** (some of interior inaccessible because of undergrowth; circuit of walls possible, with care) is fairly well preserved. Its crenellated walls and square towers rest partly on 4C foundations. The area enclosed is about 180m by 90m. There are outer and inner courts. Fragments of ancient walls, both polygonal and Cyclopean, can be traced near the middle of the S wall, on the NE side, and on the W side of the castle. There are also ancient cisterns and staircases cut in the rock. Below, to the N, is **Vöidhokoiliá** (good bathing) probable site of the Mycenaean harbour.

The steep path (red spots) leads down from the castle in 10 minutes to the mouth of the so-called **Grotto of Nestor**, on the N slope of Koryphasion (easy ascent from Vöidhokoilia). The arched entrance is c 9m wide and 3.5m high. The cave itself is 18m long, 12m wide and 12m high. Clinging to the walls are stalactites with the shapes of animals and of hanging hides, whence the legend that Neleus and Nestor kept their cows here. The grotto is identified with the cavern of the Homeric *Hymn to Hermes* in which Hermes hid the cattle stolen by him from Apollo and hung up the hides of the two beasts that he had killed. Sherds attest its intensive use in the Mycenaean period and Neolithic material has also been found.

On the promontory opposite to the N reached by walking round Vöidhokoilia Bay, is one of the earliest **tholos** tombs in mainland Greece. Recent researches have shown that it was inserted into a Middle Helladic tumulus. An Early Helladic settlement preceded the tumulus and Neolithic finds have also been made. Votive offerings of the Classical and Hellenistic periods show that a later cult grew up centred on the tholos.

A rough and largely overgrown path descends the N side of Koryphasion in 45 minutes to the Pilos–Kiparissia road (see below).

The area can also be reached from the villages of **Petrokhóri** (sign to 'Navarino'; rough track) or **Romanós**, both accessible by car (left turn 12km N of Pilos on the Kiparissia road; then follow 'Navarino' sign for Vöidhokoilia). An alternative track to Vöidhokoilia via a left turn after 9.5km is signed **Ayios Nikolaos**.

A road, engineered in 1828–29 by the French army, runs S to (12km) **Methóni** (Μεθώνη; Hotels B, C, D, E), the small fortress town of 1173 inhabitants, situated on a promontory opposite the island of **Sapienza**. The harbour is almost sanded up but the imposing fortifications still testify to its medieval importance. There is a good beach to the E.

**History**. Methoni or Mothone, perhaps ancient *Pedasos*, was said to be one of the seven cities which Agamemnon promised to Achilles. In Homer it has the epithet ἀμπελόεσσα (rich in vines). It received a colony of 'perioikoi' from Nauplia about the time of the Second Messenian War. In 431 BC an Athenian attack was foiled by the bravery of

Brasidas the Spartan. The descendants of the Argive immigrants remained here even after the restoration of the Messenians by Epaminondas. Marcus Agrippa's capture of the site in 31 BC cut off Mark Antony's supplies from Egypt. Trajan granted independence to the city.

Having become a haunt of pirates, it was razed in 1125 by the Venetians, and after a period of desolation firmly assigned to Venice in 1204. Until 1206, however, Geoffrey de Villehardouin and William de Champlitte used it as a base, establishing a bishopric. The Venetians fortified it as their main port of call on the way to the Holy Land, to which were sent an annual convoy of pilgrims. The town, known as *Modon*, was noted for its wine and bacon, and had a flourishing silk industry, but although it was a naval station and shared with its neighbour Coron the description '*Oculi capitales communis*', its public buildings were never lavish. The Venetian navy, totally defeated at the Battle of Sapienza in 1354 by the Genoese under Andrea Doria, took their revenge in 1403 off Modon, defeating a Genoese fleet commanded by the French marshal, Boucicault. Here on neutral ground in 1366 Count Amadeus VI of Savoy arbitrated in the struggle between Marie de Bourbon and Angelo Acciaiouli, Archbishop of Patras. In 1500, after resisting a month's bombardment, Methoni fell to Sultan Bayezid II when the defenders prematurely deserted the walls to welcome a relieving force sent from Corfu. An attack by the Knights of Malta in 1551 was unsuccessful, and save for a second brief Venetian period in 1686–1715, following Morosini's conquest, the town remained in Turkish hands until 1828. Chateaubriand landed here in 1806, and Ibrahim Pasha disembarked his army in 1825. The story of the captive told in '*Don Quixote*' may reflect Cervantes' own experience here as a Turkish prisoner.

The Venetian **\*fortress-town** occupies a promontory washed on three sides by the sea, except where the sand has built up. Its strongest fortifications on the landward side are separated from the mainland by a great ditch. This is crossed on an attractive bridge, rebuilt by the French in 1828, to a Venetian monumental gateway of c 1700. Within, a covered way leads through a second **gate** to a third, opening into the area occupied by the medieval town (pulled down by the French when they built the modern area on the mainland). A granite **column** with a weathered inscription probably commemorates Rector Fr. Bembo (1494). Little remains except a **Turkish bath**, the ruin of the Latin **cathedral**, and cisterns. The **curtain wall** shows masonry of all periods from Classical (exposed when a section was dynamited in 1943) to 19C. The **citadel** contains many subtleties of Venetian defence, including casemates and underground passages for counter-mining. Numerous lions of St Mark, escutcheons, and dated inscriptions survive. At the S end of the enceinte an imposing **sea gate** (restored) and causeway lead to the little islet, with the octagonal **Bourdzi** tower, where the remnant of the Venetian force was massacred in 1500 (fortifications Turkish).

Offshore lie the **Oinoussai Islands**, a group consisting of **Sapienza** (see above) and **Schiza** (caves; prehistoric occupation) or Cabrera, with the tiny islet of **Ayía Marianí** between them. The storms here are very dangerous. The bay between the islands and the mainland was anciently called *Port Phoenikos*.

# B.  From Pylos (Pílos) to Kiparissía

**Road**, 65km (40½ miles).—21km Khóra.—34km Gargalianoí.—48km Filiatrá.—65km Kiparissía. Buses several times daily; 5 times of Khóra.

From Pílos the road skirts Navarino Bay. The hamlet of **Zoúnchio** derives its names from the Venetian version of the Porte de Junch (see above). 5km **Yiálova** has shipyards, and fruit warehouses. Plans for a large port and oil refinery were abandoned, after protests, in the mid 1970s. The drained Lagoon of Osman Aga, which extended to the foot of Koryphasion, has been shown by traces of ancient occupation to be a post-Classical formation. Turns (left) to **Petrokhóri** (see above) and **Romanós** (14km from Pílos; bathing). 12km Modern **Korifásion**.

The road passes immediately below (17km) the low but abrupt hill of **Epano Englianós** (site roof prominent) on which stand the remains of the **˙Palace of Nestor**, explored in 1939 and excavated since 1952 by Carl Blegen (excellent illustrated guide-book, to which the numbering of the plan here conforms). The site, which had been inhabited in the Middle Bronze Age, was occupied from c 1400 BC, by a series of royal palaces, the last of which was destroyed by fire at the end of Mycenaean IIIB. A recent theory (K. Kilian) suggests that a predecessor (LHI–II or earlier) may have had a Minoan design (with a central court). The *Iliad* preserves a tradition of a Neleid dynasty at Messenian Pylos, of whom Nestor ruled for three generations. In the 'Catalogue of Ships' he is credited with the second largest fleet (90 ships against Agamemnon's 100); the palace of Englianos compares in size and richness with that of Mycenae and has associated tholos tombs.

**NESTOR'S PALACE**

0 _____ 20 metres

**Linear B tablets** (the first to be found on the mainland) were unearthed in the room to the left of the entrance within two hours of the first day's digging in 1939, the day Italy invaded Albania. They were stored in a bank vault in Athens throughout the war.

The perimeter seems not to have been fortified in the palace period. The latest **palace** consisted of two-storeyed buildings in three main blocks, whose construction somewhat resembled that of Tudor half-timbered buildings, with wooden columns, roofs and ceilings. As a result the superstructure disappeared during the fire depositing only non-inflammable objects from the upper floor. The exterior walls were faced in squared blocks of limestone; the inner walls were of rubble, with a plaster surface, and decorated with frescoes, and had wooden wainscots. Most of the walls stand to c 1m above floor level giving a clear ground plan. The upper storey had brick walls between the wooden beams.

The **main building** was approached across an open court paved in stucco. Jutting out (right) beyond the entrance stood a **guard tower** (Pl. 57). The simple **propylon** (Pl. 1, 2) had one column in each façade with a single door in the cross-wall between. The stone bases of the columns survive and show that the wooden pillars had 64 flutes. A **sentry-box** (left) guarded the palace door and also two small rooms (Pl. 7, 8) beside the gateway, where nearly 100 clay tablets inscribed in Linear B script were found. Here perhaps was the tax collector's office. A large interior **court** (Pl. 3), open to the sky, gives access to other parts of the palace. To the left are a **pantry** (Pl. 9), its wine jars and cups lying in ruin, and a **waiting-room** (Pl. 10) with a stuccoed bench.

A wide **portico** (Pl. 4), distyle in antis, opened into a **vestibule** (Pl. 5) and then by another door into the **megaron** proper (Pl. 6), 12.8m long by 11.3m wide. In the centre a great ceremonial hearth of stuccoed clay forms a circle 4m across and raised 20cm above the floor. Round this four great columns, each with 32 flutes, supported a galleried upper storey, probably with a lantern above to let light in and smoke out. The floor was divided into patterned squares, all abstract in design except for one with an octopus. This is directly in front of a depression in the floor against the right-hand wall where a throne almost certainly stood. Beside it in the floor is a hollow from which a channel leads to another hollow, 1.8m away. These may have been used in some libation ceremony performed from the throne. The chamber was decorated with paintings, the wall behind the throne with reclining griffins and lions.

Corridors either side of the megaron served suites of service rooms and gave access to staircases leading to the upper floor. Five small rooms (Pl. 18–22) filled with thousands of cups and pots of more than 20 types must have formed as much a central depot for issue or sale as the palace pantry. Behind the megaron are magazines (Pl. 23, 24, 27) with larger pithoi fixed in stucco. Tablets were found in one room detailing their contents as olive-oil. The **bathroom** (Pl. 43) is evocative, its fixed terracotta tub (*larnax*) still *in situ*, together with pithoi for water and its pouring vessels (*kylikes*).

On the SE side of the court a colonnade (which supported a balcony) gives access to a duplicate but smaller set of apartments (Pl. 45–53) surrounding what appears to be the **Queen's megaron** (Pl. 46). The suite includes a small room (Pl. 53) with a drain hole, either another bathroom or a lavatory.

The **South-Western Building** is thought to be an earlier and less sophisticated palace, perhaps turned into a dower house when the new palace was completed. Despite differences in plan (the arrangement is not axial and the storerooms open one from another instead of from corridors) it is a self-contained unit with most of the features of the later construction (megaron, Pl. 65, etc.). Much of its stonework has been robbed, though parts of the supporting ashlar wall survive.

The **North-East Building** may have housed the palace **workshops**, and seems to have had an altar in the court. The functions of various workrooms have been identified from fragments found in them and tablet lists; they included a chariot repair-shop and an armoury. Traces of an elaborate water-supply system are visible. Farther to the N is the **wine magazine**, a separate building, in which a large room contains 35 or more large jars. Clay sealings were found marked in Linear B with the character interpreted as 'wine', and indications of its source (or vintage?).

Outside the NE gate of the citadel (100m) is a **tholos tomb**, excavated by Lord William Taylour in 1953 and restored in 1957 by the Greek Archaeological Service. It is crude in construction compared with those at Mycenae. Three other tholoi, S of the palace, excavated in 1912, 1926, and 1939, have been filled in.

The most imortant finds from Pylos are in the National Museum at Athens; various frescoes, etc., in a small museum at Khora (see below).

2km before Khora a turning (right) leads in 4km to **Mirsinokhóri**, with important **Mycenaean tombs** in the vicinity (ask directions).

Near **Papoúlia**, c 10km E of the Palace of Nestor, is a Middle Helladic burial complex, consisting of pithoi inserted into a stone-built mound.

**21km Khóra** (Hotels B, E) formerly Ligoúdhista, has an excellent museum (1966) containing Mycenaean antiquities from Messenia, including the Palace of Nestor. The three rooms contain objects from tholos and chamber tombs, including swords, and gold cups from one of the Peristeria tholoi; *frescoes from the palace; Linear B tablets; pottery from the palace 'pantries'.

Opposite the museum is the alternative route to Kalamata via Kazarma (see Rte 34A). The town (3112 inhab.) lies at the SW foot of Kondovounia, the ancient *Aigaleon*, a mountain range which forms the backbone of the peninsula and rises in Ayia Varvara to 1219m. Turning NW into its foothills you reach (34km) **Gargalianoí** (296m; Hotels A, E; 5184 inhabitants), with a monument to Agras the Macedonian guerilla, who was born here. 48km **Filiatrá** (Hotel C), well-planned and prosperous (6062 inhab.) amid currant fields and orchards of citrus fruit. All these towns have been rebuilt since the earthquake of 1886. The recent decline in population seems now to have been reversed.

**Ayía Kiriakí**, its little port (4km SW), had more important days as *Erane*, as is shown by remains of basilica and baths (5C AD) and coins from its Frankish mint.

10km SE of Filiatra is **Khristianoí**, the *Christianoupolis* of the Byzantines and seat of an archbishop in the 11C. It lost importance in the 14C and the bishopric was transferred in 1837 to Kiparissía. The large and impressive 12C **cathedral** (locked) of Ayia Sotira, wrecked by earthquake in 1886, has been restored, and there are remains of ancillary buildings.

**65km Kiparissía** (Κυπαρισσία; Hotels B, C), the chief centre (4520 inhab.) of the eparchy of Messenian Triphylia and the seat of the Bishop of Triphylia and Christianoupolis, was called *Arkadia* in the Middle Ages. The town, with pleasant broad streets, has expanded from the foot of the acropolis down to its small harbour and beaches, which are backed by groves of trees. The acropolis is a craggy rock 152m high connected with Mt Psykhro (1116m), the NE end of the Aigaleon range. Pieces of Hellenic masonry survive in the impressive Byzantine and Frankish **castle** (road to gate; *view, including Zante, Kephalonia and the Strophades), which re-introduced the round tower to Greece. There is a modern theatre in a fine position below.

The ancient city of *Kyparissiai* was founded by Epaminondas as the port of Messene. During the Slav invasions it became a refuge of the Arcadians, whence its medieval name. It was taken after a seven-day siege by William de Champlitte in 1205. In 1391–1430 it was held by the Genoese Zaccaria. The town was destroyed by Ibrahim Pasha in 1825 and, when rebuilt, resumed the ancient name.

# C.  From Kalamáta to Kiparissía

**Road**, 72km (44½ miles).—21km Turning (left) for Mavromáti and ancient Messene (Ithome).—31km Meligalá.—35km Zevgolatió.—72km Kiparissía.

**Railway**, 67km (41½ miles), in 1½–2 hours via Zevgolatió and Kaloneró. To Válira, 21km, for Mavromáti, in ½ hour.

The route traverses the **Lower Messenian Plain**, known to the ancients as *Makaria* ('Happy Land'), and described by Euripides in a lost play, quoted by Strabo, as a 'land of fair fruitage and watered by innumerable streams, abounding in pasturage for cattle and sheep, being neither very wintry in the blasts of winter, nor yet made too hot by the chariot of Helios'. Curtius observes: 'High hedges of cactus divide the well-tilled fields; the great aloe stands in thick clumps, lemons and oranges flourish plentifully, the date itself ripens under the Messenian sun, and the superabundance of oil and wine is exported from Kalamata'. Today, in addition, bananas are grown. The shorter road, on the E slope of the valley (25km to Meligalá), is described in Rte 33.

From Kalamata to (8.5km) **Messíni**, see Rte 34A. On the outskirts of Messini you fork right, then turn N up the valley of the Pamisos. At (16km) **Tríodhos** a road leads left to (4km) **Androúsa** (Ανδρούσα; 655 inhab.) the medieval *Druges*, once a bishopric of Frankish Messenia. It is well situated on an elevated terrace overlooking the plain. To the N of the imposing Frankish **castle** on the other side of a ravine, is the small Byzantine church of Ayios Yeoryios.

In a peaceful valley 4km NW of Androusa by road, beyond the village of **Kaloyerorákhi** (key), lies **Ellinoklisiá**, with an elegant church (Samarina), supposedly founded in the 14C by Andronikos II Palaiologos. Its dedication of Zoödókhos Piyí (Source of Life) comes from a spring beneath the church. Built in horizontal layers of brick and stone, it has three apses and a dome supported by ancient marble columns. The narthex supports a square belfry. Within, the mosaic borders, part of the ikonostasis, and a mural painting are of interest. Some column drums nearby show that an earlier building occupied the site.

21km **Khánia Lábaina**. A by-road (signposted 'Ithomi') ascends (left) in 10km to **Mavromáti** (bus from Kalamata; rooms), the pretty well-watered village (419m) that occupies part of the site of ancient Messene. The spring in the centre of the village (ancient construction) is that of *Klepsydra*, mentioned by Pausanias. At the far end of the village is a sign to 'Archaeological Site' (footpath).

From the railway the best approach on foot is from Válira station (see below), whence you climb W for (1¾ hrs) the **Monastery of Vourkano** (383m), which has long been visible half-way up the N slope of Mt Eva. The convent is an off-shoot of an older foundation of the same name on the summit of Ithome (see below) and offers hospitality. On the 15C entrance gate is the escutcheon of the Knights of St John. The conventual buildings, which date only from 1712, are set round a cloistered court, with an earlier church in the centre. The beautiful situation commands a view of S Messenia and of the Arcadian mountains. In 20 minutes from the monastery you can ascend to the saddle between Mts Eva and Ithome and reach the Laconian Gate (see below).

**Messene** dates from 369 BC, when Epaminondas restored the Messenians to their country and encouraged them to build a capital. The city was built, probably on the Hippodamian system, in a hollow between three hills, Eva on the SE, Psoriari on the W, and Ithome on the N, the acropolis being on the last named which was included in the circuit. The well-preserved *fortifications are an outstanding example of 4C military architecture.

**History**. *Messene*, with Megalopolis, Mantineia and Argos, completed the strategic barrier against Sparta organised by Epaminondas after the battle of Leuktra. Diodorus says that the city was built in 85 days. In 214 BC Messene was besieged by a Macedonian general, Demetrios of Pharos, who was killed under its walls; in 202 an attack by the Spartan tyrant Nabis was frustrated by Philopoemen. After the demagogue, Dinokrates, had incited the Messenians to revolt against the Achaean League, Philopoemen attacked the rebels, but was taken prisoner by them, thrown into a dungeon in Messene, and forced to take poison. He was avenged by Lykortas, the father of Polybius, who succeeded him. The sculptor Damophon was a native.

At the far end of the village, beyond the **museum** (not open to the public), a road descends to the cemetery (parking). Immediately below is the **theatre** with fine archways in the parodos retaining walls. E are the foundations of a large Roman stoa (c 80m long), recently investigated, which enclosed the N side of the **agora**, whose format is now obscured by trees. This stoa incorporated (W) a **fountain** (perhaps that of *Arsinoe* mentioned by Pausanias).

S is the thoroughly cleared Hellenistic (2C) **Sanctuary of Asklepios**, c 69m square surrounded by a colonnade whose Corinthian columns had winged Nike figures rising from their acanthus-leaf capitals. The **propylaia** is in the centre of the E side, flanked by a small **odeion** (N) and a **bouleuterion** (S).

Recent work has shown that there was a bathing establishment on the S side in the Hellenistic period (part of heating system visible) and a priests' house or prytaneion (square with inner court; Roman). To the W are various rooms of which the most important is a tripartite **Temple of Artemis** (NW corner) with bases for the cult statue and other dedications; seats with lions' feet may point to a mystery cult. The N side, divided by a monumental staircase ascending from the court, was a **sebasteion** (temple for emperor

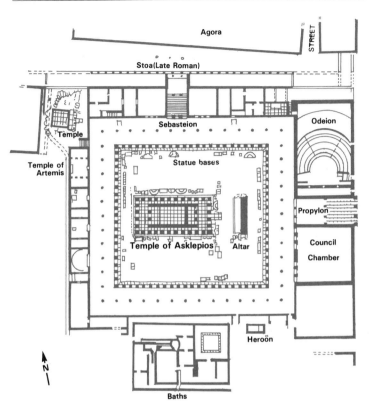

# Messene
## Asklepieion Complex

0  metres                                    40

worship) in the Roman period. At the E end is an *oikos*. In the centre of the
court is the **Temple of Asklepios and Hygiaea** (or ? the heroine *Messene*),
peripteral with 6 columns by 12. Immediately to the N of the Asklepieion
complex are the foundations of a large (80m +) Late Roman stoa which
bounded the S side of the agora. At the NW a 4–3C Temple of Artemis
Orthia and temenos of Athena Kyparissia have been discovered recently,
also a Sanctuary of Demeter (votive plaques). In a building to the SE, with
inlaid marble and mosaic floors, a fine intact statue of Artemis was discovered in 1989.

A few minutes to the SW is the **stadium** (recently cleared) which abutted
onto the city wall. Some of the seating was inscribed and stoas enclosed the
curved (N) end. Beyond the W stoa are remains of a temenos of Herakles
and, to the NW, a palaistra (40m square). At the S end and occupying a
monumental podium projecting beyond the city wall was a heröon (the
details now difficult to make out). Here, in an enormous stone-pile tumulus,
were probably the graves of distinguished (heroised) Messenian citizens.
You can follow traces of the walls W and then N beyond the stadium, or

return to the road and continue past the museum to the *Arcadian Gate, which forms, with the adjoining section of the city wall and the tower to the E, the best-preserved part of the fortifications.

The gateway, through which a road still runs, consists of an outer and an inner entrance, separated by a circular court. The **outer entrance** was flanked by square towers, 10m apart, the foundations alone of which survive. The gateway is nearly 5m wide. The open **court**, 19m in diameter, is remarkable for the perfection of its masonry, laid without mortar on a base of two more massive courses. On either side, near the outer gate, is a niche for statues of the protecting gods, one doubtless the Hermes noted by Pausanias. Under the right niche a worn inscription describes the restorations of Q. Plotius Euphemion. The **Inner Gate** has an enormous monolithic doorpost, now half fallen. A short section of **paved road** with chariot ruts is visible. Outside the gate is the stepped base of a large monument.

The main road continues W within the walls towards a line of towers standing to their original height.

The circuit of the *walls, c 9km long, follows the line of the ridge descending from Ithome and was continuous except at various inaccessible points. This vast enceinte, planned to enclose cornfields, doubtless served also as a refuge for the surrounding population in time of danger. The battlemented **curtain** consists of an outer and inner facing of unmortared squared blocks, with a rubble core; it is 2–2.5m thick and averaged 4.5m high. The steepness of the escarpment prevented the approach of siege engines. The curtain was flanked at irregular intervals (30–90m) by projecting battlemented **towers**, of which there were at least 30. These were square or, at the salient angles, semicircular. Seven are still partly extant. They had two storeys, the lower with four loopholes, the upper with six small windows. Four of the **gates** have been distinguished.

To the NE of the village, the path to Ithome passes the aqueduct which fed *Klepsydra* and reaches the recently reinvestigated shrine of **Artemis Limnatis** (or **Laphria**) (circuit wall, Ionic naiskos, cult statue base, altar, ancillary buildings). Another shrine has also been located 500m further NW. The ascent of Ithome (1½ hours from the village) is now best made by taking the track from Mavromati to the Laconian Gate (see below) and following the path from there. The summit of Ithome (Ιθώμη: 'step'; 802m) is really a ridge running SE to NW. Mentioned by Homer, Ithome figured as a refuge in the First and Third Messenian Wars. On the summit stands the small **Monastery of Vourkano**, dating from the 16C, and the mother-convent of the later monastery below (see above). It was finally abandoned in 1950 and its ikon removed from the ruined katholikon. A paved threshing floor may have been the scene of the festival of the Ithomaea, which survives to this day in an annual festival of the Panayia. The convent occupies the site of an **altar-sanctuary of Zeus Ithomatas** where human sacrifice was occasionally offered. To the S are two large cisterns. The *view embraces most of Messenia. You can descend again to the **Laconian Gate**.

Outside the Arcadian Gate a road leads via **Zerbísia** and **Neokhóri Ithómis** to **Meligalá**. About 1.5km before Meligala (see below), the road crosses the triple **Mavrozoúmenos Bridge**, built over the confluence of two rivers. The W arm spans the Upper Mavrozoumenos, the E arm the Amphitos. The N arm forms a causeway over the apex of land between them which is liable to be flooded. The bridge has seven arches (span 5.2m, height above water 4m) and one rectangular opening 2.2m high by 1.2m wide. The piers are ancient, probably contemporary with Messene; the arches mainly Turkish. The river is the Pamisos.

Returning to the main road, you cross the Pamisos then (24km) **Válira**, passing (at 28km; right) a short link (2km) to the Kalamata–Tripolis road. 31km **Meligalá** (Μελιγαλά), with a prominent clock-tower, is the largest town (1405 inhab.) in the Upper Messenian Plain, or Plain of Steniklaros, the home of the Dorian dynasty of Kresphontes. The site of the royal city is unknown. This beautiful and fertile valley, watered by many streams, enjoys a temperate climate. Its vegetation includes figs, olives, oranges, mulberries, cactus, and date palms.

Beyond the railway junction of **Zevgolatió** the road meets that from Megalopolis and turns W. The route, which is being realigned, crosses the Soulima Plain, a broad corridor through which flows the Upper Mavrozoumenos. 44km **Vasilikó** has a small museum containing objects from Malthí and a Roman mosaic found near Koroni. Above Vasilikó (turn left at sign 'Malthi 6' in village after c 2km small sign points right and left—to Tholos Tombs and Acropolis. The acropolis can be reached by a very rough track to the left a little further on) is the site of **Malthí**, doubtfully identified with the Homeric *Dorion* where Thamyris lost his eyesight. Excavations in 1927–36 by the Swedish archaeologist Natan Valmin revealed chiefly MH material. Two small **tholos tombs** (to the other side of the road below) and a sanctuary containing a bronze double-axe were discovered.

48km To the right (6km) is **Psári** with recently excavated Mycenaean tholos tombs at Metsíki. 52km **Káto Kopanáki**, on the watershed between the Arkhadéïka (Aëtos) and the W tributaries of the Pamisos, lies 5km N of **Aëtós**, a village on the N slope of Mt Sekhi (1391m) where there are Cyclopean ruins and remains of a 14C Venetian **fort**. 63km Turning (right; across the railway) for **Sidhirókastro**, a village in the hills to the NE. On a hill behind it is the 13C **castle** (no path evident) from which it takes its name.

At (65km) **Kaló Neró** you join the coastal road (see below) and turn left. 72km **Kiparissía**, see Rte 34B.

# D.  From Kiparissía to Pírgos

**Road**, 63km (39 miles).

**Railway**, 63km, 6 times daily in 1¼ hours (continuing to Patras and/or Athens); to Kaïáfa, 33km, in 40 minutes (only the slowest trains stop at Samikó).

Heading N from Kiparissia, there is a turn (5km, right; signed 'Archaeological Site') to **Mírou**.

At **Peristeriá**, 1.5km N of Mírou, important **Mycenaean tholos tombs** with rich finds (in Khora Museum) were found in 1960–65 and further recent work has revealed additional burials as well as evidence of the Mycenaean settlement.

At (6.5km) **Kaló Neró** (Hotel E) you meet the main road from the E (Rte 34C). From here road and railway follow the sandy shore. 16km The Nédha river forms the boundary between Messinia and Elis (see Rte 40). 20km **Tholó**.

A minor road (bus) serves **Lépreo** (8km), on the heights above which (turn left on edge of modern village at sign 'Ταξιάρχες'; after 2km sign in woods to right for acropolis) in a pleasant wooded setting are well-preserved walls of ancient *Lepreon*. In the SE part of the site architectural fragments from and the foundations of a **Temple of Demeter** of the 4C BC, can be seen. At **Ayios Dhimítrios**, off the main road on the N outskirts of the village (sign, right) on a prominent bluff, are some remains (LN–EH pottery; EHII houses) of prehistoric Lepreon. 20km **Káto Figalía** (see Rte 35).

25km **Kakóvatos** (Hotel D) is well-known to archaeologists for the **site** (15 minutes to the E, in the direction of **Kalídhona**) identified by Prof. Dörpfeld, following Strabo, as Triphylian Pylos, a place confused until the discoveries at Englianos with the Pylos of Nestor. Three tholos tombs and traces of a palace or sanctuary (LHI or II) were excavated in 1909–10, and the position of the lower town was identified in 1961.

Beyond (28km) **Zakháro** (Hotels C, D; 4318 inhab.) the road passes between the sea and the Lagoon of Kaïáfa, which is 5km long and contains valuable fisheries. On the lake-island of Ayía Aikateríni (cross by causeway right at 32km) are the sulphur **Baths of Kaïáfa** (Λουτρά Καϊάφα; Hotels B–E, May–October with annexes).

The waters come from springs in two large sulphurous caverns, the Cave of the Anigrian Nymphs and the Cave of Yeranion to which the ancients resorted for the cure of skin diseases. The first feeds the baths, the second is used for drinking. Local tradition ascribes the name of the lagoon to Caiaphas, High Priest of Judah, who bathed here after having been shipwrecked. To him is attributed the offensive pungency of the sulphur-laden waters.

37km Turn (right) signed again for Kaiafa Thermal Springs. 300m further on, to the left across the railway line in the area called **Kleidhí**, a low hill has some prehistoric remains. At the E foot are excavations of part of an important cemetery of tumuli (MH–LH), one covering a tholos tomb. The first tumulus to be excavated, now in a sad state, is in a lemon grove to the N of the hill. On the other side of the main road from Kleidhi, on a W spur of Mt Kaiafa (744m) is ancient *Samikon* (path from opposite Kleidhi or track by road sign for Kato Samiko). The **walls** are impressive (best view from main road to the N) but close access is difficult. The imposing enceinte in developed polygonal masonry of c 450 BC stands in places to 12 courses. Within is a less well preserved and earlier defensive wall to be dated before the 6C BC. The place was taken by Philip V of Macedon in 219 BC. 38km **Káto Samikó**.

Passing inland of the shallow Lagoon of Agoulínitsa, itself separated from the sea by a belt of dunes with pines, roads (right) lead to Kréstena (whence to Bassae, see Rte 35) and on over the Alpheios Dam to Olympia (13km; Rte 36). 50km **Epitálio** (1752 inhab.), formerly Agoulínitsa but now probably correctly recording an ancient site, straggles on the hillside, surrounded by cornfields and vineyards. The hill of Ay. Yeoryios has produced LH III remains of (?) Homeric *Thryon*. From here the road runs straight across the alluvial plain, crossing the Alpheios on a bridge 400m long that serves also as an irrigation sluice. The railway curves NE to cross the river higher up by a long iron bridge and join the branch from Olympia. 63km **Pírgos**, see Rte 40.

# 35

# Megalópolis to Andrítsaina (for Bassae) and Pírgos

**Road**, 110km (68½ miles) with spectacular scenery. 20km Karítaina.—45km Andrítsaina, turning for Bassae (mod. Vásses; 14.5km).—91km Kréstena.—110km Pírgos. **Bus** twice daily from Megalopolis to Andritsaina; twice daily from Andritsaina to Krestena; more frequently Krestena to Pirgos. **Taxis** in Megalopolis or Andritsaina for Bassae.

From Megalópolis (see Rte 33) the road runs through the ancient remains crossing the Helisson.

A minor road leads (right) in 15km, via Trílofos to **Likókhia**, near which a late Archaic and Classical **sanctuary of Artemis** (perhaps that of Artemis Kalliste, mentioned by Pausanias) was excavated in 1972 and 1975.

You follow the Alpheios at varying distances from its right bank. 11km **Katsímbali**. Here a track diverges (left) across the river to Kiparissía, between which and Mavriá, just to the N, are some remains of *Trapezous*. Ahead is seen (11km) Karítaina (winding ascent for 3km) above the junction with the road from Dhimitsána.

**Karítaina** (Καρύταινα), a picturesque medieval town, is spectacularly perched on an isolated hill at the NW corner of the Plain of Megalópolis above the right bank of the Karitaina (as the Alpheios is called at this point).

*Karítaina, Frankish bridge*

Karítaina occupies the site of ancient *Brenthe*, a deserted city which became a refuge for the people of Gortys when they were driven out by the Slavs. The name is, in fact, a corruption of Gortyna. In 1209 the Franks made Karytaina the capital of a barony of 22 fiefs. The castle was built by Hugh de Bruyères in 1254. His son Geoffrey I de Bruyères (died 1272) was the 'Sire de Caritaine' and the pattern of Peloponnesian chivalry. The castle passed by sale in 1320 to Andronikos II Palaiologos. In the War of Independence, Kolokotronis used it as a stronghold from which he defied Ibrahim Pasha.

The churches of the **Panayía** (11C), with a Frankish belfry, and of **Ayios Nikólaos** (frescoes; key from hotel), merit a visit. A precipitous path climbs in 10 minutes to the *castle (583m) which occupies the summit of a high rock, extremely steep and in places overhanging the river side. The triangular enceinte, adapted for defence by artillery as well as musketry, is a notable example of feudal fortification. In the central court is a large vaulted hall and on the W the remains of a gallery with large windows and of numerous cisterns (care needed). The *view is superb.

From the square below the castle, an asphalt road leads to **Atsíkholo** (9.5km). At **Palaiókastro** (12km further) is a large cemetery of Mycenaean chamber tombs.

From the main road below Karítaina, a branch leads N via (10km) **Ellinikó** and Stemnítsa (19km; Rte 36) to **Dhimitsána**. The road winds high in the accidented mountain range on the E side of the gorge down which the clear, green Lousios (or Gortynios) flows to its confluence with the Alpheios.

Accessible from either Atsíkholo or Ellinikó are the fine acropolis walls and Asklepieion (the two sites some 30mins/3km apart) of ancient *Gortys*, of whose history little is known but which apparently declined after the foundation of Megalopolis. Just before Atsíkholo, a rough road diverges right (small sign in Greek to Αρχαία Γόρτυς/Μονή Καλαμίου). After 1.3km, at a similar sign, turn right in the direction of Moni Kalamiou (*not* Archaia Gortys, which leads to the lower Asklepieion). About 700m along the track is a short ascent (l.) to a small steading, 100m to the N of which, on an oblong summit high above the Lousios, are the fine walls and towers (4C trapezoidal masonry: see B.C.H. 1947–48) of the **acropolis**. There is a smaller walled enclosure (? 3C) at the SE. 50m to the S of this are the remains of a second Asklepieion (inscriptions) with a stoa (abaton), spring or bath and a temple of the 5 or 4C.

To visit the main **Asklepieion** by the river below, return to the signpost (above) and descend in the direction of 'Archaia Gortys' (c 3km following the road; short cuts possible on foot). The main elements of the site (foundations of a temple of Asklepios and a bathing establishment—see R. Ginouvé, *L'établissement thermale de Gortys d'Arcadie*, 1959) are clearly visible below the last stretch of the road, which ends at the small chapel of Ayios Andréas, incorporating ancient masonry, and a pack horse bridge over the river. The **temple** (no opisthodomos) was built in the 4C and probably had sculptures by Scopas. The **bathing establishment** was built in the Hellenistic period and reconstructed in the 4C AD. Bathers entered through a portico at the E, turned left into a changing room and passed into the main central hall (warm), equipped with benches and water fountains. A small circular room off to the NE was for dry heat. A modest waiting area gave access to the circular bathroom with individual niches. The functions of the two rooms at the NE are uncertain. The hypocaust system is well preserved. The furnace, with the main water reservoir beside it, is at the far end of the complex from the entrance. Further E, across ravines, are the remains of another temple, a stoa, a watchtower and houses.

To reach the Asklepieion from **Ellinikó**, follow the sign to ancient Gortys (6km by unsurfaced road to the packhorse bridge) from the village square. The same road also gives access (turn right after 5km and then 3km (rough) + 20 min. walk) to the spectacularly situated monastery of **Ayios Ioánnis Pródhromos**, clinging to the side of the Lousios gorge, founded by Manuel Comnenos in 1167. Beyond it a rough road continues to Stemnitsa (8km further). Gortys still gives name to a modern eparchy of Arcadia.

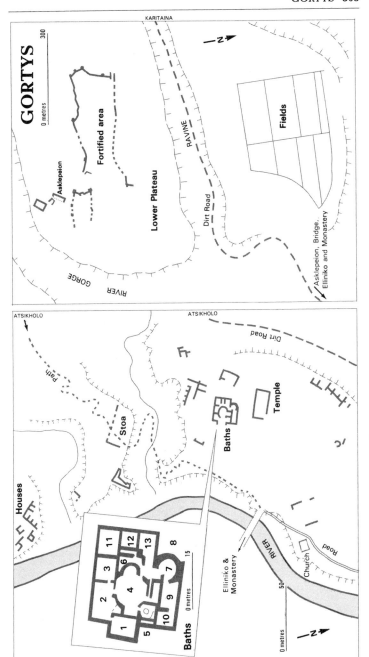

In this area in 1955 were explored three strong-points commanding the ancient route from Megalopolis to Elis: above the village of **Vlakhoráfti**, to the W, on the highest point (942m) of the W chain overlooking the gorge; at **Palaiókastro** (see above), at the W end of this chain, overlooking the Alpheios (ancient *Bouphagion*); and (smaller but probably of the Archaic period) at **Ellinikó** (see above).

The Andritsaina road crosses the river on a new bridge beside the **medieval bridge**, renovated (as an inscription once recorded) in 1439 by Manuel Raoul Melikes, a member of a noble Turkish family serving the Palaiologi at Mistra. 27km **Strongiló**. The road climbs high along the N slopes of the barren Mt Lykaion with views into the Gorge of the Alpheios. 33km **Theisóa**. The Lavdha hill above is the site (fortifications etc.) of the **ancient settlement** of the same name (under excavation).

45km **Andrítsaina** (Ανδρίτσαινα; Hotels B, D, E) an attractive ramshackle town (863 inhab.) of wooden houses, was shaken by earthquakes in 1965. It is beautifully situated on elevated ground (765m) facing NW and watered by a mountain stream. In the square stands a monument to Panayotis Anagnostopoulos, one of the Filikí Etairia who was educated at the local school. The town has an excellent **library** founded with a bequest in 1840.

A well-engineered road (14.5km; taxi; bus daily, not returning) ascends through specactular scenery to the remote Temple of Bassae. The 2½-hour walk through the valleys is rewarding. Continuation to the coast, see below.
    The celebrated **'Temple of Apollo Epikourios** at *Bassae* (at present shrouded in an obtrusive protective covering) is situated at 1131m on a narrow rocky terrace of Mt Kotilion (now Paliavlakhítsa), whose summit rises above it to the NE. The mountain is scored with ravines (βάσσαι) from which the place takes its general name; the temple site is called locally 'the columns' (στοὺς στύλους). The temple, which owes its fine preservation to its inaccessibility, is built of a cold grey local limestone that contributes to, rather than lightens, the melancholy bleakness of the landscape. The immediate surroundings are softened a little by a few oak trees and wild flowers.

The temple is attributed by Pausanias to Iktinos. Its style makes it almost certainly an earlier work than the Parthenon, and so designed c 450–447 BC, though the execution may not have been finished before 425 BC. The locality was rediscovered in 1765 by Joachim Bocher, a French architect employed by the Venetians in Zante. It was visited in 1805–06 by Leake, Dodwell, and Wm Gell. In 1811–12 the party of British and German antiquaries who had previously stripped the Aegina temple, explored the ruins and removed the sculptures. The 23 marble slabs of the cella frieze were bought by the British Government for £19,000 for the British Museum. In 1902–06 the Greek Archae-ological Society replaced some fallen column fragments and restored the cella walls. Additional fragments of the frieze were unearthed in 1961. The foundations have been shown to incorporate reused blocks from an Archaic predecessor on the same site. Some of its terracotta decoration has been found (antefixes and disk acroteria). Another Archaic building immediately to the S was originally thought to be the earlier temple.

The Classical temple is a Doric peripteral hexastyle, 38.3m long and 14.6m wide, longer, therefore, by about one fifth and fractionally wider than the Hephaisteion in Athens. The orientation is unusual, being N and S. The **peristyle**, 6 columns by 15, on a stylobate of three steps, is complete but for the SE corner column. Most of the architrave blocks are in position, but nothing of the pediments or the roof. The pediments were prepared for sculptured groups which Dinsmoor concludes were taken off in ancient times to Rome: the roof-tiles were of Parian marble. The colonnade had a coffered ceiling of different patterns.

The **interior** has the conventional pronaos, cella, and opisthodomos, but the arrangement is unusual. The **pronaos**, 5.5m long, had two columns between antae. It was decorated with a metope frieze, now in a very fragmentary state. A metal barrier, with gates, shut it off from the colonnade. A door led into the cella. The **opisthodomos**, 4.1m long, was similarly distyle in antis, open to the colonnade, but cut off by a wall from the cella. The **cella**, 16.8m long and 7m wide was in two parts. The N section, 12.2m long, had on each side a series of five half-columns engaged in buttresses that projected from the side wall, the first four pairs at right angles and the fifth pair (at the S end) diagonally inward. The half-columns are most unusually located not opposite the peristyle columns but between the intercolumniations. They had bell-shaped bases, resting on a step, 10cm high, and volutes on three faces of the Ionic capitals. The fifth pair had between them, a single Corinthian column, in marble, with 20 flutes. Its capital, now lost, is recorded as having acanthus decoration, and thus formed the earliest example of the Corinthian order yet known to us. A recent theory suggests that the Corinthian column in this curious position was in fact an aniconic representation of the deity and there was no other cult statue (no sign of base), in spite of the comments of Pausanias (see below). The height of the interior colonnade (6.3m) is greater by a foot than that of the peristyle. It supported an Ionic entablature with a frieze, richly carved in island marble and depicting the battles between Greeks and Amazons, and between Lapiths and Centaurs.

The inner **adyton**, occupying the remaining 4.6m of the cella, is also of unusual design, with a door on the left (E side). This fact prompted speculation as to whether a cult statue stood against its W wall, and whether the plan follows that of an earlier sanctuary on the site. Pausanias records that the figure of Apollo in bronze was transferred in 369 BC to the agora at Megalopolis and replaced by an acrolithic statue.

As well as the traces of an earlier Archaic temple (tiles, acroteria) votive offerings have been recovered back to Geometric times. Buildings over a wide area, especially to the N of the Classical temple, indicate that the sanctuary contained a variety of buildings and there was probably an adjacent settlement.

TO ANCIENT PHIGALEIA (AND FIGÁLIA) AND THE GORGE OF THE NÉDHA. From Bassae a road, sometimes unsurfaced before Kato Figalia, descends past (8km) Dhragóni to (11km) **Perivólia** where there are remains of a Doric temple.

A left turn in the village leads in 3kms to **Ano Figália**, which is situated within the fortifications of ancient *Phigaleia*, an Arcadian city on the borders of Elis and Messenia, which had a reputation for wizardry, witchcraft, and drunkenness. Its walls and towers occupy a high and uneven plateau, with precipitous sides, surrounded by mountains. On the S the Nedha flows far below. The antiquities on this attractive site are scattered. A sign on the edge of the village (fork right) indicates a path in the direction of **Platánia**. A short distance along this are the most accessible parts of the fortifications. Near the fork, cut by the road, are the remains of a stoa. Through the village (left fork and down hill) are the impressive remains of a **fountain house** (draw basin and columned façade) of the 4–3C BC. The church in the cemetery (above), with ancient columns, is 11C and has frescoes. A kouros from the site is in the Olympia Museum.

The main road continues from Perivolia to (25km) **Petrálona**, from which an occasional bus goes down via (34km) **Káto Figália** and Lépreon (see Rte 34D) to (49km) Figália station on the coast. Alternatively, for those on foot, a difficult but rewarding walk (preferably with a guide from Ano Figalia) follows the track into the spectacular Gorge of the Nedha to Aspro Neró, a superb *waterfall. Ancient ship-sheds were discovered lower down the river in 1972.

Beyond Andrítsaina the road, good with a few indifferent patches, runs through quiet, attractive and often wooded countryside, later with tremendous views across the Alpheios Valley towards the N heights of the Peloponnese. All along this route, which must duplicate the course of an ancient way from Olympia towards Sparta, are remains of Classical places, mostly unexcavated, seldom visited, and often not certainly identified (comp. E. Meyer: '*Neue Peloponnesische Wanderungen*', Berne, 1957). The realigned road bypasses some of the villages. 46.5km There is a turn (right) for **Sékoulas** (13km) beyond which a bridge over the Alpheios and some indifferent though passable roads give access to the N (the junction with the Tripolis to Olympia road is about 36km away). 50.5km **Míloi** (or Makhalás) lies to the right of the road. Most villages in Arkadia have a Slav or Albanian name and a readopted Greek one. Shortly after, the road swings round to the right, with a branch to Fanári (3km left). 52km Turn (right) for Sekoulas and Alifeira (see below). At the entry to (55.5km) **Káto Amygdhaliés** is another turn to Alífira (4km, right).

On this branch (dirt) after 3km is (300m left) the hospitable **Moní Sepetoú** (nuns) built against the rock face in an appealing modern style, though the original foundation is attributed by some to the 12C. 4km **Alífira**. On the edge of the village you can turn right (sign for 'Archaia Alipheira' and Miloi) for Kastro tis Dhrosítsas, where A.K. Orlandos excavated in 1932–35 (and published in 1968) the site of ancient *Alipheira*. After a short distance another sign (right) points up a track passable for 500m. The site is 20 minutes walk further up the hill and is accessible by various footpaths. Keep right at the top of the track. The buildings are laid out on a series of surprisingly large terraces. You reach first a **Sanctuary of Asklepios** (late 4C) whose small temple has an altar and statue base: a square stylobate with column fragments opposite is the remains of the peristyle court of an associated building. From the terrace immediately above are broad views both N and S. Beyond a further terrace to the E are a section of the **wall** defending the acropolis, and a tower. On the furthest terrace, at a slightly lower level, are the foundations of a Doric **Temple of Athena** (6 by 15 columns; built mid 6C), also an altar and monumental base. From the top of the track where you approached the side, another path (left) partly follows the line of the N fortifications but a good tower on this side is best seen from above. Returning to the Miloi road and turning right, after 1.4km to the right of the road is a predimented **funerary shrine** inscribed ΚΑΛΛΙΕΡΑ ΧΑΙΡΕ. Another (?), less well-preserved, is close by and both must lie on the course of an ancient route. Returning and continuing through Alifira itself, a friendly hamlet. The **Alpheios Bridge** can be reached via Dhafnoúla (passable dirt road).

57.5km The road reaches a high point with fine views N. The Moní Sepetoú is visible across a ravine. The slopes are clad in pines. 59km **Keramídhi** is 1km to the right of the road.

60km **Kallithéa** (or Zákha), a village of 1191 inhabitants, stands at 550m barely 4km S of the confluence of the Ladon with the Alpheios (Rte 36). Its situation suits the name ('Beautiful View'). You turn SW and wind down to (67km) **Barakítika**. Below the village you cross the river Temberoula. From the climb on the other side can be seen an Ottoman bridge over the river. 68km. A turn right leads to (4km) **Tripití** (or Bitzibárdi) (perhaps ancient *Stllangion*, with a Classical acropolis at Kastro). 1km through the village are the impressive remains (called locally 'To Paláti') of the Gothic **monastery of Notre Dame d'Issova**, built by the Franks and burnt by the Byzantines in 1264 (see Traquair in *Journal of the Royal Institute of British Architects* 31 (1923–24)). The smaller church of St Nicholas to the S is the successor of the original.

69km **Plátiana** is just off to the left. The hill behind the village (climbed by a dirt road leading eventually to Zakharo on the coast) is crowned by the walls of ancient *Typaneai*, in fine regular isodomic masonry (? 3C BC). Their perimeter encloses a narrow ridge, 594m long, rising at its W end to 599m. Within are remains of a theatre (withh stone throne), cisterns, two Christian churches, etc. Cars can be taken nearly 4km up the Zakharo road (keep left above the village) and parked near two wayside shrines. From here the site (the interior reasonably accessible) is 20 minutes' walk further up the track and 5 minutes up a steep footpath. About 1km farther E (on an extension of the Typaneai ridge) are some medieval ruins (Paliakumba) of *Cumba* a Frankish castle held in 1364 by Marie de Bourbon, widow of Robert of Taranto. 75km Turn for **Dhiásella** (3km right) whose old village like many in the area has been rebuilt on an adjacent site after the earthquake of 1965. It was the setting for a delightful prizewinning film (*The Flea*, D. Spirou, 1990). 79km **Grékas** lies to the left. A hill (left), above two wayside shrines is known as Kástro. Crowned now by a church of Ay. Konstandinos, it is identified with ancient *Hypana*. Another local site may be that of Homeric *Aipion*. 81km **Grillos** (formerly Múndriza). The landscape is gentle and oleanders plentiful. 84km By-road (right; 5km) for **Skilloúndia** (or Mázi). Here is the site of ancient *Skillus*. The stylobate of a Doric **temple** was proposed by Yalouris (1954) to be that of *Athena Skillountia* mentioned by Strabo, rather than that known to have been erected at the cost of the exiled Xenophon on his estate here c 444–434 BC. Recent work by I. Triandi has clarified the character of the temple (peripteral, internal colonnade) and revealed another substantial building, as well as a fortification wall and tower; also fragments of pedimental sculptures.

The main road now bypasses (86km) **Kréstena** (Hotel C), a large village (5422 inhab.) with a regular bus service to/from Pirgos. 88.5km A good road leads via Makrísia and over (8km) the Alpheios barrage to Olympia (14.5km).

1.5km before Olympia, the road passes through Flóka, to the NW of which, at **Panoúkla**, an extensive Roman **bath complex** of the 3C AD was discovered in 1972.

The route soon joins the Kiparissía–Pírgos road. Hence to (110km) **Pírgos**, see Rte 34D.

# 36

## Trípolis to Olympia (Olimbía) and Pírgos

**Road**, 156km (96½ miles). A well-engineered modern road with spectacular mountain scenery, the central section narrow and difficult driving; 3 buses daily in 4 hours.—9.5km Turning for Mantinea (see Rte 30).—26km Levídhi.—35km Turning for Kalávrita and Patras (Rte 39A).—46km Vitína.—60km Karkaloú, turning for (13km) Dhimitsána.—72km Langádhia.—86km Stavrodhrómi.—132km Olympia.—153km Pírgos.

**Railway** from Olympia to Pyrgos, 4–5 times daily in 30 minutes.

From Tripolis to (9.5km) the Mantinea turn, see Rte 30. The road follows the W side of the Plain of Mantinea close beneath the foothills of Mainalon, whose triangular summit appears at first to block the broad valley ahead. Beyond (14.5km) **Kápsas** (460 inhab.) a defile leads to the small diamond-shaped Plain of Alkimedon, immediately below the towering Mt Ostrakina (1981m), topmost peak of Mainalon. A road (18.5km; left) skirts its S side to Alonístaina (11km; Rte 30), with winter sports. Farther on, a gap (right) affords a glimpse of (22.5km) Simiádhes at the N end of the Plain of Mantinea. From the top of the next long rise you can see, crowning the next hills, the campanile of (26km) **Levídhi** (Hotel D; 1142 inhab.), native town of Alex. Papanastasiou (1879–1936), republican statesman and prime minister in 1924. A chapel of the Panayia on a low hill to the E is supposed to mark the site of the sanctuary of Artemis-Hymnia, common to the peoples of Mantinea and Orchomenos. Just beyond the town the road commands a wide view across the plain of Orchomenos (magnificently backed by the Chelmos range), into which a by-road drops abruptly towards **Kandhíla** and Arkadian *Orchomenós* (5km; Rte 26).

32km **Vlakhérna** (1000m). Khotoússa, in the valley to the N (45 minutes), stands close to the scanty remains of Hellenistic and Roman *Caphyae*: an Early Christian basilica overlies a Doric temple. At 34.5km the road to Patras (Rte 39) drops away in a valley (right) as our route climbs round the N end of the Mainalon range; the village of **Kamenítsa** is seen far below: in its valley the hill of Ay. Sotira may be the site of ancient *Torthyneion*, while Sakovoúni is a prehistoric site. 46km **Vitína** (Βύτινα; Hotels A, B, C; camping), an attractive summer resort (824 inhab.), stands in a cool and healthy upland situation (1040m) amid fir-clad slopes. It has a School of Forestry and a tradition of woodcarving. The town was Kolokotronis' supply-base. The road twists through sharp outcrops of rock. 50km. On a hill to the S are the scanty remains of *Methydrion*, a town sacrificed in the building of Megalopolis. 53km Turning to Magouli  aná (4km right) and Valtesiníko (13km).

**Magouliná**, birthplace of Theodore Kolokotronis, the klepht hero of the War of Independence, was a summer residence of the Villehardouin—hence the ruined Frankish fortress (*Argirókastro*). **Valtesiníko** lies just E of the site of ancient *Glanitsa*, where the French School found a late-Archaic bronze head in 1939. Tracks go on through the mountains and across the Ladon to Dhafni (Rte 39).

Approaching (60km) **Karkaloú** the road descends through pine-woods, with the pleasantly situated Xenia Motel (B), passing a campsite (left) with a memorial bust in bronze of Dhimitri Mitropoulos (1896–1960), the conductor, by Apartis. There are some polygonal walls near the village.

From Karkaloú a road leads (left; 8km) to **Dhimitsána** (Δημητσάνα; Hotel C), an attractive village (739 inhab.) in a magnificent situation above the Lousios, on the site of ancient *Teuthis*. A piece of ancient wall forming part of a modern house can be seen just below the more westerly of the two main churches. Some Classical walls also survive, but medieval building predominates. Dhimitsána became a centre of Greek learning after 1764, when its school was founded, and hence of opposition to the Turks; the Patriarch Gregory V and Germanos, Archbishop of Patras, were both pupils. It became a centre of activity of the Philike Etairia, and an arsenal for the War of Independence with 14 powder factories. The museum, archives, and library are worth visiting. The **Moní Filosófou** was founded in 963 but not on its present site, 2.5km SE, below Zigovisti.

The road continues to (18km) **Stemnítsa** (Στεμνίτσα; Hotel C; 495 inhab.), a beautiful mountain village (1076m) formerly known as Ipsoúnda, grandly situated against the side of Mt Klinítsa (1548m). The kastro incorporates several little churches: Ayíou

Nikoláou was repaired in 1589; the Panayía Baféro dates probably from 1640. There is a **Folk Museum**.

Beyond Stemnitsa the road forks, right for Karitaina and Megalópolis; left for (62km) **Trípolis** via Daviá (Rte 30). Off this road, at **Lipovítsi** is the Kolokotronis family home.

The road winds through rocky gorges in an increasingly barren landscape to a summit of nearly 1220m, clothed in ferns, then crosses the infant Lousios. 72km **Langádhia** (Λαγκάδια; Hotels C), native town (671 inhab.) of the Deliyianni family, appears ahead tumbling vertically down an outcrop of rock above the valley. The road winds sharply downwards to the centre of the village, where a little plateia (café) forms a superb *belvedere.

The long descent continues as the tortuous road follows a vertiginous shelf of rock a thousand feet above the gorge. Beyond (79km) **Lefkokhóri** it crosses a side valley and, surmounting a ridge, reaches the upland village of (86km) **Stavrodhrómi**.

Here a by-road (right) leads to **Trópaia** (4km; Hotel E), an attractive mountain village. About 3km E of Trópaia (turn right by sign at entrance to village) are three towers of the Frankish castle of the barony of *Akova*; and two hours W some remains of Classical *Thelpousa*, another site investigated by the French School in 1939, which had a huge 4C agora. In Tropaia the road hairpins right and continues to (10.5km) the *Ladon Dam* (Frágma Ládhonos; Φράγμα Λάδωνος), 100.5m long and c 53m high, which has formed a lake, ringed by pine trees, in the upper valley. The waters are fed to hydro-electric works, near the village of Spáthari (see below) to the W, by a tunnel, 8km long, through a mountain. It is possible to continue N round the reservoir to join the Patras road, via Dhafní (Rte 39B).

The mountains give way to rolling hills on the descent to the broad valley of the Ladon, most copious of the seven important tributaries of the Alpheios until its reduction by damming (see above). 96km Turning (right; 6km) to the hydro-electric station. Crossing the river, the road descends the right bank. Beyond (97km) **Bertsiá**, with its charming wooded stream, it climbs a ridge commanding the confluence of the Ladon and the Alpheios, where Pausanias' 'Isle of Crows' is visible. On the way up a by-road returns to the left bank of the Ladon to **Loutrá Iraías** (for Dhafnoula, Andritsaina, etc., see Rte 35), S of which, near Ay. Ioannis on the bank of the Alpheios, some remains of ancient *Heraia* were identified by the Greek Archaeological Service in 1931. A sharp hill and (113km) the Yéfira Koklamá, a concrete bridge, take us across the Erímanthos and into Elis (see Rte 40). 119km Vasiláki (400m) occupies the summit of the ridge of Sauros, a highwayman killed by Herakles. The road descends amid lush vegetation to the wide bed of the Alpheios. 124km **Mouriá**.

The Alpheios or Alfios, the largest river in the Peloponnese, rises in south-east Arkadia, close to the source of the Eurotas and flows through Arkadia and Elis, past Olympia, into the Ionian Sea. Pausanias describes it as 'a broad and noble stream, fed by seven important rivers'. These are the Helisson, Brentheates, Gortynios, Bouphagos, Ladon, Erimanthos, and Kladeos. The Peloponnesians regard the Ladon as the main stream, calling the Alfios proper the Karitaina above the confluence. In the early part of its course this runs underground. According to legend the river-god Alpheios fell in love with the nymph Arethusa. Spurning his advances she fled to Ortygia, an island off Syracuse in Sicily, and was there changed into a fountain, whereupon Alpheios flowed under the sea to join her. Shelley, celebrating the legend, calls the river a 'brackish, Dorian stream'. It was the favourite river of Zeus, and on its banks first grew the wild olive, a garland of which was the reward of victors in the Olympic Games.

129km **Miráka** (on a by-road; right), with Mycenaean tombs, is 15 minutes S of the site of ancient *Pisa*. This is on the road from Kalávrita via Lálas (Rte 39). Approaching (132km) **Olympía** (Ολυμπία; pron. Olimbía; Hotels A, B,

C, D) we see (right) the spacious International Olympic Academy, inaugurated in 1961 with the object of maintaining and promoting the Olympic spirit. Annual summer courses are held. Immediately after this (right) is a stele enclosing the heart of Pierre de Coubertin (1862–1937), who revived the games. The road passes between Mt Kronon and the excavations (left; see Rte 37), cross the Kladeos, and turn into the village, 1742 inhabitants.

**Railway Station**, 500m W of the village; 4–5 trains daily to Pirgos, for Athens etc.

**Youth hostel**.

**Buses** to Athens via Pirgos and Patras.

137km **Plátanos**. Most of the villages stand on low hills between successive small tributaries of the Alpheios, and are surrounded by orchards. Broúma, on the right beyond (139km) **Pelópio** (or Broúma), occupies the site of *Herakleia*, which once had curative springs. 146km The Eripeus, now called Lestenitza, was the scene of the myth of Poseidon and Tyro. 153km **Pírgos**, see Rte 40.

# 37

# Olympia

Approaches and hotels, etc., see above Rte 36 (end).

**OLYMPIA**, in Greek *Olimbía* (Ολυμπία; 43m) is situated in the quietly beautiful valley of the Alpheios in the territory of Pisatis, at its confluence with the Kladeos. The setting, in great contrast with most Greek sites, is pastoral, green, and lush; the ancient remains shaded by evergreen oaks, Aleppo pines, planes, and poplars, as well as olive-trees. The Kladeos bounds the site on the W and the Alpheios on the S, while to the N rises the conical Mt Kronos (123m). Olympia was not a city, but a sacred precinct occupied exclusively by temples, dwellings for the priests and officials, and public buildings in connection with the Games, and it became a sanctuary in which were concentrated many of the choicest treasures of Greek art. In the centre was the enclosure known as the **Altis**, dedicated to Zeus, in whose honour were held the quadrennial festival and the games. The best view of the site is from Mt Dhroúva above the SPAP hotel, which is also a good area for walks for those who wish to escape the now somewhat garish village.

The fame of Olympia rests upon the Olympic Games. Whatever may have been their origin, they remained until degraded by specialisation and professionalism a great national festival. A striking feature of the festival was the proclamation of the *Ekecheiria*, or Olympic Truce; still more surprising was its almost universal observance, sufficient witness in itself to the high prestige of the Olympic festival. During the week of the celebrations the competitors, while not forgetting that they were Athenians, Spartans, Milesians, Syracusans, or whatever, remembered that they were Greeks, and an Olympic victory was regarded as the highest possible honour. The simple reward of a crown of wild olive not only immortalised the victor and his family, but redounded to the glory of his native city.

The Greeks came to use the Olympiads, or periods of four years between festivals, as the basis of their chronology. The Games were held regularly in peace and in war for over 1000 years from 776 BC until their suppression in AD 393. From the first Olympiad to the time of Hadrian the embellishment of Olympia never ceased. The vitality of the festivals is reflected in the architecture and works of art that have survived.

**History**. Excavations since 1959 have shown that *Olympia* was already flourishing in Mycenaean times. The legendary foundation of the Games and the elaborated later traditions may be found recorded by Pausanias (Bk V). Homer does not mention them and the official era of the Olympiads started in 776 BC. The conduct of the games seems at first to have been disputed between *Pisa* and *Elis* and ancient authorities differ widely as to the date when the Eleans finally prevailed (between 572 and 471 BC).

Despite the vicissitudes of fortune and of war, the Olympic Games were held with the utmost regularity, the wealth of the various sanctuaries steadily accumulated, and the prestige of Olympia increased, reaching its zenith in the 5C BC. The Olympic Truce was strictly observed, with one or two exceptions. In 420 BC the Lacedaemonians were excluded from the festival on the ground of truce-breaking (Thuc. V, 49). In 364 BC, during the invasion of the Pisans and Arcadians, a battle was fought in the Altis in the presence of the crowd that had come to watch the games.

After the age of Hadrian Olympia ceased to have much religious or political significance, but was visited for sentimental reasons or out of curiosity. The games were, however, kept up until AD 393, when the edict of Theodosius I, prohibiting all pagan festivals, brought an end. In 426 Theodosius II ordered the destruction of the temples and the Altis was burnt. Soon afterwards the ruins were quarried to transform the Workshop of Pheidias into a Christian church and to build a fortification against the Vandals. In 522 and 551 the ruins were devastated anew by earthquakes, the Temple of Zeus being partially buried, while a landslip from Mt Kronos destroyed the buildings at its foot. A new settlement was swept away when the Kladeos overflowed and buried all the buildings on the W side of the precinct deep in sand and mud. Further landslips on Mt Kronos occurred and the Alpheios, changing its bed, carried away the hippodrome and part of the stadium, thus completing the ruin of Olympia, which for centuries remained an uninhabited waste covered with a layer of debris 3–3.75m deep.

The first modern traveller to visit Olympia was Dr Chandler, in 1766, though as early as 1713 Montfaucon had suggested excavation. In 1768 Winckelmann planned a restoration of Olympia. In 1811 Stanhope had a plan made of the site. A French expedition of 1829 partially excavated the Temple of Zeus. In 1852 Prof. E. Curtius revived the plan of Winckelmann for the excavation of Olympia and interested the German royal family in the project. At last, in 1874, a convention with Greece was reached, whereby the German government was permitted to carry out excavations. Their work covers three periods: 1875–81, 1936–41, and since 1952. Everything of importance has been housed in the museum, except for some bronzes (now in the National Museum in Athens). The temples of Zeus and Hera have suffered from exposure since they were uncovered.

**Administration**. The Altis proper was reserved for the gods, the dwellings of the priests and officials were in the secondary area outside. The supreme governing body was the **Olympian Senate**, elected from the Elean aristocracy, which met in the bouleuterion. The senate had control of the revenue and the Olympian officials were responsible to it. The magistrates and priests, Eleans of good family, were elected for the period of each Olympiad. They lived in the prytaneion. Though each individual sanctuary had its own staff, a superior hierarchy looked after the administration as a whole and regulated the service of the temples. At its head were three **theokoloi**, or high priests, who lived in the theololeion and dined at the prytaneion. Next were three

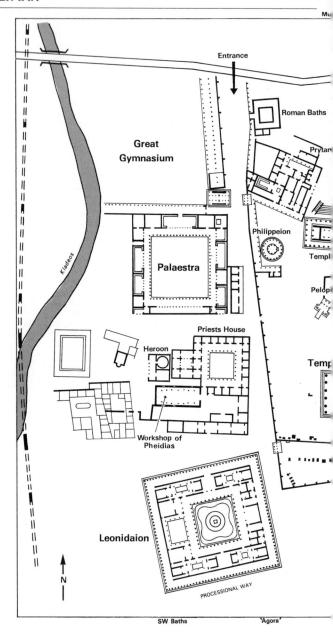

Mu

Entrance

Roman Baths

Prytan

Great
Gymnasium

Philippeion

Templ

Palaestra

Pelopi

Priests House

Heroon

Temp

Workshop of
Pheidias

Leonidaion

N

PROCESSIONAL WAY

Kladeos

SW Baths          'Agora'

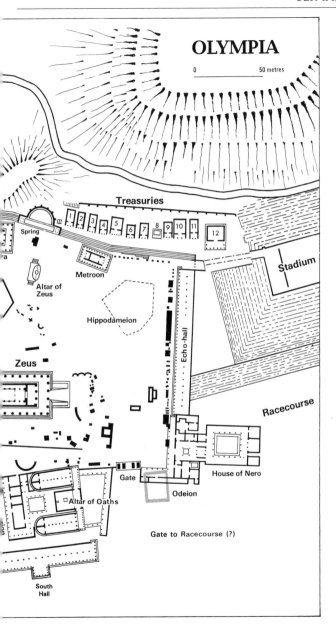

# OLYMPIA

0 _____ 50 metres

Treasuries

Spring

1 2 3 4 5 6 7 8 9 10 11

12

Stadium

Metroon

Altar of
Zeus

Hippodàmeion

Zeus

Echo-hall

Racecourse

House of Nero

Gate

Odeion

Altar of Oaths

Gate to Racecourse (?)

South
Hall

**spondophoroi**, heralds whose duty it was to travel abroad and proclaim the date of the festival and of the Olympic Truce. Finally the two (later four) hereditary **soothsayers** interpreted the oracle. In addition there was a host of minor officials such as the **kathemerothytes**, or priest of the day, the **exegetes** (who doubled the role of master of ceremonies with that of cicerone to visitors), the **epimeletes**, or keeper of the Sanctuary, three **epispondorchestai**, or dancers, a flute-player, an architect, a doctor, a chef for the prytaneion, a wood-cutter (who provided the wood for the altars), etc.

The **Quadrennial Festival**. The most important of all the festivals at Olympia was the **Festival of Zeus**, accompanied by the Olympic Games. It took place at the time of the second (or possibly first) full moon following the summer solstice, i.e. in August or September. A sacred truce fortified by severe sanctions, universally suspended hostilities during the week of the festival, forbade armed forces to enter the confines of Elis, and proclaimed the inviolability of visitors. The special representatives of the various cities and states were publicly entertained, being housed in buildings adjoining the Altis and fed at the Prytaneion. The **theoroi** or special ambassadors from foreign states, were sent at their national expense. The crowd of humbler pilgrims was accommodated in tents, or like the competitors slept in blankets on the ground.

The **Olympic Games**. The direction of the games (ἀγωνοθεσία) was, with certain interruptions, in the hands of the Eleans. Only men and boys who spoke Greek as their mother-tongue were originally allowed to compete; barbarians were admitted as spectators, but slaves were entirely excluded. No married woman might be present, or even cross the Alpheios while the games were going on, under penalty of being hurled from the Typaeon Rock. Later Romans were admitted.

Ten months before the date of the games the Elean magistrates chose a body of ten **hellanodikai**, or umpires, who supervised training and discipline as well as the actual contests. The competitors had to train for the whole ten months, the last month being spent at Elis (see below). A ceremonial procession to Olympia took place just before the festival began. The competitors took the oath at the bouleuterion on the Altar of Zeus Horkeios, swearing that they would loyally observe all the regulations of the games, and involving not only their family but their native town in the penalties consequent on any infraction.

The Eleans kept registers of the winners of the foot-race, the oldest event, after the successive winners of which each Olympiad was named; Plutarch, however, questions both their antiquity and authenticity. To the foot-race were added at intervals other competitive events, most notably the Pentathlon (in which jumping, wrestling, and throwing both spear and discus were combined with running), boxing, chariot-racing and horse racing (the 'hippic' as opposed to gymnastic contests at which tyrants and nobles competed, employing professional charioteers and jockeys), and the Pankration (a form of all-in wrestling). An Athenian took the prize for the first time in 696, and in 688 the inaugural boxing contest was won by a man from Smyrna, the first overseas city to claim an Olympic victor. Southern Italy records its first victory in 672. The Spartans were frequent winners. Events for boys were inaugurated in 632 BC.

The athletic programme was varied by the presence of historians, orators, and sophists, who read their works aloud to the assembled spectators. Herodotus here read extracts from his history. Themistocles attended the 76th Olympiad in celebration of the Persian defeat. The 211th Olympiad was postponed two years to AD 69 to allow Nero to compete and win special musical contests and a chariot-race. The records were later expunged.

After each event a herald announced the victor's name and handed him a palm. On the last day the successful competitors (Olympionikai) were each given a garland of wild olive and entertained in the Prytaneion. A victor had the right of erecting a statue in the Altis, which might represent his own features if he had won three events. By the time of the older Pliny the statues had accumulated to the number of 3000. On returning home, the victor was publicly entertained and a lyric composition was recited in his honour. Fourteen of Pindar's odes celebrate Olympionikai.

In 1896 a quadrennial international athletic festival, taking the name of the **Olympic Games**, had its inception at the stadium in Athens, when a Greek won the 'marathon'. The Games are held successively in different countries. There is no modern *ekecheiria* and the First World War prevented their celebration in 1916, as did the Second in 1940 and 1944. King Constantine II of the Hellenes (when Crown Prince) won a gold medal at the 1960 Games, held in Italy.

To reach the ancient site from the village you take the Tripolis road, pass the old museum (now closed), prominent on a hill (right), cross the Kladeos, and see (right) the entrance to the **excavations** (best guide, available at site, A. Mallwitz, *Olympia und seine Bauten*, repr. 1981, in German; shorter—A. and N. Yalouris, *Olympia. The museum and the sanctuary*, 1987, English etc). You visit first the large buildings that lie outside the Altis to the W.

On the right, immediately beyond the entrance, some remains parallel to the path mark the **xystos**, or covered running track (an Olympic stade long), which formed the E wing of the **gymnasion**, a large quadrangle extending to the Kladeos. Its propylon (? 1C BC) consisted of a Corinthian portico raised on three steps. Some capitals survive. Adjacent on the S is the **palaestra**, often called a 'wrestling school' but in fact a place for meetings and social intercourse, as well as for athletic practice of various kinds. It corresponds closely with Vitruvius' description of such a building. An open court, 41m square, is surrounded by a Doric colonnade with 19 columns on each side. Behind the colonnade, on three sides, were rooms of various sizes, entered through Ionic porches or through plain doorways. Some of them retain ancient stone benches set against the wall. On the S side the colonnade was divided into two long corridors by an inner row of 15 Ionic columns. The main entrances were at the E and W ends of the S side, through porches of two Corinthian columns *in antis*. The capitals are of unusual design, with parallels in Pompeii and Asia Minor rather than in Greece. The style generally suggests a date in the 3C BC.

A water channel, entering the palaestra at its NE corner, ran round its four sides. In the N part of the court is a pavement of grooved and plain tiles, 25m by 5.5m; its object is unknown. From the central room in the N colonnade a plain doorway gave access to the gymnasium.

To the S lies the **Theokoleion**, the official residence of the priests. The ruins belong to three periods. The original Greek structure (c 350 BC) consisted of eight rooms round a central court and covered an area 18m square. The foundations and pavement are well preserved. In the court is an ancient well lined with blocks of sandstone. Later three rooms were added on the E side and a large garden court, with cloisters and rooms, was constructed. The Romans took down the E half of the extended Greek building and enlarged the garden court. A colonnade was built round it, with 8 columns on each side.

To the W is a small round **heroön**, c 8m in diameter, enclosed within a square. The lower blocks of the circular wall are well preserved; the upper courses were probably of mud brick. Within was found an altar of earth and ashes, coated with stucco.

Adjacent on the S side is a Classical building, the sandstone walls of which are still standing to a height of 1.8m with later brickwork above. In its later form it was a **Byzantine church** divided by columns into nave and aisles with an apse on the E and a narthex on the W. Near the E end is a ruined ambo (left) with two flights of three steps, and, beyond it, a perforated marble screen of Byzantine workmanship. The original building was none other than the **Workshop of Pheidias**, described by Pausanias. This has been confirmed archaeologically by the discovery of tools and terracotta moulds used in the manufacture of the great chryselephantine statue of Zeus, and finally in 1958 by a cup bearing Pheidias' name. The building has the same measurements as the cella of the temple and a similar orientation; it probably also had a similar internal structure, being divided into two compartments with galleries supported on columns.

A long narrow building, to the S, divided by crosswalls into small rooms, is believed to have sheltered his working technicians.

To the W (not accessible) remains of Roman **baths** overlie baths of the Archaic period, near the bank of the Kladeos, together with part of a **swimming pool** of the 5C BC. This was 23m long and 1.5m deep. In the same area (S) was a Roman **guesthouse**.

Farther S, built at a slightly different angle, is the **Leonidaion**, erected by Leonidas the son of Leontas of Naxos in the 4C BC, possibly as a hostel for distinguished visitors, and adapted in the 2C AD as a residence for the Roman governor of Achaia. It stands at the crossing of the roads from Arcadia and Elis outside the processional entrance to the Altis. As originally built it had an open court, 30m square, surrounded by Doric colonnades of 12 columns per side, off which rooms opened on all four sides. The main entrance was on the S side, principal rooms on the W. Outside ran a continuous colonnade of 138 Ionic columns, the bases of which are almost all *in situ*, together with many of the capitals. Their bases and capitals were of sandstone, the shafts of shell-limestone; the whole was covered with stucco. In Roman times the rooms were remodelled, and an ornamental garden with elaborate ponds was laid out in the middle of the court. Many fragments of the colonnades were found built into the Byzantine wall (see below) and these, especially those from the terracotta cornice, show great richness of decoration.

Recent research suggests that the main (S) entrance to the Leonidaion opened on to the processional approach to the sanctuary which presumably crossed the Kladeos by a bridge. The outer boundary of the whole sanctuary complex (including the secondary area) would have been defined at the W by the retaining wall by the river. On the other side of this route, opposite the Leonidaion, an imposing **Roman building** (2C AD but some earlier construction), formerly thought to be baths (the 'southwest baths') now seems to have had a ceremonial function, with its main entrance facing the roadway. Across the court behind the N façade a doorway is surrounded by three statue niches and fronted by a swimming pool. The courtyard has an ambulatory.

Immediately W of the SW corner of the Leonidaion the so-called **spolien-haus** is probably an Early Christian structure and incorporated architectural elements from several earlier buildings in the sanctuary.

The **Altis**, or sacred precinct of Zeus, acquired its name from a corruption of the Greek word ἄλσος meaning 'Sacred Grove'. On the N it was bounded by Mt Kronos and on the other three sides by walls, the lines of which can still be traced. On the W side are remains of two parallel walls, the inner one Greek and the outer one Roman. The S wall is Roman. The original S wall, now called the South Terrace Wall, was more to the N, the Altis having been enlarged about the time of Nero. The Greek walls seem to have been merely low stone parapets and the inner precinct was probably not fully enclosed by high boundary walls until the Roman period. Within were the Temple of Zeus, the Heraion and the small Metroön, besides the Pelopion, or shrine of Pelops, and innumerable altars to Zeus and other divinities. Much of the remaining space was taken up by statues of Olympic victors and other dedications.

Entering the precinct by the **processional entrance**, a small triple opening with an external porch of four columns, we see on the right a row of large oblong pedestals, mostly belonging to equestrian statues. On the left are two pedestals bearing respectively the names of *Philonides*, courier of Alexander the Great (Paus. VI, 16, 8) and of *Sophocles*, the sculptor. Turning to the right you pass on the right a wilderness of scattered remains recovered from the Byzantine wall, but originally forming part of the Leonidaion, bouleuterion, and many other buildings. Passing between the remains of two unidentified Greek buildings with several small partitions, you reach the bouleuterion.

The **bouleuterion**, or Council House, seat of the Olympic Senate, consists of a square hall flanked N and S by larger wings of practically equal size and plan. The building was completely detached from the Altis. On its southward extension, the new S wall of the precinct was in line with the northernmost wall of the bouleuterion, which was provided with a special gateway of its own. Each wing consisted of an oblong hall with a central row of seven Doric (?) columns on separate foundations and a cross-wall cutting off its apse. Each apse was divided into two by a central wall. A triglyph frieze appears to have decorated the exteriors of the wings, whose appearance was further enhanced by the two-stepped basements on which they were raised. On the E side each wing ended in a screen of three Doric columns *in antis*. A spacious Ionic portico ran along the whole length of the E façade, providing the only means of communication between the three parts of the building. This portico had 27 columns on its front and three on each of the narrow sides; only three drums are *in situ*. The N and S wings are of the Archaic period; the central hall and the E colonnade were constructed between 373 and 364 BC.

The **central hall**, which is much later than the wings and may be contemporary with the Ionic colonnade (3C BC), appears to have had columns on its E side and blank walls without doors on the other three. A foundation in the middle may have supported the **Statue of Zeus Horkeios**, beside which competitors, their relatives, and their trainers swore that they would be guilty of no foul play in the games. At an earlier date this would have been open to the sky. Of the **N wing**, the oldest part of the building (6C BC), very little except foundations is left. The **S wing** (5C) is the best preserved. The drums of the columns of the Doric porch are still standing; the outer walls are one or two courses high; and some drums of the seven interior columns are *in situ*. The S wing differs from the N wing in that its long walls are not straight but form with the apse an elliptical shape recalling ancient structures at Sparta and Thermon: it may have been rebuilt on old foundations. In front of the connecting portico is an irregular colonnaded court of Roman date, usually called the **Trapezium Court**.

To the E of the bouleuterion, recent work (inaccessible) has identified a system of ditches which probably represent temporary defences erected by the Arcadians in the course of the battle fought in the sanctuary during the 104th Olympiad (see above). In this area have also been found a Roman **odeion** and the foundations of a gate, which may have been a minor entrance to the **hippodrome** (see below).

To the S of the bouleuterion is the **southern stoa**, over 78m long, built of tufa and raised on three limestone steps. Gardiner conjecturally identifies this colonnade with the **proedria** and assigns it to the 3C BC. It was closed on the N by a wall, with a narrow passage-way at either end. The other sides were open and had Doric columns. Within it was divided longitudinally (probably in Roman times) by a central row of sandstone Corinthian columns. The Byzantines used the stoa as the S wall of their fort.

To the S of the Leonidaion is assumed to have lain an **agora**, where temporary booths would have been erected at festival times. Pausanias mentions statues of deities with the epithet '*agoraios*'. There were no permanent buildings or statues here, at least in

Hellenistic and Roman times. The whole of the S part of Olympia is being investigated as part of a project designed to clarify the history of the sanctuary in the Roman Imperial period.

The *Temple of Zeus, dedicated to the sovereign god of Olympia, is the most important temple in the Altis and one of the largest in mainland Greece. It was built from the spoils of Pisa, after its sack by the Eleans c 470 BC, and completed before 456, when an inscribed block (quoted by Pausanias and since found) was let into the E gable to support a gold shield dedicated by the Spartans in commemoration of their victory at Tanagra. The architect was *Libon* of Elis. After an earthquake c 175 BC both façades were dismantled and rebuilt and three of the W pedimental statues replaced. In the early 6C AD the building was completely shattered by earthquakes.

The building, which is a Doric peripteral hexastyle, stands on a crepidoma of three unequal steps, itself borne on a massive platform. The foundations, which are of shell-limestone with inter-spaces filled with earth, are complete. They were sunk 90cm deep in the soil and rose 3.1m above its natural level. An embankment was raised all round, giving the appearance of an artificial hillock. Access was by a ramp at the E end. The **stylobate** is made of huge stone blocks averaging 2.6m in width. Its length, measured on the top step, seems to have been exactly 200 Olympic feet. There is no evidence of optical curvature such as distinguishes the Parthenon, though it has now been established that the columns had *entasis*.

EXTERIOR. The **peristyle** had six columns at either end and 13 at the sides; these also were made of shell-limestone, but covered with fine white stucco to give the appearance of marble. Their height was twice the axial spacing. Each of them had the usual 20 flutes and three incised rings round the neck. The echinus of the capitals was similar in outline to those of the Temple of Aphaia on Aegina. Apart from one or two drums in their original positions, none of the columns is standing. On the S side they lie as thrown down by the earthquake of the 6C.

Fragments of the entablature lie around. Above the architrave a frieze of triglyphs and plain metopes ran all round the peristyle; 21 gilded shields dedicated by Mummius in 142 BC to commemorate his destruction of Corinth were placed on the 10 metopes of the E front and on the adjacent metopes on the S side. The marks of attachment can still be seen.

The two pediments were filled with sculptured groups in Parian marble: on the **E pediment** the preparations for the chariot race between Pelops and Oinomaos; on the **W pediment** the battle of the Lapiths and Centaurs at the wedding of Peirithoös. Pausanias attributed these to Alkamenes and Paionios (see J.P. Barron in Bulletin of the Institute of Classical Studies, London University, 1984). The surviving sculptures are in the museum (see below). At the apex of the E pediment was the gold shield dedicated by the Spartans (see above), crowned sometime later by a gilt bronze Victory, by Paionios. The corner-acroteria were in the form of gilded bronze tripods.

The roof was of marble tiles, many of which are preserved in the pelopion. The earliest tiles are of Parian marble, the later ones (replacements of the Augustan period) of Pentelic. There was a continuous marble sima interrupted by 102 lion's head water-spouts, of which 39 survive (some are crude later replacements). Traces of colour found on the architectural members show that parts of the temple were painted.

The wide ambulatory surrounding the sekos was occupied by bronze statues and votive offerings. The ceiling was of wood. The pavement was of large blocks of conglomerate covered with river pebbles embedded in mortar. This was replaced in Roman times by a mosaic pavement, traces of which remain.

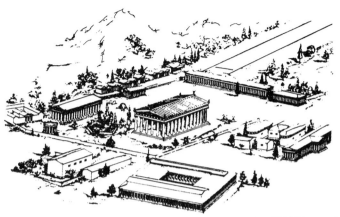

*Olympia. Reconstruction of the Sanctuary of Zeus in c 350 BC, seen from the west*

INTERIOR. The sekos had the usual arrangement of pronaos, cella, and opisthodomos. It was raised one step above the stylobate. The pronaos and opisthodomos each ended in a portico of two Doric columns between antae, surmounted (unusually) by a Doric entablature consisting of an architrave and triglyph frieze. The 12 Parian marble metopes were decorated with sculptures depicting the Labours of Herakles, six at each end. Some were removed by the French expedition of 1829 and are now in the Louvre; the rest are in the museum.

The **pronaos** was closed by three folding bronze doors. On the floor are the remains of the earliest known Greek mosaic (now covered) representing a triton with a boy seated on his tail. Pausanias noticed here the statue of Iphitos being crowned by Ekecheiria (personification of the Olympic Truce). Traces of various bases here indicate the former presence of other statues he mentions. A great door, about 4.9m wide, led into the cella.

The **cella** was 28.7m long and 13.3m wide. It was divided down the middle by two-tiered colonnades of seven Doric columns to form a nave c 6.7m wide. This colonnade supported the wooden ceiling and galleries above the aisles from which the public were allowed to view the image of Zeus. The only light came from the doorway.

The nave was divided laterally into four sections. The first formed a kind of vestibule (open to the public) extended to the second column. On either side, by the first column, was a wooden staircase leading to the galleries. The next two sections were forbidden to the public. The second, closed by a barrier, extended to the base of the statue, and had side screens made of slabs of conglomerate to divide it from the aisles. A square, the full width of the nave, was paved with black Eleusinian limestone, bordered with a kerb of Pentelic marble, to form a receptacle for the sacred oil used for anointing the statue. This probably served two purposes, both practical: mirroring light from the doorway and providing oil for the wooden core in order to prevent swelling in the damp climate which might have split the ivory. The third section, from the 5th to beyond the 7th column, is entirely occupied by the base of the statue of Zeus. The fourth section is merely a passage 1.7m wide connecting the two aisles behind the statue.

The similarity in both proportion and decoration with that of the Parthenon makes it certain that the interior arrangement was designed by Pheidias himself. If Pausanias is correct that Pheidias took as model for one of the throne figures the youth Pantarkes, who was victor in the boys' wrestling in 436 BC, the work at Olympia would seem to have been done in 436–432 after the Athena Polias was finished. This has been recently claimed as confirmed by a study of the moulds for the gold drapery, though C.H. Morgan places the Zeus before the Athena (Hesperia, 1952).

The chryselephantine **Statue of Zeus**, the masterpiece of Pheidias, was accounted one of the Seven Wonders of the ancient world.

Apart from one or two Hadrianic coins of Elis, no authenticated copies of the statue exist, and Pausanias alone of ancient writers describes it in detail, and even he devotes more attention to the throne than to the figure. It is believed to have been about seven times life-size or c 12m high. Pausanias, noting that the measurements had been recorded, says that they did not do justice to the impression made by the image on the spectator. Strabo, on the other hand, tells us that the artist is thought to have missed true proportion as the seated god almost touched the roof, giving the impression that if he rose he would knock the roof off. The ancients on the whole, however, concur in praising the extraordinary majesty and beauty of the statue. Cicero (*Orator*, II, 8) says that Pheidias made the image, not after any living model, but after that ideal beauty seen with the inward eye alone.

The **pedestal**, 90cm high, and decorated with gold reliefs of various divinities, was of blue-black Eleusinian stone, fragments of which have been discovered. Zeus was represented seated on a **throne** made of ebony and ivory overlaid with gold and precious stones. The four legs of the throne were adorned with carvings and strutted with stretchers which bore golden reliefs of combatants. Some of the great weight was taken by four pillars underneath, hidden by screens on which were paintings by Panainos, and by the footstool which had golden lions and a relief of Theseus fighting the Amazons. The **figure of Zeus** held in his right hand a chryselephantine **Victory** and in his left a sceptre with an eagle. The undraped parts of the statue—head, feet, hands, and torso—were of ivory. The **robe** was decorated with figures of animals and lilies.

The care of the statue devolved upon the descendants of Pheidias, who were called the 'Burnishers'. By the 2C BC, however, the ivory had cracked and had to be repaired by Damophon of Messene. In the time of Julius Caesar it was struck by lightning. The Emperor Caligula wanted to remove it to Rome and to replace the head of Zeus with his own, but every time his agents came near the statue it burst into a loud peal of laughter. It is believed that after the reign of Theodosius II the statue was carried off to Constantinople, where it perished in a fire in AD 475.

In 167 BC Antiochus IV Epiphanes, King of Syria, dedicated (?) behind the statue, 'A woollen curtain, a product of the gay Assyrian looms and dyed with Phoenician purple' (Paus. V, 12, 4). There are grounds for believing this to have been the veil of the temple at Jerusalem which Antiochus carried off (II Macc. VI, 2).

The **opisthodomos** had no direct communication with the cella. It was reached from the W peristyle and does not appear to have been enclosed by gratings. It had a long stone bench where people used to meet and talk.

In front of the entrance ramp to the temple are some interesting pedestals of statues detailed by Pausanias. The statues were built into the Byzantine wall (see below).

It was the custom to erect in front of the E façade of the temple the statues of the Olympionikai and the chariots dedicated by them. The latter included the **Chariot of Gelo**, by Glaukias of Aegina, and the **Chariot of Hiero**, by Kalamis and Onatas of Aegina. Near the large rectangular bases of these is the semicircular base of a group of **Nine Heroes of the Trojan War** dedicated by the Achaean cities and made by Onatas of Aegina; they are represented as drawing lots for the honour of the duel with Hector.

Opposite, on a round base, stood **Nestor** shaking the lots in his helmet. Close by is the restored triangular base of the **Nike of Paionios**, dedicated by the Dorian Messenians. Adjacent were statues of famous Olympionikai: **Telemachos the Elean** (end of 4C); **Dorieus**, and other Rhodian athletes. Rather more to the W are the base of **Diagoras of Rhodes**, his son **Praxiteles**, a Mantinean athlete (484–461 BC), and the cylindrical plinth of a **Statue of Zeus**, dedicated by the Lacedaemonians in the 6C after the second Messenian revolt. Near the NE corner of the ramp are three semicircular moulded plinths which bore statues of the **Elean Women** (1C BC). Adjacent are the pedestals of the **Eretrian Bull**, by Philesios (5C BC) with an inscription on its E margin (fragments in the museum); and of the historian Polybius (146 BC). These bases and others transferred to the new museum were within the trapezoidal area enclosed by the 6C **Byzantine wall**, which had as its N and S limits the Temple of Zeus and the S stoa. The wall, made of ancient blocks from many buildings in the Altis, was demolished by the excavators and the fragments recovered.

Moving SE you reach a heap of grey limestone blocks belonging to a pedestal that supported an equestrian group of **Mummius and the Ten Legates**. Close by on the E are remains of a Roman **triumphal arch**, erected for Nero's visit. It was largely built of older materials, including the pedestals of statues, destroyed lest the memory of their prowess should overshadow that of the megalomaniac emperor.

In the SE corner of the Altis are foundations of the **south-east building**. It had four compartments and was faced on all sides but the E by a 4C Doric colonnade with 19 columns along the front and 8 at each side. It was paved with small pebbles embedded in plaster. One suggestion as to its identity is the shrine of **Hestia**, mentioned by Xenophon. It was demolished to make way for the **House of Nero**, hurriedly built for the emperor's visit, the peristyle of which lies farther E. This house has been identified by the discovery of a lead water-pipe inscribed NER. AVG. The Doric columns of the Greek building were broken up into small pieces to form the *opus incertum* of the walls. Later a large Roman structure was constructed immediately E of Nero's house, which was partially sacrificed to the new building. This contained over 30 rooms, one octagonal, and explorations in 1963–64 showed it to have been **baths**.

Farther E lay the **hippodrome**, long since washed completely away by the Alpheios. Here was installed the 'hippaphesis' an ingenious starting gate invented by Cleoitas in the 6C BC and described by Pausanias. To the S of the House of Nero, in 1963 was uncovered the **Altar of Artemis**.

The greater part of the E side of the Altis is occupied by the foundations of the **Echo Colonnade** or **Stoa Poikile**. The former name is due to its sevenfold echo, the latter to the paintings with which it was decorated. Most of the remains are from the time of Alexander the Great when the stoa was rebuilt, those farther E from the earlier version of the 5C BC. Before this the stadium extended into the Altis.

In front of the Stoa Poikile are numerous statue bases including a long plinth bearing two Ionic columns, which supported statues of Ptolemy II Philadelphos and Arsinoe, his queen.

You reach the vaulted entrance (Hellenistic) to the **stadium**. The latter was completely explored in 1958–62 by the German Institute and restored to the form it took in the 4C BC. The artificial banks never had permanent seats, but could accommodate c 40,000 people. The track originally extended NE from near the Pelopion and was not separated from the Altis until the 5C when the Stoa Poikile was constructed. The embankments were several times enlarged and the German excavators found many older weather-worn votive offerings (helmets, shields, etc.) which had been buried during the alterations as sacred objects not to be profaned by re-use. The starting and finishing lines are *in situ*, 600 Olympic feet apart. The stone kerb round the track and the water-supply opening at intervals into basins are visible; the paved area for judges on the S side has been uncovered.

Immediately outside the entrance is a row of 12 pedestals which supported the **Zanes**, bronze images of Zeus erected out of the fines imposed on athletes in the 98th and 112th Olympiads for cheating.

A flight of ancient steps ascends to the **treasuries** which are arranged roughly in line on a terrace overlooking the Altis at the foot of Mt Kronos, the soil of which is kept back by a substantial retaining wall. Each treasury takes the form of a small temple, consisting of a single chamber and a distyle portico *in antis* facing S. They were erected by single cities, all but two outside Greece proper, for the reception of sacrificial vessels used by the *theoroi*, and possibly for storing weapons and gear used in the games. Little remains but the foundations. The description of Pausanias is problematic and the identification of several of them is uncertain. They seem to have been added roughly chronologically from E to W.

The oldest and largest, built c 600 BC and modernised about a century later, belonged to **Gela** (12). Though constructed of shell-limestone, those parts of the masonry which were most exposed to the weather, e.g. the pediment cornices, were encased in painted terracotta plaques and tiles—a survival from the days when buildings were made of wood. The terracottas were made in Gela and the building was presumably designed by Sicilian architects.

Though little more than the foundations of the **Treasury of Megara** (11) remain *in situ*, many fragments were recovered from the S Byzantine wall. It was erected between those of **Gela** and Metapontum c 570 BC as is shown by the fact that all ornamentation (fluting, mutules, etc.) was omitted where it could not be seen. The pediment may not have received its sculpture until c 510. Adjacent are foundations of the **Metapontum** treasury (10), slightly earlier in date. That of **Selinus** (9) is next, squashed in later between existing buildings, then (8) a structure which was probably not a treasury but the **Altar of Gaia**. The next three treasuries, which are very ruinous, are assigned to **Kyrene** (7), to which two sculptured fragments of African limestone probably belong; **Sybaris** (6) which must date before 510 BC when that city was destroyed; and **Byzantium** (5).

The architectural remains of the next building (4) belong to the 6C BC suggesting that it is more likely that of **Epidamnos** than (as usually proposed) of **Syracuse**. The Syracusan treasury, which contained the spoils of the victory at Himera (480 BC) may have been farther along (2), but both this building and that tentatively assigned to **Samos** (3) seem to have been obliterated in Roman times. The treasury of **Sikyon** (1), by contrast, has well preserved foundations. Many blocks of the superstructure in Sikyonian stone with identifying inscription have been recovered, and the building has been partially reconstructed. They date from c 480 BC. A Sikyonian treasury was dedicated by Myron to celebrate his chariot victory in the 33rd Olympiad, when the two huge bronze shrines also dedicated necessitated a special strengthening of the floor. This must have concerned an earlier building but the existing floor is also strengthened.

Immediately beyond is an **Altar to Herakles** (whether the Idaean Herakles or the famous Herakles Pausanias could not say) and, N of it, an ancient **shrine** with a pronaos facing S.

Descending the terrace steps you immediately reach the **Metroön**, a small peripteral hexastyle Doric temple of the 4C BC, dedicated to the Mother of the Gods. It measured only 20.5m by 10.5m. The remains include most of the foundations and a portion of stylobate with the drum of one column and a fragment of another. In Roman times the worship of Cybele gave place to that of Augustus and Rome, and the excavators discovered in the foundations a statue of Claudius and another of Titus.

To the W of the Metroön six prehistoric houses were uncovered by Dörpfeld, traces of two of which may be seen in front of the **Exedra of Herodes Atticus**. This was the termination of a much-needed supply of pure drinking water brought to Olympia between 157 and 160 by an aqueduct c 3km long. The water was stored in a large semicircular tank from which it flowed through lion's-head spouts into an oblong basin in front. The upper tank was paved with marble and backed by an apse supported by eight buttresses which rose to a half-cupola. The inner side had 15 niches which held statues of the family of Herodes and of their imperial patrons. At each end of the lower tank a small circular Corinthian temple enclosed a statue. A large marble bull bore an inscription recording that Herodes dedicated the reservoir to Zeus in the name of his wife Regilla, who was a priestess of Demeter.

The **Heraion**, the oldest but the best preserved building at Olympia, is situated near the NW corner of the Altis. It was originally a joint temple of Zeus and Hera but after the grander temple of Zeus was built was reserved to the goddess alone. The worship of Hera, which played little part in the history of Olympia, may have been introduced by Pheidon of Argos who supposedly usurped control of the festival. The temple is not earlier than the beginning of the 6C, and was originally built of wood, which was gradually replaced by stone. Even in the time of Pausanias columns of wood survived.

The temple, raised on a single step, was a Doric peripteral hexastyle with 16 columns at the sides. Thirty-four of the columns survive in part; two of them were re-erected in 1905 and another in 1970. They vary in diameter, in the height of the drums (while three are monolithic), and in the number and depth of the flutings, while the 18 surviving capitals show by the outlines of their echinus that they belong to every period from the foundation to Roman times. As no trace has been found of the entablature, it is believed to have been of wood. The roof tiles and akroteria (museum) were of terracotta.

INTERIOR. The division into three chambers was conventional, though the interior details are unusual. Both pronaos and opisthodomos were distyle *in antis*. The walls of the sekos were nearly 1.2m thick; the four courses forming the inner face are well preserved to a height of 90cm. The upper part was of mud brick with wooden door-posts. The **cella**, long in proportion to its breadth, was lighted only by the door. Four internal cross-walls, recalling the structure of the much later temple at Bassae, served to buttress the outside walls and to support the cross-beams of the roof. At a later date the cella was divided longitudinally by two rows of Doric columns, every second one being engaged with the corresponding buttress. There was a flat wooden ceiling.

Pausanias tells how, during the repair of the roof, the body of a hoplite was found between the ceiling and the roof. The soldier had apparently fought in the war of 401–399 BC between Elis and Sparta, during which a battle had swept over the Altis. Wounded, he had crawled to shelter only to die, remaining undiscovered for 500 years.

At the W end of the cella stands the pedestal of the archaic group of Zeus and Hera. The head of Hera has been recovered. Of all the other treasures and statues known to have been in the Heraion only the Hermes of Praxiteles has been found. It was lying in front of its pedestal between the second and third columns from the E on the N side. Six bases in the pronaos bore statues of noble Elean women. The opisthodomos is known to have held the cedar-wood Chest of Kypselos; the Disk of Iphitos, on which was inscribed the Olympic Truce; and the gold and ivory Table of Kolotes, on which the victors' crowns were displayed.

To the S of the Heraion, on the site of a prehistoric (Early Helladic II) tumulus, is the **Pelopion**, a grove containing a small eminence and an altar to Pelops, the principal Olympian hero, enclosed by a pentagonal wall. A Doric propylon at its SW end, of which foundations remain, appears to date from the 5C BC and to have replaced an older entrance. Immense quantities of archaic bronzes and terracottas were recovered in the enclosure as well as roof-tiles from the Temple of Zeus. Apsidal houses nearby are Early Helladic III.

Somewhere to the E must have stood the **Altar of Olympian Zeus**, the most sacred spot in the Altis, where a daily blood sacrifice was made. A heap of stone marks the supposed spot.

Turning towards the exit you pass, in the NW corner of the Altis, the foundations of the **Philippieion**, a circular monument begun by Philip of Macedon after the battle of Chaironeia (338 BC) and probably finished by Alexander the Great. Two concentric colonnades stood on a stylobate of three steps, the outer peristyle had 18 Ionic columns, the cella 12 engaged columns with Corinthian capitals. The roof had marble tiles and a bronze poppy on the top which held the rafters together. Within was a group of five chryselephantine statues, by Leochares, representing Philip, his mother and father, his wife Olympias, and their son Alexander. Finely carved fragments of their bases have been recovered.

Beyond stood the **Prytaneion**, the official residence of the magistrates, in which Olympic victors were feasted. The remains are scanty. The building, which dates in some form from the Archaic period (?), was later remodelled more than once in Roman times. The later Greek prytaneion was a square of 33m with an entrance on the S side and a vestibule leading into a central chamber, 6.7m square. On both sides of the central chamber were open courts. In Roman times a banqueting hall was added to the W. Beneath the prytaneion is what seems to be a foundation for the piers of a Geometric bridge over the Kladeos which originally took this course. Recent discoveries in the area (wells, hearths, food remains) have demonstrated that it was used as a campsite by visitors to the festival from the 6C or earlier.

On leaving the enclosure there are (right) remains of Roman dining pavilion, to which a bath was later added.

Across the road a drive leads to the **\*\*museum**, opened in 1972. Finds formerly in the old museum and many more previously in store are arranged chronologically.

In the ENTRANCE HALL, model of the Sacred Altis (a gift of the city of Essen), and another of the central area made to Dörpfeld's specifications and given in 1931 in memory of Kaiser Wilhelm II. Statue bases of Olympic victors: Kallias of Athens, by *Mikon*; Euthymos of Lokri Epizephyrii, by *Pythagoras*. Straight ahead is the CENTRAL HALL (see below).

To the left is GALLERY 1. Neolithic to Geometric, including grave goods from sub-Mycenaean chamber-tombs; Mycenaean boars' tusk helmet; \*tripods and handles of cauldrons decorated with bronze figures (Telchines); small Geometric votive offerings including miniature tripods and bronze and terracotta figures; in the centre, large Geometric horse in solid bronze.

GALLERY 2. Geometric and early Archaic **bronzes** and terracottas; orientalising bronze plaques, griffins, etc; \***armour and weapons**, many richly fashioned, displayed according to type and development: shields and corselets on the wall, cases of greaves, lances, and helmets below; one finely decorated Archaic cuirass stolen in the First World War and later recovered; shield bosses; sphyrelaton (sheet bronze hammered over wooden core) sphinx; restored terracotta pedimental acroterion and antefixes from the Heraion; colossal limestone **head of Hera**, probably from the cult statue of the same building.

GALLERY 3. Statuettes and tripods; sculptures and simas from various treasuries, including the pedimental statuary of the Megarian and a section of polychrome sima from the Gela treasury; Archaic figures from a perirrhanterion; battering ram; fine vases. In GALLERY 4 the Classical period is introduced by the arresting and vigorous group of *****Zeus carrying off Ganymede**, a late Archaic work executed in terracotta; warrior from a similar group; Persian *****helmet** taken by the Athenians at Marathon and dedicated to Zeus; the *****helmet of Miltiades**, victor at Marathon; small *****bronzes** and pottery; tools; objects from the Workshop of Pheidias, including terracotta moulds for forming sections of drapery for the cult statue and a *****cup** inscribed with the name of Pheidias.

Access to CENTRAL HALL. GALLERY 5. Large- and small-scale sculpture (not all from Olympia) in stone and terracotta, Classical and later; minor dedications in bronze and terracotta; pottery; 3C BC statue base with foot of bronze figure still in place; bronze head of a boy (plus reconstructed version) from the stadium.

GALLERY 6. The *****Hermes** of Praxiteles, a work found in the Temple of Hera in 1877 in the place where it was noted by Pausanias. Its attribution to Praxiteles rests on his summary description; he seems to have considered the work worth no more than the briefest remark. One of the best preserved Classical statues to have survived to modern times, it was protected by the fallen clay of which the upper walls of the temple had been built. The statue is of Parian marble, its original polish scarcely marked by the passage of time, though not quite complete.

Hermes, the messenger of the gods, was charged by Zeus to take his infant son Dionysos out of the reach of the jealous Hera, and to bring him to the nymphs of Mount Nysa, to whose care was entrusted the rearing and education of the child. Hermes is represented as resting on his journey. He stands in an attitude of easy grace, the left knee slightly bent, leaning his left arm on the trunk of a tree. In his left hand must have been the caduceus (missing). His cloak is carelessly thrown across his arm and falls in simple graceful folds over the tree trunk. On his left arm sits the ill-proportioned infant Dionysos, reaching up towards an object (a bunch of grapes?) which Hermes holds in his right hand. The form of Hermes, which is entirely nude, presents an ideal combination of grace and strength. The head is slightly turned towards the child. The hair is in short crisp locks, indicated rather than sculptured in detail. Both behind and before can be traced the groove of a metal wreath. Traces of paint have been detected on the hair, lips, and sandal. The date of this masterpiece is usually put between 363 and 343 BC though some authorities consider it a Roman copy.

GALLERY 7. Roman sculpture, especially pieces from the exedra of Herodes Atticus (restored drawing showing sculptures in position), including marble bull (inscribed), fine figure of Antinous (?). Several members of the imperial family. GALLERY 8. Objects directly concerned with the Olympic Games; part of starting block of earlier stadium; dedications of victors; base of statue (by Lysippos) of the Athenian Poulydamas; bronze discus; jumping weights (halteres); inscriptions; minor dedications.

Recently redisplayed after restoration is the important late 5C **Nike of Paionios**, of island marble, originally set on a tall triangular pedestal in front of the SE corner of the Temple of Zeus. The base is inscribed with the name of the sculptor, a native of Mende in Thrace, and a dedication to Zeus from the Messenians of Naupactos 'as a tithe from their enemies'. It was probably dedicated at the Peace of Nikias in 421 BC after the exiled Messenians had aided the Athenians in the Spartan defeat at Sphakteria. The winged Nike is shown swooping down to land on the pedestal, the drapery pressed against the body, almost transparent in places, but billowing out behind in thick curling swathes—a fine example of the dramatic use of drapery in the sculpture of this period.

The huge CENTRAL HALL contains the pedimental sculptures of the Temple of Zeus, together with the metopes and some fragments of the cornice, with lion's-head water spouts. The standard work on the sculptures was published by B. Ashmole and N. Yialouris in 1967. In the course of their recent transfer to this new gallery, about 300 fragments have been added and some rearrangement of the figures made. Since no description of the rearrangement has yet been published, the following account may be inaccurate in some details, especially the positions of the central figures in the west pediment.

The EAST PEDIMENT, attributed by Pausanias to Paionios, represents the start of the **chariot-race between Oinomaos and Pelops**. All the figures are sculpted in the round except the three inner horses of each team, which are in moderate relief. Not a trace of either chariot has been found, but the marks of attachment can be seen on the horses. The figures, none of which is complete, are 1½ times lifesize and in the severe style, consistent with a date in the early to mid-5C.

Oinomaos, King of Pisa, warned by an oracle that he would be killed by a son-in-law, was unwilling to give his daughter Hippodameia in marriage. Aspirants to her hand were challenged to a chariot-race from Olympia to Isthmia and given a start with Hippodameia while Oinomaos sacrificed a ram. By the fleet-footedness of his horses Oinomaos overtook his potential sons-in-law, spearing them in the back. He had thus disposed of 13 suitors when Pelops appeared as claimant. He bribed the charioteer Myrtilos to tamper with the axle-pins of his master's chariot so that Oinomaos was killed when his chariot crashed. Pelops thus won both his bride and her father's kingdom. The unedifying story of cheating and treachery (generally accepted as the root cause of the curse of the Atreides) seems to have provided one legendary version of the founding of the Olympic Games. Alternative versions have omitted Myrtilos' part and attributed Pelops' victory to his magical steeds (a present from Poseidon) and Oinomaos' death to *hubris* punished by Zeus. The pediment seems to omit Myrtilos and this may have been the Elean version of the story.

NOTE: the terms 'right' and 'left' used below are from the spectator's point of view.

The centre of the composition is the colossal figure of Zeus; to the left (according to the latest of a long series of suggested reconstructions) stand Oinomaos and his wife, Sterope; to the right Pelops and Hippodameia. Zeus, who is invisible to the contestants, is looking towards Pelops to indicate his good will. The identification of Sterope and Hippodameia and their consequent placing left or right made by Yalouris has been questioned by Kardhara (see A.J.A. 1970). On each side of the women is a four-horse chariot, that of Pelops attended by a boy, that of Oinomaos by a girl. Behind the team of Pelops is his charioteer (? Killas), a seer, and the personified Alpheios. Behind that of Oinomaos, a seer, a boy, and the personified Kladeos.

The WEST PEDIMENT, executed according to Pausanias by Alkamenes, illustrates the **fight between the Lapiths and Centaurs** at the marriage-feast of Peirithoös. Again none of the figures is complete, though the Apollo is almost perfect.

Peirithoös, King of the Lapiths in Thessaly and a reputed son of Zeus, invited his friend Theseus and the Centaurs to his wedding. The Centaurs had too much to drink and assaulted the women and boys present, one of the Centaurs, Eurytion, attempting to carry off the bride. Peirithoös, assisted by Theseus, defended the attacked, slew many of the Centaurs, and routed the rest.

The central figure is *Apollo, calmly towering above the tumult, who has come to the assistance of the Lapiths. On the right Hippodameia is in Eurytion's clutches; Peirithoös stands ready to strike with his sword. Beyond, a boy is being picked up by a Centaur. Next comes a Lapith woman, her garment torn, trying to tear herself free from a Centaur who has already been transfixed by the sword of a kneeling Lapith. They are watched from the corner by a crouching and a recumbent woman. The left hand side is similar, but less well preserved. The boy throttling the Centaur is being savagely bitten in the arm and shows his pain in a furrowed brow.

The sculptures are all of Parian marble with the exception of the two old women in the W pediment, the young woman in its left hand corner, and the arm of the other young woman, which are of Pentelic marble and are thought to be antique restorations. From traces of colour discovered it is clear that all the figures were painted.

On the end walls are the sculptured *metopes from the cella frieze, illustrating the **Twelve Labours of Herakles**. Each slab measured 1.6m by 1.5m, the figures being slightly under lifesize. The metopes were originally painted, the brush completing the details of hair, clothes, etc, which the chisel has merely indicated.

In a new building in the village is the **Museum of the Olympic Games**, which includes a collection of commemorative stamps.

# 38

# Corinth (Kórinthos) to Patras (Pátra)

**Road**, 135km (84 miles), mostly near the shore along the Gulf of Corinth.—21km Kiáto, for Síkyon (5km).—34km Xilókastro.—78km Turn for Kalávrita.—81km Dhiakoftó.—94km Aíyio.—127km Río (car-ferry to Andírrio, for NW Greece).—135km Pátras.—The alternative and much faster route, avoiding all villages, is the toll highway, parallel to (and generally inland of) the old road. Great care is needed in bad weather. **Buses** (starting from Athens) frequently (2¼ hours journey; 3½ hours from Athens).

**Railway**, 130km (81 miles), 9 trains daily in 1¾–2½ hours, all starting from Athens, whence c 2 hours should be added. To Xilókastro, 34km in c 40 minutes; to Dhiakoftó, 77km junction for Kalávrita, 6 trains daily in 1–1½ hours; to Aiyio, 91km in 1¼–1¾. The railway is seldom out of sight of the road.

This route follows the S shore of the Gulf of Corinth (*Korinthiakós Kólpos*), which reaches for nearly 130km from Aigosthena in the E to the 'Little Dardanelles' in the W. It varies in width between 2 and 30km, being widest in the centre and narrowest at the W. The E end of the gulf is divided by the peninsula of Perakhora into the Gulf of Alkionídhon and the Bay of Corinth, with the entrance to the Corinth Canal. The N and S sides are in remarkable contrast. The alluvial coast of Akhaia, with its innumerable torrents and its currant vineyards fringing the shore, runs WNW almost in a straight line from Corinth to Cape Dhrepano. The rugged and abrupt coast of Phokis, Lokris, and Aitolia, chiefly forest and pasture and sparsely inhabited, is broken by the Bay of

Aspra Spítia (Andíkiron Kólpos) and the Bay of Salona (Krissaíos Kólpos), in addition to several minor indentations. The encircling mountains are among the highest in Greece so that the gulf resembles a large inland lake. The scenery is fine.

**Corinth**, see Rte 25A. The road runs W along the coast. Across the Bay of Corinth is the long low promontory of Perakhora; farther E, behind Loutraki, rises the great mass of Yeraneia. After 3km the road passes the site of *Lechaion* (Rte 25E); on the left towers Acrocorinth. 10km **Periyiáli**, the first of many villages strung along the road, is situated amidst currant-vines and fruit trees in the fertile coastal Plain of Corinthia, now completely recovered from the earthquake of 1928. In world production of currants, Greece is second only to the United States. Corinthian lemons are naturally green but artificially turned yellow after picking to satisfy foreign demand.

You cross the Longos (or Rakhiani) near (11km) **Assos**, a village surrounded by cypress groves; hereabouts was fought the Spartan victory 'near the Nemea River' in 394 BC. Behind, the flat top of Mt Fokas (873m; the ancient *Apesas*) is prominent. Near **Zevgolatió** (1.5km left) are some remains of a late Roman bath explored in 1954. Beyond (14km) **Vrakháti** (Hotel D), a centre for sultanas on the Nemea, is the Kokkoni Holiday village. **Tarsína** (4km, left) has an important Byzantine church (of the Metamórfosis). Further (10km) inland near **Stimánga** are remains of a **Sanctuary of Demeter and Kore** whose existence is hinted at by Pausanias (II, 3). These are at Ayios Ionannis, 1km W of the village. After (18km) **Véllo**, where fruit juices are extracted, the road crosses the Peloponnesian Asopos, said by Classical tradition to be an extension of the Maeander flowing beneath the sea from near Miletus. The flutes of the presumptuous Marsyas were thrown up on its bank.

21km **Kiáto** (Hotels B, C) or Sikionia, with a prominent modern church, is a flourishing port (9100 inhab.) exporting raisins. From here Perakhora (Rte 25F) can be visited by boat. Near the railway station are some remains of an early Byzantine basilica. The modern village of **Vasilikó** (c 5km SW; bus) has readopted the official name of Sikyon, the later site of which it occupies.

*Síkyon* (Σίκυων), reputedly one of the oldest of Greek cities, was the capital of Sikyonia, a small district, anciently (as now) renowned for its almonds and olive-oil. In the Classical period the city was a centre of Greek art. Its school of bronze sculpture was made famous by Aristokles, Kanachos, Polykleitos, and Lysippos. Its academy of painting, established by Eupompos, produced Pausias and Pamphilos, the master of Apelles, and lasted into Hellenistic times. Sikyonian dress, and in particular Sikyonian shoes, had a wide reputation. Both the ancient city, which lay in the plain, and the later one founded by Demetrios Poliorketes on the acropolis, lay close to the Asopos.

**History**. *Sikyon* ('Cucumber Town' from σικύα, a cucumber) was originally named *Aigialeia*, probably from the Aigialaean ('coast-dwelling') Ionians who founded the city, and later called *Mekone*. The traditional list of its heroic kings includes the Argive Adrastus, the only survivor of the 'seven against Thebes'. The Homeric catalogue makes him commander of the Sikyonian contingent to Troy, and Homer gives to Sikyon the epithet εὐρύχορος (wide open). After the Dorian invasions it became subject to Argos.

About 660 BC Orthagoras, a popular tyrant, established a dynasty lasting a century, during which the city rose to prosperity. Its metal work and pottery were of high quality and a school of sculpture was founded from Crete. Boutades of Sikyon is credited with inventing the relief. Kleisthenes, greatest of the dynasty and grandfather of the Athenian legislator, joined the Amphictyonic League in the Sacred War (c 590 BC).

His destruction of the city of Krisa freed Delphi. After reorganising the Pythian Games there, he instituted similar games at Sikyon, abolishing the worship of the Argive hero Adrastus. His successor Aeschines was expelled by the Lacedaemonians c 556, and Sikyon lost its political independence in the Peloponnesian League. The city remained a centre of art and industry, and its coinage was in widespread use in the 5–3C.

The Sikyonians were loyal allies of Sparta during the Persian invasions, in the Peloponnesian War, and after, on more than one occasion providing a fleet. The city was conquered in 368 BC by the Theban Epaminondas, but shortly afterwards a Sikyonian citizen called Euphron achieved a brief local notoriety by seizing the government. In 303 BC Demetrios Poliorketes razed the ancient city in the plain and built a new one, temporarily called *Demetrias* in his honour on the ruins of the old acropolis. In 251 BC Aratos, son of Kleinias, united the city to the Achaean League, later becoming its leader. During the eclipse of Corinth after 146, Sikyon took over control of the Isthmian Games but, after the refounding of Corinth, gradually declined. Fulvia, wife of Mark Antony, died in exile here in 40 BC.

The **'new' city** of 303 BC is admirably situated 3km from the sea on an extensive triangular plateau between the gorges of the Asopos and the smaller Helison. Defended on all sides by precipitous cliffs, the plateau is divided by a rocky slope into a lower terrace, the acropolis of the old city, and an upper terrace, forming the apex of the triangle, which became the acropolis of the new. The city walls ran round the edge of the plateau and are least ruined on the W side. Excavations by the Greek Archaeological Society have uncovered a small part of the city, which seems to have been laid out on a rectangular plan.

The modern village stands on the lower level of the plateau. You can cross the presumed site of the agora to (10 minutes) the large Roman **baths**, built in brick in the 2–3C and restored as a **museum** for the site. In three rooms are displayed mosaics (? 4C BC); bronze mirror; painted terracotta frieze; pieces of sculpture; and pottery models of hedgehogs.

To the left are the foundations of two **temples**, one Archaic, the other Hellenistic, the two overlain by an Early Christian structure. The patron deities may be Apollo and Artemis. Pausanias mentions a Temple of Apollo as being rebuilt by Pythokles. Remains of Classical and Hellenistic altars and some sculpture have been recovered. The S end of the agora was closed by a Hellenistic **stoa** and the **bouleuterion**, an almost square hypostyle hall, the ceiling of which was supported by 16 Ionic columns. Later it was adapted to other uses. Near it are extensive remains of the **Gymnasium of Kleinias**, built on two levels; on either side of the central stairway linking them is a fountain. The **theatre**, one of the largest of continental Greece, occupies a natural depression in the slope dividing the upper and lower terraces. It was originally excavated by the American School in 1889–91. The building dates from the beginning of the 3C BC. It is known from Polybius that the Achaean League met here in 168 BC. The **cavea** is c 120m across. The lower diazoma could be reached by two vaulted passages as well as by 16 staircases from the parodoi. The fifty-odd tiers of seats, mostly hollowed out of the rock, were divided into 15 wedges, each of which forms one twenty-fifth part of a circle. The front seats have backs, armrests, and sculptured feet. The **orchestra**, of stamped earth, surrounded by a drain, had a diameter of c 20m. Foundation walls of the **stage buildings** show that they were twice altered in Roman times. They had as a façade a Doric portico of 13 columns in antis.

In a ravine to the W of the theatre are the remains of the **stadium**. The straight end had a wall of polygonal masonry, still partly standing. On the upper terrace are scanty ruins of the new **acropolis**. The dividing slope is honeycombed with subterranean aqueducts. The Classical cemetery area was located in 1976 below the track from Vasilikó to Traganá. The *view, especially lovely at sunrise and sunset, embraces Helikon, Kithairon, and Parnassos, with a verdant foreground contrasting with the blue of the Gulf.

The old city in the plain and its harbour have left little to mark their sites. The modern road follows the ancient alignment and road-construction in 1966 located a necropolis and mosaics of the old city.

FROM KIÁTO TO THE STYMPHALIAN LAKE, KASTANÉA AND PHENEOS (Feneó). Road, 68km (42¾ miles), via Soúli (13km), to Goúra (bus), mainly interesting for the landscape. It is possible to continue to Tríkkala, or the coast at Dhervéni. Skirting the N side of Mt Botsika (1300m), you turn SW between it and Killini. 35km **Kefalári** (380 inhab.) nestles below the secondary E summit of Killini (see below; the ascent from this side, in 12 hours, is difficult). At (39km) **Kaliáni** diverges a road to Nemea (32km; Rte 26). Just beyond (41km) the village of **Stimfália** (Hotel E; tavernas), to the left of the road, are the conspicuous remains of the Frankish Gothic church of the **Cistercian abbey of Zaraka** and its gate tower. Ancient architectural members were extensively used in the construction of the church and these probably came from the nearby Temple of Artemis, mentioned by Pausanias but no longer visible. Some of the medieval architectural carving, especially of the capitals, is very fine and in a completely western style.

About 500m to the S is the low acropolis of ancient **Stymphalos**, clearly marked by the foundations of the city wall. Crowned by a tower, it overlooks the dried-up lake below. To the E and N of the acropolis the Canadian Archaeological Institute has recently discovered (by electrical resistivity and proton magnetometer survey) evidence of a town, carefully laid out to an orthogonal plan in the 4C BC. The house blocks are long and narrow and the streets 6m wide. Remains of three Doric structures (probably temples) have been found in various parts of the site. On the N side, by the lake, are the remains of a curious round building and a spring house (cleared by A. Orlandos in the 1920s) which still functions. A small temple and altar to Athena Polias lie on a terrace just to the E of the acropolis. Also by the lakeside are the well-preserved remains of massive polygonal walls supporting a road, whose wheel ruts (1.5m apart) are visible in places.

At the E end of the lake are remains of a Roman aqueduct, probably built by Hadrian to take the abundant local spring waters to Corinth. It can be traced across the valley to the modern irrigation tunnel beneath the pass to Nemea.

The road climbs steeply from the W end of the valley to (52km) **Kastanéa** (Hotel B, at 1302m above the village), a mountain resort (902m) on the S slope of Killini below the saddle that separates Stymphalos from Pheneos. It is a good area for walking and for botanists. You descend to the E side of the Pedhías Feneoú, in ancient times a shallow lake or marsh, nowadays more often dry.

From (59.5km) **Mesinó** a road crosses the valley to **Kalívia**, passing the site of *Pheneos*, with remnants of a small Temple of Asklepios. The colossal head and feet of a broken statue from the site are in a small **museum** at Kalivia. The church of Ayios Yeoryios, to the NW, has frescoes. The road continues to (68km) **Goúra**; the modern village of **Feneós** lies on the W side of the valley, midway between the summits of Killini and Khelmos. Here a monument was erected in 1960 to nationalist victims of a communist massacre in 1944. Beyond Goura are Stenó, then **Ano** and **Káto Társos**, at the N edge of the Feneós basin. SW of the latter is a Byzantine **castle** and settlement. From a junction farther on you can turn E to Tríkkala or descend to the coast near Dhervént.

On the N slopes of Aroánia (Khelmos; 2354m), in a lugubrious and eroded valley, is the 'Source of the Styx' (4 hours W of Feneos). Make for **Vounariánika**, from which the waterfall is visible and the footpath apparent. From here Kalavrita (Rte 39) can be reached in a further 6½ hours (guide advisable), or you can descend via **Sólos** to the coast (see below).

30km **Melíssi** (Hotels, B, C, D) with a Mycenaean tomb (500m S).—34km **Xilókastro** (Ξυλόκαστρο; Hotels, A–D) is a popular seaside resort (5821 inhab.), agreeably situated amid luxuriant gardens at the mouth of the Sithas valley. It probably occupies the site of ancient *Aristonautai*, a seaport of Pellene, where the Argonauts put in. Along the sandy E shore towards

Sikia is a pinewood, called **Pefkías**, with a campsite. A **museum** devoted to the memory of the poet *Angelos Sikelianos* (1884–1951) has been established in a villa he once owned. To the SW on the mountainside stands **Zemenó**, (8km), where a wine festival is held in September.

TO TRÍKKALA (34km) and MT KILLÍNI. Just W of Xilokastro a road climbs into the Sithas valley. 12km **Pellíni**. The insignificant ruins of ancient *Pellene*, on the top of the mountain separating the valleys of the Sithas and the Forissa, offer an excellent view. 34km **Ano Tríkkala** (1067m; Hotels C, D), a winter-sporting resort, stands on the N slope of Mt Zíria, the ancient *Kyllene*, second highest mountain in the Peloponnese (2377m). Mansions of the Ottoman period have been restored. Climbers should obtain keys of the refuges from the Greek Alpine Club in Athens. An easy path climbs in 2½ hours to **Refuge A** (1646m; 50 beds; water), and (30 minutes more) to **Refuge B** (1737m; 20 beds), from which the W summit may be reached (2 hours further). The Yimnos summit (2134m), to the E overlooks Kefalari on the Kastania road (see above). There is an unsurfaced but driveable road to Refuge B (12kms).

The mountains come closer to the coast. Parnassos is visible 50km away across the gulf. Above (40km) **Kamári**, birthplace of *Panayiotis Tsaldaris*, opponent of Venizelos, who brought back the monarchy in 1935, rises the pyramidal Korifi (732m) with a nunnery on its summit. You cross the Forissa torrent. 48km **Likoporiá** (Hotel C). The conspicuous Cape Avgó, between Petséïka and (52km) **Stómio**, contends with Korifí for the site of *Donussa*. 56km **Dhervéni**, a small town (1060 inhab.) with a long narrow street, has a sandy beach. The road enters the nome of Akhaia.

**Akhaia**, or Achaea, the mountainous NW division of the Peloponnese, marches on the S with inland Arkadia and maritime Elis. Its capital is Patras. In the Mycenaean period the name of the province seems to have connoted almost the whole of the Peloponnese. In Classical times it meant chiefly the N coastal area. When the Romans conquered the Achaean League they gave the name to the whole peninsula.

The **Achaean League** was a confederation for mutual defence and protection of the coastal cities of Achaea, which met until 373 BC at Helike. It was refounded in 280 BC on as an anti-Macedonian organisation and admitted non-Achaeans. Aratos of Sikyon united Sikyon, Corinth, and other cities to the League, became its general in 245 BC, and made it the chief political power in Greece. The admission of Megalopolis antagonised Sparta and during the Cleomenic War Aratos allied the League with Antigonus Doson. The League went over to Rome in 198 BC under the leadership of Philopoemen (252–183 BC), the last great man of free Greece. It lost all power in 146 BC. The 'twelve cities' of the League were Aigai, Aigeria, Aigion, Boura, Dyme, Kerynea, Olenos, Patrai, Pellene, Pharai, Rhypes, and Tritaia.

59km **Mávra Lithária**. Aigés (8km inland) and (62km) **Aíyira** (ancient *Aigeira*) perpetuate the names of two of the Achaean twelve cities.

The site of Classical *Aigeira* (excavated by the Austrian Archaeological Institute, 1915, 1926, 1972–) is reached (from the old road) by turning under the railway just beyond Mávra Lithária and taking the steeply rising inland road towards **Paliés Aíges**. After c 5.5km there is a sign for the theatre. The antiquities lie to the left (theatre, etc., but not immediately visible) and right (acropolis) of the road. The Hellenistic **theatre**, remodelled in the Roman period, is the most impressive monument. Beyond it are a group of **naïskoi** arranged in a semi-circle, in one of which was found a head by the sculptor Eukleides. Naïskoi D and E (to the W, with some painted plaster) were dedicated to Zeus and Artemis-Iphigeneia respectively. A large complex (Hellenistic/Roman) lies to the N. It seems to include the bath building of a gymnasium, as troughs and channels for water control have been found.

Remains on the two main terraces of the **acropolis** (sharp climb; view) are less tangible. Mycenaean buildings and pottery have been discovered, and a Hellenistic/Roman square with shops. Architectural fragments and foundations of the 7C BC at the highest point may be from a Temple of Artemis-Iphigeneia mentioned by

Pausanias. Terracottas from the buildings are in the Aiyio Museum. There are some traces of the **wall** on the side of the hill above the road, byond the theatre.

The city was called *Hyperesia* by Homer (*Iliad* II, 573). Its inhabitants are said to have frustrated a Sikyonian invasion by collecting goats (αἶγες) after dark and tying torches to their horns, thus misleading the enemy into believing reinforcements had arrived: hence the later name of the city.

About 12kms further inland, beyond the villages of Paliés Aiyés and Monastíri, at **Seliána** (or Fellóï) the Monastery of Ayioi Apostoloi has a 17C church, with frescoes, and a carved wooden templon of 1730.

From (65km) **Akráta** station, below its village, tracks climb to **Sólos** (6 hours) providing a possible approach to the Styx (see above); its waters feed the Krathis, soon crossed by the road. For some distance now the mountains reach to the sea and the road runs higher with views ahead and across the Gulf of Corinth. To the right are rich olive groves and cypresses. 78km Turn for **Kalávrita** (32km; views; at 22km, restaurant and turn for **Megaspílion** in 1km).

81km **Dhiakoftó** (Διακοπτό; Hotels C, D), in a plain noted for its cherries, is the railway junction for Kalavrita and has a frequent bus connection with Patras. The excursion by train at least as far as Zakhloroú is a 'must'.

The **Kalávrita railway** was engineered in 1885–95 by an Italian company in the fantastic, sombre **•**gorge down which the Vouraïkós, or Kerynites, tumbles its boulder-strewn course. The replacement of the original steam rolling-stock by diesel railcars from 1960–62 has ended the former discomfort and for period enthusiasts much of the romance; but nothing detracts from the awe-inspiring scenery or from the achievement of the engineers. Sometimes pushing, sometimes pulling, the little locomotives (75cm gauge) proceed partly by adhesion (max. gradient 1 in 28), partly by rack-and-pinion (Abt system; gradient 1 in 7), rising 700m in 22.5km. The line crosses the water several times on bridges and runs in tunnels or on overhung ledges. The sites of ancient *Bura* and *Keryneia* occupy hilltops to E and W of the entrance to the gorge. Just below Zakhloroú, where the gorge is only a few feet wide an original tunnel on the E side suffered a partial collapse and after the Second World War was replaced by another, cut in the solid cliff on the W, and a new bridge constructed.

12.5km **Zakhloroú** (Hotel D, on the picturesque station). A steep zigzag ascent (•view towards Kalavrita up the cypress and fir-clad valley) leads E in 45 minutes to the **Moní Megaspéleion** (Ἱερά Μονή του Μεγάλου Σπηλαίου), or monastery of the great cavern, built against a vertical and almost smooth cliff. After a disastrous fire in 1934, when a powder magazine (said to date from the War of Independence) exploded, the monastery was courageously rebuilt in an uncompromising 20C style. It has a hostel of 50 beds.

Visitors are shown round by a monk (adm. fee). The **church** has ancient ikons. There is a miraculous ikon of the Mother of God, supposedly found in the great cavern by the shepherdess Euphrosyne in AD 362, and attributed to St Luke. The image is in relief, of wax and gum mastic. An interesting museum of sacred relics illustrates the history of the convent, including seraphim, carved in wood (c 1700); note two *epitaphioi* from Asia Minor, one of Russian workmanship; gospels on vellum (9–11C), with Byzantine enamel-work covers; reliquaries containing the left hand of the martyr Kharalambos in the attitude of blessing; the heads of the monks Simeon and Theodore, founders of the monastery; hands of the SS. Theodore; crosses, etc. There is also a 17C wooden ikonostasis.

Beyond Zakhloroú the valley gradually broadens. 22km **Kalávrita**, see Rte 39.

Beyond Dhiakofto the railway continues near the shore while the road runs farther inland amid olive and cypress groves. The villages are closer together.

At 83km a minor road (left) runs inland to **Mamoúsia** (ancient *Keryneia*), where a Hellenistic funerary building (peribolos) was excavated in 1975 and 1981. The façade is decorated with Ionic pilasters and there is a frieze with shields in relief. The structure was reused in the Roman period.

89km **Elíki** (Hotel B) recalls the name of the Classical *Helike* drowned by a tidal wave in the earthquake of 373 BC. The sanctuary of Helikonian Poseidon was the early meeting-place of the Achaean League. It stood 2.5km inland. Following a similar seismic disturbance in 1963, underwater investigation was undertaken in 1966, without conspicuous success.

Immediately before the crossing of the rapid Selinous, or Vostitsa, amid vineyards of currants, a road diverges (left) for **Ftéri**, or Ptéri (Πτέρη; 20km; Hotels C, E), a summer hill-resort with fine views which have earned it the sobriquet of the 'Balcony of God'. **Valimítika** (Hotel C) lies E on the shore.

94km **Aíyio** (Αίγιον; Hotels B, C, E), the chief town (22,178 inhab.) of the eparchy of Aigialeia and the seat of a bishop, is a small commercial port. Called *Vostitsa* in the Middle Ages, it gave name to the finest currants grown in Greece. Currants and olive-oil are exported and there are large paper-mills. It has a ferry to Ay. Nikolaos (twice daily).

**History**. According to legend *Aigion* took its name from a local goat (αἴξ) which suckled the infant Zeus. The city is mentioned in the Homeric Catalogue and extensive finds, mostly Hellenistic and Roman and from building plots, attest occupation also from Neolithic to Geometric times. The Achaean League met here in the Homarion and for a time it was the chief city of Achaia. The name *Vostitsa* is of Slav origin. After the division of the Morea in 1209 it was given by Geoffrey de Villehardouin to Hugh de Lille de Charpigny as the barony of La Vostice. After a period under the Acciaioli, it surrendered to the Turks in 1458 and except for a Venetian interlude in 1463–70 remained Turkish until 1821. It was partly destroyed by earthquakes in 1819 and 1888.

The town is built on a cliff 30m high above a narrow strip of shore and has several fountains. The suburbs are nondescript but the old core has considerable charm. The Panayía Tripití stands in an attractive nursery garden. From the **main square** is Ayía Lávra, Od. Mitropóleos, with the cathedral, ascends to the attractive **Plateía Psilá Alónia** (cafés with a fine view of the Gulf of Corinth. Near the cathedral a mosaic floor depicting the Good Shepherd, probably from the narthex of an Early Christian basilica of c AD 500, was found in 1973–74. Above Psila Alonia, at the junction of Odd. Solomoú (left at lights) and Rouvalí are substantial remains of a Hellenistic **naïskos**.

In Od. Ayíou Andréou, near (N of) the Plateía Ayías Lávras, the old market, designed by Ziller (1890), had been splendidly refurbished to house a cultural centre and the **Archaeological Museum** (opened August 1994). The centrepiece of the museum is a fine Roman marble figure, beautifully displayed at the far end of a series of galleries which contain material of all periods, from Aiyio and the eparchy of Aigialeia. ROOMS 1–2: Neolithic-Mycenaean, including finds from the Kallithea Mycenaean cemetery (Aiyio). ROOM 3: Protogeometric and Geometric from various sites including two bronze bowls from Kato Mavriki. ROOMS 4 and 5: Archaic, Classical, Hellenistic and Roman finds from Aiyio, Mamousia (ancient *Keryneia*) etc., including a gold Hellenistic necklace and diadem and a silver cup, also terracotta figurines and moulds; Roman bronzes, clay *thymiateirion* inscribed as a dedication to Isis, tile fragments stamped ΑΙΓΙΟ. ROOM 6: statue (above) of male figure with *aegis*. The MAIN HALL in the centre of the building has finds (mostly architectural fragments) laid out round the sides. These include terracotta antifixes and cornices from the Temple of Artemis (?) at *Aigeira*, c 500 BC; capitals and other frangments in various styles, chiefly from Aiyio and Mamousia; also inscriptions. A tile fragment from Mamousia is inscribed ΚΑΡΥΝ[ΕΙΟΝ] confirming the identification of the ancient site.

A pleasant excursion up the Selinous Valley can take in two **monasteries**, the Taxiárkhis beyond the river on the right bank, to which site it was transferred in the 17C from (1 hour farther on) Paliomonástiro. Another road, further W, mounts the foothills of Panakhaïkón (1925m), where at **Dháfnai** (12km) are two refuges of the Greek Alpine Club.

The coastal plain is well-watered by torrents descending from Panakhaïkon, and bamboo is grown. 97km **Rodhodháfni**. 105km **Selianítika** (Hotels B, C). 108km **Lambíri** (Hotel C), with a holiday camp, lies on the semicircular harbour of *Erineos*, founded by earthquake refugees from Boura; here an indecisive battle was fought between the Corinthian and Athenian fleets in 415 BC.

117km **Psathópirgos** (Ψαθόπυργος, 'thatched tower'; Motel B) lies in the midst of very fine scenery resembling the Italian Riviera, with a lovely coastline across the Gulf. The mountains, thickly clothed with firs, plane-trees, arbutus, oleander, and a variety of flowering shrubs, run down to the coast, while the road and railway pass immediately above the sea, crossing a number of torrents. 120km **Arakhovítika**. To the right is Cape Dhrépanon, the northernmost point of the Peloponnese. At (127km) **Ayios Yeóryios** is the turning for **Río** (3km; Hotels A, B; ELPA Car Camp) where a car ferry sails at frequent intervals (day and night) to Andírrio (20 minutes; Rte 55) on the N shore of the Gulf.

The **Castle of the Morea** or 'Kastelli' on the shore, formerly a prison, is now open to the public and well worth a visit. It was built by Bayazid II in 1499 before his campaign in the Morea. Parts of its aqueduct still exist by the roadside. Here took place the last stand of the Turks in October 1828 when Ibrahim Pasha's troops held out for three weeks against a combined Anglo-French force under Marshal Maison. The moated fortress is also impressive from the sea.

135km **PATRAS** (modern Pátra; Πάτρα; Hotels A–E), the largest town (152,570 inhab.) in the Peloponnese and the third largest in Greece, is the capital of the nome of Achaia, and the seat of a bishop (the historic archiepiscopal see was degraded in 1899). The ancient city lay some distance inland from its port, to which it was connected by long walls. The high status of Patras (a *colonia*, see below) in Greece under the Roman empire has left correspondingly exotic traces, though relatively little is visible today because of the extensive urban development of recent years. Myriad rescue excavations have uncovered public buildings and private houses, often with mosaic floors and fine objects. Streets have been traced and evidence of agricultural activity (wine presses, etc.) discovered. Numerous graves and funerary monuments lined the roads outside the city. There are also important traces of the Early Christian and Byzantine city, and of a Jewish presence. Patras is celebrated in Greek national annals as the see of Archbishop Germanos, who raised the standard of the Cross at Kalavryta in 1821, and important geographically as the W gateway to Greece. The modern city was rebuilt on a grid plan with broad arcaded

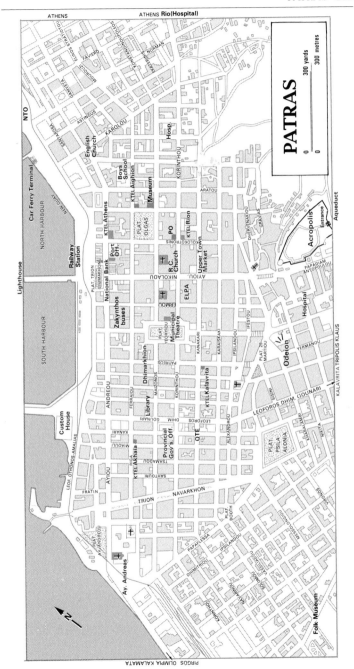

streets by Capodistrias after the Turks had burned the medieval town in 1821. Manufactures include cotton textiles and motor-tyres; among other products shipped from the busy port are currants, olive-oil, valonia, hides, and wine. The one-way street system makes exploration easier on foot.

**Restaurants**. On the quay; tavernas in the upper town.

**Post Office**. Zaími/Maízonos. **OTE**, Leof. Goúnari. **NTOG** office at Gate 6 *international terminal, at E end of quay).

**Buses** to the suburbs (including Rio) from Kolokotróni/Kanakári. **Main KTEL terminal** prominent on quay, to E of and opposite railway station. To Athens (frequent); to Aiyio and Dhiakofto (frequent); to Pirgos (regularly); to Vardha (frequent); to Kalavrita (regular); to Tripolis (daily; once via Kalavrita, once via Tripotama); to Mesolonghi and Agrinion (regular); to Navpaktos (regular); also (daily) to Levkas; to Arta and Ioannina; to Thessaloniki; to Kalamata.

**Ferries to the Ionian Islands**: daily to Kefallinía (Sami), Ithaka and Corfu); **also international** to Brindisi (car ferry), to Ancona (car ferry), and to Venice. The quays are approached by a series of Gates (ΠΥΛΗ). International departures are from Gate 6 (E end of waterfront).

**Festivals**. Carnival in February (10 days before Lent); Classical Theatre Season in summer; Procession of St Andrew, 30 November.

**Hellenic Alpine Club**, Pantanássis 29.

**History**. *Pátrai* was a substantial though not conspicuous member of the Achaean League. The idea of building her long walls came from Alcibiades (Thuc. V, 52). During an invasion of the Gauls the Patraians were the only Achaeans to cross into Phokis to help the Aitolians and they suffered accordingly. After the battle of Actium Augustus settled many of his veterans in the depopulated city which he refounded as the *Colonia Augusta Aroë Patrensis*. Hadrian is dubbed '*Restitutor Achaiae*' on coins of Patrai.

St Andrew, the first disciple, preached at Patrai and is said to have been martyred there. The town sent a bishop to the Council of Alexandria in 457 but not to earlier councils. Invading Slavs, assisted by a Saracen fleet, besieged Patras in 805 when the supposed intervention of St Andrew confirmed his veneration as the city's patron saint. The archbishop was raised to metropolitan rank about this time. In the 9–10C the city's prosperity grew, especially with the development of a silk trade and the involvement of a substantial Jewish community. In 1205 Patras became a Frankish barony and the seat of a Latin archbishop who soon ruled an almost autonomous principality. Carlo Zeno got his early military experience as a canon of Patras when it was besieged by Marie de Bourbon. In 1408 Patras was sold by its archbishop to Venice, and in 1426 the Pope appointed Pandolfo Malatesta in an attempt to hold it against the brothers Palaiologos. Constantine, however, took the city in 1429. Patras was held by his brother Thomas until 1460 when it passed to Mehmed II. It remained the commercial capital of Greece despite the political changes. Here in 1809 Byron first set foot on Greek soil. Both in the abortive rising of 1770 and in 1821 Patras claims to be the first town to have taken up arms. The Turks, however, aware of the intention of Archbishop Germanos to march on Patras from Kalavryta, occupied the citadel whence the town was bombarded and set on fire. It was not freed till 1828.

Natives of Patras are Kostis Palamas (1859–1943), the national poet; Stylianos Gonatas (1876–1966), revolutionary Prime Minister in 1922–24; and Jean Moreas (1856–1910), the French poet (born Papadiamantopoulos).

The **quay**, with the **railway station**, is generally animated. The long mole ending in a lighthouse is a favourite promenade. A little to the E, beyond the busy commercial arcades of Odhos Ay. Andreou, is Plateía Olgas. Here the **museum** is at present closed (earthquake damage): a new building is projected.

Odhós Maízonos leads SW past the Roman Catholic church to Od. Ayíou Nikoláou. Climbing to the top of this street, a broad flight of steps (view) leads to the **kastro** (08.00–17.00 (15.00 Sunday), closed Monday) built on the site of the ancient **acropolis**. This area of Patras (upper town) is appealing. It has a pleasant and relaxed atmosphere which is lacking nearer the quay. The **lower ward** of the kastro has round and polygonal towers and is planted with flowering shrubs. The N curtain wall, of early Byzantine date, incorporates Classical drums and blocks; similar elements occur in a flanking tower of the S curtain, but all periods of Byzantine–Turkish–Venetian rebuilding up to the 17C are represented. The well-preserved **keep** (no admission) has square towers but is equally indeterminate in date. The view embraces Zante and Kefallinia, the mountains of the Roumeli coast above Navpaktos, and, to the S, the peaks of Erymanthos. In Papadiamandopoúou nearby a **Temple of Augustus** has been identified.

From opposite the E gate of the castle a narrow paved road, skirting below the radio station in the park, passes (15 minute walk) through two sections of a **Roman aqueduct**, the first well-preserved, the second (ruinous) standing in places to 30m above the valley.

To the SW of the Kastro is the **odeion**, a characteristic Roman Imperial structure, which, when discovered in 1889, had 25 rows of seats (in 4 wedges) nearly entire, made of brick and faced with marble. Much of the marble was later removed by enterprising local builders. The theatre was extensively restored in 1960 and is now used for dramatic productions. The cavea faces S; the orchestra is 9.6m in diameter. In Yermanoú, just to the NW is a 3C AD **nymphaeum**. In this area of Patras the buildings seem to have been laid out on a series of terraces c 4m high. On the lower side of Plateía Ikosipénde Martíou are the remains of a substantial Roman building, which excavations (visible) in the streets below (Iféstou, Yerokostopoúlou) have suggested may be a **hippodrome** or amphitheatre. You can then take Od. Sisini, passing other Roman remains, to the Plateía Psilá Alónia. From this irregular space, planted with palms, a vigorous bronze of Archbishop Germanos raising the standard dominates the city. A substantial Roman terrace wall, typical of those needed to support buildings in this sloping area of Patras, can be seen in Od. Dhiákou, immediately below the Plateia. In Kanári (Vlákhou) a ?bath complex with nymphaeum, is being excavated.

Odhós Tríon Navarkhon descends to the W towards the huge ugly church of **Ayios Andreas**, in reinforced concrete by G. Nomikos. Here is venerated a gold *reliquary containing the head of St Andrew, returned by Pope Paul VI from St. Peter's, Rome, in 1964, where it had been since Thomas Palaiologos fled with it in 1460.

The church is supposed to be on the site of the Apostle's crucifixion, but is more likely over a Temple of Demeter. An earlier Byzantine church suffered in the fire of 1821. An inscription from the kastro commemorates the restoration of a church by Archbishop Malatesta in 1426; the composer Dufay is recorded to have written music in the same year for a consecration of his cathedral. According to a much older tradition the relics of St Andrew had already been removed in the 4C, when St Regulus, or Rule, Bishop of Patras, fled with the body to Scotland and was wrecked off Muckcross, in Fife, where he founded **St Andrews**.

You can return via Od. Korinthou or Od. Maizonos, passing the undistinguished public buildings of Patras to Plateía Yeoryíou Tou Prótou, the central square of the city, with the **theatre**, and then to the quay.

On the W side of the town in the Skagliopoúlou Park (Odd. Korítsas and Mavrokordhátou) is the **Folk Museum**.

An EXCURSION can be made to the Akhaia-Klauss wine vaults (8km; leave via Od. Goúnari, or Bus 7 to Klauss), founded 1861, where parties are given conducted tours (09.00–19.30). The buildings occupy the site of a partly excavated Mycenaean chamber-tomb cemetery.

Climbers wishing to ascend Mt Panakhaïkon (1927m) should contact the Hellenic Alpine Club in Patras. From **Romanós** (6.5km from Patras) it is three hours on foot to **Psarthi Refuge A** (1494m; 50 beds; water; ski-lift), then 45 minutes to **Prassondi Refuge B** (1798m).

# 39

# Trípolis to Patras (Pátra)

## A.  Via Kalávrita

**Road**, 165km (102.5 miles) magnificently scenic, needing care in the Erimanthos Mts. Bus daily (early morning) in c 6 hours (including ½ hour in Kalavrita); additional morning bus from Kalavrita to Patras. 58km Káto Klitoriá.—90km Turning for Kalávrita (3km right).—142km Khalandrítsa.—149km Turning for Pirgos.—165km Pátras.

**Tripolis**, see Rte 30; then to (35km) **Vlakhérna**, see Rte 36. 1km farther on, at the N end of Mt Mainalon, you turn right off the Olympia road to make a long descent into the wooded and marshy valley of the lesser (S) affluent of the Ladon. 42km **Panayítsa**. You pass below (45km) **Dháras**, where Photakos (1798–1878) lived in exile and wrote his history of the war of 1821. The narrow road enters Akhaia and runs close to the rushing stream, beyond a defile joining the wide valley of the Ladon. Turning upstream (N), the road crosses (50km) the **Aroanios Bridge** (Yéfira tou Aroaníou) to the W bank, leaving to the left the Tripótama road (Rte 39B).

58km **Káto Klitoriá** (Hotel B), locally known as Mazéïka, a market village (915 inhab.) at the junction of two valleys, lies at the SW foot of the Aroania Mts (comp. Rte 38). At the W exit of the village, a track (left; signed) leads in 500m to ancient *Kleitor*, on flat ground between two rivers, with imposing **walls** and towers and the remains of a theatre. The view opens to the W past (64km) **Ano Klitoriá**. 72.5km **Kastélli** lies below (left) under iron-bearing hills. The mountain views become immense as the road climbs in increasingly rough country to (74km) **Afkhéna tou Khelmoú** (the 'Aroania neck'; 1049m), a saddle where diverges a road to Tripótama (27.5km; see below).

The road descends in loops to (76.5km) **Priólithos** (799m) at the head of the long and pretty valley of the Vouraïkos which gradually broadens. You pass below Ayia Lavra (see below) and reach the Patras–Kalavrita road, 3km W of Kalávrita. 92km **Kalávrita** (Καλάβρυτα; Hotels B, C, D), chief town (2111 inhab.) of an eparchy and seat of a bishop, is situated at 756m on the Vouraïkos at the foot of Mt Velia. Cool mountain springs and the freshness of the air make it especially attractive in summer.

**Kalávrita** is the successor to ancient *Kynaithes*, whose inhabitants were distinguished for their independence, wildness, and irreverence. The town was destroyed by the Aetolians in 220 BC but revived under Hadrian. After 1205 the fief of *Kalovrate* fell to Otto de Tournai, and in 1301 passed to the barons of Chalandritsa. In modern Greek history it disputes with Kalamata the claim to be the first town liberated in the War of Independence (see below). It twice fell into Ibrahim Pasha's hands, in 1826 and 1827. On 13 December 1943 German occupying troops, in reprisal for the shooting of 81 of their men taken prisoner by ELAS guerillas, here massacred 1436 males over the age of 15 and burnt the town. 20 mins NE (signed 'Sacrifice of 1943') is the memorial on the hillside site of the massacre. Kalavrita is a member of the Association of Martyred Towns, whose members include Coventry, Guernica and Lidice. Since 1962 the German Federal government has re-endowed Kalavritan schools.

The clock on the **Metropolitan church** stands at 2.34, the hour of the massacre of 1943. Some antique remains may be seen between Ay. Aikaterini and Ay. Yeoryios and round the Kalavritiní spring, to the SW of the town, identified with the Classical *Alyssos*. About 1 hour E of the town on a rocky height stand the ruins of '*Tremola*', or the Kástro tis Oriás. The first name derives from Humbert de la Trémouille, the second from the beautiful Katherine Palaiologos, daughter of a Chalandritsa baron, who is said to have committed suicide rather than fall into Turkish hands in 1463.

7km SW (taxis) is **Ayía Lávra**, the celebrated monastery (09.30–13.30; 18.00–19.30, most days) where Germanos, Archbishop of Patras, raised the standard of revolt on 21 March 1821. A hermitage, started in 961, developed into a monastery many times destroyed and rebuilt. The present building, begun in 1839, has suffered by earthquake and fire and in 1943 but, again rebuilt, retains the **Church of the Dormition** from before the sack by Ibrahim in 1826. A little **museum** contains historical relics and medieval MSS. On a hill 2.5km to the W stands the imposing monument to the national uprising of 1821, erected on the 150th anniversary. On the back is a relief of the banner of the Dormition on which *Archbishop Germanos* administered the oath of revolt.

From Kalavrita, a road (signed 'Winter Sports Centre' and 'Sacrifice of 1943') leads past the massacre site. 6km Junction (right; partly surfaced) for (12km SE) **Ano Loússoi**, (13km) **Káto Loússoi**, (16.5km) the spectacular **Kastria caves** (lakes; stalactites etc.; open to visitors), (19km) **Kastría** and (27km) **Káto Kleitoriá** (see above).

At **Káto Loússoi**, there is a turning (right) which may be reached (in 4km; one bus daily in each direction to/from Kalavrita) the remains of ancient *Lousoi*. A good but unsurfaced track leads in loops up the hillside. A few hundred metres from the main road are the recent excavations (Austrian Archaeological Institute) which have uncovered a Hellenistic house with peristyle, bathroom and farming equipment. Another building includes a dining room with space for 11 couches, also two phases of a bathroom. The area was reconstructed in the Roman period and there are also signs of pre-Hellenistic occupation. Higher up the track (left), on a bluff above the valley, lies a Hellenistic **Sanctuary of Artemis** (Austrian Institute 1898–99 and renewed excavation). The temple (3C BC with a predecessor, and votives back to the Geometric period), by the roadside, is of unusual design; the pronaos, cella (with base for cult statue) and opisthodomos being flanked on either side by porticoes which replace the usual colonnade. Below are remains of a semicircular building, with propylaea, and of a fountain house. The latter was supplied by an aqueduct whose line has been partly traced higher up the valley. The acropolis of the ancient town (walls, remains of towers) is on the hill of Profitis Ilias, above the temple.

The road ahead climbs through forests to (11km) the Aroania ski lift. From the top of the lift (open in summer) the spectacular summit of Khelmos (2431m) is accessible in about 3 hours rough climb. There is a refuge at 2100m.

From Kalávrita to **Megaspíleion** and **Dhiakoftó** (Athens), see Rte 38.

The Patras road heads W across the valley to enter the winding gap between Panakhaïkón, to the N, and Erímanthos, to the S. 100km **Vrisári** (or Gouménissa; 2km, right) has a Mycenaean cemetery near the church of Ayia Paraskevi. The jagged peaks of Erimanthos are well seen from (104km) Flámboura. 108km **Boúmbouka** retains a Turkish appearance. The road climbs to nearly 1067m before descending to (116km) **Káto Vlasía** under the N face of Erímanthos. At Kastritsi, about 3km SW of the road, is the site of ancient *Leontion* with a theatre (4C BC) excavated by N. Yialouris in 1958. New engineering has removed many loops of the road, which climbs steadily up the N side of a wild gorge. The dizzy ledge runs along the S outliers of Panakhaïkon. 126km **Plátanos** and Kálanos are superbly sited facing *vistas of epic grandeur extending W to the sea.

Beyond (127km) **Kalanístra** (*view) the road reaches a further summit (721m) with a magnificent retrospective panorama. A by-road diverges (right) to **Dheméstikha** (8km) with vineyards producing well-known wines bottled by Akhaia-Klauss near Patras. Modern **Leóntio** (8km further) has some Mycenaean and other antiquities. 134km **Katarráktis** lies in an enclosed valley above which Mycenaean settlements (and traces of Middle Helladic occupation) were located in 1957 in the region of ancient *Pharai*. 142km **Khalandrítsa** (974 inhab.), once a Frankish barony and with a fine 11–12C church (Ay. Athanasios), looks over the coastal plain towards Zante.

A Mycenaean settlement has been located at Ay. Antonios and a tholos tomb at Troumbe, both nearby. 147km (right) just before the turn to **Méntzaina** is the 10C basilican church of the Koimisis tis Theotokou, on the site of a Roman complex. In and around the church is an Early Christian cemetery, also Frankish and Ottoman burials. 149km You join the road described in Rte 39B. 165km **Patras**, see Rte 38.

# B.   Via Tripótama

**Road**, 179km (112 miles), since its improvement the main link between Arkadia and Akhaia.—50km Aroánios Bridge.—83km Tripótama (ancient Psophis).—179km Patras.—**Bus**, once daily in either direction; also once daily Athens–Patras–Tripótama–Dháfni. Once daily from Tripótama to Pírgos.

From Tripolis to (50km) the **Aroanios Bridge**, see Rte 39A. Here a new road diverges W and, beyond (55.5km) Kalívia, quits the Ladon valley. At 68km a road ascends to the S to **Dháfni** (5km; Hotel E), a deme of 1287 inhabitants. in a delightful situation, with a monastery (Evanghelistrias) of the late 17C and many medieval churches. For access from here to the **Ladhon Dam**, see Rte 36. At the far end of (74km) **Páos** a dirt road (left; signed Kontovásaina) passes after 8km the chapel of Ayios Petros (views) which stands in the **Sanctuary of Aphrodite Erykina** (now published by C. Kardara) which was identified in 1967–69. It was the seat of an oracle.

The church is on the site of the **temple** and a **telesterion**. Nearer the road are the base of a monumental **altar** and a section of paved ancient **road**, also a tripartite **building**. A fountain was fed via terracotta pipes from a spring on the mountain above. The **stadium** was in the hollow immediately to the N (sections of the **judges' seats** survive). Hephaestos was also worshipped here and the sanctuary included metalworking installations. A sacred road connects the site with *Psophis*. Sanctuary finds are of the 7C and later, but the area has yielded material from prehistoric to Frankish in date.

The road crosses a saddle and joins the Seiraíos (Versiótiko). To the left the Afrodísion range divides Akhaia from Arkadia. 83km **Tripótama** (550m), a small village and bus junction, stands at the confluence of the Seiraíos and the Aroánios (Livartsinó) with the Erímanthos (Nousaïtiko), where the common frontiers of Akhaia, Arkadia and Elis meet. There is a turn (right) for Kalávrita. Here are extensive but scanty remains of ancient *Psophis*, destroyed by Philip V of Macedon in 219 BC. The situation, hemmed in by mountains, is subject to extremes of heat and violent winds.

After Tripótama the route crosses the Erímanthos into Elis, rising high above its right bank on the slopes of Mt Lámbeia. 97km **Lámbeia**, a well-watered spot with plane-trees, lies below the Ano Moní Dhívris. As Dhívri, it was the head-quarters of the Peloponnesian communist rebels in 1948.

About 5km beyond Lambeia a road diverges (left) across the extensive plateau of Pholóis, the watershed between the Alpheios and the Pineios, which ancient legend peopled with Centaurs. Some remains near Koúmanis, off the road (right) at 8km, have been identified with Classical *Lasion*. 22km **Lála** (Hotel D) was of some importance in the Ottoman period. The road makes a long winding descent to (39km) **Plátanos** (Rte 36), 3km W of Olympia on the Pirgos road.

The main road descends gradually by twists and turns above a series of ravines, passing into the basin of the Pineios. 117km N of **Kakotári** (3km, right) Kastro Orias is a Frankish fortress. 122km Turn (left) for Amaliádha (34km, Rte 40); also for ancient *Elis*, branching right in Khavári for Avyío). At (125km) **Ayía Triádha**, formerly Boukovína, with another Frankish citadel over Hellenistic remains, also a Mycenaean chamber-tomb cemetery, you turn N, crossing the Pineios into Akhaia, and run through uplands between Mts Skóllis (W) and Erímanthos. 144km By-road to **Kaléntzi** (8km right; Hotel B, April–October), a pleasant mountain base (975m), from which the Ionian Islands can be seen and the second summit of Erimanthos (2128m) climbed. Here was born *George Papandreou* (1888–1968), prime minister in 1961–65. At 164km the Kalavrita road (Rte 39A) comes in on the right. Passing below **Kallithéa**, with a Late Helladic cemetery (at Laganídhia), you descend to the olive-groves in the coastal plain. Kríni (2km right) has a Mycenaean cemetery. 179km **Patras**, see Rte 38.

# 40

# Patras (Pátra) to Pírgos

**Road**, 96km (60 miles) in flat fertile country.—23km Káto Akhaía.—62km Lekhainá, for Killíni and Chlemoútsi.—66km Andrávidha.—72.5km Gastoúni, for Loutrá Killínis.—84.5km Amaliádha (E of the road).—96km Pírgos. **Buses** c hourly. Note that road improvements allow for many of the villages mentioned to be bypassed.

**Railway**, 100km (62 miles), following the road closely all the way. 7 trains daily in 1½–3 hours.

Most of this route is in **Elis**, bordered on the N by Akhaia, on the E by Arkadia, on the S very briefly by Messenia, and on the W by the Ionian Sea. The Channel of Zante separates the area from that island, and Kefallinia lies off its N seaboard. Elis faces W towards Europe, is remote from the Aegean, and cut off from the rest of the Peloponnese by a mountain barrier intersected by easily guarded ravines.

In antiquity the region was divided into three parts: *Hollow Elis*, or Elis proper, in the N, watered by the Elean Peneios; *Pisatis*, the country of Pisa, on the Alpheios, in the centre (including Olympia; Rtes 36, 37); and *Triphylia*, between the Alpheios and the Neda, in the S. Famous for the grove of Altis and the Temple of Zeus at Olympia and for the Olympic Games, Elis was regarded as a holy land and its neutrality respected from high antiquity until the Peloponnesian War. The country was noted for its horses and especially suited to the growth of fine flax.

The place-names attest later occupation from the N and W by Avars, Slavs, and Albanians. The coastal plain became an important centre of the Frankish occupation and has always supported horses, sheep, goats and cattle. The cultivation of the currant-vine since 1850 has brought prosperity and importance, though only since the Second World War has the area ceased to be malarial.

The road (many of the villages are bypassed) leaves Patras by an unattractive stretch of shore, backed by untidy factories and workshops. 5km Itiés. 8km **Paralía Proastíou** (Hotels C). The coast now commands a view across the Gulf of Patras. The plain produces lemons and currants. 12km **Vraknéïka**. Beyond (13km) **Tsoukaléïka** a by-road ascends inland.

After 3.5km it divides, the left branch ascending to **Mazaráki** (12km), where a large Protogeometric and Geometric votive deposit belonging to the sanctuary of a female deity (?Artemis) was excavated from 1973. The right branch leads to Ano Soudhenéïka (12km) near which, at **Arla** (bus), is the Frankish **fort** at Yiftókastro which controls the passes to the S. A poor road continues to **Sandaméri** (11km further; bus) a village deriving name from a Frankish Château de Saint-Omer.

You cross the Pirros and enter (23km) **Káto Akhaîa** (4947 inhab.; Hotel C), the site of ancient *Dyme*. The Chronicle of the Morea is probably incorrect in locating here the landing of Guillaume de Champlitte in 1205.

Here a branch road goes off (right) to **Araxos** (13km), the airfield of Patras, near the marshy lagoons of the NW promontory of the Peloponnese. Above the fish-hatcheries rises the 'Kastro tis Kalogrias', a hill with an enceinte of Cyclopean walls that stand in places to 9m. This is the **Teichos Dymaion** of Polybius. Excavations of the Greek Archaeological Service in 1962–65 proved occupation in Early, Middle, and Late Helladic times. LHIIIC material shows that the site was reoccupied after a destruction c 1200 BC and before a final catastrophic eclipse in the 11C. There are impressive walls and good views—but beware of snakes.

Turning S from the town, green foothills rise ahead with the long stark arête of Skóllis (1015m), above Sandaméri, farther left. 35km **Lápas**. The road enters the nome of Elis (see above). 43km Néa Manoládha. 47km **Várdha** lies 2km E of **Manoládha**, an estate formerly held by the Crown Prince, scene in 1316 of a battle between Louis of Burgundy and Ferdinand of Majorca in which the latter was slain. It has a 12C church (the Palaiopanagia, being restored) and is noted for water-melons and yoghourt. Beyond Manoládha the by-road continues to **Loutrá Kounoupéli** (10km; sandy beach) in an area troubled by mosquitoes. 62km **Lekhainá** (Hotel E), a market town of 3137 inhab., is the birthplace of Andrea Karkavitsa (1866–1923), the novelist. 64.5km Turning (right) for Killini, Chlemoutsi, and Loutra Killinis (see below) on the extreme W projection of the Peloponnese.

The road joins a by-road direct from Lekhaina at (4km) **Mirsíni** and runs W to (8km) **Neokhóri**, where it divides. To the right is (16km) **Killíni** (Κυλλήνη; Hotels C, D), ferry-boat station for Zante (several times daily in 1½ hours; also to Kefallinía, comp. Rte 56; departures are less frequent out of season). As *Glarentza* (or Clarence) it was the chief port of Frankish Morea.

Ancient *Kyllene* was the port of Elis, a trading point with Magna Graecia, and in the Peloponnesian War served as a Spartan naval station. Here Alcibiades landed after his fugitive journey from Thurii. Kyllene was captured by Sulpicius in 208 BC. In the Middle Ages *Clarence* became the residence of the Villehardouin princes of Akhaia, and their Angevin successors here developed the court life described in the Chronicles of the Morea. 'Chiarenza' became the port of transit for Venetian and Genoese galleys from Brindisi or Taranto. In 1428 it passed to Constantine Palaiologos, who systematically destroyed it as soon as he held the last Frankish outpost (Patras).

Scattered foundations of the medieval city remain on the low plateau NW of the modern village with a large ruined church similar to that at Andravidha. A medieval castle was dynamited during the German occupation. Earlier remains may be traced near the 12C Byzantine **Moní ton Vlakhernón** (30 minutes to the E), completed by the Franks.

The conspicuous *Castle of Khlemoútsi** on the lone height to the S known to the ancients as *Cape Chelonatas* (from its resemblance when seen from seaward to a tortoise-shell) is reached from Neokhori (see above) by taking the Loutrá Killínis road to **Kástro** (8km). The site can also be approached direct from Killini itself via the coast road, with a turn inland (6km) to Kastro. Above the village towers the crenellated enceinte of the best-preserved Frankish monument in the Morea.

Khlemoutsi was built in 1220–23 with revenues confiscated from the Latin clergy by Geoffrey I Villehardouin, who called it *Clairmont*. The Venetians later dubbed it *Castel Tornese* perhaps after the coins (tournois) minted in Glarentza. The castle was held by Ferdinand of Majorca in 1314–16. It fell in 1427 to Constantine Palaiologos, who based here his campaign against Patras. The Turks refortified the site after 1460. Some traces of Middle Helladic occupation of the hill have been recognised in the castle foundations. On the lower E slopes of this hill palaeolithic implements were found in 1960.

The original recessed **entrance gate** has been obscured by the Turkish addition built flush with the curtain into the outer passage. Within to the left is a well-preserved 13C construction, but most of the buildings that backed the **curtain wall** have disappeared; their fireplaces only remain. The breach made by Ibrahim Pasha's guns in 1825 can be seen near the SW angle. The **keep**, a huge irregular hexagon, consists of a series of vast vaulted galleries arranged round a court. These were divided into two stories either by an intermediate vault (as in the N and NW) or by wooden floors (S and SW). The massive barrel-vaults, in fine ashlar masonry, were strengthened by reinforcing arches; though these have mostly fallen much of the vault has held. The double-arched windows are interesting. The *view commands the Zante channel and the whole plain of Elis.

Beyond **Kástro**, you turn left onto the coast road to **Loutrá Killínis** (6km; Hotels A, C; see below).

66km **Andravídha** (Ανδραβιδα), an uninteresting market-town of 3147 inhabitants, replaces *Andreville*, once the flourishing capital of the Frankish principate of the Morea and seat of a catholic bishop. Of his cathedral church of Ayia Sophia, two Gothic bays of the E end with the apse and E aisle chapels survive in a ruinous state. Of the Templars' church of St James, where the Villehardouin princes were buried, nothing remains. 70km **Kavásila** is the railway junction for Killini and Loutra Killinis. The road crosses the Pinios, depleted since the damming works (see below). 72.5km **Gastoúni** (Hotels C, E), the livestock market (5883 inhab.) of the plain, takes its name from the Frankish fief of Gastogne and under the Turkish occupation was the chief town of Elis. The interesting church of the **Panayia** is 12C.

Here a road diverges W to **Vartholomió**, another large village (3182 inhab.), where it meets a road from Lekhaina (see above), continuing to **Loutrá Killínis** (16km; Hotels A, C), a thermal establishment amid pine woods, near the excellent sandy Olympic Beach (holiday camp and extensive tourist development). By the **baths** are remains of their Roman predecessors.

In the opposite direction from Gastouni (occasional buses; others from Amaliádha) a good road leads NE via **Avgeío** (or Boukhióti) to (12km) ancient *Elis*, excavated by the Austrian School in 1910–14 and jointly with the Greek Archaeological Service since 1960. The bus stops by a small museum, which has a plan of the excavated remains. These are scattered and, with the exception of the theatre, largely overgrown and invisible. From the 5C the site was of considerable importance, not only as the main city of Elis, but also because of its dominant role in the organisation of the Olympic Games (see Rte 37). Athletes trained here under supervision for one month before the start of the games and facilities for them (palaistrai, gymnasia) and the officials (Hellanodikaion; Stoa of the Hellanodikai) were provided. All these buildings have been identified in the vicinity of the agora, where is also the south or 'Corcyraean' stoa, mentioned by Pausanias, although his explanation of its name which requires a foundation date in the 5C cannot be reconciled with the archaeological evidence for one in the 2 or 1C BC. A Late Roman building has fine mosaics of the Muses and the Labours of Herakles. A path leads to the **theatre**, a Hellenistic reconstruction of a Classical structure, again altered in Roman times. There are remains of parodoi, foundations in poor limestone of the paraskenion, and portions of the analemma. The cavea was banked, probably with radials in stone, but did not have stone seats. Stone 'tickets' were found. An Early Helladic tomb came to light and nine slab-covered graves attributed to the transitional period between sub-Mycenaean and protogeometric. The boundaries of the city have been fixed and two cemeteries explored. The **acropolis** was on the hill locally called Kaloskópi, a name which led to the erroneous location here of Beauregard, a lost Frankish castle.

About 5km farther up the river near **Kéndro** is the huge Pinios irrigation dam, built in 1961–62 by American engineers, forming a large lake. In a series of international 'salvage digs' in the area, the flat-topped hill of Armátova, in the angle of the confluence of the Ladon and Peneios, just NW of **Agrapidhokhóri**, upheld its claim to be the site of *Elean Pylos*.

78km **Savália**. The main road avoids **Amaliádha** (6km E; Hotels C), a modern market town with 15,232 inhabitants, served by both railway and buses. To the right extends the sandy **Paralía tis Kouroútas** (car camping; tavernas, etc.) frequented by Elians in summer. At (88km) **Khanákia** a by-road runs (right) to **Skafídhia** (5km; Hotels A, E), with a Byzantine monastery. Leaving to the right Ayios Ioannis (see below), you enter (97km) **Pírgos** (Πύργος; Hotels C), a busy market town (21,958 inhab.), occupied with the currant trade (Stafidhikó Institoúto, etc.).

A branch railway and road run W. 5km **Ayios Ioánnis** occupies the site of ancient *Letrinoi* which gives to Pirgos its official deme-name. 11km Turning (right) to **Ayios Andréas** (*Pheia*; see below). 13km **Katákolo** (Hotels A, C, D) is a small port founded for the currant trade in 1857. It is used by cruise ships as a base for the visit to Olympia. **Fía**, on the bay of Ayios Andreas, is a hamlet with a good beach. Ancient *Pheia*, once the main port of Elis, was partially engulfed by the earthquake that overthrew the Temple of Zeus at Olympia in the 6C AD. Its low acropolis (Pondikókastro) became the *Beauvoir* of the Villehardouin, and finds are of all periods from Neolithic to Hellenistic. The walls can be traced underwater, where the remains were explored by N. Yalouris and John Hall in 1957–60.

To Olympia, see Rte 36; Samikon and Kakovatos, see Rte 34.

# IV CENTRAL GREECE

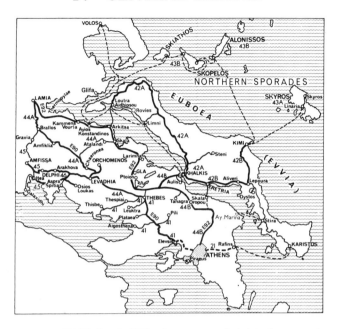

**CENTRAL GREECE (Steréa Ellás)** denotes an administrative grouping of seven nomes that extend from Attica to Akarnanía. Of these only Viotía (Boeotia), Evvia (Euboea), Fokís (Phocis), and part of Fthiótis (Phthiotis) come in this section. In antiquity **Boeotia** (Βοιωτία; in modern Greek Viotía) was a district, lying between the Euboean Straits and the Gulf of Corinth, bounded on the N by Opuntian Lokris, and on the S by Attica and Megaris. The low-lying interior is nearly surrounded by mountains. On the S is the barrier of Parnes and Kithairon. On the W are Helikon and Parnassos, and on the N the Opuntian mountains. The highest summit in Boeotia is Helikon, which rises to 1750m. Near the E coast are more isolated heights, between which the Asopos plain reaches to the sea. The Asopos, rising near Plataia, flows past Tanagra, and debouches into the Euboean Channel N of Oropos. Its plain is adjoined on the N by the plain of Thebes, beyond which extend the Boeotian Lakes. The Kopaïs, once the largest lake in Greece, is now a fertile plain growing cereals and cotton and grazing pedigree cattle. The Boeotian Kephissos, the other notable river, finds its outlets in swallow-holes. Between Helikon and the coastal ridge to the S is the plain of Thisbe.

Boeotia flourished in prehistoric times with Mycenaean centres at 'Minyan' Orchomenos, at Gla, and at 'Cadmeian' Thebes. The history of the region is summarised with the descriptions of these places. With two sea coasts and good harbours Boeotia was well placed for maritime trade. All land routes between northern and southern Greece pass through it. The soil was fertile. Despite these natural advantages the Boeotians never (save for nine short years under Epaminondas) took the leadership in Greek affairs, because, in the opinion of Strabo, 'they belittled the value of learning and of sociability, and cared alone for the military virtues'. They had in antiquity a reputation for slow-witted illiteracy and boorish manners, but their policy towards the Euripos was astute.

Among the many battles fought in Boeotia, three were of vital importance: Plataea, in 479 BC, which secured the independence of Greece at the end of the Persian wars; Leuktra, in 371, which ended the long-suffered hegemony of Sparta and gave Thebes her nine-years' period of leadership over the rest of Greece; and Chaironeia, in 338, at which city-state democracy was virtually extinguished by the victory of Philip of Macedon.

On account of its Classical interest and sparse modern habitation, Boeotia was one of the earliest regions to attract the interest of archaeologists. Some of the sites explored by earlier generations, especially those of battles, are only rewarding to dedicated antiquaries, though many of them still enjoy that romantic isolation fast being lost elsewhere. Aigósthena, Gla, and the museum at Thebes should not be missed. Orchomenos is impressive. Places of natural beauty include the valley of the Muses on Mt Helikon and the N coast of the Gulf of Corinth, the latter accessible with difficulty, but offering a number of impressive fortified sites to the energetic walker. The largest centres are Thebes and Levadhia, in both of which fair accommodation and good food can be found. Levadhia is the administrative capital of the modern nome. A rash of factories has begun to disfigure the E plains.

**Phokis** (modern Fokís) is a small region famous for containing the city and oracle of Delphi. In antiquity it was bounded on the N by Epiknemidian Locris and Opuntian Locris, on the E by Boeotia, on the W by Ozolian Locris and Doris, and on the S by two inlets of the Gulf of Corinth, the Krisaean Gulf (Bay of Itea) and the Antikyran Gulf (Bay of Aspra Spitia). At one time its territory extended across Greece to the port of Daphnous, on the Atalante Channel. The interior is unproductive and mountainous, culminating in Parnassos (2457m). None of the 22 Phocian cities was very large.

# 41

# Athens to Thebes (Thíva). Central Boeotia (Viotía)

**Road**, 74km (46 miles) undulating and sinuous over Mt Kithairon.—To (22.5km) Elévsis, see Rte 16. The town is bypassed and a right fork leads to (27km) Mándhra.—51.5km. Turning for Aigósthena.—53km Eleútherai.—61km Erithrai.—74km Thebes. **Buses** from Thissíon Terminal, also several times daily, to Villiá and Aigósthena. Direct buses (1½ hrs) to Thebes follow the National Highway (Rte 41B).

The **railway**, 100km (62 miles) to Thebes (8 times daily in 75–90 minutes) runs very close to the Lamia highway described in Rte 44B.

From Athens to the Elevsis turn, see Rte 16. You continue by the main Corinth highway, but at 24km branch right and by-pass **Mándra** (10,012 inhab.) at the base of the stony hills that shut in the plain of Eleusis on the W. The road ascends to (36km) **Ayios Sotír**, the church of the Saviour, whose silver-painted dome marks the summit of the first ridge. Entering the mouth of the valley of Palaiokhori (small Byzantine church), the road undulates across several ridges. 42km Restaurant on a col. After the descent, an ancient watch-tower marks the entrance to (47.5km) modern **Oinóï**.

To find the scanty ruins uncertainly identified with ancient *Oinoe*, an important Athenian border fortress, you take the by-road (right, signposted to the Kithairon waterworks tunnel) towards Pánakton. The sites lie right of the road after c 3km, just before a turning (left) to **Osios Melétios** (3km N), an interesting and attractive monastery with an 11C Byzantine church. The exonarthex has a decorated floor and 14C frescoes. At (10km) **Pánakton**, a medieval tower on a conical hill commanding the cultivated plateau at the W end of Parnes marks the site of a Frankish settlement and a more ancient fortress, taken by treachery by the Boeotians in 421 BC and returned to the Athenians by Demetrios Poliorketes. It was also a stronghold in Late Helladic times and there are remains of other periods from Neolithic to Byzantine. The identification of both places leaves many historical problems unexplained (see J.H.S. 1926). Some scholars would exchange the identities of Panakton and Eleutherai (see below). The road goes on to (13km) **Píli**, with a Frankish tower, and the plain of Skourta (Rte 19B).

5km Turning (left) for Aigosthena.

This road runs W and bypasses (4km) **Villiá** (Βιλιά; Hotels B, C, tavernas), a chicken-farming village of 1912 inhabitants. Avoiding a military road which goes off right up Kithairon, at (12km) **Ayios Vasíleos** you cross the line of an ancient road, explored by N.G.L. Hammond (B.S.A., 1954) and claimed by him to be the main highway from Boeotia to the Peloponnese. Near **Vathikhória**, to the SW, are the remains of seven guard-towers of Classical date, two of which stand to almost their original height.

The road descends (*view) to the sheltered bay of **Aigósthena** (22km; Hotel (summer) C; tavernas), the most E arm of the Gulf of Corinth, known before it readopted the ancient name as **Pórto Yermenó**. It is thickly planted with olives and shut in to the N by Kithairon and to the S by Pateras. *Aigosthena* (Αἰγόσθενα) belonged to Megara; it was never of great importance, but the *fortifications are among the finest in Greece. The walls enclosed a rectangle c 550m by 180m. The E wall, partly of polygonal masonry, with four square towers in regular ashlar courses, is the best preserved. The tower at the SE angle, one of the best examples of Greek defensive architecture of the 4C BC, rises over 10m above the top of the wall. Joist-holes for wooden floors can be seen in the middle towers. Within the enceinte two small churches locate the remains of late-Byzantine monastic cells; lower down is a larger basilica with floor mosaics. Long walls descend to the sea. The Lacedaemonians retreated to Aigosthena after their defeat at Leuktra in 371 BC.

52km **Kháni Káza** lies just within the entrance to the Pass of Yiftókastro between Vordositi (956m), the E outlier of Kithairon, and the W spur (930m) of Mt Pastra. It is still debated whether this or the pass farther W now crossed by a military road represents the ancient pass of *Dryoskephalai*. At the entrance on the right of the road rises a steep and rocky knoll crowned by the *fortress known as *Eleutherai* (commonly Yiftókastro), though the identification can be questioned (see above). Eleutherai, originally Boeotian, went over to Athens in the 6C BC. The defences, in excellent masonry of the 4C BC, are nearly complete on the N side. Eight rectangular towers, 35m–45m apart, are connected by walls about 3.5m high. Several of the towers cover sally-ports in the adjoining curtain. Each tower had a door to the court and three small openings in the upper storey.

In the fields opposite the Aigosthena fork (and well seen from the E wall of Eleutherai) is the substructure of a **temple** dating from c 300 BC, perhaps that of Dionysos mentioned by Pausanias. Farther E two Early Christian **basilicas** have been located.

To the W the heights of Mt Kithairon rise to 1410m. The mountain, where Oedipus was exposed and where Pentheus was torn to pieces by the Bacchantes, became the frontier between Attica and Boeotia when the

Eleutherians cast in their lot with Athens. Its pine-woods are noted for their game. At (57km) the summit of the pass, the great Boeotian plain lies below, though Thebes is hidden by an intermediate hillock. In the middle distance the two Boeotian lakes are backed by Mt Ptoön, while farther W rise the summits of Helikon and Parnassus, and on the NE horizon the pyramidal Dhirfis in Euboea. The road curves down to (61km) **Erithraí** (Ερυθραί or Kriekoúki), nowadays an enclave of Attica, with 3519 inhabitants.

At the far end of the town a road leads W to (5km) **Plataiaí** where, just before the village and on both sides of the road, are the widespread ruins of ancient *Plataea*. There is a plan of the battle. The ruined **enceinte**, with some stretches of excellent 4C ashlar masonry and other less well-preserved pieces of polygonal work, encompasses foundations of a small temple, and of the **Katagogeion**, or hotel, erected for its visitors after the destruction of the town in 426 BC, neither now visible.

*Plataea*, a small Boeotian town, near the border with Attica, early turned to Athens in an attempt to maintain its independence of Thebes. In 490 BC the Plataeans achieved fame by sending their entire army of 1000 men to support the Athenians at Marathon. During the invasion of Xerxes, they remained staunchly loyal to the Athenian cause and their city was destroyed by the Persians and Thebans. A period of peace when Plataea was guaranteed from attack followed the battle of 479 (see below). A Theban attempt in 431 to invest the rebuilt city was foiled, but in 427 after a two years' siege Plataea was razed to the ground by the Spartans and its people slain. Rebuilt after the Peace of Antalcidas (387), it was again destroyed in 373 by the Thebans. After the battle of Chaironeia, Philip, in fulfilment of his policy of humiliating Thebes, refounded the town, which lasted into Byzantine times, though without particular importance.

The **Battle of Plataea** is described in detail by Herodotus (IX, 19). In 479, after sacking Athens, Mardonius retired by way of Tanagra to Boeotia, where the terrain was better suited to his cavalry. He encamped before the Asopos near Plataea, facing the foothills of Kithairon over whose passes armies from Attica or the Peloponnese must come. The forces of the Greek league, commanded by the Spartan Pausanias, with Aristides' Athenians on the left wing, took up their first position along the foothills. They were outnumbered three to one and lacked a cavalry arm. For three weeks the opposing generals manoeuvred for favourable positions. The Greeks suffered constant harrying by the Persian cavalry, though a picked force of 300 Athenians succeeded in killing Masistius, the Persian cavalry commander. A Greek attempt to outflank the enemy and cut them off from Thebes miscarried; in the subsequent retreat the Greek forces became split into three. Mardonius attacked the Spartans, whose fighting qualities proved superior, and the Persian general was slain. The Athenians fought a pitched battle with the Boeotians, annihilating the Theban Sacred Band. When the Persian camp was stormed, no quarter was given. The battle clinched the defeat of the Persian campaign, and though its outcome was decided more by the quality of the men than the tactics of their generals, the three weeks' campaign was a notable achievement of Greek unity in the spirit of the oath taken by the League. In honour of the dead the member states instituted a pan-Hellenic festival to Zeus Eleutherios (the Liberator), which survived many centuries.

Crossing the tiny Asopos, you enter the nome of Boeotia. 74km **Thebes**.

**THEBES** (Θήβα; Hotels C, D), in modern parlance **Thíva**, a town (19,505 inhab.) with an extreme climate, has twice been rebuilt after destructive earthquakes in 1853 and 1893. The modern centre is on the summit of the ancient acropolis, or *Kadmeía*, a plateau 800m long and 400m wide, situated 60m above the surrounding plain. The Kadmeia is bounded on either side by rocky gullies; in recent years haphazard building has spilled into these, further obliterating the scanty pointers to the ancient topography. Beyond, sprawling suburbs occupy part of the area once included in the Classical city, which had a circuit of 6.5–8km.

As the birthplace or home of Dionysos, Herakles, Teiresias, and the Labdacidae in the legendary period, and of Pindar, Epaminondas, and

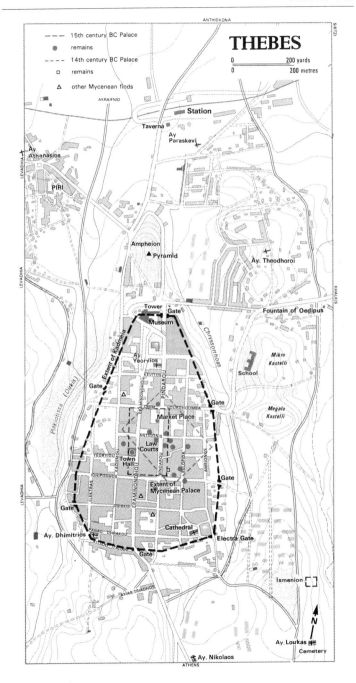

# THEBES

- – – – 15th century BC Palace
- ● remains
- - - - - 14th century BC Palace
- □ remains
- △ other Mycenean finds

0          200 yards
0          200 metres

ANTHIDKONA

SIRTZI

AKRAIFNIO

Station

Taverna

Ay Paraskevi

Ay Athanasios

LEVADHIA

PIRI

Ampheion
▲ Pyramid

Ay. Theodhoroi

KHALKIS

Tower
Gate

Museum

Fountain of Oedipus

Extent of Kadheia

Ay. Yeoryios

Chryssorhoas

Mikro Kastelli

School

KEVITOS

Gate

EPAMINONDHOU

DIRM

PINDAROU

VOURDHOUMBA

Gate

Megalo Kastelli

Pikiolissa (Dirkis)

Market Place

ANTIGONIS

YEORYIOU

Law Courts

PINDAROU

PELOPIDA

AMBIONS

Town Hall

DRIPODHOS

Gate

ILLEKTRAS

EPAMINIONDHOU

Extent of Mycenean Palace

DIRKIS

Gate

△

Gate

Cathedral

Ay. Dhimitrios

PANAC DHRAKOU

YIAS TRIADHOS

Gate

Electra Gate

Ismenion

N

Ay. Nikolaos

ATHENS

Ay. Loukas
Cemetery

LEVADHIA

Pelopidas in historical times, the 'seven-gated city' is inextricably bound up with Greek myth, literature, and history. The city of Kadmos claimed the invention of the Greek alphabet. The historical city strove to be mistress of Boeotia and, for a very short period in the 4C BC led the whole of Greece.

With the exception of the Palace excavations and the contents of the fine museum, the visible remains are unimpressive. Specialists can indulge in topographical detection of the sites of the monuments, streams and fountains that figured so vividly in Greek tragedy and in Greek history.

**History**. *Thebes* is called Ogygian by many Classical poets from the tradition that the land was first inhabited by the Ectenians, whose king was Ogygos. The traditional foundation of the city by Kadmos (or Cadmus; trad. date 1313 BC) and the sowing of the dragon's teeth begin a saga of tragedy and bloodshed paralleled at Mycenae. Among the Labdacidae, descendants of Kadmos, was Laios who married Jocasta. Thus Thebes was the scene of the tragic destiny of Oedipus, who slew his own father and became by Jocasta the father of Eteocles, Polyneices, Antigone, and Ismene. Rivalry between Eteocles and Polyneices brought about the intervention of the Argives under Adrastos (father-in-law of Polyneices) and the disastrous war of the Seven against Thebes (trad. date 1213 BC). In the reign of Laodamos, son of Eteocles, the Epigonoi (sons of the Seven) took Thebes and razed it to the ground (trad. date 1198 BC).

From the earliest times Thebes is represented as a flourishing city, with seven gates. Sixty years after the fall of Troy Thebes is said to have defeated Orchomenos and to have become the capital of a loose federation, later known as the **Boeotian League**. This federation of the greater cities of Boeotia was governed (in the 4C BC, at any rate) by eleven magistrates called *Boeotarchs*, Thebes supplying two, whereas the other members were allowed only one each. Thebes was a member of the Amphictyonic League.

An inveterate opponent of Athens, Thebes was naturally inclined to favour Athenian enemies. She medised in the Persian Wars. The Spartans are said to have forced some Thebans to help them at Thermopylae, but they deserted at the first opportunity. The fortified city of Thebes was the base of Mardonius before the battle of Plataea (479 BC) and his Theban allies shared in his defeat. Shortly before the battle of Tanagra in 457 the Lacedaemonians marched into Boeotia and re-established Thebes at the head of the Boeotian League. At the beginning of the Peloponnesian War Thebes attacked Plataea (431); as an ally of Sparta she helped to bring about the downfall of Athens. In 394, however, she joined a confederacy against Sparta. The seizure of the Kadmeia by the Lacedaemonian Phoebidas in 382 in defiance of the Peace of Antalcidas and its recovery in 379 by the Theban exiles under Pelopidas precipitated war. The battle of Leuktra (371), won by the genius of Epaminondas and the devotion of the Sacred Band, gave Thebes for a brief period of nine years the hegemony in Greece. By restoring Messenia, helping to found Megalopolis, and organising the Arcadian League, Epaminondas completed the humiliation of Sparta. After his untimely death at Mantinea in 362 the Theban supremacy, which depended entirely on himself, disappeared, and the subsequent history of Thebes is a record of disasters.

Joining her traditional enemy Athens against Philip at the instigation of Demosthenes, Thebes shared in the defeat of Chaironeia in 338, and a revolt shortly after Philip's death was ruthlessly suppressed by Alexander the Great in 336. The city was completely destroyed, with the exception of the temples and Pindar's house; 6000 inhabitants were killed and 30,000 enslaved. In 316 Cassander rebuilt Thebes, but in 290 it was taken by Demetrios Poliorketes. The Thebans sided with Mithridates in his war with Rome, but eventually went over to Sulla. In spite of this the city was finally dismembered in 86 by Sulla, who gave half its territory to the Delphians, by way of compensation for plundering the oracle. Strabo (IX) found Thebes hardly the size of a respectable village. In the time of Pausanias (IX, 7, 6) only the Kadmeia was inhabited. In AD 248 and again in 396 it was taken by the Goths, being spared (by Alaric) on the second occasion.

Thebes enjoyed a second period of renown in the Middle Ages. From the 9C it was the seat of the Strategos of Byzantine Hellas. In 1040 it surrendered to the Bulgarians after fierce resistance. In 1146 it was sacked by the Normans of Sicily led by their great admiral, George of Antioch. The city was now famous for its silk manufactures, and it was from Thebes that King Roger introduced silk culture into Sicily, from where it reached Lucca a century later, and eventually spread to the rest of Europe. The silks of Thebes, which were worn by the Byzantine emperors, were ultimately supplanted by those of Sicily, and with the decline of the silk trade the prosperity of Thebes faded. In 1205 it was taken by Boniface III of Montferrat, who granted it to Otho de la Roche. Under his house Thebes was the capital of the Duchy of Athens. Half the city subsequently passed by marriage to the family of St-Omer. Under the Turks Thebes degenerated into a wretched village, overshadowed by Levadia, which was made the seat of the pasha.

The plateau is covered by a grid of parallel streets; the main thoroughfare comprises the S half of Odhós Epaminóndhas, a short section of Odhós Antigónis, at right angles, and the N half of Odhós Pindhárou. Beneath the modern streets lie two superposed Mycenaean palaces, the extent and positions of which have been tentatively plotted.

The site was identified and partly dug by Keramopoulos in 1906–29; spectacular finds have been made since 1963 by Greek archaeologists mainly in rescue excavations on building sites. More Linear B tablets were found in 1994. The archaeological evidence, reappraised, shows that above many earlier levels, the earlier palace is placed diagonally to the present grid, while the later is set on the N–S alignment that the town has followed ever since. The megaron complex excavated by Keramopoulos on Od. Pindhárou, behind the present market place, was identified by him as the 'House of Kadmos'. Annexes of both palaces, including comparable jewellers' workshops, have been explored. The 'Kadmeion' was destroyed by fire about the beginning of LHIIIA2 (c 1375–50); the New Palace, designed for a new orientation and with foundations down to bedrock, was begun immediately but destroyed in its turn at the end of LHIIIB1 (c 1250). Linear B tablets found at 28 Pelopidhou were in the context of the earlier palace. Classical masonry, which overlies parts of the two Mycenaean palaces at the junction of Pindarou and Antigonis, and continues under those streets, is identified with the peribolos wall of the **Sanctuary of Demeter Thesmophoros** (which Pausanias placed within the House of Kadmos).

The principal excavations are located on the plan. Not much comprehensible is likely to be visible to the visitor, though the two orientations are obvious in Pindarou, where Keramopoulos' original excavations which produced the stirrup jars with Linear B inscriptions are a little N of a more recent site where the cylinder seals (see below) were found.

The *museum (excellent handbook available in English), at the N end of Pindárou, stands within the enceinte of the Frankish **castle** of Nicholas II de St-Omer, largely destroyed in 1311 by the Catalans, below its surviving 13C **tower**. The pleasant garden and courtyard are strewn with inscriptions of varying dates, sculptural remains including fine Byzantine reliefs, Turkish tombstones, architectural fragments and Early Christian mosaics (seasons). There are five rooms. In the first are important inscriptions from different parts of Boeotia, including a *stele* of the general Xenokrates, a colleague of Epaminondas at Leuktra, Nero's proclamation at the Isthmian games in AD 67, and a list of dedications at the Heraion of Khorsiai illustrating an important stage in the development of the alphabet.

In the second are displayed Archaic *kouroi from the Ptoïon; 5 and 4C funerary *stelai* from Akraiphnion, Thebes and Thespiai; Daedalic bust (mid-7C BC) from Tanagra; marble torsos and reliefs; Geometric stone tripods from Plataea. Third room in cases, *pottery, prehistoric from Eutresis and Lithares and Thebes, Mycenaean from Moustaphathos and Thebes (including stirrup jars painted with Linear B characters); 30 *cylinder seals of lapis lazuli, 14 with cuneiform inscriptions, nearly all from the east (a few are Cypriot, 15–13C BC), the greater number being of the Kassite-Babylonian period of the 14C BC, seemingly confirming the traditional connection of Thebes with Phoenicia; bronze plates and shoulder pieces from a Mycenaean corselet; granulated jewellery; carved legs (of a throne or its canopy ?), the largest pieces of worked ivory so far found in Greece; Linear B tablets; fragments of a fresco from the old palace, showing a procession of women bearing gifts; Archaic, Classical and Hellenistic *vases and *terracottas found at the Rhitsona cemetery (including rider and Priapic figure). Fourth room, sepulchral *stelai* painted and incised, representing Boeotian warriors killed at (?) Delion in 425 BC (note the shields adorned with representations of Pegasus, the Chimaera etc.); inscriptions and statues of priestesses from Aulis. Fifth room, Mycenaean painted *larnakes and other finds (pottery, terracottas, bronzes, etc.) from a large cemetery near Tanagra.

On Kastelli hill, just outside the E gate, a large frescoed chamber-tomb, approached by two long parallel dromoi, was discovered in 1971.

Other traces of ancient *Thebes* may be located in clockwise direction beginning from the museum. The Levadhia road descends below the museum through the site of the **Borean Gate**. On the left is a pleasant park on the hillock of the **Ampheion** where there is a large grave mound of Early Helladic or early Middle Helladic date. You turn right and cross the bed of the Strophia or 'Hollow Road', N of which extended the **agora** and, out towards the railway station, the **theatre**. Following the Khalkis road away from the **Proetidian Gate** (where pieces of the polygonal Roman wall, found in 1915, are partly visible by the road side), you cross the bed of the Ayios Ioannis (ancient *Ismenos?*) by a bridge. On the right of this bridge once gushed the spring of Ayios Theodoros, the ancient **Fountain of Oedipus**, where Oedipus washed off his father's blood (small pleasant park).

Following the course of the supposed Ismenos to the S, you leave to the right the wooded hill of **Kastellia**, partly occupied by an old people's home and the grammar school. For the chamber tomb, see above; Christian **catacombs** are also in evidence. You soon reach (right) the Ismenian Hill, sacred to Apollo, where in 1910 was discovered the **Ismenion** temple (4C BC), where the festival of the Daphnephoroi (laurel-bearers) was celebrated. The foundations are best preserved on the W. There are Mycenaean tombs underneath. At the side of the hill in the cemetery chapel of St Luke are fragments of a large marble sarcophagus (3C AD), locally venerated as that of the Evangelist, though its three inscriptions refer to the family of a Roman official called Zosimus. The old Athens road returns towards the Kadmeia by the line of the 'Hollow Road' and ends at the **Electra Gate**, the circular foundations of whose two flanking towers in ashlar masonry may be seen on either side of Odhós Amphíon. Near the gate was the extensive Sanctuary of Herakles, now probably occupied by the church of **Ayios Nikólaos** (Byzantine lintel in the interior). Crossing the main Athens road, you reach the medieval **aqueduct** (Kamáres) which brought water from the sources on Mt Kithairon to the Kadmeia. The Athens road enters the town through the probable site of the **Onka Gate**. To the SE is the **Kolonáki** hill with an extensive cemetery of Mycenaean chamber tombs. Further W the church of **Ayios Dhimítrios** (formerly the Megale Panagia, 1867) incorporates many fragments of ancient sculpture and architecture. To the NW of the centre is a **necropolis** of the 8C BC. The stream that flows along the W foot of the Kadmeia is the **Dhirkis** (Dirce); on the further bank the small church of Ayia Triádha is the starting point for Vlach wedding processions.

## Excursions from Thebes

TO LEUKTRA (Lévktra), 18km (11 miles). You take the Athens road and after a mile turn right. 12km **Melissokhóri** (Báltsia). 18km **Lévktra** (or Parapoúngia), is a group of three hamlets on a hill. At the **Battle of Leuktra** in 371 BC the Boeotians under Epaminondas defeated a larger force of Spartans in battle. This was the final blow to the legend of Spartan invincibility and for a short time gave Thebes the hegemony over all Greece. Visible up a valley to the right on the approach to Leuktra and signposted at the track is the *Tropaion* (locally 'Mármara'), a monumental trophy erected by the Thebans after the victory and now restored. A circular plinth of triglyphs has a dome-shaped roof of nine stone shields sculptured in relief; it probably supported a warrior figure in bronze.

A dirt road (passable by car in summer) goes on from the village down the right bank of the Livadhóstra to its mouth on the Gulf of Corinth. Here are some ashlar walls of *Kreusis*, the port of Thespiai, which was occupied by the Spartan Kleombrotos before the battle of Leuktra, and probably saw his retreating embarkation for Aigosthena.

Just under 3km NE of Leuktra are the foundations of massive walls in polygonal masonry, forming an enclosure 500m square, doubtless the Homeric *Eutresis*. About 300m SE at the foot of the ridge is the **Arkopódhi Fountain**, at the junction of the ancient ways from Thebes to Thisbe and Thespiai to Plataiai. To the E of the fountain the American School excavated in 1924–27 a series of Early Helladic, Middle Helladic, and Mycenaean **houses**. In 1958 they found traces of Neolithic occupation, including steatopygous clay figurines.

TO THESPIAI AND THISBE (Thísvi), 37km (23 miles). You take the Levadhia road, and after 5km diverge left (signposted 'Paralia Beach') up the cultivated Kanavári valley. 17km The twin villages of **Leondári** and **Thespiaí** (Erimókastro) rise to the right. Below, near the road, are scanty vestiges of ancient *Thespiaí*, excavated by the French School in 1888–91, when they demolished what was left of the walls to recover more than 350 inscriptions. The Thespians honoured Love above all the gods, and here the courtesan Phryne made her home. Her famous marble statue of Love by Praxiteles was still at Thespiaí in the time of Cicero. It was carried off to Rome by Caligula and then (after having been restored to Thespiai by Claudius) by Nero.

20km Fork. Ahead the shorter road avoids the villages but it is better to bear left through **Ellopía** and (27km) **Xironomí**.

On a dirt road running S from Xironomí to Alikí (see below) over the W shoulder of Mavrovouni are a fine **watch-tower** and foundations of two **fortresses**, one a large enclosure dating to the Spartan invasions of Boeotia in the early 4C BC, and the other small of late Roman date.

136km **Dhómvrena** (officially Koríni), was resettled here after a reprisal destruction in the Second World War. Immediately S of **Thísvi** (formerly Kakósi), its twin village to the NW, on a low plateau stand the extensive remains of ancient *Thisbe* (Θίσβη), still, as Homer says, 'the haunt of doves'. A fine length of wall with seven towers of good Classical masonry defends the S slope. On a hill to the NW of modern Thísvi are early polygonal walls.

A rough road leads SW from Dhómvrena, crossing the plain by the ancient dyke dividing it into two halves for alternate annual drainage and irrigation. It passes cliffs and an isolated shore to (6.5km) **Ayios Ioánnis** on the Bay of Dhómvrena. A difficult path round the bay leads E to **Alikí**, dominated by Mt Korombíli, on which stand the 4C fortifications of an acropolis identified with the *Siphai* of Thucydides and *Tipha* of Pausanias; other ancient remains are by the shore.

The road continues beyond Thisvi to (6.5km) **Khóstia** (or Pródhromos), then descends through rocky outcrops and olive groves to **Paralía**, a hamlet on the Bay of Saranda. A hill site with 4C BC walls on the left of the road, 4km from Khóstia, may be *Korsiai*. Recent excavations here (Canadian Archaeological Institute 1980–) have shown that this site was occupied (not continuously) from Neolithic to Roman times. Some of the walling is Archaic/Early Classical; most is 4C. Further W (poor road) is the monastery of Osios Serapheim then, 2km inland from the head of the exposed gulf of Zaltsas, the site of ancient *Boulis* on a steep hill with walling.

TO THE VALLEY OF THE MUSES AND MT HELIKON. To Thespiaí, see above. You leave the Dhómvrena road and take a road W to (24km) **Palaiopanayía**, the farthest point reachable by car. Here it is advisable to take a guide. On foot or mule-back you rise gently to the NW and come in ½ hour to **Palaiópirgos**, a medieval tower possibly on the site of *Keressos*. The tower has a fireplace, proving that it was lived in. On the slopes to the S and SE of the tower are the remains of a late medieval Turkish village, including a small church. Crossing the stream of Episkopi, to the right is a hill still crowned by the ancient Hellenic tower (Pirgáki) which Pausanias recorded as all that survived of *Askra*, a site more plausibly located by a recent survey on the saddle of land between Keressos and the tower. Here was the farm of Hesiod, who called it 'a cursed town, bad in winter, unbearable in summer, pleasant at no time'.

1¾ hours. Crossing the Permessos, you reach the Valley of the Muses. Here on the site of the chapel of Ayia Triádha (now removed) are the remains taken in 1888–89 to be a temple of the Muses, but reappraised in 1954 as a monumental **altar**. Close above is a large Ionic **stoa** of the 3C and, a little higher up, **theatre** (late 3C BC) in which were held the contests of the Mouseia. The cavea may be clearly distinguished.

The whole of the upper valley of the Permessos, with its groves and springs, was dedicated to the Muses. Their sanctuary, or *Mouseion*, stood in a sacred grove. The district is now sadly disafforested and the scanty trees that survive scarcely enable the visitor to recapture the charm and mystery of this region; its religious significance appears, however, to have lasted well into the Christian era, for ruined chapels are seen on all sides.

The cult of the **Muses** came originally from Pieria at the foot of Mt Olympos. It was inhabited by Thracian shepherds who worshipped the goddesses of the mountains and springs. They came south and founded Askra. In Boeotia Mt Helikon and the fountains of Aganippe and Hippocrene were sacred to the Muses, and in Phocis Parnassos and the Kastalian fountain. Libations of water, milk, and honey were the usual offerings.

The **Mouseia**, or Musean Games, were held every four years and comprised musical and poetic contests, to which were later added dramatic contests. The prize was a wreath of myrtle. In addition there were **erotica**, or games in honour of Love, which included athletic sports as well as musical competitions. The sanctuary became a fount of poetic inspiration. It was adorned with statues of the Muses by Kephisodotos, Strongylion, and Olympiosthenes; of Dionysos by Lysippus and by Myron; and of the great lyric poets. The sanctuary was despoiled by Constantine the Great.

From the Valley of the Muses to Hippocrene takes about 5 hours there and back. The route is comparatively easy and most of the distance can be ridden. The fountain is on Mt Zagora, an E summit of Mt Helikon, which comprises a whole range extending W to the Bay of Aspra Spitia. Its highest point is separated from Mt Zagora by the Pass of Koukoura, and called Palaiovouni (1750m). From Ayia Triadha you make for a side valley which opens at the foot of the Marandhali, an eastern outlier of Zagora. You cross a stream; on the right bank near the chapel of Ayios Nikolaos (476m) and a ruined monastery is a grove with a scanty spring. This may be the **Aganippe Fountain**. After a climb of 2½ hours you reach a glade (1360m) near the top of the N slope. Here, concealed near the mouth of the Marandhali and arbutus trees, is the mouth of an ancient well, now known as Krío Pigádhi ('Cold Water'). This was the **Hippocrene** ('Fountain of the Horse') which, so tradition tells us, gushed forth from the spot where Pegasus struck his hoofs when he landed from the skies. This point is a ½ hour below the summit of Mt Zagora (1530m). From Krío Pigádhi you can descend by the N slope of the mountain (on foot) direct to Ayia Triádha in 45 minutes.

To Akraifnio and the Ptoïon, to Khalkis and Aulis, to Anthedon, and to Larimna, see Rte 44B.

# 42

# Euboea (Evvia)

**EUBOEA** (Ευβοία), in modern Greek **Evvia**, next to Crete the largest Greek island, extends NW to SE for over 150km almost parallel to the mainland of Greece (Locris, Boeotia, Attica), from which it is separated by a strait virtually landlocked at either end. Midway along the W coast the strait contracts to a narrow channel called the Euripos. Here from the 5C BC a succession of bridges (the latest opened in 1993) has joined Euboea to Boeotia. The E coast is largely inaccessible, with abrupt and hostile cliffs; it has one port, at Kími. The other harbours are nearly all on the gentler W coast, chief of these being Khalkís on the Euripos and Káristos, near the S tip of the island. In antiquity the two principal cities were on the W coast: *Chalkis*, looking towards Boeotia, survives as the modern capital; *Eretria*, though still the ferry terminal from Attica, is a seaside village with no continuous historical tradition.

The centre of Euboea is largely occupied by an irregular mountain range, geographically the SE continuation of Ossa and Pelion, and broken by valleys. The highest point is Mt Dhírfis (1745m). In the N half the mountains are clothed with forests of chestnuts, pines and planes. In the exuberantly fertile plains are grown large quantities of corn, as well as vines, figs, and olives. Most famous is the Lelantine Plain between Khalkis and Eretria. The mineral wealth is considerable, lignite and magnesite being exported. The marble and asbestos of Karystos were renowned in antiquity; here was the source of the cipollino extensively used for building in Imperial and later Rome.

Euboea is one of the most delightful parts of Greece and still relatively unvisited though becoming popular with weekenders from Athens. For those with time the ferry from the N of the island (Ayiókambos) to Thessaly provides a quieter and much more attractive route to or from N Greece than the National Highway and cuts out the long hike round the gulf of Lamia.

A recent book describing a six-month personal journey in Evvia is Sarah Wheeler, *An island apart*, 1992.

**History**. Evidence of Palaeolithic habitation has been found at Artaki and Makrikapa. In remote antiquity Euboea was peopled by colonists from Thessaly who settled in the N (Ellopians), in the W (Abantes) and in the S (Dryopes). According to tradition the early settlers were joined by Ionians from Attica, Aeolians from Phthiotis, and Dorians from the Peloponnesus. The island, also called Makris because of its length, was divided between seven independent city-states, of which the most important were *Eretria* and *Chalkis*, rivals for the possession of the fertile Lelantine Plain. These two rich and powerful merchant cities founded colonies on the coasts of Thrace, Italy and Sicily, as well as in the islands of the Aegean. After the expulsion of the Peisistratids Chalkis joined Boeotia against Athens. In consequence, in 506 BC, the Athenians crossed the strait, defeated the Chalcidians and divided their land between 5000 cleruchs. Eretria had assisted in the Ionic revolt against Persia some ten years before the first great Persian invasion of Greece. The Persians, in retaliation, took the city by storm in 490, burned it, and enslaved the inhabitants. Although later rebuilt, Eretria never fully recovered her former power. After the Persian wars the whole of Euboea became subject to Athens. In 446 the island revolted, but was reconquered by Pericles. In 411 a second revolt, inspired by the defeat of the Athenian fleet at the hands of the Lacedaemonians, and coming at a time when Athens was weakened by the Sicilian disasters and internal faction, was more successful. The same year the inhabitants of

Chalkis, with the cooperation of Boeotia, built a bridge over the Euripos and thereby hampered the maritime trade of Athens (see below). In 378 the Athenians induced most of the Euboean cities to join their new maritime league; but, after the battle of Leuktra (371), the island passed under the suzerainty of Thebes. In 358 it was liberated by Chares, who restored it to the protection of Athens. It was incorporated in Macedonia after the battle of Chaironeia (338). In 194 it was taken from Philip V of Macedon by the Romans, who restored its cities to nominal independence. The island later came under the sway of Byzantium.

In AD 1209 Euboea was divided into the three baronies of Chalkis, Karystos and Oreos, which owed allegiance to the king of Salonika. The Venetians held the ports and numerous minor Frankish nobles occupied the interior, building several castles. By 1366 the Venetians were masters of almost the whole of Euboea. It was they who gave to the island the name of *Negroponte* ('Black Bridge'), which apparently referred to the bridge over the Euripos (see below). The name is a twofold corruption of Euripos. This had already been corrupted to *Egripo*, and Egripo was turned by the Venetians into Negroponte. Under the Venetians Negroponte ranked as a kingdom, and its standard was one of the three hoisted in St Mark's Square. After the expulsion of the Venetians from Constantinople by the Genoese, Negroponte became the centre of their influence in Romania. In 1470 the island was conquered by the Turks and came under the immediate government of the Capitan Pasha, high admiral of the Ottoman Empire. In 1830, after the War of Independence, Euboea passed to Greece. By special decree, a certain number of Moslems were permitted to remain on the island.

# A.  Khalkís and Northern Euboea

**Approaches from Athens**. To Khalkís, by **road**, 81km (50½ miles), bus every half-hour in 1½ hours, see Rte 44B. By **railway**, 83km (51 miles), 17 times daily in c 1½ hours.—Loutrá Aidipsoú can be reached by ferry via Arkitsa (Rte 44B); buses 3 times daily; or via the new coast road N of Limni 4 buses daily, three involving a change in Khalkís.

**KHALKÍS** (Χαλκίς, commonly Khalkídha; Hotels A–E), attractively situated on the Euripos at its narrowest, is the capital (51,646 inhab.) of the nome of Euboea and the seat of an archbishop. The town carries on an important trade in butter, livestock, and agricultural implements. Its industries include distilleries. It is the centre of bus communications of the island.

Ancient *Chalkis*, which is mainly known from numerous rescue excavations, was famous for its manufactures in bronze, exporting arms, vases, and votive tripods; it was the mother-city of many early colonies. The archaic site lay E of the present town, harbouring on the bay of Ayios Stéfanos, with an acropolis farther E on the lower height of **Vathrovouniá**. Here polygonal walling probably dates from 377 BC. In the 4C the city spread over the low hill on which the modern city stands; this may be the classical *Kanethos*.

**History**. According to the ancients the name of Chalkis (from *chalkos*, bronze) reflected the importance of its chief industry, though modern scholarship has suggested an alternative derivation from *chalke*, the limpet shell yielding purple dye (murex). The site of the Mycenaean city of the great-hearted Abantes (Il. II, 540) remains unknown, but the present site was occupied in late-Geometric times. The situation of the city, with two harbours on the Euripos, outlet of a rich island, made for its early development into a commercial and colonising centre. It was on the trade route between Thessaly (horses and corn), Thrace and Macedonia (gold of Thasos, timber, corn) and Attica and central Greece. In the 8C BC Chalkis colonised the Northern Sporades and so many cities (32 in all) in the Macedonian peninsula between the Thermaic and Strymonic gulfs that the whole peninsula was called *Chalkidike* (Rte 64). Later its settlers established themselves in Sicily; Naxos, Messana (now Messina); and in Italy: Rhegion (Reggio) and Cumae.

Chalkis fought many wars with Eretria for possession of the Lelantine Plain, and in the 7C emerged victorious. Its last king Amphidamos, a contemporary of Hesiod, was killed in one of these wars, and the government passed to the aristocracy, who were themselves overthrown when the Athenians overwhelmed the Chalcidians in 506 BC. Chalkis sent 20 ships in 480 to the Greek fleet and its soldiers took part in the battle of Plataea. Its subsequent history is largely that of Euboea. In 1210 it was seized by the Venetians, who fortified it with walls and made it the capital of the kingdom of Negroponte. When the Turks acquired Euboea in 1470, Chalkis became the head-quarters of the Capitan Pasha. Morosini attacked it in 1688 but had to call off his siege after 4000 of his troops and Königsmark, their commander, had died of malaria.

A new bridge (Rte 44B) crosses the strait well to the S of the Euripos. The older entry is described. The mainland approach to the Euripos is guarded by **Karabába**, a Turkish fortress of 1686; scanty rock-cuttings suggest an ancient fortress on this site, supposedly a Macedonian fort built c 334 BC. The walls afford a wonderful *view of the strait and whole town. In the mainland suburb below are (left) the town beach and (right) the **railway station** and an information office. The unusual **bridge** that carries the old road over the Euripos opens by a double action; the carriageway descends just sufficiently to allow each half-span to roll on rails under its own approaches.

The Euripos is notorious for its alternating currents, which change direction 6 or 7 times a day and on occasion as often as 14 times in 24 hours. The current flows from N to S for about 3 hours at a rate which may exceed 6 knots. It then suddenly subsides; and, after a few minutes of quiescence, it begins to flow in the opposite direction. The passage of the channel with the current is dangerous and the bridge is opened only when the direction is favourable. A red ball indicates a N–S current; a white ball a S–N current. The phenomenon is alluded to by Aeschylus (Agam. 190), as well as by Livy, Cicero, Pliny and Strabo. The cause is complex and still not fully understood. According to a popular tradition, Aristotle, in despair at his failure to solve the problem, flung himself into the Euripos.

The Euripos was first spanned in 411 BC. In 334 the Chalcidians included the Boeotian fort of Kanethos within the city boundaries. Under Justinian the fixed wooden bridge was replaced by a movable structure. The Turks replaced this with another fixed wooden bridge. In 1856 a wooden swing bridge was erected; in 1896 a Belgian company enlarged the channel, demolished the Venetian fort that had guarded the approach, and built an iron swing bridge. This gave place in 1962 to the existing structure. A new road bridge, considerably further S, was opened in 1993.

The original bridge leads to the older part of the town ('Kastro'), S of Leofóros Venizélou. Immediately to the left, across the bridge, is an interesting modern metal sculpture, after the Nike of Samothrace, by Carmelo Mendola, given by Chalkis' Sicilian twin-town, Giardini. A **mosque**, with ancient columns and a truncated polygonal minaret, is used as a store (no admission) for medieval antiquities. In front is a handsome marble **fountain**. A road from the SW corner of the square, by which the mosque stands, leads S to the church of **Ayía Paraskeví**, a basilica with pointed arches, above which runs a second row of large arches, incomplete and without a gallery. The columns are chiefly of cipollino and Hymettian marble, and the capitals are much varied. It was converted by the Crusaders in the 14C into a Gothic cathedral. Note the fine carved boss in the S choir aisle vault. Near the old Venetian **Governor's Palace**, now a prison, is the arcaded **Turkish aqueduct**, which supplied Khalkis with water from two springs on Mt Dhirfis, 25km away. At Od. Balalaíou 43 is the sole survivor of many **Venetian city towers** which once existed in Chalkis (Negroponte). Unlike other medieval towers in Euboea, it has a ground floor entry. There is a **Folklore Museum**

*Khalkis. Mosque (A.M. Chenavard, 1850)*

(open Tuesday and Thursday evenings, Sunday morning) in Od. Skalkóta, E of Ayia Paraskevi.

From the broad esplanade, Leofóros Venizélou leads past the Law Courts to the **Archaeological Museum** which has a somewhat miscellaneous but well-displayed collection (all labels in Greek). The courtyard contains some architectural members, inscriptions, grave *stelai* and freestanding sculpture, much of which is Hellenistic and Roman. Inside is interesting Neolithic material from the Skoteini Cave; and Early Helladic from Manika; also Early Cycladic finds from Euboea. Prehistoric seals and jewellery. Middle Helladic and Mycenaean pottery and Mycenaean bronzes. Good Protogeometric pottery and Geometric bronzes. Hellenic pottery and figurines. Hellenistic and Roman glass. Euboean coinage. Relief and free-standing sculpture of various periods.

An EXCURSION may be made (via Nea Artaki, see below) to (33km) **Stení** (Hotels C), the pleasant village below the cone of **Mt Dhírfis** that provides the best starting-point for climbing the highest mountain in Euboea (1745m). The ancient name *Dirphys* gave the goddess Hera her name 'Dirphya'. Many species of plant are purely local.

The **ascent** starts by road. 3km from the village, beyond springs and a large car park, the asphalt ends. An earth road (driveable in dry weather) now climbs in zigzags to a fork just above the tree-line, where a branch (left) leads in 1km to the **Fountain of Liri Refuge** (36 beds; keys from Alpine Club, Khalkis). Alternatively, 1.25km before the branch, a signed path, with painted marks, leads left to the refuge. A few yards before this path a good, but not motorable, track bears left to a col between the refuge and the summit-ridge, and onto the track from the refuge to the summit (c 1½ hours), which is clearly marked in red all the way. The *view is magnificent.

FROM KHALKÍS TO LOUTRÁ AIDHIPSOÚ, (1) 113km (70 miles), via Límni, Roviés and the W coast; (2) 153km (94½ miles), via Ay. Anna, Oreoí and the E and N coasts. The road runs N, skirting the shore. At 6km, the promontory of **Mánika** has important but unspectacular remains of an Early Helladic settlement and cemetery, at present being further investigated. 8km **Artáki** (Hotels B, C). To Stení Dhírfios, see above. From (15km)

**Psakhná** (Ψαχνά; 5649 inhab.), with a chapel containing frescoes dated AD 1245, can be visited **Kastrí**, one hour N, a hill surmounted by a Venetian castle. At **Triádha** (6.5km) are the house in which was born Nikolaos Kriezoti, the local hero of 1821, and some excavated remains of an Early Christian basilica. You climb the outlying E spur of Kandhílion (1222m), the ancient *Makistos*, a long range that now cuts you off from the Euboic Gulf; fine retrospective view to Khalkis and the Euripos.

From the summit (over 600m; café), the road descends in bold curves through the Kleisoura, a succession of wooded ravines amid scenery of great beauty; there is a magnificent *view across the forests to the islands of Skopelos and Skiathos. In a grand defile is the church of Ayios Yeoryios. This gradually opens into a beautiful wide valley, where plane-trees shade a limpid stream.

51.5km **Prokópi** (Hotel E), renamed after 1923 by refugees from Prokopion (Urgúp) in Turkey, has a chapel enshrining the relics of St John the Russian, a Tsarist soldier who died in 1730 as a Turkish slave at Urgúp. He was canonised by the Russian church in 1962 (pilgrimage, 27 May). The place is better known by its former name of **Akhmetága** for the estate of the Noel-Baker family and for their North Euboean Foundation which runs a health centre, a veterinary service, and a model farm. The by-road E traverses fine wooded country to a disappointing shore. 56km **Mandoúdhi** (1km right of the road) has magnesite quarries, a brick factory, and a little harbour at Kimási on the E coast (4km). 59.5km **Kírinthos**, where some ramparts of the 6C BC are taken for the site of *Kerinthos*. At (66km) **Strofiliá** the road forks.

(1). The left branch crosses the hills to **Límni** (17km; Hotels C), a beautiful fishing village of 2129 inhabitants. A hydrofoil service (4 times weekly) provides links with Khalkis to the S and Loutra Aedhipsou and Ay. Konstandinos to the N. The sands and pine-woods of Limni make it popular with artists. An Early Christian basilica came to light in 1960 but little to demonstrate the site of Classical *Aigai*. The hills above are quarried for magnesite.

From Limni the **Moní Galatáki**, to the SE beyond **Katoúnia**, may be reached by road (9km) or by boat in 1 hour.

N of Limni, which can be by-passed, a new fine road, sometimes at sea level, sometimes cut into the cliff, runs above the coastal villages (rooms, holiday facilities, often attractive beaches). 22km **Khrónia**. 26km **Roviés**, the site of ancient *Orobia*, is pleasant. There is a Frankish **tower**, built some time after 1255 by William de Villehardouin, in the centre of the village. 40 minutes walk away is the Byzantine monastery of **Gerónda**, with fine frescoes. 39km **Iliá**. 48km **Loutra Aidhipsoú** (113km from Khalkis).

(2). Beyond Strofiliá the right branch continues along the E slopes of Mt Xiron. At 70km there is a turning (right) to **Angáli**, where the remains of ancient *Trychas* have been tentatively identified. After (75km) **Ayía Anna** the ascent continues, with a view back along the cliffs to the E coast. The road follows a pine-clad ridge (412m) to (85km) **Pappádhes**, then winds down high above a precipitous valley with views of Skopelos and Skiathos. 97km **Vasiliká** was the subject of an anthropoligical study (E. Friedl). Just before (109.5km) **Agriovótano** a track leads in 2km to **Cape Artemision**. In the straits below in July 480 BC took place the first encounter of the Greek fleet with the Persian fleet, based on Trikeri, the peninsula opposite. Neither side could claim the advantage. Near here in 1928 was found the famous bronze Poseidon, now in the National Museum. The countryside is dotted with beehives. 129km **Istiaía** (Hotels B, E), or Xerokhóri, with 3966 inhabitants the chief town of an eparchy, is beautifully situated in an amphitheatre of hills overlooking the northern plain. This is the only habitat of storks in Euboea. A gravel road runs NW to the bathing beach of Kamatádhika (6km). 134km **Oreoí** (or Oreoús; Hotels C, D, E), with 1304 inhabitants, has a small harbour with remains of an ancient mole. Near the village square is a fine Hellenistic bull found in the sea in 1965. The **kastro** is a Venetian fort built on the foundations of a Hellenic enceinte and reusing earlier material. Finds go back to the Mycenaean period. In the valley between the kastro and the village are the foundations of a marble temple.

**History**. The Euboean city of *Histiaia* or *Hestiaia*, colonised by Ellopians of Thessaly, was called by Homer *polystaphylos* ('rich in vines'). It was conquered in 447–446 BC by Tolmides and Pericles. The Athenians, having expelled the inhabitants, founded a colony of 2000 cleruchs at *Oreos*, to the W of the deserted city. After the Peloponnesian War Oreos was subdued by the Lacedaemonians and the cleruchs driven out. The Histiaeans were recalled to their former city, thenceforth known by either name (Strabo X). Subsequently it was ruled by tyrants until the Macedonian invasion. In 207 it was surprised by Attalos II of Pergamon and the Romans; in 200 it was taken by the Roman fleet under Apustius. According to Livy, Oreos had two citadels separated by a valley; hence the modern plural *Oreoi*. The maritime acropolis, which dominated the port, was attacked by the Romans; the inland acropolis, *Oreos Apanos*, simultaneously attacked by Attalos.

The road now crosses the wooded spurs of Mt Teléthrion (1352m). 142km Approach road (right) to the car ferry (8 daily in summer) from **Ayiókambos** to Glífa in Thessaly (Rte 49A). 152km **Loutrá Aidhipsoú** (Λουτρά Αιδηψού; Hotels A–E, mostly May–October only) is a busy and popular spa well known to the ancients and patronised by Sulla. The sulphur-impregnated springs, with a temperature of 21–71°C, rise near the sea at Cape Therma (hydropathic) at the S end of the town, in powerful little jets, exhaling steam and leaving alkaline deposits. The ancients believed that they were connected with Thermopylae (Rte 44B). The waters enjoy a high reputation for the cure of stiff joints, gout, rheumatism, sciatica and other related ailments. Near the spring of Ayii Anaryiroi are the ruins of **Roman baths** which are to be preserved. There is a display of antiquities in the Spa building.

Car ferry to Arkitsa (Rte 44B; regularly in 45 minutes); buses to Athens in 3½ hours. Buses to Khalkis via Roviés. Hydrofoils on Ay. Konstandinos–Khalkis line, via Limni.

A road runs W from Aidhipsos to Líkhas (24km) on the W point of the island, passing **Yiáltra** and **Gregolímano** (Hotel A).

# B. From Khalkís to Kími and Káristos

**Road** to Kími, 93km (58 miles); bus. 23km Erétria.—46km Alivéri.—54km Lépoura, turning for Káristos (127km from Khalkís).—93km Kími.

**From Athens** the shortest and quickest approach to Erétria is by the frequent car-ferry (½ hour) from Skála Oropoú (50km from Athens; Rte 20); through buses to Kími.—By public transport Káristos is perhaps best reached via Rafína (Rte 21) by boat in 2 hours; or via the Ayía Marína to Néa Stíra ferry (Rte 21).

The road leaves Khalkis through its industrial outskirts, with Vathrovouniá (see above) rising on the left, to cross the Lelantine Plain. In the 8–7C BC this was the subject of deadly rivalry between Chalkis and Eretria. Noted in the Hymn to Apollo as famous for its vineyards, it is so still. Beyond

(6.5km) **Néa Lámpsakos**, turning (left) to **Mítikas** and **Fílla** (6.5km). Between the villages is a hill with two towers. Above Fílla, on the hill of Kastélli conspicuous even from the mainland, a **castle** (view) stands on an ancient enceinte. A cemetery of the 6C AD has been found. 10.5km **Vasilikó** also has a tower. The three **towers** above, with a fourth at **Ayia Triádha**, are Venetian and sited in combination with the castle to protect the S part of the Lelantine plain. The Vasilikó tower was occupied by the Turks in 1470 during their siege of Negroponte.

A by-road descends in 2km to **Lefkandí** (Hotel C; tavernas), a coastal resort. The flat headland ('Xeropolis') to the S, was explored in 1965–66 and 1969–70 by the British School and found to be a high occupation mound (no visible remains) with three associated cemeteries. The place seems to have barely survived beyond the Geometric period, but had been occupied from the Early, through the Middle, and Late Helladic periods, and yielded unusually informative layers of LHIIIC to Protogeometric. Lefkandi has been suggested as the site of *Old Eretria*, the city Homer linked with Chalkis in the Catalogue of Ships.

About 200m N of Lefkandí harbour, on **Toumba hill**, an important Dark Age cemetery has been investigated, as well as the largest building of that period (c 1000 BC) so far known in Greece. The structure (now covered by a prominent modern roof) was about 10m wide and 45m long, with an apsidal end. It was built of mud brick on a high (1.5m) stone socle. There was a peristyle of wooden columns. In the main chamber was a double grave, one compartment containing the cremated remains of a warrior, wrapped in a fine cloth and placed in a bronze urn, together with the body of a woman with rich accoutrements; the other, four horses. The building was abandoned and deliberately filled in in the same generation as it was constructed, perhaps as a hero-shrine to the deceased buried within.

23km **Erétria** (Hotels B, C), with 3022 inhabitants, was founded as Néa Psara in 1824 by refugees from the island of Psara. The new town overlies much of the ancient city, the ruins of which are the most extensive in Euboea. Malakonta Beach, to the W, has large bungalow hotels.

**History**. *Eretria*, next to Chalkis the most important city in Euboea, was one of the chief maritime states of Greece and is included in the Homeric catalogue. Traces of Mycenaean, Protogeometric and Geometric occupation have been found on the acropolis. Eretria contributed five ships to the support of Miletus in the revolt from Persia (500 BC), a gesture which drew upon it the wrath of the Persians ten years later, when they razed the city to the ground and enslaved the inhabitants. Nevertheless Eretria made a partial recovery, sending contingents to Salamis in 480 and to Plataea in 479. In 377 it joined the Second Athenian Confederacy. In 198 it was plundered by the Romans. After destruction in 87 BC in the Mithridatic wars, the city was never in antiquity rebuilt.

A school of philosophy was founded at Eretria in 320 BC. The ancient ceramics of Eretria were of high quality.

The Swiss Archaeological Mission (now the Swiss School) started systematic investigations in 1964. Subsequent excavations have been conducted by both Swiss and Greek archaeologists. On foot a full round of the visible ruins requires at least three hours, but the museum and lower sites can be cursorily seen more quickly.

On the NW outskirts of the village the **museum**, its contents well displayed in new cases, is arranged in chronological order, with explanatory material in Greek and French. ROOM I. Cases 1–5. Finds from Lefkandi, including fine LHIIIC pictorial pottery (1) and the outstanding PG centaur (3). Cases 6–7. Other prehistoric material from Euboea. Other cases contain Geometric and Archaic material from specific areas of ancient Eretria (Heroön, Case 10; Sanctuary of Apollo, Case 12). ROOM II. Important remains of the sculptural decoration of the pediment of the Archaic Temple of Apollo Daphnephoros: the abduction of Antiope by Theseus; Athena. The

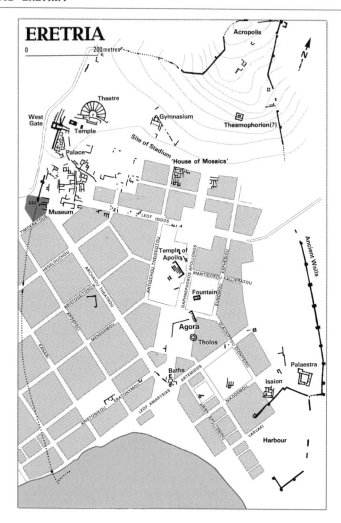

# ERETRIA

0 ___200 metres___

Acropolis

West Gate

Theatre

Temple

Palace

Gymnasium

Thesmophorion(?)

Site of Stadium

'House of Mosaics'

Museum

LEOF. ISIDOS

TIMOKRATOUS

HEGELOUCHOU

ARCHAIOU THEATROU

ARISTOGEITONOS

APOSTOLI

KAVARI

MENEDIMOU

ANTIOCHOU THEODOTOU

DAPHNEPHOROS APOLLONOS

Temple of Apollo

MANTIDOROU KALLIKRATOU

EUINOU

ALEPHEIOU

Fountain

Agora

Tholos

GLAUKIPPOU DIONYSIOU

Ancient Walls

Palaestra

Baths

ARTEMIDOS

Isaion

KRATONYMOU

ARISTONIKOU

LEOF. AMARYSIAS

NIKODEMOU

APOLLONIOU

VARVAKI

Harbour

'Athenian' subject matter may reflect political connections between the two states. Other cases contain specific sites and themes: 16 Euboean Coinage, 19 Cults of Eretria, 22 Tomb of Eros, 25 Temple of Artemis Amarisios. Outside the Museum a large area, including a covered section, is filled with architectural fragments, *stelai* etc.

Turning towards the acropolis we come first to a large area of recent excavation within the W fortifications of the city. These comprised a broad moat and a wall. The *West Gate had a barbican which extended across the moat on a corbelled arch. The masonry on a tightly interlocking trapezoidal system is impressive. Extensive remains of the **House of the Mosaics** (illustrated guidebook), a 4C peristyle hosue, with a Hellenistic extension, cover an abandoned Heroön of the 7–6C. A well-preserved clay bath remains *in situ*. To the NE are foundations of a **Temple of Dionysos**.

Beyond rises the **theatre**, excavated by the American School in 1890–95. It retains its seven lower rows of seats, much defaced; the upper tiers, which were exposed to view, have nearly all been removed, block by block, to build the modern village. A semicircular drainage channel 2m wide runs in front of the lowest row. From the orchestra steps descend through a square opening into an underground vaulted passage, leading to the hyposkenion; it was used for the sudden appearance and disappearance of a '*deus ex machina*'. The high stage is raised on seven or eight courses of masonry. Under its centre is another vaulted passage, probably a public entrance to the orchestra.

Farther E at the foot of the acropolis is a **gymnasium**, excavated in 1895 (fenced). By its W end was found an inscribed *stele* set up in honour of a gymnasiarch benefactor. Near the same spot is the pedestal of a statue bearing an inscription within a votive wreath to one who had encouraged boys in athletics. At the E end is an extensive series of water conduits which supplied the bathing troughs.

On a hill 10 minutes W of the theatre a tumulus encloses a **Macedonian tomb** (key from museum). The dromos, on the N, leads to a square vaulted chamber, containing two funeral couches in marble, with their pillows and draperies, and two thrones and a table, all coloured.

Above the theatre you can climb in 20 minutes to the **acropolis**, with ashlar walls and towers. It has a fine *view to the SW; on the left and in front, part of Attica, with Pentelikon and Parnes; on the right, Kithairon, with Parnassos in the distance. The Lelantine Plain (see above) lies to the NW.

On the descent are remains of a **thesmophoreion** and a sanctuary of a female deity, perhaps Artemis Olympia. Further S, in the town, are the bare foundations of a **Temple of Apollo Daphnephoros**, excavated by Greek archaeologists in 1900 and restudied by the Swiss in 1964, when remains of the Geometric period were found below it, also potters' workshops nearby. Superimposed are the stylobates of a Doric peripteral temple of 6 by 14 columns, with a cella in three equal parts, erected c 530–520 BC (sculpture in the museum); and an Ionic peripteral building of c 670–650, which probably had 6 by 19 columns in wood.

To the E are some remains of an **isaion** excavated in 1915 by the Greek Archaeological Society, and beyond them ruins of a **palaestra**. Close to the sea a mosaic marks an ancient bath site.

31.5km **Amárinthos** (3638 inhab.; Hotels B, C, D; tavernas) has a sandy beach and (on a hill to the E) two Byzantine churches. The hills come nearly to the shore. Near Tharoúnia (21km NE) the **Skoteiní Cave** was used from Neolithic to Roman times, partly for cult. 46km **Alivéri** (Hotels D), with 5065 inhabitants, is situated on a hill, the site of ancient *Tamynai*, where the Athenians under Phokion defeated Kallias of Chalkis in 354 BC. A mineral railway descends from an important lignite mine in the hills to Káravos, its little port, now dominated by an electricity generating station. Here was probably the landing-place of an ancient ferry. On a knoll above the E shore of the bay rises a square medieval **fortress**, with a door 6m above the ground. At Alivéri you can find taxis for the visit to Dystos. 52km **Vélos** (or Veloúsia). To the NW is a castle and to the S a square tower. At (54km) **Lépoura** the road divides.

The visit to ancient *Dystos* is only for the determined visitor, preferably carrying a machete. The best approach is to take the Karistos road (right) through **Kriezá** (3km); after a further 5km (ignore signs to modern Distos) the site can be seen (1km right). The ruins (see T. Wiegand in *Athenische Mitteilungen 24* (1899)) stand on an isolated, overgrown, and snake-infested hill overlooking the E shore of a drained lake encircled by swallow-holes. The **walls** of the 5C city, of polygonal construction, 3m high and 2m thick, with 11 towers, describe a semicircle eastward from the W cliff. The main entrance on the E, between two towers, leads to the **agora**. On the slopes of the hill, especially on the N, are terraces with remains of **houses**, important examples from the 5C BC. They had an entrance passage, an inner court, a living room, two bedrooms, and possibly an upper storey. On top of the hill, to the W, is the **acropolis**, the N part of which became a Venetian fortress (*view from the shattered tower).

## To Káristos

From Lépoura the right branch continues SE. 57km **Kriezá**. Near the village of (71km) **Zárakes** are ruined windmills and some foundations, possibly of *Zaretra*, a place captured by Phokion in 350 BC. Between (77km) **Almiropótamos** (with a ferry service from its port below to Ayia Marina on the mainland) and **Polipótamos** a rocky ridge along the narrowest part of the island has sea views on both sides. Just beyond the Mesokhória (beach) turn a Turkish stone road can be seen below (left). 96.5km A sign (left) points to **Dragon's Houses** (4km of rough road and 5 minute walk, or 2km by path from Stira), three impressive ancient buildings of uncertain function (see A.J.A. 1976). 97.5km **Stíra** has a pleasant little square. A Venetian **castle** crowns an acropolis, probably that of Homeric *Styra*. **Néa Stíra** (Hotels C), 4km SW, is a seaside resort, connected by ferry with Rafína and Ayía Marína (Rte 21). The island of Stíra, offshore, lies almost opposite Rhamnous. The road winds round the S end of the Kliosi Ridge. 118km Turning (right) via Kakagióni, to **Marmári** (Hotels C; ferry to Rafina), another seaside resort with ancient cipollino quarries.

127km **Káristos** (Κάρυστος; Hotels A, C), an attractive town of 4663 inhabitants, founded after the War of Independence near the site of ancient *Karystos*, is the seat of a bishop and of an eparch, and a pleasant summer resort on a broad bay facing S. From Attica it is more easily visited by ferry from Rafina. The ancient city was famous for its cipollino marble and for asbestos.

At the SE end of the esplanade a medieval **tower** incorporates ancient blocks. From it a road leads inland to **Míli** (3km), a hamlet (cafés) in a lush ravine. From the little plateia the left fork climbs to Graviá and by a good stone bridge across a ravine to **Kokkino Kastro** (or Castel Rosso; view), a fine Venetian fort so called from the reddish colour of its stone, probably the ancient acropolis of Karystos. In the ancient quarries are half-worked columns. On the Paximádhi peninsula to the W recent survey has identified a Classical farm site at Palaio Pithari and an ancient fortified settlement at Cape Mnima.

The **ascent** of Mt Okhi can be made from Míli in c 3 hours, by a path (difficult to follow) round the S side to the refuge (1000m) above a chestnut wood. Easier to find is a mule-path to a col (1 hour; goatherds' huts) below the W summit; this can also be reached from Melissón (guide necessary) via the Gorge of Kallianou, through magnificent country. From here the approach is up a ridge round the N side. The summit consists of a line of tors, of which the W (Profitis Ilias) is the highest (1405m). Below the tors farther E, on the S side, is a primitive building similar to those at Stira, called the 'House of the Dragon'. It may have been a watch-house of the 6C BC.

About 5 hours NE of Karístos is Cape Kafirévs (Cavo Doro), the ancient *Kaphareus*, where Nauplios, father of Palamedes, is said to have lighted torches to mislead the Greeks on their return from Troy, in revenge for the murder of his son on a false charge of treachery. About four hours SE of Karystos, near the extreme S point of Euboea, is the site of *Geraistos*, where triglyphs and an inscription have been found from the celebrated sanctuary of Poseidon. The coast facing E between these two points is probably the 'Hollows' (τά κοίλα) of Herodotus 8. 13, where in 480 a Persian squadron came to grief in a storm.

From Lépoura the Kími road runs N in a wooded valley between Dhirfis and the hills of the E coast. Some of the villages described are now by-passed by realignment. 64km Khánia, by two little streams. 65km **Avlonári** (1km right) stands on the road to **Okhthoniá** (540m), a summer resort, which appears (right; 7km) massed on its hill, beneath a pretty church and a Venetian tower (762m), built on Roman foundations. The road now enters the attractive valley of the Oxylithos, guarded on all sides by the picturesque Frankish **towers** so common in Euboea, and dotted with hamlets and chapels. 73km Monódhri. The road climbs, with many bends, to (77km) Dhirrévmata. 80km Konístrais has a long main street on a ridge amid rolling olive-clad hills. The road undulates and winds amid lush greenery and small hillside villages. At (88.5km) **Kalimeriánoi** a new road descends directly to the shore, while the old road enters a pass.

93km **Kími** (Κύμη; Hotels C, E), locally called Koumi, is a cheerful town (3223 inhab.), which owes its prosperity to its vineyards and orchards, and to the lignite mines to the W. It stands at 262m on a ridge overlooking the island of Skiros. It is celebrated for figs and honey and for its bold sailors; in 1821 it put to sea a fleet of 55 merchant ships, which earned it a bombardment from the Turks. There is a **Folk Museum**. **Paralía Kímis** (Hotel D), its small port with a merchant navy school, lies 4km away. The harbour was repaired after 1945 by one Robert Nesbit, as a plaque records.

In the vineyards round Kimi are many graves of the 4–3C BC. A road leads NE to the monastery of the **Sótiros** (1643) which may occupy the site of ancient *Kyme Phyrkontis*. Another road runs N from Kimi to springs and a café, whence a track climbs round the summit of Mt Ortári (756m) to Cape Kalámi (splendid cliff scenery from either).

At **Ano Potamiá** (6km to the S, reached via the coast road) the **kastro**, with buildings and an enceinte wall of the 4 and 3C, was once identified as belonging to ancient *Oechalia*. The ancient topography of the area is much debated.

# 43

# Northern Sporades (Sporádhes)

Grouped near the Thessalian coast are Skiathos, Skopelos, Alonissos, and numerous smaller islands; these together comprise the eparchy of Skopelos, part of the nome of Magnesia. Some way to the E is Skiros, the largest and, with its attendant islets, forming part of the eparchy of Karistia in the nome of Euboea. The whole group is called the **Northern Sporades**, though the islands have very marked individual characteristics. Most inter-island journeys can be made most days, the least easy being from Skiros to Skopelos.

## A.  Skíros

**Approaches from Athens** by bus (3½hrs) to Kími in Euboea (comp. Rte 42A), thence by daily ferry (c 2 hours), through booking from Athens.

Skiros has a direct air service from Athens in 50 minutes. Daily in summer; less frequently in winter.

**SKÍROS** (Σκύρος; pop. 2901; Hotels A, B, C, E) is the most easterly as well as the largest of the Northern Sporades, with a length of c 27km and an area of 205 sq. km. It is divided into two nearly equal parts by a low-lying isthmus with a natural harbour sheltered by islets in Kolpos Kalamitsas on the SW, and the exposed little haven of Akhili on the NE. On the S coast is another natural harbour, Trís Boúkes. The fertile N half of the island contains the capital **Skyros** and rises in Mt Olympos to 400m. The mountains of the rugged S half culminate in Kokhílas (782m) and are covered with forests of oaks, pines, and beeches. Here also are marble quarries, reopened in 1961. The variegated Skyrian marble was famed in antiquity. Crayfish are caught in large quantities off the coast. Skiros is well-watered, providing pasture for a few oxen and numerous sheep and goats, descendants of the goats that were highly prized in Strabo's time. Wheat, oranges, lemons, honey and wine are among the exports.

**Legend and History**. Achilles, disguised as a girl, was sent by his mother Thetis to the court of Lykomedes, king of Skyros, to prevent his going to the Trojan War. Her precaution was in vain; for Odysseus lured him to Troy, where he was killed before it fell. Neoptolemos or Pyrrhos, son of Achilles, was brought up in Skyros and thence taken by Odysseus to the Trojan War (Sophocles, *Phil.* 239). It was in Skyros that Lykomedes treacherously killed Theseus, king of Athens, who had sought asylum with him.

In 476 BC Kimon conquered the island, enslaved the inhabitants, and planted Athenian settlers (Thucydides I, 98). Kimon discovered the bones of Theseus in the island; he had them taken to Athens and enshrined in the Theseion. In 322 BC the Macedonians took Skyros from the Athenians. In 196 the Romans forced Philip V of Macedon to restore the island to the Athenians.

**Linariá** (rooms), the landing-place, with good fishing, is on the W coast. About 11km away (bus), on the NE coast, is the capital **Skíros**, or Khorió, (Hotels B, E), facing inland on a high terrace at the foot of a precipitious hill, on which is the ruined **kastro**. The hilltop was the acropolis of the ancient city which Homer calls αἰπύς, ('steep'). This may have been Plutarch's 'high cliff' from which Lykomedes pushed Theseus to his death. Remains of ancient walls may be traced in the foundations of the Venetian enceinte; over the gate is a lion of St Mark; within is a decaying convent (St George the Arab), founded in 962, once famous for its miracles. Also of interest is the church of **Episkopí** (895). The town has steep narrow and winding streets, and is noted for its little white cubic houses with flat black roofs, furnished with low tables and elaborately carved chairs, ancient and modern embroidery and island pottery. A small **museum** in the Town Hall contains medieval church furniture. There is a small **Archaeological Museum** and a **Folk Museum** with good embroideries. Overlooking the sea, on a conspicuous bastion, is an inappropriate **Memorial to Rupert Brooke** in the form of a bronze 'statue of an ideal poet' (1931), by M. Tombros.

Rupert Brooke (1887–1915) was buried on the W slope of Mt Kokhílas (or Konchylia), in an olive grove about 1.5km from the shore, during the night of 23 April 1915, having died of septicaemia the same afternoon in the French hospital ship Duguay Trouin. The expeditionary force, of which he was a member, sailed from Skiros at dawn for the Dardanelles. The visit to the grave, restored by the Royal Navy in 1961, can be made by motor-boat from Linariá to **Trís Boúkes**, or by taxi.

The most frequented beaches are to the N and S of **Skiros** and in the vicinity of **Linariá**, also at **Atsítsa** in the NW.

There is a recently excavated prehistoric settlement at **Palamári** in the N.

# B.  Skíathos, Skópelos, Alónissos

**Approaches from Athens** (apply Alkyon Agency, 98 Akadhimías). Daily by coach to Ayios Konstandínos (Rte 44B), whence by ferry or hydrofoil to Skíathos, Glóssa (Skopelos), Skópelos, and (less frequently) Alónnisos.— **From Volos**: several times daily to Skiathos and Glossa (Skopelos), sometimes continuing to Skopelos and Alonnisos; also hydrofoils.

Skiathos has a direct **air** service (1–5 daily) from Athens in 40 minutes; also international charters.

**SKÍATHOS** (Σκίαθος; Hotels L–E, F/A), nearest of the Northern Sporades to the Thessalian coast, resembles Mt Pelion in its beautiful scenery and thick forests. It is particularly known for its excellent sandy beaches, with exclusive summer hotels. The island has an area of 78 sq. km and a friendly population of 5096, most of whom live in the one town. There is good fishing. The fertile but ill-cultivated land yields grape-vines, olives, fruit-trees, and cereals. Tourism is now the main industry.

At *Skiathos* in 480 BC three Greek guardships of the Artemision fleet were surprised by a Sidonian squadron of Xerxes' fleet (providing Herodotus with one of his most realistic details); Pytheas of Aegina, wounded and captured, was spared for his valour and later rescued at Salamis. Skiathos became a subject ally of Athens. It was devastated by Philip V of Macedon in 220 BC. The island was the home of the novelists Alexander Papadhiamandis (1851–1911), whose house is a focus of pilgrimage, and Alexander Moraitidhis (1851–1929).

**Skíathos** (Hotels A–E), the only town, lies on the SE coast, with densely wooded hills rising behind. The ancient city on this site was deserted in the Middle Ages (see below). The picturesque pine-clad islet of **Boúrtzi** (tourist pavilion), with ancient cannon standing below the school, is reached by causeway and has a good view of the harbour. In the upper town is the **cathedral** of the Trion Ierarkhon.

A road runs SW along the shore, passing above (3km) the pleasant beaches of **Akhladiás** (Hotels A, C, F/A), then crosses the peninsula of **Kalamáki**, a large headland with elegant villas and hotels. Beyond are the two superb bays (also served by boats in summer) of (7km) **Platánia** (Hotel A) and (10.5km) *****Koukounariés** (Hotels L, B, C, D), said with some justification to have the finest beach in Greece. The monastery of Panayia Kounistra is 3km inland from this road.

In 1538–1829 the inhabitants removed to an almost inaccessible position on the most northerly tip of the island. The **Kastro**, as their deserted town is called, is three hours' walk from Skiathos town, or can be reached by boat. It is built on a rocky peninsula formerly connected to the rest of the island by a drawbridge. Of its ruinous buildings, the **Church of Christ** is the best preserved, with a wooden screen of 1695 and some of its frescoes more or less intact. An alternative route to Kastro, partly motorable over dirt roads, takes you via the **monasteries** of Taxiarkhis, Evangelistrias, with a fine Byzantine church containing frescoes and a library of MSS, and Ayios Kharalambos, to which the novelist Alexander Moraitidhis retired shortly before his death.

**SKÓPELOS** (Σκόπελος; Hotels A–E, F/A), the ancient *Peparethos*, separated from Skíathos by the Skopelos Channel, grows grape-vines, olives, almonds, pears, plums and other fruit. There is a seasonal prune factory. A well-watered island of 122 sq. km, it is more intensively cultivated than Skíathos. Its 2972 inhabitants are more scattered, less seafaring, and more conservative. Local costume may be seen on feast days and pottery is made. Tourism has become prominent.

Ancient Peparethos had become *Skopelos* by Ptolemaic times. In the Byzantine era it was used as a place of exile. In Frankish times it was taken by the Brothers Ghizi and attached to the duchy of Naxos. In 1538 Barbarossa slaughtered the entire population.

The capital, **Khóra Skopélou** (2603 inhab.) rises imposingly on slopes above a roadstead exposed to the blasts of the Meltemi. Traditional fine slate roofs have been partly superseded by tiles. Blindingly white in the sun are the many (supposedly 123) little churches, some of which (the **Panayitsa**) stand high on the steep W scarp of the town. Their ikons and screens (17–18C) are of good local workmanship, notably those in the church of **Khristó**, which has a gilded 'choros' or corona lucis. Pleasant black ware is produced by a local potter. Beyond his workshop, E of the town, on the shore are vestiges of a Classical building (Asklepieion ?), fast being eroded by the sea. Fragments remain of the church of 1078, possibly on the spot where Reginus, first bishop and patron saint of Skopelos, was martyred in 362. Farther on is the fortified **Moní Episkopí**, former seat of the bishopric of Skopelos, suppressed in the last century. Several other monasteries to the E of the town include those of Evangelistria and Prodromos and Metamorfosis, the latter disused.

A road (buses daily) crosses the island to (8km) **Agnónda**, a sheltered harbour on the S coast, passing the Bay of Stafilos (Hotel B), said to take name from Staphylos, a Minoan general. A tomb dug here in 1927 was claimed as his. It continues to the coastal villages (rooms) of **Iliós**, **Klíma**, and (30km) pretty **Glóssa** (1062 inhab; Hotel C), above the W coast facing Skiathos, with its port Loutráki at which boats call. Glossa has Venetian remains.

A narrow channel, partly occupied by two islets, separates Skopelos from Khelidhrómi, the ancient *Ikos*, known also as Liadhrómia and officially as **Alónnisos** (Αλόννησος; 2985 inhab.). It is a hilly wooded island culminating in Mt Kouvoúli (494m). Its old Khóra, (Alónnisos, or Liadhromia; Hotels B, C, D), well situated on a hill, although some houses have been renovated, has been superseded as the main centre by **Patitíri** (Hotels B, C, E), the harbour. The two are linked by an attractive calderimi, a pleasant stroll (40minutes; also by bus). Another village, **Vótsi**, lies just to the E and there are two other tiny settlements further N. The hill of **Kokkinókastro** on a bay NE of Patitiri has some remains of ancient *Ikos*. Middle Palaeolithic finds have been made on the islet of Vrákhos.

There are several rocky islets to the E and NE of Alonnisos, uninhabited save for a few shepherds and their flocks. They include **Pelagonesi**, **Gioura**, **Piperi** ('Peppercorn', so called from its shape), and **Psathoura**, the northernmost of the group, where an extensive ancient city lies submerged. Some authorities consider that Psathoura not modern Alonnisos was the ancient *Halonnesos*, the ownership of which was a bone of contention between Philip of Macedon and the Athenians; one of the surviving orations of Demosthenes is on this subject. A Byzantine wreck off Pelagonesi was examined in 1970. Cargo raised was mainly glazed sgraffito pottery (mid 12C).

# 44

# From Athens to Lamía

## A. Via Levadhiá

**Road**, 212km (131½ miles). To (74km) Thebes, see Rte 41.—119km Levadhiá.—125km Orchomenós turn.—132km Chairóneia.—180km Brállos. Steep but well engineered pass.—212km Lamía.—**Buses** daily by this route; more frequently to Levadhia, and from Levadhia to Lamia.

**Railway**, via Thebes (comp. Rte 44B), beyond which it follows closely the general course of this road; c 16 times daily to Lianokladhi (for Lamia; bus connection) in 2½–4 hours; c 9 times daily to Levadhia in 1½–2 hours.

From Athens to (74km) **Thebes**, see Rte 41. Leaving Thebes by a short curving descent, after 5km a road diverges left (comp. Rte 41) to Thespiai and Thisbe. At 80.5km, just beyond a bridge over a torrent bed, a motorable track (left; signs in Greek) leads across fields in c 1.5km to a fold in the hills in which is the **Kabeírion**, a sanctuary explored in 1887 and more fully excavated in 1956–69.

The E end of a **temple** forms the skene of a large **theatre**, twice rebuilt. A central **altar**, the focus of both temple and theatre, shows that the spectacle was a sacred rite. Three circular buildings and two water basins with pipe connections were related to the cult. Three halls form an open square at the edge of the sacred area. The site was used from Archaic to Roman times. It is notable for the amusing Kabeiran pottery produced locally apparently exclusively intended for use at the site.

The road runs across the Teneric Plain. To the N Mt Fagas (567m), or Sphingion, the reputed haunt of the Sphinx, rises above the Varikó marsh. From (91km) the low ridge of Kazarma, which separates the Theban from the Kopaic plain, Parnassos is visible ahead in the distance. On the ridge stood *Onchestos*, at one time seat of the Amphictyonic League and, in Macedonian times, of the Boeotian Confederation; the Poseidonion and bouleuterion were identified in 1972. A medieval watch-tower and grotto lie just off the road (left). The grotto produced material from the Old to Middle Stone Age. The road now follows the margin of the drained **Lake Kopáïs**.

**Lake Kopáïs** (Copais, Κοπάϊς) is named after the ancient city of *Kopai*. It was the largest lake in Greece, measuring 24km by 13km; Strabo says that it had a circuit of 380 stadia (68km). For most of the year it was a reedy swamp, while large tracts dried up completely in summer. In the rainy season the surrounding basin used to be frequently inundated and it is doubtless to some exceptionally severe flood that the tradition of the Ogygian deluge is due. The eels of Copais were very large and succulent, and the reeds which fringed its shores were the raw materials of the Greek flute.

  The natural outlets of the lake (all on the E and NE) were swallow-holes (*katavothrae*). These were not, however, sufficient to cope with a sudden inrush of water, and from early times attempts were made to increase the natural out-flow. On the dry bed of the lake have been found traces of prehistoric dikes and canals, sometimes attributed to the Minyans. They channelled the waters to various *katavothrae* with such success that the whole basin was reclaimed. Strabo repeats the tradition that it was dry cultivated ground in the days when it belonged to Orchomenos. Herakles is said, out of emnity to the Orchomenians, to have blocked up the *katavothrae*; Strabo explains that the chasms were affected by earthquakes. After the destruction of the Minyan drainage works and throughout the historic period the Copaic basin remained a lake.

Attempts were made, however, in historical times to supplement the *katavothrae* by means of tunnels. Two artificial emissaries have been discovered. The more extensive is the tunnel towards Larimna. This may have been the work of Krates, engineer to Alexander the Great. The other appears to have anticipated the modern tunnel from Kopais to Likéri. Neither of the ancient tunnels was completed. A further attempt to control the inflowing rivers was undertaken in the reign of the Emperor Hadrian. In 1887 Scottish engineers took over from a French company works started 20 years earlier. A dam was built, two canals were cut from W to E, and the Melas, the main affluent, was diverted and canalised. The **Great Central Canal** is 25km long, 23m wide, and 1.8–8.2m deep. The **Outer Canal** (32km long), to the S collects the waters of the affluents from the S side. The water of the Melas flows down the 'Great Katavothra'. The water of the Outer Canal and the winter overflow is drained through a tunnel into Lake Iliki, and then to the sea. After reclamation, completed in 1931, the ground was divided between pasture and the cultivation of cereals and cotton. The area under cultivation by the British Lake Kopais Company steadily increased to 180 sq. km by 1952, when the Greek government acquired the estate by expropriation.

At the **Battle of Lake Kopais**, in 1311, the Catalan Grand Company practically annihilated the chivalry of Frankish Greece. The battle was fought near Orchomenos (Skripou), see below.

82.5km **Alíartos**. Some scanty remains of ancient *Haliartos*, excavated by the British School in 1926, can be seen on a rocky hill (right), now known as Palaiókastro or Mázi. This was one of several fortified places that commanded the road from Orchomenos to Thebes, the only natural highway through Central Greece. Part of the Classical fortification wall of the town was found in 1976 near the main road. Medieval fortification is represented by the Moúkhli Tower which overlooks a modern canning factory, immediately S of the modern town.

At **Seínti**, 3km E of Aliartos, beside the main road, a 4C building complex (stoa and shops?) may be part of an agora.

To the S behind (97.5km) **Pétra** rises a jagged row of hills. At **Solinári** (left) is a site tentatively identified with the Temple of Tilphoussios where the seer Teiresias died. 107km Crossroads. To the left is modern Koroneia, but off the next turning (left; to **Ayios Yeóryios**), in a valley 4km S, are some remains (theatre, temple foundations, walls) of ancient *Koroneia*, where in 447 BC the Athenians suffered the defeat that lost them control of Boeotia. The Spartans under Agesilaus failed to consolidate a victory here in 394. At the spring of **Pótza**, near Ayios Yeoryios, is plausibly located the sanctuary of Zeus Laphystios and the shrine of Herakles Charops mentioned by Pausanias. The road turns N for a short distance with the railway, then parts company to run W into the plain of Levadhia.

119km **Levadhiá** (Λεβαδειά; Hotels B, C, D) is a busy town of 18,437 inhabitants, the capital of the nome of Boeotia (Viotía), and the seat of a bishop. It is pleasantly situated at the mouth of the gorge of the Erkina (ancient *Herkyna*) which runs between Mt Lafistios on the E and the hill on which stands the prominent Frankish kastro, to the W. Further W is Mt Ayios Ilias which most authorities confuse with the kastro. Levadhia is a prosperous industrial centre making gay coloured textiles. The railway station lies 7km NE of the centre.

**History**. The earliest settlement on the Herkyna was *Mideia*, known to Homer (Il. ii, 507), the citadel of which may have been on a hill, now called Tripolithári, N of the modern town. During the Classical period *Lebadeia* was not of much importance.

Minor archaeological finds have been made beneath the town. It was sacked by Lysander and later by Archelaus. Pausanias found it 'equal in style and splendour to the most flourishing cities in Greece'; its fame and prosperity were chiefly due to the oracle of Trophonios, which was the only one functioning in Boeotia in the time of Plutarch. Having a certain strategic importance **Levadia** prospered in the Middle Ages. It was the birthplace of St Nicholas Peregrinus (1075–94), a demented youth who, dying in Trani (Apulia), was canonised by the Roman church. In the 13C it passed to the dukes of Athens. In 1311–81 it was the third city of the Catalan duchy of Athens and Neopatras, its military capital, and the seat of a bishop. It withstood a siege by Walter II de Brienne in 1335, but fell by treason to the Navarrese in 1381. The town passed to Nerio Acciaioli in 1385 and Bayezid captured it in 1394. Levadhia gained importance under the Turks and at the War of Independence was still the second city of the Greek mainland.

A conspicuous feature of the town is the 18C **clock tower**. By the riverside are old fulling and spinning mills. A sign at the S end of the town points to the Oracle of Trophonios where a picturesque **Turkish bridge** spans the Herkyna just below the **Springs of Trophonios** (restaurant; tavernas; swimming pool). Modern waterworks have confused the ancient picture.

The visit to the gorge and springs of the Herkyna and to the kastro and further summit of Mt Ay. Ilias takes about two hours, probably longer without transport to Ay. Ilias. The gorge itself can be seen in a pleasant short stroll. The river, whose ultimate source is on Mt Lafistios (to the E), is fed by springs (now mostly enclosed) which gush from both sides of the gorge. Scholars have variously identified the **Spring of Memory** (Mnemosyne) and the **Spring of Forgetfulness** (Lethe).

The Oracle of Trophonios and the Temple of Zeus are now usually thought to have been situated on the summit of Mt Ayios Ilias (see below). The **Temple of Trophonios**, which was surrounded by a sacred grove, was probably on the right bank of the Herkyna, perhaps now beneath the lowest tower of the medieval fortification (one of the first landmarks you meet to the right), which is partly composed of blocks from a Classical structure. Inscriptions referring to Trophonios have been found and some other ancient blocks in nearby chapels.

Beyond the tower are votive niches cut in the rock, also a chamber 4m square and 3m high, with benches, originally employed for sanctuary ritual but later a favourite retreat of the Turkish governor. A structure encloses springs. The path up the gorge leads to a recently built open air theatre and, high up in the rock face, the chapels of Zoödhokhos Piyi and Jerusalem of the Grotto.

Returning to the tower (see above), 15 minutes climb up Od. Frouríou, is the medieval **kastro**, a fortress used by the Catalans in the 14C and partly built of ancient material. Its custody was entrusted to the most important Siculo-Catalan families and it held the previous relic of the head of St George. It was severely damaged by earthquake in 1894 but is still impressive.

The second summit visible to the W from the kastro is that of **Ayios Ilias** (402m, accessible by road), identifiable by cypress trees, aerials, a small church and ancillary buildings, and a cross at the N end. Here are some blocks of the temple of Zeus Basileios seen unfinished by Pausanias. Immediately W of the modern chapel have been found remains (now filled in) of a circular subterranean construction identified with the **Oracle of Trophonios** in its 3C AD form.

The **Oracle of Trophonios** was renowned as far back as the 6C BC. Among those who consulted it were Croesus, Mardonius, and the traveller Pausanias, who gives from personal experience a detailed account of the process (see Paus. IX, 39, 5–14) which involved various rituals followed by descent into a subterranean chamber.

FROM LEVADHIÁ TO ORCHOMENÓS, 11km (7 miles). You leave Levadhia by the Lamia road (see below), turning off after 5.5km to the right and passing cotton ginneries. The Frankish tower of *Thourion* is visible on a hill c 1km to the NW. The Battle of Lake Kopais is thought to have been fought in the immediate vicinity and the Duke of Athens to have surveyed the battlefield from this tower prior to the engagement. 11km **Orchomenós**, a town of 5525 inhabitants, combining the former hamlets of Petromagoúla and Skrípou, lies at the foot of a desolate rocky ridge, known in antiquity as *Akontion* ('Javelin') and today as Dhourdhouvana. The *church of the former convent of the Dormition (Koimesis tis Theotokou), admirably restored since its fabric was split by an earthquake in 1895, was built in 874. Designed in a Bulgar tradition of Byzantine building, it is the unique example of its type in Greece, though similar in plan to Ayia Sophia at Ohrid. The single cupola on a high drum rests on solid walls, but the proportions are good. The whole building consists of column-drums from a temple (of the Graces) and blocks from the theatre. The interior, architecturally unadorned, is frescoed but cluttered by ornate and tasteless furniture.

Ancient *Orchomenos*, occupying a strong position at the E end of Akontion, was of the richest and most important centres of Mycenaean times. Traditionally it was the capital of the Minyans. Homer compared its treasures with those of Egyptian Thebes. It appears to have been inhabited almost continuously from the Neolithic period to the time of Alexander the Great.

**History**. The Minyans were supposed to have come from the Thessalian seaboard (or, more fancifully, direct from Egypt) to Orchomenos and made it their capital. They drained Lake Kopaïs and built a series of fortresses of which the most remarkable is Gla. Their dominion extended across Boeotia, and Thebes itself came, for a time, under their sway. Minyan Ware, so-called because Schliemann first discovered it at Orchomenos, is a 'fine wheel-made ware of well refined, grey clay with a very smooth polished surface which is curiously soapy to the touch'. Its origin is a mystery, its period Middle Helladic and it comes also in yellow and other colours.

About 600 BC Orchomenos joined the Boeotian League, but did not put its emblem on her coinage until 387 BC. If she became a member of the Kalaurian League it was because of her authority over the Boeotian coast towns. She took the side of the invader in the Persian Wars. Orchomenos joined Sparta against Thebes in 395 and 394 BC, and was saved after Leuktra (371) only by the good offices of Epaminondas. In 364 Thebes seized the pretext of a conspiracy to destroy her venerable rival during Epaminondas' absence. Eleven years later the Phocians rebuilt Orchomenos, but it was again destroyed by the Thebans in 349. Under Philip of Macedon and Alexander the Great it was again rebuilt. In 87 Sulla defeated Archelaus, the general of Mithridates, under its walls. The Graces, or Charites, were first worshipped at Orchomenos.

Immediately W of the church, excavations since 1970 have revealed a probable **Mycenaean palace** built c 1350 and destroyed 1200 BC, with extensive remains of fresco decoration. Across the road are impressive remains of the **theatre** of the 4C BC. About 150m SW of the church, in a walled enclosure, is the so-called *Treasury of Minyas** (adm. restricted), a Mycenaean tholos tomb recalling the Treasury of Atreus at Mycenae. It was excavated by Schliemann in 1880–86. The stone revetments of the **dromos** were robbed in 1862 and the roof of the **tholos** has fallen in, but the gateway still has its threshold and lintel of dark grey Levadhia marble and eight courses stand of the tholos itself. The most remarkable features were the bronze rosettes, which decorated the walls, and the **thalamos**, or inner

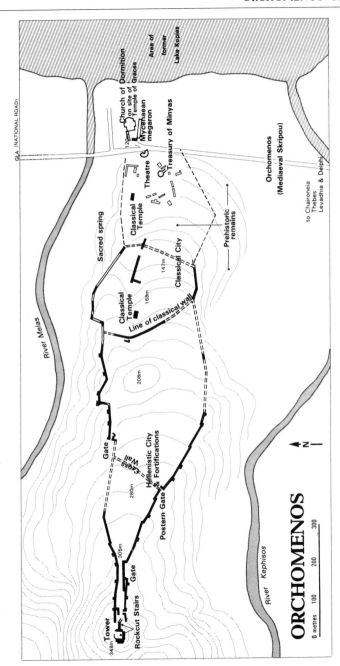

# ORCHOMENOS

0 metres   100   200   300

River Kephisos

River Melas

N

Tower
348m
Rockcut Stairs

Gate

305m

Postern Gate

Hellenistic City & Fortifications

Cross Wall

280m

Gate

208m

Line of classical wall

Classical Temple
168m

Sacred spring

Classical Temple

Theatre

147m

Classical City

Prehistoric remains

GLA (NATIONAL ROAD)

Church of Dormition
on site of Temple of Graces
120

Temple of Graces

Mycenaean megaron

Treasury of Minyas

Area of former Lake Kopaïs

Orchomenos (Mediaeval Skripou)

to Chaironeia
Thebes
Levadhia & Delphi

sepulchral chamber cut out of the rock. In its ceiling are slabs of green schist, carved with spirals interwoven with fan-shaped leaves, and surrounded by a border of rosettes. In the middle of the tholos are remains of a marble pedestal belonging to a funerary monument of the Macedonian period, once erroneously taken for the tomb of Hesiod, which was in the agora.

The **city walls** of the Archaic period ran along the N and S sides of the ridge forming a long triangle, whose apex was the acropolis. Within these walls the excavations of Furtwängler and Bulle in 1903–05 revealed a series of superimposed settlements.

To the W and E of the Treasury of Minyas are the remains of a Neolithic **settlement** (?6000–3400 BC), consisting of beehive huts built of unfired brick on stone socles. Above this was a town of Early Helladic date (3000–2000), characterised by deep circular ashpits, 6–8m diameter. Above this again appear the apsidal house and rectangular megaron common in Thessaly and Elis (2000–1750) and yielding the so-called Minyan ware (see above) of Middle Helladic date.

Near the cemetery is the substructure (21m x 85) of an **Archaic temple**, of the 9C or 8C BC, resting, as at Tiryns and at Mycenae, on much older remains. This was a part of the Middle Helladic town of 1700–1450 BC. About 350m W of the cemetery, on an intermediate terrace, are the remains of a **Temple of Asklepios**, measuring 22m x 11.5m. From there are reached the upper terraces, the location of the **Macedonian town**.

An ancient stairway mounts to the **acropolis** (308m), in size hardly more than a square keep. The cliffs on the E and N formed a natural defence; on the S and W the site was protected by massive walls, dating from the 4C BC and among the finest extant examples of ancient Greek fortification. The view is extensive including the entire Kopaic plain.

From Levadhia to Arakhova and Delphi, and to Osios Loukas, see Rte 45.

The Lamia road turns N out of Levadhia and rounds the easterly foothills of the Parnassos range to enter the broad valley of the Boeotian Kefissos. 125km Turning (right) for **Orkhomenos** (see above). You now cross the battlefield of Chaironeia at the entrance (left) of the defile of Kérata. 132km Kápraina has readopted the old name **Khairónia**. Ancient *Chaironeia* (χαιρώνεια) cannot be missed since the **\*lion** stands at the roadside. It guarded the **polyandrion**, or common tomb, in which the Thebans buried the members of the Sacred Band killed in the battle of Chaironeia. This remarkable but not very realistic sculpture, which was discovered by a party of English visitors in 1818 almost buried in the ground, was smashed during the War of Independence by the brigand patriot Odysseus Androutsos under the impression that it contained treasure. In 1902–04 the Greek Archaeological Society restored it and replaced it on its ancient plinth. It is constructed of three hollow sections of bluish-grey Boeotian marble, and is represented seated on its haunches; its height is 5.5m (8.5m, with the plinth). The ossuary which it adorned was a rectangular enclosure surrounded by a peribolos wall; inside were found 254 skeletons and various objects now in Athens. There is a small rock-cut theatre.

Adjacent is a **museum** containing Neolithic, Middle Helladic and Protogeometric ware from Chaironeia (especially the Toúmba Baloménou c 2km to the NNE, now being re-excavated); Neolithic, EH, and MH vessels from Elateia; black-figure vases from Abai; finds from Exarkhos and Ayia Marina (see below) and Mycenaean remains from Orchomenos, including a fragment of fresco from the palace; vases, terracottas, and arms from the Tumulus of the Macedonians.

The **Battle of Chaironeia** was the outcome of the sabre-rattling policy of Demosthenes, who, by rousing anti-Macedonian feeling in the Athenians and concluding an alliance with Boeotia, provoked Philip of Macedon to attack Southern Greece. After capturing

Amphissa, Philip entered Boeotian territory at the head of 30,000 foot and 20,000 horse. He found the allied army, perhaps slightly inferior in numbers, barring his way in the plain to the E of Chaironeia. The Athenians, attacking on the left wing, gained an initial advantage. The Macedonian cavalry, led by the 18-year old Alexander, overwhelmed the Theban sacred band, who fought on to the death. The Athenians (among them Demosthenes himself), taken in the rear, fled. Philip buried the Macedonian dead in a great **tumulus** (to be seen near the railway); he burned the Athenian corpses and sent the ashes to Athens. The Thebans were permitted to bury their dead in a common tomb (see above). The result of the battle was the unquestioned supremacy of Macedon, crystallised the following year at the Synedrion of Corinth. After the battle Philip treated Thebes with the utmost severity, but was unexpectedly lenient towards Athens. In the same plain Sulla won his great victory over Archelaus in 86 BC.

The ancient city, whose chief industry was the distillation of unguents from the lily, rose, narcissus, and iris, was the birthplace of Plutarch (AD 46–?127), who kept a school here, holding a priesthood for life from AD 95 at Delphi. The **acropolis** (270m) occupies two summits separated by a saddle. There are remains of Hellenic walls and fragments of earlier walls in polygonal and Cyclopean work. At the N foot of the hill is a little **theatre**.

To the left is a road to **Ayios Vlásios**, a name disguising St Blaize, above which (left) stand *walls of the acropolis of ancient *Panopeos*, the reputed home of Epeios, who built the Trojan Horse. The road crosses the railway near (137.5km) **Dhávlia** station. The village lies 7km W; and 30 minutes S of the village, in a wooded situation on an abrupt E spur of Parnassos, the ruins of ancient *Daulis*. Road and railway pass out of Boeotia into Lokris through the Pass of Belessi, anciently Pass of Parapotamoi, down which Philip marched to Chaironeia in 338 BC. At 141km the road divides by a cotton-mill.

The right branch runs NE to **Atalándi** (28km; Rte 44B). At 7km you leave to the left an asphalted by-road to modern **Elátia** (6.5km), formerly Drakhmani, with a small museum and (3km farther N by a dry-weather track) a Neolithic settlement mound and a LHIIIC/SubMycenaean chamber tomb cemetery at Alonáki, nearby. An (uncorrected) Carbon 14 dating of c 5520 BC was obtained for monochrome pottery and of c 5080 for the earliest painted pottery. The road crosses a ridge between Mt Khlomón (right; 1081m) and Mt Varvás, the E spur of Kallidhromon with a fine view of Parnassos. Beyond (13.5km) **Kalapódhi**, opposite the church of Ay. Apostoloi and just above the road, German excavators have uncovered, beneath Byzantine material, the remains of a **Sanctuary of Artemis Elaphebolia and Apollo**. The most substantial remains (the site is now overgrown, with little to see) were those of three temples, two Archaic and one Classical but there were earlier structures on the site and the numerous offerings from votive deposits suggest continuous cult activity here from the Mycenaean period. A road (left) leads to **Zéli** (with a Mycenaean cemetery and Macedonian-type rock-cut tombs), from which the ruins of *Elateia*, the capital of ancient Phokis and the city of Onomarchos, a noted general in the Sacred War of 357–346 BC, may be reached in 40 minutes. Philip made Elateia his base for the invasion of Greece. The consternation which seized the Athenians on learning of its capture by Philip in 339 BC is described in a famous passage of Demosthenes. In 198 the city was taken by the Roman general Flamininus. It was unsuccessfully besieged in 86–85 BC by Taxilas, a general of Mithridates, and c AD 176 by the robber horde of the Costobocs (from Hungary). On a hill called **Kástro Lazoú** (fine view) are the ruins of a **Temple of Athena Kranaia**, excavated by the French School in 1886. The temple, which was served by boy-priests, was in the Doric order with 6 columns by 13. To the E of Kalapodhi a bridle path leads round Mt Khlomon in 8km to **Exarkhos**, passing the remains of *Abai* and *Hyamopolis*.

The main road bears left. The long range of Kallídhromon appears ahead. At (150km) **Káto Tithoréa** (or Kifissokhóri; Hotel C) a by-road runs SW to **Tithoréa** (or Velitsa; 6.5km), a tobacco-growing village (1005 inhab.), named after the ancient city nearby. Its walls (3m thick) and towers are impressive. Ayía Marína, to the S has a Neolithic settlement. The road traverses a defile between Parnassos and Kallidhromon. 164km **Amfíklia** (Αμφίκλεια; Hotels D, E), or Dadí, with 3145 inhabitants, the largest town in W Lokris, is piled up the hill in terraces, as was its ancient predecessor to the W. The **acropolis** of the ancient site is marked by a Frankish tower, now in the middle of the cemetery. Keeping right (the left route leads to Lilaia and Gravia), you cross the river and the railway to (169km) **Lílaia** station. The citadel of *Lilaia*, with walls and towers standing to a great height, occupies the precipitous edge of a remote slope of Parnassós, 6.5km SW beyond **Polídhroso**. Beside the Classical walls, at the top of the slope, is a very large Frankish tower (13.3m x 7.6m). The road starts to climb through increasingly grand scenery.

Near (180km) **Brállos** (Μπραλλος; restaurant) a turning for Amfissa, important as connecting Lamia via the Rion ferry with Patras, drops across the valley to enter at **Graviá** a defile on the opposite side (Rte 45). Just below Gravia (3km S of Brallos station) is **Bralos British Military Cemetery** with the graves of 95 allied soldiers who died (mostly of influenza) in the 49th Stationary Hospital, transferred here in 1917. Brallos was the N end of the overland supply route from Itea for the Macedonian front. The old road and the railway now start their arduous passage of the Pass of Fournataki, the col connecting Mt Oiti on the W with Mt Kallidhromon. An alternative route descends to the National Road near Thermopylae. **Elevtherokhóri**, off this road, is the starting-point for (1½hours) the refuge-hut on Kallidhromon (organised from Lamia).

The railway threads two long tunnels, between which a long iron viaduct crosses the Asopos. Farther on another viaduct traverses the Gorgopotamos. Both these bridges were blown up in 1942–43 by British parachutists aided by Greek partisans, exploits which cut a German supply route to North Africa for six months. The Gorgopotamos Bridge was again blown by the retreating Germans and the present bridge was built by US army engineers in 1948. The anniversary of the allied exploit is usually celebrated every November; at the commemoration in 1964 an old mine exploded killing 13 people and injuring 51 others.

Just beyond the summit (619m) is (190km) the **Khání Karnásou** (refreshments), overlooking the great plain of Lamia. The descent, formerly one of the steepest and most tortuous in Greece, has been modified by road engineering. The region is steeped in legends of Herakles. Some ruins (walls, section of an acqueduct; gymnasium) above the gorge of the Asopos (left; near the point where it debouches into the plain) are taken to be *Herakleia Trachinia*, the 5C successor of *Trachis*, his last residence, from where, suffering torments from the poisoned shirt of Nessus, he ascended to his self-immolation on Mt Oite. During the Persian invasion of 480 BC the Persians had their camp at Trachis and from here the Anopaia path, betrayed to them by Ephialtes, led to the rear of the Greek position at Thermopylae. From the foot of the pass the road drives straight across the plain and the Spercheios to (212km) **Lamia** (Rte 47).

# B.   Via Kamména Voúrla

**Road**, Ethniki Odhos 1214km (133 miles), toll highway.—38km Malakássa.—61km Turning for Khalkís (20km).—85km Turning for Thebes
(6km).—110km Kástro (Gla).—170km Kamména Voúrla.—194km
Thermopylae (Thermopíles).—214km Lamía.—Buses 10 times daily in 3½ hours.

**Railway**, 219km (136 miles), see Rte 44A. The line closely follows the highway nearly to Thebes (90km, see below); then it takes the course of the old
road, via Levadhiá, described in Rte 44A. Lianokládhi station (6.5km W of
Lamía) is connected by bus (all trains) with Lamia.

To reach the National Highway you may leave central Athens by Od.
Patissión (Rte 20), by Liossíon (Rte 19B), or (best) by Akharnón, between
the two, to merge beyond **Patíssia** with the approach from Piraeus. At 20km,
past a bridge under the railway, a turning (signposted Ay. Stéfanos)
branches right for Marathon Lake which comes briefly into view near the
25km post. After crossing the railway, the highway follows a course parallel
to the old Kalamos road (Rte 22). Near (29km) **Polidhéndhri** is a road (right)
to the Amphiaraion (Rte 22). To the left rises Béletsi (841m), the NE
extremity of Parnes. Road and railway pass through the narrow gap
between Béletsi and Mavrinora in the district known in ancient times as
the *Diakria*.

By-passing **Malakássa**, which stands at the foot of the Dhekelia pass, with
(38km) the road (right) to Skala Oropos and the ferry to Euboea, you cross
the gentle rolling country that extends from Parnes to the S Euboean Gulf.
47km **Avlón**, population 6346, lies 2km left on the railway. The road enters
Boeotia and crosses the Asopos. Beyond (53km) **Oinófita** (formerly Stani-
átes), toll gate. The battle of Oenophyta resulted in a victory for the
Athenians in 457 BC. 59km Turning for **Dílessi**, a little coastal village made
notorious by the murders of 1870 (see Rte 21). It probably occupies the site
of ancient *Delion*; the Athenian defeat of 425 BC is to be placed c 5km to
the S near 'Palaiokháni'. The road crosses the Khalkis branch line just
beyond its junction with the main railway at Oinói (1.5km left). 61km
**Skhimatári** (left) in a spreading industrial zone has a small and badly lit
museum containing *stelai*, figurines, and inscriptions from Tanagra.

Ancient *Tanagra* (best reached (right; just before bridge) off the road from Oinói to
Ayios Thomás) occupied a nearly circular hill rising from the N bank of the Asopos, c
5km S of Skhimatari and a similar distance from modern Tanagra. The most prominent
feature of the plain today is an airfield of the Hellenic Air Force (identity documents
should be carried) and an aircraft factory (on the site of a large ancient cemetery).
Tanagra was the scene of a Spartan victory over the Athenians and Argives in 457 BC
and (?) birthplace of the poetess Corinna, who defeated Pindar in a musical contest at
Thebes. The ruins include an enceinte of c 385 BC and a visible but still buried theatre.
A recent survey has located and tentatively identified other buildings, also the ancient
quarries on Mt Kerykios, to the SW. The place is particularly noted for the terracotta
figurines discovered in the extensive necropolis in 1874.
  A further series of chamber tombs by modern Tanagra excavated since 1969 has
yielded Mycenaean larnakes and associated terracotta plaques of most unusual design
(see Thebes Museum).
  Across the river Asopos, to the E of the site, the 12C church of **Ayios Thomás**
incorporates much ancient material.

TO KHALKÍS (81km from Athens). A road diverges N to (7km) **Vathí**, with
shipyards, a huge radio station, and a station on the Khalkis branch line.

*'Tanagra' figurine, 250-200 BC*

To reach ancient *Aulis* (commonly Avlídha), famed in the Homeric epic as the place where Agamemnon sacrificed Iphigeneia, you take an older and poorer road E from Vathí (*not* the main coastal highway). The long narrow **Temple of Artemis** was discovered during the building of the road in 1941. Its identification is certain from the inscription on a statue base. The site was excavated by Threpsiades in 1956–61. The cella dates from the 5C but was restored in Roman times; it originally had a porch with two columns *in antis*, which was rebuilt with four columns in Hellenistic times. To the S of the temple are some remains of **potters' establishments**, with a kiln, and a third building, perhaps a hotel.

By a large cement factory (right), you diverge right to the older road (signed Παλαιά Γέφυρα). Straight ahead is an alternative crossing by the new (1993) bridge. The old road continues NW round the bay. Closer to the sea (dirt road) by Lake Glifa and the railway line **Lófos Vlíkhas** is the site of a substantial Mycenaean settlement, also with earlier remains. The road crosses the Euripos. 20km **Khalkis**, see Rte 42A.

On the mainland opposite Khalkis a road runs N to **Dhrosiá** (4km; formerly Khaliá) continuing round the coast past (7.5km) the probable site of the **Tomb of Salganeus** mentioned by Pausanias. This is at the NW end of a long ridge which has yielded EH, MH and Mycenaean material. 11km *Anthedon*, excavated by the American School, has some well-preserved remains of a quay, now thought to be of Byzantine date, and of two moles (partly submerged). The line of the city walls can be traced round the acropolis, a low hill close to the shore to the E, and around the lower town to the SW.

At 70km (right) is the old road to Khalkis (19km).

On this road, at the approach to (5km) **Rhítsona**, now a mere hamlet after its destruction as a reprisal during the German occupation, is the site of ancient *Mykalessos*, mentioned by Homer and bearing a pre-Greek name. Its existence ended in 414 BC when a body of Theban mercenaries hired by Athens fell upon the place on their way home and slew every living creature, including the animals and a school of boys just gathered for their morning lesson. The road crosses a tortuous pass (view) between Messapion and Mt Galatsidheza, then runs in the flat plain through the industrial mainland development to Khalkis.

The road continues very straight with the low grey Messapion Oros (1021m at its N extremity) to the right. The railway swings SW towards Thebes. At 85km the flyover junction, **Thebes** (4km) is well seen to the left. On the W side of **Litharés**, the next hill to the right, near the lake shore, excavations in 1971–72 uncovered a large EH settlement comparable with Zygouries. The N side of Mt Fagas crowds in on the left on the approach to the Boeotian Lakes, reduced to two since the draining of Kopaïs, and greatly reduced in size in the recent years of drought. The road skirts the rocky SW shore of Lake Ilíki (motel; restaurant), an irregular sheet of water ringed by low steep hills.

**Lake Likéri**, renamed **Ilíki** (Υλίκη), occupies a deep depression 50m below the level of the Kopaic plain. After receiving the waters of Kopaïs the level of the lake rose to 80m. In 1958, however, a new aqueduct was opened to supply water from Iliki to Marathon Lake. Iliki is 8km long and, at its widest, N–S point 3.6km broad. Jutting into the Lake, the **Klimatári** peninsula has a Frankish tower, and remains of an ancient settlement (?*Hyle*) only visible when the water is low. The ridge of Mouriki (83m), pierced by a canal, separates Iliki from Lake Paralimni (Παραλίμνη), which extends to the NE towards the sea. Oval in shape, 8km long and 1.5km broad, it is enclosed by Mt Ptoön, to the N and W, and Messapion, on the E. The ridge (95m) which separates it from the sea, is pierced by a tunnel which carries off superfluous waters to the Euboean Channel near Anthedon. Both ridges are seared by ancient cuttings. A recession of Paralimni exposed two sets of remains investigated in 1965–66 and identified with the Isos of Strabo at the NE end and with the early site of Hyle at the SW.

At 100km, to either side of the main road, several hundred tombs have been excavated in a large cemetery of the Archaic to Hellenistic periods. 102km **Akraífnio** (1462 inhab.; 1.5km right), formerly Kardhítsa, has readopted a variant name of the ancient ruined city of Akraiphia which occupied the ridge of Kriaria, 10 minutes SE of the village beyond a ravine. Here was found the inscription relating to Nero's proclamation of Greek freedom, now in Thebes museum. There are traces of fortifications (4C BC). The church of Ayios Yeoryios high above the village bears an inscription of 1311 naming Antoine le Flamenc, one of the survivors of the Battle of Kopaïs. The village is the starting-point for the Ptoïon.

From Akraifnio you take the road towards Kokkinó but at its first bend continue straight ahead on a motorable track which soon divides. The right branch crosses the valley. After c 1km, to the right of the track on the flat hill of **Kastráki** is a sanctuary dedicated to the *Hero Ptoïos*. Two altars, two buildings, and the bases of 28 tripods suggest that the cult flourished during the two periods when Akraiphia enjoyed relative autonomy (c 550–480 and 456–446). Above are remains of a 4C **temple** to an Earth goddess, mother of the hero. The left branch keeps to the N side of the valley (view back over the Ptoös sanctuary) and leads in ¾ hour to the ravine of **Perdhikovrísi** on the slope of Mt Ptoön (725m). Here, below the main summit, was the **Ptoïon**, or **Sanctuary of Ptoan Apollo**, seat of an infallible oracle. The site, cleaned in 1963–64 by the French School (new work in progress), had already suffered greatly from the depredations of men and goats since the excavations of 1885. These yielded numerous statues (chiefly kouroi), bronzes, vases, and inscriptions, now divided between the museums of Athens and Thebes.

The site occupies three terraces below a spring. W of the disused chapel of Ayia Paraskevi you come to the **lower terrace**, on which are the ruins of a large **cistern**, with seven compartments, which collected the waters of the upper spring and fed them by a conduit to an ablutionary building just below. Above the cistern lies the **middle terrace** mainly occupied by two long parallel **stoas**. The **upper terrace** bears a few courses of the foundations of a **temple** of the Doric order that had 6 columns by 13. It was rebuilt in the 3C BC over the ruins of a 7C structure. A long base in front of the temple probably supported tripods and/or statues. A little higher up is a **cavern**, perhaps the abode of the oracle. The modern **fountain** on the path above has taken the place of the ancient one at the foot of the sanctuary. From the S end of the site, fine view over the Lakes.

The main track mounts in 30 minutes to the convent of Pelayía, visible on its plateau (546m).

The Kokkino road from Akraifnio (above) can be used as an approach to Larimna. The first col affords a fine view down to Gla (see below), which on foot can be reached from the Ptoïon in one hour.

The road crosses the channelled effluents of Lake Kopais, which spreads out to the left. On a clear day Mt Parnassos is visible ahead. The road sweeps right. 110km **Kástro**, formerly Topólia, rises on a hill to the left, which was once an island; here vestiges of polygonal walling and inscribed stones in the church mark the site of *Kopai*, the city mentioned in the 'Catalogue of Ships' which gave name to the 'Copaic' lake. To the right, on a low eminence, also an island in antiquity, is the Mycenaean stronghold of **\*Gla**, a remarkable fortress many times larger than Mycenae or Tiryns, whose very identification is uncertain. The approach road, signposted Lárimna, (passable for motors; 25-minute walk) leaves the highway immediately before a large petrol station and before the Kastro exit, and makes a complete circuit of the fortress. The site was partially explored by the French School in 1883. The four gates of the city were cleared in 1956–60 by the Greek Archaeological Service under Threpsiades and work was restarted in 1979 by Prof. Sp. Iakovidhis. They were damaged by fire when the city fell. The **fortifications**, 2.8km in length, run along the edge of a precipitous low cliff. The South or **Royal Gate** had double bronze-faced doors. From here a road led directly to the vast walled '**agora**', a space enclosed by long parallel buildings. These were apparently store- and work-rooms, with limited access and provision for the manipulation of heavy loads (?sacks of grain); also some living quarters. Fragments of large storage jars encourage this identification. The best-preserved ruins are of a complex at the highest point of the site (72m above the plain) against the N wall. Usually described as a 'palace', the building, which contains two megarons but lacks the distinctive features (e.g. hearths) of other Mycenaean palaces, is now thought to have housed two high officials of equal status. The two wings allow for some intercommunication.

About 10km NW of **Kastro** (off a road to Orkhomenos), E of the village of Loútsi and between it and Pávlo, the hill of Ayios Athanásios was apprently the acropolis (walls) of ancient *Hyettos*.

The route continues N, climbing through scrub-covered hills. 119km Turning for **Lárimna**.

A road descends via (1.5km) **Martíno** to (8km) **Lárimna** (Hotel D), a friendly village on an inlet of the N Euboean Gulf. On the farther shore of the inlet are the extensive and obtrusive works of the only nickel mine in Europe lying W of the former 'Iron Curtain'. The village, built largely on ancient foundations, fronts two small bays. In the bay to the W (taverna; bathing) are considerable remains of the port installations of the 4C BC, when *Larymna* had the most easterly harbour of Lokris. Two piers forming the harbour mouth (once guarded by a chain) can be seen underwater with the line of a long protective mole; the quay, of ashlar masonry, was guarded by towers. The islet of Ayios Nikolaos has Byzantine and Early Christian remains.

124.5km **Mázi** (right) has an Early Christian basilica. 127.5km Turn for (or via Mazi) **Ayios Ioánnis Theólogos**, on the coast, the site of ancient *Halai*.

The site comprises a harbour and acropolis excavated by the Americans in the 1910s and reinvestigated from 1988. There are finds from the Neolithic to Byzantine periods. The Classical town had a grid plan. Within the acropolis are an archaic temple, circular ?granaries, late Roman tombs and the remains of an Early Christian church.

You descend through cultivated country (132km toll gate) to the Gulf of Atalandi. 137.5km (left) **Kiparíssi** has walls and an Archaic sanctuary belonging to ancient *Opius* (at Kastráki). The little port of (141.5km) **Skála** serves **Atalándi** (Hotels C, D), 5km to the W, the chief town of the eparchy of Lokris with 5456 inhabitants. It brews a popular German beer under licence. There is a long stretch of the Hellenistic fortifications at Makedhoniká in the NE outskirts. The village of **Megaplátanos** (4km N) has a fortified ancient settlement at Palaiokástra. For the route W to join the Thebes–Lamia road, see Rte 44A. 145.5km **Livanátes**. On a spur to the W is a military satellite station. By the sea, on the hill of Pírgos, are some remains of ancient *Kynos* (prehistoric–Hellenistic finds).

The road now runs in the cultivated strip between the hills of Lokris and the narrowing North Euboean Gulf (or Atalandi Channel). 150km **Arkítsa** (1km right; Hotels B, C) has a car-ferry service 8 times daily to Loutrá Aidhipsoú in Euboea. 154.5km **Ayios Nikólaos** (Hotel D) is on the shore. The landscape becomes grander as the Knimís Mountains (937m) crowd in towards the sea.

Beyond the olive groves of Cape Kálamos is (166.5km) **Ayios Konstandínos** (Hotels A, C, D), a pleasant developing resort on a little bay near the site of *Daphnous*. Ferry services to the Northern Sporades, see Rte 43. To the right is the Dhiavlos Knimidhos, the narrow channel blocked with islets that separates the W tip of Euboea from Cape Knimís.

175km **Kamména Voúrla** (Hotels A–E) is a busy, fashionable thermal resort ringed by olive trees; its salt radioactive waters are recommended to sufferers from rheumatism and arthritis. 182km Kainoúrio. The site of ancient *Thronion* is on a hill to the left. For a brief moment distant Parnassos can be glimpsed again behind the foothills of Kallidhromon. The road crosses several broad torrents. 187km Modern Skárfia, with an earth satellite station, lies to the right; the site of ancient *Skarpheia* is on a hill (left) just before the by-pass of (190km) **Mólos**. 194km Ayía Triádha (2.5km right) lies in the flat alluvial marsh that borders the Maliakos Kolpos; across the gulf are seen the distant slopes of Mt Othrys. At 199.5km a road winds back E to Mendhenítsa (9.5km).

**Mendhenítsa**, the site of ancient *Pharygai*, is occupied by the **Castle of Bodonitsa**, seat of the Frankish marquisate of the Pallavicini in 1205–1410. It survived the Catalan invasion by placing itself under Venetian protection in 1335, but fell to the Turks after a siege. The fortress has a double enceinte, the lower enclosure on ancient foundations; the upper part, better preserved, is approached by a barbican.

We approach the famous Pass of Thermopylae (Στενά τών Θερμοπυλών) between the steep N side of Kallídhromon and the sea. The pass will always be remembered for the devotion of Leonidas and his Spartans during the Persian invasion of 480 BC. The defile, which is just under 6.5km long, ran between precipitous mountains and the sea. It was extremely narrow at both ends, but widened in the middle, where were the hot springs that gave the pass its name. It was in antiquity, for a force of any size, the only practical means of communication on land between Thessaly and S Greece. To understand the ancient topography, you must imagine the sea close on the right. Today the silt brought down by the Sperkheios has advanced the coast-line by nearly 5km, though the plain is still marshy. The modern road coincides with the ancient road for most of the way, except at the critical narrows where it runs N of the old course; here you must visualise the road nearer the cliffs with the sea extending to within a few metres of their foot.

**History**. By the time Xerxes was bridging the Hellespont for his invasion forces, the confederacy gathered at the Isthmus of Corinth was planning a combined forward defence of Greece. The Pass of Tempe, in N Thessaly, was considered but found impracticable because it could be turned. The next point of defence was Thermopylae, which it was decided to hold. Like Xerxes' invasion, the defence was to be a combined operation on land and sea. While the small Greek army occupied Thermopylae, the Greek fleet lay off *Artemision* (Euboea) to prevent the Persian fleet sailing down the Euboean Gulf in support of their army. Meanwhile the Persian army had reached Trachis (Rte 44A) and the Persian fleet the coast of Magnesia, at which point the weather came to the aid of the Greek naval forces.

The Greek army was under the command of Leonidas, king of Sparta. He repaired the Wall of the Phocians and took up his main position behind it, in the centre of the pass. The total Greek force was about 7300 men. The Persians are credited by modern historians with 300,000 men, though Herodotus adduces a grand total of more than 5¾ million. The Persians made several unsuccessful and costly assaults on the improvised fortifications of the Greeks. Xerxes had almost given up hope of forcing a passage when the Malian Ephialtes indicated a means of turning the Greek position by a mountain path called the **Anopaia**. Leonidas had posted the 1000 Phocians along it so that there could be no surprise from that quarter. However, Xerxes determined to use the path. Led by Ephialtes, Hydarnes, commander of the Persian 'Immortals', set out in the evening with 2000 men and marched through the night. The next morning they routed the Phocians and reached the E end of the pass, where they took the defenders in the rear.

Leonidas, foreseeing that he would be crushed between two attacks, had already ordered the withdrawal of the main force, retaining only his 300 Spartans, the 700 Thespians, and the 400 Thebans, who 'were kept back as hostages, very much against their will' since the Thebans were suspected of medising; they deserted in a body to the Persians as soon as opportunity offered. The course of the desperate battle, the death of Leonidas, and the famous 'last stand' of the Spartans on the hillock of Kolonos is told in detail by Herodotus (Bk VII), and visitors wishing to traverse the ground in detail cannot do better than follow his vivid and dramatic account.

All save two of the 300 Spartans were killed. One atoned for his survival by his valour at Plataia; the other hanged himself on his return to Sparta. The dead were buried where they fell and later commemorated by monuments bearing two celebrated epigrams. On the hillock a stone lion, which survived to the time of Tiberius, was erected to Leonidas. Forty years after the battle his body was taken to Sparta.

Thermopylae was seized by Leosthenes in the Lamian War. The tactics of Xerxes were copied by all who wished to force the Pass of Thermopylae. In 279 Brennus, at the head of his Gauls, finding himself checked by the troops of Kallipos, used the Anopaia path to turn the Greek position; but this time the Greeks were able to escape to their ships. In 191 Antiochus III, King of Syria, with 10,000 men, tried to deny the pass to the 40,000 legionaries of the Roman consul Manlius Acilius Glabrio and his legate M. Porcius Cato. Antiochus raised a double wall, with trenches, across the defile, and built forts on the slopes of Mt Kallidromon. Cato succeeded in carrying the forts and in taking the pass from the position in the rear, while Glabrio made a frontal attack. Antiochus escaped with only 500 men.

In AD 395 Alaric entered the pass without opposition. In the 6C 'the straits of Thermopylae, which seemed to protect, but which had so often betrayed, the safety of Greece, were diligently strengthened by the labours of Justinian' (Gibbon, *Decline and Fall*). In 1204 Boniface of Montferrat came through unopposed. Retreating British troops began to take up position here in 1941, but evacuation was ordered before the Germans reached the area.

**201km Thermopylae** (Hotels C, D), modern Thermopíles. Here in 1955 King Paul inaugurated the **memorial** to Leonidas and the Three Hundred, a white marble monument, surmounted by a striking bronze figure of Leonidas (see Rte 31, Sparta). The base bears reliefs of scenes from the battle and records the famous epigrams. It was erected at American expense. On the opposite side of the road is the **grave mound**. On the left, just beyond, are hot springs, with a hot waterfall, a popular hydropathic establishment and a restaurant. The waters (43°C) are impregnated with carbonic acid, lime, salt, and sulphur, and are said to be good for the cure of sciatica, stiff joints, and glandular complaints. At the W exit to the defile a hill is probably the site of *Anthela* where the meetings of the Amphictyonic League were held in autumn (in spring they met at Delphi).

204km A road (left) ascends to Brallos (Rte 44A). 205km Another leads to Dhamásta, Iráklia and the Amfissa road. The road crosses the Sperkheios. The **Alamanas Bridge** here was heroically defended on 5 May 1821 by Athanasios Diakos and the Bp of Salona, with 700 Greeks, against a superior force led by Omer Vrioni and Mehmet Pasha (monument with mosaic). To the left the solemn mass of Mt Oiti is well seen, and, farther behind us, the zigzag descent from Kallidhromon of the road from Amfissa and Levadhia (Rte 44A). Looking up the Specheios valley we see the imposing mass of Mt Timfristos.

215km **Lamía**, see Rte 47A. The National Highway turns E, the Lamia by-pass continues straight on; turning left you enter the city from the E.

# 45

# From (Athens) Levadhiá to Delphi (Dhelfí) and Amfissa

**Road**, 189km (117½ miles). To Thebes, see Rte 41, thence to (119km) Levadhiá, see Rte 44A.—141km Turning for Osios Loukás (14km).—156km Arákhova.—166km Delphí (Rte 46).—189km Amfissa.

From Athens to (74km) **Thebes**, see Rte 41; thence to (119km) **Levadhia**, see Rte 44A. The road continues W, winding up the N side of the narrowing valley. The scenery becomes increasingly grand as Parnassos dominates the whole region, though its summit is often hidden in cloud or capped with snow. Korakólithos (pleasant restaurants) is now avoided by a tunnel. The road descends before climbing through a defile. On the older (right) road line at (141.5km) **Skhísti**, or 'Tríodhos' (424m), the meeting-place in antiquity of three roads, from Daulis, Delphi, and Ambrossos, Sophocles laid the scene of Oedipus' murder of his father (Oedipus Tyrannus). Lying in a setting of lonely grandeur between the heights of Bardana and Kastri, it is still a parting of the ways.

The branch road leads S in an open valley to **Dhístomo** (Δίστομο; 4km; Hotels D), scene of a Nazi reprisal massacre on 10 June 1944, when 218 villagers were killed (plaques on church façade). In commemoration a community in Atlantic City adopted the name Distomo. The little town occupies the site of *Ambrossos,* few traces of which are visible. Parts of the wall and classical and Hellenistic graves have been located. An Early Christian basilica with mosaic was discovered in 1981. There is an **Archaeological Collection** (1994). Most travellers will here turn left to Osios Loukas (see below). Ahead the road zigzags down a further 10km to **Aspra Spítia**, on the Bay of Andíkira, a hideous dormitory town built by Aluminium of Greece, whose works were erected in 1962–65 at Ayios Theodhoros on the E side of the bay. Here the Roman and Byzantine remains of *Medeon* were excavated by the French School and Greek Archaeological Service in 1962–63 before they were built over. A huge Mycenaean acropolis was also explored and 250 tombs dug. At the W end of the bay, 2.5km farther on, is **Andíkira** on the site of the ancient Phocian town of *Antikyra.* A five-aisled Early Christian basilica has been uncovered here (at Pelatia). Continuation to **Itéa**, see Rte 55C.

**Osios Loukás**, the Monastery of St Luke Stíris, lies 8km E of Dhístomo. The road passes through **Stíri** and then through almond groves (the blossom delightful in the early spring). The monastery, one of the most interesting ecclesiastical complexes in Greece, stands on the brow of a peaked hill facing S and commanding wonderful views of Helikon and the surrounding country. Though there are still monks, the place is more ancient monument than retreat, and is equipped with a small hotel and restaurant.

The monastery is dedicated not to the Evangelist, but to a local beatified hermit, the Blessed Luke (Osios Loukás) of Stíri. A later 10C Life of Osios Loukas, also other traditions, give information about his life and the development of the monastic complex. His family fled from Aegina on its invasion by the Saracens and Luke was born in 'Kastorion' (probably Kastri, i.e. Delphi). After many adventures the hermit came to Stíri, where he died in 953. Already between 941 and 944 a church had been founded, dedicated to St Barbara, but the establishment of a larger church (the *Eukterion*) is attributed to Romanos II in 961. This was in recognition of the fulfilment of Luke's prophecy that Crete should be liberated by an emperor named Romanos. Both the existing churches have suffered from earthquakes. Restoration and conservation work since 1958 have changed former ideas of their chronological sequence and elucidated many details. The mosaics, although incomplete and partly reset, are both attractive and important.

From the flagged terrace is seen the rebuilt **trapeza** or refectory (now an impressive museum of Byzantine sculpture), above which rises the S flank of the katholikon set off by the flowing line of its dome. Recent research and observations (e.g. of blocked earlier windows in the walls of the nave) suggest that the building is an extension of an earlier church (the **Eukterion** of 961–966, see above), whose outline followed that of the crypt which belonged to it. The *katholikon, dedicated to Holy Luke and dating from c 1011–48, is comparable with the church at Daphni (Rte 16) and with it coupled by Krautheimer as 'probably the most beautiful representatives of

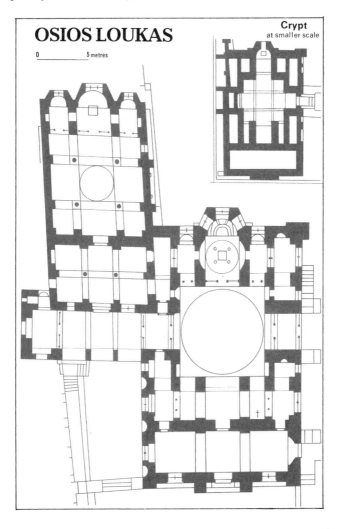

OSIOS LOUKAS

0      5 metres

Crypt
at smaller scale

the Greek-cross-octagon plan'. The foundation walls are of stone with stone and brick above. Columns of cipollino, Hymettian marble, and bigio antico divide the windows, each of which is surmounted by a large impost bearing a Greek cross. The lower parts of the windows are filled with sculptured marble. An inscription in the outer wall records the dedication by Xenocrates and Eumaridas of a fountain; the slab probably came from ancient Stiris. An exonarthex added in the 12C was demolished in the late 19C.

INTERIOR. The W door opens into a **narthex**, which has a vaulted ceiling and **\*mosaics** on a gold ground. On the arches are depicted the Apostles; in the lunettes, the Washing of Feet, the Crucifixion, and the Resurrection. On the ceiling are medallions of the Baptist, the Virgin with angels, and saints. On the pavement are slabs of verde antico.

The central domed **nave** is approached through a vestibule which, with the two transepts and the bema, form in plan the arms of the cross enclosed within the external rectangle of the walls. The angles are filled in by twelve groin-vaulted or domed bays, surmounted by a second storey of equal height to form a **matroneum**; this is frescoed (interesting graffiti of medieval ships) and carried over the transepts by open galleries. The piers have polychrome marble revetments. The **bema** and its flanking chapels are each closed off by a templon, that in the centre forming the ikonostasis, those to left and right open colonnades. There are ikons by Mikhail Damaskinos (16C).

The interplay of light and shade produced by the multiplicity of arches gives an air of solemn mystery, enhanced by reflected light from gold **mosaics**. Those in the dome were damaged in 1659 by earthquake and replaced by paintings. The mosaics are most complete in the vestibule and its aisles, and in the N transept (though these are medallions with busts of saints only). On the squinches supporting the dome mosaics of the Nativity, Presentation and Baptism. In the apse, mosaics of the Virgin and Child; above, in the vault, Descent of the Holy Ghost. The katholikon also has early 11C frescoes in the NE, NW and SW chapels, and in the gallery above the narthex.

The **crypt**, once taken to be the original church of St Barbara since it contains Holy Luke's tomb, is supported by square bevelled columns with imposts. It is lavishly decorated with 11C frescoes illustrating the Passion of Christ. The groin vaults are divided into panels containing busts of saints and monks in medallions. Beneath is a rock-cut refuge with its own water supply.

The smaller **church of the Theotókos** is attached to the N transept of the katholikon. The discovery (1964) of the fresco of Joshua as a Holy Warrior (end of 10C/early 11C) on the outer face of the N wall of the narthex, now seen in the interior of the later katholikon, has proved it be the earlier of the two churches (though not of course earlier than the Eukterion). The Theotokos itself now appears to to be the result of an extension (997–1011) of part of an earlier building, presumably the church of St Barbara, traces of whose construction have been recognised. The exterior has elaborate cloisonné masonry decorated with courses of deep dog-tooth brickwork and a cufic frieze. The **drum**, architecturally clumsy, has marble panels worked in great sculptural detail, recalling Islamic work. The church is fronted by a **exonarthex** (16C), with triple portico. Beyond, the **narthex** proper has two columns with Corinthian capitals. The church itself is a plain cross-in-square, the dome borne on four large granite columns with Byzantine capitals and imposts. The floor mosaics are fine.

The Delphi road passes through the Stenopos Zemenous, the upper ravine of the Platania, between the precipices of Parnassos and the bare slopes of Xerovouni (1554m). 146.5km **Khan of Ziméno** (700m), with a spring at the foot of a large oriental plane tree. At the head of the pass (766m) is the **Khan of St Athanasius**, with a chapel by a spring. The road winds steeply upwards: there is a good view of Arakhova, perched on a rocky spur of Parnassos above the gorge of the Pleistos.

157km **Arákhova** (Αράχωβα; 942m; Hotels B, C, D, E), a town of 3084 inhabitants, is noted for its rugs, wines and embroideries. Copious streams of water run down its narrow streets. The houses rise in terraces on the mountain spur; at the top is the church of **St George**. The town may occupy the site of a small Classical place called *Petrites*, which succeeded the two prehistoric towns of *Anemoreia* and *Kyparissos*. There are traces of these below and above the Katoptirio rock. Arakhova is the best starting-point for the climb of Parnassos. For skiing facilities, see below.

**Parnassos** is a complex mountain mass, with two main peaks: hence Ovid's *biceps Parnassus*. The higher summit is called **Lyakoura** or **Lykeri** ('Wolf Mountain', anciently *Lykorea*; 2457m) and the lower **Gerontovrachos** ('Old Man's Rock'; 2435m). To the Greeks Parnassos was sacred to Dionysos and the Maenads; it was the Latin poets who made it, with the Castalian Fountain, the home of Apollo and the Muses. During the flood, Deucalion's ship rested on the top of Parnassos.

The ski centre at **Fterólakkas** (c 1500m; car park) is reached by road (c 26km) from Arakhova via (9km) **Kalívia**. The centre is open for skiing in December–April (restaurant), when chair-lifts operate in two stages to c 180m where there are ski slopes (ski-lifts). There are higher slopes with lifts and a restaurant at **Kelária**. The lower centre functions as an excursion resort in summer. July and August are the only practicable months for climbing to the summit when the paths are free of snow. Due to recent changes in road and accommodation facilities, it is desirable to seek up-to-date information as to the most suitable approach. With a car and guide (or precise directions) it is possible to drive to within 45 minutes' walk of the summit via the access roads to the skiing installations. The traditional method of making the proper climb is to spend a night at the Hellenic Alpine Club refuge (**Katafíyion Sarantári**; 1890m, 28 beds); a robust vehicle can get to within 15-minutes' walk of the refuge. The guide lives in Arakhova, where contact should be made through the Alpine Club (preferably from Athens as the Arakhova guide can be hard to find). Only food need be taken to the refuge. The climb is usually made before dawn and takes about five hours there and back, though fell-walkers would do it in less. It is practicable for a fit climber, who does not mind the heat, to do the whole expedition in the day from Kalivia, ignoring the refuge.

The *view at sunrise, before the mists gather, exceeds in grandeur and interest almost every other prospect in the world. Little by little the map of Greece unfolds. To the NW are Timphristos and Pindos; to the N, beyond Kallidromon, are Oite, Othrys, Pelion, Ossa and Olympos. To the NE lies the Atalante Channel and the island of Euboea, with the Gulfs of Lamia and Volo, and the Northern Sporades beyond. In the far distance the grey mass of Mount Athos rises from the sea. To the SE are Helikon, Attica and the Cyclades; to the S the Gulf of Corinth, with its isthmus; beyond, the Peloponnesian mountains, Kyllene, Maenalon, Aroania, Erimanthos, and Panachaikon, with Taiyetos in the background. To the W, beyond the vale of Amphissa, the view is masked by the mountains of Lokris and Doris, two of which, Kiona (2500m) and Vardousi (2495m) are higher than Parnassos.

The road now descends gradually, skirting the cliffs of Parnassos on the right and keeping high above the Pleistos, whose ravine is hidden by vineyards. Egyptian vultures can be seen. It passes through one of the ancient cemeteries of Delphi. To the left of the road (1200m before the Castalia spring) are the remains of a square tower, probably of the 4–3C BC and one of a chain controlling the Levadhia–Delphi road. It was subsequently used as a burial place in the Roman period. On the right are the

Phaedriades, the precipices that shut in Delphi on the W. We now pass through the centre of ancient *Delphi* (Rte 46). On the left is Marmaria, with the Sanctuary of Athena. The road bears right and then makes a sharp bend to the left at the Castalian Fountain. To the S is the Papadhia Glen, through which the overflow from the spring flows into the Pleistos. Passing on the right the Pythian Sanctuary and the museum, it sweeps round to the right to enter the modern village.

166km **DELPHI** (Δελφοί; Hotels A–E), in modern Greek **Dhelfí**, at one time called New Kastri, is a modern village (1499 inhab.) built since 1892, about 1km W of the former village, **Kastri**, which stood on the ruins of ancient Delphi (Rte 46). By a special convention with the Greek Government in April 1891, the French School obtained a ten-years' lease of the ancient site, bought out the inhabitants, and arranged for their transplantation to the new village, which was supplied with water by means of an aqueduct from the Fountain of Kassotis. In Delphi is an annexe of the School of Fine Arts in Athens, where artists of all nationalities may stay, and here in 1965 was founded an International Cultural Centre sponsored by the Council of Europe. Reached by a road from the top of the village towards the NW entrance (closed) to the site enclosure is the **Sikelianos Museum**, formerly the house of the poet Angelos Sikelianos (1884–1951).

From Delphi the road descends steeply with acute bends. 175.5km **Khrissó** (now just off the road) is the modern equivalent of *Krisa* (some remains) without the importance of the ancient town. Krisa gave its name to the Krisaean Gulf (Krissaios Kolpos), on which Itea stands, and to the plain that extends for c 18km from the head of the bay to Amfissa. The plain, which is divided into two parts by the intrusion above Itea from W and from E of two mountain spurs, is exceptionally fertile in the N section (the Krisaean Plain proper as opposed to the Kirrhaean Plain), which is covered by the largest plantation of olives in Greece. At 178.5km the road divides; to the left the Navpaktos road descends in 4m through the olives to **Itéa** (see Rte 55C). The main road drives straight for Amfissa.

189km **Amfissa** (Αμφισσα; 180m; Hotels C, D), the chief town (7189 inhab.) of the eparchy of Parnassidhos and the seat of a bishop, is better remembered by its medieval name of *Salona*. Finely situated at the NW end of the Krisaean Plain on the first slopes of the Lokrian mountains, in antiquity *Amphissa* was the capital of Ozolian Lokris. The ruined but impressive Frankish **castle** (1205) is accessible by road. It has three enceintes, partly built on the walls of the ancient **acropolis**. Antique survivals include the remains of walls of Classical quadrangular and Hellenistic polygonal masonry, some reused, and of two towers. A Roman building on the E slopes was investigated in 1973. It had a large apsidal room with niches in its well-preserved walls. That and another room had fine mosaic floors. There are also a cistern of which the lower part is ancient and the upper part medieval, two ruined churches, and a circular keep. At the S foot of the castle is a fine arcaded Turkish **fountain** and the 12C **church of the Sotiros**. Mosaic floors from Roman buildings have been found in various parts of the town. On a site to the N of the cathedral is a **baptistery** of the late 4C AD, with marble facings and fine mosaics. Near the Nomarkhia are the remains of an Early Christian basilica, with mosaics.

*Amphissa* was denounced by Aeschines in 339 BC for violating the Krisaean Plain. The Amphictyonic League appealed to Philip of Macedon, who, making good use of the opportunity, invaded Greece and destroyed Amphissa. The city was rebuilt and furnished 400 hoplites in the war against Brennus in 279 BC. Destroyed again, by the Bulgars in the Middle Ages, it was rebuilt by the Franks, who renamed it *Salona*. The

Picard Autremencourt barons of Salona were feudatories of the kings of Salonika. In 1311 the Catalan Roger Deslaurs took the title of count, which passed in 1335 to Alfonso Frederichs of Aragon. In 1394 Salona fell to the Turks.

FROM AMFISSA TO LAMÍA, 73km (45 miles) (bus), magnificent road with sharp winding ascent and descent of the Pass of Gravia (870m), between Gkiona and Parnassos, celebrated for its heroic defence in 1821 by Odysseus Androutsos with 180 Greeks, against 3000 Turks. 33km **Graviá**, and thence via (41km) Brallos to Lamia, see Rte 44A.

To Návpaktos and Mesolóngi, see Rte 55B, C.

# 46

# Delphi (Dhelfí)

**Approaches** and hotels, see Rte 45. A hurried visit to the site takes c 3 hours; a reasonably thorough exploration needs at least 6. The hilly terrain is tiring though there are good paths. Changes of temperature make it advisable to carry a pullover, even in summer.

\*\***DELPHI** (Δελφοί; Dhelfí or Dhelfoùs), transformed by the excavators' skill since it disappointed Byron and Barry, is by common consent the most spectacularly beautiful ancient site in Greece and the one which, even to the uninitiated, most vividly evokes the Classical past. In antiquity Delphi was regarded as the centre of the world (ὀμφαλὸς γῆς) and to this and to its oracle the place owed its prestige, which extended far beyond the Greek world. The sacred precinct is superbly situated below the S slopes of Parnassos within the angle formed by the twin Phaedriades ('Shining Rocks', so called because they reflect the light), which form a tremendous precipice 250–300m high. The W rock is called Rhodini ('Roseate'), anciently *Nauplia*; from the E rock, Phleboukos ('Flamboyant', anciently *Hyampeia*) the Delphians used to hurl those found guilty of sacrilege. The cleft between the two, hollowed out by cascades from the upper plateau, is continued on the S by a line of ravines, by which the waters flow into the Pleistos. To the W the rocky spur of Mt Ay. Ilias (700m) completes the theatre-like setting. On the S Delphi is bounded by the ravine of the river Pleistos, in which the pipeline from the Mornos barrage near Lidhoriki is conspicuous; beyond rises the barrier of Mt Kirphys. The site is in a seismic area. On several occasions earthquakes and storms have caused the fall of great fragments of rock from Parnassos and serious landslips endangering the safety of the monuments. The \*view down the sacred plain to Itea, with its myriad olive-trees, is delightful.

**History**. The natural features of the site, in the 'centre of the world', with its springs, exhalations and crevasses, in a theatre of forbidding precipices, have helped to give Delphi its mysterious and sacred character. In the beginning it was sacred to Mother Earth and Poseidon, and was called *Pytho*, the name by which it is known in Homer (*Iliad* IX, 405; *Odyssey* VII, 80). It had an oracle where the Pythia (priestess) officiated near the cave of the serpent Python, son of Mother Earth. At an early date Delphi was colonised by settlers from *Lykorea*, which was situated on the plateau above it, but it was in the territory of *Krisa* and was therefore partially subject to that city.

The importation into Krisa from Crete of the cult of Apollo Delphinios, an island deity worshipped in the form of a dolphin, led to the introduction of his cult at Pytho, which then changed its name to *Delphoi*. Henceforward the holy place became the Sanctuary of Pythian Apollo. Later other gods were associated with the sanctuary; these included Dionysos and Athena Pronoia. The Pythian Games, one of the four great national Greek festivals, were instituted in honour of Apollo, Artemis and Leto, and at first were held every eight years (see below). The fame of the oracle, whose efficacy was fostered by its priestly administrators, spread all over the ancient world, and the festival attracted competitors and visitors from far and wide.

After the Dorian Invasion (c 1100 BC) the sanctuary became a centre of an association called the **Amphictyonic League**. This was by false etymology supposed to have been founded by Amphictyon, but really only means the league of the dwellers round a particular locality. The league was composed of twelve tribes, each of which contained various city-states, large and small, all of which had equal status within it, whatever their importance outside. This rudimentary United Nations included Thessalians, Dorians, Ionians and Achaeans. Both Athens and Sparta belonged to the league. In spite of the theoretical equality of members votes could be transferred and political power was reflected in the decisions made. The administration of the sanctuary was conducted by the council of the League together with the community of Delphi.

The city of Krisa levied dues on all pilgrims to Delphi, many of whom had to disembark at its port of Kirrha. Early in the 6C the pilgrims complained of extortionate charges, and the Delphians appealed to the Amphictyonic League. The league, urged on, it is said, by Athens, declared war against the Krisaeans. The ensuing conflict was known as the **First Sacred War** (c 595–586 BC). Invaluable assistance was given by Kleisthenes of Sikyon, and Krisa, with its port Kirrha, was destroyed. Its territory was confiscated. The Amphictyonic League took the Temple of Apollo at Delphi under its wing, and the state of Delphi was made autonomous. The Krisaean Plain was dedicated to the god and no one was allowed to till it or use it for grazing on pain of excommunication. About this time the Pythian Games were reorganised and, from 582 BC, like the Olympic Games, were held every four years (see below). Kleisthenes won the first chariot race. He later instituted Pythian Games at Sikyon. Now followed a period of great prosperity. In this century the Treasuries of Corinth, Sikyon and Klazomenai were dedicated. Croesus, last king of Lydia (560–546 BC), was a great benefactor of the sanctuary—to no avail in his case. Amasis, king of Egypt, was another. These worldwide benefactions show that, while Olympia may be regarded as an expression of Greek nationalism, the prestige of Delphi rested on its international character. In 548 BC the temple was destroyed by fire. The contract to rebuild was let to the exiled Athenian Alkmaeonidae, who gained a reputation for munificence by facing the new temple with Parian marble instead of the common stone prescribed in the specifications (Hdt. V, 62).

In the Persian Wars the oracle was inclined to medise. Nevertheless, in 480 BC, Xerxes sent a detachment to plunder the temple. The soldiers had reached the Sanctuary of Athena Pronoia when thunder was heard and two huge crags rolled down and crushed many of them to death (Hdt. VIII, 35–39; see below). After the Persian defeats, trophies, statues, and new treasuries were set up in celebration. Delphi now became involved, despite the prudence of its administrators, in the rivalries of the leading Greek states. The oracle lost much of its prestige because of charges of partiality and corruption; but offerings continued to arrive from the conflicting states and from foreign rulers such as the tyrants of Syracuse.

In 448 BC occurred the **Second Sacred War**, in which the Lacedaemonians wrested the temple from the Phocians and handed it over to the Delphians. As soon as they had withdrawn the Athenians recovered the temple and handed it back to the Phocians. The Delphians soon got it back and their possession was confirmed in the Peace of Nikias (421 BC). In 373 the temple was again destroyed, this time by an earthquake, and it was again rebuilt, by international cooperation. In 356 the Phocians, who had, on the accusation of Thebes, been fined by the Amphictyonic League for having cultivated a portion of the Krisaean Plain, retaliated by seizing Delphi with all its treasures. This precipitated the **Third Sacred War**, during which Phocis temporarily became one of the leading powers in Greece. In 346, when the conflict had been determined by the intervention of Philip of Macedon, the temple was restored to the custody of the Amphictyonic League. In the same year Philip, who had replaced Phocis in the league, was elected president of the Pythian Games. The **Fourth Sacred War** broke out in 339. This time it was the Amphissans who were accused of cultivating the Krisaean Plain. The Amphictyons appealed to Philip, who invaded Greece in 338, won the battle of Chaironeia, and destroyed the city of Amphissa.

The Aetolians succeeded the Macedonians as masters of Delphi. In 279 BC Brennus and his Gauls advanced to the attack of Delphi by the same route as the Persians in 480. They were repulsed in the same supernatural manner. Their retreat was disastrous. Some years later their discomfiture was celebrated in the festival of the *Soteria*, organised by the Aetolians. In 189 the Aetolians were driven out by the Romans. Under Roman sway the oracle lost further prestige, as the Romans did not take its utterances very seriously. The precinct was plundered by Sulla in 86 BC; by way of compensation, he gave the Delphians half the territory of dismembered Thebes.

In the imperial era the fortunes of the oracle depended on the whim of the ruler for the time being. Augustus reorganised the Amphictyonic League. Nero seized over 500 bronze statues in a fit of rage at the oracle's condemnation of his matricide. Domitian effected some restoration. Pliny counted more than 3000 statues and Pausanias found Delphi still rich in works of art. It was restored by Hadrian and the Antonines to much of its former splendour. Constantine carried off several of its treasures to adorn his new capital. The oracle was consulted by Julian, but was finally abolished by Theodosius about AD 385. Long before its extinction its authority, impaired by strong Doric prejudices, had sadly diminished. Towards the end its utterances were almost entirely concerned with private and domestic matters such as marriages, loans, voyages and sales. Cyriac of Ancona copied inscriptions here in March 1436, after which the site appears to have been ignored until rediscovered by Wheler and Spon in 1676. Flaubert records finding in 1851 Byron's name on a column of the now-destroyed Panayia.

**The Oracle**. The Delphic oracle was the most famous in Greece. Those who wished to consult it first sacrificed a sheep, goat, boar or other animal, after which (if the omens were favourable) they went into the room adjoining the **adyton**. There they awaited their turn, which was determined by lot, unless they had received from the Delphians the **promanteia**, or right of prior consultation. No women were admitted. They handed in questions written on leaden tablets, many of which have been discovered. The **Pythia**, or priestess who delivered the oracle was, at least in later times, a peasant woman over 50 years old. At the height of the oracle's fame there were three of them. Accounts say that, after purifying herself in the Castalian Fountain, drinking of the water of the Kassotis, and munching a bay leaf, she took her seat upon the tripod, which was placed over the chasm in the adyton. No archaeological evidence has been discovered to support the existence of a 'chasm'. Intoxicated by the exhalations from the chasm, or more probably by the atmosphere of the ceremony and the bay leaves, she uttered incoherent sounds, which were interpreted in hexameter verse by a poet in waiting. The interpretation, which was always obscure and frequently equivocal, was handed over to the enquirer, who not seldom returned more mystified than he had come. Even Croesus, the great benefactor of Delphi, was cruelly misled by the oracle on the eve of his war with Persia. All the same, according to Strabo, 'of all oracles in the world it had the reputation of being the most truthful'.

**Festivals**. The **Pythian Games** were instituted to commemorate Apollo's slaying of the serpent Python. At first they were held every eight years. Originally they were little more than a religious ceremony taking the form of a hymn in honour of Apollo. After the Amphictyonic League had taken over the control of the temple in the early 6C (see above), the games were reorganised and held every four years. The first Pythiad of the new regime was in 582 BC. The festival began with sacrifices and a sacred play about the fight of Apollo and the serpent. There followed, in the theatre, musical contests of cithara, flute and song, and hymns of praise in honour of Apollo; later tragedies and comedies were added. Then came athletic competitions in the stadium, and finally chariot races in the Krisaean Plain, the prize for which was a bay wreath. The Greek states sent **theoriae**, or sacred embassies, to the games, who were loaded with gifts to the god. The Athenians also sent on occasions not connected with the games a special embassy or **pythiad** for the purpose of holding a separate festival, which included athletic games and plays. After the repulse of the Gauls in 278 BC a special festival called the **Soteria** was held under the aegis of the Aetolians (see above). In the imperial era the interval between the games reverted to eight years.

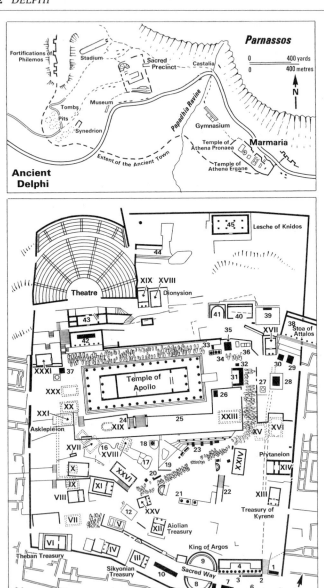

**Parnassos**

Fortifications of Philemos

Stadium

Sacred Precinct

Castalia

0 — 400 yards
0 — 400 metres

N

Tombs

Museum

Pits

Synedrion

*Papadhia Ravine*

Gymnasium

Temple of Athena Pronaea

Marmaria

Extent of the Ancient Town

Temple of Athena Ergane

**Ancient Delphi**

45 — Lesche of Knidos

44

Theatre

XIX XVIII

Dionysion

43

41 40 39

42

XVII — Stoa of Attalos

38

35

33

36

34

32

31

30

29

28

27

26

XXIII

XVI

XV

XXXI 37

XXX

Temple of Apollo

XXI XX

Asklepieíon

24

XIX

25

XVII

16

XVIII

17

18

19

20

23

XXX

Prytaneíon

XIV

XIII

Treasury of Kyrene

X

IX XI

XXVI

21

22

VIII

12

XXV

VII

V

XII — Aiolian Treasury

VI

IV

King of Argos

9

Theban Treasury

Sikyonian Treasury

10

III

Sacred Way

8

7 3 2

4

1

5

6

Epigones

Entrance

**DELPHI
Temenos of Apollo**

0 — 30 metres

N

**Excavations**. The French architect Laurent examined the site in 1838. He was followed in 1840 by Ottfried Müller, who succumbed to a fever contracted here, and E. Curtius. In 1860–61 Foucart and others did some preliminary work. In 1892 an exhaustive survey was begun by the French School, under the leadership of Th. Homolle. Work was particularly intensive until 1903 and has continued regularly since. A long series of excavation reports and studies has been published. The centenary of French work at the site was celebrated in Delphi and Athens in 1992. The figures on the plan correspond with those of the French excavation reports and guide. The French School has published two guides (1991), to the site and to the museum.

Following Pausanias (X, 8, 6 ff.), the visit begins with the attractive spot called **Marmária**, nearly 1.5km to the E of the sanctuary. A path leads down from the Arakhova road. Marmaria was the **Sanctuary of Athena**, whom the Delphians worshipped as *Athena Pronaia* (Guardian of the Temple), or, by a play upon words, as *Athena Pronoia* (Providence). Some of the finest sculptures found here are in the museum. The precinct is roughly rectangular, with the entrance on the E.

An upper terrace N of the gate supported the small **Precinct of Phylakos**; one of its two buildings was the **Heroön of Phylakos**, who, with Autonoös, routed the Persians in 480 BC. The other may have been dedicated to the saviours of Delphi at the time of the onset of the Gauls in 279 BC. An inscription on the retaining wall locates the **Altars of Athena Hygieia** and of **Eileithyia**.

Through the gateway, where a huge lintel lies on the ground, is reached the oldest part of the sanctuary, dedicated to **Athena Hygieia** and **Zosteria**. Here the excavations of 1922 revealed the existence of a Mycenaean settlement (finds in the museum). The **Old Temple of Athena Pronoia** was a Doric peripteral hexastyle structure in tufa, built at the beginning of the 5C BC on the site of a still older building (7C) from which capitals survive. The temple was damaged in 480 BC by the fall of rocks that routed the Persians and its ruin was completed by the earthquake of 373. Fifteen columns and the stylobate had been found when in 1905 another landslip demolished all but three of the columns.

The centre of the precinct is occupied by three buildings. A **Doric treasury** (490–460 BC), of marble, stood on a lime-stone foundation. The Aeolian **Treasury of Massalia**, *in antis*, built c 530 BC in Parian marble, was of remarkably fine workmanship, recalling the Treasury of the Siphnians. The third building, a Pentelic marble **\*tholos**, or rotunda, of the early 4C, was one of the finest in Delphi. Its dedication and purpose are unknown. It has a circular peristyle of 20 slender Doric columns on a platform of three steps. Three columns with their entablature were re-erected in 1938; the cornice and metopes have been restored in replica from the best surviving fragments. The entrance to the circular cella was on the S. The paved interior was decorated with Corinthian half-columns. To the W of the Tholos c 360 BC rose the **New Temple of Athena Pronoia**, a severe prostyle edifice with a portico of six columns of the Doric order. Beyond this temple, and partly beneath it, is an earlier rectangular building (5C), probably a priest's dwelling.

To the NW of Marmaria are the remains of the **gymnasium**, originally dating from the 4C BC, but rebuilt by the Romans. The slope of the ground necessitated its arrangement on different levels. On the upper level (recently cleared and re-investigated) was the **xystos**, or covered colonnade, where the athletes practised in bad weather, with a parallel track in the open air. The lower terrace was occupied by the **palaestra**. This is divided into the palaestra proper, a court 12m square surrounded by a colonnade on all four sides, and the **baths**, comprising a circular (cold) bath 9m in diameter and 1.8m deep, and, in the retaining wall at the back, a series of douche baths. The hot baths, N of the court, are a Roman addition. A column hereabouts bears the names of Byron and Hobhouse.

You return to the road. A short distance farther on, on a sharp bend, opens the ravine separating the two Phaedriades. Here is the celebrated **Castalian Spring** (538m). By this spring Apollo planted a cutting of the bay he had brought from Tempe (see Rte 57). The base of a statue of *Ge*, the goddess of Earth, shows that the spring was an early place of cult-worship.

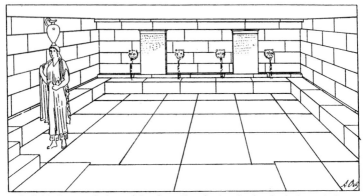

*Delphi. Restored view of the Castalian Spring in the Archaic period (by A. Orlandos)*

In this spring all who came to Delphi for any religious object whatever had to purify themselves. Bathing of the hair seems to have been the principal part of the ceremony and is one attributed to the god himself. Murderers, however, bathed the whole body. The fancy which ascribed poetic inspiration to the waters of the Castalian fountain was an invention of the Roman poets. The present form of the fountain is of Roman or Hellenistic date.

The spring had a façade of seven marble pilasters. The four niches within were presumably for votive offerings; in the largest is a column drum once used as the altar of a Byzantine chapel. The water was collected in a long narrow reservoir (9m x 1m) which fed seven jets (holes still visible). These jets fell into a rectangular court, 9m x 3m, reached by rock-hewn steps. The overflow from the fountain joins the water of the gorge dividing the Phaedriades, which plunges into a deep rocky glen, to join the Pleistos flowing in the valley far below. An Archaic square fountain house, discovered in 1957, lies nearer the road.

A wide, paved path (lavatories at the top of first flight of entrance steps) leads to the entrance of the Sanctuary of Apollo and the museum.

The **Sanctuary of Apollo** like the much more extensive Altis at Olympia, was an enclosure containing many monuments besides the temple. This sacred precinct was situated on the rising ground above the town. It was surrounded by the usual **peribolos**, or enclosure wall, with several gates. Its shape is that of an irregular quadrangle or trapezium, and it measures about 183m x 128m. The S wall is built of squared blocks and dates from the 5C BC; the W and N walls, which are polygonal, from the 6C; while the splendid E wall was rebuilt in the 4C on the old foundations by the architect Agathon. The steepness of the slope necessitated terraces, running E–W, and the provision of a separate platform for each building. The terraces, some with a gate on either side, were intersected by the Sacred Way, which wound up from the main entrance, at the SE, to the NW corner.

From the main entrance modern steps lead to a paved rectangular **square**, which was enclosed by Roman porticoes and doubtless used as a market-place for the sale of religious objects. Four steps lead up to the **main gate**, 3.7m wide, through which you enter the **Sacred Way**. This is 3.7–4.9m wide, and was paved in the Roman period with slabs taken from near-by build-ings. Some of this makeshift pavement is intact. The Sacred Way was adorned on either side with the votive monuments that are a feature of the precinct.

Immediately within the gate, to the right, stood the **Bull of Corcyra** (Pl. 1). The base, which survives, supported a bronze bull by Theopompos of Aegina, dedicated c 480 BC from the proceeds of a catch of tunny. Next, beyond a flight of steps, were the **Offerings of the Arcadians** (Pl. 2). The line of bases supported nine bronze statues of Apollo, Victory, and Arcadian heroes. They were erected to commemorate a successful invasion of Lakonia in 369 BC and placed, out of bravado, facing the Lacedaemonian monument (Pl. 6), insult being added to injury by employing the ageing sculptor Antiphanes (see below). The **base** (Pl. 3), beyond, bore a statue of Philopoemen. The grandiose **Monument of the Admirals**, dedicated by the Spartan Lysander in 403 BC after he had crushed the Athenians at Aegospotami, held 37 bronze statues of gods and Spartiate admirals, made by nine Peloponnesian sculptors including Antiphanes of Argos. The inscriptions from the statues of Lysander and Arakos, in verse composed by Ion of Samos, have been recovered.

Until 1963 it was commonly accepted that the large rectangular exedra (Pl. 4) behind the Arcadian bases was Lysander's monument but it now seems likely that this is a monument, possibly Macedonian, of the early 4C. On the S side, next to the Spartan group was the **Offering of Marathon**, dedicated by the Athenians 30 years after the battle in honour of Miltiades. The long base supported 16 statues, the original ones of Pheidias, according to Pausanias. One theory assigns the **Riace Bronzes** (two Classical Greek bronze masterpieces, recovered from the sea off southern Italy and now in the museum in Reggio Calabria) to this monument.

You pass between two semicircular exedrae, both dedicated by the Argives, that to the left erected in honour of the **Epigones** (Pl. 8) the successors of the Seven Champions, likewise loot of the spoils of Oinoë. To the right the **Kings of Argos** monument (Pl. 9) was added at the foundation of Messene, and its position near to the Spartan offering would not have gone unnoticed. This exedra was to bear 20 statues of the early kings and heroes of Argos. Ten statues only were finished, filling the W quadrant; their bases have been restored to place. The adjacent square niche is covered with personal decrees.

To the left four plinths survive, three of them with inscriptions, from the **Offerings of the Tarentines** (Pl. 10); the statues were by Ageladas of Argos. Beyond is the first of many **treasuries**, similar to those at Olympia; in them were stored cult equipment, smaller votive offerings etc., and important documents were recorded. The **Treasury of the Sikyonians** (Pl. III), a Doric edifice *in antis*, was built about the beginning of the 5C in place of those raised by Kleisthenes after the First Sacred War. In the foundations were used remains of two older buildings, a tholos of 13 columns (c 580 BC) and a rectangular monopteros (open pavilion) of 14 columns surmounted by a roof, perhaps designed to shelter the chariot of Kleisthenes; to this belong the metopes in the museum.

Opposite, to the right, behind unidentifiable bases, are some confused foundations of an unidentified Aeolian treasury. Another destroyed treasury (Pl. V) was perhaps that of the Megarians.

The **Treasury of the Siphnians** (Pl. IV) the massive foundations of which you now pass, was built in 526–525 BC with a tithe of the profits from the gold-mines of Siphnos and was intended to surpass in opulence the existing treasuries at Delphi. It was an Ionic temple *in antis*, with two columns in the form of Caryatids between the antae. Fragments of the Caryatids were found on the site (now in the museum). The treasury faced W. A sculptured frieze of Parian marble ran round the four sides (also in the museum).

You have reached the so-called 'Crossroads of the Treasuries'. A branch-road, 27m long runs to a W gate. On its S side was the **Treasury of the Thebans** (Pl. VI) built after Leuktra. At the corner some remains may be of the **Treasury of the Boeotians** (Pl. VII). Behind the Treasury of the Athenians (see below) are insubstantial traces of three further **treasuries**; the Potidaian (Pl. VIII), an older Athenian building (?; Pl. IX), and the Etruscan (Pl. X).

The Sacred Way, now at an altitude of 550m, describes a semicircle and ascends to the NE. Prominent on the left is the **˙Treasury of the Athenians** (Pl. XI), according to Pausanias built just after 490 BC with a tithe of the spoils of Marathon, but quite possibly earlier (? c 500 BC). The French School, aided by a large grant from the municipality of Athens, re-erected the building in 1904–06. The structure was reassembled from scattered stones (more than four-fifths of them recovered) to its original state, though the foundations had to be readjusted and new columns supplied. This Doric building is distyle *in antis*, and measures 10m x 6m. It stands on a terrace ending in a triangular buttress and reached by a staircase from the Sacred Way. The triglyph frieze depicted the exploits of Herakles and of Theseus; the originals are in the Museum, the sculptures *in situ* being casts in arbitrary positions.

The walls are covered with more than 150 inscriptions. Many of them, decorated with crowns, refer to the Athenian Pythaid, or special embassy; others include honorific decrees in favour of the Athenians, decrees of the Amphictyons about Dionysiac artists, and two **Hymns to Apollo**, with the musical notation in Greek letters above the text. On the S the terrace ended in a triangular space on which were displayed the trophies of Marathon with the dedication 'The Athenians dedicate to Apollo the spoils of the Medes after the battle of Marathon'. The inscription is a 3C copy of the damaged original.

Just across the Sacred Way must be located the **Treasury of the Syracusans** (Pl. 12), which (true to form) was erected here after the Athenian expedition had come to grief. This part of the sanctuary was dug into by a Christian cemetery, but some surviving foundation blocks mark the spot. Adjacent are the foundations of the **Treasury of the Knidians** (Pl. XXV), built in Parian marble before the capture of Knidos in 544 BC by the Persians. A lateral road leads E to the **Treasury of Cyrene** (Pl. XIII), probably of mid-4C date.

The **bouleuterion** (Pl. XXVI), seat of the Delphic senate, was a plain rectangular building. Higher up is the **Sanctuary of Earth** or of **Ge-Themis** (Pl. 16), part of which was destroyed to make way for the great retaining wall. This is a circle of rocks surrounding a natural cleft in the ground, and is the site (or one of them) of the primitive oracle of *Ge-Themis*, guarded by the serpent Python. One of the rocks, supported by modern masonry, was the **Rock of the Sibyl** (Pl. 17) on which, according to ancient local tradition, the sibyl Herophile prophesied. Another rock supported a statue of Leto; on a third was the **Monument of the Naxians** (Pl. 18) dedicated c 570 BC. This was an Ionic column with 44 flutings, over 9m high, surmounted by a sphinx (now in the museum). The lower part of the column is *in situ*. An inscription of 322 BC on the base renews to the Naxians the right of *promanteia*.

A little higher up the Sacred Way crosses the **threshing floor** (*Halos*), a circular place 15m in diameter, surrounded by seats. Here was presented every seventh year the *Septerion*, a morality play celebrating the death of Python. To the N was the **Stoa of the Athenians** (Pl. 23), dedicated after the end of the Persian Wars. A three-stepped limestone basement supported a colonnade, 30m long and 4m deep, consisting of 8 Ionic columns in Parian marble, set 4m apart. The architrave was of wood, as well as the roof, which leaned against the wall of the temple terrace. On the top step of the basement is an Archaic inscription recording the Athenian dedication of cables (from the pontoon bridge thrown by Xerxes across the Hellespont) and figureheads (from Persian ships).

Beneath the Byzantine paving in front of the portico was found a deposit of ivory, gold, and bronze objects (museum), which had been damaged in a fire in the mid-5C and deliberately buried. A lane branches off to the right to a small gate in the peribolos wall. On the right (S) of this lane is the **Treasury of Corinth** (Pl. XXIV), ascribed by Herodotus to Kypselos. It was not only the oldest but the richest of the buildings of this kind, thanks to the generosity of the kings of Lydia. Opposite (N) are the remains of two destroyed treasuries (Pl. XV, XVI) and of the **prytaneion** (Pl. XIV). Outside the gate, to the N, are Roman **baths**, with mosaics.

The Sacred Way now describes another curve (to the N; 561m), below and to the right of the remarkable **polygonal wall**, which supports the platform on which stands the Temple of Apollo. It is built in irregular interlocking blocks with curved joints, a style unique to Delphi. This has both practical and aesthetic advantages, giving strength in seismic shocks without appearing to be a rigid barrier across the sanctuary.

The wall, site of the first excavations at Delphi, follows the irregularities of the ground. Its height varies from 1.8 to 3.7m, and its total length from E to W is c 82m. The dressed face was covered in the 2C BC–1C AD with more than 800 inscriptions. Along the base the rough-hewn blocks project in their natural condition. The components of the upper courses were joined by double T-clamps run with lead. Towards the SE end the inscriptions are particularly numerous. Records, public and private, important and trivial, are all mixed together; they relate above all to the emancipation of slaves, and constitute an invaluable record of Delphic families and events.

The Sacred Way, here about 6m wide and well paved, climbs steeply. On the right is the site of the **Tripod of Plataia** (Pl. 27). The circular pedestal has been re-erected. This offering was dedicated by the Greeks from the spoils of Plataea (Paus. X, 13, 9). On the stone base was a gilt bronze pedestal about 5.5m high, consisting of three intertwined serpents, on which were engraved the names of the 31 city-states contributing to the victory. This was carried off by Constantine the Great and still reposes in a mutilated state, in the ancient Hippodrome, at Istanbul. The three serpent heads supported a golden tripod, which was seized by the Phocians after 356 BC.

At the top of the slope you come to the so-called 'Crossroads of the Tripods', where stand the bases of long vanished votive offerings. The most remarkable were the **Tripods of Gelon and Hiero** (Pl. 36), tyrants of Syracuse, and of their brothers. The offering which commemorated Gelon's victory at Himera over the Carthaginians in 481 BC, comprised four monuments supporting golden tripods and Victories, weighing 50 talents in all. They were some of the earliest objects to be looted when in 353 BC the Phocians needed funds for the Sacred War. The *stele* in front, adorned with a bull, bears an honorific decree in favour of a citizen of Kleitor in Arcadia. The base adjoining that of the tripods on the left is that of the **Acanthus Column** with the dancing girls, now in the museum.

Before entering the temple terrace, to the right and adjacent to the Plataian Tripod, is the rectangular plinth of a **Chariot of Helios** (Pl. 28), dedicated by the Rhodians. A detailed examination (see B.C.H. 1963) of the cuttings into which the hooves of the quadriga fitted has suggested that the missing horses may be those now adorning St Mark's cathedral, Venice, though these have been derived by other authorities from a similar group made for Alexander the Great and set up at Corinth in 336 BC. On the left are a ruined treasury (Acanthians ?), and two enormous bases, which bore statues of *Eumenes* (Pl. 29) and *Attalos* (Pl. 30) of Pergamon. Above, extending across the temenos wall, are the ruins of the **Stoa of Attalos** (Pl. 38).

The Sacred Way turns W and becomes the upper walk of the temple precinct (573m). In front of the entrance to the E is the **Great Altar of Apollo** (Pl. 31) a rectangular structure with steps in black and white marble, dedicated by the Chians in gratitude for their deliverance from the Persians. It presumably kept the orientation of its predecessor, which is slightly oblique to the present temple, but accorded with that of the temple burnt in 548 BC. The altar was piously re-erected in 1920 at the expense of the inhabitants of Chios but restored more accurately in 1960.

Between the altar and its temple is an esplanade bearing bases of other monuments. By the altar stood a golden statue of Eumenes II (Pl. 32). A big square plinth (Pl. 35) bore perhaps the Apollo Sitalcus; there follow the dual column bases (Pl. 34) of the offering of Aristaineta and the base of the Palm-tree of Eurymedon, dedicated by the Athenians after their victory of 468 BC. Behind is the restored Monument of Prusias II (Pl. 33), king of Bithynia (182–149), which bore an equestrian statue of that devious monarch.

The **Temple of Apollo**, reduced before the restorations of 1939–41 to its bare foundations, rests on its N side on the living rock, and on the S side on a huge substructure of irregular courses nearly 61m long and 3–4.6m high. The foundations consist of two concentric rectangles, the outer supporting the peristyle and the inner the sekos. The stylobate, on three steps of fine bluish local limestone, has been partially restored and many of the pavement blocks returned to place. One complete column of the 4C façade and portions of the others have been re-erected so that the building, even though in ruins, once again dominates the sanctuary as it should. A stone ramp leads up to the entrance of the temple on the E.

**History**. Discounting the legendary constructions of laurel, beeswax, and bronze, of which Pausanias gives the traditional account but which are unsupported by archaeological evidence, the existing building had two predecessors. A structure of the 7C was burnt in 548 BC, and replaced by a larger temple, started perhaps in 536, but completed in 513–505 by the Alkmaeonids, who were in exile from Athens. Of this archaic temple, which was admired by Aeschylus, Pindar, and Euripides, fragments, including some of the pedimental sculptures by Antenor, have been found (now in the museum). It was ruined in 373 BC. The existing temple was built in 366–c 329 by Xenodoros and Agathon on the old foundations. It was fired in 88 BC by Thracian invaders, and restored by Domitian after the further ravages of Sulla. The robbing of the metal clamps in the Middle Ages was the prime cause of its final dismemberment.

The temple was the usual Doric peripteral hexastyle, 60m x 22m, with six stuccoed poros columns at the ends and 15 on the sides. Both pronaos and opisthodomos had two columns between antae. The architrave was decorated with shields captured from the Persians at Plataea (E side) and from the Gauls (W and S sides). Some of the spouts and marble tiles have been discovered, but not a fragment of the pediments described by Pausanias. Earthquakes and systematic spoliation have left practically nothing of the sekos, so that there is no clear indication of the arrangement of the **adyton**, or inner shrine. This was an underground chamber, in which were the **omphalos** and, according to later authorities, the **oracular chasm**.

To the W of the temple are the foundations of a Roman building (Pl. XX), in which was found the statue of Antinous, now in the museum. From the SW angle of the temple you can descend past the **House of the Pythia** (?; Pl. XXIX) to the S walk (Pl. 25). In the SE corner was probably the Offering of the Messenians of Naupaktos (Pl. XXIII), erected to commemorate their victory at Sphakteria. Below the temple ramp was the monument of Aemilius Paullus (Pl. 26).

The Sacred Way was protected above the Temple of Apollo by a retaining wall, called the **ischegaon**, constructed c 355 BC of reused material from the Alkmaeonid temple. This was examined by the French School during the 1950–57 excavations. At the NW angle of the terrace was the **Offering of Polyzalos**, which was buried in some catastrophe (? 373 BC) and from which the celebrated Charioteer was recovered. Adjoining on the W is the **Lion Hunt of Alexander the Great** (Pl. 42), a large rectangular exedra of dressed stones.

An epigram on the back wall has established the identity of this exedra with the monument described by Pliny and Plutarch. It was dedicated in 320 BC by Krateros, who had saved the life of Alexander the Great during a lion-hunt near Susa. A bronze group by Lysippos and Leochares represented the incident (cf. also the mosaic at Pella).

You climb a Roman staircase to the *theatre, one of the best preserved in Greece, built in the 4C BC, and restored by Eumenes II in 159 and by the Romans. The cavea was contained in a parallelogram 50m broad. The N and W sides of the **analemma**, or supporting wall, coincide with the line of the peribolos. The 35 tiers of seats were divided into two uneven sections by a paved **diazoma** or landing (23 in the lower section and 7 in the upper). The seats were of white marble from Parnassos. The **orchestra** was paved with polygonal slabs and measured 18m across. It was surrounded by an enclosed conduit. The front of the **stage** (Pl. 43) was adorned with a frieze in relief depicting the Labours of Herakles (now in the museum). There is a fine *view of the sanctuary from the top of the theatre (596m).

Between the stage buildings and the Alexander exedra a pathway runs E above the ischegaon, passing a semicircular exedra (Pl. 41). Beyond is the **Monument of the Thessalians** (Pl. 40), a rectangular **exedra**, dedicated by **Daochos II** of Pharsalus, who as hieromnemon represented Thessaly in 336–332 at the Amphictyonic League, over which he presided. On a plinth 12m long (now in the museum) stood statues of his house; the inscriptions remain *in situ* and five of the statues are in the museum. Beyond is the ruined **Temenos of Neoptolemos** (Pl. 39), beneath which have been excavated remains of a settlement of the Mycenaean period. In front is a long base attributed to the Corcyraeans.

Somewhere NE of the theatre was the **Fountain of Kassotis** (595m), the water of which descended into the adyton. This was an artificial reservoir fed by the *Delphousa* (now **Kerna**), a spring which rises from a rock 70m N. The Pythia drank the waters of this spring before prophesying. Two stages of the **Kerna Fountain**, one Classical, the other Archaic, have been uncovered between the theatre and the stadium. Farther E of the theatre was the **Lesche of the Knidians** (Pl. 45). This was a club-house (used also for ritual dining) dedicated by the Knidians c 450 BC. The building formed a rectangle 18.9m by 9.8m, with a door in the middle of the S side. The walls, of unburnt brick, rested on a socle of poros. The wooden roof was held in place by eight wooden pillars. The club was adorned by Polygnotos with paintings described in detail by Pausanias.

A path winds up from the diazoma of the theatre to (5 minutes) the **stadium**. This was situated in the highest part of the ancient city (645m). The N side is cut into the rock. The S side was artificially supported, and excavations now afford a fine view of the massive supporting blocks of Classical masonry (5C BC). Four pillars remain of the Roman **triumphal arch** which decorated the SE entrance of the final form given it by Herodes Atticus. The **track** was then established at 600 Roman feet (177m). Both starting-point (**aphesis**) and finishing post (**terma**) had stone sills with posts separating the 17 or 18 runners.

The N long side had 12 tiers of seats; 13 staircases divided it into 12 rectangular blocks. A rectangular tribune, on which are benches with backs, was the stand of the **proedria** or presidents of the games. The W end of the **sphendone** had the conventional semicircular shape (unlike the stadia at Olympia and at Epidauros). Here were 6 tiers of seats divided by 3 staircases into 4 **cunei**. The S long side had only 6 tiers of seats. There was accommodation for 7000 spectators.

Above the stadium, to the W, on the slopes of Mt Ayios Ilias (700m), the **Fortress of Philomelos**, the sole fortification of Delphi, was built in 355 BC as a defence against the Lokrians of Amphissa. The hill again saw fighting in the civil war. To the S of the fortress are threshing-floors and tombs. Here was the **west necropolis**. Sepulchral relics of every period, from the Mycenaean to Byzantine, have been found in this area. The chapel of Ay. Ilias, on the road between the sanctuary and the village, stands on a rectangular platform partly built of ancient masonry. This was the site of the **synedrion** or place of assembly built by Hadrian for the Amphictyonic League. The spot was called *Pylaea*. The name was afterwards given to a suburb which came into existence here in Roman times. Above the chapel is an interesting **tomb** and, N of the tomb, is the **House of the French School**. Below this is a sepulchral crypt. Just S is the museum.

The **··museum**, rebuilt in 1959–61 and well laid out, is especially rich in Archaic sculpture from the site.

TERRACE: Sarcophagus of Meleager, discovered by Capodistrias; large panelled mosaic (5C AD) depicting animals and birds. On entry you ascend the stair (right) to the LANDING (ROOM 1), where stands the Omphalos, a sculptured stone found in the S wall of the Temple of Apollo and anciently believed to mark the point where the eagles of Zeus met at the centre of the known world. Cauldron on marble stand (7C; restored). The poor frieze of the Labours of Herakles (1C AD) on the left wall is from the proscenium of the theatre.

ROOM 2. On the walls, heavy bronze shields of Cretan or Hittite style. Small bronze kouros (Daedalic; c 650 BC); griffins.

ROOM 3. Two **·kouroi**, erected to commemorate Cleobis and Biton, who died in their sleep in the Heraion of Argos as a reward for yoking themselves to their mother's chariot; the statues, which are mentioned by Herodotus, mark the transition between the Daedalic and true Archaic styles (? 582 BC). Bronze statuette of Apollo (c 530 BC). Five remarkable **metopes** from a building preceding the Treasury of Sikyon (second quarter of 6C BC). These are Sikyonian work, in yellow limestone.

Left to right: 1. **The Dioscuri and the Argo**. Castor and Pollux, on horseback, appear on the right and left of the ship; in the midst of the warriors in the Argo is Orpheus. 2. **Europa and the Bull**. 3. **The Dioscuri and Idas, Son of Aphareus, on a Cattle-Lifting Raid in Arcadia**. Castor is leading, followed by Idas and Pollux (Lynkeus, brother of Idas, is not shown). The raiders fell out after their expedition and all, except the immortal Pollux, were killed. 4. **Calydonian Boar**. Under its belly is the silhouette of a wounded hound. 5. **Flight of Helle on the Ram with the Golden Fleece**.

In ROOM 4 are displayed the items recovered in fragments in 1939 from an apothetes, or sacred dump, in front of the Stoa of the Athenians. Archaic **·bull** (6C BC) of silver sheets, originally attached by silver nails to a copper frame; hooves, horns, and other gold-plated parts are better preserved. **·Head** of a seated male **chryselephantine statue** with elements of the gold decoration of the garments, notably two plates with repoussé animal motifs in differing styles (6C BC). Another ivory head with its golden diadem.

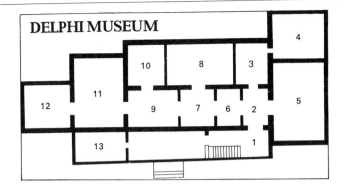

Forearm of a chryselephantine statue. Miniature friezes in ivory from a throne or casket. Ivory statuette of a god with a tame lion (7C BC). Bronzes: athletes (early 5C BC); censer held up by an exquisite female figure (c 460 BC).

ROOM 5. Scuplture from the **Siphnian Treasury**: the East Pediment; much of the **\*\*frieze**; a caryatid with polos capital; and part of the doorway with fine lotus and palmette decoration. In addition the room contains the winged \*Sphinx of the Naxians (570–560 BC), and another caryatid head with polos, of unknown provenance, once thought to have belonged to the Treasury of Knidos.

The **East Pediment** represents the dispute between Herakles and Apollo over the Delphic tripod. The **frieze**, in a mature Archaic style, foreshadows in its rhythmic quality that of the Parthenon nearly a century later. The horses are especially spirited and the fallen corpse almost natural in position. The four sides have no narrative continuity: the **E Side**, below the pediment, depicts in two panels an Assembly of Gods (supporters of Troy to the left of Zeus, of Greece to the right) who watch Homeric heroes fighting over the body of Patroclus. The **N Side** shows nine groups of Gods in battle with the Giants, grouped round three chariots. The names were painted at the bottom of the composition, as on vases. Some other elements (chariot wheels) were also painted. The chariot of Cybele and the death of Ephialtes are well preserved. The **S and W Sides** (believed to be by a different sculptor) are fragmentary.

ROOM 6 contains 24 surviving **metopes** (some very fragmentary) out of 30, from the Athenian Treasury. Pausanias' statement that the treasury was dedicated after Marathon is sometimes disputed on the grounds that the stylistic characteristics seem rather earlier (c 500?). The metopes represent the Labours of Herakles (N and W sides), the Exploits of Theseus (S side) and the Battle of the Amazons (E side). Note especially Herakles and the Arcadian Stag, Theseus and the Bull of Marathon.

In ROOMS 7 and 8 are grouped **pedimental statuary** from the Archaic Temple of Apollo. All the figures have unfinished backs, with tenons and mortises to fix them to the tympanum. Some traces of colour survive. Both pediments probably had a frontal chariot in the centre. That in the W (of ?Zeus) was flanked by a battle of gods and giants; that in the E (of Apollo, perhaps appearing to the Hyperboreans) by standing figures, with animal combat groups in the corners. Lion's head spouts; Nike acroterion, and other fragments; inscriptions. Small bronze of a walking cow.

The inscriptions concern the history of the temple: lists of subscribers to its rebuilding; re-dedication; repairs by the Emperor Domitian (AD 84); also, with musical notation, hymns to Apollo composed in the 2C BC.

ROOM 9. Grave *stelai*; bronze kalpis (early 4C); circular altar with reliefs, found in the Tholos. In ROOM 10 are metopes and other fragments from the tholos.

ROOM 11 contains sculpture of the 4C BC. Left to right: fragment of pillar. Three colossal dancing girls, grouped round a column representing an acanthus stalk, probably a monumental support (9m high) for a tripod; the figures were possibly Thyiads, who celebrated feasts in honour of Dionysos. Five *statues from the votive **offering of Daochos** of Thessaly, celebrating the victory of his master Philip in 336 BC at Chaironeia. This family monument of nine statues reproduced in marble a group in bronze at Pharsala, of which part at least was by Lysippos. The group, identified from the surviving inscription of the plinth, forms a genealogical succession of seven generations from the 6C BC. The best-preserved figures are those representing **Agias**, great-grandfather of the dedicator (depicted as an athlete), who had not only won an Olympic wreath, but had five victories at the Nemean, three at the Pythian, and five at the Isthmian Games; and Agelaos, his young brother, who won a track event at Delphi. Statue of a philosopher.

ROOM 12, contains the famous *charioteer** and the few other surviving fragments of the Auriga of Polyzalos, of which it was part. The figure was discovered in 1896 where it had fallen when the remainder was crushed during the earthquake of 373 BC. The rider, dressed in a long tunic (xystis), is represented life-size. On his head is a victor's fillet. He holds the reins in his right hand. From this calm and formal pose we may infer that he is performing his lap of honour. Taken out of its context, the figure is at first sight less than satisfactory. The disproportion of the body, often criticised, may have been a deliberate attempt to counter optical distortion when seen from below. Similarly the eyes, of magnesium and onyx, wonderfully preserved, are not symmetrical. The work, one of the few great surviving bronzes of the 5C, dates from c 475 and was dedicated by a Sicilian prince to commemorate a chariot victory in the Pythian Games in 478 or 474 BC. The sculptor may have been Pythagoras of Samos, who was in exile at this time at Rhegion.

ROOM 13. Small *bronzes** and pottery (case of excellent fragments); *Antinous, in polished Parian marble, particularly good of its genre, with an expression of gentle melancholy; head, probably of Titus Q. Flamininus, victor of Cynoscephalae (197 BC); head of an unknown philosopher, expressive (Hellenistic); young girl laughing, reminiscent of the arktoi found at Brauron.

## Excursions from Delphi

TO THE SYBARIS CAVE AND THE GORGE OF THE PLEISTOS. This excursion takes 3½–4 hours there and back, or 2½ hours if the visit to the gorge is omitted. A new earth road leads down from the main road E of Marmaria. The path descends in zigzags, crosses some retaining walls, and reaches the bottom of the gorge. Thence it ascends for c 100m, passes some caves, crosses the stream, passes near a waterfall which worked a fulling mill, and ends (1 hour) at a deep well-like hole in the rock full of water in winter. This is called **Zaleska** and was in antiquity the *Spring of Sybaris*. The approach is dangerous.

The **Cave of Sybaris** is a large cavern in a deep ravine on the hillside beyond the Pleistos. This is known also as **Krypsána** ('Hiding Place') or **Askitarió** ('Hermitage', after a hermit who is said to have lived in it). It was used as a refuge by the people of Kastri during the War of Independence. From the cavern you descend again to the torrent as far as an irrigation ditch, which is followed for 150m; you then turn right to reach a path which ascends in ½ hour to the little **Monastery of the Panayia**. On the right are the ruins of a Chapel of the Redeemer.

It is possible to descend to the Pleistos (1½ hours more), passing the spring of **Kephalovrísi**, which turns some mills, and by the **Chapels of Ayios Vasilios, Ayios Ioannis** and others, near an ancient well and a sacred wood.

TO THE CORYCIAN CAVE. With a car the cave is more easily reached from Kalívia, above Arakhova, by a signed road.

From Delphi the site fence now blocks the ancient rock-cut path starting above the stadium. The modern path (marked) begins above the **Sikelianos Museum** (see Rte 45). In c 1 hour you reach the top of the **Phaedriades**, known today as **Elafókastro** (1225m). The path continues on the **Plateau of Livadhi**, used as a pasturage by ancient and modern shepherds alike, as far as the conspicuous watering troughs. Here we turn right (E) and cross the low ridge. On the E slope a broad path will be found at the entrance to the forest, leading down the valley (this is marked with red arrows and signs). These are not easy to follow near two small tarns, where you make for the gap between two hills. From this gap a rough path climbs in zig-zags. 2½ hours. You reach (1299m) the low arched entrance to the **Corycian Cave**, now called **Sarantavlí** ('Forty Rooms'). This cave, which Pausanias thought the finest he had seen (X, 32, 2), was sacred to Pan and the Nymphs (inscriptions). Above it the Dionysiac orgies were celebrated by the Thyiades (Aeschylus, *Eumenides* 22). When the Persians were marching on Delphi, the inhabitants took refuge in the Corycian Cave (Hdt. VIII, 36); it was again used as a refuge during the War of Independence and on other occasions. Within a faint light reveals the pink and green walls of the cave, and the stalactites and stalagmites. Excavations of the French School in 1970 showed the periods of use to be Neolithic, late-Mycenaean, and 6–4C.

Ascent of Parnassos, see Rte 45.

# V  THESSALY

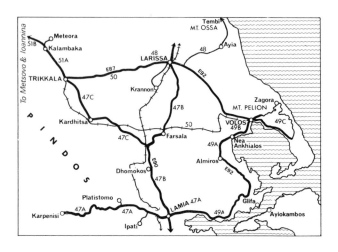

**Thessaly**, one of the most fertile areas of Greece and, in summer, one of the hottest places in Europe, consists of a vast plain surrounded on all sides by mountains. On the N the Kamvounian Mts separate it from Macedonia; on the W is the Pindos range, with Epirus beyond; to the E Olympos, Ossa, and Pelion bar the way to its sea coast on the Gulf of Thessaloniki; to the S Othrys divides it from Aitolia and from Phthiotis and Phocis. In antiquity Thessaly included also the long narrow valley of the Spercheios between Othrys and Mt Oiti, in which is the city of Lamia. In the SE the peninsula of Magnesia extends beyond Pelion almost to Euboea, and the Northern Sporades, with the sea encroaching into the Gulf of Volos. Mountain passes give access to Thessaly from outside, those through the Pindos being particularly spectacular.

In the Tertiary epoch the whole plain was under water. It is nowadays drained by the Peneios, which rises in the Pindos and, joined by substantial tributaries, flows through the Vale of Tempe into the Gulf of Thessaloniki. The surrounding mountains are covered with forests of pine, oak, and beech; the plain yields corn, rice, tobacco, and fruit. A massive new project high in the Pindos (Rte 47C) will divert part of the waters of the Akheloös to assist in the irrigation of the Thessalian plain. The horses of Thessaly have always been famous; Thessalian cavalry helped the Athenians in the Peloponnesian War. Cattle and sheep thrive on its pastures. In the mountains bears, wolves, and wild boar still roam but are seldom seen; in the plain the fauna include hares, herons, cranes, storks, and wildfowl.

The population includes Albanians and Vlachs, few of whom are still nomadic shepherds. The province has three large towns, Larissa, its political centre, Volos, its chief port, and Trikkala. Thessaly is traversed from S to N by the main line of the Greek State Railway, with branches to Volos and Trikkala; the principal towns are linked by good roads with frequent bus services. Thessaly has important archaeological remains of all periods but most attention has been devoted to the prehistoric.

Thessaly was early divided into four districts or tetrarchies, an organisation which subsisted up to the time of the Peloponnesian War. The divisions were *Hestaeotis* (region of Trikkala), in the NW; *Thessaliotis* (including Pharsalos, now Farsala), in the SW; *Pelasgiotis* (Larissa), in the E and NE, in which was Skotoussa, the original home of the Dodona oracle; and *Phthiotis* (Othrys), in the SE, which included the Homeric city of Phthia and was the country of Deukalion and of Achilles and his Myrmidons. There were also four secondary divisions: *Magnesia*, covering the peninsula of that name (Rte 49); *Dolopia*, S of Thessaliotis, inhabited by the ancient race of the Dolopians who fought before Troy; *Oetaea*, in the upper valley of the Spercheios (now part of Phthiotis and Phocis); and *Malis*, a district on the shores of the Maliac Gulf (Gulf of Lamia), which extended as far as Thermopylae.

For some time after the conquest Thessaly was governed by kings who claimed descent from Herakles. Later the kingship was abolished and the government in the separate cities became oligarchic, with power concentrated in the hands of a few great families descended from the kings. The most powerful of these were the *Aleuadai*, who ruled at Larissa, and their kinsmen the *Skopadai*, whose seat was at Krannon (c 24km SW of Larissa). Pausanias reminds us (VII, 10, 2) that the Aleuadai betrayed Thessaly to the Persians in 480 BC. The general attitude of these northern oligarchs was never cordial to the rest of Greece, although, says Thucydides (IV, 78), the common people of Thessaly liked the Athenians. As time went on, the rulers formed themselves into a kind of confederation. Each of the four main divisions remained politically independent but, to guard against the contingency of war, a chief magistrate was elected under the name of *Tagos* (Ταγός), who had supreme command. He was generally one of the Aleuadai.

Other cities of importance in antiquity besides Larissa and Krannon were Pharsalos and Pherai (modern Velestíno). About 374 BC Jason, tyrant of Pherai, was elected Tagos. His rule and that of his successor Alexander (died 357) was so unbearably harsh that the Thessalians solicited aid from the Thebans and threw off their yoke. Twenty years later, Philip of Macedon, similarly invited, annexed the whole country to his own dominions. In 275 Pyrrhus, king of Epirus, after his adventures in Italy, made himself master of Thessaly and Macedonia. In 197, the Romans took Thessaly under their protection, as part of a Roman province (Strabo, XVII). Larissa soon became the political and religious capital of the reorganised confederation, which was surrounded by a number of minor leagues.

Under the Roman empire Thessaly was united to Macedonia, but in the reign of Diocletian it became a separate province.

In the 12C, after a succession of invaders, Thessaly became the centre of a Bulgar-Vlach kingdom known as *Great Wallachia*. The Turks conquered the country in 1389 and held it for five centuries. The Congress of Berlin (1878) assigned to Greece Thessaly and the District of Arta (Rte 53A); three years later Turkey ceded to Greece the whole of Thessaly S of the Peneios. Greece retained her new acquisition despite the disastrous war of 1897, and after the war of 1912–13 obtained the remaining area of Thessaly.

# 47

# Central Thessaly

## A. Lamía and the Valley of the Sperkheiós

**LAMÍA** (Λαμία, Hotels C, D), the chief town of the nome of Fthiotis (Fthiotída) and the seat of an archbishop, is a lively and pleasant town of 44,084 inhabitants, lying below two wooded hills. It is a market centre for cotton, cereals, and garden produce. A characteristic sight is the storks' nests on the roofs.

**History.** *Lamia* is remembered for the Lamian War (323–322 BC) in which the Athenians attempted to free themselves from Macedonian domination. Leosthenes seized Thermopylae and shut up Antipater, the Macedonian viceroy, in Lamia. After Leosthenes had been killed in a sortie, the command passed to Antiphilos. A Macedonian relief force freed Antipater, and Antiphilos was defeated at Krannon. A stronghold in the Middle Ages, Lamia was known to the Franks as *Gipton* and to the Catalans as *El Cito*, whence perhaps the Turkish name *Zitouni*. Since 1961 Lamia has had 'sister town' links with Dover, Delaware. Rescue excavations have revealed many traces of the ancient city, its walls and cemeteries.

Round the central Plateía Elevtherías are grouped the Nomarkhía, the cathedral, and several hotels. Odhós Dhiákou leads to **Platéia Dhiákou**, adorned with a characteristic statue of Athanasios Dhiakos, a local patriot. From here a street ascends the hill of Ayios Loukás (restaurant) in steps. Just to the E of Plateia Elevtherias is the shaded Plateía Laoú (tavernas), where the waters of the Gorgopótamos gush from a fountain. Dominating the town on the NE is the **kastro** (views), a castle of the Catalan Duchy of Neopatras (1319–93). Traces of Middle and Late Bronze Age occupation and a Protogeometric tomb have been found. The walls stand on Classical foundations and show masonry of many later epochs (incl. Roman; Catalan; Turkish battlements). They command a fine view both to E and W. There is a road up to the main gate.

On the summit of the kastro (refreshments), a military barracks of the time of King Otho has been attractively restored to provide offices for the Archaeological Service, a lecture theatre and an excellent **museum** (opened 1994). The latter contains a wide range of prehistoric finds from Neolithic to Mycenaean, including material from Lianokládhi and Elátia, interesting Sub-Myceanean and Geometric objects, with models of tomb types, outstanding finds and architectural elements from the Temple of Apollo and Artemis at Kalapódhi; pottery, sculpture and small finds of the Classical, Hellenistic and Roman periods. There are interesting thematic presentations and the displays are excellent.

The main **bus station** is at the S end of Satoviándou, near the Railway: *Ipáti* (6 daily), *Atalándi* etc (5), *Elátia* (1), *Fársala* (4), *Dhomokós* (6) etc. Slightly nearer the town centre are offices in Papakiriazí for *Athens* (16), *Thessaloníki* (2), *Pátras* (1) and, in Márkou Bótsari nearby, for *Karpeníssi* (4, with 1 daily bus from *Karpeníssi* to *Agrínio*). At Palaiológon and Rozáki Angelí is the station for *Vólos* (1), *Almirós* (1), *Pelasyía* (5). From 2 Septemvríou, off Thermopílon, buses for *Pírgos* (1), *Delphí* and *Amfissa* (2), *Khalkís* (2), *Lárissa* (2), *Grevená* (1), *Tríkkala* (7), *Kardhítsa* (7), also other services to Thessaloníki and Patras.

FROM LAMIA TO KARPENISI, good road, 82km (51 miles). The road runs W with the railway to (8km) **Lianokládhi station**, junction for Lamia, on the main Athens–Thessaloniki line. You cross the railway and gradually ascend in the lush broad valley of the Sperkheiós. The huge mass of Mt Oiti looms to the left continuing through the village of (14.5km) **Lianokládhi**. Excavation of a mound by the Ipáti turn revealed a MH apsidal house.

At 16.5km a road diverges left across the river to **Loutrá Ipátis** (Λουτρά Υπάτης; 3km; Hotels A, B, C, D, E), a thermal establishment whose waters (25.5°C) are good for skin diseases and bronchial infections. The same road continues to (8km) **Ipáti**, the ancient *Hypata* (some finds) and the *Neo-Patras* of the Franks and Catalans, finely situated on the N slope of Mt Oiti. In antiquity it was the capital of the Aenianes, a tribe which migrated S from Ossa. During the Lamian War it was the centre of the military operations of the confederate Greeks. The remains of the Catalan castle (some ancient masonry) are slight but the situation and views are fine. It is reached via the lush area of Perivólia either by following a rough but driveable track (left; small sign includes 'Kastro'; (3km)) just before the entrance to the village, or from the church of Ayios Nikólaos (35 min walk). In the 13C it was the capital of the dominions of John Doukas who with help from Athens here defeated the forces of Michael VIII Palaiologos in 1275. In 1318 it became the second capital of Alfonso's Catalan duchy 'of Athens and Neo-Patras'. The town was taken by the Turks in 1393 and made the seat of a pasha. Here were born Leo the Mathematician (c 800) and St Athanasios the Meteorite (1305–83). The inhabitants cultivate tobacco and weave linen. At **Sarandári** (3km NW) is a Macedonian tomb and at Mexiátes (9km NE) three others. Ipáti is the starting-point for the ascent of **Mt Oiti** (Οίτη) legendary scene of the death of Herakles, whose summit (Pírgos; 2153m) may be climbed from the Trapeza refuge of the Greek Alpine Club (3½ hrs from Ipáti). The descent from the refuge may be made in 4 hrs to **Pavlianí**, c 8km W of Brállos (Rte 44A).

23km **Kastrí** takes its name from a ruined fortress with square towers. 30km Varibóbi has readopted the name of **Makrakómi** (Hotel D), a town known to Livy, the ruins of which stand on the hill to the NE of the little market town (2717 inhab.). Beyond the Sperkheiós **Sperkheiás** (2957 inhab.) is visible. To its E, on the left bank of the tributary Inakhos, is **Ayios Sóstis**, site of ancient *Sosthenis*, mentioned by Ptolemy. About 5km to the N of Makrakómi are the baths of **Platístomo** (Λουτρά Πλατυστόμου, Hotels C, D), the waters of which are recommended in cases of dyspepsia, anaemia, disorders of the stomach, and spinal complaints. Another road climbs N to Rendína and Smókovo (comp. Rte 47C).

Beyond Makrakómi a road crosses the river to **Palaiovrákha** on the N slope of Mt Goulinás (1466m; view). Between this village and its neighbour Pterí (or Fterí) are some remains of ancient *Spercheiai*. 39km **Vítoli**. The vegetation becomes increasingly temperate as the valley narrows to a gorge. Above (47.5km) **Ayios Yeóryios** the slopes become increasingly wooded and the climb gradually steeper. The valley divides. Just beyond (52km) **Kháni Panétsou** in the Dhipotoma valley by-roads lead NW to **Merkádha**, **Mavrílo**, and **Ayía Triádha** (34km), a beautiful mountain village which upheld a tradition of learning in Turkish times. You climb out of the valley by continuous turns to (60km) **Timfristós** (841km), known for its cherries. A branch to Fourná (40km N) passes through spectacular forests of fir. The road now zig-zags across the spruce-clad saddle between Pikrovouni (1503m; N) and Kokkalia (1721m; S). As you reach the road-summit (c 1430m), on the watershed of the Southern Pindos and the boundary between Phthiotis and Evrytania, there is a fine view of the peak of Mt Timfristós. Along the summit ridge a road runs S to **Kríkello** (18km) and **Dhomnísta** (26km; Hotel B) continuing to Thermon, not completely surfaced. Your road winds down to **Ayios Nikólaos** (left; 1km) in the enclosed valley of the Karpenisiotis. **Mt Timfristos** (or **Veloukhi**; summit 2315m) towers above the road to the right. On the mountain is the **Refuge of Dhiavolótopos** (1840m; 40 beds; 2 hrs walk from Karpenisi), but the area has ski slopes and can now be reached by road from the town.

82km **Karpenísi** (Καρπενίσι; Hotels A, B, C, D) is the chief and only sizeable place (pop. 5868) of Evritanía, by population the smallest nome of mainland Greece. The town was captured by Communist rebels in January 1949 and held for 18 days. Its houses occupy both slopes of a torrent that descends to a small plain, wholly enclosed by mountains and dominated on the N by the peaks of Timfristos. The older parts are attractive but some of the modern buildings are quite out of scale with their surroundings. Roads in the area have been greatly improved and hotels provided to cater for winter sports clientele. A locally available leaflet gives information about village rooms. **Koriskádhes** (SW) is one of a group of 'listed' villages. A road leads S to **Méga Khorió** (15km; Hotel D) on the N slope of **Mt Kalliakoúdha** (2100m) on another route to Thermon. Its companion village, **Mikró Khorió**, was overwhelmed on 13 January 1963 by a landslide while most of the 336 inhabitants were at a church festival in another village. Continuation see Rte 54.

For roads from Karpenísi to **Thérmon** and **Agrínio**, see Rte 54.

# B.   From Lamía to Lárissa via Fársala

**Road**, 114km (71 miles), part of the traditional S–N route through Greece, which has been only partly superseded by the new highway to Thessaloniki via the coast. 35km Dhomokós.—68km Fársala.—114km Lárissa. **Bus** several times daily in 3–3½ hrs.

**Railway** (from Lianokládhi), 127km (79 miles) in 2–2½ hrs, part of the main line from Athens to Thessaloniki. From Lianokládhi the railway climbs at a gradient of 1 in 50 for nearly 36km to surmount the barrier of Mt Othrys; its course lies W of the road. There is a succession of bridges, then follow 27 short tunnels as the line climbs out of the Sperkheios valley. It reaches the summit-level (585m) to the E of Mt Mokhlouka (892m), then descends, crossing the W end of the drained Lake Xynias.—43.5 km Angeías; the line follows the river Sofadhítikos through a gap in the hills.—Beyond (61km) Thavmakós (see below) the kastro of Dhomokós can be seen. The railway then accompanies the road in the plain to Néo Monastíri (see below).—85km Palaiofársalos is the most important junction in Thessaly; branch lines run E to Volos and W to Trikkala and Kalambaka (Rte 50). Farsala is c 13km E. The line surmounts a low ridge.—101.5km Dhoxará.—109.5km Krannón; the ruins of the ancient city are 10km W.—127km Lárissa.

You leave Lamia by Odhos Ipsilándi. The road skirts the E side of Mt Profitis Ilias, soon joining the by-pass, and begins a gradual ascent of the **Furka Pass** (850m), the main route through the brown W foothills of Mt Othrys. There are fine views to the left over the Sperkheios to Mt Oiti. On the curving descent is (16km) the **Khání Drágoman Agá**, now a taverna. You cross the level cultivated plain formed by the draining of Lake Xynias. Some walls of ancient *Xyniai* survive near its S limit (S of the modern village, 3km W of the road). On the banks, near the village of **Ombriakí**, two Neolithic settlements have been identified. The road passes chromium mine workings and surmounts another ridge.

35km **Dhomokós** (Δομοκός; pop. 1939), chief town of an eparchy and seat of a bishop, is picturesquely situated 1km above the road (left) on a rocky hill (520m). Good Classical walls can be seen on the hill near the bus station and built into various houses; parts of the 4C fortifications have been traced. The railway station, a distance away in the plain to the N, keeps the ancient name, *Thaumakoi.*

The town, which commanded the defile of Koile, was so called because of the astonishment (*thauma*) of the traveller from the S who had climbed over rugged hills and had suddenly been confronted with the vast plain of Thessaly. *Thaumakoi* was vainly besieged by Philip V in 198 BC and was taken by Acilius Glabrio in 191. During the Greco-Turkish war of 1897 Dhomokos was the last stage in the retreat of the Greek army under Constantine I (17 May). The advance of the Turks, who reached the Furka pass two days later, was halted only by the intervention of the Powers.

The abrupt descent (at the bottom, left, an alternative minor route to Kardhitsa and/or Smokovo and Rendina, Rte 47C) affords a fine *view of the Thessalian Plain, in which you continue N. The road to Trikkala (Rte 47C) and Ioannina diverges at (60km) **Néo Monastíri**. On the hill (right) of **Yinaikókastro** some well-preserved walls remain to locate ancient *Proerna*; its Temple of Demeter has been recognised in the village and prehistoric material (EH and Mycenaean) has also been found. After **Vrisiá** you pass between two isolated hills, Plake (left) and Griva (right). Beyond the turning to Stavros is a restaurant. 68.5km **Fársala** (Φάρσαλα; Hotels D, E), four-fifths destroyed in the earthquake of 1954 is now mainly noted for its 'halva' sweetmeat. Its bishopric was suppressed in 1900 and incorporated in the see of Larissa, but with 7094 inhabitants, it is still the largest place in its eparchy. It has a station, 3km N, on the railway from Volos to Trikkala. The tree-clad ridge of Fetih-Djami, SW of the town, has been occupied since Neolithic times.

The **Battle of Pharsalus** (9 August 48 BC), which took place in the plain to the W, decided the issue between Pompey and Caesar and the fate of the Roman world. Pompey, trusting to his overwhelming superiority in cavalry, led by Labienus, planned to turn Caesar's right wing and fall upon his rear. Labienus' cavalry charge was put to flight, panic spread through Pompey's army, and Pompey himself fled with an escort of only four men. His army lost 15,000 and the remainder surrendered next day. Yves Béquignon (B.C.H. 1960) concludes that the battle took place on the left bank of the Enipeus.

**Archaeological discoveries** are mostly more interesting to the specialist. Traces of the walls can be made out on Fetih- Djami (above), the ancient acropolis, a tree clad ridge to the S, and at various places, notably beneath and beside the church of Ay. Nikolaos (Od. Ay. Nikoláou) in the SE part of the town on the slopes of the acropolis. Also below, in Od. Koukouflí and, in the town centre, at two points (one with a gate) by the bus station on the Lamia road. The bus station has desecrated the ancient centre, where are the sad remains of a spring, associated with Thetis. Further out, to the left of the Lamia road is an interesting **tholos tomb** in polygonal masonry, perhaps of Archaic date; other rectangular built tombs are beside and to the S. Prehistoric material was excavated on the hill of Ayía Paraskeví.

About 2km E of the railway station, near the village of Aspróyia, is a Dervish monastery (Tekkés too Bekasí) perhaps on the site of a Byzantine foundation. The cemetery includes two domed mausoleia (the earlier ?16C). The walled complex has a tower on the E.

You cross the Volos–Trikkala railway and the Enipeus, an important tribu-tary of the Peneios, on a five-arched bridge. 82km **Khalkiádhes**. Here a by-road leads right to **Ano Skotoússa**, to the E of which are some remains of ancient *Skotoussa*, the supposed original home of the Dodona oracle.

Above to the N and E rise the mountains of Khalkodhóni or Kara Dagh, anciently called Kynos Kephalai or Cynoscephalae ('dogs' heads') and famous for two battles. The **First Battle of Cynoscephalae**, in 364 BC, was between Alexander of Pherai and the combined forces of Thessalians and Thebans. Alexander was defeated but the Theban general Pelopidas was killed. The **Second Battle of Cynoscephalae**, in 197, irreparably weakened the power of Macedonia. The Romans under Flamininus totally defeated Philip V of Macedon, the issue being decided by an elephant charge. An uneasy period followed, ending in the battle of Pydna and complete Macedonian dependence upon Rome.

92km **Záppio**. The road continues in the plain through agricultural land, passing the Xenia motel on the way into (114km) **Lárissa**, see Rte 48.

# C.   From Lamía to Kardhítsa and Tríkkala

**Road**, 118km. (73 miles). 56km Néo Monastíri.—70km Sofádhes.—92km Kardhítsa.—118km Tríkkala.

To (56km) **Néo Monastíri**, see Rte 47B. The road branches left and runs NW through the Thessalian plain, crossing torrents and streams from the Pindos (left). 70km **Sofádhes** (Σοφάδες) an agricultural centre (5415 inhab.) on the Thessalian railway, is by-passed to the W.

A by-road leads (left) in 8km to the village of **Philiá** where an important pan-Thessalian sanctuary of Itonian Athena was located in 1963. Excavations yielded fine Geometric and Archaic bronzes and the area other material from Mycenaean to Early Christian but there is now nothing to see on the site though Roman inscriptions from the sanctuary are built into the church of the Taxiarchs at Melissokhóri to the W. On a prominent hill (183m) to the N, near the hamlet of Pírgos (3km), are some remains (also partly beneath the village) identified by an inscription found at Mataranga (see below) as ancient *Kierion*, a place Stephanus of Byzantium equated with Thessalian *Arne*. At **Moskholoúri**, between Sofódhes and Pírgos, a fine bridge over the Sofadhitikos may be as early as the 13C. You pass (left) remains of an old bridge and (right) conical mounds. At (84km) **Ayios Theódhoros** you join the road from Larissa W of Mataránga. 90km A by-pass (right) leads to the Trikkala road (4km).

92km **KARDHÍTSA** (Καρδηίτσα; Hotels B, C), the capital of its nome, is an uninteresting town of 30,067 inhabitants, laid out on a rectilinear plan in Turkish times. It has no ancient associations. An important market centre attracting custom from the Thessalian plain and from the mountainous Agrafa region, it trades in tobacco, cereals, cotton, silk, and cattle, and is served by the Thessalian railway. Its buildings are liberally adorned with storks' nests. There is a pleasant park. Methane gas has been discovered in the vicinity. Kardhítsa' was the birthplace of Gen. Nikolaos Plastiras (1883–1953), leader of the revolution of 1922.

**Buses** frequently to Tríkkala; hourly to Lárissa; hourly to Fanári and Mouzáki; 7 daily to Athens; 4 daily to Thessaloníki; once weekly to Arta via Argithéa; and to other surrounding villages.

## Routes south and south east of Kardhítsa

These routes can also be approached from Tríkkala or Píli, via Mouzáki and Fanári.

I. TO SMOKOVO SPA AND RENDINA, 60kms (37 miles; bus; also accessible via variable roads from the Lamia-Karpenisi road, see below). The road runs due S.

At 5km a right fork leads to (10km) **Kallíthiro** (ancient *Kallithera*) where excavated sections of the 4–3C town have been excellently displayed (visible from street) at basement level below the modern buildings. There are several examples to the S of the main square and (in Od. 25 Martíou) an ancient tile store.

14km Turn (right) for (23km) **Katafíyi**, outside which (2km rough road) is the interesting **Moní Pétras**, dedicated to the Panayia. The church (under restoration; guard on site in summer, otherwise key from Katafiyi) is c AD 1600, with extensive frescoes (including a fine donor scene) and a carved wooden templon and other furniture. A side chapel is dedicated to Ayios Sotiros. From Katafiyi Lake Megdovo can be reached in 21km at Kastanía and this diversion combined with the following excursion.

At the Kallíthiro fork, the main road turns SE, via (12km) **Kallifóni** and (16km) **Kédhros** (for Dhomokos) to (30km) **Smókovo Spa** (Λουτρά Σμοκόβου; Hotels B, C, D, E), with alkaline sulphur springs (38.9–40°C), for nervous, rheumatic, catarrhal, and skin complaints. The spa is beautifully situated at an altitude of 450m in a shady ravine and is an excursion centre. Thence secondary roads (mostly asphalt to Rendina) continue a serpentine course through or past (60km) **Rendína**, 6km from which (rough road) is a fine and beautifully situated old monastery (said to be a 8C foundation; with good and extensive frescoes of 1662, some recently cleaned). It is possible to join (at c 86km) the Lamia–Karpenisi road (at Makrakomi, Vitoli or near Ayios Yeoryios, Rte 47A). The roads S of the monastery are rough. From the village, the route S is difficult but under reconstruction.

II. TO MITROPOLIS, LAKE MEGDOVO AND THE TAVROPOS BARRAGE. Round trip from Kardhitsa c 93km (58 miles).

The lake can be approached from several different points, including the Mouzáki direction. The roads (best to NW and NE) are mostly asphalt though sometimes narrow and deteriorated. There is a bad section (c 6km; under improvement with an EEC grant) at the SW corner.

You take the road SW in the direction of (10km) **Mitrópolis** on the site of ancient *Metropolis* which was a civic centre made up of several towns, including Ithome (see below). With Trikke, Pelinnaion, and Gomphoi, it was part of a fortified rectangle protecting the approach to the Thessalian plain. Excavation has revealed fragments of the town, including sections of the walls. The circuit was apparently 16-sided, a small acropolis within. Metropolis was captured in 191 BC by Flamininus and occupied by Caesar before the battle of Pharsalus. A Mycenaean tholos tomb was discovered to the S in 1958. Above, on the mountainside (1151m), are the little fortresses of **Voúnesi** and **Portítsa**, perhaps part of the synoecism.

The road then ascends (alternative routes) to the hydroelectric **Lake of Megdova** near (19km) **Koróni**, whose monastery has a 16C church. The lake is formed by the **Tavropos Barrage** (conceived in 1925 by Plastiras, opened in 1959) on a tributary of the Acheloös. After serving electrical generators, the water provides irrigation in the plain and finally discharges into the Peneios.

The circuit of the lake is an attractive drive, especially in the wooded landscape at the NW. There is a belvedere at **Neokhóri** to the SW about 15km above the dam which is crossed by the road (cars only). Several of the villages have rooms and restaurants.

From **Kastanía**, at the SE, is a road to Katafiyi (for Moni Petras; see above).

III. TO FANARI, 11kms (7 miles).

NW from Kardhitsa a road keeps company with the railway to (11km) **Fanári**, a village of 871 inhabitants, situated on the W side of a rocky hill called 'the Beacon' (Φανάρι). The fine Byzantine fortress which marks the summit is conspicuous for miles around. The wall is preserved to c 14m and there are six towers, a cistern and (?) church within. Its foundation date is uncertain but it was important in the 13–14C. The structure incorporates ancient masonry. This was the site of 'rugged *Ithome*' of the *Iliad*, one of the towns incorporated in Metropolis (see above). It was 'a heap of stones' in Strabo's day. The road continues to Mouzáki (for Trikkala).

From Kardhítsa to **Lárissa**, see Rte 50.

The broad level Tríkkala road drives NW from Kardhítsa. Prominent to the W is the castle at Fanári (see above). 108km **Agnanteró** has a local festival on 27 August. 116.5km A bypass leads off to the right. You cross the Peneios.

118km **TRÍKKALA** (Τρίκαλα; Hotels B, C, D), the third largest town in Thessaly, with 44,232 inhabitants, is attractively situated on both banks of the Lethaios (locally Trikkalinos), some distance from its confluence with the Peneios, at the end of a low ridge (Mt Khasia) projecting from the N limit of the Thessalian plain. The town is the capital of the nome of Trikkala and seat of an archbishop. Its population used to be increased in winter by the influx of Vlach shepherds driven from their mountains by the inclement weather. It has an important market in cereals, rice, silk, cotton, tobacco, and livestock.

**Buses** from main bus station at Odd. Othonos/Garivaldi, to Lárissa (frequently), to Kardhítsa (frequently), to Kalambáka (frequently) to Athens (regularly), to Vólos, Thessaloníki and Ioánnina (2–6 times daily), to Grevená (once daily). Local buses to Píli and Mouzáki (regularly), to some Pindos villages—Dhési, Mesokhóra (2 or 3 times per week).

**Tourist Office** in bus station.

**Police** at Odd. Kapodhistríou/Asklipíou.

**History**. Trikkala is the *Trikke* of Homer, the domain of Podaleirios and Machaon, the two sons of Asklepios, 'cunning leeches' who led the Trikkeans to the Trojan War (*Iliad*, II, 729). It was credited with the earliest of all the temples to Asklepios and in later times had a medical school of repute. Trikke was one of the four cities of Hestaiotis forming a defensive quadrilateral (see above). The plain of Trikke produced the finest of the renowned Thessalian horses, the features of which are reproduced in the frieze of the Parthenon. The name *Trikkala* first appears in the 12C. Under the Turks Trikkala was the chief town of Thessaly despite periodical uprisings such as that of Dionysios 'the Skylosophos', its bishop. After the battle for Athens in 1945, Trikkala became one of the communist guerrilla strongholds.

The road from Kardhítsa passes close to Ayios Konstandinos and the **Kursum Cami**, a mosque built by Sinan Pasha in 1550, with a fine soaring dome and (originally) an external arcade. The building is being restored. Immediately to the S is the Mausoleum of Osman Shah (d. 1567/8) who commissioned the mosque. The river Lethaios divides the town. On its banks are numerous cafés. The Plateía Ríga Ferraíou on the S bank (with a bronze group commemorating five locals hanged by the Germans in 1944) is connected by bridges with the Plateía Ethnikís Antistáseos and the large central Plateía Iróön Politekhníou both opening on the N bank.

To the S Odhós Asklipíou has shops and cafés. At Od. Garivaldi 6 is a **Folk Museum and Art Gallery**. On the N bank, Odhós Saráfis leads W to the impressive **frourion**, a Byzantine fortress on Hellenistic foundations, where the lower ward has a tourist pavilion (view) and the great keep (no

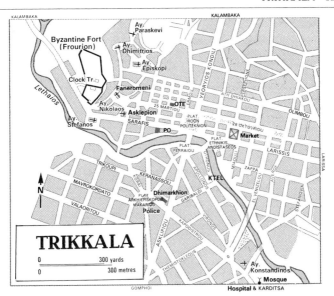

KALAMBAKA

KALAMBAKA

Ay. Paraskevi

Byzantine Fort (Frourion)

Ay. Dhimitrios

Ay. Episkopi

Clock Tr.

Faneromeni

OTE

Ay. Nikolaos

25 MARTIOU

Asklepion

Ay. Stefanos

SARAFIS

PO

PLAT. IROON POLITEKNION

28 OKTOVRIOU

OLIMBOU

PLAT. ETHNIKIS ANDISTASEOS

Market

PLAT. FERRAIOU

LARISSIS

LARISSA

TRIKOUPI

KERANASSOU

KTEL

ZAPPA

N

MAVROKORDATO

PLAT. Dhimarkhion

ARKHIEPISKOPOU MAKARIOU

Police

GARIBALDI

VALAORITOU

**TRIKKALA**

0 ———— 300 yards

0 ———— 300 metres

THEMISTOKLEOUS

Ay. Konstandinos

Mosque

GOMPHOI

Hospital & KARDITSA

adm.) a castellated clock tower. SE of the frourio (the main area adjacent to Od. Saráfis) are some remains of what may be the **Asklepieion**, excavated by the Greek Archaeological Service intermittently since 1912. In view of the legends concerning the origins of the Asklepios cult in Trikke, this site is of great potential interest. Visible buildings (badly kept, and partly overlain by the foundations of a Byzantine church, probably that of the 10C monastery of Ay. Nikolaos) include a Hellenistic stoa and a Roman bath, perhaps representing different phases of a therapeutic complex laid out round a court. Ayios Nikolaos, the cathedral church since 1967, is immediately to the W.

The Panayia Faneromeni close by was damaged by fire in 1991. Here, on the E slopes of the frourion, is **Varoúsa**, a quiet picturesque quarter of old Turko-Greek houses. The principal churches are here. While several claim to an early foundation many surviving remains are from rebuildings/redecoration in the 19 and 20C. The traditional type is two-aisled. Ay. Dhimitrios incorporates ancient blocks in its construction, has a gilded wooden templon, and 17C frescoes. Ayia Marina is 18C with frescoes. Ayioi Anargyroi was refurbished in 1575 and painted soon after: the figures include the two bishops Bessarion, both later canonised. Ay. Ioannis Prodromos is 17C, with frescoes. Ay. Stephanos, the cathedral church of Trikkala in the 14C, was probably founded by Simeon Ouros, despot of Epirus and Acarnania with his capital at Trikkala until 1355. It was destroyed and rebuilt in the late 19C and many of its contents transferred to Ay. Nikolaos and Faneromeni. In the kastro (inaccessible) have been identified the remains of a church of Archangelos, probably the cathedral before Ay. Stephanos. There is an archaeological collection (access restricted) at Od. 25 Martiou no. 31.

## Excursions from Tríkkala

TO GOMPHOI AND THE PORTA PANAYIA, 20.5km (13 miles).

Passing the railway station the road leads SW across the plain. 7km **Piyí**. 10.5km **Ligariá** stands above the Portaïkos, a torrent that often floods the plain. At 12km there is a left turn to **Gómfoi** (3km), a village on a hill overlooking the Pamisos, 5km W of **Lazarína**, with a stud farm.

Ancient *Gomphoi*, on a wooded ridge between the modern village and Mouzáki (sign to Archaeological Site on the road between them), was of considerable importance by reason of its domination of the chief pass from Thessaly into Epirus, and one of the four strongholds forming a square (see above). It was fortified by Philip II. In the civil war it supported, to its cost, Pompey against Caesar. On its site the Byzantines founded the city of *Episkope*. The situation is pleasant and some sections of the walls can be traced but there is not a great deal to see. Many ancient blocks are incorporated in the houses of the village.

Now seen ahead is the great cleft of the Stená tis Pórtas with, right, half-way up the mountain, the monastery of Dousiko (see below). 15km **Paliomonastíri**, where the road divides, the left branch for Mouzáki (see below). You keep right for (19km) **Píli** (1974 inhab.; Hotel D) which stands at the entrance to the *Stená tis Pórtas*, a beautiful defile through which the Portaïkos emerges from the Pindos.

Across the river from Pili (bridge; road) and 1.5km upstream, is the delightful church of **Pórta Panagía** (founded 1283; the narthex probably later). Within, the *figures of Christ and of the Virgin are amongst the finest Byzantine mosaics in Greece and, as ikons, unique. On the splendid marble ikonostasis the figure of Christ is on the left, a reversal of customary Orthodox ikonography. On the same side of the river, but further E (signs from bridge) is the **Monastery of Doúsiko** (5.5km; women not admitted), known locally as **Ai Vessáris**, which stands at 762m above its village amid chestnuts and limes. It was founded in 1515 by the Blessed Bessarion (later Archbishop of Larissa), and completed in 1556 by his son. The monastery is on a grand scale with 336 cells, a library of importance and an imposing church with a full cycle of frescoes and a carved wooden ikonostasis (1767).

## Routes into the Pindos (and for Arta)

The only completely asphalted routes across the Pindos at present are those from Karpeníssi to Agrínio (described under Rte 54) and from Kalambáka to Ioánnina (Rte 51B) but (2) and (3) below are regularly used, in spite of their variable state. At present they are recommended mainly for their wonderful scenery, cool summer climate and winter sports. There are some interesting but little known monuments. Buses from Kardhítsa and Tríkkala serve many of the villages, though infrequently. There is a weekly bus from Tríkkala to Arta, via Argithéa.

I. TO DHESI VIA ELATI 65km (40 miles); good asphalt road until just before Dhési.

To (19km) **Píli**, see above. 20.5km an attractive single-arched **bridge** built in 1514 by the Blessed Bessarion spans the river; a pebble mosaic decorates the rock face on the far side. 21.5km The road crosses the river. 23.5km You leave to the left a turn for **Mesokhóra**. The road climbs, at first through a broad valley. The scenery is spectacular, a combination of tree-clad slopes (firs dominating as the altitude increases) and bare towering peaks. 32.5km **Eláti** (Hotels B, D, rooms), lies on the W side of Kerketion (Kóziaka; see Rte 51). The village is delightful in the summer and a centre of winter sports. Local produce is sold by the roadside. Higher up to the right is the

**Khatzípetros Refuge** (1250m) from which the summit (1900m) of Kerketion may be climbed.

At 39.5km is a Thessaloniki University Forestry plantation (the research station is at Pertoúli). The road drops into an attractive plateau where, every May, the Sarakatsánoi hold a gathering. 43km You pass a turn (right) for **Khrisomiliá** via which Kalambáka and the Metéora can be reached by a partly surfaced route. 47km **Pertoúli**, cold even in August at nearly 1220m, lies beyond the watershed. 51km **Neraïdhokhóri**, with some unappealing new building, stands above the infant Acheloös. 55km The 18C church of Ayía Paraskeví lies to the left, with a separate upper-storey chapel. Beyond (65km) the small village of **Dhési** (twice weekly bus from Trikkala) only with great difficulty can you continue to Arta, and progress on the projected road improvement is slow.

II. TO MESOKHORA (71km) AND ARTA c 186km (116 miles); good tarmac road until just before Vathíremma, unsurfaced but said to be adequate until (c 111km) Kápsala, then tarmac to Arta.

To (23.5km) the Mesokhora turn, as (I) above. You turn left. At first the road winds along the lush valley floor. At 30km it enters a narrow gorge, to cross the river at Piyí ton Theón and climb to the substantial village of (35km) **Stournaráïka**. The ascent continues reaching (42km) a high saddle with retrospective views and a small new hill resort. Planes give way to fir trees. 46km A map by the roadside indicates routes in the area. The tarmac ends on the descent to (54km) **Vathíremma**, with a pleasant café. 69.5km **Mesokhóra** (Hotel D). 71km Major construction works mark the site of the controversial Akheloös project which will divert part of the westward-flowing river to help with the irrigation of Thessaly, east of the Pindos. The consequences for the environment of Western Greece are far from clear. The project also includes a hydro-electric scheme. The road continues via **Krifí** to (c 111km) **Kápsala** beyond which, at Palaiokhóri, is a church of the **Yennisis tis Theotokou**. At **Kipséli**, on a more circuitous route, is a Folk Collection. Otherwise a surfaced route can be followed to (c 186km) **Arta** (Rte 53A).

III. TO ARGITHEA (52.5km) and ARTA 161.5km, (100 miles; bus once weekly).

To (15km) **Paliomonastíri** (see above for Pili). You keep left for (20.5km) **Mouzáki**. The landscape of the foothills is green and gentle. Taking the Argithéa road through Mouzáki, at 23.5km you leave to the left a turn for Pevkofito and Moni Spilias (see below). The road runs through a delightful valley, rich in vegetation. Beyond (30.5km) a turn for Dhrakótripa the road climbs and there are retrospective views over the valley and Thessalian plain. 36.5km **Oxiá**. Bare peaks rise above high fir-covered slopes to a height of 1758m. 48.5km You reach the summit and descend (roadworks) to (52.5km) the pretty village of **Argithéa** nestling deep in its mountain valley.

The antiquities of this region, ancient *Athamania*, are not well known. Athamania sided with first Sparta and then Athens in the alliances of the 5 and 4C. In the 3C it was dominated by Pyrrhus, later becoming an independent kingdom, which reached its greatest extent in the 2C when it stretched into the Thessalian plain. In 191 it became a Macedonian province and in 168 gave allegiance to Rome. Ancient townships have been identified with varying degrees of certainty. Some excavation has been done recently. At **Elliniká**, 2km SW of the modern village, a settlement may be the ancient capital of Argithea: numerous tombs (4C–1C BC) belonging to the site have been examined. Near **Petrotó** (at Palaiókastro) a fortified Hellenistic site and associated cemetery have been investigated.

Beyond Argithea are 40km of dirt roads, sometimes in indifferent condition but regularly used by cars, before you can again pick surfaced routes for (161. 5kms) Arta (Rte 53A).

Intrepid explorers with tough vehicles can essay visits to two interesting churches in the Argithea area. 10km further beyond the village there is a turn right for **Anthiró** which is 3km away. 4km further is the small monastery of the **Yénnisis tis Theotókou** with 17 and 18C paintings, at present being attractively restored. The katholikon has two storeys, the upper (19C frescoes) being a double church dedicated to to Zoödhokhos Piyi and Ay. Anargyroi. Keys must be sought from the priest in Anthiro.

In the mountains to the S is the spectacularly situated 17C monastery of the **Panayía Spiliás** with 17–18C paintings (accommodation and food available in summer). The smaller church (Koimesis tes Theotokou) is 17C, the larger (Zoödhokhos Piyi) is 19C. It may be reached from Argithea by turning left (signs for Karyá, Spiliá) across the valley at the junction mentioned above for Anthiro. From this point Moni Spilias is reached after 26km over very rough roads. Return (and/or approach) is also possible (and faster if Moni Spilias is the sole objective) via **Vlási** and **Pevkófito** to the turn outside Mouzaki (see above), 42.5kms from the monastery: this route also involves about 25km of bad or indifferent roads stretches of which are being improved.

From Tríkkala to **Kalambáka** and the **Metéora**, see Rte 51.

# 48

## Lárissa and its environs

**LÁRISSA**, or **Lárisa** (Λάρισα), the chief town of its nome and capital of the province of Thessaly, with 112,777 inhabitants, is an important road centre, the headquarters of the Greek First Army, and the seat (since the 7C) of the Metropolitan 'Bishop of the Second Thessaly and Exarch of All Hellas'. Situated in the middle of the Thessalian plain on the right bank of the Peneios, with its spacious squares and busy streets it has more the air of a city than anywhere else in central Greece. Evidence of Larissa's long history is not prominent, though traces of the Turkish enceinte still survive to the S of the town. There is good local ouzo, halva and ice cream. Unusually for Greece, bicycles are much used. The presence of storks on the roofs adds a bizarre touch to the townscape.

**Railway station**, 1.25km S of the centre, for the main Athens–Thessaloniki line, and for Volos.

**Hotels** A, B, C, D.

**Zakharoplasteia** and cafés in the main square and in the Alkazar park. Konstantinídhis Zakharoplasteion at 4 Panagoúli is particularly recommended.

**Post Offices**, (1) Odd. Velissaríou and Papakiriazí; (2) Gázi and Papakiriazí.— **OTE Centre**, Od. Filellínon.

**Information**, etc. **NTO** Koumoundhoúrou; **Tourist Police**, Papanastasíou and Ayíou Nikoláou; Olympic Airways, 70 Papanastasíou and Koumoundhoúrou.

**Book** Gnósi, 37 Papakiriazí; Pardhía, 11 Kanári.

**Buses. Main Bus Station** at Yiorgiádhou/Olímbou (Larissa–Volos etc; Athens); for Kardhítsa/Trikkala (Iroön Politekhníou, in S of town); for Kozami (Karamasíou, N of river); for Grevená (Ergatikís Protomayías; for Ioánnina (Agnóstou Stratiótou, SW); for Verria (Iásonos/Palaiológou, S). To Athens (6); to Volos (12); to Trikkala (frequently), also to Ioannina (daily); to Tírnavos and Elasson (frequently); to Kozani (regularly), to Kardhitsa (regularly); to Farsala (regularly).

**History.** The name *Larissa*, meaning 'citadel', is pre-Hellenic and a settlement seems to have existed on the site from earliest times. Palaeolithic remains were discovered in 1960 on the W outskirts. An early ruler, Aleuas, who claimed descent from Herakles, founded the powerful family of the Aleuadai. The dynasty attracted to their court the poet Pindar, the sophist Gorgias, and the physician Hippocrates, the last two of whom died at Larissa. In 480 BC the Aleuadai supported Xerxes; four years later the Spartans attacked them unsuccessfully. At the end of the 5C BC their power was weakened by a democratic revolt and by the rise of the tyrants of Pherai, the most formidable of whom was Jason. The last Aleuadai injudiciously invited the aid of Philip of Macedon, who annexed Larissa and the whole of Thessaly. After the second battle of Cynoscephalae (197) the Romans made Larissa the capital of the reorganised Thessalian confederation. In 171 Perseus, king of Macedon, defeated the Romans near Larissa. Pompey passed through the city on his flight after the battle of Pharsalus.

Achilleios, Bishop and patron saint of Larissa, was present at the Council of Nicaea (325) and by the 5C the city had metropolitan rank. Larissa fell to the Bulgars in 985. Byzantine rule was restored and, though the Normans laid siege to the town in 1096, survived till the Frankish occupation of the 4th Crusade when Thessaly fell to Boniface of Montferrat. Theodore Angelos drove out the Franks and Michael II, his nephew, ruled Thessaly from Arta. Michael's illegitimate son, John Doukas, defied the emperors and his half-brother in Epirus alike. After his death in 1289, his son John II remained the ward and vassal of Guy de la Roche until 1308, when he threw in his lot with Byzantium in time to rid his territories of the Catalan Grand Company, who passed through on their way S. In 1318 John II died without an heir and Thessaly, invaded from all sides, was quarrelled over until Andronikos III restored uneasy Byzantine rule. By bloodless conquest Thessaly fell in 1348 to Stephen Dušan, who installed its conqueror Gregory Preljub, as 'Caesar' in Trikkala. After Dušan's death another period

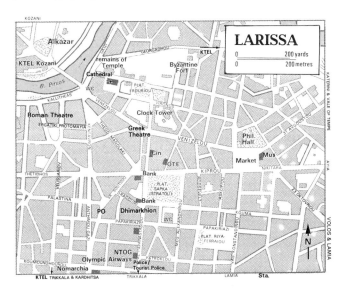

of anarchy in 1355–59 ended when Symeon Uroš established himself as 'Emperor'. His son, John Uroš, turned monk and the Serbs became little more than Byzantine vassals. By 1393 Bayezid's Turks were encamped on the Spercheios and Thessaly remained Turkish until 1881. The Turks renamed Larissa *Yenişehir* ('new town') in contradistinction to the 'old town', of Krannon. It was the headquarters of Mehmed IV during the siege of Candia in 1669 and its military garrison inhibited the participation of Thessaly in the War of Independence. Larissa did not, however, succeed Trikkala as the Turkish capital of Thessaly, until 1870.

The centre of Larissa is the huge Plateía Sápka, shaded by limes and orange trees and lively with cafés, patisseries, and cinemas. Above its NW corner, in A. Papanastasíou, the 3C **theatre** (capacity c 10,000) was found in 1968 and has lately been intensively investigated and restored. Further W, at Odd. Velissaríou and Ergatikís Protomayiás is a Roman theatre of the 2C AD, though with an earlier history. Od. Papanastasíou leads shortly to the low hill, once the acropolis of the ancient city, now crowned by a **clock tower** (To Rolóï). NE is the impressive Byzantine **frourion** (traces of an Early Christian basilica). To the W are the new **cathedral** and some vestiges of a Classical **temple**, overlooking the new bridge which replaced a medieval bridge of 12 arches across the Peneios. Beyond, along the river, extends the **Alkazár**, a fine shady park (cafés), a favourite promenade in summer.

Returning by Od. Venizélou, you pass between the **Philharmonic Hall** and the covered **market**. Opposite a small public garden is a **mosque** with a conspicuous minaret. Here is the interesting **Archaeological Museum**, containing Thessalian antiquities from the nome of Larissa. In the single hall are displayed; a menhir from Soufli tumulus (Middle Bronze Age); Archaic temple fragments, 5C Roman funerary stelai from Larissa and other sites; Classical bronzes from Tirnavos and Argiroupolis; later sculpture, typically Thessalian in character; late-Imperial stelai depicting mounted warriors (the Greco-Roman antecedents in art of the Byzantine portrayal of St George). Important are the Palaeolithic and Neolithic finds from the valley of the Peneios.

The mound (**Magoula**) **of Gremmoú**, near Dhendrá, 10.5km from Larissa off the Kozani road to the left, represents the site of Homeric *Argyssa*, though the principal antiquities excavated since 1955 by the German Institute are Neolithic.

24km SW (3km S of the main road to Kardhítsa) are the ruins of *Krannon*, once one of the foremost cities of Thessaly and the seat of the *Skopadai*, kinsmen of the Aleuadai, whose wealth was proverbial. The poet Simonides (556–467 BC), who beat Aeschylus in a competition for the best elegy on the fallen at Marathon, lived for a time at Krannon under the patronage of the Skopadai. At Krannon in 322 BC, Antipater, the Macedonian regent, defeated the confederate Greeks and so put a stop to the Lamian War. Temple of Asklepios is mentioned in inscriptions. S of the village, the low hill of Kastro, with a pleasant church of the Panayía at its N foot, was the ancient acropolis (recent excavations but little to see). Passing behind the Kastro, passable dirt tracks lead (4.5km from village) to three **tholos tombs** of the 5C BC, showing a remarkable survival in Thessaly of a Mycenaean form. The Turks called Krannon *Eskişehir* ('Old Town' or 'Old Larissa'), by way of contrast to the 'New Town' of Larissa (see above). 5km SE of Krannon, excavations at two cemetery sites in the vicinity of the village of **Ay. Yióryios** produced rich finds including weapons and huge Thessalian fibulae of c 650–550 BC. There are several tumuli in the area, as at **Dhoxará** (Mavrópetra). The finds from both sites are in the Larissa Museum. Mavrópetra also has a Byzantine site.

From Larissa a road runs NE via Omorfokhóri to (20km) **Sikoúri**, continuing to **Spiliá** (786m), 8km farther on, departure point for the mountain refuge (3 hrs) on **Mt Ossa** (see below). A group of Mycenaean tholos tombs was identified in 1969 near the village.

FROM LÁRISSA TO AYIÁ, AYIÓKAMBOS, STÓMIO AND TÉMBI 109km (68 miles, buses to various points; see Rte 57).

You take the Volos road E across the plain, and at 6.5km branch left. At (16km) **Elevthéri**, a by-road goes off left for **Marmárini** (6.5km) where many tholos tombs were examined in 1903 and there are scanty remains of ancient *Lakereia*. You pass into the Dhotion Plain. At 18km, to the S of the road, a hill **Palaíkastro** (take the turn to **Plasiá**, formerly Neokhóri, then first left, then left again up a track onto the hillside) has remains of an extensive building complex of the 5C BC. About 1km ENE of this site a fine built tomb of the 5 and 4C was found in 1972. 39km **Ayiá** (Hotels E; F/A), chief place (4014 inhab.) of an eparchy, is situated on the S slopes of Ossa above the gorge dividing Ossa from Pelion, and c 11km from the sea. It has several post-Byzantine churches with interesting decoration (see T. Koumoulides and L. Deriziotes, *Ekklesies tes Ayias, Larisses*, 1985—Greek with some English; good illustrations). The town is a base for expeditions on **Mt Ossa**, or Kissavos (1978m), a bold isolated mountain commanding a magnificent *view. From the summit, Mt Athos and, in clear weather, the Turkish coast may be seen. The Giants, in their war with the Gods, are fabled to have piled Pelion on Ossa in order to reach the summit of Olympos. The W slopes of Ossa provided verde antico and Atrax marble (serpentine) for the buildings of ancient Rome.

To the NE (2km and 1km motorable track) of Ayiá is the attractive 16C **monastery** (restored) of Ayios Pandeleimon (nuns). There are frescoes of 1721 in the narthex and of the early 17C in the refectory; also an abbot's tower, with chapel. The same road continues to (7km) **Melívia**, sometimes thought to be the site of ancient *Meliboias*, native place of Philoktetes. A recent theory however locates this at the kastro of **Káto Polidhéndri** (18km SE). Near there, on the hill of Mavrovoúni, two small churches both have frescoes: that of the Panayia (16C) originally monastic, and the Koimesis tes Theotokou (16C with 17C decoration). The royal estate of **Polidhéndri** was donated by King Paul to the State in 1962 as a training school for Greek farmers.

From Ayiá a good and attractive road descends through wooded foothills to the coast at (53km) **Ayiókambos**, a sprawling resort with modest facilities, busy in July and August. Turning left (N) the road runs mostly flat behind the beach through (60km) another resort, **Velíka**. Various roads lead inland to Melivia (see above). Beyond Velika is an unsurfaced stretch of 9km before **Paliouría**, with a long shingle beach. All the villages have rooms and restaurants. The scenery inland is attractive with tree-clad slopes. 71km **Koutsoupiá** is quiet. 75km **Kókkino Neró** is a busy resort with mineral springs producing reddish water. 79km **Káritsa**. 97km **Stómio** (Hotels C, E; F/A), formerly Tsagezi, is a peaceful seaside town with a sandy beach, trees and thermal springs, below the steepest face of Ossa. 100km **Omólio** in ancient times had a Temple of Poseidon Petraios; a tomb near the river produced an exquisite hoard of Classical jewellery in 1961 (now in Larissa Museum). Protogeometric tombs have yielded iron, bronze, and gold objects. 109km You join the main road at the E end of the Tembi pass (Rte 57).

From Lárissa to **Fársala**, see Rte 47B; to **Vólos**, see Rte 50; to **Tírnavos** and **Elassón**, see Rte 58; to the **Vale of Tempe** by main road, see Rte 57; to **Tríkkala** and **Metéora**, see Rtes 50 and 51.

# 49

# Magnesía

## A. From Lamía to Vólos

**Road**, 111km (69 miles), of which 82km by National Highway (toll). 51km. Exit for Glífa **car ferry**. 86km. Exit for Vólos. 88km Mikrothívai and 93km Néa Ankhíalos (Phthiotic Thebes). 111km. Vólos. **Buses** from Palaiológou/ Rozáki Angelí daily to Almirós and Vólos, 5 times to Pelasyía.

You leave Lamia at the E and in 4km join the National Highway. At **Megálo Vrísi**, beyond the turn to the National Road and 4km from Lamia, is a prehistoric mound site which may be Homeric *Alos*. 16km **Stilís** (Στυλίς; exit), the port of Lamia, has some coastal shipping. It occupies the site of Thessalian *Phaleron* and its population of 4993 derive their livelihood from olive culture. Just beyond **Karavómilos** (Hotels C), at 26km is (left) **Akhinós**, backed by a flat-topped hill (chapel), the acropolis of ancient *Echinos*, referred to in the *Lysistrata*. Excavations have produced ancient buildings (including parts of the city wall) and tombs. 30.5km. Exit for **Rákhes, Akhládhi** and **Pelasyía** (Πελασγία); about 1½ hours N on foot from Pelasyia (buses from Lamía and Vólos) are the remains of *Larissa Kremaste*. 34km (near 244km post, by the Agroinvest factory) are some remains perhaps of a Hellenistic fort guarding the narrows. 36km Parking area by the channel (Dhiavlos Oreon), across which is **Mt Likhás**, the W promontory of Euboea (see Rte 42A). 40km Toll gate. 51km Exit: roads to Pelasyía (17km; see above), and to **Glífa**, ancient *Androna*, (11km; car ferry to Ayiókambos in Euboea, see Rte 42A).

Here you can make a seaward detour (c 10km farther), passing first a turn to **Paralía Pelasyías**, with an Early Christian basilica. After Glífa the road runs just inland of **Akhílleo**, a popular bathing-place, then past **Ftelió** (officially Pteleós), a pleasant village lying inland of the site of Homeric *Pteleon*, marked perhaps by a medieval tower on a height nearer the sea (Mycenaean tombs to the NW). Beyond Pteleos you join the old road N and continue past **Soúrpi** (Σούρπη), a nesting-place of storks. **Magoúla Plataniótiki**, on the Bay of Soúrpi is probably the site of *Old Halos*, destroyed by the Macedonians, under Parmenion, in 346 BC. A turn (left) under the National Road leads in 7km to the **Moní Xenías**, dating from the 17C, when it moved down from a higher site, where there are ruins of the 5–13C. You may then either rejoin the National Highway or stay on the old road to visit the the ruins of *New Halos*.

Hellenistic Halos lies to the right, its acropolis on a hill to the left. The site, which has been surveyed but not excavated and partially destroyed by quarrying, was probably founded in the Hellenistic period. The town was laid out on a grid plan and surrounded by a wall with numerous towers. The small acropolis (subsequently crowned by a Byzantine fortress) was connected to the town by similar walls which ran down the hillside in a V-shape, from the summit to the NW and SW corners of the town defences. The fortifications and the absence of public buildings (though there was an agora) suggest that Halos was a military foundation. At the time of its construction, the site was closer to the sea and effectively dominated the passage between Mt Othrys and the Pagasitic Gulf. See H.R. Reinders, *New Halos*, Utrecht, 1988. **Almirós** (Hotels B, C), 6.5km beyond Halos, is the capital of an eparchy, with a population of 8502 and a small museum. It has an hourly bus connection (in 45 mins) with Volos. Benjamin of Tudela remarks on the presence of numerous Italian and Jewish merchants at Almiros, and the Emperor Alexios III in 1199 granted trading concessions here to the Venetians.

63km Toll gate. To the right is **Mt Khlomon** (893m) which guards the Trikkeri Strait (Dhiavlos Trikeriou), the landlocked entrance to the gulf of Volos, scene in 480 BC of the first encounter between the Greek and Persian fleets (see Rte 42). 70km Exit for Halos and Almirós, see above. 76.5km Xirias bridge, followed by the return spur from Almiros. At 87km take the Volos exit, leaving the Highway which continues N to join near Velestíno (c 16km on) the line of the old Volos–Larissa road (Rte 50).

You head east.

To the W the same road leads (in 39kms) to **Fársala** (Rte 47B). After 11km, to the right of the road a bronze wing on a pillar commemorates two airmen who died in a crash in 1954.

88km **Mikrothívai** stands below the flat hill of **Phthiotic Thebes**, which is ringed by ruined Classical walls with 40 towers and has remains of a temple of Athena, a theatre, and a stoa; the walls can be seen from the road (two fields' lengths away) about 1.5km beyond Mikrothívai. Finds are in the Volos Museum. 93km **Néa Ankhíalos**, a village (Hotels C, D; 4602 inhab.) by the sea, founded by refugees in 1906, and occupying the site of ancient *Pyrasos*. The name and population of Phthiotic Thebes were transferred in Early Christian times to this town, which was originally its port (some harbour installations located). This is one of the most important Early Christian/Early Byzantine sites in Greece. Nine basilicas (mid 4C to mid 6C AD), remains of the city wall, graves and parts of the settlement (including two bathing establishments, sections of a roadway and other houses and public buildings) have been excavated. The city was abandoned about 620. In five large areas of excavation (three of them along the main road) are the five most important basilicas (A, B, G (the basilica of Archbishop Peter), D, and 'Martyrios'). G had two predecessors, the first of them earlier 4C AD. Beneath this are two even earlier building complexes, one of which might be a shrine of Demeter mentioned in literary sources. Immediately SW, close to the city wall, a rich monumental baptistery of early Constantinian type, with octagonal font and elaborate facilities for the sacrament of baptism, was found in 1983. It must belong to the original phase of the basilica. Several of these buildings have produced fine mosaics, paintings and architectural fragments, some of which may be seen in the small **museum** which lies within the site enclosure to the left of the road.

The road now follows the pretty coast above little bays backed by olive-clad hills. From the summit of the last rise there is a wide panorama over the Gulf, then a fine view down to Volos, with Mt Pelion behind. The sanctuary of **Amphanai** (right) was located by the German Institute in 1972.

In the plain you pass through the sites of Pagasai and Demetrias (see below), then (right) the buildings of the Volos campus of the new University of Thessaly, turning right at a major junction (lights) with the Larissa road to enter (111km) **Volos**.

# B. Vólos and its environs

**VÓLOS** (Βόλος), a bustling town of 77,192 inhabitants, capital of its eparchy and of the nome of Magnesia and constituting a deme still officially called Pagasai, is the seat of an archbishop (Metropolitan of Demetrias) and the chief port of Thessaly. The harbour dates from 1912, but some form of maritime town has existed in the area from prehistoric times. It is the main channel of Thessalian exports: cereals, garden produce, cotton, silk, olive-oil, skins, sugar, and soap. With its mills, tanneries, and refineries, now of industrial archaeological interest, it was a potential rival of Piraeus until stricken by two disastrous earthquakes in 1954 and 1955. The recent start of a rail and road ferry to Syria has given new impetus to a large industrial area on the Larissa road. The town's attractive site between Mt Pelion and the Gulf, its excellent museum and the quality of its hotels and restaurants make it a pleasant base.

**Hotels**. B, C, D, E; many on or near quay.

**Restaurants**. Many on quay. The majority of these are Tsipourádhika, which serve the local aperitif *tsípouro*, a variety of rakí, each order being accompanied by a different mezé. Especially recommended for devotees of traditional Greek entertainment is the modest restaurant I Skála tou Milánou at Iólkou (officially El. Venizelou) and Analípseos, whose proprietors play traditional Greek music (especially rebetika) after serving the food.

**Post Office**, Pávlou Melá. **OTE Centre**, Iólkou/Sokrátous. **Tourist Office (NTO)**, Plateía Ríga Feraíou, near the Town Hall. **Tourist Police**, Koumoundhoúrou; **ELPA**, Gr. Lambráki.

**Bus Terminals**. Local (town) services, opposite Dhimarkhíon. Remainder from main bus station at A. Zákhou 1 and Gr. Lambráki.

**Bus Services** to Athens, regularly; to Lárissa, frequently; to Velestíno, regularly; to Almirós, frequently; to Pelasyía, daily; to Loutrá Aidhipsoú, daily, via Arkítsa. To Portariá and Makrinítsa, frequently; to most other villages on Pélion, 2–3 times daily; to Lekhónia, etc.

**Car Hire**. Avis, Iásonos 139; others nearby.

**Bookshop**, Omiros, Dhimitriádhos 83 (in lane). Mainly Greek.

**Boats/Hydrofoils** from Town Quay to the Northern Sporades, Euboea.

Entering the town from the junction with the Larissa road (Rte 49A) you pass (left) the rising ground where lay ancient Iolkos (see below), also with medieval buildings; beyond is the railway station. The road then enters Plateía Ríga Ferraíou, a huge triangle bordering the picturesque **fishing harbour**. The **Dhimarkíon** (Town Hall), by D. Pikionis in traditional Pelion style, has interesting doors, a series of woodcuts illustrating episodes in the history of Volos on the ground floor and, upstairs, a fascinating series of late 19C/early 20C photographs of Volos and environs. Close by are the **theatre** and, on the corner of Od. Metamorfósios, at the E end of the square, the Volos **Odeion** (Music College) in a lovely neo-Classical building with a fine interior.

East of Plateia Riga Feraiou, Odhós Vasiléos Konstandínou, or Dhimi-triádhos, the uninspiring main street, runs through the chequer-board town parallel to the waterfront. At right angles to this Od. Iólkou (officially El. Venizelou) heads NE through the centre of town, crosses Od. Analípseos, another important thoroughfare, and ascends towards Ano Vólos (see below) and the villages of Pelion.

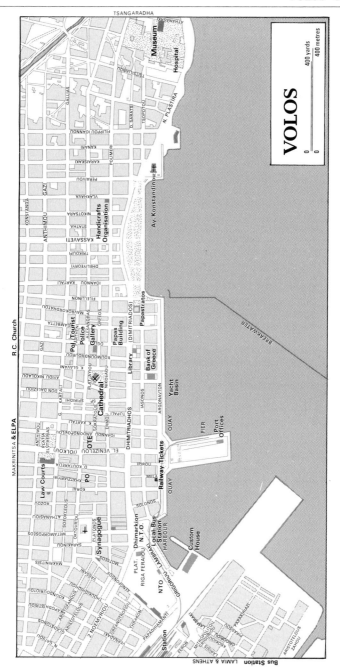

Beyond the fishing harbour, the busy quayside leads to an open space, the social centre of the town, which fronts the **landing stage** (boats for the Sporades). Here a model of the Argo forms a graceful monument to the past. The quay is continued E for nearly a mile as the Argonavton, a splendid esplanade (venue of the volta). For the **museum**, see below.

West of Riga Feraiou (see above), between the railway station and the football stadium and extending N and S of Od. Gr. Lambráki, is the older part of Volos, known as **Palaiá**. Archaeologically, the most important part of this area is the mound (412 x 320 x 9m high) of Ayii Theódhori. Excavations close by the church (in Mitropolítou Grigoríou) have revealed the remains of a Classical temple (columns reused in the balustrade of the terrace) and later remains. Pieces of ancient masonry can be seen round about. Opposite the church are the remains of an Early Christian basilica. Extensive finds have been identified (D. Theokharis, 1956) as those of ancient *Iolkos*. In the modern suburb of Néa Ionía, to the N, parts of the ancient cemetery have been excavated.

*Iolkos*, famous in legend as the place from which the Argonauts set out in quest of the Golden Fleece, had a flourishing existence. The site at Ayii Theodhori was important in Early, Middle and Late Helladic times and probably had continuity of occupation down the ages. Greek mythological personages (King Pelias, the uncle of Jason, Eumeios and Alcestis), have inevitably been associated with the site. With other towns, it was depopulated by Demetrios Poliorketes and its inhabitants moved to Demetrias. Other locations (see Dhimini) have also been proposed for Iolkos in Mycenaean times.

The main prehistoric excavations (overgrown and little to see, but thought to include Mycenaean palatial structures) are in Soulíou and, at the NW foot of the mound in Lakhaná, at which points the impressive remains of the Ottoman fortifications can best be seen. Prehistoric structures are preserved for the visitor in the basement of 68–70 Od. Papakiriazí. At the junction of Kréonos and Mitropolítou Grigoríou is a fine mediaeval cistern. At the S edge of this area (junction of M. Grigoríou and G. Lambráki) excavations on the site of *the old vegetable market in advance of rebuilding have revealed basements with pithoi. To the W a dried-up river bed may be the remains of the ancient *Anauros*.

The *museum, at the SE extremity of the town (bus no. 3 from opposite the Dhimarkhíon to its terminus; useful leaflet in English, free), was founded in 1909 by Alexis Athanasakis and, rebuilt after the earthquakes, was reopened in 1961. Its collection of c 300 painted stelai is unique.

VESTIBULE. (Theokharis Room). A changing exhibition of finds from recent rescue excavations (various periods) in the area controlled from the museum, together with a map of sites investigated in recent years. A 4C sarcophagus from Velestino has a reconstructed burial.

ROOM A, to the right: ***painted grave stelai** from Demetrias (Hellenistic); Mycenaean vases and bead jewellery from various Thessalian sites; Mycenaean and Protogeometric finds from the palace of Iolkos. Geometric pottery from Thessalian sites. In doorway, head of a youth from Meliboia (reminiscent of the Kritian Boy).

ROOM B. Walls: relief grave stelai from Phalanna, Larissa, Pherai and Gonnoi (5C BC); votive reliefs from other sites (4C). In cases: bronze votives from the sanctuary of Itonian Athena at Philia; Geometric bronzes from Thessalian sites; Palaeolithic flints and bone implements from Larissa, Sesklo and sites in the Peneus valley; Pre-pottery Neolithic tools (7th mill. BC), including a bone and flint saw.

ROOM G has excellent new displays illustrating various aspects of life in the Neolithic period: architecture, agriculture, stock rearing, implement technology, manufacture of pottery, jewellery and figurines; spinning and weaving, etc. There is also a reconstructed section through a Neolithic site demonstrating the Neolithic sequence with characteristic pottery and artefacts.

ROOM D (left of vestibule): painted grave stelai are further displayed; good model of site of Demetrias and Pagasai. In the centre, good male torso in marble (? Roman copy of original of the 5C BC). In cases: vases and figurines of Archaic to Hellenistic date; Hellenistic glass vases (tomb offerings) and gold jewellery.

ROOM E (beyond). Offerings from various graves; drawings of tombs and graves; fine case of gold jewellery.

ROOM Z. An excellent display of reconstructed burials of all periods from Mycenaean to Classical with the skeletons and grave offerings in place (in some cases, also stelai). Here also are the later stelai from Demetrias.

A stiff climb (bus) may be made to Ano Volos, the medieval town to the N, with houses built on the sides of steep hills rising to 793m. One of the houses has frescoes (1912) by Theophilos. The church of the Metamórfosis on the hill of Episkopí has a 16C ikon.

## Excursions from Volos

I. TO PAGASAI AND DEMETRIAS (bus no. 6 from opposite Dhimarkhíon). Study the topographical model of the area in the Volos Museum before you visit these sites, which may not be of great interest to the casual visitor.

*Pagasai* was the port of Iolkos and afterwards of Pherai. The port gave its name to the Pagasitikos Kolpos (Gulf of Volos). The Argo was, by the traditional story, built at Pagasai, which had a famous oracle and an altar of Apollo mentioned by Hesiod. It flourished in the 5C BC under the wing of Pherai. It was captured by Philip II of Macedon who separated it from Pherai and incorporated it in Magnesia. When Demetrios Poliorketes founded *Demetrias*, Pagasai became a dependency of the new city. Demetrias was a favourite resort of its founder and his descendants. It was the base of Philip V but tamely surrendered to the domination of Rome in 196. After the battle of Pydna (168) its fortifications were razed. The great towers of the Hellenistic ramparts were hastily strengthened in the earlier 1C BC with outer lines. Concealed in the stone plinths of these were discovered the painted stelai now in the museum at Volos. These had come from neighbouring cemeteries. In Byzantine times it was joined to the see of Thessaly. Invading Saracens sacked the town in 902. Off the coast here in 1275 the Euboean Franks were utterly defeated by the forces of Michael VIII Palaiologos.

The site was first explored in 1920–23 and excavations and survey work since 1961 have been carried out by the Greek Archaeological Service and the German Institute.

*Pagasae* is not certainly identified. Its site seems likely to have been at least partly incorporated in that of Demetrias and it is often thought that the more southerly loop of the walls belonged in origin to Pagasae. The centre may however have been further S (2.5km, at Soros, otherwise identified as ancient *Amphanai*) or in the area N and E of the theatre (Bourboulethra) where early material has been found. The walled circuit of *Demetrias* can be traced for much of its length, except on the N: a north–south diateichisma, just to the W of the 'palace' and now very badly preserved, was constructed to divide the site into two sectors in the later 3C.

The remains of the two cities lie c 3km S of Volos and can be reached in 10 minutes by car or bus, in ½ hour on foot, or in ½ hour by hired boat from Volos quay. You take the Almiros/Lamia road to the SW (Rte 49A). A turn (left, signed 'Pefkákia') encircles the promontory, on which the E part of Demetrias stands.

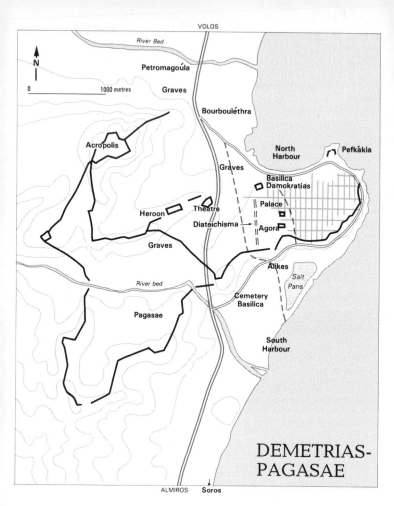

At the tip is the important prehistoric site of *Pefkakia* (deep excavation trench visible from the road), perhaps yet another candidate for ancient Iolkos. An Early Christian basilica (Demokratias), a 4C foundation with mosaic floors, was found in this, the area of the N harbour; also another important public building of the same period.

The main road continues beyond the Pefkakia turn through the middle of ancient Demetrias. The somewhat disappointing 3C theatre (bus stop) is visible to the right, an overgrown excavation site on the other side of the road. Above and to the W of the theatre is a ?heroön. The acropolis is on the heights to the NW of the theatre: there is a small fort in the W angle of the outer line of fortifications (those sometimes attributed to Pagasae).

About 300m to the E of the theatre, on a hill capped with trees, are the fenced (no admission) remains of a (fortified?) Macedonian palace still under excavation. It has a colonnaded courtyard, with massive exterior walls and four corner towers: to the W extend further courts. A short distance to the S is the site of the agora with a small temple of Artemis Iolkias. The grid plan layout of the town has been traced in this sector. Well to the S, beyond the walls and towards the S harbour are remains of another Early Christian (cemetery) basilica.

Beyond the theatre, the piers of a Hellenistic acqueduct cross the road. Further again (past a left turn to Alikés on the S side of the promontory) the road cuts through the walls, other sections of which, including towers, can be seen by inspecting the promontory on foot.

II. TO DHIMÍNI AND SÉSKLO, 6.5km and 18.5km W of Volos by road. Both (open 08.30–15.00; closed Monday) are accessible by bus. The sites are 2 hours' walk (rough road) apart, to the S of the main Larissa road (Rte 50). Finds from the sites (pottery, tools, figurines, jewellery) and background material can be seen in the Volos Museum. A descriptive leaflet in English is available covering both. Ignoring the Almiros turn, you take the Larissa road and then, still in the outskirts of Volos, an asphalted road (left; sign-posted) to the village of **Dhimíni** (Διμήνι). At the beginning of the village a track (right; sign) leads to the hill crowned by pre-historic remains of the 4th millennium BC that have given the name 'Dimini' to a culture of the period known more generally as Neolithic B. The site is attractive. It was occupied from c 4000 BC. A central courtyard with a large house (megaron) is supported by a roughly circular terrace wall. Smaller houses lie beyond the courtyard but within outer wall circuits. After a period of abandonment, the site again became an important centre in the Mycenaean period. A new megaron was built in the courtyard and extensive remains of a large township have been found on the flatter ground around the acropolis. Immediately to the NW of the Neolithic site is a Mycenaean tholos tomb. Dimíni is another candidate for ancient Iolkos.

To reach **Sésklo** (Σέσκλο) by road you follow the Larissa road for 10.5km, then turn left over a rough railway crossing. Beyond, a tarmac road continues S towards the village, but after 3km a further left turn (small sign in Greek) leads in c 1km to the acropolis which has given its name to a culture of the Neolithic A period, found widely in Thessaly and also elsewhere in Greece. The approach to the site has been attractively landscaped and has memorials to the archaeologists Christos Tsountas and Dhimitris Theokharis. The site was occupied c 6500 BC until c 5000 and later reoccupied to a lesser extent. The chief finds are Middle Neolithic (5th millennium BC). On the summit are remains of a 'palace' of megaron form (porch, main chamber with square hearth and back room). It is partly overlain by a similar but larger structure belonging to the later phase of occupation. The other houses are more modest and radiate from the centre, supported on terrace walls. One contained a potter's workshop. Traces of the Middle Neolithic settlement, thought to have accomodated upwards of 3000 people, have been found over a wide area round the central hill, for instance in an excavation 200m to the SW. About ¾ hour away is the ruined 'Palaiokastro' which may be *Aisonia*, the city of Jason's father.

# C. Mount Pélion

**Mount Pélion** (Πήλιον; 1651m), or **Pílion Oros**, the long mountain range that occupies the greater part of the peninsula enclosing the Pagasitic Gulf, forms one of the most delightful regions of Greece. Its climate, cool in summer but mild in winter, with abundant streams from the upper slopes, encourages a lush vegetation scarcely found elsewhere on the Greek mainland. It is famed for its fruit, exports chestnuts, and produces attar of roses. From its slopes the sea is rarely hidden from view. The delightful villages, well-watered and shady, have timber-framed houses with balconies; stone-paved mule paths wind between their gardens. The churches are low and wide and have an exo-narthex supported on wooden pillars, which often extends from the N and S sides of the nave in the form of a pentise.

The ancients envisaged the Giants piling Pelion on Ossa in the war with the Gods. Pelion was the home of Chiron, wisest of the Centaurs, who taught Achilles the art of music and looked after Jason in his childhood. Here the gods celebrated the nuptials of Peleus and his unwilling bride Thetis. The trees of the mountain supplied timber for the Argo.

I. TO PORTARIÁ AND ZAGORÁ, 47km (29 miles), bus to Zagora twice daily; to Portaria and Makrinitsa 10–11 times daily. Leaving the town along Iólkou, you pass (4km) **Ano Vólos** (see above), climbing steadily. The road winds steeply to (14km) **Portariá** (Πορταριά; a beautiful summer resort; Hotels A, B, C; 1093 inhab.) with a magnificent plane-tree and spring in its square. It has excellent cheese and unresinated red wine. The small **church** (1273) has frescoes of 1581. Portariá is the starting-point for the 3½ hour climb to **Pliasídhi** (1548m), one of the main heights of Pelion.

A by-road diverges round the Megarevma ravine to **Makrinítsa** (Μακρυνίτσα; 2km; Hotels A, B, E), a delightful village of 651 inhabitants. Old mansions have been made guest houses by the NTO. The picturesque little Plateia has a huge hollow plane-tree, a sculptured marble **fountain**, a small **church** with sculptural decoration in the apse, and a fine view. Higher up is the formerly monastic church of the **Panayia** (18C) with Greek inscriptions and Roman and Byzantine carvings built into the walls. A small chapel, with a school below, has frescoes. A street name commemorates Charles Ogle (1851–78), special correspondent of *The Times*, who was killed here (it is said in cold blood by order of the Turkish commander) while reporting on a fight between local insurgents and the Turks.

From Portariá the road continues to climb in zigzags, then runs along a high ledge with enormous views over the Gulf. 25km **Khánia** (1158m; Hotels B, C, E; winter sports), amid beech woods, stands at the head of the pass with a wide panorama in either direction. It has a chair-lift to Pliasídhi. Under the radar-capped crests of Pelion, you descend a tremendous valley through chestnuts, oaks, and planes, joining the road from Tsangaradha (see below) just over a mile short of (47km) **Zagorá** (Ζαγορά; 488m; rooms), a large community (2410 inhab.) of four hamlets on the E slope, facing the Aegean. In the plateia is the church of **Ayios Yeóryios** a typical Pelionic construction with an 18C ikonostasis. The countryside around is famed for the variety of its fruit (plums, damsons, pears, peaches, fraises de bois, etc.) and its aromatic red wine.

Below Zagorá on the coast is **Khorevtó** (7km), with a fine sandy beach, from which excursions can be made by boat.

II. TO MILIÉS AND TSANGARÁDHA, 55km (34 miles), buses daily to Tsangarádha, continuing to Makirrákhi; also to Miliés. You leave Volos to the SE, passing cement works and oil refineries, and skirt the Pagasitic Gulf.

On the outskirts of Volos, the road passes a prominent hill (left; access by road behind the stadium) on which is the site of *Góritsa*. The settlement, above the sea and probably of the 4C BC, is laid out on a strict grid plan and surrounded by a fortification wall with towers. There was a cemetery outside the W gate. The quarries from which the building stone was cut have been located in the vicinity.

8km **Agriá** (4544 inhab.; Hotels A, C, E; F/A) is served by town buses. 10km **Káto Lekhónia** is the terminus of a bus service (frequent). 12km **Ano Lekhónia** (tavernas). At Platanídhia by the sea is an Early Christian and Byzantine site. You pass through orchards. At (19km) **Kalá Nerá** (Hotels B, C, D, E; F/A) diverges the road to **Miliés** (8km; Hotels A), birth-place of Anthimos Gazi (1764–1828), who raised the Thessalian revolt in 1821. A charming village, it is a good base for walks in the Magnesian peninsula. Just beyond (22km) **Korópi** the road turns inland, leaving (right) a by-road to **Afissós** (Hotels A–E; F/A), a small seaside resort on the Gulf. The road climbs; the view is at first obstructed by olive-groves, then, on reaching the pass above (27km) **Afétai**, or Niáou, there is a fine *view over the whole Gulf. 35km **Miriovríti**. **Lefókastro** on the coast below has a Byzantine site. To the right is the road to **Argalastí** (11km; Hotels B, C, E; F/A), chief town (1393 inhab.) of Southern Pelion.

S of Argalasti roads lead S, in 20km, to the pleasant coastal resort of **Platania** (Hotels C, D, E) and (c 40km; unfinished) to **Trikéri**, at the SW tip of the peninsula and previously accessible only by sea.

Beyond (36km) **Neokhóri** you join a by-road from Miliés, cross a deep valley and get a first sight of the Aegean. 45.5km **Lambinoú**. The road winds vertiginously in and out of the deep clefts that fissure the E face of Pelion; the *view extends to the island of Skiathos. 55km **Tsangarádha** (Τσαγκαράδα; Hotels A, B, C, E), verdantly situated amid oak and plane forests at 472m, enjoys superb views down to the sea. A road (7km) descends to the fine beach at **Milopótamos**.

III. FROM TSANGARÁDHA TO ZAGORÁ, 29km (18 miles), one of the most beautiful roads in Greece, a splendid day's *walk in spring or autumn. The road runs fairly level at c 488m on the slopes, which are clad with oak forests and plane-trees. 7km **Moúresi**. At (13km) **Kissós**, a pretty village, the church of Ayia Marina has frescoes and a pentise 'cloister'. **Ayios Ioánnis** (Hotels B, C, D, E), its bathing-place, lies below (7km by road). 19km **Makrirrákhi**, another pleasant hamlet. You join the road from Portariá (see above). 29km **Zagorá**.

# 50

# From Vólos to Lárissa and Tríkkala

**Road**, 122km (76 miles), mainly flat. 19km Velestíno.—61km Lárissa.—122km Tríkkala. **Bus** four times daily.

**State Railway** to Lárissa, 60km (37 miles) in 1 hr, 13 times daily; to Tríkkala in 3½ hours, 4 times daily, continuing to Kalambáka; 1 through train daily Vólos to Athens (7 others involving a connection at Lárissa, in 5–6½ hours; 14 trains Lárissa to Athens in 4–6 hours.

**The Thessalian Railway** from Volos to Tríkkala (and Kalambáka), via Palaiofársalos, 164km (102 miles), follows the road to (19km) Velestíno (see below). It then turns S to cross two low passes round the E and S slopes of Khalkodhonion.—31km Aerinó stands c 5km N of Phthiotic Thebes (Rte 49A) and just N of the National Highway.—44km Rígaio. About 3km SE of the station are Erétria, with chromium mines and a mineral railway, and, on a hill (509m), the ruins of Eretria of Phthiotis, a prehistoric site with a fortified acropolis. This Eretria, according to Strabo, was one of the cities under the sway of Achilles.—At (69km) Fársala the line crosses the Lamía–Lárissa road (Rte 47B).—79km Palaiofársalos, junction for the main Athens–Thessaloníki line, is near the village of Stavrós. The line now follows roughly the course of the Lamía–Kardhítsa–Tríkkala road (Rte 47C).—98km Sofádhes.—113.5km Kardhítsa.—125.5km Fanári.—143km Tríkkala. To (164km) Kalambáka, see Rte 51A.

You leave Volos, passing over the railway, and in the next mile or so pass (left) roads to Almiros and Lamia (Rte 49A) and to Dhimini (Rte 49B). The road follows the railway, ascending the **Defile of Pilav-Tepe** (137m), named ('heap of rice') after a conical Hellenic tomb (left) disolved in 1899. The way up crosses the line of the Karla Tunnel (see below) and passes below the expanding industrial zone of Volos. Just beyond (10km) **Latomeío station**, which serves neighbouring quarries, the by-road to Sesklo (Rte 49B) goes off to the left. 19km **Velestíno** (Βελεστίνο) is a railway junction of some importance where the line to Tríkkala (see above) parts company with the branch to Larissa. From the station a road leads left into the town (3448 inhab.), which is pleasantly situated amid gardens and fountains in a ravine of Khalkodhónion. It was the birthplace of the revolutionary poet Rigas Feraios (1757–98), who was executed by the Turks in Belgrade for working towards a Balkan confederacy. There is an interesting **Museum of Agricultural Implements**.

Velestino occupies the site of *Pherai*, at one time one of the great cities of Thessaly; its port was Pagasai. Pherai was the legendary home of Admetus, whose wife Alcestis sacrificed her life for him, a story that inspired a celebrated tragedy of Euripides and an opera by Gluck. In the 4C BC the rulers of Pherai tried to dominate the whole of Thessaly and to interfere in the Greek world generally. The most notorious were Jason, elected Tagus of Thessaly in 374 and assassinated in 370, his successor Alexander who, defeated by the Theban general Pelopidas, died in 357, and Lykophron II, driven out in 352 by Philip of Macedon. Antiochus the Great (223–187) took Pherai in 191, but it was almost immediately recaptured by M. Acilius Glabrio. Some archaeological explorations were made by the Greek Archaeological Service in 1920 and 1923, and again, in collaboration with the French School, in 1925–26. In recent years there has been much rescue excavation. Rich prehistoric remains (Middle and Late Bronze Age) have been found beneath the modern village. Some aspects are reported in Υπέρεια, the proceedings of a 1986 conference (Athens, 1990).

The earliest settlement was on a hill about 1km SE of the historic city, on which the town of Velestino was built. The **acropolis** is on a trapezoidal plateau to the N of the Vlach quarter; here are the remains of the Larissan Gate and of a temple of Hercules. The city proper extended to the SW; by the church of the Panayia, prominent amongst trees above the outskirts of the town, are remains of the walls. Walls and towers uncovered on the hill of Ay. Athanasios show that this too was within the enceinte. Pherai was noted for two fountains, **Hypereia** and **Messeïs**. The former is in the centre of Velestino; the basin and conduit are covered with tiles. On the Larissa road, to the right on the edge of the town, a Hellenistic stoa (remains fenced), at least 49m long, was found in 1983. Further on (left) are the remains of a Temple of Zeus Thaulios, rebuilt in the ?4C. Archaic bronzes were removed to Athens and Geometric pottery to Volos.

There is now a choice of roads, though little difference in distance. The faster National Highway runs slightly above the W of the plain, with views across it (toll after 24km). The more interesting old road is described here. 23km **Rizómilos**. To the right are the large marshy Lake Karla, the ancient *Boibeïs*, once 24km long and 8km wide with a depth of 4–6m. Controlled and drained by a tunnel (see above) inaugurated in 1961, which takes surplus water to the Pagasitic Gulf, the lake is now a mere fraction of its former size and cannot be seen from the road. On the reclaimed and irrigated land experiments are being made with various crops, including cotton.

The ruins of several ancient cities are on the original shores: on the E is *Boibe*; on the NW *Armenion* (see below); on the SE is *Glaphyrai*, where there are foundations of a temple. The seaward side is fringed by Mavrovouni (1087m) and the saddle that connects it with Pelion.

32km **Armenió**. The site of Homeric *Armenion* is said to lie a little farther W at Kokkinés, and the huge Mycenaean circuit of walls on the promontory of Petra, projecting into the drained lake 3km N of Stefanovítiko, is equated with *Kerkinion*. The plain is dotted with prehistoric mounds. The modern villages lie mainly to the E. The range of Olympos rises ahead. 61km **Larissa** (Rte 48) is by-passed.

Beyond Larissa the road runs W through the plain, which is interrupted ahead by isolated moderate hills culminating in Mt Dobroutsi, the ancient *Titanos* (767m). At (79km) **Koutsókhero** the village fountain has been cut from a large Doric column drum. To your right, one behind the other, are the twin heights above **Goúnitsa** between which, through the impressive **Defile of Kalamaki**, the Peneios emerges into the plain.

About 1 hour SW of Koutsókhero, on a spur of Mt Dobroútsi, is the Palaiókastro of Aléfaka, the wreck of a Byzantine fortress built on ancient foundations. The ancient remains belong to *Atrax*, once inhabited by the warlike Perrhaeboi. One of the city gates, flanked by a fine piece of polygonal wall, partly survives. A number of gravestones and inscriptions from the site are in Larissa Museum and the Trikkala archaeological collection.

Beyond the village you cross the winding Peneios above its entry into the defile. A by-road (right), with a view into the defile, leads in 11km to Dhamási (see Rte 58; for Tirnavos, Elasson etc.). At (86km) **Pineiás** road and river pass between Dobroútsi and the abrupt spur of **Zárkos** (684m), the vertical W scarp of which looms over the village of **Zárkos**, 3km N of the road, with a Neolithic and EBA mound. Here was an ancient city, possibly *Phayttos* or *Pharkadon*, which in the Middle Ages became the seat of the Bishop of Gardiki (see below). At 94km, between modern **Farkadhón** (to the N) and the confluence of the Peneios with its most important tributary, the Enipeus (to the S), a road diverges S to Kardhítsa (28km). 6km N of Farkadhón is **Grizáno**, with a Byzantine fort.

The Kardhítsa road crosses the Peneios and its affluents. It follows the course of an old Turkish stone road, whose fine bridges, mostly abandoned, survive on the W side. Just S of (8km) **Vlokhós** you pass through a line of hills surmounted by ancient citadels, uncertainly identified. That rising prominently above the road (right) may be *Peirsia*; farther right Kastro of Kourtíki may be *Limnaion*; to the left is Pétrino (?*Phakion*). 10.5km **Palamá** (pop. 6010). At (20km) **Ayios Theódhoros** you join a more direct but less interesting road from Lárissa and the Lamía–Kardhítsa road (Rte 47C).

100km Crossroads. To the right is **Neokhóri** (3km), to the NW of which, in the foothills of Andikhasia, are some remains of Thessalian *Oichalia* and a Byzantine fort. Opposite (110km) **Petróporos** you pass below the hill of **Palaiogardíki** (right), its summit commanding a fine view of the plain of Tríkkala. Here the abandoned Byzantine town of **Gardiki**, which gave title to a bishop (see above), has a church (Ayía Paraskeví) reconstructed on part of the old foundations, and occupies the site of *Pelinnaion*, of which there survive sections of the walls, with gates and towers. Pelinnaion was one of four strongholds forming a defensive quadrilateral (see Rte 47C). 116km

Turn (right) for **Khrisavghí** N of which, near the remote village of **Kokkóna** is a fine Classical fort (reused in the Byzantine period). At **Palaiópirgos**, in the same direction, is a fortified Byzantine monastic complex (Palaiomonastíri). 120km A bypass skirts the town. 122km **Tríkkala**, see Rte 47C.

# 51

# The Metéora and the Central Píndos

The visit to the Metéora needs at least half a day, even if confined to the three principal monasteries, and with the use of a car.

## A.   From Tríkkala to Kalambáka. Metéora

**Road** to Kalambáka, 21km (13 miles); bus in ½ hr, continuing to (23km) Kastráki for the Metéora (through service from Lárissa regularly). The tour of the monasteries can be done by road, 21km round from Kalambáka; on foot the ancient stone paths are shorter but often steep.

**Railway** to Kalambáka, 22km in 40 minutes, 6 times daily. There are through trains from Vólos, via Fársala and Kardhítsa (see Rte 50).

You leave Tríkkala by the castle and turn NW. The road, lined with poplars, and the railway head straight across the plain, To the W rise the steep slopes of **Kerkétion**, a long range running N–S with its highest point (1900m) near the S end (ascent, see Rte 47C). 11km **Vasilikí** has a 15C cemetery church of Ayios Yeoryios. On an isolated foothill, near the village of **Peristéra** (W of the road), are some ruins to be identified with ancient *Pialeia*.

23km **Kalambáka** (Καλαμπάκα; Hotels A, B, C, E), an attractive little town of 5699 inhabitants, spreads fanwise on the green slopes at the foot of the Meteora rocks near the point where the Peneios emerges from the Pindos gorges.

**History**. Kalambáka is the *Aiginion* of antiquity, a town of the Tymphaei stated by Livy to have been impregnable. Here Caesar joined Cnaeus Domitius before marching on Pharsalus. The Byzantines called the town *Stagoi*, perhaps a corruption of εἰς τοὺς Ἁγίους, and established a bishopric here in the 10C; the see is now at Tríkkala. In 1854 a force of Greeks captured and temporarily held Kalambáka against the Turks.

The **cathedral**, dedicated to the Dormition of the Virgin, bears an inscription ascribing its foundation to Manuel I Comnenos (mid 12C). The chrysobull of Andronikos III painted on the N wall of the narthex concerns the privileges of the diocese, not the building of the church. The present building, an aisled basilica, stands on even earlier foundations; some mosaics survive below the sanctuary floor. The apse as well as the **ciborium** and centrally placed **ambo** probably belonged to the earlier building. There are several layers of paintings. From the 12C decoration have survived some frescoes on the N wall of the diaconikon. The remaining scenes were painted by Cretan artists after a reconstruction in 1573, when the narthex and cloisters were added. The church of **Ayios Ioannis Prodromos** (11–14C) is constructed of Roman materials.

A road from the town centre leads round the W end of the colossal mass of rock that looms over Kalambáka. Beyond the by-road to **Kastráki** (1289 inhab.) you enter the weird valley of the Metéora. The foot-path is shorter.

The ***METÉORA** (Τα Μετέωρα) are a series of monastic buildings perched on a cluster of detached precipitous rocks. These are composed of a stratified conglomerate of iron-grey colour scarred by erosion of wind and streaked by centuries of rainwater. 'They rise' (in the words of Dr Henry Holland who visited them in 1812) 'from the comparatively flat surface of the valley; a group of isolated masses, cones, and pillars of rock, of great height, and for the most part so perpendicular in their ascent, that each one of their numerous fronts seems to the eye as a vast wall, formed rather by the art of man, than by the more varied and irregular workings of nature. In the deep and winding recesses which form the intervals between these lofty pinnacles, the thick foliage of trees gives a shade and colouring, which, while they enhance the contrast, do not diminish the effect of the great masses of naked rock impending above.' Awe-inspiring in the most favourable conditions, the landscape in lowering weather or by the light of the full moon is daunting in the extreme.

**History.** The earliest monastic community here, the 'Thebaid of Stagoi' at Doupiani developed before 1336 among the hermits who earlier sought religious isolation and a secure retreat from the turbulent times in these caves. Their protaton, or communal church, is located by a small chapel (see below) on old foundations. Before the end of the century this skete and its protos had been eclipsed by the meteoron, which, with other communities, was encouraged and endowed by the Orthodox Serbian conquerors of Thessaly. During the Turkish conquest the monasteries became an asylum for refugees. At its largest the community numbered 13 monasteries, all coenobite, and c 20 smaller settlements. They flourished under Abbot Bessarion in the time of Suleiman the Magnificent, deriving revenues from estates on the Danube granted by the voivodes of Wallachia. The Patriarch Jeremias I (1522–45) raised several of them to the rank of imperial stavropegion. They declined in the 18C, and were already a decaying curiosity to early-19C travellers. They lost their independence to the Bishop of Trikkala in 1899. The road that now makes the visit a commonplace of tourism has shattered the solitude and isolation. There are now only a handful of monks and nuns, largely occupied in receiving visitors. However, continuing religious occupation seems assured by the Church's policy of a period of monastic service for its priests.

Access was intentionally difficult, either by a series of vertical wooden ladders of vertiginous length (20–40m), which could be retracted at night or in emergency, or in a net drawn up by rope and windlass to specially built towers, overhanging the abyss. The old methods, uncomfortable at best and often perilous, gave way in the 1920s to steps cut on the orders of Polykarpos, Bishop of Trikkala, though the rope and windlass remained in occasional use for taking in provisions. The monasteries can mostly be visited daily 09.00–13.00, 15.30–18.00, but Ayios Stephanos is closed on Mondays, Metamorphosis on Tuesdays, the Great Metéora on Tuesdays and Varlaam on Fridays. There is now no guest-house. Rules of dress must be observed (no trousers for women or shorts for men).

Beyond the Kastráki turn the road bends right. On the left stands the **Doupianí Chapel** (see above), rebuilt in 1861. The 'Broad Rock' (left), on which is the Great Metéoron, rises above several lesser pillars: the cleft rock of the **Pródromos** whose scanty ruins, already deserted in 1745, are now

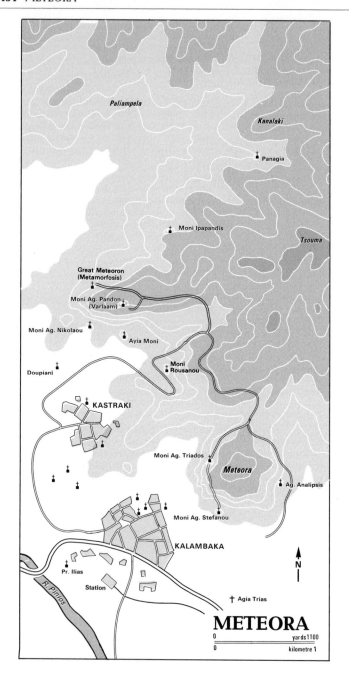

Paliampela

Kanalaki

Panagia

Moni Ipapandis

Tsouma

Great Meteoron
(Metamorfosis)

Moni Ag. Pandon
(Varlaam)

Moni Ag. Nikolaou

Ayia Moni

Moni
Rousanou

Doupiani

KASTRAKI

Moni Ag. Triados

Meteora

Ag. Analipsis

Moni Ag. Stefanou

KALAMBAKA

N

Pr. Ilias

Station

† Agia Trias

**METEORA**

0                yards 1100

0                kilometre 1

R. Pinios

inaccessible; on a higher point, near the road, is **Ayios Nikólaos tou Anapavsá** (c 1388), partly repaired in 1960 when its frescoes, by Theophanes the Cretan (1527), were restored; and the inaccessible **Ayía Moní**, dangerously perched on its slender pinnacle in 1614 and ruined in an earthquake in 1858. You leave Rousanou to the right, take the left fork, pass Barlaam (left), and arrive at the **Great Metéoron**, or coenobitic **Monastery of the Transfiguration,** the largest and loftiest of the monasteries, built on the Platys Lithos ('Broad Rock'; 534m).

The Great Meteoron was founded by St Athanasios as the poor community of the Theotokos Meteoritissa. Its privileges were guaranteed in 1362 by the Serbian Emperor Symeon Uroš and under the guidance of John Uroš, his son, who retired here c 1373 as the monk Ioasaph, it became a rich monastic house. Euthymios, Patriarch of Constantinople (1410–16), made it independent of local jurisdiction, but its head was not officially granted the title of Abbot (hegoumenos) until c 1482.

The katholikon was reconstructed by Ioasaph in 1387–88, at his own expense. His apse and sanctuary, painted in 1497–98, form the E extension of the existing church, which was enlarged after an earthquake in 1544. It is a Greek cross in square with a dome set on a drum. The paintings are well preserved. The refectory (1557), on the N side of the church, has a vaulted roof set on five pillars.

From the SE corner of the monastery (or from the path in the ravine towards Barlaam) there is a striking view of the neighbouring rock. Here among the vultures' nests can be made out two painted ikons and broken lengths of the ladders that once gave access to Hypselotéra, highest of the monasteries and dedicated to the 'Highest in the Heavens' ('Υψηλοτέρα των Ουρανών'). This convent was founded c 1390 and disappeared in the 17C, possibly owing to the danger of the ascent.

About 30 minutes N of the Broad Rock is the seldom-visited **Hypapantí**, derelict but still accessible, in a huge cavern. It deserves a visit for its brightly painted frescoes and gilded ikonostasis. The inaccessible **Ayios Dhimítrios** stands on top of a nearby rock. It was destroyed by Turkish gunfire in 1809 after having served as headquarters of a local klephtic band.

The monastery of **\*Barlaam** is approached by bridge from the road. The windlass and rope in the **tower** (erected in 1536) were much used for materials in 1961–63 when the refectory was reconstructed as a museum for the monastic treasures. The founders in 1517, Nektarios and Theophanes Asparas of Ioannina, reoccupied a site where a 14C anchorite named Barlaam had built a church dedicated to the Three Hierarchs. This they restored and it survives (repaired and frescoed in 1627–37) as a side chapel of the present katholikon erected in 1542–44. This is a good example of the late-Byzantine style with a carved and gilded ikonostasis and frescoes by Frangos Kastellanos and George of Thebes (in the narthex; 1566).

You return to the main fork. Easily accessible is **Rousánou**, a small monastery compactly set on a lower hill. The approach is by bridges, built in 1868. It was founded before 1545 by Maximos and Ioasaph of Ioannina, but by 1614 had decayed to such an extent that it was made subject to Barlaam. It is now occupied by a convent of nuns. The **church**, with an octagonal dome, is a smaller version of that of Barlaam, with frescoes of 1560.

**Ayía Triádha**, the monastery of the Holy Trinity, situated on an isolated pillar between two ravines, is entered by 130 steps partly in a tunnel through the rock. Off the passage leading into the courtyard a round chapel carved out of the rock was dedicated to St John the Baptist in 1682. The little **church** of 1476, ornamented in brick and tile, was not improved by the addition in 1684 of a large and ugly narthex. The conventual buildings are in an attractive half-timbered style with a pretty garden.

The **Moní Ayíou Stefánou**, or nunnery of St Stephen, is the only monastery visible from Kalambaka. It is easily reached since its solitary pinnacle is joined directly to the Kuklióli hill by a bridge. The convent was founded c 1400 by Antonios Cantacuzene (probably a son of Nikephoros II of Epirus), whose portrait in the **parecclesion** (the original katholikon) was defaced by Communist rebels in 1949. The **new katholikon**, rebuilt in 1798, is dedicated to the martyr Charalambos, whose head is the monastery's chief relic.

# B.   From (Tríkkala) Kalambáka to Ioánnina

**Road**, 152km (94½ miles). To (21km) Kalambáka, see above.—80.5km Katára Pass.—93km Métsovo (2km S).—152km Ioánnina. Two **buses** daily. This is a mountain road of spectacular grandeur, crossing the highest pass in Greece open to motor traffic. Although improved to a high standard, it may be closed by snow in winter and, even in early summer, the snow-line must be crossed.

The **Píndos**, or **Pindus Mountains**, an offshoot of the Dinaric Alps and an integral part of the backbone of Greece, runs from N to S and separates Epirus from Thessaly. From its S end a branch, under the name of Othrys, starting from Mt Velouchi (Timfristos), runs E to the Gulf of Volos and bounds the Thessalian plain on the S. The highest of the range's many peaks rise to the E and SE of Ioannina: these include **Kakardhitsa** (2320m), **Peristeri** (2295m) and **Kataphidhi** (2393m). Farther S the range divides: the W branch, culminating in **Tsournata** (2168m), is separated by the valley of the Agrafa from the E branch, the **Agrafa Mountains** (*Dolopia* in antiquity). In Classical times the highest peak was called *Lakmon*, a name later transferred to Mt Zygos (1555m), a peak to the E of Peristeri. The mountain sides are thickly wooded with trees of beech, oak and pine to within a short distance of the bare crests. Five important rivers have their source in the Pindos: the **Arakhthos**, flowing S through Epirus into the Gulf of Arta; the **Akheloös**, through Epirus, Akarnania, and Aitolia into the Ionian Sea, but in the process of partial diversion in the opposite direction to water Thessaly (see Rtes 47C, 54); the **Aoös**, through Epirus and Albania into the Adriatic; the **Aliakmon** and the **Pinios** into the Gulf of Thessaloniki. In many parts of the range the rivers find their way down through deep valleys or gorges. Wolves and wild boar are still common in places; brown bears survive, and, in smaller numbers, the lynx. Of the larger birds Egyptian and Griffon vultures greatly outnumber the Golden Eagle.

Journeys in the Pindos other than by the Katara Pass or the Karpenisi–Frangista route in the S (Rte 54) are often still difficult (see also Rte 47C). Off the beaten track careful planning and proper equipment are necessary (a trek led in 1963 is described by Sir John Hunt in the *Geog. Jnl*, September 1964).

From Tríkkala to (21km) **Kalambáka**, see above. The Metsovo road leads W past the Xenia motel and ascends the valley of the Peneios in company with the earthworks of an abandoned railway (to Kozáni; see Rte 58), begun by a Belgian company before 1939. At (31km) **Kháni Mourgáni** the road to Grevená (Rte 62) diverges to the right. The Peneios is crossed by a Bailey bridge. A by-road goes off (left) across a bridge of 11 arches to **Kastaniá** (18km) and **Amáranto** (21km) in a side valley to the S. The road now gains height on the slopes of the flat-topped Mt Orthovoúni (1106m). At (47km) Orthovoúni (680m) the peaks of **Notia**, usually snow-covered, are prominent to the SW, while the ranges ahead fill the horizon in a seemingly level circle. The road continues at the higher level along the S slopes of **Kratsovon** (1565m). Beyond (55km) **Trigón**, steep descent. Just after (57km) a petrol station, you pass below **Pévki** (right). Panayía is seen far ahead. 64km **Koridhallós** stands to the E of a pass into an isolated valley of the Khasia range. You cross a mountain torrent to (68km) **Koutsofianí**, a hamlet above the large village of **Panayía** which dominates the junction of the valleys. The road now climbs sharply in zigzags towards the main watershed between Khásia (right) and Notiá (left). Turning to **Malakási** (6km, left). The holm-oak gives place to pine and beech. 76km **Kámbos tou Dhespóti** (restaurant; petrol) at a height of 1300m.

There follows the ascent to (80.5km) the **Pass of Katára** (1707m; refuge). Just before the summit splendid view in both directions. The road winds round the head of the W valley, keeping nearly level for some distance. After a mile or two in disappointingly bleak and enclosed surroundings, sudden superb *view of Metsovo backed by a gigantic range of snow-clad peaks. The road makes a great loop, descending amid slopes clothed in fir, beech, and box, with fine mountain views in every direction. Turning to **Vovoúsa** (right; 35.5km), an isolated village in the Valiakalda range. At 93km you leave the main road at a saw-mill and in 2km reach Metsovo.

**Métsovo** (Μέτσοβο; Hotels A–E), has the status of deme and eparchy though little more than a large mountain village, with 2917 inhabitants, many of them Vlachs. The attractive houses are built in terraces on the steep side of a mountain separated from Mt Zygos (1555m) by two deep ravines. The town is divided by the chasm of the Metsovitikos into two parts—the 'Prosilio' (exposed to the sun) and the 'Anilio' (away from the sun)—which are connected by a bridge. All the five great rivers in the Pindos have their sources near Metsovo. The views on all sides are wonderful and the air exhilarating. The woollen rugs and local embroidered textiles are very attractive. The *museum (Mouseío Laïkís Tékhnis; visit guided), a beautiful display of the handicrafts of the region, occupies the restored 'arkhontikó' of Baron Michael Tositsa (1885–1950).

In the 17C a Turkish vizier, in disgrace with his sultan, sought asylum at Métsovo and was kindly treated. Later returning to favour at court, he repaid the generosity of his hosts when, in 1669, the town was granted special privileges, giving it virtual independence which lasted to the time of Ali Pasha. Many rich Christian families took refuge at Metsovo, which has since had a reputation for its philanthropists, among them George Averoff (1815–99). The monastery of Ayios Nikolaos has frescoes by Eustathios (1702).

**Buses** daily to Athens, via Tríkkala or via Ioánnina; to Thessaloníki, to Ioánnina.

Above Metsovo you emerge high above the Metsovitikos, longest affluent of the Arachthos, in a wild landscape of sandstone. The road here is subject to falls of rock. It descends the rugged N side of the gorge, across which, above the gentler forest-clad S slopes, tower the outlying crags and central mass of **Peristéri** (2295m). At (104km) **Votonósi**, where Tsolakoglou (first Quisling prime minister of Greece) signed an armistice with the Germans in 1941, the vegetation becomes less alpine; judas-trees, walnuts, etc. are seen again. You descend to the swift-flowing river. A by-road to Peristéri crosses the river by a Turkish pack-horse bridge. The road rises higher as the river drops below into a wild boulder-strewn gorge, while Peristéri rises to view again on the left.

There is a splendid *view down the widening river on the ascent round the S side of Mt Dhemati. Across the river on Mt Gradhetsi, above **Mikrá Gótista**, is the highest fortified enceinte of antiquity (3C BC) yet found in Greece (1562m). Ahead rises the streaked, forbidding **Mitsikeli** range (1809m) as you descend to (126km) **Baldoúmas** (café; petrol) and cross the tributary Zagoritikos on a Bailey-bridge. The road now climbs in serpentine loops over the S part of Mitsikeli, with retrospective *vistas of range upon range of the Pindos. 137km **Mázia** occupies the saddle between Mitsikeli and Dhriskos. From the summit the descent gives views across Lake Pamvotis. Monuments between here and Ioannina are described in Rte 52A. 139km (left) **Dourahán Monastery**. 145km **Stroúni** is a starting-point for climbing Mitsikeli (Refuge 2½ hrs above the village). The road descends to (148km) **Pérama**. 152km **Ioánnina** (Rte 52A).

# VI NORTH-WESTERN GREECE

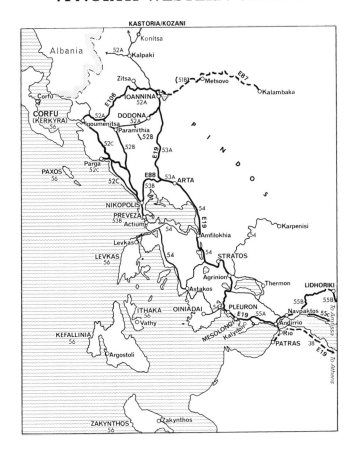

**Epirus** or **Ipiros** (Ηπειρος; 'The Mainland'), the NW province of Greece, is separated from Albania by an artificial frontier, and from Thessaly by the Pindus range. On the S it is washed by the Gulf of Arta and on the W by the Ionian Sea, with the island of Corfu lying opposite the frontier between Greece and Albania. The mountainous character of the interior and difficulties of communication have always isolated Epirus, whose inhabitants were only partly Hellenic. The few Greek colonies were confined to the coast and to the low-lying region of the S. The province, the most humid in Greece, is well wooded and produces a little corn; it has long been famous for its flocks and pasturage and for its breed of Molossian dogs. Its principal rivers are the Arta (Arachthos), the Kalamas (Thyamis), and the Mavropotamos (Acheron). Epirus is divided into four nomes: Ioannina, Preveza, Arta, and Thesprotia. The largest towns are Ioannina and Arta, both well inland, and Preveza, on the coast. The main roads are now good. In antiquity the oracle of Dodona was renowned as the oldest in Greece.

**History**. Of the 14 tribes inhabiting Epirus, the chief were the Chaones, the Thesproti and the Molossi, which gave their names to the three main divisions of the country. Each tribe was governed by its own prince. The Molossians, who claimed descent from Neoptolemos (Pyrrhus), son of Achilles, later took over the whole country as kings of Epirus. The most famous of these kings was Pyrrhus (318–272 BC). In 286 he invaded Macedonia, of which he became king for a brief period. In 280 he accepted the invitation of the Tarentines to join them in their war against Rome. After his victory at Heraclea, he came within 24 miles of Rome. A second Pyrrhic victory, at Asculum (Apulum), in 279, exhausted both sides. After adventures in Sicily helping the Greeks against the Carthaginians, Pyrrhus returned to Italy in 276; his defeat near Beneventum in the following year obliged him to leave Italy for good. But he did not remain idle. In 273 he again invaded Macedonia, becoming king for the second time, again for a short period. Afterwards he turned against Sparta and Argos, where he was ignominiously killed. After his death the kingship of Epirus was abolished, and the country divided between three generals. In the Macedonian wars, Epirus joined the Macedonians, went over to the Romans (198), and then turned against them (170). After the defeat at Pydna in 168 of Perseus, the last king of Macedon, 70 towns in Epirus were destroyed, 150,000 of the inhabitants enslaved, and the country became a Roman province.

In the Middle Ages Epirus was constantly invaded. After the division of the Byzantine empire the country was divided into **New Epirus**, with Dyrrachium (Durazzo), and **Old Epirus**, with Acarnania. After the capture of Constantinople by the Crusaders in 1204, a despotate of Epirus was set up. The first despot, Michael I, made Ioannina his capital. A later despot, Theodore Angelus, seized the Latin kingdom of Thessalonika in 1223. The dynasty expired at the end of the 13C. In 1318–35 Epirus with Cephalonia came under the domination of the Orsini, returned briefly to Byzantium, fell to the Serbs (1348–86), and returned to Cephalonia under the Tocci. The Turks captured Ioannina in 1431. In the 15C and 16C the Venetians occupied several strong points in the country. Epirus took no part in the War of Independence. In 1881 the District of Arta was freed from Turkish domination. During the Second Balkan War the Greek army took Ioannina (February 1913), and occupied all the north of Epirus; but much of the liberated territory was subsequently given to Albania. This contains a large Greek-speaking community and is usually spoken of in Greece as 'Northern Epirus'. In the Second World War the Greek army threw back the invading Italians in 1940 and, until the German intervention, reoccupied Northern Epirus.

Aitolía and Akarnanía (Αιτωλακαρνανία), together form the most westerly nome of Central Greece, lying between Epirus and the Gulf of Patras. **Aitolia**, on the E, is divided from Akarnania by the river Akheloös. Its W half, lying between the Akheloös and the Evenos, was anciently called *Old Aetolia* and included the city of Kalydon, mythologically famous for the boar hunt. **New Aetolia** or **Aitolia Epiktetos** ('Acquired Aetolia') extended to the E from the Evenos to the country of the Ozolian Locrians. The interior of Aitolia is roadless, wild and mountainous, with numerous peaks exceeding 1800m, and is accessible only to determined travellers.

*Aetolia*, originally inhabited by the Curetes, derives its name from Aetolos, son of Endymion, who fled here after having killed Apis. The five cities of Old Aetolia all took part in the Trojan War. The three tribes living in New Aetolia were barbarous, ate raw flesh, and spoke an unintelligible dialect (Thuc. III, 94). Loosely connected by a religious tie, they had a common temple at the sanctuary of Thermon. After the battle of Chaironeia (338 BC), they formed the Aetolian League which, at the beginning of the 3C BC, was strong enough to frustrate the invading armies of the Gaul Brennus. Before the expansion of the rival Achaean League under Aratos, the Aetolians reached the zenith of their power. They acquired or dominated Locris, Phocis, central Akarnania, and Boeotia, as well as numerous cities in the Peloponnesus. In the ruinous War of the Leagues (219–217 BC), Philip V of Macedon, with the Achaeans as allies, invaded Aetolia. In 211 the Aetolians allied themselves with Rome, and in 197 helped the Romans to win the battle of Cynoscephalae. Later they joined Antiochus the Great against the Romans, and in the peace of 188 their federation was virtually dissolved. In 31, after the battle of Actium, Octavian (Augustus) completed the depopulation caused by centuries of warfare by transferring most of the inhabitants to his new city of Nikopolis, on the Epirus side of the Ambracian Gulf. In the War of Independence the Aetolians defeated the Turks at Karpenisi, and Mesolongi endured three sieges.

**Akarnanía** has the sea on three sides. It is bounded on the N by the Ambracian Gulf. The W coast is joined by a causeway to the island of Levkas. There are two other Ionian Islands—Ithaca and Kefallinia—and numerous islets to the S. A mountain range (over 1500m) occupies most of the eparchy of Xiromeros between Astakós, on the S coast, and Vónitsa, on the Ambracian Gulf.

The Akarnanians emerged from obscurity at the beginning of the Peloponnesian War (431 BC). Like the Aetolians, they were uncivilised, living by piracy and robbery, and like them formed their towns into a league, which first met at Stratos, the chief town. South and central Aetolia are entirely agricultural, but the cultivation is not intensive. Currants are grown near Mesolongi, olives round Aitoliko, and tobacco near Agrinion. The mountain eparchies depend upon the produce of the forests; Xeromeros, in Akarnania, exports valonia, the acorn of the *Quercus aegilops*, used for tanning.

# 52

# From Igoumenítsa to Ioánnina, Párga and Préveza

## A. To Ioánnina (and Dodóna; also Víkos Gorge and Kónitsa, for Neápolis and the north)

**Road** 101km (63 miles), a modern highway through rugged mountainous country. **Buses** regularly.

**Igoumenítsa** (Hotels B, C, D, E; F/A), the first port of call on the Greek mainland of car ferries from Brindisi and other Italian ports, and the terminus of a local ferry (6–10 times daily; see Rte 56) from Corfu, was an insignificant village until, in 1936, it became the seat of the nomarch of Thesprotia. Rebuilt on the ruins left by the occupying troops in 1944, it is now a flourishing transit town (6807 inhab.) with a pleasant sea front.

Through the formerly marshy plain to the N the Kalamas, the ancient *Thyamis*, winds its way to the channel separating Corfu from the mainland. A barrage (1962) at the exit of the last defile now controls irrigation, and experiments are being made in rice growing. The small hills which rise above the marsh are considered by some authorities to represent the ancient *Sybota Islands*, near which a naval battle was fought in 433 BC between the Corinthians and Corcyraeans (Thuc. I, 45). Their name is now held by a group of islands between Igoumenitsa and Parga to the S. Several of the hills are crowned with ancient forts, as Pírgos, S of Kato Kalamatá.

On Mt Vriséla, near Goúmani to the N of Igoumenitsa, are the substantial remains of an ancient settlement.

From Igoumenitsa to **Preveza**, see Rte 52B, 52C: to **Parga**, see Rte 52C.

Climbing out of Igoumenitsa, the Ioannina road enters a level valley enclosed by rugged mountains. 9km Turning to Filiátes and Sayiádha.

This road runs out towards the Albanian frontier and military restrictions may be encountered. 1km You cross the Kalamas (military check at the bridge). 3km **Elaía** (the road from Elaia back to the main road near Neraḯdha, marked as good on many maps, is not so). Nearby at **Velianí** is a fortified Hellenistic settlement. 8km **Filiátes** (220m) is a lively market town. The former Turkish population dwindled in the plague of 1821 and the town was repopulated by Christian refugees. A cheese factory was built in 1963–65 by United Nations Association volunteers. **Yeroméri**, nearby, has a monastery founded in 1285. 14km Turning to **Plaísi** (5km), a decayed old town with a 17C church, which in the 19C had flourishing tanneries. It was the birthplace of Kyra Vasiliki, consort of Ali Pasha. Besieged by Albanians in 1908–13 and looted and burnt in 1943, it now has only a third of its former population. 23km **Sayiádha**, rebuilt on the coast after the hill town was destroyed in 1940–41, has a jetty opposite Corfu, and a ferry service. The ruins of the old town can be seen high above the road.

The main road turns S to cross a spur and descends again to the river, which here makes a wide loop through a gorge to the N. It follows the right bank below steep hills; the villages lie across the river. The precipitous W ranges of the Pindus rise ahead. The Paramithiá road (see Rte 52B) diverges 1km before (23km) **Menína** (officially **Neraḯdha**). The route rises continuously amid scrub, passing a turning to the 16C **Moní Pagáni**. Beyond (38.5km) **Plakotí**, it zigzags sharply up to 610m while the river threads another ravine. In the local collection of antiquities at **Polídhroso** (10km further, below) is the first complete Etruscan 'jockey-cap' helmet to be found in Greece, perhaps brought to the area by a veteran of the wars of Pyrrhos. The view opens out ahead (café) as you descend by continuous turns to rejoin the river at (52km) **Vrosína**, where an old packhorse bridge (left) crosses a tributary. The road crosses the Tyrias and undulates through cultivated hills.

At (69.5km) **Soulópoulo** you cross another affluent of the Kalamas and climb out of the river basin through countryside patterned by stone walls. 84km Turn (left) for **Zítsa** (12km; 680m), a picturesque little town (792 inhab.) locally renowned for its sweetish semi-sparkling wine (wine festival at monastery). Prosperity in Turkish times is attested by its stone houses and paved streets. The monasteries of **Profítis Ilías** and **ton Patéron** (14C), fired with nationalist zeal in 1778 by Kosmas Aitolou, fostered Greek schools. Byron sings the charms of the view in *Childe Harold* (II, xlviii): a plaque commemorates his visit.

86km Turning for **Rodhotópi** (5km) with slight remains of ancient *Passaron*, a Molossian town which survived into Roman times. The site of its Sanctuary of Zeus Areios was identified by inscriptions in 1954. At 92.5km you join the Kónitsa road in the upland plain N of Ioannina. Beyond the airport, at the N end of the lake, the Métsovo road (Rte 51B) comes in from the left.

101km **IOÁNNINA** (Τά Ιωάννινα; commonly Iánnina), a deme (56,699 inhab.) of the eparchy of Dodona, is the capital of the nome of Ioánnina, the seat of the Government-General of Epirus and of an archbishop, an army headquarters and a university town. It occupies a rocky promontory jutting into Lake Pambotis opposite the foot of the precipitous Mt Mitsikeli. The busy and friendly town lies at 475m in the midst of a plain divided between pasture and the cultivation of cereals and tobacco. Local industries include the manufacture of filigree silver jewellery. To the E and SE rise the highest peaks of the Pindus. In summer the temperature is oppressive; winters are long and cold. Motorists should note that the one-way system is impenetrable.

**Airport**, with services once or twice daily to Athens; three times weekly to Thessaloniki; weekly to Tirana (Albania). Olympic Airways in upper, main square, Mégaro Kourtío.

**Hotels** A, B, C, D.

**Post Office**, Od. Nap. Zérva/Plat. Pírrou; **OTE**, Od. 28 Oktovríou. **Information Bureau (NTO)**, Od. Nap. Zérva: tel. (0651) 25086. **Police/Tourist Police**, 28 Oktovríou.

**Bookshop**, Dhodhóni, Od. Mikhaïl Angélou.

**Car Hire**, Budget Od. Nap. Zérva 24 and others.

**Buses** from 19 Vizaníou (Plateía Pírrou) (KTEL 13 Agrinion) regularly to Arta, continuing sometimes to Agrinion, Mesolongi, and Patras; also Préveza and Dodona; from KTEL 21, 4 Zosimádhou, to Perama, Igoumenitsa, Konitsa, Metsovo; Athens, Thessaloniki etc.

**History**. *Ioannina* is first documented in 1020 and may have taken its name and site from a monastery of St John the Baptist. Taken by Bohemond, eldest son of Robert Guiscard, in the 11C, it was visited in 1160 by Benjamin of Tudela. Ioannina dates its importance, however, from the influx of refugees in 1205 from Constantinople and the Morea and its consequent fortification by Michael I Angelos. An archbishopric was established here between 1284 and 1307. In 1345 Ioannina was captured by the Serb Stefan Dušan, proclaimed in the following year Emperor of Serbia and Greece. In 1431 it surrendered to the army of the Sultan Murad II. In 1618, after an abortive rising led by Dionysos 'Skylosophos', the fanatical Bishop of Trikkala, the Christians were expelled from the citadel and their churches destroyed. Nevertheless in 1666 Spon found the town rich and populous. It reached a zenith under *Ali Pasha* (born in 1741 at the Albanian village of Tepelini), a brilliant, resourceful, and vindictive adventurer who alternately fought and served the Sultan of Turkey. Having assisted the Turks in

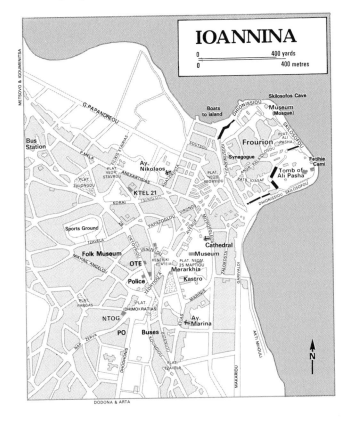

their war of 1787 against Austria, he was made Pasha of Trikkala in 1788, in which year he seized Ioannina, then a town of 35,000 inhabitants, and made it his head-quarters. In 1797 he allied himself with Napoleon, but the next year took Preveza from the French. In 1803 he subdued the Suliots. After 1807 his dependence on the Porte was merely nominal. Byron visited Ioannina in 1809, while Colonel W.M. Leake, the great topographer of Greece, was British resident, and Henry Holland was Ali Pasha's doctor. In 1817 Ali entered into an alliance with the British, who gave him Parga. At length the Sultan decided to eliminate this daring rebel. He was captured at Ioannina after a siege, and executed there in 1822. Two years before his death, besieged by Ismail Pasha, he had set fire to the town. The Congress of Berlin (1878) assigned Epirus to Greece, but it remained in Turkish hands for over 35 more years. On 21 February 1913, the Greek army entered Ioannina. The (Romaniote) Jewish community is thought to date from the reign of Alexander the Great (see Rae Dalven, *The Jews of Ioannina*, 1990). In 1904 it numbered 4000 but was practically obliterated in the Second World War.

Ioannina was long famous for its **Schools**, founded by Michael Philanthropinos (1682–1758), Leondati Giouma (1675–1725), and Meletios (1690), later Bishop of Athens and a noted historian and geographer. They were all destroyed in the fire of 1820.

The social life of Ioannina centres on Odhos Dhodhónis which connects Plateía Dhimokratías (formerly Pírrou), a beautiful belvedere laid out in front of the **Nomarkhía** (Municipal Offices; *view of Mitsikeli), and the Plateía 25 Martíou with its clock tower (To Rolóï) farther down the hill. Immediately below the Nomarkhia, Od. Mikhaíl Angélou (running W) has, in a restored Ottoman building, a good **Folk Art Museum** (Mon. 17.00–20.00; Wed. 11.00–13.00 only) with an extensive collection of Epirote costume, also ceramics and domestic and agricultural implements. Commanding the Central Square is the **Merarkhía** (army HQ) in front of which the Colours are ceremonially lowered each evening. Behind, the museum and gardens occupy the levelled upper esplanade of the kastro, which once sheltered the Christian quarter of Litharitsa: its walls were demolished by Ali Pasha and the material used to build his palace and outer fortifications of the town. The N part of the castle has been restored as a café-restaurant.

The *Archaeological Museum** (1970; 08.30–15.00, closed Mon.) has six halls. HALL A (right), cases arranged chronologically from right to left. Case 1. Stone and bone objects from Cambridge University excavations in Palaeolithic caves at Asprokhalikó and Kastrítsa. Cases 2 & 3. Neolithic and Bronze Age finds, chiefly from LHIIIB–C cist graves (swords, daggers, axes). Case 4. Protogeometric vases from the region of Agrinio. Cases 5–9 (and three centre cases), finds from the cemeteries of Vitsa, ranging from 9C Geometric to late-Classical; notable are the small stylised Geometric horse (Case 7) and a fine bronze kylix (Case 9); two superb bronze beaked *pitchers (centre). Case 10. Vases and terracotta figurines of Persephone from the Nekyomanteion of Ephyra (see Rte 52C), also the windlass mechanism. In Case 11 (various sites) note the finger ring of crystal with a sculptured bull, also elaborate gold earrings, from Ambracia; small gilded bronze plaque depicting Klytemnestra and Orestes. Case 12 includes heads of various Goddesses.

Table cases 13 & 14. Epirote coins. Some of the large bronze *vessels from the Votonosi hoard discovered in 1939 are displayed in Case 15, while Cases 16–20 and VIII–XI contain *votive bronzes (eagle, warriors, boy with dove, lion) and oracular tablets of lead from Dodona. In wall case, reconstruction of door of bouleuterion at Dodona, using original fittings.

In the CORRIDOR are grave stelai from various sites, inscriptions from Dodona, Ionic capitals from Kassope, and grave goods from Mikhalitsi (model cart from a child burial). HALL B. Marble sculptures from Mikhalitsi include female heads and an elaborate sarcophagus. HALL C (right). Finds from recent excavations at the site of the new university (Panepistemioupolis) in Cases 23, 26, 28 (right on entry) including iron tools and weapons and two 'Illyrian' helmets; three impressive Roman sarcophagi with mythological scenes, from Ladhokhori. End wall. Recent prehistoric finds from tumuli at Kato Merope etc., near the Albanian border; bronzes from Stephane (Preveza); a fine Thracian or Phrygian helmet; tools and weapons from Dodona (Case 25, left); material from the Vitsa cemetery (Case 24). HALLS D and E (left). 19–20C paintings and sculpture. HALL F (right). Fine Frankish-Byzantine *capitals from a church at Gliki; hoards of Venetian coins; an ecclesiastical collection of icons, books, church plate and jewellery.

Odhós Avérof, lined with silversmiths, descends directly to the frourion. Lower down, off to the left, the narrow streets have small traditional shops and cafeneions crowded together. The **frourion**, the fortress of the Despots, was restored in 1815 by Ali Pasha as his headquarters. The **walls**, though impressive, preserve very little Byzantine work. The landward side was protected by the 'khandáki', a moat (now filled in) joining the two little landing places (see below) and crossed by three wooden bridges. At the W, in the former Jewish quarter is a **synagogue** of Romaniote type, still in use. Towards the NW is the former **Turkish library**, restored in 1973. Enclosed by a wall in the NW corner, overlooking the lake, is the picturesque *Cami of Aslan Pasha, a conventual foundation of 1618. An implausible tradition places here the rape and murder in 1801 of Kyra Phrosyne and her 17 companions. The mosque, which continued in use until 1928, now houses the crowded **Municipal Museum** (08.00–15.00). On the way up are cannon and piles of balls. Note the recesses for shoes in the vestibule. The mosque has a well-proportioned dome. Striking among the exhibits are the Epirote costumes and adornments of the 18–19C; also a Roman sarcophagus.

The **minaret** (closed at present) has a superb *view of the lake and the surrounding mountains. You look down (SE) on the inner citadel of **Its-Kalé** (military; adm. sometimes granted) with the **Fetihie Cami**, or Victory Mosque, a circular **tower**, the **Tomb of Ali Pasha**, and the restored **palace** or serai where the 'Lion of Ioannina' entertained Byron and Hobhouse in October 1809. Nearby was the residence of the Byzantine archon. N of the palace are some remains of a Byzantine bath complex.

The shady Leofóros Dhionissíou Skilosófou runs by the lakeside beneath the walls. In the cliff is the cave where the Skylosophos was caught and flayed alive in 1611. From the S corner of the frourio, roads wind westwards to the **cathedral** (Ayios Athanasios), rebuilt in 1820, with ornate carved woodwork and the tomb of a local patriot of 1828. You continue S below the kastro to the picturesque Odhos Koungíou which ascends to Plateía Dhimokratías (see above).

The **Lake of Ioannina**, or **Limni Pambotis**, is fed by torrents from the precipices of Mitsikeli and discharges its waters into swallow-holes. It is 10–11km long, averages 3km across, and ranges in depth from 9–20m, with shallow reedy shores. After very wet weather it may join up with the Lapsista marsh to the N. There is a 2000m international rowing course. The local boats are similar in design to those on Lake Kastoria. Boats (half-hourly in summer, from Plateía Mavíli, by the frourio) cross to the island (tavernas; trout, crayfish and eels; tourist shops; rooms) in the lake, on which are numerous monasteries very prettily situated amid trees and flowers. East of the little island village is the **Monastery of the Prodhromos** (St John the Baptist). The oldest (13C) parts are the katholikon and the E aisle. It was restored in the 16C, the 18C frescoes in the 19C. In the 16C **Monastery of Pantaleímon**, nearby, Ali Pasha was killed on 17 January 1822; the bullet marks on the floor witness to his assassination. The katholikon is in the form of a basilica. There is a small **museum** of prints and costumes. The **Philanthropinón Monastery** (Ayios Nikólaos Spanós), on a rocky height to the N of the village, was built in the 13C and rebuilt in the 16C. It has a katholikon with decorated doors and outstanding 16C frescoes.

In the **apse**, Communion of Saints. In the **nave** vault, the Almighty and the Evangelists; on the walls, Life of Jesus. **Narthex**: in the vault, Annunciation; N side, the five founders of the monastery kneeling before St Nicholas; above, Head of Christ; NW corner, portraits of Greek philosophers.

The **Monastery of Ayios Nikólaos Dhílios**, or Stratigopoúlou, is the oldest (11C). It lies to the E of the Philanthropinon. In the katholikon, fresco (restored in 16C): Judas returning his pieces of silver. In the narthex, Lives of the Virgin and St Nicholas, Last Judgement. To the S the **Monastery of Eleoúses** takes its name from a 15C ikon of the Panayia Eleousa, brought here from the kastro. The katholikon (before 1584) has 18C frescoes.

At the N end of the lake, towards **Pérama** (4km; take the Tríkkala road and turn left at sign; bus) are a spectacular series of *caverns, discovered by accident when places of refuge were being sought in the Second World War. Their stalagmites and stalactites are carefully lit and well worth a visit; parties are taken through the ½-mile of galleries by guides (08.00–sunset).

Beyond Perama a road diverges (right, signed 'Amphithéa') to follow the lakeside (pleasant tavernas) reaching in 4km the monastery of **Panayía Dourahán** (Koimesis tes Theotokou), which is reputed to have been founded in 1434 by Dourahan Pasha as a thank offering to the Virgin for protecting his night ride across the frozen lake.

At the S end of the lake, on the hill of **Kastrítsa**, near an old monastery, is the site of ancient *Tekmona*. Below this, Palaeolithic remains were dug in 1966 by the British School. Kastrítsa (c 8km) is reached, via Katsiká, by taking the W lakeshore road southwards out of Ioannina and branching left.

At **Mouzakéoi**, 14km SE of Ioannina, is the **Vrellis Museum** of wax effigies of figures of the pre-revolutionary period (1611–1821). The collection will be transferred to **Bizáni** (Rte 53A).

The EXCURSION TO DODONA should not be missed. **Road** 22km (13½ miles), bus daily. (For the approach from **Paramithiá** (55km), see Rte 52B.) You take the Arta road, passing the Xenia Hotel, an artillery barracks, then (5km) the modern buildings of the university on the hillside (site of a large Archaic and Classical cemetery) to the right, and run level through tobacco fields with distant views (left) of the Pindus. At 8km you turn right and wind over a ridge (fine retrospective views of the lake and the Pindos) into the enclosed valley of Tsarkovitsa at the foot of Mt Tomaros, whose long ridge

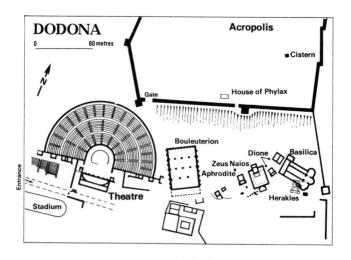

rises from the N end (1332m) to two peaks at the S (Mt Olitsikas; 1974m). 19.5km By-road (right) for Konstániani and Paramithiá (see Rte 52B).

A **tourist pavilion** (5 rooms) lies at the entrance to (22km) the ruins of *Dodóna* (08.00–17.00), beautifully sited facing Mt Tómaros amid fresh and smiling scenery. The modern village of **Dhodhóni** (Δωδώνη) stands a little farther W.

The Oracle of Zeus at Dodona, regarded as Pelasgic, was reputedly the oldest in Greece. 'Wintry Dodona' is mentioned in both *Iliad* and *Odyssey*. Strabo says that the oracle was moved from Skotoussa, in Thessaly, in obedience to the command of Apollo, but Herodotus tells of the arrival of a dove from Egyptian Thebes, which settled in an oak tree at Dodona. Homer assumes that the servers were men, called them *selloi*, prophets of Zeus, who did not wash their feet and slept on the ground. In the time of Plato, however, the divine message was given by priestesses in a state of inspired frenzy. According to Herodotus the oracle spoke in the rustling of leaves in the sacred oaks in sounds made by beating a copper vessel with a whip. The Molossian word 'peleiae' seems to have meant both doves and old women; there are trees but no oaks in the vicinity today and the main sound is the tinkling of sheep bells.

The site was identified in 1873 by Constantine Karapanos, who discovered a number of bronze objects now in the museum at Athens. More scientific excavations have been undertaken by the Greek Archaeological Service since 1952 and some judicious restoration made.

You enter along the axis of the **stadium**, of which part of the sphendone has been uncovered. The seating rises on the N side on a bank thrown up against the W retaining wall of the theatre at the end of the 3C BC. The superb *theatre was judiciously restored in 1960–63 for use at the annual festival of drama. Constructed originally in the time of Pyrrhus (297–272 BC), it was destroyed by the Aetolians in 219 BC and rebuilt shortly afterwards by Philip V out of the spoils taken from Thermon. It suffered at the hands of the Romans in 168–167 BC and was converted into an arena about the time of Augustus when the lowest seating was replaced by a protective wall (see below).

The **skene** is built in good isodomic masonry. The outer **façade** consisted of a stoa of 13 octagonal columns. An **arch** admitted to the centre of the stage. Double **gateways**, with Ionic half-columns, open into either parodos, leading to the **orchestra**. The fine horseshoe-shaped drainage channel is well-preserved.

The **cavea** is partly recessed in the side of the acropolis hill and partly supported by massive retaining walls (up to 21m high) of excellent rusticated ashlar masonry, buttressed by towers. It is divided by two diazomata, the three resulting banks of seats having 21 (reduced later to 15; see above), 16, and 21 rows (the lower two banks restored to position). Ten stairways divided the lower banks into 9 kerkides, while the topmost bank has 18 wedges. Two broad staircases added later against the façade lead up to the upper diazoma, while a **ceremonial entrance** from the direction of the acropolis opens into the topmost gallery; here cuttings show where a gate fitted. The back retaining wall is almost complete, though some wall slabs of the gallery have fallen forward.

Behind the theatre a well-preserved **gate** leads into the **acropolis**. The surrounding wall, 3–4.5m wide, is now less than 3m high. The enclosure is roughly quadrilateral with towers on three sides. The fabric is of various periods with Hellenistic predominating.

A path descends to the terrace, E of the theatre, site of the **sanctuary**. Only foundations remain. The large hypostyle hall is shown by inscribed decrees and an inscribed altar to be the **bouleuterion** of the Epirot confederacy built by Pyrrhus. To the S of the bouleuterion, a rectangular building has been the focus of recent work (Prof. S. Dakaris). Built in the early 3C and destroyed in 169, it was probably the **prytaneion**. It has a large room with benches for delegates, and a Doric colonnaded court to the E. The W wall of the peristyle was part of the original boundary of the sanctuary. Late 3C additions included dining and service rooms and an Ionic stoa to the E. Further to the E, is a small, rectangular **Temple of Aphrodite**. The **Temenos of Zeus Naios**, or **Hiera Oikia**, is a complex ruin in which four phases can be distinguished. At first worship centred upon the sacred oak-tree; fragments of votive tripods of the 8C BC have been recovered. A stone temple was not built until the 4C, when it consisted merely of cella and pronaos. This and the oak were then surrounded by a peribolos wall. The wall was replaced in the time of Pyrrhus by an enclosure of Ionic colonnades facing inwards on three sides with a blind wall on the E next the tree. After the burning of the sacred groves in 219 BC the temple was enlarged with an Ionic portico and an adyton, and the peribolos rebuilt with an Ionic propylon.

Beyond are two successive versions of a **Temple of Dione**, and a **Sanctuary of Herakles**. These are overlain by an Early Christian **basilica**, which incorporates an honorific decree of 180 BC. Dodona sent a bishop to the Council of Ephesos in AD 431, but the basilica is probably of Justinianic date.

FROM IOANNINA TO THE VIKOS GORGE: (A) via **Monodhéndri**. Road, c 80.5km (50 miles) round trip (daily bus). The Konitsa road (see below) is followed to (19km) **Kariés**. Beyond the village a by-road (signposted 'Vitsa') diverges right, climbing the slope of Mitsikeli with wide views over the main road. It soon turns E, running level through a gap into the **Zagoria**, an upland forested valley extending SE. Below Asprángeloi and again at a further junction you bear left, following signs for Monodhéndri. 36km **Vítsa** (Hotel B), an old stone-built village, has extensive views of forest-clad mountains. Further on (left) excavations have revealed a settlement and cemetery of the 9–4C BC (finds in Ioannina; published J. Vokotopoulou). Some of the graves were covered with stone tumuli and have produced rich material. 40km **Monodhéndri** (1090m; Hotels B), a traditional village somewhat spoilt by tourism. The road continues to the **Oxiá** viewpoint (car park). A path beyond the village square leads in 600m to the deserted monastery of *Ayía Paraskeví (1412), perched high on a sheer cliff above the **Vikos Gorge** (Farángi Víkou). The cells and frescoed chapel have been restored and vertiginous paths with perilous bridges lead on to caves and hermits' cells. In the lush gorge (long stepped descent) the river Voïdhomátis runs NW to Vikos.

(B) via **Víkos** or **Pápingo**, 124kms (77 miles) round trip (bus; not daily).

To the Vitsa turn (19km), as for (A). Continuing on the main road, you turn right (at 39km) for **Pápingo**. The road climbs through lush country and then, after spectacular views N over the plain of Kónitsa, descends through the pleasant village of **Arísti** (49km; Hotels B), where there is a turn to **Víkos** (4km), above the gorge. Below Aristi you cross the Voidhomatis. At **Kleidhí**, on the N bank (path, left, in ½hour), near the small deserted monastery of Ayioi Anargyroi, excavation of a Palaeolithic rock shelter began in 1981. A steep zig-zag ascent leads to **Megálo Pápingo** (62km; Hotels A, B; rooms; small restaurants), a delightful stone-built village and a base for walks on Mt Gamela. **Mikró Pápingo** (rooms) is 2km further. On the way a mountain stream has been dammed to provide a swimming pool.

## Walking in the Vikos area

The area is delightful for walking, though proper equipment and advance planning are essential (for useful book, see bibliography). The Vikos Gorge is best started from Monodhéndri. The path is reasonably clear and has been marked. The walk (7–8hrs) can be terminated by ascending to Víkos (W bank) or (further) Megálo Pápingo, or crossing the river bed and making for Mikró Pápingo, where walks on **Mt Gamela** can be started—to the refuge (1950m; 3 hrs), the high **Lake Dhrakolímni** (4hrs), the summit (2486m; 5½hrs).

FROM IOANNINA TO KONITSA AND NEAPOLIS (for Kozáni or Kastoriá). Road, 174km (108 miles); some discretion needed in view of proximity of Albanian frontier. Leaving the Métsovo/Tríkkala road to the right and that to Igoumenítsa on the left, you run N across the marshy plain of Lapsista at the foot of Mitsikeli. 17km **Asfáka** stands on the E shore of the seasonal **Lake Miradhia**. At (19km) **Kariés**, by-road (right) to the Vikos Gorge (see above). 33km **Memorial to the Fallen** of 1940–41 and museum at the junction of the by-road to the monastery of **Vélla** (2.5km SW). Vella takes its name from a ruined Byzantine town nearby; its bishopric was merged with that of Ioannina in 1842. 34km **Kalpáki** (600m; police post), a road junction of great strategic importance, commands the chief route into Greece from Albania. Here, on 1–14 November 1940, the Greek army fought a stubborn defensive battle against the Italian invaders; their counter-offensive threw the Italians back over the Albanian frontier.

Here diverges a road now effectively serving only the eparchy of Pogóni, but once leading to Aryirókastro (Gjirokastrë in Albania, recently (1993) beset by problems between the Greek community and Albanian authorities). **Dhelvináki** (22km), with 922 inhabitants, has succeeded **Pogonianí** as chief town of the region. The archbishopric of Pogoniani, founded by Constantine IV Pogonatos (668–685), may originally have had its seat at Molyvdhoskepastos (see below).

The main road makes a steep ascent with views of Mt Gamela (right), whose several rugged peaks rise to 2480m. After the junction (45km) below **Yeroplátanos**, the road descends in loops to the Voïdhomatis, crosses the river c 8km below the Vikos gorge (see above), and runs through an upland plain growing melons.

To the N and W of **Yeroplátanos**, also accessible via Dhelvináki and Pogonianí (above), **Vasiliká** (9km N, on a difficult road) has a 17C church of **Ayios Yióryios** with frescoes; **Paliópirgos** (at Koutsókrano and Palaiouríes; 17km NW) and **Káto Merópi** (13km NW) have several excavated tumuli (of many) with cist tombs and finds from the 11–4C BC, also some later, as well as a partly investigated prehistoric settlement (see Ioannina Museum).

Just before (64.5km) **Kónitsa** you pass (right) the narrow entrance to the colossal gorge through which the Aoös emerges from the Pindos. To the right of the modern road, the river is spanned by a fine one-arched bridge (1871), with a bailey bridge carrying the old road in between.

About two hours delightful walk up the gorge is the **Monastery of the Yénnisis tes Theotókou**, founded in 1774 and restored after its destruction (apart from the church) by the Germans in 1944 (key must normally be obtained from the office of the Metropolitan in Konitsa but this will not admit to the church unless a church official is present). The scenery is especially dramatic from the more arduous upper level path which has to be used when the river is high.

To the NE towers **Smólikas** (2579m), highest peak of the Pindos, to the S **Gaméla**. **Kónitsa** (2858 inhab.; Hotels C, D, E; see also Bourazani, below), a pleasant and friendly mountain market centre, commands the road from the hillside above the gorge. It is the seat of an eparchy and the birthplace of the mother of Ali Pasha and was conquered by the Turks of Murad II in 1440. The Greeks entered the town on 24 February 1913. From 24 December 1947 to 15 January 1948 its garrison withstood violent attacks of the communist General Markos, who intended to make it his capital. Above the central square can be seen the house of Hussein-Bey, a fine mansion made by local builders and, higher, the more ruinous family house of Hamkos, the mother of Ali Pasha. Above is the kastro. In the lower part of the town survives the minaret of the mosque of Sultan Suleiman the Magnificent (1536). There is also a small folk museum.

About half an hour to the W of Konitsa is the **Kókkine Panayía** (Koimisis tis Theotokou; 1412), with frescoes. From Kónitsa the road W leads towards the frontier (19km), where the Aoös below its confluence with the Voïd-homatis becomes the Vijosë (Viosa) as it flows through Albania into the Adriatic above Valona. The river is crossed by two ancient bridges **Bourazáni** and **Mertzáni**. Past the Hotel Bourazani (B), the road leads through beautifully lush and fertile country to (17km from Konitsa) the delightful and beautifully kept Monastery of the Koímisis tis Theotókou below Molyvdhosképastos. This dates to the reign of Constantine IV Pogonatos (668–685) and was restored by Andronikos Comnenus in c 1183. The frescoes were restored in 1521 and there is 14C woodwork. At **Molyvdhosképastos** (6km further) are several interesting churches. **Ayioi Apostóloi**, with frescoes, has a belvedere overlooking the river Saranda-poros and the frontier with Albania.

From Kónitsa a broad new road climbs sharply out of the Aoös Valley, then winds amid the W foothills of Smolikas. It descends to the Sarandá-poros and follows its left bank upstream. At 89km the river is crossed. Beyond (95km) **Pirsóyianni**, which is by-passed, a tributary is bridged at the confluence, and the road gradually bears E. You cross the boundary into the nome of Kastoria and leave the river for another tributary. The scenery is often wild and dramatic.

Pirsóyianni, **Kastanéa** and other neighbouring villages are known as the **Mastorok-hória** (villages of the craftsmen) from the fact that groups of their inhabitants used to travel all over Greece constructing public and private buildings.

Beyond (119km) **Eptakhóri**, where local buses from the two nomes meet and exchange passengers, a steady climb passes a spring and picnic site to a summit of 1443m at the boundary of the nome of Kozáni. Here is a wide view to the S. 135.5km **Pendálofos** (1060m), a picturesque mountain village with stone houses that formed the headquarters of the British Mission to the Greek Resistance in the Second World War. The road zigzags down to the gorge of the Pramoritsu, or Koutsomiliá, then gradually climbs into more open upland. Beyond (150km) **Morfí** it drops down again to the Koutsomi-lia, crossing the torrent to climb a long windswept ridge with extensive retrospective views near (158km) the Omalí turn. 164.5km **Tsotíli** (840m), with one of the first colleges founded during the Turkish domination. The road descends to (174km) **Neápolis**, whence to Kastoriá or Kozáni, see Rte 62.

From Ioánnina to **Métsovo** and into Thessaly, see Rte 51B.

# B. To Préveza via Paramithiá

**Road**, 112km (69½ miles) via (58km) Glikí.

For the first 24km you follow the Ioánnina road (Rte 52A), then turn right. The road crosses a ridge. 34km **Paramithiá** (Παραμυθιά; Hotel D), a large village (pop. 2144), picturesquely scattered on the slopes below the W scarp of Mt Korillas, is the chief place of the eparchy of Suli. Its name, which means 'consolation', is variously derived. It was called by the Turks *Aij Donat Kalessi* and by the Venetians *Castel San Donato*, names again variously explained as a corruption of the ancient *Aidonati* or after the 4C Donatos, Bishop of Euroia. In the 18C Paramithiá was the capital of one of the three sanjaks of Epirus. Above the town (path; or road in c 5kms via main road N, then turn towards Petousi to ΒΡΥΣΗ ΚΟΡΙΛΛΑ) is the ruined Venetian **kastro**, built on Hellenic foundations. The town was temporarily held by British forces in 1941. At **Veliani**, 6.5km SE, remains of a 7C basilica may mark the see of the Bishop of Photike.

FROM PARAMITHIA TO DODONA (55km (34 miles) of which 34km asphalted).
Just outside (N) Paramithiá, a minor road (signed **Petoúsi**) diverges right. Soon unsurfaced and quite rough it climbs in steep zig-zags via the hamlet of **Ayía Kiriakí** to the high village of **Petoúsi** (18km) and then to **Pardháli** where it continues asphalted through softer country. 47km Turn to **Konstaniani** (1km, left) with a 12C church of the Archangel Michael (frescoes). 55km **Dodona** (Rte 52A).

You now continue in the enclosed valley of the Kokkitos below the steep scarps of Paramithiás. At 38km a main road branches right to **Morfí** (for Párga, and Préveza via the coast, Rte 52C). You pass (40km) **Prodhrómio** where a rich Macedonian warrior burial in a cist beneath a mound was found in 1979. Finds included a fine bronze hydria used as the ash urn, gilded wreaths and iron weapons and armour. 57km Turn (left) for 'Souli villages', a well engineered road on the N side of the Akheron gorge (see below). **Soúli** itself is c 16km from the main road. 58km **Glikí** (Γλυκή), on the Akheron, is possibly the site of *Euroia*; there are remains of a church of the Despotate, supposed to be the burial place of Bishop Donatos.

The Akherontos, the mystic *Acheron* of mythology, was the river of the nether world. It comes down from the mountains of Suli and flows through a deep and gloomy ravine with precipitous sides, suggesting the terrors of Hades. At Gliki it enters the wide plain of Fanari, where it traverses meres and swamps, never wholly dry even in summer, which were known to the ancients as the *Acherousian Lake*. The river (boat trips from Parga) flows past Ephyra (see below) and enters the sea at the pleasant village of **Ammoudhiá** on the Bay of Fanari, S of Parga. There the Corinthian fleet put in in 433 BC and Robert Guiscard's wintered in AD 1084.

A track near Glikí (signed Σκάλα Τσαβελαίνας) leads through the gorge, and after 1 hour turns N and enters by a narrow pass into the region of Suli. The scenery is grand and impressive. 1½ hours. The **Castle of Suli** stands on an isolated hill near the village of the same name (memorials), 366m above the Acheron. It was one of the strongholds of the Suliots, a tribe of Christian Epirots, mustering about 4000 fighting men and women (see also Rte 52C, Zalóngo). Their territory, like Montenegro farther N, was a centre of stubborn resistance to the Moslems and contains several castles. From 1790 they were at war with Ali Pasha until 1803, when at great cost he captured their principal fastnesses, and they retired to the Ionian Islands. At the outbreak of the War of Independence most of the Suliots returned to the mainland where they again engaged the Turks. Among them was Markos Botsaris, defender of Mesolongi. In 1823 Great Britain negotiated their capitulation on favourable terms and they all emigrated to Cephalonia.

You descend to (69km) **Skepastó**, beyond which you join Rte 52C. 112km **Préveza**, see Rte 53B.

# C.   To Párga and Préveza

**Road**, 99km (61½ miles).—28km Margaríti.—38km Morfí, for Párga (12km).—52km Kastrí, for Ephyra. 56km Skepastó.—99km Préveza. From Morfí there is a choice of routes. That described in detail here passes through rich scenic inland country and (using the ferries at Préveza and Ríon) gives a total distance from Igoumenítsa to Athens of 476.5km (bus in 8½ hours). The **coastal road** from Morfí to Préveza, which is marked as the main route on most maps, provides an alternative route for that section. It is 7kms shorter and will be shorter still and considerably faster, when complete. There are still diversions and unfinished sections, though much is good.

The road skirts the S side of Igoumenitsa Bay. At **Ladhokhóri** (3km), near the sea, was found in 1975 a Late Roman mausoleum of brick and stone construction with four fine sculptured marble sarcophagi (now in the Ioannina Museum). A courtyard house was associated with the mausoleum. At 12km is **Platariá** (Hotel B, ferry to Corfu), with a good beach. **Sívota** (Hotels A–E) is 12km SW on the coast. You turn inland up a broad valley between mountain ranges, then descend through low hills on to a dyke road across marshes. 28km **Margaríti** (restaurant), despite its size (857 inhab.), controls a tiny eparchy of a few neighbouring villages. Important relics of its past under Venetians and Turks disappeared when the town was fired during military occupation in 1944. Remains of two fortresses crown neighbouring heights: that to the S is substantial (path); that to the N has a Turkish mansion (track). 38km **Morfí** stands at the junction of the road (right) to **Párga** (12km) which also gives access to the coastal route to Preveza (below). From this road also Ephyra (see below) can be reached most directly.

**PÁRGA** (Hotels A–E; F/A), a clean and picturesque little seaside town (1699 inhab.) backed by slopes of orange and olive groves, stands opposite the island of Paxos, 19km away. The town, considerably affected by package tourism, spreads across the neck of a rocky headland, crowned by a **frourion** of Norman origin (its keep is adorned with the lion of St Mark). The tiny bay has rocks and islets and many cafés along the waterfront. The larger bay of **Khrissoyiáli** (Hotel B), 1.5km to the W, has a superb sweep of beach.

*Parga* was already important in the 14C. In 1401 it came under the protection of the Venetians, who dominated it until 1797, except for brief intervals in 1452–54 and after 1701 when it fell into Turkish hands. Taken by the French, who left a small fort on the densely wooded islet of the Panayia, it enjoyed a brief existence in 1800–07 as an independent state under the aegis of Russia, then at the Treaty of Tilsit passed again to the French. Ali Pasha bought it from the British who had replaced the French in 1814. He drove out its people who sought refuge in the Ionian Islands. Some of them later returned, but from then until 1913 Parga was subject to Turkey, when it became Greek. Constantine Kanaris, the admiral of the War of Independence, was born here in 1790.

For Préveza, you can continue (right) along the newer road or bear left at Morfí and cross a ridge to the valley of the **Acheron**, with cotton fields. 52km **Kastrí** occupies the site of *Pandosia* with imposing Classical walls. Immediately before the Acheron crossing a turning (right; signposted) leads in 5km by a dyke-road to **Mesopótamo**. Here (road right in village), on a rocky hill above the confluence of the Kokytos with the Acheron (Periphlegethon), are the remains of the ***Nekyomanteion of Ephyra**, oracle of the dead and sanctuary of Persephone and Hades. From the site the extent of the ancient Acherousian Lake is obvious; the river (see above) flows on to the sea through willows and poplars. The acropolis of **Ephyra** (under excavation) rises at the N end of the ridge on which the Nekyomanteion stands and c 600m distant: it has a prehistoric Cyclopean wall and tumuli with LHIII burials.

The Nekyomanteion (08.30–15.00) is an astonishing construction with labyrinthine corridors and windowless rooms, both above and below ground. The remains, impressively complete in plan with standing arches, are in excellent polygonal masonry, Hellenistic in date, and were ruined by fire in 168 BC. The core of the complex is a unit with exceptionally thick walls consisting of an undivided central corridor, with three rooms off either side. There was evidence of offerings of grain and liquids (? honey), as well as the sacrifice of animals. Two terracotta busts of Persephone were also found here. The arrangements and purpose of the complex recall Homer's description (Od. x, 512) of the visit of Odysseus to the House of Hades and his sacrifice to the spirits of the dead. Remains of a bronze windlass suggest that mechanical trickery may have been employed, after a preparation involving disorientation techniques and hallucinatory drugs, in inducing satisfactory spiritual visitation.

The **coast road** towards Preveza bears right beyond Morfí, passes the Párga turn, then close to the Nekyomanteion, and turns right to reach the coast at **Loútsa** (Hotel C, 59km from Igoumenitsa). At 63km you divert from a section still under construction and pass through (65kms) **Ligiá** (beach). About 3km beyond Ligia, as the road begins to ascend again, a turn (right; unsurfaced; signed Restaurant Artolithia) leads in c 1.5km to the concealed site of an impressive Roman **nymphaeum**. Keep left at houses until the road bends sharply over a stream (culvert). The remains, surrounded by thick undergrowth and hard to see from a distance, are c 100m above the road before the turn. The main chamber (of three) has four entrances and six semicircular niches and belongs to the 3C AD. It may have been in the grounds of a private estate. The monument, which is preserved in part to its original height, is known locally as **Frangoekklissiá**.

Returning to the main road you turn right and ascend to rejoin (69km) the new highway, near **Rizá** where a site at Panagía may be ancient *Kassopaia*. At (74km) **Kastrosikiá** are hotels (B, C) and a camping site. There are long stretches of beach. The road continues along the coast, passing (78km) a turn to Nikopolis and Arta, where it is joined by the inland road (see below) to (92km) Preveza.

At 56km on the inland route, you join Rte 52B just below **Skepastó**. The road now climbs steeply, then winds S through a long valley. At 75.5km a road ascends (left) to the village of **Kamarína** (officially **Zálongo** after its mountain).

Beyond Kamarína a footpath (left; 5.5km from main road; small sign) leads in 3 minutes to the attractive site of **Kassope**. On a broad plateau facing S, with a high acropolis behind, these ruins of the 4C BC were discovered in 1951–55; excavations were resumed in 1976. The city was laid out early in the 4C BC on the Hippodamian system and protected by a polygonal wall. It was burned by the Romans in 167 BC and abandoned when Nikopolis was founded. There is a good site plan by the guard's hut.

Investigations have concentrated on the area round the **agora**. This is bounded on the N by a **stoa** with octagonal Doric columns. It has some unusual terracotta antefixes (eagles and thunderbolts; eagles and Ganymedes). A row of bases in front and to the E were originally occupied by statues of deceased citizens dedicated to the city and the Gods. The building, of the 3C, is underlain by a predecessor. On the W side of the

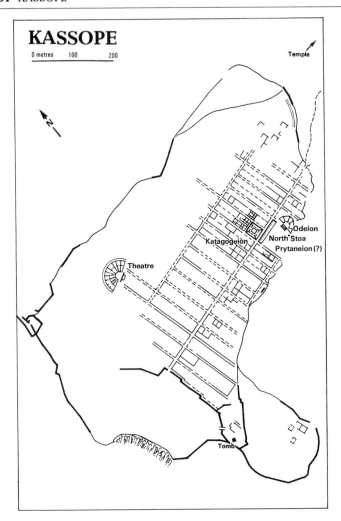

**KASSOPE**

0 metres    100    200

Temple

Odeion
North Stoa
Katagogeion
Prytaneion (?)

Theatre

Tomb

agora was a paved rectangular area bordered by orthostats, beyond which passes one of the N–S streets, which was roofed at this point to form a kind of stoa. On the other (W) side of this street, a rectangular building still under study (possibly a **prytaneion**) is centred round a small courtyard which had a Doric portico. To the E of the agora is a small **odeion**. Immediately behind (to the N of) the N stoa are the remains of a **katagogeion** (hostel) consisting of rooms (each with a table and hearth) around a court, which had a peristyle of octagonal Doric columns and an entrance porch on to the street to the S. To the N of the katagogeion a number of houses have been excavated. Most consist of rooms round a small court and were built in the Classical period, though often altered subsequently. Farther NW is the **theatre**. At the SW corner of the site is a subterranean vaulted built tomb of the 4–3C, probably a **heroön**.

Continuing up the road you see (100m, left) the remains of a **Temple of Aphrodite** (Ionic, prostyle) and, beyond that, part of a defence wall blocking the pass. The road climbs a further 400m to the **Monastery of Zalongo,** where the Suliot mountaineers took refuge when attacked by Ali Pasha. Sixty women escaped with their children to the summit, where, after performing their traditional dance, they threw themselves over the precipice. This act is commemorated by a huge sculpture above the monastery (footpath).

At 80km **Arkhángelos** you emerge on the Bay of Gomares joining the new coastal road (see above), 3km S of **Kastrosikiá** (Rte 53B). At 90km the ruins of *Nikopolis* (Hotels, B, C) lie to the left. The new road peters out 3km short of (99km) **Préveza.**

*The Souliot Women at Zalonga. Engraving*

# 53

## Ioánnina to Arta and Préveza

### A. To Arta

**Road,** 75km (47 miles), well engineered section of the main highway to Athens. **Buses** (KTEL 13) 9 daily to Arta, also regularly to Préveza.

From Ioánnina to (8km) the Dodona turn, see Rte 52. The road continues straight and level with views of the scarred heights of Mt Tómaros (right). A causeway carries the highway across a marshlake. It climbs between **Bizáni** (11km), where the **Vrellis Museum** (Rte 52A) will be transferred, and **Manolássa** (right), two heights known as battlefields in 1913. 17km **Kháni Avgoú** stands 3km left on a col (629m), the highest point on the route. The walls of *Pirtelia* are visible on the isolated hill (right) as you descend to the cultivated upper valley of the **Louros**. The road has been realigned; on the old loop is **Kháni Emín Agá**, a police post with a small museum illustrating the campaign of 1912–13; a memorial, opposite, marks the site of Constantine's headquarters during the siege of Ioannina.

You pass the principal springs that feed the infant Louros. 31km **Kháni Teróvou** (restaurants). At the entrance to the **Louros *Gorge** the road crosses to the right bank. The river, shaded by great planes, flows between **Xerovoúni** (1614m), the long range of mountains to the E, and **Zarkorákhi** (1332m; to the W). Here and there are remains of fortifications, ancient and modern. 38km **Potamiá** (restaurants). Near (40km) **Kleisoúra**, the narrowest point and the nome boundary, is a tunnel. **Panayía** (43km) is a pleasant spot for picnics. You pass **Kerasóna** (48km) and at 53km (in cliff above road to right; small sign) the **Asprokhalikó** cave which in 1965 (further work in 1981) proved to contain the first extensive stratified deposits of Middle and Upper Palaeolithic date found in Greece.

The road bends left and there is a turn to **Ayios Yeóryios**, with an ornamented church, on a hill to the left. You reach the artificial lake formed by the Louros Dam. Immediately beyond (right) is the entrance to a rock-cut conduit, part of a **Roman aqueduct** that fed Nikopolis, over 64km away. Some spectacular arches can be seen by the Ay. Yeóryios road (see above). About 1.5km farther down (left) is a hydro-electric station. To the right is the **Paidópolis Zírou**, an orphanage of the Royal Foundation. At 64km **Filippiás** (Φιλιππιάς; usually Filippiádha, accusative; 4040 inhab. Hotel C) is the excavated 13C **Monastery of the Pantánassa**, where recent excavations in the church and cloister have revealed frescoes and and *opus sectile* floor. Some of the architectural elements were probably brought from Nikopolis.

A road crosses the river to **Kambí** (5km), continuing amid the S foothills of Xerovouni to **Kastrí** (16km; bus daily), 3km from **Ammótopos**. Here, at Xerovouni (rough path in 10 minutes), is the 4C site of ancient *Horraon*, with substantial remains of walls and houses. It was destroyed by the Romans in 168 BC. About 3km farther on, by a disused factory, you leave the road to Préveza (Rte 53B), turn left across the Louros, and traverse the orange-groves of the Ambracian plain. At the approach to the Arakhthos a road enters on the right from **Salaóra** (18km; with fish hatcheries) on the Ambracian Gulf. Crossing the Arakhthos to enter Arta, you see (left) a Turkish packhorse *bridge (**the Bridge of Arta**): the legend that the mason built his wife into the foundations to strengthen the bridge is enshrined in a song that is known also among other Balkan peoples. There is a Folk Art Museum nearby.

75km (48½ miles) **ARTA** (Hotels B, C, E), pleasantly situated in a loop of the Arakhthos, is a friendly town (19,087 inhab.) interspersed with orange groves. Remains are coming to light of its ancient past as *Ambracia*, capital of Pyrrhus, king of Epirus, and there are reminders of its period of greatness as the seat of the Despotate of Epirus. A useful tourist booklet (1993) in various languages is available and, for those with some knowledge of Greek, K.T. Yiannélos, Τα Βυζαντινά Μνημεία τῆς Αρτας, 1990, published by the Town Council.

**History**. Ambracia was colonised by Corinth c 625 BC and had a grid plan at least by the 5C BC. Pausanias found only ruins. After the fall of Constantinople and of the Morea to the Franks, Michael I Angelos, with the approval of the exiled Emperor Alexios III, set up the autonomous Despotate of Epirus at Arta, or Narte. Here Euphrosyne, Alexios' empress, died in exile. The town fell to the Turks in 1449, but soon passed to the Venetians. The French held it for two years after the Treaty of Campoformio (1797) but, after a period of subjection to Ali Pasha of Ioannina, it fell again under direct Turkish rule in 1822–1912. Hoca Ishak Efendi (1774–1834), the

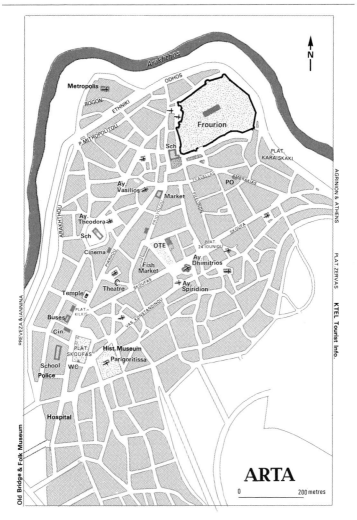

**ARTA**

0                    200 metres

accomplished linguist who first introduced western science into Turkish education, was born at Arta.

The **frourion**, a 13C castle now occupied by the Xenia Hotel, commands the bend of the river. The restored outer walls (virtually complete), with reused Classical blocks, can be followed and give pleasant views northward to Xerovouni. Some scanty remains of a Classical **temple** survive near the river bank. To the SW off Od. Pírrhou is **Ayios Vasílios**, a small 14C church with the elaborate brick and tile decoration characteristic of the area. Farther on is the 13C **Ayía Theodhóra**, properly the church of St George the Martyr, a conventual church where Theodora, consort of Michael II, took the veil and ended her days. The domed narthex, perhaps added in her lifetime, has outstanding brick and tile decoration; within stands a reconstruction of Theodora's tomb (excavated in 1873), originally erected by Nikephoros I, her son. The fine capitals are said to derive from Nikopolis. Part of the ? **prytaneion** of the ancient city was found in a rescue excavation nearby.

Odhós Pírrhou continues SW. In Od. Priovólou (50m W) in 1976 was found the **bouleuterion**, and remains of a substantial Hellenistic public building can be seen further S in a plot on the same side of the street. Remains of the 4–3C theatre are in Od. Tsakálof, between Priovólou and Skoufá. Towards the bottom of Priovólou (right) are the foundations of a large Doric **temple** of the early 5C BC, uncovered in 1964–69. Its tiles were stamped AMBP. Sections of the ancient town wall (c 500 BC) have been located on Odd. Porfiríou Mitropolítou and Rógon, also, prominently, to the NW in the vicinty of Arakhthoú 15, where there are towers and a gate. In the grounds of the bishopric Byzantine remains may be of a predecessor which was destroyed by floods in the 13C. The busy Plateía Kilkás, the main square with the bus station, has several restaurants. Beyond is the larger Plateía Skoufás (Historical Museum, opened by arrangement); dominated by the former metropolitan church of **Panayía Parigorítissa**, a huge square building crowned by six domes. It was erected in 1282–89 by Nikephoros and John, sons of Michael II. The gloomy interior, has a certain majesty; the curious sub-structure of the central dome, borne on antique columns on a primitive cantilever principle, cannot be as unsound as it appears. The mosaics of the Pantocrator and the prophets in the dome (cleaned) belong to the original decoration. There is an archaeological museum in the cloisters (charge; open Mon–Fri). On the S side of town at Odd. Komnínou/ Ayíon Apostólon burial enclosures have been found by the roadway leading to the S gate of the ancient city.

By the river 3.5km S of the town on a road which follows the E bank of the river, is the **Káto Panayía**, a nunnery founded by Michael II whose monogram can be traced on the S wall of the church. It shelters 20 orphaned girls who weave blankets and carpets (for sale). The church incorporates prophyry columns perhaps from a Syrian Temple of Aphrodite (Classical foundation blocks visible in the terrace). The exterior walls are adorned with bands of cable and meander patterns with decorative motifs worked in red tile. The frescoes within are mainly of the 18C; fragments in the apse date from the 13C.

Among the monasteries for which the region is noted are the **Moní Vlakhérnai** (NE of the town, 8.5km by car; leave on Ioánnina road and turn off immediately right for **Grammenítsa**), transformed into a convent of nuns by Theodore Angelos c 1225, not many years after its foundation. The church was embellished by Michael II. Fragments of the original marble templon are built into the narthex doorway. Within are two marble tombs, believed from their fragmentary inscriptions to belong to Michael II and to two of his sons. Near **Plisioí** (5km SW via the bridge) is the 8–9C church of **Ayios Dhimítrios Katsoúri**, the chapel of a Patriarchal monastery. The frescoes are assigned to the late 12–early 13C. The nearby church of **Ayios Nikólaos tis Rodhiás** (12–13C) also has frescoes of the early 13C. Two unusual scenes are preserved in the W corner bays—the three Hebrews in the Fiery Furnace and the Seven Sleepers of Ephesus. The **Panayía tou Bryóni**, 10km SW near **Neokhoráki** off the Amfilokhía road, was enlarged with a transept and dome during the Patriarchate of Germanos II, perhaps at the time of his visit to Epirus in 1238. The monastery at **Péta** (8km E, leave by Amphilokhía road) has a 17C epitaphios from the Morea and a monument of 1821. Further afield is the (10C or earlier) church of the Panayía at **Kovonisía** (26km SW).

# B. To Préveza

**Road**, 105km (67 miles), following the Arta road to (64km) Filippiás (see above), then branching right.—98km Nikópolis—105km Préveza. **Buses** several times daily.

From Ioánnina to (66km) the Fix orangeade factory, see above. The Préveza road turns SW and runs roughly parallel with the lower reaches of the Louros. Just beyond (70km) **Néa Kerasoús** are, left on a low hill, the impressive ruins of *Rogon*, or *Rogous* (ancient *Bouchetion*), protected by a marshy loop of the river. Access is by the next minor road left, then track—or through village. An excellent outer polygonal enceinte encloses a medieval citadel, built on ashlar foundations (end 5C BC, then three subsequent phases of alteration and reconstruction before it was abandoned after 31 BC), with a church (defaced frescoes). The place gave its name to a medieval see. At (77km) **Stefáni** at the S end of the Thesprotiká range, we join a road from **Thesprotikó** (10km N), a deme with a population of 1936. Beyond (81km) **Loúros** (refreshments), a large village (pop. 2073), the road runs straight and level in the lush plain irrigated by the Louros. At (93km) **Mikhalítsi**, off the road to the right, tombs of the 4C BC have been explored. The peninsula narrows to an isthmus. On the E is a marshy lagoon, the haunt of herons and other wildfowl.

The road passes through the extensive and overgrown site of *Nikopolis*, the city founded by Augustus after his victory at Actium. To the W is the Bay of Gomares where he had concentrated his forces before the battle.

**History**. In commemoration of his victory, Octavian (Augustus) raised the status of Patrai to that of Roman colony and founded the new *Colonia* of *Nikopolis* ('victory city') on his camp site. To populate the new city, he resettled the inhabitants of most of the towns of Aetolia and Akarnania, including Kalydon, Ambracia, and Amphilochian Argos. It was made a member of the Amphictyonic League and to it were transferred the Actian games. St Paul spent a winter (? 64) at 'Nicopolis of Macedonia', where he wrote his Epistle to Titus. By AD 67 the city was the capital of an Epirot province. The philosopher Epictetus (c 60–140) had a school here, and the city was the reputed birthplace of Pope St Eleutherios (175–189). Thriving in the time of Strabo, it was plundered by Alaric, Genseric, and Totila. Justinian rebuilt its defences, reducing their compass. At the coming of the Slavs, the Byzantines removed the seat of the theme to Naupaktos and Nikopolis decayed. Here, in 1795, John Sibthorp, the English botanist, fell ill and returned to die in Bath. The Greek Archaeological Service has excavated at intervals since 1913 and a new survey is in progress.

Parts of the widely scattered site are very overgrown and the visit arduous. The **theatre** is prominent to the right of the road. The walls of the proscenium still stand, and the auditorium rises to the upper portico, its niches and arcades the haunt of storks. In several places the holes in which the poles for the velarium, or awning, were fixed may be seen. The line of the cunei can be distinguished though the stone seats have mostly vanished.

A dirt road (signed incorrectly 'Temple of Apollo') to the left skirts the **stadium** which, unusually in Greece, was rounded at both ends like those of Asia Minor. It leads in 450m to the village of **Smirtoúla**, above which are the remains of the commemorative **monument** erected by Augustus after the battle of Actium on the site where his tent had been pitched (see Murray and Petsas in *Archaeology* 1988 (Sept/Oct). A massive podium of masonry fronted by a stepped terrace is preserved. In its face are cuttings where the bronze prow rams of captured ships were attached. The positions of 23 have been identified. There were probably originally 33–35, a tithe of the c 350 captured in the battle. The largest was two tons in weight. Above these was a long inscription (parts preserved) recording the dedication to Mars and Neptune (not Apollo as

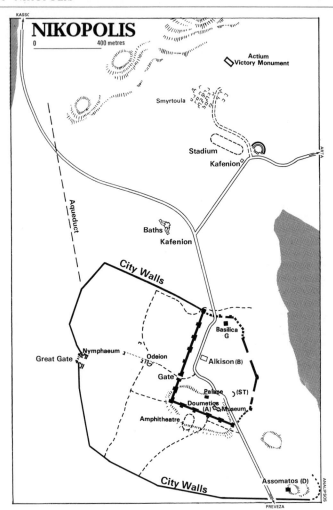

mistakenly reported by Cassius Dio 51. 1. 3). On top of the podium was a structure with Corinthian columns. The *Actia* festival (previously at Actium, q.v.), was transferred to Nikopolis by Augustus.

The road runs S, meeting the inland road from Parga (Rte 52C) near some ruined **baths**, then enters the Byzantine enceinte. To the left, just inside the circuit, is **Basilica** G (Γ). Further on are the excavated remains of the **Basilica of Alkyson** (= Basilica B), a double-aisled church with tripartite transept, founded by Bishop Alkyson (died 516). Two heads in mosaic survive from its Christian decoration. Beyond the basilica a track leads (right) through a fine **gate** in Justinian's *walls, here well preserved for c 500m. The path may be followed past the Augustan **odeion**, restored for use in the annual festival of ancient drama (Aug), to the **Great Gate** in the

**city walls** of the Augustan period. Some remains of the **aqueduct** that supplied the city with water from the Louros survive to the N as well as part of the **nymphaeum** in which it terminated.

Further along the main road is the **museum**, opened in 1972. On the walls of the lobby are inscribed stelai bases and gravestones. Two rooms display statues, sarcophagi, Roman portraits (notably Agrippa, Augustus's general at Actium, and Faustina the Younger, wife of Marcus Aurelius) and capitals; in the centre of the first room, grave *lion (3C BC); in the second, huge cylindrical base with Amazonomachia reliefs (reused as the ambo of the Alkyson basilica); large glass cinerary urn; rings and lamps.

In the field near by (phylax will guide) is the **Basilica of Doumetios** (= Basilica A), dated from its fine floor mosaics to the second quarter of the 6C. Adjacent to the W is the palace of the archbishops of *Epirus Vetus* who had their seat here. N of that are remains of baths and a cistern. To the NE, on the other side of the road, are slight remains of the 6th basilica of the area (ΣΤ in Greek numerals). Basilica D (Δ) (the 'Asomatos'; 5–6C) with a peacock mosaic floor is off the road to the left, 400m beyond the main walls. To the W of that is a church of the Ascension (Analipsis). The amphitheatre lay outside the city walls, to the S.

105km **Préveza** (Πρέβεζα; Hotels B, C, D, E), the pleasant chief town (13,341 inhab.) of a small nome, stands on the N shore of the shallow strait, here only 1km wide, through which the waters of the Ambracian Gulf reach the sea. The waterside esplanade is a favourite evening promenade. A car ferry crosses the strait (half-hourly) to Aktion, where there is an airport with three flights a week to Athens (Préveza terminal at Spiliádhou 5 and Balkoú), and charter flights from abroad, also an important military base.

Preveza occupies the site of ancient *Berenikia*, founded c 290 BC by Pyrrhus in honour of his mother-in-law Berenice, queen of Ptolemy Soter. The town was occupied by the Venetians in 1499. Ceded to the Turks by the Treaty of Carlowitz (1699), it was retaken in 1717. In 1797 Preveza passed, with the Ionian Islands, to the French, but the next year was retaken by Ali Pasha in the name of the Sultan of Turkey and remained in Turkish hands until it fell to the Greek army in 1912. In 1881–1912 the Greco-Turkish frontier ran through the strait.

On the S side of the strait the sandy promontory of **Aktion** (Latin, *Actium*) is sharper in outline than that of Preveza and almost closes the entrance to the Gulf. At the naval **Battle of Actium**, on 2 September 31 BC, Agrippa, Octavian's commander, with a smaller but more manoeuvrable fleet, routed the combined navies of Antony and Cleopatra. The royal leaders deserted the army they had massed for an invasion in Italy, and it surrendered a week later. Ships sunk in the battle have been located beneath the sea and archaeological investigation is planned. By the ferry landing-place stands a Venetian fort (not open). On the promontory, 1km N, are scanty remains of the **Temple of Apollo Aktios**.

A temple, under the protection of neighbouring *Anaktorion*, existed here in the 5C BC. From it came two kouroi now in the Louvre. Gymnastic games and horse races were held. After his victory at Actium, Augustus rebuilt the temple and consecrated in special boathouses examples of the vessels captured in the battle. The festival he transferred to his new city of Nikopolis (q.v.), adding naval and musical events. The '*Actia*', held every five years and declared sacred, thus took rank with the four great Panhellenic games.

To **Levkas** (21km from Aktion), and to **Amfilokhia**, see Rte 54.

# 54

# From Arta to Mesolóngi

**Road**, 123km (76½ miles), through the varied countryside of Aitolía and Akarnanía with its characteristic lakes and lagoons, and impressive monuments. The road, has been much widened and realigned, with main towns and villages bypassed. 43km Amfilokhía.—72.5km Strátos.—85km (53 miles) Agrínio, for Thérmon.—114km Aitolikó, for Oeniadae.—119km Plévron.—123km Mesolóngi. **Bus** via Agrímio regularly.

You leave Arta and turn SE through orange-groves. 12km **Kombóti** (1.5km left; pop. 2050) was the native town of Nik. Skoufa, one of the founders of the Philike Hetaireia. Approaching the Ambracian Gulf the road rises on the oak-clad slope of **Makrinóros**, a long mountain ridge parallel to the shore. The pass en corniche thus formed, sometimes called the 'Thermopylae of Western Greece', was guarded in antiquity by a string of forts. At its summit is **Kástro Palaiokoúlia**, defended during the War of Independence by the Greek captain Iskos. 18km **Menídhi** marks the N end of the pass; (33km) **Anoixiátiko**, the S end. Just beyond (38km) **Kríkelo** is (left) the little church of Ayios Ioannis, behind which (road signposted) rise the insignificant remains of **Amphilochian Argos**, a town of some importance in the Peloponnesian War.

46km **Amfilokhía** (Αμφιλοχία; Hotels C, D) stands at the head of the Gulf of Karvasará, the farthest inland reach of the Ambracian Gulf. The town (pop. 4392) was founded by Ali Pasha as a military station; its former name, *Karvasarás*, is supposed to be a corruption of 'caravanserai'. On the hill (189m) above are some remains of an ancient town with long walls, perhaps to be identified with *Limnaia*.

FROM AMFILOKHIA TO LEVKAS, 59km (37 miles). The road follows the S line of the Ambracian Gulf, often away from the shore amid marsh, cotton fields, or low hills. To the left Mt Bergandi rises to 1428m; **Thírio** (**museum** with Classical and Roman material, including inscriptions, from ancient *Thyreion*), on its N slope, has adopted the ancient name of a place where Cicero, sailing along the Akarnanian coast, spent two hours at the house of his friend Xenomanes. 38km **Vónitsa** (Hotels C, D; pop. 4037), chief town of the eparchy of Vónitsa and Xiroméros, has a small port below a fine citadel (access by car via Od. Grívas) with a triple line of walls and towers on the SE. The Venetian version dates to 1676, but there seem also to be Byzantine, Frankish and Turkish work. A road runs W from Vónitsa to the Aktion–Preveza ferry (12km), passing after 3km a turning to the pleasant beach (5km) at **Panayía**. At 5km, near the shore, are the conspicuous hill-top ruins of *Anaktorion*, a Corinthian colony of 630 BC. The road bears SW. Coming in to (49km) **Ayios Nikólaos** you meet another road from Aktion (10km) and beyond the village cross the outlet of the marsh-lake Voulkári to the Ionian Sea. To the left is seen the **Castle of Grivas** (or Froúrio Tekés), dating from the War of Independence.

By this castle a turn (left) is signed **Perátia**. Below Peratia, turn right (no sign) for **Playiá** and through the village to **Fort St. George**, an impressive Venetian monument with good views (8km from main road; adequate except for last 500m). There are remains of ?an Early Christian basilica in the centre of the fort and of ancient buildings in the vicinity.

The road then crosses a long causeway to the Frankish **Kastro Santa Maura** (Rte 56), guarding a gap between the mainland and the island of Levkas. The strait is crossed by a moveable bridge, whence another causeway carries the road into (59.5km) **Lévkas** (see Rte 56C).

FROM AMPHILOKHIA TO MESOLONGI VIA ASTAKOS (155km, 96 miles). Road surfaced except for sections between Mítikas and Astakós and Astakós and Lesíni. A pleasant route, coastal between Pálairos and Astakós.

From Amphilokhía to (38km) Vónitsa, as above. On the S outskirts of Vónitsa, you ignore the turn to Aktion and continue straight ahead (S). The countryside is rich and undulating, with cornfields and pasture. At 49km the road passes close to the SE limit of **Lake Voulkári** where, near the village of **Kekhropoúla** are the impressive fortifications and other remains of ancient *Palaerus* (now called **Kástro**; at 53.5km an unsigned track allows access in c 8km, roundabout, but seek directions; also possible by bad track from **Pogoniá**). 61km Modern **Pálairos** (Hotel B). You proceed along the coast to **Mítikas** (some remains of ancient *Alyzia*), by-passed by the main road, a pleasant village but busy in season. Opposite are three islets of which the largest is **Kálamos**. About 2km E of Mitikas, not far from the sea, are the substantial remains of the Early Christian basilica of **Ay. Sofía**. Further along the coast (some unsurfaced patches) is (105km) **Astakós** (pop. 2459; Hotels B, D), formerly *Dragomestre*, coastal base of Sir Richard Church's operations in Western Greece in 1828. A pleasant small town with a ferry service to Ithaca and Cephallonia, and connecting buses to Athens (twice daily). The main road bypasses the village and continues S. The road turns inland (roadworks after 10km).

At **Platiyialí** (c 12km S off the main road), is a large submerged Early Helladic settlement discovered during construction work on new shipyards.

—116km Lesíni.—121km Katokhí (for *Oeniadae*, see below), Neokhóri, Aitolikó and (155km) Mesolónghi.

An alternative route from Lesíni (turn left in village) passes near **Pendálofos**, with its prominent church, skirts the N end of the lagoon of Aitolikó and joins the main road just S of the Stená Kleisoúras, 16km from Lesíni. This route also gives access to the 5C (?) fortifications of **Palaiománina**, perhaps ancient *Sauria*, reached via Pendálofos and the village of the same name (11km further N).

You cross a low saddle behind the town between two ranges of hills. 52km **Stános**, on the W slope, overlooks the N arm of **Lake Ambrakía**, which is crossed on a causeway. The road continues along the E shore. 67km Turn (right) to Astakós. A little further on in the distance is **Lake Ozerós** (right).

75.5km **Strátos** (Στράτος), a melancholy village (left) stands in the centre of the *ruins of *Stratos*, the ancient capital and largest city of Akarnania. The walls, dating from before 429 BC and particularly well preserved, stand on a low bluff commanding the broad Acheloös. A new survey of the site is in progress. A folk-dancing festival is held annually in September.

**History**. The site was occupied in early times but first became important in the 5C BC. During the Peloponnesian War Knemos of Sparta besieged it vainly in 429 BC and in 426 Eurylochos passed below its walls without daring to attack. Agesilaos failed to take *Stratos* in 391, but it passed to Kassander in 314, and in 263, when Akarnania was partitioned, fell to the Aitolians. After the dissolution of the Aitolian League (188), the Romans held it against Philip V and Perseus of Macedon, but by the late 1C it had lost all importance. The site was explored by the French School in 1892, 1910–11, and 1924.

The **walls** embrace four parallel N–S ridges with their three intervening depressions. A transverse N–S wall divides the city into two parts. With the exception of the **theatre** (unexcavated) most of the public buildings seem to have been in the W sector. In the centre of the S wall, to the right of the track to the village, is the **Main Gate**, with a defensive interior court. The remains of the **agora** are scanty. The central wall leads up past the ancient quarries to the **acropolis**, seemingly a fortified refuge rather than a religious place. Curiously placed athwart a projecting section of the W wall is the Doric **Temple of Zeus**, built on a platform c 70m from E to W. Peripteral (6 x 11 columns) and somewhat larger than the Athenian Hephaisteion, it

dates from the 4C, probably after 338 BC. An Ionic colonnade surrounded the cella on three sides. The stylobate and parts of the cella walls survive.

There is a turn (right) for Palaiománina, Pendálofos etc (see above); also Astakós. The road passes within the E wall of Strátos, then turns to cross the **Acheloös Barrage** (Φράγμα Αχελώου). The former bridge is 5km upstream. The **Acheloös**, or Aspropotamos, is the longest river (217km) in Greece. Rising in the Pindus, it forms the boundary between Aitolia and Akarnania, and falls into the sea opposite the Echinades Islands. Since 1960 the river has been harnessed to provide power (see below) and irrigation. A by-pass to the W avoids Agrínio. A new construction project, high in the Pindus to the E (see Rte 47C), to divert part of its waters to irrigate the Thessalian plain will alter the nature of the river here, with potentially disastrous consequences for the Aitolian wetlands.

88km **Agrínio** (Αγρίνιο; Hotels B, C, D), a lively town of 39,368 inhabitants, is the capital of the eparchy of Trikhonídhos and the largest place in the nome. It is a tobacco-growing centre, and a starting-point for the visit to Thermon. The town was almost completely rebuilt after an earthquake in 1887. There is a small archaeological **museum**. The site of ancient *Agrinion* has been located above the village of **Megáli Khóra**, 4km NW of the town.

FROM AGRINIO TO THERMON (and alternative routes to Karpeníssi), 32km (20 miles), infrequent bus. Off the Karpeníssi road (see below) a branch to the right passes through the agricultural villages along the N shore of *Lake Trikhonís. There is a fine view of **Mt Vlokhos** (610m; left). At (11km) **Paravóla** are substantial remains of ancient *Boukation* (Classical and 4C with Byzantine towers). The road runs along the shore, then climbs in turns above orange groves to **Mirtéa**, with a monastery of 1491. 29km **Ayía Sofía** is a long pretty village with gushing streams; its Byzantine church incorporates blocks from a **Temple of Aphrodite**. 32km **Thérmon** (or **Kefalovrísi**; Hotel D) has a charming rural square with a modest hotel and restaurants, reminiscent of Mt Pelion. Just over 1km S (sign to 'Museum') at 'Palaió Bazári' are the remains of ancient *Thermon*, the spiritual centre of the Aitolians, who here held their elections of magistrates at an annual festival.

The festival was the occasion also for a great fair and for athletic games. Thermon became a Pan-Aitolian sanctuary centred on the temple of Apollo Thermios. Some 2000 of the statues erected here were destroyed by Philip V of Macedon when he sacked the place in 218 BC. The Greek Archaeological Service excavated the site in 1898–1916 and new work is in progress.

The **sanctuary**, with its E side against Mt Mega Lakkos, was surrounded by a rectangular peribolos protected by towers dating from the 3C BC. The largest of three temples, near the N wall, is the **Temple of Apollo Thermios** (630 BC), a narrow peripteral building (unusually aligned N–S) with five columns at the ends and 15 at the sides. A row of columns down the centre divided the building lengthwise. The

*Thermon, Temple of Apollo. Reconstruction of section of wooden entablature with painted terracotta metopes, antefixes, etc. (c 630 BC)*

walls may have been made of sun-dried brick. The entablature was of wood; the metopes, acroteria, antefixes and cornice facings of painted terracotta. At a lower level are the foundations of a temple of the Geometric period built with an apsidal peristyle. To the N, and at a still lower level are houses of a prehistoric village; one particularly large and well-built with an apsidal end. By the gate are remains of a Temple of Artemis and, to the E, of Apollo Lyseios. To the S is a **fountain**, still operating, with three spouts and, beyond, are two parallel **stoas**. These are being reinvestigated. The W was 165m long and had wooden columns; the E has interior benches. Both had predecessors. A third **stoa**, so far only partly investigated, runs at right angles to the other two across the S side of the enclosed area. Against the S wall is a building which may have been a bouleuterion. Notable in the **museum** are Archaic terracotta metopes (the best are in Athens), crucial evidence for the history of Greek mural painting, and decorative fragments from the Temple; Middle Bronze Age pottery, part of a Mycenaean helmet, and a fine pair of bronze horses mounted on a single base (Geometric).

You can return to Agrínio by the S shore of the lake, making a round of c 72.5km; or, by another road (infrequent bus) reach **Návpaktos** (Rte 55). From Thermon, there are two direct routes to **Karpeníssi**. The more westerly (78km), rather precipitous, goes by way of the spectacularly situated monastery of **Proússos** (40km) then **Méga Khorió** (Rte 47A). The easterly rout (c 100km), winding aand not yet fully surfaced is by **Neokhóri** and **Dhómnísta**.

FROM AGRINIO TO KARPENISSI, 116km (72½ miles). A tough but impressive drive over a series of ridges of the Southern Pindus with climbs up to 1219m. Bus once daily. The road winds NE in the foothills of **Panaitolikón**. Beyond (24km) **Kelanítis** it climbs in earnest to reach a saddle with the first view of Lake Kremaston. 40km **Ayios Vlásios** (1158m), a scattered mountain village (restaurant). You descend and just after (47km) **Khoúni** pass a road to **Kremastá** (6.5km, left), standing just below the confluence of the Acheloös with its two largest tributaries. Here a great dam, 172m high, and a hydro-electric power station have been constructed by an American company.

51km Fork left for **Lake Kremastón**, the largest artificial lake in Greece, which drowned several villages, rebuilt on the slopes above. The main road veers E to cross an arm of the lake by a new bridge and regains the line of the former road (which made use of a ferry crossing) near (63km) **Ayios Yeóryios**. It zigzags high above the valley to (75.5km) **Frangísta** (Φραγκίστα), at and beyond which are turns (left) to the remote N villages of the **Agrafa**, good walking country. The road suddenly reaches a small plane-shaded opening with springs, grass, and a café. It climbs steeply to 1067m, then descends to cross the Megdova by (92km) the **Markopoulos Bridge** (Restaurant). It climbs again through firs to a col (c 1220m) in the W outliers of Timfristos, then descends. 117km **Karpenissi**, and thence to Lamia, see Rte 47A.

Leaving Agrínio you turn S. The route runs straight across the irrigated plain dividing Lakes Trikhonis (left; see above) and Lysimakhia (right), crosses the canal linking the two lakes, joins the road coming from the S shore of Lake Trikhonis, then follows the SE shore of **Lake Lysimakhia** before turning S into the hills. 105km **Frangouléïka** lies in the pretty valley that leads into the **Stená tis Kleisoúras**, a long cleft in the sandstone, in which stands the monastery of **Ayía Eleoúsa**. At the exit is a pleasant prospect of the Aitolikó lagoon. 111km Turning (right) to **Angelókastro** (16km) where there are remains of a Byzantine fortress (13C; road). There is a tholos tomb cemetery at Repítsa, nearby. The coastal plain is planted with olives. The realigned road runs well above the older road (and eventually by-passes Mesolongi). 117km Turning to **Aitolikó** (7km) and (14.5km farther) **Oiniadai**.

**Aitolikó** (Αιτωλικό; Hotels D), a medieval refuge-town of 4286 inhabitants, stands on an island between its lagoon and the larger seaward Lagoon of Mesolongi, and is joined to the mainland (to which the town has spread) at either end by fine stone bridges. The local sailing boats have affinities with the Egyptian felucca and the nets are unusual. The 15C church of the **Panayía** has wall paintings. William Martin, an English deserter seaman, was one of the 600 who here successfully defied Omer Vrioni's siege in 1823.

From Aitolikó a road runs W in very flat arable country. You leave on the right a turn to Astakós (46km; see above), pass through **Neokhóri** (3471 inhab.), cross the Acheloös by a new bridge, and reach **Katokhí** (3002 inhab.) with a ruined medieval tower. Signs ('Ancient Oiniadae') through the village lead to a right turn (also signed). At **Oeniadae** (6km, left), a road ascends the acropolis, the rocky wooded hill of **Tríkardho Kástro**. Beyond the site, the road, unsurfaced, passes the ancient harbour and proceeds towards Astakós. After 200m a track (left) leads to the N (for docks, see below) and W sides of the site. *Oeniadae* was explored by the American School in 1901 and new work is in progress.

    *Oeniadae*, though unhealthily situated and inaccessible in winter, was strategically important as the key to S Akarnania. It was taken after a siege in 455 BC by exiled Messenians established at Naupaktos, and attacked in vain by Pericles in 453. Demosthenes in 424 forced the town to join the Athenian alliance. It fell to the Aitolians in 336 and, without bloodshed, to Philip V in 219. Captured by the Romans eight years later it was handed over to the Aitolian League. The town was restored to the Akarnanians in 189.

    Taking the first turn into the site, through fine fortifications in Archaic polygonal masonry (6C), you climb to near the **theatre**, cleared and used occasionally for performances. It has 27 rows of seats; inscriptions on the lowest three rows record the freeing of slaves and date the building (late 3C BC). The site, though generally wooded, is easily accessible at this point (and pleasantly filled with oak trees) but it is thickly overgrown at the periphery and some is fenced off. On all sides, except the S, it is surrounded by the marshes of Lezíni, the ancient Lake Melita. On the S a plain slopes down to the Acheloös. The main **gate** (to the S), is one of many with arched openings, a feature unusual in Greek architecture. Farther N are remarkable remains of the **docks** reconstructed by Philip V. There are a buttressed quay, porticoes surrounding a basin hewn in the rock, berths with traces of the rings to which the ships were moored,

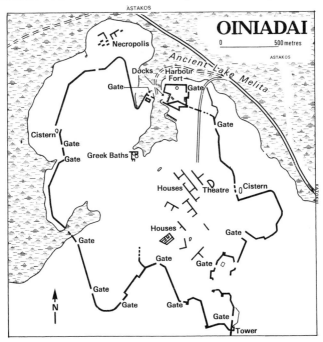

excellent ship-sheds and their slipways. To the SW of the port are some remains of **baths** of Greek construction.

Beyond Aitolikó the new road continues through rice fields. To the right are salt flats. 122km Ancient *Pleuron* (Plévron), high above the main road, is reached from the restaurant (Plevron) opposite a turning to Mesolóngi etc. Just N of the restaurant a rough track (c 5km, passable with care; poor in final stages) leads indirectly towards the site. In the early stages you pass below the two lower hills (Petrovoúni and Gyphtókastro) which have some Archaic remains of an enceinte that probably represents **Old Pleuron**, the city of the Curetes destroyed by Demetrios II, son of Antigonus Gonatas, in 234 BC. The track climbs to the enceinte of ashlar masonry (Kástro Iriniό), the **\*New Pleuron** built soon afterwards. The splendid **walls**, have 36

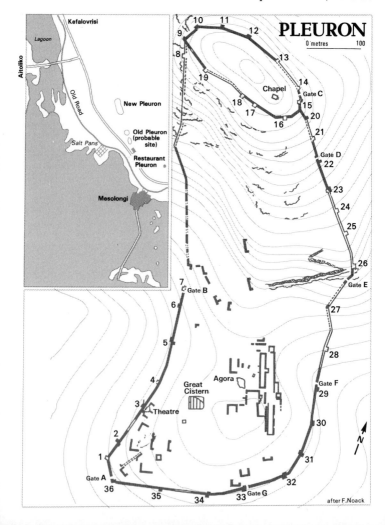

towers and 7 gates; the circuit is almost complete and stands in places to 15 courses of Hellenistic masonry.

Within are the ruins of a **theatre**, perhaps the smallest in Greece. The stage, with the proscenium, backed on to the city wall; a small doorway led through the orchestra to a square tower. In a hollow to the SE is a *cistern, 31m x 20m x 4m deep, divided into five rectangular basins by four partition walls pierced by triangular openings. Near the E wall is the **agora**, a flat rectangular terrace 145m long. It is crowded with the debris of buildings; among them a portico 60.5m x 10m, with enclosing walls still standing to a height of c 0.6m. There are also exedrae and pedestals. To the N (half an hour's steep climb; best to follow E wall) is the **acropolis**, which had square towers. Below the terrace the hill sinks rapidly E towards the city walls. At the foot of the depression is a fine gateway 1.7m wide, 2.7m high and 2m thick. The lintel is formed of two large horizontal blocks; in it and in the stone of the threshold are the holes for the gatepost.

At **Finikiá**, on the slopes below the acropolis, are the substantial remains of a three-aisled Early Christian basilica.

126km **MESOLÓNGI** (Μεσολόγγι; Hotels B, D, E; F/A), or **Missolonghi**, with 10,916 inhabitants, is the capital of the nome of Aitolía and Akarnanía, and the seat of a bishop. The town is more familiar to the English-speaking world than many others in Greece of greater importance, for here Lord Byron (born 1788) died of fever on 19 April 1824, after ten months of incessant activity in the cause of Greek independence. Mesolóngi, now by-passed by the main highway, is situated on the E shore of a vast lagoon (Limnothálassa) partly given over to fish hatcheries and the haunt of many water-birds. This has always been too shallow to allow access to vessels of any size, and a long causeway extends S to deep water at **Tourlídha**. Drainage and reclamation work is hastening the disappearance of the fishing community and their characteristic reed huts built on piles. In the local cafés the 'mezès' are varied and good.

**History.** *Mesolongi* was the W centre of resistance against the Turks in the War of Independence, and endured three sieges. In 1822 it was defended by Mavrogordato against a force of 10,000 led by Omer Vrioni and Reshid Pasha. In 1823 its commander was the Suliot, Markos Botsaris. In January 1824 Lord Byron came to Mesolongi and inspired the defenders with his enthusiasm; he died the following April before the beginning of the final siege. In April 1825 Reshid Pasha appeared before the town with 15,000 troops. The defenders numbered only 5000. Hampered by furious sorties and by a lack of supplies, Reshid Pasha could make no headway for six months. Then Ibrahim Pasha, with 10,000 Egyptians, advanced to his aid from the Peloponnese. After fluctuating struggles for the islands in the lagoon, the enemy closed round the devoted town. At the end of their resources after 12 months of siege, almost the whole population determined to break out. Their attempt (the 'Exodos') was made on the night of 22/23 April 1826. Though they managed to get clear of the town, they were frustrated by the treachery of a Bulgarian deserter, who had forewarned the besiegers. The fugitives, imagining themselves safe, were ambushed by 1000 Albanians on the slopes of Mt Zygos. Out of the 9000 who left Mesolongi—soldiers and civilians—only 1800 made good their escape to Amphissa. Meanwhile those who had stayed behind fired their magazines, overwhelming themselves and their enemies in a common destruction. In 1828 the Turks surrendered Mesolongi without firing a shot.

The town is entered through the Venetian walls by the 'Gate of the Sortie', rebuilt by King Otho to protect the hastily repaired earthen rampart through which the exodos was made. Within the gate (right) is a pleasant garden with the **heroön** (adm. free) commemorating the heroes of the town's three sieges. A large central tumulus contains the bodies of un-named defenders; to the right is the tomb of Botsaris, and, between the two, a statue of Byron erected in 1881, beneath which is the poet's heart. The centre of the town is the Plateía Bótsari, where the **Dhimarkhíon** houses the **Museum of the Revolution**, with Byron relics and several dramatic pictures of the war. Od. Trikoúpis leads W and, at the end, Od. Levídhou brings you to a small square where a **memorial garden** occupies the site of the house in which Byron died: the house was destroyed in the Second World War. Round a school is the causeway, with a bust of the poet Kostis Palamas and the reconstructed base of the historic **windmill** blown up by Christos Kapsalis on 11 April 1826.

*Capture of Mesolóngi. Engraving*

# 55

# From Mesolóngi to Athens

## A.  Via Río

**Road** to 41km (25½ miles) Andírrio, whence by frequent ferry to Río; from Rio to Athens (211km), see Rtes 38, 24. **Bus** regularly in 4 hrs; also from Mesolóngi to Patras.

The road runs E towards the dark mass of Varásova. To the right are seen the mountains that rise behind Patras. 5km Turning (left) to **Ayios Simeón**, the monastery where the people of Mesolongi made their last stand after the 'exodos' in 1826. At 8.5km a track (left; signposted) leads in a few minutes to ancient *Kalydon*, celebrated in the heroic age as the home of Oeneus and his sons Tydeus and Meleager. The neighbouring slopes, culminating at Mt Zygos (950m), were the scene of the hunt of the Kalydonian boar. Though Strabo couples Kalydon with Pleuron as an ornament to Greece, it was historically insignificant. The city received a death blow when Augustus transferred its inhabitants to Nikopolis and most of the public treasures to Patras.

After a few minutes, signs point to a **heroön** (right) and the **temple** (left). The **heroön** consists of rooms grouped round a peristyle court with a well and cistern. Under the main room is an impressive sepulchral chamber with stone furniture. The path continues to a ruined church (left) standing on ancient foundations, near the S fortifications of the ancient town. The **Sanctuary of Artemis Laphria** is impressively situated on a spur immediately to the SW, commanding the plain and gulf. The site was excavated by Danish archaeologists in 1925–32. A massive foundation platform locates the 4C **temple**, erected on a terrace supported by 6C retaining walls. Remains of painted terracotta metopes were recovered from earlier temples of c 570 and c 620 BC. Major finds are in the National Archaeological Museum in Athens.

You cross the Evinos. 10.5km Turning for **Káto Vasilikí** (4km), where the hill of **Ayía Triádha** has Hellenistic and Byzantine fortifications (? of Aetolian *Chalkis*) and an Early Christian basilica incorporating earlier masonry; also later churches. The road passes inland of **Mt Varásova** (916m), the ancient Mt Chalkis, by a low pass to emerge en corniche above the Gulf of Patras on the barren flanks of Klókova (Taphiassos; 1041m). The *views across the gulf include Patras itself and the mountains behind as far as the long crest of Erymanthos. At (32km) **Ríza** the road descends to the narrow coastal plain. Palaiókastro Mamákou (left) may be ancient *Makynia*. The torrents crossing the Patras-Rio road are conspicuous over the water. At 38km the road diverges right to **Andírrio** (Αντίρριο), where the ferry to **Río** (Rte 38) across the 'Little Dardanelles' provides the shortest approach from NW Greece to **Athens** (211km from Rio; see Rtes 38, 24).

Andírrio, like Río, has a picturesque medieval fortress. It is known as the **Castle of Roumeli**.

# B.  Via inland road to Lidhoríki and Delphí

**Road**, 370.5km (230 miles), mountainous with splendid scenery, but arduous driving between Navpaktos and Amfissa. The route can be shortened by 27.5km, and more significantly in terms of time, by taking the road across the Mornos dam and avoiding Lidhoriki.—48km Návpaktos.—135km Lidhoríki.—184km Amfissa. Then, via (206.5km) Delphí to Athens, see Rte 45. **Buses** twice daily from Návpaktos to Lidhoríki in 3 hrs; twice daily from Lidhoríki to Amfissa in 1½ hrs; also daily from Amfissa to Delphí; 5–6 times daily from Delphí to Athens (poor connections).

From Mesolóngi to (37.5km) the Andírrio turning, see Rte 55A. Beyond Andírrio the road runs a field's length from the sea, and briefly has a long view right down the Gulf of Corinth.

48km **Návpaktos** (Ναύπακτος; Hotels B, C, D) is a charming town (10,854 inhab.) though rather congested. The picturesque, mainly Venetian, **castle** (road access from W side of town; views; attractively floodlit at night), from which ramparts descend to enclose the little *harbour*, recalls the medieval past when it was known in the West as *Lepanto*. The plateia, shaded by jacaranda trees, looks across the Gulf to Mt Panakhaïkon. An old mosque E of the harbour is an archaeological store.

Here in 1571 the Turkish admiral fitted out before the decisive **Battle of Lepanto**, fought in fact off the Echinades. The allied fleet, under Don John of Austria, natural son of the Emperor Charles V, included contingents from Venice, Genoa, the Papal States,

Spain, Sicily, and Naples. The Turks were assisted by the Bey of Alexandria and the Bey of Algiers. The result was an overwhelming victory for Christendom, the Moslem sea-power suffering a blow from which it never recovered. The young Cervantes, creator of *Don Quixote*, here lost the use of his left hand.

Ancient *Naupaktos*, a town of the Ozolian Locrians, was taken in 455 by the Athenians. Here they established a colony of Messenians, who had been dispossessed by their Spartan conquerors. The place played an important part in the Peloponnesian War; it was successfully defended in 429 by Phormion and in 426 by Demosthenes against the Spartans, and became a base for the Sicilian expedition.

A by-road (buses daily) leads inland to (48km) **Thérmon**, see Rte 54.

Leaving Návpaktos, you keep left, following signs first to Amfissa then to Lidhoríki, and avoiding the new bridge and coast road. Your route first heads up the W side of the Mornos valley. 51.5km Keep straight ahead for Lidhoríki. At (52.5km) **Káto Dháfni** the road turns right onto a five-span bridge which carries the road across the **Mornos** near its mouth. The broad river valley is now completely empty of water. 54.5km **Kastráki**. 58.5km The **Moní Ay Ioánnou** is 2km to the left. At (60km) **Evpálio** (right) there is a by-road to **Monastiráki** (6.5km), on the coast. The way continues through rolling hills interspersed with orchards and little streams, climbing gradually. Prominent on a bluff to the right is a radar station commanding the Río strait. The mountains behind Patras become very prominent across the Gulf and there are splendid retrospective views southwards before the descent past (66km) **Filothéi** (or Goumaíoi). 68.5km Turning (left) for the **Varnákova Monastery** (6km), a Byzantine foundation rebuilt by Capodistrias in 1831. The road turns N, crosses a ridge, then follows a ledge high up the mountainside above a side valley of the Mornos. During the gradual descent to the main river the horizon becomes increasingly filled with peaks, those to the N barren, those to the E clothed with forests. Beyond (71.5km) a sign to **Teíkio** (right) the road drops to (78.5km; café) cross the Mornos, now virtually dry, at its confluence with the Loufolóreko.

A by-road up the valley makes for **Terpsithéa** (13km). Off this (left), at (5km) **Limnítsa**, minor roads lead into the mountains to **Khrísovo** and **Katafíyio**, once refuges from the Turks, the latter better reached by the more westerly road out of Navpaktos.

The road climbs high above the N bank of the Mornos and a series of wooded valleys open out to the east. There are dark pine forests on the higher slopes. You descend again almost to river level to cross a side stream. The valley becomes broader with views ahead towards Mt Giona (2509m). 90.5km Turning to **Krokíli** (11km), native village of Yiannis Makriyiannis, a hero of the 1821 revolt. A succession of bridges cross gulleys and minor streams. At 94.5km is the **Mornos Dam** (right; 850m long) across which a road (27.5km shorter and much quicker, also for Lidhoríki) leads along the S side of the artificial lake to rejoin your route N of Malandríno.

Continuing N, the road between this point and Lidhoriki has some very poor patches. At (97.5km) turning to **Kókkinos**. The view to the east includes **Kallípolis** (see below) crowned by its church. N up the Kókkino valley are the Vardhousia Mts (2437m). At 103km, follow a sign to **Dháfnos**. Across (108km) the Kókkino there is a by-road (at 111km) to **Dhiakópi** (2km to the left). 116.5km Rising immediately above the road to the right is a conical hill with the remains of **Kállion** or Veloúkhi (ancient *Kallipolis*). The lower part of the site was excavated in intensive campaigns from 1976 by the Greek Archaeological Service and the French School in advance of flooding for creation of the Mornos barrage. Further work is in progress. Classical remains are of the Hellenistic to Late Roman periods and include parts of the city wall, houses, public buildings and the Roman cemetery.

The site suffered destruction by the Gauls in 279 BC. More prominent on the higher slopes of the acropolis are substantial walls and buildings of a fortified medieval settlement (Loidorix), perhaps built by the Catalans who certainly occupied the site in the 14C AD. As *Loidorix*, it was one of the three Catalan strong-points of the county of Salona. The summit was occupied by a donjon. Lower down is a cistern and remains of houses. In places the medieval walls overlie the ancient. Below on the shore are some sad remains of the drowned old village of Kallion now again above water level. A short distance further along the road is the newer hamlet and there are good retrospective views of the ancient site.

135km **Lidhoríki** (559m; Hotel E), a pleasant mountain village with 985 inhabitants and an archaeological collection (1994), is the chief market centre of Doris, one of the two eparchies of Phocis. Continuing S in the shallow and comparatively populous valley of the Velá, the road is much improved. At 123km the road round the S of the lake (see above) comes in from the right crossing the valley on a short embankment. To the W, 1km beyond **Aigítion** (formerly Stroúza), a fortified acropolis may be ancient *Aegition*, with other forts in its territory (on Mts Vourokhori and Zerza). 144km **Palaiókastro** is on an ancient site. Roads branch (left) to **Malandrinó** and (right) to **Vraîla** and then **Amigdhaliá** etc. Beyond this last turn Classical walling is visible (left). The road climbs amid scrub to the summit (850m), passing (153.5km) a turn to the monastery of **Panayía tis Koutsouriótissas** (right; 7km). 154.5km To the right is a road to Eratiní on the coast (with, after 3km, a minor road to Ayioi Pándes). 159km Turn for Pendeória and Galaxídhi (comp. Rte 55C).

The road bears left, to the NE. Ahead and right rises the range of Parnassos as it descends to (167km) **Vounikhóra** (761m). The landscape is scrubby and uninteresting; beyond the village however the *view opens out to the right giving a glimpse of the Bay of Galaxidhi with Khrisó and Delphi lying on the slopes of Parnassos. 174km **Ayía Evthímia** (460m). The landscape mellows suddenly (180km) with a full view of the olive groves which fill the valley of Amphissa. The town stands at its head. There is a winding descent on the flank of Mt Kokinari to (184km) **Amfissa**, from which via (206.5km) **Delphi** to (370.5km) **Athens**, see Rte 45.

# C.  Via coastal road to Galaxídhi, then Dhesfína (or Delphi)

**Road**, 312km (195 miles), new highway to Itéa along the Gulf of Corinth, thence joining Delphi–Levadhiá road.

To (48km) **Návpaktos**, see Rte 55B. Just E of the town the ways part by the Mornos. The new road (right), crosses nearer the mouth of the river, soon approaches and then follows the coast. There are few villages and place-names often derived from beaches or isolated churches. 58km **Monastiráki**, a pretty village where Herodotos located *Erythrae*. 65km **Káto Marathiás**. Farther on a cluster of hamlets faces the Islet of Trizonia (Hotels B, C). 84km (52½ miles) **Ayios Nikólaos** is linked three times daily by car ferry with Aíyio (1 hr; Rte 38). 92km **Paralía Tolofónos** and (95km) **Eratiní** (Hotel B) are served by a minor road. Eratiní stands on the bay of **Vitrinitsa** where in 1675 Sir Giles Eastcourt died, one of the first recorded Englishmen to visit

Greece. The site of ancient *Tolophon*, with a well-preserved enceinte, lies near (104.5km) **Ayioi Pándes** (Hotel C).

The road now skirts the sheltered inner bays of the W side of the Gulf of Itea. 114km **Galaxídhi** (Γαλαξίδι; Hotels L, A, B, C, D), a well-built old seafaring town (pop. 1369), with many absentee householders, is picturesquely situated on a wooded bay with a fine view of Parnassos. The church of the **Metamórphosis** was reputedly rebuilt by Michael II Angelos in gratitude for his recovery from an illness; it has an exceptionally good altar screen. There is an interesting **Maritime Museum** (publications), with paintings, equipment and relics; also some antiquities and material relating to the Wars of Independence. The town has sections of ancient wall, which may have belonged to ancient *Chaleion*.

The coast is scarred with quarries and mines: bauxite is loaded by cableway and tipped direct into ships. The little Bay of Salona, site of Salona's medieval port, now Ormos Itéas, was also the scene of Frank Abney Hastings' exploit with the steamship *Karteria* against the Turks in 1827.

You ignore the by-pass (for Amphissa, Delphi and Athens, allowing an alternative route to that described below) and turn to (133km) **Itéa** (Hotels B, C), with 4303 inhabitants. The modern harbour of Amfissa, built round a promontory at the head of the Gulf, it is a fresh and pleasant small resort, busy at intervals with cruise ships disembarking their excursions to Delphi.

135km **Kírra**.

French (and more recently Greek) excavations show that ancient *Kirrha* flourished in Early and Middle Helladic times, though it is best known for its part in the First Sacred War. Recent work has revealed part of a Classical harbour-front building and some remains of the harbour itself can be made out beneath the sea. There is a Frankish tower on the sea front, mainly constructed of reused Classical blocks. This (rather than Galaxidhi, as usually supposed) may have been the port of medieval Salona (Amphissa). There are Early Christian and Byzantine remains at **Ayios Nikólaos** (2km N of the tower) where there was an important settlement.

Beyond Kirrha a spectacular road climbs 610m up the face of Koútsouras and across its saddle to (155km) **Dhesfína**, continuing in an enclosed valley. At (159km) the large **Moní Timíou Prodhrómou**, it divides. The right branch makes a steep descent to **Andíkira** (11km; Rte 45), while the left branch crosses another ridge to (168km) **Dhístomo** (for Osios Loukas, Rte 45). Hence to (195km) **Levadhiá** and via Thebes to (314km) **Athens**, see Rte 45.

# 56

# The Ionian Islands

The **IONIAN ISLANDS**, known also as the **Eptánisa**, from the seven principal islands, lie in the Ionian Sea mainly off the W coast of Greece. The 'seven islands', from N to S, are **Corfu** (off the coast of Albania and Epirus); **Paxoi** (off the coast of Epirus); **Levkas** (off Akarnania); **Ithaka**, **Cephalonia**, or Kefallinia, and **Zakynthos**, or Zante (at the entrance to the Gulf of Corinth); and **Kithira** (to the S of the Vatika Peninsula in the

Peloponnese). The smaller islands include the group of the Othonian Islands—**Fano, Merlera**, and **Samothraki**—to the NW of Corfu; **Andipaxoi**, S of Paxoi; **Meganisi** and **Kalamos**, between Levkas and the mainland of Akarnania; the **Echinadhes** lying E of Ithaka near the mouth of the Acheloös; and **Andikithira**, S of Kithira. A claim by Palmerston at the time of the 'Don Pacifico' incident in 1848 that the islets of Sapienza and Cervi, off Messenia, formed part of the Ionian Islands was not sustained. The grouping of the islands is a largely artificial conception of medieval and 19C politics. The group, excluding Kithira (now administered from Piraeus), still remains nominally an administrative region, divided into four nomes, but the frequency of communication between each nome and Athens is greater than between the nomes themselves. The islands are described together here, partly because of the interest to British travellers of their tenure by Britain in 1815–64 as a protectorate.

The largest of the islands is Cephalonia, with the highest mountain, but by far the most important is Corfu, with the largest town. The scenery combines the lush greenness of the English countryside (together with a rainfall spread through the year) with the characteristic Greek seascape. The high hedges that line the roads are also unusual in Greece. The total population of the four nomes is 193,734.

**Climate and Season**. The climate of the Ionian Islands is generally temperate, but subject to sudden changes. Their winter is rather rainy and their summer rather too hot, but in spring and autumn they are enchanting. The average temperature ranges from 6.7°–32.8°C (44°–91°F); the annual average of rainy days is as high as 100. The *Scirocco*, which blows from the SE, is depressing and unpleasant. Frost is rare, and snow seldom falls except on the tops of the hills. Squalls (*borasche*) are frequent. Earthquakes, especially in Zante, Levkas, and Cephalonia are not uncommon.

**History**. The name Ionian is not easily explained; Herodotus in his account of the Ionian peoples does not refer to the *Ionian Islands* as such. In Homeric times a maritime people, under the generic name of *Kephallenians*, inhabited the islands at the mouth of the Gulf of Corinth. *Odysseus* (or *Ulysses*), King of Ithaca, was the epic personification of this naval realm, which comprised the islands (or cities) of *Ithaca, Doulichion, Same*, and *Zakynthos*, as well as the islets (Od. IX, 21 ff). At the 'extreme end of the earth' was *Scheria* (? Corcyra or Corfu), where dwelt the friendly Phaeaceans. Since Classical times authorities have disagreed as to the modern equivalents. The traditional school identifies Ithaca with Ithaka, Same with Same in Cephalonia, and Zakynthos with Zante; but, echoing the perplexity of the ancients, is hazy about Doulichion. Strabo (X, 2) insists that it was one of the Echinades. Others place it at Pale, in Cephalonia. The revolutionary views of Dörpfeld, put forward in detail in 1927, that Levkas is ancient *Ithaka*, modern Ithaka ancient *Same*, and Cephalonia ancient *Doulichion*, have not received general support; though the theory removes the problem of the identification of Doulichion (which, since it sent 40 ships to Troy as against 12 from the other three cities, must have been larger than the Echinades), it poses other problems, equally insoluble. Samuel Butler reminds us that we ought not to look for the accuracy of a guidebook in a narrative that tells us of a monster with six heads and three rows of teeth in each; and, remembering that the whole region is particularly prone to seismic disturbances, we must perhaps be resigned to the geographical mysteries of the *Odyssey*. A thorough archaeological exploration of Cephalonia may eventually clarify its position in the Mycenaean world and provide new answers. Some lively views have been put forward by experienced yachtsmen on the Homeric topography of this area.

After the age of Homer the islands ceased for centuries to have any common bond of union. At the outbreak of the Peloponnesian War (431 BC) Corcyra, Kephallenia, and Zakynthos were allies of Athens, and Leucas (Levkas) of Sparta. Both the Corcyreans and the Leucadians provided fleets for their respective leaders.

Towards the end of the 3C BC the islands became Roman. In AD 890 the Byzantine emperor Leo the Philosopher (886–911) formed all seven into one province; and in this condition they belonged to the Eastern Empire after the disintegration of Italy. In the decline of the Empire they were again divided up, and various Latin princes owned the different islands. They are heard of occasionally in the struggles between the Greek emperors and the Western crusaders. They were desolated by the ravages of corsairs, Christian as well as Mohammedan. After many vicissitudes, the inhabitants of Corfu placed themselves, in 1386, under the sovereignty of Venice, the state which was to influence the destinies of the islands more than any other. During the next two centuries Venice obtained control of most of the other Ionian Islands; but two of them remained independent much longer. Levkas was annexed in 1684, Kythera not till 1717.

The rule of the Venetians, much less severe than in the Archipelago, embodied some of the principles of Machiavelli. The more prominent citizens, instead of being imprisoned or executed, were ennobled. Frequent intermarriages made for a close assimilation of races, and the ascendancy of the more cultured partner helped to consolidate the domination of Venice. Education was discouraged and Ionian youths were granted the privilege of purchasing degrees at Italian universities without having to pass examinations. Italian became the official language and the Roman Catholic religion was established. The humbler classes who formed the great bulk of the population, remained faithful to the Greek language and to the Orthodox Church.

On the fall of Venice in 1797, the Treaty of Campo Formio transferred the Ionian Islands to the French Republic, and they were occupied by a small French garrison. The French soldiers were driven out in 1798 by a combined Russian and Turkish force. By the provisions of the Treaty of 21 March 1800, between the Tsar and the Sultan, the Ionian Islands were formed into a separate state, with the high-sounding title of the **Septinsular Republic**. The republic was under the protectorate first of the Porte, later of Russia. This period of quasi-independence (1800–07) proved to be little better than a reign of terror. Within two years all seven islands had risen against their general government and each separate island against its local authorities. Horrors, resembling those of the Corcyrean factions described by Thucydides (III, 81) were of daily occurrence. In 1802, on the change of masters, the principal Ionians sent an envoy to the Tsar, imploring his interference, and as a result the Russian plenipotentiary, Count Mocenigo, a native of Zante, which had become particularly notorious for the number of its assassinations, was empowered to proclaim new forms of administration.

But in 1807, by the Treaty of Tilsit, the islands were given back to France, and incorporated in the province of Illyria. In 1809 Great Britain came on the scene, General Oswald took Cephalonia, Ithaka, Zante, and Kythera that year, and Levkas in 1810. Paxos was reduced in 1814 and after the fall of Napoleon Corfu was surrendered by its French defender, at the command of Louis XVIII, to Sir James Campbell. The Treaty of Paris (1815) made the Ionian Islands an independent state under the protection of the British crown.

Sir Thomas Maitland (?1759–1824) was first Lord High Commissioner. A constitution was drawn up at his direction, and adopted by the Ionian Constituent Assembly in 1817. The administration at Corfu comprised the Lord High Commissioner, the Senate of six members, and the Assembly. The Senate and the Assembly of 42 deputies were ciphers, for the Lord High Commissioner had the right of veto on all their acts, charge of foreign relations, and the immediate control of the police and health departments. He was represented in each of the other six islands by a British Resident, with local functions similar to his own.

Maitland was not slow to make use of his dictatorial powers and soon acquired the nickname 'King Tom'. Despite the defects of the colonial system, the next 30 years gave the Ionian Islands an era of peace and prosperity unparalleled on the mainland. The administration of justice became impartial. Direct taxation was practically abolished and the revenue, raised chiefly by import and export duties, was freed from peculation. Trade and agriculture were encouraged; educational establishments (including even a short-lived university at Corfu) were founded; and excellent roads, unknown in Greece since Roman times, were built, as well as harbours, quays, and aqueducts. The Greek Church was restored.

Nationalist feeling soon overrode material considerations. The islanders, who had at first welcomed the British, particularly resented the measures taken to enforce their neutrality in the Greek struggle for independence. The achievement by Greece in 1830 of her immediate aims increased the discontent with foreign rule. A powerful opposition, headed by Andreas Mustoxidi, agitated for union with Greece. In 1858,

Gladstone was sent on a special commission and for a few days exercised the functions of Lord High Commissioner. He vainly attempted to meet the situation by proposing a number of reforms. As late as 1861 he declared that it would be a 'crime against the safety of Europe' to give up the islands.

On the change of dynasty in Greece, however, Great Britain voluntarily ceded all rights over the Ionian Islands by the Treaty of London signed in 1864; at the same time their union with Greece was formally recognised. Edward Lear made a tour in 1863, drawing his 'Views in the Seven Ionian Islands'.

# A.  Corfú (Kérkira)

**Approaches**. **By Air**. From Athens, twice daily in c 50 minutes; from Thessaloníki twice weekly in 1 hour. From London direct c twice a week in summer.

**By Sea. Car Ferry** from Igoumenítsa, many times daily in 1½hr; from Pátras, 1—5 times daily via Igoumenítsa.

Through **buses** from Athens (2–3 times daily and Thessaloníki (twice daily) connect with boats. **Ferries** also from Sayiádha (N of Igoumenitsa) to Kérkira (twice weekly); from Platariá (S of Igoumenitsa) to Levkímmi (daily); from Igoumenítsa to Levkímmi (daily). Day trips to Albania (Sarandë) in summer.

Corfú is a port-of-call also (several times daily in summer; several times weekly in winter) of international **car ferry** services, Piraeus–Ancona, Piraeus–Bari, Venice, Patras–Brindisi, Patras–Ancona, Patras–Otranto Patras–Trieste, also others (break of journey at Corfu—no extra charge—must be notified before embarkation); and it is visited by innumerable cruise ships. Passengers without an international ticket travelling between two Greek ports can do so only by Greek shipping lines.

**CORFÚ**, in Greek **Kérkira** (Κέρκυρα), is the best known and most beautiful of the Ionian Islands. With a length of 64km and maximum width in the N of nearly 32km, it is the second largest of the seven islands, but the population (pop. 105,356) is much greater than that of more spacious Kefallinía. Its capital is likewise the most important and populous town in the group. The most northerly of the Ionian Islands, situated less than 3km off the N Epirot coast of Albania, and the nearest Greek land to Italy, Corfú has a natural importance as the gateway between East and West. Until the Balkan Wars of 1912–13 extended the Greek frontier, it had long been a Christian outpost on the very verge of Turkish territory.

The land, especially in the long S peninsula, is well-watered and fertile. Cypress, fig, orange, and lemon trees are found in magnificent profusion, but above all the olive, which is here unpruned, almost attains the size and dignity of a forest tree. About four million grow in the island, providing a large output of oil. Cactus is common. Vineyards abound, producing good white wine (unresinated) and a rather sweet heavy red wine with a short life. Apples and pears are grown and, more important, tomatoes. The broad N section is crossed by a range of hills from W to E, culminating in Pantokrator (914m). In the S a lesser range is topped by Mt Ayioi Dheka (567m), a conspicuous landmark.

The effects of the long Venetian domination are still apparent. Italian, once the official language, and strongly tinged with the Venetian dialect, is still quite commonly spoken and understood. The place-names are bi-lingual, with a preference for the Italian form. Among the legacies of British rule are cricket and ginger beer. A local speciality is the *kum-kwat*, the crystallised miniature Japanese orange. Except in Corfu town, hotels are often closed in winter.

**History**. The name Corfú is an Italian corruption of Koryphó, a Byzantine name derived from the two peaks (Κορυφαί) on which the citadel of the chief town is built. The ancient name *Corcyra* appears first in Herodotus. About 734 BC (traditional date, not yet confirmed by pottery found) a colony was planted here by the Corinthians. This rapidly became rich and powerful enough to found colonies of its own. Corinth soon became jealous and apprehensive, and c 664 BC a battle was fought between their respective fleets, the first Greek sea-fight on record. The Corcyreans took no part in the Persian wars. In 432 BC they invoked the help of Athens against the Corinthians. The consequent engagement off the Sybota Is., between the Corcyreans and their mother-city, precipitated the Peloponnesian War. During this struggle the power and importance of Corcyra was irretrievably squandered in the calamitous feuds between the oligarchic and democratic parties. The victory of the democrats in 425 BC was marked by atrocities. Corcyra was chosen by the Athenians for the final review of their fleet in 415 BC on the eve of the Sicilian expedition.

Though Corcyra never recovered her former importance, the island was by 373 BC, according to Xenophon, in a wonderful state of fertility and opulence. After a succession of masters, it became Roman in 229 BC. Here Octavian assembled his fleet before the battle of Actium, and at various times Tibullus, Cato, and Cicero all came to the island. In AD 67 Corcyra was visited by Nero, on his way to Greece. According to Suetonius, he sang and danced before the altar of Zeus at Kassiope.

During the Crusades, the geographical position of Corfu again brought it into prominence. Robert Guiscard seized the island in 1081 during his wars with the Eastern Empire. Richard I of England landed here on his return from the Holy Land in 1193, on his way to Ragusa and unexpected captivity. Passing from the Venetians to the Genoese and back again (1204–14), Corfu came under Epirus until 1267, then under the Angevins of Naples. Towards the end it suffered greatly at the hands of pirates. In 1386, the inhabitants invoked the aid of Venice, under whose sovereignty they remained until her downfall in 1797. Venice made Corfu her principal arsenal in Greece and surrounded the town with extensive fortifications, which defied the whole power of the Ottomans in 1537 and 1570 and, above all, in the celebrated siege of 1716, remarkable as the last great attempt of the Turks to extend their conquests in Christendom. In this siege the personal efforts of the High Admiral of the Ottoman Empire were frustrated by the skill and daring of Marshal Schulenburg, a soldier of fortune from Saxony.

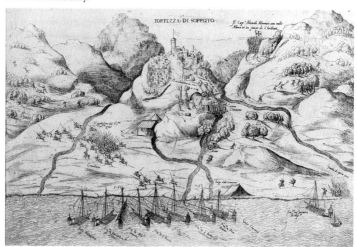

*Soppoto. Battle between Venetians and Turks, 1670. Engraving*

The subsequent history of Corfu is largely that of the Ionian Islands as a whole (see above). Count John Capodistrias, the first President of independent Greece, was a Corfiot. In 1915–16 the island was used as a base for the reorganisation of the Serbian army after its disastrous retreat, until its transfer to the Thessaloniki front. In August 1923, in consequence of the murder of Gen. Tellini, the Italian president of the Greco-Albanian Boundary Commission, Italy bombarded Corfu, and subsequently occupied the island, together with Paxos, Antipaxos, Merlera, and Samothraki, until 27 September, when the incident was closed by the payment of an idemnity of 50 million lire. As a result, however, Corfu remained a 'frontier region' with special restrictions from 1924 to 1961. In the Second World War the island was occupied in 1941–43 without much unpleasantness by the Italians and later by the Germans. There followed ten days of bombardment and fighting (13–23 September) before the city was reduced by the Germans. During this time a quarter of the town was destroyed, including the seat of the Ionian parliament, the magnificent old library of the former university with 70,000 volumes, and 14 churches with their paintings of the Ionian school. In the international channel NE of Corfu on 22 October 1946 two British destroyers hit an uncharted Albanian minefield, deliberately laid, losing 45 men.

Corfu has a tradition of musical performance dating from 1733. Edward Lear (1812–88), author of the *Book of Nonsense*, lived for some time at Corfu while painting and writing about Greece.

The town of **Corfú** or **Kérkira** (Κέρκυρα), situated on an irregular peninsula about the middle of the E coast, just S of the islet of **Ptikhía**, is the capital of the island and the largest town in the Ionian Islands. Including the suburbs of **Mandoúki** to the W and **Gáritsa** and **Sarókko** to the S, now all contiguous, it has 31,359 inhabitants. Destined by the Venetians to become the headquarters of their Greek possessions, its strong fortifications immediately catch the eye. As a busy port-of-call for vessels plying between Italy and Greece, for cruise ships, and for naval vessels, it is a favourite resort of visitors. The old town has narrow streets and tall houses, having formerly been enclosed by walls. During the British occupation it was given a good water supply and extended towards the site of the ancient city to the S. The grave damage, caused by the fighting in 1943 between Italians and Germans and worsened in 1944 by Anglo-American bombing, left scars which were slow to disappear.

**Airport**, just beyond the suburb of Sarókko. **Terminal**, Kapodhistríou 20.

**Hotels** L, A–E.

**Tavernas** near Mon Repos beach, near the Achílleion, at Kanóni, at Pérama, etc.

**Post Office** (Pl. 6), Leof. Alexándras 26. **OTE Centre** (Pl. 6), Od. Mántzaros 3.

**Informaton Offices** NTOG and **Tourist Police**, Kapodhistríou (Old Palace).
  **Police**, Alexandras.

**Buses** from the Spianádha (Pl. 3) to Mon Repos and Kanóni; from Plat Theotóki (Sarókko; Pl. 6) to Dhasiá, Ipsos; to the Achilleion, etc.; from the Néo Froúrio (Pl. 2) to Athens etc., Kassiópi and rest of island.

**Motor-Boats** in summer, from below the Spianádha to Dhasiá (out morning; return afternoon and early evening).

**Amusements**. **Casino** at Kanóni (Hilton); **Tennis Club** Od. Romanoú 4(Pl. 7); **Bathing** (nearest) at Mon Repos beach (Pl. 16); **Concerts** in the Bandstand on Sundays.

The modern **harbour** runs along the NW edge of the city, from the Adriatic ferry berths to the W (Pl. 1) to the drive-on quay of the Igoumenítsa car ferry to the E (Pl. 2). From the **Custom House** (Pl. 2) you follow the quay E beneath the untidy lower slopes of the **Néo Froúrio** (Fortezza Nuova), built in 1577–88 by the Venetians. The fortress, having served the French, was given its superstructure by the British and only ceased to be a military post after 1864. Until the Second World War it was used by a police school;

during the war its casemates sheltered the Corfiots from air raids; the barrack-block is now occupied by a naval detachment. The bastions, picturesquely overgrown by fig trees and wild flowers, may be explored (closed at midday) from the E side entrance. The W wall above the dry moat has two large lions of St Mark.

You reach the sun-drenched Plateía Yeoryíou B, with its judas trees, where even the horses of the hired carriages wear hats. The **Porta Spilia** (16C), incorporated in a later structure gives access to the main street through the heart of the town (see below). From the SE corner another narrow passage passes the Nea Yorki hotel and leads by stepped streets (*skalinádhes*) into the Kambielo (*Campiello*) quarter where constricted alleys (*kantoúnia*) wind through high tenements; here are an attractive Venetian well-head of 1699 and the churches of **Panayía Kremastí** and the **Pantokrátor** both with good altar-screens.

In fine weather it is better to follow the sea road, flanked by handsome houses along the line of the old walls and with good views of the mainland. Rounding the point (Od. Arseníou) you pass the **Museum of Byzantine and Post-Byzantine Art** in the church of Antivouniótissa and the **Archbishop's Palace**, the former **Nomarkhía** (1835), on the site of Capodistrias' birth-place, and now the seat of the **Ionian University**. The **Corfu Literary Society** has a good exhibition of material relating to the culturual life of the island. The **Solomos Museum** is devoted to the poet Dionysios Solomos (1798–1857). The point affords also a view of the citadel.

The **Royal Palace** (Pl. 3), a large Classical building constructed of Malta stone, has an elegant Doric portico of 32 columns, set forward and linking two gates (of St Michael and St George) in the form of triumphal arches; beyond these the portico curves forward to lateral pavilions. Above the cornice are seven sculptured medallions with the emblems of the Ionian islands. In front stands a bronze statue, by Prosellenti, of Sir Frederic Adam, who organised the water-supply of Corfu.

The palace was designed by Colonel (later General Sir George) Whitmore in 1819 to serve as treasury of the newly created Order of St Michael and St George, and as residence for the Lord High Commissioner. A legislative assembly was incorporated. In 1864 the building was handed intact to the King of the Hellenes; it served as a royal residence but fell into disrepair after 1913. After some damage by billeted refugees in the Civil War, the High Commissioner's private apartments were restored for the Greek government for use as a museum, while in 1954, at the instance of Sir Charles Peake, then British ambassador in Athens, the state rooms were restored as a memorial to the British connection with Corfu.

The State Rooms comprise the **Throne Room**, meeting-place of the Ionian senate, with the original throne and full-length portraits of High Commissioners; the **Rotunda**, or ballroom, with ceiling motif of the badge of the Order and the original floor; and the **Dining Room**. One wing houses the **Museum of Asiatic Art**—a collection of Chinese and Japanese porcelain and bronzes, presented by Greg. Manos, a former Greek ambassador in the Far East, while in another room is a **Collection of Christian Art**, with floor mosaics from Ayia Kerkyra (see below Palaiopolis/Mon Repos); frescoes; ikons by Hieremias Palladhes (16C), Yeoryios Kortezas, Emmanuel Tzanes, and Mikhaïl Dhamaskinos.

The **\*Esplanade** (Pl. 3, 7), or **Spianádha**, a huge open space separating the citadel from the town, served the Venetians as a parade and exercise ground. It is divided by a central avenue. The N half of the Esplanade, known as the Plateía, in front of the Palace, forms the 'field' on which in July are played the traditional cricket matches between two local clubs and visiting teams from Britain and Malta. Its former gravel surface has given place to turf but a matting wicket is still used. On the W it is bounded by the 'Liston', an imposing arcaded row of tall houses designed during the French occupation in 1807–14 in imitation of the Rue de Rivoli; here are many popular cafés. On the grass-sown S half of the Esplanade (The Spianádha proper) rise a bandstand (*Palko*) and an elegant Ionic **rotunda** in memory of Sir Thomas Maitland, first Lord High Commissioner (1815–23). At the S end the former **Ionian Academy** (now a school) faces the Nautical Club whose 'eights' row offshore.

On the central avenue stands a **Statue of Marshal Schulenburg**, erected by the Venetians in his lifetime just after the siege of 1716. Executed by Ant. Corradini in Carrara marble, it was removed here from the citadel by the British. To the N the glacis of the citadel is occupied by exotic gardens, containing a statue of the eccentric Philhellene Lord Guilford (1769–1828), founder of the Ionian Academy. Beyond the wall stands the chapel of **Panayía Mandrakína** (1700). A bridge flanked by cannon of 1684 crosses the 16C moat, where (left) motor-boats may be hired and (right) the local children usually swim. The **Pálaio Froúrio** (Fortezza Vecchia), or **citadel** (open daily, subject to some restrictions; no cameras), occupies a promontory with two heights. First heard of as '**Korypho**' in 968, it remained through the Middle Ages the fortified township. The heights are crowned by the 'Castel di Terra' with a semaphore and lighthouse, and the 'Castel de Mar', a Byzantine foundation, formerly the powder magazine. Explosions in the 18C destroyed most earlier work, but the W bastions are substantially as built in 1558 by Savorgnani and Martinengo. Below to the S is the former **Garrison Church of St George**, with a Doric portico, built by the British (1830). On the N side are the buildings of the **Military Academy**, which with some ancient Venetian barracks over-look the little harbour of **Mandraki**. On the seaward point once stood a temple of Hera Akraia.

The landward fortress, reached by a curving tunnel, has a magnificent *view, with gorgeous colouring. To the E extends the long mountainous coastline of Albania and Epirus. To the W the island rises above and beyond the town.

Leofóros Kapodhistríou runs along the W side of the Esplanade behind the Liston. The church of **Ayios Spiridón** was erected in 1589–96. The early-18C ceiling paintings of Panayotis Doxaras were tastelessly refurbished in the 19C. The marble iconostasis (1864; by the Austrian Maurs) takes the form of a complete church façade. Admiral And. Pisani's lamp, near the pulpit, dates from 1711.

Spiridon, Bishop of Cyprus, suffered during the persecution of Diocletian and was a member of the Council of Nicaea in 325. His body was brought to Corfu in 1489 and is preserved in a richly-ornamented silver **sarcophagus** (1867; Viennese) to the right of the high altar. Four times a year (11 August; first Sunday in November; Palm Sunday; Saturday in Holy Week) the remains are carried in solemn procession round parts of the town and esplanade. The routes and rites are different and commemorate miraculous deliverances, respectively from the Turks in 1716, from plague in 1673, from plague in 1630, and from famine (? before 1553). So popular is the saint that nearly half the boys in the island are named after him.

You turn left into Od. Filarmoníkis, with its animated vegetable market, and soon meet Od. Nikifórou Theotóki, the main pedestrian street since Venetian times, which runs through the town from the Liston to the Old Port. Beyond it you cross, farther on, Od. Voulgaréos, the narrow arcaded street that channels traffic from the Esplanade towards Sarókko. On the corner stands the **Dhimarkhíon**, built in 1663 as a Venetian loggia; converted (1720) into the Teatro San Giacomo, it became in 1903 the town hall.

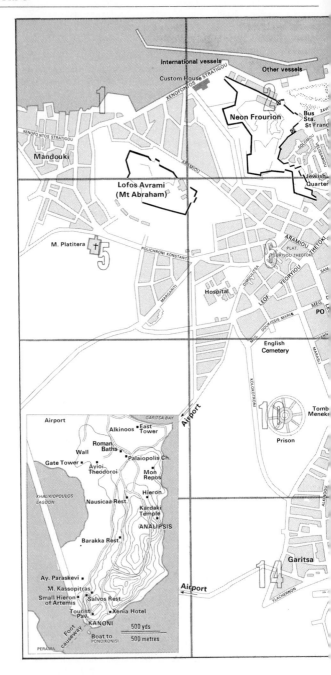

International vessels

Other vessels

Custom House STRATIGOU

XENOFONTOS

1

ZAVI

Neon Frourion

Bus
Sta.
St Franc

XENOFONTOS STRATIGOU

Mandouki

ARAMIOU

2

SOLOMOU

VESSARIONI

ELISSARIOU

Jewish
Quarter

Lofos Avrami
(Mt Abraham)

ARAMIOU

PLAT.
(YEORYIOU THEOTOKI

THETOKI

M. Platitera

5

POLICHRONI KONSTANTI

6

YEORYIOU

OIKONOMOU

SAM

LEOF.

MEG

MARGARITI

Hospital

DIMOULITSA

MIG. DOUKISSIS MARIA

PO

ROANN

English
Cemetery

MARASLI

KOLOKOTRONI

Tomb
Menekr

10

Prison

GARITSA BAY

Airport

Airport

Alkinoos    East
Tower

Roman
Baths

Wall

Palaiopolis Ch.

Gate Tower

Ayioi
Theodoroi

KHALIKIOPOULOS
LAGOON

Nausicaa Rest.

Mon
Repos

Hieron

Kardaki
Temple

ANALIPSIS

Barakka Rest.

Garitsa

14

VLACHERNON

Ay. Paraskevi

M. Kassopitras

Small Hieron
of Artemis

Salvos Rest.

Tourist
Pav.

Xenia Hotel

KANONI

500 yds

Foot
causeway

Boat to
PONDIKONISI

500 metres

PERAMA

Airport

ALKETA

TOUNDOLI

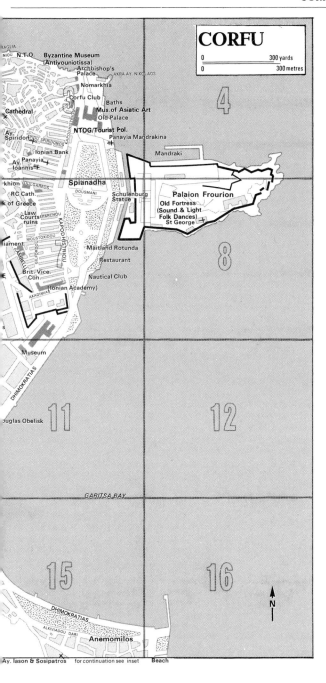

A mutilated relief of 1691 in the E façade commemorates Morosini's victories. N.C. Mantzaros (1795–1874), who directed the opera here, is best remembered as composer of the Greek national anthem. In the square, to the S, stands the elegant façade (1658) of the **Latin Cathedral** (St James), remarkably unadorned for Italian work of this period; the church, made a roofless shell in 1943, has been restored. The former Archbishop's Palace (1754; later, Law Courts) is opposite.

In the quarter within the ramparts farther S, the former **Ionian Parliament**, removed here from the palace in 1855, was given after 1869 to the British community as their Anglican church; bombed in the war, it was repaired in 1961 to house a small art gallery.

Leofóros Yeoryíou Theotóki runs SW towards the Plateía Theotóki, the centre of the modern quarter that has evolved from the former suburb of Sarokko (San Rocco). On the way is the site of the **Municipal Theatre** of 1902, ruined in 1944. It was the HQ of the Serbian army in 1915–16 and here in 1918 was proclaimed the new country of Yugoslavia. A new theatre was designed in 1963 by P. Sakellarios to replace it.

To the W (1km) of the Plateía Theotóki in the convent church of **Platitéra** (Pl. 5) are the tombs of Count John Capodistrias and of Photios Tzavellas (1774–1811), the Suliot klepht, and there are paintings by Clotzas (Last Judgement) and Poulakis (Revelation of St John). From Sarókko Leof. Alexándras runs down to the Bay of Gáritsa.

From the Spianádha Leofóros Dhimokratías (Vasiléos Konstandínou) skirts the Bay of Gáritsa. Beyond the Corfu Palace Hotel you come to the \***museum** (Pl. 11). Beneath the colonnade (A): Inscribed statue bases. GROUND FLOOR HALL (B), Sculpture, mostly Roman copies of Greek originals.

FIRST FLOOR. On the landing (Δ), left, huge pithos (6C BC); tomb monuments from the Garitsa cemetery; vigorous lion-head spouts from the Classical temple of Mon Repos; early Doric capital, with abacus bearing an Archaic inscription; funerary stele with boustrophedon inscription in Homeric hexameters honouring Arniadas, a Corcyraean general who died in battle on the Arachthos in Epirus (6C BC); (case 1) pottery (7–6C) from tombs. CORRIDOR ROOM (E): left of door (case 2), prehistoric finds from Sidhari, Ermones, and Aphiona; right of door (case 3), Archaic finds from Garitsa cemetery; along the wall, arranged chronologically, finds from the Hieron at Kerousadhes, from Rodha, and from N Epirus, as well as from Garitsa: notably Corinthian and Laconian pottery, terracotta antefixes from the Temple at Rodha (5C BC), and (case 8) inscribed bronze decrees appointing consuls (4C BC); (case 9) head of Aphrodite (c 300 BC; Praxitelean school); large Protocorinthian olpe decorated with four bands of animals; bronze komast carrying a rhyton (part of a lebes; 570 BC).

HALL OF THE GORGON (Z). \*Pediment (restored) of the Archaic Temple of Artemis (590–580 BC): the central Gorgon, with Pegasus and Chrysaor, is flanked by hybrid 'panthers', then battles of gods and giants (or titans). Other architectonic fragments of the same temple include triglyphs and metopes, the terracotta sima and antefixes, and those in Parian marble with which they were replaced c 520 BC. NORTH HALL (H). Head of a Corinthian kouros, in Naxian marble. Bronze figures of men and beasts, sculptured terracotta roof tiles, Gorgon's head, lion spout, all from a large temple (of Hera?) excavated in the grounds of Mon Repos in 1962–67. Part of a smaller pediment from Figareto with reclining figure and Dionysos etc. Lead plate showing the profile of a frieze. Painted \*sima from a smaller building, reminiscent of the finds from Thermon (Rte 54). \*Lion of

Menekrates, probably the crowning ornament of his tomb; discovered in 1843 (though not on the tomb), its date is disputed between 625 and 550 BC. Terracotta votive figurines from the Small Hieron of Artemis, near Kanoni. Archaic torso of the type of the Kassel Apollo; head of Menander, good copy of an original by Kephisodotos and Timarchos; head of an unknown philosopher (Roman copy of an original c 300 BC). Rich tomb with military equipment from Prodhromi (Thesprotia) 4–3C BC.

An **obelisk** to Sir Howard Douglas (died 1841) stands at the seaward end of Leofóros Alexándras, where a road leads towards a hill crowned by the prison. Here during the demolition of the Venetian fort of San Salvatore in 1843 was discovered an extensive necropolis. The huge circular **Tomb of Menekrates** (in the garden of the police station) (? 7C BC) was supposedly crowned by the lion in the museum. Menekrates, according to the inscription, was drowned.

The **English Cemetery**, on the N side of the Prison, has interesting memorials both civil and military. Here are buried the dead from HMS *Saumarez* and *Volagé* (1946).

The pleasant *promenade, backed with gardens, skirts the suburb of **Gáritsa**, or Kastrádhes, and curves to the left. Keeping straight on in the district called **Anemómilos**, you reach the Byzantine church of **Ayíon Iásonos kai Sosípatros**. This is an domed inscribed-cross church of the two-column type with a dome on an octagonal drum. It has bands of Cufic decoration and incorporates three ancient monolithic columns. There is an early 11C fresco of St Arsenius on the E wall of the narthex. SS Jason and Sosipater, according to tradition the disciples of St Paul from Tarsus and Iconium, were the first preachers of christianity in Corcyra, and Sosipater was martyred here under Caligula. Two 15C tombs beneath the screen are sometimes optimistically shown as those of the saints.

Here we are within the bounds of '**Palaiópolis**' or ancient *Corcyra*, which occupied the peninsula between the bay of Garitsa (ancient *Alkinoös*) and the lagoon of Khalikiopoulo (ancient *Hyllaian* harbour). The ancient city was sacked by the Goths in the 6C and later abandoned. The later Greeks and Venetians used it as a quarry in the erection of the modern town of Corfu. A large tower, forming the SE extremity of the harbour of Alkinoös was excavated in 1965 beside the church of Ay. Athanasios.

About five minutes farther on is the entrance to the royal villa of **Mon Repos** (no adm.), laid out for Sir Frederic Adam in 1824 and successively the summer residence of British Lord High Commissioners and Greek kings. Prince Philip, Duke of Edinburgh, was born here in 1921. Opposite the gates is the gutted Palaiopolis church of **Ayía Kérkyra**, where an inscription recording its foundation by Bishop Jovian before 450 and reused elements of a Doric temple have survived successive destructions in the 11C by the Saracens, in 1537 by the Turks, and in 1940. A Venetian lion of a 17C rebuilding also survives.

The basilica, which succeeded a semicircular building of the 2–1C (itself on foundations of a 6C temple), had double aisles and an exo-narthex and was comparable with Ayios Dhimitrios at Thessaloniki. After sacking by the Goths, it was reconstructed with single aisles using old materials.

A path to the right leads to further remains of the ancient lower city. Just W of the monastery of Ayioi Theódhoroi are vestiges of the Archaic **altar** and **Temple of Artemis**, from which came the pediments in the museum. The building was peripteral with 8 columns by 17. It was replaced by another temple on the same site in c 400 BC. Another hundred yards to the

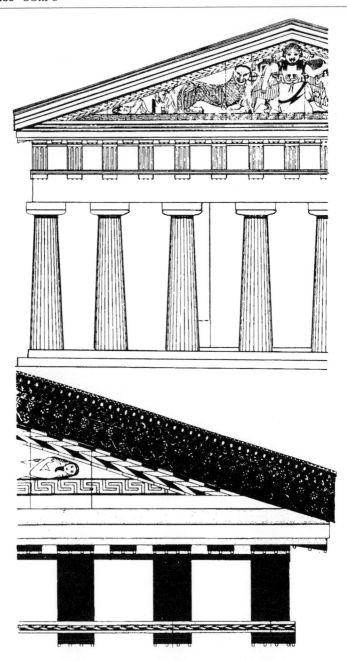

*Corfu. Temple of Artemis, E front. Top: Gorgon pediment.
Bottom: restoration of terracotta and painted decoration*

W is the ruined chapel of **Nerándzika** built over a section of the ancient city **walls**; these can be traced to the shore of the lagoon.

TO ANALIPSIS AND KANONI. The road (bus) continues S to the village of **Análipsis** (1km farther), on the site of the acropolis of the old city. Here are the meagre remains of the 6C Doric 'Kardhaki' temple and of a fountain (used in Venetian times and for watering British ships). The larger Archaic temple of the 7C (see above) lies within the grounds of Mon Repos to the N. Passing the Corfu Hilton you come to (4km) **Kanóni** (Hotels L, A, C), a semi-circular terrace, fashioned as a gun position by the French and called by the British 'One-gun Battery'. It commands a celebrated *view across the former entrance to the Hyllaian harbour. In the foreground are two little islets, each bearing a monastery. A causeway (reached by a steep path) leads to **Vlakhérna**, gleaming white beneath its red roofs, from which small boats cross to **Pondikonísi** (Mouse Island) where the monastery peeps from a thick clump of cypresses (pilgrimage to the disappointing 19C chapel on 6 Aug). It was the inspiration of Arnold Boecklin's *Isle of the Dead*, and is one of two claimants to be the ship of Odysseus turned to stone by Poseidon.

The Hyllaian harbour, once guarded by moles and a chain, is now cut off by a causeway across which (on foot only) Pérama can be reached (see below).

## Excursions on the Island

I. TO THE ACHILLEION AND BENITSES, a round of 24km (15 miles), buses regularly. You leave Plateía Theotóki on the SW, pass the airport (Pl. 13) and skirt the lagoon of Khalikiopoulos. At 5km **Vrióni** to the left is the road for Pérama and Benítses (the return route). You continue by the inland road, leaving on the right (at 6.5km) a road for **Ayioi Dhéka** (3km), starting point for the ascent in 1½ hr of the mountain of the same name (567m; *view). 8.5km **Gastoúri** (Hotels B, C) just beyond which, on the summit of a wooded eminence overlooking the sea and the town of Corfu, stands the **Achílleion**, built in 1890–91 by the Italian architect Cardilo for the Empress Elisabeth of Austria. After her assassination it was bought by Kaiser Wilhelm II, who spent every spring here 1908–14. It passed to the Greek government as enemy property and in December 1962 was leased to Baron von Richthoven as a casino for roulette and chemin-de-fer: this has now been transferred to the Hilton Hotel at Kanoni. The villa, dedicated to Achilles, favourite hero of the empress, is set in an Italian landscape garden, liberally ornamented with statuary, of Homeric subjects and proportions but mediocre inspiration. The Dying Achilles, by Herter (1884), should however be noted. The mansion, a curious pastiche within of Teutonic fin-de-siècle neo-Classicism, has been restored. The ground floor includes a **museum** of mementoes of its former owners, including fine portraits of the Empress Elisabeth by Winterhalter and the saddle-throne from which Wilhelm II dictated despatches.

The best view is obtained from the neighbouring hill of Ayía Kiriakí. Near by is a **French Military Cemetery** (225 graves) of the First World War, when the Achilleion became an allied naval hospital.

The road drops by steep bends to join the coastal road (see above) halfway between Pérama and (12km) **Benítses** (Hotels A–E; F/A), originally a pretty fishing village with a small beach. Amid an orange grove, on private land, are some remains of Roman villa baths with mosaic pavements. Continuation to the S, see below. The return to Corfu is made by the *coastal road. You turn back, leaving to the left the road to the Achilleion, and pass its

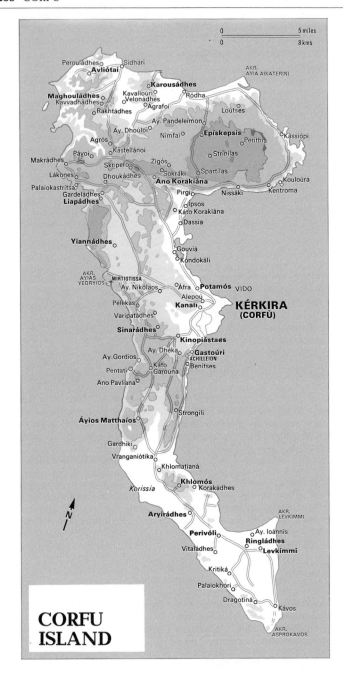

0 ___ 5 miles
0 ___ 8 kms

Perouládhes  Sidhári
**Avliótai**

Maghouládhes  Kavallouri  Ródha
Kavvadhádhes  Velonádhes
Rakhtádhes  Agrafoi
Ay. Pandeleimon  Loútses
Agrós  Ay. Dhoúloi  Nimfai  **Epískepsis**  Perithiá  Kássiópi
Páyoi  Kastellánoi  Strínilas
Makrádhes  Zigós  Spartilas
Lákones  Skripero  Sokráki  Spartilas  Kouloúra
Dhoukádhes  **Áno Korakiána**  Kentroma
Palaiokastrítsa  Nissáki
Gardeládhes  Pirgí
**Liapádhes**  Ípsos
Káto Korakiána
Dassia

**Yiannádhes**
Gouviá
Kondokáli

AKR.
AYIAS  **MIRTIOTISSA**
YEORYIOS  Ay. Nikólaos  Áfra  **Potamós**  VIDO
Alepoú
Pélekas  **Kanáli**  **KÉRKIRA**
Varipatádhes  **(CORFU)**
**Sinarádhes**
**Kinopiástaes**
Ay. Dhéka  **Gastoúri**
Ay. Gordios  ACHILLEION
Káto  Benitses
Pentatí  Garoúna
Áno Pavliana

Strongilí

**Áyios Matthaíos**

Gardhikí
Vranganiótika
Khlomatianá
**Khlomós**
*Korissía*  Korakádhes

**Aryirádhes**
AKR.
LEVKÍMMI
**Perivóli**  Ay. Ioánnis
**Ringládhes**
Vitaládhes  **Levkímmi**

Kritiká
Palaiokhóri
Dragotiná  Kávos
AKR.
ASPROKAVOS

AKR.
AYIA AIKATERINI

N

**CORFU
ISLAND**

ruined private landing-place. 16km **Pérama** (Hotels A–E; F/A). About 1km farther on, a promontory (restaurants) has views of Pontikonísi (see above) and Mon Repos. 24km **Corfú**.

## II. TO THE NORTH OF THE ISLAND: PALAIOKASTRITSA, KASSIOPI AND MT PANTOCRATOR.

Round trip of 87km (54 miles); extensions possible. Buses to Palaiokastrítsa regularly (also to Sidhári); to Kassiópi c 5 daily. This road also starts at Plateía Theotóki and after 1km divides (left to Pelekas, see below). You pass the monastery of Platitera (see above) and bear left, rejoining the coast some way outside the town. To the right is the **Lazaretto** islet, formerly the quarantine station. The road skirts the sheltered roadstead of Gouviá, where some French ships evaded pursuit by Nelson. The bay has large hotels, camping sites, a yacht marina, and a youth hostel. 8km **Kondokáli** (Hotels, A, C, D; F/A) lies at its S end. On the shore is a roofless Venetian arsenal, or galley repair shed, of 1716. Beyond (9km) **Gouviá** (Hotels, A–E; F/A), you take the inland fork at (10km) **Tsavrós**. 14km Turn (left) for the delightful *bay of **Palaiokastrítsa** (10km) (Παλαιοκαστρίτσα; Hotels A–E; tavernas). The by-road descends to the gates of the monastery, attractively sited on a promontory (92m; view) with terraced gardens. Though founded in 1228, it now has little that dates before the 18C.

From **Palaiokastrítsa**, or by returing to the main road and turning left after a further 3km, you can reach in 5km **Lákkones** which has a lovely panorama of Palaiokastritsa and its surroundings; here the Classical student can assess the merits of locating on the coast below the site of Homeric *Scheria*, with the twin ports of the Phaeacians and the gardens of Alkinoös. Beyond **Lákkones** is a good road via **Makrádhes** to **Kríni** (parking; café) from which it is a 10 minute walk to **Angelókastro**, a castle already existing in 1272 when it is referred to in the Neapolitan Angevin archives as Castrum Sancti Angeli. The view is outstanding, including the citadel of Corfu.

From **Makrádhes** you can continue through **Vístonas** on a beautiful road to (9.5km) Troumpétas on the main road.

20km **Troumpétas**, where there is a good view from the col of Ayios Pandeleimon and a turning (left, 15km) to **Sidhári**, **Perouládhes** and the NW. Both places have beaches, and good sandy coves can be reached on foot between the two.

Offshore, 11km NW, are the **Diapóntia** islands (boats from Sidhári)—(**Erikoússa**, **Othonoí**, and **Mathráki**), with 575 inhabitants between them, constituting the final limit of Greek sovereignty in the NW.

32km **Ródha** (Hotels A–E; F/A), site of another temple (5C BC) explored in 1938 by John Papadimitriou is now geared to mass tourism. 49km **Kassiópi**, an attractive fishing village, preserves its ancient name and a large Angevin **castle**, the haunt of owls. The church may occupy the site of the Temple of Zeus visited by Nero. It was rebuilt after 1537 and enlarged in 1590 by successive Venetian admirals. Note the ikon Panayia Cassiopitra by Th. Poulakis (c 1670) and 17C frescoes. 62km **Nisáki** (Hotels L, A, C; F/A, to the E). 65km **Barbáti** beach is seen below. Before (69km) **Píryi** (Πύργι; Hotels A, C, D; F/A) a road to the right mounts to **Spartíla** (8km).

From **Spartíla** an unpaved, steep and rocky road leads to the **Pantokrátor** monastery (18.5km), built in 1347 on **Mt Pantokrator** (906m), or **Monte San Salvatore**, the highest point of the island. The summit is spoilt by a radio mast, but the *view is superb. In clear weather the coast of Italy is just visible above the horizon to the NW. To the E are the Acroceraunian Mountains, the castle and plain of Butrinto, with its river and two lakes, the villages extending far into the interior of Albania. To the S the city and whole island of Corfu are stretched out like a map with Paxoi and Levkas in the distance.

**Ayios Márkos** (1.25km inland of Púryi) has a church (Ay. Merkoúrios) of 1075 with contemporary frescoes in Cappadocian style, and another (Pantokrátor), above the village, with good wall paintings of 1576.

70km **Ipsos** (Hotels B, C, D, E; F/A). At 72km a turn (right) leads in 1km to the village of **Káto Korakianá**, where the small wood-roofed chapel of **Ay. Nikólaos** dates from the 17C, though the E part of the N wall is assigned to the 11C. Frescoes of this period are now in the Corfu Museum. Nearby at **Dhasiá** (Hotels A, B, C, D; F/A) are various camping-sites and holiday complexes. To the right a by-road leads to the **Castello Mimbelli**, a hotel occupying a 19C castle in a Venetian Gothic style that once belonged to George II of the Hellenes. The road follows the attractive bay and mounts a wooded promontory. At (77km) **Tzávros** the circuit is complete and Corfu town a further 10km.

III. THE S OF THE ISLAND, returning via Gardhíki and Sinarádhes 129km (80 miles); regular buses down the spine of the island to Kávos, and to Glifádha and Vátos. The excursion could be subdivided, using the alternative inland route between Vranganiótika and Ay. Dhéka.

From (12km) Benitses (see above) a road continues S along the coast to (20km) **Moraïtika** (Hotels L, A–E), with fine sands. The road turns inland near the huge Mesongi Beach hotel (510 rooms) to pass down the middle of the long peninsula. 24km **Vranganiótika**.

An alternative inland route to (or from) Corfu town joins this road. It passes through **Strongilí**, **Ayioi Dhéka** and villages to the SW of Corfu.

To the right lies Lake Korission. 35km **Argirádhes** (pop. 820). 44km **Levkímmi** (pop. 3471) is the centre of a group of villages. Its port **Melíkia** has a ferry connection to the mainland (see above). 47km **Kávos**, near the SE tip of the island, has an attractive beach but has suffered badly from tourist development. 3km to the S of Kavos, on the promontory of **Aspró-kavos** is the charming ruined monastery of the **Panayía Arkoudhílla**. The route turns NW and loops back to Levkímmi (62km), passing various villages, of which the largest is **Palaiokhóri** and the last **Kritiká**.

Beyond Levkímmi you return by the outward route as far as **Vranganió-tika**, beyond (1km) which turn left in the direction of **Ayios Mathaíos**. 82km Turn (left) for **Gardhíki** (1.5km) with remains of a Byzantine castle and a cave with Upper Palaeolithic occupation. The Gardhíki road continues further to the **Panayía Mesavrísi** on Lake Korission and the W coast. Returning to the main road, you continue N in beautiful countryside to crossroads at (98km) **Kastelláni** (alternatively descending to the coast at **Ayios Górdhis**) and (100km) **Sinarádhes**, with a good **Ethnographic Museum**. **Aeróstato** (restaurant; view), 1km W of the village, overlooks the coast. 106km **Pélekas** (beach; buses), an attractive cluster of colour-washed houses with a famous belvedere (restaurant; view) at **Ayios Yeoryios** (392m), furnished by the Kaiser. The road leads N to **Glifádha** (beach; Hotels A, B) and (110km) **Vátos** where there are signs for the convent of **Mirtidhiótissa**, near a pleasant beach (1.5km on a poor road). 113km **Ermónes** (Hotels A, B), had Neolithic and Bronze Age occupation. Nearby is the **Corfu Golf Club**. You return across the island to (129km) **Corfú**.

Between the Gouviá road and the Pélekas road, a third runs out of Corfu town, via Potamós, to **The Village**, a reconstruction by the Bouas family of a complete community, with church, museum of bygones, local crafts and a good restaurant. The buildings, constructed with old materials, form a living replica of the Venetian era in Corfu.

# B. Páxoi

**Approaches**. From Corfú, daily **ferry** in 4 hours (this leaves Paxoi in the morning, returning in the afternoon). From Parga in summer.

**Páxos**, more correctly **Páxoi** (usually **Páxous**, accusative; 2236 inhab.; Hotels B, E; F/A), the smallest of the seven chief Ionian Islands, is 8km long and only 3km broad. It is situated 14.5km S of Corfu and 13km W of the coast of Epirus off Parga. The island produces little else than olives, almonds, and vines. The highest point is not more than 180m above the sea. Its farm houses and churches are particularly attractive. The principal village is an attractive cluster of Venetian houses at **Gáïo** (1km S; F/A) on the E side. The harbour inlet contains a small rocky islet crowned with a fort. It is a sailing centre in the summer. A road (8km; bus) links Gáïo with **Lákka** (F/A), the second little harbour at the N end of the island, with a branch to **Pórto Lóngos** on the NE.

Immediately S of Paxoi, and separated from it by a narrow channel, is the rocky islet of **Andípaxoi**, inhabited by a few shepherds and fishermen and cultivated for garden produce and wine by the Paxians. It is visited by sportsmen in the season for shooting migratory quail, and has good bathing-beaches also on the E coast (excursions in summer).

# C. Lévkas

**Approaches**. **By road**, bridge and causeway, from Akarnanía, see Rte 54.

**Ferry** connections (daily) from Nídhri to Itháki and Kefallinía; also to Meganísi. In summer also from Vasilikí to Itháki and Kefallinía.

**LÉVKAS** (Λεύκας; usually **Leíkádha**, accusative) is an island separated at its NE corner from the mainland of Akarnania by a shallow lagoon and a narrow strait, through which runs the Levkas Ship Canal. The name of the island is derived from the white cliff at its southern tip. The island is 32km long and between 8 and 13km wide; with minor attendant islets, including Kálamos, Kástos and Meganísi, it forms a nome of 21,111 inhabitants. The centre of the island is occupied by a range of limestone mountains, culminating in Mt Elati (1082m). The most populous and wooded district is that opposite the mainland, where the valleys, running down to the sea, are sprinkled with small villages. The island exports oil, wine, and salt, of which a considerable quantity is obtained by evaporation in the lagoon.

The topography of the NE end of the island is peculiar. A long narrow sandy spit (the *Yiro*) runs out from the N coast, sweeping E towards the mainland which it virtually joins in an area of marshes. This spit encloses a shallow lagoon which surrounds the modern town of Levkas on three sides and extends S between the island and the mainland. Much of the lagoon is only 0.6–1.5m deep, and to the S there are islands and sandbanks.

The evidence of ancient writers suggests that in antiquity Levkas was joined to the mainland by an isthmus, probably across the narrow strait to the SE of the modern town and roughly opposite ancient Leucas (see below). But if, as is also believed, a canal was cut by the Corinthian colonists in the 7C BC, then Thucydides (III, 81) implies that it was silted up by 427 BC when the Peloponnesians 'transported their ships over the Leucadian isthmus'. The canal was restored, probably about the time of Augustus, and a stone bridge, of which some remains are still visible near Fort Constantine (see below), was built from the ancient city of Rouga, on the Akarnanian coast. In the Middle Ages one of the Latin princes built a fort on the Yiro, midway between Levkas and the mainland and on the landward side of the channel that breaches it. This fort, which acquired the name of Fort Santa Maura, from a chapel within its walls so called, gave an alternative name to the whole island. It was remodelled by the Turks, who connected it with Levkas by an aqueduct of 260 arches, serving also as a causeway, 1190m long, which divided the lagoon into two. The aqueduct was shattered by earthquake of 1704 but survived as a dangerous causeway till 1825 (ruins in lagoon N of existing road causeway). The Venetians maintained the canal and the Venetian governor lived initially in the fort, while the town, then called *Amaxikhi*, that developed into modern Levkas grew up at the nearest point on the island.

During the protectorate of Russia **Fort Alexander** and **Fort Constantine**, a few hundred metres N of it, were built on islands in the strait to guard the S approach channel. A little farther S are the remains of Fort St. George (Rte 54). The Anglo-Ionian government constructed a harbour on the spit of sand flanking Fort Santa Maura and protected by a mole ending in a lighthouse. In 1905 the Greek government built the existing Levkas Ship Canal from Fort Santa Maura southwards past Forts Alexander and Constantine. Its length is 5km and it is kept dredged to a depth of c 4.5m.

**History**. *Leucas* was colonised by the Corinthians in 640 BC, about a century after Corcyra. The Leucadians had three ships at the Battle of Salamis, and they sided with Sparta in the Peloponnesian War. The island was devastated by the Corcyraeans in 436 BC and by the Athenians ten years later. In the war between Rome and Philip of Macedon, the Akarnanians, who had made Leucas their capital in 230 BC, rejected the Roman alliance, and were reduced after a gallant defence vividly described by Livy (XXXIII, 17). Leucas continued to be important under the Romans, its bishop being one of the fathers at the Council of Nicaea in AD 325. The island passed in the 13C to Giovanni Orsini as the dowry of his wife Maria, daughter of Nikephoros Comnenus, Bishop of Epirus. The Turks seized it in 1479. Thenceforward the island was alternately Turkish and Venetian until 1718, when it was formally ceded to Venice. It suffered four bad earthquakes in the 18C, when it shared the political fortunes of the other Ionian Islands. Levkas was captured from the French in 1810 by a force under General Oswald that included Richard Church, Hudson Lowe, and Kolokotronis.

Native to Levkas are the writers Aristoteles Valaoritis (1824–79), and Angelos Sikelianos (1884–1951). Here also was born, his father an Irish army surgeon and his mother from Kythera, Lafcadio Hearn (1850–1904) who ended his life (as Yakumo Koizumi) a citizen of Japan.

**Lévkas** (Hotels B, C, E), the capital (6344 inhab.), directly approached by the causeway, was badly damaged by earthquakes in 1867 and 1948 and is characterised by the light and temporary nature of its upper stories. The cathedral (**Pantokrator**) of 1684 has the tomb of Valaoritis. A little **museum** (ikons and antiquities) is housed below the library (weekday mornings, free). There is a **Folk Museum** off the main square. The ceiling paintings of **Ayios Mínas** are by Nicolas Doxaras (died 1761), and **Ayios Dhimítrios** has paintings attributed to Panayiotis Doxaras (died 1729). The causeway, with glimpses in the water (left) of its Turkish predecessor (see above), and followed (right) by the modern deep water canal, leads to the boat bridge which replaced a chain ferry in 1986. Beyond stands the **Castle of Santa Maura** (adm. free), erected by Orsini in 1300. It passed to Walter de Brienne in 1331 and from the Angevins to the Tocco family after 1362, but the present structure is largely due to Venetian and Turkish repairs. For the forts on the Mainland, see Rte 54.

A good view of the town, with the lagoon, causeway and canal, may be had from the convent of **Faneroméni**, high up the hill immediately W of the town (3km; road signposted Tsoukaládhes, where it peters out). On this road, in the suburbs of the town is the **Archaeological Museum** with material from the island of all periods, including finds from and photographs of excavations at Nídhri.

TOUR OF THE ISLAND, 80km (50 miles). With planning, most of the route can be covered by bus, the more distant villages (Atháni, Vasilikí) being served 2–4 times daily in summer; Vlikhó more frequently. You bear inland, then soon fork left for the E coast. The acropolis of **Nerikós** to the right (concrete track opposite Mamidhákis petrol station) is the site of ancient *Leucas*, where traces of walls remain amid the modern terracing. The road reaches the shore in sight of Forts Alexander and Constantine, with the medieval Fort of St George, (Rte 54) on the opposing shore.

16km **Nídhri** (Hotels B, E; ferries, see above) a port-of-call for yachts, stands opposite the islet of **Madhoúri**, the retreat of A. Valaoritis. Further S is **Skórpios**, property of the late Aristotle Onassis. On the peninsula of Ayía Kiriakí, across the landlocked bay of Vlikhó (5 minutes by boat), is the house in which Wilhelm Dörpfeld (1853–1940) lived during his long excavations when trying to prove that Levkas, not Ithaki, is the island described as Ithaka by Homer. His tomb is 200m from the house. He uncovered Early Bronze Age circular tumuli with graves in the plain of Nídhri. 22km **Vlikhó**. The village churches in the S part of the island have 17C and 18C frescoes. 40km **Vasilikí** (Hotels B, C, E; ferries, see above) is a fishing village on a deep bay backed by a fertile plain. From Vasilikí you can turn N and return up the W side of the island via (47km) **Ayios Pétros** and (51.5km) **Komíli**.

From **Komíli** a road, good to **Atháni** (5km; rooms), last 10km poor, leads S along the rocky peninsular to **Ayios Nikólaos Níras** and **Cape Dukáto** (lighthouse), ancient *Leukatas*, the point to the S, a precipitous white cliff (60m), which gives the island its name. A few fragments and sherds mark the once famous Temple of Apollo. The place is well-known from the sea by many passing travellers but rarely visited. Here Childe Harold 'saw the evening star above Leucadia's far projecting rock of woe'. The rock was the scene in antiquity of leaps or dives into the sea (*katapontismos*), performed as a trial, a sacrifice, or a cure for unrequited love. The leap was successfully performed in the time of Strabo and of Cicero by having live birds attached to the victim (or performer) and rescue boats handy. Sappho supposed to have leaped to her death here.

N of **Komíli** the road passes **Kalamítsi** above the coast, below the hill villages of **Exanthiá** and **Khrímonas**. There is a turn to **Ayios Nikítas** (Hotels B, C) a popular beach resort. You continue by a winding route to Lefkas.

# D.  Itháki and Kefallinía

**Approaches**. **Car Ferry** daily from Patras to Kefallinía (Sámi), in c 4 hours continuing (c 1½ hours) to Itháki; also less frequently between Sámi and Corfú. Some services continue to Italian ports. Other ferry services connect Kefallinía (Ayía Evfímia) with Itháki and Astakós (mainland) (daily; connecting bus to Athens), Kefallinía (Argostóli) with Zákynthos, Kefallinía and Itháki (Pisaëtos) with Lévkas (Nídhri and Vasilikí), Kefallinía (Póros, Lixoúri, Argostóli) with Killíni (Peloponnese). **Air** daily service to Kefallinía from Athens in one hour (airport 6.5km S of Argostóli); twice weekly from Kefallinía to Zákynthos. Also international charters.

**ITHÁKI**, or Ithaka (Ιθάκη), with an area of 114 sq. km, makes up for being the second smallest of the seven islands by its fame in the Homeric epic. 27km long and 6.5km wide at its broadest part, it is divided into two unequal peninsulas by a narrow isthmus and everywhere rises in rugged hills, which reach their highest point in the N peninsula. Ithaka is separated from Kefallinía by the Ithaka Channel, a deep strait hardly 4km across at its narrowest. Its N extremity, Cape Marmakas, is 11km from the S coast of Levkas. To the NE lie the islets of Arkoúdhi and Atokos. The island's 3082 inhabitants are administered as an eparchy of the nome of Kefallinía.

The bold and barren outline of the mountains and cliffs is impressive. There is hardly any level ground. The coasts are indented by numerous small harbours and creeks, the λιμένες πάνορμοι of the *Odyssey* (XIII, 195). Exceptions to the general barrenness are seen in the cultivated lower slopes of the ridges and in little valleys, where olive and almond trees grow; the upper slopes are clothed with vineyards or with evergreen copses of myrtle, cypress, arbutus, mastic, oleander, and all the aromatic shrubs of the Levant. Here and there among the rocks are little green patches, gay with wild flowers.

The inhabitants are hospitable and industrious. Ithakan wine is reputed the best in the Ionian Islands and the roast hare is noted. The Ithakans have always been first-rate mariners and the depopulation of the island is partly due to their roving disposition. English spoken on the island may have been acquired in Australia or South Africa.

**History**. Few architectural remains have so far been discovered to confirm the topography of the *Odyssey*, though Geometric tripods have come to light in circumstances reminiscent of Homer. After the heroic period the island retired into obscurity. By 1504 it was practically depopulated owing to the depredations of corsairs and to the furious wars between Turks and Christians. The Venetians resettled on it Ionians from neighbouring islands.

**Vathí** (Hotels B, rooms; car, scooter and boat hire; agencies), like the island officially called **Itháki**, the chief town (1714 inhab.), lies in the S peninsula at the end of a deep inlet (Bay of Vathí) opening from the **Gulf of Mólo**, which almost separates the island into two halves. The town, which dates only from the 16C, is beautifully situated, extending in one narrow strip of white houses round the S extremity of the horseshoe deep (βαθύς) from which it takes its name. Comparatively large ships can moor close to the doors of their owners. On a tiny island in the harbour is a chapel, once the **Lazaretto**. Most of the town has been repaired or rebuilt since 1953. The carved wooden screen in the **cathedral** is worth a visit. The rebuilt museum was opened in 1965. Within, owing to the efforts of Miss Sylvia Benton who salvaged the pieces from the earthquake ruins and supervised their mending, are nearly 1000 vases (mainly 8–6C) found by the British School in two shrines at Aëtos. The house of Odysseus Androutsos was ruined. Reached by a winding road 4km above the harbour is the pleasant village of **Perakhóri**, where a sign (right) indicates the footpath (15mins) to the ruins of *Palaiochora*, a Venetian foundation. Some of the churches have remarkable painted stone templons. A dirt road beyond Perakhóri leads in 3km to the **Monastery of the Taxiárkhis**.

## Excursions

A day or two's car hire is strongly recommended on Itháki, as bus services are limited (3 daily Vathí–Kióni via Stavrós; also daily taxi Stavrós–Vathí); but note that there is only one petrol station on the island—in Vathí.

I. SARAKINIKO AND FILIATRO BEACHES. From the SE corner of Vathí bay (by the Hotel Mentor) a road climbs and then descends to the beautiful double bay (pebbles) of **Sarakíniko**, originally a pirate base. The further bay is the best for swimming. 15 minutes beyond is **Filiatró**. Journey time and effort can be reduced by taking a taxi to the top of the hill beyond the town, where it becomes unsuitable for vehicles.

II. GROTTO OF THE NYMPHS. About 2.5km W of Vathí is the little **Bay of Dhexiá** (or **Dhexá**), perhaps the harbour of *Phorkys* (now signed 'Forkinos Bay'), in which the sleeping Odysseus was deposited by the Phaeacians. A dirt road (left; signed 'Nimfis Cave') leads in 2km to a copse of cypresses in which is a stalactite cave, known as **Marmarospiliá**, equated with the **Grotto of the Nymphs** (Od. XIII, 103). A narrow entrance only 1.8m high leads to a cavern 15m across, now 'enriched' with coloured lights and music. At the S end there is an opening in the roof, presumably cut to carry off the smoke of the sacrificial fires, 17m above the floor.

III. THE S END OF THE ISLAND. A poor road (signed 'Marathiá'; passable by car but not recommended) runs S from Vathí through a fertile valley. About 4km from the town a footpath (right; signed) leads immediately to the **Cave of Eumaios** reputed home of the Homeric shepherd. The setting is attractive. 200m beyond the turning to the cave, at the top of a rise, a cliff path (left) leads in 45 minutes to the spring of Perapigádhi (67m). This is identified with Homer's **Fountain of Arethusa**, where the swine of Eumaios were watered. The peasants call the neighbouring cliff **Kórax** (raven rock). The road continues for another 1km to the plateau of **Marathiá**, where it degenerates into a track. Here may have been located the pigsties of Eumaios. A path leads SW in 40 minutes to the Bay of **Ayios Andréas**, where Telemachos landed on his return from Pylos.

III. TO ALALKOMENAI AND PISAËTOS. The road passes the bay of Dhexiá (see above) and at 4km divides. The left branch climbs to the chapel of (6.5km) **Ayios Yeóryios** (130m), a small building with recently renewed roof about 50m to the right of the road. From another building by the roadside about 100m before the chapel a path leads to the sides and summit (20 minutes) of the rocky hill of Aëtós (right; 381m) on which are situated the remains of *Alalkomenai*, known to the locals as **Kástro tou Odysséos** and wrongly identified by Schliemann in 1878 as the site of the Homeric capital. There have been finds of most periods from Mycenaean to Hellenistic, and later. British School excavations uncovered remains of an early sanctuary, an Archaic temple and a large dump of vases of Geometric and Archaic Corinthian ware. Recent work has revealed (W of the church) remains of a large building, possibly a Temple of Apollo (inscription) mentioned in the *Odyssey*. A monumental circular structure to the E may be part of a larger sanctuary complex (see above). Striking are terrace walls of polygonal masonry, with flights of steps connecting the levels. The path continues upwards to reach (45min) the summit (sign to 'Cyclopean Walls' en route), a rocky and uneven plateau amazingly protected on the S side by a wall of gigantic blocks, some squared, some polygonal, normally dated to 700 BC but most closely resembling the walls of the Mycenaean fortresses and conceivably of that date. Eagles nest here and the view is fine. 7km **Pisaëtós** harbour (ferries to Kefallinía and Lévkas) has a pleasant pebble beach.

FROM VATHI TO STAVROS. The road coincides to 4km with that to **Pisaëtós** (see above). You keep right and cross the isthmus with the Gulf of Mólo on our right. Ahead rises **Mt Nírito** (806m) round which, at 12km, the road divides. Formerly called Anoyi, the mountain has taken the ancient name, the 'Neritos ardua saxis' of Virgil and Νήριτον εἰνοσίφυλλον of Homer, though its barren slopes (if correctly identified) must since have been greatly deforested. The sheer and circuitous route on the E side (dirt beyond the monastery; 12km to Stavros) passes the monastery of **Katharón** (556m; 4km from the fork), restored with a benefaction from Aristotle Onassis and Maria Callas and open to visitors in summer. There is a frescoed ikon. An ikon from here, supposedly by El Greco, is kept in Vathí (church of the Taxiarkhis). There is a *view over the Gulf of Vathí and to

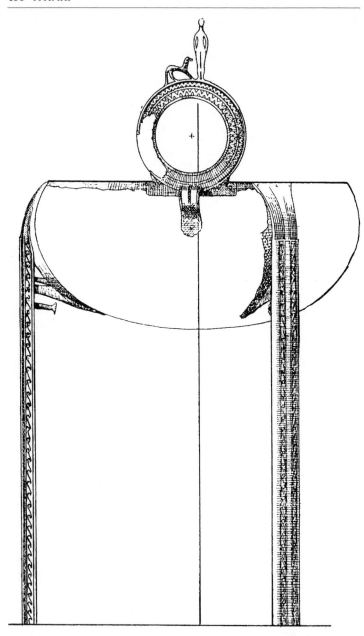

*Reconstruction of bronze tripod from Ithaki. Geometric period*

the village of **Anoyí**, whose church has fine Byzantine frescoes, located in 1953 and cleaned in 1985. The better road along the W flank above the Ithaka Channel passes above **Ayios Ioánnis**, a bathing place served by a lower by-road. 14.5km **Levkí** (160m). 18km **Stavrós** is the focal point (311 inhab.) of the villages in the N part of the island. It has several cafés and restaurants, also rooms to let and a regular morning taxi service to Vathí (return in the afternoon).

A road leads down SW to the bay of **Pólis**, the name of which recalls the Homeric capital. The beach is badly polluted except on the NW shore where a cave-sanctuary (Spílio Louízou: not accessible), was explored in 1930 by the British School. It yielded pottery of all periods from Mycenaean to Roman, and 12 Geometric tripods (Il. XIII). A late ex-voto inscribed ΕΥΧΗΝ ΟΔΥΣΣΕΙ ('my vow to Odysseus') suggests that Odysseus was the object of a local hero-cult. About 1km N of Stavrós is the Kastro on the hill of **Pelikáta** (follow signs to 'Museum'). Excavations of the British School revealed the ruins of a small settlement of the Early Bronze Age which flourished to Mycenaean times. Apart from a few Hellenic and Hellenistic tombs, the site was not again occupied until the Venetian period. A small **museum**, on the site of the now invisible antiquities, restored in 1957, contains materials from the site and from Polis, including the tripods (see above), also other local finds, rescued undamaged in 1953.

Beyond Pelikáta the road divides. The left branch leads in 3kms to **Exoyí**, another high Venetian village with, beyond (20 mins up a bad track) a deserted monastery with dramatic views. The lower road loops through several villages, eventually joining a more direct route from Stavrós at Fríkes (see below). In **Platrithiá** a path (left; signed) leads in 20 minutes to the chapel of **Ayios Athanásios** near the ruins of a tower of the 6C BC, a spot popularly called the **School of Homer**. Further on, in the direction of **Exoyí** and also accessible from there, is the so-called spring of Melanídhro, an ancient domed cistern. Beyond the cafeneion at Platrithiá a narrow asphalt road (left) soon divides. The left branch passes a monumental complex dedicated to the poor of Ithaka, to Kalamos and the now-abandoned hotel **Apólavsis** which must have been delightful in its day. The right branch terminates at the house of the doctor who has assembled a remarkable collection of folk art.

From Stavrós the road descends E to **Fríkes** (car ferry to Levkas) and **Kióni** (6.5km), attractively sited above the E coast. Both have yacht facilities and restaurants.

**KEFALLINÍA** (Κεφαλληνία), or Cephalonia, with 29,392 inhabitants, is the largest in area of the Ionian Islands. Separated from Ithaki by the Ithaki Channel, it lies between Levkas and Zante, exactly opposite the entrance of the Gulf of Patras. Of very irregular shape the island is rugged and mountainous. A high ridge runs from NW to SE, the foothills covering almost the whole island. The chief summit is the highest point of the Ionian Islands. Kefallinia is divided into three eparchies, which together with that of Ithakí, form the nome of Kefallinia. The population has halved in the 20C and is still falling. The **airport** (Olympic Airways office in Argostóli) has a daily connection with Athens and international charters.

The soil is fertile but not at all well watered, with few constantly flowing streams; and the landscape lacks the luxuriance of Corfu and Zante. Characteristic features of the fine scenery are the noble forests of a local fir-tree (*Abies Cephalonensis*) which give the mountain slopes their sombre look; the currant vineyards; and the olive groves. Perfumes are made from the flowers and pines, and there are excellent local wines. About one-sixth of the land belongs to the convents.

**History**. There were four cities in ancient Kephallenia: *Pale, Kranioi, Same*, and *Pronnoi*. Herodotus mentions that 200 citizens of Pale fought at Plataea. The Athenians

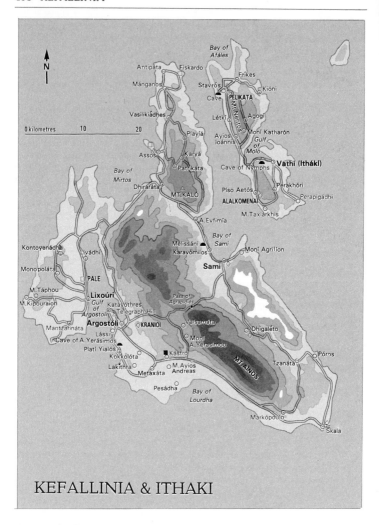

# KEFALLINIA & ITHAKI

won over the Kephallenians, without fighting, at the outbreak of the Peloponnesian War. In the Roman wars in Greece the island was reduced (189 BC); according to Strabo, C. Antonius possessed the whole island as his private estate. It was afterwards given to the Athenians by Hadrian. In the Middle Ages it was taken from the Normans of Sicily by Robert Guiscard, who died on the island in 1085. Subsequent masters were the Pisans (1099); Margaritone of Brindisi (1185), succeeded by the Orsini (1194) and the Tocchi (1323); the Turks (1485); the Venetians (1500); and the French (1797). A member of the short-lived Septinsular Republic, it was taken in 1809 by the British, who held it with the other Ionian Islands until 1864. *Sir Charles Napier*, Resident in 1822–30, built roads and did much else for the island. After his day, in 1848, a rising of the inhabitants was checked at the entrance to the town of Argostoli by a section of a British company under a sergeant. The following year another insurrection was as speedily suppressed.

In 1943 the occupying Italian force, comprising 9000 troops of the Alpine 'Acqui' Division, not only refused to cooperate with or surrender to the Germans, but for seven days fought them for possession of the island. Three thousand were forced to surrender and during three ensuing days were shot in cold blood (it is said on Hitler's personal order). Only 34 survived by shamming death. The bodies were taken in 1953 to a cemetery in Bari. Much of the island was destroyed by earthquake in 1953.

**Sámi** (Hotels B, C, D), a pleasant modern anchorage (928 inhab.) on the deep bay that indents the E coast opposite Ithaki is the main point of arrival from Patras and other Ionian islands. Here Don John of Austria anchored his fleet before Lepanto (commemorative inscription in town). At the back of the town, above the main plateia, is a Roman building with well-preserved but badly tended walls. Leaving the town by the continuation of this street you can visit the two hills of Ayioi Fanéntes and Palaiókastro, above the town, where are some remains of ancient *Same*, the island's capital in antiquity, ringed by Cyclopean and polygonal walling. The same route also leads to the monasteries of **Agrilíon** (in a fine position) and **Ay. Fanéntes** (built on the ancient town walls and incorporating one of the towers) and the beautiful **Antísamos Bay**. The furthest point (Ayioi Fanéntes) is c 6kms from Sámi: the road is mostly indifferent.

FROM SAMI TO ARGOSTOLI, 23km (15 miles), bus four times daily. On the outskirts of the town is a turning (right) to the N of the island. Beyond **Karavómilos**, 2km along this road is (right; restaurant) the pleasant **Lake Karavómilos** fed by underground sources; then (300m further; left) a turn to the remarkable semi-underground **Lake Melissáni** (200m; adm. includes short boat trip). An artificial tunnel leads to a small lake of clear turquoise and indigo water; a boat takes the visitor to an inner cavern. The site had a sanctuary of Pan in antiquity (finds in Argostoli). 2km Turning (left) for Póros and the SE of the island.

The road is being improved but much is still bad. At (8km) **Dhigaléto** (Kástro) are prehistoric fortifications, with Classical structures inside. 21km **Tzanáta** has recently discovered tholos tombs (not accessible). 24km **Póros** (24km; Hotels B, C, E; several buses a day from Argostoli) has a regular and much used ferry connection with Killíni in the Peloponnese and is becoming a tourist centre. There have been recent Neolithic finds and a Mycenaean tomb. Roads connect Tzanáta with the S coast and Póros with Skála to the SE.

3.5km The **Cave of Drogaráti** (small charge for adm.) a large, electrically lit, stalagmitic cavern, lies 500m right of the road. The road now winds up through maquis to (11.5km) the Agrapidies Pass (549m). Near the top a road leads (left) to **Mt Ainos**, climbing first to a radar post on the N crest, then continuing to a television station on the summit (1619m). 16km Col, with fine view down to Argostóli and across the gulf.

A road descends (left) to a small plain in which lies **Frangáta**. This village and **Valsamáta**, its neighbour, were built after the earthquake with funds subscribed from Britain. About 2km beyond Frangáta is the convent of **Ayios Yerásimos** (closed 13.00–15.00), with the venerated silver sarcophagus of St Gerasimos, the patron saint of the island, who founded an order of women in 1554 and was beatified in 1622. A massive new church now obscures the older establishment. It is possible to continue on a good road via Kástro (see below) to the S.

Beyond 19.5km **Razáta** a sign (left; visible from Argostóli direction 'Cyclo-pean Walls 2km') leads by track and on foot to the walls of ancient *Kranioi*. Parts of the walls, nearly 5km round, are well preserved. There is little to be seen of a shrine of Demeter and Kore, identified by an inscribed statue base (in museum). It probably consisted of a small Doric temple and functioned from the 6C to the late Hellenistic period. The cult was closely associated with a nearby spring. 21km Immediately below the road (sign) is **Ayía Varvára**, a little cave chapel. You pass turnings (left) round the Lagoon of Koutavos (see below) and (right) to Assos and the N end of the island (see below), then cross a causeway to reach (24km) **Argostóli**.

**Argostóli** (Αργοστόλι; Hotels B, C, D), the capital (6815 inhab.), seat of the nomarch and of an archbishop, has been completely rebuilt since the earthquake of 1953. The **Archaeological Museum** contains a good collection of miscellaneous prehistoric finds; Palaeolithic from excavations of Kavvadhias; Middle Helladic from Kokkolata, Mycenaean from Masakarata, Mavrata, Metaxata, Lakithra; terracotta revetments from a Doric temple at Miniá (early 6C BC); a fine bronze head from Sami of the 3C AD; material from Lake Melissani (Pan sanctuary). The excellent **public library** preserves the Venetian archives and has a fine *****museum** of local history. The town is delightfully situated some way up the Gulf of Argostoli in an inlet so shallow that a causeway and bridge 640m long have been thrown across it to shorten the road in from the E. The bridge, with its many arches, was built by the British military commander in 1813. The circuit of the shallow **Lagoon of Koutavos**, thus cut off, makes a pleasant walk (5km) and may include a visit to the ruins of *Kranioi* (see above). On the E side of the bay, along the Assos road to the N of the causeway, is a **British Cemetery** (key with cottage just before, right).

Another short excursion may be made round the tip of **Lássi** (Hotels A, C), the peninsula on which Argostóli stands. 2.5km N of the town are the marine katavothres, where the sea pours endlessly into subterranean tunnels. A team of Austrian scientists has shown that the water reappears at Melissáni (see above). The flow was used in the 19C to drive mills. It was interrupted by the earthquake but a mill has been restored. A monument to Italian soldiers killed in 1943 crowns a hill to the N of the peninsula (access road; signs). On the headland of Ay. Theódhori a lighthouse ('Sapper' Doric of 1820, rebuilt) commands the entire gulf. You can continue round Telegraph Hill and return (left) to the town, or go on S to Lássi itself, beyond which (left; sign) is the **Cave of Ay. Yerasimos**. Further are the beaches of **Makrí Yialós** and **Platí Yialós** (Hotel A), with organised facilities for bathing.

A longer excursion (c 26km) to the S of Argostóli, comprises several places of interest. It can be extended to **Skála** in the SE (36km direct from Argostoli; daily bus). You leave by the W shore of Koutavos. 8.5km **Kástro**, a village at the foot of the 13C **Castle of St George**, around which clustered the medieval and Venetian capital of the island, called **San Giorgio**. There are considerable remains of houses, churches, and of a convent. The remains of the citadel include a drawbridge, the enceinte, churches, and barracks. The town, which once had 15,000 inhabitants, was destroyed by an earthquake in 1636 and abandoned for Argostoli in 1757. The *****view** comprises the peninsula of Paliki on the W, Mt Ainos, and the island of Zante. 9km Turning for **Pesádha** (right; 7km; ferries to Zákinthos).

A short distance along the Pesádha road is a turn (left; sign) to the beautifully restored church of the **Monastery of Ay. Apóstolos Andréas** with a **Museum of Church Art** (1989) interesting and well-arranged. A new museum building is under construction.

You return SW via **Metaxáta**, where the house occupied by Lord Byron in 1823–24 was wrecked in 1953 but a plaque on the gate opposite commemorates his still-flourishing ivy, and pass **Miniá** and the **airport** before regaining Argostóli. There is an alternative route further inland, via Lakíthra.

Several other places S and W of Kástro have features of interest, especially prehistoric. The necropolis of **Masarakáta** (continue 100m on Pesádha road beyond road to monastery and turn right), excavated by Kavvadias, yielded 83 Mycenaean tombs, one of the tholos type and is interesting to visit. The tombs at **Metaxáta** are good but difficult to find on private land. Another necropolis at **Kokkoláta**, has pre-Mycenaean tombs, but is not informative. At **Lakíthra** (rebuilt by French subscriptions and in an attractive position above the fertile plain) are Mycenaean tombs in a protected archaeological area, and antique grain silos hewn from the rock. The model village of **Kourkoumeláta** (Hotel C), built after 1953 by Andreas Vergotis, whose body lies in its cemetery, has the look of a prosperous city suburb.

Beyond **Travliáta** (below **Kástro**) a main road continues E to (42km) **Skála** (Hotels B, C), with developing tourism. A project to protect the local Loggerhead turtle has been started here. 2km N on the road to Póros, under the chapel of Ayios Yeóryios, foundations have been found of an Archaic temple (6C BC) and another structure. Beneath the ruined church of Ayios Athanásios in the S outskirts of the village (200m from sea; signs), has been excavated an extensive Roman villa of the 2C AD, of which the second room was early converted to Christian use. Mosaics with metrical inscriptions naming Krateros as the artist include an apotropaic representation of Phthonos (Envy being devoured by wild beasts). From Skála it is possible to continue, via **Ayios Yeóryios** to Póros (see above), returning via (55km) Tzanáta and (68.5km) Markópoulo, where a strange (?migratory) phenomenon occurs c 6–15 August when small, harmless snakes invade the church, to Argostóli.

A ferry crosses the gulf frequently in ½ hour to **Lixoúri** (Λειξούρι; Hotels B, C; F/A), the second town (3181 inhab.) of the island, situated on the isolated peninsula of **Palíki** (by road 31km). It is served also by some boat services. Here were born Elias Meniates (1669–1714), patriotic writer, and Andreas Lascaratos (1811–1901), satirist and anti-clerical pamphleteer. There is a folklore museum and archaeological collection in the public library. The ancient city of *Pale* was situated close to the sea, c 1.5km N of Lixoúri, which was probably built in great part from its ruins. Little now remains of the city which once successfully resisted Macedonia, and Lixouri itself has suffered ruin in 1867 and 1953. At Kontoyenádha (19km NW) the chapel of Ayios Yeóryios has 10C paintings. The S part of the peninsula has unusual scenery. The monasteries of **Kipouraíon** (restored) and **Taphíou** (ruined) are interestingly situated c 17km SW of Lixoúri.

FROM ARGOSTOLI TO FISKARDO, 53km, road arduous but good, bus daily. From Argostóli it is 29km (from Sámi 16km) to a road-junction (Sinióri) in the valley that lies between the main part of the island and Mt Kaló in the northern Peninsula of Erissos. On the W side of this peninsula, 10km farther N, **Assos** (restaurants) occupies the most beautiful situation on the island. The ruined Venetian **castle** (1595) stands on a peninsula headland commanding two anchorages. The cottages and vineyards within the large enclosure are attractive, while the picturesque village on the isthmus below relieves the stern grandeur of the sea and mountains. The main road runs on to **Fiskárdo** (Hotels A, B, C; ferries to Sámi, and other islands), near the N end of the island, probably the ancient *Panormos*. The place takes its name from Robert Guiscard, who died here in 1085. One of the few places to suffer no earthquake damage, Fiskárdo still has houses typical of the island before the disaster. The curious **church** (ruined) on the headland to the NE has twin W towers of Norman type, but nothing is known of its history. There is also a small lighthouse, possibly Venetian. Much of the tiny village is owned by rich expatriates.

# E.  Zánte

**Approaches**. **Car ferry**, regularly (less frequent in winter) from Killíni (Rte 40) in 1½ hours; through buses (4 daily) from Athens via Patras. Car-drivers should obtain a priority ticket for the return from the agent in Zákinthos.— **By Air**. From Athens daily in 1 hour; weekly to Kefallinía.—**Terminal** at Róma 16.

**Zánte**, officially styled by its ancient name of *Zakynthos* (Ζάκυνθος), in modern transliteration **Zákinthos**, is the southernmost of the four central Ionian Islands. It lies 21km W of the Peloponnesian coast, and is separated from it by the deep Channel of Zante. It is 40km long and 19km broad (458 sq. km). The beauty and fertility of Zakinthos and the picturesque situation of its capital on the margin of a semicircular bay have been celebrated in all ages, from Theocritus onwards. Pliny and Strabo describe the richness of its woods and harvests, though Herodotus, who had visited the island, remembers only the pitch wells (IV, 195). The Homeric epithet 'woody' is no longer apposite, as its woods have been mostly replaced by currant vines and olives, the mainstays of the export trade. The potency of its wine merits mention by English travellers as early as 1517. Mandolato is a local brand of nougat.

The island abounds in gardens, and in spring and autumn is carpeted with fragrant wild flowers, whence the Venetian jingle 'Zante, fior di Levante'. In the W of this volcanic island the land is barren and mountainous (**Mount Yiri**, 756m); the fertile E half has no height greater than **Mount Skopos** (485m). The island has suffered from periodic earthquakes, one of the worst having occurred in 1820. Those of 1840 and 1893 were less severe, but that of 1953 wrecked the island.

As in Corfu and Kefallinia, there are many Roman Catholic families in Zante, chiefly of Italian origin. A large proportion of its inhabitants are descended from settlers brought by the Venetians from the Peloponnese (see Itháki), from Christians who emigrated from Cyprus and Crete when those islands were conquered by the Turks, and from younger branches of noble Italian families.

**History**. Homer, both in the *Iliad* and in the *Odyssey*, calls the island by the name it still officially bears, though Pliny (IV, 54) affirms that it was in the earliest time called *Hyrie*. An ancient tradition quoted by Strabo ascribed to the Zakynthians the foundation of Saguntum in Spain.

According to Thucydides (II, 66), Zakynthos was colonised by Achaeans from the Peloponnese. Herodotus (VI, 70) relates how Demaratos, the exiled King of Sparta, who had taken refuge in Zakynthos, was hospitably sheltered by the inhabitants from the wrath of the pursuing Lacedaemonians and escaped thence to Persia. Not long before the Peloponnesian War the island was reduced by the Athenian general Tolmides. An ally of Athens during that war, it appears to have been subsequently dependent on Sparta. Later it belonged to Philip III of Macedon (Polybius V, 4). During the second Punic War Zakynthos was occupied by the Romans. Afterwards restored to Philip, whose deputy Hierocles of Agrigentum sold it to the Achaeans, it again became Roman in 191 BC.

The role of Zante since has been insignificant. It was ravaged by the Vandals (in 474), Saracens, and Normans, and depopulated by the Turks (in 1479). It was Venetian from 1489 to 1797. Kolokotronis took refuge here in 1805. Richard Church conducted the landing of a small British force in 1809. During the War of Independence some of the chief families of Zante and Cephalonia distinguished themselves by their efforts on behalf of the national cause, despite official discouragement. Lord Byron, whose enthusiasm for the Greek cause had assured the success of two loans floated in London, banked the first instalment of £40,000 in Zante. Frank Abney Hastings died on Zante in 1828 of tetanus as a result of a wrist wound received the week before at Aitoliko.

Zante was the birthplace of Ugo Foscolo (1778–1827), whose Ionian nationality is generally merged in his Italian reputation; of Andreas Kalvos (died 1867), the poet, whose remains were returned to his native island in 1960 from Lincolnshire where he lived with his English wife; and of Solomos (1798–1857), the Greek national poet, who, inspired by Dante, forged Demotic Greek into a poetic idiom. Andreas Vesalius (1514–64), the founder of modern anatomy, was ship-wrecked off Zante and died on the island, while returning from a pilgrimage to Jerusalem enforced on him by the Inquisition for an experiment in human dissection.

**Zákinthos** (Hotels A–E; F/A; also at Argási, 4km S, see below), the capital (10,236 inhab.) of the island nome, faces Loutrá Killínis on the Peloponnesian coast. The town, which is the seat of an archbishop, stretches along its bay for 2.5km, but reaches back only at one point, uphill to the castle. It has been almost completely rebuilt since the earthquake of 1953 in the attractive arcaded style for which it was celebrated. A few of the old streets survive. There are two museums. In an attractive building in Plateía Solomoú is a **Museum of Byzantine Art**, mainly retrieved from wrecked churches; the local carving of various ikonostaseis is notable; here also is a sculptured relief by Thorvaldsen from a monument (1820) to Maitland. This museum also contains a fine collection of post-Byzantine ikons, and later paintings. The **public library** nearby has an exhibition of World War II Resistance and photographs of old Zante. The **Solomos Museum**, in St Mark's Square a little inland, is installed above the mausoleum of the two poets, Solomos and Kalvos, and has material connected with various prominent locals. The site of Ugo Foscolo's house is now a small garden with a marble monument. His oil lamp is in the chapel opposite. Among the reconstructed churches worth a visit are **Ayios Nikólaos tou Mólou** (on the quay), and the **Kyría ton Angélon**, beyond the Xenia Hotel. At the N end of the town is a **British Cemetery**.

Towards the S end of the town, the **Panayía Faroméni** (excellent music), before 1953 the finest church, has been rebuilt and the interior is being restored. In **Ayios Dhionísios**, farther on, are the relics of the local St Dionysios (died 1622), the island's patron, brought back in 1716 from the Strophádhes, also frescoes by Cozzari, a local pupil of Tiepolo. Both churches have conspicuous campanili.

The ruins of the Venetian **kastro** (107m) occupy the flat top of the hill above the town. The *view comprises the W coast of Greece from the Mesolongi lagoon to Navarino Bay, backed by the lofty mountains of Akarnania, Aitolia, Arcadia, and Messenia. On the headland across the Channel of **Zante** rises Khlemoútsi (Rte 40). To the W extend enormous currant vineyards.

**Mt Skopos** (485m), so called from a rock on the top resembling a sentry, may be ascended in 2½ hours. John Dallam, the English organ-builder, with two companions, climbed it on Easter Sunday 1599 while on the way to deliver an organ to Mehmet III as a gift from Elizabeth I. The road SE along the shore is followed for 3km where a path mounts to the right passing the Panayía Skopiótissa (poor road from Argási). The most striking feature of the view from the top is the gloomy peak of Ainos in Kefallinia rising abruptly from the sea. Farther SE the road runs very prettily via **Argási** (Hotels A, B, C, E) to (11km) **Vasilikó** (Hotels B, C, D; occasional bus) beyond which is **Cape Yeráki**, with quarries of sandstone.

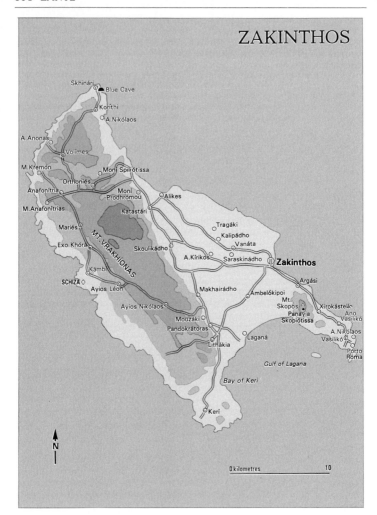

## Excursions from Zakynthos

A. TO THE NORTH, 61km (38 miles); buses to Katastári and Volímes. Near the suburb of **Bokháli**, where the Philike Etaireia took their oath, on the hill of **Stráni** is a park and monument to Solomos. Here he got the inspiration for his hymn to Liberty. You round the S of the Kastro hill, then bear NW through currant vineyards to (15km) **Katastári**, the island's largest village (1190 inhab.), at the N end of the plain. Here there is a turn to the saltpans and beach of **Alikés** (2.5km, right; Hotels D). Through the village is a turn (left) to the **Moní Ayios Ioánnis Pródhromos** (16–17C), with a good ikon by Th. Poulakis. The road winds up with views across to Kefallinia then turns W across a cultivated plateau. 26km Turning (left) for **Orthoniés** and (2km further, with a left branch) the **Moní Spiliótissa**, originally a 16C foundation with a cave church. 28km Road (right) to **Volímes** (5km), continuing to **Skhinári** lighthouse (12km) at the N tip of the island, with a branch to **Ayios Nikólaos** (13km; summer ferries to Kefallinia; boat trips to the Blue Cave). Near Volimes are two monasteries: **Ayios Andréas** 2km NW and **Ayios Yeóryios Kremón** ('of the cliffs') 3km SW. The latter is 1.5km from a spectacular seaside viewpoint (do not take your car to the edge). 30km Road (right) to **Anafonítria**, where the monastery has a medieval tower and wall-paintings and the reputed cell of St Dionysios. A track has been blasted to the sea on the Bay of Vrama. The road turns S through (34km) **Maríes** and a series of upland villages often out of sight of the sea. 36km **Exo Khóra**. On the coast 2km away is **Kámpi** (ancient *Schiza*) with cafes overlooking the sea, and Mycenaean tombs. Beyond (46km) **Ayios Nikólaos** the road winds down with views of the plain, the airport, and the Bay of Lagana. At (56km) **Makhairádo** the church has a splendid interior with a fine carved iconostasis. 61km **Zákinthos**.

B. TO THE SOUTH-WEST, 20.5km (13 miles). Leave the town by the Lithakiá road. 3km Turning to the Airport. You pass a succession of roads leading to **Laganá** (Hotels A, B, C, D), a beach c 6.5km long with restaurants (crowded at summer week-ends). At 16km you branch left and in 1km reach the shore of the Bay of Kerí, where are curious pitch springs (Píssa tou Kerioú), a natural phenomenon known to Herodotus and Pliny, and used then as now for caulking ships. One may be seen at the base of the jetty. 20.5km **Kerí** has a 17C church and a beach with small cafés.

Over 48km to the S of Zante lie the remote **Strophádhes**, visited only two or three times per year by caique from Zante. On the large island stands a Byzantine fortress-monastery, once rich and populous until it succumbed to Saracen attack; it has a handful of monks, and in 1624–1716 guarded the relics of St Dionysios of Zante. The island is a breeding-place of shear-waters; in April wild doves on their migratory passage are decimated by hunters. The smaller island takes its name of **Artonísi** from a native species of gull.

# VII NORTHERN GREECE

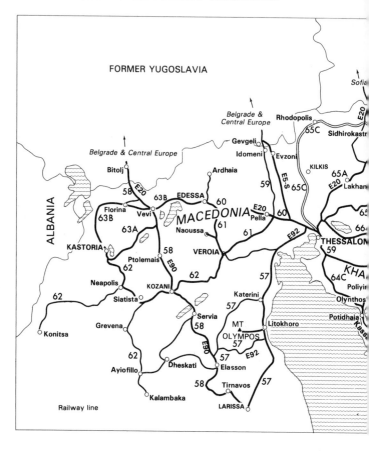

The provinces of Macedonia and Thrace, northernmost of modern Greece, are relatively recent acquisitions. Macedonia has been under Greek sovereignty since 1912, Thrace since 1920. Unknown before the First World War except to experienced Balkan travellers, and little visited as late as 1950, the region has great natural beauty and interest; it is now easily accessible, and increasingly fostering tourism, though remoter parts can still be remarkably primitive. The province of **Macedonia** (Makedhonía; 2,236,019 inhab.) is only part of the large but ill-defined area to which the name of Macedonia has been given since Classical times; much of it is now within the territory of bordering states. The Greek province is shaped like a gigantic capital L, on its side, with the short arm extending N from the Thessalian border and the long arm bounding the Aegean Sea on the N, as far as its junction with Thrace. This part of Macedonia is relatively narrow, varying in width from c 45–95km, with Yugoslavia and Bulgaria beyond the frontier. On the W Macedonia marches with Albania. In the S Mount

Olympos rises on the Thessalian border and extends into both provinces. To the W of Olympos the Kamvounian Mountains divide Macedonia from Thessaly.

Macedonia is divided politically into thirteen nomes and one autonomous region. These are: Florina; Kastoria; Grevena; Kozani; Imathia; Pella; Thessaloniki; Pieria; Khalkidhiki; Serres; Drama; Kavalla; and the Ayion Oros (Athos). The regional capital is Thessaloniki, second city of Greece and seat of the Minister for Northern Greece. Among the dozen most populous centres in the country are also Kavalla, Serres, and Drama. Of the great cities of ancient Macedonia that have no modern counterpart we may mention Pella, Dion, Pydna, Potidaia, Olynthos, Philippi, and Amphipolis.

**Thrace**, or **Western Thrace** (Dhitikí Thráki), as it is called to distinguish it from the region regained by Turkey, is the NE province of Greece. Extending from the Nestos to the Evros, which forms the frontier with Turkey, it has a population of 338,005. The interior is largely covered by the Rhodope Mountains, which rise to 2278m and lie mainly in Bulgaria. The province is divided politically into the nomes of Xanthi; Rhodhopi, with the chief town, Komotini; and Evros. Western Thrace was part of the Ottoman Empire before the Balkan Wars of 1912–13. The Treaty of Bucharest (1913) gave it to Bulgaria, but in 1920, after the Treaty of Neuilly (1919) it became Greek. From 1920 until the war of 1922 with Turkey, Eastern Thrace also was under Greek rule.

The original Thracians were Indo-European but not Hellenic; they came from the Carpathian region, and had fair or red hair and grey eyes. They spoke a language so far undeciphered. The whole area beyond the Strymon seems hardly to have been reached by the Bronze Age, and the ethnic and historical affinities of Thrace are with Bulgaria and Turkey rather than with Greece (see below).

The climate of the northern provinces is Balkan rather than Mediterranean, with extreme temperatures in summer and winter and a considerable rainfall. Their topography has few affinities with that of southern Greece. The coastline is little indented and safe anchorages are scarce. The larger rivers are perennial. The mountains are for the most part covered with dense forest or scrub. The interior is mountainous, the W regions being traversed from N to S by part of the mountain backbone of Greece. The ranges are divided at intervals by valleys through which flow five important rivers. From W to E these are the Aliakmon (Bistritsa), the Axios (Vardar), the Strymon (Struma), marking the E frontier of Classical Macedonia, the Nestos (Mesta), marking the modern boundary between Macedonia and Thrace, and the Evros (Maritsa), dividing Western from Eastern Thrace. Mountain lakes are numerous on and near the NW frontiers and the formations of an additional 40 by means of barrages is contemplated; the shallower marsh-lakes formed in the plains are slowly disappearing with the harnessing of the rivers. A noteworthy geographical feature of Macedonia is the Khalkidhikí Peninsula, with its three prongs—Kassándra, Sithonía (Lóngos), and Athos—projecting boldly into the Aegean and helping to form the Gulf of Thessaloniki (ancient Thermaic Gulf) on one side and the Gulf of Orphani (Strymonic Gulf) on the other. Off the boundary with Thrace is the island of Thasos.

The argillaceous planes have not been cultivated to the extent that might have been expected; but this is largely due to the chequered history of the provinces. Important products are tobacco, rice, beans, sesame, and poppy seed; fruit and a wide variety of vegetables are grown in increasing quantity, and a sugar-beet industry, started in 1960, has proved highly successful. Manufactures include wine, cloth, macaroni, and soap. More important are the hydro-electric schemes in construction, and the development of Ptolemaïs as an industrial area: fertilisers are manufactured on an increased scale. Though rich in minerals (copper, chrome, gold, iron, lead, molybdenum, silver, magnesite, asbestos), Macedonian mines are not yet fully exploited. There is trade in timber, livestock, skins, furs, and wool. In Thrace sunflowers are grown for their seed oil.

During the long Middle Ages the population of Macedonia became very mixed. Slavs, chiefly Bulgarian, with a strong admixture of Bosnian and Serbian elements, and Turks were predominant inland while the coast from the Aliakmon to the Strymon including the Chalcidice trident was mainly Greek. A profound change was caused by the provisions of the Treaty of Lausanne (1923), whereby 348,000 Moslems living in Macedonia were exchanged for 538,600 Greeks from Asia Minor. As a result of the events of the Second World War and the Civil Wars the greater part of the Slav population retired or was exiled across the neighbouring frontiers. In Thrace, however, the Turkish population was not exchanged after 1922 but allowed to remain (as Greeks were allowed to remain in Constantinople). This fact gives to the province a special flavour, Turkish villages alternating with Greek; here Greeks and Turks still live together, yet separately, as they did all over the Ottoman Empire until 1922. The Moslem minority comprises two-sevenths of the population; they enjoy full Greek citizenship and freedom of worship in their mosques. The N provinces are still suffering depopulation by emigration, in recent years to Western Germany, Australia, and Canada.

These areas are still rich in the variety of their flora and fauna, though excessive local hunting is rapidly exterminating many unique species, just as constant grazing of domestic goats is destroying rare plants. The formation of national parks is still under consideration. Lions, which (according to Herodotus) troubled Xerxes in Macedonia, seem not to have survived into our era, and though the brown bear is protected on the Bulgarian side of the Rhodope Mountains, its appearance in Greece seems to be limited to the Pindus near the Albanian frontier. The jackal is still seen, wild cat and wild boar inhabit Pindus, and wolves are not unknown. Roe deer and wild goat are much depleted since the war. Many of the larger European birds may be seen: vultures, hawks, and the golden eagle in the mountain regions, and storks, herons, cormorants, pelicans, and occasionally flamingoes in the coastal plains and marshes. Of the many reptiles, only two snakes are harmful: one, the adder, is common. The harmless lizards grow to a surprising size. Tortoises abound. The insect life is rich.

**Communications** now compare favourably with those elsewhere in Greece. The railways remain slow because of the terrain, but the main roads are good. The highway linking former Yugoslavia with Turkey, which crosses the entire region, has been completely renewed. For much of its length in Greece it follows the course of the **Via Egnatia** (or Egnatía Odhós), the great military road between the Adriatic and Byzantium, systematised by the Romans in the 2C BC to form, together with the Via Appia, a direct link from Rome via Brundisium with the East. Parts of it undoubtedly date from Macedonian times, at least the reign of Philip II. It had two branches starting from Apollonia (Avlona) and Dyrrachium (Durazzo), passed Lychidnus (near Lake Ochrida), Herakleia Lynkestis (Bitolj), Edhessa, Pella, Thessalonica, Amphipolis, and Philippi. Neapolis (Kavalla) was the E terminus until the conquest of Thrace in AD 46, ship being taken thence for the Troad. Later the road was extended through Thrace by Akontisma and Trajanopolis, to end at Byzantium (Istanbul). Its name may derive from its builder but not from Gnatia in Apulia. Augustus founded colonies along its route; Nero installed inns; Trajan repaired it in AD 107–112 (adding on the Italian side the Via Trajana as an alternative to the Via Appia). Milestones found on its route as far apart as Ochrid, Amphipolis, and Akontisma bear witness to repairs by Caracalla in 216–217. An epitaph discovered near the site of Ad Duodecimum, a staging post 12 Roman miles W of Philippi, commemorates C. Lavus Faustus 'institor tabernae'. From the 4C AD the Via Egnatia lost importance to the N route via Sirmium, Belgrade, Naissus (Niš), Serdica (Sofia), Philippopolis (Plovdiv), and Hadrianopolis (Edirne), as Milan replaced Rome as the starting-point. Good modern hotels are to be found in the larger towns, at recently exploited seaside resorts, and at some archaeological sites and beauty spots; elsewhere accommodation is still limited.

**History.** Archaeological research has suggested that in the earliest times *Macedonia* had affinities with the NW, its short late-Neolithic culture (c 2600 BC) stemming from the Danube. In Macedonia the Early and Middle Bronze Age (2500–1700) had Anatolian or Northern origins, and Aegean influences are felt only briefly in the Mycenaean period, soon cut short by the so-called 'Lausitz Incursions' an Iron Age migration from Central Europe, of which the 'Dorian Invasion' was part. These people from the Hungarian plains swept all before their iron swords, passing onward to the S. A return wave from Thessaly founded the historical state of Macedonia about the 8C BC.

The problem of whether Macedonians were Greeks has been endlessly debated from the time of Herodotus to the present day, usually to the accompaniment of political polemics. Some Greek tribes probably settled in the S part of Macedonia. According to one tradition their leaders were the three sons of the Heraclid Temenos, who had fled from Argos. The youngest of the three, Perdikkas, is said to have founded the Macedonian monarchy and to have made his capital at Aigai, in Emathia. Another tradition makes an earlier Heraclid, Karanos, the founder of the dynasty and Perdikkas only the fourth of the line. It seems reasonably certain that by the 7C BC a kingdom was established at Aigai, from which the whole region was subdued and unified. Hence the poetic name of Emathia for the whole of Macedonia. The Greek settlers intermarried with the aborigines and spoke a dialect akin to the Doric, but with many barbarous words and forms; so much so that the Macedonians were never regarded as genuine Hellenes, though seldom actually called Barbarians. After the 6C BC Greek influence increasingly filtered N from Thasos.

From written record little is known of Macedonia until the reign of Amyntas I (c 540–505), under whom it was virtually a satrapy of Persia. His son Alexander I (died c 455 BC) was a secret philhellene despite the fact that he accompanied Xerxes on his invasion to Greece. He later extended his kingdom to the Strymon. The reign of Perdikkas II (454–414), coinciding with the period of Athenian expansion, is characterised by scheming but not very able vacillation between Athens and her enemies. Archelaus (413–399) was a patron of Greek art and literature and established cordial relations with Greece, which remained friendly until the advent of Philip II (359–336). That king, intent on universal conquest, began by seizing various Greek cities on the Macedonian coast, such as Amphipolis, Pydna, Potidaea, Methone, and Olynthos. The well-meaning but misdirected efforts of Demosthenes (witness the Philippic and Olynthiac orations) to rouse the Athenians against the danger from Philip met with little response. The Athenians were not really aroused until Philip, invited by the Amphictyonic League (see Delphi), marched through the pass of Thermopylae on the pretext of punishing the Locrians of Amphissa. Through the influence of Demosthenes, the Athenians allied themselves with the Thebans, but the allies were defeated at Chaironeia in 338 and the independence of the Greek city states was lost. A congress held at Corinth after the victory decided on war against Persia; but, in the midst of his preparations, Philip was murdered. He was succeeded by his son Alexander the Great (336–323), who was destined to fulfil the ambition of world conquest that Philip had cherished.

On Alexander's death there was general upheaval. His regent in Macedonia, Antipater, won the Lamian War against the Greeks with the victory of Krannon. Antipater's son Cassander, who had been deprived by his father of the succession to the regency, proclaimed himself king of Macedonia in 306 and, after the battle of Ipsos (301), secured the possession of Macedonia and Greece. On his death in 297, his son Philip IV held the throne for a few months. In 294 Demetrios Poliorketes, son of Antigonus the One-Eyed, one of Alexander's generals who had become king of Asia and had been killed at Ipsos, was acknowledged king of Macedonia; but in 286 he was deserted by his own troops, who offered the throne to Pyrrhus, king of Epirus. Two years later Pyrrhus had to hand over Macedonia to Lysimachus, another of Alexander's generals, who had made himself king of Thrace in 306. In 277 Antigonus Gonatas, son of Demetrios Poliorketes, obtained the throne of Macedonia, though Pyrrhus contested it again in 273. Demetrios II (239–229), son of Antigonus Gonatas, and Antigonus Doson (229–220) tried to win the mastery over Greece. Now came the period of the three Macedonian Wars (214–205, 200–194, and 171–168), and of the last Macedonian kings. Philip V (220–179) was defeated by the Romans at Kynoskephalai in 197, and his son Perseus (178–168) at Pydna in 168. After Pydna Macedonia was divided into four republics with capitals at Thessalonica, Pella, Pelagonia (Herakleia Lynkestis), and Amphipolis. This arrangement did not last long, for in 148 Macedonia became a Roman province. In 27 BC, as a senatorial province, Macedonia was separated from Achaia, and extended N to the Danube, E to the Hebros (Evros), and S and SW to include Thessaly and Epirus. After the Roman subjugation of Thrace in AD 46, Macedonia, no longer a frontier province, recovered some of its prosperity, attracting the missionary zeal of St Paul.

The Goths invaded Macedonia in AD 252. In 289 Diocletian altered the province's boundaries by taking away Thessaly and Epirus. Constantine created the diocese of Macedonia, which took in Thessaly, Epirus, and Crete, the province becoming one of the first to receive the epithet 'Salutaris'. The Byzantine centuries saw incursions by

Goths (378), Huns (434), Ostrogoths (478), Bulgars (500), Slavs (527), Huns again (540), and Goths again (558). In the 7C the Serbs reached the gates of Thessalonica. The 9C was marked by the invasions of Bulgars and Saracens who, at the beginning of the 10C, seized Thessalonica. In 1014 Macedonia came under the rule of Byzantium. In 1185 William of Sicily sacked Thessalonica. After the capture of Constantinople in 1204 by the army of the Fourth Crusade, the Latin kingdom of Thessalonica was given to Boniface of Montferrat; but his successor was expelled in 1223 by Theodore Angelus, despot of Epirus, who called himself Emperor of Thessalonica. He was defeated in 1230 by the Bulgarian Tsar Ivan Asen II, who incorporated N and central Macedonia into the second Bulgarian or Bulgar-Vlach Empire, the remainder being absorbed in the Nicaean (Byzantine) Empire in 1246. On the extinction of the direct line of the house of Asen, the power of Bulgaria declined, and NW Macedonia again came under the despotate of Epirus. In the 14C Macedonia fell under the domination of the Serbs. Stefan Dušan (1331–55) conquered all Macedonia except Thessalonica, as well as Thessaly, Epirus, and part of Bulgaria. In 1364 Murad I, sultan of Turkey, routed the united Serbs, Hungarians, and Vlachs on the banks of the Maritsa and by 1375 the whole of the Balkan peninsula, with Macedonia, came under Turkish domination. The invasion of Timur (Tamerlane) reversed the trend of expansion. After the battle of Ankara in 1402, in which the Turks under Bayezid I were totally defeated, Timur reinstated the various principalities that had been suppressed, including the Christian ones in E Europe. Under Murad II the Turks defeated the Christians at Varna in 1444 and established Ottoman domination in E Europe. This survived till the Balkan Wars of 1912–13.

In 1900–08 the so-called 'Macedonian Struggle' took place, when armed bands (Greek 'andartes', Bulgarian 'comitajis', and Serb 'chetniks') contended for supremacy in various mountain regions. Greek Macedonia became a reality in 1912 (see below). The Treaty of Bucharest (1913) fixed the Mesta as the frontier with Bulgaria, which retained its seaboard on the Aegean until the end of the First World War. The treaties of St Germain (1919), of Neuilly (1919), and of Sèvres (1920) attempted to solve the problem of Macedonia. For some years until the war with Turkey in 1922 the whole of Thrace passed to Greece. The Treaty of Lausanne (1923) gave back Eastern Thrace to Turkey. In the Second World War Macedonia served in 1940 as the base for the successful Greek campaign against the Italians, but fell within a week to the German onslaught in 1941 (see below).

**Campaigns. Balkan Wars.** In October 1912 the Balkan League (Bulgaria, Serbia, and Greece) rose against the Turks.

By the end of the month the Bulgarians had defeated the main Ottoman armies in Thrace, and the Serbs were in possession of the whole of old Serbia and most of Albania. The Greeks, under Crown Prince Constantine, advanced through the most difficult passes of Olympus, captured Elassona, defeated Hassim Tahsim Pasha at Servidje (Servia), and occupied Verria and Vodena (Edhessa), while the Turks retreated on Thessaloniki and Monastir (Bitolj). On 1 November the Greeks won a victory at Yenidje Vardar (Yiannitsa); on 8 November (6 October O.S.; St Demetrius' Day) George I led his troops into Thessaloniki. In Epirus a small column had captured Preveza and was besieging Ioannina.

An armistice was signed, but the Congress of London, meeting on 16 Dec, had no result except to show that the Bulgarians had not abated their claims to Macedonia and were intriguing against Serbia. On 6 March Ioannina surrendered; three weeks later the Bulgarians, assisted by the Serbs, took Adrianople. Meanwhile, the Greek Navy, under Admiral Koundhouriotis, controlled the Aegean; Lesbos, Chios, and Samos were captured.

The First Balkan War ended with the Treaty of London (30 May 1913), and all territory west of the line Enos–Midia was ceded to the Balkan League as a whole. A Graeco-Serb treaty was ratified on 1 June after the Bulgarians had tried and failed to expel the Greek forces from the Mount Pangaion district to the east of the Struma mouth. Towards the end of June the Greeks were attacked by the 2nd Bulgarian Army under General Ivanof on a wide front and lost Gevgeli. On 2 July the Greeks, their infantry attacking with dash and supported by mountain guns, recaptured the town; next day Lakhanas was captured by bayonet assault. On 6 July they took the store-town of Doiran. Retreating to Strumnitsa and the Rupel Pass, the Bulgarians committed atrocities at Serres and Sidhirokastro (Demirhisar). By the end of the month the Greeks had reached the Kresne Pass, the Rumanians were threatening Sofia and the Bulgarians had lost.

In the spring of 1916, during the **First World War**, the Bulgarians invaded Macedonia. In the previous autumn the Allies had landed an expeditionary force at Thessaloniki, where Venizelos established a provisional Government. Until final victory in 1918 the inadequately equipped Allies (British, French, and Greek) could do no more than hold in check Austrians, Germans, and Bulgars on an almost static line along the N frontier and the Struma. The main battle areas were in the Monastir Gap and round Doiran, but malaria and dysentery accounted for a great part of the casualties.

**Second World War.** The Axis attack on Greece followed immediately upon the indefinite postponement of the invasion of Britain in favour of a drive for the Middle East. Mussolini, acting prematurely, and without Hitler's knowledge, delivered on 28 October 1940, an ultimatum to General Metaxas demanding the passage of Italian forces, which provoked a terse 'Όχι in reply. After the Italian attack, Greek forces soon moved forward from W Macedonia into Albania, inflicting great losses on the Italians. British air units moved to Greece, but Greece, afraid of provoking German intervention, declined the aid of British land forces until February when it was obvious that such intervention was not only inevitable but imminent. The wavering attitude of Yugoslavia and the possible effects, both on Greek morale and Turkish participation, of withdrawing from E Macedonia, had prevented any political decision being reached on which line should be defended. The available British force, commanded by General Sir Maitland Wilson, consisted of the 1st British Armoured Brigade Group (Brigadier H.V.S. Charrington), the New Zealand Division (Major-General Sir Bernard Freyberg, VC), and the 6th Australian Division (Major-General Sir Iven Mackey). The Australians were still arriving when the Germans invaded.

At 5.45 on the Sunday morning of 6 April German forces in overwhelming strength were launched simultaneously against Yugoslavia and Greece. On 7 April, the Bulgarian Army occupied Alexandroupolis and Komotini, and Von List's 12th Army crossed the frontier at Doiran and Gevgeli. The Greek hope of holding the Metaxas Line in E Macedonia was at once shown to be militarily impossible, but since the commanders in Albania could not be persuaded to give up their gains and retreat before the Italians, it was decided, against the judgement of the British commander, to try to hold the 'Aliakmon Line' (Kaimaktsalan–Vermion–Olympos). Thessaloniki fell on the morning of 9 April and a small British armoured force held the Vevi pass for three days while Greek troops withdrew from northern frontier positions. The New Zealand brigades dug in athwart the Servia pass, the Petra pass, and the gap between Olympos and the sea. The collapse of Yugoslavia and a swift enemy advance in the NW from Kastoria to Grevena, driving towards the Meteora, cut off the Greek army in Albania and threatened to turn the Aliakmon Line even before preparations were complete. The 9th Panzer Division reached the Aliakmon on 14 April and a fighting withdrawal and disengagement was ordered to Thermopylae. The Servia pass was held until 17 April when German troops were already penetrating the Vale of Tempe; rearguard actions were then fought in Tempe and at Elasson, and the New Zealand forces were extricated through the Larissa bottleneck by 19 April. In Athens Greek surrender and British evacuation were already under consideration and the campaign turned into a race for the southern beaches.

The Civil Wars of 1946–49 were waged with ideological intensity from beyond the Greek frontiers, the aim being Communist domination rather than acquisition of territory. Many civilians, particularly children, were kidnapped from frontier areas for indoctrination in Albania or Yugoslav Macedonia and though the bitterness has slowly healed and military control on movement has now been relaxed, depopulation is still characteristic of the NW frontier region.

An excellent guide to the antiquities of Thrace is—C. Bakirtzis and D. Triantaphyllos, *Thrace*, Athens, 1988 (Cultural Foundation of ETBA [National Bank of Industrial Development], Cultural Guides 1).

# 57

## From (Athens) Lárissa to Thessaloníki. Mount Olympos

**Road**, 154km (96 miles). This forms part of the main highway from Athens to Thessaloníki (c 504km), which by-passes Lárissa to the E; on the section through the Vale of Témbi (Tempe) a toll is levied.—27km Vale of Témbi.— 51km Pandeleímon.—67.5km Turning to Litókhoro (5km) for the ascent of Mt Olympos.—87km Kateríni.—120km Aiyínio.—185km Thessaloníki.— **Buses** 14 daily from Lárissa; through services from Athens in c 7 hours.

**Railway**, 171km (106 miles), the main State Railway line from Athens (510km), regular trains daily in c 2½ hours from Lárissa (4 fast through trains from Athens in c 4 hours to Lárissa, 6 hours to Thessaloníki; couchettes and sleeping-cars on night trains).—Platí (133.5km from Larissa), where the line is a few kms N of the road, is the junction for Vérria, etc. (Rte 61).

**Air Service** (Olympic Airways) from Athens to Thessaloníki regularly in 50 minutes. The route passes over Parnes and across the Euripos near Khalkís. Mt Dhirfis is seen on the right. As the aircraft passes over the strait separating Skiáthos and Skópelos, the striking coastline of Magnesía and the Gulf of Volos are well seen. During the flight up the Thermaic Gulf, Pilion, Ossa, and Olympos appear successively to the left, while reaching out on the right are the three prongs of Khalkidikí, Kassándra in the foreground, Sithonía behind, and in the far distance Athos, the Holy Mountain.

**Lárissa**, see Rte 48. You leave the town by the museum and join the by-pass. The road passes the first of the refineries for the sugar industry started in 1960, and runs parallel to the railway. Ahead (left) is the Olympos range, while the great cone of Ossa rises to the right above brown stony foothills (see Rte 48). The road crosses a flat cultivated plain, the bed of the Classical *Nessonis*, one of the lakes left by the recession of the flood that once covered the Thessalian plain. 14km **Yirtóni station** (restaurant). 27km Turnings to **Tírnavos** (left; 33km) and **Ambelákia** (right; 5km).

On the **Tírnavos** road (unsurfaced beyond modern **Gónnoi**), you reach (3km) the site of ancient *Gonnos* (or Gonnoi) which lies 2km to the S of the village, where there is a substantial archaeological collection; also a Turkish fort on a hill to the W. The remains of the ancient site are on a group of low hills to the right of the road. Gonnos was important throughout antiquity because it is situated to control both the W end of the Tempe pass and a N–S route over the E shoulder of Mt Olympos. There are signs that the site was occupied from prehistoric to Roman times but it seems to have been of particular importance in the Macedonian period.

The focus of settlement in the Archaic period was on the NE hill where the remains of a **circuit wall** can be made out. An apsidal **Temple of Athena** was built in Archaic times and reconstructed in the 4 or 3C BC. The city wall was extended in the Hellenistic period to take in the other two hills. There were 12 **towers** at the SW where there is also a **gate**; a second lying to the SW, on flatter ground where the line of the wall has almost disappeared. The **agora** has been conjecturally located on the lower slopes of the NE hill. A **Temple of Artemis**, identified from inscriptions, is near the SW gate and a **Temple of Asklepios** (Hellenistic or Late Roman) some 300m E of the walls. To the NW of the acropolis are the remains of a channel which apparently brought water from a spring on the mountain.

17km **Rodhiá**, where the entrance to the *Stená Rodhiás* is the source of an important collection of Palaeolithic tools. 28km **Tírnavos** (Rte 58).

The ascent (excellent retrospective views of the site of Gonnos and of the Vale of Tempe) to **Ambelákia** (Rooms) winds up the mountainside. The village, named after its vineyards, is beautifully situated amid oaks on Mt Kissavos.

It was already known for its cotton and silk in the 17C, and became in 1780 the centre of a 'joint partnership' of spinners and dyers of red yarn, claimed as the world's first working 'co-operative', with branch offices as far away as London. The town was ruined in 1811 by the bravos of Ali Pasha, but the **Mansion of George Schwarz** (its president) and that of his brother, Demetrios, attest their prosperity; their rococo painted interiors have been splendidly restored. The village is now a summer resort (600m).

At (29km) **Témbi**, formerly Baba, starts the toll road; the railway is across the river.

The **•Vale of Tempe**, in Greek just **Témbi** (Τα Τέμπη), is a beautiful glen, now somewhat spoilt by traffic, between Olympos and Ossa. Through it the Piniós, Thessaly's principal river, flows to the sea. The glen, called **Lykóstoma** ('Wolf's Mouth') in the Middle Ages, is 10km long and only 27–50m wide; it is the most practicable way out of the Thessalian plain to the NE. It was formed in the Quaternary Epoch by a convulsion that rent the mountains and, by providing the Larissan Lake with an outlet to the sea, allowed the Thessalian plain to emerge. The Thessalians, according to Herodotus (VII, 129), attributed the convulsion to Poseidon, the god of storms and earthquakes. This violent topographical distortion finds an echo in the legends of the War of the Gods and Giants (Gigantomachia).

The attraction of the glen is one of contrast. The stern, almost vertical cliffs, scarred by winter torrents and only partly clothed with ivy and other climbing plants, are offset by the peaceful river scenery below. The swift and turbid Piniós is overshadowed on either side by plane-trees and willows. The banks are fringed with lentisk, *Agnus castus*, terebinth, and laurel.

*Tempe*, whose praises are sung by innumerable Roman and other poets, was a centre of the worship of Apollo. The god, having killed the serpent Python, purified himself in the waters of the Piniós, and cut a branch of laurel which he replanted by the Castalian Fountain at Delphi. In memory of this event, every eight years a mission of well-born youths was sent from Delphi to Tempe, to bring back cuttings of the sacred laurel. The Vale of Tempe was one of the gateways to the interior of Greece, but it could be turned by a narrow track to the N via the Forest of Kallipeuke and the town of Gonnoi and by passes through the Olympos massif. In 480 BC a force of 10,000 Greeks occupied Tempe, to deny passage to the Persians, However, hearing that Xerxes was already turning their position by the inland roads, they withdrew to Thermopylae, abandoning Thessaly to the invader. Herodotus (VII, 128, 173) tells us that the Persians came over the shoulder of Olympos and down on Gonnoi (as did the Germans in 1941). In 168 BC the Romans entered Thessaly by way of Gonnoi, but they established a military post in the Vale of Tempe.

Beyond the **Spring of Venus** you reach the Wolf's Mouth (see above). On a rocky hillock (right) stand the ruins of the medieval *Kástro tis Oraiás* (Castle 'of Oriá', really 'of the beautiful maiden'), linked with a local legend and popular song; at the foot of the rock are the remains of an ancient fortress. At **Ayía Paraskeví** a graceful suspension bridge (for foot passengers only) crosses the river; it leads to a chapel and grotto on the opposite bank. The sea appears ahead. 36.5km The **Spring of Daphne** provides a cool and refreshing retreat.

A by-road (see Rte 48) continues on the right bank to **Omólio** (3km), **Stómio** (13km) on the coast, and **Ayiókambos** (46km; for Ayiá).

The road crosses the river and railway (37km **station for Piryetós**) and, with the mouth of the Pinios (fish hatcheries) on the right, passes through the last low foothills of Kato Olympos. **Aiyáni**, a post on the Turkish frontier of 1881–1912, can be seen on the hills c 3km left. Soon afterwards is the **Spring of Diana**. 52km **Pandeleímon**, on the site of the ancient *Herakleia Platamona*, guards the narrows between Kato Olympos and the sea. Here is the splendid *Castle of Platamóna, built by Crusaders in 1204–22 to command the entrance to the Thermaic Gulf. It was taken by Theodore Angelos in 1218 when the Lombard followers of Roland Piche fell from the walls 'like birds from their nest'. Nearby is a sandy beach, with two camp-sites. The **Spring of the Muses** is (left) between the Xenia and the castle. On the coast to the N are holiday developments. We leave the toll road. At (58km) **Leptokariás** (Hotels A, B, C, D) is the beginning of an indifferent road (see below) through the Olympos massif to Elasson. To the left, row upon row of peaks rise to the crest of Olympos, usually snow-capped or shrouded in cloud. 63.5km **Pláka Litokhórou** (Hotels B, C). 70.5km **Limín Litokhórou**, with the railway station of Litókhoro; the town (see below) is seen to the left.

The coastal plain broadens into the strip known to the ancients as *Pieria*, birthplace of the Muses. Just beyond the station is the crossing of the tiny Baphyras, a stream made navigable by the Macedonians to serve Dion, the site of which lies 6.5km NW (signposted from the main road).

You cross the Mavroneri, the *Aison* of Plutarch (comp. below), and skirt (87km) **Kateríni** (Hotels C, D, E), a market town of 43,613 inhabitants, that commands a wonderful view of Olympos. It has one of two Uniate churches in Greece. Its popular **Paralía** (Hotels B, C, D, E; F/A) lies 7km E on the Thermaic Gulf. To Elasson (71km), see Rte 58.

Ancient *Dion* may also be approached from Kateríni. A road (16km; bus) runs S, via **Káritsa** with an early Iron Age tumulus cemetery at Ayios Vassílios, to the modern village (also known as **Malathriá**). Just before the name sign of the village, in a fenced enclosure (right) can be seen the dromos and impressive façade of a Macedonian tomb. The site of **Dion** (open daily 08.30–17.00, or 19.00 in summer), a little to the SW of the village, is entered from the south gate (car park). Visitors are advised to purchase the useful leaflet with a plan of the site and information about the museum.

*Dion* rose to prominence under Archelaus (413–399), who built a temple to Zeus, a stadium for festival games, a theatre (to which Euripides contributed plays), and an enceinte wall. In Macedonian times the place was a troop concentration centre rather than a city. Here Philip II celebrated his triumph after the capture of Olynthos, and here Alexander sacrificed before invading Persia. With Dodona, the city was laid waste by the Aitolians in 220 BC, Philip V taking revenge in 218 by destroying Thermon. Dion was quickly rebuilt, for Philip made it his base before Kynoskephalai as did Perseus his before the Third Macedonian War. After the Battle of Pydna (see below) the Romans established here the *Colonia Julia Diensis*. The town had a bishop in AD 346. It was sacked by Alaric and seems not to have recovered. Explorations undertaken in 1928–31 by Thessaloniki University were renewed in 1962. The line of the walls has been traced but the remains appear to be later than the time of Archelaus. The Roman town measured c 500m by 460.

The line of the fortifications which defines the limits of the city is clear, the most intensively excavated sections being at the N, SW and E.

Opposite the entrance to the site, you cross the line of the city wall and step onto the main **S–N street**, part of the original 4C layout but paved with large blocks in the Roman period. The row of buildings immediately to the left are **storerooms** and **workshops** of the 3 and 4C AD, though the large squared blocks of earlier Hellenistic structures can be seen beneath their floors. Farther on (left) an impressive **Roman façade** has relief sculpture consisting of alternating shields and cuirasses. A side road leads off (right). The next takes you to a residential area (villas, bath buildings etc.) with splendid Roman mosaics (Dionysos in triumph) of the 2C AD. SE of the villas a viewing tower marks an oddly shaped extension of the wall at the corner of the site which may have served as a jetty for river transport. From the roadway leading off the other side of the main street a side lane (left; dead end) has remains of private houses of the 2 and 3C AD. Beyond these you turn left between the W side of the same complex and the remains (farther W) of an **Early Christian basilica**, whose predecessor on the same site had a mosaic floor. Climbing the bank (right) you can look down into the E apse and the aisle of the building. The narthex lay beyond. Architectural fragments from the buildings are visible. Turning W, you reach the **town wall**, of which a substantial section can be observed. The original structure (4C)

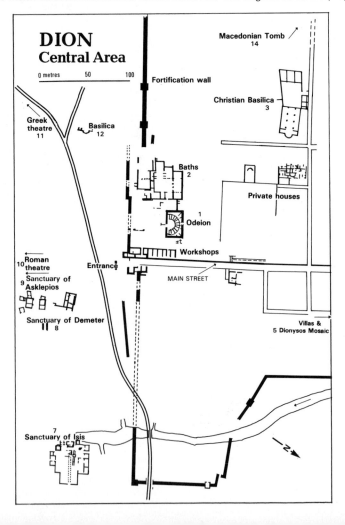

was mainly of large squared blocks; the later (Roman and Early Christian) repairs can be easily distinguished. There are projecting square towers. To the right, with an inspection tower beyond, are the remains of a substantial Roman bath building (Severan period), whose hypocaust system is its most immediately obvious feature. It was finely appointed. The bases of some of the columns which adorned the interior can be seen. Statues of the god Asklepios and his family (now in the museum) were found here and the building may thus have been part of a larger therapeutic complex. This view is perhaps supported by the existence close by to the E of an **odeion**, which can be reached by a path along the S side of the baths.

You are now close to the entrance, opposite which, in a large enclosure on the other side of the road, are the remains of a **Sanctuary of Demeter**. Some finds are as early as the 5C. The oldest architectural elements are two rectangular 'megarons' of large square blocks which can be easily made out among the rather confusing structures of the later layout. To the S of this is a small **Temple of Asklepios**.

Returning to the road, you turn right (E), cross the stream and reach (right) the **Sanctuary of Isis**, a large complex of Hellenistic origin. It is best viewed from the E side. A central passage leads to an altar. Behind this is a façade of four columns and a flight of steps, at the top of which lay the **Temple of Isis** in her guise of Goddess of Birth. To the S and N of the main temple are **smaller temples** to Isis (as Goddess of Fortune) and to Aphrodite Hypolimpidia (i.e. below Olympos). Copies of some of the votive statues, and of the cult state of Isis as Goddess of Fortune have been set up in the positions of the originals.

Back beyond the site car park are (right, close to the town wall) the remains of an Early Christian funerary basilica with a subterranean tomb and, further away, the remains of the Hellenistic **theatre** (temporary seating for performances). To the NE, at the edge of a wood, is the 2C AD Roman **odeion**, similar to that in the main site but on a larger scale.

Near the W gate is a stretch of aqueduct (outside the wall) and the central water distribution reservoir.

To the N and E of the site cemeteries have been investigated with graves of the 5C BC to 5C AD, including Macedonian tombs. To the W is an Early Iron Age tumulus cemetery.

In the village is the excellent new **\*museum** (open daily 08.30–17.00 or 19.00 in summer; closed on Monday mornings) with finds from Dion and other sites in the vicinity. It is most attractively laid out and has a particularly good collection of Hellenistic and Roman material.

GROUND FLOOR. The first section contains finds from the baths: statues, including Dionysos, the family of Asklepios, other portraits. The second section has material from the Sanctuary of Isis—including the cult statues of Isis (as Fortune) and Aphrodite Hypolimpidia, as well as other votive sculptures, stelai with carved footprints, and Roman honorific inscriptions and statues. The third section concerns the Sanctuary of Demeter—heads of Demeter and Aphrodite, three other female statues; also figures of Demeter and Aphrodite; altar of Aphrodite, case of votive offerings. There follows a case of finds from other sanctuaries, including the Sanctuary of Asklepios: small statue of Asklepios; sculpture and inscriptions from the Temple of Dionysos. Head, inscription and other statues from the Altar of Athens. Two further cases contain finds from the cemeteries, including Macedonian tombs: gold jewellery and iron weapons etc. Hellenistic and Roman grave stelai, many inscribed. Beyond are Early Christian grave stelai and a case with items of ecclesiastical equipment from the basilicas.

UPPER FLOOR. Models of Pieria and Mount Olympos. A special room contains the remains of a 2C AD water organ, with drawings illustrating its use, which matches ancient descriptions. In the main gallery a head of Faustina and other figures including philosophers from the Villa of Dionysos are displayed. Finds from Olympos and Early Iron Age sanctuaries on its slopes. Sculptures (especially grave stelai), inscriptions, pottery etc. from other parts of Pieria, including Pydna and Kitros. Interesting group of bronze votives from a rural shrine at Ritini.

BASEMENT (supported by the Pieridhes Foundation). Extensive displays illustrate daily life in Dion, various arts and craft techniques (copying of sculpture by pointing, mosaic and opus sectile, stoneworking) and particular groups of finds (coins, inscriptions etc.). The hypocaust of the baths is explained and panels illustrate the water supply system of Dion.

At 97km by the Michaelidhes brickworks Macedonian tombs have been found. At (99km) **Kítros** (1789 inhab.; 1km W of the road), a custom recalling Aristophanes survives, when, on 8 January (St Domenica), the women take control of the village, ejecting the men from the cafés; similar events occur at **Kolindhrós** (3732 inhab.; c 16km NW). Macedonian and Roman *Pydna*, transferred by Archelaus away from the sea in 410, may have been at Alónia, NW of Kitros. Most finds have been from graves. At **Alikí**, 3km E of Kítros, are the largest salt works in Greece. They surround the **Toúzla Marsh** which corresponds to the ancient harbour of *Pydna*. Though some terraces have been observed and pottery found, there is nothing here to see but a pleasant beach (tavernas and rooms). 106km Turn for **Makríyialos** on the coast with (3km S; 1.5km beyond the Hotel Panórama) at **Kástro** the acropolis of ancient *Pydna* (Byzantine *Kitros*) where the substantial remains are of the later period. A Byzantine basilica of the 10C succeeded Early Christian churches. The original fortifications were of the time of Justinian. The site was taken by the Franks in 1204 and turned into a military camp (a tower and cistern were constructed within the church.) It was captured by the Turks at the end of the 14C. Other remains of the ancient settlement (houses, a fragment of the mud-brick fortification wall) and its cemeteries have been discovered here and beneath the modern village to the N. These suggest that at least some of the population returned after the transfer effected by Archelaus (see above). Pydna gave its name to the famous battle of 168 BC.

When Lucius Aemilius Paullus took command of the Roman forces in 168, Perseus, the last king of Macedon, held an impregnable position SE of Dion. By a feigned attempt to turn the Macedonian position, the Roman general induced Perseus to retire to a point 11km S of Pydna, near the Aison (see above), where the decisive **Battle of Pydna** took place between 38,000 Romans and 43,000 Macedonians. At first the Macedonian spearmen (in the centre) carried all before them; but their close order was broken in their headlong drive over the uneven ground. Then the Roman legions counterattacked the Macedonian centre, while the two Roman wings threw themselves upon the Macedonian right wing. The Romans finally broke through the formidable phalanx. Some 20,000 Macedonians were killed and 11,000 captured; their king, who fled to Samothrace, was taken later and ended his life as a state-prisoner in Italy.

111km **Palaió Elevtherokhóri**. Hereabouts was ancient *Methone*, founded, according to Plutarch, from Eretria. The town was used on several occasions by the Athenians as a base against the Macedonians, and Philip II lost an eye besieging it.

The old road (30.5km longer) continues via **Aiyínio** (4289 inhab.) and **Kipséli**, perhaps the site of ancient *Aloros*, to join the Verria road at **Alexándreia**, see Rte 61.

The main highway branches right across the Pedhias Kampanias, crossing the Aliakmon and the Axios near their mouths, and joins the Verria road in the outskirts of (155km) **Thessaloníki**.

## Mount Olympos

**OLYMPOS** (Ολυμπος; in modern Greek **Ólimbos**), the highest mountain range in Greece, the traditional abode of the Gods, rises at the NE limit of Thessaly and falls away into Macedonia. The massif soars to 2917m and wears a crown of snow from early autumn to the end of April. On the seaward E side is a line of vast precipices cleft by tree-filled ravines. To the S the main range is separated by a depression from **Káto Olimbos**, or Low Olympos, a region of wooded hills rising to (1587m) **Metamórfosis**. It is easily accessible from **Kariá** on the Elassón–Leptokariá road (see below). To the N rises High Olympos, with the highest peaks grouped round the centre of the massif in the form of an amphitheatre enclosing the deep Mavrolongos valley. Oak, chestnut, beech, and plane trees flourish at the lower levels; higher up pine forests reach almost to the snow line. The principal summits are in three groups. To the S are **Serai** (2704m), **Kaloyeros** (2701m), and **Palaiomanastri** (2815m). The central group comprises **Skolion** (2911m), from which fine precipices fall into the Tigania glen; **Skala** (2865m); **Mytikas** ('the needle'), highest of all (2917m) the Pantheon, more broken; and **Stafani**, the 'Throne of Zeus' (2909m), a majestic curve of limestone arête. Then, separated from the central group by the Col of Porta (2682m) come **Toumba** (2784m) and **Profitis Ilias** (2787m), an easy shale-covered peak on the top of which is a tiny chapel, which used to be visited once a year by monks; hence an arête called **Petróstrounga** descends towards the valley of the Varkos.

This range is the most famous of those called Olympos, though there are mountains of that name in Euboea, Elis, Laconia, and Arcadia; also in Cyprus and in Asia Minor. In Greek mythology Olympos was the residence of the gods, whose life of pleasure there was imagined in human terms unencumbered with moral philosophy. Hesiod incorrectly reports Olympos as 'never struck by the wind or touched by snow'. Lions seem to have survived in the country about Olympos down to Classical times (Herod. VII, 126; Paus. VI, 5, 5). Evidence of a Sanctuary of Zeus of the Hellenistic period with animal sacrifices was found in 1965.

The sultan Mehmet IV is said to have attempted the highest peak without success in 1669, and in 1780 a French naval officer, G.S. Sonnini, reached Ayios Dhionisios. Leake in 1806 and Pouqueville in 1810 toured the lower area. After 1821 it became a notorious haunt of nationalist bands and bandits. Heinrich Barth, in the wake of the medieval church builders, climbed Profitis Ilias in 1862 and in 1904 Tvigic, the Serbian geographer, did some geological work on the slopes, but the difficulty of the approach and the insecurity of the region deterred all but the keenest. As late as 1910 Edward Richter, on his third attempt at the climb, was captured and held to ransom by bandits after the escorting gendarmes had been killed. In 1912 the territory passed from Turkey to Greece and the following year two philhellene Swiss artists, Daniel Baud-Bovy and Frederic Boissonas, with Chr. Kakalos, a local guide, climbed the Throne of Zeus and Mytikas. In 1921 an official mission of two Swiss topographers, Marcel Kurz and Hans Bickel, completed the exploration of the range and mapped it. A large international party explored the summits in 1927, and since the Greek Alpine Club established a shelter in 1931 the mountain has been explored by increasing numbers. Colonel John Hunt held mountain training courses here in 1945, and since 1961 the Greek Army has had a ski school on the slopes.

## A. By car from Larissa

From Larissa to (61km) **Elassón** and (70km) **Mikró Elevtherokhóri**, see Rte 58. Here you turn right and shortly, at (75.5km) **Kallithéa**, the road divides;

the left branch passes through the picturesque **Stená Pétras** between Olympos and Pieria to Kateríni (131km). You take the right branch. Beyond (84km) **Olimbiádha** a military road (18km long) branches left through **Spármos** to **Refuge B** (Vrissópoulos) below the Army Ski-Training Centre, which was moved here from Mt Vermion in 1961. The old road continues E under High Olympos to (99km) **Kariá**. Low Olympos rises to the right. The road passes below (116km) **Leptokariá** to join the Thessaloníki highway at (120km) **Skála Leptokariás** (see above), from where it is a further 58km back to Lárissa via Témbi.

## B. The ascent from Litókhoro

**Litókhoro** (Hotels A, D), a pleasant well-watered town of 6656 inhabitants connected with its railway station (8km) by bus, stands nearly 305m up on the E flank of Olympos. The inhabitants have long had a reputation as mariners and were prominent in the abortive uprising of 1878. It developed in the 1920s as a health resort for the tubercular. Notwithstanding the provision of a military road up Olympos from the W (see above), Litókhoro is the principal centre for climbing in the Olympos massif. Here from the office of the Greek Alpine Club (EOΣ) information may be obtained, guides hired, and the keys of refuges borrowed. There are fixed charges for climbing guides, mules, and food.

The ascent (arduous rather than difficult for mountaineers) is made in two days, the night being spent at a refuge. July and August are the best months.

**Route 1** (red marks). The road (asphalt to **Priónia**, 18km, see below) ascends NW passing the lower monastery of Ayios Dhionisios (the '**Metokhí**') and climbs steadily up the slopes of **Stavrós** (950m) where there is abundant water. 1½–2 hours Hut (Refuge D) of the Alpine Club of Thessaloníki (1000m). You wind along the N side of the **Mavrolongos Valley** shaded with pines, in which flows the Eníppeas. 2½ hours. Below is the ruined monastery of Ayios Dhionisios, a building of c 1500 visited by Sonnini in 1780, blown up by the Turks in 1828, but rebuilt before 1856. It was destroyed in 1943 by the Germans, who believed it to be used by guerillas. The ruins can be reached in 20 minutes by a path across a hollow, but you continue almost level on the main path (following the red marks). At (3½ hours) **Priónia** (c 1600m; car park, restaurant), the springs of the Eníppeas afford the last running water.

From this point the route rises fairly steeply amid thick beech woods in a region rich in botanic interest. You climb almost to the head of the Mavrolongos to reach (7 hours) the **Katafíyio Spílios Agapitós** (2100m; 60 beds; rain-water reservoir), the A refuge of the Greek Alpine Club, on a spur facing E towards the sea. The refuge can now be reached also from the Ski School of the Greek Army (see above). From the refuge the climb to one or other summit takes c 2½ hours; the vegetation gives out after c 1 hour. The mountain is usually shrouded in cloud at the mid-day hours in hot weather. The red marks continue to the summit of Mytikas.

**Route 2** (blue marks) diverges right a little beyond the Monastery. 5 hours. **Petróstrounga** (2254m). Here are a spring (Strangos) and, lower down, a cave. 8 hours. **Profítis Ilías**, with the King Paul Refuge (C; 18 beds) and a chapel. The traverse of the high summits from **Profítis Ilias** should be undertaken only by experienced mountaineers.

An alternative starting point for ascents is **Kokkinopiló**, 18km from Elassón on the Kateríni road (see Rte 58).

# 58

# From Lárissa to Kozáni and Bitolj

**Road**, 246km (154 miles), one of the two international routes between Greece and former Yugoslavia, leaving Lárissa by the Pínios bridge.— 17km Tírnavos. Thence W and N up the Titaríssios basin (shorter alternative is a newly improved road NE via Melouna pass).—61km Elassón.—117.5km Sérvia. Crossing of the Aliakmon.—145.5km Kozáni (turn right in the town).—174.5km Ptolemáïs.—207.5km Vévi.—233km Níki (frontier post).—248km Bitolj (Monastir).

**Buses** to Elassón, frequently in 1½ hours; to Kozáni, regularly in 4 hours. From Kozani to Ptolemáïs frequently; to Flórina regularly.

**Railway** from Kozáni to Bitolj, 120km, previously daily in 5 hours (change at Amíndaio). **No service at present**.

The road crosses the Pínios and passes an Agricultural School of the Royal National Foundation. 5km **Yiánnouli**. You travel NW, straight across the plain. 17km **Tírnavos** (Τύρναβος) on the farther bank of the Titaríssios, is the chief town (12,028 inhab.) of an eparchy and a centre of ouzo production and of textile industries. Just before the bridge which carries the road into the town, a turn (right) leads to a second bridge and a fine new road, past **Argyroúpolis** (11km NE) with Protogeometric tholos tombs and a recently discovered Classical settlement, above the **Pass of Melouna**; 540m, view) to Elassón (19km shorter than the route described). Through the town our road turns SW to enter the narrow gap between two hills, Tepes (left) and Kladhares (right), through which the Titaríssios emerges to the Thessalian plain. A ruined tower guards the entrance. Before 1912 the Greco-Turkish frontier followed the ridge. You follow the river.

The **Titaríssios** has various other names, owing to uncertainty as to which is the main stream. In antiquity it was also called *Europos*, and today is known as **Xeriás**, **Voulgára**, and **Sarandáporos**. The 'lovely Titarissios', as Homer calls it (Il. II, 748) drains both Kato Olympos and the Kamvounia range, but its longest stream rises on Mt Titaros. In the Tertiary epoch the river fed the Larissan lake; it now joins the Pinios a few miles W of the Vale of Tempe.

29km **Dhamási** lies on the other bank in the narrows. A ruined fortress crowning an isolated stony hill to the N of the village is the *Mylas* that resisted the Macedonians in 171 BC. The beautiful valley gradually broadens and the sandy river flows between thickly wooded banks. 45km **Dhoméniko** was identified by Leake with *Chyretiai* on the evidence of an inscription. **Verdhikoússa** (1100m), 13km W on the slopes of Antikhasia, with 2498 inhabitants, has abundant springs. The road makes a long curving ascent away from the river, undulating through sheep pastures to the twin villages of (55km) **Galanóvrisi** (left) and **Stefanóvouno**.

62km (38 miles) **Elassón** (Ελασσών; usually Elássona, accusative; Hotels D) stands at the mouth of a short gorge, through which flows the Elassonítikos. The town (7725 inhab.) has an annual fair on 20 August.

Elasson occupies the site of the 'white *Oloösson*' of Homer (Il. II, 739); its epithet apparently derived from the limestone rocks in the neighbourhood. Chief town of the warlike Perrhaebi, it had a Bronze Age origin, but declined after the 5C BC. The Turkish base from 1897, its capture by Greek forces in 1912 opened the way N.

A fine Byzantine **bridge** spans the river. On a steep rock overlooking the gorge (road) is the attractive 13C **Panayía Olimpiótissa**, a monastery with a Byzantine church whose plan resembles that of the Holy Apostles at Thessaloniki. It has cushion capitals and a carved wooden door of 1296, also frescoes (torch needed). Two Classical tombstones are built into the gate and there are inscriptions in the court. There are small **museums** of Byzantine material and Natural History attached to the monastery.

About 4km E of Elassón is **Tsarítsani** (pop. 2492), a village said to have been founded by a colony of Bulgarians in the 10C. Later the Slavs were replaced by Greeks, who preserved a kind of independence under the Turks. Thriving on agriculture and the manufacture of silk and cotton, their prosperity declined with the plague of 1813. About ¾ hour SE of the village is the **Monastery of Áy. Athanasios**; about 1½ hours E on a W outlier of Kato Olympos is the **Monastery of Valétsiko** ('The Child'), founded by the Bulgarians, with a legend of a royal child miraculously healed.

You cross the Elassonítikos on a bridge c 2.5km N of the town. The road winds over a hill (330m) used as a defensive position by the Turks in 1912. At (70km) **Mikró Elevtherokhóri** a road to Kateríni (c 60km) and Olympos (Rte 57) diverges right.

Along this road (17km + 6km right) **Kokkinopilós** (ancient *Pythion*) is one of the starting points for the climb of Olympos (Rte 57). Near (29km) **Ayios Dhimítrios** (Hotel B), at **Spáthes**, is a Late Bronze Age cemetery of tumuli and cist tombs. **Pétra** (c 13km further, and 7km, right), retaining the name of its Byzantine predecessor, has a castle and monastery, also a mental asylum with a Byzantine church in the courtyard. The Byzantine site, now called Karakoli lies in an isolated position between Petra, and **Fotiná** to the N.

The road crosses several arms of the Sarandáporos ('Forty fords'), an affluent of the Titaríssos, mounting higher in the rolling country that characterises its upper course. Away to the E towers Mt Olympos. At 79km is a memorial and museum of the **Battle of Sarandaporos** (see below). To the SW of the village of **Vouvála** (3km W of the road) are ruins of ancient *Azoros*. The road ascends towards the Kamvoúnia range and Títaros, which together form a natural barrier between Thessaly and Macedonia, veering W its former line.

The difficult old road (now abandoned) passed through the **Stená Sarandapórou**, or **Defile of Boloustana**, a natural cleft that opens between the two ranges. In the defile King Perseus is said by Livy to have stationed 10,000 men to deny its passage to the Romans; Hassim Tahsim Pasha failed to defend it against Prince Constantine's assault in 1912.

The new road bears W past **Sarandáporo** to pierce a gap in the Kamvounian range S of Mt Dhovrás on whose S slope Metaxás is seen to the right. 108.5km **Polírrhakho**. A steep descent takes the road through the jagged cleft of **Stená Pórtas** into the Aliakmon valley where the line of the old road is rejoined. In the gap two roads (see below) branch left; you turn right in the plain below the vertical cliffs of **Mt Borsána** (885m).

The **Aliakmon** rises in the Pindus on the Albanian frontier and flows for 175km entirely in Greek territory. The upper course (comp. Rte 62) is in gentle valleys, but narrow gorges characterise most of its middle reaches, except for a few miles near Servia where its valley widens into a plain. In 1973 this was submerged by the building of the Aliakmon Barrage some 16km downstream. Neolithic and Early Bronze Age settlements in the valley were investigated in 1971–73. Some finds from a mound excavated in 1931 by W.A. Heurtley are in Thessaloniki Museum. The mound was re-explored in 1971–73 before submersion and dated to c 4930–4650 BC. In its middle course the river is not accessible by road. In medieval times it was probably navigable to a point near Verria; today its flat lower reaches are controlled by the Vavares Barrage (Rte 61). The mountains commanding the valley on the S provide a natural defence line against invaders from the N. This can, however, be turned by the easy pass between Grevená and Kalambáka.

In the Stená Pórtas two roads branch SW. The higher and poorer winds through hilly country to the SE of the river. In a glen below (18km) **Mikróvalto** is the Panayía Stanoú (or Zidhaníou), a monastery founded in the 16C and rebuilt after destruction by the Turks in 1854. 20km **Tranóvalto**. Beyond (25km) **Lazarádhes** the road (not all surfaced) continues round the steep N side of **Vounása**, the highest peak (1615km) of the Kamvounia range, or over its E spur, to (55km) **Dheskáti** (pop. 4485; Hotels D, E) and then to (97km) **Elassón** (Rte 62). On the left bank of the Aliakmon, beneath Vounása (2 hours, or c 21km by roads (partly unsurfaced), from Lazarádhes), is the Monastery of **Osios Nikánoros Závorda**, where in 1959 was discovered a complete 13C MS of the dictionary of the Patriarch Photios (c 820–891), previously known only by an incomplete copy in Cambridge. It includes quotations from lost classics. The buildings date from 1534. Frescoes of the Raising of Lazarus, the Entry into Jerusalem, and the Crucifixion are thought from their similarity to those of Barlaam (Meteora) to be by Frangos Kastellanos.

The new lower road provides an alternative route to Kozáni (c 10km longer). It turns SW in the valley to **Rímnio** on the lakeside. Here it is carried across the lake by causeway and bridge to **Aianí**, where several churches are decorated with 15–16C mural paintings. There is an interesting **archaeological collection** by the village square, with various finds of which the most numerous are Hellenistic (pottery, good bronzes, terracottas and moulds, coins, some freestanding and relief sculpture). Also on view are interesting ikons from Aianí churches; traditional costumes, jewellery and woodcarving. A new museum is well advanced. On the Kozáni side of the village a good dirt road (right, signed) leads in 1km (keep left until further sign) to **Megáli Rákhi** and a newly excavated settlement (remains mostly Hellenistic but with occupation from the Late Bronze Age; guide in Greek and English available at museum). The site, in an attractive situation and with good views to Sérvia and the S, is well laid out for visiting, with paths and viewing platforms. Cars can be taken almost to the highest point where an impressive cistern (8. 5m deep; ?Classical) survives, in the court of a large public building. Below (at car park level) are the remains of an L-shaped stoa with Doric and Ionic features which may have been part of the agora. At the same level is the House with Pithoi. Below the stoa, a building with ashlar masonry had rooms on various levels and a stoa. It shows two distinct building phases (Classical and Hellenistic), both with fine construction, and was probably a public centre. Kilns were built above it in later times. Round the hill (S and SW on the same terrace) are two houses—the House with Stairs and the House with Spindlewhorls. The private houses excavated are irregularly shaped and usually laid out round small courtyards. The settlement, identified as the central township of ancient *Aiane*, the main city of *Elimeia*, was moved c 100 BC 2km further N to **Palaíkastro Kaisareías**.

Several cemeteries have been found in the vicinity, with burials from the LBA, Archaic, Classical and Hellenistic periods. From Megáli Rákhi the **Livádhi** cemetery is visible 700m to the NE (return to dirt road and turn right). Here the most striking features are Archaic and Classical monumental built tombs in ashlar masonry, some with very thick walls and precinct boundaries. The interiors were painted. Roofs consisted of stone slabs on wooden beams. In some cases at least there seem to have been small temple-like structures above the tombs. In here a Hellenistic country villa is also being investigated. Aianí is also easily accessible from Kozáni.

117km **Sérvia** (Σέρβια; 453m) a town of 3019 inhabitants, commands the only major route S from the Aliakmon valley. It is situated 6.5m from the river, between two sharp rocks and dominated by a Byzantine **fortress** (15 min. up track beyond car park and restaurant; views), with an impressive keep, which occupies a high hill behind the town. Below the kastro to the N is the ruined church of **Ayios Theódhoros**.

Servia derives its name from a colony of Serbs, settled here in the 7C by Heraclius as a buffer against other invaders. By the 10C it was in the hands of the Bulgarians, who defended it valiantly but in vain against Basil II. In the 13C it was a frontier stronghold, and has suffered in many wars. Bombed on 14 April 1941, it was occupied the following day by the Germans. The New Zealand 4th Brigade held a line behind the town from Kastanéa to Rímnio until 17 April. Thirty German volunteers worked for a year in 1960–61 to make good war damage. Some remains at **Palaiográtsano**, on the N slope of Piéria 11km NE of Servia, probably represent the ancient *Phylakai*. At **Velvendós**, in the valley below (by-road from Servia) the architect Stamatios Kleanthes (1802–62) was born.

The Aliakmon hydro-electric lake is crossed by the longest (2km) bridge in Greece. Beyond the bridge a private road (accessible, pleasant) of the Electricity Authority (ΔEH) branches NE in 16km to the Aliakmon Barrage (Frágma Aliákmonos). Above the road junction on the SW spur of **Patsoúra** is a fortress of uncertain date. You climb gradually. To the right is a series of isolated small hills (Skopós; Rte 62). At 140km (left) is the small airport Kozani which can be by-passed to the E.

145km **KOZÁNI** (Κοζάνη), though no longer astride the main Athens–Thessaloníki road, remains the nodal point of communication between Macedonia and Epirus and the most important strategic centre for NW Greece. It is a clean and invigorating town (31,553 inhab.) with winding streets. As everywhere there has been much recent building, but the old houses are well kept, and many attractive timber-framed cottages are set off by walled gardens and cobbled courts. The capital of a nome and the seat of a metropolitan, it was a centre of Greek culture during the Turkish occupation. Textiles and agricultural tools are manufactured.

**Airport** (see above) with 3 flights per week to Athens via Kastoriá (flights from Athens are direct). **Booking Office**, 1 Od. Dhimokratías.

**Railway Station**, 1.25km S of centre; 3 good trains daily to Thessaloníki in c 4 hours.

**Hotels** B, C, D.

**Buses** from Odhos Makedhonomákhon, off main square, hourly to Thessaloníki and to Vérria, also to Ptolemaîs; 6 times daily to Lárissa and to Grevená; 5–7 times daily to Siátista, to Kastoriá, and to Flórina; 3 times daily to Sérvia; 4 times daily to Athens; twice daily to Kalambáka and Ioánnina. 7 times daily to Neápolis.

Kozani was entered on 14 April 1941, by the 9th Panzer Division. As a centre of royalist sympathies, it was much harried by left-wing bands in 1944–45.

The centre of the town is the green Plateía Níkis, with a tall clock-tower of 1855, from which all the principal roads of Western Macedonia radiate. **Ayios Nikólaos**, the metropolitan church, is a low, wide building of 1664–1721 lit by two lanterns. Built mainly of wood, it has ornate stalls and iconostasis, and a W gallery on pillars. The frescoes are blackened with age. The **library** has valuable 16C MSS.

There is small well-arranged **Archaeological Museum** (detailed guide-book in Greek and English) in a pleasant old house at Dhimokratías no. 8. ROOM B (entrance) has prehistoric material from Kitrini Limni and other sites; finds (pottery, figurines etc.) from the Macedonian Tomb at Spilia; Hellenistic pottery from Kozani. ROOM A (right). Rich finds (silver vessels, gold diadems, bronze weapons and armour) from excavations in the necropolis of Kozani. Mostly Classical and Hellenistic. ROOMS C and D (left). Small votive stelai (some inscribed) and statuettes. Hellenistic and Roman. In the courtyard are two sarcophagi: one (3C AD) from Kentro (Grevena) is signed by Philonas Ageatis.

Nearby in Od. Ionos Dhragoúmi is the large new (1987) **Historical and Folklore Museum** (guidebook in English etc.) whose exterior is designed in traditional style. The museum, which has an interesting interior layout, contains a very wide range of exhibits, well displayed. These include botanical and geological specimens, drawings of traditional buildings (especially in Kozani), archaeological material (especially strong on Neolithic from the Aliakmon Lake sites), items used in traditional crafts, memorial displays of the Wars of Independence, the Balkan Wars and the Second World War Resistance, reconstructed rooms of traditional houses, costume.

On a hill NW of the town, the park in front of the picturesque **Metamórfosis tou Sotíros** commands a good view of the town and over the plain of the Aliakmon to Sérvia.

From Kozáni to **Thessaloníki** and to **Kastoriá**, see Rte 62.

From Kozáni the road leads N. 142.5km **Koíla**. It joins the railway and skirts the W side of the drained Kitriní Límni ('Yellow Lake', formerly called Sarigkiol), where several Neolithic sites have been located. Low hills lie to the left. 157km **Kómanos**. At **Mavropiyí** (3km, left) there is a damaged Hellenistic site at Kastro. 162km **Proástio** lies (left) in the **Stená Kománou**, a low 'pass', site of the huge Ptolemáïs thermo-electric station, opened in 1959 and later linked with the Yugoslav grid. To the E (c 17km via Ptolemaïs, or approached from further S) is **Spiliá** with a Macedonian tomb of 2–1C BC which produced interesting finds (Kozani Museum). 167km **Ptolemáïs** (usually Ptolemaïdha, accusative; Hotels C, D), a growing town (pop. 25,125) on an upland plain, has become, since the exploitation of its lignite mines, an important industrial centre, producing low-grade coal, sulphuric acid, and nitrate fertilisers. It is the chief town of the eparchy of Eordaia. Near (172km) **Perdhíkkas** a dam will provide further power. Here two elephants' tusks and stone tools have been found in a context which is probably Upper Pliocene. At (185km) near the **Mnemeía Pesónton Crossroads**, with a memorial to the fallen of the Balkan Wars, you cross the road from Kastoriá to Amíndaio (Rte 63A).

188km **Xinó Neró** (2km left) has mineral waters. **Pétres** (6km right off a road to Amíndalo, on Lake Petron) has a recently excavated Hellenistic town (signs) on a hill nearby (1.5km NW), whose **floruit** was connected with the construction of the Egnatian Way through the plain below. There are substantial remains of houses—and a defence wall, the layout of the settlement conforming to the topography of the site. There was a sophisticated water supply system. Some of the pottery and terracottas found were imported from Pella. The settlement moved to the site of the present village in c 50 BC. Other finds have also been made in the vicinity (cemetery etc.). Road follows railway (gradient 1 in 40) in the gentle curving **Stená Kirli Derven**, crossing the line at (195km) **Kleidhí station**. The pass was held for three days against the Germans in 1941 while railway installations were destroyed at Amíndaio. The road by-passes (198km) **Vévi** (Rte 63A) and leaves the old Flórina road to the left. Joining the course of the Vía Egnatia, you cross an upland plain, watered by the Gieléska, leave the new road via Flórina on the left, and continue to (224km) **Níki** (tourist pavilion) where the frontier with former Yugoslavia is marked by no natural barrier (the so-called 'Monastir Gap'). It is now more generally approached via Flórina (comp. Rte 63). The road continues between the Peristeri Mountains (W) and the marshy Tserna to (238km) **Bitolj** (Hotel C), or **Monastir**, a provincial capital of former Yugoslavia and the ancient *Herakleia Lynkestis* (site above main road to left).

# 59

# Thessaloníki

**THESSALONÍKI** (Θεσσαλονίκη), the Biblical *Thessalonica*, often known in English as **Salonica**, with 383,967 inhabitants, is the second city of Greece and the natural centre of communication with her Balkan neighbours. Its role as chief city of Macedonia is much emphasised in the present political climate. It is the residence of the Minister for Northern Greece, capital of the nome of Thessaloniki and a university city. Boasting a church of Apostolic foundation, it remains the seat of an Orthodox metropolitan and a Roman Catholic bishop. In addition to being the headquarters of a Greek army corps, it has served as Advanced HQ (SE Europe) of NATO, with an armoured division. The city rises from the Bay of Thessaloniki in the form of a theatre on the slopes of Mt Khortiatis. Its citadel, the battlemented walls, and the huddled hillside houses of the upper town create a character which remains unique despite its rapid transformation, since the devastating fire of 1917, into a modern city. Its monuments though sometimes over-restored are surpassed as an illustration of ten centuries of Byzantine architecture only by those of Istanbul. Outside the walls the huge grounds of the annual international fair divide the old town from the new. Local industries (fertilisers and animal foods, agricultural machinery, etc) have developed and oil and sugar are refined. As a result the harbour, long run down by the competition of Piraeus, has revived and several passenger shipping links have been restored. The climate of Thessaloniki runs to extremes: the winters are often severe, when the city is swept by the Vardarats, or Vardar wind from the NW; the summers can be oppressive.

A useful locally available guide to the monuments, with map, is A. Papagiannopoulos, *Monuments of Thessaloniki*, Rekos.

Streets at right angles to the sea are numbered from the seaward end; those parallel to the sea from the NW. Plan references are to the central plan.

**Airport** at **Mikrá**, 11.25km SE, with international services from London, Germany, etc.; also frequent domestic service to Athens; 1–3 times weekly to Chania, Chios, Corfu, Iraklion, Ioannina, Rhodes; 4–6 times weekly to Límnos, Lesbos; connecting buses from corner of Komnínon and Níkis. (Pl. 14).

**Hotels**, L, A–E. Mostly near Egnatías or between it and the waterfront.

**Youth Hostel**, 42 Od. Svólou (Pl. 12). **Camping Sites** at Néa Kríni (see below).

**Restaurants**. *Olympos-Naousa*, Strátis, 5 and 27 Níkis.

**Post Office**, 23 Tsimiskí; Branch Office near the White Tower. **OTE Centre**, 55 Vas. Iraklíou. **Tourist Police**, at airport and railway station. **Aliens Office**, 42 Plateía Politekhníou.

**Information Offices**. **NTOG**, 8 Od. Aristotélous; **ELPA**, Vasilíssis Olgas/Aigaíon; Olympic Airways, 1 Komnínon.

**Buses**. **Local Services** (KTEL 54): 1 (from the railway station) and 2–7 traverse Tsimiskí or Níkis and Vasilíssis Olgas; 4 terminates at Mikró Karavoúrnou. 22, 23, and 24 serve Venizélou and terminate by the Ramparts in the upper town. No. 72 to the Agricultural School, Ayía Triádha, etc., from 23 Karólou Dil (Pl. 15); to Asvestokhóri from 22 Singroú. **Country Buses** from Plat. Dhikastiríon or near by. **Long-distance buses** leave from various streets off the NW end of Odhós Egnatías: to Vérria and Náousa (KTEL 25 Imathías) from 26 Oktovríou, 10; to Kilkís from Yiannitsón 76; to Edessa, to Kozáni, from 26 Oktovríou, no. 26; to Kastoriá, from Anayenníseos 6 and to Flórina from

Anayenníseos 42; to Sérres, to Néa Apollonía and Stavrós, and to Kateríni from Irínis 17; to Evzóni from Yiannitsón 76; to Kaválla from Langádha 59; to Langádha (KTEL 39 Thessaloníkis) from 10 Frángon; to Ierissós and Khalkidikí from Karakási 68; to Ioánnina (KTEL 20) from Chr. Pípsou 19; to Athens from Monastiríou 67.

**Car Hire.** Avis, 3 Níkis; Hertz, 4 Venizélou; and many others (list from NTOG), some with offices at airport.

**Motor Launches** in summer from quay (near White Tower) to Aretsoú, Peraía, Ayía Triádha, etc. **Taxis** are painted blue and white.

**Consulates.** British Consul-General, 39 Leof. Níkis; American Consulate, 59 Leof. Níkis. **British Council**, 9 Ethnikís Amínis.

**Banks.** Bank of Greece, 12 Tsimiskí; Ionian, 3 and 7 Mitropóleos; Commercial, 21 Ionos Dragoúmi.

**Clubs and Learned Organisations.** Inspectorate of Classical Antiquities at the Archaeological Museum of Byzantine Antiquities, 114 Megálou Alexándrou; Institute of Macedonian Studies, opposite White Tower; Greek Alpine Club, 14 Venizélou.

**Booksellers.** Molho, 10 Tsimiskí; Rayiá, 54 Ermoú; Barbounákis, 156 Egnatías and 9 Aristotélous; Malliáris-Paidheía, 9 Aristotélou (for guide books).

**Theatres.** Vasilikón (Royal), Strátou (Tékhnis), Párkou (Théâtre de l'atelíer), Makedhonikón Spoudhón, all near the White Tower.

**Public Lavatories** in Plat. Aristotélous and by the White Tower.

**Sports Centre** between the university and the Kaftándzoglou Stadium. **Tennis Club**, Astir, Kíprou.

**Festivals.** International Fair in September. St Demetrius (26 October; religious processions) to Okhi Day (28 October; military parade) is a three-day holiday.

**Churches** are open to visitors 08.00–13.30 & 15.30–20.00 (but not always regular).

**History.** The unimportant ancient town of *Therme* was incorporated with 25 others in 316 BC by Kassander and given the name of *Thessalonikeia* (in Strabo's spelling) after his wife, who was half-sister to Alexander the Great. It must soon have been fortified, for Antigonus Gonatas retired here after his defeat in 274 by Pyrrhus, king of Epirus. In 146, when Macedonia became a Roman province, Thessalonica was made the capital. Its geographical position at the head of the gulf favoured development, which was accelerated by the building of the Via Egnatia. Cicero spent part of his exile in 58 at Thessalonica; Pompey took refuge here in 49 from Caesar. Literary visitors included the Greek satirist Lucian, and the historian Polyaenus. The city's support of Antony and Octavian before the Battle of Philippi promoted its fortunes. In AD 49–50 St Paul preached at Thessalonica, where he antagonised some of the Jews, who attacked the house in which he had been staying. His two letters to the church he founded here have come down to us as the Epistles to the Thessalonians; he revisited the city in 56. Thessalonica repelled repeated attacks by the Goths in the 3C. Galerius, who succeeded to the E half of the Roman Empire on the retirement of Diocletian, lived in the city. The persecution he instigated claimed as a victim St Demetrius, afterwards patron saint of the city. Constantine mustered his fleet here before his successful campaign against Licinius in 324. Under Theodosius the Great (379–395) Thessalonica became the seat of the prefecture of Illyricum, a metropolitan see, and the base of the Emperor's operations against the Goths. Here Theodosius himself, severely ill, was converted to Christianity and afterwards issued the Edict of Thessalonica (380), reversing Julian's toleration of pagan gods and condemning the Arian heresy held at Constantinople. In 390, after Botheric the Goth, military commander of the city, had been lynched for failing to control his soldier's outrages, Theodosius invited the populace to a special performance in the circus and there had c 7000 of them massacred. For this crime he was made to do penance by St Ambrose, Bishop of Milan.

Favoured by Justinian, Thessalonica rose to become the second city of the Byzantine Empire. Having endured further invasions of the Goths, and resisted five sieges by Avars and Slavs, it remained an enclave in Slav dominions until Justinian II's expedition of 689, and seems to have returned to direct Byzantine administration as a theme only after Stauricius' offensive c 783. SS Cyril (died 869) and Methodius (died 885), the brothers who converted the Slavs to Christianity, were natives of Thessalonica.

Thessalonica was stormed by the Saracens (led by the Greek renegade Leo of Tripoli) in 904, when 22,000 of its inhabitants were sold into slavery. It served Basil II as a base against the Bulgars, who besieged it without success in 1041. When the city was captured in 1185 by the army and fleet of William II of Sicily, under the command of Tancred, the celebrated Homeric scholar Eustathios, then Archbishop of Thessalonica, left a detailed account of its barbarous sack. At the end of the Fourth Crusade, the city became the capital of the Latin kingdom of Thessalonica under Boniface of Montferrat (1204). Kalojan of Bulgaria was killed here in 1207 while attacking the walls, and Henry of Flanders died in the city in 1216, perhaps by poisoning, on the eve of marching against Theodore Angelus, despot of Epirus. Thessalonica fell to Epirus in 1222 (Theodore proclaiming himself Emperor), while the rest of Macedonia came under the sway of Ivan Asen II of Bulgaria; but in 1246 John Vatatzes reappropriated both to the Byzantine empire of Nicaea. In the 14C possession of Thessalonica was the first goal of every usurper aiming for the Imperial throne. The Catalan Grand Company besieged the city unsuccessfully in 1308. Michael IX died here in 1320 and from here in 1328 his son Andronikos III launched a successful campaign against his grandfather. The same century witnessed the religious struggles of the Hesychasts, or Quietists, and the insurrection of the Zealots, a 'people's party' who murdered the nobles in 1342. The short period of reform before they were crushed coincided with the artistic Golden Age of the city. During a long period of anarchy Thessalonica fell to the Ottoman Turks in 1387 and again in 1394, but in 1403, after the Mongol Timur had crushed Bayezid I at Ankara, it was restored to the Byzantines. In 1423 Andronikos Palaeologos, son of the Emperor Manuel II, despairing of keeping back the Turks, placed Thessalonica under Venetian protection. However in 1430 Murad II stormed, sacked, and occupied the already depopulated city. Some churches were transformed into mosques.

The population was suddenly increased by the influx of 20,000 Jews banished from Spain by the Edict of the Alhambra (1492). They absorbed the Bavarian Jews who had arrived 20 years earlier. By the middle of the 16C they constituted the major part of the population, and had formed a small autonomous community speaking Ladino, a form of Castilian, which they wrote in Hebrew characters. Towards the end of the century the Greeks returned in some strength. The city suffered from fires in 1545 and 1617 and from the Jewish schism of 1659 when the sect of Donmeh broke away. In 1821, at the outbreak of the Greek War of Independence, a sympathetic movement at Thessaloniki was savagely suppressed. During the 19C the Turks made a show of reforms; the Greeks improved their schools; the Jews increased their influence. In 1876 the French and German consuls were murdered by the mob; Pierre Loti, arriving in the frigate *Couronne* in time to see the assassins hanged, found in the city's romantically squalid alleys the original of his *Aziyadé*. In 1888 the railway link with the rest of Europe was built, and in 1897–1903 a new harbour constructed.

Thessaloniki (known to the Turks as *Selaïnik*) became a centre of intrigue against the misrule of Abdul Hamid. Here in 1906 was formed the Turkish Committee of Union and Progress (Ittihat ve Terakki Cemiyeti), which secretly organised the Macedonian revolt of 1908. In 1909 Abdul Hamid was deposed and exiled here. In the First Balkan War the Greek Army made a triumphal entry into Thessaloniki on 8 November (26 October O.S.), 1912, and the city was ceded to Greece by the Treaty of Bucharest (1913). King George I was assassinated in Thessaloniki on 18 March 1913. During the First World War the Entente landed an expeditionary force here on 12 October 1915, and Venizelos set up his provisional government of National Defence. The railway link with Athens via Larissa was completed the following year. In the Second World War, German tanks, advancing down the Vardar, entered the city on 9 April 1941, three days after the start of the campaign, after Canadian engineers had destroyed installations during the night. During the occupation most of Thessaloniki's Jewish population (c 60,000) was deported to Poland, never to return.

The city was damaged by fires in 1890, 1898, and 1910, at which time it still had oil street lamps. Fire devastated the city on 5 August 1917, making 70,000 homeless, and the shanty town of refugees was swollen in 1923 by the exchange of population with Turkey. Replanning of the centre was put in hand in 1925–35, but the greatest transformation occurred after 1950. Since then Thessaloniki has become a modern city, though the upper town still retains some of the old atmosphere. In June 1978 severe earthquakes caused casualties and disruption. The early churches suffered worst and the old-established Mediterranean Palace Hotel was wrecked, but serious damage to recent buildings was not widespread.

# A. The centre of the city

Despite many changes since the fire of 1917, the ancient chess-board plan remains a feature of the town. The principal thoroughfares run roughly parallel to the sea. Ayíou Dhimitríou, Egnatías, and Tsimiskí effectively dividing the old city into four belts. The Egnatía Odhós runs from the site of the Axios Gate in the NW to that of the Kassandreia Gate in the SE (though the actual gates are no more).

The street follows an ancient line and, since it was spanned by two triumphal arches, was long assumed to represent the famous Via Egnatia. The evidence of milestones however seems to show that the Egnatian Way entered from Pella by the Axios Gate but left again by the Letaia Gate, also on the NW, without passing through the city, rather as its successor does today.

Halfway along on the upper side opens the Plateía Dhikastiríon (Pl. 10), a vast square cleared by the fire of 1917. It serves as a local bus terminal. Here was the Imperial Roman **forum**. Preparatory building work for new lawcourts immediately produced ancient finds and systematic excavations of the Greek Archaeological Service under Ph. Petsas revealed the **odeion** and two **stoas** bounding the forum, and a long double **cryptoporticus**. The projected courts have been abandoned and the lower part attractively planted with gardens. Towards the SW corner stands the **Panayía Khalkéon**, founded (an inscription on the marble lintel of the W entrance) in 1028 by Christophoros of Lombardy, and restored in 1934. The church contains an almost complete cycle of frescoes belonging to the original decoration and must have been painted very soon after its construction. The name **Our Lady 'of the Coppersmiths'** recalls the time from 1430 to 1912 when it served the Turkish smiths as a mosque (the Kazançilar-Çami). The brick church has the form of a Greek cross-in-square, extended to the E by three apses and to the W by a narthex. The central dome, with a straight cornice, is mounted on a lofty octagonal drum, and the arms of the cross have triangular pediments, which give a markedly angular appearance to the whole. On the façade, however, brick half-columns support deep round arches and the cornices of the two W domes follow the rounded lines of the windows in the Athenian manner. The contrast suggests a later date for the upper stage of the narthex although the fresco of the Last Judgement inside is placed in the 11C. Within, the dome is supported by four marble columns. Contemporary frescoes in the dome (Ascension), round the drum, and in the apse, seem to derive from the mosaics of Ayia Sophia (see below). On the opposite corner is the picturesque **˙Çifte Hamam**, a Turkish bath-house erected by Sultan Murad II in 1444, used until recently as the **Loutrá Parádheisos**. The original dedicatory inscription survives. Beneath are remains of late Roman buildings.

Off the Egnatía Odhós, in Odhós Ayías Sofías (left), is the **Panayía Akheiropoíetos** (Pl. 11), one of the earliest Christian buildings still in use. It was probably dedicated to the Virgin soon after Her recognition by the Third Oecumenical Council (Ephesus, 431 AD) as Theotókos (Mother of God) and completed c 470.

It was named (Αχειροποίητος: 'Made without hands') at some time after the 12C after a celebrated ikon supposed to have been miraculously painted. A later popular name, **Ayía Paraskeví** (Good Friday), is said to come from a mistranslation of the Turkish name Eski Djuma, meaning 'old place of worship' (Djuma also meaning Friday since that was the Moslem day of worship). The church was converted into a mosque in 1430, not without detriment to its fabric. After restoration in 1910 it suffered further damage in 1923 from the billeting of refugees. Reconsecrated, it has again been restored.

The church is a basilica of Syrian type with nave and two aisles. The atrium and exo-narthex have disappeared. The narthex opens into the nave by a 'trivilon' (τρίβηλον), a triple opening formed by two columns and closed by curtains. The arcades have monolithic columns with 'Theodosian' capitals; the mosaics on the soffits, depicting birds, fruit, and flowers, show Alexandrian influence. Frescoes of c 1225 have survived in the S aisle, above the arcade between it and the nave. Eighteen of the Forty Martyrs remain, depicted either in bust in medallions or as full-length figures. Near the S chapel (the former baptistery) are some brick walls of a Roman house and below the S aisle two layers of Roman mosaic flooring are exposed.

Farther E is **Ayios Pandeleímonos**, a pretty church with a central dome and a domed narthex, first mentioned in 1169 as a dependency of the Rossikon monastery (Mt Athos). The cloister which surrounded it on three sides disappeared during Turkish use as the **Issakié Mescid Çami**. This change (c 1500) was carried out by Kadi Ishak Çelebi, whose magnificent mosque is still the central feature of Bitolj. Damage in 1978 was severe.

Farther on, the realigned Egnatía Odhós passes to the right of the **Arch of Galerius** (Pl. 12), beneath which the road, when narrower, made a slight angle. The great triumphal arch, erected to commemorate the emperor's victories over the Persians in AD 297, was shown by the excavations (1939) of E. Dyggve, the Danish archaeologist, to have formed part of a larger design, which included a palace, hippodrome, and mausoleum. Only part

*Arch of Galerius. Photo DAI Athens, Sal. 220 rsp*

of the W section of the arch survives. Originally two further piers to the SE carried a similar span, forming a double gate crowned by a central dome. The springers of the transverse arches can be seen above the cornice of the reliefs. Beneath them ran a roadway, to the NE in the form of a porticoed avenue leading to the rotunda (see below). The structure is of brick. The piers are faced with stone *reliefs. These are in four zones, separated by bands of sculptured garlands and crowned by a cyma and cornice.

S PIER E side. In the **Scene of Sacrifice** on the second zone from the bottom, Diocletian, Augustus of the East (left), in the imperial purple, and Galerius (right), his son-in-law, and Caesar, in military uniform, celebrate the latter's victories. The altar is decorated with reliefs of Jupiter and Hercules, of whom respectively they claimed to be the reincarnation. The scene below represents the surrender of an Eastern town; those above, prisoners begging for clemency, and (top) Galerius addressing his troops. In the adjacent reliefs beneath the main arch, above a row of victories, Galerius is seen (top to bottom) riding in his chariot between two towns which receive him and bid him farewell; fighting on horse-back (crowned by an eagle on the sculptured band); receiving the surrender of Mesopotamia and Armenia. On the N PIER the various scenes of combat, some with elephants, are less well preserved.

The line of the Roman avenue (see above), leads to **Ayios Yeóryios** (Pl. 12), the oldest as well as the most conspicuous intact monument in Thessaloniki, with the only surviving minaret. The **rotunda**, built of brick on the same axis as the triumphal arch, was probably erected in the lifetime of Galerius to serve as his mausoleum. The brick dome is protected by a low-pitched timber roof borne on the outer walls, one of the first known examples of this practice in Europe. After having served as church and mosque, the building is now preserved as an ancient monument (closed by earthquake damage).

Galerius died in Serdica (Sofia) and was buried in nearby Romulianum, his birthplace, since Licinius would not permit his body to be moved to Thessalonica. The rotunda was transformed into a church before 400, when the SE recess was converted into an arch and the sanctuary constructed; the main entrance was moved from the SW to the NW, and a narthex added. At the same time an ambulatory (now destroyed) was built round the outside and the recesses in the original wall opened into it. Some time after the 10C the upper part of the sanctuary fell and the dome was repaired. The buttresses date from this time. This is possibly the church known in the Middle Ages as the **Asomaton**, or Archangels, which gave its name to the quarter and its gate. For some time in the 15C the Asomaton served as the Metropolitan church of the Greeks. In 1591, the year of the Hegira 999 (when the end of the world was expected) the rotunda was turned into the **Mosque of Sinan Pasha**; later it was renamed after Hortaci Suleïman Effendi, whose tomb (19C) stands in the courtyard (SE side). The elegant stelai surrounding the church date from the time of Mahmoud II (1807–39).

INTERIOR (closed at present). The marble stoup at the entrance is supported by columns of green Thessalian marble. The circular wall, 6m thick, has eight barrel-vaulted recesses. Over each recess is an arched window; above and between these are small lunettes; the dome is c 24m across. *Mosaics, Hellenistic in feeling and dating from the end of the 4C, decorate the dome and recesses. Eight scenes round the dome show elaborate architectural façades with saints in prayer. Their vestments are varied and their features individual; all were martyred in the East, the majority under Diocletian. Of the middle zone, which probably represented the Apostles, only some sandalled feet survive. The central figure of Christ is lost, though some heads remain of the attendant angels. In the recesses (that to the SE restored in 1885) are medallions with birds and fruit on a gold ground. In the apse which, like the bema and the ambulatory (now destroyed), was added to the original building on its conversion into a church, four truncated columns (of a ciborium?) show the original floor level. There are some badly preserved frescoes of the Ascension (second half of the 9C). Sculptural fragments and other Christian items have been collected in the building and a fine *mosaic of St Andrew has been remounted.

Seaward of the Arch of Galerius, Od. Goúnari leads to Plateía Navarínou, a large square formed by the excavations since 1970 in the **Palace of Galerius** (Pl. 16). A deep cutting is surrounded by a low wall so that the remains can be seen from various vantage points. Most impressive is an octagonal building, richly decorated within, perhaps the throne room.

A short walk NW is **Ayía Sophía** (Pl. 11), conspicuously situated in a garden, planted with palms and Mediterranean pine, that occupies the site of its former atrium. The main façade closes the end of Odhós Ermoú. The heavy exterior was not improved by the loss of the elegant Turkish portico, ruined by an Italian air raid in 1941, and the building suffered severely in 1978.

The date of Ayia Sophia (the church of the Holy Wisdom) is disputed. Imperfect pendentives and the masonry style led some scholars to think it older than its Justinianean namesake in Constantinople. More likely the building represents a transitional form between the domed basilica and the domed cruciform church and should be dated to the early 8C, perhaps to the reign of Leo III the Isaurian (717–40). Beneath are remains of a five-aisled Early Christian basilica and, below again, of a Roman building. In 1585 it was transformed into a mosque by Raktoub Ibrahim Pasha. Damaged by fire in 1890, it was reconstructed in 1907–10 and restored to Christian worship in 1912. The Greeks used its minaret (since demolished) for a machine gun post in 1913 while subduing the Bulgarian garrison barricaded in a school nearby.

The spacious INTERIOR remains impressive despite extensive scaffolding. The drum, borne on pendentives, on which the dome rests, is a square with rounded corners rather than a circle. The dome, 10m in diameter, is decorated with fine mosaics of the Ascension. In the centre, in a circular medallion supported by two angels, the Almighty is seated on a rainbow throne; in the drum are the Virgin with an angel on either side, and figures of the Apostles divided by trees. Below the angels is a Greek inscription in four lines from Acts I, 11 (Ye men of Galilee, why stand ye gazing up into heaven?). The mosaics are now attributed to the 9C or 10C. In the apse are monograms of Constantine VI and of the Empress Irene, and the Virgin enthroned. There are traces of an earlier mosaic of the cross which, during the iconoclastic period, accompanied the liturgical inscription now interrupted by the Virgin's feet; the existing mosaics, therefore, are dated to 785–97. In the arches of the W wall of the narthex, part of the original fresco decoration of the 11C remains. Fragments of full-length male and female saints can be distinguished, with busts of saints below.

To the SE, across the road, is the entrance to a subterranean chapel, dedicated to St John the Baptist. This connects with the crypt of a Roman nymphaeum. Excavations to the E of the church in 1961 revealed part of a basilica of the 4C AD adorned with mosaics and frescoes.

From the S side of the church Odhós Skholeíon Exadháktilon leads past a large school to the principal shopping street of the city, still known by its Byzantine name of Tsimiskí (Pl. 14, 15). The alternative name of Megálou Alexándrou, previously used, has now been transferred elsewhere. To the S in Od. Ay. Sofías stands **Ayios Gregóris Palamá**, built in 1912–13 to serve as the cathedral. Here is re-interred the body of Archbishop Gregory Palamas (c 1295–1359), champion of the Hesychasts. Tsimiskí crosses Odhós Karólou Dil, which honours Charles Diehl (1859–1944), the French Byzantinist, and Odhós Aristotélous (see below). On the left is the **post office**. Just beyond, the picturesque remains (right) of the **Iaoudi Hamam** are now part of a market. To the W is Eleftherías Square. You now turn up the lively Odhós Eleftheríou Venizélou, with fashion shops. At its crossing with the Egnatía Odhós (lined to the W with hotels) is the **Hamza Beg Çami**, founded in 1468, enlarged before 1592 and partly rebuilt after a fire in 1620. It is the largest mosque on Greek soil. Behind rises the **Dhimarkhíon**. Venizélou St mounts to the **Dioikitírion** (Pl. 6), administrative centre of the Ministry of Northern Greece, which occupies the same site as the Turkish Konak. The square in front is laid out as a memorial to Prince Nicolas, first military governor of Macedonia (1912). Odhós Ayíou Dhimitríou follows an ancient line.

**Ayios Dhimítrios** (Pl. 6), a basilica of the 5C with double side-aisles, and transepts flanking the apse and projecting farther E, is the largest church in Greece. The building was reduced to a shell by the fire of 1917, though the main arcades stood and the sanctuary survived to roof level. It was reconstructed in 1926–48, where possible with surviving materials, more or less as it had been before the fire. The open timber roof however was replaced by one of reinforced concrete.

**History**. Local tradition makes St Demetrius a native of Thessalonica, though Sirmium, near Mitrovitsa, also claims him. He was martyred at the command of Galerius. The saint, as the city's guardian, defended it against enemy attacks. His tomb exuded a sacred oil with miraculous healing powers. His cult fostered the opposition of Thessalonica to the 14C ikonoclastic movement. A fair, of considerable importance in the Middle Ages, accompanied his festal days (20–26 October). Immediately after the edict of toleration the Christians built a small church on the site of the martyrdom. In AD 412–13 Leontius, prefect of Illyricum, miraculously healed of paralysis, founded 'between the ruins of the Roman bath and the Stadium', a large church which was damaged by fire in the reign of Heraclius (c 629–34) and shortly afterwards rebuilt by Archbishop John with the addition of the E transepts. The plan seems to have remained unaltered despite later repairs. Here in 688 the Emperor Justinian II celebrated his success against the Slavs. The church was pillaged in 1430 but left to the Christians until 1491 when, in the reign of Bayezid II (as shown by an inscription formerly above the W door), it became the Kasimiye Çami. Between 1907 and 1912, when it was returned to Christian use, the wonderful mosaics were rediscovered, only to be largely destroyed in the fire of 1917. The rebuilding was by architects Zachos (died 1938) and Thanopoulos under the supervision of Ephor S. Pelekanides.

The EXTERIOR appears cruciform because of the transept roofs, which break the line of the aisles although they do not form a true crossing with the nave. Outside the W front, which is flanked by two low towers, stands the great **phiale**, a canopied immersion font. The usual entrance is by the S door.

The spacious INTERIOR, 43m long, has been impressively restored, though the upper surfaces have only whitewashed plaster in place of the destroyed revetment of polychrome marble (traces above the arcade). The **nave**, 12m wide and ending in an apse, is flanked by double aisles, with round arches supported by columns of green, red, and white marble. The ancient shafts (some renewed) must have been replacements from elsewhere after the first fire since they have pedestals of uneven height. The carved *capitals with their imposts repay detailed attention; many are Theodosian. The ancient marble revetment has been renewed on the piers, and the floor repaved in Thessalian marble.

At the W end are a curious wall painting with a unicorn and a calendar of movable feasts for 1474–93. On the N side is the marble tomb (1481) of Osios Loukas Spantounis, of Florentine workmanship most unusual in Greece. A domed chamber at the NW corner survives from a Roman building and probably held the tomb of St Demetrius; it is poorly frescoed. At the entrance is a damaged mosaic of the saint.

AYIOS DHIMITRIOS

On the floor of the nave remains of a hexagonal base mark the site of the silver ciborium of St Demetrius, burnt in 581. The great polygonal **choros** is a noteworthy copy. On the first pier of the S arcade is a fresco of Archbishop Palamas with the blessed Ioasaph (presumably John VI Cantacuzenus who took the habit under that name). The **ikonastasis** and the furnishings are replicas of Byzantine work in fretted marble, the **ambo** to the left, the **cathedra** to the right. On the pier behind the throne, fresco of Osios Loukas (died 953). To the right and left of the ikonostasis survive five *mosaics, three contemporary with Leo's rebuilding. Right Pier: St Demetrius and the builders of the church, presumably the prefect Leontius and Archbishop John, defender of the city in 617–619; St Sergius sumptuously attired as captain of the Imperial guard (a later work); St Demetrius with a deacon (discovered when a masking Turkish wall was removed). Left Pier: St Demetrius with two children; Virgin and (?) St Theodore (the date still disputed).

In the outer S aisle are frescoes of the saint and of the miraculous defeat of a Barbarian invasion. At the SE corner stands the dark little **Chapel of Ay. Euthymios**, with frescoes of 1303.

The **crypt** (now set out as a museum), discovered in the fire, is entered from the S transept. Here are located the **martyrion** of the saint (early 4C), perhaps an adaptation of part of the **Roman bath** in which St Demetrius was traditionally imprisoned. Beneath its apse was found a small cruciform reliquary-crypt containing a phial of blood-soaked earth. Parts of a fountain from a fish pond described by Archbishop Eustathios (died 1193) were also discovered. A stretch of paved Roman **street** shows that the martyrion was originally above the ground level.

To the NW of the church are a haphazard collection of Byzantine walls, column fragments and Hebrew tombstones. To the N rise two domes of a Turkish bath. The trifoliate church of **Profítis Ilías** (Pl. 6), which served the 14C **Néa Moní**, occupies the site of a Byzantine palace, as its Turkish name (**Eski Séraï Çamisi**) suggests. Converted to the Moslem rite of Fethi Murad, it was disfigured by massive external buttresses, the removal of which has revealed its fine brick decoration. The square narthex, with an upper storey supported on pillars, is characteristic of the monastic Katholikon (badly damaged mosaics and medieval graffiti). Internally the church needed such thorough restoration that its only original features are the four columns supporting the dome and fragmentary mosaics in the small window embrasures of the drum.

# B. The seafront and the Eastern Quarter

From the centre Odhós Aristotélous, a broad flower-planted avenue, crosses Odhós Ermoú and Tsimiskí and descends to the sea. At the seaward end (at Níkis 39) is the British Consulate-General. Leofóros Níkis (Pl. 14), a quayside esplanade with noted restaurants, replaces the 10C seaward rampart demolished in 1866–74. To the right it leads to Plateía Eleftherías, centre of banking, and to the **harbour**.

The original port, constructed by Constantine the Great, was silted up in the Middle Ages. A new harbour was fashioned by a French company in the late 19C and in 1911 Thessaloniki was the third port of Turkey. The competition of Piraeus and the through railway to Athens killed its passenger services and after the Second World War commerce was virtually non-existent. Since 1960 new Macedonian industries increased traffic to the extent that a new quay was begun in 1962. A Free Zone encouraged Yugoslav use of the port.

You turn left along the promenade. On the shore at the far end (1km), among trees, is the famous **White Tower** (Pl. 16), or **Lefkós Pírgos** (Λευκός Πύργος) (32m high) which marked the S angle of the ramparts. Built c 1430 either by the Venetians or the Turks, it served in the 18–19C as a prison for the Janissaries. Their massacre in 1826 at the order of Mahmoud II gained for it the name of Bloody Tower, forgotten since the application of whitewash. The tower is now a **Byzantine Museum** (closed Monday morning; illustrated catalogue available). GROUND FLOOR: Urban Organisation. Plan of city in Roman period; floor mosaics; coins. FIRST FLOOR: Worship in Early Christian Thessaloniki. *Mosaics from Ay. Dhimitrios; column capitals; *4C silver reliquary. SECOND FLOOR: Christian cemeteries:

˙tomb frescoes; glass. THIRD FLOOR: History and Art in Byzantine Thessaloniki. Sculpture; ˙frescoes from Ay. Sophia; pottery; ˙10C gold and enamel armlets; jewellery; coins; ikons etc. FOURTH AND FIFTH FLOORS: Economopoulos Collection of 16–18C ikons, coins, pottery.

Grouped opposite the Tower, at the corners of Leofóros Ethnikís Amínis (Rte 59C), are the **Officers' Club** and the **Society for Macedonian Studies** (Εταιρεία Μακεδονικών Σπουδών). Adjacent is the **State Theatre** (1961) and, by the sea, the **National Theatre**. Beyond, a **park** divides the old town from its huge E extension. An avenue leads (left) to the entrance of the Fair (see below).

Along the foreshore a broad **Esplanade** was laid out in 1961–62 on reclaimed land. This promenade, flanked by gardens, extends S to (4km) the new **Yacht Basin**. Beyond is the **Villa Allatini**, where the banished Abdul Hamid II, sultan of Turkey, lived in 1909–12; it is now a military hospital. 5.5km **Mikró Karavoúrnou**; on the point stands the **Kiverneíon**, or Government House, a splendidly successful Ionic neo-Classical building in white marble. A military encampment bars access to the prominent **tumulus** opposite. Beyond the point are **Arétsou** (Hotel C), a popular sea-side resort with tavernas, NTOG beach, and yacht marina, and **Néa Kríni** (camping sites). Both have fine views across the gulf to Mt Olympos.

Leofóros Vasiléos Yeoryíou tou Prótou runs E to its crossing with Odhós Ayías Triádhos, on the corner of which a marble bust commemorates the assassination here in 1913 of George I. The road continues as Leofóros Vasilíssis Ólgas (see below), off which (left) is the **Yeni Çami**, a large mosque which housed the archaeological museum in 1917–62. No. 68 houses the impressive **Folk Art—Ethnological Museum** (open mornings; closed Thursday) with costumes and artefacts and displays illustrating traditional life. Further on are two art galleries, the **Municipal Gallery** and the **Gallery of the National Bank of Greece**. Od. Konstandinoupóleos, then Leofóros Stratoú, lead back along the N side of the park past the Army Headquarters to the permanent site of the **International Fair**. The commercial fair, held in the Middle Ages as part of the festivities of St Demetrius (October), was revived in 1926.

Inland, beyond the fair, rises the university (p. 539) and farther to the NE a new **sports centre**, with a covered **swimming pool**, and the **Kaftándzoglou Stadium**, erected from a bequest of Lysimachos Kaftandzoglou (1870–1937), the diplomat, and opened in 1960 by King Paul. Beyond, in the Toúmba area, an important prehistoric settlement is being excavated by archaeologists from the University of Thessaloníki.

Across the road from the Fair entrance is the ˙**Archaeological Museum**, opened in 1963. In front of the building are two fine sarcophagi. In the entrance hall are available some useful books and minor publications about material in the museum and sites in the vicinity.

The museum consists of an inner and an outer series of rooms laid out round a court. The inner rooms (access from hall opposite entrance) house finds from **Sindhos** (see below). You begin with the outer series. It should be noted that little of the Classical material is at present on display.

OUTER ROOMS: ROOM 1 (to left of entrance) contains Neolithic to Iron Age finds from sites in Macedonia, with a map showing their location. Included is material from recent British School excavations at *Assiros Toumba*, N of Thessaloníki. Under a glass case is the outline body of a girl with grave goods and jewellery, as found near Verria (12–10C BC). ROOM 2 (up steps from vestibule). Ionic capital and other fragments from a temple at Thermi (end 6C BC). A small head, which may be part of the frieze, is

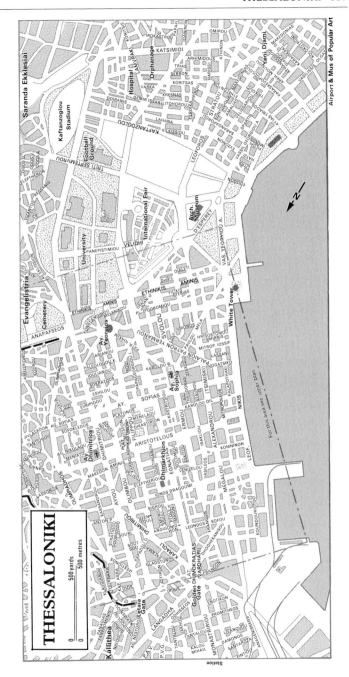

THESSALONIKI

0        500 yards
0      500 metres

just inside ROOM 3; also sculptures of various periods. ROOM 4. Portrait head of a man from a grave relief of mid 1C, and other Hellenistic works.

ROOM 5, a long hall, partially arranged as a Roman courtyard with a central floor mosaic and wall mosaics, all from a villa in Thessaloniki. The floor mosaics depict three legends: Dionysos and Ariadne at Naxos; Zeus and Ganymede; Apollo and Daphne (?). The wall mosaic of three spirited horses (right) is attractive. Statuary includes a powerful Atlas, from the agora of Thessaloniki (1C BC); a dignified bust of Dionysos, from Drama; three headless Muses (late Roman copies of Hellenistic originals). Against the right-hand wall is a marble arch with rich relief decoration, part of the Palace of Galerius (early 4C AD), discovered in 1957; on the left is Thessalonica personified; on the right, a portrait of the emperor; on the sides, Pan and a dancer. Beside are two engaged capitals with figures. Cases against the wall contain fine glass objects mainly from excavations on the site of new university buildings; also Hellenistic pottery including a mould-made 'Megarian' bowl with scenes in relief of the Trojan War. ROOM 6. Portrait statues and heads, mainly of 1C AD, with two fine figures of Augustus and (headless) possibly Claudius. ROOM 7. Later portrait heads: girl, with pendant ear-rings, a fashionable hair-style and petulant expression; other fine female heads; statue of the Emperor Hadrian (?); *bronze head of a man (the Emperor Gallienus ?) from Riakia (Pieria). ROOM 8. By the wall are two fine busts of a man and a woman (late 4C AD). In a case is Byzantine pottery.

From ROOM 7 a door to the left of the entrance leads via a corridor to a spectacular exhibition of finds from the *Royal Tombs of Verghina (see Rte 61) and other rich Late Classical and Hellenistic material. The corridor has photographs and a model of the site. Amongst the spectacular objects on display are a ceremonial shield of intricate workmanship, a gold wreath, gorytus (quiver) and casket, ivory figures of the Macedonian royal family, armour and metal vessels all from the Tomb of Philip II. Also noteworthy are a gold medallion with the head of Philip and the famous Dherveni crater (4C), a bronze vessel with appliqué statuettes and silver ornamentation. A further gallery beyond the Verghina room is at present closed.

Returning to the vestibule you enter the INNER ROOMS which are occupied by a modern display of finds from the rich Late Archaic/Early Classical cemetery discovered in 1980 in the NW suburb of **Síndhos**. Of the 121 graves excavated, objects from 36 are displayed. The tombs varied greatly in quantity of grave goods. Some had only a few vases; the contents of others (e.g. Tomb 67) occupy several showcases. The finds include gold funerary masks, silver vessels, gold and silver jewellery, bronze vessels, weapons and armour (helmets with gold trimmings). Also model furniture in iron, and carts (one exceptionally fine, with three terracotta mules, from Tomb 59). These probably reflect the expected activities of the deceased in the next world. There are many clay figurines and fine vases.

On the far corner stands YMCA Headquarters, behind which the **Municipal Library** (open 08.00–13.00, 16.00–20.00) faces on to the beginning of the Tsimiskí.

# C. Tour of the ramparts

The present course of the Byzantine *ramparts seem to have been adopted in the reign of Theodosius (AD 379–395). Whether this perpetuates an enceinte of Kassander is uncertain, but here and there well-laid courses of Hellenistic masonry remain. The length of the circuit in the 4C AD was c 8 kilometres, about half of which survives, with upwards of 40 towers, almost all square, spaced very irregularly at distances varying between 7.6m and 128m. The construction is largely of rubble with courses of brick, though in places it is entirely of brick, sometimes with rows of brick arches to give added strength. This device (which enables the wall to remain standing even if the base is sapped) was not again revived in Europe until the 12–13C. Inscriptions survive from a number of rebuildings. The walls stand to a height of 7.6–15.2m, though the upper courses are mostly 14C or 15C work with restorations. In places an outwork (proteichisma) can be traced, 3.7–5.5m from the wall. This was designed to deny access to enemy battering rams. All the major gates have now disappeared.

From the White Tower you take Leofóros Ethnikís Amínis (Pl. 16). The ancient ramparts, here almost completely vanished, followed the line of the next street to the W. The Plateía Sintrivaníou (Kalamarías), with a Turkish fountain, occupies the site of the Kassandreia Gate on the Egnatía Odhós, one of four gates in the E wall. An inscription indicates repairs by Archbishop Eusebius in the 6C. To the left you catch a glimpse of the Arch of Galerius. Odhós Ethnikís Amínis continues NE alongside gardens (left) in which short sections of the wall are preserved. To the right extends the site of the **Aristotelian University of Thessaloníki** (Pl. 12), founded in 1925 and removed here in the following year to the former Turkish Military Academy, that faces the road. The university, divided further E by Od. Panepistimíou, now occupies a huge precinct covering much of the former Jewish cemetery, systematically desecrated by the Germans in 1943. Among the more striking new buildings are the circular **Meteorological Observatory** and the huge **Polytechnic School**. The **library** contains 300,000 books. Passing between the **Chemical Faculty** and the **Central Hospital** you bear left across a square where Odhós Ayíou Dhimitríou once entered the walls by the Gate of the Archangels.

A little to the N, off Olimbiádhos, a red house in Odhós Apostólou Pávlou (next to the Turkish Consulate) is the **Birthplace of Mustafa Kemal** (Atatürk; 1881–1938), first President of Turkey. A plaque was placed here in 1933. Kemal, the son of a government clerk, spent his childhood in the city and attended the Military Cadet School. In 1907–11 he was posted to the Turkish Third Army (then in Thessaloníki), and took part in the march to Constantinople that overthrew Abdul Hamid. Further (300m) up Apostólou Pávlou (entrance in Irodhótou, to the W) is the 14C church of **Ayios Nikólaos Orfanós** with fine contemporary frescoes.

From Od. Zográfou, running N beside the **Evangelístria Cemetery**, the first lane (left) leads shortly to the walls, here partly hidden by houses. You continue N past the grounds of the **Municipal Hospital** (Pl. 4) and then to a path that runs parallel to the road where the walls become continuous, with sections surviving to the battlements. High up on the **Hormisdas Tower**, part of an inscription, 9m long in brick, reads τείχεσιν ἀρρήκτοις Ὁρμίσδας ἐξετέλεσε τήνδε πόλιν (by indestructible walls Hormisdas completely fortified this town). Hormisdas the Younger held various offices in Thessaloniki and Constantinople under Theodosius. Higher up, the **Chain Tower** (Gingirli Koule), so called from the heavy stringcourse half way up, is a circular keep of the 16C, and perhaps replaced a corner tower destroyed in 1430. To the left of its modern steps some regular masonry appears to be

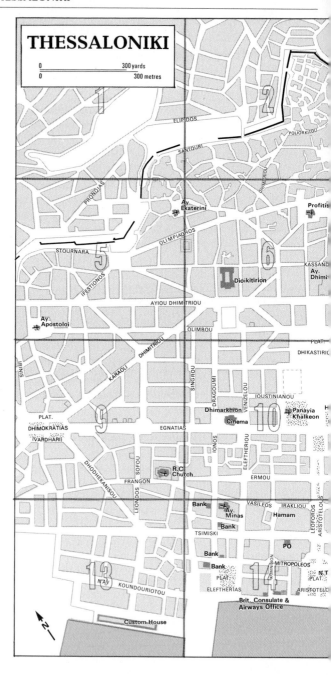

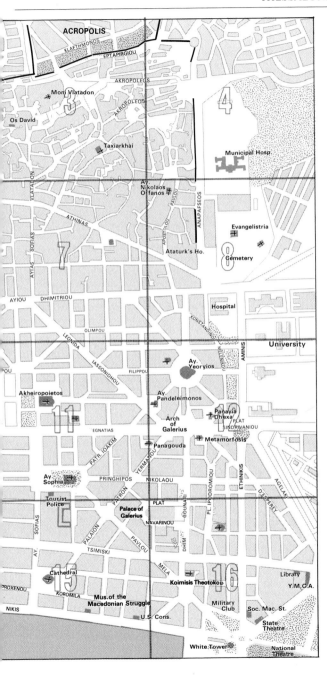

of Classical date. You can pass inside the circuit through a gap in the wall or continue W round the outside of the Acropolis.

The **acropolis** (buses 22 or 23 from Od. Venizélou) still has most of its wall, though on the E side this is largely Turkish. The long S section (facing N) is the most interesting (for an approach, see main text below). Access can also be gained from beyond the Chain Tower, via the **Gate of Anna Palaeologus**, first opened in 1355 by the widow of Andronikos III. It has a Byzantine inscription. The triangle here, where the acropolis wall meets the city wall, is probably to be identified with the **Trigonion** where the storming Turks gained entry in 1430. Within the Acropolis unremarkable suburban villas climb haphazardly to the **Eptapírghion** (Yedí Koulé; tavernas), a fortress with seven towers until recently used as a prison, that crowns the summit (also accessible via Agrafon). The massive central tower bears an Arabic inscription recording its construction in 1431 by Sungur Çauş Bey. The NW section of the acropolis wall can be reached by turning off Odhós Eptapirghíou and left into Od. Spartákou. At the end the cobbled Od. Agrafon (right) follows the wall.

Odhós Eptapirghíou follows (W) the excellently preserved *south wall of the acropolis, which is also part of the main circuit of the city. Steps mount to the top, where the walk within the inner and outer parapets, accessible for c 100m, commands the acropolis; from here in 1345 the enraged mob hurled the nobles on to stakes below. The original towers face towards the acropolis which, more vulnerable to an expected assault from the landward, might be invested first. In the 14C when the likelier danger had proven to be from the sea, four shallow towers were added on the seaward side. The second one bears the device of Andronikos II Palaeologus. A small secret **postern** survives between the second and third. A modern gate has been opened towards the W end, nearly opposite which stands the **Moni Vlatádhon** (Pl. 3), a monastery founded in the 14C by the Cretan brothers Vlatades. Since the church is dedicated to the Transfiguration, they were probably Hesychasts. Largely rebuilt in 1801, the church (originally on the plan of Ayia Ekaterini) has original frescoes in the bema and in the parecclesion to the right. Some recently uncovered paintings are dated to the 11C. The monastic buildings house a Patriarchal Academy of Patristic Studies. Farther along Odhós Eptapirghíou, the wall is partly hidden by old houses.

A lane leads (left) to **Osios Davíd** (Pl. 2), a tiny church probably dating from the late 5C, though its foundation is attributed by tradition to Theodora, daughter of Galerius. In medieval times it served the Moní Latómou. Its plan, an inscribed cross of Syrian type and unusually early date, was mutilated when it became a mosque. A *mosaic, discovered in 1921 beneath plaster in the apse and contemporary with the church, shows Christ, beardless, between Ezekiel and Habakkuk. It seems to interpret the visions of Ezekiel I and II in the spirit of the New Testament, for the two prophets can also represent SS. Paul and Peter. Late 12C frescoes of exceptional quality were recently discovered in the S vault. They show the Baptism, Nativity and Presentation. To the SE the church of the Taxiarchs is 14C.

You can leave the walled circuit again by the **Eski Delik**, an ancient gate, later blocked, then reopened by the Turks. The walls follow the rugged natural contour westwards. The two abrupt angles of the salient W of the gate are exceptionally provided with polygonal towers, one with a postern. Just beyond the second is the triangular **Tower of Manuel Palaeologus** (c 1230), on which (6m up) can be seen an inscription in four lines coupling his name with that of George Apokaukos, probably governor of the city. The ramparts facing NE and N, pierced by the Turkish **Yeni Delik** (New Gate), incorporate numerous pieces of Hellenistic masonry and one section of Roman construction. A short distance from the wall is **Ayía Ekateríni** (Pl. 5), a pretty church of similar plan to the Dhodeka Apostoloi (see below) without a narthex. The outer walk has arcades, closed externally with glass, and surmounted by a wavy cornice. The church dates from the late 13C; the contemporary paintings were much damaged during its time as the **Yakob Pasha Çami** after 1510.

The extreme NW limit of the ramparts has more frequent towers and was protected by an outwork. The **Letaia Gate**, with a hexagonal barbican, has been reduced to ruin in this century; there remains some pseudo-isodomic masonry incorporating reused Classical blocks. A few metres inside the gate is the **·Dhódheka Apóstoloi** (Pl. 5), the least restored and perhaps the most charming of Thessaloníki's churches. Founded by the Patriarch Niphou (1312–15), it was a monastic church until its conversion to the Mohammedan rite as the **Soouk Sou Çami**. The E end has richly patterned brickwork. Round three sides of the central cross-in-square runs an outer aisle with four corner domes. The narthex has an arcaded façade. The inner dome is borne on four columns with capitals from an earlier structure. The wall paintings, extensive but damaged, include a Tree of Jesse in the S aisle. The four barrel vaults that support the drum have lively mosaics. S vault: Nativity, with a bucolic shepherd and soulful animals; the handmaiden Salome prepares a bath; the midwife tests the temperature of the water, while the Child apprehensively turns away. The Transfiguration is a powerful composition.

Just below are the **Loutrá Phoenix** with an attractive dome.

You now descend Odhós Irínis, where an animated fruit market largely masks the wall, to Plateía Dhimokratías (Pl. 9), or **Vardhári**, the busy W entrance to the city. A **Statue of Constantine**, liberator of Thessalonica, occupies the site of the sculptured Golden Gate of the Flavian epoch, described and drawn by 19C travellers, but since totally demolished.

Here the two principal routes into the city converge. To the N in Odhós Langadhá stands a fine **memorial** (1962) to the 50,000 Jews of Thessaloníki who perished in the gas chambers of Auschwitz. The monument, a monolithic block of Pentelic marble, was designed by the Italian architect, Manfredo Portino. To the NW Odhós Monastiríou leads shortly to the **railway station**.

From the square, Odhós Frángon follows the line of the early Byzantine walls, to the **Vardar Stronghold** (*Top Hane*, the Turkish fort and arsenal), now restored and laid out as a park. Fragments of Byzantine walls also survive near the Roman Catholic church. Between here and the modern harbour lay the Classical port, silted up in the Middle Ages. Here is now an interesting quarter of Turkish warehouses, the streets paved with lava.

In the nearer suburbs of Thessaloniki there are two British Military Cemeteries of the First World War. The **Zeitenlik** or **Lembet Road Cemetery**, off the W side of the Serres road, contains 1648 British graves; the **Monastir Road Indian Cemetery**, 3km from the centre beyond the station, commemorates 520 fallen. Other cemeteries are situated at Mikrá (see below; 1900 burials) and near Khortiátis (see below; 586 graves).

# D.  Excursions from Thessaloníki

I. TO AYIA TRIADHA AND THE THERMAIC GULF. Road 29km (18 miles), bus in summer; also by motor-boat. You leave the city by the long Leofóros Megálou Alexándrou (once briefly renamed after John Kennedy) which, behind the waterfront esplanade, takes eastbound traffic (return by the older Leof. Vasilíssis Olgas, parallel inland). Soon a turning goes off left for **Pilaía** (20,785 inhab.) and **Panórama** (see below); between the two is **Anatolia College**, an American school for boys and girls. It was founded (as a boys' school) in 1886 in Asia Minor and removed to Thessaloniki after the First World War. The main road keeps inland of Aretsou and continues through lengthening ribbon development. At 7km a road leads left (1km) to the **American Farm School** (Amerikániki Yeoryikí Skholí), founded in 1903 by John Henry House in order to introduce modern methods into Greece (c 800 students; visit on application to the Director). You pass the **Army Staff College** and just touch the shore. 10km The Northern HQ of the Hellenic Air Force stands where the road to Políyiros diverges left (Rte 64A). 11km Turning (right) for the Airport; beside the road is the very prominent **Tsairi Toumba**. Other mounds can be seen as the road skirts the airport. At 16km the road to Nea Moudhianá and Kassándra bears left. You continue past turns to **Peraía** (Hotels B, C), with a relay station of the American radio, and **Néoi Epivátai**, both popular beach resorts. 23km **Ayía Triádha** (Hotels B, C) has a large camp site and bathing beach of the NTOG, and a Youth Hostel. Beyond Ayía Triádha is a turn for **Angelokhóri**, a centre of tomato and cucumber growing; before the village a track leads (right) to Cape Megálo Karavournoú, site of ancient *Dinaion*. The main road continues to (29km) **Néa Mikhanióna**, a busy small fishing town on the open gulf, with many shaded restaurants just above the long beach. The town is on the site of ancient *Ainia*; painted Macedonian tombs have been discovered recently.

II. MOUNT KHORTIÁTIS (1201m) rises to the E of Thessaloníki and separates the Gulf from Lake Langadhá (Koronía). The summit is in a prohibited zone, but the road can be followed to a height of 672m. The approach road quits the N suburbs of Thessaloníki (leaving the centre via Odd. Langadhá, Venizélou and Vassiléos Yioryíou) and rises to (9km) **Asvestokhóri**, a popular summer resort (270m; 3326 inhab.) on the W slope of Profitis Ilias (768m). 14km Near quarries, roads descend (right) to Panórama (see below) and, soon after (left), to **Ayios Vasílios** on the Via Egnatia by the lake (Rte 66). You pass the remains of an aqueduct and reach (18km) **Khortiátis**, facing NW on wooded slopes. From here the road climbs a further 5km to the prohibited zone, with fine views over Thessaloníki; there is also a signposted path from Khortiátis to (1¾ hours) a refuge of the Alpine Club. You can return by taking the S turn at the quarries to reach first **Néa Panórama** (with the option of bearing left and descending via Thermi, Rte 64A), then **Panórama** (Hotels A, C) just above Anatolia College (comp. above).

III. FROM THESSALONIKI TO POLIKASTRO AND GHEVGELI. Road, 82km (51 miles) and railway (79km in 2 hours). This is the main highway into former Yugoslavia and the main railway route to Belgrade, following the plain and valley of the Axios (Vardar). To (23km) **Yéfira**, see Rte 60. The road then turns N and follows the left bank of the Axios. The river is largely controlled by irrigation and anti-flood works. From Yéfira to the border the old road through the villages and the National Highway run parallel. From (39km) **Kastanás** the railway runs between the roads. To the E are the American drainage works that reduced the former **Lake Amatovon**. At (53km) **Limnótopos**, you cross one of the sluices. 60km **Políkastro** (Hotels B, C, D), formerly *Karasouli*, has an international Military Cemetery with British graves. A large ammunition dump here was blown up in a German air raid in April 1917. The town is at the SW end of **Lake Ardzan**, also drained, on the N shore of which the Iron Age site of *Chauchitsa* (Tsaout-sitza) was excavated by the British School in 1921. The railway now crosses to the W of roads and river to follow the Vardar through the **Stena Tsingane Derven**, a defile 10km long at the E foot of Païkon (with molybdenum mines in the foothills), to the frontier station of **Idhoméni**. The roads remain E of the isolated **Mt Skhóli** (354km), passing (69km) **Mikró Dhásos**, to (74km) **Evzóni** (Hotels B, D, E), beyond which is the frontier post, still on the left bank of the river. The Vardar is crossed in former Yugoslavia. 82km **Ghevgéli** (motel).

# 60

## From Thessaloníki to Edhessa

**Road**, Via Egnatia, 89km (55 miles), straight and level; dual carriageway to Khalkídhona; bus hourly. **Railway**, see Rte 61. All Vérria trains continue to Edhessa: total journey time c 2 hours.

This route leaves Thessaloníki by the Plateía Dhimokratías (Pl. 9) and the railway station, at first following the international line to former Yugoslavia through industrial suburbs. The road passes under the ring road, then above the railway on a flyover. At (7km) **Dhiavatá**, road to Kilkís (37km, right). You cross the Serres railway and pass a memorial to French soldiers killed in the First World War. At the crossing (11km) of the Gallikos, from whose sandy bed small quantities of gold are extracted, the prehistoric mound of *Gradhembório* can be seen to the N. A road branches left to Síndhos and into the central Pedhias Kampanias (comp. Rte 61).

At (7km) **Síndhos** important Archaic and Classical cemeteries have been discovered in the course of construction work since 1980. The burials which were in stone cists, stone or clay sarcophagi or simple pits, probably belong to the nearby settlement mound of Néa Ankhíalos, which is perhaps to be identified with the ancient town of *Chalastra*. Potters' kilns were constructed over the cemetery area in the 4C. For the spectacular finds see description of Thessaloníki Museum. 11km **Pírgos**, another candidate for *Chalastra*, was on the coast in Classical times. Between Síndhos and Pírgos, Xerxes' fleet waited for the army to catch up. 15km **Néa Málgara**, a huge refugee settlement amid rice-fields on the right bank of the Axios, is built on land reclaimed since ancient times. 25km **Klidhí** may represent ancient *Haloros* where, following preclassical boundaries, the nome of Imathia pushes a narrow tongue to the sea.

14km A large flat mound to the left is called Trapezoidhís. You cross over the National Highway and the railway to the frontier with former Yugoslavia. 24.5km **Yéfira** (right; Motel C), at the junction of the old road to the border (spur to the Highway), is (as its name indicates) where the Axios was bridged before being diverted to its modern bed. A prehistoric table-mound and Classical finds prove the antiquity of the site; here in 1912 was signed the agreement surrendering Thessaloníki to Greece. About 1.5km farther on irrigation canals carry water from the **Axios River Barrage** (1954–58) 3km N of the road (approach-road on top of dyke). At the crossing of the Axios is a girder bridge of 14 spans, built by British sappers (228 Army Field Company) in 1945 (plaque, left at bridge entrance).

The **Axios**, or **Vardar**, the largest river in Macedonia, rises deep in former Yugoslavia and flows for only 80.5km through Greece from the 'Iron Gates' to the sea. Before the flood and reclamation works, instituted by Venizelos in 1925, gave the river its present bed, the area was largely malarial marshes. Further irrigation works, jointly controlling the Axios and Aliakmon, undertaken in 1953–63 by C. Karamanlis, have brought the greater part under cultivation.

31km **Khalkídhona** (3144 inhab.; Hotel C, restaurants) grew up after 1923 round the old timber-framed han at the junction where the Via Egnatia and the Verria road, also of Roman origin or earlier, divided to pass Lake Loudhias. You follow the Via Egnatia. About 1.5km farther on is a turning (right) for Políkastro and the border. This road passes through Evropós, where the kouros in the Kilkis Museum was found and, more recently, a monumental vaulted tomb. To the S is a fertile plain, drained by the Loudhias, an artificial river that perpetuates the name of the Classical Lake Loudhias (later Lake Yiannitsa), drained in 1927–36. In earlier times this was connected with the sea (see below). A series of funerary mounds (left) marks the edge of the lake. 38km **Pélla** (2374 inhab.).

**PÉLLA** (Πέλλα), capital of Macedonia at the height of its greatness and birthplace of Alexander the Great, was formerly connected by a shallow navigable lagoon with the Thermaic Gulf. Chance finds in 1957 located the exact site of the city, estimated to have occupied 3.8 sq. km; and excavations by Prof. Makaronas and Ph. Petsas in 1957–68 uncovered outstanding pebble mosaics of c 300 BC. Recent years have seen spectacular further progress in investigation, under Mrs M. Karamanoli-Siganidhou, but much (agora, palace) is not yet laid out for visiting. An illustrated leaflet is available on request and the museum and site have useful explanatory panels.

An earlier settlement called *Bounomeia* by Stephanus Byzantius may have lain to the S, where prehistoric sherds have been found. *Pella* is mentioned by Herodotus and has yielded coins from the mid-5C BC. The Macedonian capital was transferred from Aigai to Pella by Archelaus (413–399 BC), whose artistic entourage included the painter Zeuxis, the poet Agathon, and Euripides. The two latter died here in 400 and 406 respectively. Philip II was born here in 382 and Alexander the Great in 356. The city flourished especially under Antigonus Gonatas. It fell to Aemilius Paulus after the Battle of Pydna, and from 148 BC lost importance to Thessalonica. At one time the Romans called it *Diocletianopolis*; the site may then have been moved to the W.

The most accessible area is across the road from the museum (see below).

The site as a whole, laid out on a grid plan, covers a large area. The extensive **agora** lies to the NE of the museum, and W of the road leading up to the village of Palaiá Pélla, from which it can be best seen via a path off to the left. It occupied five insulae of the town grid and over 60,000 sq. metres. The large square was surrounded by Doric porticoes, with shops, workshops (potters, coroplasts) etc. behind. On the N side was a **Sanctuary of Aphrodite and Cybele** incorporating ritual and dining rooms, metal workshops etc. There is also a **nymphaion**. The **main street** of the town traversed the agora, with a **monumental gateway** at the E.

On the **acropolis** which occupied a hill to the W of Palaiá Pélla, some distance to the N of the agora and the fenced site, a large and important complex, almost certainly a palace, is being investigated. It is hard to identify it with the **Palace of Archelaos**, painted by Zeuxis, where Alexander was born in 356 BC, since it seems only to have been built about that time (and substantially altered in the following century). Philip II or Cassander may have been reponsible. It comprises at least six large square units, some consisting of courtyards surrounded by rooms. The palace had a monumental façade and entrance with a ramp and Doric columns. To the N a complex with bathing facilities may have been a gymnasium.

In the village of Palaiá Pélla is a **Sanctuary of Demeter and Kore** (Thesmophorion), circular, with an altar at the centre: this is still being excavated.

By the museum are three rectangular house-blocks, cut across by the main road. The richest of the houses, occupying the whole of 'Block 1', to the right, is the **House of the Lion Hunt**, a building of the late 4C BC, 50m wide and more than 90m long, with three open courts running N and S. Three of its dozen rooms were decorated with mosaics now in the museum. Fragments of painted plaster, bronze bosses from the doors, and terracotta antefixes show it to have been a splendid building, and its stamped roof tiles suggest that it had an official function. The building is bordered by broad streets lined with clay water-pipes and stone sewers. Much of the central peristyle (six columns square) has been re-erected and the great patterned pebble mosaics of the main rooms restored.

Block 5 (two blocks to the W) has yielded a further range of mosaics, including the Rape of Helen (Pl. D), a Stag Hunt (Pl. E) and an Amazonomachia (Pl. F).

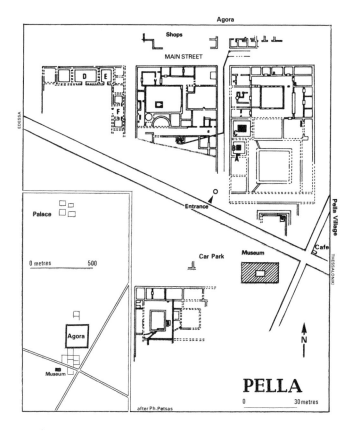

after Ph. Petsas

**PELLA**

0    30 metres

The **museum** has been rearranged with excellent new displays. In the ENTRANCE HALL are Neolithic and Bronze Age finds from the area and Bronze Age material from the tel site at Mandalo. Finds from Iron Age cemeteries at Arkhontikó and Agrosikiá. Painted wall decoration of a Hellenistic house in a style equivalent to the Pompeian First style. Panels illustrate the housing and town plan of Pella. In cases are items of domestic use, fine bronzes and terracottas, two coin hoards and other coins.

ROOM 2 (right). Material (Hellenistic to 1C) from the Agora including finds from ceramic workshops—fine (painted and relief decorated) and coarse Hellenistic pottery; figurines and moulds; large terracotta statuettes. A fine bronze of Poseidon. Finds from the Thesmophorion (3–2C BC) include terracotta figurines. Pottery and terracottas from the cemeteries, Hellenistic—3C AD. Marble statuette of Alexander as Pan. Terracottas from the Sanctuary of Aphrodite and Cybele (3–1C BC). Gold jewellery from the West cemetery, 3C AD.

ROOM 3 (beyond entrance hall). Panels describing the palace; various architectural elements. Fine *mosaics from Blocks 1 and 5. The life-size figures are fashioned with natural pebbles of various colours; special features are outlined with strips of lead or clay. The eyes (all missing) were probably semi-precious stones. The positions from which the mosaics came are indicated on the plan. Lion hunt (Pl. C), perhaps the rescue of Alexander himself by Krateros near Susa; Dionysos on a tiger's back (Pl. B); griffin attacking a deer (Pl. A); also centaurs, florals.

Other houses, and sections of the defences, have been located up to 200m to the S of the museum. Cemeteries have been excavated in various parts of the site. No trace has yet been found of the theatre where the Bacchae of Euripides received its first performance in c 408 BC.

To the S of the road, rising above the drained marsh, is a small green mound, originally the late-Helladic settlement of *Phacos*. On it was later built a fortified treasury that served the Macedonian kings and is described by Livy.

39.5km **Néa Pélla** (right) is a refugee settlement. By the road (right) are the so-called **Baths of Alexander**, a Hellenistic fountain, repaired by the Romans; Aemilius Paulus probably pitched camp here and a Roman settlement developed. 42.5km Turn (right) for **Agrosikéa** (10km) has an ancient settlement occupied from Neolithic to Early Christian times and centred on a recently excavated mound at Pelíti. Off this road, **Rakhóna** has a 4C cemetery with monumental tombs covered by a mound, and funerary sculpture. 48km **Yiannitsá** (Γιαννιτσά, or Γενιτσά; Hotel C), seat of an eparchy and the largest town (22,504 inhab.) in the nome of Pella, lies to the right of the road. As *Yeniceyi Vardar* it was a holy place of the Turks. Neolithic finds have been made in the Paliá Agora. In a dilapidated mosque are the tombs of the Evrenos family (14–15C), descendants of the conqueror of Macedonia. A bronze **monument** by the road commemorates the Battle of Yiannitsa (1912), which ensured the liberation of Thessaloniki. The battle actually took place at (53km) **Melíssi**, where the Turks fiercely contested the crossing of the Balítsa. 56km **Kariótissa**. To the N, c 10km away, **Meterízi** (1597m), the third highest peak of the **Páïkon Mountains**, rises abruptly from the plain. Mt Páïkon itself (behind right) is 1649m. You cross two of the large flood canals that channel to the Aliakmon the waters of the Vodas, the Moglenitsa, and countless mountain streams from Vermion that once inundated the plain. Edhessa and its waterfalls come into view ahead. The road meets the railway from Verria at (73km) **Skídhra** (Hotel C), a fruit grading and canning centre (4562 inhab.). At the S end of the bridge over the Vodas the road joins that from Verria (see below). 75km **Mavrovoúni** stands on the N bank. A direct route to Aridhaía (via Apsalos) leads off to the right. Off that road to the E, **Anidhro Kalí** may be the site of ancient *Meneida* and **Mándalo** has a Neolithic and Early Bronze Age settlement under excavation. You cross the railway and pass among orchards of peaches and pears. Beyond (83km) **Rizári** the valley becomes lush as you again cross the copious streams of the Vodas below Edhessa's falls. Turns (right, see below) to the archaeological site etc. There is a short steep ascent to the town.

89km **EDHESSA** (Hotels B, C, D, E) is beautifully situated on a steep bluff, facing SE, over which the waters of the Edhesseos fall into the plain of Thessaloníki. The town itself occupies a semi-circular plateau (350m), backed by the foothills of Mt Vermion. Through it flow numerous cascades which inspired the Slav name of **Vodena** (The Waters). Capital of the nome of Pella and seat of a metropolitan, the town (17,128 inhab.) is a favourite summer resort. A commanding situation on the Via Egnatia has always made it strategically important. Industries include the manufacture of carpets, and Edhessa is a prominent trading and agricultural centre. The view takes in the Pindos on the W, Olympos to the SE, and the heights beyond Thessaloníki to the E.

**History**. Until the discoveries in 1977 at Vergina, Edhessa was thought to be the site of ancient *Aigai*, a belief the local inhabitants are disinclined to relinquish. It was a flourishing place in antiquity. During the temporary Bulgarian occupation it was called *Vodena*. In October 1912 the Greek army entered the town. In the Second World War it was again occupied by Bulgarians.

The numerous streams that score the town unite on the E to fall in cascades. The area at the top of the *falls (sign 'Katarraktes') has been turned into an attractive park at the cliff's edge. The drop is 24m, after which the water flows steeply to the plain. The cliffs are covered with luxuriant vegetation, including vines, pomegranites, figs, and nut trees. There are said to be crayfish in the waters. The volume of water is diminished by hydro-electric works. Under the falls is a cave with stalactites. Edhessa also has several worthwhile industrial buildings, mostly on this side of town, including a hemp factory (some of the disused machinery still in place) below the top of the falls. To the W of the park is the old quarter of **Varóssi**. Here Odhós Makedhonomákhon has attractive old houses, also a Cultural Centre (Politistikó Kéntro), in a startling modern building, where you can buy a useful guide *Edessa, City of Waters* (English), 1993. Below in Od. Megálou Alexándrou, from the terrace near the **Archbishop's Palace** there is a splendid *view, with the monastery of Ayia Triadha in the foreground. The church of **Koimísis tis Panayías**, now the archiepiscopal chapel, incorporates antique columns (as does the smaller SS Peter and Paul nearby), probably from a temple on the site, and has a fine ikonostasis. Wall paintings have been revealed in recent investigations. Next to the church is the interesting Parthenagogeió (Girls' School; 1877), now housing a **folk museum**. Sections of the town's medieval walls can be seen in a lane descending to the right. Nearer the centre, off Egnatías, an attractive mosque, the **Yeni Çami** (1904) houses an archaeological collection (not normally open). At the N end of the town in the area of Kiouprí, reached by various pedestrianised streets (including Od. Konstantinoupóleos) from the park by the falls, is a fine single-span **bridge**, of Roman or Byzantine date. The acropolis of the ancient city was on the site of the modern town: sections of the walls have been traced and other finds made.

The walls of the **lower city** were traced in 1968 in the 'Longos' area below the falls. The recent excavations (free; phylax on site; leaflet in English available) near Ayía Triádha are interesting. They are reached by returning along the Thessaloníki road for 2.5 or 5km and then following signs (left turn) for the site or for **Ayía Triádha** monastery (1865, incorporating antique material). The site has well preserved walls, Classical in origin but with extensive Roman and Byzantine repairs and alterations. Much of the visible remains are Byzantine, reusing earlier material. A gate leads to a paved main street with a partly re-erected Ionic colonnade (inscriptions). The second road continues to the hydro-electric works (no adm.) but you can continue part the gate to the reservoir at the foot of the falls. By the huge pipe are the overgrown remains of an Early Christian basilica. A left turn before the lakes takes you to the monastery and the archaeological site.

From Edhessa a road leads N (bus 10 times daily in summer) via **Apsalos** (turning for Skídhra, see Rte 61) to (24km) **Aridhaía** (Hotel D), or **Ardhéa**, a friendly but uninteresting town (4455 inhab.), seat of the eparchy of **Almopías**, in a low well-watered plain hemmed in by the magnificent crests of the Vóras range that form the frontier with former Yugoslavia. Here are grown pimentos, tobacco, and silk. The French built a Decauville railway from Skídhra to serve the area in the First World War; this survived as a passenger line until 1935. To the SE (c 10km) just outside (c 1km on a dirt road) **Khrisí** can be seen a substantial section (wall and towers) of the fortifications of what was probably Byzantine *Moglena* overlooking the River Moglenitsa. In the centre of the site is a Middle Byzantine basilica in a bad state; to the N a cemetery basilica and some graves have been investigated. A road goes on W of Aridhaía via **Loutráki** (Rooms) to **Loutra Loutrakíou** (also known as **Loutrá Pozaríou** or, locally, just **Loutrá** (11km; Hotels B, C, D, E), a large if somewhat seedy hydropathic establishment in a pretty glen with plane trees shading the tumbling waters. Nearby caves have been discovered with ritual carvings. NE of Aridhaía, a road (no through buses) through the mountains via Foustáni, Arkhángelos and Políkastro is the locally preferred route to Thessaloníki.

To **Náousa** and **Vérria**, see Rte 61.

# <u>61</u>

# From Thessaloníki to Vérria (and Edhessa)

**Road**, 75km (46½ miles), leaving the Via Egnatia (Rte 60) at (30.5km) Khalkídhona, and continuing, flat and monotonous, to (75km) Vérria. **Bus** every ½ hour.

**Railway**, 69km (43 miles), 8 trains daily in c 70 minutes; the line branches from the Athens line at (19km) Platí and runs 1.5–5km S of the road most of the way to (69km) Vérria. Beyond Vérria the railway continues N via Náousa to (111km) Edhessa etc.

From Thessaloníki to 30.5km **Khalkídhona**, see Rte 60. The road crosses the Pedhias Kampanias, an exposed and very flat plain, that extends to the Gulf of Thessaloniki; it was once a lagoon into which both the Axios and Aliakmon drained, and as late as classical times was navigable nearly to Pella. The settlement of **Adhendro** ('without trees'), on the railway (left), is aptly named. You cross the **Loudhías**, an artificial river created in 1925 (comp. Rte 60), and enter the ancient district of *Emathia*, a monotonous country populated by herds of goats, from which the modern nome takes its name. 43.5km Turning for **Platí** (3km left), an important railway junction (see above; 2498 inhab.) with a sugar refinery. At 49km the old road to Athens forks left through **Alexándreia** (Hotels D, E), or **Yídha**, a sprawling agricultural town (pop. 12,109). 66km You cross the sluice by which the waters of the Vodas are diverted to the Aliakmon. At **Néa Nikomídhia**, 4km N, a neolithic settlement (now little to see) was excavated in 1961–64 by the British and American Schools. Radio-carbon tests have given a date of c 6200 BC, by far the earliest Neolithic known on the Greek mainland. Houses of two periods were found, arranged round a central structure which yielded female idols and serpentine axes. The settlement was fortified. At 72km we pass close to **Vérria station** (right), leave the Verghína road (see below) to the left, join that from Edhessa, and enter Vérria from the north.

75km **VÉRRIA** (Βέροια; pop. 37,858), anciently Βέροια, the *Berea* of the New Testament, is the capital of the nome of Imathia and the seat of a metropolitan. Attractively situated on a travertine terrace (188m) near the E foot of Mt Vermion (skiing facilities) and commanding the plain below. The Tripotamos, a tributary of the Aliakmon, runs through a ravine just N of the town centre. The local cloth industry using hemp and flax spun locally has declined but there is a market (Tuesday) for peaches and apples from the district. There has been much undistinguished modern building but the town well repays a visit as numerous churches, traditional houses and Ottoman buildings survive and the bazaar area (lower part of Vasiléos Konstantínou and side streets) give a good feeling of its original character. On the debit side are a rash of modern cafés (round Eleá) and poor food. A useful guidebook (*Veria*, in Greek and English) published by the Town Council, is available from some bookshops. In difficulty, enquire at Dhimarkhíon.

**Hotels** B, C, D.

**Post Office**, Leof. Mitropóleos (Pl. 1).

**OTE**, Leof. Mitropóleos (Pl. 2).

**Police**, Leof. Mitropóleos (Pl. 3).

**Town Hall (Dhimarkhíon)**, Leof. Mitropóleos (Pl. 4).

**Banks**, Leof. Mitropóleos.

**Railway Station**, 3km N.

**Buses**. Town services from Od. Venizélou, opposite Ayios Antónios. Remainder from bus station (Pl. 18) just below, off Od. Vermíou. To Verghína (9 daily), also to Náousa (frequently) Edhessa (5). To Athens (3) and Thessaloníki (frequently). Also (frequently) from the Plateía Orologíou (K. Rektivan) to Thessaloníki and to Kozáni.

**History**. *Beroea* emerges at the end of the 5C as the second city of Emathia, known from an inscription to have been dedicated to Herakles Kynagidas. It was the first Macedonian city to surrender after the Roman victory of Pydna in 168 BC. Pompey spent the winter of 49–48 BC here. St Paul and Silas, having experienced trouble at Thessalonika, withdrew to Beroea, where the Jews, more noble than those of Thessalonika, searched the scriptures daily (Acts XVII, 10–12). At an early date Beroea became a bishopric. When Diocletian reorganised the Roman colonial empire, he made Beroea one of the two capitals of Macedonia. About the end of the 10C it endured the Bulgar invasions, and in the 14C was occupied by the Serbs. The Turks, who called the town *Karaferiye*, established a military colony here. Many ancient Greek and Roman finds have come from rescue excavations in the town. Elements of the fortification system have been traced on the N, E and S. Fragments of the stadium have been recovered outside the walls to the E and temples are mentioned in Hellenistic inscriptions. Many finds have come from graves, including a cemetery of vaulted rock

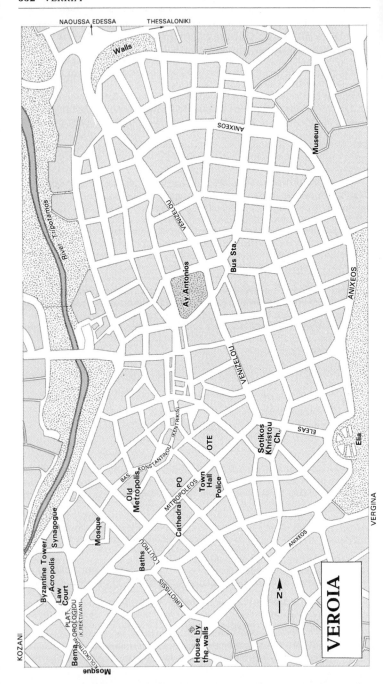

VEROIA

cut chamber tombs of the Hellenistic period just outside the ancient walls to the N, and the large Classical NE cemetery near the railway station.

Near the top of the hill at the entrance to the town (Pl. 20) remnants of the ramparts survive. A **tower**, of pseudo-isodomic construction resembling the Letaia Gate at Thessaloniki has been dated to the 3C AD; among reused blocks are grave reliefs and shield metopes. Buses continue along El. Venizélou to the terminal (Pl. 18), just off the main street opposite the enormous church of Ayios Antonios (Pl. 19), an 1860 rebuilding of a 1000 AD foundation. Venizélou continues to a junction with Leof. Mitropóleos and Eliás. A pleasanter approach to the town centre can be made via Leof. Aníxeos (left after the top of the hill, or walk down Vizaníou from the bus station) which curves round to follow the edge of the plateau (the line of the ancient fortifications) overlooking the plain. The **museum** at Aníxeos 47 (Pl. 17 08.00–15.00, closed Monday), stands in a garden lined with grave stelai of various periods (especially Roman) and other architectural fragments. Inside, ROOM 1 has a plan of Verria with the locations of ancient sites, and a model of a typical rock-cut tomb. Grave groups of the 4–2C BC include fine bronze vessels and terracottas. ROOM 2 has sculpture, mostly Hellenistic grave stelai, one of which, from the Great Tumulus at Verghina, is painted. Inscriptions include the 2C BC gymnasium rules. ROOM 3 has Roman sculpture, also cases of terracottas and glass. The sculpture consists of grave stelai, portraits and mythological figures. Marble table supports have figures of Ganymede and the Eagle, and a winged demon. A new display of the finds from Nía Nikomídhia is in prospect.

Farther on at the bottom of Leofóros Eliás is a belvedere (Pl. 16; pleasant café; view). Elías runs up to meet Venizélou and Mitropóleos at the centre of the town. At the junction is the delightful church of **Sotíras Christós** (Pl. 15; 08.30–13.00, except Mondays) which is 14C with frescoes of the same period by Kallierges. The external arcade was added in the 18C. Mitropóleos, a busy shopping street with most of the major facilities, rises gently past the modern Cathedral of SS Peter and Paul (Pl. 12), with re-used capitals in the narthex, to the Plateía Orologíou (K. Rektivan), site of the Kastro (Pl. 9) see below.

Parallel with Mitropóleos and linking Venizélou with Plat. Orologíou is Od. Vas. Konstantínou (or Kentrikís), which gives more of a flavour of old Verria with its narrow side streets and old houses sloping down to the Tripotamos. At the junction with Perikléous is the 11C **Old Metropolis** (Pl. 10), impressive in spite of its poor state (one side-aisle has been demolished), with Early Christian columns and a minaret. Opposite stands the **plane tree** from which the Turks hanged Archbishop Kallimachos in 1436. Beyond is a mosque (Pl. 11).

On the other side of Mitropóleos, Od. Loútrou leads to a delightful Ottoman bath complex (Pl. 13), well restored externally but the interior not yet accessible. Here Od. Kiriotíssis has old houses and at the very end, where it narrows and descends, a remarkable section of the Roman/Byzantine defences (Pl. 14) supporting a 'modern' house.

Off Plateía Orologíou (K. Rektivan), behind the lawcourts (Pl. 5) is the site of the ancient acropolis. The major visible structure is said to be a Byzantine tower (Pl. 9) incorporating Classical masonry. It appears at least to incorporate a cistern. Nearby is the Jewish synagogue (Pl.8). On the opposite side of the square, a few yards up the first turn off Od. Kolokotróni (Pl. 6) is the so-called **bema** (a fanciful reconstruction of 1961) from which St Paul is said to have preached. Close by is a mosque (Pl. 7; closed).

The numerous churches (about 40 survive, marked by dots on the plan) of wattle and timber construction were the most unusual feature of the lower town. Built during the Turkish domination, they were sited inconspicuously behind houses and their appearance disguised. Formerly they were hard to find. Most of the ramshackle old houses have now been replaced by modern blocks and the churches revealed. They are usually locked and enquiry must be made at the museum or the Ephorate of Byzantine Antiquities at Od. Ant. Kamára no. 3.

The PRINCIPAL EXCURSIONS are to Mt Vermion and to the Macedonian tombs at Verghína and Levkádhia.

**Macedonian tombs** belong mainly to the late Classical and Hellenistic periods. Although subterranean, they were splendid structures, built of local poros stone, with vaulted roofs. The façades of smaller tombs have a pediment or a simply sculptured cornice. Later and grander examples resemble the Classical temple, with columns, entablature, and pediment. The doors were generally of marble and hung on metal hinges. The main chamber may be preceded by an anteroom. Furniture consisted of marble couches or thrones. The walls were usually plastered and painted. The façade may also be frescoed. A substantial number have now been excavated, mostly in Macedonia. Some of the finest and most accessible are those near Veroia.

The road to Verghína (11km; bus 9 times daily) leaves Vérria near the belvedere, passing Lofos Vikellis, with the birthplace of the writer Konstantinos Vikelas (1808–86). The house is preserved. 5km **Ayía Varvára** has a spring and a café. The Pieria Mts stand out ahead. You descend to the **Aliakmon Barrage**, a graceful concrete structure, 320m long, whose 19 piers carry the road across the river. The approach on the N curves to avoid the 3C BC **Temple Tomb** (visible left; no adm.), discovered during construction work. The outer doorway has triglyphs, the inner is white with a yellow moulding. The interior is plastered and painted in bands, white below, black and red above. At the end of the bridge, turn left.

11km **Verghína** (Βεργίνα), a refugee village of 1923, named after a legendary queen of Beroia, replaces a city that existed from the beginning of the Iron Age to Classical times. This is now certainly to be identified with ancient *Aigai*, which Perdikkas, founder of the Macedonian monarchy, made his capital.

The residence of the kings until the seat of government was transferred to Pella, it remained the national sanctuary and the royal burial-place. Here Philip II was assassinated in 336 BC. A tradition that the Macedonian dynasty would perish as soon as one of the kings was buried elsewhere was given point by the chaos that followed the burial of Alexander the Great in Alexandria. The place was pillaged by Gaulish mercenaries left to guard it by Pyrrhus in 274/3 BC.

Recent excavations, directed by Professor Manolis Andronikos until his death in 1992, have had spectacular results, most notably in the discovery of the Tomb of Philip II. Other rich tombs have been excavated and progress made in locating some of the public buldings of Aigai. An excellent and well illustrated survey of the site has been provided by Andronikos in his *Vergina: the Royal Tombs*.

Most visitors will first approach the site of the Great Tumulus, now within the limits of the modern village (signs) and recently opened to the public. Above the tumulus a road leads out of the village to cross a ravine and ascend, past Rhomaios' tomb, to the palace. 'Close below the palace is the theatre. Other monuments including the Tomb of the Throne (near Rhomaios' tomb), the Sanctuary of Eukleia, and Cybele cannot at present be visited. The latter two monuments may have been located in the agora of the ancient city which probably lay in the area below the theatre and to the S of the modern village.

Until excavated, the **Great Tumulus** covered a smaller mound which overlay the Royal Tombs and was probably ordered by Antigonos Gonatas to protect his own tomb and cover the damage caused by the Gauls. Broken tombstones from the Gallic destruction were found in the fill. The four tombs and heroon which lay beneath the smaller mound are now covered by a massive domed hall which the visitor approaches as though entering the tumulus (not, or course, possible in antiquity). The hall contains various explanatory panels. Three of the tombs are of particular interest; the fourth was destroyed. Tomb I (otherwise looted of its contents) has fine wall paintings including a remarkable scene of the Rape of Persephone by Hades. Greatest interest has, however, attached to Tomb II, unlooted and with a hunting scene over the façade, which most authorities now consider to be the burial place of Philip II. Within were found two marble sarcophagi containing burial caskets of gold, and all the panoply of royal burial: purple and gold cloth (now finely restored) shrouding the bones, gold wreaths, sceptre, miniature ivory portraits from a throne or bier (apparently representing members of the Macedonian royal family), armour, weapons, a ceremonial shield with exquisite decoration, and silver and bronze vessels. The **··**finds are on display in Thessaloniki. Apart from the archaeological dating and the general character of the contents, a remarkable reconstruction of the features of the male occupant of the tomb, using forensic methods

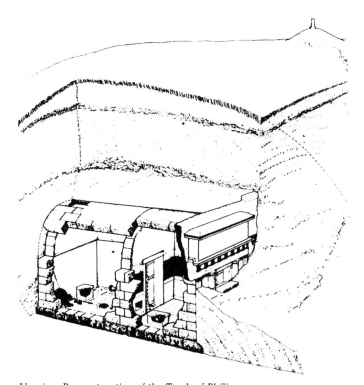

*Vergina. Reconstruction of the Tomb of Philip*

(J.H.S. 1984; A.J.A. 1990), has indicated a horrific eye wound such as Philip is known to have suffered in his lifetime. Tomb III (the Prince's Tomb) has architectural details painted in blue and red, moulded shields on the façade and, in the interior, a frieze of riders and chariots. It may have contained the remains of Alexander IV, son of Alexander the Great and Roxane who was assassinated in 310 BC at the age of 13.

East of the village extends the vast **Tumulus Cemetery** of the Early Iron Age (10–7C BC) partly excavated by Prof. Andronikos in 1952–61. Of the hundreds of mounds, many were disturbed in Hellenistic times, but intact burials have yielded iron swords, bronze ornaments (including a triple double-axe amulet), Lausitz ware, and Protogeometric pottery.

The **Palace of Palatitsa** (so-called after the old village to the NE at its first discovery in 1861 by a French expedition) is situated on a low hill to the SE marked by a large oak-tree. Excavations of the Greek Archaeological Service in 1937–40 were resumed in 1954–61. The building, roughly 90m square, dates probably from the reign of Antigonus Gonatas and was destroyed by fire. The N side, where the lower courses of the outer wall are well preserved, is littered with poros drums and capitals. A triple **propylaia** leads through the E wing to a central **peristyle** of pilasters (16 by 16) with double engaged columns. On the S side is a **mosaic floor** finely executed in polychrome pebbles. A secondary court, with ancillary rooms is situated to the SW. There is a bathing establishment to the NE.

Below the palace and 100m to the N a small 4C theatre was discovered in 1982. The location of this in relation to the palace closely accords with the account of the assassination of Philip which took place in the theatre of Aigai in 336. The theatre probably lies at the edge of the **agora**, presently being investigated. 80m N is the Sanctuary of Eukleia where an inscription marked a dedication to the goddess by Philip's mother. A Sanctuary of Cybele and other public buildings are also being studied.

By the road back to the village is *Tomb of Verghína** (or Rhomaios' Tomb; roofed; excavated in 1937), a Macedonian temple tomb with an Ionic façade closed by two pairs of marble doors. Within, a marble *throne**, 1.8m high, with a footstool, has arms supported by carved sphinxes and a back with painted decoration. Close by is the recently (1987) discovered Tomb of the Throne which contained a painted and gilded marble throne, with a painted scene of Hades and Persephone on the back panel. Also found here were rich graves (pits and cists) of the 6 and 5C. Other Macedonian tombs have been excavated further to the E, near the village of Palatítsa.

FROM VERRIA TO EDHESSA, 47km (29 miles). From Ay. Antonios the road leads N across the Tripotamos, through industrial suburbs. Road and railway run together through the plain with the mountains to the left. 13km **Náousa station** lies off the road (right). The flourishing town (19,794 inhab.) of **Náousa** (Hotels B, E; bus from the station) stands 6.5km W on a travertine terrace between two tributaries of the Arapitsa, one of which falls near by in a cascade. The town is renowned for its full red wine, its peaches, and its silk. Naousa is a corruption of **Nea Augousta** and has been known to the Turks as **Agustos**; it occupies an ancient site, perhaps that of *Mieza* (but see below). The town was destroyed in 1821 and again suffered in 1944–48 but its narrow streets remain on an old plan. In its carnival masked dancers with scimitars symbolise the oppression of the Janissaries. Near the modern church of **Ayía Paraskeví** a fine park looks out over the plain and there is a small military museum. The wooden **Ayios Dhimítrios** is built over an ancient structure. **Kefalóvrisi**, off the road from Naoussa to Kopanós, where a dressed rockface (with beam holes) backs a terrace (cave shrines etc.) overlooking the Isvoria springs, may be the site of the **nymphaion of Mieza** where Philip established the School in which Aristotle taught Alexander. The setting is fine and the site has been recently tidied.

14km **Kopanós** has an important cemetery (4C to Hellenistic, including a Macedonian tomb) which was discovered in 1977. The settlement with which it is to be associated may lie beneath the modern village. 16km **Levkádhia**, a hamlet W of the road, has given its name to three Macedonian tombs, lying near the main road before you reach the village turn. The discovery of a building with mosaics S of the village and another on a hill near the Arapitsa suggest that Levkádhia was a place of some importance, and is another candidate for ancient *Mieza* where Aristotle taught (see above). Signposted (right, on a by-road crossing the railway) is the *Great Tomb** (or Tomb of Judgement), protected by a concrete hangar. This is the largest Macedonian Tomb so far found.

On the **façade** two outer pilasters and four Doric fluted columns support an entablature with painted metopes and triglyphs and a frieze in bas-relief depicting a battle between Macedonians and Persians. A second (Ionic) story, rising above the vault, has seven false doors surmounted by a pediment (of which only fragments survive). Two life-size frescoes in vivid colours represent (left) the deceased with Hermes Psychopompos and (right) Aiakos and Rhadamanthys, the judges of the Underworld. An ante-chamber leads to a square barrel-vaulted **chamber** with painted panels between engaged pilasters. Rows of nails remain in situ where presumably garlands were hung. The tomb is dated to the beginning of the 3C BC. 200m further on is the *Tomb of the Flowers** (excavated 1971; 3–2C BC) with fine floral and figural paintings. Behind an Ionic façade are two chambers. Although the tomb was robbed, a marble sarcophagus was found and ivory fragments apparently of mythological figures decorating a casket. Returning to the main road 200m farther N (sign), is the accessible 'Kinch' Tomb, and 300m beyond this (left) the much smaller vaulted **Lyson Kallikles Tomb** of the early 2C BC, with a plain exterior. It contained the urn burials of three related families. Their names are inscribed on the niches inside, and the walls are painted with garlands and decorative panels.

At (32km) **Skídhra** (see Rte 60) the road joins the Via Egnatia. 47km **Edhessa**.

**Mt Vermion** (2027m) is the most densely forested mountain in Greece, with beech, oak, chestnut, pine, hazel, whitethorn, cornel-cherry, and evergreen maquis, in which dwell roedeer, red deer, and wild pig. It was a centre of resistance in the Second World War (see N.G.L. Hammond, *Venture into Greece*, 1983). Approach is from Verria (farther, but newer road) or from Náousa, where a steep road mounts to (18km) **Selí** (refuge, 18 beds; ski lifts; Hotel B at Káto Vérrio), a village (1420m) on the NE slope. Here winter sports are held from mid January to mid March (Greek ski championship in late February). In late spring and summer delightful walks can be taken on the mountain.

# 62

# From Thessaloníki to Kozáni and Kastoriá

**Road**, 221km (137 miles). To (30.5km) Khalkídhona, see Rte 60; then to (75km) Vérria, see Rte 61. Beyond Verria broad road through magnificent mountain scenery.—92km Kastanéa. 135km Kozáni, then through relatively flat upland country.—155km Siátista turning.—178.5km Neápolis.—209km Argos Orestikón.—220.5km Kastoriá. **Bus** frequently to Kozani; 5 daily from Kozani to Kastoria.

**Railway** to Kozáni (222km), 5 through trains daily in c 4 hours. The line follows the road to (69km) Vérria (see Rte 61), then turns N to (111km) Edhessa (comp. Rte 61), where it runs W following the road described in Rte 63 to (162km) Amíndaio. Here the line divides, the S branch following Rte 58 to Kozáni.

From Thessaloníki to (30.5km) **Khalkídhona**, see Rte 60; then to (75km) **Vérria**, see Rte 61. Beyond Vérria, which can be by-passed, the road winds up past army depots, a reservoir, with a hydro-electric station, and a restaurant with trout pools. 80km **Tripótamos**. Orchards clothe the rolling hills and stalls of produce line the road as it climbs into the Tripótamos valley, which divides the outlying spur of **Máti Poulioú** (left; 1238m) from the main Vermion range. 84km **Yeoryianí** A turning (left) crosses a ridge to **Lefkópetra** (5km) with scanty remains of an ancient temple. There are offensive signs of marble quarrying. The road clings to a shelf on the N side of the narrowing valley, beautifully clothed with oak and beech woods. 89km Spring. 92km **Kastanéa** has a magnificent position on the hillside (902m) amid orchards of apples and nuts. Above the village stands the **Monastery of Panayía Soúmela**, built by refugees who brought with them (c 1930) from the Soumela monastery in Pontus an ikon of the Virgin attributed to St Luke. It is a focus of pilgrimage on 15 August. As you cross the shoulder of Máti Poulioú, from a height of 1081m there is a tremendous **⋆⋆**view into the Aliakmon Valley; the river, just over 3km away, is more than 914m below. Beyond it the jagged heights of **Piéria** tower to 2190m. The road continues to climb, with retrospective views from the steep turns towards Kastanéa, before turning away from the Aliakmon to reach (100km) its summit (1359m) on Dhiavasis Kadovas, a S ridge of Vérmion. From (101.5km) **Zoödhókhos Piyí** (1359m; restaurants), which is named after a small church built above a spring, Mt Olympos is seen to the E behind Piéria. The road descends by a spectacular ladder and vertiginous curves. At (108.5km) **Polímilos**, with water mills, it enters a gentle upland valley with the **Skopós Hills** to the S; the villages lie off the road on their slopes. On the edge of the plain at (113km) **Voskokhorió** a small Christian basilica (? early 6C) came to light in 1935. At **Akríni** (11km right) another, with delightful animal mosaics, was uncovered in 1959. 121km **Ayios Dhimítrios** has a power station. The road descends gently with long straight stretches, running along the S edge of the drained Kítrini Límni (Rte 58) to (127km) **Dhrépano**. Signs for Ioannina (right) and, 1km further, Lárissa/Athens (left) give access to bypass routes. Joining the railway from the N (Rte 58) and the main Lárissa road, you enter (135km) **Kozáni** (Rte 58).

For Kozáni and thence to **Lárissa** and to the former Yugoslav frontier (**Níki**), see Rte 58; to **Grevená**, see below.

Beyond Kozáni the road maintains a fairly constant level just below 610m all the way to Kastoriá, keeping company to **Siátista** with an unfinished railway planned to link Kozáni with Kalambáka. 141km **Vateró**. A flat-bottomed pass opens between the **Voúrinos** and **Askion** ranges, to N and S. 155km **Kháni Bára**. Turning for Siátista (right; 3km).

Siátista (Hotel C) seems to have been settled in the 16C and to have become a caravan centre of merchants trading with Vienna. In the 18C as *Sisechte* it was noted for its wines, tanneries and for industry, but after 1821 gradually declined. Since the vineyards were destroyed by phylloxera in 1928–35, it has reverted to the fur trade. The town (5688 inhab.), made up of the two districts of **Khóra** and **Yeráneia**, is (like Kastoria) noted for its 18C houses, timber-framed with jutting balconies and gabled roofs. The **Poulikos Mansion**, with an elaborately panelled and frescoed interior, was restored in 1962, and others may also be visited. The church of **Ayios Dhimítrios**, founded in 1647, was rebuilt after a fire in 1910; **Ayía Paraskeví** dates from 1677. The **Manousákis Library**, left to the town by the 19C scholar, contains local archaeological finds.

158.5km A **restaurant** stands at the parting of the ways to Kastoriá and Grevená.

FROM THE SIATISTA FORK TO GREVENÁ AND KALAMBÁKA. Road, 98km; bus from Kozáni 6 times daily to Grevená, once to Kalambáka. The road turns S to cross the Aliakmon, continuing sinuous and undulating below the foothills of the Pindus W of the river. Beyond (16km) **Vatólakkos** you enter the valley of the Greveniotikos. 28km **Grevená** (601m; Hotels C, D) is the chief town (9345 inhab.) of a mainly agricultural nome that corresponds roughly to the ancient district of *Elimeiotis*. It has a school of forestry. The fair of Ay. Akhillios, starting on the first Monday in June, maintains an ancient tradition. The town, at the confluence of two branches of the Greveniotikos, is the focal point of numerous mountain tracks. It was a centre of Greek learning in the Middle Ages and the headquarters of the Armatoles, an irregular militia of Byzantine times, kept up by the Turks, from whose ranks arose the patriotic brigand, or klepht. A comparable situation arose in 1944–49 with the German retreat, when ELAS supporters fought the established government. Descending into a curious eroded grey gorge you cross the Venetikos. The remains of two previous bridges can be seen. The road climbs again into wooded uplands with views towards the Aliakmon. 60km Road to Dheskáti and Elassón (see Rte 58). 71km **Ayiófillo** is on the low watershed that divides the Aliakmon basin from that of the Pinios. By-road (left) to Dheskáti (see above). At 88km near the Metéora, you join the road from Ioánnina (Rte 51B). 98km **Kalambáka**.

The road turns NW into upland country, drained by the upper Aliakmon. There are many villages. 165km **Midhrókastro**. Far to the W is **Smolikas**, usually snow capped. 168km **Kalonéri**, as its name suggests, heralds a greener and more fertile countryside. A series of Bailey bridges carry the road across the Aliakmon and its tributaries. 178.5km **Neápolis** (pop. 1889; Hotel C), makes cheese.

The Kastoriá road recrosses the Aliakmon and winds amid slopes clad with oak. 195km **Vogatsikó**, a pretty small town on seven low wooded hills, below the bluish-grey mountain (1361m) of the same name, sits above a gorge. The road runs along the hillside above the beautiful valley. Beyond (201km) **Kostarázi** where there is a military garrison, a concrete bridge crosses the emissary from Lake Kastoria that feeds the Aliakmon. You by-pass (209km) **Argos Orestikón**, an important garrison town (pop. 6653) with the airport of Kastoriá and a military air-field on the late Roman site (some walls) of *Diocletianoupolis*. It is noted for the manufacture of 'flokkates' and 'kilimia', varieties of woollen carpet. The road surmounts a low rise and descends to (215km) **Dhispílio**, on Lake Kastoria, meeting the road from Edhessa (Rte 63). Kastoria is seen across an arm of the lake. There is a large military cemetery.

**Lake Kastoria** (**Límni Kastoriás**), or **Lake Orestias**, 620m above sea level, and c 6.5km long by 5km wide, is almost divided into two by a peninsula projecting from the W shore. On the neck of this the town is built. The lake, which varies in depth from 7.5m to 15m, is fished for carp, tench, and eels. In summer the waters are hot, turbid, and often covered with a green film, and frogs keep up an incessant chorus; in winter the lake is often frozen. Birds abound and adders are not uncommon round the shores. Traces of a Prehistoric lake dwelling were found on the S shore in 1940. The circuit (road, 32km, almost at lake level) can be made by car comfortably in an hour. The surrounding mountains are attractive, as are the apple orchards at the N end.

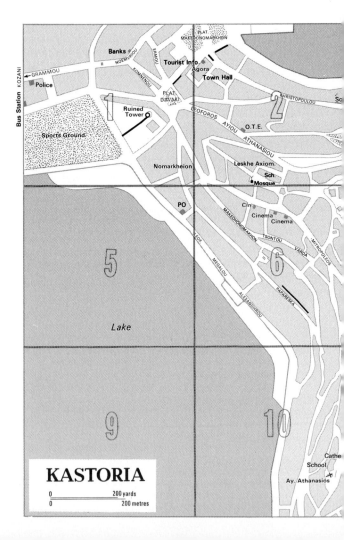

221km **KASTORIÁ** (Καστοριά), the seat of a metropolitan and capital of a nome, is delightfully situated on the isthmus of a peninsula. Many of its 14,775 inhabitants are occupied in the fur trade, and are especially skilled in matching and joining rejected pieces of mink imported from abroad. Although the character of the town has been altered by the construction of modern blocks, some of their large houses, ('arkhontiká' of the 17–18C ), with workshops on the ground floor, survive scattered amid trees and approached by narrow cobbled ways of the Turkish period when the town was known as *Kesriye*. Storks nest on the roofs. Of the 72 churches for which the town was noted, 54 survive; seven of the Byzantine period and about 30 others of medieval date were scheduled in 1924 as ancient monuments.

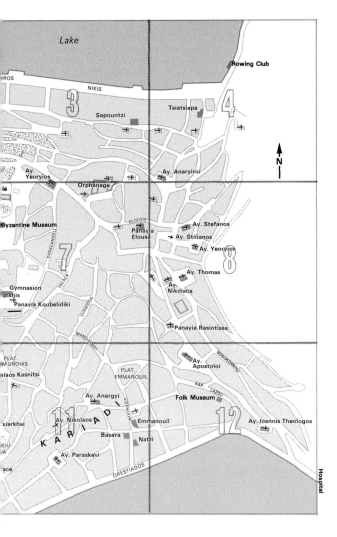

With one exception the Kastorian churches are basilican, the earliest with two low aisles while the later ones are without. The naves are barrel-vaulted. Exteriors are either decorated with crude patternwork (including chi-rho symbols) in tile, or plastered and frescoed. Most churches are kept locked. Keys are either at nearby houses or with the phylax and enquiry must be made. There are a **Folk Museum** (in Kapetán Lázou, off Orestiádhos) and a **Byzantine Museum**, with ikons (next to Xenía Hotel, off Athanasíou). The town is subject to sudden winds and changes of temperature.

**Airport**. 10km SE (at Argos Orestikón) with flights to/from Athens.

**Hotels**, A, B, C, D. **Restaurants** near the Káto Agorá.

**Post Office**, 19 Mitropóleos; **OTE Centre**, 19 Ay. Athanasíou. **Tourist Police**, 25 Grammón. **Olympic Airways Office**, Megálou Alexándrou 15; service to Athens three times weekly direct (flights in the opposite direction are via Kozáni). **Banks** in the lower town.

**Buses** frequently to Argos Orestikón; regularly to Kozáni; daily to Amíndaio; also to Thessaloníki, via Edhessa (and once via Kozáni); daily to Flórina; to Athens, etc.

**Carnival** at Epiphany (6–8 January); Anniversary celebration of liberation from the Turks, 11 November.

**History**. The ancient *Keletron*, mentioned by Livy (xxxi, 40), probably occupied the hill Vigla above the shoreward suburb. It was captured in 200 BC after a siege by the Roman consul, P. Sulpicius Galba. Removed to the present site, the town was renamed *Justinianopolis*, according to the contemporary Procopius, after its refounder, but soon called *Kastoria* after the beavers that haunted the lake. The town was occupied by the Bulgars of Tsar Samuel in 990–1018 until freed by Basil II. It was surprised and captured in 1083 by Robert Guiscard from an English garrison of 300 men. Bohemond spent Christmas 1096 here, having crossed the Pindus by a route of his own. Disputed in the 12C between the despots of Epirus and emperors of Nicaea, Kastoria enjoyed a period of prosperity under Michael Paleologus. The town continued to thrive under the Serbs who held it in 1331–80. After five years of Albanian rule, it fell to the Turks in 1385 who remained its masters until 1912. A colony of Jews continued trade with Vienna and Constantinople, and the fur industry has flourished for 500 years. It was the Greco-American base for the final campaign against rebels of the Grammos and Vitsi Mountains in the severe winter of 1949.

The **bus terminal** (Pl. 1) marks the entrance to the town. Some remains of the Byzantine **ramparts** that guarded the neck of the isthmus can be seen from Plateía Dhaváki, named after a hero of 1940 (statue). Odhós Mitropóleos, the main street of the town, runs SE past the post office. Steps mount left past the little **Taxiárkhis** (Pl. 7) by the gymnasion to the **Panayía Koubelídhiki**, an 11C triconchial church with a high central drum. The frescoes date from the 13–16C. Farther along, off the triangular Plateía Omónoias, is **Ayios Nikólaos Kasnítsis** (Pl. 6), a single-chamber wood-roofed chapel with a semicircular apse. The late 12C frescoes are in a bad state of preservation but include a large number of images from the Orthodox Festival cycle. N of the door leading to the nave is depicted the donor of the church, Nikephoros Kasnitzi the Magistros, with an inscription. S of the door is his wife, Anne.

The left fork goes on to the Plateía Pávlou Melá. The **Taxiárkhai of the Metropolis** (Pl. 11) is a small three-aisled basilica with fragments of 10C frescoes in the diakonikon and prothesis. The remainder of the interior frescoes (1359) were executed by the monk Daniel and include the Dormition of the Virgin at the W end of the nave. The external frescoes represent people buried in the church in the 15C with, over the door, a 13C Virgin and Child. In the narthex is Melas' tomb. Beyond the ornate 19C cathedral, with detached belfry, is **Ayios Athanásios** (Pl. 10; key at No. 27, to the left), built in 1384–85 by Stoias and Theodore Musaki, members of the ruling Albanian family. In the contemporary frescoes the saints are depicted in Byzantine princely or military costume; above are scenes of the Life and Passion of Christ.

Returning to Omónoia Square, take the right fork. **Odhós Mandakási**, a pretty lane to the right, descends to the unspoilt **Karíaki** quarter near the S shore. Here three excellent examples of **Arkhontiká** (the 18C Natzes house has fine painted ceilings) lie to the SE of **Ayioi Anáryiroi** (Pl. 11), an over-restored church with an unusual W gallery; its screen, carved and gilded, has panels of topographical scenes. The lakeside avenue leads to Ayios Ioánnis Theólogos, (Pl. 12) from where you can follow the main road through the town. **Ayios Apóstoloi** (Pl. 12) was frescoed by Onouphrios in 1545. Of the group of churches just to the N (Pl. 8) **Ayios Nikólaos by Ay. Thomás** has been restored since it was hit by an Italian bomb in the Second World War; the frescoes date from 1663. **Ayios Stéfanos** is a small high and narrow barrel-vaulted basilica with a semi-hexagonal apse containing some poorly preserved frescoes from the 10C in the narthex and in the W part of the nave. The remainder have been assigned to the late 12C. In the adjacent **Ayios Yeóryios** (rebuilt under the Turks) the Normans assembled to give themselves up to the Emperor Alexis in 1085. **Ayioi Anáryiroi Várlaam** (Pl. 4), a small but very high three-aisled, barrel-vaulted and wood-roofed basilica with a semicircular apse, is the oldest church in Kastoria. It contains fragments of early 11C frescoes in the narthex (Constantine, a donor; SS Constantine and Helen; SS Basil and Nicholas). The remainder of the frescoes were executed by two different painters and are assigned to the late 12C. The scene of Jesus and Nathaniel is one rarely depicted in Byzantine art. Its screen is also decorated.

Below the Xenia Du Lac (Pl. 7) in a garden overlooking the lake, stands a statue of Athanasios Khristopoulos (1772–1847), a native poet. Odhós Ayíou Athanasíou returns to the Plateía Dhaváki, whence you can follow the **Byzantine Wall** to the Káto Agorá. The covered market faces the Plateía Makedhonomákhon (Pl. 2), laid out to celebrate Gen. James Van Fleet, head of the US Military Mission to the Greek Army (1948–50). At the little quay, with a fish market, can be seen the curious wooden boats peculiar to the lake designed in an ancient tradition.

The lakeside road (or walk) provides fine *views of the surrounding mountains. Leaving the town on the NE by Leof. Níkis, it is about an hour's walk to the **Moní Panayía Mavriótissa** , which is a one-aisled wood-roofed church with a semicircular apse. The frescoes from the original decoration of the building which are on the E and S walls of the nave and on the E wall of the narthex, as well as part of its exterior wall, are assigned to the early 13C. They have an interesting miniature quality. The two headless figures in the upper register to the left of the Tree of Jesse on the exterior of the S wall are variously identified as the Emperor Alexius (1081–1118) and his son John II, or as Michael VIII (1259–82) with his brother John Palaeologus. On its SE side is attached the chapel of **Ayios Ioánnis Theólogos** in which there are 16C frescoes. You can return (slightly longer) by continuing round the rocky peninsula to the SE corner of the town and Od. Orestiádhos.

At **Omorphoklissiá**, formerly Gallista, 19km SW of Kastoriá, is the church of Ayios Yeóryios, restored in 1955. A small rectangular structure, built in the 11C, it was extended under Andronikos II (inscription). In the exo-narthex survive vigorous frescoes of seven saints from the beginning of the 14C, as well as an old wooden statue of St George.

# 63

# From Kastoriá to Edhessa

## A.   Via the Stená Kleisoúras (Amíndaio)

**Road**, 125.5km (78 miles), crossing (30km) the steep Kleisoúra Pass.—61km Mnemeía Pesónton Crossroads (4km W of Amíndaio; the km posts on this road show distance from Amíndaio). You turn left on to the main Kozáni–Níkı road (Rte 58).—69km Kírli Dervén Pass (easy). At (75km) Vévi, you join the road from Flórina (Rte 63B).—122.5km Edhessa. **Buses** four times daily in 3½ hours continuing to Thessaloníki; to Amíndaio also daily (different times).

Leaving Kastoriá by the Kozáni road (Rte 62) you bear left at (5.5km) **Dhispílio** and skirt the marshy edges of the lake. The road ascends the valley of the little Xeropótamos and, just short of (23km) **Vassileiás**, climbs out of the valley to the E by a zigzag (retrospective *views of Lake Kastoria), where it becomes narrow and mountainous. Beyond (26km) **Vérga**, a grim alpine village, the hills are eroded by water-courses. Rockfalls may be encountered. The **Stená Kleisoúras** is a steep and isolated saddle between Mt Vérbista (at the S end of the Vernon range) and Mt Moríki (the N extension of Askion). 30km The summit (1180m) is marked by a stone arch. **Kleisoúra**, where the church of Ayios Dhimítrios has a carved wooden templon of the 15C, stands a little higher to the right. The view into the Aspropótamos plain to the E is not beautiful. The descent, less abrupt, follows the slopes of Vérbista. **Varikó** (reached via Kleisoúra) is seen in a deep valley below. A low saddle takes the road into the Mesikantítsa valley. The summit of Mt Vítsi, scene of much fighting in 1947–49, is seen to the left, while ahead the horizon is closed by the Vóras range, an enormous vista of mountains rising to 2438m on the frontier, 40km away. 39km **Lékhovo** enjoys cool springs on the oak-clad slope of Vérbista. A monument to Vanghelis (died 1904), leader of a nationalist band, stands by the road near the village of **Aspróyia** (left). 47km **Sklíthro**. The road, still shut in by hills, runs straight and level in the Stara valley to (53km) **Aetós**, from which a plain with cornfields extends SE towards Perdíkkas. 61km **Mnemeía Pesónton crossroads** (Rte 58).

Ahead the road continues (with a turn for the archaeological site at Pétres, see Rte 58) to **Amíndaio** (3.5km), a railway junction (Hotel E; 2972 inhab.) and headquarters of an armoured group, supposedly named after one of Alexander's generals. It is also known by its former name, Sorovits, for the battle fought here on 22–24 October 1912. In 1941 the railway was blown up before the advancing Germans by British irregular troops led by the author Peter Fleming. The local wines are good. A prehistoric cemetery (222 tombs) yielded valuable finds in 1900. Amindaion may be the *Cellis* of the itineraries. The road continues beside the railway along the shore of the little Lake Petrón to (11km) **Ayios Pandeleímon** on Lake Vegorítis. Road and railway follow the W shore of the lake to close with our route just after **Ayios Spiridón** (see below). The road junction is beyond Arnissa (29km from the crossroads).

You turn left on to the Ptolemaïs–Níkı road (Rte 58), leaving it again (right) after c 13km for (75km) **Vévi**, there to join the road from Flórina. 126km **Edhessa**, see below.

# B.  Via Flórina

**Road**, 136km (85 miles), hilly and winding, passing within 9.5km of the Albanian frontier. (There are no restrictions on the main road, but on by-roads travellers may find police posts where they are discouraged from proceeding). Partly gravel to (35.5km) Trígouno (turning for Préspa Lakes), then asphalt.—65km Flórina. 88km Vévi.—137km Edhessa. **Bus** three times daily to Florina; also from Flórina to Edhessa, regularly.

**Railway** from Flórina to Edhessa (continuing to Thessaloníki), 85km in 2 hours, five times daily. The branch from Flórina joins the line from Bitolj (Rte 58) at Mesonísi in the plain N of the road, passes S of Vévi and traverses the Kirli Derven pass (Rte 58) to Amíndaio. Then it skirts Lake Vegoritis, passing through Arnissa.

From Kastoriá you take the lakeshore road N and quickly turn away left. Climbing into bare hills there is a good retrospective view of Kastoria and its lake. Beyond a ridge, the road descends to the oak-forested upper valley of the Aliakmon, crossed by Bailey bridge. In the river bed are stone breakwaters. 19km **Gávros Police Post**. Immediately before this is a road (right) for **Melás** (15km), formerly Státistan tou Korestíou, where the patriot Pavlos Melas was killed by the Turks in 1904. At 25km you cross the river again by a memorial of the civil war (1948–49) and, soon after, leave (left) the road to **Koritsa** (Korçë; 56km) in Albania (the frontier is closed). At 29km to the right of road is a bust of Christos Kota, a champion of Macedonian Hellenism, burnt alive by the Bulgarians; the near-by village is named after him. The road rises in the fertile small valley of the principal affluent of the Aliakmon, here called the Livadhopótamos. Just beyond (35.5km) **Trígouno** is a police post, where a road (left), signposted to **Laimós** (20km) and **Préspa**, climbs to a saddle overlooking the **Prespa Lakes**.

**Megáli Préspa** is shared between Albania, the former Yugoslavia, and Greece; **Mikrí Préspa** between Albania and Greece only. These high (850m) and remote lakes where the temperature reaches 20° below zero in winter are the habitat of migratory birds who nest especially in the reeds of **Mikrí Préspa**. There are several interesting churches, well described in an excellent booklet on the antiquities of Prespa recently published by the Ministry of Culture (D. Evyenidhou et al., 1991; English translation). 6km from the main road is a turning (left) to **Oxiá** and **Mikrolímni** (5km), the latter on the shore of the smaller lake. Villages to the right include **Platí**, near which is the 16C chapel of Ayios Nikólaos (or Ayía Sotíra) with fine frescoes. At 49km you turn right for **Laimós** (2km), with a 15C chapel of the Ipapandís (some frescoes) and **Ayios Yermanós** (4km), where traditional houses have been restored by EOT as tourist accomodation (also other rooms). In the square, the new church of **Ayios Yermanós** (1882) is joined to and dominates the old which dates from 1006 (restored and repainted in 1743). Some of the earlier fresco decoration survives including a figure of Ayios Yermanós over the original S entrance (late12/early 13C). Below the square, the basilican church of **Ayios Athanásios** (late 18C) has frescoes dated to 1816 by an inscription. The narthex is a 19C addition. The main road crosses **Mikrí Préspa** to **Koúla** where there are cafés and a military post. Beyond the second café the road divides, straight ahead for **Vronteró**, left for **Psarádhes**.

The **Vronteró** branch leads in 2km (track, left) to the jetty where boatmen (contact best made in advance by telephone) cross in a few minutes to the prominent islet of **Ayios Akhíllios**. The church of the village cemetery (Ayios Yióryios) has some 15C frescoes. About ten minutes walk over or round the hill above the landing stage are the prominent remains of the c 1000 AD three-aisled basilica. A tomb in the diakonikon with sculpted cover slab is said to be that of Ayios Akhilleios, Bishop of Larissa. In another tomb was found a piece of silk (10C) with gold embroidered eagles and natural motifs (in Thessaloniki, White Tower). Fragments of the fresco decoration are in the Florina Museum. Towards the E end of the island (the hilltop above marked by a prominent cross) is the **Monastery of the Pórphyra Panagía**. The monastic buildings have disintegrated but the church (founded early 16C) has good frescoes of 1524 (S wall of main church) and two later phases (mid 16C, including the Porphyra Panayia, above entrance to main church) and 1741.

**Psarádhes** (rooms), on a southern inlet of Megáli Préspa, is reached in 6km from **Koúla** (see above). The village is attractive, though many of its fine old houses are in a poor state of repair. From the village boats may be hired for lakeside beaches and for an excursion to view two impressive rock paintings (15C) of the Panayia and, on the shores of the open lake, the 14–15C hermitages of the **Metamórfosis**, the **Mikrí Análipsi** and **Panagía Eleoúsa** with small painted chapels in varying degrees of decay. The hillside opposite Psarádhes, disfigured by an EOT complex, provides a good view of the N and    eaches of the lake.

The road improves. 38.5km **Andartikó**. It continues to climb amid fine beech forests to (48km) the summit of the **Pisodhéri Pass** (1498m; Hotel B) between the Varnoús (Peristéri) and Vérnon ranges. Here there is another police post. On the descent is a splendid vista down the wooded Lerínska valley to Flórina and the plain beyond.

65km **Flórina** (Φλώρινα; 660m; Hotels B, C), with 12,355 inhabitants, is the capital of the nome of Florina. It has an important agricultural school and a small zoo. Near the entrance to the town is a statue of Kota (see above). Old Turkish houses, picturesque and some restored, line the river. The church of **Ayios Yeóryios**, pleasantly situated outside the town, has a view over the plain. Excavations in 1931–34, renewed recently, at **Ay. Pandeleímon**, a hill to the S marked by a large cross and the Xenia hotel (now Hotel Tottis), uncovered the remains of a town built by Philip II (c 352 BC) and burnt in 48 BC in the campaign that ended at Pharsala. The site is close to the road (left) about 200m beyond the hotel. Finds include a metal smelting furnace and a large number of iron objects. This is not *Herakleia Lynkestis*, now surely placed by inscription at Bitolj. Finds are in the museum near the railway station.

The GROUND FLOOR of the **museum** is dominated by Roman reliefs from the area, many with strikingly frontal figures in a late style. The UPPER FLOOR has displays of material from Ay. Pandeleiman and Petres, with a milestone from the Via Egnatia. The Petres finds are particularly interesting (Megarian bowls, iron objects, terracottas, painted plaster) and are accompanied by a topographic model of the site and restored drawings of houses. There is an extensive display (drawings, photographs, information panels in Greek; some original objects) of material from the churches of Prespa. Finds from Ayios Akhíllios include parts of the stone templon of the basilica.

Not far from the archaeological museum, on the other side of the rivers, is an excellent **Gallery of Modern Art** (Μουσείο Σύγχρονης Τεχνης; open daily 18.00–21.00, except Monday), with an excellent collection of works by Greek and European artists. A smaller gallery, in a building formerly used by the Railway authorities, houses a collection of paintings by artists from Florina (open Weds and Sat 18.00–21.00, Sundays 10.00–13.00). Folk material is displayed in the Aristotelis Collection, in the same part of town; and in the Café Dhiethnés.

*Florina was a coveted objective of the guerilla rebels of the Civil War. They failed to take it in May 1947, and their assault on it using 4000 men and artillery, defeated in February 1949, was their last major effort.*

The Thessaloníki road leads E across the Monastir plain. It crosses the railway to the former Yugoslavia, then at 78.5km briefly joins the course of the ancient Via Egnatia which comes in on the left from Bitolj (Rte 58). The ancient road probably turned S through the Kirli Derven pass (Rte 58) to

Amíndaio and crossed the valley now flooded by Lake Vegoritis to rejoin the modern road near Arnissa. At 84km beside an unusual memorial (1917) from the Drina Division to their Serbian brothers, you fork left. 88km **Vévi** (Βεύη). The road traverses an upland plateau in a stony, desolate landscape. Ahead rise the massive outlying peaks of Vóras; behind the nearest (Piperitsa, 1996m) towers the snow-clad **Kaimaktsalán** (2524m). 97.5km **Kélla** (960m) is a stone-built town (980 inhab.) reminiscent of the Scottish highlands; just beyond you have a view (right) down to Lake Petrón. The road winds among scrub covered hills. At a second summit (960m) on the boundary between the nomes of Flórina and Edhessa comes a sudden *view across the N end of Lake Vegoritis to Arnissa. After an enclosed descent the road joins the gorge of a torrent that feeds the lake at Ayios Spiridón to the lakeside.

**Lake Vegorítis** (540m), or **Ostrovo**, is 19km long from N to S, 8km wide (maximum), and in places 49m deep. It is well stocked with fish: lake-trout were successfully introduced from Switzerland in 1958. Off Arnissa, in the N, is an island with remains of a mosque which local tradition claims was once in the centre of a village now submerged. The level of the lake, which was formerly liable to periodic flooding, is controlled by an underground outflow that feeds the Vodas. In ancient times it was much smaller.

113km Crossroads. **Panayítsa** lies 4km N, **Árnissa** 2.5km right on the lake, where there is a trout hatchery. The main road passes behind the town, while the railway hugs the shore. Together they thread the flat Stena Edhessis, joining the canalised **Vodas**, or Edhesseos, near its exit from a marsh lake that feeds it. At (134km) **Ágras** a hydroelectric station was opened in 1954. Here is buried Tellos Agapinos, who fought under the name of Kapetan Agras in the Macedonian struggle and was killed while on a mission under truce to the Bulgarians in 1907. On the descent the valley becomes wide and lush. The railway, seen intermittently across the river between its seven tunnels, crosses a viaduct. 136km **Edhessa**, see Rte 60.

# 64

# Khalkidhikí (Chalcidice) and Mount Athos

The peninsula of *Chalcidice*, modern **Khalkidhikí** (Χαλκιδική), received its name from the number of colonies planted there by the city of Khalkis in Euboea. Geographically it is the most prominent feature of Macedonia, projecting into the Aegean between the Gulf of Thessaloniki on the W and the Gulf of Orfani on the E. It branches into three smaller peninsulas: Kassandra (anciently Pallene), Sithonia or Longos, and Athos (Akte). The Gulf of Kassandra (Toronaios Kolpos) separates Kassandra and Sithonia, and the Singitic Gulf comes between Sithonia and Athos. Other than in the W, along the S coastal plain, and in Kassandra, the interior is wooded and mountainous, the highest point Mt Athos, rising to 2033m. On the landward side the limit of Chalcidice is marked by the lakes E of Thessaloniki, though the nome boundary runs a few miles S of them. Administratively the region is divided into the nome of Khalkidhikí, which comprises the greater part of the peninsula, and Ayion Oros, coterminous with the territory of Athos, which has an autonomous constitution. The inhabitants are mainly engaged in agriculture, though the mines are important and tourism is playing a rapidly increasing role. Many kilometres of new road across the centre of the peninsula, with offshoots southwards into Kassandra and Sithonia, have been built to foster tourist holiday development of the coastal areas. The coasts in the remote past supported flourishing cities, some of them, notably Olynthos, of more than local importance. Finds from the many archaeological sites are in the Thessaloníki and Poliyiros museums. A useful guide with good maps and plans and historical information, available locally in various languages, is I. Papangelos, *Khalkidiki*, Malliaris Paidheia, Thessaloniki, 1982 and later revised editions.

# A.   From Thessaloníki to Ouranópolis

**Road**, 143km (89 miles). **Bus** at least twice daily.

From Thessaloníki to (10km) the Ay. Triádha turn, see Rte 59D (or leave by Egnatías and its eastward extensions). You bear left and pass, soon afterwards, a turning (left) to **Thérmi**, a small place bearing the name of the predecessor of Thessaloníki. The road runs in a cultivated plain dotted with factories. 19km **Loutrá Thérmis**, a small spa with hot springs. To the S **Ayía Paraskeví** has a Macedonian tomb (at Mikrí Toúmba); and a huge Archaic cemetery, largely intact, with splendid finds (in Thessaloníki); to the N, at **Peristéra**, the church of Ay. Andreas has 9C frescoes. 25km **Vasiliká** (tavernas). The village stands (right) on a by-road to **Sourotí**, 5km SW, with mineral waters. The plain changes to a wide valley as you cross the nome boundary, then climb along the N side. 31km Crossroads, with (left; 3km) the **Moní Ayía Anastasía Pharmakolítria**, founded c 888 by Theophano, wife of Leo VI the Philosopher. 39.5km **Galátista**, a mining centre (2571 inhab.), occupying the site of ancient *Anthemous*, was the scene of a Communist massacre in 1945. 48km **Ayios Pródhromos** stands in pleasant upland country. At 50km a right turn onto the old road leads (in 6km) to the Palaiókastro crossroads (for the coast and Políyiros; see Rte 64D).

The road now climbs round the slopes of **Mt Kholomón** (1165m) amid chestnut woods, rising to 1006m on a ridge just below the summit before descending to (86km) **Arnaía**, beautiful centre (2235 inhab.) of a fruit and wine-growing region. At (91km) **Palaiokhóri**, a road runs S to the equally delightful **Megáli Panayía**, a focus of pilgrimage on 15 August (8km) beyond which another descends to the Singhitikos Gulf at **Pirgadhíkia** (27.5km), where there is a possibly Byzantine wall on the peninsula and a medieval tower at Kambos. A further road diverges left at 96km to **Olimbiádha** (19km; Hotels B, C), the ancient *Kapros Limen*, on the Strymonic Gulf, and then along the shore NW to Stavrós (Rte 66). 2km to the E of Olimbiádha, on the peninsula of **Liotópi** (Classical and medieval walls), is the probable site of *Stageira*, birthplace of Aristotle.

At (99km) modern **Stáyira** (tourist pavilion) a recent statue of Aristotle stands amid the ruins of a Byzantine fortress. In the village a Byzantine hall church has been restored. 100km **Stratoníki**, represents the ancient *Stratonike*. In the hills to the S, gold and silver were mined in the 16C; probably the same mines provided the coinage of *Akanthos* in antiquity.

Today iron and magnesite are worked. New forests have been planted on the coastal slopes. 113km Turn for **Stratóni** (1km left; Hotel E; with some ancient remains) and the N.

129km **Ierissós** (Hotels B, C, D, E) is a straggling fishing village (2858 inhab.) on the shore of the bay of the same name. It is a departure point for Mt Athos and there are sightseeing cruises. The ruined medieval watch-tower outside the village to the NW has Hellenic foundations, and reused marbles. Ancient too are the remains of a mole still, in use. The town occupies part of the site of the huge Archaic, Classical and Hellenistic cemetery of *Akanthos*, which extends to the shore, with tombs in the sand. Some of them (4C) were cremations carried out in a clay-lined grave, the clay being fired in the process to create a kind of terracotta coffin. Finds are in Poliyiros Museum. Remains (Classical to Byzantine) of the ancient town lie on low hills immediately to the SE. Fortifications are visible on the E side of acropolis and another stretch (Hellenistic) and a public building, possibly a Prytaneion, have been investigated. *Akanthos* was traversed by Xerxes and seized by Brasidas in his Macedonian campaign. The town was founded from Andros.

The road continues to (133.5km) **Néa Rhódha** (Hotels A, B, C), on the N shore, and to the landing stage of (136km) **Tripití**, on the S shore of the vale of **Provlaka**, as the narrowest part of the isthmus is called. The name is a contraction of Proaulax, the **Canal** (αὔλαξ).

In 480 BC, aware of the disaster that had befallen Mardonius eleven years before, when he lost 300 ships and 20,000 men trying to round the promontory of Athos, Xerxes ordered a canal across the isthmus for the passage of his invasion fleet. The citizens of Akanthos awarded heroic honours to Artakhaies, who died while in charge of its cutting and was given a state funeral by Xerxes. The canal was apparently dug in a hollow between low banks past the town of Sane (long since vanished). Several artificial mounds and substructions of walls can be traced along its course. Its width seems to have been 12–15m. The isthmus is estimated to have risen 14m since the canal was cut. Recent research (B.S.A. 1991 and 1994) promises clarification of the nature of the canal. An alternative theory suggests that only part of the line was true canal, the central part of the crossing being in the form of a trackway.

Beyond Tripití, with views towards the attractive islet of **Amoulianí** (access from Tripití (cars) and Ouranópolis; camping; Hotels B, D), you pass a hotel (A) and reach (143km) **Ouranópolis** (Hotels A–E; tavernas), known also as **Prosfóri**, and from its 14C tower (restored) as **Pírgos**. The fishing village (771 inhab.) built by refugees in 1922, has adopted the name of a lost town founded by Alexarchos, son of Antipater, in 316 BC though it is as likely to be ancient *Dion*. The inhabitants make knotted rugs to Byzantine patterns, a 'tradition' started by an Australian (Mrs J.N. Loch) in 1928. Beyond lies the territory of the Holy Mountain. Boats leave for the S side of the peninsula and there are sightseeing trips.

# B. Mount Athos

The wild, often roadless, and picturesque peninsula of **ATHOS** or Ayion Oros ('Holy Mountain'), anciently known also as *Akte*, easternmost of the three prongs of Khalkidhikí, is connected to the mainland by a low isthmus only 2.5km across (see above). The peninsula is c 50km long and 5 to 10km wide. The area of the nome of Ayion Oros is 339 sq. km. The population, exclusively male, is given by the 1991 census as 1536. The ground rises abruptly from the isthmus to 91m and for the first dozen miles maintains a level of about 180m, for the most part beautifully wooded. Beyond the land becomes mountainous, rising immediately S of **Kariés** (properly **Kariaí**), the administrative capital, to 610m; from here a rugged broken country, covered with dark forests, extends to the foot of **Mt Athos** (2033m), a cone of white limestone which rises in solitary magnificence from the sea. The jackal is still found.

The Holy Community, a kind of monastic republic (see below), is composed of 20 monasteries, of which 17 are Greek, one Russian (Roussiko), one Bulgarian (Zografou), and one Serb (Khiliandari). There is also a Roumanian retreat, but the number of hermitages and cells has dwindled steadily along with the number of monks throughout the century, though the last few years have seen a revival of interest in the monastic life amongst the younger generation and a number of new novices have entered the orders. Divorced from distracting modernity, unaffected by hurry (the Julian Calendar, 13 days behind the rest of Europe, is still in use, and the day divided into Byzantine hours of variable length with sunset as 12 o'clock), the Holy Mountain affords to the devout a glimpse of life wholly dedicated to God, to the weary a welcome, if temporary, retreat from the world, and to the lover of nature and medieval art a treasury of beauty. That visitors are, in a sense, a contradiction of the reason for the community's existence should not be forgotten by the traveller.

**Formalities**. The visitor, who must be male and (unless a theological student) over 21 years of age, must apply through his consul to the Foreign Ministry in Athens or to the Minister for Northern Greece in Thessaloníki for a permit to visit Athos (fee). A letter of introduction from the Metropolitan of Athens or the Archbishop of Thessaloníki is an additional advantage, and members of the clergy should have a written permit from the patriarchate of Constantinople. The documents must be presented immediately upon arrival to the Nomarch at Kariés (now, more usually, at the first port of call). A residence permit (*diamonitírion*), is then issued, which has to be presented at each convent visited (take care to recover it when leaving). Members of conducted groups avoid personal formalities. A special permit is needed for photography. Filming and tape-recording are forbidden.

The gates of the monasteries are open only during the daytime. The visitor will be received with kindness and simple courtesy, lodged (for a maximum of four days), and entertained with fish, vegetables, rice dressed in various ways, cheese, sweet-meats, fruits, and very fair wine made on the mountain. Meat, which few of the monks ever taste, is not to be expected. On 159 days in the year they have only one meal and then eggs, cheese, wine, fish, milk, and oil are forbidden; on the other days they are allowed only two meals. The visitor's contribution to monastic funds on leaving should be at least commensurate with the hospitality he has received. Supplementary rations, purchased before arrival on Athos, are a great advantage.

**Approaches**. **By sea** either from **Ierissós** by boat down the N coast to Iviron or Grand Lavra (daily) or from **Ouranópolis** (at least once daily; calling also at Néa Rhóda) down the S coast to Dhafní. There are two buses daily in summer from Thessaloníki to the ports (see above). The morning bus connects three times weekly with the late-morning boat from Ouranópolis. Telephone numbers of the Limenarkheia are Ierissós: 0377 22576; Ouranopolis 0377 71248. **By land**, Kariés may be reached on foot in c 6 hours though this approach is rarely used and may lead to administrative difficulties.

On Athos, there are buses from the port of **Dhafní** to **Kariés**, and from **Iviron** monastery to Kariés, the latter connecting with the boat from Ierissós. The road from Dhafní to Kariés (bus in 1 hour) was constructed in 1962 for the millenary celebrations. Otherwise the road system is limited and unsophisticated, though some establishments (between Stavronikíta and Grand Lavra on the N coast and between Xeropótamou and Simonópetra on the S, also Ayíou Pávlou) are accessible in this way and there is some scope for hiring basic vehicles in Kariés. Many of the monasteries can be approached by boat (and a walk inland) through intermediate stops on the routes from Ouranópolis and Ierissós to Dhafní and Ivíron/Grand Lavra, and there is a service from Dhafní to Ayía Anna. Ports at the E end of the peninsula are less frequently served. Otherwise travel is on foot. The tracks and roads are confusing and directions should be sought continually. Maps are available but are not always reliable.

**History**. Strabo, echoing Herodotus, says that Pelasgi from Lemnos came to the peninsula, where they founded five cities; Kleonai, Olophyxos, Akrothoön, Dion, and Thyssos. Colonies were also planted here by Eretria. On the isthmus stood the towns of Akanthos and Sane. Of all these only Akanthos is known by any remains. In 480 BC Xerxes dug his canal (see above), and in the time of Alexander the Great Deinokrates, architect of the Temple of Diana at Ephesus, proposed to fashion Mt Athos into a gigantic statue of the world-conqueror.

The fame of Athos rests entirely on its medieval monasteries. Legends of foundation by the Virgin herself, by St Helena, or by one or other Roman emperor of the 4C or 5C, often supported by documents forged in the 18C, seem to have been tacitly abandoned with the official celebration in 1963 of the 1000th anniversary of the founding of the monastic community. It is likely that anchorites lived on the mountain at an earlier time, fugitives, perhaps, from ikonoclastic persecution in 726–842; Peter the Athonite, the most famous of the early monks, is supposed to have lived for 50 years in a cave. Existing **lavras** (λαύρα, cloister or monk's cell) were organised by Athanasios the Athonite, friend and counsellor of the Emperor Nikephoros Phokas, the first historical benefactor of the Holy Mountain. He founded the monastery of the Great Lavra (963 or 961) and instituted the strict rule of the Abbot Theodore. Thereafter foundations multiplied under the protection of the emperors (especially Alexius I Comnenus, who placed them under Imperial jurisdiction), until they reached the number of 40, with, it is said, 1000 monks in each. Andronikos II relinquished his authority to the Patriarch in 1312. The incursions of the Latins, Catalans (1307), Serbs (1346), and Turks caused the abandonment of a few outlying sites, but the importance of Mt Athos was not impaired. It reached its zenith in the 15C, after which a period of decadence set in, followed by reinvigorating reforms. After the fall of Constantinople in 1453 the monks kept on good terms with the sultans, one of whom, Selim I, paid a state visit to the peninsula. Thanks to this political dexterity, the Holy Mountain remained the spiritual centre of orthodoxy. It built its own schools, one of which, that of Vatopedhi, had a famous headmaster, Eugene Bulgaris (1753–59). At the beginning of the War of Independence the community joined the insurgents, but sank defeated under the Turkish yoke.

Despite its seclusion, Mt Athos has always attracted the attention, not necessarily disinterested, of the outside world. The Vatican has frequently, but without success, tried to exercise some influence. Russia was dominant here from 1830 to 1890. In 1912 the peninsula was occupied by Greek troops, and the Treaty of London (1913) proclaimed its independence and neutrality. During the First World War the Allies sent in a detachment and a cultural mission. In 1926 Mt Athos was formed into a theocratic republic under the suzerainty of Greece. During the Second World War a German antiquarian expedition visited the Holy Mountain.

**Organisation**. By a decree of 16 September 1926 the peninsula forms part of Greece but enjoys administrative autonomy, while in church matters it depends on the Oecumenical Patriarch. All monks, of whatever race, become Greek subjects on retiring to Mt Athos; no heterodox or schismatics are admitted. Women are excluded. The Hellenic Republic is represented by a governor having the rank of nomarch, answerable to the Ministry for Foreign Affairs, and by a police force. The administrative autonomy is centred in the Synod, or Holy Council (*Hiera Synaxis*), with its seat at Kariés, comprising 20 deputies (*Antiprósopoi*), one from each convent. The deputies are elected annually in January; and four of them, appointed in rotation, form the *Epistasia*, with executive powers. One of the four takes precedence as the First of Athos (Ο πρώτος του Αθωνος). The Holy Council also exercises financial and judicial authority.

The 20 convents are divided into two categories; *coenobite* (κοινοβιακαί; 'living in common') and *idiorrhythmic* (ιδιόρρυθμοι; 'eccentric', 'going their own way'). In the eleven coenobite convents all members are clothed alike, pool their resources, and live on the same meagre fare in the common hall or refectory (*trápeza*). The monks of the nine idiorrhythmic convents enjoy a milder rule. They live apart from their fellows, though their convents may have refectories, and they have no property in common.

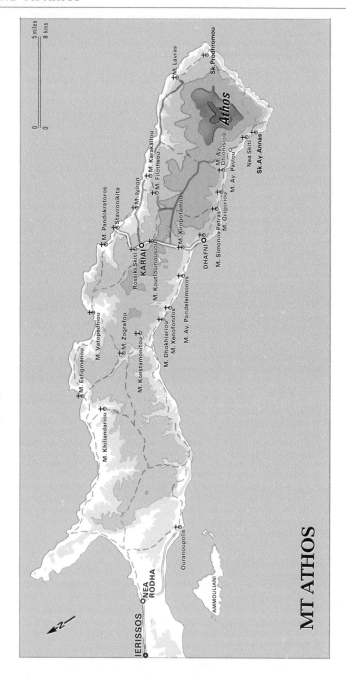

5 miles
8 kms

M. Lavras
Sk Prodhromou

Athos

M. Karakállou
M. Filotheou
M. Iviron
M. Av. Dhionísiou
Nea Skíti
Sk Ay Annas
M. Pandokrátoros
Stavroníkita
M. Ay. Pávlou
Rossik.Skíti
KARIaı
M. Xiropotámou
M. Grigoriou
M. Simonos Petras
DHAFNI
M. Koutloumousíou
M. Estigménou
M. Vatopedhíou
M. Zográfou
M. Dhokhiaríou
M. Xenofóndos
M. Konstamonítou
M. Ay. Pandeleímonos
M. Khiliandaríou
Ouranoúpolis
AMMOULIANI
MT ATHOS
N
IERISSOS
NEA RODHA

Each monk provides his own clothes and obtains his food from his own resources. All of them attend services for at least 8 out of the 24 hours. These include Mass (*Leitourgía*), Vespers (*Hesperinón*), Compline (*Apódheipnon*), and Nocturnal Office (*Nykterinón*) which may on occasion last throughout the night and even exceptionally for 24 hours. As well as the convents, there are *anchorites*, who live apart in cells, some of them well-nigh inaccessible; *sarabaites*, groups of two or three hermits living in hermitages or small houses; and *gyrovakes*, mendicant and vagabond monks. The small retreats and cells have various names, such as *skeítai* (σκήται) *kelliá*, *kathísmata*, etc.

Each convent is administered by an abbot (*hegoúmenos*), elected for life or for a definite period assisted by two or three coadjutors (*epítropoi*) and by a Council (*Synaxis*) of Elders (*Proistámenoi*). There is also a class of inferior monks (*paramikroí*), who do manual labour. The monk begins as a novice (*dhókimos*, or *rasofóros*, from the name of his black gown). In the next three years he becomes crusader (*stavrofóros*) or *mikróskhima* (wearer of short coat); then *megalóskhema* (wearer of long coat; this coat has elaborate symbolic embroidery). All the monks are bearded and wear their hair long, either hanging down or tucked into a bonnet known as a *skouphiá*; their normal dress is the *zostikón*, a black gown with a leathern girdle.

Among the oldest and most strictly observed of the rules is that of Constantine Monomachus (1060), which forbids access to 'every woman, every female animal, every child, eunuch, and smooth-faced person'. This rule, relaxed in 1345, was confirmed in 1575, 1753, and 1780, and is still officially in force, save that it is no longer incumbent upon a visitor to be bearded. She-cats and hens are however now openly tolerated; some pig-breeding is indulged in; and the ban on young boys is not always strictly enforced.

The coenobitic monastery resembles 'a compound of the walled town and the galleried inn' (Sherrard), usually in the form of a rectangle and guarded by towers. The entrance is through a door at one of the four corners. The principal building in the middle of the enclosure, is the **katholikón**, or communal church, cruciform with double narthex and several cupolas. Between the church and one of the short walls is the **phiále**, a canopied stoup containing holy water. Built into the short wall beyond is the apsidal **trápeza** (refectory), with an ambo from which a monk reads during meals, and, near the seat of the hegoúmenos, a platter for the consecrated bread. Against the opposite short wall is the **archontaría**, or guest-chamber. The monks' cells, adorned with porticoes and balconies, line the long walls.

**Art**. Though many treasures, particularly classical manuscripts, have been pillaged, burnt, neglected, or sold in the past, Athos is still rich in minor works of art. Little except charters and chrysobuls survive from the earliest times, but the archives (now jealously guarded) of Grand Lavra, Vatopedhi, and Iviron, and the library of Vatopedhi, are of the first importance. Reliquaries, chalices, and illuminated MSS survive in quantity. In the major arts of architecture and painting, if there is not much of the first rank, there is sufficient of interest and merit to give a comprehensive picture of the late-Byzantine scene. The principal features in which Athonite churches diverge from general Byzantine practice are the apsidal ends to the transepts and the double narthex, divided into **líti** and **mesonyktikón**, often flanked by side chapels. Two schools of painting are represented. The **Macedonian School** skilfully adapts painting to architectural media. Its protagonists are Manuel Panselinos (early 14C) and his contemporaries. The **Cretan School**, affected by the art of Italy and S Germany, was founded c 1535 by Theophanes and continued by Frangos Kastellanos of Thebes. Some discoloured frescoes have been repainted from time to time.

Orthodox decoration, intended to illustrate Church doctrine, has become traditional and stereotyped. The katholikon of Dokheiaríou is a complete example. In the top of the dome is the Almighty in glory, surrounded by the Virgin, John the Baptist, prophets, and angels. In the three apses and behind the ikonostasis are paintings illustrating the life of the saint commemorated. In the dome of the central apse are the Madonna and Child, with Christ below. In the left apse, Death and Resurrection of the Saviour, with Old Testament figures; in the right apse, Christ and the Trinity, and similar figures. Above the altar, the Risen Christ. In the nave and choir are depicted the great church festivals, arranged in four parallel zones. In the narthex the cupolas glorify Christ; on the walls are Church councils, lives of the martyrs, and the Last Judgement. In the refectory (e.g. at Lávra) the subject of the frescoes is food. There may be local variations of the traditional style. There are few ikons of importance.

The visitor arriving by sea at **Dhafní** (pop. 16) takes the attractive road (bus) to Kariés which at first runs close to the sea and then turns inland to the NE. After ½ hour it passes the idiorrhythmic convent of **Xeropotámou** (41 monks), pleasantly situated c 140m above the sea. It derives its name from a seasonal torrent. By forged documents the convent acquired in the 18C a 'traditional' foundation by Pulcheria, empress in 450–457. Its first genuine mention is in the 10C; it received privileges from Michael VIII in 1275 after an earthquake the previous year, and the Sultan Selim I (or, more probably, Selim II) rescued it from a period of decay. The earliest of the present buildings dates from 1763, when the paintings in the katholikon were also executed. Two ancient reliefs are built into the W wall of the court; the 'Roman' inscriptions are 18C forgeries and the two busts on the clock-tower (said to be St Paul of Athos and Pulcheria) are of the 15C. The chief treasures are a piece of the Cross (30cm long) and the so-called *Paten of St Pulcheria, depicting the Virgin at prayer standing adored by two angels with censers; in the first band is a procession of angels; in the second, the Apostles prostrate in worship. The paten was made in the 15C; the mounting showing the inscription, with the name, is an 18C addition. From the guest-chamber there is a fine view.

To St Pantaleimon and other W coast monasteries, see below.

Farther on is the coenobite convent (45 monks) of **Koutloumousíou**, situated in the most fertile part of the peninsula, amid gardens, vineyards, olive plantations, and cornfields. This convent is first documented in 1169. It is named after the princely Seljuk family of Kutlumush, of which its convent founder was a member. Bad fires in 1857 and 1870 (and again more recently) wrought havoc with all but the **katholikon**, rebuilt before 1540, and the arcaded E range, which dates from 1767. The frescoes of the katholikon have been repainted. There is a fine view of Kariés from the monastery. 2 hours **Kariés**.

   **Kariés** or **Kariaí** (Καρυαί; pop. 216; post and telegraph office; telephone) is the capital of Mt Athos; hence its other names of **Prótaton** ('Foremost') and **Mesé** ('Middle'). It is a little town surrounded by vineyards and gardens, with a few shops kept by monks and lay brothers. Its monastery was reputedly founded by Constantine and destroyed by Julian the Apostate. The restored basilican Church of the **Prótaton**, the oldest on Mt Athos, dates from the 10C. Various additions since 1508 were stripped away in 1955–57. The *ikonostasis dates from 1607. In the **Chapel of St John the Baptist** are *frescoes of the Nativity and of the Presentation in the Temple attributed to Manuel Panselinos (early 14C) and considered the finest in the peninsula; others, of a later date, are beautifully fresh and delicate. There are also silver filigree crosses and a wonder-working ikon. The **Council House** has a chamber in which the 20 deputies deliberate sitting on divans. Each of the deputies has a lodge at Kariés to accommodate himself and younger monks of his convent attending the school here. Visitors to any of the lodges are hospitably received. The **Athonite School for Novices** was established in 1950 for 60 boys.

The hazel (λεπτοκαρυά) from which the town derives its name, is common. Hazel nuts are exported.

FROM KARIÉS TO VATOPÉDHI, 3 hours. The track, passing the huge ruinous Russian church of **St Andrew**, goes N. **Vatopédhi** (Βατοπέδιον), one of the largest and most modern on Mt Athos is an idiorrhythmic convent with 103 monks. The monastery, rather like a country mansion, is built round a huge triangular court in a charming pastoral setting overlooking a little bay, with a highly picturesque harbour. The SE wing was destroyed by fire in February 1966.

Foundation traditions tell of Constantine as well as of Theodosius, the miraculous rescue of whose son Arcadius from the sea by the Virgin is supposedly commemorated by the name Vatopaidion (βάτος, bramble, and παιδίον, child). The story tells of the boy being placed under a bramble for the hermits to find. The name is more likely Vatopédhion (bramble-ground). The historical founders are Athanasius, Nicholas, and Antony from Adrianople (late 10C). The Emperor John VI Cantacuzenus retired here in 1355 under the name Ioasaph. The monastery was a cenobion in 1573–1661.

Most of the attractive buildings are of the 17C or later. The **katholikon** (Annunciation), is an 11C basilica adapted to the plan of a Greek cross. It has a massive detached belfry and a double narthex. The 15C bronze doors, from St Sophia, Thessaloniki, have panels in relief depicting the Annunciation. Over the second door is an 11C mosaic of Intercession (δέησις): centre, Christ in glory; at the sides, the Virgin and John the Baptist. The inner doors, inlaid with ivory, are dated 1567. The impressive interior, which has a polygonal apse, is decorated with frescoes of the Macedonian School (1312), restored in 1789 and 1819. Porphyry columns support the dome. In the **Chapel of St Demetrius** (N) are ikons of St Peter and St Paul (16C), in a beautiful frame; of the Panayia Odegetria, in a 13–14C frame, with reliefs of Christian festivals; of St Anne; and of the Crucifixion (13C) in a 14C metal frame. The ikonostasis is a fine work of art. The **Chapel of the Holy Girdle** contains a good Nativity. The *cup of Manuel Paleologos (early 15C) is made of a block of jasper 25.5cm across, on a silver base decorated with enamel; the engraved handles are in the shape of dragons. There are some fine crosses with silver-gilt ornamentation. The most notable relic, the 'Girdle of the Virgin', was given to the monastery by Lazar I of Serbia (1372–89).

The **library** contains 8000 volumes. Especially noteworthy are an Octateuch (first eight books of the Bible); a psalter (No. 610), autographed by Constantine IX Monomachos (1042–54); an evangelistary (No. 735), and a MS of Ptolemy's *Geographia*, with which are 17 chapters of Strabo's *Geography*, the *Periplus* of Hadrian, and 42 maps in colour. Two fragments of frescoes were discovered in the library, the first representing only the heads of the Apostles Peter and Paul. They are attributed to the painters commissioned by Stephen Nemanja and his son (c 1197–98) to decorate the Refectory.

The monks' walk is an attractive promenade. Not far from the convent are the ruins of the **Athonite Academy**, founded in 1749 with the aid of the learned Eugene Bulgaris of Corfu, but destroyed in the same century. Some arches of its aqueduct survive.

FROM VATOPÉDHI TO ESPHIGMÉNOU, 2½ hours. The convent of **Esphigménou** (coenobite; 52 monks) stands on the edge of the sea, at the mouth of a torrent in a little narrow valley (whence probably its name: ἐσφιγμένος, compressed). First mentioned in a document of 1034, it was restored in the 14C, but plundered by pirates in 1533. Except for short periods of revival, it lay abandoned till the end of the 18C. Possession of the cave of the hermit Antony of Kiev (983–1073) assured it Russian support, but, though it was restored in the 19C, it has never been of the first importance. The **church** (1808–11), overpoweringly ornate, has an ikonostasis carved with figures of Adam and Eve. There are a portable mosaic ikon of Christ (12C) and (in the library) an 11C Menologion (calendar).

About 1 hour away by track is **Khiliandharíou** (22 monks; all Slavs), an idiorrhythmic Serbian convent, northernmost of the monasteries on the E side of the peninsula. It is situated nearly a mile from the sea, in a well-watered valley surrounded by thickly wooded hills. The name is said tobe derived from its construction for 1000 monks (Χίλιοι ανδρες). Founded in 1197 by the Serbian prince Stefan Nemanja and his son Sava, it was rebuilt in 1299 by Stefan Milutin, who eventually retired, after his abdication, to Vatopedhi. Only the katholikon was undamaged by a fire in 1722, and the cell of St Sava was destroyed by another in 1961. The court has a double arcade. The **katholikon** (1293), built of brick of different colours arranged in patterns, has a richly decorated narthex of c 1380. It contains frescoes of the 13–14C, restored in 1863–64 by artists of Galatista following the original style, a marble mosaic pavement (12C), and the cenotaph of Stefan Nemanja (the Monk Simeon). The little **Chapel of the Ascension** was decorated in 1302. The **liti** is a rectangular hall in front of the church in which prayers are said on Saturdays. The **refectory** has frescoes on its walls. Noteworthy are a mosaic ikon of the Virgin and Child (13–14C), another of the Panayia Trikherousa ('with three hands'; 14C), an altar cloth of 1399, with Christ standing between two angels blessing St Basil and St John Chrysostom.

The **library** contains interesting MSS in Slavonic languages. In the **muniment room** of the library are four *ikons depicting archangels from the ikonostasis presented by Stefan Dušan, charters and deeds of gift from Byzantine emperors and princes of Serbia and Bulgaria, as well as firmans promising protection and privileges from successive sultans and viziers. The surrounding countryside offers delightful walks and the shore good bathing.

*Athos, Iviron Monastery. Christ Pantocrator in the dome of the church*

The northernmost part of the peninsula consists of hills intersected by deep valleys, down which torrents flow to the sea, the shore here indented with little bays. The hills are covered with the fragrant and feathery Isthmian pine, and with every variety of shrub and flower. The foliage of the N and S is blended in great variety, the olive with the oak, and the orange with the pine.

FROM VATOPÉDHI TO IVÍRON, 4 hours or by boat. The path runs SE and S, close to the E coast of the peninsula. After 2½ hours you reach **Pantokrátoros** (56 monks), an idiorrhythmic convent founded c 1357–63 by Alexios the Stratopedarch and John the Primicerius, whose inscribed tombs have been found in the narthex. The walls, repaired in 1536, have a massive tower. It is built on a sea-washed rock above a small cove and has a fine view of Stavronikíta. The old katholikon has been often renovated (fragmentary 14C frescoes). The library has interesting 11C MSS. An hour later you come to another idiorrhythmic convent, that of **Stavronikíta** (31 monks), perhaps founded in 1153 (or even earlier) but refounded in 1542 by the Patriarch Jeremiah of Constantinople. The monastery, with its massive tower, crowns a precipitous rock at the edge of the sea. The **katholikon** has frescoes of 1546 executed by monks. It has a mosaic ikon of St Nicholas and a psalter of the 12C. After another hour you arrive at **Ivíron** (Monastery of the Iberians), also idiorrhythmic, with 43 monks (Greeks, Russians, Roumanians, and Georgians). It was founded in 979 or 986 by three Iberians or Georgians under charter from Basil II the Bulgar-Slayer. Badly damaged by fire in 1865, it is a welter of buildings in an enclosed valley near the sea. The entrance opens into a vast court surrounded by heterogeneous buildings. In the middle is the **katholikon**, with a pavement that dates from the foundation. In a little chapel (1680–83) adjoining is the miraculous 10C ikon of the Panagia Portaïtissa which, found by one of the Georgians in the sea, enabled him to walk upon it. The **library** is rich in MSS, particularly of the gospels including one the gift of Peter the Great. The treasury (seldom shown) has a carved cross of 1607, another of carved wood (Raising of Lazarus), and remarkable vestments, including an embroidered tunic said to have belonged to the Emperor John Tsimiskis.

Near the convent is a former asylum for the mentally afflicted and lepers (good beach nearby). A road leads direct from Ivíron to Kariés (1½ hours).

FROM IVÍRON TO THE GRAND LÁVRA, 6½ hours. The path runs SE along the coast to the end of the peninsula. After 1½ hours amid green meadows you reach the idiorrhythmic convent of **Philothéou** (81 monks), supposedly founded in the 9C by three monks of Olympus (Arsenius, Denys, and Philotheos), but first mentioned in the 12C. It numbered Stephan Dušan among its benefactors. The convent was rebuilt after a fire in 1781. Round its church are workshops where the monks employ themselves in wood carving. There is a fine view from here of the convents of Stavronikíta and Pantokrátor. About ½ hour farther on through rich and fertile country, or 40 minutes direct from Iviron, is the coenobite convent of **Karakállou**, situated in hazel woods (460m). It was founded in the 15C by Peter Raresch IV of Moldavia and dedicated to SS Peter and Paul by one John Karakallos. The convent, which has 21 monks, was restored in 1548. There was a fire in 1988. The mountainside falls abruptly to the sea and the view over the Aegean embraces Samothráki, Imvros, and Ténedos.

Some 4 hours from Karakállou you reach the *Grand Lavra (Η Μονή της Μεγίστης Λαύρας), an idiorrhythmic convent, with 139 monks, including Russians, Rumanians, and Bulgarians (lavra means cloister or monk's cell).

The largest and perhaps the finest of all, partly because (alone of the 20) it has never suffered from fire, it is comparatively simple in plan, without the multiplicity of buildings characterising some of the others. It was founded in the time of Nikephoros Phokas (963–64) by Athanasius of Trebizond. Resembling a fortified village, with a fine 10C **tower**, it stands on a gently sloping spur (152m) overlooking a little harbour guarded by a fort. The entrance is by a long, winding and vaulted passage, with several massive iron gates. In the court are two ancient cypresses, said to have been planted at the foundation.

The **phiale**, erected in 1635, incorporates Byzantine relief panels between eight Turkish stalactite capitals. Paintings within the dome represent the Baptism of Christ. Below is an antique porphyry basin with a sculptured bronze fountain. The **katholikon**, completed in 1004, which externally resembles a domed basilica, consists of a triconchal Greek cross extended to the W and flanked by parecclesia in the form of two smaller cross-in-square churches. A hideous exo-narthex of 1814 now abuts the three W fronts, occupying the site of St Athanasius's cell. Painted Baroque doors of the Turkish period lead into the church, which was frescoed all over by Theophanes the Cretan in 1535–60. Representations of Nikephoros Phokas and his nephew, John I Tzimisces, benefactors of the church, dominate the nave. In the right parecclesion is the **Tomb of St Athanasius**. To the left the **Chapel of St Nicholas** has frescoes by Kastellanos. The cruciform **Refectory**, built by Gennadios, Archbishop of Serres in 1512, has *frescoes by Theophanes the Cretan. Within the apse, Last Supper. Side walls (in three bands): below, SS Athanasius, Euthymus, and Gregory Palamas; middle, scenes of martyrdom; above, illustration of the hymn Ἄξιον ἐστι. To the S, Life of Ay. Solitarios, Council of Nicaea, scenes in the life of the Virgin. To the N, Death of a just man, scenes in the life of St John. To the E, Last Judgement (centre, Second Coming; left, Paradise; right, Hell). The **Chapel of the Trinity (Ayía Trias)** has an ikonostasis of the 15–16C.

The treasures include the ikon of Koukouzelissa (12C), reliquary of Nikephoros Phokas (11C or earlier), and an enamelled ikon said to be that of John Tzinitzas (12C). The **library** has 5000 volumes and 2250 MSS, including a Bible of Nikephoros Phokas, set with precious stones; two leaves (from Galatians and 2 Corinthians) of the 6C 'Codex Euthalianus' are preserved.

Directly above the Grand Lavra rises the peak of **Mount Athos** (2033m), with its white cone and its precipices, in striking contrast to the dark foliage of the ridges below. The ascent can be made in one day from the convent via Kerassiá (see below; start in the early morning, return in the evening). It was climbed in 5 hours from Néa Skíti by Sir John Hunt in 1948. On the summit is the little **Chapel of the Transfiguration**, in which a service is held annually (on 6 August). The peak was one of the stations of the fire-beacons that carried Agamemnon's signal to Klytemnestra (Aesch. *Agam.* 284). The **view** all round is unsurpassed, embracing the whole N Aegean.

FROM THE GRAND LÁVRA TO DHAFNÍ, 10 hours, not counting halts. This itinerary follows the contour of the peninsula, rounding its extremity and going up the W coast. Hereabouts are numerous hermit's cells (σκήται), many of them almost inaccessible. Two hours **Kerassiá** is the principal halting-place (accommodation) and the closest point for the ascent of the Mountain (see above). A short distance away, on the coast, is **Kafsokalívia**, a colony of painters and woodcarvers who live in small groups. 3¾ hours **Ayía Anna**, a retreat where 126 monks live in separate houses, clings in terraces to a steep mountainside. Here is a shrine with a relic of St Anne.

About 5 hours from the Grand Lavra, the coenobite convent of **Ayíou Pávlou** (36 monks) is beautifully situated in an angle of stupendous cliff above a boulder-strewn torrent. Founded in the 11C by Serbs and Bulgars, it gets its name, not from the Apostle, but from a son of the Emperor Maurice, one of its chief benefactors. After a period of desertion, the buildings were renewed wing by wing in the 19–20C; the katholikon of 1447 was replaced in 1844–50. The library was lost in a fire in 1905. The **Chapel of St George** has good frescoes in the Cretan style, dated 1423 but probably of the 16C: figures of saints and Apostles and, in the narthex, the Virgin as the source of life (Ζωοδόχος πηγή). A difficult path leads in ¾ hour to the coenobite convent of **Dionysíou** (50 monks) founded in 1375 by Alexios III Emperor of Trebizond at the instance of Dionysios, brother of Theodosius, Archbishop of Trebizond. The convent stands on a precipitous rock where a bleak gorge reaches the sea; it is approached from its little landing-stage by 420 steps. The huge **tower** was built in 1520 and Peter IV Raresch of Moldavia restored the buildings (1547) after a fire in 1535. The **katholikon** has frescoes of 1547 by Zorzis (Cretan School). In the refectory is a Last Judgement (1603). There are the silver reliquary of St Niphon and (in the library) a superb chrysobul and c 600 MSS. About 1 hour farther, just above the sea and shut in by rocky cliffs, is the compact and attractive **Gregoríou** (coenobite, with 67 monks), founded c 1395 and rebuilt after a fire in 1762–83. Its katholikon has paintings of 1779. About 1 hour farther on is the coenobite convent of **Simonópetra** (or **Simópetra**; 59 monks), picturesquely situated over 305m up on a rock isolated on all sides save the NE, where a bridge of three superimposed arches joins it to the cliff. Its buildings, reconstructed on the old foundations in 1893–1902, with funds from Czar Nicholas II, are supported by heavy beams overhanging the precipice, recalling architecturally the Potala at Lhasa in Tibet. The view is magnificent.

The convent was founded in 1257 by St Simon and favoured by the Serbian Emperor John Ugleš. Fires took their usual toll in 1580 and 1625, and Turkish occupation in 1821–30, while the library and much else was destroyed in 1891. From Simonópetra Dhafní is 2 hours walk.

## Other convents on the West Coast

From Xeropotámou a path leads NW in ½ hour to **St Pantaleímon** or **Roussikó**, a huge coenobite convent once supporting 1500 Russian monks (now 38, and undergoing a revival). It was founded in 1169 in an earlier abandoned building, burnt down by the Catalan Company in 1309, but reendowed by Andronikos II two years later. It was occupied for about 80 years after 1735 by Greek monks, but rebuilt in 1812–14 in an exotic Russian style. It was swept by fire in 1968 when the assembly hall was destroyed. Above its scattered barrack-like blocks on the waterfront rise many towers and domes surmounted by golden crosses. It has a soapstone paten with a representation of the Virgin and Child, and an illuminated MS of St Gregory of Nazianzen. The singing of its Russian choirs was famous. At the monastery are some architectural and sculptural fragments from the **Temple of Zeus Ammon** at Kallithéa on the Kassandra peninsula.

About 1 hour farther, at the edge of the sea, is the coenobite convent of **Xenofóndos** (56 monks), founded at the end of the 10C by the monk Xenophon. The **old katholikon** has frescoes of the school of the Cretan Theophanes while the **new katholikon** (1837) has two fine 14C mosaic panels of saints. In the refectory is a good Last Judgment. Half an hour farther on, standing 46m above the sea, is the idiorrhythmic convent of

**Dhokheiaríou**, with 42 monks, architecturally one of the most charming. It was founded at the beginning of the 10C by Euthymios, who had been Receiver (δοχειάρης) of the Grand Lavra. The *katholikon is one of the finest on Mt Athos; its frescoes, by an unknown artist of the Cretan school (1568) embody the traditional style of decoration in all its completeness. Count Alexander IV of Moldavia and his countess Roxandra are depicted as founders. The convent has an interesting ikon, an epitaphios of 1605, and 11–12C MSS. The path now leads through wooded country to (1 hour farther) the little coenobite convent of **Konstamonítou** (31 monks), hidden in a deep defile. It was founded, according to the most probable account, in the 11C by someone from Kastamon, but tradition has altered the medieval spelling from Kastamonitou to accord with a legendary foundation by Constans, son of Constantine the Great. Its buildings are all of the 19C.

Finally, after another ½ hour, midway between the coasts you reach **Zográfou**, a coenobite convent of 19 Bulgarian monks founded by Slav nobles from Ochrid at the end of the 10C. The two churches date from 1764 and 1801 but the rest was largely rebuilt in 1860–96 in an ugly style.

Its miraculous ikon of St George (Italian style, 15C) is said to have come from Palestine without human aid, in the same way as the House of the Virgin at Loreto (see *Blue Guide Northern Italy*). The monks declare that it was painted by divine will and not by man; hence the dedication to the Zografos or Painter. There is a small hole near the eyes of the painting made by an unbelieving bishop from Constantinope, who (it is said) inserted his finger in derision and could not withdraw it, so that it had to be cut off.

The route from Zográfou across the peninsula to Khiliandhári is one of the finest on the Holy Mountain.

# C. Olinthos and Kassándra

Road to Paliouri, 119km (72 miles); 42km Néa Kallikráteia.—67.5km Néa Moudhaniá, for **Olinthos** (8km).—72.5km Potidaía.—92km Kallithéa.—119km Palioúri.

This route can be extremely busy, with long delays, on summer weekends. The road between Thessaloníki and Néa Moudhaniá is being improved. At present you can turn S in Néa Sílata (on to a minor road in the direction of Sozópolis), and join the new road until just before Néa Moudhaniá.

Leave Thessaloníki by Egnatías and follow signs to 'Halkidikí'. Beyond the city the road passes through an open region of well-tended fields. 33km (right) **Mesiméri**, has Macedonian tombs, as has (38km, left) **Lákkoma** where one recently excavated was preceded by a cist burial. The road skirts (42km) **Néa Kallikrátia** (site of an ancient colonial settlement) on the sea, only to turn inland again. 48.5km **Néa Sílata**. 51.5km **Elaiokhória**. The **Petrálona Cavern** (5km left; conducted tours; museum), where a Neanderthal skull came to light in 1960 and a full skeleton in 1976, may have been occupied c 500,000 BC. 55.5km **Néa Tríglia**. 67.5km **Néa Moudhaniá** (pop. 4403; Hotels B, C) has a small harbour. You skirt the town and reach a vast crossroads with traffic lights.

The road to the left runs through a flat cultivated plain across the base of the Gulf of Kassándra into Sithonía, joining Rte 64D at **Paralía Yerakína** (16km). You can make a diversion along that road to ancient *Olynthos*, turning left after 5.5km, by a mound, and at the beginning of the modern village (1.5km farther) taking a signed track (right) for another 1km and fording the river Retsinikia. The site of **Olynthos** (fenced; phylax; free) occupies twin flat-topped mounds running N and S, overlooking the Retsinikia. In the 5C and 4C BC it was the most important of the Greek cities in this part of the Macedonian coast.

Neolithic dwellings occupied the S spur of the hill in the early 3rd millennium BC. The Bronze Age settlement was at Ayios Mamas (see below), but c 800 BC the S hill was reoccupied by a Macedonian tribe. It was settled by Bottiaians in the 7C. Xerxes here requisitioned troops and ships in 480 BC (Herod, VII, 122); meditating rebellion in the following year, it was burnt by Artabazus and the site given to the Chalcidians. Their city paid tribute to Athens until, in 432, Perdikkas II of Macedon moved many inhabitants of neighbouring Chalcidian towns into Olynthos and it became the head of the Chalcidian League. The population grew to c 30,000 inhabitants, and the town spread to the N hill. It maintained its independence except for a short period of submission to Sparta (379 BC). After first siding with Macedon, Olynthos was reconciled to Athens by Demosthenes, who in his Olynthiac Orations, urged his countrymen to support the Olynthians against Philip. In 348, however, Philip took and destroyed Olynthos so thoroughly as to excite the comment of Demosthenes that a visitor to the place would never realise that there had been a city there (Phil. 3, 117). A Byzantine church later occupied part of the site.

The Classical city was built on the Hippodamian system with insulae of uniform area, measuring 300 by 120 Greek feet. Its excavation by the American School in 1928–34 provided a knowledge of Greek town-planning and domestic building comparable with that gained by Roman scholars from Pompeii. Sculptural and architectural fragments, exactly dated by the historic destruction, clarified the relationship between Classical and Hellenistic styles. Its pebble mosaics (conservation in progress), forerunners of those at Pella, have been covered over; some mosaics have been uncovered for display but these are not easy to find without help from the phylax and the site otherwise offers little to the layman. There are numerous open cisterns.

Returning to Néa Moudhaniá, you continue S and cross the narrow isthmus that joins Kassándra to the mainland. S of the canal are substantial remains of a defensive wall and towers (probably of the time of Justinian, with later additions). A shallow canal was cut across the isthmus in 1937, on a different line from its ancient predecessor. 72.5km **Néa Potidhaía** (Hotel C).

*Potidaia*, a Dorian colony founded c 600 BC from Corinth, soon minted its own coins. After Salamis the strongly fortified port led the Chalcidian revolt against the Persian lines of communication, resisting a siege by Artabazus. It became a member of the Delian Confederacy. Its revolt from Athens in 432 BC was one of the immediate causes of the Peloponnesian War (Thuc. I, 56). The city was subdued in 429 after a siege of two years; in the campaign Socrates saved the life of Alcibiades while serving as a hoplite. Potidaia remained an Athenian cleruchy until 404 when it passed to the Chalcidians. Recovered by Athens in 363–356, it fell to Philip of Macedon who gave it to the Olynthians. After destruction in the Olynthian War, the place was refounded by Kassander as *Kassandreia*, and became the most prosperous city in Macedonia. It repulsed the Roman fleet in the Third Macedonian War (171–168). It was destroyed by the Huns in AD 540 but revived by Justinian who was probably responsible for the fortification of the isthmus. The castle was destroyed by the Turks in 1430.

Visible remains of the ancient towns are limited. Graves have been excavated at Ayios Mámas to the N; about 2km S are traces of *Kassandreia*. A section of the town wall has been located.

The peninsula of **Kassándra**, the ancient *Pallene*, is the most fertile of the three prongs of Khalkidhikí. Before the War of Independence it contained a population of cattle-and sheep-farmers. When news arrived in 1821 of the revolt of the Greeks in the S, the people of Kassándra decided at first to join in but, finding themselves unprepared, tried to back out. It was too late. The Pasha of Thessaloníki, entering the peninsula, put all the inhabitants to the sword and razed all their houses. Kassándra was left untenanted for two years and only relatively recently has anything been done to restore its former prosperity.

From Néa Potidhaía the road follows the E side of the peninsula. **Saní** (Hotels A, B), 11km down the W coast, has a 16C tower on the promontory, which protected a dependency of the Athonite monastery of Stavronikíta. Ancient remains in the vicinity indicate the site of the Euboean colonial settlement of *Sane*. 84km **Néa Fókaia** (Hotels B, C) has another prominent tower. 88.5km **Áfitos** (Hotels A, B) marks the site of ancient *Aphytis*, where in 380 BC Agesipolis of Sparta died of fever while campaigning against Olynthos. A sanctuary of Zeus Ammon (4C BC) with an associated Sanctuary of the Nymphs and Dionysos (Xen. Hell., 5, 3, 13) were found and excavated in 1969–71 (finds in Políyiros museum and at the monastery of St. Pandeleimon on Mt. Athos). At (92km) **Kallithéa** (Hotels A, B, C, D), the road divides to form a circuit of 76km round the peninsula.

The pleasant E coast road continues close to the shore through wooded hamlets. 5km **Kriopiyí** (Hotels A, B, C, E) has an NTO camp site. 10km **Políkhrono** (Hotels A, B, C, D). Between here and Kassandhrinó to the NW, on the hill of Yeromíri, are remains of an ancient settlement and cemetery, possibly *Neapolis*, a colony of Mende. 15km **Khaniótis** (Hotels A, B, C). 19km Pefkokhorió (Hotels B, C, D, E). By the sea, 3km short of (29km) **Palioúri** (Hotels B, E) is a Xenia hotel (B) and a large NTO camp site. To the SE the peninsula ends in Cape Kalogriá, the ancient *Kanastraion*.

From Palioúri the road turns inland through **Ayía Paraskeví**, with a large Archaic cemetery, to the W coast at (40km) **Loutrá** (Hotels B, C) with hot springs. At (47km) **Néa Skióni** (Hotels C, D), chance finds in 1956 included coins and walls, relics presumably of *Skione*, once the chief town of Pallene. 2km to the E the church of Panayía Faneroméni has early 17C frescoes. Farther on is **Kalándra** (Hotels A), the site of ancient *Mende*, noted for its wine and as the birthplace of the sculptor Paionios. The ancient town lies on a hill called Xefotó, with a walled acropolis (Mycenaean to Geometric periods) on the summit of Vigla to the SE and, near the Hotel Mende, the ancient cemetery and the **proasteion** (suburb) mentioned by Thucydides (IV 130). An excavated area of the latter has yielded material of the 9–4C. On the promontory of Poseídhi (4km SW) a Temple of Poseidon, with inscribed votives from the archaic period, has recently been located. The road recrosses the peninsula through (72.5km) **Kassándra** (Hotels B, D), properly Kassandreia, an unattractive little town (2314 inhab.), to (76.5km) **Kallithéa**.

# D.  Políyiros and Sithonía

104km (65 miles), with, beyond, a circuit of 111km (69½ miles). A faster route would follow Rte 64C to Néa Moudhaniá and meet the road from Políyiros at the coast, 15km to the East.

From Thessaloníki to (56km) the Palaiókastro turn, see Rte 64A. You bear S through the village (533m), situated amid oak-woods, and wind through shaly hills. 65km **Políyiros** (Πολύγυρος; 535m), the chief town (pop. 4501) of Khalkidhiki and seat of the Bp of Kassandra. The **Archaeological Museum** is to the right at the entrance to the town. Opened in 1970, it houses finds from all over Khalkidhikí. Of particular interest are those from the sanctuary of Zeus Ammon at Aphytis and a head of Dionysos from the associated sanctuary; early black-figure pottery from Olynthos; and a Late Archaic Clazomenian larnax. Three silver coins displayed were found in the hand of a skeleton at Akanthos.

Beyond Políyiros the road winds down through rounded hills, passes large quarries, and reaches (81km) the coast at a T-junction. The road to the right leads past Ancient Olynthos (8km; see above) and joins Rte 64C at Néa Moudhaniá. You turn left. 85km **Psakoúdhia** (Hotels B, C). The site of ancient *Sermyle* should be on the coast S of Ormília or Vatopédhi, inland villages served by by-roads (left). 98km **Metamórfosis** (right; Hotels B, C, D; F/A). Beyond a camp site we reach (104.5km) **Nikítis** (2185 inhab.) at the base of the Sithonía peninsula, a town rebuilt after destruction by the Turks in the early 19C. At Ayios Yeóryios on the coast (2km SW) are substantial remains of an Early Christian settlement. The early 5C **Basilica of Bishop Sophronios** (the name recorded in a mosaic floor) has good mosaics, opus sectile and paintings. It is two-aisled with a colonnade to the W and a baptistery nearby. 100m to the N is a bath building, while 60m S is a 5C cemetery basilica with a modern church of St George in its ruins. About 1. 5km futher on the road divides.

With its trees, sharp hills, and rocks, **Sithonía** is more attractive than Kassándra and still largely unspoilt though a coast road encircles the peninsula. The right branch follows the W coast with occasional accessible but deserted coves. 7km **Eliá** (2km right) has remains of a basilica of the 5C. 17km **Néos Marmarás** (Hotels L, A, B, C, D) is a pleasant village with good seaside restaurants. Inland, near (5km) **Parthenó**, there is a sanctuary (perhaps of Zeus Koryphaios) on the summit of Mt Kostas. Beyond extend the estates (c 18 sq. km) of John C. Carras, run as a model farm to produce olives, citrus fruits, almonds, and excellent wines for **Porto Carras** (Hotels A, B), a village expressly built in a modern but unappealing Mediterranean idiom as a resort for 3000 guests (two vast hotels) and 1800 permanent residents. It has full sporting and cultural facilities, including a theatre for 4500 spectators, and a yacht marina. Fine scenery with sandy coves and beaches run below the wooded slopes of Melítonas (494m). 42km **Toróni** has rooms and a good beach. At the S end of Toroni Bay, on the 'lekythos' promontory and the hills behind, are the extensive remains of ancient *Torone*, where excavations (Greek Archaeological Society, Australian Archaeological Institute in Athens, Políyiros Ephorate of Byzantine Antiquities) since 1975 have produced important finds from the prehistoric to Ottoman periods.

*Torone*, the name supposedly derived from a daughter of Proteus (or Poseidon) and Phoenike, was founded as a colony by the Chalcidians in Hellenic times but recent excavations have revealed an important and long-lived Bronze Age settlement. In the Classical period the city gave assistance to Xerxes in his invasion of Greece (Herod. vii. 22). After the Persian wars it became subject to Athens. In 424 the gates were opened to the Spartans, under Brasidas, but the Athenian Cleon retook it two years later (Thuc. iv. 110; v. 2). Later the site was dominated by Olynthus until again recovered for Athens by Timotheus (Diod. Sic. xv. 81). It became part of Philip's Macedonian Empire (Diod. Sic. xvi. 53). In 169 BC it was unsuccessfully attacked by the Romans in the war against Perseus (Livy xliv. 12). In the 14C it is mentioned in records of Mt Athos and remains of a synthronon in Basilica A suggests that it was the seat of a bishop.

Most striking on the promontory (called the 'lekythos' after Thucydides; entry forbidden to visitors) are the walls of the Byzantine and post-Byzantine fortifications, largely built of blocks from earlier structures. Further inland the double summits of Vigla are crowned by Hellenistic fortifications with towers and a linking wall. Some of the fortifications between Vigla and the 'lekythos' are of Classical date. There are three Early Christian basilicas, the most important being that of Ayios Athanasios, a short distance NE of the main site, close to the road to Pórto Koufó. The 'lekythos' has produced evidence for settlement, more or less continuous, from the Early Bronze Age until the Ottoman period; especially interesting was a Late Geometric (c 700 BC) structure with storage pithoi, found beneath a Byzantine tower. Archaic architectural fragments probably belong to the Temple of Athena, mentioned by Thucydides. A rectangular cistern was used mainly in the Hellenistic period. Excavated remains outside the lekythos include Classical houses and a large cemetery (sub-Mycenaean to Early Geometric), whose pottery shows connections with Euboea. The well-kept remains of the basilica of Ayios Athanasios (5C; see above) is three-aisled, with parts of a mosaic floor and a synthronon surviving; in a later phase a single-aisled church was built above the earlier remains. The other two basilicas (B—between Ayios Athanasios and the promontory and G, inside the walls of the city), are less well preserved.

A small fishing fleet works from (43.5km) **Pórto Koufó**. The peninsula ends in Cape Dhrepanon, the ancient Derrhis Promontory.

The road climbs over a spur with splendid views down towards (54km) **Kalamítsa** (Hotels A). 62km Turning to **Sikéa**, seen 2km left in a bowl of hills. On a hill above the village is the fortified Early Iron Age settlement of *Koukos* (under excavation), with associated cemetery. The site may have been concerned with the exploration of copper/iron mines some 5km away. The road runs nearer sea level. 62km **Sárti** (Hotels B, C). The road runs en corniche with fine *views up and down the coast and across to Mt Athos. 100.5km **Vourvouroú** (Hotels B, D) lies on the sea. At (106.5km) **Ormos Panayías**, a tiny rock-strewn bay, a settlement of the 6C AD has come to light with a basilican church. As you turn across the peninsula towards Nikítis, a road branches right to **Ayios Nikólaos** (4km; Hotel C), where another continues to Pirgadhíkia (16km; Rte 64A).

# 65

# From Thessaloníki to Sérres

## A.  By road via Lakhanás

**Road** 95km (59 miles), the shortest route, coinciding for the first 90km with the main road to Bulgaria. Hilly winding road through varied upland country; careful driving necessary. A newer and faster road between Dorkas and the Strymon bridge may be taken in place of the older route described here. In 1916 this was the main supply road for the right wing of the allied army and was remade by British engineers. **Buses** hourly (new road) in 2¾ hours.

We leave Thessaloniki by its dreary N suburbs. The busy highway carries traffic for Lakhanás, Nigríta, and Kaválla through a gap (290m) in the **Khortiatis** range that shuts in the town to N and E. 11km **Dhervéni** (signs to 'Macedonian Tomb' and 'Ancient Cemetery'). Burial mounds of the 4C BC covering cist graves were explored here in 1962; they yielded iron weapons, a pair of gilt bronze greaves, a unique embossed krater of gilt bronze, vases of silver and alabaster, and the burnt remains of a papyrus roll (4C BC), all now in Thessaloníki Museum. To the right diverges first the Kaválla road (Rte 66), then that to Nigríta (see below), and c 1.5km farther on (left) a road to Kilkís (Rte 65C). The road crosses a cultivated plain. By the side of the road are (18.5km) a spring and (20km; left) the **Toúmba Assiros**, a prominent mound, excavated by the British School from 1975 and occupied from c 2000 BC to c 800 BC. The former Turkish name of (22.5km) **Ássiros** (right of road) was Giovesnak. We begin the long climb into the foothills of the **Krousia Mountains** (Turkish: Beşik Dağ), the ancient *Dysoron*, which separate the Axios basin from the Strymon. From the ridges fine views of the plain take in Lakes Korónia and Vólvi and the heights of Khalkidhikí. 32km We diverge onto the old road to (35km) **Dorkás** (taverna), beyond which the road crosses a declivity with pine clad slopes. At the top of the next rise, by-road (right) to **Vertískos** (8km access to Rte 65B), which gives its name to the mountains to the SE. The road undulates to (45km) **Xilópolis** at the head of another wooded valley.

52km (32 miles) **Lakhanás** was the farthest point reached by the Bulgarians in 1913. We pass first a **memorial** of the bayonet charge that checked their advance, with a small **museum**. 1km W of the village is a **British Military Cemetery**, in which are buried 270 soldiers who died on this front in 1916–17. The panorama extends to the Kerkini or Beles Mountains (2032m; comp. below) on the Bulgarian frontier. 55km **Evangelístria** stands on an irregular spur projecting into the Strymon plain. 59.5km **Kefalokhóri** has wayside tavernas.

The **Strymon**, or **Struma** (250km long), called by the Turks Kara-Su, rises in the Bulgarian mountains, enters Greece through the Rupel Pass, and flows generally SE through a broad and fertile plain enclosed by parallel chains of mountains. Its upper reaches have been dammed to form a new lake (comp. Rte 65C). Its lower course has been controlled and the former **Lake Akhinos**, anciently called *Prasias*, drained. At the SE end of the lake lay the city of *Myrkinos*, founded c 510 by Histiaias. The river empties into the Kolpos Orfanou or Strymonic Gulf. At one time it formed the boundary between Macedonia and Thrace. In the First World War the river demarcated the static front line until the break-out of July 1918.

The road descends gradually amid scrubby hills. 71.5km **Kalókastro**, where in 1917 Stanley Casson recognised Byzantine walls and the remains of a Roman town, looks out from a low ridge towards Sérres. To the left of the road is the **Struma Military Cemetery**, established in 1916 by the 40th Casualty Clearing Station; it contains the graves of 932 officers and men of the British, Indian, and Maltese forces who died on the Strymon front. At 72.5km is a turn (right) for Nigríta. At 76.5km you rejoin the new road and cross the artificially embanked Strymon by a long bridge. 81km **Provatás** (1510 inhab.) produces ouzo. **Monokklissiá** (2.5km S) is notorious for its practices of 8 January (comp. Rte 57), when the women confine the men to domestic chores while they revel in street and tavernas. The inhabitants brought the custom from E Thrace in 1922; it may derive from the Dionysiac rites of ancient Thrace. Crossing the Belitsa, a tributary of the Strymon, and the railway, you join (90km) the road to **Sidhirókastro** (19km; see below) and Bulgaria, but turn S.

After Sidhirokastro, the road (buses daily from Sérres; Konstantinídhis Agency Merarkhías 28) and railway (daily to Sofia in 9 hours from Thessaloníki) to Bulgaria follow the river through the formidable Rupel Pass, guarded by the conspicuous **Rupel Fort**. 40km **Koúla** and (43.5km) **Kuláta** are the frontier posts, beyond which the Bulgarian highway continues in the Struma valley. 153km **Sofia**.

Passing the huge Kolokotronis Barracks the road enters (95km) Serres. **Sérres** or Sérrai (Σέρρες; Hotels B, C, D) is the capital of its nome and one of the most important commercial cities (45,213 inhab.) in Macedonia. Situated at a low elevation (50m) at the foot of mountainous country (to the NE), it overlooks the fertile plain to the SW through which the Strymon flows some 24km away. Busy and with a lot of new building, Serres is nonetheless a pleasant town, with wide streets, surrounded by abundant woods and luxuriant gardens. It has a covered swimming-pool and athletic centre on the road to the kastro. A street plan is available from the Hotel Elpis (at 66 Merarkhías), and a guidebook is being prepared by the Municipality.

**History**. *Siris*, or *Serrhai*, was already chief town of its district in the time of Herodotus; in its plain Xerxes left the sacred mares of the Chariot of the Sun. It became the seat of a bishop and later of a metropolitan, and played a strategic role throughout the Middle Ages. It was ravaged in 1195–96 by the Bulgarians who defeated a Byzantine army and took prisoner Isaac Comnenus, the sebastocrator. In 1205 the marauding Vlach, Johannica, besieged Serres; Hugues de Coligny was killed and the surrendered Frankish garrison slaughtered; Boniface de Montferrat, hastening from the Morea, recaptured and refortified the town. It resisted the attacks of Cantacuzenus but fell in 1345 to Dušan, who here promulgated his legal code (1354). Helen, his widow, retired here under the religious name of Elizabeth. Though Manuel recaptured Sérres for the Byzantines in 1371, it attracted the attention of the Ottoman Turks the following year and in 1383 fell decisively into the hands of Lala Shahin. It remained Turkish (as *Siruz*) until 1913, when it was seized by the Bulgarians who set it on fire in their retreat. On 29 June the town celebrates its freedom from the Bulgarians.

The town, almost entirely rebuilt since the Bulgarian fire, is best seen from the ruined 14C **kastro** (refreshments) that crowns the round wooded hill to the N (take the road from the E of town in the direction of Oriní). To the NE is a pretty cypress-planted cemetery; to the NW an ancient aqueduct spans a gully. On the slopes below, in the NE part of the town, lay the Christian quarter (Varoch). Just below the café on the summit of the kastro is the restored **Ayios Nikólaos**, an attractive cross-in-square, with an exonarthex wider than the building. Its octagonal drum and small domes are ornamented with brick decoration. In the same general area but accessible from the town itself is the Old Metropolis, also restored, dedicated to St Theodore. It is a large aisled basilica of the 11C, rather too high for its length, with a pretty domed chapel at one corner. In the apse was a huge 11–12C wall mosaic of the Last Supper, now in the museum. Close by, in Od. Ionos Dhragoúmi, and soon to be housed in a new building at no. 62 is a **Folk Museum of the Sarakatsanoi**. The W gate of the Byzantine town has been found on Ionos Dhragoúmi, and other parts of the Byzantine fortifications located elsewhere. Between here and the busy **Plateía Emboríou**, to the S, can be seen houses of the old town. Two interesting **mosques** lie on streets leading out of Plateía Emboríou, the Tsitsirli on the Drama road, and another on the corner of Anatolikís Thrákis and Andrianopóleos.

In the attractive central Plateía Eleftherías (gardens), a short distance NW of Emboríou, a huge Turkish market with six domes, which has also seen Moslem and Christian worship in turn, is now an **Archaeological Museum**. In the attractive interior are a 12C mosaic of St Andrew from the Old

Metropolis, ancient sculpture and other finds: also the marble doors and part of a couch from the Macedonian tombs at Argilos. Accompanying the finds are excellent descriptions, with photographs, of ancient sites in the area, especially Amphipolis and Argilos; also Neos Skopos, Nea Promakhonas, Eion, Ennea Odoi, Tragilos, Dhimitra (Neolithic), Gazoros, Terpni, Verghi, Kerdhillion, Stathmos Angistas.

**Oinoússa**, an attractive village with an old church, stands (6km E) at the mouth of the Kazil Tsai valley, in which there are asbestos mines. Higher up the valley (12km), in a cool wooded site, is the **Moní Timíou Prodhrómou** (1275), with the tombs of the founders and of Gennadios II Scholarios (died 1472), first Patriarch of Byzantium under the Turks, and wall paintings.

From Sérres a steep but beautiful mountain road crosses the pass between the Vrontous Mountains and Menoikion to (48km) **Káto Nevrokópi** (Rte 68).

FROM SÉRRES TO DRAMA, 70km (43¾ miles), asphalt, bus. The road keeps to higher ground 1.5–5km N of the railway, affording superb views of the mountain chains that ring the Strymon valley and the Drama plain. 17km Near the village of **Toúmba** (right) has been located a large Neolithic settlement with Karanovo-type pottery. 21km **Ayios Khristóforos** (left) is on the site of ancient *Gazoros* (some remains on the hill of Ay. Athanasios); the modern town (by-passed) is to the right of the road. Beyond it the new road continues S. The older line passes through (29km) **Néa Zíkhni** (259m), the seat (2726 inhab.) of the small eparchy of Phyllis. NW (6km) is the Byzantine fortress of *Zichna*. At (33km) **Mesorrákhi** (189m) diverges the road to Amphipolis (Rte 66). Through the broad valley of the Angitis, for a short distance, road, river, and railway run close together. 41km (right) **Stathmós Angístas** has an ancient site at Palaiokastro to the E, with a Macedonian tomb. The road climbs to (50km) **Alistráti** (261m), a village of 2622 inhab. on an ancient town (tombs), once the seat of a bishop, on the easternmost spur of Menoikion. The descent commands a view N to the Falakron range across the Drama plain. At 56km we cross the Angitis and see (right) the Sitagroí tumulus excavated by the British School in 1968–69 (finds in Philippi museum). 59.5km **Sitagroí**. At 67km we join a road from Kato Nevrokopi. 70.5km **Drama** (Rte 68).

# B.   By road via Nigríta

Though this road is narrower and slightly longer (104km), it has less traffic and more varied scenery.

Leaving the Lakhanás road (see above) at (11km) Dhervéni, you turn E, passing (16km) between the **Saratse Toumba**, a Bronze and Iron Age tumulus, and the derelict **Perivoláki station**, once the terminus of the Stavros Military Railway (comp. Rte 66). 19km **Langadhás** (Hotels B, D), the seat of an eparchy, with 5890 inhab., has alkaline warm springs (2.5km SE). Here the Anastenaria, a ritual fire-walking ceremony, takes place on the feast of SS Constantine and Helen (21 May).

Tradition asserts that c 1250 in the Thracian village of Kosti, the church of St Constantine caught fire. The sacred ikons were heard groaning in the flames, whereupon certain villagers dashed into the fire and rescued them without suffering harm. The ikons have been handed down by the families concerned from one generation to the next and the descendants honour their saints each year by walking barefoot on fire in a state of ecstasy carrying the ikons. The walkers are called Anastenarides from their imitative groaning (αναστενάζω). In 1914, when their territory was transferred from Turkish to Bulgarian rule, they fled with their ikons to Ayia Eleni (Serres), Mavrolefki (Drama), Meliki, and Langadhas, where, until 1948, their rituals were held in secret owing to opposition from the Greek Orthodox Church. Clerical objections in 1960 caused the ceremonies to be held that year only in Ayia Eleni. The orgiastic dance to drum and lyre with attendant chorus, together with the sacrifice of a bull decked with garlands, suggests an origin far earlier than the 13C, and the ceremony probably survives, shorn of attendant excesses, from the pre-Christian worship of Dionysos.

The road winds pleasantly among low hills—rolling countryside with cornfields and fair tree cover. Near **Ossa** (33km, left) are some remains of ancient *Bisaltia*, at Kouri. The road climbs into the wooded foothills of **Mt Vertískos**, passing close beneath the steep S side of Kharvata (1103m). The chief town of the S slopes is (49km) **Sokhós**. You skirt an upland plain with the marshy **Vromolímnai** ('stinking lakes'), a once notorious breeding-place of malaria; the Greek army began draining them in 1961. 61km There is a turn (right) for Aréthousa and Rendína. The road climbs the W spur of Mt Kerdhilion and makes a winding descent. To the NE extends the area once occupied by Lake Prasias (see above), the extent of which is betrayed by the prehistoric mounds that lined its shores. 81km **Nigríta**, a pleasant and friendly town of 6531 inhabitants and the seat of the eparch of **Visaltia**, overlooks the Strymon valley. It is a centre for tobacco. The Bulgarians took the town in April 1913 and destroyed it on retiring two months later.

At **Terpní**, 2km NW, is an ancient acropolis at **Ayios Mandéios** (see Sérres Museum). At **Dhimitrítsi**, 13km NW on the same road, the Greek general Branas defeated the retreating Normans in 1185, putting an end to their expedition. **Vérghi**, between the two, has a site at Palaikastro to the N.

90km A long bridge crosses the Strymon. 95km **Skoutári**. 104km **Serres** is approached from the S past the railway station.

# C.   By railway via Sidhirókastro

**Railway**, 162km (101 miles), 8 trains daily in 1¾–3 hours. This is part of the through route to Turkey (see Rte 69B). Between Thessaloníki and Sérres the line makes a wide detour to the N via (42km) Kilkís, (97km) Rodhópolis, and (130.5km) Sidhirókastro, so that the distance covered is much greater than by road.

Good **roads** follow the course of the railway. From Thessaloníki one route to Kilkís (48km) branches left from the Sérres road (comp. Rte 65A); otherwise, and certainly better from the direction of Edhessa, you can turn up the Gallikos at Dhiavatá, following the railway. From Kilkís its continuation crosses the Krousia Mountains to (88.5km) Rodhópolis. From Néa Sánta the newer of two routes to the W is faster but by-passes the villages. By road Sidhirokastro is better reached from the Lakhanas road (see Rte 65A) or visited from Sérres.

The line runs NW but after 8km diverges from that to Ghevgheli and Central Europe. Before (22km) **Filadhélfia** you cross from the E to the W bank of the Gallikos. From **Xirokhóri**, 7km to the E, is reported a skull of Ouropithekos Makedonikos, 9-12 million years old. 30km **Gallikós**. 42km **Kilkís Station** (198m) is situated on the Thessaloníki–Kilkís road by the village of **Kristóni**, 5km SW of the town. Just SW of the station is **Sarigöl Military Cemetery**, with the graves of 659 British soldiers who died here in 1917–18 of wounds received in the attacks on the Grand-Couronneé and 'Pip' ridge, the strongpoints of the Bulgarian defence of Doiran. **Kolkhís** (5km SE), has an early Christian settlement and basilica (fragments of 12C frescoes) 2km further E at Zoödhókhos Piyí. (Keep right through the village onto dirt road, crossing the river by a ford just by the site.) To the W (17km by road from Kilkis) is the village and Byzantine castle (14C) of **Palaió Yinaikókastro** (for castle go through the village and take dirt road to left immediately after bridge). The castle (built 1326–41 by Andronikos III), so strong that it could be defended by women, dominates the surrounding plain. Restoration is in progress including a 3(?)-storied tower. There is a cistern. An EIA cemetery has been excavated below to the SE (fenced). **Kilkís** (formerly Avrathisari; Hotels C, E), capital of the nome of the same name, with 11,148 inhabitants, was the scene of the defeat of a Bulgarian attempt on Salonika on 21 June 1913. To the S of the town a conspicuous monument crowns a wooded hill and a museum records the battle. It is busy and pleasantly spacious, if undistinguished. In the higher part of the town, by the Nomarkhia, is a well-arranged **museum**. It contains LBA and EIA finds (pottery, figurines, stone tools, bronzes) from various tell sites in the area (Gallikos, Kolkhis, Kalindria, Chauchitsa; finds and reconstructions of graves from the recently excavated EIA cemetery at Palaio Yinaikokastro; the archaic kouros found at Evropós in the Axios Valley; impressive 2C AD statues from the heroön at Palatiano (and other finds from the site); fragments of Roman sarcophagi and other interesting funerary sculpture, including an *imago clipeata* with three portraits; pottery, figurines, jewellery and small finds from various other sites.

Behind the museum rises a hill crowned by a church. There are good views of the town and surrounding countryside and a spectacular cave.

The lines crosses the road from Kilkís to Doïráni at (52km) **Metallikó**. An inscribed base for statues of Hadrian and Sabina erected by the city of *Bragylae*, found in 1952, gives for the first time the ancient name of the place.

To the NE (19km by direct road from Kilkís) is the village of **Palatianó**. On a nearby hill (3km by dirt road) overlooking the plain is a row of Roman funerary enclosures one, presumably a heroön, with a series of statues on a common base. The statues can be seen in Kilkís Museum; casts are shortly to be installed in situ. The location is impressive. There are other ritual buildings; also a Macedonian tomb nearby.

The railway descends the Ayák, or Doiránis, to the shore of Lake Doiran. The flat, green landscape, quite rich in trees, contrasts with the forbidding mountains which rise steeply to the N. 71km **Doiráni station** is now separated by the frontier of former Yogoslavia from the town whose name it bears. **Lake Doiran** (10km by 6.5km), well stocked with fish, is shared between Greece and former Yugoslavia. It formed part of the Vardar-Doiran front in various actions of the First World War.

On 'Colonial Hill' above the station (1.5km S) is the **British Salonika Force Campaign Memorial**, an obelisk, 12m high, guarded by two carved couchant lions, with panels bearing the names of 2160 fallen who have no known grave. In the **Doiran Military Cemetery**, adjoining to the E, lie 1300 dead (875 British).

The railway-line follows the SE shore, then bears NE across the foothills of the Kerkini Mountains. Parallel, to the N, runs the main range, whose steep crest, rising in **Demir Kapon** to 2032m, forms the inhospitable frontier with Bulgaria; it is better known by the Slav name of Belasica. Beyond (87km) **Kastanoússa** in the narrow **Dová Tepeá** pass (270m), the views become extensive on all sides. 97km **Rodhópolis** is the centre of the alpine area.

The railway now veers E through marshy country watered by the Koumoulis. Beyond (111km) **Mandráki** we enter the valley of the Strymon, which to the S has been transformed into **Lake Kerkinis** by a dam. 120km **Viróneia**, a Greek headquarters during the war of 1913. Between here and the right bank of the Strymon were the silver mines of the Macedonian kings. At 128km the line crosses the Strymon on a long bridge near its emergence from the Rupel Pass, then turns SE, leaving the line to Sofia (opened 1965). 133.5km **Sidhirókastro town station**, 4km S of the town.

**Sidhirókastro** ('Iron Castle'; Hotel C; cafés in the Plateia), a town of 6157 inhabitants, capital of the eparchy of Sintike, is picturesquely situated at the foot of a hill on which is a 14C Byzantine kastro, with the remains of a newly discovered basilica. This (1.5km from the centre of town) can be reached by taking the road in the direction of the interesting monastery of SS Kirikos and Ioulittis. 300m beyond a track (left) leads in 7 mins to the site. The town is better remembered by its Turkish name Demir Hisar and is improbably to be identified with the ancient *Herakleia Sintike*. It is watered by the Chrysovitikos, a tributary of the Strymon. The town carries on a brisk transit trade. The church of **Ayios Dhimítrios** incorporates the pedimental façade of a Macedonian tomb as its templon. Road to Serres, see Rte 65A. There are springs and a therapeutic establishment (Hotels) near the mouth of the Rupel Pass.

The line traverses a bare landscape with cotton fields. Beyond (145.5km) **Skotoúsa** lies the broad valley of the Strymon. 162km (101 miles) **Sérres**. The station lies c 2.5km from the town centre.

# 66

# From Thessaloníki to Kaválla

**Road**, 166km (103 miles), on the course of the Via Egnatia to (101.5km) Amphípolis. **Buses** hourly to Kaválla (from Langadhá 59; hourly to Stavrós and Asprorválta (from Plateía Dhikastiríou).

At 101km, beyond the modern Strymon bridge, the **new coast road** continues straight ahead, providing an alternative way to **Kaválla** (176km) via **Néa Péramos**. This route is 10km farther than the older road described. It is much faster to Néa Péramos but slower thereafter. 126km Turning (left) to **Loutrá Elevthéron** (Hotels C, D, E), a summer resort, near the mouth of the pretty Marmara, with hot springs. Just beyond the 130km post there is a Byzantine fort, with well-preserved tower, on a cliff top immediately to the right of the road. 156km **Néa Péramos** (Hotels C, E). The fortress of the Byzantine city of *Anactoroupolis* is prominent on a hilltop to the S of the village. On the neighbouring hill, immediately to the SW is the acropolis of ancient *Oisyme*, a Thasian colony of the late 7C BC. A temple (?of Athena), founded in the Archaic period but later rebuilt, has recently been excavated and the walls investigated; finds from its cemetery by the shore are in Kavalla museum. 160km **Iraklítsa** (Hotel C). The road continues past beaches and coves. The Tosca Beach (select and not cheap) is backed by its Hotel, (A); there are an NTOG beach (restaurant) and camp site. 172km **Kalamítsa** (Hotel B) is the site of ancient *Antisara*, of which a 4C Asklepieion and an earlier wall have come to light also has the Batis beach.

You leave Thessaloníki as in Rte 65, and at (10km) **Dhervéni** leave the Sérres road to the left. Beyond (13km) lies **Layiná**, with a spring. A railway (60cm gauge), now derelict but visible a field's width left parallel to the road, was built by the Allies in 1916–17 from Sarakli (now Perivoláki; Rte

65B), just N of (16.5km) **Kavallári**, to Stavrós (see below). Lake Koronia, 14.5km long but maximum depth only 6m, is of great ornithological interest. Near the W end of the lake is a typical prehistoric mound. 24km **Ayios Vasílios**. To the right rises Mt Khortiátis with its prominent observatory and radar station; you cross a series of torrent beds. 38km **Langadhíkia**. The road runs above the S shore of the much prettier Lake Volvi (19km long) enclosed on its N side by the Volves hills or **Mt Besikíon** (658m). At (51km) **Loutrá Vólvis** are the hot sulphur springs of **Néa Apollonía** (2.5km; Hotel D), a local spa. Beyond the Kotza Potamos and a tumulus (right), (59km) **Apollonía** preserves the name of a station on the Via Egnatia, perhaps founded by Chalcidians c 432 BC on land given them by Perdikkas II of Macedon, and mentioned in the Acts of the Apostles (xvii, 1). An Ottoman complex, with a mosque, bath, khan and fortification wall and earlier Byzantine remains has been investigated on the edge of the village. 70km (right) is the attractive church of **Ayía Marína Modhíou**.

71km **Rendína** lies at the E end of the lake at the mouth of the **Stena Rendinas**, a pretty ravine sometimes called the 'Macedonian Tempe', leading to the sea. An ancient site with scattered architectural and other remains on a hill above and to the E of Ayía Marína Modhíou (and SW of the Byzantine settlement) is identified as *Arethousa*, where the 'Tomb of Euripides', who died there after being torn to pieces by the hounds of King Archelaus, became known to Roman travellers as a staging post. Through the village (just before the sign signalling its end), a prominent hill in a dominant position to the right has an impressive fortified **Byzantine settlement**. A track leads shortly to a footbridge over the river Rikhios. Near the river is a pool with warm springs which discharges into the Rikhios. It has produced traces of ancient use (Roman–Byzantine) and been dubbed the Spring of Arethusa. Beyond the bridge a path passes an Early Christian bath building (left) and cemetery structures (right) and ascends to the site (views) which is attractively laid out for visitors. It has produced Neolithic finds and material of the Classical and Roman periods but seems to have gained importance from the time of Justinian. In the 10C it became the seat of the bishopric of Liti and Rendina and expanded accordingly. The impressive fortifications (with extensions to the N and E) have several towers. At the point of entry are houses and workshops. In the centre, beyond the (?) bishop's quarters is a remarkable church constructed in the 10C round a previously existing (Justinianic) cistern. The spaces at the sides were used for burials; the church appears to have been in the upper storey. It was frescoed. To the E is a church of Palaiologos times and, at the E limit of the walls, a historically evocative secret passageway (rope rail) leads steeply downward to cisterns at the foot of the hill. From here you can return round the S side of the hill to the footbridge.

A little farther on is a by-road (right) to **Stavrós** (3.5km right; Hotels C, E), a small bathing resort (2641 inhab.) and roadstead, continuing S along the coast to **Olimbiádha** and **Stratóni** (Rte 64A) for **Ierissós** and **Ouranópolis**.

You reach the sea at the head of the Strymonic Gulf (formerly the **Gulf of Orfani**), one of the two great inlets bordering the Khalkidhikí peninsula. The foothills of **Mt Kerdhilion** (1091m) approach close to the sea. 83km **Asproválta** (Hotels C, D; F/A), sprawling along the busy main road, has a (?) Byzantine xenon (excavation planned) as well as a fine sandy beach and an NTOG camp site. At (88km) **Akroyiáli** four Roman milestones have been found. 95km The hill of **Paliókastro** (excavations) is identified with ancient *Argilos* and has Macedonian tours. At (98km) **Néa Kerdhíllia** (with further traces of ancient settlement, including Macedonian tombs) a by-road runs inland to **Aïdonokhóri**, where a site outside the village round the monastery Timíou Prodrómou is probably ancient *Tragilos*. The original fortified area was extended with buildings arranged on a grid plan. A heroön has been dug and a shrine of Leda and Aphrodite, with finds going back to the 6C BC; also part of the ancient cemetery. Finds show this site (excavations in progress) to have antedated Amphípolis.

You approach the new Strymon bridge but turn left keeping to the line of the older road (following signs to Nigrita, Amphipolis). The **Lion of Amphípolis** guards the old bridge over the Strymon. This colossal animal, reassembled from fragments in 1936–37, has been mounted on a pedestal built on the ancient foundation with blocks of the 2C BC dredged from the Strymon, where they may have been reused in a medieval dam. Originally the lion perhaps honoured Laomedon, the sailor of Mytilene who later became governor of Syria. Beyond the bridge, amid low hills (left), are the scattered remains of ancient *Amphipolis*; the outline of the acropolis walls can be seen above. The site is well worth the short diversion up the Drama road (1km farther on). The city was built on a commanding eminence (154m) above the E bank of the Strymon, just below its egress from Lake Achinos (now drained), c 5km from the sea. A loop of the river flowed round the W half of the city walls.

The place, which belonged to the Edonians of Thrace, was originally called *Ennea Hodoi* ('Nine Ways'; the original site c 1km N of Amphipolis), for which reason, according to Herodotus (VII, 114), Xerxes on crossings its bridges buried alive nine local boys and nine girls. It was colonised as *Amphipolis* by the Athenians in 437 BC after an abortive attempt 28 years earlier. Deriving its wealth from the gold mines of Mt Pangaion, Amphipolis was one of their most important N possessions: hence the consternation when it surrendered to the Spartan Brasidas in 424. The historian (and general) Thucydides saved its port of *Eion*, at the mouth of the Strymon, but, for failing to save Amphipolis as well, he was exiled for 20 years by his countrymen (Thuc. IV, 104–6; V, 26). In 421 the Athenians made an unsuccessful attempt to retake the city; in the cavalry battle both Kleon, the Athenian demagogue and general, and his opponent Brasidas were killed. Amphipolis was seized by Philip II of Macedon in 358. After the battle of Pydna (168) it became the capital of one of the four republics provisionally set up by the Romans. St Paul passed through Amphipolis on his way to Thessalonica (Acts, XVII, 1). The city was a station on the Via Egnatia and the seat of a bishop in the Early Christian period. Excavations have been made since 1956 by the Greek Archaeological Service. For those with limited time the walls and bridge (by the old railway station, see below) and the gymnasium are the most exciting of the remains.

For Amphipolis (signs) you turn left onto the Drama road which climbs, and soon there is a small sign in Greek (**Macedonian tomb**). Two tombs lie on the hill right of the road (the nearer only a few yards away): one had been plundered, but the other yielded precious articles now in Kaválla Museum. Further up the road, another sign (left) points to ancient walls and parts of the defences can be seen. Opposite the road sign which indicates 200m to the Amphipolis turn a track leads round the acropolis (c 400m) to the recently excavated **gymnasium**. This interesting complex was built in the 3C BC and continued in use, with various alterations, until the 1C AD when it was violently destroyed. At the SW is a *palaestra* with rooms round a colonnaded court. There was a monumental stepped entrance on the E, later replaced by an Ionic propylon to the N. In the NW and NE corners were washrooms of which the basin stands and water conduits and drains survive. Some exercise areas were tiled. There are several statue bases. In a room to the S of an entrance on the W side was a statue of Apellas, a Gymnasiarch of the 1C AD. Outside the N entrance was found an inscription containing an ephebic law of 21 BC, perhaps incorporating an earlier system of regulations, and referring to parts of the ancient city (agora, theatre) as yet undiscovered. Here too are an altar and late structure of reused blocks (triglyphs and metopes). N and E stretch the *xystos* and *paradromis* (covered and fair-weather running tracks; comp. Delphi). The xystos was fronted by a Doric colonnade. In both the starting blocks have been found and arrangements for supporting string lines dividing the tracks identified. From the gymnasium a track leads up the hill to the main site.

Returning to the main road you can continue to the turn (left) for the modern village. On the hill opposite the turn is a Hellenistic cemetery of rock-cut tombs. In the village a newly constructed museum is due to open in the near future. Excavations nearby have located a 4C heroön. The church contains a relief of Totoes, the Thracian equivalent of Hypnos. Signs direct up the hill to the main archaeological area, on the acropolis of the ancient city (phylax in attendance for much of the day). The principal remains so far excavated are not of the Classical period but of five **churches** of the 5 and 6C AD, four basilical and one with a hexagonal internal layout. Some of the mosaics (including fine and varied representations of birds) can be seen, protected by wooden shelters; others remain semi-permanently covered. E of basilica A huge Early Christian **cistern** was later subdivided and finally filled with houses and workshops. S of the basilicas is a section of the wall. The gymnasium is below on the hillside. A short distance further up the track are the remains of a Roman house, again under a shelter to protect its mosaics. It has a paved courtyard with a well in addition to mosaic floors and an apsidal room which originally had painted plaster decoration. Beside the house and not yet fully investigated is a building with statue dedications in front. 100m below these structures, down a track, is a remarkable Hellenistic house (covered) with fine painted decoration employing architectural motifs of the kind which formed the basis for the First Pompeian style. A **Shrine of Clio** borders a deep ravine to the SE.

Returning again to the Drama road the next turning left leads in 400m to a derelict railway station below a ruined Byzantine tower, which once bore an inscription stating that it was built in 1367 for the monastery of the Pantocrator on Mt Athos. Here and farther on three long sections of the *city walls* stand in places to a height of 7m. These have now been proved by soundings at 64 places to form a circuit of nearly 7km, with the inner acropolis wall of 2km. Built in fine coursed masonry, with towers, gates, sluices for flood waters resembling archery embrasures, and walkways, the walls extend to guard a crossing of the Strymon. Farther on (500m), within a fenced enclosure are further sections of the wall and the interesting fossilised wooden piles of the *ancient bridge*. If the site is closed, these can be adequately viewed from the track which runs alongside the river.

FROM AMPHIPOLIS TO DRAMA, 53km. After 8km the road divides, the older road (left) running N to join the Sérres–Dráma road (30km; Rte 65A) at Mesorrákhi. The right branch runs in upland country with views W across the Strymon plain and with the mass of Pangaion to the E. Near (17km) **Mikró Soúli** is the probable site of Byzantine *Zabernikeia*, with a tower and small church whose altar is supported by a milestone from the Via Egnatia. 20km **Rhodholívos** (2981 inhab.) is the most populous village of the eparchy of **Phyllis**. Neolithic houses and remains of a Temple of Diana have been unearthed here. 25km **Próti** (2033 inhab.). 31km **Néa Báfra** (see Tour of Pangaion, below). 53km **Dráma**, see Rte 68.

To resume the route to Kaválla you turn left at the crossroads below Amphipolis onto the older road (for the new coast road via **Néa Péramos** see heading to Rte 66). The silted up harbour of *Eion*, with the walls (10–14C) of Byzantine *Khrysoupolis* on the far side, is visible to the right between the road and the sea. There is a good view from the new road which passes closer to the harbour's edge. The acropolis of ancient *Eion* is on the hill of Profítis Ilías, to the left of the road, 6km beyond the Strymon bridge and 900m NE of Khrisoupolis. A turn (right) leads in 500m to the fine beach and summer resort of **Toúzla**. Below (111km) Boúrnali, an isolated little hill, the road swings inland. 115km **Galipsós**.

Here a road leads S to (2km) **Orfáni**, the village that gives its name to the gulf; the prominent walls (not yet archaeologically explored) are Turkish and perhaps Byzantine. On the prominent Kanóni hill are remains thought to be those of ancient *Phangri*. 8km **Karianí**, 4km to the E of which Gaïdhourókastro may represent the site of ancient *Galepsos*, where Perseus of Macedon touched in his headlong flight to Samothrace after his defeat at Pydna (Livy, 44–5).

The road enters the beautiful valley between Mt Pangaíon on the N and Mt Símvolon on the S, following the ancient road taken by Xerxes in 480 BC; by Roman times the Via Egnatia had been diverted round the N of Pangaion in order to pass through both Amphipolis and Philippi. 123km **Podhokhóri**, which has a three-aisled Early Christian basilica, excavated in 1973, is connected by road with Karianí (see above). To the N, on Pangaion, N of the abandoned village of Palaió Podhokhóri, the **Arkoud-hótripa Cave** has produced EBA and Classical finds, the latter perhaps to be associated with a cult of Dionysos. The villages are mostly to the left (N) of the road on the S slopes of Pangaion. 137km Turn (left) for **Kípiá**. 200m past this turn, in a fenced enclosure immediately to the left of the main road is a 5C Early Christian basilica (Karnátza). On the rising ground behind c 250m E and slightly N is a shrine (dining rooms etc, round a court) of the rider-hero Auloneites (Ἥρως Αυλωνείτης), with an Early Christian basilica in its ruins. It has produced reliefs. The site is best approached from the N, via a track beside the Karnatza basilica. At 143km **Panayía** (or Akrovoúni) is a turning for Néa Péramos (13km), which provides an alternative coastal run into Kaválla (see below). 146.5km **Elevtheroúpolis** or **Právio**, a flourishing town of 4879 inhabitants, mainly engaged in tobacco culture, is the capital of the eparchy of Pangaios and the seat of a bishop. It is the usual base for the ascent of Mt Pangaion. A site on the hill of **Palaiámbela** is another candidate for ancient *Phangri*.

## Tour and ascent of Mount Pangaion

A road (64.5km; bus daily to Mesolakkiá from Kaválla) traverses the bare N side of the mountain, joining the Amphípolis–Dráma road at **Néa Báfra** (see above). 3km **Khortokópi** (left) has rock carvings to the S of the village, and other antiquities. 6.5km **Andifílippoi**. Palaiokhóri lies in a valley to the left. 15km **Nikisianí** nestles in a broader valley 3km to the left. Traces of ancient mines and metallurgical establishments have been observed. Hereabouts, according to some authorities, was *Skaptesyle*, where Thucydides had an estate incorporating gold mines, to which he retired in exile after the fiasco at Amphípolis. Here he collected materials for his history and here he died. Other scholars place the estate near Stavrós or near Khrisoúpolis. A large **tumulus**, 1km right of the road, was excavated in 1959–60 by D. Lazarides, when six shaft graves yielded vessels and coins (4C BC) now in Kaválla museum. 25km Turn (left) for the Moní Ikossifoiníssis (5km; see below). 29km **Kormísta**. For the ascent of Pangaion, see below. 34km **Néa Báfra** stands on the Dráma–Amphípolis road (see above).

The ascent of the mountain can be started from **Kormísta**. **Mount Pangaion** was celebrated for its oracle of Dionysos, for the roses that grew on its slopes, and for the gold and silver mines in its neighbourhood. Here the Maenads tore Orpheus to pieces for comparing Apollo with Dionysos. The higher slopes are of crystalline white marble so the metal deposits must have been lower down. Its riches attracted the cupidity of the ancient world and led to constant strife between neighbouring states until Philip II of Macedon gained control.

A climb of 2 hours brings you to the busy **Monastery of the Ikosifoiníssis** (Μονή της Εικοσιφοινίσσης), beautifully situated 753m up in the midst of plane woods. The monks welcome visitors (donation expected). The monastery is said to have been founded in the time of Sozon, metropolitan of Philippi (443–54) but is probably not earlier than the 10C. It suffered much under the Turks, notably in 1823, when it was charged with having sheltered partisans in the War of Independence. The **katholikon**, a fine Byzantine building (restored 1954) has good modern frescoes. The library is rich in treasures, including a MS Gospel on vellum (1378), with a cover inlaid with precious stones.

The ascent is generally made early in the morning in order to see the sunrise. The route up is via the **Cavern of Askepótrypo**, past a secondary summit (1705m) to the highest peak, **Pilaf Tepe** (1958m). Above the tree line the path commands the whole Strymon valley.

At 159km you join the road from Drama (Rte 68) and wind up through the gap in the barrier ridge that separates Kaválla from its hinterland; the old Turkish paved road is clearly visible below (right). From the summit (210m), with a sanatorium, a large tourist pavilion and post office, and the **Monastery of St Silas**, you get a superb sudden *view of the Bay of Kávalla, with the town framed between the hills and the sea; in the middle distance is the island of Thasos, and on a clear day Samothrace and even the Dardanelles can be seen. The road zigzags down to the town.

166km **KAVÁLLA** (Καβάλα), beautifully situated at the head of its bay and best seen from the sea, rises like a shallow theatre on outlying slopes of Mandra Kari, one of the chain of hills that link Mt Simvilon with the Lekanis massif. The old citadel occupies a rocky promontory jutting into the sea. The second largest city (56,571 inhab.) of Macedonia, it is the chief town of the small nome of Kaválla, the seat since 1924 of the metropolitan of Philíppi, Neápolis, and Thásos, and the headquarters of an army corps. Kaválla is the exporting centre of Macedonian tobacco. It is the best base for visiting Philíppi and the main embarkation point for the island of Thásos.

**Airport**. At Khrisóupolis (30km E) with daily flight to Athens. **Terminal** on quayside, Ethnikís Andistáseos 8 (Pl. 6). Connecting **bus** from long-distance bus station.

**Hotels** A, B, C, D; many in Venizélou and Erithroú Stavroú.

**Restaurants** of good quality in the centre and by the old harbour.

**Post Offices** (Pl. 3), Omonías and Khrisostómou Metropolítou 8. **OTE Centre** (Pl. 6), Ethnikís Andistáseos (sea front).

**NTOG office** at Plateía Eleftheriás (very good). **Tourist Police/Police**, Omonías 119. **ELPA**, Khrisostómou Smírnis 8a.

**Buses** for local destinations from Plat. Karaóli Dhimitríou; long-distance bus station at the quayside. Frequent services to all main towns in Macedonia and Thrace.

**Ferry** frequently to Príno. Daily to Tímenas (Thásos); occasionally to Limenariá. Other steamer connections to Samothráki, Límnos, Lésvos, Khíos, Rafína, Piraeus; also to the Dodecanese.

**Ancient Drama Festival** in August at Philippi and Thasos.

**History**. Kavalla occupies the site of *Neapolis*, the port of Philippi and apparently of its predecessor, and is said to have been a colony of Thasos. At the time of the Battle of Philippi the fleet of Brutus was stationed here. Neapolis was the usual port of disembarkation for travellers to Europe from the Levant. St Paul landed here on his way to Philippi (Acts, xvi, 11). In the Byzantine era the town seems to have adopted the name of *Christoupolis*. The burning of the town by the Normans on their march towards Constantinople in 1185 is recorded by an inscription from the kastro wall.

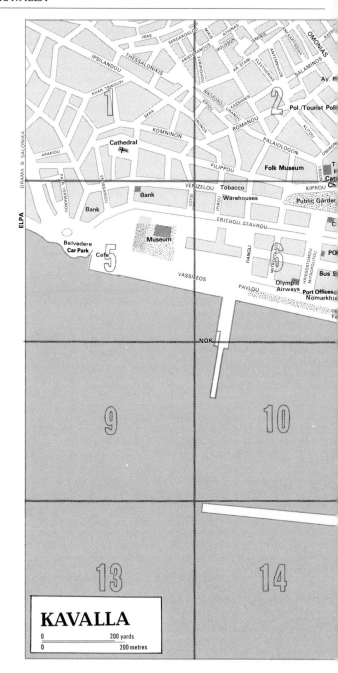

**KAVALLA**

| 0 | 200 yards |
| 0 | 200 metres |

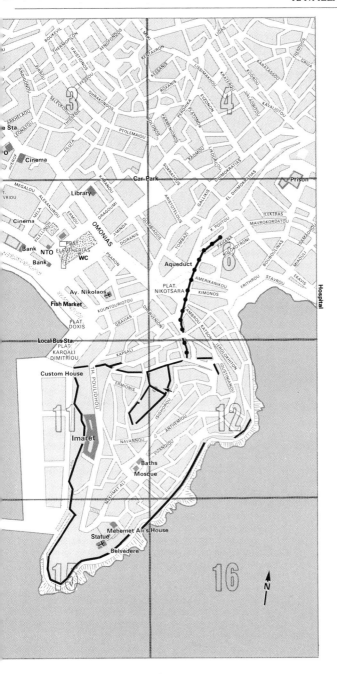

Here Ramon Muntaner and the Catalan Grand Company landed from Gallipoli (1306) at the start of their march to Athens. Kavalla was under Ottoman rule until 1912, since when it has suffered three Bulgarian occupations in 1912–13, 1916–18, and 1942–44. Here was born Mehmet Ali (1769–1849), the son of an Albanian farmer, who became pasha of Egypt and founder of the dynasty that ended with King Fuad II in 1953.

The business centre of the city occupies a depression shoreward of the citadel, a situation which necessitated the **Kamares aqueduct** (Pl. 8), the town's most prominent feature. Built in a style that derives ultimately from Roman models, this fine structure on three tiers of arches appears to date from the reign of Suleiman the Magnificent (1520–66), and carried water to the citadel. Odhós Ellenikís Dhimokratías, to the N, and neighbouring streets retain some old Turkish houses and shops, but these are fast disappearing. From Plateía Nikitára, below the aqueduct, Odhós Omonías runs NW to become the main shopping street. It passes across the landward end of the long Plateía Elevtherías (Pl. 7), which extends to the inner harbour. This is a small artificial basin within the large **harbour**, formed by the construction of two long moles since the war. Extensive land reclamation has provided a new seafront to the W (see below).

To the E, on the promontory, the **Old Citadel** is surrounded by well-preserved Byzantine walls, restored after an earthquake in 926 (inscription) and again in the 16C; they incorporate ancient blocks. The attractive multi-domed **Imaret** (Pl. 11), an almshouse for 300 softas, was founded by Mehmet Ali after his native town had unwisely rejected the alternative suggestion of a harbour. The seminary was endowed with the revenues of Thasos, and membership brought free pilaf and exemption from military service; it was known locally as Tembel-Haneh, the lazy man's home. The most interesting monument in the city, it is in a melancholy state of decay, although part has recently been restored as a café. Elsewhere in the town other Ottoman and Neoclassical buildings have been repaired: the Tokos Mansion, formerly the town hall and now the Ephorate of Byzantine Antiquities; the Ioannides mansion (Od. Ermióni 14, Panayía); the Peleke house (Od. Méhmet Alí 16).

Excavations by Ephor Lazarides in 1959–61, N of the Imaret, uncovered the peribolos of a **Sanctuary of the Parthenos** (6C BC); the pottery found included examples from all over the Aegean (see below).

In the Seraídaris Garden is **Mehmet Ali's birthplace** (Pl. 15), a pleasant Turkish house with good panelling, admirably cared for by the Egyptian government until 1961 and since by the Greek authorities. Below are the stable and kitchen; above, the harem and the pasha's quarters. In the little square, beyond, is a lively equestrian **statue of Ali** in bronze, by Dimitriades, below which a **belvedere** has a view towards Thasos. The rocks on the E side of the peninsula provide excellent swimming. The ruined Byzantine **kastro** (Pl. 12) that crowns the promontory is submerged on the E flank of the hill by old houses (mosque, baths, etc); the central keep is approached from the E side and its walls have a fine view of the harbour.

From Plateía Elevtherías, Odhós Khrisostómou Smírnis (Venizélou) leads W past the **public garden** (Pl. 6), then passes between tall **warehouses**, where tobacco is graded and stored. These formerly backed directly on the shore. Kaválla once had 200 of them. Just to the right is the **cathedral** (Pl. 1), with a complex marble iconostasis.

In gardens at the W end of the sea front stands the **Archaeological Museum**. Built in 1965 it comprises two ground-floor rooms linked by a wide corridor, an upstairs room, and courtyards. Exhibits are labelled in English.

GROUND FLOOR. The ENTRANCE HALL has Hellenistic and Roman sculpture from Amphipolis. ROOM I contains some Early Christian and Byzantine sculpture and architectural fragments from Neapolis (Kavalla). Finds from the Kavalla Sanctuary of Parthenos (6–5C BC), including Ionic capitals, figurines, a votive naïskos in the form of a treasury, and pottery (both local and imported). Along the CORRIDOR, with a large map showing ancient sites in Eastern Macedonia, are displayed Late Neolithic and Early Bronze Age objects, mainly from Dikili Tach, though the best finds from this site are in the Philippi Museum. Also a collection of sculpture including, at the far end, a metope (5C BC) from Aïdhonokhóri (ancient Tragilos), showing a fight between two hoplites.

ROOM II, finds from the cemetery at Amphipolis: polychrome glass; gold wreaths and diadems, and *jewellery; coloured busts of goddesses; grave stelai (one painted); figurines; and pottery, clearly from a local workshop, as yet undiscovered. At the end of the room: partial reconstruction of a double funeral chamber (3C BC) with paintings; its stele stands to the left. Nearby are gold and other articles (male and female) from the same tomb, including a polished silver mirror in a folding case and a man's ring bearing the picture of a youth.

The FIRST FLOOR ROOM (access from entrance hall) houses finds of Archaic–Roman date, mostly from colonial foundations in the area (Abdera, Oisyme, Galepsos, Tragilos). Most of the extensive explanatory material relating to the colonies is in Greek, but some of the labels are in English. Material from Abdera includes the Dolphin mosaic from a Hellenistic house, a painted Clazomenian sarcophagus from the earliest period of settlement, architectural terracottas and terracotta figurines from a sanctuary. From Nikisiani, pottery, polychrome figurines, silverware and coins of Philip II (gold staters) and Alexander the Great. From Drama, a lamp and chain in the form of a slave (2C AD). From Aïdhonokhori (Tragilos), a massive painted larnax (3C BC) and votives from a sanctuary of Aphrodite and Leda. In the COURTYARD are various marbles and inscriptions.

There is a **Folk Museum** in Od. Filíppou, to the N.

# 67

# Thásos

Car ferry from Kaválla regularly to Prinó, also four times daily from Néa Péramos; also from Keramotí (Rte 69A) frequently to Límenas. Hydrofoil regularly in summer from Kaválla to Límenas. The island deserves more than a day trip, Límenas itself meriting at least a whole day's exploration.

**Thásos**, the northernmost of the islands of the Archipelago, is of volcanic origin, mountainous, and of great natural beauty. Situated close to the mainland, its nearest point is only 10km from the mouth of the Nestos, and it thus faces the boundary between Macedonia and Thrace. Politically the island forms an eparchy of the Macedonian nome of Kaválla. Its area is 399 sq. km; almost circular in shape, it is c 24km long from N to S and c 19km wide. The highest point is **Mt Hypsárion** (1142m), nearly in the centre. The mountainsides are covered with forests, pines, planes, and chestnut trees predominating; the timber has always been in demand for shipbuilding.

The population of 13,527 is distributed between the capital and ten other villages, of which the most developed is **Limenariá**, with substantial tourist facilities, on the SW coast, where zinc workings are exploited. In the coastal areas tobacco and olives are cultivated. A road encircles the island, with branches into the interior. There is good water. The marble of Thasos has always been famous and is still in demand; the gold mines earned in antiquity for the island the epithet of 'golden'. Minerals worked today include silver, antimony, and zinc. Oil platforms visible at sea bear witness to a substantial contribution to Greece's energy needs.

**History**. The tradition of an early Phoenician occupation, recounted by Herodotus (VI, 47), is not confirmed by excavation, though the Parian colonists of c 710–680 BC seem to have had commerce with Tyre. The Parians, among whom was the poet Archilochos, excused their annexation of the island by calling it the command of Herakles, and the Phoenician myth probably dates from the time of Theogenes (mid-5C), the boxer-politician who claimed Herakles as his father. The colonists prospered by exploiting the Thasian gold mines and later took control of Skaptesyle on the mainland. Their zenith of prosperity was in the 6C BC. Early in the 5C Histiaios, tyrant of Miletus, unsuccessfully besieged the island. In the Persian wars, despite the famous walls of their city, the Thasians submitted tamely to the invader. A dispute with Athens about the mainland mines led to the reduction of the island in 463, but in 446 Thasos seems to have taken over again the mineral wealth of Galepsos. From Thasos in 424 Thucydides set out on his unsuccessful attempt to break the Spartan siege of Amphi-polis. Lysander massacred its Athenian partisans in 404, but Thasos again allied with Athens in 389 and became a permanent member of the second Athenian league.

About 340 the island was seized by Philip II and it remained Macedonian until the Romans arrived in 196 BC. During this period it developed a flourishing export of wine, and Thasian merchants carried on the trade between Thrace and Southern Greece. Under the Empire Thasian marble and oil enjoyed an international reputation. The medieval history of Thasos is obscure; the capital was removed to the interior because of pirates. Before passing under Turkish domination in 1455, the island was a fief of the Genoese Gattilusi. In 1760 it was given by Mahmud II to the family of Mehmet Ali, and became in consequence in 1813–1920 a quasi-independent appanage of Egypt, with its own president. In 1770–74 it was occupied by a Russian fleet which made great inroads into its timber. In October 1912 it was occupied by the Greek army, in 1916 by the Allies, and in 1941 by the Bulgars.

Thasos was the birthplace of Polygnotos, the painter, of the rhapsodist Stesimbrotos, and of Theogenes, son of Timoxenos, who is said by Pausanias to have carried off no fewer than 1400 athletic crowns. The physician Hippocrates lived for three years in Thasos, whose climatic variations he recorded. Excavations since 1910 have been undertaken by the French School, which has produced an excellent detailed guide.

The island capital is **Límen**, normally **Límenas** ('The Harbour'; Hotels A–E; F/A), or **Thásos**, on the N coast, on the site of the ancient city of Thasos. As well as being the administrative headquarters with 2600 inhabitants. Límen is the seat of a bishop and popular as a summer holiday centre with Greeks and Southern Europeans.

*•**Tour of the walls**, minimum of 2 hours. Note that the route described is not the only one possible and some of the important areas (e.g. the theatre) can be reached by more direct (and sometimes signposted) routes from the old harbour.

The earliest circuit of fortifications was demolished by order of Darius (492–1), the second by Kimon (464–3); the existing wall, on the old founda-tions throughout, dates mainly from a reconstruction in 412–411 BC. Two styles of masonry, polygonal and ashlar, can be distinguished. From the modern landing-place at Limenas you first visit the ancient **naval harbour** to the NE, which, although silted up, still shelters small caiques. The two moles, once protected by walls forming a marine extension of the enceinte, have been raised to the level of the water, in which can be seen the foundations of a large round tower at the angle of the S mole.

From this harbour a road branches off left from the direct route to the theatre. Passing (right; access via orchard) the **Sanctuary of Poseidon**, you reach (below, left) the ancient **Chariot Gate** adorned with an Archaic relief of Artemis in a chariot, whose horses are held by Hermes, contemporary with the date of the circumvallation (494 BC). The road ends at the **Dimitriades Quarter** (right) an area of the ancient town's housing between the 8C and 5C BC and (left) the **Gate of Semele**, with a mutilated relief of Hermes and the Graces.

The road continues as a path ascending gradually inland (E). To the left can be seen, submerged in the sea, the remains of the moles of the **commercial harbour**. On the promontory is a medieval castle (Evraió-kastro), also an ancient sanctuary and a church of the Apostles. **Thaso-poúla**, the small island to the N, now inhabited only by birds and snakes, has slight ancient and medieval remains. The path now bears S along the walls, here of fine polygonal blocks, to a wood of holm oaks, amid which (below right) is the cavea of the **Greek theatre** (easiest access by direct route from Old Harbour, via the **Sanctuary of Dionysos**, for which see below). The remains have been arranged to show architectural members of the 4C BC, recovered from the late remodelling of the orchestra (by the Romans for wild beast shows). New investigations are in progress. The theatre is sometimes used for performances of ancient drama.

You continue to climb, following the scarp (the wall here has been destroyed) to the **acropolis** (also with more direct access from the town, off the theatre path), a ridge with three summits. The first is known by inscriptions to have held a **Sanctuary of Pythian Apollo** (the god who told the Parians to colonise Thasos). The existing remains, except for sections of the foundations, are of the **Genoese citadel**. This dates partly from a reconstruction by Tedisio Zaccaria (c 1310) and partly from the Gattilusi era. At the S angle is the guard-room, built of ancient materials; nearby, in the outer wall, is an elegant relief of a funeral feast (5C or 4C BC). The wall now runs SW through remains of a medieval village to a high terrace of fine construction on which are the foundations (all that survives) of the 5C **Temple of Athena**, identified in 1958 by the discovery of sherds inscribed to Athena Poliouchos (in the museum). The path now descends to a little col where there is a rock-hewn **Sanctuary of Pan**, with a worn Hellenistic bas-relief of the god piping to his goats. Just beyond this a high rock forming the third summit commands an extensive *view of Samothrace and the mainland.

Descending steeply to the SW by a secret **stairway** hewn from the rock in the 6C BC, you regain the line of the walls. Beyond a tower a large stone has a carved **apotropaion**, two enormous eyes to protect the enceinte from the evil eye. Just before a sharp bend in the wall to the W, is the **Gate of Parmenon**, with its lintel still in place and nearby a block signed with the name of the craftsman: 'Parmenon made me'. You pass through the gate and descend into the town. The **Gate of Silenus**, is at the fork where the road to Makrí Ammos branches off left from the main road to Panayía. It is an unusual oblique postern, with a colossal mutilated *bas-relief of Silenus holding a kantharos; below is a niche for votive offerings. The sculpture, which is of Ionian workmanship and unique for its style and size, survives from the earliest circuit. A short distance further up the Panayía road is an archaic **Sanctuary of Demeter**. From the Silenos Gate a path leads on to a tower, then the **Gate of Dionysos and Herakles**. An archaic inscription still in place records that these two gods were the patron divinities of Thasos.

Acropolis

Temple

Theatre

Artemis

Dionysion

Dimitriadis
Quarter

Poseidonion

Gate

Chariot Gate

Harbour

HARBOU

Sanctuary

Evraiokastro

**THASOS**

0             150 metres

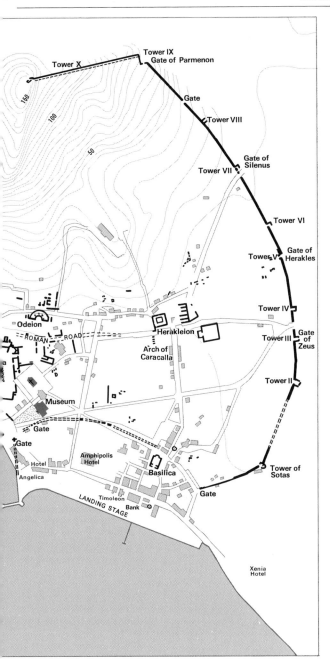

The relief of the archer Herakles is in Istanbul; that of Dionysos is missing. The path to the **Gate of Zeus and Hera** is blocked and access must be gained off the Panayía road (or from the centre of town). It has 5C bas-reliefs in the Archaic manner: before the seated Hera stands Iris; before Zeus, Hermes (this panel not in situ). A few metres away is the Roman **Sarcophagus of Poliades**. The line of the walls continues NW, crossing the village square (see below) to reach the harbour.

**The Lower Town**, 1 hour. A few yards E of the two gates near the naval harbour (see above) is a group of ruins, the chief of which is the **Sanctuary of Poseidon**. This is a large quadrangular terrace with the remains of a circular and a square altar. At the gate of the sanctuary are two bases with inscriptions (beginning of 4C); a little in front, almost intact, is the **Monumental Altar to Hera Epilimenia** (Protectress of Harbours), which had an inscription (now in the museum) reciting the sacred law forbidding the sacrifice of she-goats. To the S is the **Sanctuary of Dionysos**, a triangular temenos, re-explored in 1957–58, and covered again except for the remains of a 3C choregic monument. On its semicircular base are engraved the names of victors in a theatrical competition; the categories in which they competed were represented by statues; the statue of comedy is in the museum together with the colossal head of Dionysos from the centrepiece of the group.

The **agora** (entered from the square by the museum) is bordered by porticoes. Its layout has been clarified by judicious restoration of the foundations since 1955. The place was entered from the harbour by **propylaia** in the NW corner, and from the town side by several passageways which led into the **south west stoa**, a Doric colonnade of 33 columns (1C AD). In the S angle of the square is a monumental **altar**. The **south east stoa**, also of the 1C AD, had 31 columns of which three have been re-erected at the E end. This fronted a long hypostyle gallery, entered by four doors; the wall which they pierced still stands to a height of 1.8m. Beneath the E end is the base of a **Monument of Glaukos** (7C BC). In the centre of the agora is a **heroön of Lucius Caesar** and another of **Theogenes**; and in the N angle a **Sanctuary of Zeus Agoraios** surrounded by a balustrade, later interrupted by a **tholos** (3–2C BC). On the NE side, next to the propylaia, is a building with projecting wings (c 330 BC), similar to the Stoa of Zeus at Athens; this survived to the 5C AD when it gave place to a Christian **basilica**.

Outside the E angle is the unexplained flagged **Passage of the Theoria** (c 470 BC) from which came reliefs now in the Louvre, and inscriptions with lists of magistrates (in the museum). Farther to the E (best access off road from Dionysion to Odeion) is the disappointing **Artemision**; ex-voto objects dedicated to Artemis have been recovered dating from 7C BC. The Hellenistic sanctuary had a square temenos, traced in 1959, though most of its statuary was carried off to Istanbul in 1909.

A new museum will open during the currency of this guide. The contents of the old **museum** (closed Monday) are described. The CENTRAL HALL (I). Colossal Kriophoros (= ram-bearer; early 6C; unfinished), found in the acropolis wall; head of Pegasus, part of the architectural decoration of the Herakleion; torso of a kouros, found in the sea off Cape Pachys; funerary stele (late 6C); painted terracotta plaques and heads, including a frieze of riders; head of Silenus (c 525 BC); kouros of the school of Pythagoras from the Herakleion; head of a horse from the same (c 460 BC), much less Archaic in style. Finds from the Temple of Artemis, including a bronze statuette of the goddess and an exquisite lion's head in ivory (6C BC); coins of 5–4C BC from a necropolis hoard; finds from the Sanctuary of Athena Poliouchos, including inscribed sherds and various votives, some Cycladic; sculptures, including a Marsyas and a 4C archaising Zeus Agoraios or Dionysos. ROOM TO LEFT OF ENTRANCE. Statues of Dionysos and Tragedy; Architectonic fragments, including a metope and triglyphs; inscriptions, including a dedication to Pan by the guards of the ramparts (3C BC); three Thracian rider reliefs; Roman statuette of Orestes and Electra; offering chest from agora for collecting offering for the athlete Theogenes; various votives.

ROOM TO RIGHT OF ENTRANCE: two heads, school of Skopas; relief decoration of an altar to Cybele (2C AD); head of young Dionysos (3C BC); Aphrodite on a dolphin with Eros clinging to its tail; reliefs including grave stelai, some with funerary banquets; votive reliefs and works from the theatre; 3C statue of Comedy from the Dionysion; reclining youth, beautiful but mutilated; Roman imperial *heads, among them a negroid head and portraits of Claudius, Julius Caesar, Lucius Caesar and Hadrian; Hermes (headless copy of Hermes of Andros, Roman); two statues of Nemesis; Boustrophedon funerary inscription of Glaukos, son of Leptine, of Paros (companion of Archilochos); other inscriptions, including one governing the sale of wine; wine measures; cases of pottery. In the **courtyard** are various sculptures, including a large bird (date?).

Outside the S corner of the agora a paved street, uncovered for 50m, leads SW, passing a well-preserved **exedra** (1C AD), the remains of an **odeion** (left), and the so-called **Court of 100 Flagstones** (covered). Continuing, you reach the slight remains of the **Triumphal Arch of Caracalla**, identified by its inscription, and the **Herakleion**, or **Sanctuary of Herakles**. All these monuments can be reached from a road running between them from the Panayía road to the theatre.

The monumental entrance to the sanctuary was a Propylon, with a staircase, leading to the COURT. On the N side is an **Ionic Temple**, a peripteral edifice with 6 by 8 columns surrounding a single chamber (early 5C). In front of it is a ruinous **altar**. To the S, partly covered by the modern road leading to the Silenus Gate, is a building divided into rooms, which incorporated or replaced a 6C Temple in polygonal masonry. In the S corner is a **triangular court**, which had a circular monument. Farther to the S the site of the **Monument of Thersilochos** (excavated in 1913 and filled in again) houses a collection of marble fragments.

In the village square are a few fragments of an Early Christian **basilica** (?6C), probably ruined in 904 when Leo of Tripoli occupied the island. To the E of the apse is a mosaic belonging to a building of the Hadrianic period.

At **Tsoukalarió** on the N coast, to the W of the ancient town, is an early Christian complex, with Middle Byzantine tombs.

## Excursions

3km SE of **Límenas** is **Makrí Ammos** (Hotel A, summer only), a pleasant beach (charge) with tavernas.

Other excursions can be made independently or form part of a **round trip** of the island (95km; buses make the whole circuit but some coastal villages are served independently; also inland to **Theólogos** etc.). Two delightful inland villages are close to Limenas: the road (SE) rises through pine-woods, and, crossing a ridge, emerges on a ledge (*view of the beautiful bay of Potamiá). 8km **Panayía** (Hotels B, D, E) has a square with two gushing fountains, shaded by a plane-tree. 9.5km **Potamiá**, slightly larger, with steep stone streets and old Turkish houses, is a starting-point for the ascent of Ipsarion (Hypsarion; 1142m) in 2–3 hours. A museum has works of the local artist Polignotos Vayis. **Skála Potamías** on the coast has a pleasant beach, hotels (B, C, D, E) and tavernas. On **Cape Pirgos**, to the NE, are some remains of an ancient lighthouse inscribed as his own tomb and memorial by one Akeratos.

The main road continues down the E coast. The island abounds in unexcavated Hellenic and medieval remains (an account of which in J.H.S., vol. 29, 1909 is supplemented in B.C.H., vol. 54, 1930). 17.5km **Kínira** (Hotels C, E). Vestiges of ancient *Koinyra* are nearby. 28.5km **Alikí** has ancient marble quarries, an Archaic sanctuary, and two excavated basilican churches—all of some interest. Ancient mines have been located at several points in the S of the island. The best preserved of many Hellenic **towers** is near **Thimoniá** (a short distance inland from Alikí), the greatest concentration of them near Astrís; they were probably for defence against pirates. At 34.5km is the impressively situated **Moní Arkhangélou**. Beyond (41.5km) **Astrís** (Hotel C) is (48.5km) **Potós** (Hotels A, B, C, D), with an Early Christian basilica, and the turning for finely situated **Theológos** (Hotels B, C), 10km inland in the Dipotamos valley below the S slope of Ipsárion. The town was the medieval capital of Thassos. There are some attractive houses: that of Mehmet Ali's youth survives. Remains of a castle (**Kouphó-kastro**) crowns a hill to the south-east. At **Kastrí** is a prehistoric and early Iron Age fortified settlement. Returning to the coast road you reach (52.5km) **Limenariá** (1488 inhab.; Hotels B, C, D, E), now a substantial tourist centre, formerly important for cadmium mining. A road leads inland in 15km to **Kástro** with an Early Christian refuge settlement reused in the 15C (about 30 houses). 65.5km Turnings for **Mariés** (8km inland) and its **Skála** on the coast. Ancient kilns and ceramic workshops have been found in the vicinity. An ochre mine in the **Tsíni** area was apparently used in the Palaeolithic period. The road follows the shore, passing many small pensions and camping places amid the pines. 79km **Prinó**. **Skála Prínou** (Hotels B; ferry for Kavalla), is 2km away on the coast. 95km **Límenas**.

# 68

# Philíppi and Dráma

**Road**, 37km (23 miles), passing (15km) Philíppi. Frequent **bus** (20-minute ride to Philíppi).

You leave Kavalla by the Thessaloníki road (Rte 66) and beyond the coastal range take the right fork. **Amygdaléonas** may be the site of the **Mansion Fonsca** on the Via Egnatia. The road passes the old airfield of Kavalla. 9km **Dáton**, a village on the edge of the marshy plain of Philíppi (left), bears the name held by the district even before the foundation of Philíppi. The modern road (restaurant at 12km) runs to the West of the Roman. On the latter, 1km before it rejoins this route at the approach to Philíppi, is the **Khan of Dikili Tach**, where a monument erected by a Roman officer, C. Vibius, has Latin inscriptions on each face. Opposite, on the S side of the Roman road, is a hill where the French School and Greek Archaeological Service have unearthed an important prehistoric settlement. Its Neolithic and Early

Bronze Age pottery is dated to the period of the foundation of Troy; and there is some later material. Finds are in the Philíppi and Kavalla museums. Where the two roads meet, ancient stone fragments strewn about the tobacco fields show that a large suburb extended to the E of Philíppi. At (15km) **Krinídhes** (Hotels C, E) are important remains belonging to ancient Philíppi. In Od. Merarkhías, right of the main road, is a large 'extra-muros' cemetery basilica: part of a second with a mosaic floor has been uncovered close by. Left of the main road (below Jetoil petrol station) is an enclosure with built tombs, and a mortuary compelx including a church and stoa—part of the East Cemetery of Philíppi.

15.5km **Philíppi** guarded the narrow gap between hill and marsh through which the Via Egnatia has to pass. The highway formed the *decumanus* of the city and the modern road, on the same course, passes the theatre and through the excavations. To the left, is the larger archaeological area with the forum of the Roman city and, opposite (i.e. on the same side of the road as the theatre), Basilica A. The museum is a short distance further on (right). Bus travellers should disembark at the forum; cars may be better parked below the museum rather than in the large car park. The theatre has a large car park and tourist pavilion for the festival. Dominating the plain, the Greek acropolis with its prominent medieval towers occupies the last outcrop of the Lekanis range which extends E to the Nestos. In general visible remains are Roman or Early Christian.

**History**. The ancient town of *Krenides* ('Fountains') was colonised by Thasians in 361 BC led by the exiled Athenian Kallistratos, on the site of a native settlement possibly called *Daton*. It was taken over in 356 by Philip II of Macedon, who renamed it *Philippi* after himself. The place was of little importance until the establishment of the Via Egnatia as a military road. After the momentous battle of 42 BC (see below), the city was refounded with veterans of the battle by Octavian and from 27 BC bore the name *Colonia Julia Augusta Philippensis*. Philippi was the first stage on the journey westwards from its port, Neapolis (Kavalla). In AD 49 St Paul, having sailed from the Troad to Neapolis, spent some time at Philippi, where he first preached the gospel in Europe and where, with Silas, he was cast into prison (Acts, xvi, 9–40). Six years later St Paul again visited Philippi (Acts, xx, 6). From his prison in Rome in 64, or possibly earlier from Ephesus, he wrote his Epistle to the Philippians, for whom he seems to have had a special affection. Christianity throve at Philippi, which had a large basilica as early as the 5C. It was occupied by the Goths in 473. It gave the title to a Byzantine metropolitan and (though the city was deserted by c 950) remained his seat until, in 1619, the see, renamed 'Philippi and Drama' was transferred to Drama. Since 1924 the title has passed to the Metropolitan residing at Kavalla. The site has been excavated by the French School (1920–24 and since 1927) and by Greek archaeologists. A new guidebook is in preparation by the Archaeological Service.

**Battle of Philippi**. Following the assassination of Julius Caesar in 44 BC, the republicans Brutus and Cassius made for the East. By the time Antony and Octavian, great-nephew of Julius, had temporarily assuaged their own rivalry by the device of the triumvirate (43), Brutus, who had seized Macedonia, and Cassius, who had secured Syria, were in control of all the Roman provinces E of the Adriatic, and commanded 19 legions and numerous cavalry. Leaving Lepidus behind to rule Italy, Antony and Octavian, with an equivalent force, marched against Brutus and Cassius. The armies met in the plain of Philippi in October 42. The republicans were encamped to the W of the town athwart the main road (where traces of their field works have been noted). In the ensuing two battles Brutus and Cassius made the same mistakes as Pompey had at Pharsalus. Having command of the sea at Neapolis and shorter communications, their obvious policy was to exhaust the enemy by avoiding action. A hazardous frontal attack by Antony forced a pitched battle, and muddled generalship contributed to the defeat of Cassius, who committed suicide. Brutus, who had been victorious over Octavian, was three weeks later forced against his better judgement to fight again in the same place, where the legions of the Triumvirate were executing a dangerous infiltration between his troops and the marsh. The outcome was disastrous and Brutus, too, killed himself.

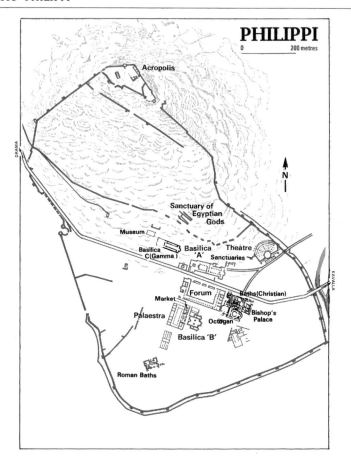

The poet Horace fought on the republican side and joined in the 'headlong rout, his poor shield ingloriously left behind' (*Odes*, II, 7).

The **forum**, a paved rectangle 99m by 50m, had uniform porticoes on three sides approached by steps. The plan is quite clear, though the remains do not stand much above the foundations. On the N side monumental **fountains** flanked a **tribune** and monuments to citizens and emperors; the decumanus passed along and above its rear wall (remains parallel with and below the modern road), leaving a view towards the acropolis. The rear walls of all four sides make an enclosing rectangle, and this replanning of the general ensemble can be dated by inscriptions to the reign of Marcus Aurelius. At the NE and NW angles stood two **temples**; on the E side a **library**. The S side replaced houses of the Augustan period.

To the S of the forum rise the conspicuous remains of the 'Direkler' (Turkish: 'Pillars') or **Basilica B**, one of the failures that marked the slow transition from the true basilica to the cruciform church with dome. The 6C architect attempted to cover the E end of a basilica with a brick cupola. The E wall collapsed under the weight before the altar or synthronon could be assembled, so that the sanctuary was never dedicated. The W end, still standing in 837 when the invading Bulgars carved an inscription in it, fell in turn, leaving only the narthex to be converted into a small church in the 10C by the addition of an apse made out of earlier materials. The pillars, formed of reused antique blocks, have interesting capitals with acanthus-leaf decoration. The central arch of the W wall shows the springing of the narthex vault. Chunks of the fallen dome survive and a fine *capital. The Bulgarian inscription was removed in 1943. Two contemporary annexes to the N form the **baptistery**; two to the S, designed perhaps as the diakonikon, probably constituted the sanctuary itself after the collapse of the chancel.

The remains, particularly interesting to students of architecture, are exhaustively discussed by Paul Lemerle in *Philippes et la Macédoine orientale à l'époque chrétienne et byzantine* (1945), and in more recent literature. To make way for the basilica a covered market and the greater part of a **palaestra** were levelled; much of the material went into the church. The most interesting part surviving (below the SE corner) is a monumental **public latrine**, almost perfectly preserved, which is approached by a descending flight of steps and a double portal. Many of the 50 marble seats are still in place. Farther over are **Roman baths**, built c AD 250 and destroyed by fire soon afterwards (mosaics destroyed by the Bulgarians in 1941–45).

Excavations by Prof. Pelekanides since 1960 E of the Forum (the area is fenced off but can be seen from the road) uncovered remains of an **octago-nal church**, comparable in size and plan with San Vitale at Ravenna, except that the octagon is inscribed in a square. Excavation is complete and publication in progress. It had an inner colonnade of 20 columns on seven sides with a marble screen closing the bema on the eighth. The church was approached from the Via Egnatia by a great gate (perhaps that described by Eusebius). On the N side it had a **baptistery** communicating with **baths**. Beneath the octagon a Macedonian tomb has yielded gold finds: the massive stone at the entrance is still in position. More recent excavation has shown that there was an earlier octagonal structure on the site and that a 4C basilican church dedicated to St Paul preceded that, in turn. S of the octagonal building is the **bishop's residence**.

On the N side of the road is **Basilica A**, erected c 500 on a prepared terrace. It was probably ruined in an earthquake in the same century, then used as a quarry. Its plan was recovered before 1939 and its N walls stand to a considerable height.

The terrace is reached by **propylaea** and a broad **stairway** (to the left of the modern entrance). Half-way up on the right was a **crypt** of Roman date, taken by the 5C to be the prison of St Paul and later frescoed with scenes from his life and crowned by a chapel. On the terrace the foundations of a Hellenistic temple were converted into a **cistern**. A huge paved **atrium**, with a W façade with fountains and three porticoes, extended E to the **church**, which is entered by three doors. The **narthex** gave access at the N end to a separate **baptistery** (well preserved, with mosaic floor) and by three openings to the church itself. This is an aisled basilica with E transepts and semi-circular apse, comparable in size with Ayios Demetrios at Thessaloniki. Within can be traced the position of an **ambo** and the **screen**. The E wall, unusually, had two doors.

The **museum** is above the road to the W of the entrances to the forum and Basilica A. Outside are Early Christian mosaics from a country house at Piyes tis Voiranis near Bournabasi; also architectural fragments from Philippi. Beside is another basilica (Gamma), three-aisled and built in the early 6C, with ancillary structures. Within, most of the exhibits (except those from the British excavations at Sitagroi!) are labelled in English as well as Greek. In the vestibule are finds from the French School's Neolithic site at Dikili Tach. The main ground floor room contains Early Christian material from Philippi: fine capitals and other architectural members, many with sculptural decoration; also a mosaic, inscriptions and a case with coins from excavations in the octagonal church. An alcove at the far end has finds from Sitagroi. The upstairs room has chiefly Roman finds from the site. At the far end are Nike figures and an Athena from a temple in the forum. Restored drawings show their original position on the building (acroteria). A case of finds from Roman tombs includes glass and pottery. A small group of earlier items has a fragmentary inscription of a plan for the city of Philippi by Alexander the Great.

From the museum a path ascends to the **acropolis** (311m) with its three massive medieval towers built on the ruins of the Macedonian walls. The climb is recommended more for the view of the forum, the octagonal church, the battlefield, and the plain than for the remains, though the hill is remarkable also for the variety of its insect life (butterflies, dragonflies, etc.). On the way up are some Christian signs carved in the rock, and a terrace with the remains of a **Sanctuary of Egyptian Deities** (Isis, Serapis, Harpocrates).

Returning to Basilica A and continuing E round the base of the rocks, you find a series of **rock sanctuaries**. Farther on are numerous lengthy Latin inscriptions (2–3C) recording benefactors of a religious college, dedicated to Silvanus. There are also scores of reliefs cut in the rock (extending above the theatre), mainly dedicated to Bendis, the Thracian equivalent of Artemis. Below is the **theatre**, built against the slope of the hill, which dates back to the foundation of Philippi. Of the original building there survives some well-built masonry of the analemma and parodoi. In the Roman era (2C AD) the theatre was remodelled; the orchestra was paved, the paradoi vaulted. Remains of the Roman *frons scaenae* show it to have resembled the type of Asia Minor, with its rubble wall pierced by five doors. The Roman stage disappeared in the last alterations (3C) into an arena. To this period belong three bas-reliefs of Nemesis, Mars, and Victory, found in the W parodos. Recent excavations have shown that the cavea had an upper tier, probably added during the Roman period. Visible are the lateral passageway dividing lower tier from upper, the front wall of the upper tier, with draining vents, the rubble foundations for the seating and the vaulted substructure. The building remained virtually whole till the 16C. The seating of the cavea was restored in 1957–59 to allow the staging of dramatic performances.

To regain the road, you follow the Byzantine enceinte, which was built on the top of the 4C walls. Although ruinous, its line can be traced along the slope of the acropolis and for most of its course in the plain. It is equipped with towers and redans. No trace remains of the arch which early travellers describe as bestriding the road.

By-passing (24.5km) **Dhoxáto** (114m), a deme of 3594 inhabitants, engaged in tobacco cultivation, you join the road from Paranésti (see below) on a low plateau and cross the railway. The isolated **Korílovo** (623m) stands out on the right, while **Bóz Dág** (2231m), the summit of the Falakrón range, towers to the N.

37km **Dráma** (Δράμα; 105m, Hotels B, C, D), a thriving town of 37,604 inhabitants, is the capital of the nome of Dráma, the seat of a metropolitan, and the headquarters of an army corps. It is ringed but not overshadowed to the N by the heights of Falakrón, and commands the 'golden plain', the tobacco from which provides its livelihood. The town has a **Tobacco Research Station** and some timber production. Though it holds no particular interest for the tourist, the large shaded squares and restaurants make it a pleasant place to pause and there are attractive old houses and shops.

An archaeological museum, in Patriárkhou Dhíonissíou to the S of the park, is built but unoccupied. There is a small folk collection in the Nomarkhía.

**History.** *Drama* is thought to occupy the site of an Edonian town called *Drabeskos* by Thucydides (I, 100), where the Athenians in 465 BC were cut to pieces in their first and unsuccessful attempt to colonise Amphipolis. The Edonians, a Thracian people who dwelt between the Strymon and the Nestos, were notorious for their orgiastic worship of Dionysos. Drama was of some importance in the Byzantine era and its original walls may be as early as the 9C. Boniface de Montferrat fortified the town in 1205 and here in 1317 died Irène de Montferrat, second wife of Andronikos II. The Turks occupied it in c 1371. Briefly in the 14C Dráma (previously in the see of Philippi) was raised to the status of metropolitan see, only to be incorporated with Serres. In 1619 the see of Philippi (which already included Kavalla) was removed to Drama, the metropolitan taking the dual title 'Philippi and Drama'. In 1924 this was divided, the title of Philippi passing to the new see at Kavalla.

FROM DRÁMA TO XÁNTHI BY THE INLAND ROAD, 88.5km. You leave the town by the Kaválla road (Rte 68), but turn left at (5km) **Khoristí**, and follow the course of the railway all the way to Stavroúpolis. Beyond (16km) **Nikifóros**, a centre of tobacco cultivation, are remains of an aqueduct. The road traverses rugged country with wild mountain views all round as it crosss the watershed between the Angistis and the Nestos. 26km A right fork leads to the villages of Pteléa and Mirtoúsa. Beyond (4km) the latter, towards Paranésti, is a fort (?4C) at Aerikó. Just before (36km) **Paranésti** (Hotel E), the railway crosses the Nestos by Bailey bridge to the left of the road bridge and follows the left of the river valley to the SE, passing through the most attractive country of the route.

The **Néstos**, or **Mesta**, rises in the Rhodope Mountains in Bulgaria and divides Macedonia geographically from Thrace, though the modern nome boundaries rather reflect local convenience. Under the Treaty of Bucharest (1913), the river formed the frontier with Bulgaria, which for two or three years enjoyed an Aegean seaboard extending from the Mesta to Dedeagatch and beyond. Above Paranesti the river is enclosed in inaccessible gorges that rival in wildness that between Stavroupolis and Toxotes, and the whole of its basin N to the Bulgarian frontier is hemmed in by the Rhodope chain, the rolling heights of which, swathed in beech forests, constitute much of the nome of Drama. The area, which has a good climate and fertile soil, has not found favour with Anatolian Greeks, and since 1923 has remained practically uninhabited. The lower course of the Nestos lies through the alluvial plain of Khrisoúpolis.

52km **Neokhóri** has an Early Iron Age fort 1km SE at Mourkana, in an arm of the river. At **Kalíva** 10km N of Neokhóri is a 4C fort (signed path to left of road), reused in the 6C AD. There are remains of the wall and houses. At (61km) **Stavroúpolis**, a deme of 1043 inhabitants, in the fairest part of the Nestos valley, a kafenion in the attractive little plateia has an interesting collection of bygones.

To the SE of Stavroúpolis, reached from the station by minor road (after 3km towards Komniná, take sign-posted motorable track left for 1.5km), is a remarkable vaulted **tomb**, excavated in 1953. The chamber is 3m square and the vaulted dromos 4.9m long. The tomb was constructed in local marble with paintings done directly on to the marble surface (a technique unusual in Macedonia). Within are two handsome marble funerary couches.

From Stavroúpolis the road turns E, climbing through a low pass to the N of Akhlat Tsal (1401m). At (80km) the junction of two predominantly Moslem valleys you meet the road from Plovdiv in Bulgaria (buses twice weekly from Komotiní, via Haskovo and continuing to Sofia, 10 hrs). The road (41km to the border) holds no particular interest though near **Gláfki** (c 13km) are remains of a Byzantine fort. 88.5km **Xánthi**, see Rte 69.

FROM DRAMA TO KATO NEVROKOPI, 45km (28 miles). The road at first goes NW as far as (24km) **Prosotáni** (pop. 3683), the ancient *Pyrsopolis*, which it leaves on the left. Then turning N into the Falakron Mountains, it climbs the **Stená Granítou**, a defile between Mavro Longos (1404m) and Vothlitsi (1201m). The valley broadens and divides, the main road following the W opening in thick woods (the right branch goes on to the Bartiseva refuge from which Boz Dag is climbed). From (33km) **Granítis** (793m) we descend into an intensely cultivated flat depression, where (45km) **Káto Nevrokópi** (Hotel D; pop 2158) guards the road to the Bulgarian frontier (no crossing), 11km to the N. The area E of this road, between Drama and the frontier, was a preserve of the nomadic Sarakatzanoi.

From Dráma to **Sérres** see Rte 65A.

# 69

# Alexandroúpolis and the Turkish frontier (Istanbul)

## A. By road

**Road**, 735km (457 miles), of international standard all the way. To (166km) Kaválla, see Rte 66.—222km Xánthi.—290km Komotiní.—355km Alexandroúpolis.—388.5km Ardhánio. Here the main highway into Turkey diverges via Ipsala and Keşan (Istanbul, 264km; Gallipoli–Çanakkale ferry, 162.5km, for Izmir).—454km Dhidhimótikho.—494km Kastanéai (frontier).—504km Edirne, whence 232km to Istanbul (**Bus** daily exc. Thurs from Xánthi: Taródhis Tours, Stoá Noúsi).

From Thessaloníki to (166km) **Kaválla**, see Rte 66. You leave Kaválla by its E suburbs, passing a huge stadium. Beyond (176km) **Néa Karváli**, where scanty remains of a large enceinte have been equated with ancient *Akontisma*, the road turns away from the coast and at 183.5km passes (right) a square (?) Roman fort. 187km **Pondolívadho** is an industrial suburb. An ancient site (right) may be *Pistyros*, a point of Xerxes' march mentioned by Herodotus. To the left indented foothills of the **Lakánis Mountains** (home of the Edoni) rise to 1298m; to the right the flat plain of Khrisoupolis extends to the Nestos. 191km **Gravoúna**.

About 1.5km beyond the village a by-road runs S to (4km) **Khrisoúpolis** (Χρυσούπολις), seat (7208 inhab; Hotel C) of the eparchy of Nestos and in Byzantine times a town of some importance on the high road. It was known to the Turks as Sari Saban, meaning Yellow Plain. 3km SW of Khrisoúpolis is the new airport which, although officially described as 'Kavalla' is almost equidistant between Kaválla and Xánthi. 18.5km **Keramotí** (Hotels B, C, D, E; campsite; tavernas) is linked by frequent car-ferry with Thasos, 5km offshore. The successful culture of oysters was started in 1959 in the little inlet on which the harbour stands, and the bird life is varied.

The villages lie off the road in the foothills to the left. 203km **Kríni** has a small medieval fortress. 206km **Parádheisos**, a prettily terraced village (cafés), overlooks the tree-grown banks of the Nestos. The river is crossed by a barrage which controls the irrigation of the whole delta. The Via Egnatia appears to have crossed the river nearer its mouth. To the right of the road, towards the river, are some scattered remains of Byzantine *Topeiros*, including a three-aisled Middle Byzantine church. The road joins the railway (see Rte 69B), and enters Thrace. 210km **Toxótes** (left), with a minaret, and **Tímbano**, with wooden balconies, are typical villages of the S slope of Akhlat Tsal (left), where Turkish growers still produce the prized Xanthíyaka, the finest quality of Turkish tobacco. The picturesque irregularity of these villages with their gardens and decaying mosques is emphasised by neighbouring Greek refugee settlements, planned in rigid lines with churches in the functional style of the 1920s. A huge sugar factory typifies a current product.

222km **Xánthi** (Ξάνθη; Hotels B, C, D), seat of a metropolitan and the prosperous capital (34,889) of a nome, stands at the opening of the narrow upper valley of the Esketze, the ancient *Kosintos*. The main road by-passes the town which, however, should not be missed. The main attraction is the beautiful traditional houses of **Old Xánthi** (Παλαιά Ξάνθη; tavernas) which cluster on the hillside to the N of the modern town and below the Byzantine **kastro** (sections of fortifications visible), built to defend the defile from Bulgar incursions. There is a **Folk Museum** (Λαογραφικό Μουσείο; open evenings and Sunday mornings) in Od. Antíka, containing local costumes, traditional implements, etc. The **cathedral** has a collection of ikons, manuscripts and church plate. On the higher slopes are some monasteries, one of which, the **Moní Megíston Taxiárchon**, houses the **Ecclesiastical College of Xánthi**. Byzantine *Xanthea* grew up below the kastro. Under the Turks a mere summer resort, Xánthi, with the coming of the railway, superseded Yenije (see below) as the centre of the fine tobacco growing area. A local brand of cigarettes (Kiretsiler) has a wide reputation. The lower town has been considerably rebuilt in recent years, but as well as sections of Byzantine structures, there are some delightful streets of old low buildings with small shops, cafés, etc. The new **airport** at Khrisoúpolis (see above) serves Xánthi, as well as Kaválla, and buses connect with the flights, starting from the Olympic Airways office at Michael Vógdhou 6a.

At **Dhiomídhia** (6km S of Xánthi) there is an important prehistoric (especially Late Neolithic) settlement on the hill **Tepés** to the N of the village.

FROM XANTHI TO AVDHIRA, 26km (16 miles; bus). From the Porto Lagos road (see below) you take the right fork at (8km) **Vaféïka**. 11km **Yeniséa** long the centre of the tobacco trade and the local Turkish capital (Yenije), has declined in importance. Continuing beyond the modern village of (19km) **Ávdhira**, the road bypasses excavations and you reach the sea at (27.5km) **Ayios Pandeleímon**. Just before reaching the sea, there is a sign (left) to the **Archaeological Site** and the road leads in a few metres to the remains of ancient *Abdera* (Ἄβδηρα).

**History**. The city, traditionally founded by Herakles on the spot where Abderos was killed by Diomedes' horses, was in fact colonised c 656 BC from Klazomenai. Refounded c 500 BC by refugees from a Persian occupation of Teos (SW of Smyrna), it became a prominent member of the Delian League and famous for the beauty of its coinage. Democritus, the 5C philosopher who expounded an atomic theory, Protagoras (c 481–411), the first of the Sophists, and Anaxarchos, the counsellor of Alexander the Great, were all born here, but despite the celebrity of its school of philosophy, the inhabitants generally were proverbial for their dullness. Hippocrates and Juvenal inveigh against its sickly air. Abdera shared the fortunes of Macedonia and, despite a sack in 170 BC by an over-zealous general, remained nominally free of Rome down to Imperial times. Abdera was important in the Early Christian and Byzantine periods when a fortress (*Polystylon*) was built on the Classical acropolis. Roads connected Polystylon with *Xanthea* and *Peritheorion*. It is known to have been the seat of a bishop in the 9C.

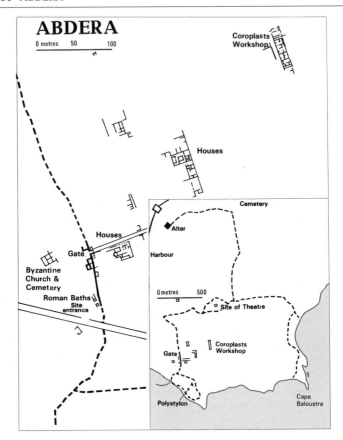

Systematic excavations began in 1950 directed by D. Lazarides for the Greek Archaeological Service. A museum, in the modern village, is now nearly complete. The nature of the site is probably best appreciated by climbing first the track immediately opposite the gate to the fenced site, which leads in a few metres to Polystylon, site of the acropolis of the city from the Classical period. The first conspicuous monument is a small single-aisled **church** of the 12C, with the remains of a contemporary **cemetery** beside it. Below are good sections of the **defences**, the Byzantine built over the Classical, with the masonry of the two periods clearly distinguishable. A square **tower** of the Classical system is preserved. Within the wall some parts of a **bath building** with hypocaust can be made out. In the sea beyond, within the lines of the modern breakwater, can be seen the scattered remnants of the ancient **harbour** mole. On the highest point of the promontory, its position indicated from below by a triangulation block, is a fine three-aisled Middle Byzantine church on the site of an Early Christian **basilica** of c 600, with an octagonal **baptistery** (from the earlier period) at the NW. Beyond are the remains of the bishop's palace. From this point, the broader extent of the Greek and Roman city can be best surveyed. It lay in a depression N and E of the acropolis. In antiquity the sea reached much further inland, approaching the W arm of the walls. The fortified circuit, almost 5.5km in total, has been fully traced. The Archaic acropolis, focus of the earliest part of the fortifications (7–6C) and predecessor to Polystylon, was on the high ground to the NW. The whole of the valley seems to have been settled and the E limit, as defined by the wall, extended to a second (smaller) harbour out of your sight beyond the furthest visible promontory. This can be reached, if desired, by following the road beyond the archaeological site to Pórto Molós (good beach).

You may now descend and enter the gate to the main site. To the right is a Roman **bath** building and, beyond, the **city wall**. Past the path are Late Roman **houses**. A large square structure was a **forward tower**, into which Roman burials (fragments of sarcophagi visible) were later inserted. N of this is the **gateway** to the city, protected by two square **towers**. The wall (and towers) in fine masonry belong, in origin, to the Classical period, but the wall itself underwent many later repairs, and differences in construction style are evident here and there. The main structure has an inner and an outer face, with rubble filling. Within the gate, the remains are less impressive. They belong almost exclusively to **blocks of houses** of the Hellenistic and Roman periods, sometimes with Classical buildings shown to underly them, as in the first units visible, where a paved Roman floor is at the top and Classical house remains at the bottom of the excavated sequence. In general the house remains are disappointing to the visitor, though it is possible to make out paved courts with wells and drainage channels, column bases, threshold blocks, the outlines of rooms, etc. The town was laid out on a grid system from the 4C, with several houses in blocks of uniform size. At the far NE of the site are buildings which included a **figure-maker's workshop**. Beyond this, and best reached by a track off the Pórto Molós road, is the **theatre**, of whose remains there is little to be seen.

At the NW extremity of the site, reached by returning for c 1.3km towards modern Avdhira and striking E by tracks, is a fenced enclosure where the Archaic acropolis, the Archaic wall (7–6C) is partly overlain by the N sector of the late Classical. Here, in the 4–3C, ground altars, probably to Demeter and Kore, were approached by steps. 2000 miniature votive vases were found. Remains of ship-sheds against the wall here are associated with an early harbour when the shore line was different. Remains of a public building of the Archaic period have been located c 100m from the NW corner of the fortifications. Graves of various periods have been excavated outside the walls. On the other side of the same track is an exacavated section of the wall in a fenced enclosure and there are tumuli to the N.

From Xánthi there is a choice of two routes: the main road (see below) leading SE to Lagos on the coast or the Via Egnatia, which, although here a secondary road, is an adequate and historically rather more interesting alternative; it is also c 10km shorter.

FROM XANTHI TO KOMOTINI BY THE VIA EGNATIA, 48km (30 miles). The road strikes due E, followed by the railway (Rte 69B). About 1.5km beyond **Amaxádhes**, a track (right) leads in 5km to the best-preserved part of *Anastasioupolis* (Byzantine *Peritheorion*).

The town was a station on the Via Egnatia, probably taking its name from Anastasius I (491–518): it lies on the N shore of Lake Vistonis. After destruction in the early 13C, it was rebuilt and renamed under Andronicus III (1328–41). At the edge of the lake, among trees, is a fenced archaeological area. The site is very overgrown but the spectacular remains make the effort involved worthwhile. Preserved nearly to its original height is the *S gate of the city, which gave onto the harbour (marble plaques to each side have monograms of the Palaiologues). Also to be seen here are a tower and sections of the fortification wall. Most of the wall circuit can be traced and different periods of construction distinguished.

Returning to the main road, there is a further sign to Anastasioupolis after 3km. Here the road passes through a section of walling which also served as an aqueduct and dates to the time of Justinian. The archaeological area can also be reached via this track (c 30 minutes on foot; the track is blocked to vehicles at the railway line).

Beyond (28km) **Iasmós**, you cross (32km) the **River Kompsátos**. Just beyond the bridge (signs) a rough path leads in 5 minutes to a delightful medieval bridge with two arches, a central pier and the original surface partly preserved. Returning to the main road you soon pass (left) the fenced remains of a Byzantine church and shortly (33km) enter **Políanthos** which has a Byzantine castle and, to the N, at **Kedík Kazín**, the remains of a Hellenistic fort. A Hellenistic cemetery has also been excavated in the vicinity. 38km **Linós** (left) 6km to the N of which on Mt Papikion (adequate dirt road) is a Byzantine cemetery and a recently excavated 10–11C Byzantine church with an opus sectile marble floor. This was part of a more extensive and impressive monastic complex (refectory, baths, cistern etc.) 38km Sóstis (left). A sign (right) to Prehistoric Settlement can be safely ignored: there is nothing to see.

An alternative and rather more pleasant route into Komotiní (13km) is to turn into Sóstis and proceed via (5km) **Mískhos**, with an attractive silver-capped minaret.

42km Track (left; signposted; rough but passable) to the site of medieval *Mosynopolis*, the limit of Norman penetration in 1185.

Originally Porsula, the town was granted city rank by Diocletian with the name *Maximianopolis*, and sent a metropolitan to the Council of Ephesus. Geoffroy de Villehardouin, a chronicler of the Fourth Crusade, accepted it as his fief. The best-preserved section of the walls, with square and round towers, is by the track after 1km, but other remains can be seen over a wide area. Inscriptions and architectural fragments from the site are in the Komotiní Museum. (The track continues 2.5km farther to join the alternative route to Komotiní just beyond Mískhos; see above.)

Returning to the asphalt road, there are signs to **Paradhími**, known for its prehistoric tomb (finds in Kaválla and Komotiní Museums). At 44km you join the main road.

FROM XANTHI TO KOMOTINI VIA PORTO LAGOS (main road) 57km (35 miles). The **main road** leaves Xánthi to the SE, crossing the railway. The well-watered country to the right grows excellent tobacco. At (230km) **Vaféïka**, by-road (right; see above) to Avdhira. Between Vaféïka and **Koutsoú** (at c 4km) an extensive Hellenistic and Roman site was discovered to the S of the main road in 1973. There are also remains of the Classical period. 248km **Pórto Lágos**, the port of Komotiní, stands on a tongue of land separating the Vistonian Gulf from Lake Vistonis. The remains of a Byzantine basilica of the 10C lie right of the road (sign) just beyond the town. The church is an early example of the inscribed-cross type and was built over the remains of an Early Christian structure. It stands within a fortified Byzantine settlement (?*Poron*). Remains of the defences are particularly evident towards the sea, where they include towers. They can be seen also on the other side of the road. The place still has a bishop. Worth a glance are the old Genoese fort and an attractive church. Beyond the channel through which the lake drains into the sea, the road is carried on a causeway with a marshy lagoon on the right. Fish and eels are caught in great numbers and the area is celebrated for the variety of its water-birds. The eels are almost exclusively exported live in tanks to Germany and Central Europe. The fish traps can be visited.

A low hill rising to the SE (off the by-road to Fanári; Hotels B, C) may be the site of ancient *Dikaia*. Graves have been excavated (1977). Near the village is an NTOG camp site. Some ruins, identified with *Stryme*, once famed for its wine, were explored by Thessaloníki University (1957–59) at **Mitrikó** on the remote coast c 16km farther E. A city wall was traced with houses, which yielded a hoard of Maroneian tetradrachms of the 4C BC.

At 278.5km is Messoúni airport. You join the direct road from Xánthi (see above) between Paradhimi and Maximianoupolis, then cross the Akmar. 289km **Komotiní** (Κομοτηνή; Hotels B, C, E), a garrison town only 22.5km from the Bulgarian frontier, and the capital of the nome of Rhodópi Greek Thrace, has pleasant broad streets and squares and a delightful old quarter centred round the Plateias Iféstou (metal-workers) and Irínis. It is a flourishing market centre (37,036 inhab.) for tobacco, cattle, hides, and agricultural goods (annual livestock fair in Holy Week). About half of the inhabitants are Turks, who know the town as **Gümülcüne**, and many are Bulgarian speaking (Pomaks). Here are a college of the University of Thrace and a Moslem secondary college. The city is linked by bus (daily) with Istanbul. An Olympic Airways bus connects with one flight a day from Alexandroúpolis (Komotini terminal at Vasiléos Yioryíou 2). The seasonal Boukloutza on which Komotiní stands has been diverted since the town was flooded in 1960. The walls of the Byzantine fortress are to the left on entering the town. The excellent **Archaeological Museum**, opened in 1976, on the S side of the inner ring road (Od. N. Zoîdhou) houses attractively displayed finds from the whole of Thrace. Outside is a fine Roman sarcophagus with garlands and bucrania. Within, outstanding is the unique gold imperial `bust of Marcus Aurelius found at Plotinoupolis. Also displayed are a remarkable phallic altar; a Clazomenian sarcophagus from Abdera and fine objects from graves at the same site; Archaic pottery and a grave stele from Dikaia (part formerly in Athens); interesting votive plaques from the Sanctuary of Demeter at Mesembria; finds from the Paradhimi tomb and tombs at Ardhani and Orestiadha; honorific decrees from Doriskos and Maroneia (4C BC); also from Maroneia, an inscribed marble block (3C) with impressions of feet and a fine relief of a Thracian rider (4C); case of Greek, Roman and Byzantine coins; ground plans of Stryme, Mesembria and Maroneia. There is also an excellent **Folk Museum** (10.00–13.00, except Sundays) in Od. Ayíou Yioryíou which occupies the restored 19C Peídhis Mansion. It contains furniture, embroideries, costume, domestic and agricultural utensils and implements (including fine bronzes), and ecclesiastical plate. A large Byzantine Collection in the Papanikoláou Foundation building, near the Nomarkhía, is opened only by private arrangement. A useful guide to Komotiní is obtainable from the Dhimarkhion which has an office of public relations (Δημόσιων Σχέσεων).

N of Komotiní, a road leads towards **Nimféa** (15km). After 5km the road enters an attractively wooded area, with unobtrusive amenities for picnicing. An unsurfaced road diverges (right) to **Pandhrósos**. The main road continues to climb and (3km beyond the Pandrósos turn) reaches the impressive Byzantine fort of **Kalés tis Nimféas** with splendid views over the plain of Komotiní. Access to Nimféa itself is restricted by the military.

9km further W (on a different road) is **Símvola** with a good Macedonian tomb of the 3C or earlier.

The principal archaeological sites of this region, the ancient *Kikones*, lie to the SE of Komotiní on the coast. They are cut off from the hinterland by barren limestone hills scored by ravines and torrents. A road (bus from Komotiní) crosses the railway and the Filiouri to (18km) **Xilayaní (Ergáni**, 3km E, has a prehistoric and Byzantine fort at Abar-Tepe), **Proskinités** (24km), with a Neolithic settlement at **Kokkinókhoma** and (31.5km) **Marónia** (pleasant square and cafés). From here the road descends, with occasional signs to antiquities, through the middle of the ancient site, to the coast (4km).

The site of *Maroneia* was a city of importance from Homeric times to the Genoese period. The Classical site of the 4–3 BC occupied an enormous area, the wall circuit being 10.5km in extent, running from the sheer-faced acropolis of Ay. Athanásios above the village down to the coast (Ayios Kharálambos). The extensive ruins, visited by Reinach in 1880, when the walls were still up to 12m high, have been partially explored since 1973 and investigations continue. The area is thickly wooded and, although several interesting features can be easily approached by roads and tracks, a full exploration of the remains requires time, determination and a knowledge of the literature (in particular D. Lazarides, *Maroneia kai Orthagoria*, Athens, 1972, in Greek.)

You follow the road from the village towards the coast. A dirt track (left) leads to the **theatre** and **sanctuary** (IEPO), in 1.3km and 1.6km respectively. The theatre (right of the track) which has been recently reinvestigated was a Hellenistic construction, altered in Roman times. Some of the seating survives, part of the stage building (re-using material from earlier buildings) and the foundation for the proskenion columns, with a number of architectural elements. The seating was provided with a protective barrier (thorakion) in the Roman period for contests involving wild animals. The theatre was built across the ravine and was protected from damage by storm water by an enormous built drainage channel which can be seen to have passed beneath.

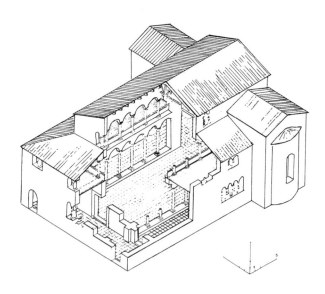

*Reconstruction of Early Christian basilica by P. Xidhas, taken from the book Sinaxi Maroneias by Ch. Bakirtzis and G. Hadjimichalis, Agra Publications, Athens*

200m NE of the theatre is a substantial section of walling with towers. The foundations of the sanctuary complex (probably dedicated to Dionysos), farther on, can be made out. The main temple had a pronaos and cella (with hearth or base for cult statue) and ancillary structures but the surviving remains are hardly worth more than a glance.

Returning to the main road, a short distance further down (left) is the most accessible part of the city wall, with two square towers. The wall in general is 2.3–3m thick and has square or round towers at irregular intervals; more frequent on flat ground. A sign to 'Mosaic' (left) takes you to a recently restored Hellenistic mosaic. 300m farther down the road, a second sign ('Mosaic', left) leads to the Byzantine fortifications which have been partly cleared and are impressive. They were constructed on an earlier (Classical) system which protected the harbour. You reach a parking space above the harbour. In an enclosure immediately to the right are the well-preserved remains of a double monumental gateway with three openings in each face, possibly Hadrianic and the entrance to the agora. Farther right (200m) excavations are in progress. Left from the car park, beside a restaurant, are the fenced remains of the Byzantine church of Ayios Kharalambos. A 9C structure, 8m below modern ground level, was succeeded by an inscribed-cross building, the cathedral of a Middle Byzantine bishopric (synthronon in apse).

The acropolis of **Ayios Yióryios** (3km NE) has walling and was used in prehistoric and probably archaic times.

At **Sínaxi**, 7km E of Maroneia, an important Middle Byzantine monastery complex (furnished refectory, tombs etc.) was constructed partly over an Early Christian basilica of the time of Justinian.

Near the village of **Petrotá** byond Sínaxi, are millstone quarries used till the 1930s, with some pieces partly cut still in situ.

Travelling E, from Komotiní, at 294km there is a turning (left) to **Gratíni** (Γρατύνη; 13km), with a by-road to **Páterma** (17.5km).

7km after leaving the main road is a turning (left) to **Iámpoli** (ΙΑΜΠΟΛΗ; small sign; road unsurfaced, rough in places but passable). Beyond Iámpoli (9km) the road continues to the poor Turkish village of Páterma (17.5km) which depends for its livelihood on tobacco cultivation. 2km after Páterma a track leads off (left), just beyond a roadside well (right), to the fenced remains of a one-aisled Byzantine church of the 11–12C. Returning to the road and continuing, you reach (3km from the village) a fine three-arched medieval bridge, carrying its narrow track across the river. The wooded surroundings are delightful.

**Gratíni** (Byzantine *Gratianos*) is reached by ignoring the Iámpoli turn and continuing along the asphalt road. The pleasant village lies at the foot of a steep hill (20–30 minute climb; path overgrown in places) crowned by the ruinous remains of a Byzantine fortress of the Palaeologue period. A fine Byzantine cistern (with some modern repair) is still in use and accessible, by the little chapel on the summit. Just off the village square, in a neglected plot, is a subterranean funerary chapel of the 13C.

302.5km **Aratos** has an attractive minaret. At (306.5km) **Arísvi**, to the left of the road, are six arches of a Roman bridge that carried the Via Egnatia over the Filiouri. The road turns SW at (317km) **Sápes**, a pleasant town of 2247 inhabitants.

From here there is a road to **Arianá**, 3km to the N of which, at the river **Filiouri**, is a Roman bath of the 2C AD and a Late Roman cemetery. This road continues NE to **Mikró Dherió** (67km) where it turns E to rejoin Rte 69, 9km N of **Souflí** (90km from **Sápes**). W of **Mikró Dherió** burial tumuli of the 8 and 9C BC, covering megalithic and other tombs, have been excavated.

323.5km **Vélki**. Crossing a stream and the railway by a double bridge (1961) the road climbs amid scrub-covered hills noted for quail, woodcock, and snipe. 331km By-road (right) for **Pérama**, beyond which, is **Petrotá** (c 10km see above Sínaxi). 339km By-road to **Mesembria** (Mesimvría).

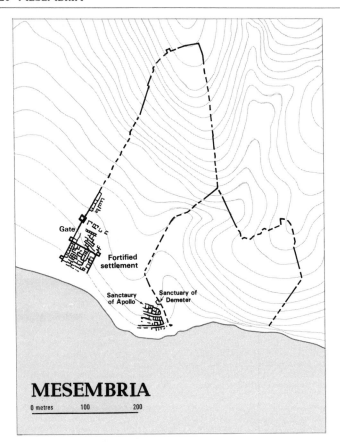

**MESEMBRIA**

0 metres    100         200

The road passes through **Dhíkella** (1.5km) and continues to the site of *Mesembria* (Mesimvría) (6km further). The town was a Samothracian colony of the late 7C and is mentioned by Herodotus. It is sometimes called 'Aegean' Mesembria to distinguish it from another site of the same name on the Euxine.

To the left, beyond the site entrance, the S section of the central leg of the wall crosses the road and can be traced to a tower above the sea. A structure (three-roomed) of fine large blocks which abuts on the wall c 20m inland from the tower and other buildings belong to the 4C **Sanctuary of Demeter** from which came an inscribed base and the fine votive plaques which are in the Komotiní Museum. To the right of the main path, inside the E arm of the main fortifications, an Archaic sanctuary of Apollo consists of buildings grouped round a paved open court. There are remains of a prostyle temple and a stoa. The torso of a kouros and many vases inscribed to Apollo were found.

The most conspicuous part of the site is an unusual **fortified settlement** which occupies only the SW corner of the whole walled area which included an **acropolis** to the N. The defensive circuit can be traced at many points on the ground but is most easily appreciated in the area of the fortified settlement, against which it is built. The E part of the fortifications of the city (which have **three** N–S arms) may belong to the first period of settlement, with an acropolis at that time on the E hill.

The thickness of the walls of the fortified settlement can be clearly discerned, as can the fact that the earlier buildings excavated outside the limits of the fort (N) and partly underlying its walls are on a different alignment from those within. The fort therefore belongs to a secondary phase of the life of the settlement. Within the complex small one-and two-room units (workshops?) lie against the W and part of the N walls. The buildings are laid out on the Hippodamian system, with **streets** on an orthogonal grid—three running E–W and two N–S. At the SE the houses are, unusually, separated from the wall by a road, probably because there was no room for this outside between the wall and the sea. In the centre are house blocks and against the W wall two **houses**. The rooms of that at the NE corner (below the tower) can be easily distinguished, with court, threshold block, etc. Three different phases of construction have been noted between the 5C and 2C BC. Most of the visible remains belong to the second of these, though evidence for the different periods can be seen here and there, with underlying walls on different alignments and layered surfaces to the streets. A large building in the centre of the site may be a public building of some kind. A substantial block of houses outside the fortified settlement has been excavated c 80m to the N. The city **fortifications** are best seen at the W side, where there are three towers. The second (from the S) bears inscriptions, the third (beyond the fortified settlement) guards a **gate** into the town with two marble steps and an unusual circular passage in its N side. The masonry of the walls is in a variety of styles, often of fine quality.

There is a good beach and a fine view W to the mountain spur that hides Maroneia (path; 3½ hours).

The road descends to the coast amongst the dense vineyards of (343km) **Mákri**, built on the site of a Byzantine settlement which was the seat of a bishop from the 9C. Sections of the fortification walls can be seen and various churches have been investigated in or near the village. Near the modern Ayios Anastasios is a Middle Byzantine church, largely covered by a mosque, and Ayios Yioryios is built over its Byzantine predecessor 349km **Néa Khilí** (Hotel D).

355km (220½ miles **ALEXANDROÚPOLIS** (Αλεξανδρούπολις, often written abbreviated to Αλεξ/πολις), the pleasant chief town (36,994 inhab.) of the nome of Evrou, was known to the Turks as *Dedeagaç*. It was renamed after King Alexander in 1919. With air services to Athens, a station on the Thessaloníki–Istanbul railway, and a sea connection with Samothráki, it is the best centre from which to explore Thrace. It is noted for its fish; caviar and mussels are specialities.

**Airport**, 6.5km E, with daily service to Athens. **Air Terminal** on sea front E of lighthouse, Colétti and Ellis 8.

**Railway Station**, E of centre of town.

**Hotels** A–E; F/A.

**Restaurants**. Near the Dhimarkhíon and the lighthouse.

**Post Office** Anatolikís Thrákis. **Tourist Police**, Od. Karaïskáki.

**Buses** to Xánthi, Kaválla, and Thessaloníki daily; to Dhidhimótikho and Orestías, 7 times daily; to Mákri, 5 times daily.

**Ferry** to Samothráki daily in summer, less frequently to Kaválla.

**Wine Festival** in July–September.

**History**. Alexandroupolis is probably on the site of ancient *Salis*, parts of whose Roman cemeteries have been excavated under the modern town. The Turkish name (Dedea-ğaç; Tree of the holy man) derives from a colony of dervishes established in the 15C. The place remained a fishing village until reached in 1872 by the railway from Edirne, after which it rapidly usurped the importance of Ainos (Enez). The Greek archbishopric was transferred in 1889. Ancient *Zone* is placed hereabouts.

The main road, parallel with the sea, forms the principal boulevard of the town, Od. Dhimokratías (formerly, and still on several signs, Leof. Vasiléos Yioryíou B), venue of the 'volta' which necessitates the evening diversion of traffic. On the shore facing the large artificial harbour is a conspicuous lighthouse, to the W of which a broad promenade has been laid out above the beach. The huge modern cathedral of St Nicholas farther inland is prominent. It has an important 13C carved wooden ikon of the Virgin from Ainos. There is an archaeological collection in the **Old Dhimarkhíon** (Town Hall) in Plateía Polyteknhíou (also called Eleftherías; good restaurant), reached via Od. Kíprou (KYΠPOY) the entrance unsigned and well-concealed in an arcade, with sculpture from the area and finds from the Sanctuary of Demeter at Mesembria, also plans of the Sanctuary of the Great Gods on Samothrace.

Beyond Alexandroúpolis road and railway continue E together, passing the airport. 368.5km You cross the Tsáï. On the far bank was the Roman and Byzantine staging-post of *Trajanopolis*, which succeeded *Doriskos* (see below). It was the scene in 161 under Marcus Aurelius of the spectacular miracles of St Glyceria, a Roman maiden later martyred in the Propontis. After a long period as a Metropolitan see, the town seems to have been ruined in the wars of 1205 and lost importance to Demotika; the see was removed c 1353 to Peritheorion. To the left of the road is a magnificently preserved **hána** or staging-post built for use in the 14 and 15C when the town itself had gone into decline. The adjacent thermal springs (Hotels C, D) help treat kidney ailments. The hills visible to the S are across the Turkish frontier.

379km Turning (right, in the opposite direction to the modern village) for ancient *Doriskos*, a Persian fortress town established in 512 BC by Darius I, where Xerxes numbered his armies in 480 (modern scholarship suggests that Herodotus' inflated figures be reduced to 200,000). Some remains (not so far identified as earlier than 4C BC) stand on the flat-topped hill of Sarayia overlooking the railway. The by-road goes on into the Evros delta (see below; permit necessary).

382.5km **Férai** (Φέραι usually Féres; Hotel C), with 4637 inhabitants, was known to the Turks as Farecik. A turn doubles back into the town. In the angle is a picturesque water gate. In the centre of the town, at the highest point, is the church (signed 'Byzantine Temple') of **Ayía Sophía**, katholikon of the monastery of the **Theotokos Cosmosoteira**, built by Isaac Comnenus in 1152. It is of the domed-inscribed cross plan. The interesting frescoes (in need of cleaning), much defaced by the Turks, are of the same date. There are fine carved capitals. The monastery was provided with defences, parts of which are visible: in the 14C it became a fortified civilian settlement. At (388.5km) **Ardháni** you leave the main highway to Turkey which follows the ancient course of the Via Egnatia, crossing the Evros by a long bridge (1962) to **Ipsala** (11km; ancient Kypsela), the Turkish frontier town.

The ancient *Kypsela*, greatest city of the Thracians, lost importance by the 4C BC and in Livy's time was only a fort. Returning towards Thessalonika from his meeting here with Henry of Flanders in 1207, Boniface of Montferrat was intercepted and decapitated by a Bulgarian ambush.

The **Evros** (Εβρος; ancient *Hebros*; Turkish Meriçi; Bulgarian Maritza), of which there are periodic glimpses, rises in Bulgaria S of Sofia and, after a course of c 500km, enters the Aegean opposite the island of Samothrace through a delta 11km wide. Since 1923 its lower course through the flat Thracian plain has formed the boundary between Greece and Turkey, save where the suburbs of Edirne make a Turkish enclave W of the river. It is navigable for small boats as far as Edirne, below which it is crossed by bridges only at Pithio and Ipsala. Its waters abound in fish and water fowl; rare geese and eagles may be seen. Round its twin mouths, noted by Strabo, are several swamps and lakes, of which the largest is Gala–Gölu, the ancient *Stentoris* of Herodotus, on the Turkish side. Some way SW of this lake is the town of Enos, familiar to diplomats as one end of the Enos–Midia line and the ancient *Ainos*, the foundation of which Virgil ascribes to Aeneas. The river has given its name to the nome of Evrou whose capital is Alexandroúpolis. The hill slopes that rise in the W of the province to 914m are clothed with oak forests; cereals, vines and tobacco are cultivated in the plain.

397.5km **Provató** is a local communication centre, with (2km beyond the village) a memorial to General Asimakópoulos. 421km **Souflí** (Σουφλί; Hotels C, D, E) is a pleasant town (4489 inhab.), engaged in the cultivation of vines and silk worms. It has old timber-framed houses, the best of which are up the hill to the left of the main road. One of these, the **Arkhontikó Kourtídhi**, contains the interesting **Silk Museum**. The house itself is a fine example of a traditional upper-class family house (*arkhontikó*) with rooms opening off a large *salóni* upstairs, workrooms on the ground floor and a summer kitchen and other utility rooms off the courtyard. The ground floor has a display of equipment and illustrative material to demonstrate the process of silk production (the original function of this part of the house). Upstairs are examples of local costumes and silk items. The side rooms contain memorabilia of the original owner, a restored kitchen, etc. In the church of **Ayios Yióryios** is a fine 18C carved ikonostasis. At (432km) **Mándra** you meet a by-road that descends a wooded valley from **Mikró Dherió** (22.5km NW, see above), a group of villages near the Bulgarian frontier.

454km **Dhidhimótikho** (Διδυμότειχο; Hotels B, D; cafés and National Bank in the Plateía; public lavatory facing the Dhimarkhion), a market town (8336 inhab.) of Turkish timber-framed houses, clusters round an abrupt hill over-looking the Erithropotamos or Kizil Remma. An inscription, found in 1937, identifies the site with *Plotinoupolis*, founded by Trajan in honour of his wife, Plotina.

**History**. The fortress-town of *Demotika* played an important part in Byzantine history. In 1189 during the **Third Crusade** Frederick Barbarossa held the town hostage while negotiating with the Emperor Isaac II Angelos. The wounded Michael IX fled here after his defeat by the Catalan Grand Company at Aprus (1305), and here in 1341 John VI Cantacuzene had himself proclaimed emperor. The town fell to the Turks in 1361 and Murad I made it his capital for four years before transferring to Adrianople; his son Bayezid was born here. Charles XII of Sweden lay at Demotika in 1713–14, a virtual prisoner of Ahmed III, to whose dominions he had fled after the Battle of Poltava.

To the right, on crossing the bridge, is the sheer-sided hill of **Ayía Pétra** crowned by an aerial mast. This was the core of Roman *Plotinopoulis*. Recent excavations, mainly on the NE flank and including some of the fortification wall, have revealed little of interest for the casual visitor, though one must recall the fine gold bust from here in the Komotiní Museum. The road climbs into the town. In the Plateia (off the main road to the left) is a large square mosque with a pyramidal roof. It was begun by Murad I and completed by his son, Bayezid. It has a fine interior (wooden ceiling, calligraphic inscriptions) and the minaret has two fretted balconies. The town has other interesting Ottoman buildings (including hamams) which have recently been studied.

A short distance above the Plateia, in a fine old house, is the outstanding *Folk Museum (open regularly in the evenings and at most other times by request), begun by a co-operative of local school-masters in the 1970s and supported by the local authority. It is well laid out and organised. Particularly interesting are items in the BASEMENT connected with agricultural, domestic and industrial activities (threshing sledges, liquor still, dyeing equipment, ironworker's furnace). On the GROUND FLOOR is a large range of material, including women's costumes from various parts of Thrace. Amongst the domestic items are wooden flasks and vessels. The

FIRST FLOOR has more costumes (including men's), furniture, a prisoner's stone ball, reconstructed kitchen, etc. The SECOND FLOOR has equipment related to the production of wool, and weaving (vertical and horizontal looms).

Above the Folk Museum are the walls of the **kastro**, much of the interior of which is occupied by post-Byzantine buildings, including the cathedral of **Ayios Athanásios**. The most impressive section of Byzantine walling is to the left, on the ascent (view across to Plotinopoulis, see above). Within the settlement with its delightful old houses, is the cathedral, a 19C structure on Byzantine foundations. Beside it are the conspicuous though partial remains of an arched Byzantine building, probably a *hana* (hostel). Below is a rock-cut cavern, popularly supposed to have been the prison of Charles XII. Another close approach to the fortifications may be made by ascending Od. Ermou (EPMOY), a narrow street c 100m N of your original point of entry into the kastro. At first concrete, this soon reverts to its ancient surface and climbs the N face of the fortifications. The walls give a good view of the **Evros**; there is a military post on the summit. By the river, below is a tower-cistern.

On the far side of Dhidhimótikho, a fork (right; asphalt, deteriorated in places) off the main road leads to (10km) **Petrádhes**, (16km) **Píthio** and rejoins the highway at (23km) **Thoúrio**. From Petrádhes, a frontier village, a road runs to (11km farther) Uzunköprü in Turkey.

At **Píthio** (Byzantine *Empython*), well seen on a low hill above the Evros as the road begins to descend towards the village, are the outstanding remains of a *Byzantine* **fort** of the 13C, used by John Cantacuzenus as a headquarters. The central tower is preserved to a height of two storeys and probably had a third. The interior architecture (arches, brick vaults, stairways) is impressive and it was probably a partly domestic establishment. Linked to this by a section of wall with a fine gateway is a smaller tower,

*Castle of Pythion, 13C. Restored drawing by M. Korres*

probably exclusively military in character. Other sections of the defences survive close by and part of the outer system can be seen in the village.

Another road leads W up the Erithropotamos valley to (31km) **Zóni**, on the Bulgarian frontier, where it continues via (48km) **Filáki** and down the right bank of the Arda to (62km) **Kastaniés** (see below). From Zóni an old Ottoman road (now in Bulgarian territory) traverses the mountains to Komotiní (107km). These roads are generally subject to military control and permit on both sides of the frontier.

The highway continues N, rejoining the railway (which makes a wide loop to the E through Píthio) at (464km) **Thoúrio**. At (475km) **Orestiás** (commonly Orestiádha; Hotels B, C, D), seat of an eparchy (12,691 inhab.) and the only refugee settlement in the North to be founded as a town, sugar is refined. At **Leptí** (6km E) are some tumuli with Hellenistic cist burials. The minarets of Edirne can be seen in the distance (right) from the road into (494km) **Kastaniés** (Custom House).

The small triangle of Greek soil lying between the Arda and the Evros is served by a road from Kastanées and by railway to **Orméni**, its principal village.

503km **EDIRNE**, formerly *Adrianople*, both names being successive corruptions of *Hadrianopolis*, a city which has lost its former importance, stands beyond the frontier. Refounded by Hadrian in AD 125 from *Uscudama*, chief town of the Bessi, it remained a strategic stronghold until the decline of the Ottoman Empire. The period of its zenith in 1367–1458 as the Ottoman capital left many fine buildings though the later Selimiye Cami by Sinan is its masterpiece. It remains the market town of the area and is much visited by local Greeks.

# B.   By railway

**Railway** to Alexandroúpolis, 442km (274 miles), two trains daily in 7½–8¾ hours and Píthio, 555km (344 miles) in 9½ hours, one (the daily through train from Piraeus to Istanbul) continuing via Uzunköprü to 834km (518 miles) Istanbul in 26 hours from Athens. To Sérres, see Rte 65; to Dráma, 6 trains daily in 4–7 hours. One extra train daily between Dráma and Alexandroúpolis (in c 4¾ hours) and two from Alexandroúpolis to Píthio (2½ hours), continuing to Edirne (3½ hours) and Orméni (4 hours); or to Dhíkaia and Svilengrad.

The railway was designed by the Turks as a strategic route and built by a French company in 1892–95. It was deliberately laid at least 19km from the coast so as to be beyond the range of naval bombardment, and at the two ports where for convenience it approached the coast (Dedeagatch and Thessaloniki) was provided with inland by-passes (now abandoned). The section E from Alexandroúpolis dates from 1869–72.

From Thessaloníki to (162km) **Sérres**, see Rte 65. The railway now follows the N limit of the former Lake Prasias, winding across the plain. The landscape is peppered with tumuli. Many of the settlements were established after 1923 as refugee colonies. For some distance the only interest is provided by the changing perspective of the Menoikion range to the N and the more distant views, to the S, of Kerdhilion. Between (187km) **Tholó** and (194km) **Mirrínis**, where the line crosses the Amphipolis road, a branch line (no passenger service) diverges to Tzágezi. It keeps company with the Serres–Drama road through the Angitis valley, and beyond (206km) **Angístis**, where a fine but looted Macedonian tomb near the station was excavated in 1972, threads the **Tasliki Stena**, the narrow gorge by which the river forces its way out of the Drama plain between Menoikion and Pangaion. It crosses the 'golden plain' of Drama, extensively cultivated with tobacco.

232km **Dráma**, see Rte 68; the station lies 1km S of the centre. Beyond Drama the line runs E, followed closely as far as Stavroúpolis by a secondary road described in Rte 68. It ascends the valley of the Xeropotamos (maximum gradient 1 in 40) to reach, at (257.5km) **Plataniás**, the watershed (322m) between the Angitis and the Nestos. An equally steep descent leads to the Stena Korpilón and at (269km) **Paranésti** and a crossing of the Nestos which is then followed. Beyond (292km) **Stavroúpolis** is a spectacular defile with numerous tunnels. At (312.5km) **Toxótes** the Kavalla–Xanthi road is crossed. 327km **Xánthi**, see Rte 69A. Beyond Xanthi the line runs E, following the low ground to the S of the Via Egnatia. The railway passes SW of (373.5km) **Komotiní** (Rte 69A), the station of which is 2.5km from the centre. For a while the railway keeps well S of the road to Alexandroúpolis, then, at (405.5km) **Méstis**, just S of Vélki, crosses it at right angles, continuing E to a summit of 278m and (420km) **Kírki** in the valley of the little Iren. The hills to the N have tin and silver mines. The railway descends the stream to (441km) **Alexandroúpolis** (Rte 69A).

From here to (539km) **Dhidhimótikho** the line is never more than 3km E of the road (see Rte 69A); in places they run together. 553.5km **Píthio** (Πύθιο), on a loop to the E of the road, is an important frontier where the Hellenic and Turkish State Railways meet. The little town occupies the site of an ancient fortified city with an acropolis (see Rte 69A). To the SE the line crosses into Turkey. 563km **Uzunköprü**. 833.5km **Istanbul**.

The W branch from Pithio, which once joined the international line from Turkey into Bulgaria, is now virtually defunct since there is a newer link entirely within Turkish territory.

# 70

# Samothráki (Samothrace) and Límnos

These two islands, which geographically form part of the Eastern Sporades (Rte 74), are described here as they can be easily reached from the Thracian coast. Límnos is often approached by air from Athens or Thessaloniki, or by foreign charters.

## A.  Samothráki

**Car Ferry** from Alexandroúpolis (34km in 2 hours) daily in summer, twice or 3 times weekly in winter. Less frequently to Kaválla (summer only). The island is also visited by occasional steamer services (some from Kími in Evvia) which tend to change each year.

**Hotels** B, C, E.

The island of **Samothráki** (Σαμοθράκη, in English **Samothrace**), lies some 32km SW of Alexandroúpolis and almost equidistant from the Gallipoli peninsula. The surrounding sea, swept by the prevailing N winds, is often rough and stormy. There is only one anchorage. Apart from a narrow coastal plain in the N and a region of rolling hills to the SW, the island, elliptical in shape and only 176 sq. km in area, consists of eroded granite mountains, rising in Mt Fengári to 1600m. Wild goats roam the mountainsides. Winters are hard, with heavy rains and thick snow. The island enjoys copious springs, and in Classical times was probably much more fertile. Fruit is abundant. Politically the island belongs to Thrace as an eparchy of the nome of Evros. Half of the population (3083 inhab.) is divided between Khóra and Kamariótissa.

**History.** In the Neolithic and Bronze Ages Samothrace was occupied by people of Thracian stock. From 'the topmost peak of wooded Samothrace' Poseidon watched the fighting on the plains of Troy (*Iliad*, xiii, 12), a city supposedly founded from the island, though in fact more likely from Lemnos (see below). The non-Greek Thracian language and religion survived the arrival of Greek colonists c 700 and in cult ritual to the 1C BC. Archaeological evidence contradicts the Classical tradition that the colonists were earlier and came from Samos; Strabo indeed suggests that the Samians invented the story for their own glory. The colonists' dialect has been shown by inscription to have been Aeolian rather than Ionian, and probably derived from Lesbos or the Troad. In the 6C Samothrace had a silver coinage, the city reached its greatest extent, and colonies were established on the mainland. The Samothracian navy was represented at Salamis. In the 5C her power declined, though the fame of her cult increased until the island became the chief centre of religious life in the N Aegean. At the Sanctuary of the Great Gods Herodotus and King Lysander of Sparta were initiated. Aristophanes and Plato refer to its Mysteries. Here Philip of Macedon met and fell in love with his wife Olympias of Epirus, mother of Alexander the Great. The Macedonian dynasty continued to adorn the sanctuary until their downfall. Though the presence of the sanctuary assured the independence of the city, the island was used as a naval base by the Second Athenian League, by King Lysimachos of Thrace, and by the Ptolemies, Seleucids, and Macedonians in turn.

After the Battle of Pydna, Perseus, the last king of Macedon, sought refuge in the island, only to be taken prisoner by the Romans. Aristarchus (fl. 155–143 BC), editor of Homer, was a native. In 84 BC the sanctuary was pillaged by Corsairs, but soon revived under Roman patronage. The legend that Dardanos, the legendary founder of Troy, had come from Samothrace and that his descendant, Aeneas, had brought the cult to Rome, gave Samothrace a particular interest to the Romans. Varro and Piso (father-in-law of Julius Caesar) were initiates. The island, a natural port of call between the Troad and Neapolis (Kavalla), saw St Paul on his way to Philippi. Hadrian visited Samothrace and though an earthquake c AD 200 began its decline, the ancient religion survived to the 4C. In 1419 the island was visited by Buondelmonte, and in 1444, when it had passed into the hands of the Genoese Gattilusi, princes of Enos and Samothrace, by Cyriacus of Ancona. It was taken by the Turks in 1457, passed to Greece after the First World War, and suffered a Bulgarian occupation in 1941–44.

The landing-place of **Kamariótissa** (Hotels B, C, E), on the W coast, is close to the promontory of Akrotiri. The church of the **Panayia Kamariotissa** is on the site of an Early Christian basilica of which some architectural fragments can be seen. In the craggy fold of the mountains above (bus) is the village of **Khóra**, or **Samothráki**, with 719 inhabitants and a medieval castle. On the N coast, reached by road (6km; bus) from Kamariótissa, is the ancient *Palaiopolis*, marked on the W by a grove of plane-trees and the small Xenia Hotel (B, + another, B). The ancient city, now a confusion of rocks and wild olive trees, occupies the shoulder of Ayios Yeóryios, a ridge extending N towards the sea from the central massif of Fengári. From the acropolis on the ridge the colossal **city wall**, Archaic (polygonal) and Hellenistic, runs W across a ravine and takes in a smaller hill before reaching the shore by a small chapel. Two ruined medieval **towers**, built of antique materials by Palamede Gattilusio in 1444, command the sea, beneath which lie remains of the harbour mole and of a Byzantine church. Between the ancient city and the Xenia Hotel a river descends to the sea. The torrents that feed it bound the **Sanctuary of the Great Gods**. A path leads past the museum (see below) to the site.

The religion of the Great Gods was a pre-Greek Chthonic cult. The Great Gods comprised the Great Mother of Axieros (related to Cybele and later identified with Demeter), an ithyphallic fertility god called Kadmilos (later identified with Hermes), the powerful Kabeiroi (Dardanos and Aetion), twin demons later fused with the Dioskouroi, and Axiokersos and Axiokersa (Hades and Persephone). In later times Hekate, Aphrodite, and Kadmos and Harmonia were added by assimilation or confusion. Ancient writers fought shy of saying much about the Kabeiroi, whose wrath was considered implacable. They were Anatolian in origin and, save at Thebes, hardly known in mainland Greece. Towards the end of the Archaic period Samothrace overtook Lemnos in importance as their principal place of worship.

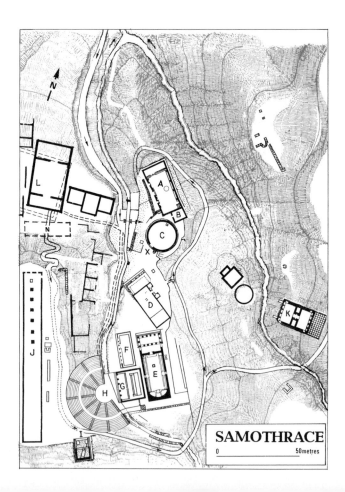

**SAMOTHRACE**

0                    50metres

The sanctuary had an extra-territorial character, apparently independent of the city-state that adjoined it, since at festivals this sent envoys like any other polis. Initiation into the mysteries, which was not essential for attendance at the sanctuary (unlike Eleusis), was open to anyone, regardless of nationality, sex, age, or social status. Initiation could be obtained at any time, and its two degrees (myesis and epoptia) could be taken without interval. A moral standard seems to have been required for the higher degree (which was not obligatory but, rather, exceptional) and some form of confession and absolution preceded it. Ceremonies apparently took place by torchlight.

The early sanctuary, approached from the W, occupied the promontory between the E and central torrents. A sacrificial area of the 7C BC underlies the Temenos, and utilitarian structures were added piecemeal in the 5C and early 4C. The temple area was lavishly renewed in marble by the Ptolemies. A new access from the town side was provided by Ptolemy II Philadelphus, after which the site was extended to a typically Hellenistic planned design on the promontory between the central and W streams.

Excavations were begun in 1863 by Champoiseau, French consul at Adrianople, who discovered the famous Victory now in the Louvre in Paris. A French mission mapped the site in 1866. Austrian expeditions, directed by A. Conze in 1873 and 1875, uncovered the Ptolemaion; its marbles were divided between Austria and Turkey, but only a few of those shipped to Gallipoli arrived at Istanbul. A Swedish team worked on the site in 1923–25. In 1938 systematic exploration was begun by the Institute of Fine Arts, New York University, under Karl Lehmann and Phyllis Williams Lehmann and continues at present under James R. McCredie. Guide in English to the excavations and museum, by the excavators.

To the left of the path, the **anaktoron** (Pl. A) served as a hall of initiation into the Mysteries (myesis). Built of good polygonal masonry the present building dates to early Imperial times, but its design is nearly identical to its predecessors of the 4C and 3C BC. Its walls still stand in places to a height of 3.6m. The interior (27m by 11.5m), reached by three doors, from the W terrace, was divided by a partition into a main hall and an inner sanctum (on the N). This was guarded by bronze statues and marked by a warning stele. Limestone bases show where a wooden grandstand occupied the E and part of the N wall of the hall. In the centre was a circular wooden platform; in the SE corner a libation pit. Built on to the S end of the anaktoron was a **sacristy** (Pl. B; Iera Oikia), dating to the 3C or 4C AD, which replaces an early Imperial building. Here, it seems, the novice was vested and hither he returned to receive a document certifying his initiation.

The **rotunda** (Pl. C), the largest circular building known in Greek architecture (more than 20m across), was dedicated to the Great Gods by Queen Arsinoe between 289 and 281 BC, from which it takes its name **Arsinoeion**. Numerous marbles that survived the destroying earthquake have been arranged to show the structure of the building. A marble wall, crowned by a beautiful marble stringcourse, was surmounted by a gallery of pilasters supporting a Doric entablature. Within, the gallery had Corinthian half-columns with an Ionic cornice.

In the interior of the rotunda are some walls of the **orthostate structure**, the early 4C predecessor of the anaktoron.

Farther S (Pl. x; reached from the path) a **sacred rock** of blue-green porphyry has a yellow tufa pavement from which libations were poured.

The **temenos** (Pl. D) is a rectangular precinct, open to the sky; surviving courses of masonry represent only the foundations of its latest state in the 4C BC. It was entered on the NE side by an Ionic **propylon** of Thasian marble, of which many fragments can be seen both here and in the museum. Within the precinct probably stood a famous statue of Aphrodite and Pothos by Skopas. Abutting is an artificial terrace with a good view towards the sea.

To the S are the imposing remains of the **Hieron** (Pl. E; the sanctuary), a Doric edifice used for the Epopteia, or higher initiation ceremonies. Begun in the last quarter of the 4C BC, it was not finished until c 170 years later and was extensively restored in the 3C AD. The limestone foundations are complete and most of the euthynteria in Thasian marble still in situ. The **façade** consisted of a double porch of 14 columns standing before antae; five columns and one architrave block were re-erected in 1956 and the steps restored with modern blocks. The capital on the corner column was re-turned from Vienna, where the pedimental statues still remain.

A marble ceiling beam is preserved in the pronaos. The marble floor has disappeared, leaving the limestone under-pavement exposed. The spectators' benches on either side date from the Roman restoration, as does the marble floor of the apse. Here foundations of limestone blocks and irregular fieldstones (5C and 6C BC respectively) show that the building had precursors. Outside the foundations, on the E side, two sacred stones flank a torch-holder; here the hierophant may have heard the candidate's confession before admission.

Along the W side of the Hieron were two buildings. That to the N, dubbed the **Hall of Votive Gifts** (Pl. F), took the form of a rectangular stoa with a Doric limestone colonnade of 6 columns between antae. Built c 540 BC, it survived with minor repairs for close on a thousand years. Adjacent, to the S, is the better-preserved substructure of the **Altar Court** (Pl. G), a hypae-thral enclosure entered through a colonnade. The unequal spacing of its columns is shown by the surviving drums. Fragments of the architrave bear a dedicatory inscription by (?) Arrhidaios, half-brother of Alexander the Great.

The outline of the **theatre** (Pl. H) is recognisable though all but two of its seats of white limestone and red porphyry vanished in 1927–37. The river is channelled under the orchestra in a late-Roman concrete culvert (restored).

A path winds up to the WESTERN HILL. The N part of this is occupied by the so-called '*Ruinenviereck*' (Pl. L), a medieval structure, probably a fortification, built entirely of antique material from the sanctuary. To the S, on a terrace, recent excavations have revealed the remains of a **neorion** (Pl. N) or ship-display building of the early 3C BC. Measuring 30 x 14m, with two doorways (Doric entablature) in the N wall, the structure was divided internally by a row of columns, the intervals closed by grills. The ship stood in the S aisle—one of the pairs of marble supports (curved to support the hull and allowing space for the keel) is still in situ. The boat was probably a trireme captured in a sea battle by the fleet of Antigonos Gonatas. Immediately to the N is a **hestiatorion** of the later 3C, with space for 15 dining couches in the main room. Over this a Byzantine industrial structure (removed) was constructed about the 10C AD. This complex also overlay a Roman building (to the S) with wall-benches and marble supports, thought to be for the display of votive offerings. From here a stairway probably ascended to the terrace above the theatre. There a **stoa**, its foundations (Pl. J) 90m long and originally laid bare by the Austrian expedition, was examined in 1963–64. Hundreds of blocks with elements of Doric and Ionic orders from outer and inner colonnades survive. It was probably of the early 3C BC. Farther on is the **Nike monument** (Pl. I) with the foundations of the precinct or building in which the statue stood. There was a shallow upper and a deep lower basin; in places the clay pipelines that fed and drained them can be traced.

The Parian marble 'Winged Victory', that formed the centrepiece of the monument, was removed to Paris in 1863 and the ship's prow on which it stands in 1891. The right hand, recovered in 1950, is on permanent loan to the Louvre.

The path leads across the river and over the hill where the crowded **South Necropolis** (6C BC–2C AD) was excavated in 1957 to the E ravine, beyond which stood the **Ptolemaion** (Pl. K), a monumental gateway to the sanctuary, dedicated to the Great Gods by Ptolemy II Philadelphus. The substructure is pierced by a barrel-vaulted tunnel through which at that time the river was channelled. The foundations carried an Ionic portico on the E and a Corinthian portico on the W. The Austrians carried off many decorative elements of its two pediments; other blocks lie in the ravine. Abutments for a wooden bridge (with a span of c 18m) that crossed the river after its course had been altered by an earthquake can still be seen. Immediately opposite are a flagged circular Area and a later Doric structure dedicated by Philip and Alexander, successors to Alexander the Great.

The **museum** is arranged as an aid to the understanding of the site. In HALL A typical sections of each building have been reconstructed from available fragments, though these are not necessarily in their original juxtaposition. Also in this room are two stelai, from the anaktoron and the Hieron, prohibiting entry to the uninitiated. HALL B is devoted to scuplture. Fragments from the propylon of the temenos (c 340 BC): monolithic Ionic column of Thasian marble; necking with anthemion ornament and fragmentary capital; portions of the frieze of over 80 dancing maidens and musicians, probably depicting the wedding of Kadmos and Harmonia (in deliberately Archaistic style). Two figures retrieved from the central river bed of the sanctuary, probably parts of a pedimental group (c 460–450 BC): bust of the blind seer Teiresias, which owing to a misidentification by Cyriac of Ancona became a model for Renaissance portraits of Aristotle; the eyes were recut in the 19C when the bust was used as an ikon on a house in Khora. Headless statue of (?) Persephone.

Case 1 contains religious and votive objects, including iron finger rings (one of the outward signs of initiation commented upon by Pliny); **Case 2**, coins and stamped roof tiles; in **Case 3** are small architectural fragments; water-spouts, antefixes, mouldings, sections of floor, ceiling, etc. **Case 4** displays sculptural pieces (4C BC–1C AD), including a marble portrait head of Queen Arsinoe III; bronze statuette of Herakles; fragments in high relief representing Centaurs.

HALL C. Acroterial Victory from the Hieron (c 130 BC), reconstituted in 1950 from fragments buried after the statue fell in the earthquake c AD 200. Cases on the right side of the hall contain finds from the sanctuary (the pottery reflects its long history and the cosmopolitan origins of its pilgrims); those on the left side objects from tombs round the city. **Case 2**. Bronze decorations from the propylon of the temenos; votive gifts, including fragments of an iron chain-mail cuirass of the 3C BC (? Gaulish La Tène workmanship). **Case 3**. Local ware of the 7C BC. **Case 10**. Terracotta statuette of a young winged god (3C BC) from the S necropolis; fine blown glassware; complete contents of a Roman tomb chamber of AD 135; terracotta figurine of a girl (early 1C BC). **Case 11**. Stele of c 400 BC with an inscription in Greek characters but in an undeciphered (presumably Thracian) language. Further inscriptions, set up in the courtyard, include lists of initiates, dedications, etc. HALL D. Grave goods, pottery, and jewellery from the cemeteries.

ASCENT OF MT SAOS (FENGARI), 5–6 hours from **Khóra**, or (preferable) in 4 hours from **Thermá** (or Loutrá; bus; camping to W of village), a place on the N coast with hot sulphur springs, 8km E of Palaiópolis. Another 9km beyond Thermá is the beautiful River Phoniás with a tower at its mouth and a fine waterfall c 1.5km upstream. **Mount Saos, Saoce** or **Fengári** (1560m) was the peak from which Poseidon gazed upon the plains of Troy; the modern traveller can do the same. The *view is all-embracing. N to W, the coast of Thrace and Macedonia as far as the Khalkidhikí peninsula and Mt Athos, with the island of Thasos in between; S, the islands of Imvros and Limnos; E, the Dardanelles, the plain of Troy, and Mt Ida in the far distance.

At **Mikró Voúni** on the S coast a prehistoric settlement is under excavation.

# B. Límnos

**Approaches. By Air**, from Athens 3–4 times daily, in 60 minutes; also daily in c 40 minutes from Thessaloníki; less frequently to Lésvos. **Terminal**, Od. N. Garofallídhi, Myrina.

**By Sea**. Connections 2–7 times weekly with Piraeus or Rafína; also to Kími (Evvia), Ayios Konstandínos, Kaválla, Alexandroúpolis, Lésvos, Samothráki, Ayios Evstrátios, Thessaloníki.

The island of **Límnos** (Λῆμνος or Lemnos) is situated in the middle of the N Aegean, midway between Mt Athos and Asia Minor. Intervening on the Asian side are the Turkish islands of Imvros and Tenedos. To the N rises Samothráki; to the SE is Lésvos, to the nome of which Límnos belongs, together with the islet of Ayios Evstrátios which lies due S. Límnos, with a population of 16,017 and an area of 453 sq. km, is almost bisected by two deep inlets of the sea the Gulf of Moudhros in the S and the Bay of Pournia in the N the isthmus between them being only 3km across. Valerius Flaccus (*Argonautica*, II, 431) calls the island 'tenuis Lemnos', though the W half is rugged and hilly, rising in the NW corner to 430m. The bare plains of the E yield small quantities of cereals, sesame, cotton, and tobacco. The local wine is good. Numerous hot springs attest to the island's volcanic origin. It has excellent beaches. Turtles breed at Avlonas, N of Mírina.

**History**. According to Homer the inhabitants of Lemnos were of Thracian stock; Herodotus and Thucydides, however, call them Pelasgi or Tirrheni (the same Tyrrhenian pirates that Dionysos transformed into dolphins). This may well represent two stages of pre-Greek history. Archaeology has shown that Lemnos had an advanced Neolithic civilisation, and a Bronze Age culture of Minoan–Mycenaean type, connected with Troy and Lesbos, which continued without a sharp break into the Geometric period. In the 8–6C the island seems to have had contact with the Greeks, though it is certain from inscriptions that before the 6C the inhabitants were not Greek; their language is undeciphered and their burial customs show affinities with Villanovan (Etruscan) burials in Italy. The island is said by Polybius to have borne the more ancient name of *Aithaleia*, it possibly took the name Lemnos from a goddess identifiable with the Great Mother. The principal cults, however, were those of Hephaistos (said to have been thrown down to Lemnos from Olympos for intervening in a quarrel between Zeus and Hera, his parents) and of the Kabeiroi.

Among many legends is that of the curse of Aphrodite upon the Lemnians for impugning her virtue. This alienated the men from their wives, who murdered their husbands. Only king Thoas escaped, saved by his daughter Hypsipyle. When the Argonauts put in at Lemnos, some of their number stayed behind to marry the Lemnian widows, becoming by them the fathers of the Minyans. The Minyans were driven out by the Pelasgians to Elis Tryphilia in the Peloponnesos. Homer tells of Philoktetes, the most celebrated archer of the Trojan War, who spent ten years on Lemnos with a wounded foot. The proverbial expression 'Lemnian deeds' for atrocities is attributed by Herodotus (VI, 138) to an episode in the Persian Wars. The Lemnians carried off some Athenian women from Brauron. The children of this enterprise looked down on their Lemnian half-brothers, whereupon the Lemnians slaughtered both them and their Athenian mothers.

Lemnos fell to Persia c 513 BC and changed hands more than once before the end of the Persian wars. Hippias is said to have died here after Marathon. From 477 BC the island formed part of the Delian League, and later received cleruchies from Athens (they dedicated the famous Lemnian Athena of Pheidias on the acropolis of Athens). Lemnian troops fought for Athens at Sphakteria (425) at Amphipolis (422) and at Syracuse (413). Apart from brief periods of domination by Sparta (404–393), by the Macedonians, and by the Seleucid Antiochus the Great, Lemnos remained under Athenian influence to the time of Septimius Severus. The island was twice visited (AD 162 and 165) by Dioskorides. In the 2C and 3C the Lemnian Philostratus family achieved fame in Rome as sophists. The island was plundered by the Heruli and later passed to Byzantium. It had a bishop in the 4C and became a metropolitan see in the reign of Leo VI. In 924 the Saracens under Leo of Tripoli were defeated by a Byzantine fleet off the island. Venetian merchants settled in the 11C and 12C, establishing sovereignty after 1204 under the Navigaiosa grand dukes. In the 13–15C the island was disputed between Venetians, Genoese, and Byzantines, and after 1462 between Venetians and Turks. John of Selymbria spent some years in exile here after 1344 and Gregory Palamas took refuge in 1349. After 1670 the Turks in their turn used it as a place of exile for disgraced notables. Orloff's Russians occupied the island in the war of 1770, only to be driven out by Hassan Bey. Lemnos became Greek for a few months in 1829 before being exchanged with the Turks for Euboea. It fell to Greece in 1912, and was the British base for the Gallipoli campaign. Its connection with Turkey ended by treaty in 1920.

The island capital and chief port **Mírina** or **Kástro** (Hotels L, A, B, C, D; F/ A) is situated on the W coast. The verdant town (4342 inhab.) is the seat of the Metropolitan of Lemnos. Ancient *Myrina* stood on the promontory which separates the good, sandy beach on the N side from the island's main harbour on the S. The present kastro stands in part on ancient foundations and was built and rebuilt, after sieges and earthquakes, by Byzantines, Venetians and Genoese. The circuit is almost complete and still stands to its full height on most of the S, E and NE sides. There is a complex zig-zag entrance on the E and a concealed gate near sea level on the N. Inscriptions attest a Sanctuary of Artemis, and houses and streets (mostly medieval) can be traced. There are also arsenals, cisterns and a tunnel about 100m long at the W. On the first floor of the **museum** are prehistoric finds from Poliokhni (two rooms) and Mirina; later sculpture and inscriptions. On the second floor, displayed by period, are finds from Ifestia and the Kabeirion; also material from other sites and displays of bronzes, and Hellenistic ceramic workshops.

Two roads lead towards Moúdhros (28km). The better, inland one to the N passes near a **bath house**, built by Hassan Bey and proceeds via **Thermá** (6km), **Livadhorkhóri** (15km), and the **airport** (17km) after which it curves S. The more southerly road passes the beaches of **Platí** and **Thános** (impassable to large vehicles) and continues round the coast to attractive **Kondiás**. To the SE, at **Vriókastro** and **Trokhaliá**, are some Bronze Age remains. The roads join at **Livadhokhóri** and continue to **Moúdhros**.

In the First World War, the **Gulf of Mudros**, one of the best natural harbours in the Aegean, became the base of the Mediterranean Expeditionary Force. Sir Ian Hamilton launched his attack on the Dardanelles (25 April 1915) from here. In the same harbour the armistice with Turkey was concluded on 30 October 1918 on board HMS *Agamemnon*. **East Mudros Military Cemetery**, to the NE of the town, with c 900 British Commonwealth dead, contains also a French memorial, though the French graves were removed in 1922. At **Portianós**, on the W side of the inner harbour, lie a further 350 dead of the Gallipoli campaign.

The most important archaeological remains of Lemnos are at **Poliókhni** on the E coast below Cape Voroskópos (ancient *Droskopos*). This presumably represents the Homeric 'Lemnos'. From Moudhros the site is reached by the road E past the military cemetery to **Roussópoli** where you turn right for **Kamínia**. Beyond the village (by-passed) a motorable track (left, sign) leads in 2km to Poliokhni. Excavations in 1931–36, by Alessandro della Seta of the Italian School, uncovered four settlements in stratigraphic sequence, the latest an unfortified town of the Late Bronze Age (c 1500–1000 BC). Beneath lay a city of the Copper Age (pre-Mycenaean and probably earlier than Troy VI), and beneath that again remains of two Neolithic cities. The later of these was equipped with stone baths, the earliest found in the Aegean. The **town walls** (c 2000 BC), with towers and gates, stand in places to a height of 5m. The city seems to have been destroyed by an earthquake. The main street and a number of houses were explored. The earliest city (4th millennium BC) is believed to be earlier than Troy I. The site has been recently tidied and plans provided.

A third road runs from Moudhros to the NE tip of the island. **Kómi**, between Moudhros and Kondopoúli, is known from an inscription to have had a sanctuary of Herakles, but only slight Byzantine remains are visible today. The **Bay of Pournia**, to the N of the road, has several ancient sites. The medieval castle of Kokkino, or *Kotchinos*, now **Kótsinas**, rose to importance with the decline of Hephaistia (see below), though the site was abandoned after the silting up of the harbour and no remains are visible. Here in 1442 the Empress of Constantine XI Palaeologus died in childbirth while under siege by the Turks; the castle was successfully defended by the Venetians against the Turks in 1476. Between the castle and the village of **Repanídhi** lay *Mosychlos*, famous in antiquity and in the Middle Ages for Lemnian earth, a red bole containing a large percentage of silica, used as a tonic and astringent medicine. It was extracted on only one day in the year (latterly 6 August) to the accompaniment of religious ceremonies and exported (anciently under the seal of Artemis; 'terra sigillata') right up to the 19C.

The hamlet of **Palaiópolis**, on a rocky peninsula above the sea, occupies the site of *Hephaisteía* (Ηφαιστία). Access is off the road running NE from Moudhros to **Pláka** via the village of **Kondopoúli** (33km from Mirina), beyond which a road (sign 'Ifestia') leads in 5km to the site. In Classical times this was the principal city of Lemnos, paying the larger tribute to Athens. It had pre-Greek origins. It became seat of a Byzantine bishop, fell to the Venetians in 1204, and c 1395 was wrecked by a landslide and abandoned. Excavations in 1926–30 and 1937–39 by the Italian School uncovered a necropolis (8C BC) and a sanctuary destroyed in the last years of the 6C BC. Hellenistic material, including potters' kilns, has been found in recent excavations. The local pottery carried Minoan–Mycenaean traditions into the Geometric period; imported ware proves a lively trade with Macedonia, Corinth, and Athens. Among traces of later Greek occupation are a **theatre**, remodelled in Roman times, and Byzantine churches.

Opposite Hephaisteia, on the other side of the bay (at **Khlóï**) is the attractively situated **Kabeirion**, excavated in 1937–39 by the Italian School. With a vehicle, it is necessary to return to Kondopouli; then, 6km further, a turn (left, sign 'Kaveirio') provides a rough track in 5kms to the site. In early ('Pelasgian') times this sanctuary (plan in Mírina Museum) had precedence over that of Samothrace. It occupies two level tracts divided by a rocky spur. Archaic foundations have been ascribed to an **anaktoron**, a **telesterion**, and a **stoa**, but the surviving remains are Late Roman. The N level is occupied by a huge edifice, probably the Hellenistic **telesterion**, with a façade of 12 Doric columns and internal colonnades. Among many inscriptions listing officials of the cult was found a letter from Philip V requesting initiation as epoptes. Below the site is a cave, sometimes called the **Cave of Philoctetes**.

From the Kabeirion turn the main road continues to **Pláka** (another 7km). **Evraiókastro** c 3km E, has ancient walls.

*Hermaeon*, on the NE coast but not certainly located (?Mt. Alepotrypes SW of Plaka), was, according to Aeschylus, one of the series of hills on which fire-beacons were lit at the instance of Agamemnon to signal to his wife Klytemnestra at Mycenae the fall of Troy (*Agamemnon*, 283), possibly an anachronism suggested by a similar system used in the opposite direction by Xerxes during the invasion of Greece (?).

Submarine research in 1960 in the **Charos Reef**, 16km offshore, located blocks of marble belonging to an Archaic Temple of Apollo that once stood in the ancient town of *Chryse*. One of the prehistoric centres of the island, Chryse is mentioned by Herodotus as having been engulfed by the sea as the result of an earthquake. Here (according to the *Iliad*) Philoktetes, the exiled Achaean general, died.

About 32km S of Lemnos is the small island of **Ayios Evstrátios** or **Aistrátes** (27km$^2$) used periodically as a deportation settlement for political offenders. Its highest point is Mt Símádhi (296km). Small quantities of iron, coal, and oil are found. The island village, **Ayios Evstrátios**, lies on the NW coast. The site of the ancient city, on a hill between two streams, shows traces of Mycenaean, Greek, Roman, and Byzantine occupation. Nowadays the island is dry and waterless and food is scarce. The beaches are unattractive.

# VIII ISLANDS OF THE AEGEAN

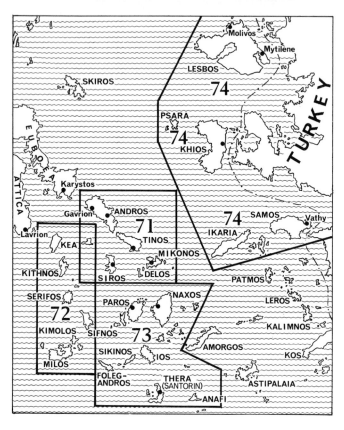

The **Aegean Sea** is bounded on the N by Macedonia and Thrace, on the W by the mainland of Greece, on the E by Asia Minor and on the S by Crete. Ancient writers divided it into the *Thracian Sea*, in the N; the *Myrtoan Sea*, in the SW, so called after Myrtos, an obscure island off the coast of Argolis; the *Ikarian Sea*, in the E, named after the island of Ikaria; and the Cretan Sea, in the S. The derivation of the word Aegean (Αἰγαίον) is uncertain; it may be from αἰγίς, in its secondary meaning of squall, in reference to the sudden gales that affect the area. The Byzantines and Venetians called it the *Archipelago*, and the Turks, the *White Sea*.

In the centre of the Aegean are the **Cyclades** (Κυκλάδες), a group of islands forming a rough circle (κύκλος) round Delos. In antiquity only 12 or 15 islands were regarded as belonging to the Cyclades (Strabo, X), and they depended on Delos. Today some 30 islands and islets are comprised within the nome of the Cyclades (**Kikládhon**), with its capital at Ermoúpolis (Siros). This political division, which includes Delos and the S Sporades, as well as the Cyclades proper, is divided into eight eparchies and has over 94,005 inhabitants. The **Sporades** are three island groups 'scattered' in the

Aegean, to the N, S, and E of the Cyclades. The Southern Sporades are described with Delos and the Cyclades in the first three routes of this section; the Eastern Sporades, excluding the Dodecanese, in the remaining route. The Northern Sporades are described for convenience in Rte 43; the Dodecanese are described in a separate section (IX) and Amorgos with them; Crete, which partly closes the Aegean on the S occupies a separate volume.

The **Aegean Islands** are the peaks of a submerged plateau now 90–200m below the surface and bounded by deeps of 600–900m. In the N they are formed of limestone, gneiss, schist, and marble; in the S of volcanic rock, lava, basalt, and trachyte. These mountainous and largely arid islands have lost their once luxuriant forests, but the larger ones produce olives, figs, and vines. The wines of Santorini and Naxos are renowned; likewise the marble of Paros and Tinos. Milos has long been noted for obsidian. Iron is found in Serifos, Kithnos, and Andros. The limpid air and the equable climate are a great attraction and the heat of summer is alleviated by the periodic N winds (Tramontana; ancient Boreas) and later by the more predictable Etesian winds (Meltémi), which, blowing also from the N, prevail from early July to mid-September, sometimes very strong.

The little seaside villages, with their clean white houses and sparkling streets, sometimes paved with marble, vary widely in atmosphere from island to island as the temperament of the islanders varies with local resources. They often contrast markedly with the villages inland, where terraced cultivation is a feature of the landscape. Windmills, formerly characteristic, are now very rare. The inhabitants, partly Roman Catholic, claim a purer Greek strain than those of the mainland: they have, perhaps, been more influenced in the past by contact with the Italian peninsula and less by contact with the Turks.

Virtually all islands now have some degree of foreign tourism, though the intensity of this phenomenon and the sophistication of the facilities vary greatly. The islands most oriented towards visitors tend to be very quiet out of season. Local agricultural activity has declined rapidly in recent years and much food is imported.

**Communications**. Most of the islands can be reached by regular vehicle ferries, which serve the islands in groups, travelling outward and returning in inverse order. Some Cycladic routes have a common port-of-call in Siros and on some days (especially in summer) other islands (Mikonos, Paros, Naxos) provide further interchange points between the Cyclades and the Dodecanese. To reach an island on a different round from that on which you set out it is often necessary to return to Piraeus. Some small craft ply between islands in the summer. In general services are less frequent and provide fewer connections outside the summer season. The services outlined in the route headings were those in force in summer 1993. Sailing times are subject to change at short notice and should always be checked on day of sailing (tel. 143, in Athens; elsewhere at the local port office or *Limenarkheíon*). The Eastern Sporades and several of the Cyclades are individually linked by air with Athens.

**Cruise Ships** operating from Piraeus usually combine the most popular islands into a round trip of 3–7 days, calling nearly always at Mikonos, Delos, Rhodes, Heraklion (Crete), and Santorini. Additional calls may be made at Patmos and Kos. More ambitious rounds include Istanbul, Troy, Izmir, Ephesos, and Halicarnassos in Turkey.

Travellers who wish to go from island to island according to their fancy must hire a caique, an expensive and often arduous business, or a yacht, which (though not less expensive) is more easily arranged. Details of the many yacht brokers in Athens and Piraeus may be had from the Greek Yacht Brokers and Consultants Association, 7 Filellínon, Athens. Of over 80 Greek harbours and anchorages now equipped with facilities for servicing of yachts, some 25 are in the Aegean island area. The Aegean is an uncertain and capricious sea and experience is essential.

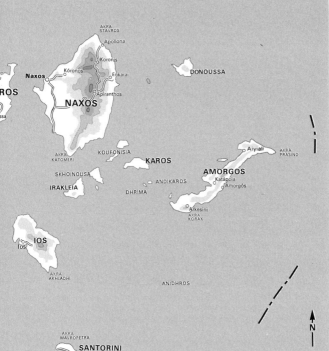

# THE CYCLADES

IKARIA

AKRA
PAPAS

AKRA
EVROS

**Mikonos**
**MIKONOS**

DILOS

AKRA
STAVROS

Apollona

Koronis

Kóronos

Enkarai

**Naxos**

**NAXOS**

Apiranthos

DONOUSSA

ROS

ssa

AKRA
KATOMERI

KOUFONISIA

**KAROS**

Aiyiali

AKRA
PRASINO

**AMORGOS**

Katápola

Amorgós

SKHOINOUSA

**IRAKLEIA**

ANDIKAROS

DHRIMA

Arkesini
AKRA
KORAX

**IOS**

Iós

AKRA
AKHLADHI

ANIDHROS

AKRA
MAVROPETRA

**SANTORINI**

THIRASIA

**Thira**

Karterádhos

**ANAFI**

Akrotiri

Emborio

Anáfi

N

**History**. The Cyclades were said to have been originally populated by Carians. Thucydides tells us (I, 4) that King Minos conquered the Cyclades and expelled the Carians. Herodotus (I, 171) says that in ancient times the Carians, who went by the name of Leleges, were subjects of Minos and served in the ships of his navy; and that, long after the time of Minos, they were driven from the islands by Ionians and Dorians and settled on the mainland of Asia Minor.

So far there have been relatively few Neolithic discoveries in the Cyclades. They enjoyed a flourishing Bronze Age civilisation which was at first independent and later had affinities with Crete and then Mycenae. The Cycladic Bronze Age has been divided into the Early, Middle and Late Cycladic, each stage with further subdivisions. The nine periods, roughly corresponding to those into which Sir Arthur Evans divided the Minoan civilisation in Crete, cover about fifteen centuries from 3500 to 1100 BC. Perhaps the most important single evidence of the wide-ranging contacts of Cycladic civilisation is the volcanic mineral obsidian. The principal though not the only place in the Aegean where obsidian is found is Melos, where it is abundant. This mineral was of great importance before the discovery of copper and bronze and even for some time after they had come into use. The prehistoric trade in obsidian from Melos was considerable, and it has been found in Crete and other Aegean islands, on the mainland of Greece, in Thessaly, and on the coast of Asia Minor. This dispersal proved the existence of sea communications as early as Mesolithic times.

Before the end of the Early Cycladic Period people lived in houses often grouped in villages. Some of the pottery had elaborate designs of spirals and painted decoration was introduced. Melos made pottery with white designs on a dark ground, perhaps inspired by Early Minoan examples. Model boats of lead prove not only the use of this metal but the commonplace of navigation. Marble figurines were placed in graves and occasionally exported (e.g. to Crete). Many cemeteries of small stone-built cist graves have been excavated. At the end of the EBA the Cycladic culture went into decline, possibly as the result of invasions. In the Middle Cycladic Period there was considerable progress. The second city at Phylakopi on Melos had larger and better-built houses, and was probably protected by a wall; Ayia Irini on Kea certainly was. Pottery designs showed a naturalistic tendency, flowers and animals being freely represented. During this period fine Middle Minoan pottery was imported into Melos and Kea, and local vases sometimes imitated the Cretan polychrome designs on a black ground (Kamares ware). Contemporary Melian vases have been found in the Temple Repositories at Knossos. Contact with the mainland is proved by the discovery in the Cyclades of Minyan ware of the Middle Helladic Period. By the end of the Middle Cycladic Period (c 1600 BC) the Cyclades appear to have been completely under the domination of Crete, thus confirming the tradition that they were conquered by Minos (see above). This view is borne out by the fact that many features of Cretan material culture (pottery, bronzes, frescoes, architecture) are found in the islands. Such features are particularly evident on Thera. After the volcanic explosion of Thera (probably c 1500 BC, but possibly a century earlier) the influence of the mainland became stronger and Mycenaean imports rivalled Minoan. At the end of the 15C, when the centre of Aegean civilisation passed from Knossos to Mycenae mainland contacts replaced those with Crete. The local pottery declined in quality. The decline of Bronze Age culture in the Cyclades mirrored that of the mainland after the fall of the Mycenaean palaces. There was a dramatic loss of population and the following Protogeometric period shows relatively little continuity from earlier times.

In the 10C and 9C Ionians colonised the islands and Delos became the religious centre of the Greek world. There were important artistic developments in the Cyclades in the Geometric and Archaic periods. The islands were overrun by the Persians in the invasion of 490 BC. In 478/477 they were included in the Delian League and so imperceptibly became incorporated into the Athenian Empire. They remained tributary to Athens till 404, after which they had a few years of independence. In 378 they joined the Second Athenian League and again came under the influence of Athens. In the Social War (357–355) they revolted, only to become subject to Macedon. In 308 they passed to Antigonus, who founded the League of Islanders; then to the Ptolemies who, vanquished at Andros in 228, were supplanted by the Macedonian, Antigonus Doson. He was succeeded by Philip V. After Philip's defeat at Cynoscephalae in 197, the Cyclades passed to the Rhodians, and later to the Romans. Temporarily conquered by

Mithridates in 88, they were returned to Rome. They were abandoned by the Eastern Empire to the raids of the Goths, Saracens, and Slavs.

In 1204 the islands were given by the Crusaders to Venice, who handed them over to adventurers as hereditary fiefs of the Republic. The result was 20 small vassal states. Members of the Ghizi family held Tenos, Mykonos, Skyros, Skopelos, Skiathos, and Astypalaea, as well as parts of Keos and Seriphos, of which the Giustianini and Michieti had the remainder. The Sanudi held Naxos and Paros, and many smaller islands, and called themselves dukes of Naxos; the Navigajosi aspired to the title of grand dukes of Lemnos; the Venieri were marquesses of Cerigo (Kythera); the Viari had Cerigotto; the Barozzi, Santorini (Thera); the Dandoli, Andros; the Quirini, Amorgos, and the Foscoli, Anaphe. Most of these island dynasties were suppressed by the Turks after the fall of Constantinople in 1453; but some survived for another century. Among them were the dukes of Naxos, who had almost from the start broken with Venice and gone over to her enemies. In 1210 Marco Sanudo, first Duke of Naxos, took an oath of fealty to the Latin emperor Henry of Flanders and, as a reward, was made feudal superior of the other Aegean barons, with the grandiose title of Duke of the Archipelago and Sovereign of the Dodecanese.

Early in the 17C the islands were ransacked by English adventurers looking for antiquities. Admiral Sir Kenelm Digby acted as the agent of Charles I, who is said to have amassed 400 pieces of sculpture. The rival collection of the Duke of Buckingham was enriched by the efforts of Sir Thomas Roe, ambassador to the Porte. More successful than either was the Rev. William Petty, chaplain to the second Earl of Arundel (1580–1646), whose daring adventures in the pursuit of the antique became a byword. The famous Parian Chronicle was one of his prizes. Lord Arundel can be said to have provided the foundation for Classical archaeology in England; his collection of ancient sculptures was presented in 1667 to the University of Oxford by his grandson Henry Howard, afterwards sixth Duke of Norfolk. It is now in the Ashmolean Museum, Oxford.

The Civil War brought these archaeological forays to an end. In the month that Naseby was fought (June 1645) the Turks invaded Crete. During the 24 years of the Candian War the islands were alternately occupied by Turks and Venetians. On its termination in 1669 the Archipelago enjoyed a century of comparative peace, broken by the outbreak in 1770 of war between Turkey and Russia. The Russian fleet spent the winter of 1770–71 at Paros and annexed eighteen of the Cyclades to the Russian Empire. The Russian domination lasted however, for only four or five years. Thereafter no event of importance disturbed the tranquility of the islands till the Revolution of 1821.

In both world wars the Aegean was tragically prominent. In 1915, during the first, the natural harbour of Moudros, on the island of Lemnos, was made the Allied base, and the island of Imbros the GHQ of the ill-fated Dardanelles Expedition. In the Second World War the Germans had for a time air and local naval superiority which enabled them to occupy Crete after Greece had been overrun and, later, to thwart the British landings at Kos and Leros.

# 71

# Northern Cyclades (Kikládhes)

## A. Síros

**Car Ferry** from Piraeus, 127km in 3½–5½ hours several times daily, continuing either via Tínos to Míkonos; or via Páros to Náxos, often then to Ios, Santoríni and sometimes Crete and Rhodes; or via Páros to Sámos. There are several services to Síkinos, and Folégandros; also to the Dodecanese, less frequently to some other islands. From Rafína, regular service via Andros, Tínos and/or Míkonos in 4–5 hours.

**Note**: Síros is a main centre of Aegean (and especially Cycladic) sea communications; it is often possible to travel from one island to another via Síros when there are no direct services.

**Air Service**, 2–3 daily to Siros.

**Síros** (Σύρος, in English often **SYROS** or **Syra**), situated in the centre of the Cyclades, owes its development to its port and its manufactures. The island, 22.5km long with a maximum width of 9km, is pleasant but not spectacular and no longer deserves the eulogy of Homer, who calls it rich in herds and flocks and having plenty of wine and corn. It does, however, produce barley, wine, oil, figs, and green vegetables. Síros is the nursery of Roman Catholicism in Greece; about half the population of its capital and nearly all the inhabitants outside it are Catholic.

**Ermoúpolis** (Hotels A, B, C, E; restaurants on the quay), capital of the island and of the nome of the Cyclades (Kikládhon), is situated on the E coast. The clean town has fine 19C mansions adorned with wrought-iron balconies. The 13,030 inhabitants represent two-thirds of the island population. It is the seat of a Greek archbishop and of a Roman Catholic bishop. The older quarters are built on two conical hills, that to the S, crowned by the Roman Catholic cathedral, being the medieval **Ano Síros**, still a separate deme of 1652 inhabitants. The hill of **Vrontádho**, to the N, is the Orthodox quarter. The port is the traffic centre of the Cyclades, with services to many islands. An interesting volume in English describing the town's development in the early 19C is J. Travlos and A. Kokkou, *Ermoupolis*, Athens, 1984 (Commercial Bank of Greece).

**History**. Nothing survives of the ancient city of *Syria*. In the Middle Ages the inhabitants, in fear of pirates, withdrew from their seaside town to a lofty hill about 1.5km inland, where they built Ano (Upper) or Old Syros. This became the quarter of the Roman Catholics, descendants of the Genoese and Venetian settlers who, during the Turkish rule after 1566, were under the protection of the King of France. The inhabitants took no active part in the War of Greek Independence, but took refugees from Psara and Chios, who founded Ermoupolis. The port became the coal-bunkering station for packet ships of the E Mediterranean and the chief port of Greece, but declined when oil-burning became general to its present role as mercantile junction of the Aegean. Syros has a significant industrial history (cotton mills and tanneries).

Protected by the Asses' Isle (Gaidhouronísi) and by a long breakwater, and bounded on the S by the old **lazaréto**, or quarantine station, the port is generally crowded with cargo ships laid up or under repair. It has a hydraulic slip capable of lifting large vessels. Round the outer harbour are former ironworks and tanneries. The lower town is built round the inner or **commercial harbour**. To the left, behind the waterfront, is the conspicuous belfry of the church of the **Koímisis**.

The **quay**, bustling and animated, is lined with cafés, tavernas, and shops selling loukoumi (Turkish delight), and farther W enlivened by caiques and fish markets. Odhos Ermoú, or Od. Khíou (the fruit and grocery market) farther on, lead to Plateía Miaoúlis, the town centre. This dignified square, paved with marble and shaded by trees, contains a bandstand and an obelisk to Andreas Miaoulis (1768–1835), the admiral and patriot. It is dominated by the **Town Hall**, an elegant building of c 1870, and round the square are grouped arcaded cafés, clubs, and the public library. Behind this is the **Apollo Theatre** (opened 1864, altered 1970, last performance 1953).

In the side street to the left of the Town Hall, below the **clock tower**, is the entrance to the small **museum**. Here three rooms contain important pottery and other finds from the Early Cycladic fort at **Kastrí** (see below), casual finds from Syros (including a phallic idol similar to those on Delos), and a small relief of a boar hunt from Amorgos. To the W is the Orthodox **cathedral** (Metamórfosis), with the tomb of Anthimos Gazis (1758–1828), the Thessalian patriot.

From here, partly by 800 steps (stiff climb; c 1 hour), Odhós Omírou passes between the French **École des Frères** (right) and **St Sebastian** (left), and mounts to **Ano Síros** (180m), which may be reached by bus or taxi via the fashionable quarter of **Neápolis**. Halfway up is the **French Hospital**, served by sisters of mercy. In the upper town are many Catholic churches and the cathedral of St George, **Ayíou Nikoláou** of the Orthodox faith, and tier upon tier of whitewashed houses. Next to Ayios Yeóryios and shaded by pepper-trees is the **British Military Cemetery** where lie 108 British and other dead from the Aegean Islands, more than half of whom were drowned when the transport ship *Arcadian* was torpedoed on its way from Thessaloníki to Alexandria on 15 April 1917. Ano Síros was the birthplace of Markos Vamvakáris who achieved fame as a singer of **rebétika**, the Greek equivalent (in content, if not style) of the American blues. The view of the port and of neighbouring islands is striking. Another splendid viewpoint is the church of the **Anástasis** on the hill of **Vrontádho**.

The favourite summer evening promenade is the E wall of the commercial harbour. In the **Vapória** quarter, with its elegant villas, is the blue-domed church of **Ayios Nikólaos** and, higher up, the **Tríon Ierárkhon** and its orphanage. A road leads N from the first along the cliffs in 30 minutes to **Ayios Dhimítrios**, a fair example of modern 'Byzantine' style (1936).

**Kíni** (11km; Hotels B, D) on the W shore and **Galessás** (11km; buses from the Custom House; Hotels A, B, C, E), farther S on the slopes above the coast, are pleasant villages with tourist facilities. There is a frequent bus service on the road via (3.5km) **Mánna** to **Poseidonía** (Hotels B, C); and **Fínikas** (Φοίνικας), situated a mile apart on an inlet of the SW coast. They bear the names of the two cities ruled, according to the *Odyssey*, by Ktesios, father of Eumaeus the swineherd (Od. xv, 406); minor finds have been unearthed in both places. Poseidonía, better known by its popular name **Dellagrázia** (Ντελλαγράτσια), is the favourite summer resort of the islanders, with attractive villas and small tavernas. Beyond Manna a by-road leads S to **Vári** (10km; Hotels C, D), a developing resort in a pretty bay, where Dellagrazia may be pleasantly reached on foot in 2 hours round the S coast.

The N quarter of the island, rising in Mt Pirgos to 450m, is accessible only on foot. Here is the so-called **Cave of Pherekydes**, recalling the teacher of Pythagoras (fl. c 544 BC). Farther N near **Khalandrianí** (at least 2 hours walk from Ermoúpolis; seek directions) was an Early Cycladic cemetery with over 400 graves (finds from the 19C excavations in Athens; new survey and planning in progress) and a settlement (unexcavated). At **Kastrí**, a sheer and isolated hill above the sea beyond Khalandrianí, is an impressive refuge settlement of the late 3rd millennium BC with fortifications and towers.

# B.   Andros and Tínos

**Ferries**, at least daily, leave Rafína (50 minutes from Athens by frequent bus; comp. Rte 21) for Gávrio (2½ hours), the main harbour of Andros, regularly continuing to Tínos (4 hours) and sometimes to Síros (4½ hours). There is a hydrofoil service to Andros town.

Tínos is served by daily **boats** from Piraeus direct (4–5 hours) also via Síros.

**ANDROS** (8781 inhab.), or **Ándhros** (Ἄνδρος), the northernmost and one of the largest of the Cyclades, is 34km long and 13km wide with an area of 303 sq. km. It is separated from Euboea by the dangerous Doro Passage and from Tinos by a strait only 335m wide. The well-wooded island produces figs, oranges, lemons, oil, silk, and wine. Andros was sacred to Dionysos and there was a tradition that during the festival of the god a fountain in his sanctuary flowed with wine. Characteristic of the island are the stone field-walls, which are given rhythm and visual interest by triangular orthostats set at intervals, and the medieval dovecotes, square towers ornamented in patterned tilework. The latter are also found on Tinos, and seem to have marked a Venetian craze for dove-keeping combined with the competitive mania for tower building which swept Italy (comp. Bologna, San Gimignano, etc.).

**History**. The island is said to have been settled by Andreus, a general of Rhadamanthos of Crete, and later colonised by Ionians. Andros joined the fleet of Xerxes in 480 BC, for which Themistocles attempted to impose a heavy fine on the islanders; on their refusal to pay, he laid siege unsuccessfully to their city (Herod. viii, 111). Later Andros became subject to Athens and then to Macedon. In 200 BC it was captured by the Romans and handed over to Attalos I of Pergamon. In the Byzantine era it suffered from piratical raids. From 1207 the Dandoli held it under Venice as a hereditary fief. Seized by the Turks in 1556, Andros was ceded to Greece after the War of Independence.

The boats dock at **Gávrio** (Hotels B, C, D), a village on a sheltered bay (sandy beach to the NW), from which there is a connecting bus to the capital (1½ hours).

About ½ hour inland (or by road branching left from route to **Khóra**) at Ay. Pétros is a fine round **Hellenic tower**, of five floors, c 20m high. It is built on a base of large stones 4m high and has an inner hall 5.5m in diameter with a corbelled dome pierced by lunettes. A shaft dug into the wall above the entrance gave access by means of ladders to the upper storeys, served also by a winding staircase. The window has a projecting ledge with a rope-slot.

8km **Batsí** (Μπατσί; Hotels C, D), a seaside village farther along the coast, is attractively grouped round its little harbour, sometimes served by boats. The road rises steadily along the S slope of Mt Petalon (994km), the central culmination of the island, with views toward the unimportant island of **Yiáros**, several times used as a detainee camp. The promontory of **Ipsilí** has a Geometric settlement and temples. You pass above (16km) **Palaió-polis**, with an archaeological collection, whose scattered houses drop amid steep cultivated terraces to a wide bay. Near the shore remains (wall and towers, gateway, mole, street, house, basilica) of the ancient city of *Andros* have been identified, some as the result of work still in progress. The road divides, the right branch continuing to **Kórthí** (36km; Hotel C), a small landing-place on a deep bay (good beach) near the SE corner of the island.

On the promontory of **Zagorá**, c 2.5km beyond the fork, an important Late Geometric settlement was excavated by the University of Sydney in 1967–69 and subsequently. The neck of the sheer promontory is closed by a fortification wall. Within are the remains of blocks of houses and a small freestanding temple which continued in use after the site was abandoned. Finds from the site are in the museum in Andros (see below) and a guidebook (English) is available there.

The road turns inland on the slopes of Pétalon to run high above the beautiful valley of **Mesariá** which divides the island into two unequal parts. The villages multiply, fig-trees abound, and the countryside is dotted with dovecotes. 24km **Ménites**. A stiff climb of 1 hour in the direction of Phállika

(SE) leads to the **Moní Panakhrántou** supposed to have been visited by Nikephoros Phokas. 27km **Mesariá** has a church (1158) of the Taxiarchs, with paintings (12C). You descend through **Lámira** to (32km) **Andros** or 'Khora', the main centre.

The town (Hotels B, C, D), seat of a bishop with 1370 inhabitants, is situated on the E coast and subject to cool winds even in summer. It occupies a low eminence between two exposed beaches and extends picturesquely along the rocky tongue of land that juts out between them. There is a poor anchorage to the N. The main street (no cars), paved in marble and overhung by little balconies, descends past the **post office** (within is a large-scale map of the island) to the little **Plateia Kaïrís** overlooking the sandy S beach. Off the Plateia is a well-equipped **Museum of Modern Art**, with library, (built by the Basil and Elise Goulandris Foundation in 1979; extended 1984), which houses sculptures of Michael Tombros (1888–1970) and outstanding temporary exhibitions of the work of major international modern artists. Beyond it continues along the spine of the promontory in the **Kato Kastro** past the Metropolis to terminate before the little maritime **museum** in the windswept Plateia Riva. Here a modern bronze to the Unknown Sailor faces the eroded ruins of a Venetian castle, built on a detached outcrop of rock joined by a narrow bridge.

The new **Archaeological Museum** (good guidebook to the Zagora finds available in English) houses material from all over the island, including Palaiopolis, but the most prominent displays are of material from the Late Geometric settlement at Zagora. After an introductory section, these rooms illustrate (successively) Architecture (the fortification wall and domestic); Coarse Pottery; Fine Pottery; Personal and Household Objects; The Temple; The Cemetery. There is also a collection of ancient sculpture and Byzantine and later architectural fragments.

On the slopes, 3km NW, stands **Apoíkia** (Hotel B) with mineral springs, the water of which is celebrated throughout Greece. The road passes the medieval tower of Montelos. To the E is **Steniés**, with a restored tower house at Apatoúria, nearby.

**TINOS** (Τήνος), lying between Andros and Míkonos and NE of Síros, is 27.5km long and 12km wide. The port and capital is on the S coast; there is also an anchorage at Pánormos on the N coast. Elsewhere the island rises abruptly from the sea, especially in the NE where Mt Tsiknia attains 713m. In the centre it is peppered with white villages, compactly built on the hillsides. Their characteristic churches have an Italianate look with many-storied open-worked belfries, attractive W façades and lateral arcades. Conspicuous also in the green and pleasant landscape are the medieval dovecotes (comp. Andros). Tiny terraces are intensely cultivated with vines, figs, and vegetables. The wine of Tinos, famous in antiquity, is still good, both retsina and sweet unresinated. The Tinians are skilful marble workers. The island is the birthplace of a remarkable number of artists (see **Pírgos**).

**History**. The island was anciently called *Ophiousa*, as it was said to abound in snakes; for the same reason the name *Tenos* may derive from the Phoenician word tenok. A celebrated temple was dedicated to Poseidon who was credited with sending storks to exterminate the snakes. In 480 BC the Tenians were forced to serve in the fleet of Xerxes against Greece, but one of their ships deserted to the Greeks before the Battle of Salamis with news of the Persian intentions. For this service the name of Tenos was inscribed on the Tripod of Delphi (Hdt. VIII, 82). Tenos was captured by the Venetians under Andrea Ghisi in 1207. It withstood assaults for over 500 years, not falling to the Turks till 1714. The long Venetian domination made Tenos the most Catholic of the Cyclades. In the War of Greek Independence, while the Orthodox inhabitants took an active part, the Catholics held aloof. Today they have their own bishop, churches, convents, and schools. The Ursulines have a noteworthy girls' school at Loutra (see below). In 1822 the discovery of a wonder-working ikon of the Virgin made Tenos into a place of Orthodox pilgrimage. On 15 August 1940, before the port of Tenos, during the celebration of the Feast of the Assumption (see below), the Greek cruiser *Helle* was torpedoed by a submarine of unknown nationality, on the eve of the outbreak of the war between Greece and Italy.

**Tínos** (or **Khóra**; Hotels B, C, D), the capital, is an attractive town of 3754 inhabitants, dominated by the great pilgrims' church. The cheerful water-front is busy with hotels, restaurants, and cafés. A broad avenue climbs in 10 minutes to the church of **Panayia Evanghelístria** (Our Lady of Good Tidings), which, with its conventual buildings, forms a picturesque group. The white marble, of which it is built, includes reused material from the Temple of Apollo at Delos, as well as local and Parian stone. A gateway with an ogee arch, preceded by a floor of pebble mosaic, admits to the great **court**, shaded by trees and surrounded by porticoes. A monumental stair-case mounts to the **church**, where, surrounded by innumerable gold and silver ex-votos, the celebrated ikon is displayed. Twice a year, on the feasts of the Annunciation (25 March) and of the Assumption (15 August), thou-sands of pilgrims from all over Greece come here, many in hope of a cure. Off the courtyard are several exhibition halls, with displays of ikons and religious furniture, sculptures by A. Sókhos, paintings including works by famous local artists (Ghízis, Lítras etc).

About 250m above (and to the W and E of) the church, rough roads encircle the fortifications (walls and towers, 5C with later repairs; some-times incorporated in modern structures) of the acropolis of the site of ancient *Tenos* in the Classical and later periods. The occasion for the transfer of the settlement here from its earlier site at Xómbourgo (see below) is unknown.

On the right of the descent from the church is the **museum**, built in 1969 in the island's dovecote style. It contains a colossal pithos of the 7C BC with five bands of frieze figures in relief; another (2.5m high) with geometric designs; sculpture of various periods, especially from the sanctuary at Kiónia (see below); and a sundial attributed to Andronikos Kyrrhestes in the 1C BC. In a room above are modern paintings and sculpture.

At Kiónia, ½ hour W along the shore (bathing here and beyond), just before the Tinos Beach hotel, is a **Sanctuary of Poseidon and Amphitrite**, first dug by Belgian archaeol-ogists in 1900. Recent work by French scholars (published R. Étienne, 1986) has clarified its nature and history. Although there are some signs of previous activity, the earliest monumental development (temple, altar, dining rooms, double-fronted stoa 170m long, fountain) belongs to the late 4C and early 3C BC and was continued in the Roman period. Sculptures from the site (in Tinos Museum) include fragments of colossal figures of Poseidon and Amphitrite, the altar frieze with garlands, bucrania and rosettes, marine monsters thought to be from the pediments of the temple and statues of Roman emperors (some cuirassed) and other figures. The altar also had freestanding works (Eros, Anteros, Nike figures) by Agasos of Ephesos.

## Excursions

Buses from the quay to most of the island villages. Cars and scooters for hire.

1. To MONÍ KEKHROVOUNÍOU (10km) and XÓMBOURGO (13km). The route is described as a round trip of about 26km (with possible extensions to Kómi, Kalloní (21km from Khóra) and Kolimvíthres), returning via Voláx, Krókos, Loutrá, Xinára and Tripótamos. With a car the excursion can be easily completed in a day; by public transport, it may be better divided.

Leaving **Khóra** on the **Pórto** road, keep left after 1km and right after 3km. 1km further ignore the left turn which by-passes the villages of **Triantáros**, **Dhío Khoriá** and **Arnádhos** via which however you may reach the attractive monastery (nuns) of **Moní Kekhrovouníou** a 12C foundation where in 1822 Ayia Pelagia (canonised in 1971) saw visions which led to the discovery of the famous ikon. Beyond the monastery the road continues to **Mesí** (turn left, leaving **Falatádho** to the right). At 13km from **Khóra** a narrow road ascends (left) to the Catholic monastery of the Sacred Heart, a short distance below the impressive Venetian walls of the prominent citadel of **Xómburgo** (565m), with a fine view of the Cyclades. Below the castle are some remains of the site of ancient *Tenos* in the Geometric, Archaic and Classical periods—Classical built tombs, a Geometric sanctuary of Demeter and a fine section of the Archaic city wall (above the church of **Zoödhókhos Piyí**, reached by a path round to the W side of the hill). Returning to the main road and continuing N, you meet a sign (right) to **Voláx** (2km along an unsurfaced road), a charming village in a curious lunar landscape, with a flourishing tradition of basket making. The main road continues N, via pretty **Krókos** to **Kómi** (18km) and **Kalloní** (21km). From **Kómi** a right fork leads in 2.5km to the exposed bay of **Kolimvíthres**.

Returning to **Khóra** by a different route (following signs to **Tínos** after **Krókos**), short diversions from the main road take you to **Loutrá**, with a girls' school run by Ursuline nuns and **Xinára**, seat of the Catholic archbishop. Above **Xinára**, the road skirts **Tripótamos** and descends to **Khóra**.

2. TO ISTÉRNIA (26km), PÍRGOS (32km) and PÁNORMOS (35km). Leaving **Khóra** on the same road as for (1), a left turn after 500m ascends to **Tripótamos** (6.5km). Following signs to **Pírgos**, the road runs along the S flank of the hills with views to **Síros**. At 13km there is a rough descent to the village of **Ayios Romanós** on the coast. At 18.5km a square Hellenistic tower can be seen below the road. 20km a fine new road descends left to (4.5km) the coastal hamlet of **Kalívia**, below the attractive village of (21km) **Kardhianí**, clinging to the hillside. 26km **Istérnia** whose church has a dome incoporating part of an ancient column (rooms; see below). On the coast below is **Ayios Nikítas**. 32km **Pírgos** (formerly *Pánormos*, the name now abrogated to the port), the largest village (342 inhab.) on the island, has an old grammar school built by Capodistrias in 1830, and a School of Fine Arts. It is the birthplace of several noted modern Greek artists (a small museum houses some of their works), amongst them the sculptors *Y. Halepás* and *D. Phillipótes* and the painter *N. Lítras*. The house of Halepás next to the museum can be visited, that of Lítras is closed. 35km **Pánormos** (rooms) is an attractive harbour, formerly used for loading marble.

The road to **Marlás** (2km from the **Pírgos** fork) and beyond (where quarries produce fine white, black and green marble) has a narrow turning on the outskirts of the village, signed to the Monastery of **Kíra Xéni** (Our Lady of the Strangers), reached in 1km. The 17C foundation is appealing (open only early morning; otherwise key must be obtained in **Pírgos**). Below it is the monastic church of **Káto Monastíri**, above, that of **Ayía Thékla** (with a modern counterpart). Just below the junction of the approach roads to **Kíra Xéni** and **Ayía Thékla**, cut by the road construction, are the modest remains of the first Mycenaean-type tholos tomb to be discovered in the Cyclades. Small, rock cut and lined with neatly laid slabs, it contained pottery of the 14C and 13C BC.

3. TO PÓRTO (7km). This small resort, to the E of **Khóra** has good swimming. Below the road at **Ayía Varvára** (3.5km) is a round Hellenistic tower. The coastal road further S (via **Ayios Fokás**, Hotel C) also has good beaches.

# C. Míkonos and Delos (Dhílos)

**Car Ferries** from Piraeus 1–4 times daily to Míkonos in 5–7½ hours. The return journey is made in the afternoon or overnight. A round trip (allowing a view of Tínos and Míkonos) can be made in a long day. Also from Rafína. From Tínos twice daily in c ½ hour. From Síros in c 1 hour.

There are also occasional connections (some summer only) to other Cycladic islands, to Rhodes and the Dodecanese, and to the N Aegean. Smaller craft make summer trips to and from Náxos, Páros, etc. Caiques daily from Míkonos to Delos.

**By Air.** 4–10 flights a day in 50 minutes; also 2–3 times weekly to Crete and Rhodes; daily to Thíra, Rhodes; less frequently to Sámos, Khíos; also international charters.

**Míkonos**, more familiarly in English **Mykonos**, is a rocky island of 60 sq. km producing manganese and a little barley, wine, and figs. Four-fifths of the 5365 inhabitants live in or around the capital, which, from being solely the point of departure for Delos, has developed into the most popular tourist centre of the Cyclades, welcoming cruise ships daily.

**History**. In antiquity the island had two cities, *Mykonos*, on the W coast, and *Panormos*, on the N coast. Strabo notes that baldness was prevalent here so that bald men were sometimes called Mykonians. The Persian commander Datis touched at Mykonos in 490 BC on his way to Greece. After the Persian wars the island became an Athenian colony. In the Middle Ages it belonged to the dukes of Naxos and later was incorporated in the Venetian province of Tenos. In 1822, under the leadership of the heroine Manto Mavrogenous, the islanders repulsed an attack by the Turks. Mykonos is now part of the eparchy of Syros.

The town and port of **Míkonos** (Hotels A–E) is situated on the W coast on the site of the ancient city, a curving bay ending in a low promontory and backed by an amphitheatre of hills. Its small churches and chapels, and its glittering white houses, with their arcades and marble staircases, give it a special charm, and its narrow lanes seemingly inexhaustable scope for losing your way (a deliberate defence against pirates). The less attractive esplanade, lined with cafés, is a favourite promenade and the pelicans, which have become mascots of the island, a constant curiosity. In summer artists from all countries frequent the *Skholí Kalón Tekhnón*, a branch of the Athens School of Fine Art. The locally woven linens are colourful.

Of the many little churches erected from the proceeds of fishing and piracy, the **Paraportianí**, near the quay, is typically picturesque. Near by is the **local museum** with a floor of black Tinos marble and bygones from demolished houses. The Metropolis and the Roman Catholic church, bearing the Ghizi escutcheon, are on the way to the promontory where three celebrated windmills catch the wind in their small triangular sails. Below them picturesque houses rise straight from the sea.

At the other end of the bay, beyond the Leto hotel, the **Archaeological Museum** contains important finds from the necropolis of Rheneia, used in 425 BC during the purification of Delos. Notable are a statue of Herakles in Parian marble; cinerary urns, ossuaries in lead, and a quantity of pottery from all parts of the Aegean found on Delos. Of unusual interest is a fine 7C *pithos (found in Míkonos in 1961; restored) showing relief scenes of the Trojan horse and the massacre at Troy.

To N and S of the town several beaches are accessible in 20–40 minutes on foot, or by bus; **Ayios Stéfanos** has a bungalow and other hotels (A, B, C, D).

**Excursions**. These are of minor interest but may be combined with visits to more distant beaches. There are reasonable bus services, and many boat excursions to beaches. Cars, scooters and cycles may be hired. Taxis (fixed charges displayed) from the square.

1. **Garden of Rapháki**, ½ hour E. This garden, with its fine trees, was bequeathed by the patriot sailor Sourmales, who ran the blockade of Crete in 1862.

2. **Mt Ayios Ilías**, 2 hours N. This hill (364m), the highest point of the island, is supposed to be the *Dimastos* of Pliny. You can return via the sandy bay of **Pánormos**. At Palaiókastro, near by, the ruined medieval castle of **Darga** occupies the site of the ancient city of Panormos.

3. **Lenós**, 1 hour SE, has the remains of a round Hellenic tower and of a gatehouse.

4. **Ano Méra** or **Tourlianí**, 4km E, has a convent and a Hotel (A). On the sea beyond is **Kalafáti Beach** (Hotels B). About 1.5km out to see is the islet of **Dhragonísi**, with remarkable caves haunted by seals, and crumbling cliffs.

FROM MIKONOS TO DELOS, caique (charge, also for archaeological site and museum) c 08.30–09.00, returning from 12.00 The crossing (c ½ hour) is often choppy and cold; in rough weather (not infrequent when the N wind blows) it cannot be made. On leaving Mikonos you pass the islets of Ayios Yeoryios and Kavouronisi and head for Cape Kako, the N point of Delos. On a clear day Tinos stands up grey and black to starboard with the Panayia Evanghelistria white above the town and the villages prominent below Xombourgo. Siros is seen for a time ahead (beyond Rheneia) and, far to port, Paros. The cloud effects above the islands are often enchanting. We double Cape Kako and enter the strait separating Delos from Rhenia.

The island of **DELOS** (Δήλος), or Lesser Dhílos (η Μικρή Δήλος), is 5.5km long and 1.2km wide, and has an area of only 5 sq. km. It is separated from Rheneia or Greater Dhílos by a channel 900m wide, running from N to S. Two rocky islets, Little Rhevmatariá and Great Rhevmatariá (ancient Isle of Hecate), rise from the middle of the channel. The W coast is indented by three small havens the Bay of Skardhaná; the Little Harbour, the ancient Sacred Harbour, adjoined by the ancient Commercial Harbour; and the Bay of Foúrni. On the other side of the island, on the NE coast, is the anchorage of Goúrna, used by caiques in rough weather. The interior of the island is sharply undulating, reaching a height of 113m in the bare conical Mt Kinthos. To the SW is the dry gorge of the Inopos.

Delos, though the smallest of the Cyclades, was once the political and religious centre of the Aegean, with a teeming population. Birth-place of Apollo and Artemis, it boasted an oracle second only to that of Delphi and a famous temple of Apollo, raised by the common contribution of the Greek states. Today it is virtually uninhabited except by site guardians and members of the French School and their staff, whose houses and offices are clustered near the ruins of the Sanctuary of Apollo. The work of the French School, begun in 1873 and still in progress, has revealed a complex of buildings that bear comparison with those of Delphi and Olympia. The site includes the great Panhellenic sanctuary and the area of the Sacred Lake; the maritime and commercial city, with its docks, harbours, and warehouses; and finally a town of the 3C BC, the streets of which invite comparison with those of Pompeii. The **··**ruins extend for over 1km; to explore the site thoroughly more than one visit is necessary. There is a **tourist pavilion** on the site with a restaurant and bar but there is no accommodation. The other houses in the vicinity of the museum are those of the resident attendants.

**History**. *Delos* was anciently called *Ortygia*, or Quail Island. The remains of a prehistoric settlement on the top of Mt Kinthos prove that Delos was inhabited in the 3rd millennium BC. From a very early period it was a religious centre and a busy port.

The Ionians who colonised the Cyclades in the 10–9C brought to Delos the cult of Leto, who was said to have given birth here to Artemis and Apollo. By the 7C the sacred island, under the protection of Naxos, became the headquarters of a league of Aegean Ionians, who held a great festival, the *Delia* (see below) in honour of Apollo, celebrated in the Homeric Hymn. The Athenians took advantage of their kinship with the Ionians to enter the league, of which they became the ruling spirit. They sent religious embassies annually to Delos (see below) and purified the sanctuary on more than one occasion. The first purification was by Peisistratos in 543 BC. Polykrates, tyrant of Samos (died 522 BC), having conquered the Cyclades, attached Rheneia to Delos with chains and dedicated the larger island to Apollo.

In 490 BC, the Delians fled from their island to Tenos, but the Persian commander Datis, who had sent his fleet to Rheneia, left Delos inviolate. Delos was the centre of the **Delian** or **First 'Athenian' Confederacy**, the maritime league founded in 478 BC under the leadership of Athens, and its treasury was established in the island until its transference to Athens in 454.

In 426 the Athenians ordered a second purification of Delos. They removed to Rhenia all the coffins of the dead which were in Delos and passed a decree that thenceforward no one should die or give birth in the sacred island, and that all who were near the time of either should be carried across to Rheneia. After the purification the Athenians restored the Delian Festival, which had lapsed in the course of years (see below) and instituted the Delian Games. In 422 the Athenians banished the remaining Delians on the pretext that they were impure and unworthy of the sacred island. Later, however, at the bidding of the Delphic oracle, they let the Delians return. Athenian overseers called *Amphictiones* administered the temple, with the nominal concurrence of the Delians. Plutarch tells us that in 417 Nikias, head of the Athenian embassy, disembarked in Rheneia and crossed to Delos in procession on a temporary wooden bridge that he had brought with him.

After the defeat of Athens at Aegospotami in 404, Delos appealed to Sparta and from 401 to 394 enjoyed a short independence until the Athenians regained possession. In 378 they instituted the **Second Athenian Confederacy**, notably different from the first, as it was purely defensive and not an instrument of imperialism. The Delians were not satisfied, as only two years later they attempted to regain control of the sanctuary, and the Athenians had to reassert their authority.

By 315 BC the command of the Aegean had passed to Egypt. Delos, again independent, became the centre of an island confederacy, and entered on the most prosperous period of its history. Rich offerings flowed into the sanctuary. Honours decreed to foreign benefactors attest to the variety and importance of the island's diplomatic and commercial relations. From the mass of contemporary inscriptions that have survived can be drawn a detailed picture of the temple administration and of the island economy. Delos was a democracy with an archon, a senate and an assembly. The care of the sanctuary was in the hands of four *Hieropes* elected annually, each of whom combined the office of priest and administrator.

By 250 BC the first Romans had settled in Delos, and Roman merchants soon dominated other foreign immigrants. In 166 the Roman senate allowed the Athenians to reoccupy the island, and in order to counterbalance the commercial power of Rhodes, made Delos into a free port. The Delians were expelled, never to return and the island became a cleruchy under the control of an Athenian *Epimeletes*. The Romans, however, remained the true masters of the island. In 146 the importers of Corinth moved from their devastated city to Delos. Strabo says that the great religious festival was now in essence a trade fair on a heroic scale, and reminds us that Delos acquired the grim reputation of being the slave-market of Greece, as many as 10,000 slaves changing hands in a single day. The sanctuary continued to attract its devotees, but it was trade that filled the island coffers. An association of Italian merchants, with the backing of Rome, was formed under the title of *Hermaists*, and made itself prominent. Commercial houses and syndicates of merchants from Tyre, Beyrout, Alexandria, and elsewhere formed trade associations. The town was embellished with monuments of every kind.

In 88 BC, during the First Mithridatic War, in which Athens had supported Mithridates and Delos repudiated Athens in favour of Rome, Menophanes, a general of Mithridates, descended on the island. He killed natives and foreigners alike, enslaved the women and children, seized the sanctuary treasure, looted the merchandise, and razed the city to the ground. Regained the following year by Sulla, Delos was returned to the Athenians and partly rebuilt with Roman aid. In 69 the island was sacked by Athenodoros. About 66 BC the Roman legate Triarius built a wall round the city to protect it from further piratical attacks. But its day was done. In the 2C AD we find Pausanias observing that, were the temple guard withdrawn, Delos would be uninhabited. Philostratus (3C) says that the Athenians put the island up for sale but there were no offers. The emperor Julian is said to have consulted the Delian oracle. Ravaged by successive masters of the Cyclades, barbarians, pirates, Knights of St. John of Jerusalem; used as a marble quarry by Venetians and Turks, and even by the inhabitants of Mykonos and Tenos; the sacred island sank into insignificance.

In the 17C Sir Kenelm Digby removed marbles from Delos for the collection of Charles I.

**The Delian Festivals**. Festivals called *Delia* in honour of Apollo and Artemis and their mother Leto were celebrated in Delos from remote antiquity. The Athenians took part, sending ambassadors called *Deliastae* and later *Theoroi*. The sacred vessel, called *Theoris*, in which they sailed, was said to be the one which Theseus had sent after his adventures in Crete. In the course of time the ancient festival ceased to be held, and it was not till 426 BC that the Athenians revived it (see above). They not only restored the *Delia* but instituted the Delian Games. Festival and games were held every four years. By virtue of their leadership of the Delian Confederacy, the Athenians took the most prominent part in the ceremonies. Though the islanders shared in providing choruses and victims for the sacrifices, the leader *Architheoros*, was an Athenian. On arrival in the island, the embassy from Athens marched in procession to the temple, singing the *Prosodion*, the hymn recounting the story of Leto and the birth of the divine twins, and intoning chants in honour of Apollo. The procession then made a solemn tour of the sanctuary. After that, the victims were sacrificed, and the games began. The games comprised athletic sports, horse-racing, and musical contests. The *geranos*, or sacred dance, was performed before the altar of Apollo. Proceedings ended with theatrical plays and banquets. The *Lesser Delia* were simpler but an annual festival. For this the Athenians sent the Theoris every year to Delos. Before embarking, they offered sacrifice in the Delion at Marathon, to ensure a happy voyage. During the absence of the sacred vessel, the city of Athens was purified and it was forbidden to execute criminals.

**Plan**. The numbered references correspond with those in the definitive Guide of the French School, though not every building is described in this text.

## I. Harbour area

Landing is at a mole (made of debris removed during the excavations) at a point between the Sacred Harbour (left) and the Commercial Harbour (right). The **Sacred Harbour**, which by the 2C BC was also used as a commercial port, was protected on the N by a breakwater of granite blocks, 150m long, built in Archaic times. Most of its remains are underwater and the harbour is sanded up. From the 2C BC the **Commercial Harbour** extended S for c 800m, divided by moles into five basins. Some mooring stones are visible. At the base of the modern mole is an open space called the **Agora of the Competialists** (Pl. 2), which divides the maritime and residential quarters to the S (see below) from the Sanctuary to the N. The Competialists were the heads of associations of freedmen and slaves who celebrated annually the Roman festivals of the Lares Compitales, gods of the crossroads. In the centre are parts of a circular shrine, and a larger square base, both offerings of the Hermaists to Hermes and his mother Maia. They probably also built c 150 BC the **Ionic Naiskos** (left) before which stands a marble offertory box, adorned with a relief of two snakes.

You turn left into a paved road, 13.8m wide, known as the **Dromos**, or **Sacred Way**. It is lined with exedrae and statue bases, notably (right) that of an equestrian statue of Epigenes of Teos, a general of Attalos I of

Pergamon (241–197 BC). On the seaward side are the remains of the **Stoa of Philip** (Pl. 3), dedicated to Apollo by Philip V of Macedon, who was master of the Cyclades until his defeat at Kynoskephalai in 197 BC. The dedicatory inscription on the architrave is clear. The stoa in grey marble, 71.3m by 11m, had 16 Doric columns, fluted on the upper part only, of which one remains standing. The building was doubled on the W some 30 years later by a stoa with 25 columns that faced the sea. To the right of the Sacred Way is the so-called **south stoa** (Pl. 4), built in the 3C BC.

A passage through this portico led into the **Agora of the Delians** (Pl. 84), which before the three stoas were built had direct access to the shore. It is bounded N and E by an angled 2C portico, over which is an Ionic storey, and S by another portico (3C), set obliquely. A white mosaic survives from the Imperial epoch when Roman baths were installed here. To the S and E of the agora are the ruins of houses; one of them has been called the **House of Kerdon**, from a sepulchral stele now in the museum. Near the SE corner of the Agora, at a crossroads, is the **Shrine of Tritopator**, ancestor of the Attic family of Pyrrhakides. This is a little circular enclosure, with an opening to the NW. Behind it, reached by a few steps, are the ruins of the **Basilica of St. Quiricus** (Pl. 86), a 5C Byzantine apsidal church.

## II. The Hieron of Apollo

At the end of the Dromos in a little square (right) are a small sanctuary, and the marble **Exedra of Soteles**. Three marble steps lead up to the **south-west propylaia** (Pl. 5), erected in the mid-2C BC by the Athenians to form the main entrance to the sanctuary of Apollo. It had three doorways and four Doric columns. A statue of Hermes was erected in front of its predecessor in 341 BC. You enter the **Hieron of Apollo**, a huge precinct enclosing temples, altars, votive offerings, and remains from a thousand years of worship. Within to the right is the **Oikos of the Naxians** (Pl. 6), a 7–6C building with a central colonnade. It replaced a Geometric structure and may take its orientation from 'Building Γ' (Pl. 7), the most ancient temple (perhaps of Mycenaean date), respected throughout antiquity; the remains of this lie 5.5m E. Against the N wall of the Oikos is the rectangular base of the colossal **Statue of Apollo** (Pl. 9), made of Naxian marble. It bears the celebrated inscription in Archaic letters (7C BC) 'I am of the same marble, statue and pedestal'; a 4C dedication 'The Naxians to Apollo'; and numerous graffiti of Venetian and 17C travellers.

The god was represented as a kouros in characteristic Archaic posture, nude, standing, with hands on thighs; he wore a metal belt. Plutarch relates that Nikias, sent in 417 BC from Athens in charge of the sacred embassy, brought with him a bronze palm tree among the votive offerings (the base of which survives; see below). A gust of wind blew over the palm tree, which carried with it the statue of Apollo. It was then probably re-erected in the present position. Two fragments of the statue that the Venetians tried in vain to remove (part of the trunk and part of the thighs) are now behind the Temple of Artemis (see below); a hand is in the museum; part of a foot is in the British Museum.

On the right of the Sacred Way are three important temples. The first is the **'Great' Temple of Apollo** (Pl. 13), begun at the time of the foundation of the Delian Confederacy in 477 BC. Construction languished after the transfer to Athens of the treasury in 454, and was not resumed until the 3C BC. Erected on a high base of granite blocks, and approached by steps of Delian marble, it was a Doric peripteral building (29.6m by 13.4m) with 6 x 13 columns. These were fluted only at the base and neck. The metopes were plain and the architrave was decorated with palm leaves and lion-mask spouts placed above each triglyph. The cella had pronaos and opistho-domos.

Adjoining is the **Temple of the Athenians** (Pl. 12), a Doric amphiprostyle building of 425–417 BC with six columns in front. It measures 17.8m by 11.4m, and had a **prodomos** with four columns in antis. In the **cella** were the statues, probably chryselephantine, which gave the temple its alterna-tive name of 'House of the Seven'. They were placed on a semicircular pedestal of Eleusinian marble, the base of which has been reconstituted behind the temple. The roof sloped to a ridge presumably to accommodate the Archaic statue of Apollo, by the Naxian sculptors Tektaios and Ange-lion, previously in the Porinos Naos. Fragments of the corner acroteria are now in the museum.

The third temple, in poros and dating from the 6C, is the **Porinós Naós** (Pl. 11) of the inscriptions. It is 15.7m long and 10m wide. Here was originally deposited the treasure of the Delian Confederacy.

In front, on the Sacred Way, a long base bears a 3C inscription in honour of Philetairos, first King of Pergamon (280–263 BC). An adjacent base has a Doric frieze with roses and bulls' heads alternating with metopes. The buildings arranged in an arc to the N have been called **treasuries** by analogy with similar structures at Olympia and Delphi. Beneath this group are remains of a Mycenaean settlement sometimes thought to include a palace.

To the W of the Sacred Way, in a paved square, is the angled **Stoa of the Naxians** (Pl. 36). In its SW corner are the granite foundations, with a cylindrical hollow in the middle, of the **bronze palm tree** (see above) dedicated by Nikias. On one of the fragments (replaced) of the lower marble course of the monument can be read the name of Nikias, beginning the dedicatory inscription. Near by some courses of a column on which was a statue of Antiochus the Great (223–187 BC) have been set up. To the NW of the column are two late 6C houses (Pl. 43, 44) called the **Hieropoion** and the **Oikos of Andros**. To the N of the houses, near a portico, three of whose columns have been replaced, is a **temple** (Pl. 42) preceded by a colonnade, perhaps the **keraton** built by the Athenians. Portions of its sculptured frieze have been set up on a neighbouring wall. Close by are the foundations of an apsidal building (Pl. 39) which may have enclosed an altar.

The **Artemision** or **Sanctuary of Artemis**, farther N, is bounded by Ionic porticoes on the E and N. To the left is a semicircular platform hewn in the rock, which seems to have been a cult object from the Late Helladic II period, perhaps the **sema** or tomb of the two Hyperborean maidens who brought the first offerings to Apollo. The Ionic **Temple of Artemis** (Pl. 46), on a high granite base, was rebuilt c 179 BC on the site of an Archaic predecessor, itself orientated to a Mycenaean forerunner. Behind it are two fragments of the kouros (see above) abandoned here by 17C collectors. Many statues of Artemis have been found here (see museum), including that dedicated by Nikandre now in Athens.

To the E and S of the Apollo temples was an open space bounded by an Archaic building with a central colonnade, perhaps the **bouleuterion**, and the **prytaneion**, where a votive herm has been reerected. Farther E is the **'Monument of the Bulls'** (Pl. 24), a misnomer derived from its decoration. It is an oblong building, 67m long and 8.8m wide, of Hellenistic date and unusual design, which had a granite peribolos. The foundations, all that remains, are in gneiss and granite. A pronaos, at the S end, led into a long gallery with a hollow floor placed over a partitioned framework and surrounded by a pavement 46cm above it. It probably housed a trireme dedicated after a naval victory, perhaps by Demetrios Poliorketes, and is

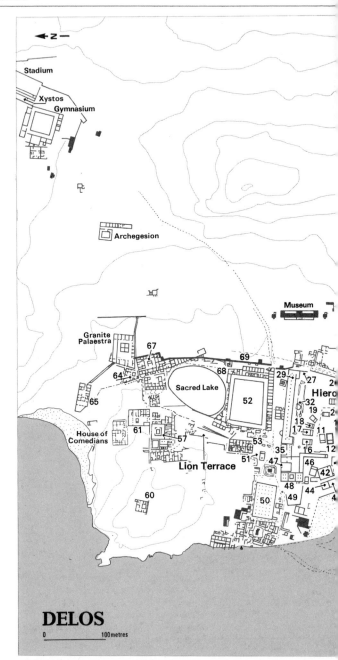

**DELOS**

0       100 metres

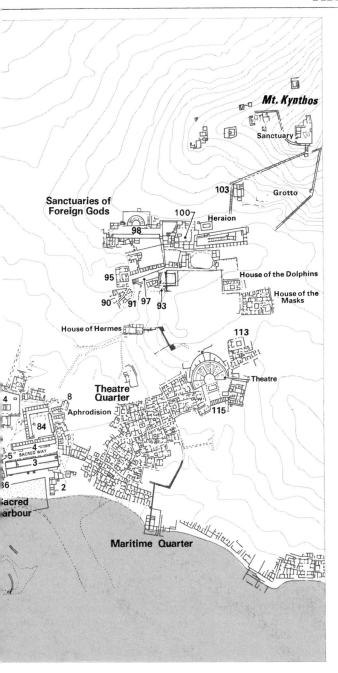

Mt. Kynthos

Sanctuary

103

Grotto

Sanctuaries of
Foreign Gods

100

Heraion

98

95

House of the Dolphins

House of the
Masks

90

91 97 93

House of Hermes

113

Theatre

Theatre
Quarter

4

8

Aphrodision

115

84

SACRED WAY

5

4

3

86

2

Sacred
Harbour

Maritime Quarter

therefore to be identified with the **neorion** named in inscriptions (cf. Samothrace). A cella at the N end has a trapezoidal base or altar.

The Hieron is bounded on the E by a late enceinte wall (Pl. 26), with an entrance gateway (Pl. 27) through which you can quickly reach the museum (see below). Just outside the gate vestiges of a small **Sanctuary of Dionysos** are characterised by several choregic monuments in the form of a huge phallus with Dionysiac reliefs on the pedestal, one erected by Karystos c 300 BC.

Extending westwards to form the N boundary of the Hieron is the **Stoa of Antigonus** (Pl. 29), dedicated, according to its mutilated inscription, by a king of Macedon, son of Demetrios (Antigonus Gonatas). The portico, 124m long, has two longitudinal galleries with a salient wing at either end. On the S side were 47 columns; within were 19. The triglyphs of the frieze are decorated with bulls' heads. In the E wing a statue of C. Billienus has been replaced on its base. In front of the stoa are two parallel lines of statue bases, including the **base of the Progones**, on which stood some 20 statues of the ancestors, real and mythical, of Gonatas. This may have been modelled on the Monument of the Eponymous Heroes in the agora at Athens.

Near by in a circular abaton (Pl. 32) is a Mycenaean ossuary, comprising small chamber tombs, reached by a dromos, in which were found skeletons and Mycenaean and earlier vases. This may be the **theke**, where Arge and Opis, two of the Hyperborean maidens, were buried and where some curious sacrificial rites were performed (according to Herodotus) by the women of the island. In the street outside the Hieron, behind the stoa, is the **Minoe Fountain** of the inscriptions. Farther on, adjoining the S end of the Stoa of Antigonus, is an **oikos** (Pl. 47) of 402–394 BC. The gap beyond was a passage admitting to the Hieron, beyond which are some remains of the **ekklesiasterion** (Pl. 47), several times enlarged, and of a 5C edifice comprising two hypostyle halls with a peristyle court between, doubtfully identified as the **thesmophorion** (Pl. 48).

## III.  Region of the Sacred Lake

The **Agora of Theophrastos** (Pl. 49; often muddy), raised on an embankment and dating from c 166 BC, is named after the Epimelete Theophrastos, whose statue-base survives. Another base commemorates L. Cornelius Sulla. To the N is the little **Sanctuary of Poseidon Nauklarios**, identified by an inscription on its 4C altar. Adjacent is a large hypostyle hall (Pl. 50), which resembles in form the Telesterion at Eleusis and has been given the name **'Stoa of Poseidon'**; it seems, however, to have been built c 208 BC as an exchange or merchants' hall. The original inscription 'The Delians to Apollo' was altered in 166 BC to read 'The Athenians to Apollo'. Forty-four Doric and Ionic columns supported a roof sloping to a ridge with a central lantern. The S side comprised an open Doric colonnade.   Returning E past a modern house you see the foundations of the **Dodekatheon** (Pl. 51), a small hexastyle Doric temple of the 4C BC, dedicated to the Twelve Gods. Turning left there are (right) the remains of a small **Temple of Leto** (Pl. 53) of the 6C, and (left) a granite building with a double court. The ground floor was divided into small rooms, perhaps sculptors' workshops, while above was an assembly room. A ruined Doric **propylon** leads to the **Agora of the Italians**, a huge open court, 101m by 69m, surrounded by a Doric peristyle of white marble columns on red bases with an Ionic colonnaded gallery above.

The agora was built by Italian residents of Delos; the peristyle by individuals or trade groups known as Hermaists (see above). Begun c 110 BC, it was repaired after Mithridates' sack, but abandoned before 50 BC. On the inner side is a series of cells or exedrae containing votive monuments, statues, and mosaics. Noteworthy cells on the W side are those of L. Orbius, O. Cluvius, and C. Ofellius, the last with a fine nude statue by the Athenian sculptors Dionysios and Timarchides, now lying overturned by its base; the cell of P. Satricanius, on the N side has a good mosaic. In a cell on the E side was found a statue of a fighting Gaul. Outside, on the E, S, and W sides, are lines of shops opening into the street.

The avenue leading N is bordered on the left by the **Terrace of the Lions**. Here at least nine lions in Naxian marble of the 7C BC guarded the sacred area. Similar monumental approaches are found in Egypt (e.g. Karnak). Five remain in situ; at least one more, removed in the 17C, adorns the Arsenal at Venice. The lean animals are represented 'sejant', that is, sitting on their haunches with their front legs upright, and face the Sacred Lake.

The **Sacred Lake**, dry since 1926, is an oval depression surrounded by a modern wall, which represents its extent in Hellenistic times. This is the lake called 'The Hoop' (Τροχοειδής) of which Herodotus was reminded when describing the Sacred Lake of Sais in Egypt (II, 170). In it were kept the sacred swans and geese of Apollo. The marshy ground that extended to the S before the construction of the Agora of the Italians was probably part of the domain of Leto. This lake, possibly formed by an overflow of the Inopos which, a little to the N, fell into the Bay of Skardhana, was closely associated with the cult of Apollo. A palm tree has been planted in the centre in memory of the sacred palm to which Leto clung when giving birth to Apollo (*Odyssey* IV).

Beyond the Lion Terrace a street ascends to the **Institution of the Poseidoniasts of Berytos** (Pl. 57), an association of Syrian shipowners and merchants from Beirut, who worshipped Baal, a god they identified with Poseidon.

The vestibule leads into a court bounded W by a portico into which opened four chapels. One of these, later than the others, was dedicated to the goddess Roma and contains her statue. On the E side a colonnade leads to peristyle court, with a cistern. To the W of this court is another, with a mosaic pavement, which was probably used as a meeting-place. To the S were reception rooms and, in the basement below them, a series of shops. Statues found in this building included the group of Aphrodite and Pan (in Athens).

Beyond the Institution a road runs N–S alongside four houses bearing apotropaic symbols. To the N is the **House of the Comedians** and two other houses. It had an unusual peristyle of two stories, Doric and Ionic, in marble.

To the W, situated on the promontory overlooking the Bay of Skardhana, is **Hill House** (Pl. 60), well-preserved but unremarkable.

Returning along the N flank of the Institution in the direction of the Sacred Lake, you reach the **House of the Diadoumenos** (Pl. 61), so called from the discovery here of a replica of the celebrated statue of Polykleitos. The house had an elaborate water-supply system. Turning E and leaving on the left a Hellenistic altar, you next enter the **Lake House** (Pl. 64), which occupies a trapezoidal island with doors on streets to E and W. On the other side of the farther street is the **granite palaestra** (Pl. 66), built partly of granite blocks some time after 166 BC. In the middle of this building is a large cistern of four compartments, with a poros roof; it is surrounded by a Doric peristyle. To the N was a granite colonnade. To the E is a granite retaining wall, between which and the city wall, is the **Well of the Maltese**, the only well known in Delos before the excavations. Adjoining is the **Lake Palaestra**, ruined when the city wall was built.

The **city wall** (Pl. 69), called also the **Wall of Triarius**, was built by the Roman legate Triarius c 66 BC to protect Delos from the attacks of the pirate Athenodoros. It was partly built over houses and shops which were demolished and filled with rubble to form a foundation. The S part of the wall was demolished in 1925–26. It skirted the E side of the Sacred Lake and of the Agora of the Italians. On a bastion of the wall, a little to the S, was found a small **prostyle temple** (Pl. 68), with four columns, open to the E and with an altar in front.

The **tourist pavilion** and the **museum** are now close by.

Enthusiasts who wish to explore farther to the NE can make for the **archegesion** (Pl. 74), sacred to the worship of Apollo in the guise of the legendary king Anios. The latest part of the structure dates from the 6C BC. Farther on are the square Ionic peristyle of the **gymnasium**, and the **stadium**, both built before the **xystos** (covered track) was added (c 200 BC) between them. Beyond the stadium is a cluster of ancient houses and near the E shore the remains of a **synagogue**.

## IV. The Museum

The **museum** contains most of the finds from the island except the finest sculpture which is in Athens. CENTRAL HALL. Many Archaic kouroi and korai, sanctuary dedications of the late 7C and 6C BC, all manufactured of marble from Naxos or Paros, the most important centres in the early development of Greek monumental sculpture; triangular base, one corner adorned with a ram's head, inscribed with the name of the sculptor and dedicator, Euthykartides of Naxos, which orginally supported a huge kouros; sphinx on column, 6C; small archaic seated figures; statues of Olympian gods, late 6C. ROOMS TO RIGHT OF ENTRANCE. (1) Dedications from many parts of Greece, Geometric, Orientalising and Archaic in date: pottery, terracottas, some bronzes. The Orientalising pottery is particularly fine. Case 7 contains the important votive deposit from below the Artemision, with Mycenaean objects, including outstanding ivory plaques, with both incised and relief decoration. Noteworthy are an animal combat and a warrior with boar's tusk helmet and figure-of-eight shield. Case 17 has Archaic polychrome plates. (2) Hellenistic wall paintings and mosaics, pottery and terracottas, including ornate braziers. ROOMS TO LEFT OF ENTRANCE. (1) Classical sculpture of the 5C. Especially striking are the akroteria compositions from the Temple of the Athenians, in a delicate late 5C style. The main central group from the E end of the building is Boreas and Oreithyia, the W group of Eos and Kephalos is fragmentary. Nymphs from the corners of the building; various torsos, including athletes; a lion from the Artemision. (2 corner room) Late Classical and Hellenistic sculpture. Deities, including Artemis with a hind, figures of Pan with sack and tambourine, base of bronze statue with sandalled foot still adhering, herms, portraits; (3). Hellenistic and Roman sculpture. Deities, Imperial and private portraits. Votive stele from the Temple of Good Fortune with inset bronze relief plaque showing Artemis with torches, an altar, satyrs.

## V. The Theatre Quarter and Mt Kínthos

From the museum you turn S into the **ancient town**, in the direction of the starting point. Here is the quarter where Delos is comparable with Pompeii. In sharp contrast with the spacious sanctuaries and public buildings, the crowded residential area, with twisting narrow streets, huddles behind the shore establishments on rising ground. With the increase of population it spread right up to the sanctuaries.

The **Delian House** of the Hellenistic and Roman period had its rooms grouped round a central courtyard which was reached from the street by a corridor. Richer homes had a peristyle round the court, with marble columns, and the walls plastered and painted. The court had a mosaic floor serving as an impluvium, beneath which a cistern stored rainwater. The Rhodian Peristyle is also found on Delos; a large hall fronted by a taller colonnade occupied one side, and one or two storeys of rooms the others.

The road of the theatre, paved and drained, ascends between houses and shops giving directly on to the street. Here and there niches show that the street was lit by lamps. To the right is a house with a stove and built-in basins, probably a **dyer's workshop**. A small passage and steps lead up past a dolphin mosaic covering a cistern to the **House of Cleopatra**. The marble colonnade has been restored and in the courtyard stand two elegant statues representing Cleopatra and Dioscourides, the Athenian owners (2C BC). On the opposite side of the road is the **House of Dionysos**, where part of the staircase to an upper floor remains. In one room the rough plaster has graffiti (triremes, horseman, etc.), perhaps done by the plasterers before they added the surface layer for the painted marbling. The courtyard contains a mosaic of Dionysos (in *opus vermiculatum*), wreathed in ivy leaves and holding a thyrsos, mounted on a vine-clad panther. Farther along, the **House of the Trident**, one of the largest on the island, has a 'Rhodian' peristyle and an elegant well-head. The mosaics are simple but striking, and include an anchor with a dolphin and a trident with a ribbon tied in a bow.

There is some resemblance between this design and the trademarks on amphorae found in a sunken ship off Marseille, suggesting that the house belonged to the Delian wine-merchant who owned the ship. Another mosaic depicts a Panathenaic amphora indicating that a member of the house-hold had won a victory in a chariot-race.

Next is the **theatre**, built in the early 3C BC to hold c 5500 spectators. It is surrounded by a fine analemma of local marble but the theatron is ruinous except for the lower tiers. The **orchestra** has been restored. The **skene** had engaged Doric columns and was flanked by paraskenia, each with two columns in an upper storey. From the highest point of the theatre, 17m above the orchestra, there is a fine *view over the excavations and the shore.

To the W is a huge **dexamené** (Pl. 115), or cistern, with nine compartments, which collected water from the theatre and partly supplied the town. Nearby is the great foundation which supported the Altar of Dionysos, with, behind it, remains of a little **Temple of Apollo** in antis, dated by an inscription to 110–109 BC. Two adjacent temenoi were dedicated to Artemis-Hekate (W) and Dionysos, Hermes, and Pan (E).

Abutting the theatre on the SE is a building known as the '**Hotel**' (Pl. 113). It had three storeys and a large cistern and is thought to have accommodated visitors to the festival. The **House of the Masks** (Pl. 112) is notable for its *mosaic pavements with designs inspired by the cult of Dionysos or directly by the drama. It may have been used as a hostel by visiting troupes of actors. The walls were plastered and painted to represent marble. One mosaic has comic and satyric masks. The best known depicts Dionysos seated on a panther. The god holds the thyrsos and a tambourine; the detail shows even the whiskers of the animal. The **House of the Dolphins**, across the street, is named from another fine mosaic (Erotes on dolphins) signed by the artist.

An ancient path ascends **Mt Kinthos** (112m) which has a wonderful view of the Cyclades. The height furnished a surname for both Apollo and Artemis, who must have been worshipped here in the 7C BC. The site has yielded remains of Cycladic houses of the 3rd millennium, but it was abandoned for long periods and became an important sanctuary only in 281–267 BC when existing buildings were rebuilt and the peribolos constructed. On the flattened summit stood the **Sanctuary of Kynthian Zeus and Athena**; here niches for votive offerings, statue bases, and a dedicatory mosaic were found. The little distyle vestibule of 208 BC was replaced in 94 BC by a marble propylon.

Nearby, on the S summit, are the remains of a small **Sanctuary of Zeus Hypsistos** and other gods. To the E, on a barely accessible terrace (58m) has been excavated a **Sanctuary of Artemis Locheia**. There are the foundations of a temple with a doorway in the middle of the long S side. On the way down to the N (traces of an ancient road) are the ruins of several other sanctuaries.

You descend by the Sacred Way, pausing to look at the **Grotto of Herakles** which is roofed to a peak with inclined slabs of granite in a Cyclopean fashion reminiscent of the Sybil's Cave at Cumae, though probably of Hellenistic date. On a platform outside stands a circular marble altar of the Hellenistic period, while within is the pedestal that bore a statue of the hero. Farther down is a sanctuary attributed by the Athenians to Agathe Tyche (good fortune), in reality the **Philadelpheion** (Pl. 103) dedicated to the cult of Arsinoë, sister and wife of Ptolemy II Philadelphos, who was deified after her death in 270 BC. You reach the terrace of the Heraion.

The **Heraion** is firmly identified by the dedication to Hera of vases and terracotta figurines found beneath the imposing marble **altar** to the S. The **temple**, of the early 5C, was also of marble and had a pronaos of two columns in antis. It replaced a 7C structure in poros some of whose foundations are visible below the later pavement.

Below to the left extend the **Sanctuaries of the Foreign Gods**, which occupy a long terrace; the S section is reserved for Egyptian, the N for Syrian divinities. Against the granite retaining wall of the Heraion terrace is the E portico of an enclosure with a central **avenue** bordered by alternating little sphinxes and massive altars. To the N is **Serapeion C** (Pl. 100), the most important of the three Egyptian sanctuaries at Delos. The main entrance was on the S side. Serapis had powers of healing and of foretelling the future.

The paved court was bounded on the S and partly on the W by an angular Ionic portico. To the N is the carefully constructed small **Temple of Serapis** (first half of 2C BC). To the E, on a higher level, is the marble façade of the **Temple of Isis**. At the end of the cella is a statue of the goddess, on a rocky bench serving as a base. In front of the temple, lower down, is a **perfume altar**, the upper part of which is decorated in front with four slabs of marble in the form of horns.

From the Sanctuary Court is approached the great **Sanctuary of the Syrian Gods** (Pl. 98), whose cult started c 128 BC. Here were worshipped Adad and Atargatis, introduced from Bambyke-Hierapolis, and after ten years regularised under an Athenian high priest. Atargatis was then identified with Holy Aphrodite and the worst orgiastic rites of the fertility cult abandoned. The **theatre** (400–500 spectators) in which its rites were performed was protected from view by walls which surrounded the precinct. This was entered by a portal with Ionic columns. Sacred fish were kept in a tank in the sanctuary.

From the S end of the terrace a long flight of steps descends to the bed of the **Inopos**, a torrent only a few hundred metres long which even in ancient times must have had a long dry season. It flowed from a source on Mt Kynthos past the Sacred Lake into the Bay of Skardhana, and is mentioned in the Homeric Hymn. The Delians imagined that its waters came from the Nile, an association perhaps endorsed by the resemblance of the local lizards to baby crocodiles. A **reservoir** (Pl. 97) in white marble, provided with a staircase, sluice-gates, and outlet channels, collected the waters. Today it is inhabited by terrapins.

On the farther bank, S of the reservoir, are the ruins of the **Samothrakeion** (Pl. 93), dedicated to the Kabeiroi, built on two terraces. On the upper level was a **temple** of the 4C BC with a Doric portico; on the lower a circular shrine (2C BC) for the reception of offerings to the Chthonic divinities, together with a monument to Mithridates (120–63 BC). This had two Ionic columns and a frieze of medallions depicting his generals and allies.

Turning N you enter a street running between the reservoir (left) and a row of shops. Between two of the shops is an alley, with a bench (left) carved with dedicatory inscriptions to Serapis, Isis, and Anubis. At the end of the alley a staircase leads to the ruins of **Serapeion B**. The court of this sanctuary is bounded on the E by a covered portico, under which is a rectangular crypt. The little **temple**, placed in the NW corner of the court, faces S.

The street bears left in front of the **House of the Inopos** (Pl. 95). Beyond the reservoir, to the left, are the circular **Shrine of the Nymphs of Pyrrhakides**, and **Serapeion A** (Pl. 91), the oldest sanctuary of Serapis on the island. Its temple stands on a stepped basement in a paved court; under its cella is a rectangular crypt, reached by a staircase and supplied with water by a conduit. Descending the ancient road you pass the **House of Hermes** with three storeys built against the hill. The colonnades of the ground and first floors have been restored. Here were found a number of Herms. Farther on is a small **Temple of Aphrodite**, built of irregular marble blocks in the 4C BC. Behind it is the descent to the Agora of the Competialists (Pl. 2).

## VI.  The Maritime Quarter

Along the seashore, S of the landing-place, a series of **magazines** or **warehouses** have their backs to the Theatre Quarter. They opened on to a quay bordering one of the four basins of the Commercial Harbour. Continuing S, across the line of the city wall (see above), which here ran down to the sea, you reach a second group of magazines.

There was no communication between these warehouses and the Theatre Quarter behind them, an indication that the trade of Delos was essentially a transit trade between E and W. Island blocks, divided by streets running parallel to the sea or at right angles to it, each had a central court surrounded by large structures used as bonded warehouses. A typical example is the **Magazine of the Columns**. The building adjoining it has a fine marble basin in a vestibule.

About 800m farther S is the **Bay of Foúrni**, sheltered from the N winds by a rocky promontory on which are the ruins of a **Sanctuary of Asklepios**, with three buildings in line. The northernmost is a prostyle Doric temple with four columns, measuring c 15m by c 6m. Beyond it is a large hall of granite with a door on its E side; and finally the propylaia to the sanctuary, paved in white marble.

**Rhéneia**, or **Greater Delos**, now uninhabited, on the W side of the Channel of Delos, is 10km long and has a maximum width of c 4km. It is almost divided into two by a narrow isthmus about its middle. It has a ruined **lazaret** for ships in quarantine bound for Síros, with an anchorage facing Delos (25 minutes by caique). That part of the shore which faces the Rhevmataria islets (10 minutes from the Sacred Harbour) was reserved as a birthplace for pregnant, and as a necropolis for dying Delians expelled from their island by the Athenians. Rheneia was the landfall of Nikias in 417 BC, when he crossed in state to Delos on the bridge that he had brought with him. The island town was on the W coast, facing Síros.

In the area for expectant and dying Delians are a series of tombs, circular sepulchral altars and sarcophagi with holes for the insertion of steles, and numerous ruined little houses, probably for the reception of the evicted people.

In the village of **Herakleion** a sanctuary was discovered, with a well and a portico. Opposite Great Rhevmataria, on the seashore below the chapel of **Ayía Kiriakí**, is the **necropolis**, discovered in 1898, in which the Athenians during the purification of 426 BC, placed the coffins exhumed from Delos. This is a walled enclosure c 65m square, divided into small rectangular sections. It contained a mass of human bones and vase fragments of every period down to the 5C. A little to the S, in the small bay of **Porto Generale**, is a curious Greek columbarium. This is a rectangular vault, reached by a staircase, and containing on either side two tiers of niches for coffins, closed by stone slabs.

The island was intensively cultivated in antiquity with farmsteads belonging to the sanctuary (J. H. Kent in *Hesperia* 17 (1948)).

# 72

# Western Cyclades (Kikládhes)

Despite its proximity to Attica, this is the least visited group of the Aegean islands.

## A.   Kéa

**Ferry** daily from Lávrion (comp. Rte 17) in 2 hours, sometimes continuing to Kíthnos; some services also from Rafína (Rte 22), sometimes also for Kithnos.

**Hydrofoil** daily (1–2) for Kéa and Kíthnos from Zéa.

**KÉA**, the ancient *Keos*, locally known as **Tziá** (1787 inhab.), is the nearest of the Cyclades to Attica, only 21km from Cape Sounion and 64.5km from Piraeus. Oval in shape, 19km long from N to S and 10km wide, the island has a hilly interior, rising to 568m. It is well watered (hence its early name of *Hydroussa*) and one of the most fertile of the Cyclades (Virgil, *Georgics*, I, 14). The eparchy of Kea includes the islands of Kíthnos, Sérifos, and Makrónisos.

**History**. In early times *Keos* was populated by Ionians. Kean ships fought on the Greek side at Artemision and Salamis (Hdt. VIII, 1, 46). The island had four cities; Ioulis, with its port Koressia, Karthaia, and Poiëessa. Ioulis was the birth-place of the lyric poets Simonides (556–468) and Bacchylides (481–431), of the sophist Prodikos, the physician Erasistratos, and the peripatetic philosopher Ariston. The Keans were noted for their modesty and sobriety: hence the adage οὐ Χίος ἀλλὰ Κεῖος (Aristophanes, Ran. 970).

Boats dock at **Livádhi** (Hotels B, C), officially **Korissía**, pleasantly situated amid trees on the bay of Ayios Nikólaos in the NW of the island. Ancient *Koressia* occupied a site a little to the W, with a temple of Apollo Sminthios, from which the kouros in the National Museum was recovered in 1930. About 1.5km E round the bay is **Vourkári**, an attractive fishing hamlet which attracts summer visitors.

Opposite, on the pretty promontory of **Ayía Iríni**, are the remains of an important prehistoric settlement excavated in the 1960s and 1970s by a team from the University of Cincinnati under the late J.L. Caskey. Several volumes of the final publication have now appeared and an excellent short guidebook is available. Most of the building remains that can be seen belong to the early Late Bronze Age (the largest complex, to the S of the site, is called 'House A'). Nearby can be seen the **gateway** into the settlement and, close to that, a long, narrow free-standing building which was a **temple** and yielded fine large terracotta figures in a Minoan style. In the N part of the site, some well built houses of regularly laid thin slabs belong to the Early Bronze Age. Two sets of **fortifications** can be seen. The inner (only a short section visible) is Middle Bronze Age in date and has horseshoe-shaped towers. The outer belongs to the end of the same period and is more substantial. A **spring chamber** beyond the defences was reached by a covered passage. The site is one of the most important in the Cyclades, especially for demonstrating interconnections between these islands, on the one hand, and Crete and the Greek mainland, on the other. The site came under strong Minoan influence from c 1600 BC. It was wrecked by an earthquake c 1450 BC by which time mainland features are equally prominent. Subsequently the town was rebuilt but less intensively occupied. Although it was abandoned as a settlement during the 11C, the temple seems to have remained in continuous use until later antiquity. Amongst later finds are a 5C dedication inscribed to Dionysos.

A road continues NE to the delightful bay of (5km) **Otziás**, then turns E to (10km) the monastery of **Panayía Kastrianí** (18C; rooms).

A road (bus) climbs to the depopulated town of **Khóra** (Hotels B, E), the island capital with 569 inhabitants, on a hill (349m) once occupied by the ancient city of *Ioulis*. The **kastro** of Domenico Michelli (1210), demolished in 1865, incorporated material from a Temple of Apollo situated on its acropolis. A small **museum** has antiquities from the island and particularly finds from Ayia Irini. About 15 minutes E of the town is a colossal Archaic **lion** carved out of the rock, 6m long and 2.7m high.

The bays of **Písses** (7km; bus) and **Koúndhouros** (Hotel B), to the S, have good bathing and the interior of the island, often tree-clad, is attractive. The extensive ruins of ancient *Poiëessa* (Ποιήεσσα), are on the W coast near **Písses**. By foot the site may be reached in c 2 hours from Khóra, via **Astra** and **Káto Meriá**. You can return via the ruined monastery of **Ayía Marína** (off the more direct route to **Khóra**), built around a Hellenic *tower, probably the finest of its kind in Greece. About 7.5m square it is built of rectangular blocks of schist, finely joined without mortar. There are three storeys supported by stone joists.

On the opposite coast, c 1½ hours SE of Káto Meriá (and approached from there or **Elliniká**) is **Póles**, where are the ruins of ancient *Karthaia*: houses, Temples of Apollo and Athena, a theatre, and the considerable remains of an enceinte wall and gate One building is conjectured to have been the choregic school of Simonides.

# B.   From Piraeus to Mílos

**Ferry** daily, calling at Kíthnos, Sérifos, Sífnos, less frequently Kímolos and sometimes continuing to Folégandros, Síkinos, Ios, Thíra (Rte 73; Crete and Rhodes).
   There are usually weekly connections to Síros. Kíthnos is also served from Lávrion and Rafína, usually via Kéa.

**Air Service**, twice daily to Mílos.

**KÍTHNOS** (Κύθνος), separated from Kea by a strait 8km wide, owes its alternative name **Thermiá** to its hot springs. It is 75 sq. km. in area. All but a handful of the population is divided between two villages, Since 1940, when the iron mines went bankrupt, the Thermiots (1632 inhab.) have been largely dependent on agriculture and traditional ways survive here to a greater extent than on many islands. Tourism (including Athenian weekenders) is playing an increasing part in the island's economy.

*Kythnos* supplied two ships to the Greek fleet at Salamis. It was a member of the Delian Confederacy and became tributary to Athens. After the death of Nero in AD 68, an imposter claiming to be the emperor was driven ashore at Kythnos in a storm; he was seized and put to death by Calpurnius Asprenas, the proconsul of Galba. Pliny notes that the island produced excellent cheese; it still does, other products being barley, wine, figs, and almonds. Copper was mined and worked on the island from the Early Bronze Age.

The boat puts in at **Mérikhas** (Hotel C) on the W coast. A road leads inland, passing the beach of **Episkopí** and (2.5km) the site of ancient Kythnos at **Vryókastro** (or Rigókastro), to (6km) **Kíthnos**, known also as **Messariá** or just **Khóra**, the little capital (672 inhab.), where several churches have ikons by Skordili (c 1700). **Ayía Sába** (1613) bears the arms of Ant. Gozzadini, a descendant of the Italian medieval governors. Descending from **Khóra** to the E coast, the road passes turnings to **Aiolikó Khorió**, site of a wind-generated electricity project and to **Profítis Ilías**. 4km The tiny harbour of **Loutrá** (Hotels C; Rooms) has warm iron-bearing springs which cover the ground with a reddish deposit. The Turks used them for bathing and King Otho built a **hydro** for invalid visitors. One spring (37°C) provides drinking water; another is hot (52°). The waters are used in the cure of eczema, gout, sciatica, and nervous complaints. In the quiet bay of Ayía Iríni, a short distance to the S, marble slabs behind the church commemorate the killing by soldiers of King Otho of three leaders of the revolution in 1862, On Cape Kephalos (154m), the NW point of the island (1½ hour walk from Loutra), stands the **Kástro tou Aí Yióryi** (or 'tou Kataképhalou' or 'tis Oriás'), the medieval citadel, abandoned c 1650; the ruins include towers, monasteries, and the Byzantine church of Our Lady of Compassion with wall-paintings.

A pleasant walk (c 1hr) from **Khóra**, alternatively by road (in 3km) from **Mérikhas**, is to Dhriopís (Δριοπίς), or **Dhriopídha**, formerly **Síllaka**, the other village (591 inhab.) and former capital. There is a traditional pottery. Nearby is Katafíki, the best known of the island's many caves. 6km further, on a headland of the SE coast stands the **Panayía tis Kanálas**, a monastery with a holy ikon of St Luke. The hamlet has some facilities in the summer. Off this route a dirt road leads to **Flamboúria** on the W coast, a small summer resort, with the castle of Kastellas on a promontory to the S; also to Ay. Dhimítrios at the SW tip of the island.

**SÉRIFOS** (Σέριφος), a small rocky island (65 sq. km), with 1095 inhabitants, lies almost equidistant between Kíthnos and Sífnos and c 13km from either. Passengers land at **Livádhi** (Hotels B, C, D, E; Rooms), the hot little land-locked harbour from which a road (bus) rises through market gardens to (1.5km) **Khóra** (312 inhab.; rooms), a white village built precipitously on a commanding spur where accommodation must be found in private houses. **Psilí Ammos**, 20 minutes walk to the NE, is the best sandy beach. **Livadhákia** to the SW has camping. A road runs inland from Khóra. After 3km it divides; the W branch (unsurfaced after 2km) passes a round Hellenistic tower and an unattractive private monastery then avoids (6.5km) **Megálo Khorió**, said to be the site of ancient *Seriphos*. In 1880–1912 it was the centre of a mining district, with outlets to the sea beyond at (9km) **Méga Livádhi** (good swimming), and Koutalá to the W. A little iron ore is still shipped.

The right branch (asphalt) goes to (10km) **Kéntarkhos** (bus to Panayía in school term only) via Panayía, called after its 10C church with ikons by Skordilis, then Pírgos, Galaní and **Moní Taxiárkhon**, an interesting building of late medieval date. An alternative approach is by the old path from Khóra (c 1¼ hrs) via the pretty village of **Kallítsos**. Beyond the monastery a dirt road leads to the fine beach of **Platí Yialó**.

Perseus and Danaë were washed ashore on ancient Seriphos, and here later Perseus turned King Polydeuces to stone with Medusa's head. The Roman emperors used the island as a place of exile for political prisoners.

**SÍFNOS** (Σίφνος), situated 19km SE of Sérifos, is a fertile island with a delightful climate and an abundance of excellent water. The interior is mountainous, with Mt Profítis Ilías rising to 680m. Much of the countryside is terraced for the production of olives, grapes, citrus and other fruits, almonds and vegetables, and for the grazing of animals. The island is dotted with monasteries and churches, local tradition claiming 365 in all, one for each day of the year.

In pre-Classical times Siphnos was famous for its gold and silver mines, which Herodotus says made the Siphnians the wealthiest of the islanders by the late 6C BC. When the mineral deposits were exhausted in the Classical period the deceitfulness, greed and poverty of the people became a byword, and Pausanias relates a characteristic tale to the effect that the mines were flooded by Apollo after the Siphnians had attempted to renege on their customary annual tithe to Delphi. Numerous ancient mines are to be seen on the island, most notably at the peninsular of Ay. Sóstis on the NE coast (some prehistoric). Also of interest are the remains of nearly 50 circular towers located at strategic points throughout the island, and dating from the Classical and Hellenistic periods.

The ship berths between high cliffs in the bay of **Kamáres** (Hotels B, C) on the more rugged W coast. On the N slopes are two monasteries, the larger that of Ay. Simeón. A bus ascends under the cliffs of Profítis Ilías on the S to (5.5km) **Apollónia** (Hotels B, C,), the island capital (689 inhab.). Its flat-roofed white houses rise in an amphitheatre on three terraced hills. At **Stavrí**, the town's principal quarter and main square, are a library and folklore museum built in 1967. In the N quarter of Péra Yitoniá are the house of the poet Kleánthis Triandáfillos (or Rabagás) (1849–89) and the church of **Panayiá Yeraniofóra**, where the external figure of St George was restored in 1767. The foundations on which this church was constructed may be those of a 7C BC temple to Apollo. The frescoed church of **Sotíra** has a carved wooden ikonostasis.

About 1.5km to the N is **Artemóna** (669 inhab.; Hotel C), the second village of Sífnos. It is believed Artemona's main church, **Panayía Kókhi** was built on the site of an ancient temple to Artemis. From this village there are central paths (surfaced road under construction) to the N of the island and the small settlement on the bay of **Kherrónisos**.

SE from Apollonia, through the village of **Exámbela**, roads run to the bays of **Fáros** (6.5km) and **Platí Yialós** (9.5km; Hotels B, C, D), both excellent bathing places with sandy beaches. Below Apollonia to the E lies the hamlet of **Káto Petáli** (1.5km) on the road leading to **Kástro** (a further 1.5km; Rooms), a delightful but decaying medieval village on the E coast, occupying the site of ancient *Siphnos*. Part of the 14C wall built by the Venetian Corogna family survives, and there are many old churches, also a **museum** (see below). On the way to Kástro, to the S, is the nunnery of **Khrisostómou** built in 1550, it was adorned by the Bavarians and used as a school from 1834–44. On the SW coast is the charming bay of **Vathí**, best reached by boat, but also accessible by foot along pathways from Platí Yialós (60 minutes) and Exámbela (90 minutes).

Three ancient acropolis sites have been identified on the island. To the S of Apollonia paths lead past **Mt Ay. Andréas** (427m), on the summit of which is a walled settlement inhabited from the third millenium BC, excavated on behalf of the Greek Archaeological Service in the 1970s. The visible sections of the fortifications are of the Mycenaean and Geometric periods. At **Kástro** (ancient *Siphnos*, see above) sections of white marble walling of the 6C BC were discovered in the 1930s by the British School, along with foundations of houses of the Geometric period and the site of a temple of the 7C BC, with a votive deposit. Most of the archaeological artefacts from the island have been collected in a small but interesting museum in Kástro. A third acropolis is situated at the church of **Ay. Nikítas**, some 5km N of Artemóna. The site has not been excavated, but the walls probably date to the Archaic period.

**KÍMOLOS** (Κίμωλος), an island barely 8km across with 728 inhabitants, lies between Sífnos and Mílos, from which it is separated by a strait only 1km wide. Pliny says that it was once called *Echinousa*, from echinus, a sea-urchin; it owed its Italian name, *Argentiera*, to the silver mines formerly worked here. The island has long been noted for its Fullers' earth, used in the preparation of cloth and in barbers' shops in Athens (Aristophanes, *Ran.*, 713). Kimolos was incorporated by Marco Sanudo into the duchy of Naxos; it later became a notorious pirates' nest. Its olive trees were felled by the Venetians during the Turkish wars and it is now barren, but given colour by the variety of its rocks.

**Kímolos**, the only village, crowns a hill 1km from **Psáthi**, its harbour, which is on the SE coast. The little houses open on to an inner court. The church of the **Evangelístria** dates from 1614. **Prássa**, 15 minutes N by boat, has radioactive springs. On the W coast **Palaiókastro**, on a steep rock 396m high, has remains of strong fortifications. Excavations in 1937 on the islet of **Ayios Andréas**, off the SW shore, revealed remains of an ancient settlement which, with its necropolis (on the mainland opposite) lasted from Mycenaean to Early Christian times.

The uninhabited islet of **Políaigos** lies off the SE extremity of Kímolos.

**MÍLOS** (Μήλος), or **Melos**, the SW outpost of the Cyclades, with 4390 inhabitants, is divided almost into two by a deep gulf, forming a spacious natural harbour. The entrance is on the N. The coast is much indented. The island has an area of 153 sq. km and is roughly 21km long by 13km wide. Mt Profitis Ilias (751m) rises to the SW of the gulf, but the rest of the island is arid low hills, much gashed by mines and quarries. The volcanic nature of the soil is expressed in the hot springs, the mines of sulphur and alum, and the obsidian that gave the island its importance in prehistoric times. Bensonite, barium, perlite and kaolin are also mined. A geothermal energy station is in operation. Melos was the first island to yield detailed information about the sequence of occupation in the Cyclades in the Bronze Age, through the key site of Phylakopi. From the island came also the famous Venus di Milo, now in the Louvre in Paris. The eparchy of Milos includes the islands of Sífnos, Kímolos, Síkinos and Folégandros. Tourist facilities are concentrated in Adhamata, though rooms are also available in Pláka and Pollónia. There is a small airstrip with two or three connections a day to Athens.

**History.** *Melos* was an important centre in the Bronze Age. By c 1600 BC Melos, with the rest of the Cyclades, seems to have been absorbed in the Cretan 'empire' associated with King Minos. When power passed from Knossos to Mycenae, the source of influence on the islands changed also. After the Dorian invasion (c 1100 BC) Melos was colonised by Dorian Lacedaemonians. In the Peloponnesian War it declared itself neutral, but, provoked by Athens, inclined towards Sparta. Athens, having command of the sea, determined to coerce the Melians into submission (416 BC). Before taking action, the Athenians sent envoys to Melos. Thucydides has preserved in his 'Melian dialogue' (V, 85–111) the gist of the speeches made on either side. The Melians declined the terms and the Athenians besieged their city. After several months they surrendered unconditionally. The Athenians killed all the males of military age, enslaved the women and children, and repopulated the island with 500 Athenian colonists. In the Middle Ages the island was under the Franks. During the Turkish domination (here very lightly felt) and afterwards, the Melians acquired and kept a reputation for intrepid seamanship which they still enjoy. Here in 1628 Sir Kenelm Digby began his memoirs. From Melos in the 1680s a party under Archbishop Georgirenes migrated to London where they built the first Greek church there on a site assigned to them by James, Duke of York. The memory of this survives in 'Greek Street', Soho. During the First World War the island was an Allied naval base.

The port of Mílos is **Adhamas** (commonly **Adhámata**; Hotels B, C, D; Rooms; pop. 1168), founded on the E side of the harbour by Cretan refugees fleeing Turkish reprisals in 1912. Their ikons can be seen in the small and attractive church of **Ayía Triádha**. Both this and the church of **Christ and the Virgin** (with prominent clock tower) at the highest point of the town have pebble mosaics; the latter also has a fine painted iconstasis. On the shore to the W of the town stands a small monument to French soldiers and sailors who died on Milos in 1897. A geological museum is under construction.

A winding road ascends NW, through the lower villages of **Triovásalos** and **Karódhromos** (leaving **Tripití** to the W and **Plákes** to the E), to (3.5km) **Pláka**, officially **Mílos** (660 inhab.), the island capital, constructed in a defensive position about 1800 as a protection against piratical raids.

The village can also be reached by a path from the N side of Adhámata which skirts the obsidian quarry of Sta Nychia above the village and later joins the old roadway, stone-paved in part, to ascend to **Tripití** (pleasant cafeneion with small terrace overlooking valley), just below Plaka. Between Tripití and Pláka, a long ridge (**Piriántes**) was the acropolis of the ancient site, which occupies the slopes below Tripití down to the ancient harbour (now the pretty fishing hamlet of **Klíma**). A road down from Tripiti gives access to the most important parts of the site. To the SW are extensive and impressive Early Christian **catacombs**. The long narrow entrance leads into a low-pitched room, beyond which run tunnels, lined with tombs, some with the remains of frescoes. N of the catacombs are good sections of the **city wall** (other parts traceable over a wide area) part with fine polygonal masonry adjoining a round bastion of regularly coursed stonework. The Venus di Milo was discovered close by in what seems to have been the **gymnasium**, whose running track was laid out on the flat ground immediately below. Farther on is the **theatre** (excavated in 1917 and partially restored; reinvestigation in progress), probably Roman. Its situation is impressive and the view may have distracted attention from the performances. Nearby is an Early Christian baptistery. To the NW (paths) is a prominent low conical hill crowned by a small church of Profitis Ilias. On the flat ground to the E of this may have been the ancient **agora**. The remains of a substantial building, perhaps a Roman temple, can be seen. From Profítis Ilías paths ascend to Pláka (more sections of the city wall visible).

Pláka is attractive with its typically Cycladic houses and narrow alleyways. The church, dedicated to the Virgin and built in 1810 of materials brought from the abandoned Zefiría (see below), is finely situated to the N, with a terrace at the top of a sheer cliff (view to Andímilos; pleasant at sunset). There is a small **Folk Museum** close by which includes some interesting relics of the pilots (telescopes, etc.) for which the island was at one time famous. To the E is the small catholic church of the **Rosaria**, with a memorial to Louis Brest, the French consul on Melos who removed the Venus to France. Above the village rises the **kástro** (980m) whose Frankish remains enclose the beautiful 13C church of **Thalassítra**. The antiquities were much destroyed by German gun emplacements in the Second World War. From the summit there are excellent and extensive views, much to be recommended both for themselves and for appreciating the complex geography of the island.

On the lower edge of Pláka a small neo-Classical building (formerly a school) has been restored (1984) and contains the **Archaeological Museum**. The vestibule and room to the right have sculpture and inscriptions from Classical and Roman Melos; the room across the vestibule Archaic, Classical and Roman material (pottery, etc.) mainly from tombs; the room to the left important finds (mainly pottery) from the 1911 excavation season at Phylakopi (finds from the main campaign are in the National Archaeological Museum in Athens).

A road leads E to the N coast (occasional buses to **Pollónia**, starting from Adhámata) and (7km) the ruinous site of *Phylakopí*, excavated by the British School in 1896–99, 1911 and 1974–7. The remains of three successive Bronze Age cities were discovered. The **first city** dates from the Early Cycladic period; the **second** is Middle Cycladic; the **third** had two main phases, in the first of which strong Minoan influence is evident in the pottery and frescoes (including that of Flying Fish, in Athens), while in the second Mycenaean is dominant. This latter is reflected in the construction of a Mainland-style **palace** with megaron which can be recognised on the N side of the site, by the sea, by its massive threshold block, now broken. It was preceded by another large building, in which fragments of a Linear A tablet were found, possibly the administrative centre in the 'Minoan' stage. In 1974–77, a **Mycenaean shrine** (LH IIIA–C) yielded many finds including a tiny gold mask and a terracotta cult figure probably of Mainland manufacture. The shrine can be seen close to the city wall, to the right of the path leading from the main road into the site. There were two elements, East and West, with a paved court between containing a stone bench and ceremonial standing stone. The **city wall** is also well preserved at the W end of the town. Interesting too are the natural hexagonal basalt pillars, originating from the Glaronísia (see below). The road continues to (10km) **Pollónia** (Rooms; restaurant), an attractive fishing village facing the island of **Kimolos** (daily caique).

To the NW (boat from Pollónia) are the curious volcanic islets known as the **Glaronísia** (Gull Islands). They have remarkable caves and crystalline rocks.

From Adhámata, a road runs SE along the shore. After 3km there is a by-road (left) past the electricity works to (1km) **Zefiría**, the capital of the island from the 8C to 1793, when the survivors of an epidemic moved to the Pláka area. The village is still known locally as **Khóra** (the term for an island capital) and all the major church festivals are celebrated there. The double church (to Christ and the Virgin) is delightful. Many architectural fragments from the once prosperous village, which had numerous churches and monasteries, can be seen in the fields around.

From Zefiría a rough road (ask for directions) leads W (4km farther) to the beautiful shingle beach of **Palaiokhóra** backed by multicoloured rocks.

Immediately beyond the Zefiría fork, by the coast road, small rings of bubbles can be seen a few metres out to sea. These mark the eruptions of hot springs. The road passes salt pans, the airstrip, and continues through **Próvata** to the pleasant monastery of **Ayía Marína** (formerly rich) continuing, rougher, to **Emborió** (taverna; boat from Adhámata) on the coast. Before Ayía Marína a road leads W to the deserted but intact monastery of **Ayios Ioánnis Sidherianós**. Beyond here the roads serve mines and quarries in the S and W of the island (**Khálakas**) where there is virtually no permanent settlement.

To the NW of Mílos is the uninhabited islet of Andímilos, a reserve for a rare species of chamois.

# 73

# Southern Cyclades and Southern Sporades

**Ferry** direct or via Síros, 2–3 times daily to Páros and Náxos, continuing at least once daily to Ios and Santoríni, (Thíra) and returning in reverse order. Once or twice weekly the boat calls at Anáfi. Síkinos and Folégandros may also be included once or twice weekly (but see Rte 72B). Thíra can be reached in summer once a week from Mílos and the W Cyclades also from the N Aegean via other Cycladic islands on a route to Irákleion.

A **hydrofoil** service from Rafína serves Páros and Náxos via the N Cyclades. Amorgós, the most easterly of the S Sporades, included in the nome of the Cyclades, is served also by boats to the Dodecanese and is described with them; see Rte 75.

A regular local service connects Náxos with Amorgós, via Irakliá, Schoinoússa, Ano Koufoníssi and (sometimes) Dhonoússa. Other routes (including to Míkonos) are worked in the summer by small craft.

**By Air.** To Páros several times daily in 45 minutes. To Náxos twice daily (except Tuesday) in 50 minutes. To Thíra three times daily in 40 minutes; connections to Crete and Rhodes; also international charters.

**PÁROS** (ΠΑΡΟΣ), is one of the most attractive of the Cyclades, though the charm of the main centres has now been considerably modified by tourist development. It has 9591 inhabitants, an area of 166 sq. km and is oval in shape. The interior is almost entirely taken up by **Mt Profítis Ilías** (771m; road to summit; views), on the slopes of which are the famous marble quarries. The mountain slopes evenly down to the maritime plain which surrounds it on every side. Barley and wheat are grown and the red wine is full and palatable, but there are few trees. Paros was the birthplace of the lyric poet Archílochos (fl. 714–676 BC), inventor of Iambic verse. The island had a bishop before 431; the present joint see with Naxos dates from 1683.

**History.** *Paros* was colonised by Ionians. In the 7C it sent a colony to Thasos, the poet Archilochos accompanying the expedition (see Rte 67). In 490 BC Paros sent a trireme with the Persian fleet. After Marathon Miltiades led a retaliatory expedition against the island but failed to take it, receiving an injury that, becoming gangrenous, proved fatal (Hdt. vi, 133). After the defeat of Xerxes, in 480, Paros became subject to Athens.

In the Middle Ages Paros formed part of the duchy of Naxos until 1389. In 1537 it passed to the Turks, who held it until the War of Greek Independence. In the early 17C the 'Parian Chronicle' was discovered in the island by William Petty, chaplain to the Earl of Arundel. This is a chronological account of the principal events in Greek history (biased on the side of art rather than politics), from Kekrops (traditional date 1582 BC) to the archonship of Diognetos (264 BC). The greater part of this inscription is in the Ashmolean Museum at Oxford. Hugues Creveliers, the original of Byron's 'Corsair' operated from Paros in the 1670s (he was eventually blown up in his flagship by an offended servant). The Russian fleet spent the winter of 1770–71 at Paros. The German Archaeological Institute has had a special interest in the island.

Backed by distant hills beyond the coastal plain **Parikía** (Hotels A–E), or **Páros**, the capital (2932 inhab.), lies on the W coast. The town extends along the shore, the line of its white flat-roofed houses broken only by the blue domes of churches. The ship moors close to the bus terminal.

The **Panayía 'Ekatontapilianí'**, traditionally the cathedral church of Our Lady 'with a hundred doors', a corruption probably of *Katapolianí* ('below the town'), was greatly altered externally, by restoration (1960–63; Prof. A. Orlandos) from Venetian Baroque to a primitive Byzantine style. The church had needed attention since the earthquake of 1733. Said to have been founded by St Helena, mother of Constantine, while she was on her way to the Holy Land in search of the True Cross, it occupies the site of a secular Roman edifice of c 300 (mosaics of the Labours of Hercules). Altered in the 10C after an earthquake, it has the form of a Greek cross, sombre and impressive, with an unusual triforium and a dome carried on pendentives. The apse is flanked by 'parekklesia', of which one at any rate antedates the main building, for **Ayios Nikolaos** (left) dates at least from the time of Justinian I; it has Doric column shafts and a marble ikonostasis of 1611. The **baptistery**, off the S transept, has a sunken immersion font, cruciform in plan. In the pleasant **Archaeological Museum** (near the gymnasion) are a winged victory of the school of Skopas, an inscription relating to Archilochos, and part of the 'Parian Chronicle'; also Melian amphorae. It houses the finds from Saliagos and the prehistoric settlement in Parikia.

The narrow main street, or the parallel shore promenade, leads to a hillock, crowned by the ruined Venetian **castle** built in 1260 with material from a Temple of Demeter. The temple site is occupied by the church of **Ayíou Konstandínou** and overlies a prehistoric settlement partly excavated earlier this century. By the school a bust commemorates Panayiotis Kallierou (1861–1937), the Pestalozzi of Greece, who taught here for 30 years. Farther on, the hill of Ayía Anna, with wind-mills, affords a pleasant sea view.

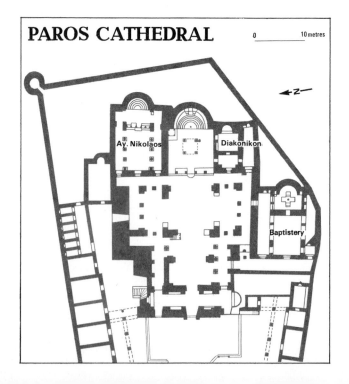

PAROS CATHEDRAL

0 — 10 metres

Ay. Nikolaos

Diakonikon

Baptistery

To the S of Parikía, just beyond the Xenia Hotel, are a **Grotto of the Nymphs** and, on the terrace of a small hill (left), some remains of an **Asklepieion**. Farther S are the site of the **Pytheion** and the **Moní Khristós Dhásous**, attractively surrounded by trees. The road, not very interesting, continues with views of Andíparos to **Poúnda**, the airport and the villages at the S end of the island. Near (10km) **Piskopianá** the Grávari estate is known as **Petaloúdhes** from the migratory butterflies seen there (comp. Rhodes).

TO NÁOUSSA, 10.5km (6½ miles), bus. The road leads NE past the park. Nearer the shore an extensive ancient cemetery is being excavated. At 2km road (right; c 3km) to the **Monastíri Zoödhókhos Piyí Longobárdhas** (women not admitted) with a library and wall-paintings. At the next fork you bear left and cross the little Helytas, c 180m beyond which are (left) the excavated remains of a 7C basilican church on the site of the **Heroön of Archilochos** (4C BC). There are traces of a **Sanctuary of Delian Apollo** (or Delion) on the hill of Kástro to the W. Fragments of the cult statue and base have been collected and partly reassembled in the museum. The road passes small churches to the right and left in a pleasant valley between rolling green hills.

8.5km On a concealed plateau on top of unpromising cliffs at the head of **Náoussa Bay** (W) is the important site of **Koukounariés**, still in the course of excavation by Dr D. Schilardhi. There are extensive remains of a fortified settlement of the Mycenaean (LHIIIC) and Geometric periods but other material, both earlier and later, has also been found. About 100m SE is a Geometric Sanctuary of Athena with a 7C temple (non-peripteral), altar and boundary wall: nearby are houses of the same period. There are tombs (undated) on the W side of the hill. 10.5km **Náoussa** (Hotels A–E; F/A), a picturesque, though touristy fishing village with 1685 inhabitants, has a small caique harbour, interesting churches, and a half-submerged Venetian fortress. Harbour installations are submerged in the bay, as are a number of wrecks including one Russian of the late 18C. Remains of an early Geometric fortified site lie on the Oikonomos headland to the E.

To reach the famous **Parian Marble Quarries**, you take the Náoussa road out of Parikía and fork right beyond the park up the Helytas valley. On the other side of the valley (left) rises Profitis Ilias with a cave of Eileithyia and a sanctuary of Aphrodite. We continue to (5km) **Maráthi**. The quarries (sign) lie some way beyond the main track to the monastery of Ayios Mínas. The numerous excavations are underground. The largest is 100m long and nearly 9m wide with a chamber on either side of the central passage. The marks of the wedges used by the ancient quarrymen are visible everywhere; also to be seen is a sculptured tablet. The quarries had lain idle for centuries until 1844 when marble was required for the tomb of Napoleon. The road goes on to (17km) **Márpissa** (Hotel C; F/A) and other E coast resorts. **Píso Livádhi** (Hotels B, C, E) has a summer boat connection with Náxos (and Míkonos).

**Andíparos** (Αντίπαρος; 819 inhab.; Hotels C, D, E; excursions from Parikia in summer) is now separated from SW Paros by the 'Fourteen-foot Channel' but was joined to it in prehistoric times. Its ancient name was *Oliaros*. The principal attraction is the stalactite **cavern** at the S end of the island.

In 1964–65 excavations by the British School on the islet of **Saliagós** (between Páros and Andíparos) uncovered a Neolithic site, the first to be excavated in the Cyclades. Stone building foundations, obsidian arrow-heads, a 'fiddle' idol, and a marble figurine of a fertility cult were found, the relics of a sheep-farming people of the 4th millennium BC. On **Dhespotikó**, an islet to the W of Andíparos, the *Prepesinthos* of ancient times, early Cycladic cist-graves were explored in 1960 by the Greek Archaeological Service.

**NÁXOS** (Νάξος), the largest and most beautiful of the Cyclades, made an indelible impression on the youthful Byron. The island, 30km long and 19km wide, forms a complete eparchy. The interior of Naxos is traversed by a mountain range, rising to 1004m in Mt Zévs, or Zas, the highest summit in the Cyclades. Other peaks are Kóronos (1000m) in the N of the island, and Fanári (930m) between it and Zas. The island is divided by fertile valleys, well-watered until the recent years of drought. Groves of olive, orange, lemon, pomegranate, and fig trees abound, and fruit, oil, corn, and wine are exported. Local wine can be good, the honey is excellent, and the cheeses varied. Citron, a local liqueur, is distilled from leaves. Emery is found in abundance. The marble of Naxos, scarcely inferior to that of Paros, was much used by ancient sculptors, especially in the Archaic period. The 14,838 inhabitants are Orthodox except for a few Roman Catholic descendants of medieval Venetian settlers, who have their own archbishop (of Naxos-with-Tinos). There are a number of little-known small Byzantine churches (see AJA, 1968): since these are usually locked it necessary to make advance arrangements for admission.

**Náxos** (Hotels A–E; F/A), the **Khóra**, with 4334 inhabitants, occupies the site of the ancient and medieval capitals on the W coast. The Mycenaean settlement has been shown by recent excavations to have been at Grotta, just to the N, where a large site (covered) near the orthodox cathedral (**Mitrópolis**), has produced an apparently continuous sequence of use from the Mycenaean to Roman periods, with features including a Mycenaean fortification wall of baked brick on a stone socle and Protogeometric and Geometric burials and ritual structures. The ancient **agora** (stoas etc) has also been located in this area, towards the sea. Much of the modern development on the outskirts is unappealing but the narrow lanes and small shops of the so-called 'agora' (off the small coastal plateia) are attractive, though the people are in general less spontaneously friendly than is usual in the Cyclades. The island has become very popular with tourists in recent years. Most visitors stay in the Khora, where the hotels are concentrated, but it is not hard to find quieter places elsewhere. An aiport (2.5km S of the town) opened in 1992. The bus station (reasonable services to most villages and main beaches; printed timetables available) is at the N end of the quay. There are bus tours of the island in the summer and cars, scooters and bicycles can be rented.

**History.** *Naxos* is perhaps best known in myth as the place where Theseus deserted Ariadne on his way back to Athens from Crete, a story celebrated in one of the most accomplished poems of Catullus and an opera by Richard Strauss. Herodotus says that the Naxians were Ionians of Athenian stock. In 501 BC Naxian exiles, living in Miletus, enlisted Persian aid against the island's ruler. The failure of the Persian expedition precipitated the Ionian revolt (Hdt. v, 30). The Persians sacked the island in 490. The Naxiots sent four ships to join the Greek fleet at Salamis, and in 471 were the first of the allied states to come under the dominion of Athens. At the battle of Naxos in 376 BC the Athenians routed a Lacedaemonian fleet. In 1207 Naxos was seized by Marco Sanudi, who founded a Venetian duchy. Breaking with Venice, he put himself under the protection of Henry of Flanders, the Latin emperor, and was rewarded in 1210 with the titles of Duke of the Archipelago and Sovereign of the Dodecanese, making him feudal superior of the other Aegean barons. His house, and the succeeding dynasty of the Crispi, ruled over much of the Cyclades for 360 years. Naxos fell to the Turks in 1566 but became a seat of Greek learning. In 1770–74 it was occupied by the Russians.

On the quay is a statue, erected in 1963, of Petros Protopapadhakis (1858–1922), the politician, a native of Apíranthos. A causeway crosses to the islet of **Palátia** where the huge doorway of the **Temple of Apollo** stands on a partially restored stylobate. The temple may date from the days of Lygdamis, tyrant c 530 BC. The harbour mole, rebuilt by Marco Sanudi, corresponds with an ancient breakwater. At the landward end of the causeway a stretch of prehistoric road is exposed in an excavation.

The walls of the town have mostly disappeared. From the little square, lanes climb to the outer enceinte of the **kastro**, within which are picturesque houses of Venetian character, many bearing coats of arms. The **Panayía Theosképastos** preserves a remarkable 14C ikon of the Crucifixion. The Latin **cathedral**, founded in the 13C, is paved with heraldic tombstones, many still claiming titles centuries after the Duchy of the Archipelago had fallen to the Turks. It has a (recently cleaned) 10C ikon of the Virgin and

Child, a unique example of a full-length representation in its period. Nearby is the building which until recently was the French Ursuline convent and a house, at one time a school, at which Nikos Kazantzakis was a pupil for two years, now the **museum**. It contains Early Cycladic figurines, marble vases and bead jewellery, from Naxos and Koufonisi; Mycenaean pottery, including octopus style stirrup jars from tombs at Aplomata amd Kamini; Geometric finds from sites within the town, also Tsikalario and the island of Donoussa; Archaic pottery, including fragments of a large pithos decorated in relief with chariots and riders (note the 'Homeric' figure-of-eight shields); small Classical torsos and sculptures; fragmentary kouroi from Sangri; a Roman mosaic and a Roman cuirass statue from Iria (see below), perhaps of Marcus Antonius. The cuirass is decorated with scenes of the punishment of Dirce etc.

## Excursions

TO ENGARÉS 8km (5 miles). Just outside the town to the N rises the hill of **Aplómata**, with Mycenaean chamber-tombs (on the very edge of the cliff) and a memorial to a local resistance hero of 1944. Here was the ancient fort of *Delion*, where occurred the events in the Naxo-Milesian war, related by Plutarch. The **Moní Khrisostómou**, above, was built c 1760 by Bishop Anthimou. You turn inland to (8km) **Mitriá** in the fruit-growing Engarés valley. From Mitriá, a road runs NE to the Mélanes area. The main road (very rough) continues on or near the E coast to the beautiful **Faneroméni** monastery (1606) and Apollona (see below).

TO APÍRANTHOS, 28km (17 miles). The main road of the island leads SE across the fertile plane of **Livádhi**. On the outskirts of the town is a turn (right) for the airport and the beaches of **Ayios Prokópios** and **Ayía Anna**.
   At **Iria** are the slight remains of a series of Temples (?to Dionysos) used from the Geometric to Late Roman periods (see also museum). 2km A turn (left) leads to **Mélanes** (9km) beyond which are the quarries of **Fleríó** (12km) where two unfinished Kouroi of the 7C lie abandoned. This road also gives access to the attractive villages of **Potamiá**. 4.5km A fork (right) leads to a cluster of villages, of which **Trípodhes** (also Vívlos) is the most important. An hour's walk from it towards the sea are towers of various periods. Further down the coast are **Mikrí Vígla** and **Pirgáki** (both with beaches), where the proper road ends.

*Iria: the Archaic Temple. Restored drawing by M. Korres*

5km **Galanádho,** just beyond which is the fine **Bellónia Pírgos** (tower house) with a double church, orthodox on one side, Catholic on the other. 8km You reach a col, from which can be seen below **Ayios Mámas** (9C), once the cathedral of Naxos (access easier from the valley below **Potamiá** road; see above). To the right is **Sangrí,** with many relics of the Middle Ages in its vicinity (towers, churches, monasteries), together with (at **Yíroulas,** a 30-minute walk SW) the site of ancient *Aulonos* (recent excavations), where a temple of Demeter and Kore has been superseded by a Byzantine church.

About 3km N of Sangrí, opposite the tower of **Vaséon,** the small single-aisled chapel of **Ay. Artémios** has aniconic frescoes of the 9C. Beyond Sangrí there is a turn (right, unsurfaced) for **Ayiassós** (10km; beach, restaurant, rooms). After a short distance, on the hillside to the left (Mt Profitis Ilias) is visible the abandoned monastery of the **Kaloritissa** (locally **Kalorítsa**) which has a **Cave Church of the Nativity** with some aniconic frescoes of the 9C and two later layers from the early 10C and 12/13C.

You enter the olive-growing plain of **Tragaías.** 14km (left) the village of **Tsikalarió** (also known as Apáno Kástro) lies below an interesting Geometric cemetery (20 minute walk through village, keeping left after 5 minutes; sign) with a standing stone at the approach and stone built grave circles over a wide area. A further 20-minute climb up the main path is Epáno Kástro (walls, towers, cisterns, churches), built by Marco Sanudi II (1244–63).

15km **Khalkí** is the principal village in a group. Its Byzantine churches have wall-paintings; of the Venetian tower-houses the Pírgos Frangopoúlou is the most striking.

In **Khalkí** the domed church of **Protóthronos** (9–10C) has fragments of an early basilica in the apse, where there is also a stone synthronon. An inscribed marble lintel built into the wall was probably taken from the **templon** of the church. The legible part records the date 1052 and the names of the donors, the bishop Leo and the protospatharios Nicetas. Beneath the dome frescoes, the remains of a similar composition were exposed, probably part of the first (10C) decoration. These were detached and are now housed in the ducal palace in the town of Naxos. Assigned to the restoration before 1083 is the existing dome decoration—the Deesis in the conch in the apse, the S vault and the surviving frescoes in the NW corner of the church, i.e. the compartment of the narthex, organised as a separate parekklesion in the 11C.

Near Khalki is **Ay. Yíoryios Diassorítis** (11C), with three layers of frescoes, those of the 11/12C recently restored. Off the road from Khalkí to **Moní** in the village of **Kalóxilos** is the **Panayía Dhamiótissa,** of free-standing cross type with a dome. The frescoes are dated to the 12/13C and include the Crucifixion and the Dormition of the Virgin. Nearer Moní is the **Panayía Dhrosianí** in which some fragments of pre-ikonoclastic decoration have recently been exposed in the N apse and dome. 13C frescoes have been removed.

19km **Filóti,** the island's largest village (1576 inhab.), a former Frankish fief, stands on the N flank of Zas (1004m), the highest point of the Cyclades. The Cave of Zas (steep climb; ask directions) has produced substantial prehistoric and some later finds. 28km **Apíranthos** (Απείρανθος; post office), called locally **Aperáthou,** an attractive village (762 inhab.), was rebuilt by the Sommaripa and Crispi in the 14C on an ancient site. There are small **Archaeological** and **Folk Museums** and a geological collection in the school. By the bus stop the shop of a local womens' co-operative sells embroideries etc., with traditional designs.

Just outside Apíranthos is the church of **Ay. Yióryios,** with, attached to the NW corner, **Ay. Pakhómios** with its twin apsidal recesses. The inscription of 1253/54 on the templon of Ay. Yióryios probably relates to the frescoes of both churches. Also near the village is the three-aisled basilica of **Ay. Ioánnis Theólogos** with remains of three layers of frescoes. The earliest are assigned to the 10C, while the major part of the decoration dates from the beginning of the 11C and the 12C. To the SE of Apíranthos is the interesting church of **Ay. Kyriakí** which contains some of the earliest aniconic decoration in Greece, dated to the 9C. Some remains of a later decoration can be seen in the S aisle.

Buses (via Apeíranthos) serve the villages in the N of the island, notably (13km) **Koronís** (359 inhab.) centre for the rich emery quarries (to the E), which are linked by aerial ropeway with a bay on the E coast and (21km) **Komiakí**, a pretty village, and (21km) **Apóllona**, on the NE coast. Here there is a colossal *kouros, broken and unfinished, showing the working methods. The area was extensively quarried in antiquity.

The Hellenistic *Tower of Kheimárrou** in the SE (due S of Zas) can be reached in 3½ hours on foot from Filóti or by a very rough road. It stands to 45 courses of masonry.

Four islets to the E and SE of Naxos (but in the eparchy of Thera), **Irakliá**, **Skhinoússa**, **Ano Koufoníssi** (**Káto Koufoníssi** close by is barely inhabited) and **Dhonoússa** are served by ferries once or twice a week (more frequently in summer) and a local service from Naxos (variable). They have little in the way of visible antiquities (several prehistoric sites have been excavated) but are quite charming. Rooms tend to be difficult to find in the summer. **Dhonoússa**, or Denoussa, has a Geometric fortified settlement explored in 1969–72. In a bay off the island on 9–10 August 1914 S.M.S. *Goeben* and *Breslau* coaled during their successful escape to Constantinople. The uninhabited islet of **Kéros**, S of the Koufoníssa, has produced important prehistoric finds (in National Archaeological Museum, Athens) and was evidently an important centre.

**IOS** or **Nió** (119 sq. km), lying E of Síkinos (see below) and between Páros (N) and Thira (S), belongs to the eparchy of Thíra. As the name implies, this beautiful little island was Ionian. An apocryphal *Life of Homer* relates that, during a voyage from Sámos to Athens, the poet was driven ashore on Ios, died there and was buried on the seashore. Ios was a fief of the Venetian Pisani, but was captured by the Turks in 1537. The hilly interior has twin peaks Pirgos (722m) and Megálo Vounó (714m). The island yields corn, dairy produce, and oil. The oak forests of Ios were once a considerable source of wealth. The only advantage that tourism has brought to the island has been financial.

Landing is made at **Ormos Iou** (Hotels C, D, E), an excellent harbour on the W coast, with a good beach (Yialós) near by. A short distance inland the low hill of **Sárkos** has a newly excavated prehistoric settlement, with Early Cycladic houses. There is another, better beach in Milopótamos bay (Hotels B, C, E) to the S. The island capital, **Ios** (1234 inhab.), lies 1km inland near the site of the ancient city. Ios is remarkable for the large number of attractive chapels, said to amount to 400; **Ayía Ekateríni** incorporates fragments of Classical sculpture. The ruined **Palaiókastro**, built by the Crispi in the 15C, stands on a commanding height above the beach of **Ayios Theodhótis** (bus in summer). At the N tip of the island (2 hours walk) is the creek of **Plakotós**, where the Dutch traveller Paasch van Krienen claimed to have discovered the tomb of Homer in 1770; all he did was to open some prehistoric graves. At the S end of the island (boat excursions in summer) is the sandy bay of **Manganári** (Hotel B).

**THÍRA** (Θήρα), or **SANTORÍNI** (Σαντορίνη), is the most important of the southern Sporades and the most southerly of the islands included in the nome of the Cyclades. It owes its alternative name to its patron, St Irene of Thessaloníki, who died here in exile in 304; officially it has readopted the ancient name *Thera*. The island, one of the great natural curiosities of Greece, is a huge volcano, the centre of which disappeared in a terrific explosion in prehistoric times. Today it has the form of a crescent 75 sq. km in area, the horns projecting westward, with an intrusion of the sea now

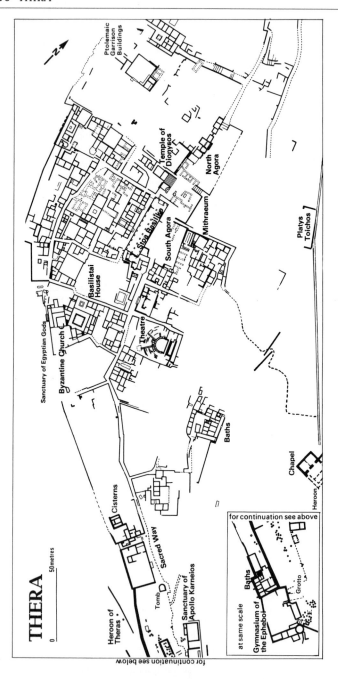

THERA

0     50 metres

Heron of
Theras

Sanctuary of
Apollo Karneios

Tomb

Sacred Way

Cisterns

Sanctuary of Egyptian Gods

Byzantine Church

Basilistai
House

Theatre

Stoa Basilike

South Agora

Temple of
Dionysos

Mithraeum

North
Agora

Ptolemaic
Garrison
Buildings

Baths

Platys
Toichos

Chapel

Heroon

for continuation see above

Gymnasium of
the Epheboi

Baths

Grotto

at same scale

for continuation see below

forming a roadstead where once the crater rose. In the middle of this lagoon, which is 208 fathoms (380m) deep, are the Kaiméni ('Burnt') Islands, still actively volcanic. On its NW side the island of **Therasía** partly continues the circular outline. Between its S coast and the S horn of Thira is an opening of the sea, in the middle of which is the tiny islet of Aspronísi.

The inner side of the crescent of Thira has weirdly shaped precipitous cliffs up to 305m high. To the E, the ground, covered with lava and pumice, slopes down gradually to the sea, the surface being interrupted by conical hillocks and a few hills, the highest being Megalos Ayios Ilias (566m), Mikros Ayios Ilias (337m), and Mesa Vouno (338m), all in the SE, and Megalo Vouno (333m) in the N. On the volcanic soil only vines and tomatoes are cultivated, but an experiment is being made with growing pistatchios. The potent Santorini wine has a great reputation. The mining of pumice ash is the island's main industry. Apart from one or two wells, the island is waterless, and rainwater is collected in cisterns. The light is famous for its intensity. By air the island can be reached directly from Athens twice daily in 55 minutes.

**Geology**. The island, originally a volcano of marble and metamorphic schist with its main crater in the middle of what is now the roadstead, has from earliest times changed its shape as the result of eruptions. One, analogous to that of Krakatoa in 1889 and placed c 1500 BC (or 1628, see below), ended in an explosion which blew out the centre of the island. In the SW only the islet of Aspronísi survives of the original land surface. In 236 BC another eruption separated **Therasía** from the NW of Thera. In 196 BC, the islet of **Hiera** or **Old Kaimeni** made its appearance. In AD 46 another islet, **Thia** appeared and vanished. In 1570 the S coast of Thera, with the port of Eleusis, collapsed beneath the sea. Three years later **Mikrá Kaiméni** appeared, and in 1711–12 **Néa** or **Great Kaimeni**. In January 1866 there began a violent eruption that lasted two years, observed by Fouqué, the French geologist and archaeologist. This eruption produced the George I Volcano, in the S of Great Kaimeni, and the islet of **Aphtoessa**, which disappeared in 1868. Another eruption began in July 1925, and lasted till May 1926; this joined Mikrá and Néa Kaiméni. Further disturbances occurred in 1928. An earthquake in July 1956 caused great damage; over half the buildings on the W coast were destroyed.

**History**. *Thera*, anciently known as *Kalliste* ('most beautiful'), was populated before 2000 BC and its colonists are said to have founded the African city of Cyrene. The great eruption that transformed its shape and which, together with the preceding earthquakes, destroyed its settlements, was once thought to have been the same catastrophe that overwhelmed the Cretan palaces but this theory no longer stands. Thera has been suggested as the site of Metropolis, the destroyed capital of the lost 'continent' of Atlantis. In legend it was colonised by Cadmus who had stopped at the island during his search for Europa. In the Peloponnesian War Thera and Melos were the only two of the Cyclades that declined alliance with Athens, but Thera escaped the fate of Melos. It was eventually, however, absorbed into the Athenian empire. The Ptolemies made the island into a naval base. In 1207–1335 it was held by the Barotsi as a fief of the Sanudi, and was thereafter included (till 1537) in the duchy of Naxos. The ancient city of Thera was situated in the SE of the island; the medieval capital *Skaros* to the NW of the modern capital. The island has been used in the present century as a place of exile for political prisoners. Vampires were once said to be especially prevalent in Thera.

**Excavation**. In 1869 the French School discovered on the S coast of Therasia the remains of a prehistoric town overwhelmed by the great eruption of c 1500 BC and covered with pumice and ash thrown up by it. This discovery proved that Thera, like Melos, was a centre of Cycladic civilisation. In 1896–1903 the German archaelogist Baron Hiller von Gärtringen excavated the ruins of ancient *Thera*; the neighbouring necropolis is still being excavated. In 1867 the French started investigations near Akrotiri; current excavations on this site were begun in 1967.

Ships berth at **Athinió**, a tiny haven beneath towering volcanic cliffs on the inner side of the crescent; a bus and taxis take passengers to Firá, the island's capital. In unfavourable weather, ships anchor offshore below Firá, whose dazzling white houses and domes extend along the clifftop nearly 210m above. Motor-boats take passengers to **Skála Firá**, from which Firá is reached by funicular railway, on foot or by mule up a steep, zig-zagging, paved track. Many cruise ships use **Skála Firá**. Transport on the island is by bus or taxi.

**Firá**, officially **Thíra** (1524 inhab.; Hotels A–E) has an Orthodox and a Roman Catholic cathedral, French schools, and a Dominican convent. From the terraces there is a magnificent view of the Kaiméni islets and Thirasía. The damage of 1956 has been made good with modern variations in new materials on the traditional barrel-vaulted style of building. At the Orthodox cathedral is a Byzantine Museum. A cultural centre nearby has material illustrating the history of the island. Immediately to the S of the town are the pumice mines, with ship-loading chutes. In the N part of the town, near the Roman Catholic cathedral, is a school founded by Queen Frederika where local girls are trained in carpet weaving. Near by is a small factory making spectacle frames. Just below is the **museum**, founded in 1902 and moved to the present new building in 1970. (Another museum is projected near the Orthodox cathedral to house all prehistoric material. The Classical exhibits will remain in the present building).

VESTIBULE. LM1A jars from the French excavations at Akrotiri in 1867; case of Early Cycladic figurines and small objects from the pumice mines; vases from recent excavations at Akrotiri. L-SHAPED HALL. In the long arm: Geometric and Archaic finds, mainly pottery. On a pedestal is an outstanding 7C Archaic *vessel, with relief decoration including a pelican and charioteers with Pegasus. Four Archaic kouroi; statuette of a woman combing her hair. In the shorter arm: pottery (6C and later), including three intact Attic black-figure vases; case of small figurines and animals; Hellenistic and Roman sculpture, continued in the SMALL ROOM, beyond, and in the COURTYARD. Here are also inscriptions, Archaic to Roman. BASEMENT. Late Roman and Early Christian glass, lamps, etc.

FROM FIRA TO AYIOS ILIAS AND ANCIENT THERA. By taxi direct to Ayios Ilías and on to ancient *Thera* (the easiest option, with subsequent descent to Kamári). By bus to Pírgos, then on foot to Ayios Ilías (45 minutes) and ancient Thera (30 minutes more); or by bus to Kamári, then on foot with a steep climb c 4km up the road to the ruins.

ROAD, 12km (7½ miles). The course is SE through vineyards. 5km Turning (left) to **Monólithos**, a conspicuous isolated outcrop by the shore which has produced traces of Mycenaean occupation in the 13C BC, the first attested on the island after the volcanic catastrophe of the 15C BC. Soon after a road forks right to **Pírgos** (Hotel C), with picturesque old houses and a Venetian fort. From here a road ascends to the top of **Megálos Ayios Ilías**, the highest point on the island (566m). The *view is magnificent, extending to the mountains of Crete. On the summit are a radar station and a small monastery of 1711, with a museum of ikons, MSS, and vestments. The road continues SE, passing **Episkopí** (right), a Byzantine church of 11C; there are two chapels, at one time used simultaneously by the Orthodox and Roman Catholic faiths. Beyond **Kamári** (Hotels A–E; F/A), ancient *Oea*, with its black beach, you climb in steep zig-zags to (12km) the **Selládha**, the high saddle where the road ends. A short way up a path (left) is the entrance to the ancient city.

Before entering the ruins, near the top of the road, are the Classical and Archaic cemeteries; also (left) a section of ancient paved road. Below the Selládha, to the SW, is the Geometric necropolis; here have been found some of the famous 'Santorini Vases', fine pottery and bronze tripods.

Ancient *Thera*, covering an area 800m long from NW to SE and 140m wide, occupies a rocky spine of Mesa Vouno and was built on a terrace supported by massive foundations. In the Byzantine era it was surrounded by a wall. The main street, crossed by numerous side streets, ran along its entire length.

Archaic tombs show that *Thera* was in existence before the 9C BC. The ruins, however, largely date from the time of the Ptolemies (300–145 BC), who made Thera into an advanced naval base from which they could control the Aegean, and from the Byzantine era. The port of Thera, *Oea*, was situated at Kamári at the foot of Mesa Vouno.

From the entrance gate the path leads up to the tiny chapel of **Ayios Stéfanos**. This was built over the ruins of the Byzantine **Basilica of the Archangel Michael** (4C or 5C). About 200m farther on is the **Temenos of Artemidoros of Perge** (right), an admiral of the Ptolemies. The enclosure, with a black lava floor, has an Altar of Concord and, in relief on the wall, the Eagle of Zeus, the Lion of Apollo Stephanephoros, the Medallion of Artemidoros, and the Dolphin of Poseidon. Beyond, a narrow stepped road leads up to the Ptolemaic garrison buildings, with the **gymnasium** and the **governor's palace**. Back from these towards the N is a little grotto converted into a Chapel of Christ, and N again, the **votive niche of Demeter and Kore**, with a throne carved out of the rock, at the entrance to a large cave called Pitaros.

The main street enters the **agora**, 110m long by 16.5–30m wide and divided into two. The N part, with a row of shops, overlooks the **Platís Teíchos** ('broad wall'), a fine quadrangular bastion of unknown function. Beyond (right) are the **Altar of Ptolemy Philometer** and the terrace of the **Temple of Dionysos**. The S part of the Agora is bordered by the Stoa Basilike, or **Royal Portico** (40m by 10m) with an interior Doric colonnade and rows of columns against the walls. It was probably founded by one of the Ptolemies. The roof was restored in the time of Trajan, and further alterations were made in AD 150. Above and behind it are four blocks of Hellenistic houses, decorated with mosaics and provided with cisterns and lavatories. Each block stands in a little square. One of the houses has a wall-medall ionin relief bearing a phallus inscribed 'To my friends'. Beyond the Agora are (right) **Roman baths**, complete with well, wood oven, and water conduits, and (left) the **theatre**.

A track leads up W past the **Basilistai House**, or Residence of Ptolemaios the Benefactor, to the ruins of Byzantine churches (earlier the Temple of Pythian Apollo). Just beyond is the **Sanctuary of the Egyptian Deities** (Isis, Anubis, Serapis) with small niches carved in the rock.

You descend towards the promontory, following the Sacred Way past the small **Temple of Ptolemy III** and the **Column of Artemis**, partly engaged in the rock, to the **Temple of Apollo Karneios**. This dates from the 6C BC and occupies a rectangle 32m by 10m. The gate, on the SW, opens into a square court with a cistern. On the E side is a room; on the W are the paved **pronaos** and the **cella**, flanked on the SW side by two little rooms with walls and doors intact. On the W side of the temple are the foundations of the **Heroön of Theras**, the eponymous coloniser from Sparta. Below, to the N, is the **Chapel of the Annunciation**, near which are remains of a Heroön and a rotunda.

You reach next the **Terrace of the Festivals**, with a fine view across the beach of Perissa to the promontory of Akrotiri. This terrace, dating from the 6C BC, has impressive retaining walls in two styles (best seen from below at the end of the promontory) and it overlooks further Roman baths.

This terrace was the religious centre of the oldest Dorian cults. On it were celebrated the gymnopaediai, dances of nude boys in honour of Apollo Karneios. Scratched on the rocks are names of the gods inscribed by the faithful, and of favourite dancers, with erotic appreciations by their admirers. Some of these graffiti are as early as the 7C BC.

At the extreme S of the City is the **Gymnasium of the Epheboi**, with a spacious court and many more graffiti, including numerous outlines of feet. Off the court are a staircase, a rotunda, and rooms; and, in the N corner, the Grotto of **Hermes and Hercules**, the gods of the epheboi.

On foot, instead of returning the same way, it is possible to descend from the Selládha to (½ hour) **Veríssa** (Hotels A–E) on the coast (buses to Firá). A white church, built in the 19C as a result of the miraculous vision of a peasant, occupies the site of a Byzantine basilica. The flying buttresses were added after an earthquake. In the S corner are the foundations of a circular **Heroön** converted in the 1C AD into the tomb of a certain Herasikleia. You turn inland. 4km **Emboreió** (Hotels A, D, E), or **Nimporió**, a village of 1365 inhabitants, situated on the foothills of Mesa Vouno, has a regular bus to Firá. In the cemetery is a statue of Polyhymnia surrounded by a wall. Beyond Emboreio, beside the road (right), is the chapel of **Ayios Nikólaos Marmarinós**, converted from a marble **Temple of Thea Basilica** (the Mother of the Gods) of the 3C BC (note the coffered ceiling). Near the S tip of the island (30 minutes S of Emboreion) are some remains of ancient *Eleusinos*. Passing the turning (left) for Akrotíri (see below) the road continues N past Pírgos (right) to (16km) Firá.

FROM FIRA TO AKROTIRI, 12km (7½ miles) to the village (bus), thence 1km to the site (bus; taxis). The road runs high above the bay, passing turnings (right) to Ormos Athiniós and (left) to Pírgos and Veríssa. 12km Akrotíri (333 inhab.) has a ruined medieval castle. At the entrance to the village a road leads left in 1km to the excavations, begun in 1967 by the late Prof. Sp. Marinatos (who died at work here in 1974) and continued under Prof. C. Doumas. The site may be compared with Herculaneum, in that it is both buried beneath volcanic material and of exceptional importance.

The •site is in a ravine below the village, the roofs which cover the remains being about level with the ground surface at the sides. The visitor follows a marked route. Although Akrotíri has produced an enormous number of outstanding finds (especially the frescoes), these can at present only be viewed in Athens (National Archaeological Museum), though a new museum is planned for the island to house them. The attraction of the site is its architecture, the best-preserved of any prehistoric settlement in the Aegean and, in some cases, surviving up to the third storey. The buildings date to LMIA, though evidence for occupation at least as far back as the Early Cycladic period has been recovered. The site was probably destroyed c 1500 BC, though a a recent proposal of 1628 BC is being debated. This is based on scientific analysis of ash residue which may not however be related to Thera. There is no regular plan: the town being composed of house-blocks and independent 'villas' (Xesté = villa), divided by narrow streets. Some of the construction is of simple rubble masonry but some of the villas are magnificently built of fine ashlar masonry. The basements were a result of raised street levels created during repairs of earlier earthquake damage. Noteworthy are stone staircases, the slab paving of some of the upper stories and the threshold, lintel and jamb blocks of intact doors and windows. A few finds have been left in situ: millstones for grinding grain and large storage vessels (in the N part of the site). From

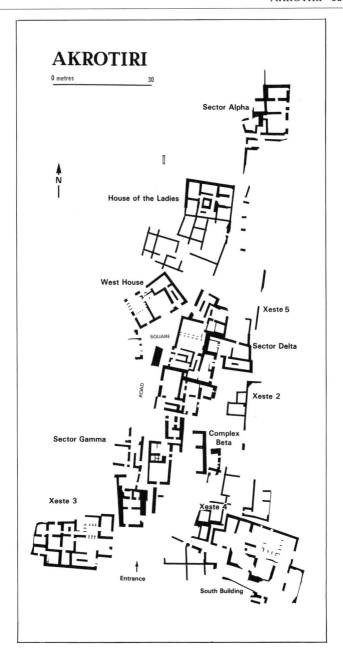

# AKROTIRI

0 metres                    30

Sector Alpha

N

House of the Ladies

West House

Xeste 5

SQUARE

Sector Delta

ROAD

Xeste 2

Sector Gamma

Complex
Beta

Xeste 3

Xeste 4

Entrance

South Building

the West House, with a broad window in the first floor, came the Ship Fresco and from Xeste 3 scenes of women gathering saffron in honour of a deity.

FROM FIRA TO OIA, 13km (8 miles), bus or taxi. On foot in c 2½ hours. As far as Foinikiá the road runs inland of the path. The path leaves Fira on the N and follows the cliffs through white hamlets. ½ hour **Merovígli** (taverna), a village on a height; its name Ημεροβίγλι means 'watch tower'. On the left is a promontory (304m) bearing the ruins of *Skaros*, the medieval capital of the island, with a castle of the Crispi. The path continues to skirt the shore as far as (1 hour) a track fork on the slopes of **Megálo Vounó** (333m). The turning to the right leads in ½ hour to **Cape Koloumbos**, on the NE coast, near which some rock-hewn tombs have been discovered. Keeping left, you reach (1¾ hours) the hamlet of **Foinikiá**, near here joining the road. 2½ hours **Oía** (439 inhab.), the official but incorrect name adopted by Apáno Meriá; for ancient *Oea* see above. The village was ruined by the 1956 earthquake. It has some tourist shops and a small **Maritime Museum**. Below to the S is the little port of **Ayios Nikólaos**, facing the island of Thirasía (boats available).

**Thirasía** (excursions in summer), once part of the island of Thera before the great prehistoric eruption, is now an island c 5km long and 2.5km wide. It has a landing-place at **Manolás**, in the middle of the E coast. The ancient city of *Therasia* was in the N of the island. In the S, between Capes Kimina and Tripiti, are pumice ash quarries, which supplied much of the material for building the banks of the Suez Canal. In these quarries a Middle-Late Cycladic settlement was accidentally discovered in 1869. Nothing remains to be seen.

EXCURSION TO NEA (GREAT) KAIMENE. A motor-boat from Skála Firá crosses in 20 minutes to the island. From the landing stage a walk across cinder leads in 30 minutes to the Metaxá Crater where gases and hot vapours sometimes issue from fissures.

**Anáfi** (Ανάφη), or **Anaphe**, is a small island (37.5 sq. km) to the E of Santorini, to which politically it belongs. It was celebrated in legend as having been raised out of the sea by Apollo as a refuge for the Argonauts when overwhelmed by a storm. Landing is at **Ayios Nikólaos** in the centre of the S shore. **Anáfi**, or **Khóra** (261 inhab.), the only village, lies 15 minutes inland. Paths lead E to (80 minutes) **Katelimátsa**, where there is an ancient site, and on to (100 minutes) the attractive monastery of the **Kalamiótissa**, site of a temple of Apollo of which there are remains. Other traces of ancient habitation can be seen to the N of Katelimátsa, at **Kastélli** (20-minute walk). Many antiquities were removed by the Russians in 1770–74 to St Petersburg.

Síkinos and Folégandros lie between Ios and Mílos and belong to the eparchy of Thíra. **Síkinos** (Σίκινος; 37.5 sq. km; 267 inhab; Hotel B) is said to have once been called *Oinoe* ('Wine Island') from the fertility of its vines. The S coast is rocky and barren, but elsewhere the island produces wine, figs, and wheat. The Skala at **Aloprónoia**, on the SE coast, is exposed and often inaccessible. About 1 hour inland (or minibus), in the middle of the island, is the village capital, called **Kástro** or **Khóra**, at the foot of a rock crowned by a fortified monastery (Zoödhókhos Piyí), now ruinous. To the SW (1¾ hours), at **Episkopí**, stands an impressive Heroön, or temple-tomb (3C AD), converted in the (?) 7C into the church of Koimisis Theotokou, and remodelled after earthquake damage shortly before 1673. At the NE tip of the island (1½ hours from Kastro) is **Palaiókastro** with ruins of another ancient sanctuary.

**Folégandros** (Φολέγανδρος; Hotels B, C, E) is one of the smallest of the Cyclades (35 sq. km; 558 inhab.). From Karavostásis, the harbour, a narrow road leads in 40 minutes to the pretty Khóra (244 inhab.), with a medieval portion called Kástro. The ancient city crowned the hill above. The beautiful church of Panayía stands on a head-land to the N. Apáno Meriá (296 inhab.), a scattered village, lies 1 hour to the NW of Khóra; from the windmills on the way a wide view embraces Sífnos and Kímolos and the coast of Crete.

*Embroidery from Foíegandros, Cyclades*

# 74

# Eastern Sporades (Sporádhes)

The **Eastern Sporades**, generally more fertile and greener than the Cyclades, lie off the coast of Asia Minor. Imbros and Tenedos belong to Turkey; most of the remainder, which extend S to the Dodecanese, are under Greek sovereignty. Samothrace and Lemnos, the most northerly, are described for convenience with Thrace (from which they are most easily accessible; see Rte 70A, B).

## A. Ikaría and Sámos

**Ferries** from Piraeus, 1–3 daily (direct or via Páros, Náxos, Síros or Míkonos), to Ikaría (in 8½–11 hours) and to Sámos (Vathí in 9½–15 hours; Karlóvasi in 8–17 hours), where arrival may be very early in the morning. On Sámos most boats call first at Karlóvasi and then Vathí. At Ikaría the usual port-of-call is Ayios Kírikos, but some steamers call regularly at Evdhilos. Infrequently boats call also at Foúrnoi, to which there is a daily caique from Ikaría, also sometimes Karlóvasi. Sámos is also connected with Khíos, Líemnos and Thessaloníki, and with the Dodecanese.

There are connections (frequent in summer, including day trips) to Pátmos; also Kušadasi (for Ephesus) on the Turkish mainland.

**By Air** (to Sámos) several times daily in 45 minutes. The air-field lies between Pithagório and the Heraíon. **Main Terminal**, Kanári and Smírnis, Vathí.

**Ikaría** (Ἰκαρία), a delightful, green, well-watered island with many scattered hamlets among the orchards and vineyards, is noted for its honey, as well as its radioactive hot springs. Part of the island was tragically devastated by fire in 1993, with loss of life. With **Foúrnoi** it forms an eparchy (8926 inhab.) of the nome of Samos. The name, possibly deriving from the Phoenician 'ikor' referring to an abundance of fish, attracted to itself a legendary past in which Ikaros and Daedalus figure prominently (a modern sculpture based on the myth adorns the harbour mole at Ayios Kírikos). In antiquity the island had other names, notably *Doliche*. The S coast rises to a ridge (**Atheras**), the highest point of which (1880m), SW of the capital, was known to the ancients as Pramnos or Drakanon.

The little capital, **Ayios Kírikos** (Hotels; Rooms) with 1797 inhabitants, lies on the SE shore. Neighbouring to the E is **Thérma** (Hotels B, C, D, E summer only), the principal spa, whose name and fame were similar in antiquity. Some Roman remains can be seen. An unidentified Archaic acropolis and Classical tombs have been noted at **Katafíyi** c 6.5km E. Remains of *Drakanon*, another Classical town, lie near Fáro at the E end of the island. Most impressive here is the circular *tower of the 3C. Some finds are on show in the Gymnasion of Ayios Kírikos.

40km from Ayios Kírikos (daily bus; impressive views) is the pretty village of **Evdhilos** (Εὔδηλος; Hotels B, E; rooms), in the middle of the N coast, which can be used as a base for the W half of the island. At **Kámbos** (3km W), with a small **museum**, are the remains of ancient *Oinoe*. The Byzantine town on this site readopted the name of Doliche, and left the ruins called 'Palatia', which incorporate a Roman odeion (visible), and the attractive 11C church of Ayía Iríni.

Farther W (11km) is **Armenistís** (Hotels C; Rooms; good beaches), destination of the daily bus, and beyond (4km), reached by a poor road, the beautifully situated sanctuary of **Artemis Tauropolos** at **Na**. The stone of the temple and various other buildings has been mostly fed to the lime kilns. The site, lying opposite Míkonos and on the direct route from Ionia to Delos, was the starting point for processions to the Delian sanctuary. Inland the most interesting excursion is to the **Kástro tis Nikariás** a small fort of the 10C. This is best reached via the village of **Stelí** (occasional bus; 1 hour on foot from Evdhilos, with a further hour or more for the ascent, which involves a steep climb).

**Foúrni** consists of a small group of islands, of which only two are inhabited. The daily caique (from Ayios Kírikos; weather often rough) calls first at the smaller of these, **Thímaina**. By the harbour of the village of Foúrni (rooms), the largest island, are the substantial remains of a Hellenistic (and Roman) fortified town. Inscriptions can be seen carved on the rocks. At **Khrissomiliá** (c 10km N, best reached by boat), a prettily situated village, are the remains of an ancient building of marble (a temple or tower) with a Byzantine church built above.

**SÁMOS** (Σάμος) lies closest of all Greek islands to the coast of Asia Minor, to which it was connected in prehistoric times, being separated from Cape Mykale by a strait 1.8km wide. A range of mountains (a continuation of the mainland chain) runs through the island from E to W, rising to peaks at Karvouni (or Ampelos; 1153m) in the centre and Kerkis (or Kerketevs; 1433m) in the extreme W. Samos, with an area of 492 sq. km, supports 41,965 inhabitants. The N coast is precipitous and rocky, while the S coast opens on little plains and beaches excellent for bathing. The capital Vathí (in the bay of the same name) is on the N. Although Vathí is now most commonly called simply Sámos, or Samos town, the official name is retained in this text to avoid confusion with the island as a whole. The island is thickly wooded, except at the drier E end, and abounds in springs and winter torrents. At all times it has been known for its fertility, which gave rise to many of the names by which it was known in antiquity (Anthemousa, Phyllas, Dryousa, etc.), and which led Menander to claim it could produce even birds' milk (Strabo xiv). The main products are wine (the Samian Moskháto, a sweet reddish wine, is widely exported and has a high reputation), honey, tobacco, shipbuilding timber, and olive oil. Several villages have potteries. The mean winter temperature is warmer than that of Athens.

**History**. That *Samos* was inhabited least as early as the 4th millennium BC is proved by Neolithic finds at Pithagório. The island's name is said to derive from a Phoenician word meaning 'high'. Pelasgians introduced the cult of Hera, and the Classical writers endowed the island with an eponymous hero, son of an Argonaut colonist. Later Samos was settled by Ionians. In the 8C or 7C Samos came into the possession of territory on the opposing mainland, which gave rise to continual boundary disputes with Priene. About 638 BC the Samian Kolaios voyaged through the Pillars of Hercules and returned with wealth that soon become proverbial. After the overthrow of the tyrant Demoteles in the early 6C Samos was ruled by a landed aristocracy (the Geomoroi).

About 540, Polycrates and his brothers Pantagnotus and Syloson became tyrants (it is possible that the dynasty was established earlier by their father Aeaces). Polycrates soon ousted his brothers and ruled alone, bringing Samos to the height of its prosperity. He built up a great naval force, annexed many of the neighbouring islands and concluded alliances with Cyrene and with Amasis of Egypt. His court attracted many eminent artists and poets, among them Anacreon of Teos, and Polycrates was responsible for what Herodotus describes as the three greatest works to be seen in any Greek land—the aqueduct constructed by Eupalinos, the mole of the harbour, and the temple of Hera (the largest known to Herodotus) built by the architects Rhoikos and Theodoros. During this century, Samos founded many colonies, especially in the Propontis, and as far afield as Zancle in Sicily. In 522 BC Polycrates was tricked and captured by the Persian satrap Orontes and crucified on the mainland opposite.

Syloson, Polycrates' brother, now became tyrant with Persian support, although anti-Persian feeling in the island led to Samian participation in the Ionian revolt against Persia. In the battle of Lade however, in 494, the Samian fleet deserted to the Persians. Samos fought on the Persian side at Salamis, but finally turned against Xerxes at the battle of Mycale. In 479–440, Samos was an independent member of the Athenian League, contributing ships instead of tribute. Following a revolt, Samos was crushed by Pericles after a nine-month siege—a feat which received favourable comparison with the capture of Troy. Some time between 440 and 412 an oligarchic régime took over, perhaps installed by the Athenians. The island was faithful to Athens during the Peloponnesian War, and was captured by the Spartan Lysander in 404 BC. In 394 BC the Athenian admiral Konon recaptured Samos, which seceded from Athens in 391. The Athenians retook the island in 365 and replaced the entire native population with colonists. The Samians returned from exile only in 321 BC as the result of an edict of Alexander the Great, put into effect after his death by his regent Perdikkas. In the same year Antigonus Monophthalmus gained control of Ionia, and probably of Samos which he certainly controlled some time before 306. After his death Samos fell to Lysimachus of Thrace, and when he was defeated and killed in the battle of Corupedion in 281, passed under the influence of the Ptolemies of Egypt who used the island as a naval base. Later in the century Kallikrates of Samos became Ptolemy's admiral, a position amounting to viceroy of the sea. Ptolemaic control of the island lasted until 197 BC, with a short interruption in 259–246 when Samos came under the rule of Antiochus II. After a brief occupation by Philip V of Macedon, Samos came under the influence of the Pergamene dynasts, and became part of the Roman province of Asia in 129 BC. The works of art of the city and sanctuary were plundered by Verres in 82 BC and further suffered from pirates' raids between c 70–67 BC. It recovered somewhat under the proconsulship of Quintus Cicero in 62 BC, but was plundered again by Antony, who with Cleopatra visited the island in 39 BC. Relations between Augustus and Samos were more friendly. Having wintered on the island in 20–19 BC, he restored its autonomy and had many works of art returned. This status was annulled by Vespasian in AD 70 and Samos became part of the *Provincia Insularum*. The emperor Gaius is said to have contemplated rebuilding the palace of Polykrates.

In the Byzantine era Samos belonged to the eparchy of the Cyclades. It was from here that Nikephoros Phokas embarked on his expedition against Crete in 960. This period marks the decline of Samos. After the invasion of the Turks in 1453 it was depopulated until the 17C, when it was re-occupied and ruled by an archbishop. Samos was occupied by the Russians in 1772–74. In 1821 the island played a leading part in the uprising and proved such a valiant adversary that 'to go to Samos' became the proverbial expression used by the Turks to mean certain death. The Samians won a series of victories, but the island was restored to the Turks at the end of the war. They were, however, accorded special privileges amounting to autonomy. They were governed by a Greek prince, the first being Stephanos Bogaridas (1834–59). In 1912 the Turkish fleet at Vathy was bombarded by two Italian warships, and Samos was reunited with Greece. In 1943 Samos was temporarily occupied first by Italians, then by the British, and heavily bombarded by the Germans, who later seized it. After the war it was a partisan stronghold.

Several village names reflect the arrival of immigrants from other parts of Greece.

See G. Shipley, *A History of Samos 800–188 BC*, 1987, Oxford.

**Vathí** (Βαθύ; Hotels B, C, D, E; F/A), the capital of the island and usually now called simply **Sámos** (see above), consists of the port of **Sámos** (or **Limín Vathéos**), with 5792 inhabitants, situated in a deep bay on the N coast, and the attractive suburb of **Ano Vathí** (2440 inhab.; now sometimes simply Vathí) on a hill to the S of the bay. This affords a wonderful view of the port itself, the bay, and the coast of Asia Minor. The town dates from the 19C when it was named *Stephanoupolis* after the first autonomous governor. Tourist facilities (car hire etc.) are readily available. The best local bathing is to be found in shingle coves c 5–8km W (buses).

The fine **Archaeological Museum** (in two buildings) lies behind the public garden, next to the Town Hall and the post office. Housed in it are outstanding finds mostly of the 6C BC from the ancient city of Samos and the Heraion. These include sculptures (among which are the three remaining statues of the Archaic group by Geneleos) and grave reliefs, votive bronzes, with a large collection of griffin-heads; pottery and ivories; and inscriptions. The centrepiece of the new building is an enormous kouros (5m tall), the body discovered in the Heraion sanctuary in 1980, the face in 1984. The figure is inscribed as a dedication and dates to 570/60 BC. There is much fine miniature sculpture in various materials (including wood). A special display in the older building describes and illustrates the history of the Heraion.

In Od. Asklipiádhou, above the N end of the harbour, the Archbishopric houses a small **Byzantine and Ecclesiastical Museum** with church plate and some interesting icons from the monasteries of Samos.

SHORTER EXCURSIONS. The monastery of **Zoödhókhos Piyí**, founded in 1756 on the hill Pabaidhóni, is 7km from Vathy to the E. It is noted for its wood-carving, its hospitality, and for the spectacular view it affords of the strait of Mykale. A visit to **Ayía Zóni** (1695), another monastery, in the plain of Vlamári, c 3km from Vathí, can easily be included in the excursion.

A visit may be paid to the lighthouse of **Kótsikas** c 5km N of Vathí at the mouth of the bay (fine view).

About 2.5km S of the town, off the Pithagório road (see below) by-roads lead to **Palaiókastro** (6km from Vathí; the ancient site, with some good walls, is c 2km before the village on a bluff to the right of the road) and to (12km) the Strait of Mykale (Stenon Kouzantazi) close by the bathing-beach of Psíli Ammos.

**Mitilíni**, on the high road to **Khóra**, has a small **Palaeontological Museum**.

Regular **boat** excursions to Pátmos, Ikaría and Foúrni; Caiques to Kušádasi, the Turkish port opposite Sámos which is close to the ruins of Ephesos. Also to various beaches. From Karlóvassi to Ikaría and Foúrni.

The PRINCIPAL EXCURSIONS on the island are to ancient Samos at Pithagório and the Heraion and to Karlóvasi. By car they can be combined into a round TOUR OF THE ISLAND, 92km (57 miles), in a day.

**Taxis** for hire (legally fixed prices displayed in Plateia); **Buses** daily to Karlóvasi, either direct (7) or via Pithagório (2); frequently to Pithagório, either by the main road or via Mitilíni and Khóra. Cars, scooters, cycles for hire.

The road climbs out of Vathí and continues S over a ridge with fine views of the Strait of Mykale and of the islands of the Dodecanese. 14km **Pithagório** (Πυθαγόρειο; Hotels A–E; boat excursions locally and to Turkey), a busy but attractive tourist centre, lies on the S coast of the island. Formerly called Tigáni, it was given its present name in 1955 in honour of Pythagoras. It has 1405 inhabitants and occupies the site of ancient *Samos* (a useful though now dated guide is R. Tolle, *Die antike Stadt Samos*, 1969). A small **museum** contains sculptures, among them an Archaic statue of Aiakes; Archaic grave stelai bearing anthemia; Hellenistic grave reliefs; and Roman remains. A new museum (excavations on the projected site on the Vathí road) is planned to house these and other stored objects. Numerous rescue excavations in the town have revealed fragments of the ancient settlement and its religious and public buildings.

The **Castle of Logothetes** (1824), with a church of the **Transfiguration** (1833) occupy the hill to the W of the harbour. This was the site of the prehistoric settlement, later *Astypalaia*, subsequently incorporated into the town of Samos. The area to the E of the church has remains of a 2C Hellenistic villa with two peristyle courts. This was modified in Roman times when Antony and Cleopatra and various emperors are said to have stayed here. In the 5C AD the N court was overlain by an Early Christian basilica with a small chapel (foundations well preserved; mosaic) on its S side. Remains of other periods are less evident. Although this was presumably the acropolis of ancient Samos, no sign of the palace of Polykrates has come to light.

The mole of the harbour is built on the foundations of the ancient mole of the period of Polycrates, described by Herodotus (3, 60) as one of the greatest works of any Greek land. There are three miles of good pebble and sand beaches to the W.

2km out of the town on the main road to Vathí a road branches (left) to the traces of the ancient **theatre** (right); below the road are Hellenistic and Roman houses. Here a right branch ascends to the small monastery of **Panayía Spilianí** which hides the mouth of a series of underground caves and cisterns used as a place of refuge during the Turkish occupation and during more recent wars. The left branch continues to the Eupalineion (Evpalínion), or *Tunnel of Eupalinos (open mornings in season), completed during the tyranny of Polycrates in 524 BC.

The tunnel may have been started during the tyranny of Aiakes and probably took 15 years to complete. It was hewn through the mountain, under the direction of Eupalinos of Megara, its architect, from the N side (outside the walls) to a point within the walls, working being begun from both ends. Besides assuring the water supply during time of siege, the tunnel provided an escape route in emergency. It was so used by Maeandrius during Darius' attack. A low and narrow entrance from a small white building gives place in the tunnel proper to a ledge beside the deep water channel.

Beyond the tunnel you can continue W to reach the **city wall**. This wall runs spectacularly up the side of the mountain, turns E along the top and returns towards the sea at a point E of the Panayía Spilianí. Its whole extent of 7km with 35 towers has been traced. It is excellently preserved at the top, and the views over Mykale and over the inland plain are superb.

FROM PITHAGORIO TO THE HERAION, 8km (5 miles); c 5 buses daily; taxi; bicycles (the road is flat and an easy ride) for hire in Pithagório. Taking the road for **Khóra** and the airport, about 500m out of town the archaeological site (left) at Thérmes (Monday, Wednesday, Sunday 10.00–14.45) contains interesting discoveries of three main periods. An Early Christian basilica went through several phases of which the most striking remains are three of the buttresses added to the structure for support. From these the site takes its name Tría Dhóntia, 'three teeth'. The basilica was part of a larger building complex. At an earlier period Roman Baths were built over the E part of an enormous Hellenistic gymnasium. Several features of this, including a palaistra and the starting line of the running track, have been investigated. These buildings lie in the SW angle of the town walls. Between here and the harbour to the E, sections of the ancient and Byzantine walls can be seen close to the sea. 500m beyond the site the Lake of Glifádha lies to the left of the road. Opposite, on a low hill, the church of Panayítsa overlies an Early Christian basilica (mosaic). Between it and the road other ancient structures include Early Christian cemetery buildings. Nearby an Archaic sanctuary of Artemis has been excavated. Continuing, take the left fork, pass the airfield, and (at 6km) again bear left.

The **Heraion**, or **Sanctuary of Hera** (08.30–15.00; closed Monday), lies on the coast at a place called **Kolónna** after the one surviving column of the great temple. It is close by the torrent Imbrasos, which is said to have seen the birth of Hera, and is a few minutes' walk on the Pithagório side of its small village, frequented as a bathing resort. Few Greek sanctuaries can boast a history of such length that can be traced in such detail. There is an excellent guidebook, in German and Greek.

Excavations undertaken by the German Archaeological Institute in 1910–14, 1925–39, and since 1952 have revealed that the history of the site begins in the Bronze Age. Among buildings uncovered is a tholos tomb of the late-Mycenaean period. The

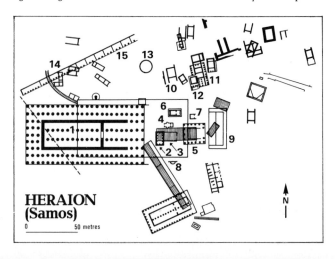

**HERAION
(Samos)**

0          50 metres

N

continuous history of the sanctuary during the next centuries is attested by altars and two temples earlier than the first great temple. The early 8C structure was developed into the first true Greek temple by the addition of a peristyle (7 x 17); after its destruction c 670 BC, it was replaced by another (6 x 18 columns). During the 6C the sanctuary was widely extended, activity beginning probably a generation before Polycrates and being continued by him. To this period belongs the great temple. Further buildings belong to the Hellenistic and Roman periods and include a Christian basilica of the 5C AD.

The first **Great Temple** was built c 575–560BC by the celebrated Samian artist Rhoikos, in association (according to some authorities) with the architect Theodoros. Herodotus claims it was the largest temple of its day. In the Ionic order, 97.5m long by 49m wide, it was a dipteron, with 8 columns by 20 (rectangle on plan). The first structure was relatively short-lived because of its inadequate foundations. Its successor (40m to the W and making use of many pieces of the older building, notably the column-bases; Pl. 1) was begun c 530, under Polykrates, but work was interrupted, perhaps on his death, and not continued until c 500. In front of the **pronaos**, at the E end, were three rows of eight columns, at the W end, three rows of nine. Its construction was again suspended, resumed in the 3C but was never completed. A single column, itself incomplete, stands at the present time.

The complex of buildings immediately to the E includes an **altar** (Pl. 2), a late building with buttresses (Pl. 3), a small **bath** (Pl. 4), a peripteral **temple** (Pl. 5) belonging to the Roman period, a second Roman **temple** (Pl. 6), dating from the 2C AD, and an Early Christian **basilica**. All that remains of the last today is the N aisle with the foundations of the nave, and the apse (Pl. 7). To the S lies the base (Pl. 8) on which stood statues of the orator Cicero and his brother Quintus. Beyond this group, to the E, is the large **altar** (Pl. 9) which is said to have been erected by Rhoikos. This was constructed on the site of a cult area of the 2nd millennium BC above a more recent altar which had been restored in the Geometric period.

To the N of this group of buildings, the whole area is now overgrown and inaccessible. In it were found another complex of constructions dating from various periods. These include two small **temples** in antis (Pl. 10, 11), the second of which overlies a peripteral temple, and a third Temple (Pl. 12) of late date. To the W of this group were the foundations of a circular building (Pl. 13), and farther to the W an Archaic **stoa** (Pl. 14). A number of members of the temple of Rhoikos were found beneath this stoa, where they were buried after its destruction, thus proving it to belong to the late Archaic period. Between this stoa and the great temple is a **stoa** (Pl. 15) of the Hellenistic period.

In the extreme E area of the site have been uncovered the foundations of a number of buildings, including treasuries, temples, and administrative offices. Also, four wells were discovered here full of vases dating from the Geometric period to the 7C. A late-Mycenaean wall and the remains of several Mycenaean buildings were also found in this area.

The village of **Iréo** is a tourist centre with hotels (B, C, D). About 1.5km W of the site and 10 minutes walk from the village is the **Pírgos Sarakíni**, a tower dating from the Turkish occupation (late 16C).

At the W end of the plain **Míli** has an attractive square. From below the turn to Míli the main road continues to **Pagóndas** (cafés, view). Hence a forest track runs high round the S side of the island to **Spatharaíoi**, rejoining the main road at **Pírgos** (see below).

The round tour continues from the right fork before the airfield (see above) to (22km) **Khóra** (1316 inhab.), before 1821 the island capital, then winds across the rugged but often tree-clad centre of the island. 25km turn (right) for **Mavratzéi** (3km), one of several villages specialising in pottery. On the way is the pleasant monastery of **Timíou Stavroú** (Holy Cross). 31km **Koumaradhéi**, below which is the 16C monastery of **Megáli Panagía**, with fine carvings and frescoes. 35km **Pírgos** (653 inhab.; Hotel D). 50km turning (left) for (4km) **Marathókambos** (Hotels B, C, D), with a splendid view of the S coast. From here several attractive villages (**Plátanos**, **Niokhóri** etc) are accessible. The road continues to the coastal resort, beyond which are quiet villages including **Kalithéa** and **Dhrakéi**. 58km **Karlóvasi** (Καρλόβασι; Hotels A, B, C, D; excursions by sea to Foúrni etc. in summer) is a small port (5250 inhab.) on the N coast (2 hours by sea from Vathí, at which most boats to and from Piraeus call. An Olympic Airways bus service connects with one flight a day from the main airport. The area inland of the town is rich in vines which contribute to the reputation of the Samian wines. From Karlóvasi the visitor can make many walks on **Mt Kerkis**, from the summit of which a magnificent view of the Aegean and the neighbouring islands may be obtained. It is best approached from the village of **Kosmadhéi** (or from Marathókambos). From here, too, the villages of Léka (largely deserted) and Kastanéa may be visited. A short distance to the W is the attractive shingle beach of the bay of **Potámi**, with an interesting modern church.

The road from Karlóvasi to Vathí skirts the coast all the way, offering spectacular views of the rocky coastline. Beyond the huge plane-tree of **Ayios Dhimítrios**, it runs high along the cliffs. 71.5km **Ayios Konstandínos** is a fishing hamlet. Just beyond is a tourist pavilion (**Ta Platanákia**) and a branch road through woods to Manolátes in an area growing cherries and nuts. 76km Turning to **Vourliótes**, a centre of vine-growing, from which may be visited the interesting 15C mountain monastery of **Vrondianí**, the oldest on the island, founded in 1566. 82km **Kokkári** (Hotels A–E) has a small harbour. From here we approach Vathí along the W side of its gulf through **Malagari** (Hotel A), a region of many pine trees. 92km **Vathí**.

# B.  Khíos

**Approaches**. **By Air** from Athens at least four times daily in 1 hour, twice weekly to Lésvos and Thessaloníki.

**Ferries** 1–4 times daily from Piraeus to Khíos direct in 9–11 hours (some overnight; very early arrival), continuing to Lésvos (comp. also Rte 74C also Límnos and Kaválla (or Thessaloníki); also connections to Sámos and Pátmos.

**KHÍOS** or **Chíos** (Χίος, famed for its fertility and with a delightful climate, lies 64.5km NW of Sámos and 56km S of Lésvos. A strait only 8km across separates it from the peninsula of Karaburnu in Asia Minor. With Psará and some dependent islets it forms a nome of 52,184 inhabitants. Khíos, 48km long and with a width varying from 13 to 24km, deserves Homer's epithet Παιπαλόεσσα (craggy). A mountain range crosses the island from N to S. The highest point is Mt Pelinaion, or Profitis Ilias (1297m), in the N. The volcanic origin of the island is evident in the frequent earthquakes, some of which have been catastrophic. There are numerous springs but no rivers and cultivation of the eastern plains is dependent upon irrigation. Khios is the chief source of mastic, a resin of the lentisk tree, once used in making picture-varnish, but now almost entirely in the flavouring of a favourite

Levantine liqueur and in chewing-gum. The villages where the tree is 'milked' are called Mastikhokhória. Lemons, oranges, and tangerines are exported; olives and almonds are grown. Khian wine, famous in antiquity, is produced on the NW coast. The Khians of the Classical era were overfond of it, according to Aristophanes, who contrasted them with the sober inhabitants of Keos (comp. Rte 72A).

**History**. According to some authorities the name Chios is of Phoenician origin and means mastic. Excavations have demonstrated occupation in the Neolithic and Bronze Ages (see below). Wherever the earliest settlers came from, tradition held that Chios was colonised by the Ionians. Neleus and Androklos, younger sons of Kodros, King of Athens, after a dispute about the succession to the throne, crossed the Aegean in search of a new home 140 years after the fall of Troy. They settled on the W coast of Asia Minor between the rivers Hermus and Maeander and in Chios and Samos, the two islands off this coastal strip. In historical times we find twelve cities united into the Ionic Confederacy. These cities were, from N to S, Phokaea, Erythrae, Klazomenae, on the Gulf of Smyrna (Izmir), the city and island of Chios, Teos, Lebedos, Kolophon, Ephesus, the city and island of Samos, Priene, Myus, and Miletus. Smyrna, which was situated in this district but was of Aeolic origin, was added c 700 BC to the confederacy. Its common sanctuary was the Panionion, on the promontory of Mykale, opposite Samos; here was held the *Panionia*, or great national assembly of the confederacy.

These cities soon attained a high degree of civilised prosperity. The arts and literature prospered. Among the lengthy list of artists and authors after Homer (claimed as a native of Chios) are the philosophers Thales of Miletus, one of the Seven Sages, and Pythagoras of Samos, the poet Anacreon of Teos, and the painters Apelles of Kolophon, Zeuxis of Herakleia (Miletus), and Parrhasius of Ephesus. Other natives of Chios were the tragic poet Ion, the historian Theopompos (born c 378 BC), and the sophist Theocritus (4C BC). The chief cities of Ionia had an international reputation, which lasted into our era, and they occupied a special place in the early history of Christianity: witness the Acts of the Apostles, the Epistles of St Paul to the Ephesians, and the Revelation of St John to the Seven Churches of Asia, two of which were Ephesus and Smyrna.

In the 6C and 5C BC Chios had a celebrated school of sculpture. One of its artisans, Glaucus (fl. 490 BC), invented the art of soldering metals. Chios was the first Greek city to engage in the slave trade, later so profitable in Delos. Towards the end of the 5C the Chians had more domestic slaves than any other Greek state except Sparta.

The Ionians were first conquered by Croesus, king of Lydia (reigned 560–546), and then in 545 by Harpagus, a general of Cyrus, king of Persia. In 499 BC, instigated by the wayward Aristagoras, Governor of Miletus, the Ionians revolted against Persian domination. Aristagoras canvassed help for the rebels from Athens and Eretria. Athens sent twenty ships 'the beginning of mischief both to the Greeks and to the barbarians' (Herod, V, 97). At the Battle of Lade in 494, the Greek fleet was worsted, despite the valour of the Chiot Squadron, and Miletus sacked.

In 477, after the defeat of the Persian invasions, Chios joined the Delian Confederacy and remained a member till 412. Thucydides says (III, 10) that Chios and Lesbos were the only free allies of Athens, the remainder being subordinate in lesser or greater degree. In 412 Chios revolted against Athens. Though she was joined by other Ionian cities, including Miletus, Teos, and Mytilene, the Athenians defeated the Chiots and ravaged their country. In 378 Chios joined the Second Athenian Confederacy; in 354 she revolted again and her independence was recognised. In 333 the island was captured by a general of Alexander the Great. In the 3C BC Chios joined in alliance with Aetolia. Later, as an ally of Rome, she took part in the war with Antiochus. Her wealth excited the cupidity of the legionaries and the island was pillaged by Verres and by the forces of Mithridates. In 86 BC, after its recapture by Sulla, independence was regained. This was at first respected by the Roman emperors. After the earthquake of 17 BC Tiberius contributed towards the rehabilitation of the island. Vespasian incorporated it in the province of the Islands.

From now on the history becomes obscure. St Paul 'sailed over against Chios on his way to Miletus' (Acts XX, 15). A Christian church was established in the island. In the 8C it was ravaged by Saracens. Occupied by Zachas, a pirate chief, it was freed in 1092 by Alexander Comnenus. In 1172 it was captured by Doge Vital Michialli; and in 1204, occupied by Venetians. They were replaced in 1261 by the Genoese. There followed incursions of Franks, Catalans, and Turks. By the middle of the 14C, however, Genoese domination was secure under the aegis of the Giustianini. In 1344 they formed a kind of chartered company, the *Maona*, which administered the island and was responsible for its defence. Chios again became prosperous. As early as 1513 a consul for the English was appointed to look after the affairs of the Levant Company who were engaged in trading cloth for wine. In 1566 the Turks under Piali Pasha captured the island. Thereafter, until 1821, despite several risings, it enjoyed under the Turks a measure of semi-independence. At the beginning of the War of Greek Independence in 1821 the Samians induced the Chians to join them in the revolt. In 1822 the Turks inflicted dreadful vengeance. They massacred 25,000 and enslaved 47,000. Only the mastic towns were spared. In the same year the Greek admiral Kanaris avenged his compatriots by destroying with fireships the Turkish flagship, with its commander Kara Ali; but his was a hollow victory. Those Chiots who had escaped the massacre had fled abroad. The more fortunate of the Chian refugees later made a name for themselves as merchants in London (the Rallis brothers), Liverpool, Manchester, Paris, Marseilles, Leghorn, Palermo, Odessa, Alexandria, and India. Chios never fully recovered from the events of 1822. The earthquake of 1881 did great damage; over 3500 of the islanders perished. In 1912 the island was liberated by the Greek fleet. Many of the best-known shipping families are Chiot. From Chios came Leo Allatius (1586–1669), scholar and librarian of the Vatican.

**Khíos**, or **Khóra**, the capital of the island and a seaport with 22,894 inhabitants, is situated in the middle of the E coast, facing Asia Minor, and is known to the Turks as **Sakiz**. It occupies the site of the ancient city. The town lies within a fertile coastal strip; behind are wooded hills, with the bare mountains of the interior beyond.

**Airport**, 4km S. **Terminal**, Prokimaía.

**Hotels** A, C, D.

**Post Office**, Od. Omírou, behind S end of quay.

**NTOG**, 11 Od. Kanári.

**Buses** from Od. F. de Coúlans to most villages.

**Ferry** daily to Çešme in 1 hour (May–October); weekly in winter.

The **harbour** is smaller than in antiquity, as landward building has encroached upon it. Close by is the **Plateía Vounáki**, the town centre, laid out on the W with gardens containing a statue of Kanaris, by Tombros, and vestiges of a 16C church. On the opposite side of the square is a former Turkish mosque (open mornings, except Monday), with some antiquities. To the N rises the ruined 14C **froúrio** which commanded the harbour. There survive a few towers, gates, and case-mates, some bearing the arms of the Giustianini. Within is the old Turkish quarter, established in the 16C over the ruins of Genoese houses, and the marble tomb of Kara Ali. There is a small **Byzantine Collection**.

The **gymnasion** dates from 1792. The **library** was founded in 1817 by Adhamantios Koraï (1748–1833), the great scholar, who bequeathed to it his own collections, including works on Egypt given to him by Napoleon. It was further enriched in 1962 by the collections of Dr Philip Argenti, well known in London as a scholar and philatelist. Above the library is a small ethnological and costume museum (open mornings daily, except Sunday) and the picture gallery of the Argenti family. There is a copy of Delacroix's painting of the massacre at Chios (1824, original in the Louvre).

The **Archaeological Museum** in Od. Porfirá (closed for long-term repairs in 1994) contains finds from excavations on the island, including Emborio, Fana and Ayio Gala (see below); also a large collection of inscriptions, including a letter to the people of Chios from Alexander the Great; architectural fragments from the Temple of Apollo of Fana.

Though swamped by modern building, scanty remains of walls and of a theatre may be traced on a hill to the N of the town. Outside the town (N) are the Tabákika behind which are remains of an Early Christian basilica, and an imposing Leper Hospital founded in the 16C. Another Early Christian basilica, Ay. Isidhóros, was built in the 4 or 5C and several times altered, finally with the addition of a minaret in the Ottoman period.

EXCURSION TO NEA MONI, 14km (8½ miles) (bus once a week; daily as far as Kariés then 8km mountain walk; or by taxi). The convent of **\*\*Néa Moní** was founded between 1042 and 1054 by the Emperor Constantine IX Monomachos after the discovery by a peasant of the miraculous ikon. The 11C church, which has a marble pavement, was badly damaged in the earthquake of 1881, when the main dome fell, but has been restored. The contemporary **\*mosaics** include a Dormition of the Virgin, Raising of Lazarus, a Deposition from the Cross, the only known mosaic example in Greece, etc. There is a small ecclesiastical museum.

TO ANÁVATOS 24km (15 miles) (bus once weekly, as for Néa Moní). Perched high on a rocky elevation to the NW of Néa Moní, this evocative Byzantine village now has a tiny population of old people. The grey, tower-like houses are well preserved and the church on the acropolis has been renovated. In 1822 hundreds of the inhabitants were massacred by the Turks.

TO KARDHAMILA, 28km (17½ miles) N (several buses daily). The road (signposted) leaves Plateía Vounáki, passing (right) a bronze **Memorial to the Unknown Sailor** by Apartis. 4km **Vrontádhos** (Hotels A, B, C), a town of 4429 inhabitants, straggles along the coast. On its N outskirts is the Stone of Homer, or Dhaskalópetra, an enormous block of dressed stone on a spur, probably a country shrine connected with the cult of Rhea or Cybele. 7km (right; on a promontory) Tomb of Yianni Psychares (1932), son-in-law of Renan. Beyond (10km) the little bay of **Milínka**, with a spring, the road zig-zags up, then descends again to the sea. View across to the five Oinoussai Is. (see below). 16km **Langádha**, a fishing village (simple restaurants). The road passes the Plain of Delphinion. In antiquity the city of *Delphinion* was a strong point with more than one harbour. The Athenians fortified it in 412. The site of the harbours was explored by the British School in 1954. 28km **Kardhámila** (Καρδάμηλα; Hotels B, C) is made up of the picturesque upper town (830 inhab.) and **Mármaro** (1335 inhab.), especially noted for the skill and daring of its sailors. Nagós and Vlikhádha, on the shore to the N, have beaches and tavernas (excellent fish and local fruit).

TO VOLISSOS, 40km (25 miles) NW (bus twice weekly). You leave Khóra by the Kardhámila road, but diverge left after a mile. The road climbs round Mt Aipos. 9km **memorial** to the fallen of 1912. 18.5km **Ayios Isídhoros**. The view opens out over the W coast to Psará. 40km **Volissós** was once the home of the Homeridai, a clan that claimed descent from Homer. The so-called Castle of Belisarius was probably built by the Genoese. Beyond Volissós the road continues W to the **Moní Ayías Markéllas**, named after a local 16C saint and, at the NW of the island, the site of **Ayio Gála**, excavated by the British School in 1938. There are two caves, the upper containing two Byzantine churches and remains of a Neolithic settlement, the lower more Neolithic finds.

TO PIRGI AND MESTA, 35km (22 miles; several buses daily). You leave by the inland southern road, passing a turning (right) for **Lithí**, a fishing village on the W coast, birthplace of the philanthropist, Andreas Singros. 8km To the right is **Váviloi**, a village with a church frescoed in 1963 by a Hawaiian artist. Beyond Vaviloi is **Sklaviá** (2km) with Byzantine and medieval remains, and, farther N, the **Panayía tis Krínis**, a church of 1287. 10km Small col, with two windmills. Ahead (left) on its hill can be seen **Naós tis Sikeliás**, a church of the 13C with characteristic tile ornament. 20km **Armólia**, with turning (left) for Kalamotí (see below). Soon after is a kastro on a hill (right). 23.5km Road (left) to Emborió (5km; see below). 25km **Pirgí** (Πυργί), a medieval fortress **\*town** of 1164 inhabitants, is the most interesting and attractive place on Khios, with churches and houses having curious sgraffito decoration. Good examples surround the main square, off one side of which is the tiny church of **Ayioi Apóstoloi**, with 12C frescoes. The narrow streets have many round-roofed houses, and arches span the streets as a protection against earthquakes. Today Pirgí is the main mastic town. 31.5km Olímboi; turning (left) for Kato Fana (see below). 35.5km Mestá, formerly the principal mastic centre, has ramparts and tortuous streets. The church of Palaiós Taxiárkhis has recently revealed painting of 1503.

At **Emborió** on a promontory of the SE coast beyond Pirgi, an Early Bronze Age settlement was unearthed near and at sea-level. Four phases of occupation were identified, the last with a fire destruction. It has been equated with *Leukonion*, a rival to Troy. The town survived the fire and in the Middle and Late Bronze Ages spread up the hill, subsequently crowned by a late-Roman fortress which was ruined c AD 660. A Greek city of the 8–6C BC was discovered on the higher hill (Profitis Ilias), N of the harbour. Traces of 50 houses were revealed, as well as a megaron and a temple of Athena within a walled circuit. Nearer the harbour an Archaic temple (6C) was discovered, replaced in the 5C by a Classical building; both were used in the 6C AD as quarries for the building of a Christian basilica. The only visible remains are of the megaron and Temple of Athena on Profitis Ilias (a steep climb), and an Early Christian baptistery S of the harbour. A votive deposit yielded a kylix signed by the potter Nikesermos, now in the Khios museum. The black pebble beach has good bathing. Underwater exploration brought to light numerous amphorae not only of Chian origin but also from Attica, Rhodes, Kos, and Thasos, an indication of the extent and importance of the wine trade to Chios.

At **Káto Faná** some ruins of a Temple of Apollo (late 6C) mark the site of ancient *Phanai*, which existed as early as the 9C. Both this site and Emborió were excavated by the British School in 1951–54.

You can return to Khóra by branching right at Armólia through **Kalamóti**, then continuing N along the road closer to the coast. The road passed **Ayios Mínas** (c 1590), where in 1822 the Turks massacred 3000 Chiots (ossuary), then crosses the Kambos plain, a rich citrus-growing area, with (right) **Kondári**, where the liberators disembarked in 1912. The **Kámbos** region is worth visiting, with its old Genoese houses, one of which, a beautiful mansion in gardens, has become a taverna.

Off the NE coast of Khios, in the strait separating it from Asia Minor, are the five small **Oinoussai Islands** (daily boat from Khóra; Hotel D; rooms; post office; good bathing). The inhabitants (636) are renowned sailors and fishermen and have produced some leading shipowners. The Navtikó Gymnásio is the only nautical boarding school of Greece. In the bay of Çeşme in 1770 a Russian squadron destroyed a huge Turkish fleet.

About 19km W of the NW coast of Khios lies the island of **Psará** (Ψαρά; Hotel A; rooms), whose inhabitants won renown in the war of Greek Independence. It is reached by caique three times weekly from Volissós and three times from Khíos town. Rocky and mountainous it has an area of 41.5 sq. km and a population of 438, all in one town. At **Arkhontikí** is a Mycenaean cemetery and settlement of the 14–13C BC. The monastery of the **Panayía** is 10km N of the main village.

After the fall of Constantinople in 1453 the islanders fled to Khios, where some of their descendants returned to mingle with refugees from Euboea and Thessaly. In the Russo-Turkish war Psarian ships harried the Turks. The Psarians escaped reprisals because the Turkish governor was prevented from landing by bad weather, and after the Treaty of Kutchuk Kainardji achieved a certain protection and prosperity by sailing under the Russian flag. Psara was the birthplace of Konstantinos Kanaris (1785–1877) and many other noted sailors. In the war that began in 1821, Psara (with Hydra and Spetsai) was among the first to revolt, Psara in particular causing the Turks great annoyance. In 1823 the Psarians raided the coast of Asia Minor. In revenge the Turks under Hosref Pasha attacked the island from Mytilene in June 1824. Influx of refugees from Chios, Lesbos, and Smyrna had swollen the population to 20,000. The Turks silenced the batteries of Kanalos on the N side of the island, and stormed the island with 14,000 Janissaries. The islanders blew up their own powder magazines at Ftelia and Palaiokastro, and only 3000 souls escaped the subsequent massacre by the Turks. Ruined houses, a simple white memorial (1956), and six famous lines of Solomos bear witness to the event. The refugees fled to Monemvasia and later founded Néa Psará in Euboea. In 1844 Psara was given special electoral privileges, but the island has never recovered.

# C. Lésvos

**Approaches**. **By Air**: from Athens 3–4 times daily in 45 minutes; to Khíos twice weekly; to Límnos three times weekly; to Thessaloníki 5–6 times weekly.

**Ferries** from Piraeus daily overnight via Khíos; 1–2 weekly direct. Occasional connections with Límnos, Kaválla and Thessaloníki to the N, and Sámos and Rhodes to the S.

**Caique** service daily in summer round the island; occasionally from Mólivos, via Mitilíni, to Ayvalik on the Turkish mainland (c 56km to Pergamon).

**LÉSVOS** (Λέσβος, or **Lésbos**; more generally called **Mitilíni** after its capital), ancient *Mytilene*, is after Crete and Euboea the largest of the Aegean islands, 70km long, up to 45km wide, and 1632 sq. km. in area. It lies close to Asia Minor, the NE coast facing the Gulf of Edremit (Adramyti), and is 301km from Athens. To the N is Límnos and to the S Khios. Oval in shape, Lesvos is deeply indented by two arms of the sea: the Gulf of Kalloni in the S and the Gulf of Yera in the SE. The interior is mountainous, fertile with dense olive plantations in the E, bare in the W, where much of its former vegetation has been remarkably petrified. The climate is temperate, with mild winters and cool summers, especially at Molivos, where the temperature tends to drop sharply at night; in Mitilini it is usually warmer and sometimes humid. The island is subject to earthquakes and there are numerous hot springs. The population (87,151 inhab.) is mainly occupied in producing the olives and olive oil for which the island has long been celebrated; there are over 100 refineries. The vineyards also are productive though less famed than they were in antiquity. The chief manufacture is soap; there are also tanneries and textile mills, and in the W tobacco is cultivated. The roads were built during the Turkish occupation by an English engineer. The island's fauna include the rare star shrew, called locally 'blind mice', and a species of salamander. Notable also are the herds of horses that graze round the Gulf of Kalloni, connected perhaps with the ancient horse-breeding traditions of the Troad. Though there is little of great archaeological importance, the cultural associations, both ancient and modern, and beautiful scenery and beaches of the island are increasingly attracting visitors.

**History**. Its geographical situation and many harbours made *Lesbos* a centre for trade and communications from the earliest times and it is only recently that the division between Greece and Turkey has, by severing connections with Asia Minor, frustrated its natural role as an intermediary between the mainland and the Aegean. Prehistoric finds indicating occupation from c 3300 BC until the end of the Mycenaean period relate closely to those at ancient Troy. According to Homer, Lesbos, siding with Troy, was invaded by both Achilles and Odysseus. The inhabitants were probably Pelasgian, but in the 10C BC the island and the mainland opposite were colonised by Aeolians under the leadership of the Penthelides, the last of whom was murdered in 659 BC. A struggle developed between Methymna and Mytilene for the leadership of the island, and although Mytilene won and has remained the capital, a tradition of independent resistance was fostered in the W part of the island, which was to recur at critical moments. Lesbos was governed oligarchically with increasing chaos until Pittacus, one of the Seven Sages (589–579), calmed the island and as Aesymnetes (dictator) induced this period of greatest prosperity and cultural importance. A large fleet and wide mercantile interests (especially in Egypt) were combined with a high standard of education and a comparative freedom for women, two traditions still noticeable today. Terpander, the father of Greek music, and Arion, who invented dithyrambic poetry, had already made Lesbos famous in the 7C, but it was with Alcaeus and Sappho, both aristocrats and enemies of Pittacus, that the island reached its cultural climax. In 527 Lesbos fell under Persian domination and was not freed until 479, when it joined the Athenian League.

In 428 soon after the Peloponnesian War started, Mytilene tried to break away with Spartan help, but the plan was betrayed by Methymna to Athens. The Mytileneans were severely punished (Thuc. III, 36–50). This was the dramatic occasion when a second galley with a reprieve was sent after the first had left with orders for wholesale massacre, and arrived in time. In 405 Lesbos fell to the Spartans and thereafter changed hands frequently, being ruled by Persia, Macedonia, and the Ptolemies until Mithridates occupied it (in 88–79 BC) only to be ousted by the Romans. According to Suetonius, Julius Caesar 'won his spurs' during the Roman storming of Mytilene. It was much favoured by Pompey. St Paul, on his way back to Jerusalem from Greece (c AD 52), spent a night at Mytilene before passing by Chios and Samos. By the 5C Lesbos had many fine basilicas.

As a Byzantine dominion, the island was used as a place of exile, notably for the Empress Irene in 809. It suffered Saracen invasions in 821, 881, and 1055, which prompted the inhabitants to leave the coast for the mountains. In 1085 it fell to Tzachas, the Seljuk conqueror of Izmir, although Alexius Comnenus retook the island which remained under Byzantine control until 1128, when it passed for a time to the Venetians. In 1204 Lesbos became part of the Latin empire, but fell to the Greeks of Nicaea in 1247. At the end of the 13C it was devastated by Catalan mercenaries and in 1334 Dom. Cataneo made an attempt on it. In 1354 it was given to Francesco Gattelusio, a Genoese adventurer who had helped John Paleologus regain the Byzantine throne, as a dowry for John's sister Maria, who married Francesco; the island then enjoyed a century's untroubled prosperity under the Gattelusi who established an important trading principality in the N Aegean. Lesbos fell to the Turks in 1462 and, despite attempts to free it by Orsano Giustiniano in 1464, by Pesaro in 1499, and by a Franco-Rhodian fleet in 1501, remained under Turkish domination till 1912, though enjoying considerable privileges and prosperity in the 19C (despite a revolt in 1821). Large numbers of refugees from Asia Minor were absorbed after 1912. In 1941–44 the island was occupied by German forces.

The chief town, near the SE corner of the island, is **Mitilíni** (Μυτιλήνη), capital of the nome of Lesvos, which includes the islands of Limnos and Ayios Evstratios. It is the seat of a metropolitan. The modern town (23,971 inhab.) is spread over the slopes overlooking the harbour and the isthmus that joins to the mainland the wooded promontory on which the kastro stands. Still retaining much of its Levantine flavour, Mitilíni is a bustling entrepôt port but without particular interest.

**Airport**, 10km S of the town. **Terminal**, Kavétsou 44.

**Hotels**, A, B, C, F/A.

**Post Office** W of quay.

**Village Buses** from Od. Venizélou, near S quay.

In antiquity the castle hill, with the Classical town, was separated from the mainland by a channel joining the N and S ports. Later the city overflowed from the island and the channel was crossed by marble bridges (mentioned by Longus in *Daphnis and*

*Chloë*): one of these was recently found opposite the Yeni Tzami. According to Vitruvius the new town was built on the Hippodamian (grid) plan, a fact he deplored since the streets caught the full blast of the N and S winds. Recent archaeological work in the town has confirmed this. Mytilene was a favourite place with the Julio-Claudian emperors and more dedications to them have been found than in any other Greek imperial city.

The ancient S port has become the main **harbour** with the boat agencies along the N and E quay, the hotels, restaurants, cafés, and town theatre on the W quay. The main shopping street or Agora runs parallel behind to the N harbour. An old harbour master's office has been turned into a **folk museum** at the N end. By the Italianate church of Ayios Therapón is a fine new **Byzantine Museum** housing a good collection of well displayed ikons.

There is a new archaeological museum under construction on the road up to the castle. Beyond the old **museum** (recently refurbished and with new displays) at the foot of the pines planted in the First World War is an EOT beach. A road runs round the edge of the peninsula to the N harbour whose ancient remains are visible under water. In this **Epáno Skála** area are visible here and there through salvage excavations various ancient buildings, including a fine archaic apsidal structure behind the mental hospital and some Roman houses. Between Odd. **Nikomidhías** and **Dhikilí** a large site (later an Ottoman cemetery) contains sections of the Classical city wall in fine polygonal masonry, and the remains of a Roman peristyle building (possibly a tavern/brothel) above a sequence of earlier buildings.

The **kastro**, which has a fine view over the town and across to Turkey, was constructed (according to a Latin inscription above the W gate) by the Gattelusi in 1374 on the site of a Byzantine castle. The Turks added towers for artillery and outer walls and a dry moat, as well as fortifications running down to the N harbour. They also built a medresse, or theological college, which is still well preserved inside the upper bailey and numerous other structures, now in ruins, inside the castle. A 19C mosque replaced a Byzantine church, probably the burial chapel of the Gattilusi. Excavations in the upper bailey since 1985 have revealed, beneath later Turkish houses, remains of a sanctuary of Demeter or **Thesmophorion**—altars and votive pits, ritual dining rooms and architectural elements of an Archaic temple of mixed Doric and Ionic style—also sacrifical debris, numerous votive figurines and a curse tablet mentioning Demeter.

The main entrance is on the S side through an inner and outer gate, where you pass through the upper bailey to the Gattilusi innermost stronghold, a keep-like arrangement of high walls and massive towers originally surrounded by a dry ditch. Built into the gate tower are the arms of the Gattilusi with the Paleologue eagle, scales and the monogram of the imperial family (other such heraldic devices are to be seen throughout the castle) as well as reused Roman funerary reliefs of gladiators and wild beast fighters. In the SE corner of the upper bailey are extensive crypts.

The ancient **theatre** lies on the side of a hill at the W edge of town amid pine trees (clearly visible some 2km from the kastro). Excavations at various times this century have revealed the orchestra, stage and some seating as well as clearing the collapsed vomitoria. Some restoration in 1968 stabilised the theatre in its Roman form, when it had been converted for gladiatorial combat and wild beast fights by building a high wall around the orchestra. The Roman general Pompey is said to have used the theatre at Mytilene as his model for the first stone-built theatre in Rome in 55 BC although the two structures are not alike.

To the N of the theatre above Ayía Kyriakí cemetery are remains of the city **walls** in polygonal masonry of the 5C BC. These ran from the N breakwater of the N port (Maloeis) to the S end of the S port, encompassing all the theatre hill. Lower down was the site of a late-Roman **villa**, whence came the Khorafa mosaics (4C), depicting scenes from the comedies of Menander.

To the S of Mitilíni a road runs along the coastal plain. At (4km) **Vareiá**, inland of which at **Akrotíri** (1.5km), are a museum of paintings by Theophilos and the Teriade Gallery of Modern Art. Just to the S of (6km) **Neápolis** (Hotels B, C) are remains of the Early Christian basilica of Argala. Beyond the airport and (10km) **Krátigos** the road continues round Cape Argilios at the SE corner of the island. At 20km a lane branches left to Cape Ermouyenis (1km) at the entrance to the gulf of Yéra (chapel, café, and beach); keeping right, you reach (22km) the site of the Early Christian basilica of Loutrá with a mosaic. 25km **Loutrá** is an old thermal station. From here a road returns to Mitilíni (8.5km) over a saddle of Mt Amali, affording superb views both E and W, or (if you keep left) another descends to Skála Loutrón and Koundhouroudhiá on an inlet of the gulf of Yera, across which a regular passenger ferry plies to Pérama (see below). For the N outskirts of Mitilíni, see below.

TO YERA AND PLOMARI, 41km (25½ miles; several buses daily). The island's main road runs W from Mitilíni and crosses a low ridge. Soon after reaching the shore of the Gulf of Yera it passes the hot springs of (9km) **Thérmai Yéras** (below the road, left). About 1.5km farther on Pelasgic walls can be found on a steep hill. At 12km you turn off to the left through a region thickly populated in antiquity. Soon after a river bridge and before the big olive refinery at (14km) **Dípi** (Ντίπι) are some remains of an ancient harbour (partly submerged). Near (15km) **Káto Trítos** (1km right) are ruins of ancient houses. The road crosses a ridge and descends to (23km) **Palaió-kipos**, with an underground church (Taxiárkhon). From (25km) **Pappádhos** a road leads (right; 1.5km) to **Mesagró** and the remains of the medieval Castle of Yera. At the far end of Pappadhos are turnings to Pérama (1.5km) and to Skópelos (1km right).

**Pérama**, with a tannery and oil refineries, stands on the Gulf of Yera, near the site of ancient *Hiera*, said by Pliny to have been destroyed by earthquake. **Skópelos** (1861 inhab.) has catacombs (Lagoúmis tis Ayías Magdhalínis) and a Turkish fountain.

The road winds across the E shoulder of Mt Olympos, then descends through a narrow valley to Ayios Isidhoros on the shore. 41km **Plomári** (Πλωμάρι; Hotels B, C, D), a centre (3450 inhab.) created as *Bilmar* in the 19C when the inland villagers returned to the S coast, is now the second largest town of the island, famed for its ouzo, with a small port. From here a road leads N to **Megalokhóri** (8.5km) and through chestnut forests round the slopes of Olympos to Ayiassós (see below).

TO AYIASSOS AND POLIKHNITOS, 45km (28 miles; 2–3 buses daily). You follow the main road W (see above), pass the turn to Plomári, then after another mile turn left. Just beyond (15km) **Keramía**, turning (left; 1.5km) for **Ippeio**, with remains of ancient houses. 22km Fork left for Ayiassós (4km).

**Ayiassós** (Αγιασός; Hotel B), a shaded and well-watered hill-town of 2890 inhabitants, stands on a slope under Mt Olympos (966m). It is noted for weaving and pottery. The Byzantine monastery of the **Koimísisis Theotó-kou** has a good collection of ikons and a big festival on 14–15 August. On **Kastélli**, a pine-clad hill to the NW, are the walls of a medieval castle. The remains of *Penthile*, 4km S on the Plomári road, now ploughed out, supposedly date from the Aeolic migration.

The major road continues W through beautiful pine woods with views of Mt Olympos to (40km) **Vasiliká**, supposed place of exile of the Empress Irene. 43km **Lisvóri** has thermal springs. 45km **Polikhnítos** (Πολυχνίτος;

Hotel E), a little town (3008 inhab.) with hot saline springs. A road goes through the town W to **Skála Polikhnítou** and the salt flats on the Gulf of Kalloni; another road (left) goes S to **Vríssa** (5km; Hotel E), with a Genoese tower nearby, and down to **Vaterá** (8km; Hotels C), a long beach with cafés ending to the W in Cape Phokas, site of a Temple of Dionysos and probably of the ancient city of *Brisa*, earlier known as *Lyrnessos*.

FROM MITILINI TO MANDAMADHOS (bus daily) (and Mólivos, see below), 37.5km (23 miles). Coast and inland roads. Taking the road NW, at (4km) **Koúrtzes** the hot baths (Thermakiás) date from Roman times. About 1km farther on a road branches (left) to **Mória** (1.5km), a village W of which stand several impressive arches of a Roman aqueduct that brought water to Mytilene. Also near the village is a large Roman marble quarry, now being studied. 8km **Pámfilla**. You cross the base of a small promontory. 10km **Pírgoi Thermís**, 17C Turkish towers, just beyond which a track leads (left) to the **Panayía Tourlotí**, a Byzantine church of the 15C or earlier. 12.5km **Loutrá Thermís** (Hotel B on the sea). You arrive opposite the **Sarlitza Hotel** (E), immediately left of the entrance to which are the baths. The therapeutic qualities of the hot saline and chalybeate springs (49°C) were recommended by Claudius Galen. By the modern spring is the site of an ancient temple to Artemis and an adjoining complex of baths.

The prehistoric site of *Thermi*, to the E of the road, was excavated in 1929–33 by the British School under Miss Winifred Lamb. It was first occupied at the beginning of the Bronze Age (c 2750 BC) evidently by colonists from the Troad since there is a close resemblance between the black pottery found here and that of Troy I. Cycladic influences then began to outweigh those from Asia Minor and c 2000 BC the city was depopulated, despite the construction of considerable fortifications. The city was reoccupied c 1400 until its destruction by fire some 200 years later (by Greek armies in the Trojan War?). There is little to see.

Beyond (16.5km) **Mistegná** (Hotels B, C), where are traces of ancient *Aigeiros*, a by-road ascends (left) to **Néai Kidhoníai** with a ruined medieval castle. 25km **Vatíka** (cafés) has a good beach. 32km **Aspropótamos** lies to the right of the road, on the Bay of Makriyialos. You turn inland to (37km) **Mandamádhos**, a village (1245 inhab.) amid low hills, where the church of the Taxiárkhon, 800m N, possesses a remarkable black ikon of St Michael, carved in wood and smelling of spring flowers. At a festival soon after Easter bulls are sacrificed and eaten, a rite of likely pagan origin (see below).

The road continues to (43km) **Kápi**, where it divides to pass either side of Mt Lepedimnos (969m). To the S a passable road leads via (52km) **Ipsilométopo**, where (30 minutes S) an Early Christian basilica of c 550, with columns, mosaic, and tombs, was excavated in 1925 (Greek Archaeological Service), to (55.5km) **Stípsi** (Στύψη) and then joins the main Kalloni–Petra road (see below). On the N road is (45km) **Klió**, where a track leads down to the Gulf of Tsonia (good beach; cafés); on a wooded hill are remains of a fort, perhaps the historic castle of **Ayios Theódhoros**, where Giustiniano encountered the Turks in 1464. A road continues W of **Klió** to (49km) **Sikamiá**, the beautiful little port of which (4km right) is known locally as 'Little Egypt' because of its warmth in winter. 52km **Argennós**. 62km **Mólivos** (see below).

FROM MITILINI TO KALLONI AND MOLIVOS, 62km (38½ miles), by the main road (4 buses daily). To the Plomári and Ayiassós turns, see above. Keeping to the right you cross pine-wooded hills. 30km Kakadhélli bridge, N of which, at a locality called **Mésa**, are remains of an Ionic pseudo-dipteral temple of Aphrodite (8 by 14 columns). You reach the **Gulf of Kalloni** at (33km) the turning (left; 3km) for ancient *Pyrra*, or Pyrrha, set in a little valley. The remains of an earlier Pyrra (destroyed by earthquake c 231 BC) are believed to have been located some 8km SW beneath the gulf. Near the first site has been excavated the Early Christian basilica of 'Akhladeris'. The by-road continues to **Vasiliká** on the Ayiassos–Polikhnitos road. The main Kalloní road now skirts salt-flats. 36km Turning (right) to Ayía Paraskeví.

About 1km up this turning some vestiges of ancient *Gerna* are marked by a chapel. 3km **Ayía Paraskeví**, a large village (2457 inhab.) is noted for its festival of St Charalambos soon after Easter. A bull sacrifice is followed by an equestrian parade and races.

There are many attractive excursions in the district. About 45 minutes E is the Early Christian basilica of **Khalinádhos**, built in the 6C on the Syriac plan; columns and capitals have been restored to place and other columns have been observed in a chapel on the hill of Tsikniá overlooking the Kalloní–Mólivos road. About the same distance NW on the road to Stípsi is the **packhorse bridge**, built by the Gattilusi, with a fine arch across the two affluents of the Tsiknias; 5km W of Ayía Paraskeví on a track which leads to the main Kalloni–Petra road, near **Klopédhi**, ruins of two archaic temples, one to Apollo Napaios, yielded numerous Aeolic capitals of the 6C BC now in the Archaeological Museum at Mitilíni.

You cross the Tsikniás. 39.5km **Arísvi**; vestiges of ancient *Arisbe*, ruined by earthquake in 321 BC, can be reached by track to the right; on its acropolis are remains of the Byzantine castle of Kalloní, rebuilt by the Turks but abandoned in 1757. 40km **Kalloní** (Καλλονή; Hotels B, C; F/A; 1604 inhab.) stands at an important crossroads. Its **skála**, 2km S on the gulf, is the centre of the sardine-fishing and a good red wine is also locally produced.

You turn N, leaving the Antissa road (see below), and shortly pass the track to (15 minutes, left) the Byzantine **Moní Myrsiniótissas**, with the tomb of Bishop Ignatius (d. 1568); the nuns do embroidery. You climb out of the Plain of Kalloní, meet at 49km the road from Stípsi (see above) and, topping a rise, descend to **Pétra** (Hotels B, C) on the NW coast. It is notable for the church of the **Panayía Glykofiloússa** (1747) built on top of a high rock near the fine beach. The 16C church of **Ayios Nikólaos** is frescoed; festival 15 August. The road meets the shore at **Khiliopigádha**, supposedly the landfall of Achilles.

62km **Mólivos** (Hotels A, B, C; tourist office by the bus stop) has officially resumed its ancient name *Methymna* (Μέθυμνα), pronounced Míthimna, a word of pre-Greek derivation. Picturesque tower-houses face S over a small fishing harbour and a long beach. On a steep hill above the maze of narrow stepped streets, a Genoese **castle** of the Gattilusi dominates the town and has a fine view N across the strait to Cape Baba in Turkey. Remains of polygonal walls (8C BC), of an Archaic temple, and of a Roman aqueduct are visible.

*Methymna*, the second city of Lesbos, was the birthplace of the poet Arion (fl. 625 BC) and the historian Hellanicus (c 496–411 BC). The celebrated Lesbian vine grew in the neighbourhood. The city refused to join the great Lesbian revolt (428 BC); in 406 it was sacked by the Spartans.

Along the coast, 3km E, is **Eftaloús**, with radioactive springs and good bathing. From this his native village Kleanthes Michaelides, the 19C short-story writer who died in Hull, took his pen name Argyris Eftaliotis.

THE W PART OF THE ISLAND (2–3 buses daily to Antissa, Sígri, Eressós) is best approached from Kalloni (see above). Bear left outside Kalloní. 5km The monastery of **Leimónos** (left), built in 1523 by St Ignatius, metropolitan of Methymna, has a museum and library with 450 MSS, including an 8C evangelistery; festival 14 October. On 'Tyrannídha' hill (690m), to the right of the road, took place the Turkish last stand in 1912 (memorial). The terrain is rough and volcanic. Climbing there are fine retrospective views over the Gulf of Kalloni and its salt pans. 9km Col. The road descends above the little plain of **Fília**. The road passes just above (16km) **Skalokhóri** (religious festival on 23 August). From here a track leads down to the coast near ancient Antissa (see below). Soon after the NW coast comes into view. 25km **Vadhoússa**. 30km (right; just below the road) the Byzantine **Perivóli** monastery (1590, restored 1962) has good frescoes of the Second Coming. 32km Turning to **Gavathá** (right) with a fine beach (cafés). 34km **Andissa** (1068 inhab.; Hotel E).

The remains of ancient *Antissa* (see above) lie on the coast near a ruined Genoese castle. The ancient acropolis was excavated by the British School in 1931; its life extended from the Bronze Age until the Romans destroyed it for harbouring the Macedonian admiral Antinora in 168 BC.

Beyond modern Antissa the road divides. The left branch turns S to Eressós (see below) and Skála Eressoú. The right branch continues W, passing (40km) a stepped pathway (left) up to the Ipsilon monastery on Mt Ordimnos (view). Just beyond is a sign (left) to the Petrified Forest (see below). 52km **Sígri** (Σίγρι; Hotel B; Village G.H.), lies at the W end of the island. The red-roofed village has a small Turkish castle of 1757 on a low rocky promontory and a fine beach. The region of Sigri is famous for the **petrified forest** (Απολιθομένο Δάσος), well seen on the track that leads SE to Eressós. This unique phenomenon was caused by various trees (mainly conifers and sequoia) being buried in volcanic ash (when is not certain) and then petrified by the action of hot waters containing silicic acid and iron pyrites.

49km **Eressós** (Ερεσός; Hotels B, C, E), known to the Turks as *Herse*, has 1247 inhabitants and a local archaeological **museum** with sculpture and mosaics. The modern inhabitants, as in many other villages, migrate down to the coastal plain in summer, where (3km S) **Skála Eressoú** (Hotel B) occupies the site of ancient *Eressos*, birthplace of Sappho and of the philosopher Theophrastos (d. 287 BC). The village lies at the E end of a long beach underneath a rocky acropolis (Vígla) on the E side of which are to be seen the remains of a Byzantine-Genoese castle, some Roman cisterns, and a fine example of Archaic polygonal walling. In the village are the ruins of a large 5C basilica of St Andrew with mosaics; along the beach by the mouth of the Khalandras, are remains of a similar basilica of Aphendélli (also 5C) in the Syriac style.

To the SE of Lesvos, near the Asiatic shore, are the three islets of **Arginusae**, off which in 406 BC the Athenians won a naval victory over the Lacedaemonians. The Spartan admiral Kallikratidas was killed and 70 of his ships sunk or captured. The Athenians lost 25 ships and were prevented by the weather from rescuing the crews. For this omission eight of the Athenian commanders in the battle were recalled to Athens, tried, and six of them executed. This drastic action was a major factor in the Athenian annihilation at Aegospotami.

# IX THE DODECANESE
## (Dhodhekánisa)

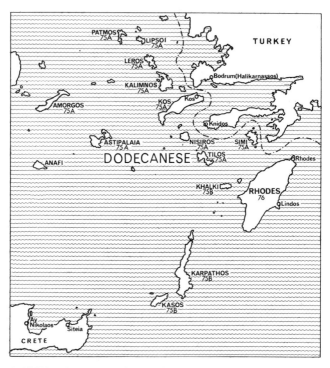

The **DODECANESE** (Δωδεκάνησα; 'Twelve Islands') are politically a group of islands, lying in the SE Aegean, off the coast of Asia Minor, of which they are geographically a part. Their name is a misnomer, for 14 islands have independent local government status and a few of their dependent islets are inhabited. The nome is divided into four eparchies: Kalymnos, including Patmos, Lipsos, Leros, and Astypalaia; Karpathos, including Kasos; Kos, including Nisiros; Rhodes, including Telos, Syme, Chalki, and Megisti, the last some way E of Rhodes. They are strictly the SE continuation of the Eastern Sporades, and are sometimes rather confusingly called Southern Sporades. Their total population is 163,476.

The rather misleading term Dodecanese is relatively recent. It was adopted in 1908, when 12 'privileged' islands of the Eastern Aegean, excluding Rhodes, Kos, and Lipsos, but including an intruder, Ikaria (see Rte 74A), united in protest against the deprivation by Turkey of the special privileges that they had enjoyed since the 16C under Suleiman the Magnificent (1495–1566). The term has since come to include the island of Rhodes and other islands not on the list of 1908: indeed Rhodes is now regarded as the chief of the Dodecanese and its city is their capital.

During the Italo-Turkish war of 1911–12 the islands were seized by Italy and were retained by her as a pledge for the fulfilment of the first Treaty of Lausanne (1912). After the First World War the Treaty of Sévres (1920) gave the islands to Italy but, by an agreement between Italy and Greece, they were all to be passed on to Greece. This agreement was repudiated by Italy after the disastrous Greek campaign of 1922. The second Treaty of Lausanne (1923) gave the Dodecanese to Italy. In 1944–45 the islands were occupied as opportunity occurred and put under British Military Administration. On 7 March 1947 they were officially united to Greece. By far the largest of the islands is Rhodes.

**Approaches. By Air** from Athens to *Rhodes*, 3–5 times daily in 55 minutes; also in summer from Iráklion daily. To Kos twice daily in 50 minutes. To Léros 5–7 weekly in 55 minutes. To Astipália twice weekly in 65 minutes. In addition, Kos is connected with Rhodes and Rhodes with Thessaloníki, Míkonos, Síros, Thíra, Kásos, Kárpathos, Kastellórizo and Sitía (Crete). Some services are summer only. Rhodes and Kos are also served in summer by direct flights (mainly charter) from some European countries. For other connections,see under Rhodes and Kos.

**By Sea**. From Piraeus the departure is usually made in the afternoon or early evening, and the voyage takes 14–27 hours according to route and ports of call. The fastest boats (3-4 weekly) go direct to Rhodes. There are c 10–20 services weekly. Apart from the direct boat, they may be divided into those taking the long S route (Rte 75B), c. 2–6 times weekly, calling at some of Síros, Míkonos, Páros, Náxos, Mílos, Ios, Folégandros, Thíra, Ayios Nikólaos and Sitía in Crete, Kásos, Kárpathos, and Khálki; and those which take the N route (Rte 75A), c 5–9 times weekly. These call sometimes in the Cyclades, often at Pátmos, then at Léros, Kálimnos, and Kos (also, infrequently, at Nísiros, Tílos, and Simi); in addition sometimes at Amorgós and Astipálaia. Most boats are car ferries. Routes and frequencies vary slightly according to season and from year to year. There are some services from Rafína via Andros, Tínos and Míkonos.

From Thessaloníki there is a weekly service via the Eastern Sporades and Ikaría to Pátmos, Léros, Kálimnos, Kos, and Rhodes and return.

A local vessel based on Kálimnos connects (once or twice weekly) all Dodecanese and Sámos in two circuits, the more southerly as far as Kastellórizo. There are other local caique services (some summer only) connecting the smaller islands with each other and/or with the nearer of the two main islands, Kos and Rhodes. There are some hydrofoils in summer, based on Kos and Rhodes with services as far N as Sámos, S as Khálki; also to Turkey. Kastellórizo, see Rte 76.

There are connections from Rhodes and Kos to Turkey (Bodrum and Marmaris, respectively; most frequent in summer). Rhodes is on routes to Cyprus and the East Mediterranean and to Egypt.

The Dodecanese enjoy special, though no longer very valuable, exemptions from customs duties and returning visitors must clear customs before leaving even for destinations in Greece.

A recent collection of articles about archaeological research in this area is S. Dietz and I. Papachristodoulou, *Archaeology in the Dodecanese*, 1988, Copenhagen, National Museum of Denmark, Department of Near Eastern and Classical Antiquities. A volume on Rhodes and the Dodecanese in the Blue Guide series is in preparation.

# 75

# From Piraeus to Rhodes (Rhódhos)

## A. The Northern route

**Ferries** from Piraeus, see above; also some other local services, including hydrofoils, based on Kálimnos, Kos and Rhodes.

An alternative route (from Rafína), via the Cyclades, may call at Páros, Míkonos and Amorgós.

**AMORGÓS** (Αμοργός), the most easterly of the Cyclades (but in some ways more closely linked with the Dodecanese) and part of the eparchy of Naxos, is a narrow island, 18km long from SW to NE, with 1632 inhabitants. It has three mountain peaks: Krikelas (780m) in the NE, Profitis Ilias (735m) in the centre, and Korax (576m) in the SW. Krikelas lost its forest in 1835 in a fire that lasted three weeks. The cliffs on the S coast are scenically magnificent. In antiquity there were three cities, *Aigiale*, *Minoa*, and *Arkesine*, all situated on the N coast. Amorgos was the home of Semonides (fl. 664 BC), who came here from Samos. The local waters were the scene of the decisive defeat of the Athenian fleet in the Lamian War, from which Athenian naval power never recovered.

The main landing-place (some boats also call at **Aiyiáli**) is **Katápola** (Hotels C; Rooms), on the W coast, about the middle of the island. On the hill above are the considerable remains of *Minoa*, including Hellenistic fortifications, a gymnasium, a stadium, and a temple of Apollo, excavated by the French School in 1888. Renewed excavations in the last few years (Prof. L. Marangou) have considerably added to knowledge of the site, discoveries including a Hellenistic distyle temple, a probable Serapeion with crypt, and the likely site of the theatre and/or bouleuterion (the last three all mentioned in inscriptions); also, on the summit, a Geometric enclosure wall, cult building and traces of prehistoric occupation. A road (4km; bus) leads to **Amorgós** (361m), or **Khóra** (Rooms), the pleasant little capital, with a small but attractively housed collection of antiquities. About ½ hour NE of Khora, at the base of a precipitous rock, is the celebrated **Khozoviótissa**, or Convent of the Presentation of the Virgin, founded by the Emperor Alexis Comnenus. It contains an ikon of the Virgin 'miraculously' conveyed hither from Cyprus.

About 3 hours SW of Khora (or occasional bus) is the hamlet of **Vroútsi** from which a path leads in 1 hour to the ruins of ancient *Arkesine* at **Kastrí** on the N coast. Further S at **Ayía Triádha**, near modern **Arkesíni**, is a well-preserved Hellenic tower. The rough road continues S to the plain of **Kolofána**. At **Markianí**, almost due S of Kastri but near the opposite coast, is a recently excavated fortified early Cycladic settlement. N from Khóra, a path (also occasional minibus by rough road; or boat from Katápola) reaches **Aigiáli** (94 inhab.; Hotels B, C), above which three attractive villages ring the coastal plain. Nearby the church of **Exokhorianí** incorporates a temple of Athena. Near here was found in 1906 a tablet on which were inscribed 134 verses relating to the laws of Amorgós (now in the Epigraphical Museum in Athens). At the NE extremity of Amorgós are the scanty ruins of ancient *Aegiale*, most easily visited by boat. The tombs excavated here have yielded pottery and other objects dating from the Early Cycladic period.

**ASTIPÁLAIA** (Αστυπάλαια; the accent is impartially placed on any of the last three syllables, and in local dialect the name becomes **Astropaliá**), the westernmost of the Dodecanese, is said to be the only Aegean island without snakes. It lies 40km SE of Amorgos and about the same distance W of Kos. There is a small **airport** with two flights a week to/from Athens in c 65 minutes. By the Venetians in the Middle Ages and again during the later Italian occupation it was called *Stampália*. The island consists of two peninsulas connected by a long slender isthmus and has a length of 18km. The coastline is much indented and has high cliffs. The hilly interior rises to 506m on the W peninsula and to 335m on the E. The traditional women's costumes are varied and elaborate. The long Venetian occupation has left its mark on the dialect and outlook of the inhabitants, who number 1073.

**History**. The island, which had some importance in antiquity, was called Ichthyoessa from its abundance of fish and the 'Table of the Gods' because of its flowers and its fertility—today not much in evidence. An interesting though unproven theory (M. Ovenden) sets the naming of the constellations here in the Early Bronze Age. There are Mycenaean remains. In later times the island received colonists from Epidauros. The most colourful Astipalaian was the strong-man Kleomedes, who killed his opponent Ikkos of Epidauros in a boxing match during the 71st Olympiad and was disqualified. He returned mad with rage and grief to Astipalaia and pulled down the local school about its children's ears, killing them all. The Romans used the island bays in their operations against Aegean pirates. From 1207 to 1522 Astipalaia was ruled by the Venetian family of Quirini, who introduced settlers from Mykonos and Tinos. In 1522 it fell to the Turks who slightly altered its name to *Ustrupalia*. Except during the Cretan War (1648–68) and during 1821–28, they held it until 1912, when it was the first of the Dodecanese to be occupied by the Italians and the springboard of their expedition to Rhodes.

The port of **Periyialó** (Hotels D), situated on the W side of the Bay of Maltesana, is virtually one with the island capital **Kastéllo** (80m), named after its Venetian castle. The streets of the town are steep and narrow and many of the houses have wooden balconies. The **castle**, built by John Quirini in the 13C, has its entrance on the W. Over the vaulted entrance, which bears the Quirini arms, is the restored Church of the **Madonna of the Castle**; on the outer wall of the apse the Quirini arms are repeated. On one occasion the defenders of the castle are said to have repelled assailants round the gate by throwing down on them beehives full of previously maddened bees. The interior of the castle is a complex of narrow lanes, dilapidated houses and covered passage-ways. Here is another church, of **St George**.

Of the many attractive seaside hamlets, the prettiest is Livádhi, just SW of the town. Nearby is an Early Christian basilica of **Ayios Vassílios**. NE a road leads to **Vathí** (11km) via **Análipsi**, with Roman baths.

**PÁTMOS** (Πάτμος), home of the Revelation of St John the Divine, is the northernmost of the Dodecanese. Though the area is only 39 sq. km, it has a long and irregular coastline with many little bays. Its three sections are joined by two narrow isthmuses, of which that nearest the centre forms the focal point of the island. Here was the ancient city, here is the modern port, Skála, dominated from the S by Patmos Town and its fortified monastic crag. The rocky and volcanic soil is moderately hilly, rising to 270m. The climate is healthy, but the arid soil yields only a small quantity of cereals, vegetables, and wine, not sufficient for the needs of the 2715 inhabitants. The water is brackish. Sponge-fishing used to be the main occupation but is now defunct.

**History**. *Patmos* receives passing mention by Thucydides, Strabo, and Pliny. The first inhabitants were Mycenaeans, then Dorians, who later received Ionian colonists. The Romans made it a place of exile for political prisoners. Here, in AD 95, during the reign of Domitian, was banished St John the Divine, by tradition identified with the Apostle John, though the identification has been disputed. For centuries the island was deserted owing to incursions of Saracen pirates. In 1088, the blessed Christodoulos, a Bithynian abbot, obtained permission from Alexis I Comnenus to found a monastery at Patmos in honour of St John. The island was captured by the Venetians in 1207. In 1461 Pope Pius II took both island and monastery under his protection. The Turks captured Patmos in 1537, and exacted from the monks an annual tribute. In 1669 the island received Venetian refugees from Candia (Crete).

Boats dock at **Skála** (Hotels B, C, D, E; F/A), the commercial centre (1442 inhab.) of the island, situated in a sheltered bay facing E. The animated Plateia, with arcaded buildings in the Italian colonial style, opens off the quay. Near by on the shore is a pleasant church with twin domes. A road (2km; taxis) has all but superseded the ancient paved mule-path (20 minutes) to Patmos Town. On the ascent there are fine *views of the surrounding islands and rocks. Half-way up are the new buildings of the **Theological College**, founded in 1669 and attended by students from all Greece, and the Convent of the Apocalypse (Μονή της Αποκαλύψεως), a cell of the monastery. Here are three small churches, and the **Cave of St Anne**, where by tradition St John dictated the Revelation to his disciple Prochoros.

**Pátmos**, or **Khóra** (670 inhab.), has pleasant 16–17C houses spread round the foot of the monastery, 152m above the sea. The fortified *Monastery of St John, founded in 1088 by the Blessed Christodoulos, has the appearance of a great polygonal castle, with towers and battlements. It is visited by the faithful on 21 May, the saint's day, and celebrates Easter week with some pomp. An excellent illustrated guide is available in English. To the left, as you enter by the fortified gate, is the tomb of Gregory of Kos, Bp of Dhidhimotiko (d. 1693). The **entrance court**, built in 1698, is attractive. Its E side forms the exonarthex of the church, which incorporates elements from an earlier chapel and perhaps from a Temple of Artemis. Between the arches hangs a huge wooden simantron.

You enter the **church** by the right-hand door, which admits to the **Founder's Chapel**; his marble sarcophagus is surmounted by a reliquary covered with repoussé scenes in silver-gilt (1796). A low doorway with an ancient lintel and a medieval door leads into the **narthex**. The church proper is a Greek cross-in-square. The floor, of grey and white marble, dates back to the foundation. The Ikonostasis (1820) is heavy and ornate, and some of the furniture has inlaid work in a Saracen style. Above the door of the Outer Treasury is an ikon on a gold ground, signed by Emmanuel Tzanes (1674). The 12C **Chapel of the Theotokos**, to the S, contains near-contemporary *frescoes, brought to light in 1958, when later paintings were stripped away. Behind the altar, the Holy Trinity, represented as three angels being given hospitality by Abraham; below, the Virgin, flanked by the archangels, Michael and Gabriel, wearing Byzantine imperial robes.

Outside the S door is the **inner courtyard**, from which opens the **refectory**, a modified 11C building equipped with long stone tables. The walls have remains of late 12C frescoes, executed in two phases. They represent scenes of Christ's Passion, his miracles, an illustration of Psalm 102, etc. A stair leads up to the *library (c 2000 printed books) in which are displayed a selection from the collection of 890 MSS. The greatest treasure, since the 9C Plato codex was removed in 1803 (now in Oxford), is 33 leaves of the **Codex Porphyrius**, comprising most of St Mark's gospel. The greater part of the book (182 ff) is in Leningrad. It was written in the early 6C on purple vellum, in uncials of silver and the holy names in gold. Important textually also are an 8C Book of Job, with commentaries drawn from 19 scholars; and the Discourses of St Gregory, written in 941 in Calabria. This is one of the works listed in 1201 in a surviving Catalogue of the Library. Some exquisite illumination in the Byzantine tradition can be seen in various Gospels and Cartularies (12–14C). Also displayed are charters and deeds from the **Monastic Archives** (13,000 documents), including the foundation chrysobul of Alexis Comnenus.

The *treasury, the most important monastic collection in Greece outside Mt Athos, contains embroidered stoles (15–18C); ikons, notably a miniature mosaic framed in silver of St Nicholas (11C) and a celebrated St Theodore (13C); church furniture, including a handsome chalice of 1679, a superb crozier (1677) with gold relief decoration and pale blue enamel work, ornamented with diamonds; benediction crosses in wooden filigree; pendant model ships (16C) in enamelled silver set with precious stones, worn by the wives of rich ship-owners. The windows command a fine view of Skála and the W roof terrace the finest *panorama of the greater part of the Aegean.

Some vestiges of ancient *Patmos* crown the hill **Kastélli** behind Skála to the NW. Launches depart at frequent intervals in July–August for various beaches, of which **Gríkou** (Hotels B, C, D; F/A) lies to the SE; **Kámbos** (Hotel B; taverna) to the NE (25 minutes); and **Lampí**, bright with coloured stones, on the N coast.

**Arkoí**, to the NE of Patmos and N of Lipsoi, is a dependent islet with 50 inhabitants.

**Lípsoi** (Λείψοι), situated E of Patmos and N of Leros and surrounded by numerous islets, is one of the smallest of the Dodecanese with an area of 15.5 sq. km. Its outline is irregular and indented, especially on the SE coast, in which is the little harbour. The only centre of population is the village (606 inhab.) of **Lipsoi** (Hotel D) above the harbour. A little food is produced and there is some fishing.

**LÉROS** (Λέρος), like Patmos, consists of three peninsulas joined by two isthmuses, and its coastline is deeply indented. The largest of these, safe anchorages, are the Bay of Alinda on the E coast, on which is the island capital, and the bays of Gourna and Porto Lago, on the W coast. The island is well wooded and its hills accessible by Italian military roads. The fertile valleys in the centre yield olives, figs, carobs, tobacco, fruit, and wine. The **airport** (at **Parthéni** in the NW; office in Plátanos) has a daily service to Athens.

**History**. *Leros* and Kalymnos are believed to have been the Kalydnian Isles mentioned by Homer. Leros is said to have been colonised by Miletus. The inhabitants had a reputation for being unprincipled. The island was famed for its honey and for a Temple of Artemis, associated with the story of Meleager and his sisters. Leros shared the medieval history of its neighbours. In 1916 the Royal Navy set up a base at Porto Lago, which was greatly developed by the Italians after 1923. Here on 3 February 1926 Admiral de Pinedo ended his pioneer flight from Australia. In the Second World War British forces temporarily occupied Leros. In more recent times of political stress it has known internment camps.

**Island Customs**. During the Carnival men and women compose satirical verses which children, dressed as monks, recite at parties given in houses where a marriage has taken place during the previous year. This custom seems to derive from the ceremonies in honour of Dionysos at Eleusis. A peculiarity of local law is that all real property passes in the female line, with the result that virtually all the houses and landed property belong to women.

The ship enters Porto Lago bay and docks at **Lakkí** (Hotels B, C, D, E), with 2366 inhabitants and a prominent and now infamous mental asylum. A road mounts to (3km) **Plátanos** which, with **Ayía Marína** (3km NE), its other port on the Bay of Alinda and the site of ancient *Leros*, forms the capital, with 2493 inhabitants. The houses rise on the hillside below the **kastro**, situated on a height inaccessible from the E and precipitous on the other sides. The castle, originally Byzantine, was rebuilt by the Knights of St John. A cross on the hillside marks the **British Military Cemetery**, where lie the casualties of the battle in November 1943.

From Plátanos a road leads round the bay to the summer resort of **Alinda** (Hotels B, C, D, E), continuing to the airport at **Parthéni**, while a path descends to **Pantéli**, with a beach, 500m SE of the castle. In the S of the island, 3km from **Lakkí**, is **Xirókambos** (rooms), with a caïque connection to Kálimnos.

Léros is surrounded by numerous islets. About 19km E is **Pharmáko**, or Pharmakousa, where Julius Caesar, returning from his notorious sojourn in Bithynia, was captured by pirates and detained for 38 days until his ransom arrived; he later caught and crucified his captors.

**KÁLIMNOS** (Κάλυμνος) lies immediately S of Léros and W of the Asiatic peninsula of Bodrum (Halicarnassus). The island is approximately rectangular in shape, with a peninsular extension to the NW separated by a channel of only 2.5km from Leros. Its greatest length is 21km and its width 13km, giving an area of 109 sq. km. The surface is mountainous and barren, except in the valleys. A range extending along the peninsula joins the northernmost of three transverse ranges in the main part of the island. The central range is the highest, with Mt Profitis Ilias (686m); it is continued on the W by the hills of the islet of Telendos. These three ranges are separated by two fertile valleys, that of Vathí between the N and the central range, and that of Pothiá and Brostá between the central and S range. The coastline is much indented, with precipitous cliffs and small coves. The population of 15,842 is mainly concentrated in the island capital **Pothiá**. Until recently the chief industry, as in ancient times, has been the fishing and marketing of sponges but this is now much reduced. The produce includes figs, oranges, olives, grapes, and cereals. Kalimnos was once famed for its honey, which rivalled that of Attica.

**History**. *Kalymnos* is believed to be one of the Kalydnian Isles of the Homeric Catalogue of Ships, the other being Leros. The island was inhabited from the Neolithic period; later it was colonised by Dorians from the Argolid. In antiquity its fortunes tended to follow those of Kos, and in the Middle Ages it underwent Venetian, Rhodian, and Turkish domination. It was most actively opposed to Italian rule, using blue and white paint everywhere in the Greek national colours. In 1935 there were riots against an attempt to suppress Greek in schools and to set up an autocephalous Church of the Dodecanese. In the Second World War most of the Kalymnians took refuge in the Asiatic peninsula opposite the island, where they dispersed to various places, including Gaza in Israel.

The capital **Pothiá** (Hotels B, C, D, E) or **Kálimnos**, is also the chief port and the industrial and commercial centre of the island, a town (10,543 inhab.) comparable in size with Ermoúpolis in Síros. It is situated at the head of a bay of the S coast. To the SE of the town, which holds little interest for visitors, is a small thermal establishment. There is a small **Archaeological**

**Museum**. Kálimnos has good sea connections with its neighbours, including a regular service to Mastikhári on Kos.

A motor-boat may be taken in 35 minutes to the **Cave of Kefalás**, near the SW promontory of the island. The cave (adm. fee) was a sanctuary of Olympian Zeus.

A road (bus; cars for hire at Pothiá) leads up the fertile and beautiful valley. Soon after leaving the town, you pass on the left a hill with three disused windmills on its slopes and on its summit a ruined **Castle of the Knights** (or **Khrisókhira**), with a little church and rock-cut Mycenaean tombs. 3km **Khorió** (3259 inhab.) is the former capital of Kalimnos, built below a **castle** (views) which served as a refuge in the Middle Ages. Farther on the valley narrows. Near (4km) **Dhámos** you pass a ruined church, of which only the apse (with an inscription to Apollo) remains, near which are the remains of a Temple of Apollo and a theatre. The road now bears SW and descends. 5.5km **Pánormos** (Hotels C, D), on the W coast, and **Mirtées** (Hotels B, C, D), 1.5km farther on, are summer resorts. A Byzantine chapel on the S side of Mirties Bay has a mosaic floor (inscription). To the N is the castle of **Kastélli**. Masoúri has a good beach. The road continues to the farthest village of **Emborió**.

To the N, close to the shore, is the islet of **Télendos** (regular ferry from Mirtées), with ancient remains the most important being Roman and Early Christian (baths, basilica), and the ruins of the **Monastery of Ayios Vasíleios**, dominated by a medieval castle. Since the Middle Ages the coastline has receded; for about a mile from the shore the remains of medieval houses can be seen under water.

FROM POTHIA TO VATHI, by coast-road or inland (bus). Just beyond the entrance to the inlet is seen the mouth of the **Grotto of Daskaleiós**, the largest of the caves in the island. It is accessible only with difficulty from the sea. Immediately inside is a chamber 25m long, from which opens on the right another chamber, at a lower level, with stalactites and stalagmites and a cavity full of brackish water. Many prehistoric objects were found, ranging from the Neolithic to the Bronze Age. At the head of the inlet is the district of **Vathí**, consisting of three villages, **Rhína**, the little port, **Plátanos**, named after a huge plane tree, and **Metókhi**, farther inland. 100m N of the harbour are the remains of an Early Christian basilica, with a small church of **Ayía Iríni** built over the NE corner. At **Ayios Pandeleímon**, to the N of Vathí, is an ancient settlement with an Early Christian basilica (**Palaio-panayía**). There is another basilica 500m to the N. The Valley of Vathy is the most attractive part of the island, its luxuriant vegetation thriving on the volcanic and well-watered soil. At its mouth are orange and tangerine orchards and occasional olive groves; farther inland are figs and vineyards. The barrenness of the enclosing hills is in sharp contrast to the fertility of the valley. It is rich in antiquities. At Rhína is a rock-hewn throne; near Plátanos are cyclopean walls and a little chapel in an enclosure of Hellenic walls.

Between Kálimnos and Kos is the islet of **Pserimós** (10 sq. km), with a monastery and 79 inhabitants.

The island of **KOS** (Κώς), or **Cos** (26,379 inhab.) is the second most visited of the Dodecanese, though, with an area of 282 sq. km, it is only one-fifth the size of Rhodes. It is a long narrow island, with a length of 45km from NE to SW, and a width varying from 11 to 1.5km, its narrowest part being the isthmus leading to the Peninsula of Kefalos at the SW. It lies at the entrance to the deeply indented Gulf of Kos, the Ceramic Gulf of antiquity, between the Asiatic Peninsula of Bodrum (Halicarnassus) only 5km away to the N, and the Peninsula of Knidos on the S (16km distant). A long mountain chain runs near the S of the island from Cape Foka, at its E end, to the neighbourhood of Pilí, in the centre. Its highest point is Mt Oromedhon or Dhikaios (847m), gently sloping on the N, precipitous on the S. In the NW there is a plateau, where the ground slopes towards the sea. The Peninsula of Kephalos is moderately hilly, with Mt Latra rising to 428m, the hills sloping down to Cape Krikelos, the southernmost point of the island. The coastline is scarcely indented, and there is only one real harbour, Mandraki, at the city and port of Kos, which is situated at the NE end of the island. Kos produces an abundance of juicy grapes, as well as fine water melons and oil, cereals, vegetables and tobacco. Among local wines are Glafkos (white) and Apellis (red).

The island is better watered than any other of the Dodecanese. It is especially rich in warm and tepid ferruginous springs celebrated even before the time of Hippocrates, the greatest physician of antiquity, who was born at Kos c 460 BC and is said to have died in 357 at the age of 104. Another native was the poet Philetas, a contemporary of Ptolemy II Philadelphos (285–247 BC). The bucolic poet Theocritus, born at Syracuse c 310 BC, lived for a time in Kos as a disciple of Philetas. His 7th Idyll has a Koan setting. The painter Apelles, whose Aphrodite Anadyomene adorned the Asklepieion, is claimed as a native of Kos, though he may have been born in Ionia at Kolophon or Ephesus. He flourished in the time of Alexander the Great (336–323 BC).

**History**. The island has had several names. Thucydides and Strabo called it *Kos Meropis*, Pliny *Nymphaea*, and Stephanos of Byzantium *Karis*. In the Middle Ages it was known as *Lango*, perhaps because of its length, and later as *Stanchio*, a corruption of 'stin Ko', whence the Turkish *Istanköy*. Kos was inhabited in Neolithic times, as is proved by discoveries in the Cave of Aspripetra, near Kephalos. It was colonised by Carians and, in the Homeric Age, by Dorians from Epidauros. In the Persian wars it was under the sway of Artemisia, queen of Caria, and so fought on the losing side. Kos was at first a member of the Dorian hexapolis and of little importance. Its city (later remembered as Astypalaia, 'old city') was situated in the SW of the island and was destroyed by the Lacedaemonians in the Peloponnesian War. The new city of Kos was founded in 366 BC and rapidly prospered to become one of the greatest maritime centres of the Aegean. Its sanctuary of Asklepios and school of medicine made it famous all over the ancient world. The city was adorned with a plethora of artistic monuments. Its wines and silks had a great reputation; the light silk dresses called *Coae vestes* were well known to the Romans for their transparency.

Kos was occupied by Alexander the Great in 336 BC, and on his death in 323 passed to the Ptolemies. Ptolemy II Philadelphos was born in the island in 309. Cleopatra is said to have used the island as a store for some of her treasures. Later Kos was allied to Rome before becoming part of the pro-consular Province of Asia. In the Byzantine era Kos was the seat of a bishop and many Early Christian basilicas (5–6C) have been uncovered. In the 11C Kos was ravaged by Saracens. Later it passed to the Genoese, becoming in 1304 a fief of the Zaccharia family. Two years later it was ceded to the Knights of St John, who did not take possession till 1315. The Knights made it into a strong-point. It was attacked by the Turks in 1457 and 1477, and fell to them, with Rhodes, in 1522. Hadji Ali Haseki, voivode and tyrant of Athens, was finally exiled to Kos and there on 23 December 1795 beheaded. In 1912, after nearly four centuries of Turkish domination, it was occupied by the Italians in the course of their war with Turkey. In the Second World War British forces temporarily occupied the island until driven out by the Germans.

Note S.M. Sherwin-White, *Ancient Cos: an historical study from the Dorian settlement to the imperial period*, 1978, Göttingen.

The city of **Kos** lies in a plain at the NE end of the island, just S of the Kos Channel (here at its narrowest; 5km), which separates it from the Anatolian coast. Despite undistinguished modern buildings and suburbs, it is a pleasant town, though busy in season, with tidy open streets, resplendent gardens and orchards, and extensive Classical and Roman remains. Of the 14,714 inhabitants, about half are Muslims and most of the remainder of the Orthodox faith. Kos has some importance as a trading port, and has given its name to a variety of lettuce adopted from its shores.

**Airport**, 26km W near Andimákhia; daily services to Athens in 50 minutes, to Rhodes 1–3 weekly in 45 minutes; also to Frankfurt, and (by charter) elsewhere. **Terminal** at Leofóros Vasiléos Pávlou 22.

**Hotels** A–E; F/A. **Restaurants** on the waterfront.

**Tourist Police**. **Police** on Aktí Koundouriótou, near Castle. **EOT office**, Aktí Koundouriótou. **Post Office**, El. Venizélou. **OTE**, 8 Víronos.

**Bus Station**, Kleopátras/Pisándrou. **Bicycles** for hire by the hour.

**Excursion Boats** daily in season to neighbouring islands. Regular service from Mastikhári to Kálimnos.

**Admission** to Museum, Castle, and Roman House at standard museum hours; to the Asklepieion at standard site hours.

**History**. There is a settlement of the Minoan and Mycenaean periods beneath the modern town of Kos and a number of Mycenaean tombs have been discovered to the SW as well as Protogeometric and Geometric graves within its walls. The ancient city, founded in 366 BC, had a perimeter of c 4km. Devastated by earthquakes c 5 BC, in AD 142, and again in 469, it was virtually destroyed in 554. The old materials were largely reused in each new rebuilding and later pillaged for the medieval defences. The **City of the Knights**, bounded by an enceinte, erected in 1391–96 to counter the menace of Bayezid, occupied only the agora and harbour quarter of the old city. Traces remain opposite the castle, whence the course of the wall may be traced to the SW tower (see below). The Schlegelholz Bastion, adorned with arms of the bailiff and of Grand Master Heredia, survives at the SE corner; within the walls remain three small Byzantine chapels and a house bearing the arms of Bailiff Francesco Sans (1514). Archaeological explorations, begun in 1900 by Rudolf Herzog, were undertaken after 1928 by Luciano Lorenzi of the Italian School, and given impetus by the havoc caused on 23 April 1933 by a severe earthquake. Extensive excavations took place in 1935–43 and there has been much recent work (1980s) by the Greek Archaeological Service. Many of the mosaics recovered were removed to adorn the castle in Rhodes. An excellent guidebook is C. & C. Mee, *Kos*, 1979 (Lycabettos Press).

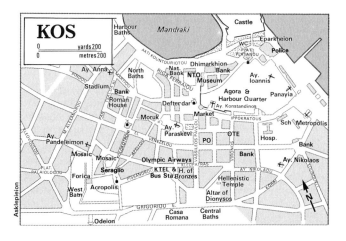

The picturesque harbour of **Mandráki**, with a good yacht station, has the same name as its counterpart in Rhodes. Ferries dock at a new quay further NE. Opposite the Mandráki quay the former **Palace of the Regent**, by F. di Fausto (1928), houses the Town Hall, Custom House, and Port Offices. Turning left you can mount to the terreplein of the castle, now Plateía Platánou. In the centre grows the so-called **Plane-tree of Hippocrates**, a gigantic tree with a trunk 14m in diameter and branches propped up by antique marble fragments. Inevitably tradition insists that Hippocrates taught under its shade, though it is not more than 500 years old. To the right stands the **Mosque of Gazi Hassan Pasha**, or **of the Loggia**, a three-storeyed building of 1786, entered on the first floor by a graceful staircase with a double portico or loggia. An elegant **minaret** stands at the corner. Beneath the tree a **fountain** has for basin an antique sarcophagus. A little grove shades the cemetery.

From the terreplein a stone bridge leads across the outer moat (now a palm-shaded avenue) to the **Castle of the Knights**, the city's principal monument. The fortress has two enceintes, one within the other. You enter by a drawbridge and a gateway in the S curtain wall of the outer enceinte. Above the gate are a Hellenic frieze and the quartered arms of Amboise and the Order.

The original castle, roughly rectangular in plan, was begun in 1450 by the Venetian Fantino Guerini, governor of Kos (1436–53), and completed in 1478 by the Genoese Edoardo de Carmadino (governor 1471–95). After the unsuccessful Turkish assault of 1480, an outer enceinte was begun in 1495 by Grand Master Pierre d'Aubusson and completed in 1514 by G.M. Fabrizio Del Carretto. In its construction Italian architects and craftsmen were employed. Both enceintes incorporate masonry from the Asklepieion and other ancient Greek buildings. There is a deep fosse between the two lines of walls.

A passageway leads to the S terrace, from which a flight of steps gives access to the **antiquarium**, containing Coan marbles, inscriptions, sculptural fragments, sepulchral monuments, and a number of fine knightly escutcheons carved in marble. One of the inscriptions commemorates the physician Xenophon, who helped to poison the Emperor Claudius (Tacitus, *Annals*, xii, 67, 2).

The heavy cylindrical **Bastion Del Carretto**, at the SW angle of the outer enceinte, resembles the bastion of the same name in the walls of Rhodes. The corresponding **north-east tower**, which projects somewhat, commands a good view over the sea towards Anatolia. The NW tower, or **Tower of Aubusson**, overlooking the harbour, is polygonal. It bears the arms of Aubusson quartered with those of the Order, and an Italian inscription of 1503.

From the terrace a staircase descends to the left of the antiquarium and reach a horseshoe ravelin in front of the inner enceinte. On its right is the entrance. All four angles of the inner enceinte have cylindrical towers, with battlements and embrasures, and appropriate escutcheons. The inner curtain wall is similarly adorned. On the **inner south-west tower** are the fleurs-de-lis of France.

Turning S again we enter the partially walled area of the Chora, or city of the Knights (see above), excavated since the earthquake of 1933 to show Roman levels of the agora and harbour quarter.

The N sector of the excavations lay outside the Hellenistic city walls. From E to W may be distinguished a Hellenistic sanctuary, orientated to the N; next, a **stoa** (4–3C), of which 6 columns with acanthus capitals have been re-erected. These were recovered from the foundations of the **Harbour Basilica**, built over the stoa in the 5C AD. Its ruins lie immediately S of the Mosque of the Loggia (see above). Farther W are extensive fragments of the **Sanctuary of the Port Quarter**, probably an Aphrodision. The S sector of the area represents the N extremity of the ancient city proper, which is divided by a broad road running N–S. To the E are insulae of houses and shops. To the W lies the **agora**, just within the Knights' W gate, which in the Middle Ages was called 'Porta tou Forou'. A fine stretch of rusticated ashlar masonry marks its E boundary and some columns have been re-erected.

The site exit is by a gate leading to Plateía Eleftherías, the main square of the town. The **museum** contains interesting sculpture of the Hellenistic and Roman periods; upper galleries (pottery) are not open at present. Across the square is the 18C **Defterdar Mosque**. Odhós Vas. Pavlou leads to the S side of town and another area of excavations with a large **Roman house** (rebuilt by the Italians to protect its many mosaics) and the **central baths**. From here you can turn W to visit the **odeion**, approached by an avenue of cypresses; of its 14 rows of marble seats, seven are original. The near-by church of **Ayios Ioánnis Pródhromos** is the baptistery of the largest Early Christian church of Kos.

Opposite are the *Western Excavations, a huge L-shaped area below the acropolis (see below), a low hill crowned by a minaret. A section of the **Decumanus Maximus** is exposed with the houses on its N side, many of which retain mosaics (3C AD) and frescoes. The large **House of the Europa Mosaic** is the best preserved, and yielded many complete statues. The **cardo**, beautifully paved and recalling the streets of Pompeii, leads N. To the left are extensive **Roman baths**. The calidarium is well preserved; the frigidarium was transformed into a Christian **basilica** at a later date. The marble immersion font and much of the mosaic door survives of the baptistery, the marble doorway of which has been re-erected. Farther W the colonnade of the **xystos** of a Hellenistic gymnasium (2C BC) has been restored. To the right of the road, beyond a row of antique taverns, stands the restored **forica** of the baths, a sumptuous latrine built round a peristyle court. Beyond, a shelter protects a large mosaic showing gladiatorial scenes.

A flight of steps by the forica leads up to the acropolis, from where the picturesque Odhos Apéllou, an old street of the Turkish quarter, returns NE. The area is still known as the **Seraglio**. Excavation suggests that this was the centre of prehistoric Kos. Farther NW (below the church of Ayía Anna on Od. 25 Martíou) are some remains of the **stadium**, principally the curious aphesis, or starting-gate. Recent excavations have shown that the stadium was in immediate contact with the gymnasium (above).

The PRINCIPAL EXCURSION is to the Asklepieion, 4km by road. You take the Kefalos road and, beyond the town, fork left. 3km **Ghermí**, or Khermetes, a Muslim village, officially **Platáni**. By an avenue of cypresses you approach the **Asklepieíon**, or **Sanctuary of Asklepios**. It occupies the site of a grove sacred to Apollo Kyparessios, mentioned in the 4C, but it was not built until after the death of Hippocrates (357 BC) and dates from the Hellenistic period.

The sanctuary was one of the main seats of the Asklepiadai, supposed descendants of Asklepios, who were a hereditary close order of priests, jealous guardians of the secrets of medicine. The technique of healing differed from that at Epidauros and elsewhere, where cures were effected by suggestion. At Kos, as is revealed by inscriptions, patients underwent positive treatment at the hands of physicians on lines laid down by Hippocrates. Herondas in his fourth mime describes a sacrifice at the Asklepieion. The sanctuary had the right of asylum. It throve in the days of the Ptolemies and later under Nero. The rich court physician Xenophon (see above), on his return to Kos, lavished on the sanctuary the statues he had amassed in Rome. Even in the late-Imperial period great baths were built. In the 6C AD all was overwhelmed, either by an earthquake

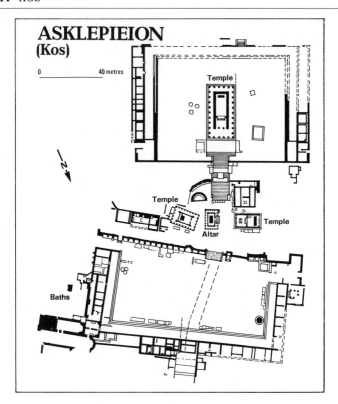

or in 554 when Anatolian hordes ravaged the island. The Knights of St John used the ruins as a quarry. A local antiquary, G.E. Zaraphtis, identified the site; in 1902 the German Herzog began systematic excavation, and the work was completed by the Italians with extensive restorations.

Passing (left) remains of **Roman baths** (1C AD), where the hypocaust and plunge bath are well preserved, you ascend to the lower terrace of the sanctuary. This was surrounded on three sides by porticoes. On the fourth side was a retaining wall of massive proportions, part of which survives. Near the middle of the wall are a fountain, which still plays, the staircase leading to the Middle Terrace, and several reservoirs fed by conduits from ferruginous and sulphurous springs and drawn upon by invalids taking the cure. Between the reservoirs and the staircase are the remains of a small **temple**, with the pedestal of a statue of Nero as Asklepios (the inscription records its dedication by the physician Xenophon). On this terrace were probably held the Asklepian festivals, which, on the evidence of inscriptions, included athletic games and other contests.

Steps lead to the middle terrace. On the right is an Ionic **temple in antis**, dating from the late 4C or early 3C BC, and so the oldest temple in the sanctuary. The capitals, of painted marble, are exceptionally fine; the rest of the building was in white or black marble. In the floor of the cella was a coffer of marble slabs for the reception of votive offerings. The temple was adorned with paintings by Apelles, including the celebrated Aphrodite

Anadyomene, removed by Augustus to Rome. Behind the temple is a **Roman house** on a Greek foundation, probably the priest's dwelling. In front of the temple, to the left, is the **great altar**, similar to that at Pergamon; it is in the form of the Greek letter Π, with a central staircase. Its ceiling, partly surviving, was coffered; between the columns of the portico were statues of Asklepios, Hygieia, and members of their family, attributed to the sons of Praxiteles. To the left of the altar is a **Roman temple**, orientated aslant. It is a peripteral Ionic building, with half-fluted columns and a magnificent entablature with floral decoration, part of which remains. In the wall at the end of the terrace is a **monumental staircase**, to the left of which is an **exedra**, with niches for statues.

The upper terrace occupies the site of the sacred wood. On it is the great Doric **Temple of Asklepios**. This is peripteral, with six columns by eleven. It stands on a base of three carved steps, the lowest of which is of black marble. The well-preserved **pronaos** is in antis; its threshold is a black limestone monolith. In it was installed in the Christian era a chapel of the **Panayía tou Társou**, the altar of which survives. Three sides of the terrace were lined with porticoes, on which houses were later built.

From the upper terrace there is a magnificent ˙view. Below is the town of Kos, with its harbour, surrounded by gardens and orchards. In the distance, across the sea, are the Peninsula of Knidos to the SE, the deeply indented Gulf of Kos to the E, the Promontory of Bodrum (Halicarnassus) to the NE, and the islands of Pserimos and Kalimnos to the NW.

The Asklepieion is situated near the foot of **Mt Oromedon**, the highest peak of which is **Dhikaíos** (847m). The mountain has many springs, one of which supplies the town of Kos with water via an aqueduct. This is the ancient *Vourina*, the sacred spring of Theocritus. It is enclosed in a domed building approached by a corridor. Another fountain has the name of **Kokkineró**, or 'Red Water'.

FROM KOS TO KEFALOS, road, 43.5km (27 miles), crossing the island lengthwise. You leave on the left the turning for the Asklepieion, which is visible 1km farther on, with Mt Dhikaíos behind it. To the right, reaching to the sea, extends an agricultural plain. At (9km) **Zipári**, which had an early basilica dedicated to St Paul (mosaics and early font) a road leads left for **Asfendíou** (3km; 244m), on the slopes of Dhikaíos, where a Byzantine basilica and a small temple of Demeter and Kore were explored by the Italians. Dhikaíos can be ascended in 1 hour. On the left is the mountain ridge forming the backbone of the island; on the right, over the sea, are the islands of Pserimos and Kalimnos (ferry service to the latter from **Mastikhári**, 6km below, on the coast). You pass a ruined Roman aqueduct. From (15km) **Pilí** (2435 inhab.) a track, passable by car, leads to **Old Pylae** (Palaiopilí; 4km), a ruined village dominated by a hill (320m) on which are the remains of a concentric Byzantine **castle**. Within the lowest enceinte is the church of the **Purification of the Virgin Mary** (Ipapandís), incorporating ancient masonry and decorated with well-preserved 14C frescoes.

From Pilí a winding road descends to **Kardhámaina** (Hotels A–E), ancient *Halasarna*, on the S coast, a centre of massive tourist developments. There are remains of a Hellenistic theatre and of an Early Christian basilica (Ayía Theótis). A secular Early Christian building, incorporating ancient material and probably destroyed in the earthquake of 544 AD overlies the Hellenistic Temple of Apollo Halasarnas. It has a caique service to Nísiros.

After passing a large windmill, the road rises to a plateau and begins to descend. 24km Turn (right) for **Mastikhári** (4km) with a boat to Nísiros. Near (25km) **Andimákhia** (128m; Hotel C), a straggling village of 2089 inhabitants, is the airport of Kos. A track leads left in 3km to the battlemented **Castle of Antimachia** (144m), dating from the time of the Knights. It is triangular in plan and has a drawbridge in front of its only gate, which bears the quartered arms of Amboise and of the Order. Inside are ruins of houses, cisterns, and two churches. Another road descends to Kardhámaina.

Further on there is a view of the end of the island, dominated by Mt Latra (428m), and known as the Peninsula of Kefalos. The road gradually descends to cross a stream and then rises steeply to a bare plain, where the island contracts into an isthmus only

1.5km across. The road approaches the N coast and then descends to (34km) the shore of the Bay of Kamares, on the S coast. In the bay is the picturesque **St Nicholas Rock**. The area has considerable tourist facilities. At **Ayios Stéfanos** are the impressive ruins of two Christian basilicas (through hotel grounds, opposite the rock). 43.5km **Kéfalos** (106m; 228 inhab.; Hotels A, C, E) dominates the Bay of Kamares. On a neighbouring height is a ruined **castle**. About 5 minutes to the S of the village, on a metalled road, the **Panayía Palatianí** (rebuilt 1988), elevated to the left, seems to be on an ancient site (blocks in field walls). 10 minutes further (sign left 'Palatia'), delightfully situated amongst pines, are the remains of a Hellenistic Doric **temple** *in antis*, its stylobate and some column drums survive. Lower down (5 mins) towards Kefalos, are another **temple** *in antis* and a **theatre**. These may belong to the ancient town of *Astypalaia*. Immediately beyond the site entrance the road forks, right to the sea at Ayios Ioannis Theologos (5km), left to the **Cave of Aspripetra** (3.5km), which has produced Neolithic finds.

**Nísiros** (Νίσυρος), a small pentagonal island of 41.5 sq. km, is an extinct volcano, whose hot sulphurous springs have been celebrated since antiquity. Pumice is quarried on the island of **Yialí**, also a source of obsidian in later prehistoric times. The attractive port of **Mandráki** (661 inhab.; Hotels B, C), on the N coast, is dominated by the ruined bastion of the Castle of the Knights (1312) which, with a 14C subterranean church (Panayía Spilianí), is situated on a small steep headland to the W. This is linked by a low saddle to a hill (Palaiókastro) S of the village, where there are extensive remains (towers and a massive gateway) of the 4C, and later city walls.

From Mandráki (erratic bus service), a road follows the N coast to (**Loutrá**, 1.5km E), a small spa (baths open in summer). Farther on, after abandoned pumice quarries high to the right, is (at 4km) a junction where the left branch proceeds (0.5km) to **Páloi**, a fishing hamlet, with remains of Roman (and modern) baths. A traditional building is being restored as a hotel: 3km further is **Liés** and the good beach of **Pakhiá Ammos**. The right branch winds up among oak and almond trees to (13km) **Emboriós** on a hill, where there are scanty remains of a Venetian castle, destroyed by an earthquake in 1933. The road continues climbing (views of Turkey and Tílos to the S) to (17km) **Nikiá**, a pretty village on the rim of the central depression, which is 4km across. The central cone within rises to 692m. Near the village is the monastery of **Ayios Ioánnis Theólogos**. In summer there are daily excursions from Kos (boat 2½ hours and bus). A geothermal plant is under construction to provide power for the island and for Kos and Kalímnos.

**Tílos** (Τήλος), lying between Nísiros on the N and Khálki on the S, is accurately described by Strabo as long, high, and narrow. The Italians, reviving a medieval name of uncertain origin, called it *Piscopi*. Apart from a coastal plain in the N, the interior is hilly, rising in the NW to 654m. Most of the 172 inhabitants are engaged in agriculture. The women stil sometimes wear traditional costume. The rugged coastline is indented with bays. **Livádhia** (Hotels C, E), the island landing-place, on a bay of the NE coast, is connected with **Mikró Khorió**, a hamlet just below a central saddle, by a road (c 1.5km), continuing N to (7km) **Megálo Khorió**, which through the ages has been the island capital. There are remains of Archaic-Classical walls; the church of the Archangel Michael is on the foundations of a Greek temple on the acropolis; and the whole site is crowned by a ruined castle of the Knights built of ancient masonry and incorporating a Classical gateway. A 15C monastery of **Ayios Pandeleimon**, 7km away at the W extremity of the island, incorporates Early Christian and Byzantine material.

**Sími** (Σύμη), or **Syme**, is situated at the mouth of the Doridis Gulf, between two Asiatic peninsulas—that of Knidos on the N and that of Dorakis on the

S. It is only 10km from the latter, which was called Cynossema Promontory in antiquity. The island is 24km N of Rhodes, across the Strait of Marmara, and there is a daily connection. Irregular in shape, it has an area of 67 sq. km. The arid interior is hilly, but the once deficient water supply is now augmented by a solar still. The coasts have high cliffs and are difficult of access, but there are inlets in which small ships can find shelter. Except in the fertile valley of Pedhi and Panaidhakia and on the plateaux, the soil is allergic to cultivation. The climate is mild except in the height of summer, when the temperature may exceed 38°C. The population (23,000 in 1912; 6300 in 1937), much reduced by emigration, is 2332, all but a few in the capital. Small quantities of cereals, wine, olives, honey and tobacco are produced. The main industry used to be sponge-fishing and Simian divers the ablest in the Aegean; they recovered the Ephebos of Antikithera. Their ships passed by inheritance in the male line, houses in the female line with the dowry.

**History**. The Homeric Catalogue of Ships records a contribution of three vessels from Syme to the Trojan expedition. Later Syme was colonised by the Carians, who abandoned it during a drought. In 411 BC the Lacedaemonians, after a successful engagement off Knidos with an Athenian naval detachment, set up a trophy on Syme. This action led to the revolt of Rhodes from the Athenian Confederacy. The islanders have always been renowned shipbuilders. They built fast skiffs for the Knights of St John and were employed in the same capacity by the Turks, under whom they enjoyed numerous privileges and extensive estates on the mainland. Much of their timber was used up during the War of Independence.

The town of **Sími** (Hotels A, B, C; rooms), in the N of the island, is divided into **Yialós**, on its bay, and **Khorió**, above. There is a daily boat to Rhodes. Most of the inhabitants live in the upper town, where a small **museum** includes antiquities and photographs of frescoes from the island's churches, many inaccessible. There is also a small **Nautical Museum**. On a height above the town is a **Castle of the Knights**, partly built of blocks from the walls of the ancient acropolis which once surrounded the hill. Over the entrance gate are the arms of Aubusson quartered with those of the Order (1507). Inside the castle are the remains of a **Temple of Athena**, and a **Church of the Panayía**, rebuilt after its destruction in 1943. The nose cone of the bomb that destroyed it is now a bell. Below the houses of upper Sími is the ancient Greek necropolis.

The **Bay of Nimborió**, 2.5km NW of lower Syme, once the island's commercial harbour, is now a summer resort. The church of **Ayía Iríni** lies on an Early Christian basilica and includes some of its material. In the **Bay of Pédhi**, 2.5km E, is an isolated village normally occupied by farm labourers and fishermen and frequented by summer visitors. In the vicinity are Greek and Roman remains.

The 18C **Monastery of St Michael Panormítis** (Rooms; donation expected; restaurant) is 15km from **Khorió** by rough road (or boat in 1¾ hours), on the Bay of Panormitis at the S extremity of the island. It was used as a staging camp in 1945 for refugees returning from Turkey. The church has fine frescoes and an ikon of St Michael. The sanctuary contains offerings from Simians all over the world. The chief festival, on 7–9 November, attracts pilgrims from far and wide. In the church is a magnificent ikonostasis by Mastro Diaco Tagliaduro of Kos.

# B. The Southern route

**Ferries** etc., see above. By this route a visit to the Dodecanese can be conveniently combined with a tour of Crete.

**By Air.** Daily connections between Rhodes and Kárpathos, less frequently via Kásos to Sitía (Crete); 5 weekly from Rhodes to Iráklion.

**Kásos** (Κάσος) is the most southerly of the Dodecanese. It lies c 48km E of Zákro in Crete, across the Kasos Channel, and is separated from Kárpathos by a channel of 11km. The island, elliptical in shape and with an area of 49 sq. km, has an overall length of 18km with precipitous and inaccessible coasts, except on the NW side where the few villages are scattered. The sea is often rough. The hilly interior rises in Mt Priona to 549m. The population (1088) has been greatly reduced by emigration, in the past particularly to Egypt. More than 5000 Kasiots are said to have helped build the Suez Canal.

*Kasos* is mentioned in the Homeric Catalogue of Ships. It was made subject to the Venetian family of Cornaro in 1306, when they acquired Karpathos, and was lost to the Turks only in 1537. In 1824 the Egyptians ravaged the island, an event remembered as 'the Holocaust' by the Kasiots, and for some years afterwards the island was deserted.

**Emborió** (Hotels C), the port, midway along the N coast, lies just E of the capital, **Frí** (Φρύ), an abbreviated form of **Othrys**. It has many abandoned houses and is uninteresting save for the fine view of Kárpathos to the E. Nearby to the W is **Ayía Marína**, 1km to the SE of which the cave of **Ellinokamará** seems to have housed prehistoric as well as later cult. The walling at the entrance is probably Classical. Linear A and B inscriptions have been identified. Inland is **Póli**, the former capital, on the site of the acropolis of the ancient city.

**KÁRPATHOS** (Κάρπαθος), better known by its medieval name *Scarpanto*, is the chief of the group midway between Crete and Rhodes. Long and narrow, it is 48km from end to end with a maximum width of 11km and has about the same area as Kos. The coastline is steep but little indented: there are bays, but only the Bay of Tristoma at the N end gives much protection from the prevailing winds. A mountain range traverses the island from N to S, rising to Mt Profitis Ilias (1014m) and Mt Kalolimni (Lastros; 1120m): the twin peaks in the centre virtually divide the island in two. The long N section, covered with stunted pine trees on the E and bare on the W, is sparsely populated, preserves many ancient customs, and has few springs; the more populous S section (known as 'European' Karpathos) is well watered and its valleys are productive. The 5323 inhabitants are mostly engaged in agriculture and pasture. There are said to be more Karpathiots in Piraeus than in Scarpanto. A great concourse of emigré islanders assembled in 1966 to discuss the island's future economy. The small airport is 10km SW of **Pigádhia**.

**History.** In antiquity, as officially today, the island was called *Karpathos*, though Homer has it as *Krapathos*. Its medieval name of *Scarpanto* was revived by the Italians and is still in common use. The Turks called it *Kerpe*. Despite its size, Karpathos has had an uneventful existence. The Latin Empire gave it in fief to the Genoese Andrea and Lodovico Moresco. In 1306 it was acquired by the Venetian family of Cornaro, who yielded it to the Turks in 1538. In 1835 Sultan Mahmoud II gave it certain financial privileges.

The chief port and 'capital' is **Pigádhia** (Hotels A–E; F/A), or **Kárpathos**, a modern town (1692 inhab.) on the wide sandy bay of **Vrónti** in the SE of the island. Gardens and olive-groves fringe it on the NW. The rocky citadel to the E is the site of Classical *Potidaion* and equally of a Minoan settlement (tombs near by). Minoan and Mycenaean remains (chiefly tombs) have been found at various sites.

TOUR OF THE S PART OF THE ISLAND, 34.5km (21½ miles; buses to Voládha, for Spóa, and to Arkása). The road leads NW to (7km) **Apéri** (149m), the former capital (402 inhab.), divided into two by a stream. It is the seat of the Metropolitan of Karpathos and Kasos. The streets are steep and narrow, many of them stepped. The road ascends SW to (9km) **Voládha** (450m), with a castle on a prominent hill. 11km **Othos** (399m). 14km **Pilés** (399m), with pleasant gardens, looks towards the W coast, to which you descend and turn S. 19km **Finíki** is a little fishing harbour in a fertile region growing citrus fruits and vegetables. At the S end of the same bay is (22km) **Arkássa** (Hotels B), a picturesque village, with fruit orchards. It has remains of a 5C Byzantine Church (Ayía Anastasía), the mosaic pavement of which is in Rhodes museum. On a steep-sided promontory to the SW are some remains of Classical *Arkaseia*. A road, climbs inland to (28km) **Menetés** (Hotels B, C), a village served 20 minutes by bus from (34.5km) Pigádhia (see above).

The centre of the island is reached by a track from Othos round the W side of Mt Kalolimni or a road (bus) via **Píles**. 14km **Mesokhorió** is built on a precipitous rock on the W coast. Here a stream gushes out of the pavement of a church. In the environs are the church of **Ayía Iríni**, with frescoes, and many Byzantine ruins. On the islet of **Sókastro**, close inshore, is a ruined Frankish castle. From Mesokhorió the road leads across the island to **Spóa** (351m) above the little E coast harbour of Ayios Nikólaos. From Spóa, where the pine forests are bent double by the wind, Olimbos can be reached (see below).

The N part of the island is approached more easily (in 2 hours) by boat from Pigádhia. Landing is made at **Dhiafáni** on the NE coast, whence a road ascends to (9km) **Ólimbos** (304 inhab.), perched on the flank of Profitis Ilias, overlooking the W coast. On the slopes of the mountain are more than 40 windmills. Olimbos is supposed to be the oldest settlement in Karpathos. Some inhabitants still wear traditional costume. Their dialect retains many ancient Doric words. The well-built houses are in three sections and have handsome doors with wooden locks and keys said to be of a pattern dating back to Homeric times. The Byzantine village church has some frescoes. In the vicinity are the remains of an ancient temple. About 3 hours N is **Trístoma**, with a landing-place on a relatively sheltered bay. A headland about half-way to Trístoma is taken as the site of *Brykous*.

Immediately N of Karpathos and separated by a channel only 27m wide is the islet of **Sariá** (10.5 sq. km), inhabited in summer only by shepherds. On it are the ruins of a Byzantine church.

The island of **Khálki** (Χάλκη), the ancient *Chalke* and medieval *Charki*, lies 16km W of Rhodes (daily boat to/from Kámiros Skála). The bare and hilly interior culminates in Mt Merovigli (596m). There are no springs and few wells. The population (281 inhab.) has been greatly reduced by emigration though limited tourist development has taken place. The landing-place is **Emborió**, or Skála, at the NE corner of the island. A road climbs inland in 30 minutes to the village of **Khorió** (274m), now virtually abandoned. Its church is partly built of Hellenic materials. One mile inland, on top of a bare hill, formerly a Greek acropolis, is the Castle of the Knights, built on Greek foundations and incorporating much ancient masonry. Inside is the church of Ayios Nikólaos, with late Byzantine frescoes. About 8km NW of Emborio the church of

**Taxiárkhis Mikhaílis o Panormítis** has 10–12C frescoes. In the vicinity of Ayios Ioánnis in the W of the island, about 2 hours walk from Emborió, is a deserted mediaeval settlement where the church of Ayios Nikítas has frescoes of 10–15C.

# 76

# Rhodes (Rhódhos)

The island of **RHODES** (Ρόδος), in Greek **Rhódhos**, with 98,456 inhabitants, is separated from the SW coast of Asia Minor by the Strait of Marmara, about 11km wide. By far the largest of the Dodecanese with an area of 1398.5 sq. km, Rhodes is diamond-shaped, 77km long from N to S and with a maximum width of 35.5km. It is traversed from N to S by a range of hills rising from either end towards the W centre, where Mt Ataviros shoots up to 1215m. The other summits do not exceed 823m. Much of the island is very fertile, with a wide variety of plants and trees; vegetation grows to some of the mountain-tops. There are oranges, lemons, figs, pears, pistachio and olives. Broom, myrtle, heath, spurge and laurel grow in profusion, as well as aromatic plants such as lavender, sage, marjoram and styrax. The rock-rose is so exuberant that Rhodes is often called the 'Island of Roses'. The fauna include deer (reintroduced by the Italians), foxes, hares, badgers, martens, and hedgehogs; partridges, vultures, jackdaws, and jays. In antiquity the island was infested with snakes (its name may derive from 'erod' a Phoenician word for snake), and farmers still wear leather boots to the knee as protection against a small species which is poisonous. The larger snakes are harmless. Some of the lizards are large: the 'Rhodes dragon' (*Agama stellio*) grows to 35.5cm. There are so many butterflies that Rhodes has been called 'Butterfly Island'.

The climate of Rhodes resembles that of eastern Sicily. The temperature varies from 10°C in winter to 30–32°C in summer. The winds are constant and occasionally violent, though the E side of the island is usually sheltered. Windmills are a feature of the landscape. The year is divided between a dry season, from April to the end of October, and a wet season, from November to the end of March. The best months for a visit are April–May and September–October. From spring to autumn the island is crowded with tourists from every country in Europe and hotel accommodation is at a premium.

**History**. In antiquity the island was called *Aithrea*, *Ophioussa* (from its snakes), *Telchinia* and several other names. The name of **Rhodes** is of uncertain etymology, but is probably not derived (as so often stated) from the Greek word for rose, ρόδον. Pindar tells of the birth of Rhodes, offspring of the love of Helios, the Sun God, for the nymph Rhoda. Neolithic remains have been found at various cave sites and Ialysos and Trianda, in particular, have produced important Bronze Age finds. In that period, the island was influenced first by Minoan and then by Mycenaean culture. Homer mentions three cities in Rhodes–Lindos, Ialysos, and Kameiros (*Iliad*, II, 656). These three cities, with Kos, Knidos, and Halicarnassus, formed the Dorian hexapolis in the SW corner of Asia Minor.

The three Dorian cities of Rhodes attained great prosperity, with trade routes throughout the Mediterranean, and founded colonies in the neighbouring islands and on the coasts of Asia Minor and Europe. In the 6C BC they were governed by tyrants. Having submitted to the Persians in 490, in 478 the Rhodians joined the Delian

Confederacy as subject-allies of Athens, but in 411, late in the Peloponnesian War, they revolted in favour of Sparta. In 408 the three cities united to found the capital *City of Rhodes*, which they populated with their own citizens. The overall layout, attributed to Hippodamos of Miletus, the most famous town-planner of antiquity, has been traced by archaeologists.

The new city, whose planning Strabo praises extravagantly, immediately became prominent. At first it had an oligarchic government and in 396 submitted to Sparta. Later a democratic constitution was adopted and its citizens joined the Athenians, whom they helped, in conjunction with the Persian fleet, to defeat the Spartans at the battle of Knidos (394). In 378 Rhodes joined the Second Athenian Confederacy, but in 357 she revolted again, this time at the instigation of Mausolus, king of Caria, who placed a Carian garrison in the island. As allies of Persia the Rhodians gave help to the city of Tyre when it was besieged by Alexander the Great. In 332 a Macedonian garrison was installed but this was expelled after the death of Alexander. In the wars that followed, the Rhodians allied themselves with Ptolemy I, who assisted them in 305 when their city was besieged by Demetrios Poliorketes. When, after a year, Demetrios was compelled to raise the siege, he was so impressed by the defenders' valour that he left them his siege artillery, from the sale of which they defrayed the cost of the Colossus. The Rhodians accorded divine honours to Ptolemy as their saviour: hence his name Soter.

Soon afterwards with heightened prestige, Rhodes reached the zenith of her prosperity. Her port became the centre of trade between Italy, Greece and Macedonia, and Asia and Africa. She became the first naval Power in the Aegean. Her currency was everywhere accepted. Rhodian law, the earliest code of marine law, was universally esteemed: Augustus adopted it as a model, an example followed by Justinian, and its provisions are still quoted today. With a population of 60,000–80,000, the city was lavishly adorned and entered an artistic golden age. Devastation by the great earthquake of 222 BC inspired an international programme of aid in money and talent. Even as late as the 1C AD, when the city had been despoiled of most of its treasures, Pliny counted no fewer than 2000 statues, many of them colossal. The Rhodians were enthusiastic admirers of athletics, music, and oratory. The orator Aeschines (389–314 BC), after his discomfiture at the hands of Demosthenes, founded at Rhodes a school of rhetoric, which was later to be attended by famous Romans, including Cato, Cicero, Julius Caesar, and Lucretius. Apollonius (fl. 222–181 BC), a native of Alexandria, taught rhetoric at Rhodes with so much success that the Rhodians awarded him the cognomen Rhodius.

By the 2C BC the Rhodians were allies of Rome. Their help against Philip V of Macedon, which led to his defeat at Cynoscephalae in 197, gained them the Cyclades, and the participation of their fleet in the war against Antiochus the Great, king of Syria, won them in 188 BC the former Syrian possession of S Caria, where they had from an early period made numerous settlements. The Rhodian espousal of the cause of Perseus brought swift Roman retribution. After Pydna Rhodes had to surrender her possessions on the mainland of Asia Minor and, in 166, her trade was injured when the Romans declared Delos a free port. In the Mithridatic wars Rhodes recovered the favour of Rome. Mithridates unsuccessfully besieged the city. Sulla restored to Rhodes her lost Asiatic possessions. In the civil war Rhodes sided with Julius Caesar and suffered in consequence at the hands of Cassius, who plundered the city in 43 BC and destroyed or captured the Rhodian fleet. This was a fatal blow to the naval power of Rhodes.

Augustus accorded to Rhodes the title of Allied City. Vespasian (emperor AD 70–79) incorporated it in the empire. Reattached to the province of Asia, it became under Diocletian (284–305) capital of the province of the Islands. It was visited by St Paul during his second or third journey (Acts, xxi, 1) and it had a bishop at a very early date. In the 4C the bishops of Rhodes were granted the title of Metropolitan, with jurisdiction over 12 of the dioceses of the Archipelago. In the 9C the Rhodians deserted the Roman church. In 1274, however, we find the Metropolitan of Rhodes attending the Council of Lyons and a signatory of the short-lived reunion of the Eastern and Latin churches.

After the division of the Empire in 395, Rhodes naturally became part of the Eastern Empire and followed its destiny. From 654 it was frequently pillaged and for a time occupied by the Saracens. In 1082 Alexander Comnenus gave the Venetians important privileges in the island. In the Crusades Christian ships used the ports of Rhodes as a convenient stopping-place. During the Fourth Crusade, which established the Latin empire of Constantinople, the Greek Governor of Rhodes, Leo Gavalas, declared the independence of the island. Later the Genoese obtained control of it and in 1306 received as refugees the Knights of St John of Jerusalem. The refugees soon became the masters of Rhodes.

The **Knights of St John of Jerusalem**, otherwise Knights of Rhodes and later Knights of Malta, were originally **Hospitallers**, charitable brotherhoods founded for the care in hospital of the poor and sick. They originated c 1048 in a hospital which merchants of Amalfi had built in Jerusalem for pilgrims to the Holy Sepulchre. Their first rector,

Coats of arms of the Grand Masters of the Order of St John

Gerard, formed them into a strictly constituted religious body subject to the jurisdiction of the Patriarch of Jerusalem. The Order soon became predominantly military and the Hospitallers were sworn to defend the Holy Sepulchre to the last drop of their blood and to make war on infidels wherever met. In 1191, after Saladin had captured Jerusalem, they retired to Acre. Bitter rivalry arose between them and the Knights Templar, ending in hostilities in which the Templars got the upper hand. Clinging to Acre, the Hospitallers were driven out in 1291 after a terrible siege, and they sailed to Cyprus. In 1306 they fled from Cyprus to Rhodes. Having in vain demanded from the emperor the fief of Rhodes, they took it by force in 1309, after a two years' siege.

The brethren were divided into three classes—knights, chaplains, and serving brothers or fighting squires who followed the knights into action. In the 12C the Order was divided into seven 'Tongues' or Languages—Provence, Auvergne, France, Italy, Spain (later subdivided into Aragon and Castile), England and Germany. Each 'Tongue' had a Bailiff, and the Bailiffs, under the presidency of the Grand Master, elected for life by the Knights, formed the chapter of the Order. The modern British Order of St John of Jerusalem, founded in 1827, may be regarded as a revival of the 'Language' of England.

Having conquered Rhodes, the Knights of St John built a powerful fleet which protected the island's trade. Pope Clement V assigned to them part of the property of the Templars who had been suppressed in 1312. For two centuries the Knights of St John defied the Turks. For his assistance to the Knights during the siege of 1313, Amadeus V, count of Savoy, was rewarded by a grant of the arms of the Order with a collar bearing the letters F.E.R.T. (Fortitudo eius Rhodum tenuit). The Knights took part in the capture and later in the defence of Smyrna, and withstood two great sieges in 1444 by the Sultan of Egypt, and in 1480 by Mehmet II, at which time their infantry general ('turcopolier') was an Englishman, John Kendal. At last, in June 1522 Suleiman I, having captured Belgrade, attacked Rhodes with a force said to have numbered 100,000 men. The Knights mustered only 650, with the addition of 200 Genoese sailors, 50 Venetians, 400 Cretans and 600 of the inhabitants. Pope Adrian VI vainly implored the Christian princes to come to their aid. The Turks had the city blockaded by sea. They eventually secured the heights above it and thence shelled the fortifications. Several times the besieged repaired the breaches in the walls, but their numbers daily diminished. They had spent their strength and traitors had infiltrated into their ranks. In December the Turks made another and final breach in the walls. The Knights capitulated on honourable terms. On 1 January 1523, the Grand Master, Villiers de l'Isle Adam, with 180 surviving brethren, left the island. They first retired to Candia (Herakleion), Crete, and in 1530 to Malta.

After their departure the churches were converted into mosques. Not till 1660 were the Fathers of the Mission able to return to Rhodes and administer to the Christian slaves. In 1719 they were placed under the protection of the Apostolic Prefecture of Constantinople. In 1873 French Franciscan Sisters established schools and in 1889 the Brothers of the Christian Doctrine founded the College of St John. In 1877 the island was created an apostolic prefecture.

In 1912, during their war with Turkey, the Italians captured Rhodes after a short siege. In the latter part of the Second World War the Germans took over from the Italians. In 1945 the island was freed by British and Greek commandos, and in 1947 it was officially awarded to Greece.

**Rhodian Art**. Rhodian artefacts of the 2nd millennium BC show marked influences of Crete and Mycenae. No palaces have yet been discovered, but chamber tombs have yielded sepulchral furniture, notably pottery, jewellery and weapons. Pottery, when not imported, follows Minoan and Mycenaean prototypes, although with some local features. Jewellery includes articles of glass paste (Mycenaean), engraved gold items, filigree work, precious stones and incised scarabs. Among the weapons are bronze swords and daggers. There is evidence that the island was affected by the eruption of the Thera volcano.

As elsewhere in the Aegean, the Mycenaean Age was succeeded by the Geometric and Orientalising periods (1100–650 BC). The excavations at Lindos, Ialysos, Kameiros, and Vrulia have given rich yields of pottery. Rhodian vases of the 7C and 6C are decorated with animal figures, including goats and fugitive hares, palm, and vine leaves, and geometric designs (roses, circles, and swastikas). With the native ware are found vases from Corinth, Attica, Cyprus, and the Orient. Some votive objects including figurines, scarabs, and engraved stones, from the Temple of Athena at Lindos and at Ialysos are of Phoenician origin.

The foundation in 408 BC of the city of Rhodes brought an influx of famous artists. Lysippos of Sikyon, the sculptor attached to the court of Alexander the Great, produced at Rhodes his famous Chariot of the Sun. Under the influence of Lysippos was founded the **School of Rhodes**, which flourished for three centuries and of which Pliny gives an account. Leaders of the school included Protogenes, the painter from Caria who lived in poverty until acclaimed by Apelles, Chares of Lindos, creator of the Colossus of Rhodes, and Bryaxis, responsible for at least five statues of note. These were followed by a host of other artists, both native and immigrant, of whom little is known save their names, many of which appear on statue bases uncovered on the Acropolis of Lindos. The sculptors, from Chares downwards, worked chiefly in bronze. We know something about Philiskos, author of a group of the Muses, which was carried off to Rome, perhaps by Crassus, and placed in the Porticus of Octavia. Inspired by Lysippos, Philiskos was especially skilled in the treatment of drapery. Heliodoros of Rhodes produced a group of Pan and Olympus, now believed to be in the Museum at Naples.

The loss of her independence did not halt the artistic activity of Rhodes. One of her sculptors made a Colossus 12m high, dedicated to the Roman people and placed in the Temple of Athena Polias and Zeus Polieos on the Acropolis of Rhodes. There followed Boïthos of Chalcedon, and Apollonios and Tauriskos of Tralles, who made a group of Dirce which was found in the Baths of Caracalla in Rome and is now at Naples. Pliny mentions Aristonidas, who executed a statue of Atamos bewailing the death of his son Learchos. The group of Menelaus and Patroclus, a fragment of which is now in Rome under the name of Pasquino, came from Rhodes. Best known of all is the Laocoön, found in 1506 in the Golden House of Nero in Rome; this group was produced in the 1C BC by the Rhodian sculptors Agesander, Polydorus, and Athenodorus. After the creation of this masterpiece Rhodian art declined.

There are a number of Early Christian basilicas and interesting painted Byzantine churches. With the arrival of the Knights of St John the art of Rhodes becomes westernised. The Grand Masters, most of whom came from France or from Spain, naturally favoured the style of their native countries, and French or Spanish Gothic predominated. Two periods can be distinguished: from 1309 to 1480, and from 1480 to 1522. In the earlier period the Knights depended on local labour unfamiliar with the Gothic style, and the work was heavy and maladroit, with intrusive Byzantine elements. In the second period, which was inspired by d'Aubusson (1476–1503), one of the most eminent of the Grand Masters, can be seen the hand of the Western craftsman. The Gothic character of the work remains, but the forms are more harmonious, the execution more accurate, and the decoration natural or cleverly stylised. Towards the end of the period a few Renaissance motives were introduced, alleviating the severity of the monastic Gothic. These included marble cornices to doors and windows, elaborate escutcheons, and inscriptions carved in superb Latin characters. Here and there are forms deriving from Sicily and southern Italy.

The walls of Rhodes, with their succession of towers, bastions, lunettes, ravelins, and barbicans, are a magnificent example of military architecture of the 14C, 15C, and 16C. The inscriptions and escutcheons that adorn the walls enable one to follow the history of their development. Up to the time of the siege of 1480 the emphasis was on the architectural aspect; later building and modification relied less on the architect than on the engineer. Many Italian engineers were employed on the work.

Gothic influences persisted into the Turkish period, which added little but an Oriental veneer, some elegant minarets and fountains, and the introduction of pottery from Anatolia. The brief Italian period left a mixed legacy of bombastic architecture, over-restoration, and well-engineered roads.

The **City of Rhodes** (42,400 inhab.), situated at the N end of the island, today consists of two distinct parts. The **Old City**, hemmed in by walls built by the Knights, is clustered round the Central or Commercial Harbour, and is itself divided into two. In the NW is a walled enclosure called the **Castle of the Knights or Collachium**. The rest of the city is known as the **Khóra**. The **New Town**, built since the Italian occupation of 1912, and consisting largely of hotels, extends to the N of the Old City as far as the N extremity of the island, and westwards to the foot of the acropolis of ancient Rhodes. It includes two quarters of the Greek city, Marasi and Neochori. On its E side is Mandraki, the second and smaller harbour of Rhodes, generally used by yachts and caiques calling at the island. The gardens of Rhodes are noted for their oleanders, bougainvilleas, and hibiscus. The city has suffered greatly from earthquakes. That of 225 BC overthrew the Colossus. Others occurred in AD 157, 515, 1364, 1481, 1851, and 1863. Of the ancient city few traces remain, though much of its street plan has been plotted under the present town. One side of its tourist appeal is represented by the existence of a golf course (at Afandoú) and a casino.

**Airport**, 16km SW near Paradhissi. Weekly to Rome. Several services a day to Athens; 4 weekly to Iráklion; less frequently to Thessaloníki, Síros, Thíra, Kós, Sitía, daily to Kárpathos, Kásos, Kastellórizo.

**Hotels** A–E, F/A.

**Post Office** (Pl. 7), opposite the cathedral. **OTE**, 25 Martíou. **Olympic Airways**, 9 Ieroú Lókhou.

**Tourist Police**, **NTOG**, Makaríou/Papágou; on right through archway at entrance to 'Museum Square'; **Police** Od.Eth. Dhodhekanissíon.

**Buses** from Od. Papágou, S of the Agora to the island villages to the E, Lindos etc. also local buses. Local Tourist Office, Plateía Rímim (Sound and Light Square); from Od. Avérof (W side of Néa Agora) to villages in the W of the island. Also Excursions to Lindos, Kameiros, etc.

The **modern city** is laid out along the waterfront of **Mandráki** (Pl. 7), the northern of the two natural harbours, now equipped as a yacht anchorage. The harbour entrance is guarded by two bronze deer (that to seaward replacing the former Italian she-wolf). On the mole protecting the E side of the basin stand three windmills and Fort St Nicholas, a cylindrical tower dating from 1464–67, topped by a lighthouse (view).

The word Mandráki, used elsewhere in the area for small enclosed harbours, means a small sheepfold. The alternative name **Harbour of the Galleys**, is a misnomer; Mandráki was always secondary to the equally misnamed Commercial Harbour, and under the Knights was occupied by small boat builders. Here probably stood the **Colossus of Rhodes**, a bronze statue of Helios, the sun god, set up by Chares of Lindos c 290 BC and considered one of the seven wonders of the world. Its erection was financed by the sale of the siege artillery that Demetrios Poliorketes had presented to the city at the end of his unsuccessful siege (305–304 BC). It was 60 cubits (c 27m) high. Helios, the protector of the city of Rhodes, was represented with his head framed in sunrays and dressed in a chlamys; in his right hand he held a torch, which served as a beacon to mariners. The tradition that the statue bestrode the harbour entrance and that ships passed beneath it is without foundation. The earthquakes of 225 BC overthrew the statue. For eight centuries its huge fragments lay undisturbed, respected by the superstitious reverence of the Rhodians. At last, in 653, Saracen corsairs collected them and brought them to Tyre. There they were sold to Jewish merchants of Emesa, who carried them away on 900 camels to be melted down and resold. Reports of the discovery of a piece in 1987 proved groundless.

The public buildings lining the waterfront all date from the Italian occupation and were designed in various monumental styles by Florestano di Fausto. Dominating the harbour mouth is the square campanile of the **cathedral** (Pl. 7), or **Church of the Evangelist**, built in 1925 on the model of the church of St John in the Old City, destroyed in 1856. The **fountain** outside the W end is a copy of the 13C Fontana Grande at Viterbo; the main **post office** stands opposite. Linked to the cathedral is the **Nomarkhía**, or Prefecture, formerly the Governor's Palace, the most considerable monument of the Italian period, built in a Venetian Gothic style. Its picturesque arcaded façade, with marble decoration, closing the seaward side of the

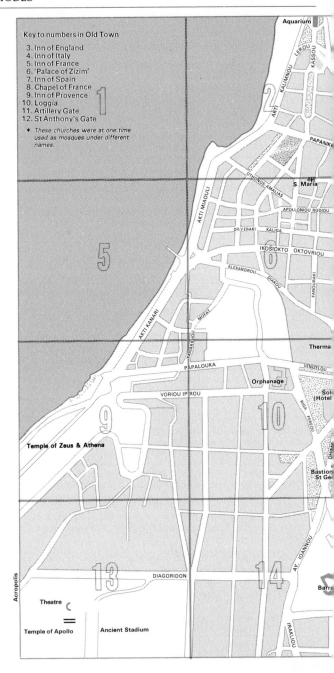

Key to numbers in Old Town

3. Inn of England
4. Inn of Italy
5. Inn of France
6. 'Palace of Zizim'
7. Inn of Spain
8. Chapel of France
9. Inn of Provence
10. Loggia
11. Artillery Gate
12. St Anthony's Gate

∗ *These churches were at one time used as mosques under different names.*

Aquarium

LEROU

KASSOU

AKTI

KALIMNOU

PAPANIK

OTHONOS AMALIAS

S. Maria

APOLLONIOU RODIOU

AKTI MIAOULI

DILVERAKI    KALIGA

IKOSIOKTO  OKTOVRIOU

ALEXANDROU    DIAKOU

FANDURAKI

AKTI KANARI

MOZAT

KAVARTIOU

Therma

PAPALOUKA

VENIZELOU

Orphanage

Sol
(Hotel

VORIOU IPIROU

RIGA  FEROU

OHMI

Temple of Zeus & Athena

Bastion
St Ge

AV. IOANNOU

Acropolis

DIAGORIDON

Barra

Theatre

Temple of Apollo    Ancient Stadium

IRAKLIOU

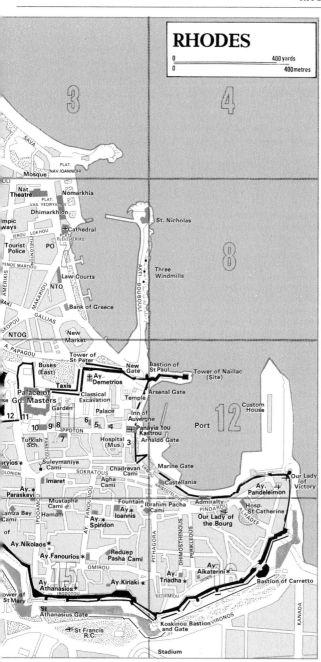

**RHODES**

0 — 400 yards

0 — 400 metres

3

4

SAVA

PLAT. NAV.IOANNIDHI

Mosque

ULI

Nat. Theatre

Nomarkhia

PLAT. VAS. YEORYIOSII

Dhimarkhion

mpic ways

IEROU LOKHOU

Cathedral

PLAT. ELEVTHERIAS

Tourist Police

PO

St. Nicholas

 PENDE MARTIOU

AMERIKIS

Law Courts

NTO

Three Windmills

AKI

MAKARIOU

Bank of Greece

SKOPOU

GALLIAS

8

NTOG

New Market

A PAPAGOU

Tower of St Peter

Buses (East)

Ay. Demetrios

New Gate

Bastion of St Paul

Tower of Naillac (Site)

Taxis

Palace of se Gd. Masters

Classical Excavation

Arsenal Gate

Temple

Custom House

12 11

10

9 8

Garden

Palace

6 5 4

Inn of Auvergne

Panayia tou Kastrou

Port

IPPOTON

7

Turkish Sch.

Hospital (Mus.)

3

Arnaldo Gate

12

PANETLIOU

ryios

Suleymaniye Cami

SOKRATOUS

Chadrevan Cami

Marine Tower

Castellania

Our Lady of Victory

OLONION

Agha Cami

ERIOU

ARISTOTELOUS

Ay. Pandeleimon

Ay. Paraskevi

Imaret

Mustapha Cami

Fountain

Ibrahim Pacha Cami

Admiralty

PINDAROU

Hosp. St Catherine

IPODAMOU

FANOURIOU

Ay. Ioannis

Our Lady of the Bourg

amza Bey Cami

Hamam

Ay. Spiridon

PITHAGORA

DHIMOSTHENOUS

PERIKLEOUS

ALHADEF

of

Ay. Nikolaos

Ay. Fanourios

Reduep Pasha Cami

Ay. Aikaterini

Bastion of Carretto

OMIROU

ower of St Mary

Ay. Athanasios

Ay. Kiriaki

Ay. Triadha

IRINIS

10

KANADA

IRODOTOU

St Athanasius Gate

EFTHIMIOU

Koskinou Bastion and Gate

VIRONOS

St Francis R.C.

Stadium

15

Plateia, is set off by the severity of the **Dhimarkhíon** and the **theatre**. To the N is a popular public beach (fee).

Beyond the theatre rises the elegant minaret of the **Mosque of Murad Reis** (Pl. 3). In front stands a circular turbeh enclosing the tomb of Murad Reis, admiral of the Turkish fleet during the siege of Rhodes. In the cemetery flanking the mosque are the tombs of many noble Turks who died in exile in Rhodes, including a Shah of Persia and a prince of the Crimea. Farther on, beyond the Villa Cleobohus featured in Lawrence Durrell's *Reflections on a Marine Venus* and Hotel des Roses (1927), the road follows the shore to **Akrotíri Ammou** (Sandy Point), the N extremity of the island. Here the **Hydrobiological Institute** (Pl. 2) houses a remarkable collection of preserved marine creatures caught in local waters (sharks, sun-fish, manta, sword-fish, etc.) and an **aquarium** unusually rich in octopods, molluscs, crustacea, etc.

The W shore, overlooked by many hotels, is still freely accessible.

Returning S along Mandráki, here fronted by gardens, you pass in succession the Limenarkhion, then, on the other side of the narrow Od. Makaríou, **Law Courts**, popular cafés under a neo-Gothic loggia, and the **Bank of Greece**. Contrasting with their golden stone is the flat whiteness of the **Nea Agora** (Pl. 7), a huge polygonal market in a Turkish style, which is the focal-point of the modern town. Beneath the N wall of the medieval city extends the **Garden of the Deer**, ablaze with sub-tropical flowers.

You enter the **˙˙Old City** by the **New Gate**, or **Gate of Liberty** (or Pilí Eleftherías), opened in 1924, and enter the Plateía Símis or Arsenal Square. You are now in the **Collachium**, or **Castle of the Knights**, the preserve of the Knights of St John, divided from the remainder of the city by an inner wall. In it are the Palace of the Grand Masters and the 'Inns' or residences of the 'Tongues' (see above). In Arsenal Square, which communicates with the commercial harbour (see below) are the Pîli Navárkhou, are the remains, discovered in 1922, of a **Temple of Aphrodite** (Pl. 11) dating from the 3C BC. They include foundations, bases, and shafts of columns, and fragments of the entablature. To the right is the **Municipal Gallery** (Mon to Sat 08.00–14.00; Weds 17.00 20.00; closed Sun), whose airy rooms containing an excellent collection of works of Greek artists. Behind the temple is the **Inn of the Tongue of Auvergne** (Pl. 11), a 15C building restored in 1919, the side of which overlooks the attractive Plateía Argirokástrou. In the centre of this square a Byzantine font serves as fountain; the heaps of cannon-balls were amassed during the siege of 1522. On the right the Institute of History and Archaeology (with the ephorate of antiquities) occupies the **Palace of the Armeria**, built in the 14C under Roger de Pins and used as the first hospital of the Order. Also in this square is the **Museum of Decorative Arts and Folklore** (08.00–15.00 daily). You pass beneath an arch. To the left is the office of the **Tourist Police**. Beyond (on the same side of the square) is the 13C Byzantine churech of the Panayía ton Kástron which, as St. Mary's, became the first cathedral of the Knights. After 1522 the Turks converted it into a mosque called **Enderoum**, and it now serves as a **Byzantine Museum** (08.00–15.00; closed Monday). In the courtyard of the Commercial Bank opposite is an amusing modern mosaic of black and white pebbles in a style that has survived unchanged in Rhodes from Byzantine times.

Leaving to the right the Street of the Knights (see below) you enter Hospital Square. Here on the left is the **Inn of the Tongue of England** (3; Pl. 11), built in 1482, despoiled and almost destroyed in 1850, rebuilt on the original plan by Colonel Sir Vivian Gabriel, and repaired by the British in 1949. Opposite stands the **Hospital of the Knights** (Pl. 11), begun in 1440 over the remains of a Roman building and completed in 1481–89. During the War of Greek Independence the Turks used it for their sick and wounded, but later degraded it into barracks. It was skilfully restored under Amedeo Maiuri in 1913–18. Bomb damage sustained to the S side in the Second World War has again been made good. The **façade**, set forward from the plain E wall above, consists of eight deep arches of unadorned severity. Seven, surmounted by a wall relieved by two string-courses lead into open magazines, while the one to the right of centre shelters the main gate-way and supports a projecting apsidal chapel (see below). By skilful use of vertical moulding this arrangement is given the appearance of a gate-tower. The **portal** is decorated with a rope design. The original door of cypress was presented by Sultan Mahmoud to Louis-Philippe in 1836 and now reposes at Versailles.

Since 1916 the building has housed the *****Archaeological Museum** (08.00–15.00; closed Mondays). The **Great Court** is enclosed by a double portico, of which the lower storey is vaulted. Beneath the lower colonnade are various fragments; in the centre crouches a marble lion (1C BC); in the corners are cannon balls and catapult shot. An outside stair leads to the upper gallery where are ranged funerary stelai and altar-bases. The entire E wing is occupied by the **Infirmary Ward**, a rectangular hall divided length-ways by an arcade borne on seven columns; its ogee arches support a ceiling of cypress-wood.

The ward held 32 beds with brocaded canopies, and the patients ate from silver plate. Two surgeons were on duty at all times. The dark cubicles that open from the hall have been variously explained as confessionals, isolation wards, and wardrobes.

Beneath a flamboyant arch in the long wall opens the vaulted exedra, with three Gothic windows, that projects above the main gate. This held an altar where mass was said daily. Round the walls of the hall are ranged **memorials** of the Knights from the destroyed church of St John. Notable are a classical marble sarcophagus used in 1355 as the tomb of Grand Master Pierre de Corneillan (lid in the Cluny Museum, Paris; copy here) and tomb-slabs of Thomas Newport (1502), of Nicholas de Montmirel (1511), commandant of the Hospital, of Tomaso Provena (1499), and of Fernando de Heredia (1493). Heraldic devices include the royal arms of England.

Off the Ward opens the former staff refectory with reliefs (several from Nísyros) on the walls—those in a frontal, simplified late Roman style are particularly striking. Off this are reached the three (two of them small) rooms of **sculpture**. Although the display is rather cramped, the works give a good idea of the variety in subject and treatment and often the delicacy of Rhodian Hellenistic sculpture. There are several examples of the **Nymph seated on a rock** (Room 1 etc). In Room 2, other works of note are a 1C **Crouching Aphrodite**, after the famous work of Doidalsas (and the inspiration for the title of Lawrence Durrell's book), a torso of **Artemis**, a copy of the **Tyche** (Fortune) of Antioch, an example of the **Artemis Hekate** type, an **Asklepios**, a **Hygieia**, a **Zeus**, a bearded **Bacchus**, a **Satyr** reclining on a wineskin, several elegant female statues (note the drapery). In Room 3 are included an **Aphrodite Pudica**, a 3-sided **Hekataion** in Archaising style, and a fine **Nymph (or Aphrodite)**, with arm resting on the knee.

At this point you can enter a garden overlooking the **Little Court**, excavated in 1907, with a 6C mosaic pavement from Arkassa in Karpathos. In an alcove to the left a funerary naiskos contains memorial sculpture; a mosaic is laid in front. Amongst the sculpture in the garden is a fine Hellenistic dolphin.

Off the corner of the garden opposite the sculpture galleries, two further interconnected rooms include a **funerary stele of young Timarista** taking her last farewell of Crito, her mother, a delicate work of the 5C BC; Crito's hair was recut after damage in antiquity; two headless Kouroi (6C BC) found at Kameiros, but which appear to come from Paros and Naxos; two fragmentary heads; sculptured perirrhanterion stand of the 7C BC.

From here you return to the gallery round the main central court to visit its surrounding rooms, some of which may be closed. The first three contain Geometric—Archaic pottery mainly from tombs in the territory of ancient Ialyssos. On the W side three rooms have prehistoric (mainly Mycenaean) pottery and other finds, while six more rooms (on the N) have a large selection of mainly Archaic pottery (and some other material). There are good examples of both Rhodian and Attic black-figure, fine Rhodian amphorae and oinochoai, including examples decorated in the 'Wild Goat' style, also some Corinthian imports.

Leaving the museum you turn left from Hospital Square to ascend the cobbled *Street of the Knights (Odhos Ippoton; Pl. 11), the main thoroughfare of the Collachium which it crosses from E to W, rising towards the Palace. Its noble buildings, plentifully adorned with coats-of-arms, were restored with care and accuracy in 1913–16, so that the street provides a faithful picture of late medieval architecture, though the overall effect is perhaps too tidy to evoke the full spirit of the Middle Ages. To the right are offices of the Archaeological Service and a Bookshop.

The knightly houses and inns follow the same general pattern, having two storeys with a flat ornamental façade and a terrace roof. Vaulted store-houses, or stables (?), occupied the lower floor while the upper storey was reached by an open stair and gallery from a central court. The rounded arches, the horizontal emphasis given by string-courses, and the large square windows suggest that the Renaissance was already affecting even a military order of medieval chivalry.

On the left is the N façade of the Hospital (see below) with a good portal at the far end. Opposite is the **Inn of the Tongue of Italy** (4; Pl. 11) rebuilt in 1519 when Del Carretto was Grand Master. Beyond a house bearing the arms of de l'Isle Adam quartered with those of his mother (d. 1462) is the *Inn of the Tongue of France** (5; Pl. 11), architecturally the most harmonious building in the street. It was built in 1492–1509, disfigured by the Turks, and carefully restored at the expense of Maurice Bompard, French ambassador to the Porte. The escutcheons include that of Pierre d'Aubusson (Grand Master 1476–1503). The crocodile gargoyles recall the legend of Gozon (see below). The building opposite, with an Aragonese portal and an attractive garden court, bears the Spanish arms of Villaraguts. Next to it is a charming building with an upper floor in the Turkish style.

In a side street (right) is the so-called **Palace of Zizim** (6; Pl. 11), pretender brother of Bayezid II, given asylum here for a short time in 1482 before being conveyed to France.

Farther on (right) the small **Chapel of the Tongue of France** (8; Pl. 11) bears a statue of the Virgin and Child and the lilies of France. The adjacent **Chaplain's House**, dated by the arms of Béranger (Grand Master 1365–74) on the façade, is occupied by the Italian consulate. An arch spans the road. Two buildings, to the left of the street, before and beyond the arch, constitute the **Inn of the Tongue of Spain** (7; Pl. 11); the first (Aragon and Castile) dates from the mid-15C, the second from c 50 years later. The **Inn of the Tongue of Provence** (9; Pl. 11) of 1518, to the right, has an elegant portal surmounted by four coats-of-arms set in a cross-shaped niche.

At the top of the street you enter Citadel Square beneath the **Loggia of St John** (10; Pl. 11), a modern reconstruction of a portico of unknown purpose. Already in ruins before the explosion of 1856, it used to join the entrance-court of the Palace to the **Conventual Church of St John** which lay parallel to the palace. A fragment of wall is all that remains of the church, and a Turkish school now occupies the site.

Built in a plain 14C style, more or less faithfully copied in the church on Mandraki, it contained the tombs of the Knights. After 1522 it was turned into a mosque. In 1856 it was destroyed when lightning struck the minaret and exploded beneath it a forgotten underground cache of gunpowder, killing c 800 people.

On the N side of the square in the highest part of the Collachium stands the **Palace of the Grand Masters** (Pl. 11; 08.00–15.00; closed Mondays), rebuilt in 1939–43 from old drawings of the original 14C building.

Son et Lumière in English, French, German, and Swedish (entrance from municipal garden outside the walls). The tour of the walls (see below) begins from the main entrance of the Palace.

The Palace stands on the site of an ancient temple of Apollo. Begun soon after the arrival in Rhodes of the Knights, and completed at the end of the 14C, it was a superb building on a rectangular plan, 79m by 75m, and was in effect an independent fortress designed with underground store-rooms to withstand a siege. It served in time of peace as the residence of the Grand Master and the place of assembly of the Order. Repaired after the earthquake of 1481, it suffered little damage in the siege of 1522. The Turks turned it into a prison. It was badly damaged by the earthquake of 1851 and the remains were further shattered by the explosion of 1856. Some of the material was used by the Turks to build a military hospital (since razed) in the grounds. The Italians, intending it as a summer residence for Victor Emmanuel III and Mussolini, rebuilt the exterior as far as possible in the old style, but redesigned the interior for modern occupation, including central heating, disguised lifts, and electric chandeliers. The preparations were barely completed when Italy relinquished the island.

The **courtyard** is decorated with Roman statuary and elements from a Byzantine church at Arnitha. Off the court are exhibitions of recent archaeological work and of Byzantine objects. The **interior** achieves grandeur though sometimes at the expense of taste. The spacious halls have timber ceilings supported on Roman and Byzantine columns and are paved in coloured marbles or with vast antique *mosaics brought from Kos. Some are lit by alabaster windows. The furniture, of many styles and periods, includes good Renaissance woodwork from Italian churches. The windows afford charming views of the city and sea. The garden contains sarcophagi of Masters, and a bronze she-wolf of Rome that once adorned the E mole of Mandraki.

Some of the ground floor and basement rooms of the Palace now house two outstanding permanent exhibitions, installed to commemorate the 2400th anniversary of the City of Rhodes in 1993 and drawing mainly on archaeological discoveries since the Second World War (earlier material is in the Archaeological Museum). The first, **Ancient Rhodes. 2400 years**, illustrates the earlier history of the island; the second covers **Rhodes from the 4C AD to the Turkish conquest (1522)**. The material is beautifully displayed, without crowding, and treats the past of the island mainly according to themes, which are illustrated by the objects shown. In the earlier exhibition, the first two rooms illustrate the history of Rhodes from the Neolithic Period until the synoecism and the foundation and organisation of the town thereafter. There follow galleries illustrating public buildings and sanctuaries (3), the Rhodian house (4), implements of domestic use (5), cosmetics and daily life (6), artistic and spiritual life (7), Rhodian ceramic workshops (8), the manufacture of bronze, glass and terracotta sculpture (9), trade, the economy, coinage (10), the cemetery (11), burial customs (12). The later displays are of crafts and trades (including the refining of sugar), fine pottery (local and imported), table ware, military equipment and organisation, intellectual life (including books), ritual (including icons), wall paintings, the early Christian basilicas and their art.

At the W end of the square you pass through the Collachium wall by a double arch to Plateía Kleovoúlou, then Od. Orféos, a long tree-lined 'piazza' with small shops and cafés. To the right an arch and a shaded walk (see below) lead to the Amboise Gate and then over the moats (deer in the outer moat) out to the new town. You turn left towards the ugly **Clock Tower**, which replaced a 15C tower (overthrown in 1851) at the SW corner of the Collachium. Ascent (fee) is permitted to see the view over the town. A few yards farther on Odhós Apollonío leads (right) to Ayios Yioryios, adapted by the Turks into the Kurmale Medresses (Pl. 11; 'College of the Date-Palm'). The dome, set on a drum of 21 blind arches, preserves its ancient tiles. The street ends at St George's gate.

The **Mosque of Suleiman** (Pl. 11; closed), erected soon after 1522 on the site of a Church of the Apostles and rebuilt in 1808, is preceded by the customary court with a fountain. It has a double portico, a portal in a Venetian Renaissance style, and an elegant minaret with a double balcony. Opposite is the **Turkish Library** (1793) with illuminated 15–16C Koran. From here you descend **Odhós Sokrátous**, the former **bazar**, now full of tourist shops. Its balconied houses, open shops and coffee-houses still preserve a Turkish atmosphere. Beyond the **Mosque of Aga** (Pl. 11), curiously raised on wooden pillars, you reach Plateía Ippokrátous. Here the Municipal Library and Island Archives occupy the so-called **Palace of the Castellan** (Pl. 12), a square building of 1507 bearing the arms of Amboise. It was probably the commercial court of the Knights and was restored by the Italians after use as a mosque (above) and a fish-market (below). The upper hall, supported by an arcaded loggia, is reached by an external stair and a sculptured marble portal; the windows are delicately moulded. To the E of Od. Pithagóra, the long street that runs S towards the Koskinou (also Ay. Ioánnou) Gate, lies the former Jewish quarter, once noted for its animation compared with the Turkish streets.

Odhós Aristotélous continues E past houses with Turkish wooden balconies to **Martyrs' Square**, damaged in the Second World War. A fountain adorned with bronze sea-horses, stands in front of the misnamed **Admiralty** (Pl. 16), whose inscriptions in Latin and Greek suggest that it was the palace of either the Orthodox metropolitan or the Latin archbishop. Odhós Pindhárou passes (right) the impressive ruins of the Gothic church of Our Lady of the Bourg, now split in two by a road with an arched exit to the waterfront, and ends before the **Hospice of St Catherine** (Pl. 16), founded by Fra Domenico d'Alemagna in 1392 to shelter Italian pilgrims travelling to the Holy Land; it was enlarged in 1516. A large excavation here has revealed a long section of the 4C town wall. At the most easterly corner of the town is the small church of Ayios Pandeleimon, beyond which, on the ramparts (left) are the ruins of the church of **Our Lady of Victory** (Pl. 12), built to commemorate the heroic defence of this rampart in 1480 and destroyed c 1522. To the left **St Catherine's Gate** leads to the **Commercial Harbour**, the larger of the two harbours of Rhodes. The Carrelto Gate at the SE corner leads to the Moat Theatre, where summer performances and concerts take place against a backdrop of the medieval walls.

This, the 'Grand Harbour', was protected by two moles, defended with artillery, between which was stretched a chain. The N mole bore the **Tower of Naillac**, a key-point during the siege, but overthrown in 1863 (reconstruction planned); that to the E, separating the harbour from the Bay of Akandia and once adorned with 15 windmills, has been enlarged to form the modern quay where inter-island boats moor. The defences round the harbour consist of a high curtain-wall with a **Marine Gate** (1478; sometimes by confusion called St Catherine's Gate, see above) that recalls the Fort St André at Villeneuve-lès-Avignon in Provence; it figured prominently in the film *Guns of Navarone*. Following the wall you may re-enter the old city by the **Arsenal Gate**, or reach Mandráki by traversing the NE salient by the **Bastion of St Paul**.

The interest of the old city has by no means been exhausted, and visitors staying in the city may explore the narrow alleys of its S sector at their leisure. The small houses and occasional churches, the unexpected archways and courtyards, and the mosques (for the most part derelict and stripped) present a colourful mixture of medieval and eastern styles.

You may begin in the SE with two churches which were converted into mosques, the 14C **Ayia Aikaterini** (or **Ilk Mihrab Cami**, whose Turkish name marks it as the first shrine at which Allah was worshipped in 1522), and the neighbouring 15C **Ayia Triadha** (**Dolapli Mescidi**, or Oratory of the Well). Both are decorated with frescoes. Farther W in the pleasant Plateia Doriéos off Omirou, beyond a characteristic windmill, is the **Redjeb Pasha Cami** (1588), the most notable mosque built by the Turks on Rhodes, with Persian faience decoration. This is sometimes open (Fridays). **Ayios Fanourios** became the **Peial ad Din Mescid**. Its frescoes were restored by the Italians in 1938.

Grouped near the centre of the town are the **Ibrahim Pasha Cami**, a spacious mosque of 1531 opening onto Plateia Dhamagítou, off Od. Plátonos. Its plane-tree is said to have provided a place of execution for the Turks. A short distance to the W once a Gothic church which later became the **Demirli Cami**, has been shown to overlie the important Early Christian **Basilica of the Archangel Michael**. Other excavations are taking place in the area. Nearby is the charming Byzantine church of **Ayios Spiridón**, converted into a mosque (the **Kavakli Mescidi**) after 1523. The church (recently restored) has a complex architectural history back to at least the 6C. Frescoes in the apse are 6—7C and 13C. In the Plateia Arionos are the **Mustapha Cami** and the remarkable **Turkish Baths** (1765, rebuilt and undergoing restoration for continued public use (1994)). Off the square is a **Folk Dance Theatre**. From here the Mosque of Suleiman (see above) may be regained via the church of **Ayía Sotíra**, once the **Takkeci Cami**. In the SW corner of the town is **Ayios Nikólaos**, later the **Abdul Djelil Mescid**, with cable ornament and vaulting, damaged in the Second World War.

## Tour of the Walls

No visitor should omit the tour of the walls, which is conducted on Tuesday and Saturday at 2.45 (later in summer), from the courtyard of the Palace (see above). A complete circuit takes 1½ hours generally the guided tour ends at the Italian Tower, reached in ¾ hour. From the top a good defender's view is obtained; a visitor who has already seen the harbour defences is well advised to return (mostly by shaded walks) along the outside of the same section to obtain an attacker's view.

The **\*Walls of Rhodes**, a masterpiece of 15–16C military architecture, are well preserved throughout their extent of 4km, having successfully withstood the siege of 1480 and for a long time that of 1522. They bear 151 escutcheons of Grand Masters and knights.

In places the walls have ancient or Byzantine foundation blocks, but little is known of the Byzantine enceinte save that it resisted the Knights for three years. The remaining towers probably date in part from before 1330, as does the moat. Reconstruction began under Grand Masters Heredia (1377–96) and de Naillac (1396–1421), who built a massive tower on the N mole of the main harbour. In 1437–71 the walls were rebuilt to incorporate a number of detached towers. After the siege of 1480 and the earthquake of 1481, Pierre d'Aubusson (1476–1503) began a systematic and thoroughgoing reconstruction; the curtain-walls were thickened, parapets widened, the gates reduced in number from five to three and made more difficult of access, and the ditches doubled in width. The work was completed by del Carretto (1513–21), with the technical help of Italian architects. In 1522 Villiers de l'Isle Adam, again with Italian help, organised the final defences. In 1465 the enceinte had been divided into eight sectors, each allotted to one of the 'Tongues', and this arrangement was in force at the time of the final siege.

The fortifications, strongest on the landward side, comprise a continuous vertical or scarped wall, on which is a platform or walk, 13.7m wide, also continuous, protected by battlements and embrasures sited for firing in any direction. In many sectors there is also a lower walk. This circumvallation is surrounded by an external fosse, 32–46m wide and 15–20m deep, provided with scarp and counterscarp.

The exit from Citadel Square is by the **Artillery Gate** and **St Anthony's Gate**. You then cross the dry moats of the Palace to reach the wide parapet above the **Gate of Amboise** (1512). A bridge of three arches spans the outer moat. The main gate, which bears the arms of the Order and of Amboise, opens below between massive cylindrical towers. In the thickness of the wall the vaulted road makes an S-bend, then passes beneath a second gate, over an inner moat, and through a third gate to a **Terreplein**, now a shaded avenue (see above). This was exposed to fire on all sides and still separated from the Palace and the town by a third moat with further bridges and gates.

To the S is the short sector of the **Tongue of Germany**, the least numerous defensive group. On the left are Suleiman Square, the Clock Tower, and the mosques of Hurmale and of Suleiman. The **Bastion of St George** has a relief of St George on the original square tower, with the arms of Pope Martin V, of the Order, and of Grand Master Antonio Fluvian (1421–37). A polygonal bulwark was added later, and in 1496 the roadway through it was closed when the final bastion was erected. The next sector is that of the **Tongue of Auvergne**, ending at the circular **Tower of Spain**.

Beyond the tower is the sector of the **Tongue of Aragon**, one of the most picturesque, which bears SE and then S. From it there is a comprehensive view, taking in the mosques of Suleiman, of Mustapha, of Ibrahim Pasha, and of Redjeb Pasha, the Tower of the Windmills, the Commercial Harbour, the Tower of St Nicholas, the port of Mandraki, the new town and the coast of Anatolia. The ravelin was completed in 1522 which did not prevent the Turks in December making here the breach that enabled them to capture the city.

The **Tower of St Mary** bears a relief of the Virgin and Child and an inscription dated 1441. Round the tower in 1487 a great polygonal bastion was added for the protection of the **Gate of St Athan** by d'Aubusson; later he closed the gate. Reopened for a sortie in 1522, it was closed again by Suleiman in 1531 and remained so until 1922. The wall turns E to one of its most striking sectors, that of the **Tongue of England**. Along it are numerous windmills. The **Gate of Koskinou**, or Gate of St John, shows clearly the difference between early and later military architecture. The earlier wall has a square tower with small embrasures and battlements, while the additions of c 1480 take the form of a huge bastion of horseshoe plan with ravelins and embrasures for larger artillery. Its defence was shared between the Tongues of England and **Provence**, whose sector follows a zigzag line marked by three towers.

The large **Bastion del Carretto**, or of Italy, is a blend of an older tower and a semicircular bastion of 1515, 50m in diameter and of three storeys. The sector skirting the Bay of Akandia, fronted by a ravelin, was defended by the **Tongue of Italy**. Nearing the mole on which is the Tower of the Windmills the wall makes a right-angled turn to the left. Just beyond the

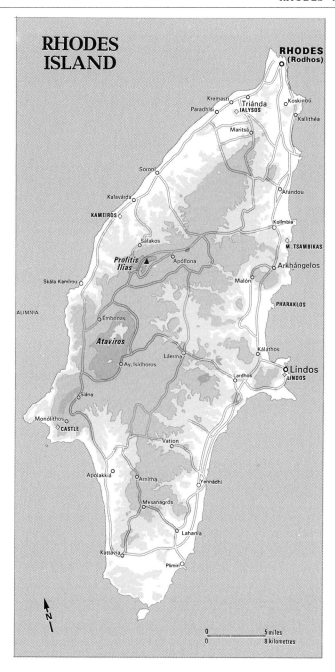

# RHODES
# ISLAND

**RHODES**
(Rodhos)

Kremastí
Paradhísi
Triánda
◇ IALYSOS
Koskinoú
Kallithéa

Maritsá

Soroní

Kalavárda

KAMEIROS ◇

Sálakos

Profítis
Ilías ▲
Apóllona

Afándou

Kolímbia

M. TSAMBIKAS ◇

Arkhángelos

Skála Kamírou

Malón

PHARAKLOS

ALIMNIA

Émbonas

*Atáviros*

Ay. Isidhoros

Láerma

Kálathos

Siána

Lardhos

Líndos
LINDOS ◇

Monólithos
◇ CASTLE

Vation

Apólakkiá
Arnítha

Yennádhi

Mesanagrós

Laharía

Kattaviá

Plimíri

| 0 | | 5 miles |
| 0 | | 8 kilometres |

tower is the Gate of St Catherine. The new sector, that of the **Tongue of Castile**, skirts the Commercial Harbour (described above). Half-way is the picturesque **Marine Gate**, with large guardrooms. Beyond it the wall coincides for a time with the E wall of the Collachium. Beyond a square tower with a chapel (frescoes), the **Arnaldo Gate** leads into Hospital Square. After the **Arsenal Gate** is the **Gate of St Paul**, where the wall runs both W and E along the mole. This is commanded by a tower and protected without by a low triangular curtain with a parapet. At a late period the defence of the Naillac mole was allotted to the Captain of the Port.

From the Gate of St Paul to the Gate of Amboise (where the tour began) is the sector of the **Tongue of France**. This runs in a general E–W direction, passing above the Gate of Liberty. At the circular **Tower of St. Peter**, which bears a figure of St Peter and the arms of Pope Pius II, the wall turns abruptly S and then again W. Skirting the Palace of the Grand Master, you reach Citadel Square.

TO THE ACROPOLIS, 20 minutes. From the centre of town take Odhós Arkhiepiskópou Makaríou. You pass the Soleil Hotel, in the grounds of which excavations (1960) revealed a cellar containing more than 100 intact amphorae, possibly buried in the earthquake of 227–226 BC. Along Od. A. Dhiákou (right at roundabout) is the **Cultural Centre of Rhodes** (exhibitions; teaching in music and the arts; café) in an attractive house with large gardens. Off Leofóros Dhimokratías pleasant streets climb to the right. Up one of these Kheimarrás, at the junction with P. Melá, the remains of one of the most important Early Christian basilicas discovered in Rhodes have been preserved (visible from the street) in the basements of blocks of flats. Further along P. Melá, you turn right into Od. Dhiagorídhon which rises towards **Mt Ayios Stefanos** (111m), a ridge called also **Mt Smith** after Adm. Sir Sidney Smith (1764–1840), who occupied a house here in 1802 while keeping watch on the French fleet. The **acropolis**, identified in 1916 and partly excavated in 1924–29, occupies its gentle S slope. Amid olive groves (left) are a **stadium** (restored) and a small **theatre**, of unusual square plan (only the orchestra and three seats are original work). A massive retaining wall supports a higher terrace where the stylobate of a **Temple of Pythian Apollo** bears three corner columns tastelessly fabricated from fragments. A small fountain-house, below, has a plaster-lined cistern and feed channel with draw-basin behind. At the N end of the ridge is the site of a **Temple of Zeus Polieus and Athena Polias**, marked now only by some foundations and a few column drums, the latter lying close to the main road. Odhos Voríou Ipírou winds back down into the town. Subterranean chambers to either side of the main road round the first bend are thought to belong to **nymphaia** (on the left is a plastered cistern).

## Excursions in the Island

**Road Conditions**. The coastal circuit is almost entirely surfaced. The roads crossing the island from W to E tend to be somewhat deteriorated but are adequate. Below are described only excursions to places of particular interest.

TO RHODINI, 3km S on the Líndos road (frequent buses). This is a pleasant ancient park, where, it is said, was once the School of Rhetoric of Aeschines. The park, frequented by peacocks, is shaded by plane-trees and has a stream and ponds. There are remains of a Roman aqueduct, and about 20 minutes' walk SW is the so-called **Tomb of the Ptolemies**, a Hellenistic rock tomb with a decorated façade (restored 1924).

IALYSOS AND MT PHILEREMOS, 15km SW (buses only as far as Triánda). From the Néa Agorá you take any road leading W and on reaching the sea turn left and follow Leofóros Triándon, the coast road, past the huge Rodos Palace (L) and a succession of other hotels. 3km Turning (left) to **Malpasós**. On the right of this road is the **Cave of the Dragon** with a cypress in front. The legend concerning the dragon said to have been killed here by Dieudonné de Gozon, a Provençal knight who later became Grand Master (1346–53), was convincingly exploded by F.W. Hasluck ('BSA', Vol. XX). 5km **Ixia** (Hotels L, A, B, C, D; F/A). 9km **Triánda** (Hotels L, A, B, C, D; F/A), with 7193 inhabitants, has an interesting little church. A good road rises to the left to (15km) **Mt Phileremos**, an isolated wooded hill (267m) whose level summit (•view) was the site of **Iálysos** (08.00–15.00; closed Mon), one of the three ancient cities of Rhodes. The strategic value of this hill, dominating the plain, has been recognised from Phoenician times; John Cantacuzene was besieged here by the Genoese in 1248, and from here Suleiman directed the siege of Rhodes in 1522. It was contended in 1943 between the Germans and Italians. Of the Classical acropolis there remain the foundations of a 3C **Temple of Athena Ialysia**. Later remains include some ruins of a Byzantine church. Imposing, though over-restored in 1931 and given a new tower, is the Knights' church of **Our Lady of Phileremos**, with Catholic (left) and Orthodox altars. Above is the restored **monastery**, from which a path leads E to a ruined castle of the Knights. To the W, below the temple, is an underground chapel of St George with 14 and 15C frescoes. Lower down are a **fountain** of the 4C BC, reconstructed in 1926, and the **necropolis** where c 500 tombs have been excavated in Late Mycenaean, Geometric, Archaic, and Classical cemeteries. Excavations (from 1982, and earlier this century) in the prehistoric settlement, within the area of Trianda village, suggest that it was an important centre. A thick (30cm) layer of ash from the Thera volcano has been found.

TO KALLITHEA, 10.5 km. From Arsenal Gate you follow the shore road, then, by a large cemetery (left), turn left over a bridge. Soon after (right) are a British War Cemetery (1943–45) and the caves of the Hellenistic and Roman necropolis (1C BC–1C AD). 6.5km **Rení Koskinoú** (Hotels A, B, C, D). 10.5km **Kallithéa**, a strange hydropathic establishment comprising mock-Moorish buildings, gardens, and grottoes, all placed amid the natural shore rocks. The waters are recommended for various internal ailments.

FROM RHODES TO LINDOS (55km), LAKHANIA AND KATAVIA, 95.5km (59 miles); regular bus service to Lindos, also excursion coaches daily; 3 times weekly to Katávia; daily as far as Yennádhi. The old road is described, ignoring newer bypasses. 3km **Rhodhiní** (see above). The road passes through varied scenery of hills interspersed with fertile plains and orange groves. White cubic houses and date palms give the villages a Saharan appearance. 7km **Sgoúrou** has a Hellenistic cemetery site to the E of the road. 13km **Faliráki** (Hotels L, A–E; F/A). Several roads lead down to beaches. 21km **Afándou** (Hotels A–E; F/A; golf course), the first 'Saharan' settlement (5317 inhab.). Near by is a US transmitter that broadcasts the *Voice of America*. To the SE, near the coast, is **Katholikí**, where the 16C church of **Panayía Katholikí**, built over an Early Christian basilica, has elements from Classical times. 26km Immediately after a river bridge, turning (right) to **Eleoússa**, passing (3km) the **Eptá Piyés**, seven springs which form a little lake in a gorge of pine trees. The road now passes through a narrow gap with **Mt Tsambika** (326m) to the left. **Moní Tsambíkas** (signposted) has an ancient tree in the courtyard and a good carved screen in the church. You cross a ridge (233m) and descend to **Arkhángelos** (Αρχάγγελος; Hotels C, D), another village (5781 inhab.) of African appearance, dominated by a spectacular castle. Near by the church of Ayioi Theodhoroi (1377) has wall paintings. The road turns inland, then descends steeply to a fertile valley with nut and orange groves. 38.5km **Malóna**, from which a road (5km) descends to the coast and the pleasant resort of **Kharáki**. On the promontory stands the fine **Castle of Pharaklos**, one of the strongest built by the Knights. It is well seen from the road a little further S. Just beyond (50km) **Kálathos** (Hotels C, D, E), with an Early Christian basilica at Palaioekklesia, the road divides, the right branch continuing to the S of the island. After a left turn, from the top of a low but rocky pass is a sudden *view of Lindos as we descend to the village.

*Líndos (Λίνδος), now a village of 724 inhabitants, was the chief of the three cities before the foundation of Rhodes, and in the Middle Ages was the most important place in the island after Rhodes itself. Its delightful situation, with a beautiful beach (Hotels A, B, C, D; F/A; restaurants), its old houses and trafficless streets, and its superb acropolis give it a charm altogether unique.

**History**. The site was occupied in the 3rd millennium and a temple to Athena existed from at least the 10C BC. Thanks to a geographical position between two harbours it became the most important of the three ancient cities of Rhodes. Colonists from Lindos founded Parthenopea (forerunner of Naples) and Gela, in Sicily, during the 7C. In the 6C Lindos was governed by tyrants, the most celebrated of whom was Kleoboulos (fl. 580 BC), one of the 'Seven Sages', who had a weakness for setting and solving riddles. After the foundation of the city of Rhodes, Lindos remained the religious centre of the island. St Paul is said to have landed at Lindos on his way to Rome. In the Byzantine era the acropolis was turned into a fortress, which the Knights of St John made into the headquarters of a castellany, with twelve knights and a Greek garrison. In 1317 Grand Master Foulques de Villaret took refuge in the castle after the Knights had deposed him. The Turks continued to use the acropolis as a fortress. In 1902–14 and in 1952 a Danish mission excavated the acropolis, but the restorations were done by the Italians before 1938.

**Domestic Architecture**. In Lindos there are numerous 15C houses built in a style derived from the Gothic of the Knights with Byzantine and Oriental decoration. They have a gatehouse, a courtyard with staircase, and the main building, usually with doorways and windows elaborately carved with rope designs, doves, roses, etc. The

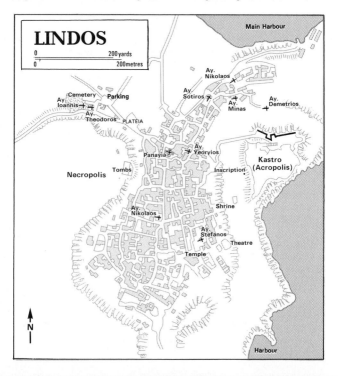

floors are paved in black and white pebble mosaic. The reception room usually contains Lindos ware, either medieval or in modern reproduction. The ceilings are often painted.

**Lindos pottery**. There is a story, without foundation, that in the 14C a Grand Master captured a Levantine ship in which some Persian potters were travelling, and that he forced the potters to work for him at Lindos: this is supposed to have been the origin of the Lindos dishes. Manufacture of the ware is said to have stopped after the Turkish occupation. In fact there were no native potteries, and all the dishes and vases came from the mainland of Asia Minor. Instead, however, of the stylised Persian decoration, the Lindos ware had floral motives, such as tulips, carnations, hyacinths, and roses in bud or in bloom, with a green back-ground picked out in red. Since the Second World War very attractive copies of this ware have been made in Rhodes itself.

At the W end of the village is the small Plateia (no parking), shaded by mulberry trees, with an old fountain and two restaurants. Near the Plateia donkeys may be hired for the acropolis. In the village most of the streets are only just wide enough to take a donkey with panniers. Following the arrows for the acropolis, to the left is the Church of the Panayía (see below). The path climbs steeply.

The **acropolis** (08.00–18.00 daily) occupies a triangular outcrop of rock (116m) accessible only from the N side. From below it is seen as a huge medieval *castle remodelled and enlarged by the Knights from an earlier stronghold. Passing under the outer gate you reach a terrace, where a rock-hewn exedra bears a *relief, 4.6m long and 5.5m high, of the stern of a ship, with its lateral rudder and the helmsman's seat; the deck served as the base of a statue of a priest of Poseidon called Hagesandros (inscription). To the right of the relief are the remains of the ancient **sacred way**. A long staircase leads to the main gate which gives entry to a vaulted passage. Above (spiral stair) is a medieval chamber, which formed part of the **Governor's Palace**. Within the battlemented enceinte is the ruined Byzantine chapel of **St John**.

The **Sanctuary of Athena Lindia** occupies the greater part of the area to the S, which is strewn with bases of statues inscribed with the names of

*Model of the acropolis, Lindos, in the Hellenistic period*

local artists. From a huge double-winged stoa (added c 208 BC) a monumental staircase leads to a higher terrace with foundations of the **propylaea** built after 407 BC. The small **temple** (23m by 7.5m) beyond, stands at the edge of the cliff near the S point of the acropolis. The existing remains, including the W wall of the cella, date from a rebuilding after a fire in 348 BC. They overlook the smaller rock-girt harbour associated by tradition with the supposed visit of St Paul. The SE end of the stoa has a splendid *view of the **great harbour**, with the two islets at its entrance and the promontory beyond.

**The village**. Descending from the acropolis and entering the village, are (right) the **House of Phaedra Moschorídes**, with a doorway of 1642. You can now leave the main road and explore the maze of unspoilt streets to the S, with their many old houses, courtyards, and staircases. Particular houses are not necessarily marked nor easily identified, but worth seeking out are the **House of Ioánnis Krékas**, for its wooden ceiling, and the *House of Papás Konstandínos, the most elaborately decorated of the Lindos houses. Its gatehouse has an ogival doorway and the courtyard an elegant staircase, while the main façade is pierced by ogival and rectangular windows. At the S end of the village is (left) an ancient wall of well-made limestone blocks, part of the peribolos of a **Temple** of the 2–1C BC.

Alongside, set in the hill, is the **theatre**. Its cavea is divided into two by a landing and into five cunei by four staircases; some 27 steps remain. On the return towards the Plateia is the church of the **Panayía**, bearing the dates 1484–90 but probably earlier. It has the form of a Latin cross, with an octagonal drum and cupola. The interior has frescoes executed in 1779 by Gregory of Syme (restored 1927) and the floor is of black and white sea pebbles.

On the promontory of Ayios Aemilianós, near the NE end of the great harbour, is the so called **Tomb of Kleoboulos**, a pre-Hellenic cylindrical structure formed of square blocks of masonry, recalling the Lelego-Carian tombs on the mainland. The sepulchral chamber is approached by a dromos. In the Middle Ages the tomb was converted into the church of St Aemilianos.

Beyond Lindos village the road follows the coast, then turns inland to (63km) **Lárdhos** (Hotels B, C, D).

A good road runs W to **Láerma**, where there is a rough road (signed **Profiliá**) to the impressive **Moní Thári** (12C and frescoes of 11C–17C). Beyond Láerma the roads are poor.

Further down the coast (good beaches; rooms) at 69km is a turn to the **Moní Ipsíni**. 71.5km **Khiotári** has a monastery of the **Metamórfosis**. 75km **Yenádhi** (Hotels B, C). At 77km you can follow the coast or turn inland to (84km) **Lakhaniá**, rejoining the shore road at (88km) **Khólakhas**, 2km to the S of which is the good beach of **Plimíri** (tavernas), with a church of **Zoödhókhos Piyí** and some ancient remains. The main road continues E via **Ayios Pavlos** to (95.5km) **Katávia**.

FROM RHODES TO KAMEIROS (36km; 5 buses daily), MONOLITHOS (73.5km; 1 bus daily) AND KATAVIA (see east coast route) 101.5km (63 miles). This excursion may be combined with that to Ialysos (see above). Beyond (9km) Trianda you continue along the coast with views across the sea to the coast of Turkey. 12km **Kremastí** (Κρεμαστή; Hotels A, B, C, E; 3604 inhab.) is noted for its annual festival held on 14–23 August, which, like those of antiquity, combines religious ceremonies (here centred on a miraculous ikon of the Virgin) with athletic games, music, and dancing. Inland, near **Máritsa** (5.5km) is the church of St George with 14C frescoes. 16km The airport is to the N of the road near **Paradhissi**. Beyond, close to the shore, was found a collection of amphorae of the 2C BC, nearly all with the craftsman's name and mark, stacked and awaiting shipment. 18km, a turning (left) leads to the wooded area of Kalamon with a cattle breeding station and an Agricultural School. Beyond a Boy Scout village extends the **Valley of Butterflies (Petaloúdhes)**. The myriad butterflies (actually moths), best seen in July–August, are attracted by the thick growth of storax with its pungent scent. 20km (right) **Theólogos** had a shrine of Apollo Erithimios and there are Early Christian remains. The main road continues through fig orchards and past numerous wind pumps. On the outskirts of (30km) **Kalavárdha** (Hotel D), you bear right along the coast.

From Kalavárdha it is possible to turn inland, either (1) to make for the E coast at **Kólimbos** (41km from Kalavárdha) or (2) to rejoin the coast road 31km further S at **Amartos**.

From the Kalavárdha fork you ascend the lower slopes of **Mt Profítis Ilías** via **Sálakos** and after 13.5km reach the turn for **Kólimbos**.

(1) This well-engineered but steep and winding road ascends continually, with fine retrospective views of the sea. It soon enters the Wood of the Prophet, luxuriant thanks to a local superstition that the prophet will slay anyone cutting down a tree. The trees are mainly pines, including umbrella pines and cypresses. 20km Hotels (A), in a wonderful situation 701m above the sea. The hotels are appropriately named ('Stag' and 'Doe') because of the number of deer in the neighbourhood. The road passes N of the summit (799m; path) of **Mt Profítis Ilías** and continues (gravel section of 7km) via (25km) the church of **Ayios Nikólaos Foundouklí** (frescoes) to (28.5km)**Eléoussa**, with an Italian governor's palace. 41km **Kólimbos**.

(2) Ignoring the **Kólimbos** turn, **Embona** (435m), 22.5km from **Kalavárdha**, a village growing wine and tobacco, is the starting-point for the ascent of **Mt Ataviros**, the highest mountain in the island (1215m).

The ascent takes 2 hours, and the descent about the same time. The mountain is bare of vegetation and has no springs. From the summit the whole of the island of Rhodes can be seen. On it are the scanty remains of the **Temple of Zeus Atabyros**, said to have been built by Althaemenes, founder of Kretinai (see below). It is certainly one of the oldest temples in Rhodes. It was adapted in the Byzantine era into the Church of St John the Baptist. The site was excavated in 1927 but the cella could not be found. About 100m NE are the remains of a stoa or propylaeum. Votive offerings found on the site and now in the Rhodes Museum include bronze, lead, and terracotta statuettes of oxen, goats, and other domestic animals.

E of **Embona** is the **Monastery of Artamíti** (380m). At (57.5km) **Amartos** the inland road meets the coastal route.

34km Turning (left, signposted) to ancient **Kámeiros** (1km; 08.30–15.00; closed Mon), the third of the ancient cities of Rhodes, called 'chalky' by Homer. It was rediscovered in 1859 after centuries of oblivion and excavated in 1929. The extensive remains, undisturbed in the Middle Ages, occupy a gentle slope overlooking the sea. The city had neither fortifications nor acropolis. You come first to an imposing **temenos**, or court, of the 3C BC, with scanty remains of a Doric temple, beyond which rises the main street of the town. Here a number of houses have come to light including one with a peristyle court. Above, the **agora** consists of a long row of shops bordered by a Doric **stoa** (3C). It covered a 6–5C **cistern** made redundant by a new system of wells, a row of which may be seen behind. A few traces remain among the trees higher up of a peripteral **Temple of Athena**.

Leaving Kameiros along the coast road you pass the ruins of *Kretinai*, a city said to have been founded by Althaemenes from Crete. 43km **Mandrikó**. 50.5km **Kámiros Skála** (daily caique to Khalki). About 6.5km out to sea is a group of islets, of which the largest is **Alímnia** (8 sq. km), with a ruined castle of Greek origin, rebuilt by the Knights, also some Neolthic remains. To the SW of Alimnia is Khálki. 53km sign ('Kamiros Castle') for **Kastéllos** (road in 2km, rough but passable), an important castle of the

Knights, perched on a rock (130m) and dominating the sea. Probably built in 1480, it is on three levels, each assigned to a different Grand Master. It is ruinous on the precipitous NE side (*view). 55km **Kritínia**. At (60km) **Amartos** you meet the inland road (see above) and continue through sparsely inhabited hills to (69km) **Siána** (443m). 73.5km **Monólithos** (Hotel D) has a daily bus from Rhodes. A steep track, ending in a dangerous descent, leads to the *Castle of Monolithos, situated on the top of a precipitous rock called **Monopetra** (236m) and accessible only by a single path. Inside it are two cisterns and the modernised church of **Ayios Pantaléonos**, with another structure beside it. There is a magnificent *view over the sea towards Khálki and another landwards of Mt Akramytes. 83.5km turn for **Apolákia** (2km; Hotels C, E), 1km to the S of which at **Arnitha** are Early Christian (at **Ayía Iríni**) and Byzantine remains.

A rough but spectacular mountain road continues S (25km) from **Arnitha** to **Katávia** via **Mesanágros** where Early Christian basilicas and other buildings underlie a 13C church of the **Dormition** (at Palaioekklisíes). A poor by-road (W) approaches the 14C **Moní Skiádhi** (3km), also accessible from the coast road.

The coast road (being improved) continues S and turns (97.5km) E for **Katávia** (101.5km; rooms). The area to the S is undeveloped but has remote beaches.

## Kastellórizo

**Ferry** from Rhodes, twice weekly in 6 ½–8 hours.

**By Air**. Connections 3–4 times weekly with Rhodes and E Crete.

**Kastellórizo** (Hotel B; rooms), officially **Megísti**, the Italian *Castelrosso*, once celebrated for its medieval castle, belongs to the Dodecanese on ethnological rather than geographical grounds, for it is in the E Mediterranean rather than the Aegean. It is 116km E of Rhodes. Largest of a miniature archipelago lying close to the coast of Lycia, Asia Minor, it is a small triangular island 6.5km long by 3km wide, with an area of 9 sq. km and thus the smallest of the 14 islands of the Dodecanese. Of its 11 dependent islets none are now inhabited. The coastline is precipitous and inaccessible except on the E side, where it forms a bay on which is the only centre of population. The interior is hilly. Cape Ayios Stefanos, at the N end of the island, is only 2.5km from the Anatolian coast. A desalination plant augments tanks of rainwater collected during the winter rains. The chalky soil yields only olives, grapes, and vegetables in insignificant quantities.

The 275 inhabitants are mainly concentrated in the little port and village of **Kastellórizo**, or **Megísti**, on the E coast. Many thousands of Castellorizans, however, live abroad, and the island is largely supported by the remittances of its emigrants who retire here when their fortunes have been made. The port of Kastellorizo provides the only safe shelter on or near the Asiatic coast between Makri and Beirut, and the island's caiques do a lively transit trade. The island was the setting for the film *Mediterraneo*.

**History**. In antiquity the island was called *Megiste*, that is, the largest of the small archipelago. Another name for it appears to have been *Kisthene*. The Turks called it *Meis*. In 1306 it was occupied by the Knights of St John, who strengthened the existing castle and used it as a place of detention for recalcitrant knights. The island was captured in 1440 by Djemal ed Din, Sultan of Egypt, who destroyed the castle. In 1450 Alfonso I of Aragon, king of Naples, reconquered the island and rebuilt the castle. Kastellorizo remained in possession of Naples, except for short intervals, until it was captured in 1512 by the Turks. It was temporarily occupied by the Venetians in 1570 and again in 1659, when the castle was again destroyed. From 1828 to 1833 it was held by the Greeks. During the First World War it was bombarded from the Anatolian coast. Since 1920 it has shared the fortunes of the Dodecanese.

Boat passengers land at the island capital **Kastellórizo** (Hotel B; rooms). The Plateia is the centre of the small town. From it ascend narrow lanes, in which are houses with characteristic wooden balconies, and windows of Anatolian type. In another square is the modern church of Ayios Yeóryios built over an Early Christian predecessor with mosaics. Nearby is the **cathedral** of SS Constantine and Helena whose interior is divided into nave and aisles by monolithic granite columns from the Temple of Apollo at Patára, in Lycia; the columns support ogival arches. From the end of this square is a good view of Mandraki harbour and the Anatolian coast. A delightfully restored **museum** (sign) contains Hellenistic and Roman inscriptions, a Lycian relief from Antifilo and pottery from wrecks of 9–13C. From a small square near Mandraki the Street of the Knights follows the line of the promontory guarding the harbour. Leaving the street, turn right onto a steep and partly stepped path, which leads to the **Lycian Tomb**. This is cut out of the rock and has a Doric façade and a rectangular interior. Many similar but less elaborate tombs are to be found on the Anatolian coast opposite (see below). Higher up are the ruins of the **Castle of the Knights**. This was built by Juan Fernando Heredia, 8th Grand Master of the Knights of St John. Its vicissitudes up to its second destruction are noted above. There survive parts of the curtain wall, and of three towers. A Doric inscription found on the site proves that a fort existed here in Classical times.

A concrete road on the right of the harbour takes you to a paved path (left), which passes the **Monastery of Ayía Triádha** to join an asphalt road (turn left). After 150m steps (left) ascend to the **Palaiókastro**, on the top of Mt Viglo (270m; 40 mins from the village). This is an ancient Greek stronghold built on a rectangular plan (81m by 61m). Inside are numerous cisterns and an ancient tower of squared blocks. To the E are the remains of propylaea, with a Doric inscription of the 3C or 2C BC on which is recorded the name Megiste and its dependence on Rhodes. There is a good view of the town and the Anatolian coast. To the E of Khora, the large church of Ayios Yióryios Santrapí is on the site of an Early Christian basilica.

TO THE BLUE GROTTO, 1½ hours by boat. This is the most attractive excursion in the island. Leaving the harbour and heading SE you follow the inaccessible coast to a slight curvature of the coastline, in which is the narrow mouth of the grotto. The *Blue Grotto, locally known as **Fokeáli** ('Refuge of Seals'), recalls the Blue Grotto of Capri, but it is more extensive. Its length is 40–46m, its breadth 24–30m, and its height 20–24m. As at Capri, the gorgeous colouring is said to be caused by the reflection and refraction of the sun's rays through the water. The roof on the left side has collapsed, the debris forming a little island. At the end of the cave, on the right, is another grotto.

On the Anatolian coast, opposite Kastellorizo, is the town of **Kaç (Antifilo)**, with a Roman theatre, numerous Lycian tombs and other ancient remains. A shipwreck of the 14C BC has been excavated here by Prof. G. Bass and colleagues.

# GLOSSARY OF ART TERMS

AEGIS. Cuirass or shield with Gorgon's head and ring of snakes.

AGORA. Public square or market-place.

AMAZONOMACHIA, GIGANTOMACHIA, TITANOMACHIA. Battle between Gods and Amazons, Giants, Titans.

AMBO (pl. *ambones*). Pulpit in a Christian basilica; two pulpits on opposite sides of a church from which the gospel and epistle were read.

ANTHEMION. Flower ornament.

APOTROPAION. A protective symbol to turn away evil.

BATTER. Sloping apron in front of wall or tower (also called talus).

BASTION. Part of fortification wall projecting from the wall itself.

BEMA. Raised platform (*anc.*); apse of a basilica (*Byz.*)

BRECCIA. A composite rock (pudding-stone).

CHITON. A tunic.

CHLAMYS. Light cloak worn by epheboi.

CHOROS. A hanging circle in metal or wood for the display of icons.

CHTHONIC. Dwelling in or under the ground.

CLOISONNE. Building technique where stones are individually framed with bricks or tiles.

COROPLAST. Maker of small figurines, usually of terracotta.

CYMA (recta or reversa). A wave moulding with double curvature.

DIACONICON. (*Byz.*) Sacristy for sacred vessels on S side of sanctuary (cf. prothesis).

EPHEBOS. Greek youth under training (military, or university).

EPITAPHIOS. Ceremonial pall.

EROTES. Figures of Eros, god of love.

ESCHARA. Sacred hearth.

EXEDRA. Semicircular recess in a classical or Byzantine building.

FORICA. Latrine.

GLACIS. Broad sloping area of natural rock, or of earth, in front of defences, on which attackers are exposed.

GYMNASION (in Mod Gk.). Grammar school.

HERM. Quadrangular pillar, usually adorned with a phallus, and surmounted by a bust.

HERÖON. Shrine or chapel of a demigod or mortal.

HIMATION. An oblong cloak thrown over the left shoulder, and fastened over or under the right.

HOPLITE. Heavily armed foot-soldier.

HYPAETHRAL. Open to the sky.

ICONOSTASIS. Screen bearing icons.

KORE. Maiden; Archaic female figure.

KOUROS. Boy; Archaic male figure.

MACHIOLATION. Openings in floors of projecting galleries, for dropping missiles on attackers.

MEGARON. Hall of a Mycenaean palace or house.

NAOS. Main room of temple, containing cult statue (*anc.*); central section of church, between narthex and iconostasis (*Byz.*).

NARTHEX. Vestibule of a Christian basilica.

NAUMACHIA. Mock naval combat for which the arena of an amphitheatre was flooded.

NYMPHAION. Sanctuary of the Nymphs.

ODEION. A concert hall, usually in the shape of a Greek theatre, but roofed.

OIKOS. A house.

OMPHALOS. A sacred stone, commemorating the 'centre of the earth' where Zeus' two eagles met.

OPUS ALEXANDRINUM. Mosaic design of black and red geometric figures on a white ground.

PANTOKRATOR. The Almighty.

PARECCLESIA. Chapel added to a Byzantine church.

PENDENTIVE. Spherical triangle formed by intersection of dome with two adjacent arches below.

PEPLOS. A mantle in one piece, worn draped by women.

PERIBOLOS. A precinct, but often archaeologically the circuit round it.

PETASOS. Broad-brimmed felt hat worn by epheboi.

PHIALE. Saucer or bowl.

PINAX. Flat plate, tablet, or panel.

PODIUM. Low wall or continuous pedestal carrying a colonnade or building.

POLYANDREION. Communal tomb.

POROS. A soft, coarse, conchiferous limestone (tufa).

PROPYLON, PROPYLAEA. Entrance gate to a temenos; in plural form when there is more than one door.

PROTHESIS. (*Anc.*) Laying out of a corpse; (*Byz.*) The setting forth of the oblation, or the chamber N of the sanctuary where this is done.

PUTEAL. Ornamental well-head.

QUADRIGA. Four-horsed chariot.

RAVELIN. Freestanding, usually triangular, fortification outside and separate from main wall.

REDAN. Triangular bastion projecting from main fortification wall.

SCARP. Retaining wall of moat or moss nearest fortification wall; retaining wall on far side is counterscarp.

SIMANTRON. Block of wood or metal bar beaten as a call to divine service.

SPHENDONE. The rounded end of a stadium.

SQUINCH. Straight or arched structure across angle of square building, to support dome.

STOA. A porch or portico not attached to a larger building.

SYNTHRONON. Seat for bishop or elders in apse of a Byzantine church.

TALUS. See batter.

TEMENOS. A sacred enclosure.

TERREPLEIN. Space behind parapet, rampart or bastion, itself consisting of inner and outer walls with an earth or rubble filling.

THEME. (*Byz.*) A province.

THOLOS. A circular building.

THYMELE. Altar set up in a theatre.

TRANSENNA. Openwork grille at the entrance to a Byzantine chapel.

TRILITHON. Gateway made up of two jambs and a lintel.

TRIREME. Greek galley rowed by 3 banks of oars.

XOANON. Wooden image or idol.

XYSTOS. Roofed colonnade in gymnasium, often equipped with starting blocks, for indoor athletic training.

# INDEX

Ancient names are printed in CAPITALS; personal names in *italics*.

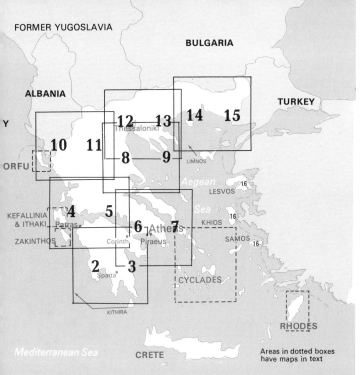

FORMER YUGOSLAVIA

BULGARIA

ALBANIA

TURKEY

Y

**10** **11**

**12** **13** **14** **15**

Thessaloniki

**8** **9**

ORFU

LIMNOS

*Aegean*

LESVOS

16

KEFALLINIA
& ITHAKI

**4** **5**

Patras

**6** Athens **7**

*Sea*

KHIOS

16

ZAKINTHOS

Corinth

Piraeus

SAMOS

16

**2** **3**

Sparta

CYCLADES

KITHIRA

RHODES

*Mediterranean Sea*

CRETE

Areas in dotted boxes
have maps in text

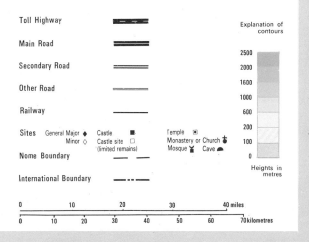

# Key page to Map numbers

| | | |
|---|---|---|
| Toll Highway | ▬▬▬ | |
| Main Road | ▬▬▬ | |
| Secondary Road | ▬▬▬ | |
| Other Road | ▬▬▬ | |
| Railway | ▬▬▬ | |

Explanation of
contours

2500
2000
1600
1000
600
200
100
0

Heights in
metres

Sites  General Major ◆  Castle ■  Temple ▣
Minor ◇  Castle site □  Monastery or Church ⛪
(limited remains)  Mosque ☪ Cave ⬤

Nome Boundary ▬ ▬

International Boundary ▬·▬·▬

| 0 | 10 | 20 | 30 | 40 miles |
|---|---|---|---|---|
| 0 | 10  20 | 30  40 | 50  60 | 70 kilometres |

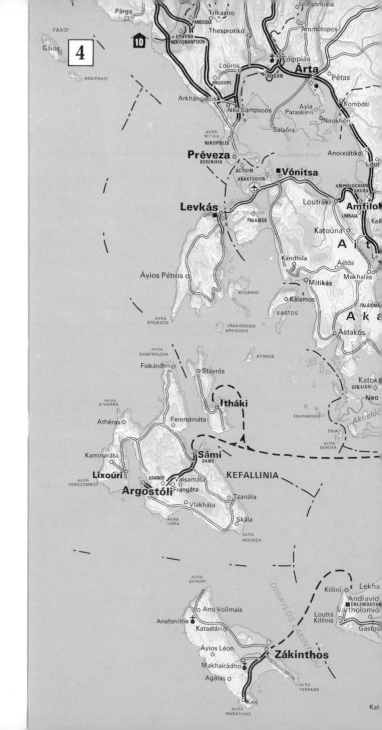

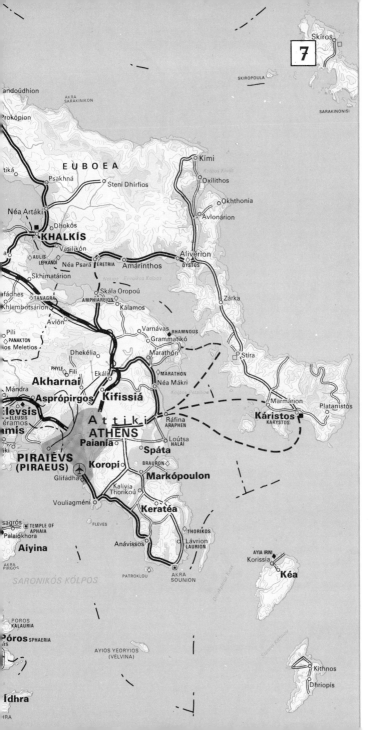

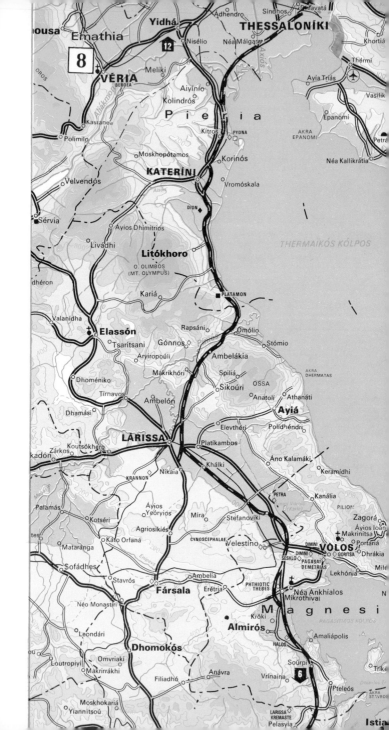

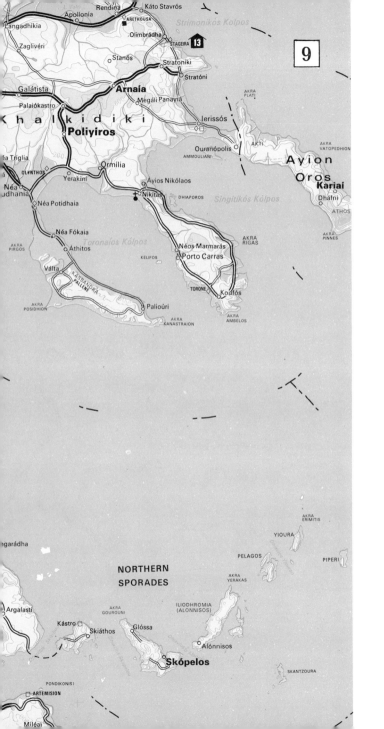

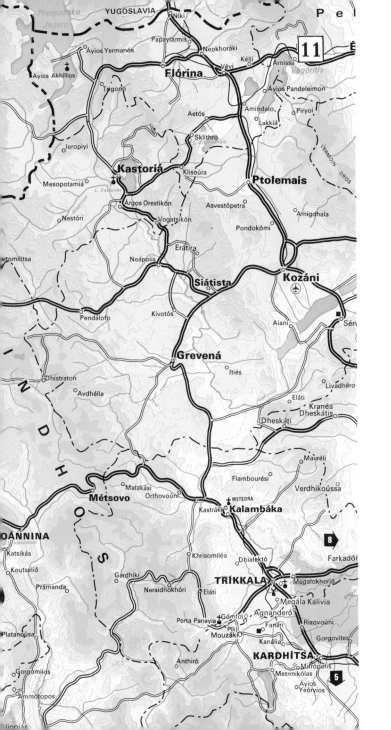

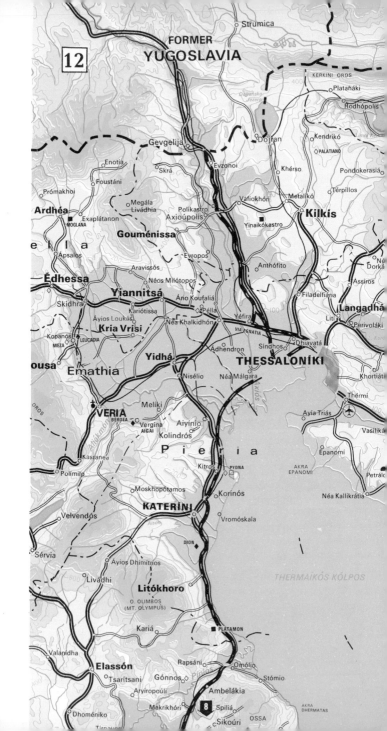

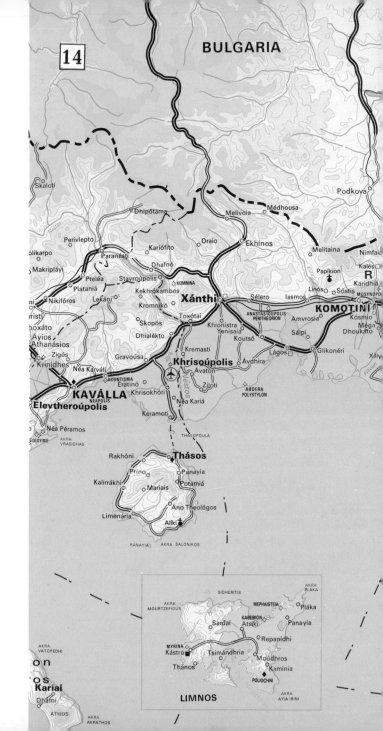

**14**

BULGARIA

Skaloti

Podkova

Dhipótama

Médhousa

Melívoia

Perívlepto

Oraío

Ekhínos

Melitaina

Nimfaía

olíkarpo

Kariófito

Papíkion

Kalés

R

Paranésti

Dhafnó

Makripláyi

Ptelóa

Stavroúpolis

KOMNINA

Sélero

Iasmos

Linós

Sóstis

Karidhiá

MOSYNOPO

Plataniá

Kekhrókambos

Xánthi

KOMOTINÍ

Nikíforos

Lekáni

Kromnikó

ANASTASIOUPOLIS
PERITHEORION

Amvrosía

Kósmio

rísti

Skopós

Toxótai

Khionístra

Méga

hoxáto

Dhialékto

Yenisaía

Sálpi

Dhoukáto

Áyios
Athanásios

Koutsó

Xíliv

Zigós

Gravoúsa

Kremastí

Lágos

Glikonéri

Kriníthes

Néa Karváli

Khrisoúpolis

Ávdhira

ACONTISMA

Avaton

Eratinó

Zilóti

ABDERA
POLYSTYLON

KAVÁLLA

Khrisokhóri

NEAPOLIS

Elevtheroúpolis

Néa Kariá

Keramotí

Néa Péramos

THASOPOULA

OISYME

AKRA
VRASIDHAS

Rakhóni

**Thásos**

Príno

Panayía

Kalirrákhi

Mariais

Potamiá

Limenária

Áno Theológos

Allíki

PANAYIA

AKRA SALONIKOS

AKRA
VATOPEDHI

SIDHERITIS

AKRA
PLÁKA

AKRA
MOÚRTZEFLOUS

MEPHAISTEIA

Pláka

Sardaí

KABEIRION
Atsiki

Panayía

Repanídhi

on

MYRINA
Kástro

Tsimándhria

Moúdhros

os
**Kariaí**

Thános

Kamínia

Dhafni

POLIOCHNI

ATHOS

AKRA
AKRATHOS

AKRA
AYIA IRINI

**LIMNOS**

16

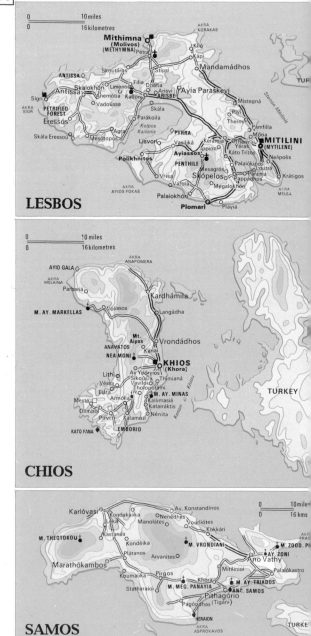

**LESBOS**

0 — 10 miles
0 — 16 kilometres

AKRA KORAKAS

**Mithimna**
(Molivos)
(METHYMNA)  Pétra  Klió
Kápi
Skoutáros  Stípsi  **Mandamádhos**
**ANTISSA**  Fília  Dháfia
Skalokhóri  Limonos  Arísvi  **Avía Paraskeví**
Antissa  Anemótia  Kallóni  **ARISBÉ**  Mistegná
Sigrí  Vadoússa  Píyi
**PETRIFIED**  Skála  Thermí
**FOREST**  Parákoila  Pámfila
AKRA  Eressós  Kolpos  Móría  **MITILINI**
SIGRI  Kalloni  **PYRRA**  (MYTILENE)
Skála Eressoú  Agra  Vasiliká  Kerami  Othermí  Néapolis
Mesótopos  Lisvorí  Ippíon  Yéras  Káto Tritos  Loutrá
**Ayiassos**  Palaiókipos  Paramái
**Polikhnitos**  Mesagrós  Pappádhos  Krátigos
**PENTHILE**  Skópelos  AKRA
Vrisa  Megalokhóri  MELEA
AKRA  Valéra  Palaiokhóri
AYIOS FOKAS  Plomári  Playiá

**CHIOS**

0 — 10 miles
0 — 16 kilometres

AKRA ANAPOMERA

**AYIO GALA**
AKRA  **Kardhámila**
MELAINA  Parbariá
Volíssos  Langádha
**M. AY. MARKELLAS**
**Mt.**  **Vrondádhos**
**Aipos**
**ANAVATOS**  Kariaí
**NEA MONI**  **KHIOS**
Lithí  Ay Yeóryios  (Khora)
Véssa  Sikoúsia  Thimianá
Eláta  Vavíloi  Tholopotámi
Mestá  Armólia  **M. AY. MINAS**
Olimbi  Kallimasiá
Pirví  Katarráktis  **TURKEY**
Kalamóti  Nénita
**KATO FANA**  **EMBORIO**

**SAMOS**

0 — 10 miles
0 — 16 kms

Karlóvasi  Ay. Konstandinos
Kondakaíika  Nenédhes  AKRA
Léka  Manolátes  Vourliótes  PRAS
Kastanéa  Kokkári  **M. ZOOD. PI**
**M. THEOTOKOU**  Kondéika  **M. VRONDIANI**  **AY. ZONI**
Plátanos  Arvanítes  Áno Vathy
Marathókambos  Mitiliníoi  Palaiókastro
Koumaíika  Pírgos  Khóra  **ANC. SAMOS**
Statharaíoi  **M. MÉG. PANAYIA**  **M. AY. TRIADOS**
Pithagório
Pagóndhas (Tigáni)
**HERAION**  **TURKE**
AKRA
ASPROKAVOS